American Reference Books Annual

2000 VOLUME 31

AMERICAN REFERENCE BOOKS ANNUAL

2000 VOLUME 31

Bohdan S. Wynar EDITOR IN CHIEF
Shannon M. Graff ASSOCIATE EDITOR

EDITORIAL ASSISTANT
Cari Ringelheim

Comprehensive annual reviewing service for
reference books published in the United States and Canada

2000

LIBRARIES UNLIMITED
ENGLEWOOD, COLORADO

Copyright © 2000 Libraries Unlimited, Inc.
All Rights Reserved
Printed in the United States of America

No part of this publication may be reproduced, stored in a retrieval system, or transmitted, in any form or by any means, electronic, mechanical, photocopying, recording, or otherwise, without the prior written permission of the publisher.

LIBRARIES UNLIMITED, INC.
P.O. Box 6633
Englewood, CO 80155-6633
1-800-237-6124
www.lu.com

Library of Congress Cataloging-in-Publication Data

American reference books annual, 1970-
  Englewood, Colo., Libraries Unlimited.

    v. 19x26 cm.

Indexes:
  1970-74. 1v.
  1975-79. 1v.
  1980-84. 1v.
  1985-89. 1v.
  1990-94. 1v.
  1995-99. 1v.

    I. Reference books--Bibliography--Periodicals.
I. Wynar, Bohdan S. II. Graff, Shannon M. III. Ringelheim, Cari
Z1035.1.A55 011'.02
ISBN 1-56308-837-1(2000 edition)
ISSN 0065-9959

Contents

Introduction xiii

Contributors xv

Journals Cited xxvii

Part I
GENERAL REFERENCE WORKS

1—General Reference Works

Acronyms and Abbreviations 3
Almanacs 3
Bibliography 4
  National and Trade Bibliography 4
    International 4
    United States. 4
    Canada. 5
    Great Britain. 5
Biography 6
  International 6
  United States 9
  Canada 10
Dictionaries and Encyclopedias 11
Directories. 16
Handbooks and Yearbooks. 22
Indexes 23
Periodicals and Serials 23
Quotation Books. 25

Part II
SOCIAL SCIENCES

2—Social Sciences in General

Social Sciences in General 31

3—Area Studies

General Works 35
United States. 38
  General Works 38
  Florida. 39
  Illinois. 40
  Texas 41
Africa 42

Asia. 44
  General Works 44
  China 44
  Japan 45
  Thailand. 46
Australia and the Pacific Area 47
Canada. 48
Europe 48
  General Works 48
  Austria. 49
  Basque Region 49
  Bulgaria 49
  Croatia. 50
  Former Soviet Republics 50
  Former Yugoslavia 51
  Great Britain 52
  Greece. 53
  Netherlands 54
  Sicily 54
Latin America and the Caribbean 54
Middle East 56
Polar Regions 57

4—Economics and Business

General Works 59
  Bibliography 59
  Biography 60
  Chronology 61
  Dictionaries and Encyclopedias. 62
  Directories. 64
  Handbooks and Yearbooks 69
  Quotation Books. 70
Business Services and Investment
   Guides 71
Consumer Guides 72
Finance and Banking 74
Industry and Manufacturing. 76
  Dictionaries and Encyclopedias. 76
  Directories. 76
  Handbooks and Yearbooks 79
Insurance 82
International Business 82
  General Works 82
    Dictionaries and Encyclopedias 82
    Directories 83

4—Economics and Business (*continued*)

International Business (*continued*)
  General Works (*continued*)
    Handbooks and Yearbooks. 86
    Asia 91
    Canada 91
    Europe 92
    Latin America and the Caribbean. 92
Labor. 93
  Career Guides 93
  Dictionaries and Encyclopedias. 98
  Directories. 98
  Handbooks and Yearbooks 99
Management 100
Marketing and Trade 101
Taxation 105

5—Education

General Works. 107
  Bibliography 107
  Dictionaries and Encyclopedias 108
  Directories 109
  Handbooks and Yearbooks 110
Alternative Education 111
Computer Resources 113
Elementary and Secondary Education . . . 114
Higher Education 114
  Biography 114
  Directories 115
  Financial Aid 118
  Handbooks and Yearbooks 123
**International Exchange Programs
  and Opportunities** 127
Nonprint Materials and Resources 129

6—Ethnic Studies and Anthropology

Anthropology and Ethnology 131
Ethnic Studies 133
  General Works. 133
  Arab Americans 133
  Asian Americans. 134
  Blacks 136
    Atlases 136
    Bibliographies. 136
    Biographies 137
    Dictionaries and Encyclopedias 141
    Directories 142
    Handbooks and Yearbooks 142

  Indians of North America 145
    Bibliography 145
    Biography 147
    Dictionaries and Encyclopedias 147
    Directories 151
    Handbooks and Yearbooks 151
  Jews 152
  Latin Americans 154

7—Genealogy and Heraldry

Genealogy 157
  Dictionaries and Encyclopedias 157
  Directories 157
  Handbooks and Yearbooks 160
Heraldry 160
Personal Names 161

8—Geography and Travel Guides

Geography 163
  General Works. 163
    Atlases 163
    Bibliographies. 165
    Biography 166
    Chronology 167
    Dictionaries and Encyclopedias 168
    Handbooks and Yearbooks 168
Travel Guides 170
  General Works. 170
  United States. 174
  Asia 179
  Australia 180
  Europe 181
  Latin America and the Caribbean 184
  Middle East 185

9—History

Archaeology 187
American History 188
  Almanacs 188
  Atlases. 190
  Bibliography 190
  Biography 191
  Chronology 192
  Dictionaries and Encyclopedias 194
  Handbooks and Yearbooks 197
African History 201
Asian History. 204
  Azerbaijan 204

China	205
Japanese	206
Korean	207
Pakistan	208

Australian History 209
Canadian History 209
Cuban History 210
European History 210
   General Works 210
   Austrian 212
   Belgium 213
   Dutch 213
   French 214
   German 215
   Greek 216
   Italian 217
   Polish 217
   Russian 217
   Slovakia 218
   Spanish 219
   United Kingdom 219
   Yugoslavia 222
Middle Eastern History 223
World History 224
   Bibliography 224
   Biography 224
   Chronology 228
   Dictionaries and Encyclopedias 229
   Handbooks and Yearbooks 233
   Quotation Books 236

10—Law

General Works 239
   Dictionaries and Encyclopedias 239
   Directories 240
   Handbooks and Yearbooks 242
Criminology and Criminal Justice 247
   Biography 247
   Handbooks and Yearbooks 248
Environmental Law 252
Human Rights 254

11—Library and Information Science and Publishing and Bookselling

Library and Information Science 257
   Reference Works 257
      Bibliographies 257
      Directories 259
      Handbooks and Yearbooks 260
   Special Topics 262
      Archives and Manuscripts 262
      Information Science 262
      Information Systems 265
      Library Management 266
      Periodicals and Serials 267
      Philosophy and Theory 267
      School Library Media Centers 268
      Special Libraries 269
Publishing and Bookselling 270
   Bibliography 270
   Biography 270
   Catalogs and Collections 271
   Dictionaries and Encyclopedias 271
   Directories 272
   Handbooks and Yearbooks 274

12—Military Studies

General Works 275
   Atlases 275
   Bibliography 275
   Biography 276
   Dictionaries and Encyclopedias 277
   Directories 279
   Handbooks and Yearbooks 280
Air Force 281
Navy 282
Weapons and Equipment 283

13—Political Science

General Works 285
   Biography 285
   Dictionaries and Encyclopedias 286
   Directories 287
Politics and Government 290
   United States 290
      Almanacs 290
      Biography 291
      Dictionaries and Encyclopedias 292
      Directories 295
      Handbooks and Yearbooks 297
   European 307
   Middle Eastern 307
Ideologies 308
International Organizations 309
International Relations 310
Public Policy and Administration 312

14—Psychology, Parapsychology, and Occultism

Psychology 315
   Bibliography. 315
   Biography 316
   Dictionaries and Encyclopedias 316
   Directories. 319
   Handbooks and Yearbooks 320
Occultism. 321
Parapsychology 322

15—Recreation and Sports

General Works. 325
Baseball. 327
Basketball 332
Bodybuilding. 333
Football. 333
Golf 335
Hockey 335
Olympics 336
Running 337
Soccer. 337
Tae Kwon Do. 337

16—Sociology

General Works. 339
Aging 340
Disabled 340
Family, Marriage, and Divorce 341
Gay and Lesbian Studies 344
Philanthropy. 345
   Directories. 345
   Handbooks and Yearbooks 347
Social Welfare and Social Work 348
Substance Abuse. 349
Youth and Child Development 350

17—Statistics, Demography, and Urban Studies

Demography 353
   General Works. 353
   Dictionaries and Encyclopedias 354
   Directories. 354
   Handbooks and Yearbooks 354
Statistics 356
   General Works. 356
      Dictionaries and Encyclopedias . . . 356
      Handbooks and Yearbooks 357
      Indexes 360
      United States. 361
Urban Studies 365

18—Women's Studies

Bibliography 367
Biography 367
Chronology. 369
Dictionaries and Encyclopedias. 370
Handbooks and Yearbooks 371
Indexes 374

Part III
Humanities

19—Humanities in General

Humanities in General 377

20—Communication and Mass Media

General Works. 379
Authorship 380
   General Works. 380
   Style Manuals 384
Radio, Television, Audio, and Video . . . 385

21—Decorative Arts

Collecting. 389
   General Works. 389
   Antiques 390
   Autographs. 391
   Books 392
   Coins (and Paper Money) 392
   Memorabilia. 394

22—Fine Arts

General Works. 397
   Bibliography. 397
   Biography 398
   Dictionaries and Encyclopedias 400
   Directories. 401
   Handbooks and Yearbooks 402
Architecture 403
Graphic Arts 407
Photography 407

23—Language and Linguistics

General Works 411
English-Language Dictionaries 414
   General Usage 414
   Eponyms 418
   Etymology 418
   Euphemisms 419
   Homophones and Homographs 419
   Juvenile 420
   New Words 421
   Sign Language 422
   Terms and Phrases 422
   Thesauri 423
Non-English-Language Dictionaries 425
   General Works 425
   Albanian 426
   Chinese 426
   Dutch 427
   Finnish 427
   French 427
   Gaelic 428
   Irish 428
   Italian 429
   Japanese 429
   Polish 430
   Russian 431
   SerboCroatian 431
   Spanish 432
   Yiddish 432

24—Literature

General Works 435
   Bibliography 435
   Bio-bibliography 437
   Dictionaries and Encyclopedias 439
   Directories 443
   Handbooks and Yearbooks 444
Children's and Young Adult Literature . . . 448
   Children's Literature 448
      Bibliography 448
      Biography 453
      Handbooks and Yearbooks 455
      Quotation Books 456
   Young Adult Literature 457
Drama 458
Fiction 461
   General Works 461
   Crime and Mystery 463
   Historical Fiction 465
   Romance 466
   Science Fiction, Fantasy, and Horror . . . 467
   Short Stories 470
National Literature 471
   American Literature 471
      General Works 471
        Bibliography, 471; *Bio-bibliography*,
        471; *Biography*, 474; *Dictionaries*
        and Encyclopedias, 475; *Handbooks*
        and Yearbooks, 476
      Individual Authors 477
        Maya Angelou, 477; *James Dickey*,
        478; *William Faulkner*, 479; *F. Scott*
        Fitzgerald, 479; *Ernest Hemingway*,
        480; *John Crowe Ransom*, 480; *John*
        Steinbeck, 481; *Mark Twain*, 481;
        Anne Tyler, 482; *Walt Whitman*, 482
   British Literature 483
      General Works 483
        Biography, 483; *Dictionaries and*
        Encyclopedias, 485; *Handbooks*
        and Yearbooks, 486
      Individual Authors 486
        Geoffrey Chaucer, 486; *Patrick*
        O'Brian, 487; *William Shakespeare*,
        487; *Dylan Thomas*, 490
   Australian and New Zealand Literature . . . 490
   French Literature 492
   Irish Literature 493
   Italian Literature 493
   Latin American Literature 494
   Middle Eastern Literature 494
   Russian Literature 495
   Scottish Literature 496
   Spanish Literature 497
Poetry 498

25—Music

General Works 503
   Bibliography 503
   Biography 504
   Dictionaries and Encyclopedias 505
   Directories 508
   Discography 509
   Handbooks and Yearbooks 510
   Indexes 511
Individual Composers and Musicians . . . 511

25—Music (continued)

Instruments 515
   Guitar 515
   Organ 516
   Piano. 516
Musical Forms 517
   Blues. 517
   Choral 518
   Classical 519
   Country Music. 519
   Jazz 520
   Operatic 521
   Orchestral 523
   Popular. 524
   Sacred 528

26—Mythology, Folklore, and Popular Culture

Folklore. 529
Mythology 532
Popular Culture 533

27—Performing Arts

General Works. 539
   Biography 539
   Directories. 540
   Handbooks and Yearbooks 541
Dance 542
Film, Television, and Video 542
   Bibliography. 542
   Bio-bibliography. 543
   Biography 545
   Dictionaries and Encyclopedias 547
   Directories. 550
   Filmography 552
   Handbooks and Yearbooks 559
   Indexes. 562
   Quotation Books. 563
   Videography 563
Theater 566

28—Philosophy and Religion

General Works. 571
Philosophy 571
   Dictionaries and Encyclopedias 571
   Directories. 575
   Handbooks and Yearbooks 576

Religion. 578
   General Works. 578
      Bibliography 578
      Biography. 580
      Dictionaries and Encyclopedias 581
      Handbooks and Yearbooks 584
   Bible Studies. 586
      Atlases 586
      Dictionaries and Encyclopedias 587
      Handbooks and Yearbooks 590
   Christianity 593
      Almanacs 593
      Bibliography 593
      Biography. 594
      Chronology 594
      Dictionaries and Encyclopedias 595
      Handbooks and Yearbooks 599
   Islam. 599
   Judaism 600

Part IV
SCIENCE AND TECHNOLOGY

29—Science and Technology in General

Bibliography 603
Biography 604
Dictionaries and Encyclopedias. 607
Directories 611
Handbooks and Yearbooks 611

30—Agricultural Sciences

General Works. 615
Food Sciences and Technology 615
   Bibliographies 615
   Dictionaries and Encyclopedias 616
   Directories. 617
   Handbooks and Yearbooks 618
   Indexes. 620
Forestry. 620
Horticulture 621
Veterinary Science. 622

31—Biological Sciences

General Works. 625
Biology 627
   Dictionaries and Encyclopedias 627

Handbooks and Yearbooks 629	Eating Disorders 678

Botany 631
   General Works. 631
      Dictionaries and Encyclopedias 631
      Handbooks and Yearbooks 633
   Flowering Plants. 634
   Succulents 637
   Trees and Shrubs. 637
Natural History 638
Zoology 640
   General Works. 640
   Birds. 641
   Domestic Animals 643
   Fishes 643
   Insects 644
   Mammals 645
   Marine Animals 647
   Reptiles and Amphibians 650

Eating Disorders 678
Endocrine and Metabolic Disorders . . . 678
Gynecology and Human
   Reproduction. 679
Sexually Transmitted Diseases 679
Skin Diseases 680
Sleep Disorders 680
Sports Medicine 681
Nursing 681
Pharmacy and Pharmaceutical Sciences . . . 682

34—High Technology

General Works 687
Computing 688
Internet 690
Telecommunications 693
   Dictionaries and Encyclopedias 693
   Directories 694
   Handbooks and Yearbooks 695

32—Engineering

Chemical Engineering 653
Civil Engineering 654
Electric Engineering and Electronics 655
Environmental Engineering 656
Materials Science 657
Mechanical Engineering 658

33—Health Sciences

General Works 659
   Bibliography 659
   Dictionaries and Encyclopedias 659
   Directories 661
   Handbooks and Yearbooks 663
Medicine 667
   General Works. 667
   Alternative Medicine 669
   Forensic Medicine 671
   Geriatrics. 672
   Pediatrics. 672
   Poisoning 674
   Specific Diseases and Conditions 675
      AIDS 675
      Alzheimer's Disease 676
      Blood and Circulatory Disorders 676
      Brain Disorders 676
      Burns 677
      Diabetes. 677

35—Physical Sciences and Mathematics

Physical Sciences 697
   General Works. 697
   Chemistry 698
      Dictionaries and Encyclopedias 698
      Directories 701
      Handbooks and Yearbooks 702
   Earth and Planetary Sciences 704
      General Works 704
      Astronomy and Space Sciences. 707
      Climatology and Meteorology 711
      Geology. 711
      Mineralogy 711
      Oceanography. 712
      Paleontology 713
      Volcanology 714
   Physics. 714
Mathematics 715

36—Resource Sciences

Energy Resources 719
Environmental Science 719
   Bibliographies 719
   Dictionaries and Encyclopedias 720
   Directories 721
   Handbooks and Yearbooks 722

37—Transportation

General Works................ 725
Air...................... 725
Ground.................... 726

Author/Title Index 727

Subject Index 757

Introduction

PURPOSE AND SCOPE

American Reference Books Annual, a far-reaching reviewing service for reference books, is now in its 31st volume. The 1,543 books and CD-ROMs reviewed in this volume cover imprints from 1999 and some from 1998 that were received too late to be reviewed in the previous volume. Titles not reviewed in ARBA 99, have been reviewed in ARBA 2000. In the 31 volumes of ARBA published since 1970, a total of 53,319 titles have been reviewed. Six cumulative indexes for ARBA cover the years 1970-1974, 1975-1979, 1980-1984, 1985-1989, 1990-1994, and 1995-1999. These indexes expedite the use of the annual volumes.

ARBA differs significantly from other reviewing media in its basic purpose, which is to provide comprehensive coverage of English-language reference books published in the United States and Canada during a single year. The categories of reference books reviewed in ARBA and the policy regarding them can be summarized as follows: (1) Dictionaries, encyclopedias, indexes, directories, bibliographies, guides, concordances, atlases, gazetteers, and other types of ready-reference tools are routinely reviewed in each volume of ARBA; coverage of this category of reference materials is nearly complete. (2) General encyclopedias that are updated annually, yearbooks, almanacs, indexing and abstracting services, and other annuals or serials are usually reviewed at intervals of three, four, or five years. The first review of such works generally provides an appropriate historical background. Subsequent reviews of these publications attempt to point out changes in scope, editorial policy, and similar matters. (3) New editions of reference books are ordinarily reviewed with appropriate comparisons to older editions. (4) Traditionally, foreign reference titles have been reviewed only if they had an exclusive distributor in the United States. In 1987 coverage was expanded to include Canadian publications that do not have U.S. distributors. Prices for such titles are in Canadian dollars unless otherwise indicated. Substantial coverage of Canadian reference publications has been achieved and will continue until it is as complete for Canada as it is for the United States. Other foreign-title coverage is restricted to English-language publications from Great Britain, as well as a few select sources from Australia and other countries. (5) Reprints are reviewed in ARBA on a selective basis as they often are produced in limited quantities. (6) Titles produced for the mass market in the areas of collectibles, travel guides, and genealogy receive selective coverage.

Certain categories of reference books are usually not reviewed in ARBA: those of fewer than 48 pages, those produced by vanity presses or by the author as publisher, and those generated by library staffs for internal use. Highly specialized reference works printed in a limited number of copies and that do not appeal to the general library audience ARBA serves may also be omitted.

Because there has been a significant increase and interest in electronic publishing, ARBA has begun reviewing this medium. More than 62 CD-ROMs receive comprehensive and lengthy evaluations in this edition. Future volumes will continue to include reviews of these state-of-the-art information storage devices in a variety of subject areas.

New to this edition are reviews of sources intended specifically for the library professional. These include monographs and handbooks that address the concerns of library and information specialists. Much like the acclaimed *Library and Information Science Annual*, these reviews provide critical analyses of library literature. These reviews can be found in chapter 11, titled "Library and Information Science and Publishing and Bookselling."

REVIEWING POLICY

To ensure well-written and erudite reviews, the ARBA staff maintains a roster of more than 400 scholar, practitioners, and library educators in all subject specialties at libraries and universities throughout the United States and Canada. Because ARBA is not a selective reviewing source, such as *Choice* or *Library Journal*, the reviews are generally longer and more critical, to detail the strengths and weaknesses of important reference works. Reviewers are asked to examine books and provide well-documented critical comments, both positive and negative. Coverage usually includes the usefulness of a given work; organization, execution, and pertinence of contents; prose style; format; availability of supplementary materials (e.g., indexes, appendixes); and similarity to other works and previous editions. Reviewers are encouraged to address the intended audience but not necessarily to give specific recommendations for purchase. An adequate description and evaluation of the reference book are sufficient. All reviews in ARBA are signed.

ARRANGEMENT

ARBA 2000 consists of 37 chapters, an author/title index, and a subject index. It is divided into four alphabetically arranged parts: "General Reference Works," "Social Sciences," "Humanities," and "Science and Technology." "General Reference Works" is subdivided by form: bibliography, biography, catalogs and collections, dictionaries and encyclopedias, handbooks and yearbooks, indexes, and so on. Within the remaining three parts, chapters are organized by topic. Thus, under "Social Sciences" the reader will find chapters titled "Economics and Business," "Education," "History," "Law," and "Sociology."

Each chapter is subdivided to reflect the arrangement strategy of the entire volume. There is a section on general works followed by a topical breakdown. For example, in the chapter titled "Performing Arts," "General Works" is followed by "Dance" and "Film, Television, and Video." The latter is divided into sections by format, which include "Biography" and "Filmography." Subdivisions are based on the amount of material available on a given topic and vary from year to year.

ACKNOWLEDGMENTS

In closing, we wish to express our gratitude to the many talented contributors without whose support this volume of ARBA could not have been compiled. We would also like to thank the members of our staff who were instrumental in its preparation: Pamela J. Getchell and former staff member Susan D. Strickland.

Bohdan S. Wynar, Editor in Chief

Editorial Staff

Bohdan S. Wynar, Editor in Chief
Shannon M. Graff, Associate Editor
Cari Ringelheim, Editorial Assistant

Contributors

Gordon J. Aamot, Head, Foster Business Library, Univ. of Washington, Seattle.

Stephen H. Aby, Education Bibliographer, Bierce Library, Univ. of Akron, Ohio.

Anthony J. Adam, Reference Librarian, Prairie View A & M Univ., Coleman Library, Tex.

January Adams, Asst. Director/Head of Adult Services, Franklin Township Public Library, Somerset, N.J.

Sandra Adell, Asst. Professor, Dept. of Afro-American Studies, Univ. of Wisconsin, Madison.

Bev Cummings Agnew, Reference Librarian, Univ. of Colorado Law School Library, Boulder.

Bryce L. Allen, Assoc. Professor, School of Information Science and Learning Technologies, Univ. of Missouri, Columbia.

Walter C. Allen, Assoc. Professor Emeritus, Graduate School of Library and Information Science, Univ. of Illinois, Urbana.

Donald Altschiller, Reference Librarian, Boston Univ.

Elizabeth L. Anderson, Part-Time Instructor, Lansing Community College, Mich.

Frank J. Anderson, Librarian Emeritus, Sandor Teszler Library, Wofford College, Spartanburg, S.C.

Robert T. Anderson, Professor, Religious Studies, Michigan State Univ., East Lansing.

Charles R. Andrews, Dean of Library Services, Hofstra Univ., Hempstead, N.Y.

Susan B. Ardis, Acting Head Science Libraries Division, Univ. of Texas, Austin.

Melvin S. Arrington Jr., Assoc. Professor of Modern Languages, Univ. of Mississippi, University.

Susan C. Awe, Asst. Director, Univ. of New Mexico, Albuquerque.

Mary A. Axford, Reference Librarian, Georgia Institute of Technology, Atlanta.

Susan D. Baird-Joshi, Database Programmer/Analyst, Rho, Redmond, Wash.

Christopher Baker, Professor of English, Armstrong Atlantic State Univ., Savannah, Ga.

Jan Bakker, Resource Center Director, North Central Regional Educational Laboratory, Oak Brook, Ill.

David A. Baldwin, Assoc. Professor, Interim Director, Fine Arts Library, Center for the Arts, Univ. of New Mexico, Albuquerque.

Jack Bales, Reference Librarian, Mary Washington College Library, Fredericksburg, Va.

Robert M. Ballard, Professor, School of Library and Information Science, North Carolina Central Univ., Durham.

Helen M. Barber, Reference Librarian, New Mexico State Univ., Las Cruces.

Suzanne I. Barchers, Author/Consultant, Denver, Colo.

Daniel C. Barkley, Asst. Director, Government Informations Department, Univ. of New Mexico, Albuquerque.

Craig W. Beard, Reference Librarian, Mervyn H. Sterne Library, Univ. of Alabama, Birmingham.

Sandra E. Belanger, Reference Librarian, San Jose State Univ. Library, Calif.

Carol Willsey Bell, Head, Local History and Genealogy Dept., Warren-Trumbull County Public Library, Warren, Ohio.

George H. Bell, Assoc. Librarian, Daniel E. Noble Science and Engineering Library, Arizona State Univ., Tempe.

Adrienne Antink Bendel, Medical Group Management Association, Lakewood, Colo.

Kenneth W. Berger, Team Leader, Reference/ILL Home Team, Perkins Library, Duke Univ., Durham, N.C.

Bernice Bergup, Humanities Reference Librarian, Davis Library, Univ. of North Carolina, Chapel Hill.

Teresa U. Berry, Reference Coordinator, Univ. of Tennessee, Knoxville.

John B. Beston, Professor of English, Santa Fe, N.Mex.

Barbara M. Bibel, Reference Librarian, Science/Business/Sociology Dept., Main Library, Oakland Public Library, Calif.

Terry D. Bilhartz, Assoc. Professor of History, Sam Houston State Univ., Huntsville, Tex.

John D. Blackwell, Reference Librarian/Collections Coordinator, Brandeis Univ., Waltham, Mass.

Richard Bleiler, Reference Librarian, Univ. of Connecticut, Storrs.

Laura K. Blessing, Personnel Librarian, Univ. of Texas, Arlington.

Daniel K. Blewett, Reference Librarian, Cudahy Library, Loyola Univ., Chicago.

Edna M. Boardman, Library Media Specialist, Minot High School, Magic City Campus, N.D.

Bobray Bordelon, Social Science Reference Center, Firestone Library, Princeton Univ. Libraries, N.J.

William Bright, Research Assoc. in Linguistics, Univ. of Colorado, Boulder.

Georgia Briscoe, Assoc. Director and Head of Technical Services, Law Library, Univ. of Colorado, Boulder.

Simon J. Bronner, Distinguished Professor of Folklore and American Studies, Capitol College, Pennsylvania State Univ., Middletown.

Sue Brown, Reference Librarian, Louisiana State Univ., Shreveport.

Patrick J. Brunet, Library Manager, Western Wisconsin Technical College, La Crosse.

Betty Jo Buckingham, (retired) Consultant, Iowa Dept. of Education, Des Moines.

John R. Burch Jr., Technical Services Librarian, Hagan Memorial Library, Cumberland College, Williamsburg, Ky.

Frederic F. Burchsted, Reference Librarian, Widener Library, Harvard Univ., Cambridge, Mass.

Robert H. Burger, Head, Slavic and East European Library, Univ. of Illinois, Urbana-Champaign.

Joanna M. Burkhardt, Head Librarian, College of Continuing Education Library, Univ. of Rhode Island, Providence.

Ingrid Schierling Burnett, Reference Librarian, Univ. of Southern Colorado Library, Pueblo.

Hans E. Bynagle, Library Director and Professor of Philosophy, Whitworth College, Spokane, Wash.

Diane M. Calabrese, Freelance Writer and Consultant, Silver Spring, Md.

Joseph L. Carlson, Library Director, Vandenberg Air Force Base, Calif.

Ruth A. Carr, Chief, U.S. History, Local History and Genealogy Div., New York Public Library.

Joseph Cataio, Manager, Booklegger's Bookstore, Chicago.

G. A. Cevasco, Assoc. Professor of English, St. John's Univ., Jamaica, N.Y.

Bert Chapman, Government Publications Coordinator, Purdue Univ., West Lafayette, Ind.

Boyd Childress, Reference Librarian, Ralph B. Draughon Library, Auburn Univ., Ala.

Heting Chu, Assoc. Professor, Palmer School of Library and Information Science, Long Island Univ., N.Y.

Dene L. Clark, (retired) Reference Librarian, Auraria Library, Denver, Colo.

Juleigh Muirhead Clark, Public Services Librarian, John D. Rockefeller, Jr. Library, Colonial Williamsburg Foundation, Williamsburg, Va.

Paul F. Clark, Assoc. Professor, Pennsylvania State Univ., University Park.

Stella T. Clark, Professor, Foreign Languages, California State Univ., San Marcos.

Harriette M. Cluxton, (formerly) Director of Medical Library Services, Illinois Masonic Medical Center, Chicago.

Gary R. Cocozzoli, Director of the Library, Lawrence Technological Univ., Southfield, Mich.

Joshua Cohen, Director for Outreach and Continuing Education, Mid-Hudson Library System, Poughkeepsie, N.Y.

Donald E. Collins, Assoc. Professor, History Dept., East Carolina Univ., Greenville, N.C.

Barbara Conroy, Career Connections, Santa Fe, N.Mex.

Kay O. Cornelius, (formerly) Teacher and Magnet School Lead Teacher, Huntsville City Schools, Ala.

Paul B. Cors, Catalog Librarian, Univ. of Wyoming, Laramie.

Deborah Cottin, Staff, Libraries Unlimited, Inc.

Gregory A. Crawford, Head of Public Services, Penn State Harrisburg, Middletown, Pa.

Mark J. Crawford, Consulting Exploration Geologist/Writer/Editor, Madison, Wis.

Milton H. Crouch, Asst. Director for Reader Services, Bailey/Howe Library, Univ. of Vermont, Burlington.

Gregory Curtis, Director, Northern Maine Technical College, Presque Isle.

Joseph W. Dauben, Professor of History and History of Science, City Univ. of New York.

Donald G. Davis Jr., Professor, Graduate School of Library and Information Science, Univ. of Texas, Austin.

Dominique-René de Lerma, Professor, Conservatory of Music, Lawrence Univ., Appleton, Wis.

Gail de Vos, Adjunct Assoc. Professor, School of Library and Information Studies, Univ. of Alberta, Edmonton.

Barbara Delzell, Research and Development Center Manager, Hewlett-Packard, Vancouver, Wash.

Margaret Denman-West, Professor Emeritus, Western Maryland College, Westminster.

Margaret F. Dominy, Head, Mathematics-Physics-Astronomy Library, Univ. of Pennsylvania, Philadelphia.

Karen Markey Drabenstott, Asst. Professor, School of Information and Library Studies, Univ. of Michigan, Ann Arbor.

Christine Drew, Reference Librarian, Babson College, Wellesley, Mass.

John A. Drobnicki, Asst. Professor/Reference Librarian, City Univ. of New York—York College.

Joe P. Dunn, Charles A. Dana Professor of History and Politics, Converse College, Spartanburg, S.C.

David Eggenberger, Freelance Writer and Editor, Vienna, Va.

Marianne B. Eimer, Interlibrary Loan/Reference Librarian, SUNY College at Fredonia, N.Y.

Marie Ellis, Librarian IV Emeritus, Univ. of Georgia Libraries, Athens.

Jean Engler, Reference Librarian, Koelbel Public Library, Englewood, Colo.

Edward Erazo, Head of Reference, Florida Atlantic Univ., Boca Raton, Fla.

Jonathon Erlen, Curator, History of Medicine, Univ. of Pittsburgh, Pa.

Patricia A. Eskoz, (retired) Catalog Librarian, Auraria Library, and Asst. Professor Emeritus, Univ. of Colorado, Denver.

G. Edward Evans, Univ. Librarian, Charles Von der Ahe Library, Loyola Marymount Univ., Los Angeles, Calif.

Elaine Ezell, Library Media Specialist, Bowling Green Jr. High School, Ohio.

Andrew Ezergailis, Professor of History, Ithaca College, N.Y.

Ian Fairclough, Technical Services Manager, Yakima Valley Regional Library, Wash.

Roberto C. Ferrari, Arts and Humanities Reference Librarian, Florida Atlantic Univ., Boca Raton.

Judith J. Field, Senior Lecturer, Program for Library and Information Science, Wayne State Univ., Detroit.

Jerry D. Flack, Professor and President's Teaching Scholar, Univ. of Colorado, Colorado Springs.

Patricia Fleming, Professor, Faculty of Library and Information Science, Univ. of Toronto.

Michael Florman, Staff, Libraries Unlimited, Inc.

James H. Flynn Jr., (formerly) Operations Research Analyst, Dept. of Defense, Va.

Michael A. Foley, Honors Director, Marywood College, Scranton, Pa.

Harold O. Forshey, Assoc. Dean, Miami Univ., Oxford, Ohio.

Lynne M. Fox, Information Services and Outreach Librarian, Denison Library, Univ. of Colorado Health Sciences Center, Denver.

A. David Franklin, Professor of Music, Winthrop Univ., Rock Hill, S.C.

David K. Frasier, Asst. Librarian, Reference Dept., Indiana Univ., Bloomington.

Susan J. Freiband, Assoc. Professor, Graduate School of Librarianship, Univ. of Puerto Rico, San Juan.

David O. Friedrichs, Professor, Univ. of Scranton, Pa.

Ronald H. Fritze, Assoc. Professor, Dept. of History, Lamar Univ., Beaumont, Tex.

Paula Frosch, Assoc. Museum Librarian, Thomas J. Watson Library, Metropolitan Museum of Art, New York.

Thomas K. Fry, Assoc. Director, Public Services, Penrose Library, Univ. of Denver, Colo.

Sandra E. Fuentes, Public Services Librarian, Vanderbilt Divinity Library, Nashville, Tenn.

Ahmad Gamaluddin, Professor, School of Library Science, Clarion State College, Pa.

Vera Gao, Catalog Librarian, Auraria Library, Univ. of Colorado, Denver.

Zev Garber, Professor and Chair, Jewish Studies, Los Angeles Valley College, Calif.

Joan Garner, Staff, Libraries Unlimited, Inc.

Pamela J. Getchell, Staff, Libraries Unlimited, Inc.

Gerald L. Gill, Assoc. Professor/Business Reference Librarian, James Madison Univ., Harrisburg, Va.

John T. Gillespie, College Professor and Writer, New York.

Lois Gilmer, Library Director, Univ. of West Florida, Fort Walton Beach.

Elizabeth A. Ginno, Coordinator of Library Computer Information Resources, Univ. Library, California State Univ., Hayward.

Barbara B. Goldstein, Media Specialist, Magothy River Middle School, Arnold, Md.

Anthony Gottlieb, Asst. Clinical Professor, Univ. of Colorado School of Medicine, Denver.

Allie Wise Goudy, Professor, Western Illinois Univ., Macomb.

Shannon M. Graff, Staff, Libraries Unlimited, Inc.

Pamela M. Graham, Latin American and Iberian Studies Librarian, Columbia Univ., New York.

Rachael Green, Reference Librarian, Noel Memorial Library, Louisiana State Univ., Shreveport.

Richard W. Grefrath, Reference Librarian, Univ. of Nevada, Reno.

Laurel Grotzinger, Professor, Univ. Libraries, Western Michigan Univ., Kalamazoo.

Susan B. Hagloch, Director, Tuscarawas County Public Library, New Philadelphia, Ohio.

Blaine H. Hall, English Language and Literature Librarian, Harold B. Lee Library, Brigham Young Univ., Provo, Utah.

Deborah Hammer, Head, History, Travel, and Biography Div., Queens Borough Public Library, Jamaica, N.Y.

Gary Handman, Head, Media Resources Center, Univ. of California, Berkeley.

Roland C. Hansen, Readers' Services Librarian, the School of the Art Institute of Chicago.

Constance Harding, Retired High School English, Journalism, and Drama Teacher, Independence, Kans.

Kimberley D. Harris, Public Librarian, Newman Riga Library, Churchville, N.Y.

Ann Hartness, Asst. Head Librarian, Benson Latin American Collection, Univ. of Texas, Austin.

Ralph Hartsock, Senior Music Catalog Librarian, Univ. of North Texas, Denton.

Karen D. Harvey, Assoc. Dean for Academic Affairs, Univ. College, Univ. of Denver, Colo.

Joy Hastings, Toyota Research Library, Toyota Motor Sales, Calif.

Fred J. Hay, Librarian of the W. L. Eury Appalachian Collection and Assoc. Professor, Center for Appalachian Studies, Appalachian State Univ., Boone, N.C.

Lucy Heckman, Reference Librarian (Business-Economics), St. John's Univ. Library, Jamaica, N.Y.

David Henige, African Studies Bibliographer, Memorial Library, Univ. of Wisconsin, Madison.

Carol D. Henry, Librarian, Lyons Township High School, LaGrange, Ill.

Diana Tixier Herald, Librarian, Freelance Writer, Grand Junction, Colo.

Susan Davis Herring, Reference Librarian, Univ. of Alabama Library, Huntsville.

Mark Y. Herring, Dean of Library Services, Winthrop Univ., Dacus Library, Rock Hill, S.C.

Janet Hilbun, Student, Texas Woman's Univ., Denton.

Marquita Hill, Cooperating Professor of Chemical Engineering, Univ. of Maine, Orono.

V. W. Hill, Social Sciences Bibliographer, Memorial Library, Univ. of Wisconsin, Madison.

Susan Tower Hollis, Assoc. Dean and Center Director, Central New York Center of the State Univ. of New York.

Paul L. Holmer, Reference Librarian, Buley Library, Southern Connecticut State Univ., New Haven.

Leslie R. Homzie, Asst. Reference Librarian, Univ. of Delaware, Newark.

Sara Anne Hook, Assoc. Dean of the Faculties, Indiana Univ., Purdue Univ., Indianapolis.

Shirley L. Hopkinson, Professor, Div. of Library and Information Science, San Jose State Univ., Calif.

Marilynn Green Hopman, Librarian, NASA Johnson Space Center, Scientific and Technical Information Center, Houston, Tex.

C. D. Hurt, Director, Graduate Library School, Univ. of Arizona, Tucson.

Jonathan F. Husband, Program Chair of the Library/Reader Services Librarian, Henry Whittemore Library, Framingham State College, Mass.

Ludmila N. Ilyina, (retired) Professor, Natural Resources Institute, Winnipeg, Man.

David Isaacson, Asst. Head of Reference and Humanities Librarian, Waldo Library, Western Michigan Univ., Kalamazoo.

Barbara Ittner, Staff, Libraries Unlimited, Inc.

Eugene B. Jackson, Professor Emeritus, Graduate School of Library and Information Sciences, Univ. of Texas, Austin.

D. Barton Johnson, Professor Emeritus of Russian, Univ. of California, Santa Barbara.

Florence W. Jones, Librarian, Auraria Campus Library, Denver, Colo.

Kelly M. Jordan, Middleburg, Va.

Suzanne Julian, Public Services Librarian, Southern Utah Univ. Library, Cedar City.

Elaine F. Jurries, Coordinator of Serials Services, Auraria Library, Denver, Colo.

Sue Kamm, Head, Audio-Visual and Stack Maintenance Divisions, Inglewood Public Library, Calif.

Thomas A. Karel, Assoc. Director for Public Services, Shadek-Fackenthal Library, Franklin and Marshall College, Lancaster, Pa.

John Laurence Kelland, Reference Bibliographer for Life Sciences, Univ. of Rhode Island Library, Kingston.

Dean H. Keller, Assoc. Dean of Libraries, Kent State Univ., Ohio.

Barbara E. Kemp, Asst. Director, Dewey Graduate Library, State Univ. of New York, Albany.

Jackson Kesler, Professor of Theatre and Dance, Western Kentucky Univ., Bowling Green.

Robert H. Kieft, Coordinator for Reference Services and Collection Development, Magill Library, Haverford College, Pa.

Vicki J. Killion, Asst. Professor of Library Science and Pharmacy, Nursing and Health Sciences Librarian, Purdue Univ., West Lafayette, Ind.

Sung Ok Kim, Senior Asst. Librarian/Social Sciences Cataloging Librarian, Cornell Univ., Ithaca, N.Y.

Norman L. Kincaide, Citation Editor, Shepard's/McGraw-Hill, Inc., Colorado Springs, Colo.

Bruce Kingma, Assoc. Professor, State Univ. of New York at Albany, Albany, N.Y.

Janet J. Kosky, Mukwonago Community Library, Wis.

Lori D. Kranz, Freelance Editor; Assoc. Editor, *The Bloomsbury Review*, Denver, Colo.

Betsy J. Kraus, Librarian, Lovelace Respiratory Research Institute, National Environmental Respiratory Center, Albuquerque, N.Mex.

Carol Krismann, Head, William M. White Business Library, Univ. of Colorado, Boulder.

Marlene M. Kuhl, Library Manager, Baltimore County Public Library, Reisterstown Branch, Md.

Edward Kurdyla, Staff, Libraries Unlimited, Inc.

Robert V. Labaree, Reference/Public Services Librarian, Von KleinSmid Library, Univ. of Southern California, Los Angeles.

Linda L. Lam-Easton, Assoc. Professor, Dept. of Religious Studies, California State Univ., Northridge.

Lizbeth Langston, Reference Librarian, Univ. of California, Riverside.

Binh P. Le, Reference Librarian, Abington College, Pennsylvania State Univ., University Park.

Charles Leck, Professor of Biological Sciences, Rutgers Univ., New Brunswick, N.J.

Hwa-Wei Lee, Dean of Libraries, Ohio Univ., Athens.

R. S. Lehmann, Rocky Mountain BankCard System, Colorado National Bank, Denver.

Polin P. Lei, Assoc. Librarian, Information Services, Arizona Health Sciences Library, Tucson.

Richard A. Leiter, Director, Law Library, Howard Univ., Washington, D.C.

John A. Lent, Drexel Hill, Pa.

Tze-chung Li, Professor, Graduate School of Library and Information Science, Rosary College, River Forest, Ill.

Charlotte Lindgren, Professor Emerita of English, Emerson College, Boston.

Larry Lobel, Virtuoso Keyboard Services, Petaluma, Calif.

Koraljka Lockhardt, Publications Editor, San Francisco Opera, Calif.

Jeffrey E. Long, Interlibrary Loan/Photocopy Services Library Assistant, Lamar Soutter Library/Univ. of Massachusetts Medical Center, Worcester.

Marit S. MacArthur, Reference Librarian, Auraria Libraries, Univ. of Colorado, Denver.

Sara R. Mack, Professor Emerita, Dept. of Library Science, Kutztown Univ., Pa.

Theresa Maggio, Head of Public Services, Southwest Georgia Regional Library, Bainbridge.

Judith A. Matthews, Physics-Astronomy/Science Reference Librarian, Main Library, Michigan State Univ., East Lansing.

John Maxymuk, Reference Librarian, Paul Robeson Library, Rutgers Univ., Camden, N.J.

George Louis Mayer, (formerly) Senior Principal Librarian, New York Public Library and Part-Time Librarian, Adelphi, Manhattan Center and Brooklyn College.

Peter H. McCracken, Odegaard Undergraduate Library, Univ. of Washington, Seattle.

Christopher Michael McDonough, Lecturer, Dept. of Classics, Princeton Univ., N.J.

Dana McDougald, Lead Media Specialist, Learning Resources Center, Cedar Shoals High School, Athens, Ga.

Glenn S. McGuigan, Reference Librarian, Penn State, Abington.

Peter Zachary McKay, Business Librarian, Univ. of Florida Libraries, Gainesville.

Robert B. McKee, Professor, Mechanical Engineering, Univ. of Nevada, Reno.

Marian B. McLeod, Professor of Speech Communication and Theater, Trenton State College, N.J.

Margo B. Mead, Technology Instruction Librarian, Louis M. Salmon Library, Univ. of Alabama, Huntsville.

Lillian R. Mesner, Mesner Information Connections, Lexington, Ky.

Michael G. Messina, Assoc. Professor, Dept. of Forest Science, Texas A & M Univ., College Station.

G. Douglas Meyers, Chair, Dept. of English, Univ. of Texas, El Paso.

Robert Michaelson, Head Librarian, Seeley G. Mudd Library for Science and Engineering, Northwestern Univ., Evanston, Ill.

Bogdan Mieczkowski, Professor of Economics, Ithaca College, N.Y.

Seiko Mieczkowski, Cocoa Beach, Fla.

Ann E. Miller, Federal Documents Librarian, Perkins Library, Duke Univ., Durham, N.C.

Bill Miller, Director of Libraries, Florida Atlantic Univ., Boca Raton.

Richard A. Miller, Professor of Economics, Wesleyan Univ., Middletown, Conn.

Carol L. Mitchell, Southeast Asian Bibliographic Services Librarian, General Library System, Univ. of Wisconsin, Madison.

James Moffet, Head, Reference Dept, Baldwin Public Library, Birmingham, Mich.

Paul A. Mogren, Head of Reference, Marriott Library, Univ. of Utah, Salt Lake City.

Janet Mongan, Research Officer, Cleveland State Univ. Library, Ohio.

Terry Ann Mood, Head of Collection Development, Univ. of Colorado, Denver.

Anne C. Moore, Electronic Resources Librarian, New Mexico State Univ., Alamogordo.

Gerald D. Moran, Director, McCartney Library, Geneva College, Beaver Falls, Pa.

Betty J. Morris, Staff, Libraries Unlimited, Inc.

K. Mulliner, Asst. to the Director of Libraries, Ohio Univ. Library, Athens.

Walt Mundkowsky, Freelance Film and Music Critic, Beverly Hills, Calif.

Craig A. Munsart, Teacher, Jefferson County Public Schools, Golden, Colo.

Paul M. Murphy III, Director of Marketing, PMX Medical, Denver, Colo.

James M. Murray, U.S. Courts Library, Spokane, Wash.

Charles Neuringer, Professor of Psychology and Theatre and Film, Univ. of Kansas, Lawrence.

Kerie L. Nickel, Librarian, St. Mary's College of Maryland, St. Mary's City.

Joseph Z. Nitecki, Professor Emeritus, School of Information Science and Policy, State Univ. of New York, Albany.

Eric R. Nitschke, Reference Librarian, Robert W. Woodruff Library, Emory Univ., Atlanta, Ga.

Christopher W. Nolan, Head, Reference Services, Maddux Library, Trinity Univ., San Antonio, Tex.

Carol L. Noll, Volunteer Librarian, Schimelpfenig Middle School, Plano, Tex.

O. Gene Norman, Head, Reference Dept., Indiana State Univ. Libraries, Terre Haute.

David G. Nowak, Asst. Professor and Reference Librarian, Mississippi State Univ. Libraries, Mississippi State.

Marshall E. Nunn, Professor, Dept. of History, Glendale Community College, Calif.

Herbert W. Ockerman, Professor, Ohio State Univ., Columbus.

Lawrence Olszewski, Manager, OCLC Information Center, Dublin, Ohio.

Ray Olszewski, Independent Consultant, Palo Alto, Calif.

Berniece M. Owen, Coordinator, Library Technical Services, Portland Community College, Oreg.

Mark Padnos, Humanities Reference Librarian, Mina Rees Library, Graduate School and Univ. Center, City Univ. of New York.

Robert Palmieri, Professor Emeritus, School of Music, Kent State Univ., Ohio.

J. Carlyle Parker, Librarian and Univ. Archivist Emeritus, Library, California State Univ., Turlock.

Gary L. Parsons, Reference Librarian, Florida Atlantic Univ., Boca Raton.

Gari-Anne Patzwald, Freelance Editor and Indexer, Lexington, Ky.

Harry E. Pence, Professor of Chemistry, State Univ. of New York, Oneonta.

Karin Pendle, Professor of Musicology, Univ. of Cincinnati, Ohio.

Julia Perez, Biological Sciences Librarian, Michigan State Univ. Libraries, East Lansing.

Glenn Petersen, Professor of Anthropology and International Affairs, Graduate Center and Baruch College, City Univ. of New York.

C. Michael Phillips, Asst. Reference Librarian, Robert Scott Small Library, College of Charleston, S.C.

Diane K. Podell, Professor, C. W. Post Campus, Long Island Univ., N.Y.

Phillip P. Powell, Asst. Reference Librarian, Robert Scott Small Library, College of Charleston, S.C.

Ann E. Prentice, Dean, College of Library and Information Services, Univ. of Maryland, College Park.

Pete Prunkl, Freelance Writer, Hickory, N.C.

Randall Rafferty, Reference Librarian, Mississippi State Univ. Library, Mississippi State.

Varadaraja V. Raman, Professor of Physics and Humanities, Rochester Institute of Technology, N.Y.

Jack Ray, Asst. Director, Loyola/Notre Dame Library, Baltimore, Md.

Nancy P. Reed, Information Services Manager, Paducah Public Library, Ky.

Diane B. Rhodes, Life Sciences and Agriculture Librarian, Arizona State Univ., Tempe.

Robert B. Marks Ridinger, Head, Electronic Information Resources Management Dept., Univ. Libraries, Northern Illinois Univ., De Kalb.

Constance Rinaldo, Ernst Magr Library, Museum of Comparative Zoology, Harvard Univ., Hanover, N.H.

Cari Ringelheim, Staff, Libraries Unlimited, Inc.

Randy Roberts, Professor of History, Purdue Univ., Ind.

Anne F. Roberts, Adjunct Professor, School of Education, State Univ. of New York, Albany.

William B. Robison, Asst. Professor, History, Southeastern Louisiana Univ., Hammond.

John M. Robson, Institute Librarian, Rose-Hulman Institute of Technology, Terre Haute, Ind.

Deborah V. Rollins, Reference Librarian, Univ. of Maine, Orono.

John B. Romeiser, Professor of French and Dept. Head, Univ. of Tennessee, Knoxville.

Samuel Rothstein, Professor Emeritus, School of Librarianship, Univ. of British Columbia, Vancouver.

Michele Russo, Acting Director, Franklin D. Schurz Library, Indiana Univ., South Bend.

Nadine Salmons, Technical Services Librarian, Fort Carson's Grant Library, Colo.

Edmund F. SantaVicca, Librarian, Information Commons, Estrella Mountain Community College Center, Litchfield Park, Ariz.

Diane Schmidt, Asst. Biology Librarian, Univ. of Illinois, Urbana.

Steven J. Schmidt, Assoc. Librarian, Indiana Univ./Purdue Univ. at Indianapolis Libraries.

Willa Schmidt, Reference Librarian, Univ. of Wisconsin, Madison.

John P. Schmitt, Regis Univ. Library, Denver, CO.

Ralph Lee Scott, Assoc. Professor, East Carolina Univ. Library, Greenville, N.C.

Robert A. Seal, Univ. Librarian, Texas Christian Univ., Fort Worth.

Margretta Reed Seashore, Professor of Genetics and Pediatrics, Yale Univ. School of Medicine, New Haven, Conn.

David Selden, Law Librarian, National Indian Law Librarian, Boulder, Colo.

Karen Selden, Catalog Librarian, Univ. of Colorado Law Library, Boulder.

Ravindra Nath Sharma, Library Director, West Virginia State College, Institute.

Deborah Sharp, Head Librarian, Lexmark Information Center, Univ. of Kentucky, Lexington.

John A. Shuler, Documents Librarian, Univ. of Illinois, Chicago.

Leena Siegelbaum, Bibliographer of Eastern European Law, Harvard Univ., Cambridge, Mass.

Esther R. Sinofsky, Library Media Teacher, Alexander Hamilton High School, Los Angeles, Calif.

Robert M. Slade, Independent Consultant, North Vancouver, B.C.

Mary Ellen Snodgrass, Freelance Writer, Charlotte, N.C.

Steven W. Sowards, Head of Main Reference Library, Michigan State Univ. Libraries, East Lansing.

Jerri Spoehel, Freelance Writer and Editor, Las Cruces, N.Mex.

Jan S. Squire, Reference and Instructional Services Librarian, Univ. of Northern Colorado, Greeley.

Karen Y. Stabler, Head of Information Services, New Mexico State Univ. Library, Las Cruces.

Victor L. Stater, Assoc. Professor of History, Louisiana State Univ., Baton Rouge.

Kay M. Stebbins, Coordinator Librarian, Louisiana State Univ., Shreveport.

Lillian Jane Steele, Historian, Old Salem, Inc., Winston-Salem, N.C.

Norman D. Stevens, Director Emeritus, Univ. of Connecticut Libraries, Storrs.

John W. Storey, Professor of History, Lamar Univ., Beaumont, Tex.

Susan D. Strickland, (formerly) Staff, Libraries Unlimited, Inc.

William C. Struning, Professor, Seton Hall Univ., South Orange, N.J.

Bruce Stuart, Professor and Parke-Davis Chair, Univ. of Maryland, Baltimore.

Mila C. Su, Senior Asst. Librarian, Pennsylvania State Univ., Altoona.

Timothy E. Sullivan, Asst. Professor of Economics, Towson State Univ., Md.

Richard H. Swain, Reference Librarian, West Chester Univ., Pa.

James H. Sweetland, Assoc. Professor, School of Library and Information Science, Univ. of Wisconsin, Milwaukee.

Nigel Tappin, (formerly) General Librarian, North York Public Library, Ont.

Martha Tarlton, Head, Humanities and Social Sciences, Univ. of North Texas Libraries, Denton.

Glynys R. Thomas, Sawyer Library, Suffolk Univ., Boston.

Katherine Margaret Thomas, (formerly) Biologist, Long Point Bird Observatory, Toronto.

Paul H. Thomas, Head, Catalog Dept., Hoover Institution Library, Stanford Univ., Calif.

Peter Thorpe, Professor Emeritus, Univ. of Colorado, Denver.

Linda D. Tietjen, Senior Instructor, Instruction and Reference Services, Auraria Library, Denver, Colo.

Bruce H. Tiffney, Assoc. Professor of Geology and Biological Sciences, Univ. of California, Santa Barbara.

Andrew G. Torok, Assoc. Professor, Northern Illinois Univ., De Kalb.

Mary L. Trenerry, Media Specialist, Millard Public Schools, Omaha, Neb.

Dean Tudor, Professor, School of Journalism, Ryerson Polytechnical Institute, Toronto.

Elias H. Tuma, Professor of Economics, Univ. of California, Davis.

Diane J. Turner, Science/Engineering Liaison, Auraria Library, Univ. of Colorado, Denver.

Robert L. Turner Jr., Librarian and Asst. Professor, Radford Univ., Va.

Michele Tyrrell, Media Specialist, Arundel Senior High School, Gambrills, Md.

Arthur R. Upgren, Professor of Astronomy and Director, Van Vleck Observatory, Wesleyan Univ., Middletown, Conn.

Nancy L. Van Atta, Reference Librarian, Dayton and Montgomery County Public Library, Dayton, Ohio.

Phyllis J. Van Orden, Professor, School of Library and Information Science, Seattle, Wash.

Susanna Van Sant, Librarian, Michigan State Univ., East Lansing.

Debra S. Van Tassel, Reference Librarian, Univ. of Colorado, Boulder.

Vandelia L. VanMeter, Professor and Library Director, Spalding Univ., Louisville, Ky.

Dario J. Villa, Reference Librarian/Bibliographer, Ronald Williams Library, Northeastern Illinois Univ., Chicago.

Graham R. Walden, Assoc. Professor, Information Services Department, Ohio State Univ., Columbus.

Richard S. Watts, Coordinator, Technical Processing Dept., San Bernardino County Library, Calif.

J. E. Weaver, Dept. of Economics, Drake Univ., Des Moines, Iowa.

Karen T. Wei, Head, Asian Library, Univ. of Illinois, Urbana.

Michael Weinberg, Reference Librarian, Ronald Williams Library, Northeastern Illinois Library, Chicago.

Emily L. Werrell, Reference/Instructional Services Librarian, Northern Kentucky Univ., Highland Heights.

Andrew B. Wertheimer, Librarian, Woodman Astronomical Library, Univ. of Wisconsin, Madison.

Lee Weston, Assoc. Professor/Reference Librarian, James A. Michener Library, Univ. of Northern Colorado, Greeley.

Lucille Whalen, Dean of Graduate Programs, Immaculate Heart College Center, Los Angeles, Calif.

David L. White, Professor, History Dept., Appalachian State Univ., Boone, N.C.

Robert L. Wick, Asst. Professor and Fine Arts Bibliographer, Auraria Library, Univ. of Colorado, Denver.

Agnes H. Widder, Humanities Bibliographer, Michigan State Univ., East Lansing.

Albert Wilhelm, Professor of English, Tennessee Technological Univ., Cookeville.

Frances C. Wilkinson, Director, Acquisitions and Serials Dept., Univ. of New Mexico, Albuquerque.

Connie Williams, Information Manager, Merrick & Company, Aurora, Colo.

Frank L. Wilson, Professor and Head, Dept. of Political Science, Purdue Univ., West Lafayette, Ind.

Mark A. Wilson, Professor of Geology, College of Wooster, Ohio.

Glenn R. Wittig, Director of Library Services, Criswell College, Dallas, Tex.

Bohdan S. Wynar, Staff, Libraries Unlimited, Inc.

Eveline L. Yang, Manager, Information Delivery Programs, Auraria Library, Univ. of Colorado, Denver.

Hope Yelich, Reference Librarian, Earl Gregg Swem Library, College of William and Mary, Williamsburg, Va.

Henry E. York, Head, Collection Management, Cleveland State Univ., Ohio.

Arthur P. Young, Director, Northern Illinois Libraries, Northern Illinois Univ., De Kalb.

Louis G. Zelenka, Jacksonville Public Library System, Fla.

Magda Želinská-Ferl, Professor/Faculty Advisor, Union Institute, Los Angeles, Calif.

L. Zgusta, Professor of Linguistics and the Classics and Member of the Center for Advance Study, Univ. of Illinois, Urbana.

Xiao (Shelley) Yan Zhang, Cataloger, Mississippi State Univ. Library, Mississippi State.

Anita Zutis, Adjunct Librarian, Queensborough Community College, Bayside, N.Y.

Journals Cited

FORM OF CITATION	JOURNAL TITLE
BL	*Booklist*
BR	*Book Report*
C&RL	*College & Research Libraries*
C&RL News	*College & Research Libraries News*
Choice	*Choice*
EL	*Emergency Librarian*
JAL	*Journal of Academic Librarianship*
LJ	*Library Journal*
RBB	*Reference Books Bulletin*
RQ	*RQ*
RUSQ	*Reference & User Services Quarterly*
SLJ	*School Library Journal*
SLMQ	*School Library Media Quarterly*
TL	*Teacher Librarian*
VOYA	*Voice of Youth Advocates*

Part I
GENERAL REFERENCE WORKS

1 General Reference Works

ACRONYMS AND ABBREVIATIONS

1. **Acronyms, Initialisms, & Abbreviations Dictionary.** 25th ed. Mary Rose Bonk, ed. Farmington Hills, Mich., Gale, 1999. 3v. $610.00/set. ISBN 0-7876-2423-3. ISSN 0270-4404.

Earlier editions of the *Acronyms, Initialisms, & Abbreviations Dictionary* published by Gale have been reviewed many times in previous ARBA volumes and there is no need to repeat former comments. The 25th edition, published in 1999, is no different from older editions. According to the publisher, there is an increased coverage in most areas with some 15,000 new terms and updates. Readers considering this title for purchase should keep in mind that review in ARBA 97 of the 21st edition (published in 1996) shows that edition sold at $285. Now the price has more than doubled.—**Bohdan S. Wynar**

2. **International Acronyms, Initialisms, & Abbreviations Dictionary: A Guide to over 169,000 International Acronyms....** 4th ed. Mary Rose Bonk and Regie A. Carlton, eds. Farmington Hills, Mich., Gale, 1997. 3v. $190.00. ISBN 0-8103-7437-4. ISSN 0743-0523.

This standard guide covers some 150 countries with most terms of current interest. The major criterion for inclusion is that a term be clearly international in scope or be continental, regional, national, or local to an area. A very broad range of subjects is covered, including abbreviations for societies, military terms, political parties, trade and commercial terms, government, research centers, and so on. Many terms have been enhanced by the addition of English translations. All in all, it is a useful source for most larger libraries and research institutions.—**Bohdan S. Wynar**

ALMANACS

3. **The Cambridge Factfinder.** 3d ed. David Crystal, ed. New York, Cambridge University Press, 1998. 891p. maps. index. $16.95pa. ISBN 0-521-63770-8.

Divided into broad areas of knowledge, this volume appears to be a hybrid genre containing the best elements of an almanac, a desk encyclopedia, and a mini atlas. Facts are presented regarding the universe, Earth, the environment, natural history, human beings, history, human geography, society, religion and mythology, communications, science and technology, arts and culture, knowledge, and sports and games. The largest section presents profiles of individual nations of the world, indicating time zone, area, population total, history, and so on. Small black-and-white profile maps are included, highlighting major cities and geographical features of each nation.

Although the world chronology ends in 1997, and some of the world records and prizes need to be updated, the majority of information included remains valid and factual. A great deal of the information has been culled from other Cambridge reference tools, and is merely repackaged here in a more portable and condensed version. A full index of some 110 pages supplements the work. This work is recommended for any ready-reference collection, either as a complement to or replacement for other almanacs.

—**Edmund F. SantaVicca**

4. **The World Almanac and Book of Facts 2000.** millennium ed. Mahwah, N.J., World Almanac Books; distr., New York, St. Martin's Press, 1999. 1024p. illus. maps. index. $24.95; $10.95pa. ISBN 0-88687-848-9; 0-88687-847-0pa.

For 132 years *The World Almanac and Book of Facts* has been keeping people up-to-date on politics, employment, technology, entertainment, sports, and many other subjects. This millennium edition features new Internet information (including many Websites), up-to-date maps and flags, winners of awards and prizes in 1999, crime statistics, and advances in health and nutrition. Three prominent men of our day contribute essays to this work: Robert Reich writes about technology and tribalism, John Updike lists the 10 greatest works of literature, and Arthur Schlesinger Jr. discusses the most influential people of the 2d millennium. There is a section on memorable quotes of the century, as well as a list of predictions that failed. As always the most important news of the past year is discussed, including the Clinton impeachment trial, the war in Kosovo, and obituaries of the deceased. Because this almanac will find readers among both those fascinated by trivia and those doing important research, this all-encompassing reference source will be a welcome addition to any public, school, or academic library.—**Shannon M. Graff**

BIBLIOGRAPHY

National and Trade Bibliography

International

5. **Guide to Microforms in Print 1998: Incorporating International Microforms in Print.** New Providence, N.J., R. R. Bowker, 1998. 2v. $430.00/set. ISBN 3-598-11365-X. ISSN 0163-8386.

The *Guide to Microforms in Print* provides comprehensive information on international microform publications. The form and content of entries in the guide include title, author(s) or editor(s), place of publication, date of publication, collation information, type of microform code, price, ISBN, extra distributor or co-publisher information, further title information, publisher code, and subject classes.

The guide is divided into a subject guide, an index of persons as subject, and an alphabetic index to publishers and distributors. The section on publishers and distributors contains full ordering information for the microforms in the guide. The subject guide provides subject access to international microform publications. The subject classification used in the subject guide is based on Dewey Decimal Classification, with some modified classes that are explained in the foreword to the guide. A finding aid for subject numbers is also included. The index of persons as subject can be consulted when looking for a collection or a nonfiction title dealing with a specific individual.—**Frances C. Wilkinson**

United States

6. **Books in Print 1998-99.** 51st ed. New Providence, N.J., R. R. Bowker, 1998. 9v. $525.00/set. ISBN 0-8352-4026-6. ISSN 0068-0214.

The 51st edition contains over 1,449,000 active titles and features over 179,000 new titles and more than 183,000 new ISBNs. Bound in 9 volumes, the set includes 4 volumes arranged by title and 4 by author. The 9th volume is devoted to publisher information and includes names, addresses (including e-mail and Website addresses), and ordering information for all of the publishers mentioned in the author and title volumes. *Books in Print* is also available in several electronic versions—*Books in Print on CD*, online access through American Library Services, CARL, Dialog, DRA, EBSCO Publishing, and others, as listed on page vii in the preface to the 1st volume. Descriptions on how to use this standard title familiar to most libraries are provided on pages ix-xi. Earlier versions of *Books in Print* have been reviewed in previous ARBA editions.—**Bohdan S. Wynar**

Canada

7. **Canadian Books in Print 1999: Author and Title Index.** Marian Butler, ed. Buffalo, N.Y., University of Toronto Press, 1999. 1352p. $165.00. ISBN 0-8020-4924-9. ISSN 0068-8398.

8. **Canadian Books in Print 1999: Subject Index.** Marian Butler, ed. Buffalo, N.Y., University of Toronto Press, 1999. 806p. $145.00. ISBN 0-8020-4925-7. ISSN 0315-1999.

Canadian Books in Print is a standard reference tool. The 1999 edition, as with previous editions, was compiled from listings obtained from Canadian publishers whose information was received before August 31, 1998. This title contains two volumes—author and title index and subject index. The *Author and Title Index* contains 44,157 entries, including 3,842 entries with a 1998 imprint. It is divided into 4 parts: author index, title index, publisher index, and publisher ISBN prefixes. The *Subject Index* covers 44,157 publications that appear in 51,047 individual entries. This volume is divided into three sections. The subject list contains a complete alphabetic list of all subject headings used in the index and lists all books in the author and title index of *Canadian Books in Print*. The subject headings used in the index are based on the Library of Congress List of Subject Headings. The publisher index is an alphabetic list of all publishers. Because listings in this book are based on information supplied by publishers before the books are published, the editor cannot always claim absolute accuracy in bibliographic detail. The editor also reminds readers that by the time this book is published, some titles listed will be out of print and prices will have changed. *Canadian Books in Print* has bridged the gap between Bowker's *Books in Print* (see entry 6) and *Whitaker's British Books in Print* (see entry 9). It is a good reference resource for all kinds of libraries and for anyone who needs information about Canadian books or is interested in the Canadian publishing industry.

—**Xiao (Shelley) Yan Zhang**

Great Britain

9. **Whitaker's Books in Print 1999: The Reference Catalogue of Current Literature.** New Providence, N.J., R. R. Bowker, 1999. 4v. $700.00/set. ISBN 0-85021-274-X. ISSN 0953-0398.

Published in 4 volumes, *Whitaker's Books in Print* is a standard title in the British book trade with a well-known and long tradition going back to 1874. Joseph Whitaker, creator of *Whitaker's Almanac*, also publishes the *Reference Catalogue of Current Literature* and, since 1968, has maintained the system of Standard Book Numbers. *Whitaker's Books in Print* lists titles published in the United Kingdom and available to the general public through the book trade. English-language titles published in continental Europe are also recorded along with titles that have a sole distributor in the United Kingdom, including American Books.

The current edition contains publishing details for some 887,000 titles from 34,000 publishers. The updating procedures are continuous. Each title that is recorded week by week in the *Bookseller* goes forward to *Whitaker's Books in Print*, including price ranges and deletions of out-of-print titles. The information on several segments of the structure of British bibliography is provided in "Guides to Books Available in the UK and Their Publishers" (pp. 10–11), describing weekly, monthly (the British Bibliography), bimonthly, quarterly, biannually, annual, and multi-year services. *Whitaker's Books in Print* is a standard source for all university and larger public and scientific libraries.—**Bohdan S. Wynar**

BIOGRAPHY

International

10. **Abridged Encyclopedia of World Biography.** Farmington Hills, Mich., Gale, 1999. 6v. illus. index. $495.00/set. ISBN 0-7876-3904-4.

This set is an abridgement of Gale's *Encyclopedia of World Biography* (2d ed.; see ARBA 99, entry 23). It provides complete biographical sketches for more than 2,000 well-known individuals and brief sketches on approximately 5,000 others. Each sketch includes key biographical data, such as date and place of birth, date of death (if deceased), nationality, and occupation. The "complete" or lengthier sketches are accompanied by portraits and suggests for further reading.

The encyclopedia is organized into six volumes covering the areas of American history, world history, literature, science and mathematics, arts and entertainment, and social sciences. Each volume contains a master name index, a nationality index, and an occupation index to the entire set.

The stated purpose of this set is to serve as "a comprehensive source of information on over 7,000 of those people who, for their contributions to human culture and society, have reputations that stand the test of time." Its greatest strength is its coverage of contemporary figures, particularly women and minorities. In some cases, this appears to be at the exclusion of prominent earlier figures provided only brief sketches. Because the set seems to be primarily intended for students, it would benefit from the addition of cross-references for names with variant spellings, such as Muammar Al-Gaddafi. One inaccuracy is the substitution of a photograph of Japanese Admiral Togo for a picture of Hideki Tojo. It is apparent that the editorial staff attempted to make the content as up-to-date as possible, given that the sketch on William Jefferson Clinton includes events of the first half of 1999. [R: LJ, 15 Nov 99, p. 58]—**Martha Tarlton**

11. **ARBA Guide to Biographical Resources 1986-1997.** Robert L. Wick and Terry Ann Mood, eds. Englewood, Colo., Libraries Unlimited, 1998. 604p. index. $60.00. ISBN 1-56308-453-8.

Inasmuch as biographical information is probably the subject most requested of reference librarians, they will certainly welcome this guide to the most useful collective biographies of the period from 1986 to 1997. As will book selectors, since biographical dictionaries are not only expensive but also often of questionable quality.

The *ARBA Guide* offers 1180 reviews, succinct but critical, of titles that were favorably reviewed in the *American Reference Books Annual* or "selected due to the importance of the work." (p. xvi). The reviews in the guide are all signed (the list of contributors impressive) and, where appropriate, have been updated or otherwise revised. Each entry provides full bibliographical information and includes citations to reviews that have appeared in the standard selection journals such as *Choice* and *Booklist*.

The *ARBA Guide* is divided into two major parts: International and National Biographies and Biographies in Professional Fields; the former is subdivided by geographic area (20), the latter by subject field (24). Thus, for example, readers can find conveniently grouped together collective biographies regarding Romania or the performing arts. Finer classifications can be obtained through the quite comprehensive subject index.

The *ARBA Guide* is a well-made book, featuring large type, generous margins, and a sturdy binding; physically it is a good value for the price. It is textually valuable as well, even for libraries already owning the ARBA volumes from where most of this material has been culled. This compilation will offer a convenient arrangement and useful revision. For libraries lacking ARBA the guide is almost a necessity. [R: Choice, May 99, p. 1587]—**Samuel Rothstein**

12. **Chambers Biographical Dictionary.** 6th ed. Melanie Parry, ed. New York, Larousse Kingfisher Chambers, 1997. 2008p. $55.00. ISBN 0-550-16060-4.

This edition of the standard *Chambers Biographical Dictionary* is a valuable and reliable single-volume collection of about 17,300 biographical entries. Previous editions were published in the United States as *Cambridge Biographical Dictionary* (see ARBA 95, entry 25). Recent Cambridge titles and editions have muddied the bibliographic waters.

Although concise and somewhat formulaic, the writing is still intelligent and readable, incorporating some interesting analysis among the facts. Several hundred individuals receive closer scrutiny in larger, boxed biographies, which contain quotes and abbreviated bibliographies. The book's subjects, however, are overwhelmingly male. Parry edited the *Larousse Dictionary of Women* (see ARBA 98, entry 24), and one would think she would be more aware than anyone of remarkable women's lives that belong in this volume. Unfortunately, the entries here are about 87 percent male; a truly comprehensive biographical dictionary needs a better balance.

Chronological coverage is heavily biased toward the present day. Based on death dates, 34 percent of the subjects died in the twentieth century, 19 percent in the nineteenth century, and 19 percent are still living. The remaining 28 percent cover the rest of time, from Adam and Eve to the eighteenth century. Individuals from all disciplines and all fields of enterprise are included, and the volume, although overwhelmingly Anglo-American, includes subjects from other cultures as well.

As a single-volume work, the *Chambers Biographical Dictionary* should be a useful source, but readers seeking more than a paragraph on an individual will likely need to look elsewhere. Its small size and price, plus its extensive, although biased, coverage make it a useful addition to any library.

—**Peter H. McCracken**

13. **Encyclopedia of World Biography on CD-ROM.** [CD-ROM]. Farmington Hills, Mich., Gale, 1999. Minimum system requirements: IBM or compatible 386. Double-speed CD-ROM. DOS 5.0. Windows 3.1 or higher. 8MB RAM. 5MB hard disk space. SVGA graphics card and monitor (256 colors). Mouse. $975.00. ISBN 0-7876-2944-8.

Using a myriad of ways to search the database, the *Encyclopedia of World Biography on CD-ROM* provides researchers with information on 7,200 of the "most frequently studied individuals from ancient times to the present." The program reflects the content of the newest edition of the print version, as it incorporates the twentieth-century supplements into one easy-to-use version. Searches can be conducted by entering a name, a subject, a place, a title of a work, or using a timeline; the software also allows for full-text searching and customized searches. Each search results in a list of hits, relevancy ranked. The user is thus immediately provided with cross-referenced information. Photographs accompany the articles.

Installation of the program using the Windows 95 platform was quite simple, and as long as the program will not be used by more than 30 users simultaneously or be used in conjunction with dial-in access, the installer will not have to go through the more tedious "unlock" process. Gale provides for a 30-day review period, but unless a full installation is done (which requires invoice and customer numbers), printing and downloading functions are blocked. Help is provided onscreen, and Gale provides a comprehensive user's manual and help card.

Navigation within the program presented no difficulties; the toolbar is easily understood and uses familiar icons. Entire articles can be printed or the user may print selected text; photographs can be printed without text. Saving text is also familiar; the TXT extension is used for the default. Information regarding correct bibliographic citation is given in the user's manual and on the help card.

The print version of this work has long been a basic resource for reliable biographical information. The CD-ROM version provides an alternative way to provide this information, but unless the library or media center will be networking the product, its cost (about half of the cost of the 19-volume set) may be prohibitive. [R: BR, Sept/Oct 99, p. 86; Choice, Dec 99, p. 684]—**Michele Tyrrell**

14. **Encyclopedia of World Biography Supplement.** Farmington Hills, Mich., Gale, 1999. 561p. illus. index. $99.00. ISBN 0-7876-2945-6. ISSN 1099-7326.

The 1st edition of this encyclopedia was published 25 years ago and the 2d edition was published in 1998 (see ARBA 99, entry 231). This standard work contains information on nearly 7,000 internationally known individuals who made substantial contributions to our society. It should be noted that the 2d edition includes all entries from the 1st edition and its 3 supplements, with some updating, along with 530 new biographies especially prepared for the 2d edition. This new supplement to the 17-volume set covers 198 new biographies as well as 2 obituary entries for individuals appearing in volumes 1-17. It includes such figures as Tony Blair, the British prime minister, and military figures who died many years ago, such as Walter Bedell Smith (1895–1961), chief of staff to General Dwight D. Eisenhower, and Anne Boleyn, Queen of England (1504–1536). The coverage of important personalities, dead some years ago or alive, will continue in subsequent supplements. [R: BL, 15 Nov 98, p. 610]—**Bohdan S. Wynar**

15. **International Who's Who 1998-99.** 62d ed. London, Europa; distr., Farmington Hills, Mich., Gale, 1998. 1726p. $340.00. ISBN 1-85743-040-9.

After 62 years of consistent publishing, the venerable *International Who's Who* annual edition remains the standard for every biographical reference source attempting to accomplish a global perspective within 2,000 pages. The entries are short, accurate, and cover the multitude of international names from all walks of life—politics, academia, philanthropy, business, and literature, to name only a few. An excellent source to keep around for a quick lookup of an unfamiliar name, and nothing on the World Wide Web can beat its organization, reputation, or rapidity of access.—**John A. Shuler**

16. **Who's Who in the World 1999.** 16th ed. New Providence, N.J., Marquis Who's Who/Reed Reference Publishing, 1999. 19559. index. $389.95. ISBN 0-8379-1121-4. ISSN 0083-9825.

17. **Who's Who 1999: An Annual Biographical Dictionary.** 151st ed. New York, St. Martin's Press, 1999. 2239p. $240.00. ISBN 0-312-21952-0.

Patterned after previous editions, these two alphabetically listed, biographical tomes have many similarities. Both books are geared to the researcher or historian who wants "access to basic data on so many of the world's currently prominent citizens" (see ARBA 97, entry 29). This year's editions of *Who's Who* (WW) contains more than 30,000 biographies, and the biennial, *Who's Who in the World* (WWITW), contains 45,000 globally noteworthy persons from almost every professional field. Both references include a preface, abbreviations used, and biographies. WWITW also includes standards of admission, key to information, and alphabetic practices as well as excellent coverage of public officials. WW features historical notes, an obituary of biographees who died from September 1997 to October 1998, the present British royal family, and an editor's note.

Each entry is in the same format—full name and present post or occupation, vital statistics, family details, education, career in chronological order, publications, avocations, and address. Among some of the many additional features in WWITW are information on military service, awards, professional and association memberships, and political affiliations. Reliance on questionnaires for factual data, and in some instances the staff, is made to compile each entry in WWITW. An anonymous editorial board selected the "people who, through their careers, affect the political, economic, scientific and artistic life of the country" in WW. Not all similarities, however, are positive. Cross-references are nearly nonexistent in both books. An attempt is made with the 1,008-page professional index in WWITW. Both volumes' print size is minuscule and requires a magnifier to read easily. And as stated in a review of WW in ARBA 96: "The entrants [continue to] hail disproportionately from Great Britain" (see entry 34). These expensive reference works are valuable and rich in detail, but other biographical sources should be consulted in order to fill in gaps.—**Nadine Salmons**

United States

18. **Dictionary of Missouri Biography.** Lawrence O. Christensen, William E. Foley, Gary R. Kremer, and Kenneth H. Winn, eds. Columbia, Mo., University of Missouri Press, 1999. 832p. index. $49.95. ISBN 0-8262-1222-0.

This dictionary provides detailed biographical sketches of more than 700 people with a connection to Missouri, including a number of individuals not included in *American National Biography* (Oxford University Press, 1999). And, in cases where individuals are covered in both sources, the Missouri dictionary appears to provide more details. To their credit, the editors appear to have encouraged their contributors to employ a lively and accessible style. Although not applied with total consistency, the style is a noticeable improvement on the dry, formulaic approach used in many biographical sources. The articles are signed and include references. There are, however, no illustrations. Although this omission is understandable, both in terms of space and cost, it limits the attraction of this source for younger users. A somewhat idiosyncratic subject index is included. For example, it lists Native Americans under that heading, yet refers to "Indian Diplomacy" and "Indian Wars." This will be an essential acquisition for libraries in the Midwest. Of course, many librarians and their users interested in finding biographical information on a particular individual may not know if that person had a connection to Missouri. If and when this source is indexed in the *Biographical and Genealogical Master Index* (1999 ed.; see ARBA 99, entry 404), its usefulness will be greatly enhanced for all libraries.—**Bryce L. Allen**

19. **The Scribner Encyclopedia of American Lives, 1986-1990: Volume 2.** Kenneth T. Jackson, Karen Markoe, and Arnold Markoe, eds. New York, Charles Scribner's Sons/Macmillan Library Reference, 1999. 967p. illus. index. $125.00. ISBN 0-684-80491-3.

Although Scribner's highly regarded *Dictionary of American Biography* is no longer in print, *The Scribner Encyclopedia of American Lives* fills that void. A 2-volume biographical reference to note Americans no long living, this encyclopedia covers the years 1981 to 1985 and 1986 to 1990. The same high standards of excellence in content and expertise of contributors are maintained. Each volume covers more than 500 Americans who left an imprint on history, including some who were infamous, as well as those whose contributions are held in high esteem. Each entry, accompanied by a portrait when available, opens with a brief summary statement of that person's most important achievements. The essay that follows is a compilation of information gathered from various sources, including original research, family interviews, professional associates, and from other contemporaries. The editors' introduction to the volume refers to the eclectic nature of those persons selected for inclusion. They range from politicians to poets, from chemists to criminals, from magicians to musicians, and from businessmen to ball players. All races, religions, and ethnic and cultural backgrounds are included. The reader will find interesting essays on those born in poverty as well as those from privileged homes, on the famous and infamous, on quiet heroes as well as glamorous and newsworthy figures. Indexes, cumulative for both volumes, are by occupation and entry names. It is important to keep in mind that should a reader be concerned about the ratio of men to women, the persons selected reflect the formative years in which women were only beginning to be more accepted as integral to the business and scientific worlds, rather than the result of sexual bias.

Those familiar with the *Dictionary of American Biography* will find the format of this series more reader-friendly, essays more conversational in approach, and the style and content less prodigious. Laypersons and scholars will enjoy browsing through the text, in addition to using it as a valuable research tool. It should be a priority purchase for college, university, research, and public libraries. [R: BR, Sept/Oct 99, p. 65]—**Margaret Denman-West**

20. **Who's Who in America 1999.** 53d ed. New Providence, N.J., Marquis Who's Who/Reed Reference Publishing, 1998. 3v. index. $549.00/set. ISBN 0-8379-0191-X. ISSN 0083-9396.

This most venerable of the Marquis stable of publications was last reviewed in ARBA in 1996 (see entry 37). That 50th edition included 92,000 entries, whereas the present edition contains approximately 105,000 biographies. The preface states that "selection is based solely on reference value. Individuals become eligible for listing by virtue of their position and/or noteworthy achievements that have proven to be of significant value to society. An individual's desire to be listed . . . [or] wealth or social position [is not sufficient reason for inclusion]." Volume 3 of this edition lists names of the biographees by 38 professional categories as well as by geographic location. However, the geographic list is not completely satisfactory as many individuals do not wish an address to be published. There are a "Retiree Index" and a "Necrology of Biographees." The latter category's entries move to the Who Was Who in America series. Additionally, a new feature of this edition is the inclusion of some enhanced entries in which the biographee provides a description of career accomplishments or family life in his or her own words. More information about avocations is also present. A key biographical reference source, *Who's Who in America* belongs in most libraries.—**Lee Weston**

21. **Who's Who of American Women 1999-2000.** 21st ed. New Providence, N.J., Marquis Who's Who/Reed Reference Publishing, 1998. 1156p. $259.00. ISBN 0-8379-0424-2. ISSN 0083-9841.

This is the 21st edition of this standard biographical resource, which has been published since 1958. This latest edition contains more than 26,000 entries, slightly less than the 30,000 listed for the 19th and 17th editions reviewed in ARBA 1996 (entry 38) and ARBA 1993 (entry 56). Like other Marquis Who's Who publications, individuals to be included are identified by Marquis staff and a board of advisors, based on "current reference value" and "conspicuous achievement," and information is solicited from each person selected. Each entry gives basic data such as name, occupation, birth date, education, career history, publications, professional activities, awards, and home and office addresses. Although a random check showed that some women whom one might expect to be listed are missing from its pages, this publication belongs on the reference shelf of nearly every library.—**Susan Davis Herring**

Canada

22. **Canadian Who's Who 1999.** [CD-ROM]. Toronto, University of Toronto Press, 1999. Minimum system requirements (Windows version): IBM or compatible. CD-ROM drive. Window 95 or Windows 3.x. Minimum system requirements (Macintosh version): CD-ROM Drive. System 7.0 or later. $195.00; $275.00 (with book).

23. **Canadian Who's Who 1999, Volume 34.** Elizabeth Lumley, ed. Buffalo, N.Y., University of Toronto Press, 1999. 1386p. $170.00. ISBN 0-8020-4931-1. ISSN 0068-9963.

Now in its 90th year, *Canadian Who's Who 1999* is still a comprehensive and authoritative source on notable living Canadians. With 1,500 new entries since the last edition, this new edition features 15,000 biographical entries on Canadian elite. Entries feature date and place of birth, education, family history, career information, memberships, creative works, honors, and awards. Influential Canadians from the fields of business, science, politics, government, education, sports, and the arts are featured herein. Libraries will find this a valuable guide for fact-checking names and areas of expertise as well as researching other biographical facts that library patrons might need. *Canadian Who's Who* is also available on CD-ROM and includes the complete text of the paper volume. Searches can be conducted by using a name, address, title, occupation, date of birth, place of birth, or recreation. The two can be purchased together for $275. This standard reference work will be a valuable addition to academic, public, and some special libraries.

—**Shannon M. Graff**

24. **Dictionary of Canadian Biography: Volume XIV, 1911 to 1920.** Ramsay Cook, ed. Buffalo, N.Y., University of Toronto Press, 1998. 1247p. index. $100.00. ISBN 0-8020-3476-4.

The *Dictionary of Canadian Biography* is part of a continuing series on Canadians started in 1966. Each volume contains biographies of famous people starting with the year 1000 and continuing to the present volume, 1920. The aim of this biography is to be a literary work that tells the story of Canadians through the medium of biography, and a highly reliable, indispensable source of information about individuals and events.

Volume XIV includes the biographies of Edward Blake, Sir Charles Tupper, and other people who flourished in the Victorian era, and brings to a close, for all practical purposes, the nineteenth century. More and more, the realities of the twentieth century provide the stories' framework: the development of the Canadian west; the industrialization of central Canada; the massive immigration that changed the ethnic composition of this country; the population shift toward big cities (both Canadian and American); and the progress in public education, in technical and post-secondary training, and in literature and the arts.

This volume includes 622 biographies that have been produced by 459 authors selected for their special knowledge of events and personalities. They have made every effort to maintain the high standards that have earned the *Dictionary of Canadian Biography* its reputation for accurate and precise information, for originality and fairness of interpretation, and for elegance and lucidity of expression. Through their research into primary sources, they have built on secondary studies, enriching and sometimes revising or superseding them.

This biography, whether as a single volume or as a complete set, allows American readers to understand more about their northern neighbors. This would be a good purchase to have on hand in a school where students are studying Canada.—**Barbara B. Goldstein**

DICTIONARIES AND ENCYCLOPEDIAS

25. Crump, Andy, comp. Ellwood, Wayne, ed. **The A to Z of World Development.** Oxford, England, New Internationalist Publications; distr., Sterling, Va., Stylus Publishing, 1998. 293p. illus. maps. $34.95pa. ISBN 1-869847-46-6.

This dictionary of international development provides an overview of the principal issues and concepts preoccupying non-governmental organization (NGO) Third World development activists over the last quarter century in 624 entries. It is a project of the innovative international editorial and graphic design cooperative behind *New Internationalist* magazine. This well-produced reference work lives up to the lively and engaging style of the periodical. It will appeal strongly to school, public, and academic librarians seeking resources on its topic.

Articles are organized alphabetically by title. The writing is straightforward and accessible. Entries range in length from a paragraph to more than a triple-column, 8½-by-11 page. They divide into sections by initial letter. The general contents list these letter sections, while section contents list articles. There is no index. Topics range from people (Willy Brandt, Che Guevara, Mahatma Gandhi) and organizations (Caribbean Development Bank, Grameen Bank) to concepts (ecotourism, genocide) and places (East Timor).

Photographs, charts, tables, graphics, and a map provide lavish illustration. Cross-references are emboldened within entries. A table of comparative statistics by country, with regional and world summary statistics, gives figures, including mortality and life expectancy, per capita GNP, population, proportion of government spending on social issues, and debt servicing as a portion of export earnings. The bibliography lists over 40 United Nations and commercial reference series and works.

Wayne Ellwood is a Toronto-based *New Internationalist* magazine editor. Andy Crump is a Geneva-based ecologist, teacher, writer, photographer, and videographer with extensive experience in development issues. The foreword is by Oxford professor Norman Myers, editor of the *Gaia Atlas of Planet Management*. Endorsing quotes come from the social studies coordinator at the Toronto Board of Education and an Oxford University geographer. This book belongs in most medium-size to large collections. It will be especially attractive to school librarians. [R: Choice, Nov 99, p. 516]—**Nigel Tappin**

26. **DK Concise Encyclopedia.** By John Farndon. New York, DK Publishing, 1999. 512p. illus. maps. index. $16.95pa. ISBN 0-7894-3948-4.

This brief source, designed for children, contains selected basic facts, combined with DK's usual colorful illustrations and photographs, on nine general topics: space, planet earth, the living world, the human body, science and technology, transportation, the world (subdivided by region), people and society, and a history timeline. A reference section concludes the work. Although the occasional error creeps in—for instance a photograph of a Jersey cow is identified as a Guernsey—the brief treatments are commendably succinct and accurate. Although the source is most suitable for a small private collection where children are present, it may also serve as a popular reference or circulating item in a library's juvenile collection.
—**Lee Weston**

27. **Elsevier Dictionaries on CD-ROM.** 1998/99 ed. [CD-ROM]. New York, Elsevier Science, 1997. Minimum system requirements: IBM or compatible 386DX processor with 20MHz. Double-speed CD-ROM. Windows 3.1, Windows 95, Windows 98, or Windows NT 3.51. 4MB RAM. Color monitor with 256 colors. $750.00.

The numbers for the 2d, expanded edition of this electronic dictionary are truly staggering—the full-text of 76 dictionaries, 1,200,000 concepts, and 4,200,000 terms. The database is divided into eight subject segments, or groups, of terminological databases: agriculture, food, and animal sciences; business; chemistry; computing; earth and space sciences; engineering; medicine; and science and technology. These dictionaries are all multilingual, allowing each language to be used as a source as well as target language. The master record consists of English terms in alphabetic order, but the user can search for terms in any of the languages covered. Definitions are skeletal, in keeping with the major purpose of providing translation equivalents. These bare-bones definitions explain the major reason for the astronomical number of terms included.

Searching is fairly standard and straightforward and requires minimal documentation. Users can of course search by source or target language. Global searches allow for searching for terms across several dictionaries. Searchers can search every word and term, including articles and conjunctions. Records can also be exported into word processing documents.

The publisher offers two purchase options. A title version option gives access to one or more dictionaries for an unlimited period of time. The segment version option is more like a lease, allowing subscribers the option of subscribing to any or all of the segments at graduated pricing for an annual license fee, ranging from $115 for the chemistry segment to $1,646 for the entire package. Subscribers must choose which option they want, since it is not possible to combine segments and individual titles on one CD-ROM.

The primary audience for this product would be writers and especially translators. Its flexibility in searching and pricing, however, makes it attractive for academic libraries with extensive foreign language-materials in science and technology.—**Lawrence Olszewski**

28. **Encyclopaedia Britannica CD-ROM 1999.** multimedia ed. [CD-ROM]. Chicago, Encyclopaedia Britannica, 1998. Minimum system requirements: IBM or compatible. Four-speed CD-ROM drive. Windows 95, Windows 98, or Windows NT 4.0. 16MB RAM. 80MB hard disk space. SVGA monitor (256 colors). Sound card and speakers. Mouse. Printer recommended. $119.00.

Be assured that the editorial integrity of the venerable *Encyclopaedia Britannica* (EB) is maintained in the 1999 CD-ROM edition. The articles are well written and well edited. The authors of signed articles, in general, possess impressive credentials attesting to their expertise in their fields. Many of the illustrations are nothing short of stunning and they contribute significantly to both the look and utility of the work. As with many multimedia encyclopedias, EB greatly supplements and complements information in the text of articles with information in the multimedia format. Indeed, as with all such encyclopedias, EB on CD-ROM presents certain material in multimedia format that could not be presented equally as well in print format.

Although EB has succeeded in many ways with its integration of text and multimedia to create a valuable and useful reference resource, and learning resource, it has also fallen into the trap of too much reliance on, or belief in, technology. The system just does not live up to expectations set by EB in the hyperbolic marketing and user information. Installation of the work, on a system that exceeded the recommended hardware and software requirements, took more than 20 minutes. The initial screens and navigation designs are attractive but not as easily understandable as they should be. The user guide and other material touts the full-text search capability of the product, even inviting the user to type in very broad and open-ended questions.

Some of the editorial features are nice and adequate, what is expected from any multimedia encyclopedia on the market today. "Spectrum" is similar to Grolier's *Knowledge Tree* and represents the classification of subjects and knowledge in a hierarchical listing. The timeline section was a bit disappointing, although being able to compare two categories side-by-side is worthwhile. The timeline categories, however, might be rethought. Currently they are architecture, literature, medicine, music, religion, science, technology, visual arts, and women's history. The last, while important, does not compare in scope to the other categories and this is shown in the actual listings; many of them are a far stretch for something relating to women and women's achievements, contributions, and so on. This is not the place to debate political correctness versus new approaches to learning, but it is evident that there are some imbalances in approach and coverage. This, of course, is true of all encyclopedias, whether electronic or printed.

EB has the requisite links to the Internet for updates and one feature that is quite interesting, with more appeal for older and more serious users. *Britannica Classica*, part of the "Spotlights" section, presents classic articles from past editions of EB, written by very noteworthy authors, including Albert Einstein, Harry Houdini, and H. L. Mencken.

Encyclopaedia Britannica CD-ROM 1999 is a useful and fact-filled tool, useful for students as a reference work or for learning exercises. If one is going to buy a multimedia encyclopedia, EB, Grolier, World Book, and Encarta offer much the same material in similar fashions and users will not go wrong with any of them. [R: Choice, April 99, p. 1431]—**Edward Kurdyla**

29. **Encyclopedia Americana on CD-ROM.** [CD-ROM]. Danbury, Conn., Grolier, 1998. Minimum system requirements (Windows version): IBM or compatible 386. MPC-rated 150 KB/sec CD-ROM drive. Windows 3.1 or Windows 95. 4MB RAM. 4MB hard disk space. SVGA card & color monitor. Mouse. Windows-supported printer. Minimum system requirements (Macintosh version): 68020 CPU, 16 MHz or faster. 150 KB/sec or higher CD-ROM drive. System 7.0 or higher. 2.5MB RAM. 4MB hard disk space. 12-inch color monitor (256 colors). Macintosh-compatible printer. $179.00. ISBN 0-7172-3404-5.

Suitable for adults and high school students alike, this remarkable reference tool contains the complete and updated text for all 30 volumes of Grolier's *Encyclopedia Americana* as well as *Merriam-Webster's Collegiate Dictionary, Tenth Edition*, Helicon Publishing Company's *Chronology of World History*, the *Dictionary of Science & Technology* from Academic Press, and a software installation program designed to accommodate a variety of systems and platforms. This breadth of scope, coupled with ease of access and change between databases, allows the user to access at least basic information on virtually any topic.

The encyclopedia includes 9 searchable indexes: an article title index (main index), full-text index, bibliography index, contributor index, subject index, geography index, article form index, date index, and maps index. If a user creates notes while using the encyclopedia, an additional user notes index is accessible. The user has the option of choosing one of these indexes from the entry window (available each time one opens the program) or by utilizing an advanced search window that allows users to search multiple indexes and to use Boolean searches. After this initial choice, the user can easily navigate between search results; bookmark, print, or save search results; and make notes regarding particular entries. Another plus is the interface capability with Internet sites through links provided by the editors. Using the other reference tools included is equally easy and straightforward.

Special features included with the set are truncation searching, sentence searching, a subject classification system, field searching, filters, wildcards, proximity searching, and case sensitivity. A brief troubleshooting guide with technical support telephone number and a networking guide are found in the user's guide that accompanies the CD-ROM.

With the usual limitations inherent in a dated, packaged product, this set nonetheless is a valuable complement to any reference collection designed to integrate electronic and print information. Cost savings are another consideration not to be overlooked. [R: BL, 15 Sept 99, p. 284]—**Edmund F. SantaVicca**

30. Mirwis, Allan N. **Subject Encyclopedias: User Guide, Review Citations, and Keyword Index.** Phoenix, Ariz., Oryx Press, 1999. 2v. index. $135.00/set. ISBN 1-57356-199-1.

The first volume is a collection development librarian's dream—a list of 1,129 subject encyclopedias published between 1990 and 1997. Each entry includes complete bibliographic details, suggested Library of Congress first line classification number, suggested Dewey decimal classification number, price, series notes, number of OCLC holdings, number of book awards from a selected list of awarding entities, and review citations. The review citations are limited to the following publications: *American Reference Books Annual, Booklist, Reference Books Bulletin, Choice, College and Research Libraries, Guide to Subject Encyclopedias and Dictionaries, The Journal of Academic Librarianship, Library Journal, RQ,* and *Wilson Library Bulletin with Rettig on Reference*. The entries are arranged by LC number and access is provided through five indexes: title, LC subject heading, DDC classification number, publisher, and rating.

The author has devised a complex rating system comprised of numerical rankings assigned to the written reviews, then factoring in the number of awards and the number of OCLC holdings. Using this system, the *Encyclopedia of Bioethics* received the highest rating of 18.83 and *The Spycatcher's Encyclopedia of Espionage* received the lowest rating of 1.01. These ratings were used to construct a rating index; the top 98 titles were then used to develop the 2d volume, the keyword index.

The keyword index is quite impressive; it provides subject access to the contents of the 98 highest-ranking titles. The keywords are alphabetically arranged with the abbreviated title of the encyclopedia listed underneath. Along with the title, the page number and volume number (as necessary) for the applicable article are noted. Keywords from "Aboriginal Storytelling" to "Zydeco" are included in the index. One drawback is that the derivations of relatively similar terms are not collapsed into one category; for example, occult, occult science, and occultism. For large reference collections owning a good number of the 98 keyword indexed titles, this book is a must-have. [R: Choice, Dec 99, p. 684]—**Susan D. Strickland**

31. **The New Book of Knowledge.** 1999 deluxe ed. Danbury, Conn., Grolier, 1999. 21v. illus. maps. index. $659.00/set. ISBN 0-7172-0530-4.

The New Book of Knowledge, designed specifically for school-age children in grades 3-8, has long been regarded as one of the top encyclopedias catering to researchers in this age group. With its large print, bright photographs, and easy-to-understand entries, this set will be a popular choice in schools, public libraries, and homes with young children.

The content of this set has been selected by educators and librarians familiar with the unique needs of children as well as familiar with curriculum requirements of schools across the nation. This encyclopedia has the added feature of providing games, illustrations, and activities that will captivate the interest of its intended audience. All articles in the work are signed and each is written by an expert in the field who also writes with the children's interest at heart. The publishers guarantees the accuracy of the articles and illustrations in the preface of the work where it is stated that the book is based on fact, not opinion, and that where there are discrepancies of opinion among experts in the field it is noted in the entry.

The set's accessibility is one its most noted features. It is arranged in alphabetic order. There is an index at the back of each volume (indicated by blue pages), which provides cross-references to the entire set. Furthermore, each volume contains a short section just before the index that provides "dictionary entries," which serve to provide users with short informational terms that may be of interest. The entries also contain important words in bold typeface that will refer readers to other entries in the encyclopedia for further information on that topic. The maps and illustrations throughout the work (often as many as three per page) are designed specifically with children in mind, and many of the illustrations are commissioned specifically for this encyclopedia. A special paperback volume that comes with the set, titled "Home and School Reading and Study Guides," provides a bibliography to other works that may be of interest to young readers. The guide is arranged into primary, intermediate, and advanced categories. New to this 1999 edition is an activities section.

There is no doubt that this encyclopedia will find much use in school libraries, public libraries with a large child clientele, and homes with children. It will give young readers with inquisitive minds just enough of a challenge to continue reading and researching its many pages of worthwhile facts and activities. [R: BL, 15 Sept 99, pp. 294-296]—**Shannon M. Graff**

32. **World Book: Millennium 2000.** deluxe ed. [CD-ROM]. Chicago, World Book, 1999. Minimum system requirements: IBM or compatible 486 with 100 MHz. Double-speed CD-ROM drive. Windows 95 or Windows NT 4.0. 16MB RAM. 40MB hard disk space. 16-bit sound card. 16-bit color. Mouse. $69.95.

The editors have followed a philosophy similar to that of classroom teaching in structuring this new version. Articles on major topics are designed to give a solid foundation on the topic, to engage the senses through multimedia, to encourage further study through links to other articles and to the Web, to organize thinking through outlines, and to reinforce understanding by posing questions. In addition, all sorts of enhancements and extras pervade this reference tool.

Two major categories divide the homepage: search and browse. The search functions focus on searching for specific topics, an atlas, a dictionary, time frames, and Web links. Browse functions allow one to cruise through various access points, including a series of sites that cover each century of the current millennium. This version contains thousands more articles than are in the print set, as well as basic and full-length video sets, pictures, sound clips, panoramas, accurate maps, simulations, animations, a distance calculator, and a free year of online updates. A series of "Wizards" allow the user to create reports, timelines, charts, Web pages, and quizzes.

As an interactive reference tool, this set offers the user a lot of information at one-tenth the price of the print set. An abridged CD-ROM version is available for almost half the price and the enhanced four–CD-ROM set is available for slightly more money. Perhaps the only aggravation of this two–CD-ROM set is the need to switch discs over and over.

This resource is recommended for high-tech collections whose users can profit from the core information and the enhancements. This is a high-quality work at a reasonable price.
—**Edmund F. SantaVicca**

33. **The World Book Encyclopedia.** 1999 ed. Chicago, World Book, 1999. 22v. illus. maps. index. $769.00/set. ISBN 0-7166-0099-4.

In an age when multimedia encyclopedias have become standard reference tools it is refreshing and reassuring to use the printed version of *The World Book Encyclopedia*. The 1999 edition, consisting of 22 volumes, some 30,000 articles, more than 28,000 illustrations (some 24,000 in color), and an index with more than 150,000 entries, is a joy to use. The articles are selected for their appropriateness to school curriculum and they are written for age and level appropriateness. The intended audiences include elementary, junior and senior high school students, and the inquisitive adult. The needs of all audiences appear to be met.

World Book engages some 3,700 consultants, advisors, and authors to produce the annually revised set. Most of those 3,700 are recognized or credentialed experts in their areas of study and authorship. The set is as up-to-date as any annual publication can be and, in fact, for most users, it is sufficient. Current events can be monitored in other works (newspapers, television, the Web); the encyclopedia has much historical information that dates very slowly, if at all, and it has value as a complete work, placing each article in context and in relation to others. Encyclopedias are a great example of classification and a great avenue for understanding the body of knowledge and the relative importance of its many components.

Perusing the printed version is an exciting and serendipitous way to discover new facts and knowledge, particularly for young persons and students. Viewing a two-page spread of several articles and illustrations almost forces users to go beyond their immediate information need and learn something new. The printed version can also be read for enjoyment. There is a 64-page article on painting, for example, which contains some 100 illustrations. This is like having a book within a book and for many persons reading a book (a traditional printed volume) is far more enjoyable than reading the equivalent on a computer screen.

Although multimedia encyclopedias have added value of additional information in audio or video formats, the printed work has the added, albeit less tangible added value of being comfortable and inviting. All libraries should have at least one printed multi-volume encyclopedia and *The World Book* should be one of their first choices. [R: BL, 15 Sept 99, pp. 298-300]—**Edward Kurdyla**

34. **World Book Multimedia Encyclopedia: Macintosh Edition.** 1999 ed. [CD-ROM]. Chicago, World Book, 1998. Minimum system requirements: Centris 650, 25 MHz 68040 processor. Double-speed CD-ROM drive. Mac OS System 7.1 or higher. 16MB RAM. 42MB hard disk space. 8-bit color monitor. Mouse. $744.00. ISBN 0-7166-8538-8.

With more than 18,000 articles (1,800 of which do not appear in the print set), this multimedia encyclopedia will satisfy introductory research needs on a variety of topics. Also included are some 8,000 illustrations, including maps (20,000 fewer images than the print set). Of these, 300 are unique to the CD-ROM. All maps have been redesigned for enhancement through electronic viewing.

Special features include the addition of two new homework Wizards—the Quiz Wizard and the Web Wizard—in addition to the Report, Chart, and Timeline Wizards of previous editions. A joint venture of World Book and the San Diego Zoo is a new Cyber Safari disc that includes stories, sounds, 360-degree views, facts, and videos regarding zoo habitats and their animal occupants. Access is also provided to the World Book Website, as well as to the 225,000-entry *World Book Dictionary* (see ARBA 98, entry 996, for a review of the print version).

A high-performance search engine and intuitive interface allow the user to access information through "Time Frame," "Just Looking (a browse function)," "Around the World" (map navigation), "Browse Media," and "World Book Online." All of these are in addition to the standard search functions that also provide for Boolean searching.

This is a well-designed, easy-to-use product that should form the base of any home reference collection, as well as the encyclopedia sections of school, public, and college library collections.

—**Edmund F. SantaVicca**

DIRECTORIES

35. **African Americans Information Directory 1998-99.** 4th ed. Kenneth Estell, ed. Farmington Hills, Mich., Gale, 1998. 560p. index. $95.00. ISBN 0-8103-9117-1. ISSN 1099-3908.

This standard resource, formerly the *Black Americans Information Directory* (see ARBA 94, entry 407), states this is "a guide to approximately 5,430 organizations, agencies, institutions, programs, and publications concerned with Black American life and culture." More than simply a list of names and addresses of associations, however, this work's 19 sections cite contact and other significant information on awards, colleges and universities, governmental programs, libraries and museums, newsletters and magazines, mass media, religious organizations, scholarships, studies programs, research centers, videos, and Internet databases. The name and subject index, much like that found in the *Encyclopedia of Associations* (see ARBA 99, entries 50 and 51), is an excellent quick resource guide to start any material search. Entries themselves are brief but well organized and easy to read due to the typeface and paper stock quality.

Of special interest is the depth of local reporting found within this text. Rather than focusing entirely on national coverage, this directory includes numerous state and local entries, subdivided by state. Surprisingly for a collection of this size, however, many useful entries are missing altogether (e.g., Black

Business Journal Online, the online version of *The Final Call*) or incomplete, but these problems can be resolved with subsequent editions. For its amount of information, this is a major acquisition for most academic and public libraries of any size.—**Anthony J. Adam**

36. **Associations Unlimited.** [CD-ROM]. Farmington Hills, Mich., Gale, 1999. Minimum system requirements: IBM or compatible 386. ISO-compatible CD-ROM drive. DOS 5.0. Windows 3.1. 8MB RAM. 10MB hard disk space. SVGA color graphics card and monitor. Mouse. $3200.00/yr (2 users); modular pricing available. ISBN 0-7876-2651-1.

This directory is the electronic version of the very popular reference standard, the *Encyclopedia of Associations* series. Included are 23,000 U.S. associations; 20,000 international associations; 100,000 U.S. regional, state, and local associations; and newly added are 300,000 associations based on IRS data on 501(c) nonprofit organizations. There are seven categories of data that break down along the divisions of nonprofit and for-profit: U.S. national, state, and local; international or multinational; and informal or untraceable associations. Searches can be done on the association's name, geographic area, industry code or description, budget figure, number of members, year founded, and any word found in the text of the entries. There is an extended search feature so that multiple fields can be searched simultaneously and an expert search feature that allows the searching of every field of the entry using field codes and Boolean operators.

The menu bar and command buttons are fairly easy to read and navigate. The opening screen allows users to search by name, by keyword, by location, do an extended search, do an expert search, or search for data in IRS nonprofits. Depending on the kind of search one is conducting, dialog boxes come up. This allows users to type in a search and end up in an alphabetic list from which they are able to choose a particular association or range of associations. Some dialog boxes provide a list of available choices, as is the case when a search by SIC codes or descriptions is conducted. A search by location allows users to search a particular city, state, country, province, postal code, or area code.

The extended search feature allows for searching across multiple categories. File folder tabs at the top allow for selecting to fill in information on name, subject, location, scope, publications, meetings, and services. Under name, users can search for the association or a contact person. Users can also check for a telephone, toll-free, or fax number or a listing of association materials. The subject search can be entered as a keyword search, a controlled subject search, a category search, an SIC code search, or a full-text search. The scope search allows for searching based on numeric values—greater than or equal to, less than or equal to, equal to, or between. Choices are the number of members, staff, budget, year founded, and number of associations in the region, state, or local area. Publications can be searched on the title, frequency, and type of publication. A search on meeting allows users to look up information by the name or type of association and geographic location. The services index allows users to look up information in an awards index by types or names, and the computer services index for available databases and mailing lists. The telecommunications services index provides a way to search for Websites, hotlines, and TDD; and the library index allows users to search by types of holdings in the association, books, software, film, or the subject areas held within the library. Records can be displayed in either a brief or full record or a label.

The online version offered through GaleNet provides many of the features offered in the CD-ROM version, with the advantage of being able to connect straight to an organization's Website. This source also contains all of the features of the print version and more, with the flexibility to cross-search certain fields. If the pricing is comparable to the print, all libraries should consider purchasing.—**Jan S. Squire**

37. **Awards, Honors, & Prizes 1999.** 15th ed. Valerie J. Webster, ed. Farmington Hills, Mich., Gale, 1999. 2v. index. $465.00/set. ISBN 0-7876-1500-5. ISSN 0196-6316.

Containing basic information on more than 26,000 awards administered by some 8,400 organizations worldwide, this set divides volumes by geography. Volume 1 is limited to the United States and Canada, while volume 2 focuses on international and foreign prizes. All fields of human endeavor are covered, from advertising to transportation, the arts and humanities, to sciences and social sciences. Diskette and magnetic tape versions are available from the publisher.

Volume 1 is arranged alphabetically by administering organization, complemented by a subject index, organization index, and award index. Each organization and award are given an entry number, used for indexing and cross-references. A typical entry includes name of organization (sometimes in alternate languages as well), mailing address, telephone number, toll-free number, fax number, e-mail address, homepage or URL information for Internet access, former name of organization, award entry number(s), award name(s), purpose of award or eligibility criteria, nature of the award (medal, monetary, certificate), frequency of award, year established, sponsor (if other than the organization), status (if discontinued), and any former name(s) of the award. Indexes mentioned above provide multiple access and search capabilities, and are keyed to both volumes. Volume 2 is arranged alphabetically by country name and provides similar information to volume 1. Awards are listed first by their English name at the end of each organization entry; the same indexes complement the volume.

Information included results from survey mailings, correspondence, and electronic mail. Although the degree of detail varies from award to award, basic directory information allows the user to pursue additional information by contacting an organization using a variety of options. Recommended for most large public and academic reference collections.—**Edmund F. SantaVicca**

38. **Directories in Print: A Descriptive Guide to Print and Non-Print Directories, Buyer's Guides, Rosters and Other Address Lists of All Kinds.** 17th ed. Dawn Conzett DesJardins, ed. Farmington Hills, Mich., Gale, 1999. 2v. index. $499.00/set. ISBN 0-7876-1513-7. ISSN 0899-353X.

The 17th edition describes 15,456 active print and non-print address lists published in the United States and some foreign countries. It provides the usual information—name, complete address with telephone and fax, a brief paragraph describing the coverage of the directory, name of the editor, price, and alternative formats. In the present volume there is more emphasis on computer-readable formats, and it incorporates 712 new and recently identified directories added from the supplement to the 16th edition. The arrangement is by broad subject categories from "General Business" to "Hobbies and Leisure Activities." The 2d volume incorporates a user's guide, abbreviations, and 3 indexes—alternative formats index, subject index, and title and keyword index. This is a good source for larger libraries and organizations.
—**Bohdan S. Wynar**

39. **Fulltext Sources Online, January 1999: For Periodicals, Newspapers, Newsletters, Newswires, & TV/Radio Transcripts.** Donald T. Hawkins and Mary B. Glose, eds. Medford, N.J., Information Today, 1999. 622p. index. $195.00/yr.; $118.00/single issue spiral-bound. ISBN 1-57387-075-7. ISSN 1040-8258.

Volume 11 of this familiar reference is the first to be published by Information Today, Inc. "Online," for the most part, refers to conventional online vendors including Burrelle's Broadcast Database, Datastar & Dialog, Dow Jones, FT Profile, Lexis-Nexis, Nikkei Net Interactive, Ovid, Questel, Reuters Business Briefing, Westlaw, and several others. The only Internet sites listed are those sponsored by those same vendors and allow free access (although not necessarily to archived articles). Librarians and patrons should consult other sources to identify other Websites that provide full-text access to materials.

Journals with free archives available on the Internet are listed in the shorter 1st section. This alphabetic listing of journals includes the Web address, span of coverage in the current file, and back issues available in the archives. For example, the entry for American libraries indicates the specific Internet address on ALA's Website and indicates that issues from December 1997 to the present are available.

The main section of this reference work is the alphabetized periodicals listing. For each of more than 8,000 journals or television programs (e.g., *20/20*, *60 Minutes*), the entry includes a list of vendors and search services providing access in full text and the specific database or section to access. The time period for when the periodical is available on the service, frequency of database update, time lag between publication in print and availability online, coverage (whether it is selective or includes all articles) and whether an archive is available is also noted.

A subject index, with 47 topics ranging from agriculture to education to medicine and health to television and radio transcripts, helps researchers locate relevant sources. The last section of this comprehensive work includes contact information for all the database vendors.—**Jan Bakker**

40. **Guide to American Directories: A Guide to the Major Business, Educational, Scientific, Technical & Professional Directories....** 14th ed. Barry Klein, ed. West Nyack, N.Y., Todd Publications, 1999. 465p. index. $95.00pa. ISBN 0-915344-67-X.

Published for more than 40 years, this guide is intended to assist business and industry in locating new markets for their products and to help organizations, researchers, and those in advertising and public relations to find reliable sources of information. It also purports to aid in finding new sources of products and services. The editors of this new 14th edition have added more than 1,000 new directories (some in new categories) and deleted some 500 that are no longer published. There are close to 200 categories of directories listed alphabetically at the beginning of the volume, covering not only academic, social service, and business-related fields, but also more unusual areas, such as collection agencies and alternative culture, lifestyle, and future research. Although the primary focus is on U.S. directories, some foreign directories are included. These are particularly helpful in fields such as education and government. Entries for each directory typically include title with brief description; number of directories; addresses with telephone, fax, e-mail, and Website information; the cost; whether it is available to the public; and whether a mailing list can be purchased.

Following the main listings are sections titled "Index—Subject" and "Index—Alphabetical," neither of which is a real index. The first simply lists the categories with the titles of the directories included in each category. The second, an alphabetic list of all directories included, would seem to be of little use even if the subject happens to be the first word of the title. For example, the word "environmental" shows 16 directories, but going directly to the category of environment and conservation yields more than 30 directories. Much more helpful would be one subject and keyword index.

In spite of the limitations regarding indexing, the guide contains a lot of information on more than 10,000 directories, many of which cannot be found elsewhere, and is presented in an easy-to-use format. It is recommended particularly for business libraries and large academic and public libraries. [R: Choice, July/Aug 99, p. 1915]—**Lucille Whalen**

41. **International Research Centers Directory 1999.** 11th ed. Michelle E. Eads, ed. Farmington Hills, Mich., Gale, 1999. 1289p. index. $470.00. ISBN 0-7876-2192-7. ISSN 0278-2731.

Since the last review of this directory (see ARBA 96, entry 55), it has increased its entries to more than 8,400 government, university, independent nonprofit centers, and commercial research and development centers. This includes institutes; laboratories; bureaus; test facilities; experiment stations; research parks; data collection and analysis centers; and foundations, councils, and other organizations that support research. This edition indicates that there have been thousands of changes and updates in order to supply current information. Most of the information is obtained from questionnaires, but secondary sources such as Websites are also consulted.

Information is provided for more than 150 countries, not including the United States. For information regarding the United States, consult Gale's *Research Centers Directory* (24th ed.; see ARBA 99, entry 333), *Research Services Directory* (see ARBA 97, entry 170), and *Government Research Directory* (Gale, 1999).

The directory is divided into 6 broad categories arranged into 17 sections. Life sciences encompasses three sections: agriculture, food, and veterinary sciences; biological and environmental sciences; and medical and health sciences. Physical sciences and engineering encompasses four sections: astronomy and space sciences, computers and mathematics, engineering and technology, and physical and earth sciences. Private and public policy and affairs encompasses four sections: business and economics, government and public affairs, labor and industrial relations, and law. Social and cultural studies encompasses four sections: behavioral and social sciences, education, humanities and religion, and regional and area studies. Multidisciplinary and research coordinating centers encompasses two sections: multidisciplinary programs and research coordinating offices and research parks.

Entries are easy to read, alphabetically arranged by the institution name, and have a sequential entry number that is used in the four indexes at the end of the book. When the information is available, entries provide the following information: street and e-mail addresses; telephone, fax, telex, and 800 numbers; and Website address. The date founded, a brief description, head of organization, staff, research areas, publications, research budget, and who provides financial support are also included. Any unique resources; library holdings; meetings and educational activities; memberships, scholarships, and awards; persons to contact; and affiliated centers are also listed.

There are four useful indexes: subject, country, personal name, and a master index. Within the alphabetic subject index, countries are listed in alphabetic order by abbreviation and then entry number. Numerous *see* references are provided. The alphabetic country index lists each section in numerical order where a reference can be found, and then entries within that section. The personal name index lists the contact names and personnel listed in the directory. The master index is arranged by the research center name and includes English and non-English names. Indications are provided for former and alternative names, acronyms, and defunct and inactive centers.

The directory is also available in four electronic formats—diskette/magnetic tape, online through DIALOG, through GaleNet, and on CD-ROM. Although the price has increased steadily, this directory is highly recommended for purchase by academic or special libraries where research programs are located or conducted.—**Jan S. Squire**

42. **Public Interest Profiles 1998-1999.** James J. DeAngelis, ed. Washington, D.C., Congressional Quarterly, 1998. 899p. index. $215.00. ISBN 1-56802-424-X. ISSN 1058-627X.

Congressional Quarterly, working with the Foundation for Public Affairs (FPA) and the related organization the Public Affairs Council, has produced a new edition of *Public Interest Profiles*. The book is a directory of the most influential public affairs groups in the United States.

The groups are divided into 12 categories, including business, constitutional rights, community, consumer/health, environmental, international affairs, political, religious, and think tanks. Entries for each group include the name of the group, the date they were founded, contact information (including e-mail and Web addresses if available), purpose, number of staff, director's name and brief biography, tax status, budget, funding sources, scope, affiliated PACs, method of operation, current concerns, publications, newsletter, conferences, board of directors, and representative quotes from newspaper and journal articles about the effectiveness and political orientation of the group.

One expects a Congressional Quarterly publication to be of high quality, and *Public Interest Profiles* confirms the expectation. The preface lists other terms for public interest groups, such as special interest groups, advocacy groups, pressure groups, and public policy organizations. The criteria used to select groups are the extent of the group's influence on national policy, the number of inquiries about the group fielded by FPA staff, the volume of news coverage about the group, and the representative nature of the group in its field of interest and activity. Sources of information about groups included questionnaires, annual reports, publication catalogs, financial statements, and more.

Included groups cut across the political spectrum. The editors make no attempt to assess the effectiveness and political orientation of the groups. If there are no representative quotes from the media, the information is listed as unavailable; such a nonpartisan approach increases the level of trust in the reliability of the information.

The topic may be too specialized for smaller libraries. Otherwise, *Public Interest Profiles* is highly recommended for academic libraries and other organizations with a strong interest in political science and public policy. [R: Choice, Sept 99, p. 122]—**Mary A. Axford**

43. **Toll-Free Phone Book USA 1999: A Directory of Toll-Free Telephone Numbers for Businesses and Organizations Nationwide.** 3d ed. Jennifer C. Perkins, ed. Detroit, Omnigraphics, 1999. 1348p. index. $120.00pa. ISBN 0-7808-0361-2. ISSN 1092-0285.

Toll-Free Phone Book USA 1999 is a useful source with more than 37,000 toll-free telephone numbers, from all carriers, that is geared to the business and professional community but will be equally helpful to the consumer market. The 1999 edition is divided into 3 principal sections, each of which includes the full company, organization, agency, or institution name; its complete mailing address; regular telephone number; toll-free telephone number; fax number; and World Wide Web and e-mail addresses. If the toll-free number is intended for a specific use, the directory describes this use in the listing.

The 1st section is an alphabetic listing by company or association name. The 2d section is a geographic arrangement in which firms and associations are listed by state and then broken down by cities and towns. The 3d section is a classified presentation in which firms and associations appear under an alphabetic (classified) subject listing. The final portion of the volume is an "Index to Classified Headings," which provides the page number for each class heading. The alphabetic listing and the geographic listing also provide the page number for the class heading for the appropriate business or association.

Toll-Free Phone Book USA 1999 provides 3 approaches to locating the toll-free number for a firm or association. The *Business Buyer's Guide: AT&T Toll-Free Directory* (1998 ed.; AT&T, 1998) provides only a yellow-page listing approach and covers only AT&T numbers. This yellow-page listing also provides only city and state, not a full address. Neither directory appears to be 100 percent complete. Of two well-known window manufacturers, Pella Corporation is listed only in *Toll-Free Phone Book USA* and Andersen Corporation is listed only in *Business Buyer's Guide*. Large academic libraries with business collections and large public libraries will wish to acquire both titles.—**Dene L. Clark**

44. **Washington 1999: A Comprehensive Directory of the Area's Major Institutions and the People Who Run Them.** 16th ed. Tiffany M. Jones, Sarah E. White, and Andrew G. Wood, eds. Washington, D.C., Columbia Books, 1999. 913p. index. $85.00pa. ISBN 1-880873-36-2. ISSN 0749-9736.

This directory is billed as a comprehensive directory to the Washington, D.C. metropolitan area's most important institutions and the people who run them. The directory could be used to contact government officials, find employment or sales prospects, and research Washington-based organizations. The directory is divided into several sections that cover 5,256 organizations. There are 17 chapters that cover major subject divisions, such as the national government, local government, international affairs, national affairs, the media, businesses, national associations, labor unions, the bar, medicine and health, foundations and philanthropy, science and policy research, education, religion, cultural institutions, clubs, and community affairs.

The entries are listed under the major subject division chapter, and then under sections and subsections. Each chapter has a 2-page introduction to the information included and an overall explanation of how the chapter is structured. Most of the entries are alphabetically arranged within the section and subsection. Each entry includes the name, date founded, address, phone, fax, Website, employees, a historical note, executives, board members, and trustees. The directory is also easily navigated despite the small print of the entries. There is a chapter and section running title at the top of each page in a bolder and larger font, and each chapter is marked in black in succession on the page's edge. Entry titles are in bold typeface and critical pieces of the entry information have bold titles and spaces to make the type of information readily identifiable. There are two indexes. An organization index that lists the entries in alphabetic order by name and includes the page number in bold and parentheses. The individuals index lists 24,862 executives, officers, and board members. Alphabetic listings include the name, title, and affiliation with the page number in bold typeface and parentheses. For those individuals with multiple affiliations, executive positions are listed first.

There are other directories available that cover different components featured in this directory in more detail, like the *Washington Information Directory* (see entry 640), which includes national government information. This comprehensive 1-volume directory provides more information than a phonebook entry and is worthwhile for large academic and public research libraries and for those needing an in-depth directory of the Washington, D.C. metropolitan area.—**Jan S. Squire**

HANDBOOKS AND YEARBOOKS

45. **The Economist Desk Companion: How To Measure, Convert, Calculate, and Define Practically Anything.** 3d ed. New York, John Wiley, 1998. 272p. index. $27.95. ISBN 0-471-24953-X.

Among the many ready-reference tools in publication, this volume offers an impressive array of information. A brief introduction explains the three major world measurement systems (i.e., metric, British, and American), followed by a major section that gives subject-by-subject definitions, measurements, formulae, and calculations pertinent to a number of disciplines and commodities and natural resources. A third section presents conversion tables that range from the simple (length, area, volume, weight) to the complex and specialized (pressure and stress, energy, finance). The final section includes abbreviations, rough conversions, historical weights and measures, and measurement systems used in countries of the world other than the United Kingdom and the United States. A full and detailed index provides easy access to most any topic.

Although this work has a distinct British slant, the quantitative information presented is objective, clear, and easily accessible. This work is highly recommended for all ready-reference collections, as it is likely to provide answers that are not easily retrieved from other sources.—**Edmund F. SantaVicca**

46. **The *Life* Millennium: The 100 Most Important Events and People of the Past 1,000 Years.** Robert Friedman, ed. New York, Life Books; distr., New York, Bulfinch Press/Little, Brown, 1998. 192p. illus. $29.95. ISBN 0-8212-2557-X.

Devising a list of important events and people of the last millennium, narrowing them down to 100, and ranking them are a daunting task. Two dozen *LIFE* editors consulted many experts to compile the initial list. From 100 (least important) to 1 (most important), these events are discussed in brief essays and accompanied by captioned photographs (some from *LIFE* magazine, some commissioned). The degree and range of impact constitute what is "important." Along the bottom of some pages is a timeline of other events related to the one depicted. For instance, under 27, the Wright Brothers, are listed as the first airmail, Lindbergh crossing the Atlantic, Yeager breaking the sound barrier, and the first jet service. The 100 most important people of the millennium are also ranked and are portrayed in small portraits with birth and death dates and a brief description of impact. At the end of the book is a timeline that also serves as an index. *The Life Millennium* is an attractive book that will delight the browser.—**Lori D. Kranz**

47. **The New York Public Library Desk Reference.** 3d ed. New York, Macmillan Library Reference/Simon & Schuster Macmillan, 1998. 1040p. illus. maps. index. $34.95. ISBN 0-02-862169-7.

The 1989 edition of this work was reviewed in the 1991 edition of ARBA 91, entry 48, by Susan Baughman, a university librarian at Goddard Library at Clark University. The review of this important reference source created by the New York Public Library was mixed, pointing out some good features along with negatives. The present edition is significantly enlarged and is now published by Macmillan, with a very reasonable price. It has landed on such prestigious best-seller lists as *Publisher's Weekly* and the *New York Times*. This new edition is quite similar to the previous one; it covers thousands of small items arranged under broad subject categories such as the physical world, the biological world, the physical sciences, mathematics, and technology—a total of 26 subject categories. An atlas and a general index conclude the volume. As was pointed out in the previous review, the information is not always accurate (see the section entitled "The World" on p. 929 for information on Ukraine) but in many uses it will answer some basic questions.—**Bohdan S. Wynar**

48. **The Yearbook of Experts, Authorities, & Spokespersons 1999: An Encyclopedia of Sources.** 17th ed. Washington D.C., Broadcast Interview Source, 1998. 674p. index. $39.95pa. ISBN 0-934333-33-5. ISSN 1051-4058.

Probably without intending to, this book prompts one to ask just exactly what an "expert" is. The editors offer little by way of definition. Their title-page note states their purpose: "to provide bona fide interview sources to working members of the media." A disclaimer is significant for readers to note: No warranty is offered "that every listed contact will be appropriate for a reader's particular purpose." There is no indication that the experts listed have been screened or vetted in any way. In short, this is an anthology of self-selected individuals and organizations who have paid to be listed in the volume. Some will be familiar (Dr. Joyce Brothers, the National Education Association), while many will not. A large number boast in their listings of having appeared on radio and television talk shows; media professionals will likely be the largest users of this volume.

The sources are indexed alphabetically, topically, and geographically. Other charts and tables include U.S. area codes and telephone numbers for foreign diplomats in the United States.—**Christopher Baker**

INDEXES

49. **The Wellesley Index to Victorian Periodicals 1824-1900.** new ed. [CD-ROM]. Walter E. Houghton, ed. New York, Routledge, 1999. Minimum system requirements: IBM or compatible. Quad-speed CD-ROM drive. Windows 3.x or Windows NT 3.51. 16MB RAM. 8MB hard disk space. 14-inch VGA monitor (256 colors). Mouse. $2,975.00. ISBN 0-415-19345-1.

At one time or another virtually all Victorian specialists have used the *Wellesley Index* (WI). A premier research tool for nineteenth-century studies, it provides access to periodical sources of Victorian thought and opinion on literature, art, science, politics, economics, and philosophy to a degree no other publication can offer. Additionally, it can serve as a major deposit for research in women's writing since it includes a wealth of material on some 1,500 Victorian women writers. Seeing as how over 90 percent of the periodical writing during the nineteenth century was done anonymously or under a pseudonym, it has made it difficult to evaluate the significance of articles not knowing their full provenance. The WI identifies the vast majority of material in the 45 journals and magazines it covers and indicates the reasons for such attributions. This new electronic edition, furthermore, includes corrections, recent research (over 2,000 in total), and numerous additions published in the *Victorian Periodicals Review* up to the end of 1997. A 40-page printed user guide supplies a helpful introduction to the program; specific features; and ways to search quickly, flexibly, and efficiently. Despite its cost, this CD-ROM can be recommended to reference collections where it will be put to sufficient use.—**G. A. Cevasco**

PERIODICALS AND SERIALS

50. **Bacon's Magazine Directory 1999: Directory of Magazines and Newsletters.** 47th ed. Chicago, Bacon's Information, 1998. 1950p. index. $285.00pa. ISSN 1088-9663.

This directory targets public relations officers, advertising departments, and organizations that need information about media outlets in all parts of the United States and Canada. It lists more than 31,000 print outlets and 160,000 editorial contacts. It includes names of publishers and editors, locations, telephone numbers, e-mail addresses, circulation numbers, advertising and subscription rates, and profiles of the publications as to content. Both print and Internet publications appear.

Compilers list more than 12,000 magazines according to 90 "market classifications" or subject areas with 240 subgroups. There is a numerical index of the classes and an alphabetic cross-index. Classifications cover the broad gamut of publications available, from entertainment to beverages to building trades to hospitals to computers to industries to pets to waste management to woodworking and so on. Following the classifications section where full details about each publication appear are several indexes, including multiple magazine publishers, African American magazines, Hispanic magazines, newsletters, and an alphabetic list of titles.

Each profile has easy-to-see symbols and abbreviations to help identify their usefulness to prospective advertisers or contributors. For example an "R" shows that the publication has a local, state, or regional editorial emphasis. The format is easy to read. Now in its 47th edition, this directory appears to be an invaluable resource for companies or organizations that wish to tell their story or sell their product to the right audience.—**Berniece M. Owen**

51. **Bacon's Newspaper Directory 1999: Directory of Daily and Community Newspapers and News Services and Syndicates.** 47th ed. Chicago, Bacon's Information, 1998. 1534p. $285.00pa. ISSN 1088-9639.

Bacon's Newspaper Directory is designed to help public relations professionals find outlets for press releases and announcements. Most of the directory provides information for more than 1,650 daily newspapers in the United States and Canada and more than 9,100 U.S. community newspapers. Entries are arranged alphabetically by state and province, and then by city. Each entry includes postal, e-mail, and home page addresses; telephone and fax numbers; circulation and issuance; geographical coverage; ownership; online availability; advertising and subscription rates; names of editors, reporters, and columnists; and feature sections. Contact notes given for some editors and reporters include useful information, such as preferred days and times to contact them, methods preferred, and areas of special coverage. Entries for weekly newspapers are brief and less detailed than those for the dailies. Many weeklies are owned by publishers of multiple newspapers, so Bacon's groups those titles under the publisher so that the user can easily see which newspapers can be reached through a single contact. Bacon's also includes a number of special lists, such as news services and syndicates, syndicated columnists by subject specialty, Sunday supplements, state newspaper associations, and African American and Hispanic bilingual newspapers. There are also locators for daily and weekly newspapers that serve as a title index.

Bacon's continues to expand its listings with each edition. Acknowledging the impact of the Internet, it tripled the number of e-mail addresses and claims to include publications that are only available online, although that fact does not seem to be indicated in the entries. Bacon's provides more detailed information than the newspaper volume of *Working Press of the Nation* (R. R. Bowker), although *Working Press* includes more special–interest, religious, ethnic, and foreign-language newspapers. Thus, there is a significant difference between the two to justify purchasing both, but the level of detail available in Bacon's makes it essential for all libraries.—**Teresa U. Berry**

52. **Hudson's Subscription Newsletter Directory.** Joan W. Artz, ed. Rhinebeck, N.Y., Hudson's, 1999. 518p. index. $189.00pa. ISBN 1-891489-01-1. ISSN 1046-8110.

By restricting its entries to subscription publications, Hudson's contains only about 4,900 items. This figure pales miserably beside the other two recognized newsletter directories: *Oxbridge Directory of Newsletters* (see ARBA 95, entry 954) with 21,000 entries and *Newsletters in Print* (see ARBA 98, entry 880) with 11,000 entries. This selectivity places the responsibility on the user of knowing beforehand whether the particular newsletter in question meets the publisher's definition of subscription. The editors have eliminated journals; reporting services; association, league, club, and foundation publications; and newsletters that are free, have controlled circulation, are published irregularly, or depend on advertising or newsstand distribution. A larger quibble involves its organization. The subject categories index deceptively lists 160 topics, but because of concatenation really totals only 52. Yet this index is indispensable because users have no dependable way of determining under which broad subject a specific topic will be found. Libraries fall under computers and information processing; radio, television, and video fall under communication; but motion pictures are under amusements. The decision to place certain titles under arbitrary topics poses several perplexing questions. Why is "Connecticut Libraries" under education and not the more obvious libraries? Why is "Database Alert" under communication and not information processing? Why is "Library Hotline" under general interest? In addition, the directory claims international coverage, but very few actually hail from overseas. As with previous editions (12th ed., see ARBA 96, entry 978; 13th ed., see ARBA 98, entry 76), the bare-bones entries contain standard directory-type information.

Some include annotations and a sizeable number have e-mail addresses, though it is hard to imagine that all of them do not have e-mail addresses given their for-profit status. Online sources are not included.

The directory is appended with five indexes, though the practical purpose for including multiple newsletter publishers and suppliers to the newsletter industry (only one clipping service and three printers) is questionable. The editor states that one or more newsletter publishers recommend these "service" organizations. The other indexes—geographic, title, and editorial—are more useful in a library environment. Because this directory overlaps considerably with the two mentioned above, as well as Ulrich's, there is little need to acquire it; based on its idiosyncratic organization and limited information, if you already own it, there is little need to use it.—**Lawrence Olszewski**

53. Milton, Suzanne, and Elizabeth Malia. **Index Guide to College Journals.** Lanham, Md., Scarecrow, 1999. 651p. $65.00. ISBN 0-8108-3569-X.

The *Index Guide to College Journals* provides an alphabetic list with indexing information for approximately 16,000 scholarly and popular periodicals that serve undergraduate academic programs. The emphasis is largely on English-language periodicals, although a few foreign-language periodicals are included, and the scope is generally limited to journals that were published in the 1990s. In addition to indexing codes, each journal title entry includes an ISSN number. A total of 48 standard bibliographic sources were consulted for indexing information, including the popular Wilson indexes, Sage abstracting services, *America History and Life*, and *PsycLit*. For each title on the source index list, the compilers have indicated whether it is available electronically.

Reference librarians and students often need to determine the indexing for a periodical in order to verify a bibliographic citation. Although *Ulrich's International Periodicals Directory* (36th ed.; see ARBA 99, entry 74) also provides indexing information, its classified arrangement makes it somewhat cumbersome to use for the purpose. One must first consult the index volume to obtain a page number, then go to the appropriate classified volume for the entry with indexing information. The *Index Guide to College Journals* allows one to obtain indexing information on commonly held periodicals using a simple, alphabetic list. It is highly recommended as a ready-reference source for all academic libraries and is potentially a good resource for larger public library collections.—**Martha Tarlton**

QUOTATION BOOKS

54. **Dictionary of Contemporary Quotations, Volume 9.** 4th rev. ed. John Gordon Burke and Ned Kehde, eds. Evanston, Ill., John Gordon Burke, 1998. 313p. $55.00. ISBN 0-934272-45-X. ISSN 0360-215X.

As indicated in the introduction, the ongoing purpose of this series of volumes is "to record contemporary quotations which are historically, sociologically, and politically significant." Added to this purpose is the exclusion of quotations from historically significant persons that might have appeared in contemporary media. As volume 9 of the series, this latest compendium serves as a supplement to volumes 5 through 8, with at least 15 percent of the quotations from volume 8 being replaced with new quotations.

The compilers have scanned approximately 175 periodicals and newspapers from 1995 to 1998, the time scope of the current volume. Quotations are arranged in two general alphabetic sections: author and subject. Information provided in the author section includes the name of the speaker, description, annotation (when appropriate), quotation, explanatory amplification, and quotation sources (title, volume, page, and date). In the subject section both speaker and source of publication are indicated.

For students and others needing a ready source of contemporary quotations culled from the leading historical, political, and cultural figures of our times, this work will serve as a beginning. In looking over the quotations, some might suggest questionable use; however, the speaker has significance. Considering the time period involved, it is also curious that the work is full of quotations from the 1970s and 1980s. This volume is recommended as a complement to quotation collections found in standard reference collections. [R: Choice, Nov 99, p. 502]—**Edmund F. SantaVicca**

55. Gaither, Carl C., and Alma E. Cavazos-Gaither, comps. **Practically Speaking: A Dictionary of Quotations on Engineering, Technology, and Architecture.** Philadelphia Pa., Institute of Physics Publishing, 1999. 367p. illus. index. $39.00pa. ISBN 0-7503-0594-0.

Sometimes a book is published to fill a niche people never knew existed. Not unlike the collections of cartoons about lawyers or doctors, the calendars devoted to dogs or cats, this is a very subject-specific work. The quotations range from Roger Bacon to Sherlock Holmes, Leonardo da Vinci to Norman Mailer, and are all pertinent to one of the three disciplines. The work is alphabetic by topic and has two thorough indexes, one by subject and one by author. As readers would expect, there is an extensive bibliography and, interestingly, an equally extensive list of permissions. It is doubtful that the compilers' claim that the general reader, with no knowledge of the fields, could form an accurate image of them, nor would it really serve to enrich the experience of the student. However, it would be a most pleasant gift for any engineer or architect. [R: Choice, June 99, pp. 1760-1761]—**Paula Frosch**

56. Gerhart, Eugene C., comp. **Quote It Completely! World Reference Guide to More Than 5,500 Memorable Quotations from Law and Literature.** Buffalo, N.Y., William S. Hein, 1998. 1362. index. $95.00 (with disc). ISBN 1-57588-400-3.

International in scope, Gerhart's compilation expands upon his previous legal quotation dictionaries: *Quote It!* (Clark Boardman Co., Ltd., 1969) and *Quote It II* (William S. Hein & Co., Inc., 1988). Unlike in most other generalized or specialized collections of notable sayings, quotations selected for inclusion in this work often appear embedded within extended passages, thereby providing the reader a more telling context and a clearer persona. These passages are subsumed beneath such alphabetically arranged topic designations as "Arbitration," "Elections," and "Royal Courts." Some of the more cryptic categories are "Strangling Time," "Barefoot," "Bow Ties," and "Giggle Test."

Predictably, this dictionary's name index reveals that many of the entries have been drawn from the mouths and pens of past and present high-profile lawyers from the United States (Clarence Darrow, F. Lee Bailey, William O. Douglas, and Alan M. Dershowitz). Aside from the omissions of Hoover, Taft, and McKinley, all twentieth-century U.S. presidents are herein represented. An impressive cross-section of statesmen, orators, and philosophers from other countries and centuries is also in evidence (e.g., Churchill, Seneca, Machiavelli, Lao-Tzu). Novelists and writers of verse are not lacking here (e.g., Dickens, Vonnegut, Maurois, Shakespeare, Pope, and Charles Osgood). Unexpected sources of bon mots include Ann Landers, Kojak, John Barrymore, and Frank McGee.

Curiously, the pronouncements of many lawyers associated with this century's most celebrated court cases are absent from this reference's pages: John Sirica, Melvin Belli, Vincent Bugliosi, Johnny Cochran, and Gerry Spence. Notwithstanding the inclusion of Margaret Chase Smith, Margaret Mead, Sandra Day O'Connor, and Indira Gandhi, a surprising number of influential female leaders and role models—whose many, varied, and articulate views on legal matters remain on record elsewhere—find no voice in this dictionary. For example, Eleanor Roosevelt, Barbara Jordan, Geraldine Ferraro, Elizabeth Dole, and Margaret Thatcher are not included.

Although the overwhelming preponderance of included quotations either remark on or otherwise refer to particular legal principles, issues, and decisions, many others bear little or no relation to matters of law. For instance, Barbara Bush's two entries seem to have as much to do with activity in a courtroom as they would with activity in a cloakroom. Dozens of quotations, excerpted from various composition and rhetoric texts, simply offer advice regarding the general improvement of one's writing skills.

Although usually accurate and helpful, cross-referencing within the subject list is at times inaccurate or insufficient. Only five see references have been included (for "Ancient Law," "Distemper," "Environment," "Perjury," and "Sports"). No cross-references are provided between the pairs "Madness" and "Insanity," "Quotations" and "Don't Quote Me," "Censorship" and "Lady Chatterley's Lover," nor between "Limericks" and "Humor." Moreover, in at least two cases, a quotation has been duplicated within this collection: Lynch's complimentary remark on Gerhart appears on both pages 648 and 890; Napoleon's quotation on toys is on both pages 1074 and 1107. Copyediting deficiencies are also noticeable: "Elliot" appears for "Eliot" (p. 528), "trail" appears for "trial" (p. 1308), and the "Contents" page contains a lapse in capitalization ("Name index"). All in all, although this volume is more comprehensive than *The Quotable Lawyer* (see ARBA 99, entry 572) or *The Oxford Dictionary of American Legal Quotations* (see ARBA 94, entry 584), it must be used judiciously. [R: Choice, July/Aug 99, p. 1915]—**Jeffrey E. Long**

Part II
SOCIAL SCIENCES

2 Social Sciences in General

SOCIAL SCIENCES IN GENERAL

57. **The Gallup Poll Cumulative Index: Public Opinion, 1935-1997.** By Alec M. Gallup. Wilmington, Del., Scholarly Resources, 1999. 596p. $150.00. ISBN 0-8420-2587-1.

This is a comprehensive index to the 25-volume Gallup Poll Annual Series, one of the largest compilations of public findings available. It covers all Gallup Polls conducted between 1935 and 1997. The index is alphabetic by topic. Topics are blessed with many subheadings to help narrow a search. Entries indicate the year and page number of the series volume. This is a must purchase for academic and public libraries with the Gallup Poll Annual Series. [R: BL, 1 Sept 99, p. 180; LJ, 1 Sept 99, p. 178; Choice, Nov 99, p. 516]
—Esther R. Sinofsky

58. **Humanitarians and Reformers.** New York, Macmillan Library Reference/Simon & Schuster Macmillan, 1999. 433p. illus. index. (Macmillan Profiles). $75.00. ISBN 0-02-865377-7.

This new volume in the Macmillan Profiles series profiles more than 125 notable international social activists and humanitarians in areas such as civil rights, anti-slavery, suffragists, human rights, Nobel Peace Prize winners, education, and philanthropy. However, only 20 of the entries are newly written. The rest are drawn from Macmillan's *Encyclopedia of African-American Culture and History*, *Encyclopedia of the American West*, *Encyclopedia of Latin American History and Culture*, and *The Nobel Laureates*—albeit edited for a young adult audience. The brief biographies, ranging from one to four pages, usually include a black-and-white photograph or illustration of the person discussed and a timeline in the margin helps place the person into a historical context. Sidebars also amplify topics, as do boxed explanations. The table of contents lists the people covered in alphabetic order, but since the name is listed first name first, scanning for a particular name is a bit slow. Special boxed explanations covering terms (such as settlement houses) and organizations (such as African National Congress) are also listed in the table of contents. Those profiled include Ralph David Abernathy; Jane Addams; Aung San Suu Kyi; Dalai Lama; Diana, Princess of Wales; Martin Luther King, Jr.; Adolfo Perez Esquivel; Andrei Sakharov; Sojourner Truth; and Elie Wiesel. Eight primary source documents are included (e.g., the Anti-Slavery Declaration of 1833), the Seneca Falls Declaration of 1848, the Civil Rights Act of 1964). "Ways to Help" (a list of volunteer opportunities), suggested reading (including Websites), a glossary, article sources, and an index help complete the volume. Although aimed at a high school audience, the briefness of the entries raises questions about its suitability at research report writing time. Other reference materials provide more in-depth information about many of the personalities included here. The lack of a series cumulative index makes it hard to find a specific entry in the series for quick reference. The price says reference, but the contents say circulating collection.
—Esther R. Sinofsky

59. **Social Issues.** Robert D. Benford, ed. New York, Macmillan Library Reference/Simon & Schuster Macmillan, 1998. 942p. illus. index. (Macmillan Compendium). $125.00. ISBN 0-02-865055-7.

Late twentieth-century industrialized societies, like the United States, are confronted by an array of complex social issues and institutional problems. These include poverty and inequality, crime, the evolution/dissolution of the nuclear family, drug abuse, population growth and migration, and race and ethnic relations. Though often experienced as personal troubles, these issues can also be understood as social problems rooted in the structure and functioning of our institutions. As the old sociological example goes: If one person is unemployed, that is a personal problem; if thousands are unemployed, that is a social issue. This 1-volume encyclopedia addresses many of our society's most compelling social issues, presenting some of the best social science insight and research into their causes, functioning, and effects.

The approximately 180 topical essays included here are drawn primarily from the 4-volume *Encyclopedia of Sociology* (see ARBA 93, entry 847) and, in a few cases, the *Dictionary of American History* (see ARBA 97, entry 419). The signed entries are arranged alphabetically by subject and address social institutions (e.g., family, education, work), social problems (e.g., crime, poverty, divorce), social processes (e.g., socialization, urbanization, social change, social movements), and contemporary issues (e.g., affirmative action, religious fundamentalism, terrorism, sexually transmitted diseases). Essays range from two to eight pages in length and are accompanied by extensive bibliographies for further reading. Though overly statistical or theoretical topics are not included, the entries that are here are nonetheless fairly advanced in their treatment of the subjects. A detailed subject/name index provides more than adequate access to the content of the entries.

This encyclopedia would be an excellent starting point for students trying to gain an overview of a subject before developing a paper or class project. Similarly, individuals interested in important policy issues could get a quick understanding of key research and its implications. This is a recommended and affordable purchase for public, school, and academic libraries that do not already own the *Encyclopedia of Sociology*. [R: Choice, July/Aug 99, p. 1929; SLJ, Aug 99, p. 181]—**Stephen H. Aby**

60. Spira, Thomas. **Nationalism and Ethnicity Terminologies: An Encyclopedic Dictionary and Research Guide. Volume 1.** Gulf Breeze, Fla., Academic International Press, 1999. 757p. $125.00. ISBN 0-87569-205-2.

In every field one title emerges as the voice that becomes recognized as the authority. This volume is such a work. The encyclopedic dictionary has 7,000 entries, provides a 75-page works cited section with 2,862 entries, and is the culmination of 25 years of scholarship in this area. The dictionary is comprehensive, with the entries predominately in the English language and 85 percent of the literature from the post World War I era (the latest entry is from 1996). A supplement is to follow this 1st volume to cover material left out and also to cover the most recent scholarship. At the beginning of the book there is a 41-page section listing all of the entries defined.

Spira is professor emeritus of history at the University of Prince Edward Island, Charlottetown, Canada, and brings to the project years of experience as the editor-founder of a comparative interdisciplinary journal dealing with regional, topical, theoretical articles, and review essays in English, French, and German.

Walker Connor notes in his foreword the "systematic scheme of classification, and its sophisticated analyses and synthesis" as key values of Spira's work along with being "Weberian in its comprehension." The dictionary is intended for scholars and students of nationalism and ethnicity. However, the scope of inclusion is so wide that general social scientists and those in the humanities will find it useful.

The nearest similar work is from 1990 by Louis L. Snyder titled *Encyclopedia of Nationalism* (see ARBA 91, entry 766). Although this is a useful tool, the breadth and depth of the works are quite different. Much of the space in Synder's work is devoted to biographical entries (these are excluded from the Spira book). Snyder provides 208 references versus 2,862 in Spira's book. The Spira contribution is simply in a class of its own with no comparisons and is highly recommended.—**Graham R. Walden**

61. **The 21st Century: Selections from the Two-Volume** *Encyclopedia of the Future.* George Thomas Kurian and Graham T. T. Molitor, eds. New York, Macmillan Library Reference/Simon & Schuster Macmillan, 1999. 999p. illus. index. (Macmillan Compendium). $125.00. ISBN 0-02-864977-X.

The subtitle readily identifies the roots of this 1-volume reference book. The goal of this compendium is to distill "the thoughts and forecasts of hundreds of the world's leading intellectuals," thus presenting "a unique perspective on the most critical problems of our times" (p. xi). Information is current through 1995, giving the book more of a "back to the future" slant. For example, the entry on intellectual property discusses the basics but does not address how new technologies like the World Wide Web are impacting this legal field. Of course, in 1995, the World Wide Web was just a glimmer on the horizon. Signed entries of varying lengths are arranged alphabetically, from abortion and acid rain to working conditions. Some biographies are included, such as those for Isaac Asimov and St. Thomas More, but none for Bill Gates. The bibliographies at the end of the entries reflect adult sources, with the most recent from 1995. The appendix offers a list of the "One Hundred Most Influential Futurist Books" from the past 65 years. These are not necessarily the best and greatest, but "have had the most impact on the development of futurism or that have expressed seminal futurist ideas" (p. 969). There is also a "Chronology of the Future" that focuses on predictions reflecting the various dimensions of futurism (e.g., astronomy, demographics, medicine, and the end of the world). It divides the future into 9 periods from short-term (starting in 2000) to after 1 trillion C.E., but does not document all the entries offered. Libraries should seriously consider their need for future-related resources before deciding to purchase this volume. [R: SLJ, Aug 99, p. 184]

—**Esther R. Sinofsky**

62. Young, T. R., and Bruce A. Arrigo. **The Dictionary of Critical Social Sciences.** Boulder, Colo., Westview Press, 1999. 351p. $50.00. ISBN 0-8133-6672-0.

This dictionary is not neutral; it is written with a "socialist edge," rejects conventional interpretation, and includes words from "socialist, progressive, radical, humanist, and left-liberal thought." Written for North American students, the entries are intended to cover both terms of interest as well as those that they should know about but lack enthusiasm for. Subjects covered include sociology, philosophy, economics, history, social psychology, political science, criminal justice, anthropology, education, theology, and law. Both the emotional and political contents of terms are explored using critical inquiry.

Young and Arrigo have an agenda for this dictionary. They seek to have the words presented move the reader, and by extension, society, toward social justice and social peace. Through critical inquiry the authors hope to "signal what work is left to be done if real peace, authentic justice, and true humanity are to flourish." Cross-references or "pointers" are included for most selections and many *see* references are used for related terms. Biographical entries occur for significant or "important luminaries."

Given the stated purposes of the book, the authors provide some interesting and provocative definitions and descriptions. The goals are lofty and the subject inclusiveness is very broad. As to whether the agenda can be attained is somewhat beyond the scope of standard book reviewing to evaluate. When authors attempt to cover such vast areas of intellectual real estate, it is inevitable that opportunities will exist to point to elements of omission, such as including St. Francis of Assisi but excluding the Jesuits, similarly including homosexuality but excluding homophobia (even though the word is used in the preface). For the clearly stated objectives and value system presented, this dictionary is highly unusual and should be a part of mid-size to large libraries collections. A clear bias is labeled, permitting students easy recognition of a particular point of view.—**Graham R. Walden**

3 Area Studies

GENERAL WORKS

63. **Cities of the World: A Compilation of Current Information on Cultural, Geographical, and Political Conditions....** 5th ed. Farmington Hills, Mich., Gale, 1999. 4v. illus. maps. index. $322.00/set. ISBN 0-8103-7691-1. ISSN 0889-2741.

With the exception of the United States, this set provides coverage of more than 2,000 cities in 193 countries. Each volume covers a broad geographic area; within the volume, information is arranged alphabetically by country. Within the entry for each country, major cities are covered in some detail, followed by brief information regarding minor cities. A "Country Profile" concludes each section, treating geography and climate, population, government, arts, science, education, commerce and industry, transportation, communications, health, clothing and services, local holidays, recommended reading, and notes for travelers.

Much of the information that forms the basis of this set comes from the *Post Reports* issued by the U.S. Department of State. As these reports are not updated annually, the information included in this set is not consistently current, although the editors claim to have updated some entries with more current information where necessary. Some entries do, in fact, have Department of State updates current through 1998. Others do not. A map of major streets is included for the major city for each country, and mediocre black-and-white photographs are scattered throughout. A table of contents and an index for each volume provide ease of access to city and country information.

Although the set provides some valuable information, it duplicates much of what can be found in a standard encyclopedia complemented by almanacs, travel guides, and other annual country profiles. This set is recommended for the collection that aims to be exhaustive, and that does not mind the costs of duplicating information.—**Edmund F. SantaVicca**

64. **Culturgrams: The Nations Around Us.** Provo, Utah, Kennedy Center Publications, 1998. 2v. maps. $80.00pa./set. ISBN 0-89434-260-6.

Culturgrams is a reference book for finding brief information on various aspects of life in all countries of the world. It has been published in two volumes and includes a glossary of terms used in the book. Volume 1 includes all countries of the Americas and Europe and is arranged alphabetically, covering Albania to Yugoslavia. Volume 2 covers Africa, Asia, and Oceania. All entries are four pages long and have been arranged under broad headings and subheadings, such as background, history, people, customs and courtesies, lifestyle, society, and information about travelers. Special attention has been given to Canada, which has three entries—Canada-Atlantic; Canada-Ontario; and West, Canada-Quebec. The book has a few entries with wrong information and old information. For example, under India the map is old with many wrong names, such as Mumbai for Bombay, Pune for Poona, and Tamil Nudu for Madras. New names have not been shown in the map. The Muslims ruled over India from the eleventh century, not the eighth century. No dates have been given for British rule in India, and the name of France has not been mentioned under foreign powers in India. The information for all countries should be checked for accuracy before printing it. The book certainly gives a broad picture of the lifestyles of people in many countries and their history. [R: RBB, 1 May 98, p. 1532]—**Ravindra Nath Sharma**

65. **EXEGY: Current Country Profiles 2000.** [CD-ROM]. Santa Barbara, Calif., ABC-CLIO, 1999. Minimum system requirements: IBM compatible or Pentium-compatible processor with 75MHz. Four-speed CD-ROM drive. Windows 95, Windows 98, or Windows NT 4.0. 16MB RAM. 120MB hard disk space. SVGA monitor 800x600. 16-bit sound card with Windows drivers. Mouse. $399.00 (stand alone); $599.00 (lab pack); $799.00 (site license). ISSN 1076-8653.

This interactive CD-ROM is an updated edition of the original 1994 product from ABC-CLIO (see ARBA 96, entry 49), whose purpose was the provision of current data on global issues through detailed files on individual countries. Significant features in the September 1999 subscription edition (which will be updated twice yearly) are a revised country index, a new subject index (ranging from history, politics, government, economics, law, and statistics to biographies, flags, and maps), and the addition of advanced Boolean searching. *EXEGY* also offers a Website (accessible by subscription only) covering lesson plans and information files emphasizing international issues designed for both instructors and students. Two optional modules on culture and environment expand coverage to fields as diverse as religion, music, art, literature, biodiversity, and endangered species, all subjects of international concern that should have been included in the basic format. Given the broad scope of this resource and its emphasis on meshing well with a structured curriculum, it may usefully be considered for acquisition by school and public library reference collections. Academic reference librarians should be aware that much of the basic data are available via other paper sources already present in their collections, such as the *Europa World Year Book* (39th ed.; see ARBA 99, entry 66) and individual country government and international agency homepages, which may be added to their array of electronic resources at no cost.—**Robert B. Marks Ridinger**

66. **Fiesta! 2.** Tessa Paul, ed. Danbury, Conn., Grolier, 1999. 16v. illus. index. $265.00/set. ISBN 0-7172-9324-6.

Each of the16 slim books in this set, titled with a country name, is a resource for middle-grade students who study nations of the world and who like to learn about formal celebrations and cultural traditions. Each cover has a colored picture of an 8– or 10–year–old in traditional dress (for the United States it is western). Inside, an outline map identifies location, and a box contains "first impressions" (basic facts). In each volume there are traditional stories, recipes, songs with music (just the melody), about six words from the country's language, and pictures of items unique to the country (e.g., dishes, clothing, symbols, ritual items). Two crafts for each, which are doable by children under supervision, will make great classroom display items. Religious festivals, central in popular and national celebrations in much of the world, are included, and there is often a box briefly outlining a religion's basic tenets. This set will be a welcome addition to the multicultural studies shelf. Set 1, titled *Fiesta!* (see ARBA 98, entry 1262), has similar material for16 other countries.—**Edna M. Boardman**

67. **Lands and Peoples.** Danbury, Conn., Grolier, 1999. 7v. illus. maps. index. $269.00/set. ISBN 0-7172-8021-7.

This set is organized by continent, and the individual volumes by countries. It could be argued that as a whole it deals with neither "lands" (in the sense of geographically, historically, or culturally distinct regions) nor "peoples" (in the sense of language or ethnic groups), but only with modern nation-states. Inasmuch as many current junior high school social studies texts have abandoned the artificially constricting criterion of United Nations membership as the most productive approach to understanding the world we live in, this set will not provide adequate support for students' work outside the classroom. On the other hand, because of its competent entries, written by a battery of capable scholars, its handy summaries of facts and figures, its flags and maps, and its generally representative photographs, it will be of great help to students eager to gather materials efficiently for school reports. All entries include materials on the landscape, language, religion, history, and government; countries deemed significant include topical discussions. If this set is intended for use in teaching beginning library skills, it will certainly serve. But programs that might consider it for use in reinforcing social studies lessons would do well to look elsewhere.—**Glenn Petersen**

68. **The Least Developed Countries 1998 Report.** New York, United Nations, 1998. 210p. $40.00pa. ISBN 92-1-112434-4. ISSN 0257-7550. S/N E.98.II.D.11.

The year 1998 marked the 50th anniversary of GATT (General Agreement on Tariffs and Trade). Among the developing countries of the world are 29 designated as "least developed." This annual report examines the economies of those countries in relation to the global economy and looks at the state of their multilateral trading systems.

Major issues covered in the report's overview chapter include an analysis of how a multilateral trading system affects opportunities for least developed countries (LDC) to participate in the world economy and the challenges that implementing World Trade Organization agreements present. Two major sections follow the overview chapter that discuss global economic developments and trade, investment and the multilateral trading system, and the relation to and impact on LDCs. Color charts, graphs, and topical fact boxes supplement the text. The fact boxes provide examples of the benefits and problems resulting from trade agreements, such as a discussion of the potential for the tourist industry in Nepal and the environmental effects of shrimp farming in Bangladesh.

The statistical appendix includes numerous tables covering basic data on the LDCs. There are demographic figures and statistics on mortality, life expectancy, low birthrates, exports, main markets, and agriculture. There are also more technical tables dealing with finance and trade issues. These are prefaced by an introductory paragraph explaining how to interpret the data.

Economists and experts in world trade wrote the report, yet the text is clearly written and well organized, making the information understandable to the interested general reader. A real coup for a government report. Business school libraries and universities offering courses in international business will find this an informative source.—**Marlene M. Kuhl**

69. Mitchell, B. R. **International Historical Statistics: Africa, Asia, & Oceania 1750-1993.** 3d ed. New York, Stockton Press/Groves Dictionaries, 1998. 1113p. $350.00. ISBN 1-56159-234-X.

70. Mitchell, B. R. **International Historical Statistics: Europe 1750-1993.** 4th ed. New York, Stockton Press/Groves Dictionaries, 1998. 959p. $350.00. ISBN 1-56159-236-6.

71. Mitchell, B. R. **International Historical Statistics: The Americas 1750-1993.** 4th ed. New York, Stockton Press/Groves Dictionaries, 1998. 830p. $350.00. ISBN 1-56159-235-8.

A librarian's search for historical statistics has been aided immensely by Mitchell's effort to compile these figures. The 1st edition of this work appeared in 1982 (see ARBA 83, entry 72) and subsequent editions were reviewed in several volumes of ARBA. In all three volumes the arrangement of material is similar: population and vital statistics, labor force, agriculture, industry, external trade, finance, prices, and national accounts. All in all, this is an important and convenient source for reference inquiries dealing with historical aspects of a specific area.—**Bohdan S. Wynar**

72. Ness, Immanuel. **Encyclopedia of World Cities.** Armonk, N.Y., Sharpe Reference/M. E. Sharpe, 1999. 2v. maps. index. $179.00. ISBN 0-7656-8017-3.

This handy 2-volume encyclopedia covers 132 major world cities. For each city 10 key areas of urban life are explored. Geography, demographics, politics, government, culture, and social issues are discussed in short essays. Each entry also includes a map showing the city's location in relation to other cities within the country and other countries. Statistical charts showing such things as growth rate, education levels, and the population's vital statistics are provided. The introduction gives the user a succinct course in urban development by explaining how the key areas affect a city's growth and development over time and how, in turn, development has impacted such things as health care and education. There is also an explanation of how to interpret statistical data. Five comparative tables make up the appendix. Among them are tables showing population rankings as well as increase and change over time. An alphabetic index and a bibliography are provided.

The encyclopedia does suffer from sins of omission. Examples from the London entry include a lack of any mention of the National Health Service, and only a sketchy description of the British educational system is included. A student looking at the entry may not have the breadth of knowledge that is assumed here. The negatives are balanced by the scope of information, its currency, and the context within which it is presented. Most statistics are from the 1990s, and information as recent as 1998 appears in some entries. Comprehensive information on cities is often hard to find, and this set will fill a need in secondary school and public libraries. [R: BL, 1 May 99, p. 1624; LJ, July 99, p. 83; Choice, Oct 99, p. 315; SLJ, Aug 99, p. 186]
—Marlene M. Kuhl

73. **The World Factbook 1999.** By the Central Intelligence Agency. Herndon, Va., Brassey's (U.S.), 1999. 639p. maps. $39.95. ISBN 1-57488-163-9.

The first review of the original version of this title noted the lack of a hard cover and the absence of an index (see ARBA 84, entry 293). Brassey's has now published the 7th reprint of this title. The cover is hard but indexing has not been added. Earlier reviews of the work (see ARBA 97, entry 80; ARBA 93, entry 105) both mention the availability of the federal government document version at a lower price. The CD-ROM format was reviewed in ARBA 95 (see entry 8) and interestingly the 2 reviewers found the paper tool quicker to use when trying to find "specific factual information." If a library does not participate in the federal documents depository program and anticipates frequent use of the volume, then this Brassey's version is adequate. All others will want to rely on the version from the Government Printing Office.
—**Graham R. Walden**

UNITED STATES

General Works

74. **Cities of the United States: A Compilation of Current Information on Economic, Cultural, Geographic, and Social Conditions.** 3d ed. Linda Schmittroth, ed. Farmington Hills, Mich., Gale, 1998. 4v. illus. maps. index. $375.00/set. ISBN 0-8103-6435-2. ISSN 0899-6075.

There are 164 urban centers considered in terms of brief population characteristics, geography, climate, history, municipal government, economy, education, research, health care, recreation, convention facilities, transportation, and communication in this work. Each entry has at least one black-and-white photograph, with many locations containing multiple scenes, some of which are a full page. The 4-volume set consists of "The South," "The West," "The Midwest," and "The Northwest," and addresses the largest cities in each state. For smaller states cities selected might actually represent rather small communities in terms of total population; for example, Vermont's state capital, Montpelier, has a 1996 estimated population of 12,848. Three states have only one city listed—Boise, Idaho; Charleston, West Virginia; and Cheyenne, Wyoming. With 10 entries, California has the most cities presented, followed by Pennsylvania with 7, and 6 each for Connecticut and Florida. The volumes are useful, and the set is a convenient single source for a variety of information, which would take some considerable effort to bring together independently. Given these observations it is easy to recommend the set to first-time purchasers. The set would complement a general reference collection well, and can be used for a surprising array of questions.

The challenging question is whether those now holding the 2d edition should purchase the 3d edition, and if such an action would constitute a sensible use of collection funds. A side-by-side comparison of the 2d and 3d editions suggests that it would be prudent to use the $375.00 elsewhere. The actual text of the compared cities is identical in word and photograph, the only changes being in the numerical updating of the initial part of each entry (including data such as population, and some economic and social statistics) as well as the population profile and some other sections with date-specific statistics. Most of this sort of data is readily available elsewhere, and although it is convenient to have it displayed like this, the price per entry for this luxury becomes high. Perhaps Gale will completely update the format, expand and revise the content, and revisit the illustrations for the 4th edition. In the event of such an overhaul, it is likely that the set would be met with great interest and would find a place in a wide variety of libraries.—**Graham R. Walden**

75.   **Congressional Quarterly's Desk Reference on the States.** By Bruce Wetterau. Washington, D.C., Congressional Quarterly, 1999. 328p. index. $49.95. ISBN 1-56802-444-4.

This volume presents historical information about states, along with information about government, current status, and practices. There are seven chapters: The States, Governorship, Legislatures, Campaigns and Elections, State Courts, State of the States, and What About My State? Chapter 7, "What About My State?—The State Profiles," takes up about 20 percent of the book and gives brief factual information about each one of our 50 states. Various questions are posed and answered. The final question in each chapter, "Where can I find…," cites and annotates various pertinent reference works. Numbered cross-references refer to item numbers within the text, and not to page numbers. So initially it is a little confusing. There are subject and name indexes. Checking under "Abortion," one is referred to item 432, "What did the court rule in *Roe vs. Wade*?" with a brief discussion. Under "*Roe vs. Wade* (1973)" readers are referred to items 418 and 432. Under 418 users find "What proportion of cases the Supreme Court decides affects states?" where *Roe vs. Wade* is mentioned as a controversial case. There is no entry under Wade. Under "Supreme Court" readers get "See also specific cases." There are entries under "Women" but no references there to *Roe vs. Wade*. There is also no entry under "Reproductive Rights," and there are no references to Roe or Wade in the name index. It seems to be a rather superficial treatment of the topic. The preface does not indicate an intended audience, but it seems to be for high school level.—**Frank J. Anderson**

76.   Renehan, Edward J., Jr. **Great American Websites: An Online Discovery of a Hidden America.** New York, Osborne/McGraw-Hill, 1997. 470p. illus. index. $24.99pa. ISBN 0-07-882304-8.

In this reference guide, Renehan identifies and cleverly annotates a collection of Websites. Readers can explore categories such as "American Sports," "Architecture," "The Great Outdoors," "Individual Americans," and "Kingdom of Kitsch." However, today one must question the usefulness of printed directories of Websites considering the instability of Web page maintenance. These sites may have short life spans. Yet, all things considered, the author does annotate a number of interesting sites. Some of the sites are clearly biased toward the author's choice in music (folk).

The author includes an overview of the search engines Yahoo! and Alta Vista. This is a nice addition for neophytes to World Wide Web searching.—**Leslie R. Homzie**

Florida

77.   Philcox, Phil, and Beverly Boe. **The Sunshine State Almanac and Book of Florida-Related Stuff.** Sarasota, Fla., Pineapple Press, 1999. 354p. illus. $16.95pa. ISBN 1-56164-178-2.

This almanac is an informal guide to Florida and is organized in a somewhat haphazard fashion. Chapter titles reflect an assortment of themes, which include animals, people, birds, bugs, health, fish, hobbies, food, house and garden, legal issues, sports, water, weather, wildlife, and vacations. Within the chapters are myriad articles—some of general interest, some humorous, and some strange. A miscellaneous chapter has several articles featuring cemeteries (e.g., early Florida cemeteries, political cemeteries, gravestone rubbings). These are unique articles and contain information of help to genealogical researchers. The first is especially noteworthy in that it contains information concerning burials of slaves and free persons of color during Florida's pioneer days. Elsewhere in the book, readers will find articles that will be ideal for reading out loud from the passenger side of the car, and some contain facts and toll-free telephone numbers for emergencies. A few articles have absolutely nothing to do with Florida. Various contributors to the work have their Internet addresses given so that additional information may be found. Although there is a detailed table of contents in the front of the text, the book could benefit greatly if a full index were added.—**Louis G. Zelenka**

78. Servies, James A., and Lana D. Servies. **A Bibliography of Florida. Volume 3: 1881-1899.** Pensacola, Fla., King & Queen Books, 1999. 559p. index. $165.00. ISBN 0-9636370-2-9.

The time frame covered by this bibliography, 1881 to 1899, was an exciting period of rapid growth in population, tourism, and development in many areas in the state of Florida. The cultivation of oranges, other citrus fruits, and field crops was beginning to move southward along the East Coast; several thousand miles of railroad tracks were constructed; and the Flagler era of resort hotels was luring winter tourists to the warm climate. St. Johns River steamboats could take the traveler inland and smaller steamers navigated the twisting stream into Silver Springs. By this time, Florida could be reached by the inhabitants of the great cities of the northeastern part of the United States by train in less than 24 hours or in just a few days by ocean. Volume 3 of this bibliography series is a continuation of the record of publications by and about the state. Included are government publications originated by state, county, and city agencies; maps; almanacs; yearbooks; and city directories. It also contains a list of books covering a vast range of topics, such as agriculture, education, health, history, hunting, the sciences, travel, and curios. Libraries, bookstores, and private collections around the nation were researched in the compilation of this work. Few of the nearly 800 newly published Florida newspapers of this time survive even in partial collections, but where possible these have been noted with entries. Of particular interest to researchers of this era is the listing for the numerous standard guides and directories of the time. There are a number of entries relating to church convocations, councils, and sessions. Topics of concern toward the end of the century—troubles with Spain and recurrent yellow fever epidemics—are evident.

Arrangement is chronological, with a chapter for each of the 19 years covered by the text. Each entry is alphabetic by author, but a thorough index by author, title, and subject provides ready access to the information. Citation numbers for each entry enhance the work, and libraries holding the items are identified by library location symbols. Nearly 80 library collections are so identified. Although this is a well-researched and quite scholarly reference, the authors have an enjoyable writing style that conveys the pleasure they must have felt during the years of research that went into the making of this bibliography. This work fulfills a great need in Florida libraries and is a valuable resource for many libraries elsewhere.—**Louis G. Zelenka**

Illinois

79. **ResourceLink Illinois.** [CD-ROM]. Santa Barbara, Calif., ABC-CLIO, 1999. Minimum system requirements (Windows version): IBM or Pentium-compatible processor at 75MHz or faster. Four-speed CD-ROM drive. Windows 95. Windows NT 4.0. Windows 98. 16MB RAM. 10MB hard disk space. SVGA monitor (640x480). Mouse. Minimum system requirements (Macintosh version): 68040 or faster processor. Double-speed CD-ROM drive. System 7.5.3. 16MB RAM. 10MB hard disk space. SVGA monitor (640x480). $49.00 (individual); $240.00 (network). ISBN 1-57607-173-1.

The title for this CD-ROM database is somewhat confusing; it should be "Electronic Encyclopedia of Illinois." Like any general encyclopedia, a wide variety of information is included. One can find articles on the environment, economy, culture, government, law, population, organization profiles, important events, and interesting features of society. Both recent and older events are covered. There are helpful reprints and excerpts of historical documents and speeches that may be hard to find elsewhere, such as the "Declaration of Purpose of the National Grange," along with more important court cases. Also included are statistical tables, with figures taken from other (usually government) sources, such as "Educational Indicators, 1990-1997" and "English Proficiency Rates, 1990." More up-to-date data can be found on agency Web pages or the *Illinois Statistical Abstract* (University of Illinois, Bureau of Economic and Business Research, 1987-). The quotations and excerpts from other sources have a brief bibliographic citation, but no page numbers. This is exasperating when one is trying to find the full-text of something partially quoted on this CD-ROM. The text entries do have a short list of sources, which includes author, title, and year of publication, for further information. Not every picture in this product has a caption explaining what the user is looking at; sometimes there is only a general title. There are 10 maps, but they are not very detailed.

The software seems more complicated than perhaps it needs to be. From the first screen, one can click on the "New" button to get the main list of 624 resources that can be chosen from. Users can restrict the search with drop-down menus by topic and by the type of information required, or just type in some keywords in the search box. From there it is not clear how to open up a selected resource; one must close out of the search page to get to a page where the resource can be opened up. Irritatingly, the text shows up in a small box down in the left corner, although the pages can be enlarged to full size for easier reading. Pages can be exported to diskettes, other drives, a network, and printers. Users can also gather a number of the resources from this disc together for exporting, or adding to. They can create their own resource files, and edit the information provided from the disc for incorporation into a paper or for a projected presentation. The system installs a copy of "Windows Media Player" and "Adobe Acrobat 3.01" onto the computer's hard drive; it would be easier if they were able to just run off the compact disc. The software also has an "uninstall" feature. If users want to do all of this fancy manipulation of text, then they should read through all of the help screens first (which seem to be pretty good) in order to fully exploit this product to its full capability. This series also has similar discs for seven other states (with more sure to be added), along with eight separate discs for long periods of U.S. and world history.

This product does not have enough information for academic libraries; it is probably more appropriate for public and school libraries, particularly if it can be mounted on a local area network for multiple-user access. There is also an option to purchase a package of five discs for use in a computer lab. A print version might be easier to use, and might even sell more copies. An Internet subscription database could also be brought online because the contents are already digitized. Such an arrangement would also allow for easier updating and expansion of the content. Some libraries will already have the *Encyclopedia of Illinois* (Somerset, 1994), the *Illinois Biographical Dictionary* (Somerset, 1998), and other Illinois reference books that would be faster to use for quick-answer reference work. The low price certainly makes this product attractive for individual purchase. [R: LJ, 15 Nov 98, p. 101]—**Daniel K. Blewett**

Texas

80. **Texas Almanac, 2000-2001.** 60th ed. Mary G. Ramos and Robert Plocheck, eds. Dallas, Tex., Dallas Morning News; distr., College Station, Tex., Texas A&M University Press, 1999. 672p. illus. maps. index. $12.95pa. ISBN 0-914511-28-9.

For ready-reference information on the state of Texas, the *Texas Almanac* has been a standard source since 1857. This 60th edition covers all the usual topics. It begins with a brief statistical profile of the state, including rankings in comparison with other states. This information is followed by a large section individually profiling Texas's 254 counties and supplying such facts as ethnicity, geographical area, climatological information, and economic activities. Another section lists cities and towns of Texas alphabetically under the county where they are located along with their 1998 population. Ghost towns and town name changes are also listed in italics. Detailed information is provided about environment and weather, state and local government, education, agriculture, and business and industry. Special sections provide brief histories of the Texas Rangers, the Texas oil industry, and a short survey of Texas history. An attractive and useful guide to Texas, this edition is billed as the millennium edition. It is too bad that the editors did not wait until 2001 for the true millennium and the 2000 census information in order to use that potent label properly.—**Ronald H. Fritze**

AFRICA

81. **Africa South of the Sahara 1999.** 28th ed. London, Europa; distr., Farmington Hills, Mich., Gale, 1999. 1185p. $415.00. ISBN 1-85743-046-8. ISSN 0065-4896.

This is an annually revised guide to sub-Saharan Africa. The first part provides background to the region and includes essays on colonial role, economic trends, and reform. With regard to commodities produced in these African countries, information and data are given about production (in the context of world production and trade) along with recent prices. Names and addresses of research institutes studying Africa worldwide come next. A selected, slightly annotated bibliography of relevant periodicals with editor, street address, telephone and fax numbers, and e-mail addresses ends this section. Part 2 provides information on approximately two dozen multinational organizations operating in sub-Saharan Africa. Most of these are United Nations agencies, but also include the likes of the Commonwealth and the Islamic Development Bank. For each of these, information is given about the activities, the extent of which (financing, publications, addresses) depends upon the specific organization. The 51 individual country surveys comprise the mass of the book (part 3). For each country, there are sections on physical and social geography, recent history, economy, statistical survey, a directory, and a bibliography. While the extent of the data varies with each country, it is generally on population, economic activity, finance, external trade, transport, education, and tourism. The dates of the data vary but are usually from the 1990s. The directory provides information (name, address, phone number) for government offices, political organizations, diplomatic representation, judicial system, religious organizations, the press, banks, and trade organizations—with specific ones mentioned again changing with each country. For those considering doing business in sub-Saharan Africa or wanting to develop the African content of a particular industry, this volume can provide useful information. Names, addresses, and other information about specific ministries and organizations can be difficult to acquire. This book makes them easily available.—**J. E. Weaver**

82. DeLancey, Mark W., and Mark D. DeLancey, comps. **Cameroon.** rev. ed. Santa Barbara, Calif., Clio Press/ABC-CLIO, 1999. 207p. maps. index. (World Bibliographical Series, v.63). $67.00. ISBN 1-85109-301-X.

The 1st edition of this bibliography was published in 1986 when Cameroon's economic future looked promising. By 1994 the country's per capita Gross Domestic Product (GDP) had dropped by almost 50 percent. This change is documented in the selection of titles covering the country's economic development.

The 654 annotated entries are organized into 25 chapters covering the history, geography, politics, and culture of the country. Sources include books, journal articles, and videotapes. Annotations are clearly written and give a comprehensive assessment of a title's contents. Researchers can pick and choose with confidence knowing that the works they select will be pertinent to their needs. The literature and arts and music chapters are outstanding in their breadth of coverage. The literature section contains 47 entries covering fiction, bibliographies, folklore, and essays. There are 64 entries under arts and music covering architecture, specific crafts, fine arts, and traditional and contemporary African music. Particular attention is paid to Cameroon's ethnic groups in these and all sections of the book.

Most titles are in English but given that both French and English are the country's official languages, it is not surprising that a fair number are in French (7 of the 12 archaeology entries are in French). There are title, author, and subject indexes and a substantive introductory essay that gives an overview of Cameroon's history to date.

As with other titles in this series, the information has been carefully selected, usefully annotated, and well organized. The bibliography will provide a good starting point for researchers studying Cameroon as a whole or for those focusing on a specific topic related to the country.—**Marlene M. Kuhl**

83. Harris, Gordon. **Central and Equatorial Africa Area Bibliography.** Lanham, Md., Scarecrow, 1999. 209p. index. (Scarecrow Area Bibliographies, no.18). $58.00. ISBN 0-8108-3606-8.

This highly useful work is the latest in the Scarecrow Area Bibliographies series, which provides access to sources on various regions of the world. The book deals with both Congos, Chad, the Central African Republic, São Tomé and Principe, Equatorial Guinea, Gabon, Rwanda, Burundi, Zambia, and Malawi. The author is a British–based academic librarian with scholarly, consulting, and bibliographic credentials on the region under study.

The series format resembles that of Clio Press's World Bibliographical Series. Both series include lengthy introductory essays on the subject by the compiler. Harris provides a thorough and readable, 32–page bibliographic essay divided into eight subject sections from general works and anthropology to historical and political citations. Sections are further subdivided by state or region. The essay provides a most helpful orientation to the region and its literature.

The bibliography is divided into 12 subsections, 1 for the region as a whole and the rest covering the 11 states. Each subsection is further split by subject. The overview section, for example, has about 50 sub-headings, from agriculture and animals to religion and women. The country sections' organization is not alphabetic but geographic, meaning one has to use the contents.

There are 1,763 citations listed. Entries are not annotated. English and French (the main colonial languages) dominate citations, but other European languages appear as well. There is an author index, but no title index. This index refers only to the bibliographic entry; there is no mention of the introductory essay, making the context provided by the essay for some works less easy to access. This is an excellent guide to publications on its region of Africa. Its long introduction may make it of interest to larger public libraries as well as to strictly research institutions.—**Nigel Tappin**

84. Kagan, Alfred, and Yvette Scheven. **Reference Guide to Africa: A Bibliography of Sources.** Lanham, Md., Scarecrow, 1999. 262p. index. $49.50. ISBN 0-8108-3585-1.

The last decade has seen a wide variety of reference tools published to aid those conducting research about the African continent. The 25 chapters of this work are divided into 2 parts. The first covers general reference sources, such as bibliographies and indexes, guides, handbooks, directories, dictionaries and encyclopedias, statistics, and biographical tools. This reviewer was happy to see that there are separate chapters for primary sources and government publications (the latter field is one of Kagan's specialties); unfortunately, these are frequently overlooked by researchers. There is also a chapter for Internet sources. Part 2 has sources logically arranged by broad subject categories: communications, literature, religion, women, music, folklore, environment, visual arts, publishing, politics, libraries and librarianship (not a subject that is often given its own chapter), languages and linguistics, history, geography and maps, development, agriculture and food, and cultural anthropology. A typical chapter has entries arranged into sections for surveys, directories, statistics, indexes, bibliographies, dictionaries and encyclopedias, and more specialized sections depending on the subject. At the end of the chapters can be found several selected Library of Congress subject headings, which are helpful for when one is searching for more sources. The 944 numbered entries are annotated, some with only a sentence (but that is all they need). Internet addresses for particular works or agencies are included as needed (this should be a standard feature of all future bibliographies of reference works). Monographs, surveys, and more general works are included when necessary. Scheven has other reference books on Africa to her credit, such as *Bibliographies for African Studies, 1987-1993* (see ARBA 95, entry 113). The standard author/title and subject indexes are included. Kagan is the present and Scheven is a past African studies bibliographer at the University of Illinois at Urbana-Champaign, which has a large African studies collection. This book has many more sources than the *Guide to Reference Sources* (11th ed.; American Library Association, 1996). This work is recommended for the reference collections of academic and large public libraries. [R: LJ, 1 Mar 99, p. 74; Choice, June 99, p. 1754]

—**Daniel K. Blewett**

ASIA

General Works

85. Nwanna, Gladson I. **Do's and Don'ts Around the World: A Country Guide to Cultural and Social Taboos and Etiquette: Asia.** Baltimore, Md., World Travel Institute Press, 1998. 254p. $24.95pa. ISBN 1-890605-01-8.

This book is part of a series listing a number of actions and activities that travelers should or should not engage in when traveling to a foreign country. The book consists of a large checklist of the countries in Asia, from Afghanistan to Japan and from China to Indonesia. The checklist indicates whether a number of actions are allowable, are not customary, or are even forbidden. Among the behaviors considered by the author are smoking, eating, and drinking alcohol in public; kissing, spitting, and dancing in public; haggling and giving money to beggars; using a Walkman or possessing a Bible; females drinking or smoking; females wearing lipstick, bikinis, or trousers; and tipping. The book considers each country and includes sections on particular "do's and don'ts," such as whether pedestrians have the right-of-way and the punishment for drug trafficking. "Additional country information," such as safe topics for discussion and whether there is a basic color with negative connotations, is included as well. The book contains much useful information, but its reliability is suspect when the reader is informed that in Pakistan begging is not customary, yet giving money to beggars is. It also states that both "guilty until proven innocent" and "innocent until proven guilty" are the law. The book indicates that spitting in public is not customary in India, which would surprise millions of paan chewers. The book concludes with a useful appendix containing a country-by-country guide to tipping; electricity requirements; telephone dialing codes; banking, business, and shopping hours; and international emergency telephone codes. The book should be used with care.—**David L. White**

China

86. **Dictionary of the Politics of the People's Republic of China.** Colin Mackerras, with Donald H. McMillen and Andrew Watson, eds. New York, Routledge, 1998. 267p. illus. index. $100.00. ISBN 0-415-15450-2.

Contributed to by 34 China scholars from Australia, Hong Kong, India, Korea, Singapore, and the United States, this dictionary assesses the dynamic nature of Chinese politics from 1978 to 1997. It is aimed at providing students, government, media and business personnel, and nonspecialist academics with useful and accessible information about the People's Republic of China (PRC). The dictionary begins with eight introductory essays, which present an overview history of the PRC, its people and government, ideology, political figures, politics and economy, the region, and the overseas Chinese. This section is followed by the main body of the dictionary, which consists of 114 descriptive topics, alphabetically arranged and carefully chosen in accord with their importance to China's political culture, economy, foreign relations, society, and the political identity of the Chinese people. The signed entries are generally well researched and well written in an essay format, with cross-references at the end of each article. The volume concludes with a selected reading list and an extensive subject index. The Pinyin romanization system is employed throughout the text with the exception of a few names, such a Sun Yat-sen, which has its own established non-Pinyin form. Since more than one-third of the book is devoted to significant persons or events, it would have been useful if the dates were noted immediately following the names and events. It would also have been useful if a glossary of English equivalents of Chinese names or terms was appended for easy reference. This work is suitable for academic and public libraries. [R: LJ, 1 May 98, p. 92]

—**Karen T. Wei**

87. Perkins, Dorothy. **Encyclopedia of China: The Essential Reference to China, Its History, and Culture.** New York, Facts on File, 1999. 662p. illus. index. (A Roundtable Press Book). $95.00. ISBN 0-8160-2693-9.

This introductory 1-volume reference work contains more than 1,000 entries, arranged alphabetically, on China's past, present, and future. Using an essay-length format to provide up-to-date and comprehensive background information, the encyclopedia has succeeded in offering general readers a source to understand this emerging superpower. The work covers all aspects of the history and culture of China, exploring its geography, population, and lifestyle; religion and popular culture; arts and crafts; literature; performing and martial arts; history; current politics and economics; and foreign relations and trade. The Pinyin romanization system is emphasized in this book but Wade-Giles equivalents are noted and references made. Most entries are also heavily cross-referenced. For example, under the heading "Qing Dynasty" there are more than 100 *see also* references. The book is further enhanced by more than 50 black-and-white photographs and illustrations. A list of suggested readings and an extensive subject index linking concepts, people, and events conclude the volume. The adequate index makes the work extremely easy to use.

A number of similar works have been published in the past 15 years. The competitive *Cambridge Encyclopedia of China* (2d ed.; see ARBA 93, entry 125) is more authoritative but lacks cross-references. Perkins's work is also more current and more adequately indexed. The expensive 3-volume reference set *Information China* (see ARBA 90, entry 121) represents the official view of the Chinese government and is far more extensive in coverage than Perkins's work but desperately needs updates. Finally, *Modern China: An Encyclopedia of History, Culture, and Nationalism* (see ARBA 99, entry 109) begins with the outbreak of the Opium War in 1839 and ends with events up to 1997. Depending on the user's needs, these volumes complement each other well. Perkins's encyclopedia is highly recommended for both academic and public libraries. [R: BL, 1 Feb 99, pp. 995-996; BR, May/June 99, p. 78; Choice, June 99, pp. 1765-1766]—**Karen T. Wei**

Japan

88. Eades, J. S., comp. **Tokyo.** Santa Barbara, Calif., Clio Press/ABC-CLIO, 1999. 288p. maps. index. (World Bibliographical Series, v.214). $85.00. ISBN 1-85109-292-7.

Number 214 in the World Bibliography Series claims the distinction of being the first annotated English-language bibliography of Tokyo. The 1,200 items covering the Edo period to the twentieth century are divided into 27 major sections covering Tokyo's history, such as geography, economy, politics, and culture. Almost all are English titles, although there are a few in French and German. Appropriate fiction, juvenile, and classic reprints are included.

Entries are numbered sequentially and are listed within sections by date of publication. *See* references are used if information on a specific subject is contained in a title whose main entry is located elsewhere. For example, titles on the Pacific War and occupation do not have their own section. Pertinent titles appear under one of the major headings.

Annotations are concise, but give a clear picture of a title's content and perspective. For example, materials printed for the postwar occupation forces and official publications of Tokyo's city government are included. In the geography section, materials published before and after the devastating 1923 earthquake give insight into the significance of the landmark disaster on the city. Painting and woodblock printing are strongly represented by numerous titles on specific artists, including those who specialized in Shunga. Literature and performing arts, both traditional and contemporary, are represented. Pachinko, Karaoke, and Sumo are covered in the popular culture section. Aum Shinrikyo is included with titles on more traditional religions.

The substantive introduction gives a narrative overview of Tokyo's history and geography, and includes tables for area and population by ward and municipality. There are indexes of authors, titles, and subjects, and maps of Central Tokyo and the Tokyo Prefecture.

The comprehensive work will be of value to a range of users. Scholars, secondary and postsecondary students, and general travelers will find it helpful. It will be especially beneficial to those involved in international relations and trade since it offers a broad spectrum of titles that give an in-depth picture of the forces that have shaped one of the world's major cities.—**Marlene M. Kuhl**

89. Kamachi, Noriko. **Culture and Customs of Japan.** Westport, Conn., Greenwood Press, 1999. 187p. illus. maps. index. (Culture and Customs of Asia). $45.00. ISBN 0-313-30197-2.

For years, most Japanese leaving the country for a long trip somehow ended up with a copy of Nippon Steel's *Nippon: The Land and Its People*. Now in its 20th edition, it continues to answer a variety of typical questions about Japanese history and culture with facing English and Japanese texts. However, as Japan became more of an economic powerhouse, a number of popular handbooks to understanding Japan for Americans emerged, some by writers whose Japanese knowledge was limited to brief visits and thus were full of whimsical impressions and factual errors. To counter this, "experts" were brought in to create newer guides. *Culture and Customs of Japan* is another example of this trend, written by University of Michigan, Dearborn, professor Noriko Kamachi. The book, although written by a historian, is not an academic one from both a positive angle (in that it is very readable) and a more critical one (there are few footnotes and the four pages of suggested readings are neither descriptive nor evaluative). Indeed, the table of contents reflects the series' aim of introducing Asian culture (religion; literature; art; housing; food; clothing; women, marriage, and family; festivals; entertainment; and social customs) to general Western audiences. From this perspective it could be seen as a cultural counterpart to the CIA country handbook, especially as Kamachi largely relegates post-war political Japan to three pages in the historical introduction. From the perspective of a ready-reference work, *The Kodansha Encyclopedia of Japan* (see ARBA 84, entry 305) or *Japan: An Illustrated Encyclopedia* (see ARBA 94, entry 115) are strongly suggested. Komachi's selection of topics and explanations are a good, readable (junior high and above) introduction to the vanishing world of Japanese traditional culture. If Greenwood comes out with a 2d edition, the editor should not to be afraid of the political aspects and perhaps should choose a less stereotypical cover photograph than the current one of a woman in kimono and bamboo umbrella.—**Andrew B. Wertheimer**

Thailand

90. Smyth, David, comp. **Thailand.** rev. ed. Santa Barbara, Calif., Clio Press/ABC-CLIO, 1998. 226p. maps. index. (World Bibliographical Series, v.65). $91.00. ISBN 1-85109-254-4.

The World Bibliographical Series continues to produce high-quality guides to research literature of the world, and the revised edition of *Thailand* is no exception. The many new and recent entries reflect the considerable growth in English-language scholarship from and about Thailand since the 1986 edition. The compiler demonstrates his knowledge of evolving research trends with the inclusion of new subject categories—"Women and Gender" and "Environment." In addition, the inclusion of works about prostitution, homosexuality, and AIDS, along with the increased number of entries for minorities, modern Thai history and politics, and literature, provides an accurate overview of research and publishing in the field.

Those seeking up-to-date information, especially on the recent economic crisis, can be assured of finding recent publications—many as recent as 1997 and 1998. At the same time, Smyth has not neglected the seminal works that form the foundation of Thai studies. Although the majority of citations refer to published monographs and research papers, the author includes a few dissertation and journal article citations, leaving one to wonder about the criteria for their selection. At a time when computers make it easy to generate endless lists of citations, Smyth's careful selections and his well-written annotations are especially important for those being introduced to the study of Thailand. As with any bibliography, there are omissions. References to CD-ROM and nonprint resources that are increasingly important to the research and teaching community would be a valuable addition. This bibliography not only serves as an excellent guide to the new student of Thailand but also serves to make us aware of the changing nature of scholarship and publishing in area studies. This work is highly recommended for college and research libraries. [R: Choice, Sept 99, p. 122]—**Carol L. Mitchell**

AUSTRALIA AND THE PACIFIC AREA

91. Daly, Martin, comp. **Tonga.** Santa Barbara, Calif., Clio Press/ABC-CLIO, 1999. 185p. maps. index. (World Biographical Series, v.217). $62.00. ISBN 1-85109-293-5.

This selective, annotated bibliography of Tonga is the 217th work in the World Biographical Series. 452 items are listed. The compiler has found it necessary to deviate from the series policy of giving preference to recent books, commercially published and generally available, because, for Tonga, many subject areas have few, if any, recent books, and the bulk of the material is found in academic journals. The Kingdom of Tonga, located about 1,800 kilometers north of New Zealand and about 800 kilometers east of Fiji, contains around 150 islands, grouped mainly in 3 clusters. It is a traditional Polynesian kingdom, mostly Christian in religion, with a total population of 97,446. Most aspects of life in the kingdom are covered in the bibliography. The usual series outline of subjects is followed by a special section on the drinking of kava and its social significance. Daly's annotations are descriptive rather than evaluative. They give excellent synopses of the content of each article or book. Even when the writings are not available to the researchers, they can obtain much valuable information on Tonga from the annotations. An introduction summarizes the Tongan geography, history, political system, foreign relations, economy, and society. Supplementary sections contain a chronology of important events in the history of Tonga, a list of doctoral theses, and a black-and-white map. Three indexes provide access by author, title, and subject. The compiler is the publication and research manager at the School of Oriental and African Studies, University of London; married to a Tongan; and has spent much time in the islands. Daly has built up an important collection of books on the area.—**Shirley L. Hopkinson**

92. **The Far East and Australasia 1999.** 30th ed. London, Europa; distr., Farmington Hills, Mich., Gale, 1998. 1337p. $450.00. ISBN 1-85743-048-4. ISSN 0071-3791.

Contributed to by more than 40 leading authorities on the region, this comprehensive guide to political events and economic developments of the past year in eastern Asia, Australia, New Zealand, and the Pacific Islands is packed with concise, accurate, and up-to-date information. There is plenty of factual material for both general readers and area specialists in this well-written volume of more than 1,300 pages. This latest edition follows the same format as previous editions. It begins with a calendar of political events, covering November 1997 to October 1998, highlighting the important activities during the past year. The main body is divided into 3 parts. Part 1 is a general survey, containing essays on the region's population, environmental issues, religions, current economic trend, and the "Pacific Century." Part 2, which consists of country surveys, is geographically organized from Afghanistan to Vietnam. It profiles each country's physical and social geography, history, and economy, and is followed by a statistical survey and directory. The coverage of information in the main text portion is of consistently high quality. Full references are given in the bibliography at the end of each country. Part 3 consists of active international organizations, major commodities, and research institutes in the area. Finally, select bibliographies of the books and periodicals conclude the volume. Except for its high price, this is an excellent reference work that is updated annually, and is invaluable for all academic, government, or public libraries as well as for general readers seeking current information on the region.—**Karen T. Wei**

CANADA

93. Gagnon, Alain-G., comp. **Québec.** Santa Barbara, Calif., Clio Press/ABC-CLIO, 1998. 350p. maps. index. (World Bibliographical Series, v.211). $105.00. ISBN 1-85109-290-0.

The World Bibliographical Series' goal is to compile a bibliography of country information for every country in the world. *Québec* is volume 211 of this series. The province of Québec has propelled itself into the national forefront by the Québec Referendum of October 1995 and its active participation in the North American Free Trade Agreement (NAFTA). These two reasons are why the editors decided to include a volume about Québec in its World Bibliographical Series.

The format for this volume is identical to the other country studies volumes. The volume is a bibliography of works about Québec and its people. The succeeding chapters are bibliographies of print, electronic, and nonprint resources categorized by topics. The topics begin with geography and history, moving into social trends, a special chapter on the women of Québec, transportation, education, art and literature, and sports and leisure. It has three separate indexes—author, title, and subject. It has a pen-and-ink map at the end of the book.

This book is recommended to special and academic libraries that have special collections of country information. This will be a valuable handbook for the government libraries that focus on international business and politics.—**Kay M. Stebbins**

EUROPE

General Works

94. **The European Union Encyclopedia and Directory 1999.** 3d ed. London, Europa Publications; distr., Farmington Hills, Mich., Gale, 1999. 520p. $450.00. ISBN 1-85743-056-5. ISSN 1363-7045.

The European Union is evolving so rapidly in terms of new regulations, policies, and personnel, that it is difficult to stay current with the latest developments. One possible way to do so is to use the many fine resources on the Internet. However, there is currently no central Web-based clearinghouse for such information. Researchers, economists, and politicians must consult numerous sites in order to collect the data they need. A practical solution to this problem is to return to traditional print media and to use *The European Union Encyclopedia and Directory 1999*, now in its 3d edition.

One particular advantage of this publication is the wealth of information that it immediately puts at the disposal of the reader. The results of the June 1999 European Parliamentary elections are here, as is the latest information on how to contact the major European Union institutes, bodies, and high-level employees. Telephone and fax numbers of these key individuals are also given, but it would be especially helpful to include e-mail addresses in future editions. In addition, there are many pages devoted to Union statistics related to trade, employment, and industrial production. As the majority of the statistics are current as of 1997, researchers who need more up-to-date information may have to turn to the Internet.

Most North Americans are unaware of the history of the European Union and how this economic powerhouse evolved out of an agreement in 1951 that set up the European Coal and Steel Community (ECSC) with six member countries: France, the Federal Republic of Germany, Italy, Belgium, the Netherlands, and Luxembourg. To a large extent, today's European Union materialized as a result of the efforts of visionary leaders in the 1950s to bind Europe together economically after the devastation and enmities of World War II. The useful chronology of the European Union in this volume charts these important developments with great clarity and specificity.

The European Union Encyclopedia and Directory 1999, while extensive, is a work that belongs in every public or university library. Hopefully, Europa Publications and the Gale Group will continue to update this important reference work on an annual basis.—**John B. Romeiser**

Austria

95. Mitchell, Michael, comp. **Austria.** rev. ed. Santa Barbara, Calif., Clio Press/ABC-CLIO, 1999. 271p. maps. index. (World Bibliographical Series, v.66). $81.00. ISBN 1-85109-297-8.

Mitchell, a British scholar and translator of German literature, follows a familiar formula in this thorough revision of the World Bibliographical Series volume on Austria that first appeared in 1986 (see ARBA 87, entry 126). Annotated citations cover 793 publications on Austrian history, culture, and society. A table of contents presents 43 topical chapters. There is also a concise introduction to the concept of Austria and an outline map. The volume concludes with author, title, and subject indexes.

Mitchell retains less than 15 percent of the titles in the 1986 edition. He emphasizes current studies; more than one-half of the selections appeared in the 1990s and another one-third in the 1980s. This is both commendable and problematic. Readers will benefit from awareness of recent work, but some key older studies are no longer mentioned. This particularly affects the chapter on history. In the absence of many works written in the 1950s, 1960s, and 1970s, readers may not appreciate the lengthy and hesitant process by which modern Austria emerged from its ambivalent relationship with Germany and with authoritarianism. This revision includes twice as many German-language titles as the 1st edition did—more than 40 percent of the total. This decision enriches many chapters, but assumes familiarity with German. The vast majority of entries describe books. Besides a few articles, periodicals, and maps, Mitchell commendably notes a half-dozen CD-ROM publications and Websites (but does not include URLs for the online versions of some cited newspapers). No other bibliography offers advice to general readers about such a wide range of things Austrian. The ABC-CLIO bibliography on Vienna (see ARBA 99, entry 119) covers the capital city, not the country. The 1986 edition remains useful for its coverage of works published before the 1980s.

—Steven W. Sowards

Basque Region

96. West, Geoffrey, comp. **The Basque Region.** Santa Barbara, Calif., Clio Press/ABC-CLIO, 1998. 148p. maps. index. (World Bibliographical Series, v.212). $55.00. ISBN 1-85109-258-7.

The Clio Press/ABC-CLIO World Bibliographical Series now covers more than 200 countries, cities, and regions. This one on the Basque region provides a valuable resource to research and writings on this often troubled area on the border between France and Spain. It includes 410 entries on Basque topics.

Entries are organized by categories and cover such topics as the history of Basque's people, flora and fauna, tourist guides, folklore, press, and literature. They include a brief summary of the contents. Most Clio Press/ABC-CLIO bibliographies emphasize literature in English. This collection has an unusually large number of foreign-language (usually Spanish or French) entries. Separate indexes assist the reader in finding entries by author, title, and specific subject matter.

This is a useful bibliography for research libraries. Continued conflict in Basque lands makes understanding the Basques and their culture important.—**Frank L. Wilson**

Bulgaria

97. Otfinoski, Steven. **Bulgaria.** New York, Facts on File, 1999. 118p. illus. maps. index. (Nations in Transition). $19.95. ISBN 0-8160-3705-1.

This is another volume in the Nations in Transition series, which is intended for middle school and high school students (see ARBA 99, entry 124, for a review of the volume entitled *Russia*). Bulgaria receives the standard attractive, easy-to-digest treatment. The history and politics of the country is divided into three chapters: prehistory to 1919, 1919 to 1989, and 1989 to the present. Other chapters address the economy, culture, religion, daily life, the cities, and present problems. The concise text is supplemented by photographs, drawings, maps, and biographical sketches (e.g., Simeon I and II, Todor Zhikov, opera singer Ljuba Welitsch, the artist Christo). A chronology of important events and a selective bibliography are useful reference aids. This book is most suitable for public and school libraries; undergraduates will need more substantial resources. [R: BR, May/June 99, p. 78]—**Thomas A. Karel**

Croatia

98. Carmichael, Cathie, comp. **Croatia.** Santa Barbara, Calif., Clio Press/ABC-CLIO, 1999. 194p. maps. index. (World Bibliographical Series, v.216). $90.00. ISBN 1-85109-285-4.

This comprehensive annotated bibliography of works about Croatia is arranged in broad general subject categories. Most of the books annotated are in English, but several are included that are written in Western European languages and in Croatian and Serbian. In an introductory essay, Carmichael provides a brief history of Croatia from the fifth century to the present day. Aware of political bias that accompanies any publication on Croatia and Serbia, Carmichael warns that the aura of nationalism conveyed by many of the titles is not unusual for this part of the world, even though it may seem slightly odd or old-fashioned in a greater European context. In order to provide a broad view of the country and its people, she included works that she personally did not agree with and also some that may be considered as anti-Croatian. Her aim was not to take sides, but to present a broad range of information about Croatia.

Like other volumes in this series, the various subject categories that are used to arrange the annotations cover the expected topics of history, geography, language, religion, society, politics, foreign relations, the economy, education, literature, and the arts. In addition, Carmichael provides several topics that are unique to Croatia, such as the national question, minorities, Croatians abroad, and the Croatian War of Independence (1990-1995). This is an excellent source for all levels of users who are looking for up-to-date information about Croatia. Author, title, and subject indexes provide good access to the contents.

—**Robert H. Burger**

Former Soviet Republics

99. Otfinoski, Steven. **Ukraine.** New York, Facts on File, 1999. 122p. illus. maps. index. (Nations in Transition). $19.95. ISBN 0-8160-3757-4.

The Nations in Transition series, published by a well-known publisher of reference works, Facts on File, is devoted to descriptions of the independent countries in Eastern Europe that formed after the fall of the Soviet Union. Previous titles include Hungary, Romania, the Czech Republic, and Poland. The present volume discusses, in handbook form, several aspects of Ukrainian history, culture, and economics. Written by a freelance writer and a former newspaper reporter, unfortunately this little book is rather disappointing. For example, the chapter entitled "The Price of Freedom" deals with the government in Ukraine. The author shows little understanding about the historical role of Kravchuk, the first president of Ukraine; his description of the second president, Leonid Kuchma, is too simplistic; and information on the prime minister is dated. Leonid Brezhnev (1906–1982) was not Ukrainian by birth and on page 31 we read that he has made his homeland (Ukraine) a "junior partner" of Russia. Chapter 8 on culture is limited to brief descriptions of several writers, occasionally with misspellings (see information on Lesya Ukrainka on page 72) and about Shevchenko joining "a nationalist organization" (p. 73). The appended bibliography is very poor, with not a single book on Ukrainian history or culture but instead, listings of poor dictionaries of the Ukrainian language and two writers—Chekhov and Gogol. This is a disappointing workbook on Ukraine, the second largest republic after Russia.—**Bohdan S. Wynar**

100. **The Territories of the Russian Federation.** London, Europa Publications; distr., Farmington Hills, Mich., Gale, 1999. 286p. maps. index. $95.00. ISBN 1-85743-070-0. ISSN 1465-461X.

The breakup of the Soviet Union in 1989 produced, among other things, a flurry of reference books that provided directories and background surveys of the newly established republics. The best of these sources, David T. Twining's *Guide to the Republics of the Former Soviet Union* (see ARBA 95, entry 166) and *Russia and the Commonwealth A to Z* by Andrew Wilson and Nina Bachkatov (see ARBA 94, entry 525), are now seriously outdated, so this major new publication on Russia is welcome. The volume opens with an introductory essay on the economics of the Russian Federation, with a chronology, statistics, and a government directory. The main portion of the book consists of "territorial surveys" and examines the 89 constituent units of the federation: the autonomous republics, provinces, administrative regions (oblasts), autonomous districts, and federal cities (Moscow and St. Petersburg). For each of these areas brief information on the geography (with a small map), history, and economy are provided, along with a directory of top officials. This will be an extremely useful reference source for students of the region and it nicely supplements *The Newly Independent States of Eurasia: A Handbook of Former Soviet Republics*, by Stephen and Sandra Batalden (see ARBA 98, entry 125). [R: Choice, Nov 99, p. 520]—**Thomas A. Karel**

Former Yugoslavia

101. Matulic, Rusko. **Bibliography of Sources on the Region of Former Yugoslavia.** New York, Columbia University Press, 1998. 441p. index. $63.00. ISBN 0-88033-402-9.

Anyone who can profit from a comprehensive general bibliography of Yugoslavia will welcome the appearance of Matulic's work. This general, non-annotated bibliography covers 16 main subjects, primarily in Western languages, regarding the region of former Yugoslavia. Approximately one-sixth of all the entries deal with the dissolution of the country during 1991 and 1992. The entries are arranged according to main subjects, ranging from agriculture, archaeology, arts, history, languages, and literature to politics and government, religion, social sciences, and expatriates. There is further division into 64 specialized subheadings such as Macedonian, Serbo Croatian, Slovene, and minority languages. The entries are numbered consecutively in order to facilitate author and subject identification in the indexes. Most of the entries are not cross-referenced and appear only once under the most predominant category, which potentially slows down the search. The book and monograph entries are arranged alphabetically by the author's name, followed by the title of the book or the pertinent chapter, city and state or country of publication, year, number of pages, and related categories. If any entry consists of a chapter, then the pertinent publication source with its editor(s) is also noted. Periodicals are entered under their name, alphabetically arranged, and presented in chronological order under the particular heading or subheading. Preceding the main entries are explanatory notes that clarify conventions used throughout. Serbo-Croat-Slovene diacritic marks that are necessary for pronunciation are also provided. Following the main entries is a listing of unpublished sources covering microfilms and other documents deposited in U.S. and British archives. These comprise, among others, military and political events around and during World War II. The geographical essay shows black-and-white maps of tribal and ethnical boundary shifts from the time the Slavs came to the Balkan Peninsula (395 B.C.E.) until the present. Also presented is a sampling of video sources dealing with the scientific, literary, artistic, and other aspects of life in former Yugoslavia. These entries contain bracketed, explanatory notes and numbers indicating the subject category as used for printed entries. An index of authors and editors as well as an index of entries by headings and subheadings is provided.

Because this well-organized and comprehensive volume covers many aspects of the different regions of Yugoslavia, it can serve as a reference on many levels. This resource is a valuable tool for Slavic scholars and will be an important edition for university libraries.—**Magda Želinská-Ferl**

Great Britain

102. **Britain 1999: The Official Yearbook of the United Kingdom.** 50th ed. By the Office for National Statistics. London, Stationery Office; distr., Lanham, Md., Bernan Associates, 1998. 564. illus. maps. index. $80.00. ISBN 0-11-621037-0.

Which women's magazine has the highest circulation in Great Britain? (*Take a Break*). Who won the Benson & Hedges Cup in Cricket in 1997-1998? (Essex). What is the largest British pharmaceutical company? (Glaxo Wellcome). This is the sort of handy information—and much, much more—that can be found in *Britain 1999*. In its 50th year of publication, this combination yearbook and encyclopedia provides a detailed overview of life and politics in Great Britain (see ARBA 95, entry 156, and ARBA 91, entry 112, for reviews of earlier editions).

As in recent editions, the book is organized into 5 main parts: Britain and its people, government and foreign affairs, social and cultural affairs, environment and transport, and economic affairs. Each part is further broken down into subsections (30 in all), though these have been reworked slightly and do not compare to the exact arrangement in previous volumes. The section on sustainable development has been reinstated in this volume and substantially expanded. Each of the subsections contains charts, diagrams, statistical tables, and short bibliographies (with Websites). Most of the content, however, is in the form of brief descriptive articles. All of the information has been updated, drawing from over 250 official government sources.

The text is interrupted by nine colorful photograph inserts (more than in earlier editions) that offer a selective look at aspects of British culture (e.g., postage stamps, gardens, museums, arts awards, and domes). Appended to the text are a directory of government departments and agencies, a discussion of recent legislation, brief obituaries, a list of abbreviations, and a list of public holidays. This continues to be a very useful reference source for current information on Great Britain and is most suitable for academic libraries.
—**Thomas A. Karel**

103. **The Encyclopedia of Britain.** Oxford, England, Helicon; distr., Farmington Hills, Mich., Gale, 1999. 1015p. illus. maps. $75.00. ISBN 1-85986-275-6.

There are few editorial tasks as daunting as assembling a single-volume encyclopedia on the culture and history of a country, much less a country as diverse and complex as Britain. In just over 1,000 pages, this book succeeds in presenting the United Kingdom in an "A-Z guide," accessible to the casual reader and useful to the professional researcher. This book should be in every library because of its comprehensiveness (more than 6,000 entries), efficient organization, and readability. It is also very up-to-date, with the latest entries from December 1998.

Encyclopedias often suffer from uneven editing, since numerous experts write entries in styles ranging from artistic to scientific to popular. This volume had a strong editorial hand that facilitates an even, unencumbered flow of information though the nearly infinite number of threads that can be followed by the extensive cross-referencing. There are hundreds of illustrations, including color and black-and-white photographs, maps, charts, and diagrams. Inset quotations related to nearby entries often tug the reader in unexpected directions, making this more than a simple reference book. An additional strength of this encyclopedia is its set of 45 special essays ("features") on both predictable topics ("The Vikings of Britain") and the unexpected ("British Food"). There are also dozens of chronologies to help plot the changing fortunes of the monarchy, the history of British higher education, the British publishing industry, British scientific advances, and much more. True to its contemporary form, the book even has a long list of relevant Websites in an appendix.

All collective volumes require choices as to which topics become entries and how much space each entry is given. The editors are quite specific about their criteria in the preface (when the Irish are included or not, how much of the former Empire is mentioned and under what circumstances, and so on). However, a book that combines popular culture with history, geography, and science will inevitably show some incongruities. The Austrian-invented postcard, for example, gets more space than the Falklands War. Nevertheless, most of the time the balance of emphasis is good, making the encyclopedia as much a pleasure to peruse as to use. [R: LJ, 1 Oct 99, p. 78]—**Mark A. Wilson**

Greece

104. Edwards, Adrian, comp. **Crete.** Santa Barbara, Calif., Clio Press/ABC-CLIO, 1998. 134p. maps. index. (World Bibliographical Series, v.215). $58.00. ISBN 1-85109-173-4.

The goal of books in the World Bibliographical Series is to provide annotated entries on works that deal with the history, geography, economy, politics, people, culture, customs, religion, and social organization of the countries of the world. This recent volume on Crete fulfills this goal, although it also has some weaknesses.

Edwards provides a serviceable history of Crete in his introduction. This is followed by a good chronology of major events in the history of Crete and a brief listing of the rulers of Crete. Most of the book is composed of the annotated entries themselves. Edwards has collected and annotated 386 entries, including books, journal articles, and Websites. Although a few sources in French, Italian, Greek, and German are included, the works are predominantly in English. Most sources are of recent publications, although major older works are also included.

The entries are organized into 27 thematic chapters; for example, geography, geology and paleontology, tourism and travel guides, archaeology, religion, health, coins and stamps, and food and drink, among others. Each entry gives the full bibliographic citation to the work as well as a brief annotation. Indexes for authors, titles, and subjects conclude the work.

The greatest weakness of the work is its exclusions. For example, although several standard works on coinage are included, others are absent, such as *The Coinage of Modern Greece, Crete, the Ionian Islands & Cyprus* by S. Gardiakos (Obol International, 1969) and *The Coinage of the Arab Amirs of Crete* by George Miles (American Numismatic, 1960). In addition, a quick search on the Historical Abstracts database, which indexes material dealing with 1450 and later, yielded more than 160 entries, many of which are missing from the bibliography.

With these weaknesses noted, Edwards has done a good job in bringing together material on an area of study that deserves greater attention. The work should be included in all libraries that strive to maintain collections on European history.—**Gregory A. Crawford**

105. Veremis, Thanos, and Mark Dragoumis, comps. **Greece.** rev. ed. Santa Barbara, Calif., Clio Press/ABC-CLIO, 1998. 388p. illus. index. (World Bibliographic Series, v.17). $70.00. ISBN 1-85109-286-2.

The latest installment in Clio Press's World Bibliographic series is *Greece*, compiled by Thanos Veremis and Mark Dragoumis, an updated revision of the 1980 edition by Mary Jo and Richard Clogg. Major political and cultural changes have taken place in Greece (as throughout Europe) since 1980, of course, and so this new edition is most welcome. Veremis, in particular, is an eminent political scientist of modern Greece, and his interests are greatly reflected here. There are expanded offerings in history, population studies, society, and foreign relations, and an entirely new section on defense and security. In these areas, this guide is an indispensable work of reference. The sections on literature and art, however, cannot be wholeheartedly recommended. Why, for instance, do the authors include one or two new scholarly works on the ancient poets Homer and Pindar alongside modern Greece's great laureates Kavafy and Seferis? There are separate bibliographies (e.g., *L'Année Philologique*) to consult for classical literature. Puzzlingly, the authors also include novels about modern Greece (e.g., British author Louis de Bernières's excellent *Corelli's Mandolin*) in the section on Greek literature. But aside from this uneven treatment of cultural works, Veremis and Dragoumis have filled an important hole in the scholarship, and libraries that cater to Greek and European studies will want to spend the $70 to obtain it. Plans are afoot, however, by the Modern Greek Studies Association—publishers of the prestigious *Journal of Modern Greek Studies*, upon which the authors heap scorn (p. 345)—to soon bring out a bibliography that will be the work of numerous experts in various disciplines, and that may be more useful for literary and artistic references.

—**Christopher Michael McDonough**

Netherlands

106. Huussen, Arend H., Jr. **Historical Dictionary of the Netherlands.** Lanham, Md., Scarecrow, 1998. 237p. (European Historical Dictionaries, no.32). $59.50. ISBN 0-8108-3514-2.

There are relatively few reference books dealing specifically with the Netherlands, so this historical dictionary is welcome. Huussen, from the University of Groningen, indicates in the preface that he intends to provide the English-reading public with "basic information on persons and topics from Dutch political, intellectual, and colonial history and culture." He includes the elements characteristic of this series: a detailed chronology, a summary of Dutch history, more than 500 dictionary entries, and a lengthy bibliography. The brief historical overview, which opens the volume, is readable and is reasonably successful in the difficult task of presenting enough historical details to inform without making the text unreadable. The dictionary entries are helpful and clear, but sometimes so brief that they lack interest and give short shrift to important topics. For example, Huussen devotes one short paragraph to the East India Company; in the *Lexicon Geschiedenis van Nederland & Belgie* (Kosmos, 1994), this topic rates a full page of small type. Because most English-speaking readers know so little about the Netherlands, more lengthy entries would have been helpful. In addition, the text of the entries is constantly interrupted by *see* references using the Latin abbreviation "q.v." traditional for this series instead of the more readable italics or bold typeface. These references appear frequently (nine in the paragraph on "Parliament"), and often refer the reader pointlessly to another entry. In the paragraph on William I (1772-1843), for example, the appearance of the word "government" is followed by a "q.v.," even though the article on government referred to describes the makeup of the Dutch cabinets after World War II. There are other English-language bibliographies on the Netherlands, including one in the World Bibliographical Series by Peter King and Michael Wintle (see ARBA 89, entry 120), but this dictionary fills a gap by providing detailed historical information in English. This work is recommended for academic and large public libraries.—**V. W. Hill**

Sicily

107. Olivastri, Valentina, comp. **Sicily.** Santa Barbara, Calif., Clio Press/ABC-CLIO, 1998. 188p. maps. index. (World Bibliographical Series, v.213). $63.00. ISBN 1-85109-291-9.

This title, another in the voluminous ABC-CLIO World Bibliographical Series, treats Sicily, the largest island of the Mediterranean. After an introduction that sketches very briefly Sicily's history, a chronology dating back to 20,000 B.C.E. is provided. These sections are followed by an annotated bibliography with 155 pages and 456 entries. It is divided into 36 chapter headings with some further divided into subheadings. Among the major topics covered are geography; history; and social conditions, including organized crime, politics, religion, economy and industry, education, literature, the arts, sports and recreation, and agriculture. The annotations are concise yet quite descriptive in their summaries of the works. The compiler attempts to emphasize English-language material, but, out of necessity, must also include many Italian sources. Separate indexes of authors, titles, and subjects as well as a map of Sicily conclude the volume. This source is recommended to any academic or public library attempting to collect the entire series, or that has a special interest in Sicily, Italy, or the Mediterranean.—**Lee Weston**

LATIN AMERICA AND THE CARIBBEAN

108. Crane, Janet, comp. **French Guiana.** Santa Barbara, Calif., Clio Press/ABC-CLIO, 1998. 160p. maps. index. (World Bibliographical Series, v.210). $59.00. ISBN 1-85109-241-2.

The World Bibliographical Series' recently published volume on French Guiana is their first devoted to this area of South America, officially a department of France. The bibliography follows the usual format for the series: an introductory essay; approximately 400 annotated bibliographic entries organized into topical chapters; and separate indexes of authors, titles, and subject terms. The compiler also includes one map of the territory.

The introduction is longer than those usually found in this series and provides necessary background for this understudied region. Crane emphasizes the dearth of scholarly English-language publications on French Guiana, noting that fewer than 40 percent of the entries in this volume refer to such publications. She also comments upon the tendency of much research to focus on a limited number of themes in the department's history, such as its penal colony, failed attempts at European settlement, and adventurers' accounts. While including references to standard works that deal with major themes in French Guiana's history, Crane also attempts to document scholarship on lesser-studied topics and to point out gaps in the literature. The annotations are detailed and informative. Although the bibliography includes a sizeable number of entries, especially given the sparse amount of research that as been done on some topics, there seem to be some significant omissions. A subject search of the online version of the *Handbook of Latin American Studies* brings up several citations that are not included in this volume: for example, general histories of French Guiana published in the 1990s and older travel accounts. It would be helpful to know more about the compiler's parameters for inclusion of materials, given the necessary limits that must be set when preparing a bibliography. There also seem to be few materials listed that were published in French Guiana, and it would be interesting to see more background on this trend and its implications for scholarship.

Despite these omissions, this volume will be of much use to new and more advanced researchers. The lack of any other recently published bibliographies on French Guiana further increases its value. Crane has charted a needed course through the relatively inaccessible terrain of scholarship about this "complicated and therefore poorly understood place." [R: Choice, Dec 99, p. 700]—**Pamela M. Graham**

109. Foster, David William, Melissa Fitch Lockhart, and Darrell B. Lockhart. **Culture and Customs of Argentina.** Westport, Conn., Greenwood Press, 1998. 173p. illus. index. (Culture and Customs of Latin America and the Caribbean). $45.00. ISBN 0-313-30319-3.

This debut volume of a new series is a thoughtful, in-depth examination of Argentina's culture. It considers the country's social customs, media, literature, cinema, and performing and visual arts within the context of the history, politics, and religion that shaped them. Two major influences discussed are immigration and military regimes.

The influence of the political climate is woven throughout each of the eight topical sections. Chapters on the arts discuss important authors, artists, and performers. Critical analysis of specific works is given especially in the case of films and works of fiction, which are analyzed in terms of their political commentary. Traditional visual arts are covered along with nontraditional subjects, such as the Silhouettes movement in which anonymous artists have painted outlines of the bodies of Los Desaparecidos (the "disappeared"). There is a comprehensive history of Argentine newspapers and radios, which examines the influences of the Catholic Church and the political regimes in power in specific time periods. Immigration is identified as having had a major impact on religious tolerance, social customs, food, and sports and is considered by the authors to be a primary cause of the Argentine "identity crisis."

This first volume in the series succeeds in accomplishing the stated goal of helping readers understand the factors that have shaped Argentina's culture. It should be noted that the book is narrowly focused, dealing with events that occurred after the country became independent, and may not be useful to those needing a basic source on Argentina. For example, except for a brief chronology, there is no information about the indigenous peoples or the Indian Wars.

The vocabulary used and concepts presented are geared toward post-secondary students. The subject index does not facilitate finding information quickly. Public and school libraries will be better served with standard sources such as *WorldMark Encyclopedia of Nations* (Gale, 1999) and the *WorldMark Encyclopedia of World Cultures and Daily Life* (see ARBA 99, entry 364) or *Culturgrams: The Nations Around Us* (see entry 64).—**Marlene M. Kuhl**

110. **Social Panorama of Latin America.** 1997 ed. New York, United Nations, 1998. 231p. $25.00pa. ISBN 92-1-121224-3. ISSN 1020-5160. S/N E.98.II.G.3.

This annual publication of the Economic Commission for Latin America and the Caribbean (ECLAC) of the United Nations provides an "assessment of the most salient aspects of social development in Latin America, with particular emphasis on the question of equity. Among the issues it examines are poverty, education, the situation of children and young people, gender and social expenditure. It also presents on overview of how Governments are implementing their social agendas and reviews new policy directions in various social sectors" (p. 13). This 1997 edition gives particular attention to the situation with regard to children's rights, analyzes gender-based role differentiation early in life, and evaluates the frequency and implications of teenage pregnancies.

Information is presented by country in text, statistical tables, and charts; the statistical appendix summarizes data for Latin America as a whole. Just as the countries that are included in each table of the main text vary depending upon whether or not relevant data are available, the tables in the appendix are based on data varying from 9 to 15 countries. Sources for all statistics are identified. There is little information about the Caribbean islands, in spite of the fact that they are included in the area of ECLAC's coverage. Although some of the statistical data can be found in other annual sources, such as the *Statistical Abstract of Latin America* (University of California at Los Angeles) and the *Statistical Yearbook for Latin America and the Caribbean*, issued by ECLAC since the mid-1980s, the focus of this publication on the statistical facts impacting the contemporary social situation in the region and analysis of that data makes it a valuable source for any library whose users need information about current Latin America. It is even more valuable because social statistics and analysis of them are much harder to locate than detailed data about economic conditions.—**Ann Hartness**

111. Williams, Raymond Leslie, and Kevin G. Guerrieri. **Culture and Customs of Colombia.** Westport, Conn., Greenwood Press, 1999. 148p. illus. maps. index. (Culture and Customs of Latin America and the Caribbean). $45.00. ISBN 0-313-30405-X.

This reference is part of a series on Latin American countries and provides a broad introduction to Colombian culture for the general reader. The authors concisely outline Colombian geography, history, religion, social customs, television, radio, newspapers, and arts (including literature, theater, music, cinema, photography, and architecture). The narrative demonstrates the authors' premise that Colombia is unique in Latin America with its extreme regionalism, its deeply founded traditionalism, an ingrained presence of the Catholic Church in daily life, and the country's political institutions, which surpass those of other South American nations. Features include an historical chronology, chapter notes, a glossary, a bibliography, and an index. The text is well written and effectively projects the authors' appreciation and affection for Colombia, its history, its literature, and its culture.—**Adrienne Antink Bendel**

MIDDLE EAST

112. Clements, Frank A., comp. **United Arab Emirates.** Santa Barbara, Calif., Clio Press/ABC-CLIO, 1998. 248p. index. (World Bibliographical Series, v.43). $73.00. ISBN 1-85109-274-9.

This is the revised edition of the World Bibliographical Series volume, by the same author, that came out in 1993. The United Arab Emirates comprise the seven Persian Gulf states of Abu Dhabi, Dubai, Sharjah, Ajman, Umm al-Qaiwain, Ras al-Khaimah, and Fujairah. This federation, sometimes known as the Trucial States or Trucial Oman, came into being in 1971 as the result of the British withdrawal from the Gulf. Since that time, of course, successive conflicts have focused U.S. attention on an area that was once of interest only to scholars. For the same reasons, this revision will be attractive to a wider audience. There are 690 annotated entries arranged by broad subject headings, further broken down by author and title. Readers who are computer-literate will be especially happy to see a separate category for Internet sites. Cross-references are used when necessary and there is an admirable series of indexes by author, title, and subject. The restriction to English-language materials makes this especially appropriate for college libraries, while the high quality of entries ensures that even area experts will find it useful. Librarians who have the 1st edition will want to retain it since the revision complements rather than replaces the earlier version. They will also want to supplement it with other tools since the bibliography is narrowly focused and does not address itself to many larger Gulf issues. This is highly recommended for any serious college or university library.—**Paul L. Holmer**

113. Quilliam, Neil, comp. **Syria.** rev. ed. Santa Barbara, Calif., Clio Press/ABC-CLIO, 1999. 284p. maps. index. (World Bibliographical Series, v.73). $87.00. ISBN 1-85109-317-6.

This revision of the 1987 edition (see ARBA 88, entry 148, for a review of the 1st edition) includes significant changes in content and reconfiguration of chapters and indexes. Sections have been reorganized and updated to reflect changes in the region during the last decade and the impact on Syria from events such as the Gulf War and the collapse of the Soviet Union. The 859 entries cover a broad range of topics within the social sciences, sciences, and arts and include some Arabic and French materials. A substantial number of titles cited were published in the 1990s. Researchers should find this annotated compilation useful.

—**Ahmad Gamaluddin**

POLAR REGIONS

114. Mills, William, and Peter Speak. **Keyguide to Information Sources on the Polar and Cold Regions.** London, Mansell/Cassell; distr., New York, Continuum Publishing, 1998. 330p. maps. index. $140.00. ISBN 0-7201-2176-0.

First published in Great Britain in 1997, this guide comes to the United States as the Shackleton exhibit is drawing record crowds as it tours the country and as more tourists opt for tours to polar regions. The compilers are specialists in polar and cold region information sources. Sources selected for inclusion in the guide include print publications, bibliographic databases, and Internet resources. Selected special and general, primarily English-language sources are included.

The book is organized into three sections, a survey of the polar and cold regions, key reference sources, and organizations engaged in polar research. The survey section covers the principal physical features of the regions and the development of scientific interest in them. The work of major international and national research groups is also covered. For those who dream of one day working in a polar region there is an informative section on education and career paths leading to such employment. The neophyte scholar will find a chapter on information searching, research strategies, relevant libraries, archives, and museums. Throughout this section *see also* references guide the user to related entries in the bibliography, and Internet addresses are given.

The bibliography is an introduction to key reference works. General and regional sources are covered. Subject resources are listed for a broad range of disciplines such as earth and life sciences, human and social sciences, arts and humanities, travel expeditions, and engineering and related subjects. Each subject area begins with an introductory essay. "Comfortable" is not an adjective usually applied to reference sources, but it describes perfectly the tone of these essays. The reader feels as though he or she is sitting with a favorite teacher discussing an approach to research.

The directory of selected organizations includes international and national research organizations. Complete addresses are given with Web and e-mail addresses provided. There is a list of libraries and archives that have significant holdings related to polar and cold region research. The SPRI Website also has this list, with collection size and focus given. Publishers located in polar regions or publishing monographs on the topic are listed, as are specialized rare and used book dealers.

This is an outstanding resource on a timely topic. Researchers, serious students, tourists, and even armchair travelers will find the guide a comprehensive source for research or the pursuit of a personal interest. Highly recommended.—**Marlene M. Kuhl**

4 Economics and Business

GENERAL WORKS

Bibliography

115. **Bibliographic Guide to Business and Economics 1998.** New York, G. K. Hall/Macmillan Library Reference, 1999. 3v. $795.00/set. ISBN 0-7838-0192-0. ISSN 0360-2702.

This bibliographic guide is a compilation of recent publications cataloged by the Research Libraries of the New York Public Library. The selection of titles is based on titles cataloged with Library of Congress Classification HA-HJ. Therefore, the *Bibliographic Guide to Business and Economics 1998* is comprehensive and includes the latest publications in the areas of business administration, economic theory, public finance, labor, insurance, transportation, communication, demographics, and statistics.

The arrangement is alphabetic by main entry (e.g., personal author, corporate body, name of conference). The scope is international and the guide is presented in a 3-volume set. It is easy to use, with *see* and *see also* references throughout the bibliography. This volume is recommended to large academic libraries and special business libraries to use as a collection development guide for business and economic collections.
—**Kay M. Stebbins**

116. **Encyclopedia of Business Information Sources.** 13th ed. James Woy, ed. Farmington Hills, Mich., Gale, 1999. 1114p. $320.00. ISBN 0-7876-2441-1. ISSN 0071-0210.

This latest edition of the *Encyclopedia of Business Information Sources* (EBIS) is quite similar to the earlier editions and will continue to serve as a useful source for business collections. EBIS is a bibliographic guide to more than 32,000 citations covering 1,100 subjects of interest to business personnel. The "Outline of Contents" lists all topics and *see* references, which allows for quick access to the exact heading. Sources for each topic are subdivided by type of material (e.g., directory, periodical, handbook, online source).

The entries include (as appropriate) title, author, publication frequency, price, URL, and a brief description. Contact information for the publishers is found in the "Sources Cited" section, which includes the publisher's address, telephone and fax numbers, and URL.

The strength of EBIS lies in its breadth of topics, which allows users to locate sources on obscure subjects not found in most libraries. There are drawbacks to using this title, however. Although there are materials listed with publication dates as recent as 1998, there are many that are much older. For example, the only three general works listed under "Computer Security" (which includes works about computer viruses) have publication dates of 1990, 1992, and 1993. The criteria for selection is not discussed, although a statement in the introduction indicates that a few out-of-print titles have been retained if they were considered to be unique or of particular interest. Perhaps the 1984 publication found under "Library Automation" is of historical interest, but it is doubtful that one would use EBIS to find classics. In general, EBIS can be useful as a starting point, but one should use it with caution.—**Michele Russo**

Biography

117. **American Business Leaders.** [CD-ROM]. Santa Barbara, Calif., ABC-CLIO, 1998. Minimum system requirements: Pentium-compatible processor at 75MHZ or faster. Four-speed CD-ROM drive. Windows 95. 8MB RAM. 30MB hard disk space. SVGA monitor 640x480 (256 colors). 16-bit sound card with Windows drivers. $49.00 (standalone); $129.00 (lab pack); $249.00 (site license). ISBN 1-57607-020-4.

This is a helpful electronic reference work that is structured around 413 biographies of significant business leaders over the course of American history. From the colonial era through the end of the twentieth century, this work outlines the lives and times of both famous and lesser-known men and women who have helped shape American business history. Individual entries provide a concise and straightforward summary of the events and achievements of particular business leaders and collectively create the sort of reference work that can be used to find not only specific information but can also be enjoyable to simply browse through. It provides specific and comparative information for these business leaders and can be used by a variety of users. Individual entries have a brief bibliography of practical works, but many of these bibliographies will probably be too brief for advanced users.

ABC-CLIO has also published a 2-volume book that contains these same 413 biographies (ISBN 1-57607-002-6), but this electronic version may be easier to use for some since it allows for searches by text and other attributes. Indeed, the principal advantage to using a CD-ROM version of the reference work is that it provides easier cross-referencing and more detailed indexes. This reference work also provides 64 linked maps and a glossary of 198 defined terms. This reference work can be searched by name, subject, text, and a variety of attributes. These attributes include occupation, birth year, death year, gender, ethnicity, and even place of birth. Unfortunately, by searching through this work, users may find that some groups and categories are underrepresented. Despite the fact that since the colonial era white males have historically dominated the top rung of the American business ladder, this work lists only 24 women out of the 413 biographies. Likewise, there is an underrepresentation of race and ethnicity with biographies of only four African Americans, one Asian, and one Hispanic. Increasing the number of featured women and minorities would make this reference work more representative of American business history. Despite any shortcomings, this is still a useful and practical guide to the economic lives and times of a number of manufacturers, merchants, financiers, business executives, and developers.—**Timothy E. Sullivan**

118. **Business Leaders for Students.** Sheila M. Dow, ed. Farmington Hills, Mich., Gale, 1999. 914p. illus. index. $95.00. ISBN 0-7876-2935-9. ISSN 1520-9296.

The purpose of this new book in Gale's popular line of business products for students is "to provide readers with a comprehensive resource of business biographies, giving them easy access to information on past and resent business leaders." This goal is met with 248 alphabetically arranged, engaging entries of historical and popular business leaders. It is, of course, impossible to be comprehensive in one volume. The advisory board of five teachers and librarians of young adults from diverse geographic locations did an excellent job of selecting the leaders for inclusion. The first entry is illustrative of the selections—Scott Adams, creator of the *Dilbert* comic strip. Historical figures such as Alexander Graham Bell, Benjamin Franklin, and Samuel Morse balance modern business leaders like Bill Gates, Charles Schwab, and Ted Turner. Many different areas of business are included, from food processing (e.g., Colonel Sanders, Oscar Mayer, Will Kellogg) to cosmetics (e.g., Mary Kay, Estée Lauder) to entertainment (e.g., Jane Fonda, George Lucas, Michael Jordan). Minority leaders are well represented with businesspeople such as Wally Amos, Akio Morita, and Barbara Proctor.

The entries are 3 to 4 pages in length, usually with a black-and-white photograph. Each begins with a one-paragraph overview, including the leader's major contributions to business, industry, and society. Next comes a summary of their personal life, with family history, vital statistics, education, affiliations, and awards, among other items. The section on career details focuses on career highlights and often reports their management style, business philosophy, or development of a product. The final sections are titled "Social and Economic Impact," which contains more in-depth analysis, and "Sources of Information," which lists mailing addresses and Websites. A basic bibliography provides suggested readings in monographs, periodicals, and databases. The separately boxed chronology features an easy-to-read list of major dates in the leader's life.

A master index provides easy access to business leaders, companies, and industries. This book is fun to peruse and stop off at any stimulating name. Its value as a basic reference tool for students seeking quick data on business leaders is great. This one volume will be much easier to use than the traditional biographical research tools and it is suited for high school and undergraduate students as well as public library patrons. [R: BR, Sept/Oct 99, p. 65; SLJ, Aug 99, p. 182]—**Georgia Briscoe**

119. Hamilton, Neil A. **American Business Leaders: From Colonial Times to the Present.** Santa Barbara, Calif., ABC-CLIO, 1999. 2v. illus. index. $150.00/set. ISBN 1-57607-002-6.

This practical and informative reference work is a collection of concise encyclopedic entries for 413 influential American business leaders. Beginning in the colonial era and continuing to the end of the twentieth century, this work chronicles the lives and times of a good number of the influential men and women of U.S. business history. Despite the fact that many of these men and women helped shape and determine the path of business development, not all of them are commonly recognized for their achievements and contributions. Consequently, this book provides an accessible, valuable, and even enjoyable guide to a number of historic business figures. It is the sort of reference book that can be a joy to read and browse through. It is a reference work that will also appeal to a wide range of users. More advanced researchers will find it a useful guide for checking facts and dates, whereas more novice users will benefit from reading and browsing through its concise and candid articles. A lot of interesting details and comparative facts are provided for both the renowned and relatively obscure business leaders who are outlined in this work. In addition, each entry has a useful, although too often brief, bibliography of practical works where interested users can turn for more information.

Examining the helpful indexes of the entries reveals that the largest number of business leaders outlined in the pages of these volumes are manufacturers, merchants, financiers, and publishers. But there are also entries for various business executives, industrialists, and developers. Because the entries in this reference work are arranged alphabetically, it reads like an encyclopedia of American business history. However, because each of the individuals outlined in these two volumes obviously lived and operated in a historic context, reading through and comparing various entries can provide a relative understanding of various social, economic, and political conditions. [R: LJ, 1 Sept 99, p. 178]—**Timothy E. Sullivan**

Chronology

120. **Notable Corporate Chronologies.** 2d ed. Kimberly N. Hunt and AnnaMarie L. Sheldon, eds. Farmington Hills, Mich., Gale, 1999. 2v. index. $390.00/set. ISBN 0-8103-9500-2. ISSN 1078-3865.

This work is an expanded, updated, and effective reference book that outlines the business histories and timelines of more than 1,500 prominent corporations. It is a valuable and compelling reference work that provides a concise profile of the historic milestones and events that have shaped the activities and performances of corporations operating in the United States and worldwide. Each of these alphabetically arranged timelines concisely outlines 30 or more significant events in the histories of industrial, commercial, and financial firms. The types of events included within these timelines have been broadly defined so that a variety of users will find useful, meaningful, and even entertaining information within them. These events include the founding and any subsequent reorganization of the firm, the introduction of new products and product lines, mergers and acquisitions, stock offerings, key financial events, the tenure of its leading managers, and even a few notable scandals within the firms. The easy-to-use and engaging chronologies provide a context and appreciation of the growth and evolution of many of the world's leading corporations. Moreover, by evaluating and contrasting comparative individual histories, this reference work also provides a more comprehensive understanding of business organization and commercial activity.

The events outlined within individual corporation timelines are concise and informative. Each entry provides not only contact information for each firm but a short list of further readings to assist in additional research. This detailed reference work includes four useful indexes: an indexed chronology that highlights 400 years of business activity, an anniversary index that lists significant forthcoming anniversaries for these corporations to the year 2021, a geographic index that identifies the corporate headquarters for these firms, and a master index that is particularly useful because many of these firms have reorganized and changed names over time. This is a useful and engaging reference work that will appeal to novice and experienced researchers alike.—**Timothy E. Sullivan**

Dictionaries and Encyclopedias

121. **The Elgar Companion to Consumer Research and Economic Psychology.** Peter E. Earl and Simon Kemp, eds. Northhampton, Mass., Edward Elgar, 1999. 649p. index. $200.00. ISBN 1-85898-554-4.

This fine scholarly reference work analyzes and surveys consumer research and economic psychology. It includes more than 100 commissioned entries, which run from "acculturation" to "work effort." The editors, both university professors in New Zealand, have assembled an impressive, international group of more than 110 scholar/researcher contributors. Each entry includes a brief overview of an area of research and interest in addition to a brief listing of some important journal articles and books in that area. Some of the especially interesting and varied topics covered in this work are brand loyalty, gambling, culture shock, shoplifting, tax evasion, children's savings, vanity, the psychology of poverty, and the history of economic psychology. All entries are signed and include bibliographies. An extensive index readily locates related topics not found in the alphabetic list of topics. Several well-done tables and figures are also provided. The editors state that the work will meet the needs of undergraduates, graduates, and researchers alike from various disciplines—business administration, economics, marketing, and psychology, to name a few. Edward Elgar Publishing has several other notable titles on economic psychology. This work is expensive, but highly recommended for large academic and public libraries.—**Edward Erazo**

122. **Encyclopedia of African American Business History.** Juliet E. K. Walker, ed. Westport, Conn., Greenwood Press, 1999. 721p. index. $115.00. ISBN 0-313-29549-2.

Containing essays by more than 100 contributors, this encyclopedia covers a wide variety of topics from the seventeenth century through the 1990s on black business history, biographies of notable business people, and surveys of black participation in selected industries. Each entry includes a selected bibliography. An introductory chapter provides an overview of the topic followed by more than 200 alphabetically arranged entries, ranging from one to several pages. The work concludes with a chronology of black business history, a select bibliography, and an index. A fine ready-reference source, this work culls a vast amount of material covering an eclectic range of subjects, including insurance companies, black slave owners, sports enterprises and entrepreneurs, women business enterprises, and biographies of publisher John H. Johnson and black business scholar Joseph A. Pierce. The selected bibliography at the end of each entry provides invaluable citations for students and scholars looking to pursue further research.

This work, however, is not without its flaws. The entry on the "Nation of Islam Enterprises," for example, contains erroneous material and also omits significant information (i.e., the history of the sect—Farrakhan's death threats against Malcolm X are omitted as are the use of federal money to subsidize questionable housing project security and the unconscionable marketing of quack AIDS drugs at drastically inflated prices). Nevertheless, this unique work is generally an outstanding reference source on the various aspects of the history of African American business.—**Donald Altschiller**

123. **Encyclopedia of Political Economy.** Phillip Anthony O'Hara, ed. New York, Routledge, 1999. 2v. $265.00/set. ISBN 0-415-15426-X.

Political economy has emerged as the cutting edge of research in several disciplines, including economics, political science, and sociology. The multiple disciplinary interest in this topic suggests correctly that political economy is open to many different approaches, paradigms, and methodologies. Marxists and neoliberal scholars claim political economy as "their" field. This encyclopedia attempts to identify and explain key concepts, terminologies, theories, and contributors in the broad field of political economy. The editors and article authors represent a wide range of preferences in their approach to political economy. As a result, the encyclopedia represents well the diversity of ideological and paradigmatic approaches to political economy. The editors, associate editors, and most contributors are economists by training and background. As a result, the economic dimension for political economy is emphasized. Key concepts and issues in political science and sociology are ignored or given short treatment. For example, corporatism, economic planning, industrial policy, and trade unions are not given separate entries, although some information on these important areas of political economy can sometimes be gleaned by use of the index. However, the editor should be commended for his inclusion of the new and rapidly growing feminist political economy in its different dimensions. This set is recommended for college and research university libraries. [R: LJ, 1 Feb 99, p. 76]—**Frank L. Wilson**

124. Foldvary, Fred E. **Dictionary of Free-Market Economics.** Northhampton, Mass., Edward Elgar, 1998. 307p. $85.00. ISBN 1-85898-432-7.

This is the first dictionary of free market terms. It includes entries on the theory of market economy, empirical studies of economic freedom, and informative biographies of free-market economists. The dictionary provides definitions of terms that other economic dictionaries omit, such as "intervention," "regulation," and "public goods." It also includes topic terms used in law, finance, and classical liberal philosophy as well as basic terms used in economics. Well-known economists' biographies, such as Keynes and Friedman as well as obscure ones such as Gerard Debren, a Nobel Prize winner for economics, are also included.

The dictionary is sorted alphabetically with extensive cross-referencing. A solid bibliography of source materials is also provided. This book is valuable to the student of economics and to the professor as well. Librarians will love it too for the short concise definitions. [R: Choice, June 99, p. 1764]

—**Kay M. Stebbins**

125. **The MIT Encyclopedia of the Japanese Economy.** 2d ed. By Robert C. Hsu. Cambridge, Mass., MIT Press, 1999. 523p. index. $60.00. ISBN 0-262-08280-2.

This book explains the structure of the Japanese economy and how it works. It contains 180 essays and 145 short definitions, which are listed alphabetically. The essays discuss the important issues for each topic, provide statistics, and give addresses of relevant companies or government bodies as well as references for additional reading. There is a detailed index referencing the Japanese and English terms for each concept.

The author has gone beyond the expected discourse to show how Japan's unique social and cultural heritage affects its economic functioning. For example, the author points out that mergers are less common in Japan than in the United States because of the strong community feeling among Japanese workers. The idea of a CEO selling a company for financial gain is seen as a betrayal of one's employees. Also, the interlocking relationships with suppliers and distributors, which are so common in Japan, lessen the push for integration.—**Adrienne Antink Bendel**

126. **The New Palgrave Dictionary of Economics and the Law.** Peter Newman, ed. New York, Stockton Press, 1998. 3v. index. $550.00/set. ISBN 1-56159-215-3.

The field of law and economics, although rooted in the contributions of David Hume and Adam Smith and subsequently of Jeremy Bentham and Friedrich Hayek, experienced its main stimulus from the writings of Ronald Coase, and began with what the editor of these volumes regards as a "meteoric rise" in the 1970s and 1980s. The field has developed interconnections, one of which is demonstrated in the companion *New Palgrave Dictionary of Money and Finance* (see ARBA 93, entry 242), while several indicate the practical applications in the transforming post-Communist economies and in the less developed countries. The new field takes account of conventions, customs, and norms in the mix of formal and intellectual problems and solutions.

In the 3 volumes under review the "List of Entries" includes cross-references. A "Subject Classification," which is divided into 7 main categories of society, economy, policy, law in general, common law systems, regulation, and biographies, is subdivided into subheadings, and those are in turn (in a separate listing) helpfully divided into the subjects of the essays found in the 3 volumes under review. This reviewer missed the inclusion of "Subject Classification" in the "List of Entries," which might have helped a general user of the dictionary in finding areas of interest. Classifications are found at the end of each essay, together with cross-references and exhaustive bibliographies. Volume 3 also contains a list of relevant "Statutes, Treaties, and Directives" (many of them emanating from the European Community Council), and a 10-page, double-column list of "Cases." In addition to their usefulness as a focused reference source, these volumes could be used as a textbook, or as a source of individual readings in a course on law and economics, crafted according to the interests or needs of the instructor. About 300 contributors to these volumes hail from many countries, most from the United States, Canada, the United Kingdom, Italy, Germany, Holland, Greece, and international organizations. Their essays are uniformly excellent, informative, and helpful for deeper research. [R: BL, 1 Oct 98, pp. 364-365; LJ, Dec 98, pp. 92, 94; RUSQ, Spring 99, pp. 310-311]

—**Bogdan Mieczkowski**

Directories

127. **American Big Businesses Directory, 1999.** Omaha, Nebr., InfoUSA, 1998. 3v. $595.00/set. ISBN 1-56105-997-8. ISSN 1061-2173.

American Big Businesses Directory, 1999 provides a comprehensive compilation of some 193,000 businesses in the United States. The term "big businesses" is used in a broad sense to include any organization with 100 employees that purchases supplies, services, materials, or products. For example, government entities and educational institutions are included. Two of the three volumes included in the set list businesses alphabetically. Each entry provides address, telephone and fax numbers, lines of business by SIC code, parent or branch relationships, employee size category, annual sales volume category, credit rating based on estimated ability to pay, and key executives. The 3d volume contains a list of businesses by U.S. city, a list of businesses by SIC code, and an alphabetic list of executives. Compilation of the directory required exhaustive examination of telephone directories, annual reports, SEC reports, government data, and postal information. Data collected were verified by telephone calls to listed businesses.

The directory would be useful to a wide range of practitioners, teachers, and students—particularly those who would like to market a product or service, or those who are engaged in market research or planning. The directory is also available in CD-ROM format (see entry 128), which will enable sorting by characteristics of interest to the user. The publisher can provide additional services, such as prospect lists and mailing labels. The directory offers essential information on large U.S. organizations in a single, authoritative source. Perhaps the publisher will consider including e-mail addresses in the next edition.

—**William C. Struning**

128. **The American Big Businesses Disc.** 2d ed. [CD-ROM]. Omaha, Nebr., InfoUSA, 1999. Minimum system requirements: IBM or compatible PC. Double-speed CD-ROM drive. Windows 3.1 or higher. 8MB RAM. 15MB hard disk space. $595.00.

The American Big Businesses Disc is a searchable CD-ROM directory of 193,000 public and private businesses and other organizations in the United States and their 703,000 executives compiled from yellow page telephone directories and public company filings. The directory claims to include all U.S. businesses with more than 100 employees. Each record contains company name and complete address including, zip code, telephone and fax numbers, type of business (both yellow page heading and expanded SIC code), multiple executive names and titles, number of employees, estimated sales volume, headquarters/branch identifiers, stock exchange and ticker symbol for public companies, and a credit rating code. Company Websites are not part of the record. The database may be searched by any of the foregoing criteria as well as by city, state, zip code, county, metro area, area code, telephone prefix, or the entire United States.

There are some anomalous search results that users would not ordinarily associate with "big business." When searching by city, for example, the results include sheriffs' departments, county commissioners, local schools, hospitals, nonprofit agencies, and other entities. Because these organizations are often large employers and significant purchasers there is some justification for including them. It appears that branch relationships for public companies are accurate. For nonprofit organizations and private companies relationships are not always specified.

The layout of the search screens is simple and clear, with tabs across the top for each main search category: company, type of business, geography, business size, and special. Along the right-hand side are additional search criteria for each category. For example, companies may be searched by name, contact person, telephone number, or ticker symbol. The help contents is straightforward, answering basic questions on the scope of the database, searching, displaying and exporting records, and contacting technical support.

The software for the library edition permits downloading up to 75 records at a time into a spreadsheet format. However, users can only pick the first 75 records the first time they download a set. Afterwards each record must be tagged individually and then downloaded in sets of up to 75 records into a separate file. The obvious intent of these limitations is to discourage users from downloading the database. The procedure makes it very cumbersome to create files of companies larger than 75 records. *The American Big Businesses Disc* is reasonably priced in comparison with other business directories available on CD-ROM.

—**Peter Zachary McKay**

129. **Business Organizations, Agencies, and Publications Directory.** 10th ed. William H. Harmer, ed. Farmington Hills, Mich., Gale, 1999. 1774p. index. $405.00. ISBN 0-7876-0766-5. ISSN 0888-1413.

The 10th edition of *Business Organizations, Agencies, and Publications Directory* (BOAPD), under the editorial direction of William H. Harmer, provides convenient access to some 37,000 sources of business information. Although U.S. entries are the most numerous, international entries are well represented. A broad spectrum of organizations and facilities are included (e.g., associations related to commerce and business, commodity and stock exchanges, labor unions, chambers of commerce, state and federal government agencies, diplomatic offices, business and trade services, as well as research and educational facilities). On the publications side, there are listings of directories, periodicals, newsletters, computer databases, and business libraries. Most entries contain address, phone, fax, e-mail, URL, key contacts, languages, and a concise description. Data were compiled from other Gale research directories, government sources, and Websites of organizations included in this volume. To facilitate searching and cross-referencing, a comprehensive name and keyword index of all organizations, agencies, publications, and information services is included in the directory. Listing in the index is alphabetic with references to each entry by entry number. BOAPD is divided into 32 sections, as listed in a table of contents. A brief overview of each section is provided in a preface. In addition to hard-copy format, BOAPD is available on magnetic tape, diskette, or online. The publisher can provide mailing labels for all or part of the entries. BOAPD provides convenient and authoritative access to a broad spectrum of business information.—**William C. Struning**

130. **Business Phone Book USA 1999: The National Directory of Addresses and Telephone Numbers.** 21st ed. Jennifer C. Perkins, ed. Detroit, Omnigraphics, 1999. 2v. index. $160.00/set. ISBN 0-7808-0357-4. ISSN 1091-3955.

Formerly called the *National Directory of Addresses and Telephone Numbers*, this directory's purpose is to be a one-stop, quick reference resource at the reference desk. This 21st edition provides 132,000 company listings with name; mailing address; city; five-digit zip code; telephone, fax, and toll-free numbers; Website and e-mail addresses; an indicator whether this site is a company headquarters; and a cross-reference notation that leads the user to the corresponding subject heading in the subject volume. Entries are in word-by-word order. The first 200 pages of volume 1 list sources of information, such as government, lodging, restaurants, major malls, hospitals or medical centers, colleges, events, and attractions for the nation's largest 81 cities. Also included are the Fortune 500, Hispanic 500, Forbes 500, Canadian 200, and Black Enterprise 100 business lists as well as airport and area codes. The area code list is updated as of 1998. Volume 2 is a subject list of the entities from volume 1 tied to the code number at the end of the line for each company in volume 1. Some groupings are useful for quick reference like consulates, newspapers, museums, libraries, hotels and motels, government offices (federal, state, county, and city), Chambers of Commerce, and Better Business Bureaus.

This is a quick and convenient resource, although the print is too small and, like most titles from Omnigraphics, it is overpriced. Omnigraphics also publishes the *National Consumer Phone Book* (see ARBA 99, entry 153) in the exact same format but with only 54,000 companies. The consulate, Better Business Bureau, Chamber of Commerce, government office, and Convention and Visitors Bureau data are virtually the same in both titles. Fax numbers and e-mail addresses are provided and the typeface is larger. Priced at $65, most libraries will find the *National Consumer Phone Book* a more focused and thus better reference tool and a better value. The *Business Phone Book* has earned good reviews in the past and can still be mildly recommended for its content and utility, but it is a title whose size and price have bloated over the years, reducing its once great value. [R: Choice, Sept 99, pp. 116-117]—**Patrick J. Brunet**

131. **Company Profiles for Students.** Donna Craft, ed. Farmington Hills, Mich., Gale, 1999. 2v. illus. index. $150.00/set. ISBN 0-7876-2936-7. ISSN 1520-2938.

With stock projects proliferating in high schools, students and teachers will be attracted to this multi-function resource. For 270 companies, each profiled on 5 to 7 pages, the editor provides company history and chronology, expenditures, analysts' opinions, current trends, employment, and a brief bibliography. General features of the set include a chronology of key business events; industry profiles, including overview, historical sketch, significant events, global presence, and key competitors in the field; and an annotated directory of business-related Websites. One senses a full range of types of companies, with the emphasis on popular service industries. Some major product names are listed in the index; for example, Kenmore and Craftsman lead to the Sears entry. *Hoover's Handbook of American Business* (1998 ed.; see ARBA 99, entry 169), the standard bearer that more briefly profiles 750 companies, tends to have straight lists in the general features whereas this resource provides context. As there are about 11,000 publicly owned companies, the editor's challenge was to choose a manageable amount of information to squeeze into 1,600 pages. On the plus side, Craft includes several foreign automobile companies and a few others, which *Hoover's* does not. Updating is already a problem, however. Despite its 1999 copyright date, months-old mergers such as Daimler/Chrysler and MCI/ WorldCom are not noted. Teachers may want to ask students to read Craft, then supplement with online sources such as the Electric Library and the individual companies. [R: Choice, Nov 99, p. 514; SLJ, Aug 99, pp. 181-182]—**Bobray Bordelon**

132. **Hoover's MasterList of Major U.S. Companies 2000.** Austin, Tex., Hoover's, 1999. 1034p. index. $99.95. ISBN 1-57311-054-X. ISSN 1066-291X.

Previous editions of this title (see ARBA 97, entry 166) included all U.S. companies traded on the New York Stock Exchange, American Stock Exchange, and the NASDAQ National Market, as well as the largest private companies, enterprises, and various high-profile companies. The criteria for inclusion in this 6th edition are all U.S. companies with sales of $125 million or more on the previously mentioned exchanges, the NASDAQ Small-Cap Market, and the Over-the-Counter Companies. These companies make up 3,499 of the 5,533 firms profiled. The remainder are comprised of the largest privately held companies, the largest mutual insurance companies, agricultural co-ops, foundations, sports teams and leagues, universities, not-for-profits, major subsidiaries of U.S. corporations with strong individual identities, and major government-owned enterprises. The data are pulled from Hoover's own database and supplemented with sales information from Media General Financial Services.

The format is an alphabetic, two-column arrangement with six companies per page. Entries include basic directory information—Website address, a description of the company's products and operations, ownership and market position, names of chief officers and a human resources contact, company status, and sales. Standard Industrial Classification codes are not used in this work. Indexes by industry description, headquarters location, and stock exchange symbol provide additional access. Tables of rankings by sales, employees, 5-year sales growth, and market value are provided for the top 500 in each category.

For a more comprehensive source, *Ward's Business Directory of U.S. Private and Public Companies* (see ARBA 93, entry 198), which includes almost 90,000 companies, includes many more companies but offers less detail on each firm. However, this work's inclusion of large enterprises that are not traditional businesses is useful. A number of errors were found (one that leaped out was Princeton University's employee size increasing by 150 percent in one year) that more careful editing would have caught. This title is also available on CD-ROM. For those needing more information on companies profiled, the editors refer the user to Hoover's Online or its other print products. If a library has the other Hoover's products, this one is not necessary. If the goal is one inexpensive source that covers the largest companies in the United States, whether public or private, this source is a bargain.—**Bobray Bordelon**

133. **Research Services Directory 2000: Commercial & Corporate Research Centers.** 7th ed. Gottlieb, Richard, ed. Lakeville, Conn., Grey House Publishing, 1999. 1089p. index. $420.00; $395.00pa. ISBN 1-891482-31-9; 1-891482-30-0pa.

Research Service Directory, now in its 7th edition, is a comprehensive source for information on independent commercial research firms, laboratories, and corporate research centers in the United States and Canada that offer contract services for hands-on, basic, or applied research and testing, data gathering, analysis, and synthesis. This volume is intended to be a complete update of the 6th edition and now includes e-mail addresses and URLs.

There are 6,296 companies included in *Research Services Directory*. These companies span a wide range of research and testing activities, from analysis of biomedical materials and consumer products to verifying computer security and hazardous waste management. Marketing research and consulting firms, information brokers, and document delivery services are also included. The arrangement of the entries is alphabetic by company name. Although up to 23 fields of information may be available for each entry, a typical entry might include company name, address, telephone number, fax number, e-mail address, Web address, contact or president name, brief description, research and technical fields, principal clients, memberships, affiliated companies, founding date, staff size, and annual revenue. Additional information may be given on special research capabilities and publications. Some entries merely provide basic directory information. Entries are compact but easy to read and the layout is both attractive and functional.

Three indexes are provided in *Research Services Directory*: a geographic index (arranged by state), a subject index of 2,000 terms with cross-references, and an index of chief executives and other key contacts. The introduction covers the scope of the volume, the method of compilation, and the availability of diskette and magnetic tape versions and customized mailing labels. There is also a user's guide that provides a key to the different fields that may be included in an individual entry.

Research Services Directory will be a popular source in many types of libraries. Although it seems most appropriate for corporate and special libraries, it will also be useful in public libraries that serve the small business community. Although entrepreneurship is growing, few small- and even medium-sized companies have the luxury of their own research departments and must rely on contracting this work to other organizations. *Research Services Directory* will provide the needed link to locating these services.—**Sara Anne Hook**

134. **The Top 5,000 European Companies 1999/2000.** Jane Bradley and Janet Thomas, eds. London, Graham & Whiteside; distr., Farmington Hills, Mich., Gale, 1999. 1143p. index. $630.00. ISBN 1-86099-158-0.

This reference work is arranged in 3 sections for easy access and will be a useful addition to libraries supporting international business studies. It is also available on CD-ROM. The 1st section ranks the top 5,000 European manufacturing and service companies by size of sales revenues, banks by total assets, and insurance companies by premium income. These figures are in U.S. dollars. Countries and companies within each country are alphabetic in the 2d section. Each company entry provides location and communication information, the names of board members and company officers, business activities, financial information for the past two years, principal shareholders, and number of employees. A business activities index comprises the 3d section. All of the companies are listed in categories according to the 4-digit 1987 U.S. Standard Industrial Classification code. An alphabetic index by company name concludes this volume.—**Sue Brown**

135. **U.S. Business Directory, 1999: 1.1 Million Businesses with 20 or More Employees.** Omaha, Nebr., InfoUSA, 1998. 2v. $795.00/set. ISBN 1-56105-995-1.

The *U.S. Business Directory* is a 2-volume reference work that lists businesses in the U.S. with 20 or more employees. The directory includes the name, address, telephone, SIC code, credit rating code, number of employees, and estimated annual sales of over 1.1 million businesses. The listings are organized by city and state, making them easy to access. Sources for the information contained in the directory include phone directories, the Securities and Exchange Commission, other government agencies and publications, company annual reports, trade journals, business magazines, and newspapers. The directory is a potentially useful reference tool for businesspeople, academic researchers, job hunters, and others. Its cost might make it prohibitive for smaller libraries, but it is recommended for libraries that can afford such a publication.—**Paul F. Clark**

136. **Who Knows What: A Guide to Experts.** 17th ed. Rockville, Md., Washington Researchers, 1999. 549p. $245.00pa. ISBN 1-56365-090-8. ISSN 0894-8801.

Washington Researchers was founded in 1974 to provide publications, workshops, and seminars for clients seeking information on various organizations and institutions. Their expertise in the field of research is utilized daily by professionals all over the world. This book is a compilation of information that has been culled, by these experts, to provide a directory for public use in the investigation of specific topics. In most cases, listings contain several different authorities (displayed as name and position occupied with telephone numbers) on subjects studied. Though the introduction states clearly that this book is designed as a telephone directory to government offices, there is a section at the beginning that catalogs "parent" or main organizations. These entries are complete with Web addresses, building addresses, and brief descriptions of functions performed by these offices, as well as telephone numbers, for help in tracking any moved, changed, or deleted positions. It is a tool designed for use, whether by librarians, scholars, businesspersons, or the general public, to quicken the outcome of subject-specific searching. Topics are arranged alphabetically and, in some cases, indexed more than once (example given: "advanced ceramics" can be found under both "A" and "C"). It is a user-friendly directory that is well organized, accurate, and divided into sections that support each other in research of specific topics. With the changes that frequently occur in government offices, some of the information may need further research, but all in all this is a good resource to have on hand. Recommended for large public and academic libraries, and government document collections.—**Kimberley D. Harris**

137. **World Directory of Business Information Websites.** Chicago, Euromonitor International; distr., Farmington Hills, Mich., Gale, 1998. 191p. index. $590.00pa. ISBN 0-86338-836-1.

This directory supplies addresses of major business information sources worldwide. Only sites with substantial, freely accessible content are included. It will be highly useful for corporate information specialists. Many of the same resources are available through Euromonitor's Website at http://www.Euromonitor.com.

Entries give site name; publishing organization with postal, fax, and e-mail addresses; the URL; and paragraph-length, point-form summaries of types of information. Most sites are those of institutions, such as central banks and government bodies, trade associations, media organizations, polling and consulting groups, think tanks, and international bodies. Media outlets are only included if their sites archive back runs.

The initial 12-page, double-columned section covers international sites. These range from the Association of British Insurers and the CIA through Ernst and Young to the World Bank and World Resources Institute. The 2d part is grouped by 7 regions, from Asia to Oceania. The 3d and longest section is arranged by country. Sites are listed for 94 countries. For some smaller ones, only one site is listed. Most countries seem to have 1 or 2 pages devoted to them—America has 25; the United Kingdom and Canada have 5 each; China has 1 column; and Japan, Germany, India, France, and Mexico have 2 to 3 pages. This reflects the United States' dominance of the Internet. A decision to list only major sites reduces dating problems of any URL list.

The two indexes are not listed in the contents. The substantial 39-page index by industrial sector ranges from "Advertising and Marketing" through "Wholesale and Retail Trade." This valuable resource will be a useful addition to collections with the budget to afford it. [R: Choice, Sept 99, p. 124]

—**Nigel Tappin**

Handbooks and Yearbooks

138. **Small Business Sourcebook: The Entrepreneur's Resource.** 13th ed. Amy R. Suchowski and Theresa J. MacFarlane, eds. Farmington Hills, Mich., Gale, 1999. 2v. index. $325.00/set. ISBN 0-7876-2121-8. ISSN 0883-3397.

This 2-volume sourcebook provides a wealth of information for persons interested in starting a small business. Part bibliography and part directory, its over 55,000 entries direct readers to resources for specific small businesses, general small business topics, and local, federal, and Canadian sources of assistance for entrepreneurs. Each entry includes, as appropriate, the name of the organization, institution, or product; contact information; author and editor, date, and frequency; availability, including price; a brief description; e-mail addresses; and Web addresses.

The majority of the work's 4,065 pages are devoted to small business profiles and general small business topics. The profiles section covers 336 different types of small businesses. The arrangement is alphabetical and includes such varied businesses as "Aerial Surveying," "Gourmet Coffee/Tea Shop," and "Web Site Design." Entries for each small business are organized into standard categories. These categories can include start-up Information, associations and other organizations, licensing information, directories of educational programs, reference works, sources of supply, statistical sources, trade periodicals, videocassettes and audiocassettes, trade shows and conventions, consultants, franchises and business opportunities, computerized databases, computer systems and software, Internet databases, libraries, and research centers.

The section on general small business topics consists of 95 chapters covering topical business functions of interest to a wide variety of small businesses. Some examples are "Benefits," "Hiring," "International Trade," "Publicity/Advertising," and "Small Business Software." Besides information on specific and general small business topics, researchers may use this work to identify government sources of assistance and support. Arranged geographically, it includes listings by state, Guam, Puerto Rico, the Virgin Islands, and Canadian provinces. Some of the standard types of sources for each geographical area include small business assistance programs, better business bureaus, chambers of commerce, and financing and loan programs.

The fourth, and smallest, section includes entries for sources of U.S. federal government assistance. The 966 listings provide information for nearly 50 federal agencies and offices. Finally, an alphabetic master index provides name access to the volumes.

The *Small Business Sourcebook* continues to be an invaluable reference source. It is recommended for academic and public libraries, as well as any other library serving users with an interest in small business.
—**Gordon J. Aamot**

139. **The Value of a Dollar 1860-1999: Prices and Incomes in the United States.** 2d ed. Scott Derks, ed. Lakeville, Conn., Grey House Publishing, 1999. 493p. illus. $90.00. ISBN 1-891482-49-1.

The purchasing history of the U.S. dollar for the last century and a half is interesting to most of us. We can see what the cost of food and clothing in our grandparents' and parents' childhood and young adult lives were, as well as our own lives. This 2d edition of *The Value of a Dollar* records the actual prices of thousands of items purchased from the Civil War to the present time, and provides information about investment options and income opportunities. It has been revised and updated to include chapters on the four-year periods of 1990 to 1994 and 1995 to 1999.

Each five-year chapter contains a chronology of key economic and historic events from each year, a report on per capita consumer prices of the day nationwide, and a selection of investment returns excerpted from Federal Reserve reports. Data in the chapters also include a selection of jobs listed in major newspapers' want ads and a list of national average wage paid for representative jobs traced annually and based on the Bureau of Economic Analysis. There is also a regional report of food prices compiled from the Bureau of Labor Statistics, a selection of prices chosen from the advertisements of the day, a selection of representative items tracked annually, and a selection of anecdotal prices and income reports from publications of the period.

There is an appendix that tracks the prices of the federal gasoline tax rate, the public debt of the federal government, the postal rate for first class mail, public elementary and secondary expenditure per pupil, federal hourly minimum wage, average cost of electricity, college tuition costs and expenditures, and other interesting historical prices.

This book is for high school and college students who are doing historical economic research. It is recommended for high school, college, and public libraries for their social history collections. [R: Choice, Oct 99, p. 316]—**Kay M. Stebbins**

Quotation Books

140. **The Wiley Book of Business Quotations.** By Henry Ehrlich. New York, John Wiley, 1998. 430p. index. $30.00. ISBN 0-471-18207-9.

Could the proliferation of books of business quotations be related to the strong economy? Titles published in the past five years include *Bartlett's Book of Business Quotations* (Little, Brown, 1994), *The Ultimate Book of Business Quotations* (AMACOM, 1998), *Forbes Book of Business Quotations* (Black Dog & Leventhal, 1997), and *Quotable Business* (2d ed.; Random House, 1999).

Now comes another compilation of more than 5,000 quotes taken from the business press, books, television, and speeches. The focus is on themes that have developed over the past 20 years. Topics such as workplace diversity, the Information Superhighway, globalization, business education, e-commerce, deregulation, and the Asian market are included. The importance of the global economy is reflected in sections on Europe and Asia (subdivided by country), NAFTA, and the role of developing countries.

The quotes are organized under 45 main subjects with subcategories under most of them. For the most part, quotes are arranged chronologically. Sections begin with a few historical quotes to illustrate how things have changed. For example, the "glass ceiling" category opens with a turn-of-the-century quote by James Fargo, president of American Express, where he threatens to close the company rather than hire a female employee. The quote is followed by numerous 1990s quotes by women executives. The scope of the quotations is broad, from well-known names such as Bill Gates, Peter Drucker, Ross Perot,

Ted Turner ("You're toast") and Bill Clinton to statements by eight-year-olds, college students, and cartoon characters (although Dilbert is not quoted).

Do not look here for the traditional epigrammatic one-liner. Ehrlich admittedly takes liberties with the term "quotation." He includes vignettes, paragraphs from articles and speeches that may contain an idea, lists, and statistics. The context for entries is given, and sometimes crucial, to the meaning of the quote. This is especially true of those quotes that are responses to questions (i.e., "Are you kidding? We reserve that right for the poor, the young, the black and the stupid"). These quotes would be meaningless without elaboration.

The author's approach makes for interesting and entertaining browsing. Speakers at the local Chamber of Commerce searching for an idea for a speech will find the collection useful. But researchers, speechwriters, and students looking for a specific quote or quotes on a topic will be better off using periodical, speech, and transcript databases or Websites that will give more complete bibliographic information. There are a name index of people quoted and a company index, but the table of contents is the only guide to topics. An alphabetic keyword index would have been useful. This is a fun collection but there is nothing here that cannot be found elsewhere.—**Marlene M. Kuhl**

BUSINESS SERVICES AND INVESTMENT GUIDES

141. **The CRB Commodity Yearbook 1998.** By Bridge Information Systems America. New York, John Wiley, 1998. 316p. $99.95. ISBN 0-471-24705-7.

Researchers seeking commodities data generally must consult many sources to obtain a thorough overview. Sources such as Catherine Friedman's *Commodity Prices* (see ARBA 92, entry 159) and Karen Chapman's *Commodity Prices Locator* (see ARBA 90, entry 274) are excellent bibliographic guides, but do not provide data. Since 1939, the Commodity Research Bureau has been a leading source for commodities statistics and market overviews. Special topics are profiled in each edition (1998 featured El Niño). The bulk of this work is devoted to market surveys and data in both table and chart form for over 100 commodities and futures. While historical information is usually provided, frequency varies. Sources are always cited; this practice allows the researcher to go to the original source for more detailed information. Additional features, such as volume for international futures exchanges and a table of conversion factors, further aid the researcher. For those needing more frequent data, the yearbook is also available on compact or floppy disk with quarterly updates.—**Bobray Bordelon**

142. **Directory of Alternative Investment Programs.** 1998 ed. Steven P. Galante and Keith W. Moore, eds. Wellesley, Mass., Asset Alternatives, 1998. 552p. index. $495.00pa. (with software); $395.00pa. ISBN 0-9652137-7-3.

Institutional investors, and to a far lesser extent a catch-all category called other investors, invest small portions of their assets in the alternative investment field as a long-term investment strategy. Institutional investors consist of pension funds (both public and corporate), endowments and foundations, banks, finance companies, and insurance companies. The type of alternative investments these investors make varies, including private equity, natural resources, managed futures, hedge funds, and options. Alternative investments are discussed in much detail by authorities in the field in an introductory "Articles" section in this directory. The alternative investments field naturally has many different players ranging from advisors and placement agents to the investors themselves. The remainder of the directory is devoted to these players. One part is a directory of advisors and agents, another a directory of close to 600 institutional investors broken down by category. Still another part analyzes and ranks the assets (and allocations of those assets) of the investors. The final part consists of five useful indexes to the entire directory.

The *Directory of Alternative Investment Programs* is a unique source. It is a companion volume to *Galante's Venture Capital & Private Equity Directory* (1998 ed.; see ARBA 99, entry 200), a directory of fund managers who put the institutional capital to work. The *Directory of Alternative Investment Programs* is a required purchase for the libraries of all institutional investors who either invest or intend to invest in the alternative field. It should also be acquired for the business collections of large public libraries as well as large academic libraries.—**Dene L. Clark**

143. Ryland, Philip. **Pocket Investor.** New York, John Wiley, 1998. 213p. (The Economist Books). $14.95pa. ISBN 0-471-29597-3.

As its name implies, *Pocket Investor* is a compact volume that is loaded with helpful information about the intricate and sometimes baffling subject of investments. It is one of a series of "pocket" books on management from *The Economist*, a long-standing and highly respected journal. The author is the deputy editor of *Investors Chronicle*. The purpose of *Pocket Investor* is to bring clarity to the complexities and jargon of the investment world. It achieves this purpose by providing a wealth of information in a convenient format that is easy to read. A unique aspect of *Pocket Investor* is that it reflects both U.S. and UK terminology.

Pocket Investor is divided into 3 parts. The 1st presents 4 essays on investing: the returns that can be expected from the market; whether excess returns are really possible; lessons from the most successful investors, such as Warren Buffet and Sir John Templeton; and the flaws in conventional stock market wisdom. These essays are concise, informative, and easy to read. A brief 5th essay describes differences in investment terminology between the United States and the United Kingdom. This is helpful because *Pocket Investor* includes information reflecting both countries' systems. The 2d part comprises the bulk of the volume and is a glossary of investment terms. Definitions are generous, sometimes providing a page or more of text. Figures and tables are included, although the content is primarily text. Interspersed throughout the glossary are quotes from famous people, from both within and outside of the financial world. Some of the terms included are quite advanced and reflect the worldwide investment arena, making *Pocket Investor* a unique and important reference source for patrons who need more than just the basics, although basic terms such as *asset* and *common stock* are also covered. Commonly used abbreviations are cross-referenced, as are country-specific terms. The 3d part is devoted to appendixes, with tables on stock and bond returns, market data, investing formulas, accounting terminology differences between the United States and the United Kingdom, and two pages of references of recommended readings. *Pocket Investor* is small enough for a briefcase, yet the typeset is clear and not too small.

In spite of a wealth of other choices, *Pocket Investor* would be a unique and appropriate addition to any public library's reference collection. Information included in *Pocket Investor* is succinct and easy to read, yet still comprehensive enough to reflect the complexity of the investment field. In addition, *Pocket Investor*'s inclusion of more global terms is useful in an investment environment that is no longer confined by geography. *Pocket Investor* would also be a good addition to collections supporting academic business programs and in libraries serving banking, investment, accounting, and consulting personnel.

—**Sara Anne Hook**

CONSUMER GUIDES

144. **The Catalog of Catalogs VI: The Complete Mail-Order Directory.** Edward L. Palder, ed. Bethesda, Md., Woodbine House, 1999. 567p. index. $25.95pa. ISBN 1-890627-08-9.

The 6th edition of this biennial and respected publication of American mail-order companies includes almost 15,000 entries. This is an increase of over 1,000 listings from the previous edition. The reader will find companies listed under 920 subject categories including 70 that are new to this edition, such as tandem bicycles, pasta sauces, totem poles, paintball, and yo-yos. Each listing includes the name of the company, address, a brief description of the product line, telephone number, and e-mail or Internet address. This title will see a lot of use in public library reference departments for those clients attempting to identify buyers for their product lines or suppliers for their stores. Shoppers will also find this a very tempting book to browse through.

This type of publication is never completely comprehensive or accurate since businesses come and go. The choice of subject categories can be debated, but with 920 subject categories, the editor has attempted to be specific in a way that would be useful to consumers.

Because we do hear about fraudulent mail-order operations and companies changing their names or moving, the compiler requests that users inform him of any problems so that they can be addressed in the next edition. The compiler also provides a few tips on how to shop online.—**Judith J. Field**

145. **Consumer Sourcebook.** 12th ed. Sonya D. Hill, ed. Farmington Hills, Mich., Gale, 1999. 1165p. index. $265.00. ISBN 0-7876-3344-5. ISSN 0738-0518.

The first *Consumer Sourcebook* (CS) came out in 1974 just after the Consumer Protection Agency was formed by Congress. The organization, content, and entries have all been modified several times since then. However, the outstanding highlight of this edition is the inclusion of the Internet Database Subsection for each of the 17 fields with 360-plus online information sources. Therefore, today's edition of the CS is a very comprehensive guide to more than 17,500 free or low-cost programs, publications, multimedia sources, and services offered by a variety of public and private groups. For this update, some 7,000 of these groups were contacted.

Each chapter includes descriptive listings for live (media), electronic, and print resources; and within the chapter, listings are arranged in subsections by type of resource. The "User's Guide" is lengthy and thorough, giving users high-school age and above easy access to a variety of current, reliable information on consumerism. A unique feature of this guide is the inclusion of an issues list within the description of each chapter.

Another important section is the "Consumer Tips." Useful subsections here include "Getting the Most for Your Money and Avoiding Consumer Problems," "How to Write a Complaint Letter," "The Typical American Shopper," and more. Two appendixes, "Hotlines and Clearinghouses" and "Testing Laboratories," and a combined alphabetic and subject index complete the volume. Most libraries will want to provide this excellent resource for their clients.—**Susan C. Awe**

146. Norrgard, Lee E., and Julia M. Norrgard. **Consumer Fraud: A Reference Handbook.** Santa Barbara, Calif., ABC-CLIO, 1998. 338p. index. (Contemporary World Issues). $45.00. ISBN 0-87436-991-6.

Part of ABC-CLIO's award-winning Contemporary World Issues series, this work reveals the spectrum of consumer fraud, from work-at-home and investment scams to credit issues and high tech merchandising. By learning what consumer fraud involves, how society is affected, and what tactics are used to combat it, readers may be able to understand their own vulnerability and avoid being taken. However, everyone pays for consumer fraud in the increased prices businesses must charge to recover their loses.

This vast, ubiquitous topic begins with a chronology starting from Hammurabi in 1800 B.C.E. and continues through telemarketing and car leasing on the brink of the twenty-first century. Brief biographical sketches of men and women, including three presidents, who either made consumer issues a career, or in the case of the presidents, played a critical role in governmental policy and legislation are included. Chapter 4 is titled "Documents, Laws, and Regulations"; "Directory of Agencies and Organizations," which is arranged alphabetically by state, is the 5th chapter. The final two chapters are annotated bibliographies of print and nonprint resources. Especially noteworthy are the 29 Websites listed.

A short glossary, a print advertisement that has the appearance of a news story or editorial, and a detailed index complete the volume. This unique, authoritative reference resource should be found in most public libraries and in business collections. Citizens, activists, students, and researchers will find a lot of information here. [R: Choice, June 99, p. 1765]—**Susan C. Awe**

147. **Orion Blue Book: Power Tool 1998.** 1998 ed. Scottsdale, Ariz., Orion Research, 1998. 376p. $94.00. ISBN 0-932089-55-0.

Orion Blue Book: Power Tool is one of 13 guides to the wholesale and retail prices of used equipment. The main purpose of the book is to assist the staff of used equipment stores to determine value. Entries are arranged by manufacturer. Under each in bold typeface are the types of tools made by that manufacturer. The years of manufacture for each particular model are then given, with new list price, retail used price, and mint and average wholesale prices. For example, a Black & Decker electric hand drill, model 1070, made between 1985 and 1987, cost $175 when new and should bring $20 used. The dealer might offer the seller $12 if in mint condition or $7 if in average condition. Users are cautioned that the prices given and national averages; local markets will vary. For the consumer, the data are useful if they wish to buy or sell through a store or for the purposes of setting a price for a classified advertisement or yard sale. For those libraries with a need for this information, this book is a good benchmark of value.

—**John M. Robson**

FINANCE AND BANKING

148. Allen, Larry. **Encyclopedia of Money.** Santa Barbara, Calif., ABC-CLIO, 1999. 328p. illus. index. $75.00. ISBN 1-57607-037-9.

Written for the general reader rather than for the scholar, this compilation of some 300 brief essays (500 to 1,000 words in length) presents a variety of historical information regarding important monetary experiences that have influenced the evolution of money and banking. Although the author indicates an intent not to dwell on proving or disproving any specific theories of monetary economics, it is evident that certain exceptions prove the rule. Likewise, theories are brought into discussion only when they result in bringing some order out of chaos. In essence, the guiding principle is identification of the common characteristics that are shared within and between various monetary systems.

The work opens with an alphabetic list of entries, followed by a brief preface and introduction. Some entries include illustrations and all include cross-references and a brief bibliography of resources. A full bibliography and index supplement the main text.

To trained economists, this work might prove too vague and unrewarding. However, to the general reader, armchair historian, and seeker of curious facts, the work should be quite fulfilling. High school, public, and college library users might benefit from the clarity of discussions. [R: BL, 15 Nov 99, pp. 649-652]—**Edmund F. SantaVicca**

149. Clark, John. **International Dictionary of Banking and Finance.** library ed. Chicago, Glenlake and Chicago, Fitzroy Dearborn, 1999. 352p. $55.00. ISBN 1-57958-160-9.

This title provides short definitions for an estimated 4,500 acronyms, keywords, terms, and proper names in the broad field of banking, finance, investments, savings institutions, and stock exchanges. Selection of entries is based heavily on UK terms with some U.S. terms and a very few continental European terms thrown in. It is strong for acronyms but weak for insurance. Any library with active business clientele will benefit from updated subject dictionaries and this one is clearly written, and UK terminology aside, easily understandable. At $55, however, it is overpriced for U.S. libraries who would find Thomas Fitch's *Dictionary of Banking Terms* (see ARBA 99, entry 186) at $12.95 and Jerry M. Rosenberg's *Dictionary of Banking* (see ARBA 94, entry 207) at $19.95 provide better coverage for less cost. In addition, the *American Bankers Association's Banking and Finance Terminology* (1999) costs $49 but is twice as long. Edward Hinkelman's *Dictionary of International Trade* (World Trade Press, 1997) at $16.50 is an acceptable choice for international banking terms. If Canadian banks use UK terminology, then this would be an acceptable purchase for larger academic and public libraries in Canada or for U.S. libraries that feel the need for a British take on banking terms. Otherwise, the other titles mentioned are better for U.S. libraries.

—**Patrick J. Brunet**

150. **Directory of Venture Capital Firms, 2000: Domestic & International.** 4th ed. Lakeville, Conn., Grey House Publishing, 1999. 1227p. index. $295.00. ISBN 1-891482-95-5.

The *Directory of Venture Capital Firms*, formerly published by Fitzroy Dearborn and titled *The International Directory of Venture Capital Funds*, has been extensively updated since its last publication in 1997. The directory lists 1,800 venture capital firms—1,270 domestic firms and 574 international firms. The data provided for each firm include contact information, education and professional background of the firm's management, a mission statement, when the firm was founded, geographic preferences, fund size, average amount of investment, portfolio companies, and investment criteria. Not all firms listed provide all of the information; some firms are more thoroughly represented than others. The 5 indexes offered here will help researchers explore the directory to their best advantage. They include a geographic index, an executive name index, a portfolio company index, an industry preference index, and a college and university index. This work will find much use in business libraries and the finance collection of many public libraries.—**Shannon M. Graff**

151. Rider, A. J. **The International Dictionary of Personal Finance.** Harrogate, England, Take That; distr., North Pomfret, Vt., Trafalgar Square, 1999. 188p. $11.95pa. ISBN 1-873668-54-6.

The number of financial and business dictionaries published each year can be overwhelming. Since most libraries cannot buy them all, finding the ones that are best for specific clientele can be very challenging. Many focus on the United States or try to cover the international scene comprehensively. Rider's new paperback dictionary focuses on two major markets: the United States and the United Kingdom. However, common terms exclusive to other parts of the world are occasionally included. It is written for the consumer and focuses on annuities, banking, bonds, business, equity-based investments and mutual funds, insurance, pensions, taxation, and wills. If a term is used exclusively in one country, it makes this distinction. The definitions are concise and sometimes include usage, but can be overly simplistic. While a number of less familiar financial terms (contango, kangaroos, peppercorn rent) are covered, some that appear regularly in the business press (hedge funds, poison pill) are not. A peculiarity is using British spellings when referring to exclusively American terms. A more comprehensive, albeit more dated and expensive alternative is *Handbook of International Financial Terms* (see ARBA 98, entry 184). Recommended only for comprehensive investment research collections or libraries requiring an inexpensive international financial dictionary.

—**Bobray Bordelon**

152. Shook, R. J. **Wall Street Dictionary.** Franklin Lakes, N.J., Career Press, 1999. 506p. $11.99pa. ISBN 1-56414-402-X.

This is a necessary reference book in any library's collection. Shook has written a complete reference tool for those interested in the definitions of basic to advanced financial terms. Recommended for anyone in need of a reference tool on financial terms.

However, this book is not recommended for financial analysts or special libraries in businesses. This is not a good reference tool for patrons who need complete and detailed explanations of financial terms. Shook's description of terms is frequently short and sometimes inaccurate. Definitions of some terms are no more than a few words. For example, "interest" is defined as "the amount of money a lender loans a borrower to pay for using the borrower's principal." What the author means is that interest is the amount of money a borrower pays to use a lender's principal. It is also the amount of money a lender or bank patron receives for loaning money to a borrower or a bank. "Intangible cost" is defined as "a business cost that is tax deductible." In fact, intangible cost are costs that are difficult to define, such as employee productivity. Finally, many economists would disagree with Shook's definition of the Friedman Theory. Most economists would define the Friedman Theory as a theory of how the money supply influences long-term inflation rates and, while it may have short-term impacts on a country's economy, the money supply has little to do with a country's economic condition in the long term.

More than 5,000 terms are defined in this text. Overall it is a good text for beginning business students or the general population interested in business terms. However, some terms are not fully defined or are misrepresented. This is unfortunate for a reference text that patrons rely on to provide complete and accurate information. [R: LJ, 1 May 99, p. 70]—**Bruce Kingma**

INDUSTRY AND MANUFACTURING

Dictionaries and Encyclopedias

153. **Encyclopedia of Emerging Industries.** Jane A. Malonis and Holly M. Selden, eds. Farmington Hills, Mich., Gale, 1998. 580p. illus. index. $249.00. ISBN 0-7876-1863-2. ISSN 1096-2433.

Encyclopedia of Emerging Industries (EEI) is the 1st edition of a planned annual series identifying, describing, and assessing the outlook for U.S. industries that show the greatest potential for growth. Twenty-one contributors, whose efforts were guided by the skilled editing of Jane A. Malonis and Holly M. Selden, have detailed essential facts on 88 U.S. industries. Some of the included industries, cigars for example, have been active in the economy for many years, but have recently experienced a resurgence of growth. Others, like artificial intelligence, have exploited recent technological developments in capturing or promising rapid growth. Industries are arranged alphabetically, listed in a table of contents, and cross-referenced in a comprehensive general index. Also, industries are indexed by SIC codes, with a conversion guide to NAICS codes. Thus, it is quite convenient to search for specific business sectors and major organizations. Each industry profile averages 3,000 words and includes current size, present status, and organization, as well as historical background and prospects for the future. In addition, leading companies are sub-profiled, industry pioneers recognized, and employment opportunities provided. Suggestions for further reading accompany each profile. Nearly 200 charts, graphs, and tables increase readability and understanding. Although a reference volume, the book should interest a broad audience—certainly business students and practitioners, but students from other fields as well, seeking trends in current U.S. business activity. [R: RUSQ, Summer 98, p. 352]—**William C. Struning**

Directories

154. **American Manufacturers Directory, 1999.** Omaha, Nebr., American Business Directories, 1999. 2v. $595.00/set. ISBN 1-56105-998-6.

Making things is out of fashion. Yet companies that manufacture products are the backbone of the economy. Everything from the food we eat and the appliances we use to prepare it, to the clothes we wear, the cars we drive, and the pumps used to fill their tanks with gasoline to power them are made by someone. The *American Manufacturers Directory* lists everyone in the U.S. supply chain, from printers to publishers to pulp and paper mills. More than 168,000 manufacturers are included.

The 2-volume print directory is arranged into 3 sections: alphabetically by company name, manufacturers by city, and manufacturers by SIC code. A final section provides counts by SIC code. Main entries are brief. A typical entry lists the manufacturer's name, address, telephone and fax numbers, a contact name and position, number of employees, estimated sales, SIC codes, a credit score, and a year code. Among the significant omissions are URLs for company Websites and company/subsidiary/affiliate/location relationships. There are no indications whether a company is publicly traded or if it is a headquarters location.

The directory's origin as a source for mailing lists compiled from yellow pages and business white pages telephone directories limits its usefulness as a reference work for manufacturing companies. Unlike Thomas Register of American Manufacturers (http://www.thomasregister.com), there is neither a trade name nor an alphabetic product name index. The entries do not offer any detail on the specific products made. To find companies that make a product one must first figure out the appropriate SIC code. The SIC definitions provided are minimal. The price advertised on InfoUSA's Website (http://www.infousa.com) is $595.00 for a subscription to the print directory with a CD-ROM version. The company also sells the data on mailing labels, magnetic tapes, and diskettes.—**Peter Zachary McKay**

155. **American Manufacturers Disc.** 2d ed. [CD-ROM]. Omaha, Nebr., InfoUSA, 1999. Minimum system requirements: IBM or compatible PC. Double-speed CD-ROM drive. Windows 3.1 or higher. 8MB RAM. 15MB hard disk space. $595.00.

American Manufacturers Disc is a searchable database of companies that report themselves as manufacturers in the SIC classification system. The package is a two-CD-ROM set. The database itself is contained on the second disc, while the first is only used to install the package's software on a hard drive.

Despite extremely skimpy printed documentation, installation of the application software goes smoothly. Installation on a Pentium 233 running Windows 95 followed the standard Windows installation procedure and required no real look at the documentation. Actual operation was a bit less obvious. The separation of the product into installation and database discs is not mentioned in the documentation (although it can be inferred from tiny labels on the CD-ROMs themselves). As a result, users may be unaware of the need to change CD-ROMs after installation.

The search routines are simple to use and straightforward to interpret (assuming users have an understanding of the Standard Industrial Code system). The database gives results quickly and are acceptably comprehensive. For a library, the biggest weakness is the division of the product into an installed application plus a CD-ROM database. Because the database itself is only 220MB and the installer only takes up 5MB, it is not at all apparent why the publisher chose this approach. A standalone, single-CD-ROM version, with the actual application executable from CD-ROM, would be handier for libraries, simplifying both onsite use and temporary use by patrons who check out the CD-ROM. Aside from this limitation, the product is well designed and an excellent example of the transfer of databases from hard-to-use paper format to searchable computer format.—**Ray Olszewski**

156. **American Wholesalers and Distributors Directory: A Comprehensive Guide Offering Industry Details on Approximately 27,000 Wholesalers....** 7th ed. Rebecca Marlow-Ferguson, ed. Farmington Hills, Mich., Gale, 1999. 1668p. index. $195.00. ISBN 0-7876-2430-6. ISSN 1061-2114.

The subtitle of this book characterizes it as "a comprehensive guide offering industry details on approximately 27,000 wholesalers and distributors in the United States." Covering 61 major product categories, with extensive cross-listings of product types, plus both geographic and SIC-code indexes, it earns the "comprehensive" portion of this claim.

It is, however, somewhat sketchy on the "details" part. The typical entry is a company name, address, and telephone, combined with a vague description of the product lines offered, one or a few SIC codes, and sometimes some miscellaneous information (officers' names, date founded, and so on).—**Ray Olszewski**

157. **Brands and Their Companies: Consumer Products and Their Manufacturers with Addresses and Phone Numbers.** 18th ed. Jennifer L. Carman and Christine A. Kesler, eds. Farmington Hills, Mich., Gale, 1998. 2v. $805.00/set. ISBN 0-7876-2286-9. ISSN 1047-6407.

Who makes Wonderbras? (Sarah Lee). What are Wooly Boogers? (tires). Gale's *Brands and Their Companies* (BTC) answers these questions and 365,000 more about consumer brand names and who makes them. Branding distinguishes a product in the marketplace, provides assurance of consistent quality, and serves as a focal point for advertising and marketing. Glancing through the entries, one is struck by the many uses to which a name can be put. For example, "American Beauty" is a pasta and also a candy, a cigarette, giftware, greeting cards, seafood, soldering irons, wallpaper, and wet mops all made by different companies. BTC covers only consumer products.

There are so many brand names it is necessary to publish them in 2 hefty volumes at a hefty price ($805 per year). This edition includes more than 365,000 consumer brands by over 77,000 manufacturers and distributors (20,000 brands are new). The work is updated with a midyear supplement and is revised annually. The sources used to compile it are company literature, the United States Patent and Trademark Office (PTO), and trade journals and directories. BTC is arranged in two separate sections: brand listings and company listings. Numerical brands precede an alphabetic listing by brand name. Entries include the trade name, description, and manufacturer or distributor. Symbols indicate companies that are out of business, brands that are no longer produced, and brands that are currently considered generic. Brands not registered with the PTO as well as imported products are included. Company listings include name, address, phone, and fax. URLs, e-mail, and toll-free numbers are included as available.

BTC is the most comprehensive listing of consumer brand-name products in print. It is derived from a database maintained by Gale and is available on tape or diskette, CD-ROM, online, and through GaleNet. Other sources for brand names commonly held by libraries include the *Standard Directory of Advertisers* (1993 ed.; see ARBA 94, entry 296) and the *Thomas Register of American Manufacturers* (87th ed.; see ARBA 98, entry 196). If readers want to know all of the brands a company makes, they will have to consult Gale's companion volumes, *Companies and Their Brands* (see entry 158).—**Peter Zachary McKay**

158. **Companies and Their Brands: Manufacturers, Their Addresses and Phone Numbers, and the Consumer Products They Produce.** 18th ed. Jennifer L. Carman and Christine A. Kesler, eds. Farmington Hills, Mich., Gale, 1998. 2v. $515.00/set. ISBN 0-7876-2527-2. ISSN 1047-6407.

This massive set is an alphabetic list of U.S. companies, containing under each company entry contact information for the company (e.g., address and telephone numbers) and the brand names of the products it produces. If the user knows a company name and wants to find out what it makes, this is a key reference. It is extensive, apparently comprehensive, and includes entries for defunct companies and product lines. If one knows a brand name and wants to find the company that makes it the companion to this volume, *Brands and Their Companies: Consumer Products and Their Manufacturers with Addresses and Phone Numbers* (see entry 157), will need to be consulted

For more specialized users, such as investors, market researchers, and providers of business services, the book can contribute usefully to the development of company profiles. Overall, this is a database that invites delivery as a searchable, computer-based product, not a paper text, and most libraries would find a CD-ROM-based product of similar scope more useful than this set. The set also includes a brief directory of industry-specific information sources.—**Ray Olszewski**

159. **Directory of Contract Electronics Manufacturers, 1999.** North American ed. Kathleen Fitzpatrick and others, eds. San Francisco, Calif., Miller Freeman, 1998. 368p. index. $295.00pa.

Listing almost 1,400 electronics manufacturers who work under contract, this directory provides information necessary to identify companies with the capabilities to match specific needs. It opens with a review of the contract electronics manufacturers industry, followed by a state-by-state list of companies. Each listing has the address; year founded; top officers; types of board assembly; production data (e.g., plant size, capacity, specifications on work done, end products); assembly equipment; test equipment; materials procurement (e.g., consignment, turnkey); and other services. Several indexes organize manufacturers regionally by type of component preparation. There is a list of associations and trade shows as well as an alphabetic list of companies.

This directory is a straightforward list of and information on contract electronics firms that do customized work to specifications. However, the terminology used for individual companies is technical, and it is assumed that the reader is familiar with it. This source will be valuable in settings where users, probably local technology firms, will need to identify possible suppliers. *Directory of Contract Electronics Manufacturers, 1999* is recommended for libraries that serve a high technology clientele from the local community.

—**Gerald L. Gill**

Handbooks and Yearbooks

160. **Dun and Bradstreet/Gale Industry Reference Handbooks: Hospitality.** Stacy A. McConnell and Linda D. Hall, eds. Farmington Hills, Mich., Gale, 1999. 722p. $99.00pa. ISBN 0-7876-3776-9.

This survey is one of nine planned to be published covering the most popular industries. Each will be updated annually. The information is a compilation of other Dun and Bradstreet and Gale reference books and as such represents material that is already owned in many libraries, but is collected here for convenience.

The opening chapter is an overview that describes the industry, its history, its key players, its workforce, and the relevance of the data collected. Particularly useful are the surveys of trends and future expectations of the industry. Next are the performance indicators and industry norms that compare a variety of data (employees, solvency ratios, profitability, and so on) by SIC code (Standard Industrial Classification). Data are from 1995 to 1997.

The largest section is an alphabetic company directory with address information, sales, employees, and private and public status. The data are similar to those of any Dun and Bradstreet directory. This is supplemented with ranking lists by sales (from 1st to 4,859th) and by employment. Next is a section chronicling merger and acquisition activity during 1997 and 1998, arranged by company, with a citation of the announcement from *Nation's Restaurant News*, *PR Newswire*, and other sources.

The associations list is selected from the *Encyclopedia of Associations* (see ARBA 99, entry 50) and seems unnecessary here. The usual hotel and restaurant associations and unions are suitable, but the Bob Crane Memorial Fan Club seems to be a curious inclusion. The consultants and trade publications sections are adapted from more of Gale's commonly available reference books.

The indexes are essential for a collection like this, and the master index does cover each of the above sections. The geographic index is by state, not city and state, and there are very useful conversion lists of SIC to NAICS (North American Industrial Classification System, the successor to Standard Industrial Classification) and from NAICS to SIC.

This work is a useful compilation combining many features from two of the best-known reference publishers, and can be recommended for libraries that are willing to acquire it annually, either selectively or as an entire series. However, the majority of this information will already be available in a reasonably equipped reference collection, and each library will have to decide the ultimate cost of convenience.
—Gary R. Cocozzoli

161. **Handbook of North American Industry.** 2d ed. John E. Cremeans, ed. Lanham, Md., Bernan Associates, 1999. 644p. maps. $89.00. ISBN 0-89059-157-1.

In 1998, the 1st edition of the *Handbook of North American Industry* appeared (see ARBA 99, entry 220). The work has now been updated and, although the amount of new information is relatively small, all that made the 1st edition win prestigious library awards remains true. While the focus is the impact of the North American Free Trade Agreement (NAFTA), the benefit of this work is its pulling together of industry and employment data from numerous U.S., Canadian, and Mexican sources to present a unified and comparative statistical analysis of the North American economy.

This edition updates some of the features found in the 1st, such as a review of NAFTA; employees, benefits, and wages in North America; and the "Free Trade Area of the Americas Initiative." The added feature is on labor unions in North America. The majority of the work is statistical in nature. Standardized chapters make it easy to gain a grasp of industry. Textual analysis is based on the statistics. With the United States being the dominant economy, more information is available on it than on its partner countries. A useful feature is a comparative table at the end of each chapter showing NAFTA's impact on each nation. Although the North American Industrial Classification System (NAICS) scheme is included in the appendix, the United States Standard Industrial Classification System (SIC) is used to present data since NAICS data are not yet available. With data from the 1997 Census not yet available, much of the data for the United States are derived from the 1992 economic census. Various statistical agencies help update the data to 1997 (with some key data as recent as 1998) and in some cases projections to 2006. Canadian data tend to end with 1996 and Mexican data usually end around 1997. In all cases, data back to 1988 are available. Additional appendixes include an overview of NAFTA's predecessor—the Maquiladora program and governmental infrastructure information.

Although more current information can be obtained from other sources, this inexpensive work makes it easy for the researcher to get a quick overview and know which sources to turn for further information. If one has the 1st edition, this is a nice but not essential update because it only has one more year of information. All business collections could benefit from this work, whether the current or the 1st edition.

—**Bobray Bordelon**

162. **How Products Are Made, Volume 4: An Illustrated Guide to Product Manufacturing.** Jacqueline L. Longe, ed. Farmington Hills, Mich., Gale, 1999. 489p. illus. index. $90.00. ISBN 0-7876-2443-8. ISSN 1072-5091.

How Products Are Made: An Illustrated Guide to Product Manufacturing provides concise descriptions of the manufacturing process for 103 common products. The products include foods (e.g., rice cakes, licorice), toys (e.g., kazoos, model trains), household items (e.g., shellac, vinyl floor covering), vehicles (e.g., motorcycles, armored trucks), clothing (e.g., spandex, wet suits), and a number of other assorted products. The descriptions are clearly written and nicely illustrated so that little, if any, technical knowledge is needed to understand the processes. This volume is part of a series of similar volumes. The index in this volume gives references on the products included in this publication as well as the products discussed in other volumes. This reference work will be a useful inclusion in any engineering, science, or business collection. It will have limited usefulness in more general collections.—**Paul F. Clark**

163. **Manufacturing Worldwide: Industry Analyses, Statistics, Products, and Leading Companies and Countries.** 3d ed. Arsen J. Darnay, ed. Farmington Hills, Mich., Gale, 1999. 885p. index. $210.00. ISBN 0-7876-2447-0. ISSN 1084-8738.

The 1st edition of this title was issued in 1995 as a companion title to Gale's established series on U.S. industries. This edition provides industry statistics for 190 countries gathered from the United Nations Industrial Development Organization Industrial Statistics Branch. The United Nations Statistical Division's *Industrial Commodity Production Statistics* was the source for the commodity data. Some of the company information was also retrieved from Gale's *World Business Directory*. These data cover the period from 1990 through 1995 except for commodity data, which are current through 1996. Only 133 manufacturing countries from the above databases had information current enough to be included for the general statistical profile section. Part 1, which is 90 percent of the book, includes nearly 500 product categories produced by more than 4,000 companies. In addition to providing statistical summaries of each product category, there is a list of representative companies for each sector, which provides standard contact information.

The country profile section provides a half-page summary of the manufacturing activities for the years 1990 to 1995 in 16 categories, such as number of establishments, total employment, and capital investment. The index provides both country and company references. For libraries fielding questions about doing business overseas, this book will be a useful addition. It will serve as a beginning point in understanding the size of the markets in other countries.—**Judith J. Field**

164. **Market Share Reporter, 2000: An Annual Compilation of Reported Market Share Data on Companies, Products, and Services.** Robert S. Lazich, ed. Farmington Hills, Mich., Gale, 1999. 595p. illus. index. $245.00. ISBN 0-7876-2449-7. ISSN 1052-9578.

This volume (the 10th edition) presents 2,000 entries in 500 SIC codes on "market" shares as reported in numerous sources (979), such as trade journals and Internet sites. All of the data are either new or updated from the 9th edition and cover North America, although the entries are primarily for information pertaining to the U.S. rather than Mexico and Canada. Entries are by firms; by products, commodities, and services; and by geographic areas. The coverage is wide: snowboard makers, agriculture banks, hotel companies, casket makers, charitable donations, gasoline stations by state, and largest grocers in various cities. Data are also provided for the 1997 Internet browser market (Netscape Navigator, Microsoft Internet Explorer, AOL, and others) and the 1998 operating systems market (Windows 98 and Windows NT). The excellent indexes include sources (979); place-names (more than 250); products, services, names, and issues (1,980); companies (4,000); brands (1,250); SIC coverage; SIC to NAICS conversion; NAICS to SIC conversion; and an annotated list. This resource is available on tape, diskette, online (LEXIS-NEXIS), and on CD-ROM. It is not a substitute for data available from the Bureau of the Census.—**Richard A. Miller**

165. **WEFA Industrial Monitor 1999-2000.** Priscilla Trumbull and Frantz R. Price, eds. New York, John Wiley, 1999. 1v. (various paging). $59.95. ISBN 0-471-33320-4. ISSN 1093-6580.

Wharton Econometric Forecasting Associates (WEFA) is part of the PRIMARK organization and is one of the country's foremost economic forecasting and consulting firms. The *WEFA Industrial Monitor* covers more than 130 major industries. Each 3– to 5–page industry chapter gives an industry overview, sales data for the past 10 years, and estimated annual industry growth rates to the year 2007. Information in each chapter is presented using a mix of narrative and graphics and follows a uniform organizational scheme.

The introduction provides brief reviews and forecasts of U.S. and world economies. It also has a useful table with forecast highlights for the top growth industries. Parts 1 through 6 of the work contain the industry chapters. They are organized into the following categories: agriculture, forestry, fishing, and the environment; mining, construction, and energy; light and heavy manufacturing; transportation and communications; wholesale and retail trade; finance, insurance, and real estate; and healthcare, education, entertainment, law, and other service industries. An industry index provides access to individual industry entries.

The 1st edition of the *WEFA Industrial Monitor* was published in 1997 (see ARBA 98, entry 198). This 2d edition, published in March 1999, also provides outstanding value at a surprisingly modest price. Its combination of solid coverage and affordability should make it quite appealing to business librarians, especially if the publisher continues to update it on a regular basis. This work is recommended for all reference collections serving clientele with business information needs. [R: Choice, Oct 99, p. 316]

—**Gordon J. Aamot**

166. **Yearbook of Tourism Statistics.** 50th ed. Lanham, Md., Bernan Associates, 1998. 2v. $150.00pa./set. ISBN 92-844-0259-X. ISSN 1011-8977.

This comprehensive summary of world tourism presents its contents pages and explanatory notes in English, French, and Spanish. The titles and headings of the tables are in English only. Countries are classified in English in alphabetic order. The information, which the World Tourism Organization has been gathering annually for 50 years, comes from data obtained by questionnaires sent to governments and from official national publications. Volume 1 presents an overview of worldwide trends in tourism, with country rankings for top destinations, earners, and spenders, among other things. These are followed by regional summaries for Africa, the Americas, East Asia and the Pacific, Europe, and the Middle East. Volume 2 presents details for selected countries and territories on total arrivals and overnight stays by country of origin.

This publication is a standard reference for tourism officials. Large urban public libraries and colleges and universities that provide public administration courses may want to consider its purchase, but it is probably too arcane for most.—**Susan B. Hagloch**

INSURANCE

167. Clark, John. **International Dictionary of Insurance and Finance.** library ed. Chicago, Glenlake and Chicago, Fitzroy Dearborn, 1999. 341p. $55.00. ISBN 1-57958-161-7.

This dictionary provides definitions of thousands of terms from insurance, banking, and finance. The definitions are firmly from the perspective of the United Kingdom financial services industry. The target audience is financial services professionals and students.

The arrangement is alphabetic and entries are brief, mostly one or two sentences. More complex terms have a longer paragraph or two devoted to them. The thorough cross-references are indicated by bold typeface in entries.

Although the dictionary is billed as international, many definitions of general terms are definitely focused on the United Kingdom. For example, *whistle blowing* is shortly and narrowly defined with respect to the *1995 Pensions Act*, and *tax return* is characterized as a document submitted annually to the *Inland Revenue*. UK *individual savings accounts* are defined, but U.S. *individual retirement accounts* are not. The institutions listed, such as the Confederation of British Industry, also have a clear UK bias, although some U.S. and many international bodies are included. Although the status of the city of London as a major financial and insurance market makes UK usage and organizations important, lack of broader context is a major limitation in a purportedly international tool. Still only a minority of terms suffer from this obvious UK bias.

Prefatory materials are limited to a paragraph-length preface and a three-paragraph blurb on the back cover. No characterization of the author's qualifications or affiliations is given, although the copyright being held by the Chartered Institute of Bankers provides a clue. This dictionary is recommended for libraries and individuals collecting material on the UK financial and insurance industry, or the international sectors where its uses are important. More narrowly focused business collections will find it less appealing.

—**Nigel Tappin**

INTERNATIONAL BUSINESS

General Works

Dictionaries and Encyclopedias

168. Hinkelman, Edward G. **Dictionary of International Trade: Handbook of the Global Trade Community.** 3d ed. San Rafael, Calif., World Trade Press, 1999. 412p. illus. $32.00pa. ISBN 1-885073-82-8.

Precise communication and understanding are essential to the conduct of international trade. To enable transactions to flow efficiently and rapidly, specialized terms and concepts have evolved. It is necessary to understand those terms and concepts in order to engage in foreign commerce or to evaluate international transactions. *Dictionary of International Trade* by Hinkelman, an international economist, author, and experienced importer/exporter, provides a concise, yet comprehensive, reference for locating appropriate terms for verifying one's understanding of concepts. More than simply a dictionary, the book contains useful appendixes that include data on acronyms, abbreviations, international dialing codes, maps, world currencies, types of business entities engaged in international trade, weights/measures, incoterms (i.e., terms of trade), letters of credit, and ocean/air freight containers. The author has included extensive lists of resources for those requiring more detailed information as well as lists of service providers. The dictionary represents a single source for obtaining much basic information on international trade. It should prove useful to importers, exporters, insurers, bankers, shippers, students, economists, and government officials, as well as readers who have a general interest in world commerce.—**William C. Struning**

169. **International Encyclopedia of the Stock Market.** Michael Sheimo, Andreas Loizou, and Alison Aves, eds. Chicago, Fitzroy Dearborn, 1999. 2v. illus. $270.00/set. ISBN 1-884964-35-4.

This encyclopedia covers stock markets and subjects germane to them worldwide. Topics include institutions, financial instruments and terms, people, and historical events. It will be a welcome addition to business and general reference collections and relevant special libraries.

Source materials for the entries derive from information supplied by exchanges and regulatory bodies as well as secondary sources. Major banks, brokerages, and other players in markets are also covered, as are commodity and other related markets and international bodies like the International Monetary Fund (IMF). The main text covers 1,191 double-column pages. Alphabetic entries range from a paragraph to more than 15 pages. Estimating from the entry list, there seem to be about 1,800 headings. Stock markets are listed under the country where they are located. Under Canada, for example, there are extensive listings for four stock exchanges—Toronto, Alberta, Vancouver, and Montreal—including directory information, listing requirements, brokerages, and more. A few major stock exchanges have *see* references from their names, but most do not. Commodity and other non-stock exchanges are listed under their name and under the country heading. Entries range broadly, from people like George Soros or Nick Leeson through specific instruments on Italian exchanges, banking in the ancient world, chaos theory, and scandals to NAFTA and Dresdner Bank. The selection of topics is eclectic and interesting, including such topics as the Japanese organized crime organization, the Yakuza.

In addition to the alphabetic sequence, there are a number of access points besides the list of headings and contents. These include *see also* references in articles and an index. The index has some quirks. It does not include page references for main entries. For example, in the index under "Galbraith, John Kenneth," only other references to him, not the actual article, are cited. The first appendix is an essay on emerging markets. The second provides a world currencies listing (from Afghanistan through Zimbabwe) with the name of the main unit, its abbreviation, and the number of subunits (e.g., 1 pound sterling is 100 pence). An annotated bibliography concludes the work.

This encyclopedia belongs in all major business and economics reference collections. It would be a useful acquisition for appropriate special libraries, individuals in financial services, and smaller libraries where funds and needs warrant. [R: BL, June 99, p. 1881; Choice, Sept 99, p. 119; RUSQ, Fall 99, pp. 93-94]—**Nigel Tappin**

Directories

170. **Directory of Consumer Brands and Their Owners 1998: Asia Pacific.** Chicago, Euromonitor International; distr., Farmington Hills, Mich., Gale, 1998. 527p. index. $990.00. ISBN 0-86338-785-3.

This title is new to Euromonitor's collection of business directories and replaces in part the previous title, *International Directory of Consumer Brands and Their Owners* (see ARBA 98, entry 200). This regional directory focuses on brand names and the Asian or Pacific companies that own them. Euromonitor also produces a CD-ROM that includes all of the regional brand name directories. The Asia Pacific directory lists more than 15,000 brand names and more than 2,500 companies that control those brands. There is a definite emphasis on manufacturing and retailing consumer products throughout the Asian market. The directory itself is divided into two main sections. One section lists individual brands under broader product categories and subcategories. The second section serves as a directory listing for the companies and is arranged alphabetically by country. Information such as mailing address, Website location, e-mail, parent or holding companies, key personnel, and brand name portfolios are all given. Hong Kong is treated as a separate political entity from China for this edition only. Several Asian countries such as Laos and Sri Lanka are not covered. Some of the information may also be found in Gale's *Brands and Their Companies* (see entry 157) and *Companies and Their Brands* (see entry 158), but neither is as broad nor as deep as Euromonitor's publication. Also a plus for Euromonitor is the market share data they provide for the brand names. Because of its relatively high price tag, however, this resource is recommended only for major business collections in academic and public libraries. It is essential for special libraries involved in Pacific Rim or Asian business or marketing activities. [R: Choice, June 99, p. 1762]—**Stephen W. Green**

171. **Major Companies of Africa South of the Sahara 1999.** 4th ed. D. Butler and V. Bentley, eds. London, Graham & Whiteside; distr., Farmington Hills, Mich., Gale, 1999. 1075p. index. $530.00. ISBN 1-86099-141-6. ISSN 1365-4845.

This latest entry in the Major Companies series from Graham & Whiteside covers 44 countries in Africa except the primarily Arab countries on the Mediterranean and Atlantic, plus Mauritania and Sudan. The clear, easy-to-understand format is consistent with other titles in the series. A 1-page introduction is followed by an alphabetic-by-country list of approximately 6,000 businesses (about one-third more than the last edition) and indexes. The introduction does not detail inclusion criteria more specifically than "the most important." Data for companies may include name; address; phone; fax; telex; e-mail or Web address; chairman, major officers, and board members; principal activities, brands, trademarks, and trade names; parent companies and subsidiaries; percentage of ownership of the subsidiaries; major auditors and legal firms; brief financials for two years; principal shareholders; public, private, or state-owned status; year established; and number of employees.

Company names and official titles appear in their native language. Not every company has each of these data elements, but business data for companies in the Third World is very hard to find and there is no other print source that can compare. Companies from the Republic of South Africa comprise one-third of the company-by-country pages. The three indexes are alphabetic by company name, alphabetic by country and then by company name, and by business activity (i.e., by SIC). Although NAICS has been available for two years, it is not used. Particular strengths of the guide are the large number of individual names (estimated at 22,000), the extensive list of subsidiaries and branch offices, and the strong indexing. Users desiring economic or political coverage might find Europa's *Africa South of the Sahara* (26th ed.; see ARBA 98, entry 108) helpful. At $530, it is a pricey item that will limit the number of libraries that can afford it. Highly recommended for graduate school, public, corporate, and academic libraries with a sub-Saharan interest.—**Patrick J. Brunet**

172. **Major Companies of South West Asia 1999.** 3d ed. Sandra James and Y. McLelland, eds. London, Graham & Whiteside; distr., Farmington Hills, Mich., Gale, 1999. 841p. index. $530.00. ISBN 1-86099-140-8.

This directory is part of a series of publications covering businesses in all parts of the globe and is updated annually. Information is provided on more than 5,000 companies in Bangladesh, Bhutan, India, Iran, Nepal, Pakistan, Sri Lanka, and Turkey. Data listed include company name, street address, telephone and fax numbers, e-mail and Web addresses, names of key contacts from the board and senior management, principal activities of the company, branch offices, any subsidiaries, trademarks held, private versus public status, associated bankers, auditors and legal counsel, date the entity was established, the number of employees, and financial indicators for the 2 most recently available years (1996 and 1997). Firms are listed alphabetically for each country. Entries are selected on the basis of sales volume, premium income, or total assets.

The volume is indexed alphabetically by company name regardless of the country of origin, alphabetically by nation, and by Standard Industrial Classification. This reference is useful to identify potential customers, joint venture partners, and possible acquisitions.—**Adrienne Antink Bendel**

173. **World Cosmetics and Toiletries Directory 1999.** Chicago, Euromonitor International; distr., Farmington Hills, Mich., Gale, 1999. 589p. $990.00pa. ISBN 0-86338-808-6.

Marketing information is supplied on 6,000 leading cosmetic companies in nearly 60 countries along with statistical marketing information data in this volume. This book has an introduction with world and area rankings of the major companies according to sales. This is followed by major companies separated into country categories and contains such information as company name and full headquarters address, telephone and fax numbers, Website and e-mail addresses, year established, main activity of company, parent holding and ultimate holding company together with details of shareholding, major subsidiaries at home and abroad with details on any shareholding, key personnel, number of employees for latest year, details of main products and brands of the manufacturing and marketing companies, number of trading names, and size of outlets for retailers. Financial data, including financial year-end turnover and profit in the last three to four years, details on sales geographically and manufacturing capabilities, general notes covering company news and development, and company products and brands market shares are included where available. This is followed by a section on official organizations, again subdivided into countries, and another section including major trade and business associations followed by a section on major trade and business journals. There are several indexes that break down the countries of the world and give sales figures on various commodities, usually from 1992 to 1996. These are followed by a general index and information source sector index. The book should be useful for personnel trying to locate potential partners, identify and find competitors, generate sales leads, and access expert insights into new markets. It also provides useful information on finances, brand and company shares, and recent developments. This should be an essential book for people interested in the toiletries and cosmetics marketing industries.

—**Herbert W. Ockerman**

174. **World Drinks Marketing Directory 1999.** Chicago, Euromonitor International; distr., Farmington Hills, Mich., Gale, 1999. 859p. index. $990.00. ISBN 0-86338-807-8.

This latest Euromonitor directory expands on material found in the well-received *European Drinks Marketing Directory* (see ARBA 97, entry 240). The new title covers 4,000 companies, approximately twice as many as the earlier version, costs twice as much, but covers the drinks industry worldwide. Drinks are broadly defined as mineral and sparkling waters, fruit juices, soft and carbonated drinks, iced tea, sport drinks, beer, wines, and spirits. Most of the companies are from 60 First World countries, but tables providing various rankings list up to 150 countries. It is divided into four parts. The first and largest part lists companies by country with some or all of the following data: company name, full address, phone, fax, telex, year established, main activities, parent and subsidiary holdings, key personnel, number of employees, outlets/operations, brands (with notes on important brands), market share, and brief financials (i.e., turnover, profit, operating revenue). Also included are general notes that can run up to 500 words of text, though most notes are only a few sentences long.

The second section gives approximately 800 sources of information such as associations and statistical locations or sources. Of particular value is the inclusion of leading market research companies for non-U.S. or U.K. markets, though it is surprisingly weak for U.S. market research companies. Other minor sections include trade and business journals, Web addresses, and nongovernmental statistical sources. The 3rd section is 37 pages of tables on per capita value and sales volume by type of drink for 50 or so of the largest economies. The last section consists of company name and type of beverage indexes, but does not include a brand name index.

This work, like other Euromonitor directories, is notably strong in non-U.S. and U.K. companies, weak in financials, and pricey. To be fair, getting accurate financial data for non-European businesses is very difficult. Although it is published in England, virtually all the terminology is understandable. Readers may also want to look at the *Food and Beverage Market Place* (1997/98 ed.; see ARBA 99, entry 1339). It is an excellent complement to the more costly and more detailed worldview provided by the equally fine and unique *World Drinks Marketing Directory 1999*. Libraries serving the drinks industry would do well to have both.—**Patrick J. Brunet**

175. **World Food Marketing Directory 1999.** Chicago, Euromonitor International; distr., Farmington Hills, Mich., Gale, 1999. 2v. index. $990.00/set. ISBN 0-86338-809-4.

In this extensive directory, the publisher expands the scope of an earlier publication, *The European Food Marketing Directory* (1994 ed.; see ARBA 95, entry 279), from regional to worldwide coverage. The directory has 4 sections. Section 1 includes profiles of approximately 6,000 major food companies in some 60 countries. Most company entries contain company name and headquarters address; telephone and fax numbers; Website and e-mail addresses, if available; year established; main activity of the company; parent or holding company, if applicable; major subsidiaries; key personnel; number of employees; main products and brands; number, trading names, and size of outlets for the retailers; financial data; sales geography and manufacturing capacity, if applicable; general notes on company news and developments; and company product and brand market shares, if available. Volume 1 lists rankings of leading international food manufacturers and retailers in the front of the volume, and each country has a similar ranking prior to the country's listing. The last three sections of the directory contain supportive material on food marketing and can be located in volume 2. Section 2 lists more than 2,000 sources of information related to food marketing, including journals, online sources, and business information Websites. Section 3 provides the reader with useful statistics, such as total consumer expenditures as well as expenditures on specific food products, for the past 5 years. Section 4 enhances access to the publication with general and sector indexes. This directory on food marketing comprises a comprehensive source of information for pertinent business and large public and academic libraries that have a demonstrated a need in this area. [R: Choice, Sept 99, p. 124]

—O. Gene Norman

Handbooks and Yearbooks

176. **Exchange Arrangements and Exchange Restrictions 1998: Annual Report.** Washington, D.C., International Monetary Fund; distr., Lanham, Md., Bernan Associates, 1998. 1008p. $95.00pa. ISBN 1-55775-744-5. ISSN 0250-7366.

This specialized resource does just as its title states. It is a directory of 115 standardized data elements on how funds can be exchanged, held, transferred, or paid by individuals or institutions covering 183 nations. For example, it states whether a nonresident may hold a bank account in Namibia, whether Moldava has controls on gold trade, or how long an export payment collection in Slovenia can be held up before it must be registered as credit payment with the Bank of Slovenia. The 115 elements are divided into 8 categories: exchange arrangements, resident and nonresident accounts, arrangements for payment and receipts, import and import payments, export and export payments, payments and proceeds for invisible transactions and current transfers, capital transactions, and changes during the last year. The title under review is the 1998 edition, therefore most data are from 1997. The 1999 edition has already been published. Only a small portion of the data is available on the IMF Website at http://www.imf.org as of October 1999. The report has been published since 1950, and for a reference work of more than 1,000 pages the price is reasonable. Faculty can purchase the title at half price. This volume is suitable for large public, academic, and business libraries serving an international banking or business clientele or where import and export clients are served.—**Patrick J. Brunet**

177. **International Financial Statistics Yearbook 1998.** Washington, D.C., International Monetary Fund; distr., Lanham, Md., Bernan Associates, 1998. 961p. $65.00pa. ISBN 155775-749-6. ISSN 0250-7463.

This yearbook contains both worldwide and country-specific financial data for the years 1968 through 1997. The available data from 1948 through 1967 are maintained in the International Monetary Fund's Economic Information System. The yearbook is arranged in four sections, preceded by a detailed introduction that explains the arrangement and compilation of the tables. Section 1 consists of time-series charts on international reserves, interest rates, exchange rates, prices, unit values and commodity prices, and trade and national accounts. Section 2 presents world financial statistical tables on exchange rates, fund accounts, international reserves, measures of money, interest rates, real effective exchange rate indexes, prices, wages, production and employment, international trade, balance of payments, national accounts, and commodity prices. Section 3, the largest part of the volume, has individual country tables and section 4 contains country notes. The publisher indicates that additional country notes are contained in the monthly issues of *International Financial Statistics*.

This is an essential economics and business reference work for any library that serves a clientele interested in international affairs and world trade. Although the presentation of data is clear and readable, some novices may be put off by the seemingly arcane annotation system that the IMF uses throughout the volume. In addition, the country notes provide essential, useful information about the history of international liquidity, interest rates, government finance, monetary authorities, and banking institutions that gives context to the data presented.—**Robert H. Burger**

178. **International Marketing Data and Statistics 1999.** 23d ed. Chicago, Euromonitor International; distr., Farmington Hills, Mich., Gale, 1999. 659p. $370.00. ISBN 0-86338-822-1. ISSN 0308-2938.

This is the 23d annual edition of a work that, in many cases, shows 21-year trends to permit the analysis of socioeconomic factors over a considerable time span and gives more validity to the basis of forecasting. It covers the countries of the Americas, Asia, Africa, and Oceanic. Most of the data are expressed in spreadsheet fashion and, in some sections, extrapolated tables have been included as well as illustrated graphs. Included is information from more than 160 countries that is broken down into marketing information sources, marketing geography, demographic trends and forecasts, economic indicators, banking and finance, external trade, labor force indicators, industrial resources and output, energy resources and output, defense, environmental data, consumer expenditure patterns, retailing and retail distribution, advertising and media patterns, consumer market sciences, consumer prices and costs, housing and household facilities, health and living standards, literacy and education, agricultural resources, communications, automobiles, transportation, travel and tourism, cultural indicators, incomes and earnings, and an index.

In the geography section the book lists capital city along with population, total population, urban population, land area, languages, religion, currency, head of state, head of government, ruling party, and major urban areas along with population, constitutional foundations, ruling government politics, microeconomic performance, and general economic outlook. The oversized book is on average paper with printing large enough to be useful when one is only looking at one area. This book should be in all libraries that are interested in international marketing. It is an excellent source of statistics.—**Herbert W. Ockerman**

179. **International Yearbook of Industrial Statistics 1998.** By the United Nations Industrial Development Organization. Northhampton, Mass., Edward Elgar, 1998. 722p. $195.00. ISBN 1-85898-777-6.

This is the fourth issue of this annual publication from the United Nations Industrial Development Organization (UNIDO). Its predecessors were the *Handbook of Industrial Statistics* (a biennial published by UNIDO until 1992 [see ARBA 92, entry 196]) and the UN's *Industrial Statistical Yearbook* (see ARBA 94, entry 216), volume 1, discontinued after its 1991 edition, published in 1993. Its purpose is to provide statistical indicators to facilitate international comparisons relating to the manufacturing sector. The first part deals with the manufacturing sector as a whole and with its branches. It contains such items as distribution of world manufacturing value added (MVA), MVA selected branches, growth of world MVA, leading producers in selected branches, and selected characteristics of branches (value added per employee, wages per employee and percent of output of cost of unit materials and utilities, cost of labor and operating surplus). The years vary with each table, but most are the mid-1990s. Some tables make comparisons back to 1980, though not annually. Countries and country groups included also vary by table. The second part consists of country tables where the data go to the four-digit level of the ISIC code. Data on the number of establishments and employees, wages and salaries paid, output, value added, gross fixed capital formation, and an index of industrial production are given. As with UN statistical publications, careful notes, explanations, definitions, and sources are provided. This is a basic sourcebook for worldwide manufacturing data.—**J. E. Weaver**

180. **Trade and Development Report, 1998.** New York, United Nations, 1998. 229p. $45.00pa. ISBN 92-1-112427-1. ISSN 0255-4607. S/N E.98.II.D.6.

The series from the United Nations Conference on Trade and Development (UNCTAD), of which this is the 1998 edition, provides an annual overview of the state of the international economy, with emphasis on prospects for developing countries. It and the series belong in larger business and government document collections.

This 1998 report has a foreword from UN Secretary General Kofi Annan. This indicates that, in response to a 1997 General Assembly resolution, it emphasizes research on ways to avoid and correct international financial crises. This was in consequence of concern at the crises in "emerging markets" starting in 1997 and 1998. It was issued in September 1998. This work has two sections, each with multiple chapters. The first provides an overview of global economic trends, the implications of the Asian crisis, background on post–Bretton Woods financial crises, and analysis on prevention and management of such events. The second presents background and analysis of the African economy and its development prospects. The report combines text with 57 statistical tables and 28 charts. No index is provided. There are detailed contents and listings of statistical tables and charts.

The analysis of financial crises and methods of preventing them will make this edition of value to those interested in international financial flows and their effects and regulation. As this has been a high–interest topic of late, this aspect will enhance the attractiveness of the issue. The series and this edition add a valuable overview, with emphasis on the development of poor countries, emerging markets, and the former communist countries, to any collection. It belongs in larger research, academic, and general collections, as well as appropriate special ones where funding permits.—**Nigel Tappin**

181. **The Washington Almanac of International Trade and Business, 1998.** Gary P. Osifchin and William O. Scouton, eds. Washington, D.C., Almanac; distr., Lanham, Md., Bernan Associates, 1998. 840p. illus. $225.00pa. ISBN 1-886222-10-X.

The almanac, primarily a directory of information on international trade and foreign policy, is sponsored by the Greater Washington Board of Trade, and includes a brief introductory section describing that organization and extolling the virtues of the Washington, D.C., area as a place to do business. This is the 4th edition of a work originally published in 1994 as *The International Washington Almanac* (see ARBA 95, entry 760). It was issued for the first time under the current title in 1995 (see ARBA 97, entry 230).

It consists of 3 main parts: Foreign Diplomatic Corps in the United States, The U.S. Government: Who Does What?, and Other Entities Dealing with Foreign Trade. In addition there is an index and a five-page section on advertisements. The 1st part is divided into 4 sections: a directory of foreign ambassadors and staff arranged in alphabetic order by country, a directory of commercial contacts at foreign embassies in Washington, a list of foreign consular offices in the U.S., and a list of local holidays (i.e., the national holidays of other countries) alphabetically by country with a two-page world timetable, listing the time in each country when it is noon in Washington, D.C.

Part 2 is divided into 3 sections. The 1st section on general export information includes 4 nondirectory subsections: export services, export regulations, customs benefits and tax incentives, U.S. export and the economy, and also an export glossary. The 2d section covers the federal legislature, and it is essentially a series of directories of U.S. congressional contacts. The 3d section is a series of directories for the Executive Branch.

Part 3 has 13 sections, including directories of multinational banks, the International Monetary Fund, international interest groups, foreign agents, Washington's international press, world trade centers, international business learning opportunities in the Greater Washington area, and chambers of commerce.

In the foreword the editors say, "Somewhere in this book every user can find an idea, a name, a telephone or fax number that will be useful." This is undoubtedly true; the almanac contains an enormous amount of information, but it is presented in the complex organization described above. There is an index, but it lists only organizations, countries, and general topics. The index does not list states, cities, products, or people. This means it is relatively easy to find information for general topics. However, it requires intimate familiarity with the complex arrangement of the sections, parts, and subsections to find information related to a particular product or to find agencies, organizations, and contacts relevant to international business interests in any specialized area of complex situation.

This work consolidates information found in a wide variety of other sources. However, nothing contains all the information gathered here. The almanac should provide practically all the information needed by anyone interested in international business. An electronic version would be superb, but even in its current less-than-user-friendly print version, it is recommended to any library with an interest in international business.—**Richard H. Swain**

182. **World Development Indicators, 1998.** Washington, D.C., World Bank; distr., Lanham, Md., Bernan Associates, 1998. 389p. index. $60.00pa. ISBN 0-8213-4124-3.

This is the 2d edition of the annual *World Development Indicators*. Most of the tables cover 148 countries with populations of more than 1 million. Generally, the indicators are given for a recent year (often 1996) and an earlier year. Time series of primary data can be found on the *World Development Indicators* CD-ROM, going back to 1960 when possible. The information is divided into 6 sections, each with an introductory essay of less than 10 pages that focuses on a few issues relevant to that section. The 1st section, "World View," reports on progress toward international development goals. A section follows on people, which includes population and labor force, income, education, and health data. The 3d section on environment has data primarily on water and air pollution, energy, land use, agriculture, and urbanization. "Economy," the 4th section, includes data on, but not limited to, the structure of output, exports, imports, and demand; government finance; monetary indicators and prices; and external debt. Next comes a section on states and markets. It has information on credit, the stock market, portfolio regulation and risk, tax policies, defense expenditures, state-owned enterprises, transport, and information among others. The final section, "Global Links," emphasizes merchandise trade, tariff barriers, global financial flows, and aid. The data come from a variety of sources. Every table has detailed information about the data—its source, collection, and definition of terms. This volume is a comprehensive source of data on most of the countries in the world. It is convenient and a valuable first (or only) resource to the desired information on a topic or country. It is likely to become a basic and much-used source.—**J. E. Weaver**

183. **World Economic Factbook 1998/99.** 6th ed. Chicago, Euromonitor International; distr., Farmington Hills, Mich., Gale, 1998. 457p. $420.00. ISBN 0-86338-817-5.

This source provides the user with economic and political data on 207 countries in a well-organized, easy-to-use format. After an introduction explaining the various features and data elements, the *Factbook* proceeds to maps of the major regions of the world followed by country rankings in 15 demographic and economic areas. These include population, birth rate, household size, GDP, GDP growth, inflation, imports and exports, and tourism receipts.

The main body of the reference is devoted to a country-by-country analysis and statistical presentation. Each country occupies two facing pages. The 1st page is a narrative section of 13 paragraphs, including political structure, political risk, last election, international disputes, economy, main industries, and energy. The second page is a statistical portrait of the country. This includes most of the same measures found in the country rankings located at the beginning of the volume with the added benefit of a three-year retrospective. To those are added more GDP figures such as consumption, death rate, and tourist spending. A demographic table follows with such characteristics as urban population, age breakdown, life expectancy, and adult literacy. The analysis ends with a table of export and import trading partners.

Because of the differing state of statistical data gathering in individual countries, not every country has a complete set of data. Many of the same statistics may be found in other sources, such as *Europa World Year Book* (39th ed.; see ARBA 99, entry 66), the CIA's *World Factbook* (1996–1997 ed.; see ARBA 97, entry 80), and Euromonitor's own duo, *International Marketing Data and Statistics* (1994 ed.; see ARBA 95, entry 252) and *European Marketing Data and Statistics* (33d ed.; see ARBA 99, entry 254). The distinguishing features of the *World Economic Factbook* are that it is easier to find the information—it is all in one place and it includes narratives on such things as political risk that are hard to find elsewhere. Libraries that cannot afford many of Euromonitor's other more expensive sources will find this one well worth acquiring. It is recommended for undergraduate and more advanced collections.—**Gerald L. Gill**

184. **World Investment Report 1999: Foreign Direct Investment and the Challenge of Development.** New York, United Nations, 1999. 541p. $45.00pa. ISBN 92-1-112440-9. S/N E.99.II.D.3.

This series from the United Nations Conference on Trade and Development (UNCTAD) provides an annual overview of foreign direct investment emphasizing the relationship between transnational corporations (TNCs) and economic development. The series will interest selectors for larger business or government document collections.

This 1999 report has a foreword from UN Secretary General Kofi Annan dated July 1999. He indicates this issue focuses on investment's impact on key aspects of development, including availability of capital, employment prospects, technical and skill levels, competitiveness, and environmental protection. It has 2 sections, each with multiple chapters. The 1st provides an overview of global and regional trends in investment; listings and statistics on the largest TNCs from the developed and developing countries and from the Central European transition economies; discussions of mergers, acquisitions, and strategic partnership trends; and policy changes, both international and national. The 2d presents background and analysis on the roles of TNCs in economic and social development processes and ways to maximize positive, and minimize the negative, impacts on host societies. Topics include discussions of environmental, technological, skills, competitiveness, and employment issues. The report combines extensive text with approximately 75 topical boxes of text, 76 figures, and 63 statistical tables. No index is provided, but there are detailed contents with lists of boxes, figures, and tables.

For suitable collections, this series and volume add valuable overviews of often ambiguous relationships between economic development, foreign investment, and TNCs in various regions of the world. This work belongs in larger economics research, academic, and general collections, as well as appropriate special ones, funding permitting.—**Nigel Tappin**

185. **World Retail Data and Statistics 1999.** Chicago, Euromonitor International; distr., Farmington Hills, Mich., Gale, 1999. 277p. $590.00pa. ISBN 0-86338-830-2.

This is a new handbook of statistical information on retail trade worldwide for 1992 to 1997. There is a companion volume, *Retail Trade International* (1998 ed.; see ARBA 99, entry 230). In the first two sections summary data on socioeconomic parameters and on world retailing trends are given. Data are not included for all 50 countries in all of the tables. The third section has specific country information on such categories as population, average size of household, retail sales, number of retail outlets, retail sales by form of organization and type of outlet, retail prices, number of grocery retailers and their turnover number, and number of EPOS and EFTPOS installations (EPOS is electronic point of sales systems, EFTPOS is electronic funds transfer at point of sales). The last section has world retail rankings. A variety of types of stores have been included, such as chain store, discount superstore, home shopping, and cooperatives. The data come from government and nongovernment sources. Currency values are given in U.S. dollars. While the publisher has tried to check accuracy and standardize the date, care is urged when using the information. Cross-country comparisons can be difficult. For those interested in retailing, this could be a convenient source of data. It could be a main source or supplement what is known from other sources. [R: Choice, Sept 99, p. 124]—**J. E. Weaver**

Asia

186.   De Mente, Boyé Lafayette. **NTC's Dictionary of Korea's Business and Cultural Code Words.** Lincolnwood, Ill., National Textbook, 1998. 462p. (NTC's Dictionaries of Cultural Code Words). $22.95. ISBN 0-8442-8362-2.

De Mente, who compiled Chinese and Japanese code words, also wrote Korean code words. With this book, De Mente completes dictionaries of code words for three Far East countries. China, Japan, and Korea share many cultural characteristics because of neighboring geographic locations and long historical relations. Despite the close cultural contact, Korean people retained a unique character and personality that is different from Chinese and Japanese cultures. This book is designed to help foreigners understand the uniqueness of Korean culture and national characteristics. De Mente's insights make this book valuable.

In this book, De Mente explores the historical and cultural background of 231 most important "code words" of Korean language. Each entry is numbered and has a Korean character with its pronunciation. The meaning of each entry is given in the form of explanatory phrases in English. The length of definition of each word ranges from one to two pages, while more important words that convey the uniqueness of Korea take up to 15 pages. In this way, De Mente provides readers with sharper understanding of the customs of Korean people.

To make this book more valuable, there are a few things that could be improved. It would be very useful if the book included a subject guide index in English. The book has a subject guide that is indexed to the numbers of words, but it does not help foreigners to find specific words. The publisher may also want to print an errata slip to fix typos. There are typos in both Korean characters (numbers 14, 21, 36, 41, 69, 100, 161, 164, and 179) and Romanized words (107, 143, 147, 159 and 164). The Romanization system is also inconsistent: some words are Romanized according to the McCune-Reischauer Romanization System, while some are not.—**Sung Ok Kim**

Canada

187.   **Scott's Directories 1999: Greater Toronto Business Directory, Volume 1.** 6th ed. Don Mills, Ont., Southam Information Products, 1999. 1v. (various paging). index. $199.00. ISBN 1-55257-029-0.

This annually revised tool meets the demand for sales leads—it is a directory to manufacturing, wholesale, distribution, medical, government, and educational markets in the Greater Toronto area. The first volume covers the base city of Toronto and the second volume covers the dozen or so other municipalities that encircle Toronto. Between them, both volumes have references to 31,800 businesses. Half of the companies have undergone some kind of change since the previous edition in 1998.

The first section is an alphabetic listing with street addresses and a reference to the main entry. The second section is a geographic listing. This is the main section where (under street) users can find the full name of the company, phone and fax numbers (but no e-mail), names of the major executives, products produced and Standard Industrial Classification code numbers, number of employees, sales generated, size of the headquarters, and year established. The last section is an SIC listing, in numerical order, with page references to the main entry. Scott's has a whole line of directories as well as CD-ROM products; it is a reliable company with a century or more of service providing leads. A useful acquisition if you need this type of data.—**Dean Tudor**

Europe

188. **European Marketing Data and Statistics 1999.** 34th ed. Chicago, Euromonitor International; distr., Farmington Hills, Mich., Gale, 1999. 483p. maps. index. $370.00. ISBN 0-86338-821-3. ISSN 0071-2930.

This is the latest annual edition of a statistical yearbook on business and marketing information for 49 countries in Western and Eastern Europe. There are four possible data periods: a 21-year trend table, 1977 to 1997 with data for some years not included; a shorter trend period; the latest year available differing by country through often 1997; and a single year. The currency denominated data are either in U.S. dollars or the national currency. The subject coverage, with a varying amount of information and data in each section, includes topics such as marketing, geography, demography trends and forecasts, economic indicators, banking and finance, external trade by destination and commodity, and labor force indicators. Much of this information is available elsewhere. This book is aiming to provide easier access to this marketing data. It also provides relevant information such as name, street address, telephone and fax numbers, e-mail address, and so on for relevant official organizations (international, pan regional, and national), national trade development bodies, and major business information libraries in the area. Although coverage is not complete in all areas, especially for countries outside of the European Union and the European Free Trade Area, this is a good source of data for the region. Each table includes its source and has endnotes where appropriate.—**J. E. Weaver**

189. Yuill, Douglas, John Bachtler, and Fiona Wishlade. **European Regional Incentives, 1999.** 18th ed. New Providence, N.J., Bowker-Saur/Reed Reference Publishing, 1999. 480p. maps. $130.00pa. ISBN 1-85739-272-8.

This annual review and analysis of regional aid policies in the EU15 (and Norway) is an easy-to-use guide to all the grants and other aid available to industry within the designated "problem regions" of the European Union. Supported by funding from 10 European governments, this edition has been expanded and enhanced to provide examination of regional disparities and give a full discussion of Agenda 2000 and the March 1998 Guidelines on National Regional Aid as well as detailed comparative analysis of regional incentive spending over the past 10 years. Also included is an in-depth study of the impact of competition policy on national regional aid policies as well as an overview of the operation of the structural funds, focusing on the current position. This definitive guide on European regional aid is invaluable to understanding European funding. Its analysis includes practical information on application procedures as well as detailed statistics, charts, and maps. Used by regional policy makers and development organizations, companies considering investing in these European countries will want to consult this reference. This work is recommended for large international business collections.—**Susan C. Awe**

Latin America and the Caribbean

190. **Consumer Latin America 1999.** 6th ed. Chicago, Euromonitor International; distr., Farmington Hills, Mich., Gale, 1999. 395p. $900.00pa. ISBN 0-86338-828-0.

The content of this series continues to improve with each edition, due in part to improved data collecting in Argentina, Brazil, Chile, Colombia, Mexico, and Venezuela. The user will find recent facts and figures useful in conducting business in the region as a whole and in depth for each of the above countries. The book includes nine sections and a complete listing of the tables that can serve as a table of contents. Section 1 provides a written commentary on those factors that impact the economy in Latin America; the other sections only provide statistical tables. Sections 2 and 3 provide overall compilations based on the information from the individual countries. In section 2, regional marketing parameters are provided and appropriate international sources are included to provide regional comparisons. In section 3, individual country consumer market material has been combined to provide a comparative overview. The remaining sections profile each of the countries separately.

Information tabulated for the individual countries varies but each table provides information regarding the source for these figures. The general categories include demographics, economic indicators, standard of living, household characteristics, retail distribution, consumer expenditures, service industries, and consumer markets. General economic figures reflect the period from 1992 to 1998 and consumer market data are from 1992 to 1997. The material in this book is now available on a CD-ROM entitled *World Consumer Markets* (Gale, 1998). Since it is difficult to find this information, this book would be a great value for any library with international business interests in Latin America.—**Judith J. Field**

191. **Economic Survey of Latin America and the Caribbean 1997-1998.** 50th ed. By the Economic Commission for Latin America and the Caribbean. New York, United Nations, 1998. 368p. $75.00pa. (with disks). ISBN 92-1-121230-8. ISSN 0257-2184. S/N E.98.II.G.2.

This 50th edition (see ARBA 98, entry 210) provides an overview of the economy in 1997 and the first half of 1998, examines the economic performance of the region in 1997, analyzes some aspects of the economic situation during the first half of 1998, reports on 20 countries of Latin America and on the situation in the countries of the English-speaking Caribbean, and a final section reviews the 50 years of the *Economic Survey of Latin American and the Caribbean*. With the book is a set of two diskettes, which provide ready access to data for recent years and permits the preparation of spreadsheets covering a longer time period.

The regional economic survey reviews macroeconomic policy; economic performance; policy lessons from the Asian crisis; and structural reforms, including general trends, banking sector, capital markets, labor reforms, and trade reforms. Economic activity, inflation, investment and saving, employment and wages, and the external sector of the region are reviewed as well. Each country survey reviews general economic trends, economic policy, the main variables of economic activity, prices, wages and employment, and the external sector.

The study of the *Economic Survey* is an important and essential part of the text for academic libraries whose curriculums include Latin American studies. It is essential to a broad understanding of the regional and global economies.—**Gerald D. Moran**

LABOR

Career Guides

192. **Career Exploration on the Internet: A Student's Guide to More Than 300 Web Sites!** Elizabeth H. Oakes, ed. Chicago, Ferguson, 1998. 208p. index. $15.95pa. ISBN 0-89434-240-1.

The Internet is transforming many facets of life. Its impact on the job search is dramatic for those in business, technical, and professional fields. This volume is a comprehensive narrative directory opening abundant information resources for anyone with access to the World Wide Web. Throughout the book, sites are listed and given helpful annotations that include scope, approach, and deficiencies where they exist.

Aimed primarily at the student or newly graduated job-seeker, these resources are most helpful for the job search, with chapters on how to find out about companies, nonprofit and public organizations, and international careers. Volunteer, internship, and summer job information and listings are covered also. Employment agencies, professional recruiting firms, and professional associations, as well as Websites of individual companies, are listed.

The opening chapters focus on sites for career exploration—sources of information on various fields and occupations. Some sites, frequently academic, offer self-assessment tools as well as occupational information. Clearinghouse sites are offered as "headquarters" for searching for career information. An individual's decision-making process may be made more difficult by such an abundance of information.

This guide assumes the reader is computer-proficient, particularly with the Internet. The style is lively and fast-paced, muck like where the listings lead. The only problem is that this means of job searching takes time and effort and diligence is clearly provided. This volume and others like it are essential tools for libraries and career centers. Anything in this venue will be outdated the minute after it is written, much less published, but the key resources and links will most likely linger even after newer and better sites come online. Thus, it provides an excellent base. [R: BR, Nov/Dec 98, p. 66]—**Barbara Conroy**

193. **Career Opportunities in Television, Cable, Video, and Multimedia.** 4th ed. New York, Checkmark Books/Facts on File, 1999. 274p. illus. index. $35.00; $18.95pa. ISBN 0-8160-3940-2; 0-8160-3941-0pa.

This book offers coverage of a wide variety of career opportunities in the popular and expanding fields of broadcasting (radio aside), video technologies, and multimedia production of entertainment and information resources. It is an update of the 3d edition published nine years ago under the title *Career Opportunities in Television, Cable, and Video*. Nine years is a long time in these fields, and an update is welcome. The industry has expanded, and job responsibilities and titles reflect this. The whole new area of multimedia, including its Web aspects, has been added.

The introductory overview that precedes each section has been significantly updated to reflect changes in the field, new terminology, and to bring the numerous and varied statistics up-to-date.

Well organized and well laid out with better typography than the 3d edition, the material is basically divided into a television broadcasting and a cable, video, and media section. Within each of these two areas, the book is arranged by job function within a few broad areas of expertise. Each includes a job description, salary range, the education and skills required or expected, and information on unions. Within each of the two areas the book offers broad coverage of job opportunities. Nontechnical jobs as they relate to the electronic media industry are covered.

The television section is divided up by function within the areas of management, programming, production, engineering, performance, advertising, and news reporting. The functions are listed alphabetically within each area and are also included in the subject index at the back. In the 2d section, the functions or areas of competency are organized more under subject areas in which cable, video, and multimedia are used. Employment in private industry, government, the health field, the education field, commercial technical products, training, and producing (e.g., managing, engineering, programming, writing) are specified, and specific areas of competency are then arranged under each.

This guide is highly recommended for both public and academic libraries. Readers should find it comprehensive, readable, and a good place to start in seeking vocational information in electronic media production.—**Florence W. Jones**

194. **Certification and Accreditation Programs Directory: A Descriptive Guide to National Voluntary Certification and Accreditation Programs for Professionals and Institutions.** 2d ed. Michael A. Pare, ed. Farmington Hills, Mich., Gale, 1999. 626p. index. $99.00pa. ISBN 0-7876-2843-3. ISSN 1084-2128.

Certifications, required for many professions and occupations, are designed to regulate individuals. Requirements and procedures that certify individuals are developed by professional, trade and specialty fields, and sometimes the law. These standards become the basis for accrediting organizations that are then established and charged with the task of ensuring the practitioner's competency, training, and credibility. This process has expanded greatly in recent years to embrace new fields, technologies, and practices that require regulation or standardization.

This volume brings together 1,700 current and voluntary certification programs listed in occupational chapters similar to the *Occupational Outlook Handbook* (1996-97 ed.; see ARBA 98, entry 238). Each program details the title awarded, requirements, exam information, fees, number of individuals certified, and accreditation information, along with contact information for the certification granting organization.

Some 250 accrediting organizations at the national, regional, or state level are listed. These organizations must be for individuals and must be current, voluntary, and available throughout the U.S. No state licensing agencies are included. Of the many continuing education programs available, only medical programs are included. Information for each listing includes full contact information (including Website), membership, application procedures and accreditation requirements, renewal, state requirements (i.e., licensure), and fees.

This volume can be of value to consumers, individuals seeking professional advancement or development, and parent and students identifying educational institutions. Businesses can review the benefits of certification for the organization and its employees. Access is relatively direct, with one index profiling certifying bodies with a list of the positions certified, another giving acronyms, and a third listing positions and accrediting organizations.—**Barbara Conroy**

195. **The Complete Guide to Environmental Careers in the 21st Century: The Environmental Careers Organization.** Kevin Doyle, ed. Washington, D.C., Island Press, 1999. 447p. illus. index. $39.95; $17.95pa. ISBN 1-55963-585-1; 1-55963-586-Xpa.

The Complete Guide to Environmental Careers in the 21st Century is a thoroughly updated, revised, and re-titled 3d edition of the *Complete Guide to Environmental Careers* (1993). This is an outstanding resource that is produced by the Environmental Careers Organization (ECO), an important nonprofit group dedicated to protecting and enhancing the environment through development of professionals, promotion of careers, and inspirational sharing. The book supports these goals very well. There is a 3-chapter overview of the environmental job field that is complete with statistics, major drivers behind trends, and useful advice. The remainder of the book provides detailed information in each chapter on where the jobs are, what is growing and what is not, earnings, education requirements, excellent resources in print and on the Web, case studies of active professionals, and profiles of people making a difference.

The "at-a-glance" section at the beginning of each detailed chapter is a valuable resource on its own. For example, in the chapter devoted to the planning segment of environmental professionals, the number of planners nationwide is given, along with the percentage of growth per year and predictions about future growth; a public, private, and nonprofit sectors breakdown; a list of 18 key job titles; a list of influential organizations; and a salary overview. Useful as an encyclopedia, dictionary, and bibliography, this is a resource highly recommended for all types of libraries.—**Barbara Delzell**

196. Cubbage, Sue, and Marcia Williams. **National Job Hotline Directory: The Job-Finder's Hot List.** River Forest, Ill., Planning/Communications, 1999. 376p. illus. $16.95pa. ISBN 1-884587-12-7.

Intended for job hunters and based on the authors' queries, this directory identifies 6,500 job hotlines operated by employers in the United States and Canada. An introduction discusses the search process, use of the telephone as part of a strategy, and its relationship to Internet and more traditional employment resources (e.g., newspapers).

Arranged alphabetically by state, chapters provide key state contacts and information. They are divided into as many as 10 topical categories, with alphabetic entries consisting of name (e.g., companies, agencies), city, and telephone number. Additional sections offer national and toll-free number hotlines, Canadian listings, free World Wide Web updates (http://www.jobfindersonline.com), and discount coupons. The separate resource lists refer job seekers only to other publications available from the publisher rather than important works available elsewhere.

This volume contains a lot of valuable information and deserves the attention of the serious job seeker. It has the makings of an excellent reference tool; however, several flaws should be noted. The lack of descriptive abstracts identifying types of jobs used by an employer and more specific topical divisions increases both time and monetary costs. An alphabetic list of all companies and agencies would improve access and assist those who have identified an employer but not a location. These limitations make it less useful for basic reference collections. [R: LJ, 15 Mar 99, pp. 66-68]—**Sandra E. Belanger**

197. Farr, J. Michael. **America's Top Jobs for College Graduates: Detailed Information on 112 Major Jobs Requiring Four-Year and Higher Degrees.** 3d ed. Indianapolis, Ind., JIST Works, 1999. 532p. index. $16.95pa. ISBN 1-56370-493-5.

This handy reference work is filled with information that anyone thinking of going to college or currently attending college will want to be familiar with. It lists and describes the top jobs for graduates with professional degrees, master's degrees, and bachelor's degrees, as well as those jobs that are often held by college graduates but do not necessarily require a degree.

The 1st section simply lists the top jobs in several different categories, including jobs with the fastest growth, those with the highest pay, and those with the largest number of openings. Section 2 lists the 112 top jobs for college graduates, describing working conditions, skills required, growth projections, training and education required, and typical salary, as well as other facts associated with each career choice. This is the largest part of the work and contains a great deal of information that readers will need. The 3d section provides advice from experts on writing résumés, getting interviews, and defining one's perfect job. The final 2 sections provide articles on the future of the job market and the outlook for college graduates up to the year 2006. The book concludes with a useful bibliography containing hundreds of career-related books, software, and Websites.

This book will be a valuable resource in any high school or university library. The information is both up-to-date and forward projecting, which adds to the books reference value. [R: Choice, Oct 99, pp. 312-314]—**Shannon M. Graff**

198. Farr, J. Michael. **America's Top Medical, Education, and Human Services Jobs: Detailed Information on 73 Major Jobs with Excellent Pay and Advancement Opportunities.** 4th ed. Indianapolis, Ind., JIST Works, 1999. 341p. $16.95pa. ISBN 1-56370-492-7.

This informal, pragmatic, and lively presentation focuses on 73 occupations and trends in rapidly growing fields. The lively introduction, "top job" lists, and sections on employment trends, earnings, and growth for the major occupations and industries offer a handy overview. An advantage to this work is the organization, the bibliography (with its limitations), and the brief overview of job searching, with tips on networking and how to track contacts.

Aside from passing mention in the introduction, no acknowledgment is offered to reveal the specific Department of Labor published sources that have been incorporated in this volume. Occupational descriptions and tables are wholly included from the *Occupational Outlook Handbook* (1996-97 ed.; see ARBA 98, entry 238) and other series, with no change or interpretation. However, no citation is offered to assist the individual who wishes to pursue a search.

The section on career planning and job search—essentially a short course on the job search—outlines essentials in a breezy fashion. This section serves as a reminder for the savvy and a hint for the naïve. Here, indeed, along with the brief introduction is the author's sole original contribution.

The 27-page selected bibliography includes key published and Internet resources grouped in useful categories to pinpoint quickly subjects like government jobs, interviewing, international jobs, and displaced workers. Unfortunately, citations are incomplete, omitting publishers other than JIST Works. This poses a barrier to easy and independent access by the reader and seems self-serving. Although useful for the individual, most libraries and career counselors would have the original sources incorporated in this volume.—**Barbara Conroy**

199. Field, Shelly. **Career Opportunities in the Sports Industry.** 2d ed. New York, Checkmark Books/Facts on File, 1999. 280p. index. $18.95. ISBN 0-8160-3794-9.

Essential information on career opportunities in most aspects of sports is detailed for professional athletes, sports teams, and for individual sports such as boxing, wrestling, and horse racing. Positions in sports business and administration, coaching and education, officiating, sports journalism, recreation and fitness, sports medicine, and wholesaling and retailing are also described. Even though comprehensive, there are gaps, such as the position of team psychologist and the sport of auto racing.

Entries give a brief overview of the position and then expand that brief information into a longer narrative of two to three pages. Each entry describes the nature of the position together with its salary range and the employment and advancement prospects that can be anticipated. Strategic tips for entering the position are given. Entries also detail the characteristics, experience, and training required. Information about relevant unions and associations is included.

Helpful appendixes supplement the directory. One lists academic degree programs for sports administration and physical education. Sponsors of relevant workshops, seminars, and symposiums are cited in another. Leagues, associations, and unions offer contact points for information and a diligent job search. Listings of promoters and cable/network television sports departments will be helpful for the more specialized seeker.

This update of the 1991 edition evidences the rise in sports interest and participation. The field is, in many ways, informal and the diversity of titles and positions pronounced. This volume presents a useful framework for viewing scope and possibility. The approach is somewhat promotional, blending pragmatic information with enthusiasm for the field. The information has been gathered from interviews, questionnaires, and publications, so it is largely informal.—**Barbara Conroy**

200. Field, Shelly. **Career Opportunities in Theater and the Performing Arts.** 2d ed. New York, Checkmark Books/Facts on File, 1999. 257p. index. $35.00; $18.95pa. ISBN 0-8160-3798-1; 0-8160-3799-Xpa.

Although this book was written for "the many thousands of people who aspire to work in theater and other performing arts," it is very basic and would probably not be useful beyond the high school level. It is divided into nine sections according to type of career, such as performing artist or educator. Within each section are descriptions of individual careers (e.g., actor, playwright), which include duties, salary, employment prospects, prerequisites/preparation, advancement, unions/associations, and tips for entry into the career. Position descriptions are generally adequate, but information on education, skills, training, and experience is often vague and frequently states the obvious (e.g., dancers "need to be flexible, agile, and coordinated").

There are several appendixes of varying usefulness. Useful are lists of educational opportunities in the performing arts and of theater and music companies that employ performing arts professionals. Less useful are a list of New York City–area theaters, a list of performing arts periodicals (not annotated), and a rather randomly selected bibliography. Although entries in the list give addresses and telephone numbers, it would have been helpful for the compiler to have included Website addresses, as many organizations and companies listed have excellent Websites that include e-mail addresses as well as information about auditions, educational programs, and job opportunities. In spite of its several flaws, this book covers an unusually wide range of careers, from secretarial to management, and may be appropriate for larger high school and public libraries or where there is particular interest in the performing arts.

—**Gari-Anne Patzwald**

201. **Job Hunter's Sourcebook: Where to Find Employment Leads and Other Job Search Resources.** 4th ed. Kathleen E. Maki Potts, ed. Farmington Hills, Mich., Gale, 1999. 1079p. index. $90.00. ISBN 0-7876-2645-7. ISSN 1053-1874.

This valuable, comprehensive presentation identifies employment leads and key resources for job-seekers, students, and career counselors. The resources address all levels of employment (executive, technical, professional, and support), enabling individuals to pinpoint essential sources for 193 broadly representative jobs. Organized by occupation, entries include publications, organizations, audiovisual and electronic resources, and other tools to use in designing an effective job-search strategy. These resources provide full citations for print sources, directories, job banks, clearinghouses, employment agencies, and executive search firms and organizations that lead to employment opportunities. Handbooks relevant to a particular occupational field are offered as guides to the job-hunting process particular to those fields. An extensive index offers broad access.

In addition, a 2d section (about 15 percent of the volume) gives citations and brief, informative descriptions of those resources focused on special job-hunting considerations for specific situations. For example, sections cover interviewing skills; government employment; international opportunities; résumés; relocation; and address special populations, such as the disabled, ex-offenders, independent contractors, and minorities.

All aspects of this guide have tapped useful, current, and reliable resources for the ever-challenging and competitive job search. Some of these will be available in local libraries and guidance centers; some might be feasible to purchase. As with any such compilation, it will be outdated quickly with more recent Internet and print resources, but it provides an excellent starting point for anyone exploring employment possibilities, motivating and guiding the pursuit of work.—**Barbara Conroy**

Dictionaries and Encyclopedias

202. Murray, R. Emmett. **Lexicon of Labor: More Than 500 Key Terms, Biographical Sketches, and Historical Insights Concerning Labor in America.** New York, New Press, 1998. 207p. $13.95pa. ISBN 1-56584-456-4.

The *Lexicon of Labor* is basically a short, 1-volume encyclopedia of the American labor movement. It has more than 500 entries and provides concise definitions of commonly used labor terms, sketches of important labor figures, descriptions of labor organizations, and information about key events in labor history. Although not comprehensive, this volume's listings are representative and, taken together, they provide a reasonable introduction to American labor. Its value would appear, however, to be greatest to those with little knowledge or background in the subject. In this sense the book would seem to be most useful as a reference work for high school and college students, news reporters, and members of the general public, as opposed to scholars and professionals involved in labor-related work.—**Paul F. Clark**

Directories

203. **Plunkett's Employers' Internet Sites with Careers Information 1999-2000.** Jack W. Plunkett and others, eds. Galveston, Tex., Plunkett Research, 1998. 701p. index. $149.99pa. ISBN 1-891775-01-4.

This book is intended to facilitate online job searches by identifying which companies are posting the most useful career information on the Internet. The primary audience is the job seeker with little or no Internet experience. There are 517 companies covered. To be included, a company must have user-friendly, useful career information on its company site, must be a public U.S. company, and must be a mid- to large-size employer.

The introductory matter includes basic advice on applying for a job online and a directory of important World Wide Web job sites. Most of the work is devoted to company-specific information. Each entry is one page and companies are arranged alphabetically. A typical entry includes basic directory information, a brief description of the business, and the company's URL. A table at the top of each page tells readers if the site contains job opening data, company data, college internship or recruiting data, benefits information, and if the site is searchable. Another section provides information on how to most effectively navigate through the Website. The entry also provides information on the types of career opportunities the company generally offers. For example, under "Management" it indicates whether or not the company typically looks for "management trainees," "experienced management," "international business," or "MBA graduates."

The volume also contains some useful indexes, including industry, geographical (by state and region), and a listing of firms with international operations. Purchasers may also write to the publisher for a free diskette version of the database. As with any print directory that accepts the challenge of documenting Web resources, a reader should be concerned about the currency and accuracy of the information. This is especially true for a work whose primary intent is to provide guidance to novice Internet users about company Websites. However, the information contained in this work is useful and well organized and, with the caveat mentioned above, is recommended for libraries serving job seekers. [R: Choice, Sept 99, p. 122]—**Gordon J. Aamot**

Handbooks and Yearbooks

204. **American Salaries and Wages Survey.** 5th ed. Helen S. Fisher, ed. Farmington Hills, Mich., Gale, 1999. 770p. $120.00pa. ISBN 0-7876-2428-4. ISSN 1055-7628.

This work is a compilation of 2,660 occupations and their corresponding salaries. Job titles and wage information were obtained from more than 190 federal and state government sources, trade associations, and journals. This book will be useful to those seeking jobs, employment counselors, economic planners, industry, and sociologists. It includes 48,000 entries. It covers the U.S., individual states, 113 cities, and 14 regions.

The book contains an introduction explaining its use and purpose. This is followed by an outline of contents—an alphabetic list of job titles. Next comes a geographical outline—job titles in specific geographic locations. The following section comprises the bulk of the volume. An eight-column chart lists job title, secondary occupation or industry designation, geographical locations for this title, intervals at which a wage is paid, low-mid-high wages for that job title, the source of the information, and the date the data were collected. The abbreviations key appears at the bottom of each page. There are four appendixes: organizations that contributed information, wage conversion table, abbreviations, and employment by occupation from 1996 projected to 2006. In general, job titles follow federal naming conventions. No fringe benefits are included in salaries listed. The editor provided the caveat that the data are compiled from a large number of sources. No attempt was made to standardize the data. Fisher warns readers to use care in making data interpretations. Information is clearly presented and easy to use. Having all these data compiled in one place is very convenient. Geographical listings and projections into the future make this an excellent planning tool.—**Joanna M. Burkhardt**

205. Dienhart, John W., and Jordan Curnutt. **Business Ethics: A Reference Handbook.** Santa Barbara, Calif., ABC-CLIO, 1998. 444p. index. (Contemporary Ethical Issues). $39.50. ISBN 0-87436-863-4.

The goals of the authors, both members of the Philosophy Department at St. Cloud University, were "to write a comprehensive reference book for business ethics by providing brief discussions of major topics in the field and to provide a theoretical orientation to integrate these topics." The book is organized into 5 broad thematic areas and then broken down into 18 chapters. For example, in "The Employee" section one finds chapters on "Terms and Conditions of Employment," "Health and Safety," "Privacy," "Discrimination and Affirmative Action," "Sexual Harassment," and "Whistleblowing and Loyalty." Each chapter is 15 to 25 pages long and is organized into standard subsections. These include "Ethics," "International Issues," "Economics," "Law," "Selected Cases," and "Statutes and Regulations."

In addition to covering a wide range of business ethics topics, the authors provide supplementary reference material. These include a discussion of Codes of Ethical Conduct; brief biographical sketches of 41 business ethics scholars; a 10-page directory of business organizations and associations related to business ethics; a bibliography of relevant print and nonprint materials; a 27-page glossary of terms; and a list of court cases, federal statutes, and agencies. An index is included.

This work provides a valuable service by pulling together a wide range of business ethics themes and issues into a format accessible to students and laypersons. *Business Ethics* is recommended for academic business libraries and others whose patrons have an interest in business ethics.—**Gordon J. Aamot**

206. **Handbook of U.S. Labor Statistics 1999: Employment, Earnings, Prices, Productivity, and Other Labor Data.** 3d ed. Eva E. Jacobs and Kendall J. Golladay, eds. Lanham, Md., Bernan Associates, 1999. 380p. index. $65.00pa. ISBN 0-89059-182-2. ISSN 1526-2553.

In its 3d edition, the *Handbook of U.S. Labor Statistics* provides a lot of information on population; employment and unemployment by industry; hourly and weekly earnings; consumer and producer prices; export and import prices; consumer expenditures by household type; employment costs; productivity; employment benefits; and other labor data that will be useful to those in business, labor, health care, or the social sciences. Besides current data, the handbook contains both historical data (some back to 1913) on labor market trends and projections of future employment by industry and occupation to 2006. Among the new features in this edition are annual data on employment and unemployment in families, data on employee tenure with current employer, wages and employment by detailed occupation, and union affiliation by industry.

The introductory articles summarize the new Standard Occupational Classification and the revision of the standards for the classification of federal data by race and ethnicity. The tables are organized by subject matter, with each section preceded by descriptions of data sources, definitions, and methodology. The primary focus is on national data, but some of the statistics are by state and city. There are also some international comparisons. The scope and depth of information provided make this an indispensable volume for any library.—**Michele Russo**

207. Lencsis, Peter M. **Workers Compensation: Reference and Guide.** Westport, Conn., Greenwood Press, 1998. 173p. index. $59.95. ISBN 1-56720-174-1.

Workers compensation in the United States is a simple concept in theory, but complex in practice. State, territorial, and federal laws are not uniform and questions frequently arise as to whether "payments are due from workers compensation as opposed to general liability insurance, health insurance, disability insurance, automobile no-fault, Social Security, Medicare, and other sources." In this guide to workers compensation, the author does a superb job of sorting out these distinctions. He writes in a simple, direct manner that is comprehensible to the layperson yet respectful of the legal principles and their ramifications.

Lencsis begins his work by tracing the history of workers compensation in Europe, England, and the United States and follows this with forerunner legislation on the federal level in the United States. From here he goes on to discuss current coverage in state and federal workers compensation laws as well as benefits and claims. He then covers related topics, such as the actual insurance policy, endorsements, rates, and experience and retrospective rating. Besides discussing rating and advisory organizations, he devotes a full chapter to special funds and residual markets. The final chapter covers current trends and issues.

Jack B. Hood, Benjamin A Hardy Jr., and Harold S. Lewis Jr. authored the 2d edition of *Workers Compensation and Employee Protection Laws in a Nutshell* in West Publishing's esteemed Nutshell series in 1989. Recent developments in the field suggest that many libraries need an updated source, and Lencsis's book fills this need very well. This work is highly recommended for all law libraries, large public libraries, academic libraries with business programs, mid-size and large business firms, and students and practitioners in the workers compensation field.—**Dene L. Clark**

MANAGEMENT

208. **Codes of Professional Responsibility: Ethics Standards in Business, Health, and Law.** 4th ed. Rena A. Gorlin, ed. Washington, D.C., BNA Books, 1999. 1149p. index. $95.00. ISBN 1-57018-148-9.

This collection of 59 codes of ethics covers a variety of professions and organizations, primarily in business, health, and law. Most are full-text, but seven present only the important sections of the text with the remaining portions summarized. An information section that details the goals and enforcement policies of the organization accompanies each code. There are also the expected address data, with e-mail and Website, and a history of the adoption of the code. While the scope of professions is not all-encompassing, what is included covers a wide range of the most commonly sought associations.

The appendixes are a convenient source of a variety of ethics resources. The 1st section covers organizations, but is grouped into 3 subsections (the U.S., elsewhere, and U.S. government). This may confuse some users, as the page headers do not reflect the subdivisions. The 2d section deals with informational resources: ethics-oriented periodicals arranged by title, reference works arranged by publisher, and Websites. The periodical listing uses shortcuts by referring users elsewhere for information on certain publications. But these *see* references are rather unclear, and it is inconvenient as well as confusing. The reference works section lists only title (and author where relevant), with no further publication date or annotation. An arrangement only by publisher (including address date) is odd, as the individual titles are not retrievable through any of the indexes. The 3d section brings together hard-to-find electronic resources. It is divided into bibliographies available online, Internet listservs, and discussion lists with information on how to subscribe.

The index is grouped into sections. The 1st is an index of ethics issues that have appeared within individual codes. The 2d is a listing of professions, along with an index of subjects covered in the corresponding code. This is useful for codes with many pages and subsections, but less important for shorter ones. The final segment is an index of organizations mentioned within the text of the codes. The multi-index format is complex, and users will need to take the time to become familiar with it.

The convenience of having in one place the actual codes of ethics for diverse organizations and professions makes this volume worthwhile for any public, academic, or corporate library and a recommended purchase. Having the information on organizations, the Websites, and other contact data as a source will be much appreciated by anyone seeking updated versions, corrections, or supplements of the codes.

—Gary R. Cocozzoli

MARKETING AND TRADE

209. **Consumer USA 1999.** 4th ed. London, Euromonitor; distr., Farmington Hills, Mich., Gale, 1999. 371p. $800.00pa. ISBN 0-86338-834-5.

The introduction notes the impressive strength, size, and growth of the consumer market in the United States. The purpose of *Consumer USA 1999* is to capture a wide range of data about the U.S. consumer market and to present these data in a logical fashion. In addition to past data, the volume presents trends and projects future levels of production and spending on a wide variety of goods and services. Published by Euromoniter, the data are drawn from a number of credible agencies, including the Census Bureau of Economic Analysis.

Consumer USA 1999 is divided into 3 sections. The 1st section provides a careful overview of the U.S. economy in general, along with specific commentary on consumption patterns and trends in a variety of sectors including catering, tourism and travel, retailing, and personal finance. The text is clear, easy to read, and supplemented with numerous tables of data. The 2d section, on marketing parameters, presents 223 tables covering economic indicators, gross domestic product, employment, education, demographics, and other systemic marketing data. The 3d section is the heart of the book, with 833 tables of data on specific product groups. These tables include sales of a particular product from the last 5 years, but also forecasts for these products up through 2003. For example, for oral hygiene products there are tables for sales of toothpaste and toothbrushes, forecasts for both of these items, manufacturer shares, and brand shares. Additional tables are provided for mouthwashes, mouth fresheners, and dental rinses. This is powerful information, not only for the manufacturer or marketing of these products, but also for the entrepreneurs, scientists and researchers, investors, and students. Detailed, current information for specific products is often difficult to find, particularly for some classes of consumer goods. The opportunity to have such information readily at hand makes this a particularly good reference tool. Tables are attractively presented and easy to interpret. A list of tables is provided at the beginning of the volume that will be a time-saver at the reference desk.

At a cost of $800, *Consumer USA 1999* is an expensive text. However, the detailed data contained would be useful in a variety of types of libraries, particularly those in the corporate arena, as well as public libraries that serve small businesses, entrepreneurs, and investors. It would also be a good addition to an academic library's reference collection. Although the intent of the volume seems to be to help non-U.S. companies find a niche in the U.S., it is also an excellent tool for U.S.-based patrons to find out detailed information about their country's products, services, and buying patterns.—**Sara Anne Hook**

210. **Direction of Trade Statistics Yearbook, 1998.** Washington, D.C., International Monetary Fund; distr., Lanham, Md., Bernan Associates, 1998. 477p. $32.00pa. ISBN 1-55775-748-8. ISSN 0252-3019.

This International Monetary Fund yearbook presents statistics on trade among countries and trading entities of the world on an annual basis for 1991 through 1997. Values of merchandise imports and exports are provided in tabular form for 182 states. Individual county information is broken down to show figures by major trading partners. Also included are aggregate figures for the world, major regions, and two other groupings. A quarterly version is also available. All figures are in U.S. dollars whether or not supplied in national currency by participating states and entities.

The brief introduction is repeated in English, French, and Spanish. It gives details on methodology, terminology, definitions, and other issues. There is a detailed table of contents. A table of country and area codes purports to give page references for the entries in the yearbook and the latest quarterly, but all the entries are listed as "X." The usefulness of the later is far from apparent.

The work is divided into 3 main table sets. The first covers world and regional data. The later divides into tables on industrial countries, developing countries, and those not covered elsewhere (effectively North Korea and Cuba). The developing countries section has aggregate figures and breakdowns for Africa, Asia, Europe, the Middle East, and the Western Hemisphere. Tables provide exports and imports for the world or region to or from the countries listed. The second part provides similar tables for the European Union, oil exporting countries, and non-oil developing countries. The longest section provides tables for the 182 countries or entities listed and is arranged alphabetically. Taiwan has no entry (under China, Republic of China, or Taiwan) nor is it included in the list of "not included elsewhere" entities in the introduction.

This useful source supplies detailed world, regional, national, and thematic trade statistics. It should be acquired by business or economics collections with the relevant client interests and budget.

—**Nigel Tappin**

211. **Foreign Trade of the United States 1999: Including State and Metro Area Export Data.** Courtenay M. Slater and James B. Rice, eds. Lanham, Md., Bernan Associates, 1999. 444p. index. $65.00pa. ISBN 0-89059-160-1.

This comprehensive overview of the participation of the United States in the global economy provides detailed data on U.S. trade in services; time series data on U.S. exports and imports, by industry and country; state-by-state data on total good exports by industry and destination; and goods exports by major metropolitan areas. Also included is complete annual balance of payments data from 1960 to 1998, data showing U.S. exports and imports as a percentage of gross domestic product, and detailed listings of exchange rates for individual national currencies. These data were gathered from the U.S. Bureau of the Census, the International Trade Administration, and the Bureau of Economic Analysis of the Department of Commerce.

Edited by Slater, a former chief economist for the Department of Commerce, this work's introductory article analyzes trends in foreign trade, and its appendix gives detailed notes on sources, definitions, and methodology. The "Using this Book" chapter will help users understand the various charts, tables, and graphs, and the "Notes and Definitions" section provides sources, definitions, and specific notes for each section. A detailed index allows readers to access the data from many additional subject areas. This well-designed book will quickly become a standard access point to data on U.S. imports and exports of both goods and services for researchers, students, and economists.—**Susan C. Awe**

212. **Handbook of International Trade and Development Statistics 1996/1997.** New York, United Nations, 1999. 1v. (various paging). $80.00. ISBN 92-1-012042-6. ISSN 0251-9461. S/N E/F.98.IID.16.

The *Handbook of International Trade and Development Statistics 1996/1997* contains statistical data related to the analysis of world trade, investment, and development. The data are intended for use by the United Nations Conference on Trade and Development; government officials; and university researchers, faculty, and students. The data are derived from existing international and national data sources and are presented analytically, including special classifications such as growth rates, rank orderings, and shares. The text is presented in English and French.

Countries covered have been classified within three main regions: Developed Market Economy Countries (e.g., United States, Canada, Japan, Israel, Western European countries); Countries in Eastern Europe (e.g., Poland, the Czech Republic, Russian Federation); and Developing Countries and Territories (e.g., all other countries in Africa, America, Asia, Europe, Oceania). Statistics provided include annual average growth rate of exports, export structure by destination and by major commodity groups, import structure by origin and by commodity groups, balance of payments, value of exports and imports, balance of payments, and gross domestic product by type of expenditure and by kind of economic activity.

This handbook is a thorough, comprehensive source of world trade data. It belongs in the business collections of academic and research libraries.—**Lucy Heckman**

213. **Major Marketing Campaigns Annual 1998.** Thomas Riggs, Elizabeth Oakes, and Patrick Hutchins, eds. Farmington Hills, Mich., Gale, 1999. 525p. illus. index. $125.00. ISBN 0-7876-3043-8. ISSN 1521-6683.

Gale's *Major Marketing Campaigns Annual 1998* (MMC) is the first of what should be a series of useful and interesting reference and research tools. MMC includes a description and analysis of 100 major marketing and advertising campaigns that appeared, at least partially, in 1997. Listed alphabetically by company, not product, the entries include an overview of the campaign, historical context, target market, competition, marketing strategy, and outcome. Short lists of further readings are found at the end of each entry and sidebars are used effectively throughout.

Gale states three criteria for selecting a campaign for inclusion: "its conceptual value or innovation (sometimes represented by the winning of awards); the importance of the company or brand for which it was run; and its effectiveness in selling the advertised product or service." For the most part, companies represented are a "who's who" of corporate America, particularly corporate America with large advertising budgets.

The depth of coverage and analysis is somewhat erratic and some of the background material is quite basic corporate information. The 100 entries take up just over 500 pages; the resulting 5-page average per entry seems inadequate to cover the intended key elements. Perhaps Gale should consider selecting a smaller number of key campaigns for more in-depth coverage, and condensing the remaining entries to a more space-saving format, including tabular or statistical material.

Illustrations depicting key graphic components of campaigns are included, although the quality of the reproduced photographs could be improved. Contact information for each company, including Website, is provided. A general index and a subject index are useful, but if the former were more detailed the book would be more useful as a reference source. As with many annuals, the dating of MMC is a bit confusing. The 1998 annual, with a 1999 copyright, covers marketing campaigns from 1997.

Overall, *Major Marketing Campaigns Annual 1998* is a good start to the series. It should be useful to business and marketing students as a starting place for research and as a basic primer, to marketing and advertising professionals doing basic competitive research and brainstorming, and to curious consumers. [R: Choice, Sept 99, p. 120; RUSQ, Fall 99, p. 97]—**Edward Kurdyla**

214. **U.S. Market Trends & Forecasts.** Andrea L. deJong, ed. Farmington Hills, Mich., Gale, 1999. 1418p. index. $295.00. ISBN 0-7876-3007-1.

This book is the 1st edition of a reference work containing market statistics and forecasts for U.S. industries. The directory is arranged alphabetically, first by industry grouping and then by individual industry within groups. The groups range from "Amusement and Leisure" through "Industrial Machinery," "Office Equipment," and "Timber and Joinery" to "Transport." It uses the older U.S. government Standard Industrial Classification (SIC) definitions of industries rather than the North American Industry Classification System (NAICS) being phased in by Canadian, Mexican, and U.S. governments, but provides conversion listings between the two. Each industry group is introduced by a brief characterization. Individual industry names have SIC codes in brackets by the heading. The format is mainly graphic, with information in tabular and chart form as well as point form highlights. Each class of information (e.g., market value) has a page to itself with all three formats on it for ease of scanning for reports. The information provided varies by industry. Many (including "Book Publishing" and "Title Insurance") have four pages each, sectors, value, and shares, while some (e.g., "Home Furnishings" and "Surety Insurance") omit market share. Some industries also have growth rates for 1993 to 1997. More than 1,300 graphs and tables are presented.

Access points include a detailed contents and a general index. The index lists market sectors as well as groups and industries. There are also an introduction and notes on research methods and sources. This valuable work is aimed at economic and market researchers and will be of interest to appropriate special libraries and larger business collections. [R: Choice, Nov 99, p. 520; RUSQ, Fall 99, pp. 101-102]

—**Nigel Tappin**

215. **World Marketing Forecasts 1999 on CD-ROM.** 2d ed. [CD-ROM]. Chicago, Euromonitor International; distr., Farmington Hills, Mich., Gale, 1999. Minimum system requirements: IBM or compatible 486. Double-speed CD-ROM drive. Windows 3.1. Windows 95. 8MB RAM (16MB RAM for Windows 95). 10MB hard disk space (20MB hard disk space for Windows 95). $2,190.00. ISBN 0-86338-824-9.

World Marketing Forecasts is a valuable tool. Projected market data have been collected for the years 1997–2010 for 49 countries in 5 geographic regions (Asia, Australia, Latin and North America, the Middle East and Africa, and Western Europe). Coverage is slightest in the Middle East and African regions (only South Africa data are provided), but coverage for the other regions is reasonably good. There are 950 data types to choose from, including forecasting predictors (such as demographic or expenditure data) as well as market forecasts for 695 different consumer goods. Projections are created using product groups (domestic electrical appliances) or the individual products therein (microwaves).

The initial workspace screen is straightforward—users select a range of years, choose a region or country, select the data type, and push the "Find Data" button on the toolbar. Results are delivered in Excel worksheets and every executed search nets four worksheets. The default worksheet is for "selected results," displaying the data in their component parts. The more useful default would be the "all results" worksheet containing the total report, by all data sets requested. Two additional blank worksheets are created to allow users to drag data over to create tables for their own use. The resulting display could use a little redefining. The headings need to be resized in order to fit more data on the screen and the workspace windows need to be resized to view the worksheets, but the data are readily accessible by scrolling. Figures can be selected by projected sales or in volume sales. The chart icon on the toolbar allows users to create a chart to display selected data. What is not obvious is that this function is much more useful once the data are "pivoted," meaning the user will need to move the product group into another workspace on the far left of the "results" screen in order to create sensible charts.

A useful function, offered at the "results" screen, is the market driver's icon on the toolbar. By clicking on this icon, a drop-down list of drivers (gross domestic product, population, or various expenditure projections) can be toggled on or off individually for comparison to the data sets selected.

The functions that are completely unclear are the remaining icons on the toolbar. These functions are only available in the selected "results" worksheet, and while this is confusing, it explains somewhat why the default spreadsheet display is the "selected results" sheet. In a "selected results" worksheet, users can click on these icons to convert the sales figures to U.S. dollars, plot the percentage of growth, convert the data to an index, show data in per capita figures, or adjust figures for projected inflation. All information from here can be selected and charted using the chart icon.

This is clearly a tool developed for professional market researchers, but is invaluable as a one-stop shop for international market projections. It is simple enough to use for undergraduates and thorough enough for faculty. Recommended for libraries serving the intense needs of international marketing professionals and students.—**Gerald L. Gill**

TAXATION

216. **The Encyclopedia of Taxation and Tax Policy.** Joseph J. Cordes, Robert D. Ebel, and Jane G. Gravelle, eds. Washington, D.C., Urban Institute, 1999. 452p. index. $75.00. ISBN 0-87766-682-2.

This is a compilation of the best essays on taxes and taxation policy published to date. The three editors gathered the best tax specialists and financial thinkers to write these taxation essays. This is the first publication of this kind and the editors plan to update it regularly and expand it internationally.

Each part of the book is in alphabetic order, from the table of contents to the entries and the index. Therefore, it can serve as a glossary of taxation terms. Each entry has an initial short definition of the term or phrase. The definition is followed by an essay and a bibliography for further research and cross-references. This is an essential addition for the taxation collection in academic, special, and public libraries. Every person interested in taxation will want to refer to this book.—**Kay M. Stebbins**

5 Education

GENERAL WORKS

Bibliography

217. **Bibliographic Guide to Education 1998.** Thorndike, Maine, G. K. Hall/Macmillan, 1999. 949p. $385.00. ISBN 0-7838-0209-9. ISSN 0147-6505.

G. K. Hall publishes subject bibliographic guides annually. They bring together recent publications cataloged by The Research Libraries of The New York Public Library and the Library of Congress for thorough subject coverage. The *Bibliographic Guide to Education* is the list of recent publications cataloged during the past year by Teachers College, Columbia University. It also contains publications in the field of education cataloged by The Research Libraries of The New York Public Library, selected on the basis of subject headings. This guide covers all aspects and levels of education. Areas include U.S. elementary and secondary education, higher and adult education, early childhood education, history and philosophy of education, applied pedagogy, international and comparative education, educational administration, education of the culturally disadvantaged and physically handicapped nursing education, and education of minorities and women. The guide is arranged alphabetically by main entry, added entry, and subject headings. Full information on an item is listed under the main entry. Because every record has Library of Congress and Dewey Decimal Classification numbers, the material can be easily located by educators, education major students, and others who are interested in this subject area. However, this guide would be easier to use if it had separate author, title, and subject indexes.—**Xiao (Shelley) Yan Zhang**

218. **El-Hi Textbooks and Serials in Print 1999: Including Related Teaching Materials K-12.** New Providence, N.J., R. R. Bowker, 1999. 2v. index. $149.00/set. ISBN 0-8352-4081-9. ISSN 0000-0825.

Access to information about 110,765 textbooks, pedagogical books, and serials for elementary through high school grades is made possible with this 2-volume set. The entries were compiled from more than 1,275 catalogs of textbook publishers and are classified and cross-referenced within 21 categories and 231 subdivisions. Besides textbooks, the work describes reference books, maps, periodicals, tests, teaching aids, and programmed learning books. Supplemental reading and AV materials not connected to a specific textbook are not covered.

The first volume contains a subject index, a how-to-use section, and a key to the many abbreviations used in the work. Each textbook entry typically provides the author, grade level, publication date, ISBN, related teaching materials, and publisher, plus other relevant information such as reading level, illustrations, binding, and price.

The second volume has an author, title, and series index for the books and a subject and title index for the serials. Serial entries contain the mandatory information on title, frequency of publication, publisher address, country code, and Dewey Decimal Classification number. Much more information is usually given, such as a description of the serial's contents, fax and e-mail data, CODENs, circulation figures, and copyright clearance information. A key to the publishers' and distributors' abbreviations gives addresses, telephone numbers, and SANs.

Besides its obvious use, *Textbooks and Serials in Print* may also be helpful to teachers planning curriculum, especially in classes that do not have state-mandated texts (like career education or library and information skills), or those that allow teacher preference when selecting materials (such as novels used in a literature-based language arts program).—**Janet J. Kosky**

Dictionaries and Encyclopedias

219. Baker, Colin, and Sylvia Prys Jones. **Encyclopedia of Bilingualism and Bilingual Education.** Washington, D.C., Multilingual Matters, 1998. 758p. illus. maps. index. $150.00. ISBN 1-85359-362-1.

Written in a style that would be accessible to a wide audience, the *Encyclopedia of Bilingualism and Bilingual Education* contains much information in 4 major sections: individual bilingualism, language and society, language contact around the world, and bilingual education. Within these 4 sections nearly 120 main topics are treated, with each topic having a central text often supplemented and illustrated by a variety of textbook excerpts and attractive color photographs, maps, graphs, and diagrams. A glossary of 375 key terms is included at the end of the book as well as author and subject indexes and an impressive bibliography of more than 2,000 references.

Treating bilingualism on two levels—sociologically and psychologically—this encyclopedia explores how issues of culture and identity intersect in learning a second language. Academically sound but not sounding academic, it is also distinguished by a format that is stimulating and visually appealing. The fact that approximately two-thirds of the world's population is bilingual speaks to the value of this fine work and the need for it becoming available in a wide range of libraries. [R: BL, 1 Feb 99, p. 995]

—**G. Douglas Meyers**

220. **Historical Dictionary of American Education.** Richard J. Altenbaugh, ed. Westport, Conn., Greenwood Press, 1999. 499p. index. $95.00. ISBN 0-313-28590-X.

This historical dictionary provides factual information about important persons and significant topics related to the development of American public, private, and parochial schools. Both elementary and secondary school levels are covered. In addition to major state and regional leaders and reformers, the volume includes biographies of significant national educators, philosophers, psychologists, and writers. The broad array of subjects includes core ideas, events, institutions, agencies, and pedagogical trends that have shaped American policies and perceptions regarding education. The more than 350 entries are arranged alphabetically and written by expert contributors. Each entry closes with a brief bibliography, and the volume ends with a list of works for further reading.

This volume is one of the best historical dictionaries that this reviewer has found on the subject. The entries are relevant, clearly written, and include key bibliographic references for further reading. The index is a model of completeness and facilitates access to the man individuals, concepts, and other information points contained in the individual entries. The *Historical Dictionary of American Education* is recommended for all libraries supporting a curriculum in K-12 education and the history of education.

—**Arthur P. Young**

221. Mitchell, Bruce M., and Robert E. Salsbury. **Encyclopedia of Multicultural Education.** Westport, Conn., Greenwood Press, 1999. 304p. index. $65.00. ISBN 0-313-30029-1.

Multicultural education, sometimes termed multiethnic or multiracial education, refers to educational efforts that attempt to inculcate more positive values toward human diversity. Its goals are to reduce bias by teaching respect for the rights of others to be culturally different, to ensure equity, and to develop school and social structures that help students and teachers to cross racial and ethnic boundaries. This 1-volume encyclopedia contains some 400 alphabetically arranged entries related to multicultural education. They include key terms, events, concepts, notable persons, and court cases, each followed by references used for that article. The items in the references are usually not found in the general bibliography at the end of the volume. Except for certain classics in the field, such as Alex Haley's *Roots*, most of the works cited are from the 1990s.

The entries, selected by the two authors and an advisory group representing various areas of multicultural education, were chosen for their relationship to the content and method of education and not just for their importance in general. Thus, Will Rogers, well-known movie actor and humorist, was included because he was a Cherokee and one of the first Native Americans to gain fame in the entertainment field. The article points out that he provides an excellent example for teachers to use for contributions of Native Americans. Many of the articles contain statements of how the material can be used in helping students acquire a positive attitude toward diversity.

In addition to the bibliography at the end of the volume, there is a general index. As might be expected, it shows the incongruity of some of our politically correct terminology. The article on African Americans, for example, is properly found under that term, but most of the related articles are found under "Black"—black education, black colleges, etc. Likewise, with Native Americans, one must look under "Indian" for some of the related material. Because there are very few *see also* references in either the articles or the index, it is important to be aware of this fact.

The work as a whole is an excellent source of information and teaching suggestions on this increasingly important topic. The format, arrangement, and straightforward, well-written text and references make it a worthwhile addition to any academic library, particularly on the secondary school level. [R: Choice, Dec 99, p. 703]—**Lucille Whalen**

Directories

222. **Educators Resource Directory, 1999.** 3d ed. Richard Gottlieb, ed. Lakeville, Conn., Grey House Publishing, 1999. 591p. index. $170.00; $145.00pa. ISBN 1-891482-76-9; 1-891482-75-0pa.

The book, formerly *The Encyclopedia of Education Information*, is a list of sources arranged in 13 categories, namely association and organizations, awards and honors, conference and grade shows, databases and online services, employment opportunities, financial resources, government agencies, professional development, publications, publishers, research centers, school library services, and suppliers. Categories are further divided by topics or geographic areas, such as international, regional, national, and state.

Each entry consists of name, address, telephone and fax numbers, and a brief description. Many entries provide e-mail and Website addresses, but there are omissions. For instance, URLs of Dialog, Hoover's, and Peterson's are not given. Many entries of serials do not provide year of first issue published, year of publication, frequency, ISSN, and pagination.

The book lists more than 5,400 entries with a few duplicated listings. Access ERIC, Bodman Foundation, *Cabell's Directory of Publishing Opportunities in Education* (3d ed.; see ARBA 94, entry 663), Edmark, and *World of Learning* (49th ed.; see ARBA 99, entry 295) are listed twice.

Coverage is extensive and adequate. However, other useful resources could have been included, such as AskEric, *Current Index to Journals in Education*, *Resources in Education*, LEXIS-NEXIS, *American Universities and Colleges* (15th ed.; see ARBA 99, entry 348), and *U.S. News and World Report* (its annual list of colleges and graduate schools). The book will enhance its usefulness if a category of bibliographic services is added in the next edition.

There are three appendixes: conferences and shows by state, school and state listings, and statistics and state numbers. Indexes include entry name, geographic, and publisher. In general, the book is well compiled, providing an important reference for finding resources in education.—**Tze-chung Li**

223. **Guide to American Educational Directories: A Guide to the Major Educational Directories of the United States.** 8th ed. Barry Klein, ed. West Nyack, N.Y., Todd Publications, 1999. 286p. index. $75.00pa. ISBN 0-915344-9-6.

Metabooks, or books that describe other books and information resources, have always enjoyed a secure position on the library reference shelf. This particular directory of directories offers a gold mine of information. Approximately 5,000 U.S. and major foreign directories are categorized under more than 100 educational headings, which cover the gamut of subjects from accounting to electronics, optometry to zoology. Each record contains the directory's title and a concise description of its contents. Publisher and distributor information, including telephone and fax numbers, is provided along with a current price. Alphabetic subject and title indexes append the guide.

This interesting and easy-to-use resource is aimed at educational organizations, educators, and researchers, but could be useful to anyone. It is particularly useful to librarians, who may find its greatest value lies in putting users in touch with unique resources they never knew existed, and which their particular library may not own. Where else might one find out about such resources as the *Pattern Designers Directory* or the *Registry of Drama Therapists*? Of course such entries share the pages with the many well-known, classic directories one would expect to locate in any respectable research library.

This 8th edition has been weeded of 500 directories no longer published, and includes more than 1,000 new entries. In this reviewer's opinion, the nature of the data included in this guide makes it an ideal candidate for distribution via CD-ROM, or better yet, on the World Wide Web. The ability to perform keyword searching online would enhance access to this information and permit continual updating.—**Judith A. Matthews**

224. **The Princeton Review Guide to Performing Arts Programs: Profiles of over 600 Colleges, High Schools, and Summer Programs.** By Muriel Topaz and Carole Everett. New York, Princeton Review/Random House, 1998. 638p. index. $24.95pa. ISBN 0-375-75095-9.

This guide is directed to prospective secondary school graduates interested in pursuing careers in the performing arts—dance, acting, and music. It is basically comprised of 2 sections. The 1st section deals with preliminary considerations: career considerations, application processes, financial aid, and 3 chapters that cover special advice for each of the unique features of the 3 performing arts areas. This covers approximately 60 pages and contains some valuable information, especially for students without proper guidance counseling. The 2d section contains profiles of more than 600 colleges, high schools, and summer programs and comprises the majority of the guide. Arranged by state and identified with appropriate icons, each program description contains pertinent data, including address, telephone and fax numbers, contact person, type of institution, enrollment, curriculum, students and faculty, renowned alumni, facilities, and audition and performance information. The data presented here tend to be somewhat general. The programs list is not comprehensive and includes only institutions that are members of the National Association of Schools of Music and of Dance and others that responded to a questionnaire. Some international programs are also profiled. There is an index followed by appendixes that list books, periodicals, organizations, and sample résumés. Although somewhat awkwardly organized and vague in data, this would be useful for high school students, especially before their graduating year, aspiring to careers in the performing arts. [R: BL, 15 Feb 99, p. 1092]—**Jackson Kesler**

Handbooks and Yearbooks

225. **Education Statistics on the United States 1999.** Mark S. Littman and Deirdre A. Gaquin, eds. Lanham, Md., Bernan Associates, 1999. 643p. index. (U.S. Databooks Series). $65.00pa. ISBN 0-89059-066-4. ISSN 1524-394X.

This volume, from the Bernan's award-winning U.S. DataBooks Series, pulls together education-related data from numerous sources, including the U.S. Bureau of the Census (Census) and the National Center from Education Statistics (NCES). The book is divided into 4 parts. The data exhibited in part A (school enrollment) and part B (educational attainment) are no longer available in print from the Bureau of the Census. The data tabulations in part D (school enrollment and financial data by county) have been arranged for the first time from computer files of the NCES.

Part A of this book provides the most recent national school enrollment data from the U.S. Census Bureau, October 1996. Historical tables on school enrollment are provided covering the period from 1947 to 1996, when obtainable. Part B of this volume includes national-level data on educational attainment measured by the highest grade completed and degrees received based on the March 1997 Current Population Survey.

Part C of this book includes an assortment of state-level tables that can be compared with other parts of the book. Tables were collected mostly from the National Center of Education Statistics' Digest of Education Statistics 1997. When more recent information has become available, the tables have been updated to reflect the changes. For example, the private school enrollment figures are more recent than the 1997 Digest. Part D of this publication includes education data tabulated for each county or its equivalent in the United States collected by the National Center for Education Statistics for those users who are interested in education statistics at the county level. Of the 14,700 regular public elementary and secondary school districts in the United States, there is a substantial difference in the number and size among states.

An educator looking for information about total enrollment, minority enrollment, number of schools by level, number of teachers, number of dropouts, students eligible for free lunch, and indicators of school revenue and expenditures will find this book a valuable resource. Geographic codes are appended to these data, such as the Federal Information Processing Standards and the Beale codes, to allow readers to relate the statistics to their own local information. Immediately following each group of tables are notes and definitions important to each group.

Because this book contains many statistics and detailed tables created by the Bureau of the Census that are not readily available elsewhere in print, this book is a valuable resource for obtaining data on educational attainment by age, race, employment status, and occupation, as well as income and earnings. The school district data taken from the National Center for Education Statistics and developed into county- and state-level totals on enrollment, expenditures, class salaries, and more, should serve as a useful tool for district-level administrators and state education officials to use as they plan for future educational programs. This volume is recommended. [R: BL, Aug 99, p. 2104; Choice, Nov 99, p. 516]—**Betty J. Morris**

226. **The Handbook of School Psychology.** 3d ed. Cecil R. Reynolds and Terry B. Gutkin, eds. New York, John Wiley, 1999. 1200p. index. $157.00. ISBN 0-471-12205-X.

This 3d edition of *The Handbook of School Psychology* updates the 1982 edition by including topics that have become well established since the last publication, as well as reconceptualizing and updating other chapters. The list of contributors includes experts from a wide range of American universities. The volume is divided into sections dealing with current perspectives: school psychology and the scientific study of behavior—contributions to theory and practice, psychological and educational assessment, school psychological interventions—focus on children; and school psychological interventions—focus of staff, programs, and organizations. Both an author and a subject index are included. Each article within the volume has an extensive bibliography and authors are identified by university affiliation. Topics for what differing opinions are prevalent are presented in an unbiased manner. The book is designed to be used by both graduate students and practicing professionals. It is a scholarly compendium of relevant issues, attempting to "provide the most up-to-date knowledge base and cogent thought in the various fields represented."
—**Janet Hilbun**

ALTERNATIVE EDUCATION

227. **Barron's Guide to Distance Learning: Degrees, Certificates, Courses.** By Pat Criscito. Hauppauge, N.Y., Barron's Educational Series, 1999. 537p. index. $18.95pa. ISBN 0-7641-0725-9.

The Internet has breathed new life into the concept of "distance learning" during a time when many adults are demanding high-quality college courses for career advancement and personal enrichment. Traditional modes of delivery, such as correspondence courses and educational television, have been supplemented or even replaced by content delivered through Websites, e-mail, and real-time chat groups. Distance learning has grown to meet the needs of today's world and is being offered by established colleges and universities as well as new entities like the University of Phoenix. With so many choices available, potential students need an accurate and comprehensive source of information. This is the niche that *Barron's Guide to Distance Learning* is trying to fill. It covers nearly 800 colleges and universities in the United States and Canada that offer some form of distance learning, either degrees, certificates, or individual courses.

Barron's Guide to Distance Learning begins with an overview of distance learning, with chapters covering accreditation and accrediting agencies, transferring credits, financial aid, and Internet resources. There is a very good chapter on the history, status, and future potential of distance learning. Chapter 7, the bulk of the volume, is devoted to the profiles of institutions offering distance learning. The profiles are arranged in alphabetic order and include such specialized organizations as the Hypnosis Motivation Institute and the International Aviation and Travel Academy, along with highly respected universities from around the country. Seminaries and community colleges are particularly well represented among the profiles. Each profile contains directory information, including Website and e-mail addresses, lists of degree and certificate programs, lists of class titles, teaching methods, how credits are granted, admission requirements, on-campus requirements, tuition and fees, financial aid, accreditation, and a narrative description. Several indexes are provided: state and province, on-campus requirements, undergraduate degree programs, graduate degree programs, doctoral degree programs, certificate and diploma programs, and individual classes.

Barron's Guide to Distance Learning is one of several possible sources that a public, school, or academic library might include in its reference collection. Similar publications are offered, including *The Oryx Guide to Distance Learning* (see ARBA 98, entry 280), *The McGraw-Hill Handbook of Distance Learning* (1999), *The Best Distance Learning Graduate Schools* (see ARBA 99, entry 304), along with several others that are not from big-name publishers. One problem with all of these volumes is the tendency for information to be quickly outdated, because most institutions are only beginning to fashion permanent programs and courses through distance learning.—**Sara Anne Hook**

228. Krebs, Arlene. **The Distance Learning Funding Sourcebook: A Guide to Foundation, Corporate, and Government Support for Telecommunications and the New Media.** 4th ed. Dubuque, Iowa, Kendall/Hunt Publishing, 1999. 419p. index. $48.00pa. ISBN 0-7872-4980-7.

Distance learning is an offspring of information technology. It is an integral part of the digital education development of the millennium. In order to provide programs for distance learners, educators seek funding to implement their proposed projects. According to the author, "this funding sourcebook offers the latest research on grants for telecommunications, multimedia, curricula development, and teacher training for private and public schools, higher education, museums, libraries, arts and culture organizations, health and social service agencies, and grassroots community organizations." The printing of the 4th edition signifies its popularity. Both Sony and Ameritech support the research of this unique resource.

The introduction of this book includes a list of foundations grouped by subject, such as business and management, curriculum development, education policy, and funding trends. The foundation chapter lists 38 foundations. Each foundation has full postal address, contact name, e-mail address, Website address, history, strengths, philosophy, supports, limitations, application, and previous recipients. The chapter on corporate giving programs lists 18 corporations that would provide distance learning funding. The descriptive format is similar to the foundation chapter. The third chapter is titled "Regional Bell, Local and Long Distance Telecommunications Companies." A total of 12 foundations are listed in this chapter. The fourth chapter is on the cable television industry. A chapter on federal government agencies that fund distance learning follows. The rest of the chapters are on intellectual property and distance learning, grant writing for success, Internet and multimedia resources, and print references. The grant writing chapter gives pointers on how to put a grant together. The appendixes on equipment donations and Internet resources for funding and grant information and the "Goal 2000: Education America Act" are worth noting. There is a Website at http://www.technogrants.com/ for those who wish to find out more about this book.—**Polin P. Lei**

COMPUTER RESOURCES

229. Andriot, Laurie, comp. **Uncle Sam's K-12 Web: Government Internet Resources for Educators, Students, and Parents.** Medford, N.J., CyberAge Books/Information Today, 1999. 244p. illus. $24.95pa. ISBN 0-910965-32-3.

This useful guide to more than 400 online government Websites is divided into sections for students, parents, and teachers. The section for students is the longest, with 11 chapters on such topics as the natural world; work; money; the mail; and math, science, and space. Each chapter lists a number of Web pages or sites appropriate for the stated audience, giving the title, URL, suggested grade level, and a paragraph describing the content. A long chapter on research resources gives sites that, although not designed specifically for students, will prove useful for background information. It is divided into broad subject areas (e.g., African American history and culture, military history, statistics) that are not listed in the table of contents or at the beginning of the chapter, making this section a bit frustrating to use. Examples of sites from all sections include NASA's "How Things Fly," the "CIA Kids Page," the EPA's "Student Center," "ArtsEdge," "Renewable Energy for Teachers," and "Marijuana: Facts Parents Need to Know." The nonevaluative descriptions note the agency or site's purpose and the topics or presentations found online. These can be a bit difficult to read when 10 or more topics are run together in paragraph format; an item list would have made it easier to read and pick out something of interest. Fortunately, users can use the detailed index to look up most of the topics found within site descriptions. For example, "earthquakes" in the index leads to the "American Memories" entry for "Great Earthquake and Fire: San Francisco." The appendix for finding government information online offers advice on using Boolean strategies and Web and government (general and agency-specific) search engines. The Website at http://www.fedworld.com gives updated links for all entries in the book. This will make a convenient bookmark for teachers since URLs do change frequently, and its also easy to make a mistake when typing in long URLs. A couple of major resources of value to educators are omitted from the book such as http://usgovsearch.northernlight.com, the Northern Light database that is free to school and public libraries. This commercial site that indexes government Web pages should probably be part of the appendix on finding government information. Another is the National Library of Education's "Gateway to Educational Materials," (http://thegateway.org), a government consortium project that indexes more than 7,000 lesson plans and teacher guides on the Internet. It is comparable to, but more extensive than, the "AskERIC Lesson Plans" site listed in the section for teachers. Librarians who serve children, parents, and teachers will want to consider adding this unique and inexpensive guide to government Internet resources to their collection.—**Deborah V. Rollins**

230. Miller, Elizabeth B. **The Internet Resource Directory for K-12 Teachers and Librarians.** 1999/2000 ed. Englewood, Colo., Libraries Unlimited, 1999. 438p. index. $27.50pa. ISBN 1-56308-812-6.

This is the 6th edition of this well-written, very popular, and extremely useful directory. This edition includes 55 more Websites than the previous edition, to bring the number of entries included up to 1,497, of which 400 are new (see ARBA 99, entry 307). There is still a free publisher's update Website, which is updated every month in order to maintain currency and accuracy of Website information and location. Entries remain selective and evaluative based upon several criteria, among which are their contribution to the K-12 curriculum, free or minimal expense, and designed with the educator in mind. Entries are arranged alphabetically by the name of the Website under the broad subject or curriculum area, and are assigned an entry number. Following the Website name are the URL and an annotation describing the Website's features and content. An introduction is also provided for each subject or curriculum area section.

This source continues to be used by librarians, teachers, and students as an aid in supplementing curriculums with up-to-date online information resources. Several changes are included in this edition. There is an addition of national and state standards for each curriculum area. The foreign languages chapter has been expanded and completely updated. Early childhood and special education have been added to the education chapter, and mathematics and computer sciences have been split into separate chapters. The social studies chapter has added more resources on immigration and twentieth-century U.S. history. The school library chapter has included more pages created by media specialists. There are two indexes, a Website index, and a subject index that refer to the entry number. This resource is highly recommended for school media centers, academic libraries (especially those with a teacher education program), and public libraries.

—Jan S. Squire

ELEMENTARY AND SECONDARY EDUCATION

231. **Funding Sources for K-12 Education 1999.** 2d ed. Phoenix, Ariz., Oryx Press, 1999. 710p. index. $34.50pa. ISBN 1-57356-198-3.

The introduction to this hefty volume states that it covers "more than 1,500 funding opportunities available in the United States and Canada, the directory includes all of the information necessary to help individuals and organizations secure funding by submitting grant proposals to the right people at the right time." This is a grand statement, but for both the novice and experienced grants writer, the directory delivers on its claim. The previous volume (see ARBA 99, entry 290) was named the Best New Directory by the Simba Awards for Excellence in Directory Publishing; the excellence has continued.

For those who are new to or perhaps heretofore unsuccessful in securing funding for their programs or projects, there are carefully executed directions for effective and efficient use, a user-friendly and convenient format, realistic examples, extensive entries, invaluable indexes, and time-saving Websites. A sample proposal and the "Guide to Proposal Planning and Writing" provide sound and practical guidance. Further, the introduction, written by a seasoned "resource developer," is insightful, dispelling grants writing as some kind of magic. Her advice is based upon real experience.

Anyone who is attempting to find the "right people" for their particular needs will appreciate the numerous indexes that make navigating this extensive resource exceptionally manageable. Included are a subject index, sponsoring organizations index, grants by program type index, and geographic index. Honestly, it is difficult to imagine what else the prospective "resource developer" might need other than perhaps successful experience.

Oryx's electronic GRANTS Database is suggested as an additional resource that is updated daily, and several other electronic resources are also indicated. Again, for those novice or experienced grants writers who are determined to seek and obtain funding for their school programs, this is an excellent resource.

—Karen D. Harvey

HIGHER EDUCATION

Biography

232. **Who's Who in International Business Education and Research.** William Shepherd, Iyanatul Islam, and Sankaran Raghunathan, eds. Northhampton, Mass., Edward Elgar, 1999. 461p. $200.00. ISBN 1-85898-290-1.

The editors of this book are professors of international business. They conducted a survey of 1,200 scholars engaged in international business education to find out who were the leaders in the field. The criteria for inclusion were research productivity, citational analyses, executive officers, fellows of the Academy of International Business, the management of U.S.-based centers for international business education and research, and peer-based nominations. The finalists numbered 159.

The entries for *Who's Who in International Business Education and Research* are in alphabetic order by their names. The information about each of the scholars includes addresses, telephone numbers, fax numbers, e-mail addresses, Web page addresses, current and past positions, degrees, offices, prizes, fellowships and honors, professional associations, memberships, editorial duties, and principal fields of interests and expertise. It also lists the languages spoken, publications, chapters and articles, and principal contribution to the field of international business education.

This *Who's Who* can be used as a directory for finding international business consultants as well as scholars in the corporate and university arenas. This work is recommended for corporate libraries whose companies are involved in international business, and for academic libraries affiliated with colleges of business. [R: Choice, Nov 99, p. 521]—**Kay M. Stebbins**

Directories

233. **Barron's Profiles of American Colleges.** 1999 ed. [CD-ROM]. Hauppauge, N.Y., Barron's Educational Series, 1998. Minimum system requirements (Windows): IBM or compatible 486. Double-speed CD-ROM drive. Windows 95. 16MB RAM. 640 x 480 display (with 256 colors). Soundblaster compatible sound card. Minimum system requirements (Macintosh): 68040 (Power PC recommended). Double-speed CD-ROM drive. System 7.1 or higher. 16MB RAM. 640 x 480 display (with 256 colors). $34.95. ISBN 0-7641-7273-5.

For the high school or continuing student, this product provides a quick and easy method of searching for institutions of higher education that meet personal requirements and expectations. A link to general information provides the user with an explanation of how to use the CD-ROM, frequently asked questions, and a list of abbreviations. This is followed by brief essays concerning finding the right college, how to score high and get into the college of choice, finding necessary financial aid, and surviving the freshman year. A separate essay details aspects of the degree of competition for entrance into colleges.

The user can also create a search profile, choosing location, major, cost, competitiveness, and enrollment size as limiting factors. Results retrieved match search parameters. Profiles for individual colleges are quite extensive, providing enrollment statistics, calendars, application deadlines, quality of life, housing, activities, sports, services for disabled students, campus safety and security, programs of study, admission requirements, financial aid packages, computing facilities, and various other categories of interest to prospective students. Locator maps provide the user with college location, and photographs and brief videos are provided for some 300 campuses. Affordable and easy to use, this handy guide should be in almost all reference collections, especially in high school and public libraries.—**Edmund F. SantaVicca**

234. **The Best Graduate Programs: Engineering.** 2d ed. By the Staff of the Princeton Review. New York, Princeton Review/Random House, 1998. 439p. index. $21.00pa. ISBN 0-375-75205-6.

This book, the only one bearing the seal of approval from the American Society for Engineering Education (ASEE), presents a detailed yet easy-to-read guide to graduate programs in engineering. The Princeton Review starts off with basic information on the status of engineering and engineering education, how to choose an engineering program, applying and getting in, and paying for school. Readers can learn about the hot engineering degrees and jobs of today, tips on getting through the application process, and how to negotiate financial aid.

The rest of the work is devoted to profiles of engineering programs found in the United States. Each profile includes standard data on the number of Ph.D. students, addresses of departments, application deadlines, and so on. However, unlike most program guides, this one does something unique by including what students currently enrolled in the programs really think of their studies, school, and area in which they live. This is where the reader can find out just how rural a school is; about crime, housing availability; and information on happiness and satisfaction of students with their programs. The combination of general information and student insight makes this book a welcome addition to any science and engineering library or career center.—**Kelly M. Jordan**

235. **Christian Colleges & Universities 1999.** Princeton, N.J., Peterson's Guides, 1998. 189p. illus. index. $14.95pa. ISBN 0-7689-0050-6. ISSN 1521-9070.

This edition continues the "official guide to campuses in the Coalition for Christian Colleges [and] Universities," first published in 1982 under the title *A Guide to Christian Colleges*. Later editions have been published by Peterson's Guides with variant titles (see ARBA 89, entry 285; ARBA 94, entry 334; ARBA 96, entry 1474). Schools that meet eight criteria for membership as enumerated in the "How to Use This Book" section are included (see also http://www.gospelcom.net/cccu). Short essays about the benefits of Christian higher education and ways of financing a college education introduce the book. For each of the 93 schools, including 3 Canadian, there is a 1-page profile alphabetic by name with data supplied by the institution. The profile includes information on enrollment, academic offerings, costs, athletic programs, admission procedures, international admissions, and financial aid. Lists serving as indexes include by state, by religious affiliation, majors by school, schools by major, athletics by sport, and graduate majors. Another list indicates by country the schools that offer study-abroad opportunities. The guide also gives brief descriptions of other special programs sponsored by the coalition, such as Chinese and Russian studies. This guide cannot be considered a comprehensive directory to denominationally affiliated schools. Depending on a library's clientele, this nominally priced guide may be appropriate for the college directory collection.
—**Margo B. Mead**

236. **College Blue Book.** 27th ed. New York, Macmillan Library Reference; distr., Farmington Hills, Mich., Gale, 1999. 5v. maps. index. $215.00/set. ISBN 0-02-865300-9. ISSN 1082-7064.

The *College Blue Book* has been a standard professional reference on higher education since it was first published in 1923. The work is now also available in a CD-ROM format. It provides comprehensive, up-to-date information on more than 18,000 colleges, universities, trade, technical and proprietary schools, state departments of education, and other sources throughout the United States and Canada. The 1999 edition includes descriptions and data from more than 3,000 4-year institutions, more than 2,000 sources of financial aid, a guide to some 7,500 institutions providing occupational education, and more than 4,500 subject areas in which degrees are offered. Each entry contains the name of the institution, address, essential telephone numbers and fax numbers, e-mail and Web addresses, a description of the institution, entrance requirements, tuition and fee costs, a description of the collegiate environment, and a description of the community environment. In addition, there are state and province maps showing the locations of the institutions. Separate indexes of U.S. and Canadian institutions are provided.

The *College Blue Book* is a well-established reference source for information on institutions of higher education. The information is obtained from responses to more than 18,000 questionnaires sent to the institutions. The editors point out in the introduction that "the information, especially in the areas of tuition, room and board, enrollments, and library holdings, is constantly changing [and because of this] it is difficult to maintain up-to-date figures in these areas, especially since our data is gathered early in the year of publication" (p. ix). Even with this caveat the *College Blue Book* is probably the most reliable reference source in this area. It is highly recommended for all academic libraries and for larger public libraries. It is a logical purchase for academic advising offices and other areas where counseling of students occurs as well.—**Robert L. Wick**

237. **Colleges that Encourage Character Development: A Resource for Parents, Students, and Educators.** Radnor, Pa., Templeton Foundation Press, 1999. 408p. illus. index. (The Templeton Guide Series). $16.95pa. ISBN 1-890151-28-9.

Individuals and institutions identified in this work were chosen by the John Templeton Foundation based on replies to a nomination packet sent to all 4-year accredited colleges and universities in the United States and to higher-education associations and centers that promote character development. In addition, the Institute on College Student Values at Florida State University conducted a search to identify strong programs for which the information packets were not returned. More than 1,000 institutions and 2,500 programs were reviewed.

The resulting guidebook is divided into 3 major sections: 405 exemplary programs listed in 10 categories, 50 presidents, and 100 colleges and universities that inspire students to lead ethical and civic-minded lives. The categories of exemplary programs are first-year programs, academic honesty programs, faculty and curriculum programs, volunteer service programs, substance-abuse prevention programs, student leadership programs, spiritual growth programs, civic education programs, character and sexuality programs, and senior year programs. The 50 men and women presidents profiled illustrate what a leader can do to establish priorities and programs to help prepare students to accept personal and civic responsibility. The 100 public and private profiled schools are listed alphabetically by category and by state. The book also contains a glossary and a resource directory of higher-education organizations.

Most, not all, states are represented by the 555 profiles of exemplary programs, presidents, and institutions. There are, doubtless, those who would disagree with the selections made, but deserving institutions not included in this edition could be included in a future edition. The Foundation encourages suggestions and input. Enough information is provided in this guidebook to assist parents, counselors, and students interested in character building with the process of selecting an appropriate institution of higher education.—**Lois Gilmer**

238. Custard, Edward T., Christine Chung, Tom Meltzer, and Eric Owens. **The Best 331 Colleges.** 2000 ed. New York, Princeton Review/Random House, 1999. 746p. index. $20.00pa. (with disc). ISBN 0-375-75411-3. ISSN 1093-9679.

The Princeton Review gives profiles of 331 colleges and universities in print format and also contains a CD-ROM with an additional 1,500 colleges and universities. Profiles include information provided by the institutions and by students who go there. The data are fresh and original, aiming to "provide a (relatively) uncensored view of life at the particular college, and acknowledge that even the best of the best of America's 3,600 or so colleges have their drawbacks." The Princeton Review prides itself on its approach: qualitative and anecdotal rather than quantitative and scientific. But they do allow colleges and universities to respond to their entries before they are printed. Each entry has a double-page spread with similar components: addresses; statistics; campus life; academics; admissions; financial facts; student voices; and interesting bits of information such as colleges they also applied to, popular majors, and pointed comments on life on campus. The front and back matter also offers interesting reading, including quotes from individual students and a rationale for the survey. This review is timely, lively, easy to read, and informative. High school counselors as well as parents and students will want to look at this when considering colleges and universities.—**Anne F. Roberts**

239. **Directory of American Scholars.** 9th ed. Rita C. Velázquez, ed. Farmington Hills, Mich., Gale, 1999. 5v. index. $495.00/set. ISBN 0-7876-3859-5. ISSN 0070-5101.

First published in 1942 by the American Council of Learned Societies, the *Directory of American Scholars* continues to be the foremost biographical reference to American humanities scholars. The 9th edition, published by the Gale Group, continues this tradition with more than 24,000 profiles of scholars in the United States and Canada. The directory is published in 4 subject volumes (e.g., vol. 1: History; vol. 2: English, Speech, and Drama; vol. 3: Foreign Languages, Linguistics, and Philology; and vol. 4: Philosophy, Religion, and Law). Volume 5 contains an alphabetic index, an index by discipline, an index by institution, and a cumulative geographic index.

The criterion for inclusion is carefully spelled out in the preface. To be included in the *Directory of American Scholars* an individual must show achievement "by reason of experience and training, of a stature in scholarly work equivalent to that associated with the doctoral degree coupled with current activity in such work, or achievement by publication of scholarly works" (p.vii).

Each entry contains the name of the scholar, personal information including marital status and children, educational attainment, career positions, a list of research topics currently being studied, and a selected list of publications. Also, the current address and e-mail address for each individual are listed. The volumes are easy to use and the indexes provide convenient access. This work is highly recommended for all academic and larger public libraries. [R: LJ, 1 Nov 99, p. 74]—**Robert L. Wick**

240. **Graduate Study in Psychology 1998-1999.** 32d ed. Washington, D.C., American Psychological Association, 1998. 545p. index. $21.95pa. ISBN 1-55798-589-8. ISSN 0742-7220.

Anyone planning graduate study in psychology will want to check out this essential directory. Covering 500 departments and schools in the United States offering programs in psychology, this directory lists admission requirements, tuition, financial assistance, goals, enrollment, and degrees awarded. Programs can also include interesting features that might be attractive to candidates, such as objectives of the department, women-oriented courses, special facilities, internships, and even physical disabilities information. In many cases, e-mail and Website addresses are given. Another nice feature is the subject directory where programs are categorized by fields, such as child development, aging, behavior therapy, and so on. The directory is made up-to-date with a 1999 addendum. This is a sensible purchase for any library seeking graduate school information.—**Carol D. Henry**

241. **Higher Education Directory, 1999.** Mary Pat Rodenhouse and Constance Healy Torregrosa, eds. Falls Church, Va., Higher Education, 1998. 660p. index. $53.00pa. ISBN 0-914927-28-0. ISSN 0736-0797.

This directory lists postsecondary, degree-granting institutions in the U.S. and its outlying areas that are accredited by bodies recognized by the U.S. Secretary of Education and the now dissolved Council of Postsecondary Education (COPA)/Commission on Recognition of Postsecondary Accreditation (CORPA). The Council for Higher Education (CHEA) accreditation recognition policies and procedures will be used for future editions when they are fully developed.

Addresses and other methods for contacting the institutions, some institutional history, enrollment, Carnegie class, accreditation, and other information are provided through short, uniform descriptions of large and small, public and proprietary institutions arranged in alphabetic order by state. Included also are names of key administrative officers. A detailed index provides the sections of the pages, the page numbers, and the telephone numbers for key administrators. Another index, arranged alphabetically by acronym of accrediting bodies, lists institutions accredited by regional, national, professional, and specialized agencies. A third index lists institutions by name. Although this commercially published work claims to have served as the "official" directory of higher education institutions since 1982, when the U.S. Department of Education ceased publishing their directory, there are other, similar directories available.—**Lois Gilmer**

Financial Aid

242. Bauer, David G. **The Teacher's Guide to Winning Grants.** San Francisco, Calif., Jossey-Bass, 1999. 150p. $24.95pa. ISBN 0-7879-4493-9.

Although written for educators, *The Teacher's Guide to Winning Grants* lays out an excellent game plan for anyone seeking grant money. Bauer is a former teacher who turned his successful gift for writing grants into a 20-year career as a consultant and public speaker. He demystifies the grant process, taking the reader through the process step–by–step. Chapters cover writing an effective needs statement, researching the potential founders, making the first contacts, developing objectives, and writing government or corporate proposals. Submitting a federal grant application and dealing with the final outcome are also included. Sample letters and worksheets illustrate his ideas and provide models for beginners. Keywords and terminology are suggested to help in the writing of the grant. *The Teacher's Guide to Winning Grants* will help grant seekers with the steps they must follow for successful grant writing. This will be a good purchase for any school or library looking for grant advice.—**Carol D. Henry**

243. Schlachter, Gail Ann. **How to Find Out About Financial Aid and Funding: A Guide to Print, Electronic, and Internet Resources Listing Scholarships, Fellowships.** San Carlos, Calif., Reference Service Press, 1999. 439p. index. $37.50. ISBN 0-918276-75-6.

This volume is a new and improved edition of a 1987 Reference Service Press guide to financial aid resources. In the dozen years since the original guide was published, there have been numerous changes in the areas of financial aid and funding. Today, for instance, there are more publicly funded loans and fewer publicly funded scholarships, more grant-making institutions, and more opportunities for funded internships. This bibliographic guide provides a listing, assessment, and ordering information for some 750 financial aid publications. Each of the reviewed publications directs readers to the sources that award some $100 billion in scholarships, fellowships, loans, grants, and internships every year.

In 1987 few of the publications about financial aid resources were available in digital format. In this volume, however, about 40 percent of the listed sources are available in electronic form or on the Internet. Internet addresses are provided for these items. The titles described in the present volume include those publications that have been issued or updated between 1994 and February 1999. Recognizing the rapid changes in these source materials, Reference Service Press plans to update this volume with a new edition every two years.

The publications listed in this bibliographic guide are presented in six chapters: "Scholarships," "Fellowships & Loans," "Grants for Individuals," "Grants for Organizations," "Awards and Prizes," "Internships," and "Federal Government Bookmarks." The items within each chapter are conveniently arranged by discipline (i.e., social sciences, humanities), geographical region, and intended audience (i.e., ethnic groups, women). Also included are five indexes that offer access to the entries by title, author, and publisher as well as geographical coverage and subject focus. Reference librarians, financial officers, career counselors, researchers, and parents of college students will find this informative volume to be well worth its moderate price.—**Terry D. Bilhartz**

244. Schlachter, Gail Ann, and R. David Weber. **College Student's Guide to Merit and Other No-Need Funding 1998-2000.** San Carlos, Calif., Reference Service Press, 1998. 470p. index. $32.00. ISBN 0-918276-62-4.

This is a directory that will be an excellent resource for both prospective college students and those who will most likely be paying for this college education, their parents. Listed are nearly 1,600 sources for college financial aid. The types of sources in the volume include scholarships, forgivable loans, and research grants. According to the introduction, numerous examples are given on how the authors have conducted a thorough revision from the previous edition.

The vast majority of the entries reflect the types of sources described in the book's title—financial aid that does not require repayment. These entries are arranged alphabetically within general areas—humanities, sciences, and social sciences. Within each entry is a surprising amount of information for the user. Each entry can include the following information in addition to the name of the awarding organization and the organization's address: purpose of the financial aid, eligibility requirements, duration of an award, special features (variables unique to the award), limitations, the number awarded, and the application deadline. The authors present this large amount of information in succinctly worded and clearly formatted entries.

Additionally, there is a short section titled "State Sources of Information on Educational Benefits" that lists state financial aid programs, including guaranteed student loan programs. Following the "State Sources" section is an annotated bibliography titled the "Financial Aid Library," which lists additional directories of financial aid. One addition is the inclusion of Websites, making this a directory providing both paper and electronic sources. Finally, there are numerous indexes to access the book. Besides the usual subject and program title indexes, there are indexes listing those awards requiring fulfillment of residency and tenability stipulations. Also, a most unique, but perhaps helpful index is that which is called a calendar index, which lists the months when each letter of application must be submitted.—**Phillip P. Powell**

245. Schlachter, Gail Ann, and R. David Weber. **Financial Aid for Research and Creative Activities Abroad, 1999-2001.** San Carlos, Calif., Reference Service Press, 1999. 484p. index. $45.00. ISBN 0-918276-63-2. ISSN 1072-530X.

Intended for Americans seeking financing for travel, study, or research abroad, this source lists more than 1,300 entries, arranged by level of study (e.g., high school/undergraduate, graduate, postdoctorate, professionals and other individuals). Many of the entries are duplicated because they are listed repeatedly in more than one level. Each annotated entry includes the following information: title, contact information (with e-mail, Web address, and fax if available), purpose, eligibility, financial data, duration, special features, limitations, number of awards available, and deadlines. Because some of the awards listed are very specific, such as the James A. Swan fund intended for research of the Batwa peoples of Africa, the subject index is essential. A future enhancement could be an electronic file (CD-ROM or diskette) to facilitate searching. A selective annotated bibliography lists some 50 entries leading users to other potential resources. With its international focus, this resource is unique enough to warrant purchase by libraries that are in need of this type of information. It is worth updating if you have an earlier edition as well. *The Annual Register of Grant Support* (32d ed.; Gale, 1998) and *Grants Register* (see entry 258) provide more costly but better coverage of U.S. and international nonrepayable financial support.—**Christine Drew**

246. Schlachter, Gail Ann, and R. David Weber. **Financial Aid for Study and Training Abroad 1999-2001.** San Carlos, Calif., Reference Service Press, 1999. 372p. index. $39.50. ISBN 0-918276-64-0.

This directory is a response to the National Security Act of 1991 and other programs that emphasize the importance of foreign language study and undergraduate scholarships for study abroad. Included in the information provided for both structured and independent study are eligibility requirements, financial data, duration of the funding, special features and limitations, number of awards given, and application date. While other financial aid directories exist, this one is recommended for current and comprehensive coverage of more than 1,000 programs.

A currency conversion table identifies currency used in key countries covered by this directory and is to be used as a guide to the approximate value of the support offered. Additional assistance is provided by an annotated bibliography of general financial aids such as scholarships, fellowships, loans, grants, internships, awards and prizes, and financial assistance to special population groups.

Programs are identified and listed in 5 separate indexes: program titles, sponsoring organizations, geographic, subject, and calendar (deadline dates). The calendar index is divided into 4 major sections (the 4 categories addressed by this work), high school and undergraduate students, graduate students, postdoctorates, and professionals and other individuals. Other sections also indicate level of study covered.

—**Lois Gilmer**

247. Schlachter, Gail Ann, and R. David Weber. **Financial Aid for Veterans, Military Personnel, and Their Dependents 1998-2000.** San Carlos, Calif., Reference Service Press, 1998. 332p. index. $40.00. ISBN 0-918276-66-7. ISSN 0896-7792.

According to the information presented in the introduction to this book, more than one-third of the U.S. population today has either direct or indirect ties with the armed services and billions of dollars a year have now been set aside for financial aid to these veterans, military personnel, and their dependents. Obviously there is a need for a comprehensive and user-friendly resource to enable those qualified for these funds to locate and access them. This directory is designed to meet that need and does so in a way that is indeed both convenient and sufficient for most users. It provides the right information, complete and accurate (to the degree that is possible in such a rapidly changing environment). To meet the challenge of escalating change, an online source is listed for updates and new information.

A clear explanation of how to use the directory and a sample entry are given. The directory is divided into 4 major sections: financial aid programs for veterans, military personnel, and their dependents (scholarships, fellowships/grants, loans, grants-in-aid, and awards); state sources of information on benefits; annotated bibliography of financial aid directories; and indexes. The indexes are worth noting. They are intuitive and greatly increase the convenience of the directory. Included are a program title index, a sponsoring organization index, a residency index, a tenability index, a subject index, and a calendar index.

It seems as though this particular resource would be exceptionally useful for high school counselors and college advisors in schools where there is a high proportion of students searching for financial aid. It provides information on sources that are not as widely known as others and, of course, if it does not provide desired information, the directory provides an annotated bibliography of financial aid directories.

—**Karen D. Harvey**

248. Schlachter, Gail Ann, and R. David Weber. **Money for Graduate Students in the Humanities 1998-2000.** 2d ed. San Carlos, Calif., Reference Service Press, 1998. 332p. index. $40.00. ISBN 0-918276-68-3.

Graduate study can be an expensive proposition, forcing many prospective students to seek funding to pay for or defray costs. This directory aids that effort by identifying scholarships, grants, loans, and awards for graduate study, training, research, or creative activities in the humanities, including such disciplines as art, architecture, music, filmmaking, journalism, dance, creative writing, religion, and philosophy. More than 900 funding sources are described, with the only requirements for inclusion being that they must target humanities graduate students and have a minimum funding level of $750.

The funding source descriptions are arranged alphabetically in 2 major sections: study and training (619 entries), and research and creative activities (305 entries). For each source there are an address, telephone number, and e-mail and Website addresses (if available), as well as descriptive categories for the purpose, eligibility, financial data, duration, limitations, number awarded, special features, and deadline. Limitations on the funding may include such factors as the applicant's group affiliation, the residency of the applicant, the field of study, and a geographic limit on where the funds may be spent. Some of these variables, as well as the subject, sponsoring organization, and program title, comprise the six indexes provided to aid in locating the most appropriate funding sources. Also included are lists of state financial aid offices and student loan programs as well as an annotated list of useful financial aid reference books.

This book's strengths are its extensive number of entries, its detailed descriptions of the grants and loans, and its thorough indexing. The fact that it is updated biennially ensures that it will remain reasonably current. It compares more than favorably with similar directories, and also has a companion volume for the social sciences (see entry 249). This should be invaluable for college and university libraries.

—**Stephen H. Aby**

249. Schlachter, Gail Ann, and R. David Weber. **Money for Graduate Students in the Social Sciences 1998-2000.** 2d ed. San Carlos, Calif., Reference Service Press, 1998. 364p. index. $42.50. ISBN 0-918276-70-5.

Schlachter and Weber report that 70 percent of the programs included in this book had substantive changes since the 1st edition. Additionally, some 200 new entries have been provided for a total of 1,032 entries. The 1st edition was well received in published reviews, and the 2d edition with the upgrades continues to be a highly useful tool. Students will find information on fellowships, grants, awards, loans, and forgivable loans. Areas covered include graduate study, training, and research as well as creative activities. Only "portable programs" are included (those that can be used at "any number of schools," with institution-based funding options specifically excluded). Programs for use in the United States are considered, with opportunities for noncitizens and nonresidents left uncovered.

No secondary sources were used to gather the data. Up to four letters and three follow-up calls were placed, with nonrespondents not presented in the compilation. There are four sections to the volume: funding opportunities, state sources, bibliographic resources, and indexes. The funding portion is divided into two categories, namely "Study and Teaching" and "Research and Creative Activities." Within each entry the following information is included: name, address, telephone and fax numbers, e-mail address, purpose, eligibility, financial data, duration, limitations, number awarded, and deadline. These categories seem to be the ones of immediate need to prospective applicants. The text is simply presented with just enough information to clarify a particular funding option without providing unnecessary detail.

The "State Sources" section lists the state financial aids and student loan programs for each state. Some 400 directories for financial aid and funding programs have been published in the past 10 years. The authors selected 40 for inclusion in their "Financial Aid Bookshelf." Indexing for the volume is available for the following categories: program title, sponsoring organization, residency, tenability, subject, and calendar.

This title provides a simple, easy-to-use format giving the prospective graduate student in the social sciences many options to pursue. Without the financial means to study, many a career would be halted. Schlachter and Weber have performed a valuable service and generated a product that will be well placed in academic as well as public libraries. This resource is highly recommended.—**Graham R. Walden**

250. **Scholarships, Fellowships, and Loans 1999: A Guide to Education-Related Financial Aid Programs for Students and Professionals.** 14th ed. Valerie J. Webster, ed. Farmington Hills, Mich., Gale, 1999. 1142p. index. $231.00. ISBN 0-7876-2647-3. ISSN 1058-5699.

Sources of financial aid for secondary, higher, and continuing education are increasingly important as the need for and costs of learning escalate. This comprehensive print directory is invaluable to discover education-related financial aid available. Covering 4,100 awards for formal and nonformal programs of study, this directory addresses high school education through undergraduate education and professional development opportunities.

Both need- and merit-based awards are listed from institutional, private, and governmental sources. Some are broad in scope, others very narrowly focused. Awards administered and funded by individual colleges and universities are not included since the most current information is available there. The main section of the directory details essential information and is accessed by six expansive indexes that enable the user to target special interests, needs, and criteria.

The main directory, arranged by awarding organization, describes each award program offered, with its purpose, required qualifications, available funding, and application and deadline information. One index offers a vocational goals access by the level of study (i.e., graduate, postgraduate) sub-arranged by the field of study (i.e., mathematics, life sciences). Another provides all awards under each field of study. Others list required state of legal residence, where required, and the place of study sought. Another designates awards targeting special qualifications such as ethnicity, religion, and association. This directory provides prospective students, parents, academic advisors, libraries, and career counselors an opening wedge to offer information and hope for individuals who require financial assistance for their education. [R: BL, July 98, p. 1903]—**Barbara Conroy**

251. Vuturo, Christopher. **The Scholarship Advisor: Hundreds of Thousands of Scholarships Worth More Than $1 Billion.** 1999 ed. New York, Princeton Review/Random House, 1998. 835p. $23.00pa. ISBN 0-375-75207-2.

The promotion on the cover of this Princeton Review paperback proclaims that Chris Vuturo, "the student who won $885,000 in scholarships," has produced a scholarship advice book that is "your complete guide to the application process." In addition to listing "hundreds of thousands of scholarships worth more than $1 billion," the guide includes "sample essays and interview tips that will make you an undeniable candidate" for one of the "countless awards that consider more than just grades." According to the *Boston Post-Gazette* blurb that is splashed on both the front and back covers, "you must—I repeat MUST—get this book. It may be the best money you ever spent."

Buyers should be aware, however, that the promotion promises more than it delivers. This 835-page, $8\frac{1}{2}$-by-11-inch volume does include 62 pages of chatty advice, a portion of which some students may find entertaining and useful. These words of wisdom are followed by a brief description and contact address for 4,658 alphabetically listed awards. The numbers and names for the awards can be accessed by using one of the indexes that sort the scholarships into the following categories: Majors/Academic Interests, Career Interests, Hobbies/Leisure Activities, Work Experience, GPA, Athletics, Minority Students, Ethnic Background,

Religious Affiliation, Disabilities, Gender-Based, Military Service, Residence, and Colleges. Unfortunately, there is no index that allows incoming freshmen, upperclassmen, and graduate students to search quickly for those awards that are available for their classification only. Moreover, the information provided about each award (i.e., award type, amount and number of awards given, minimum qualifications, deadlines) is too brief to be of great value. Notwithstanding the promotion's claim that "no other scholarship book is as easy to use," this Princeton Review publication is more hype than help.—**Terry D. Bilhartz**

Handbooks and Yearbooks

252. **The College Board College Costs & Financial Aid Handbook 2000.** 20th ed. College Board, New York; distr., New York, Henry Holt, 1999. 709p. index. $21.95pa. ISBN 0-87447-628-3.

Next to buying a home, the money paid toward college costs may well be the largest investment people ever make in their lifetime. Anyone who has ever financed a college education, or is hoping to do so, recognizes this challenge with trepidation. Not only is the cost of higher education daunting, but the search for financial assistance is difficult and confusing. This reference is designed to organize and make readily available the information that is needed to make informed decisions about this major investment.

This volume is organized into three major sections: using the book effectively and detailed information about financial aid, college descriptions, and college indexes. Because the information is complicated, it is critical that the first part is reader-friendly and comprehensive. As the authors point out, to improve chances of getting help, readers must know what they have to do, when they have to do it, and how to do it right—the first time. The handbook helps readers understand what constitutes the cost of attending college (much more than just tuition), the language and acronyms, the complexity of standard forms, the variety of funding opportunities, and the unique features of various federal programs and individual colleges. The tables and worksheets, a glossary, and an explanation of the information included in the college descriptions are most helpful.

The comprehensive college descriptions (community, state, private, and proprietary) are listed by state and include detailed cost facts—tuition and fees, out-of-district/state tuition, room and board figures (as well as costs for dependent students living at home), books and supplies, and estimates of personal expenses.

These two sections are well-researched by the College Board, as realistic and accurate as possible, and, so importantly, written in a way that makes complex and often confusing information quite understandable. As a reference for high school and college counselors, it is invaluable. Further, the cost is reasonable for determined individuals and their families. Finally, the indexes include listings for academic scholarships, art scholarships, music/drama scholarships, ROTC scholarships, and athletic scholarships, as well as an alphabetic list of all colleges profiled.—**Karen D. Harvey**

253. **The College Board College Handbook 2000.** 37th ed. New York, Henry Holt, 1999. 1882p. index. $25.95pa. (with disc). ISBN 0-87447-625-9.

The current edition of this college guide provides detailed information for more than 3,200 institutions of higher learning. Four-year and two-year colleges are grouped in separate sections alphabetically by state. Background information is provided about each school, along with facts about variables such as basis for sections, high school preparation, 1999–2000 annual costs, financial aid, application procedures, academics, majors (including most popular majors), computing on campus, student life, athletics, and student services. Contact information is often provided in the form of the address of a specific campus administrator, phone and fax numbers, and e-mail addresses. The book's consistency in format facilitates access to information and makes for easy comparative analyses of institutions.

A variety of indexes—college types, colleges with special characteristics, undergraduate enrollment size, admission selectivity, admission and placement policies, student life, NCAA sports, and ROTC—make the book user-friendly. There is useful generic information provided in "Guidance at a Glance" tabs. This includes a guide to using the *College Explorer* CD-ROM enclosed with this book that contains video clips and links to college Websites and College Board Online. This is a thoroughly documented and well-organized guide that would surely help college-bound individuals or those trying to assist them.—**G. Douglas Meyers**

254. **The College Board Scholarship Handbook 2000.** 3d ed. New York, Henry Holt, 1999. 590p. index. $24.95pa. (with disc). ISBN 0-87447-627-5.

The College Board Scholarship Handbook has information for more than 2,000 undergraduate scholarships, internships, and loan programs. It is designed to direct users toward specific award programs that match the user's personal and academic qualifications. The introductory pages include useful information on the components of the cost of attending college and some ground rules for college planning. Awards are listed in the eligibility indexes according to corporate and employer sponsors, disabilities, fields of study, gender, military participation, national and ethnic background, organization and civic affiliation, religious affiliation, returning adult, state of residence, and study abroad. Additionally, there are indexes that list award programs by internships, loans, sponsor name, and program name. Not included are local awards programs or programs offered by colleges themselves. A personal characteristics checklist is included to aid the user in determining eligibility in various categories. Accompanying the volume is a CD-ROM that quickly matches awards based on the user's eligibility.

The main part of the volume contains the program descriptions in alphabetic order. Included in each entry is the type of award (public or private scholarship, internship, or loan), eligibility requirements, application requirements, amount of award, number of awards given, deadline, and contact information including a URL. Although there is no mention of how the information for this title is gathered or how often it is updated, students and parents will nonetheless find it valuable as they seek funding to pay for college.

—**Michele Russo**

255. **Commonwealth Universities Yearbook 1999: A Directory to the Universities of the Commonwealth and the Handbook of their Association.** 74th ed. London, Association of Commonwealth Universities; distr., New York, Grove's Dictionaries, 1999. 2v. index. $265.00pa./set. ISBN 0-85143-164-X. ISSN 0069-7745.

This standard annual was reviewed in ARBA on several occasions and, indeed, it is the most useful source about the universities of the British Commonwealth of Nations. The present edition notes more than 150,000 senior personnel and 25,000 academic departments. About 480 universities and other institutions are covered in this useful publication.—**Bohdan S. Wynar**

256. Gilbert, Nedda. **The Best 80 Business Schools.** 2000 ed. New York, Princeton Review/Random House, 1999. 318p. index. $20.00pa. (with disc). ISBN 0-375-75463-6. ISSN 1067-2141.

Readers do not expect a reference book about business schools to be extraordinarily informative and relevant but also interesting, engaging, and even a little humorous now and then. The organization of the book, topics addressed, information presented, and style of writing answer the real-world needs of adults who are hoping to make a sound personal and career decision. For those who recognize the importance of the decision they are making, it is undoubtedly frustrating to find sound advice. As graduate students, these are people who are without high school guidance counselors and probably without unbiased and comprehensive advice.

This reference is based upon data collected from 18,500 students, hundreds of admissions officers, dozens of recruiters, and business school graduates. While reporting many critical statistics such as demographic information on students and faculty, other more subjective opinions that are important in the selection process are provided; for example, the opinions of students on topics such as academics, pressure, social life and fellow students, facilities, and placement and recruiting.

For those determined to seek admission to one of these top 80 business schools, there is a wealth of useful information. Common essay questions; case examples of admissions officers from Dartmouth, Harvard, Stanford, and other prestigious institutions who critique winning essays; and 15 surefire ways to torpedo your application are included.

This type of reference usually provides correct information, if you are willing to dig for it, but it is often data without the richness that allows individuals to examine their own lifestyles, needs, and professional goals to make sound, informed, personal and educational decisions. Surely it is important to know faculty-to-student ratios and average starting salary of graduates, but readers might also like to know pertinent information on student life. For those who want guidance and support for selecting and being admitted to a recognized business school, this book is likely to be fascinating and helpful reading. Once the decision has been made (or as part of the decision process), there is also a CD-ROM that contains 59 MBA and 63 LAW program applications.—**Karen D. Harvey**

257. **Graduate School: The Best Resources To Help You Choose, Get In, & Pay.** Jane Finkle, ed. Issaquah, Wash., Resource Pathways, 1998. 271p. index. (Higher Education & Careers Series). $24.95pa. ISBN 0-9653424-7-6.

This Resource Pathways guidebook is written like a bibliographic essay, focusing on the challenges of pursuing an advanced degree. It contains reviews of more than 170 resources chosen to help prospective students understand the factors involved in pursuing an advanced degree and learn how to evaluate programs as well as identify opportunities unique to minority and handicapped individuals. Practical advice is also presented on how to obtain financial aid and how to create winning applications. Recommendations are based on all available resources—books, CD-ROMs, and Websites.

This paperback book, part of the Higher Education & Careers Series, is reasonably priced. It is divided into 7 sections. The introduction seeks to explain why such a guidebook is needed and why and how Resource Pathways chose to publish it. Most helpful is an explanation regarding the organization of the book. Sections 2 through 4 contain short reviews of resources on the following topics: "Graduate School: The Best Resources To Help You Choose, Get In, and Pay"; "The Single Best Resource for Selected Graduate and Professional School Topics"; and "Resources of Interest to Specific Groups."

Section 5, longer than all of the other sections combined, is the heart of the book. It contains full-page reviews of all resources recommended for the publication. The reviews are arranged by subjects and within subjects. Most are ranked from 1 to 4. Recommended resources, from a great range of publishers, cover the following topics: obtaining a Master's degree or Ph.D.; choosing, applying to, and excelling in such different schools as business, medicine, and law; financing graduate or professional school; scholarship directories and search services; and resources of general interest.

The book concludes with five indexes and two appendixes. Access points in the indexes are title, author, publisher, media, and subject. The subject index is in rank order. The appendixes contain additional information about Resource Pathways and about the editor of this particular guidebook.

The guidebook should be helpful to anyone contemplating graduate school. The unvarnished truth about what is involved in advanced study could discourage some, but at the same time, others may have their fears of the unknown alleviated by this work and by the resources it reviews.—**Lois Gilmer**

258. **The Grants Register 2000.** 18th ed. Sara Hackwood, ed. New York, St. Martin's Press, 1999. 982p. index. $125.00. ISBN 0-312-22520-2. ISSN 0072-5471.

Higher education, even at state-supported institutions, is expensive, and the deferred income and costs involved in pursuing postgraduate study are even more daunting. The reality in today's higher-education market is that students' ability to pay educational expenses may limit their opportunities to pursue advanced study. Students' options are either to go into massive, long-term debt, to continue working and delay completion of their education, or to seek grants and fellowships. Fortunately, many sources of funding exist, and directories like this one help students identify the most appropriate sources. This volume lists over 3,500 awards for postgraduate funding in most disciplines and in over 80 countries. Covered are such activities as graduate study, postdoctoral work, professional development, and research.

The directory's arrangement is straightforward. The largest section is the grants register, an alphabetic listing of granting organizations, accompanied by addresses, phone numbers, fax numbers, contact names, e-mail addresses, and Web addresses. For each organization there is descriptive information on each of its grants arranged alphabetically by title. This information includes the broad subject of the grant, eligibility requirements, level of study supported, type of grant, number of awards offered, frequency of the awards, value of the awards, country of study, application procedure, closing dates, and additional information. Further access to these entries is provided by a subject index that lists grants hierarchically according to their subject, country of study, and name of grant (with page reference). There is also an index of discontinued awards, as well as an alphabetic list of granting organizations.

This directory's strengths are its straightforward arrangement, multidisciplinary coverage, and regular publication schedule. However, libraries should also carry grant and scholarship directories for students of other levels and group affiliation (e.g., women, minorities). That said, this should be considered part of a core collection of grant directories.—**Stephen H. Aby**

259. **International Handbook of Universities.** 15th ed. By the International Association of Universities. New York, Grove's Dictionaries, 1998. 2474p. index. $245.00. ISBN 1-56159-222-6.

This standard source for about 6,000 universities is prepared by the International Association of Universities and the UNESCO Information Center on Higher Education is published in the United States and Canada by Grove's Dictionaries. Entries are selected on the basis of their inclusion in *The World List of Universities and Other Institutions of Higher Education*, which in turn are provided by appropriate institutions of higher education in a given country. The individual entries within each country provide the name of each institution (first in English), followed by the name of the national language, administrative structure, academic year, admission requirements, fees, degrees and information about library facilities, publications, and other similar matters. In most cases information about academic staff and student enrollment is also provided. The *International Handbook of Universities* is one of the most useful sources on this subject.

—**Bohdan S. Wynar**

260. **The Princeton Review African American Student's Guide to College.** 1999 ed. By Marisa Parham, with Manie Barron. New York, Princeton Review/Random House, 1998. 250p. index. $17.95pa. ISBN 0-679-77878-0.

This specialized source is divided into four parts emphasizing African American students' approach to college: getting in, staying in, resource guide, and college profiles. The getting-in part offers advice from choosing a school based on personal factors, to the admissions process, to the cost involved, along with suggestions for acquiring financial aid. A two-year plan, describing what should be done when, is outlined in considerable detail. In addition, marginal notes are provided as reminders throughout the chapters. Worksheets complete the chapters.

Almost as much attention is devoted to staying in as to getting in. The makeup of the chapters is the same as for the 1st section. The staying-in section contains such topics as learning to live with roommates, choosing classes, and working with advisors. Staying on top of academics and staying healthy are emphasized. The resource guide by its nature deviates from the format of the two previous sections. It contains sample letters to be used in applying for admissions and scholarships, contact information in relation to the ACT and SAT and College Board offices, and suggested readings. By far the largest part of the guide is the college profiles section. It is an alphabetic listing of 150 predominantly black institutions and other U.S. institutions that offer programs in African studies. All states are not represented, while some are represented many times. Each college or university profile consists of one page. In addition to contact information, admissions procedures, and financial aid advice, there are statistical descriptions of the student body, faculty-to-student ratio, admissions ratings, most popular majors, and financial information relating to tuition and room and board.

Any college-bound student could benefit from the sound, practical advice provided in this guide. For the African American student interested in African studies or environments that enhance the African American experience, however, the guide is indispensable.—**Lois Gilmer**

261. **The Princeton Review Student Athlete's Guide to College.** By Hilary S. Abramson. New York, Princeton Review/Random House, 1999. 227p. illus. $12.00pa. ISBN 0-375-75426-1.

If one is good enough at sports to play at the intercollegiate level and one's grades are acceptable, then it is possible to win a scholarship or other grant-in-aid worth many thousands of dollars. Drawing upon the author's own experience as a student-athlete and having worked for a company that prepares students for college-admission tests, Abramson offers students help with writing letters of application and résumés (including sample letters), gives information on the complicated eligibility rules enforced by regulatory bodies, and demonstrates techniques for scoring well on entrance tests such as the SAT. In addition to this essential information, Abramson gives useful advice on how to attract attention from college coaches, how to evaluate institutions and athletic programs, and the like. The book also provides some vignettes of college coaches and a number of drawings.

Abramson's writing is straightforward and effective in conveying its points. The arrangement of material makes it easy to work through it; thus the lack of an index is no great loss. And, commendably, the coverage in this book is thoroughly nonsexist, being directed as much to women as to men.

There are a few deficiencies. Some of the text, which is printed on a dark background intended for color contrast, is so dim as to make for uncomfortable reading. The author does not shrink from touting the publications of her former employer (The Princeton Review). And one suspects that coaches and college officials may get weary of receiving many identical copies of those form letters. Otherwise this book serves its purposes very well.—**Samuel Rothstein**

INTERNATIONAL EXCHANGE PROGRAMS AND OPPORTUNITIES

262. **Academic Year Abroad 1999/2000: The Most Complete Guide to Planning Academic Year Study Abroad.** Sara J. Steen, ed. New York, Institute of International Education, 1999. 716p. illus. index. $44.95pa. ISBN 0-87206-247-3.

A detailed table of contents and indexes by field of study, consortia, and sponsoring institutions make this comprehensive volume easy to use. This well-organized directory is a thorough guide to options for international study at the postsecondary level. Programs included here are designed for completion within the September to June time frame and are at least 8 to 10 weeks in length. Each of the 2,694 entries includes information on program site, dates, eligibility, sponsoring agency, contacts, deadlines, subjects, and languages and form of instruction. Entries are grouped by geographic region, such as Western Europe, and then by country.—**Ahmad Gamaluddin**

263. **International Exchange Locator: A Resource Directory for Educational and Cultural Exchange.** 1998 ed. New York, Institute of International Education, 1998. 249p. index. $11.95pa. ISBN 0-87206-244-9.

The Alliance for International Education and Cultural Exchange is a nonprofit association of organizations comprising the international exchange community in the United States. Its mission is to formulate and promote public policy that supports the growth and well-being of international exchange between the people of the United States and other nations and to provide information on such exchanges. The locator provides a comprehensive and accessible inventory of government agents and private organizations involved in international education and cultural exchange. This book provides the most extensive collection of information on international exchange programs available. The book lists the Alliance member organizations and an extensive index dividing organizations into those involved in international exchange, industry-specific exchanges, research/support organizations, foreign affair agency and exchange programs, other federal government exchanges, and key congressional committees and members of Congress involved in international activities.

The paperback book is printed on average paper, sufficient in size, and has an average binding. The work should be useful to anyone interested in obtaining information about exchanges on a global, national, or individual basis and also to those interested in international relationships between various areas of the world. The book should be in all public and university libraries where students are looking for exchange opportunities.—**Herbert W. Ockerman**

264. **Media Courses UK 1999.** 6th ed. Lavinia Orton, ed. London, British Film Institute; distr., Bloomington, Ind., Indiana University Press, 1998. 262p. index. $15.95pa. ISBN 0-85170-683-5.

The modern sobriquet of media covers a wide range of subjects today, including film, television, radio, journalism, graphic design, animation, and multimedia. As the presence of media has become an ever-increasing part of our everyday lives, more and more schools and universities have started offering courses to prepare people for careers in this area. *Media Courses UK 1999*, now in its 6th edition, offers itself as a guide to courses currently available in the United Kingdom.

The lists are broken into four groups: undergraduate courses; postgraduate course; short courses; and "Courses in Further Education," which consist of primarily vocational programs. Each entry identifies the school, its address, a contact person, and a telephone number. Programs are identified by type, with the degree type listed before the program title, which makes the directory a little hard to read. Most entries offer a short overview of the program's curriculum and identify the percentage of the curriculum that is focused on practical experience. The appendix contains an index for school name, location, and subject specialties.
—**Steven J. Schmidt**

265. **Peterson's Summer Study Abroad 1999: The Complete Guide to More Than 1,400 Summer Academic and Language Programs.** Princeton, N.J., Peterson's Guides, 1999. 614p. illus. index. $29.95pa. ISBN 0-7689-0152-9.

Basic information on more than 1,400 summer academic and language programs is given in this comprehensive guide to study programs held in countries around the world, from Argentina to Zimbabwe. Entries for each program are arranged under country, then by the city they are located in or where they mainly take place. Finally, they are alphabetically listed under the program or the sponsor's name. Each program description describes the academic focus; student profile; living arrangements or accommodations; and gives information on eligibility requirements, onsite student support, and costs. Other information includes the program's founding date, background and history, credits given, class sizes, and methods of instruction. Addresses and Websites where further information can be obtained are provided. A separate chapter describes multicountry programs. Direct access to each program's entry is provided by four indexes: fields of study, program sponsors, host institutions, and internship programs. Helpful, well-written introductory chapters give realistic and common sense information and recommendations on the essentials of travel abroad, getting around on a budget, choosing the right country and program for personal satisfaction, and health and safety precautions. Other chapters are devoted to volunteering abroad and options in international exchange for people with disabilities. This extremely thorough and carefully prepared guide will be a necessary addition to any collection that serves persons who are interested in summer study abroad.—**Shirley L. Hopkinson**

NONPRINT MATERIALS AND RESOURCES

266. **NICEM Reference CD-ROM.** [CD-ROM]. Albuquerque, N.Mex., National Information Center for Education Media, 1999. Minimum system requirements: IBM or compatible 486 at 66MHz. Four-speed CD-ROM drive. Windows 95, Windows 98, or Windows NT 4.0. 16MB RAM. 4MB hard disk space. VGA monitor. $349.00. ISBN 0-89320-201-0.

There is no one-stop shopping when it comes to finding bibliographic and ordering information for media. Typically, one might have to check a number of print or electronic resources, Websites, or vendors before having sufficient information to order or correctly identify a nonprint media title. *NICEM Reference CD-ROM*, although not comprehensive, should be a standard tool in this process. With approximately 454,000 bibliographic records included, and a directory of some 25,000 AV producers and distributors, it constitutes a major bibliographic resource for media.

For each bibliographic record there is information including the title, length, language, subjects, audience, media type (with order number and price), abstract, producer or distributor, status, language, and publication year. When searching the database on these categories, the user may either browse choices (i.e., scan the index) or execute a search. There is also a global search option. Boolean operators can be used to combine together search terms in various fields. Beyond this, one may also sort the results of a search by up to five fields. The software interface is reasonably straightforward, if not always intuitive, and is aided by context-specific help screens. There are some quirks and limitations that are not immediately apparent, however. For example, although there are options for reporting information, these may be accompanied by limits on sorting. Also, there are noticeable inconsistencies in the application of subject headings, which can affect one's search results. At a broader level, it is difficult to discern the criteria for inclusion in the database.

Quirks and modest limitations notwithstanding, the *NICEM Reference CD-ROM* is a useful tool for identifying nonprint educational media. In addition, the publisher and distributor directory should be valuable to acquisitions librarians. This product is recommended for public and academic libraries, particularly for their professional staff.—**Stephen H. Aby**

6 Ethnic Studies and Anthropology

ANTHROPOLOGY AND ETHNOLOGY

267. **Anthropological Literature on Disc 1999.** [CD-ROM]. Thorndike, Maine, G. K. Hall/ Macmillan, 1999. Minimum system requirements: IBM or compatible 386. CD-ROM drive. Windows 3.1 or Windows 95. 8MB RAM. $995.00. ISBN 0-7838-0400-8.

Anthropological Literature is an international citation index to periodicals, journals, and edited works dating back to the late nineteenth century that are contained in the collection of the Tozzer Library at Harvard University. The 1999 annual CD-ROM includes more than the entire run of the print *Anthropological Literature*, which began in 1979. Primary emphasis is given to the following fields: archaeology, anthropology (biological and physical, cultural and social), and linguistics. Articles from sociology, history, ethnohistory, demography, geography, international development, and human genetics are also indexed. More than 50 percent of the materials indexed are not in English because articles of 2 or more pages are included if the title is in a Germanic, Romance, Scandinavian, or Slavic language. Obituaries with at least a partial bibliography are also indexed. According to the database description, book, film, and video reviews; interviews; and conference reports are not indexed. However, the source index lists 1,453 conference reports. The search capabilities are powerful and flexible. Function keys streamline all activities for experienced searchers. The searcher toggles between the history and index's drop-down menu or by clicking the desired radio button at the bottom of the display. History tracks all searches for the session, but search strategies may be saved on diskette for later use. Search sets may be combined between the two views using the Boolean operators "and" and "or." Results may be sorted by author, title, journal title, citation, or reverse date. Marked records may be printed or saved. Searchable indexes include author, title, subject, source (journal or book title), Tozzer call number, record number, and any word. Each index is capable of being browsed as well as searched. Once the user types a letter, word, or phrase into the "Go To" box, he or she is then placed at that point in the index, and can scroll the entire index in both directions. Every index entry lists the number of items contained in the database. The subject index, however, does not serve as a thesaurus and does not contain strictly Library of Congress headings. A weak point in the structure of the database is that if the user wishes to see the items under an entry in an index, three steps are required: double-click on the entry, click the search button, and then click the display button. Another notable defect is the absence of a language index.

The CD-ROM installs quickly and without problems. The CD-ROM may also be placed on a network within a single building for access by multiple workstations at no additional charge. It is written in RomView for Windows, version 1.5, by Inforonics, Inc. A succinct but thorough technical reference booklet accompanies the CD-ROM. This 14-page document explains search capabilities, printing and exporting features, and how to save and recall search strategies. The booklet clearly outlines installation procedures, licensing issues, and contact information. The Help menu contains a database description, but there is no information on the number of journals indexed or the span of coverage of the current CD-ROM. The list of journals and books indexed in *Anthropological Literature* is located at http://www.hcl.harvard.edu/tozzer/journals. All materials listed in the database are available for a fee through Tozzer library at tozillb@fas.harvard.edu. Some libraries may wish to purchase the Internet-based version of the database called

Anthropological Literature through the Research Libraries Group CitaDel service. The contents of the online database are updated on a quarterly basis as opposed to the annual update and replacement of the CD-ROM. *Anthropological Literature* is also available in print format for $250 per year. Since CD-ROM databases are rapidly declining in popularity because of remote access restrictions, the cost of the database is too high for smaller libraries. In the era of full-text databases, it is difficult for smaller academic libraries to justify this expense for a database that does not even include abstracts. The online version will be more attractive to larger libraries. The CD-ROM database is highly recommended for academic and museum libraries.
—**Anne C. Moore**

268. **Anthropological Resources: A Guide to Archival, Library, and Museum Collections.** Library-Anthropology Resource Group, comp. Lee S. Dutton, ed. New York, Garland, 1999. 517p. index. (Garland Reference Library of Social Science, v.864). $135.00. ISBN 0-8153-1188-5.

This uniquely valuable reference volume (the latest work coordinated by the Chicago-based Library-Anthology Research Group) fills a major gap in the research literature of anthropology by addressing a long-standing need for in-depth data on primary artifactual and documentary materials in all formats held in museums, archives, and libraries. Geographic coverage emphasizes Canadian and American holdings, but also profiles major collections in 15 other nations from western Europe, Central and South America, east and southeast Asia, Australia, and New Zealand. The 246 entries present full contact information on each institution (including Internet access when available), areas of specialization, collection contents (ranging from archival and manuscript holdings—both agency records and personal papers—to classes of objects, audio, and visual recordings), and related articles, books and guides. Of particular value are the histories of the inception and development of individual collections, often written by their curators. Indexing is by personal name and selected ethnic group names. Useful for undergraduate reference collections in college and university libraries (particularly those supporting baccalaureate and master's programs in anthropology), museums and historical societies, special collections in the social sciences, and all public library reference collections.—**Robert B. Marks Ridinger**

269. **Encyclopedia of Canada's Peoples.** Paul Robert Magocsi, ed. Toronto, University of Toronto Press, 1999. 1334p. $200.00. ISBN 0-8020-2938-8.

Like many countries today, Canada's peoples are represented by a variety of nationalities that constitute a wide range of cultural traditions. This encyclopedia explores the many different ethnic backgrounds of Canadian history and describe how they interrelate to shape Canadian society. As opposed to other immigrant countries, including the United States, this is the first comprehensive encyclopedia devoted to the ethnic make up of Canada. This great undertaking includes the expertise of 182 advisors who assisted on the editorial board, and 132 authors who compiled information and wrote the entries. The entries are arranged in encyclopedic format with 119 ethnic groups represented; the aboriginal peoples are further broken down into 13 groups (e.g., Siouan, Algonquians/Eastern Woodlands, Iroquoians). Every possible group is discussed here, from Acadians to Welsh, from Arabs to Spaniards. The topics discussed within each entry include the peoples origins, migration, arrival and settlement, economic life, community life, family, culture, education, religion, politics, intergroup relationships, and ethnic commitment. A bibliography is provided for each ethnic group discussed.

Nearly a decade in the making, this work is a truly scholarly contribution to the literature on Canada and especially Canadian peoples. It will be a worthwhile contribution to all academic libraries and many public libraries.—**Shannon M. Graff**

ETHNIC STUDIES

General Works

270. **Junior Worldmark Encyclopedia of World Cultures.** Jane Hoehner, ed. Farmington Hills, Mich., Gale, 1999. 9v. illus. maps. index. $225.00/set. ISBN 0-7876-1756-X.

This new encyclopedia is modeled after *Junior Worldmark Encyclopedia of the Nations* (see ARBA 97, entry 79). Although the information contained in its predecessor is general in scope, this work focuses on the culture of 295 ethnic groups outside of the United States. It is designed for use by upper elementary students; however, it is suitable for readers of all ages because it contains much information that may not be readily available elsewhere.

The format is attractive. The type is easy to read and there are black-and-white illustrations, including location maps. There are a reader's guide and a cumulative table of contents at the beginning of each volume, a glossary, and a cumulative index at the end of each. The arrangement is alphabetic by country and is continuous in the nine volumes. Within each chapter, cultural groups are treated individually. Information about each group follows the same pattern in 20 subheadings, which include language, religion, holidays, living conditions, and a bibliography. An interesting feature is the inclusion of ethnic recipes.

Political problems and ethnic conflicts are addressed only briefly under social problems. A critical omission, in the light of current events, is the lack of inclusion of Yugoslavia and its ethnic groups. However, Bosnia-Herzegovina and Croatia are included. It is hoped that the former omission will be rectified in subsequent editions.

This set is recommended as a worthwhile addition to a children's library collection or a supplement to social studies classes. If budgetary restrictions necessitate a choice between this set and its predecessor, one would probably choose the earlier work, although each deserves consideration. [R: BL, June 99, pp. 1881-1882; SLJ, Feb 99, p. 136; RUSQ, Fall 99, p. 95]—**Patricia A. Eskoz**

271. **Peoples of the Americas.** Tarrytown, N.Y., Marshall Cavendish, 1999. 11v. illus. maps. index. $329.95/set. ISBN 0-7614-7050-6.

Dense with facts, this compact multivolume geography and demography of the Americas is a meditation on survival. The nature of our land and its resources, who came first, what has been our social history, and where are we now are all told in scholarly paragraphs at the junior high school reading level. Topics include ethnic foods and folk celebrations, traditional patterns, education, and urban industrialization. But the authors neglect to discuss our debt to European intellectual civilization, which influenced American modernism with arts and sciences made public in museums, concert halls, theaters, libraries, engineering, government, and the law. Most pages have old prints of scenes of former generations or modern-day candid photographs. The indexes are effective and the glossaries are rudimentary. The maps, sidebars, and timelines are essential. Further study is facilitated by the bibliographies and text. Besides helping junior high school students, this work could be informative and interesting for American history and sociology enthusiasts.

—**Elizabeth L. Anderson**

Arab Americans

272. Hall, Loretta, and Bridget K. Hall. **Arab American Biography.** Farmington Hills, Mich., U*X*L/Gale, 1999. 2v. illus. index. $63.00/set. ISBN 0-7876-2953-7.

Defining an Arab American as an individual who traces his or her ancestry to 1 or more nations belonging to the League of Arab States, this 2-volume set profiles 75 persons who have made noteworthy achievements in a variety of fields, including politics, business, entertainment, science, and religion. Each entry includes date and place of birth (most of the individuals are currently alive), a narrative biographical description, often a black-and-white photograph, and a bibliography. Frequent sidebars provide interesting facts related to the individual. Each of the two volumes includes a table of contents, indexes by occupation and country of ancestry, and a cumulative alphabetic index for names and subjects.

Like some other ethnic reference publications, the criterion for inclusion is the individual's ancestry, not necessarily a professed commitment or involvement in the culture of his or her heritage. While many essays in this volume do describe individuals with strong Lebanese or other Arab background, some entries (such as race car driver Bobby Rahall, football star Doug Flutie, or high school teacher-turned-astronaut Christa McAuliffe) reveal little information pertinent to a student consulting a specialized reference work on Arab Americans. A future revised edition would be better as a 1-volume work, limited to individuals who were genuinely shaped by their ethnic background. The elementary level of the glossary and timeline demonstrate that this work is aimed—like other volumes in the U*X*L imprint of the Gale Group—at students in grades 5 and up. [R: BR, Nov/Dec 99, p. 71; RUSQ, Fall 99, p. 86]—**Donald Altschiller**

Asian Americans

273. **Asian-American Experience on File.** Carter Smith III and David Lindroth, eds. New York, Facts on File, 1999. 1v. (various paging). illus. maps. index. $125.00 looseleaf w/binder. ISBN 0-8160-3696-9.

This major new reference work from one of America's most respected publishers deserves special attention and recognition. Part of Facts on File's Ethnic Minorities in America set, it joins other titles on African and Hispanic Americans. It appears in a sturdy looseleaf, three-ring binder so that users may remove individual pages for copying, reference, or overheads. The publisher freely grants permission for copying of individual pages for educational purposes. The volume is self-contained and there are no evident provisions to add additional pages.

The arrangement is chronological. The introduction gives an overview of Asian American immigration and compares it with immigration from other regions. Chapter 1, "Background," examines political and cultural factors that have influenced Asian American immigration from 1820 to the present. The next four chapters are arranged into historical areas: pre-1900, 1990 to 1945, 1946 to 1974, and 1975 to the present. Chapter 6 contains valuable and fascinating information on Asian American cultural contributions (e.g., Chinese medicine, Asian-Indian cooking).

The book is strong on accessibility and visual resources, including maps, charts, black-and-white photographs, and diagrams on every page. It is printed on heavy paper and its quality is outstanding throughout. It includes valuable data on Asian Indians and Southeast Asian refugees in addition to the well-known Chinese, Japanese, Korean, and Filipino immigrants. Sources for each chapter and an unannotated bibliography list books, journal articles, and online references. The index is complete and well constructed.

This is an incredibly rich resource for anyone interested in the Asian American experience. It is especially valuable for students and teachers at all levels.—**Marshall E. Nunn**

274. **Distinguished Asian Americans: A Biographical Dictionary.** Hyung-Chan Kim and others, eds. Westport, Conn., Greenwood Press, 1999. 430p. illus. index. $65.00. ISBN 0-313-28902-6.

Distinguished Asian Americans presents the lives and achievements of 166 well-known Asian Americans who have contributed to American society. Although not all of the persons discussed were born in the United States (some have immigrated to America), each has made their mark here. By using the term "Asian Americans" the authors of this work are referring to descendants of China, India, Japan, Korea, Pakistan, the Philippines, Cambodia, Laos, and Vietnam. The people featured include businesspeople, journalists, artists, community leaders, political leaders, authors, and celebrity personalities (e.g., Connie Chung, Kristi Yamaguchi), among others. Each entry averages one to two pages and provides birth and death dates (if applicable), a brief life story, major contributions to their field, and a bibliography. Many of the entries provide a black-and-white photograph. The two appendixes at the end of the work list the individuals featured by professional field and by ethnic subgroups. A name/subject index completes the volume.

This work is intended for middle to high school age children doing research on significant Asian American figures. It will be a good purchase for school libraries or larger public libraries.

—Shannon M. Graff

275. Ng, Franklin. **The Taiwanese Americans.** Westport, Conn., Greenwood Press, 1998. 163p. illus. maps. index. (The New Americans). $39.95. ISBN 0-313-29762-2.

Chinese Americans are the largest Asian American group, only slightly outnumbering Filipino Americans. Taiwanese Americans are the second largest subgroup of Chinese Americans, following in size immigrants from mainland China and outpacing those from Hong Kong and Singapore. These figures add more importance to this book because it is the first one published on Taiwanese Americans. It is another title in The New Americans series, which is "designed for high school and general readers" (p. x). It focuses on community organization, information networks, religion, culture, and the nature of the second generation. Even though it does provide helpful historical background information, its main emphasis is on the cultural and sociological aspects of Taiwanese American life.

The author covers his subject in 4 parts. The introduction gives basic background information on Taiwan's land, people, language, religion, and history. "Coming to America" discusses early Chinese and Taiwanese immigration, composition of the new immigrants, and family and youth patterns. "Living in America" is concerned with associations, newspapers and the media, religion, and festivals. The last part, "An Evolving Taiwanese American Identity," gives valuable information on conflicts with mainlanders, politics in Taiwan, the second generation, intergroup relations, and Taiwanese Americans' "complex and evolving identity" (p. 126). Black-and-white photographs illustrate scenes from contemporary cultural life and activities. Two appendixes profile biographies of six successful Taiwanese Americans and provide eleven statistical immigration tables. There is also an unannotated bibliography that includes Internet Websites.

Ng is a professor of anthropology at California State University, Fresno, and has authored and edited several notable books on Asian American studies, including *The Asian American Encyclopedia* (see ARBA 96, entry 394) and *Chinese American Struggle for Equality* (Rourke, 1992). He writes with clarity and authority, and this book, although not strictly a reference work, belongs in all libraries. [R: SLJ, Nov 98, p. 141]—**Marshall E. Nunn**

276. Posadas, Barbara M. **The Filipino Americans.** Westport, Conn., Greenwood Press, 1999. 190p. illus. maps. index. (The New Americans). $39.95. ISBN 0-313-29742-8.

Historically, Filipino Americans have been known as an invisible minority, and there has been a real need for a comprehensive, up-to-date, reliable guide to their immigrant experience. Posadas' book admirably fills this need. Even though the books in the New Americans series are designed for high school and general readers, they are quite valuable for college students and teachers as well.

The book is tightly and logically organized into two parts and nine chapters. Its emphasis is on immigration, particularly after 1965; social and cultural issues, including values, customs, and economic and political power; identity in a multicultural society; contemporary issues for adults and elders; and the future of Filipino immigration.

A map, 5 statistical tables detailing Filipino immigration from 1920 to the present, and 18 black-and-white photographs effectively supplement the text. There are two appendixes: "Filipinos in the U.S. Census, 1910-2000" and "Notable Filipino Americans" (with eight short biographies). A glossary of cultural and immigration-related terms; a bibliography of films, videos, and distributors; and an unannotated bibliography of books and articles are also included. This is a survey but more information on certain aspects or the subject, especially on Filipinos in Alaska and Hawaii, would be helpful.

With this book, Posadas has established herself as the leading authority on Filipino Americans. She is eminently qualified as a professor of history at Northern Illinois University, as a member of the editorial boards of *Amerasia* and the *Journal of American Ethnic History*, and as the director of the Filipino National Historical Society.—**Marshall E. Nunn**

Blacks

Atlases

277. Asante, Molefi K., and Mark T. Mattson. **The African-American Atlas: Black History and Culture—An Illustrated Reference.** New York, Macmillan General Reference/Simon & Schuster Macmillan, 1998. 251p. illus. maps. $34.95. ISBN 0-02-864984-2.

From ancient African origins to present-day status, this reference, an update of the 1991 *Historical and Cultural Atlas of African Americans* (see ARBA 92, entry 343), examines African American history and culture with maps, photographs, statistics, and narratives. Arranged chronologically, chapters are given thematic titles based on spirituals that represent various aspects of African American history and life.

Although it is called an atlas, this work is much more. There are clear, detailed maps that provide graphic representation of events and information. The text integrates the history and culture of African Americans. There are also graphs, statistical charts, photographs, and drawings. One of the strengths of this work is the biographical information of leading African Americans, enhanced by clear, captioned photographs. Other appealing features include discussions of famous court cases significant to African Americans and insets that provide interesting tidbits, such as the Reconstruction Amendments, selected African American inventors, traditional African American colleges and universities, and African American servicemen awarded the Medal of Honor. Appendixes offer dates to remember, a reference list, and a comprehensive index. The oversized format allows for wide margins, generous type size, and easy-to-read maps and graphs. Bold chapter headings on every page allow easy access.

This reference should be a welcome addition to most libraries in that it provides a concise, chronological history of African Americans. The maps and other graphic materials serve to enhance the text and to provide statistical data, including that on the current status of African Americans. [R: Choice, Oct 99, p. 311]
—**Dana McDougald**

Bibliographies

278. **African-American Newspapers and Periodicals: A National Bibliography.** James P. Danky and Maureen E. Hady, eds. Cambridge, Mass., Harvard University Press, 1998. 740p. index. (Harvard University Press Reference Library). $125.00. ISBN 0-674-00788-3.

This current guide, originating from the State Historical Society of Wisconsin, identifies 6,562 titles by and about African Americans published between 1827 and the present, as located by the editors in publicly accessible collections between 1989 and 1998. The editors note that some publications, particularly those of a religious nature, are held only privately and are thus not included. However, the depth and range are truly impressive—805 titles from New York City alone, with representation from all states and Canada save Idaho, Wyoming, and North and South Dakota. Titles cover literary, historical, and political journals as well as general newspapers and magazines. Entries are arranged alphabetically by publication and title and include run dates, publication frequency, place of publication and publisher, OCLC accession number, and holdings information by library. When available, information on where the title is indexed is also provided. Excellent concluding indexes for subject/features, editors, publishers, and locations simplify access. The sole complaint is a lack of contact information for holding libraries, which will slow down the retrieval process.

As the most comprehensive African American national bibliography to date, this resource will long remain the primary research guide for locating materials in this area. This work takes the place of the earlier *Black Periodicals and Newspapers* (2d ed.; State Historical Society of Wisconsin, 1979) and serves as a companion volume to *Reference Guide to Afro-American Publications and Editors 1827-1946* (see ARBA 94, entry 1009). This volume is highly recommended for all research libraries and multicultural collections. [R: LJ, 15 Nov 99, p. 58]—**Anthony J. Adam**

279. **Interdisciplinary Bibliographic Guide to Black Studies 1998.** Thorndike, Maine, G. K. Hall/Macmillan, 1999. 480p. $295.00. ISBN 0-7838-0409-1. ISSN 0360-2710.

The latest edition of this work lists current publications cataloged during the past year by the New York Public Library (NYPL) and serves in part as an annual supplement to the *Dictionary Catalog of the Schomburg Collection of Negro Literature and History, The New York Public Library* (G. K. Hall, 1962). Although this work represents only NYPL holdings, Schomburg's dominance as a research center for black studies means that practically no other library collects at a more comprehensive level. As is the case with most G. K. Hall bibliographic guides, this volume provides complete Library of Congress cataloging information for each title, as well as ISBN and identification of NYPL holding. However, many of the international titles, especially from Africa and the Caribbean, only cite author, title, place of publication, publisher, and date. Arrangement is alphabetic by main entry, added entries, title, series titles, and subject headings. As a general listing of new items added to the Schomburg Collection, this guide has value for large research libraries, but as a finding aid for all materials on a subject or by an author, this volume and similar guides are of limited value. In a few minutes online with CATNYP (NYPL's research libraries catalog), researchers can retrieve all holdings by an author or on a subject, in addition to locating specific items through keyword searching or browsing call numbers. Considering the high price of this single volume, all save research libraries might want to rely on CATNYP as a finding guide.—**Anthony J. Adam**

280. **Strong Souls Singing: African American Books for Our Daughters and Our Sisters.** Archie Givens, ed. New York, W. W. Norton, 1998. 145p. illus. index. $22.00; $11.00pa. ISBN 0-393-02745-7; 0-393-31780-3pa.

A companion to *Spirited Minds: African American Books for Our Sons and Our Brothers* (W. W. Norton, 1997), also edited by Archie Givens, this annotated bibliography provides descriptions of more than 100 titles recommended for young readers. The volume is divided into 5 sections—History, Drama, Novels and Short Stories, Autobiographies and Biographies, and Poetry—with Novels and Short Stories being the lengthiest. One title is listed on each page and includes publication year, author, names of other contributors and awards received (if applicable), and number of pages. The descriptions are a paragraph in length and are followed by a suggested reading level. The typeface and layout are appealing and woodcut illustrations add to the appeal. The book includes title, author, and reading level indexes. Although a number of books have been published recently to offer reading lists to African American children, such as Pamela Toussaint's *Great Books for African American Children* and Donna Rand's *Black Books Galore!*, this title is designed particularly for female readers and incorporates the broadest spectrum of reading levels and interests. [R: BR, Nov/Dec 98, p. 84; SLJ, April 99, p. 45]—**Susanna Van Sant**

Biographies

281. **African American Biography, Volume 5.** By Judson Knight. Lawrence W. Baker, ed. Farmington Hills, Mich., U*X*L/Gale, 1999. 255p. illus. index. $39.00. ISBN 0-7876-3562-6. ISSN 1522-2934.

The 5th volume of the *African American Biography* continues as an excellent source for middle school and junior high school students. This new volume includes 40 biographies; 22 are new and 18 are updates from earlier profiles. The new biographies include historical figures such as Cinque and the Delaney sisters; sports heroes such as Tiger Woods, Dominique Dawes, and Venus Williams; entertainers; political leaders; and authors. Each biography includes a picture of photo, a readable narrative that also includes controversial aspects of the person's life, a quotation summarizing their philosophy, and a short bibliography. The bibliographies consist of Web pages, books, and popular magazines. Special features include extensive cross-references and a timeline of significant African American events from 1731 through 1998. Some of the terms in the glossary are curious (e.g., Halley's Comet, Soviet Union, and Yoga). There is a comprehensive list of all entries indicating volume and page number. Also included is a general bibliography of books and magazines. This series is not as comprehensive as other Gale publications, such as *Reference Library of Black America* (94th ed., 1994), *Notable Black American Women* (see ARBA 97, entry 34; see ARBA 93, entry 52), and *Who's Who Among African Americans* (1998/99 ed.; see ARBA 99, entry 379). This volume is highly recommended for school and public libraries.—**Karen Y. Stabler**

282. **Black Women in America.** New York, Macmillan Library Reference/Simon & Schuster Macmillan, 1999. 384p. illus. index. (Macmillan Profiles). $104.25. ISBN 0-02-865363-7.

Featuring 176 profiles of African American women from the eighteenth century to the present, this work is almost entirely culled from the *Encyclopedia of African American Culture and History* (see ARBA 97, entry 331). Only 14 new biographies were newly written for this volume. All the other profiles were rewritten for this work and tailored for high school students and younger. Most profiles range between one or two pages. Aimed at complementing the high school curriculum, this volume contains entries on women artists, scientists, journalists, educators, and legislators, but there seems to be an overrepresentation of entertainers and celebrities. The work is visually appealing; individual entries appear in easy-to-read type and feature notable quotations and timelines in pleasingly shaded color. In addition, the work contains about 75 black-and-white photographs. The volume concludes with a timeline, a bibliography of suggested readings, and a glossary of terms. This volume is a nice, but pricey, addition to the previously neglected but now burgeoning genre of biographical dictionaries on African American women. Similar to many other works that view their mission as providing biographies of "role models," the selection of entries does not adequately distinguish between vastly different types of accomplishments—acclaimed popular culture figures and talented individuals in intellectual and cultural spheres are randomly placed together in one volume. Readers may prefer the Distinguished African American series published by Oryx that organizes notable individuals who have excelled in specific fields in one volume.—**Donald Altschiller**

283. **Contemporary Black Biography, Volume 18: Profiles from the International Black Community.** Shirelle Phelps, ed. Farmington Hills, Mich., Gale, 1998. 286p. illus. index. $57.00. ISBN 0-7876-1274-X. ISSN 1058-1316.

Containing 62 biographies ranging in length from 2 to 5 pages, this latest edition includes profiles of neurosurgeon Keith Lanier Black, vocalist Ella Fitzgerald, sports commentator Ahmad Rashad, and nineteenth-century historian and legislator George Washington Williams, among many other individuals. See ARBA 99 (entry 376) and ARBA 96 (entries 400 and 401) for reviews of previous volumes. Each entry includes the name, occupation, a section entitled "At a Glance" for a brief summary, a narrative biography, and a bibliography. Cumulative indexes by name, subject, and occupation provide easy access to the contents of all 18 volumes. Although this series explicitly states its purpose as profiling "important and influential persons of African heritage," the volume occasionally has overly exuberant descriptions of individuals. Unfortunately, this treatment compromises the objectivity and reference value of the work. Furthermore, the series use of the word "contemporary" in the title is somewhat misleading; this volume, along with earlier editions, includes a few historical figures. Nevertheless, this series is an important and useful source for information on individuals not included in other biographical reference works. [R: BL, 15 Dec 98, p. 765]
—**Donald Altschiller**

284. **Contemporary Black Biography, Volume 19: Profiles from the International Black Community.** Shirelle Phelps, ed. Farmington Hills, Mich., Gale, 1999. 293p. illus. index. $57.00. ISBN 0-7876-1275-8. ISSN 1058-1316.

With a wide variety of biographies, bibliographies, and Websites available for those who seek all types of research material and resources on African Americans, *Contemporary Black Biography* offers dozens of interesting and influential personalities who have not only overcome tremendous odds but who continue to achieve and to inspire people of color worldwide. Consisting of 19 volumes, each individual volume also contains some individuals who, although a part of the late nineteenth- and early twentieth-century scenes, continue to inspire and create interest in all walks of life today.

Each individual biography contains basic information on the person being profiled, selected writings about the person, and other sources that readers can consult for further information. Parents and students looking for quick biographical information need look no further than the sidebar entitled "At a Glance," which is included with each narrative. Also, at the end of each volume there is an excellent cumulative nationality index, occupation index, and name index. These resources lead readers to various volumes in the set for more information on the persons being profiled. This volume is recommended for large school systems, large urban public libraries, and post-secondary institutes of higher learning.—**Lillian Jane Steele**

285.   **Contemporary Black Biography, Volume 20: Profiles from the International Black Community.** Shirelle Phelps, ed. Farmington Hills, Mich., Gale, 1999. 303p. illus. index. $57.00. ISBN 0-7876-2417-9. ISSN 1058-1316.

The 63 biographical portraits included in volume 20 of this successful Gale reference series are presented in the same format and style as in previous volumes and need not be described again here. As with earlier volumes, this one concludes with cumulative indexes for nationality, occupation, subject, and name. Interestingly, all 63 subjects are described in glowing terms ("successful," "multi-talented," "distinguished,") except 2 of the 4 non-Americans: Laurent Kabila, the dictator of Congo, and Charles Taylor, the controversial Liberian president. The two other non-Americans mentioned are Jamaican leader P. J. Patterson and the first African cardinal, Laurean Rugambwa. Phelps continues her predecessor's policy of including some earlier subjects (e.g., Charlie Parker, Anna Julia Cooper).

The writing and research are of a high quality throughout, and the coverage of blues and R&B musicians (e.g., Fats Domino, Roosevelt Sykes, Rufus Thomas) is more even-handed and well informed than in some earlier volumes. Yet, 12 volumes after this author's earlier review of this series, Charlie Patton, Blind Lemon Jefferson, and Tampa Red have still not been given their due—much less Ma Rainey, Muddy Waters, Sonny Boy Williamson, Memphis Minnie, or many other creators of the blues, Black America's greatest contribution to world culture.—**Fred J. Hay**

286.   Haskins, James. **Distinguished African American Political and Governmental Leaders.** Phoenix, Ariz., Oryx Press, 1999. 314p. illus. index. $54.95. ISBN 1-57356-126-6.

Arranged alphabetically, this biographical work includes 104 individuals who were selected for their careers in public service, either as appointed or elected officeholders. The volume includes entries starting with African Americans who served in Congress from the mid-nineteenth century (Reconstruction) through elected officials and appointees in 1998. Most entries are illustrated and contain, among other items, information on birth, education, awards and honors, offices held, family data, and a narrative description of each individual's career. Every entry contains a list of sources and many include Websites. The work concludes with a general bibliography, index, and appendixes arranged by type of office held, geographical location, party affiliation, and a chronological list of entries by birth date. Although the only other comparable reference work, *Black Americans in Congress, 1870-1989* (DIANE, 1996), contains some better bibliographic sources, the biographical entries are usually much shorter, and the coverage ends almost a decade earlier and is restricted to only members of the U.S. Congress. However, some problems can also be found in *Distinguished African American Political and Governmental Leaders*. Too many Websites are listed and they change too frequently to serve as useful sources. Furthermore, some important works, such as *Black Faces, Black Interests: The Representation of African Americans in Congress*, by Carol M. Swain (HUP, 1993), are omitted; the addition of more book-length biographical sources and citations to manuscript collections would also enhance the reference value of this volume. Nevertheless, this volume is a handy and useful source for African American biographical material not usually found in most standard reference works. [R: BL, 15 Nov 99, p. 646; Choice, Dec 99, p. 702]—**Donald Altschiller**

287. Haskins, Jim. **African American Military Heroes.** New York, John Wiley, 1998. 182p. illus. index. (Black Stars Series). $19.95. ISBN 0-471-14577-7.

Haskins, a prolific writer of African American young adult books, highlights the careers of 30 black military figures, both male and female, from Private Peter Salem's service at the Battle of Lexington in 1775 through the contributions of General Colin Powell and Commander Robert O. Goodman Jr. Few of these names will be familiar even to older students, and although the volume is aimed toward a young adult audience, readers of all ages will find something new here. The well-written essays are brief, sometimes no more than 300 words long, but all include a photograph or artist's rendering of the subject. Sidebars throughout further explicate the milieu of the individuals (e.g., buffalo soldiers). The author also makes it a point to highlight the subjects' educational backgrounds, which parents and teachers will appreciate. Unfortunately, although Haskins includes a brief bibliography at the end of this work, there are no references for further reading tied to specific essays.

This work is the only up-to-date work on this subject with a younger audience in mind. Students seeking more detailed information should refer to Michael Lee Lanning's *The African-American Soldier* (Birch Lane, 1997) and Gerald Astor's *The Right to Fight* (Presidio, 1998), in addition to the numerous recent works on specific military branches and units. This work is highly recommended for all young adult and undergraduate collections. [R: SLJ, Nov 98, p. 136]—**Anthony J. Adam**

288. Kranz, Rachel, and Philip J. Koslow. **The Biographical Dictionary of African Americans.** New York, Facts on File, 1999. 310p. index. $35.00; $18.95pa. ISBN 0-8160-3903-8; 0-8160-3904-6pa.

This is a revised and expanded edition of Kranz's work of the same title issued in 1992. The book is intended for young adults, but would be useful to any age group. Entries are well-written and substantial (most entries being about 1,000 words in length), and there are cross-references and suggestions for further reading. Entries are initialed to indicate authorship. The selection of people for inclusion was intended to be representative and not all-encompassing. It includes as many black "firsts" as possible. A sampling of key figures in the development of Black American history and those involved in its major movements from the eighteenth century into the 1990s. The authors tried to include persons that many readers will know, or will find inspiring. The initial entry is for Henry Louis (Hank) Aaron, the all-time home run king. The final entry is for Charles Young, an army officer, who was the third black person to graduate from West Point. Between these 2 names are an additional 235 entries with numerous portraits, some full-page. Entries include civil rights activists and leaders, actors, artists, athletes, educators, musicians, soldiers, and writers. Judge Thomas has an entry, but not Anita Hill. O. J. Simpson is included, but not Johnnie Cochran. Naomi Campbell, Della Reese, Redd Foxx, Dennis Rodman, Al Sharpton, and Mike Tyson did not make the book. Back matter includes a 4-page bibliography of source books on African American studies, most published in the 1980s and 1990s. Also, appendixes include entries by area of activity, entries by year of birth, and a chronology. The index not only includes the biographies, but also book titles and references to other persons and events. Rachel Kranz is an award-winning radio and video journalist who has written numerous books for young people. Philip Koslow has taught modern history and political science at the university level, and written and edited many books for young people. [R: SLJ, Aug 99, p. 184]—**Frank J. Anderson**

289. **Notable Black American Men.** Jessie Carney Smith, ed. Farmington Hills, Mich., Gale, 1999. 1365p. illus. index. $90.00. ISBN 0-7876-07633.

Ever since the publication of Smith's excellent *Notable Black American Women* (see ARBA 93, entry 52), patrons have demanded a similar volume covering men. *Notable Black American Men* (NBAM) in every way measures up to the quality of that work, offering 500, 1- to 5-page biographies of African American men, both living and dead, from poet Jupiter Hammon to golfer Tiger Woods. Nominees for inclusion represent all fields of endeavor and meet at least one or more strict criteria, such as a leading businessman, noted orator, government official, or leader for social justice. Each signed essay includes essential biographical information and a brief secondary bibliography; most feature black-and-white portraits, current addresses, and collection locations. Separate geographical, occupational, and subject indexes conclude the volume, although each of these could have used more work.

With so many different essayists, quality varies widely, but Smith's editorial team achieves an overall uniformity of tone and scope. However, controversial matters tend to be glossed over. Additionally, the difficult task of choosing only 500 representative men forces many well-known names off the list. Duke Ellington and Michael Jackson are included, but Count Basie and Marvin Gaye are not. General Frank Peterson made the cut, but not General Calvin Waller. The lesser-known and forgotten individuals who are included (e.g., Rex Ingram, William DeHart Hubbard, Robert Purvis) make NBAM a major biographical reference for all libraries. [R: BL, 15 Feb 99, p. 1085; Choice, July/Aug 99, p. 1915]—**Anthony J. Adam**

290. **Who's Who Among African Americans.** 12th ed. Ashyia N Henderson and Shirelle Phelps, eds. Farmington Hills, Mich., Gale, 1999. 1626p. index. $155.00. ISBN 0-7876-2757-7. ISSN 1081-1400.

Containing entries on more than 20,000 men and women, this 12th edition follows the format of the earlier volumes. The alphabetically arranged name entries contain a considerable amount of biographical information, including occupation, education, career information, honors and awards, organizational affiliations, military service, and home or business address. The volume features both a geographic and an occupation index and a necrology of recently deceased newsworthy African Americans. The criteria for inclusion range from election or appointment to public office, noteworthy careers, or community service. Black persons who are not American citizens but who have contributed to American life are also included. Although *Contemporary Black Biography* (see entries 283-285) contains long narrative essays on some individual achievers, this work is the most comprehensive biographical directory of African Americans currently available. Because the prefaces to the 10th and 11th editions also noted that the volume contained about 20,000 entries, it is not clear how many additions, deletions, or revisions were made in this 12th edition. In a random unscientific sampling, almost all the entries selected from the 10th, 11th, and 12th editions were identical. In future editions, the editors should explicitly indicate the approximate number of revisions made since the earlier edition. It is important information for libraries that have previous volumes because this costly later work might not be needed.—**Donald Altschiller**

Dictionaries and Encyclopedias

291. **Africana: The Encyclopedia of the African and African American Experience.** Kwame Anthony Appiah and Henry Louis Gates Jr., eds. Reading, Mass., Basic Civitas Books Perseus Books, 1999. 2095p. illus. maps. $100.00. ISBN 0-465-00071-1.

At long last, W.E.B. Du Bois's dream of an *Encyclopedia Africana* has come to fruition, thanks to the efforts of editors Appiah and Gates, along with an international team of 220 scholars. More than 3,500 signed articles cover the full scope of Africa and the Diaspora, with approximately two-fifths of the text devoted to Africa and the rest primarily covering North and South America. The editors also chose to focus on the entire continent of Africa rather than just "Black Africa," giving a broader perspective on the various cultures and peoples. The articles in this rather heavy volume range from a brief paragraph to five tri-column pages and aim to provide both fact and interpretation whenever warranted, particularly on socioeconomic topics (e.g., "Islam and Fundamentalism"). Each country study receives a general article and a ready-reference follow-up with almanac-type data. *See also* references abound, although some of the subject headings are awkward and some topics (e.g., education) are given short shrift. However, the numerous stunning black-and-white and color charts, maps, and photos alone are worth the purchase price. Geared toward a mainstream audience, this encyclopedia is extremely well written, although some Afrocentrist scholars deplore its Eurocentric basis.

Africana has also been expanded in a CD-ROM format as *Microsoft Encarta Africana 2000* to include a library of Black America, a music timeline, and other special features. Even with its arguably philosophical flaws, *Africana* is a must purchase for all academic and public libraries. [R: LJ, 15 Nov 99, p. 58]

—**Anthony J. Adam**

292. Pyatt, Sherman E., and Alan Johns. **A Dictionary and Catalog of African American Folklife of the South.** Westport, Conn., Greenwood Press, 1999. 188p. illus. index. $75.00. ISBN 0-313-27999-3.

African American folklife and lore has been a rich field of study throughout the past century, from the pioneering work of Lomax, Hurston, Hughes, Herskovits, and others up until the present. Pyatt and Johns attempt to not only catalog basic secondary resources in the field but to forward the field of southern African American folkways through personal interviews. The results are mixed, although useful. The 1st section of the book is perhaps the most interesting, being a dictionary of topics and subjects sometimes based on personal interviews with individuals currently or recently living in South Carolina or Alabama. The 2d section is the unannotated catalog of print sources (and some recordings), divided into 7 broad chapters (e.g., folk music). The categories are so broad, however, that it is difficult to find specific topics, and the index is only helpful to a point (a spot check revealed numerous print sources without relative indexing). The 3d section is the additional material, including a list of festivals, libraries and archives, and state folk cultural programs.

Despite its faults, the present volume is a handy introductory guide to the field. It is a good supplement to Donald Waters' *Strange Ways and Sweet Dreams* (Macmillan, 1983) and the numerous specialized works in the field.—**Anthony J. Adam**

Directories

293. Fitzpatrick, Sandra, and Maria R. Goodwin. **The Guide to Black Washington: Places and Events of Historical and Cultural Significance in the Nation's Capital.** rev. ed. New York, Hippocrene Books, 1999. 240p. maps. index. $16.95pa. ISBN 0-7818-0647-X.

In the last two decades, there has been a publishing boom of local and regional African American history. A WorldCat search on the subject keywords "African American" and "guidebooks" yields several dozen titles, ranging from a state government booklet entitled *African American Heritage Guide to New Jersey* to a publication titled *Black Heritage Trail and Tales of Tucson and Old Fort Huachuca near Sierra Vista, Arizona*. At least a half dozen works, including picture books and pamphlets, exclusively survey black history in Washington, D.C. This revised *Guide to Black Washington* provides an overview of historic sites in what a historian once called "the secret city," covering more than 150 places and institutions that have shaped African American history in the nation's capital.

Arranged by neighborhood and illustrated with sectional street maps, the work also provides a brief introductory essay on black history in the District of Columbia. Unfortunately, this work has not rectified some of the problems found in the 1st edition published in 1990 (see ARBA 91, entry 458). The entries on national historic sites do not list telephone numbers, hours, or contact individuals. Quotations within entries do not list the source and even checking the bibliography is frequently fruitless. Although the bibliography does contain some recent citations, the entries for the *Washington Post* and *Washington Times* omit the article titles and page numbers. Some index entries include multiple references; however, the main text needs cross-references to facilitate easier access. Most problematic is the fact that many entries lack basic historical facts, further diminishing the reference value of this work. In short, this work is mainly suitable for casual travelers. One hopes that a future edition will more adequately fulfill its role as a reference work.

—**Donald Altschiller**

Handbooks and Yearbooks

294. **African-American Culture and History.** [CD-ROM]. New York, Macmillan Library Reference/Simon & Schuster Macmillan, 1999. Minimum system requirements: IBM or compatible 486. CD-ROM drive. Windows 3.1 or Windows 95. 16MB RAM. VGA color monitor. $450.00. ISBN 0-02-865364-5.

African-American Culture and History (AACH), the latest CD-ROM product from Macmillan Library Reference, uses the excellent 5-volume *Encyclopedia of African-American Culture and History* (see

ARBA 97, entry 331) as its core. All of the articles have been reviewed and updated, and new articles have been added, with additional content drawn from the *African-American Atlas* (see entry 277) and *Macmillan Encyclopedia of World Slavery* (see ARBA 99, entry 535). The full-text of dozens of historical documents and speeches, a black-and-white photo gallery linked to related articles, an interactive timeline, and visual tours of key events in African American history (e.g., the Harlem Renaissance) enhance the overall design.

Libraries may mount AACH for single-user workstations or LANs with unlimited simultaneous users, but the product may not be mounted on a WAN or in more than one physical building. AACH is fully searchable through general subject, in-depth keyword, and "people search" interfaces. This latest selection allows the user to search the database by name, sex, birthplace, occupation, or time period. Articles may be saved, printed, or added to the clipboard.

AACH is remarkably fast and simple to use. A keyword search on "Prairie View" resulted in eight hits, including references in articles on football and architecture. Narrowing the search to "education" resulted in one hit, but it was exactly on the mark. The search interface is clean, help buttons are always available, and navigation is fluid, especially via the embedded links within articles. These links to other articles, maps, and documents significantly enhance the usefulness of this product over the paper edition. The only negative is the lack of audio and video. This resource compares favorably with the more expansive (and cheaper) Encarta Africana from Microsoft, which takes advantage of multimedia. All academic and public libraries will find AACH a major addition to their collections.—**Anthony J. Adam**

295. **African-American Experience on File.** C. Carter Smith Jr., ed. New York, Facts on File, 1999. 1v. (various paging). illus. maps. index. $125.00 looseleaf w/binder. ISBN 0-8160-3607-7.

This is an interesting but unusual publication in format, style, content, and presumed readership. Its looseleaf pages in a binder suggest that it is a work in progress and more pages will be added. Its style of one page per subtopic, based mainly on one reference, in small print and always signifying a given era or event, represents a highly selective chronicle of experiences of African Americans. Its contents are divided into six phases, from the background, which goes as far back as the beginning of humanity, through slavery, antebellum, the Jim Crow period, the early twentieth century, the civil rights era, and the continuing struggle of the present day. In less than 200 pages segmented into dates, charts, maps, and captions, the reader can get only glimpses of what those phases are supposed to cover. Potential readers will find it less useful than its publishers seem to expect. It offers little to the researcher, and hardly enough to the uninitiated, to whom it may be more confusing than enlightening. The shortcut to learning embodied in this volume does not do justice to the topics covered or to the appetite of the interested reader, its maps, dates, index, and bibliography notwithstanding. [R: BR, Sept/Oct 99, p. 79]—**Elias H. Tuma**

296. **African-American History.** Jack Salzman, ed. New York, Macmillan Library Reference/Simon & Schuster Macmillan, 1998. 1153p. illus. index. (Macmillan Compendium). $125.00. ISBN 0-02-864979-6.

A 1-volume abridgment of the 5-volume *Encyclopedia of African-American Culture and History* (see ARBA 97, entry 331), this work contains selected entries that are presented in their entirety with more than 100 illustrations. The preface indicates this volume omits entries on individual states, diplomats, black identity, and many other topics. Unlike the complete set, this abridged volume uses call-out quotations to highlight the statements and also add visual appeal. The volume concludes with an appendix of tables and statistical data and an index. Although an abridgment of a 5-volume work is necessarily selective, the editor's choice of entries seems particularly arbitrary, such as the inclusion of accused murderer O. J. Simpson instead of major civil rights leader and notable orator James Farmer. Furthermore, the selection of the 10 statistical tables with topics such as persons arrested and legal abortions is puzzling. Although this compendium is significantly less expensive than the full set, the extent of shortcomings in this work may not justify this saving. [R: SLJ, Aug 99, p. 187]—**Donald Altschiller**

297. **Black Studies on Disc 1999.** [CD-ROM]. Thorndike, Maine, G. K. Hall/Macmillan, 1999. Minimum system requirements: IBM or compatible 386. CD-ROM drive. Windows 3.1 or Windows 95. 8MB RAM. $995.00. ISBN 0-7838-0401-6.

Black Studies on Disc (BSD) combines the Catalog of the Schomburg Center for Research in Black Culture and G. K. Hall's annual *Index to Black Periodicals*, 1988 through 1998. The combined database features approximately 148,000 bibliographic records of all material formats and includes information by and about people of African descent worldwide.

The most distressing aspect of BSD is its archaic user interface. The user faces a search command box, another box for index lists (e.g., date, name, source), and a viewbox to display indexes and search histories. The interface will seem familiar to longtime search specialists, as it uses search strategies developed in the early days of library CD-ROMs. The user types in search terms or selects from the index lists (the easiest method, although it requires an additional "add to command" step), hits "search," and gets a brief bibliographic display. Oddly, the default brief display for articles cites only year, author, and article title; the user must ask for "full" display to find the dates, journal title, and page numbers. Users can mark citations for printing and sorting. Help buttons are featured throughout, but there is no "back" key. Customization is available and recommended, especially for monographs.

Despite its user interface problems, BSD is an important research acquisition for black studies programs forced otherwise to consult both the online Schomburg catalog and print indexes. This CD-ROM is recommended as a mediated search tool for large academic libraries.—**Anthony J. Adam**

298. **The New York Public Library African American Desk Reference.** New York, Songstone Press/John Wiley, 1999. 606p. illus. index. $34.95. ISBN 0-471-23924-0.

This new addition to the New York Public Library's series of desktop references derives from the extensive collections of the Schomburg Center for Research in Black Culture, one of the largest and best sources for African American studies. As with earlier almanacs in this series, the *African American Desk Reference* includes brief information, lists, contact information, and special terms (e.g., recipes) on all aspects of African American life, from the transatlantic slave trade to the present. Given the potential scope of this work, it is not surprising that the 17 chapters range over history, law, the performing arts, sports, media, health, science and technology, education, religion, and business. However, as is the nature of almanacs, the information is rarely in-depth, although the editors wisely included numerous bibliographies and Websites for further research.

Although most of the information here will have a relatively long shelf life, some of it, particularly addresses and lists, will date rapidly. The editors have attempted to feature the latest available data (e.g., *Black Enterprises*'s top companies for 1999), and updates should be included in future editions, along with corrections of minor errors (e.g., Prairie View A&M University was founded in 1876, not 1878 as listed). More illustrations, especially charts and graphs, would help future editions also. However, this well-edited inexpensive volume is one of the best in the series and is highly recommended for all public, academic, and school libraries. [R: LJ, 15 Sept 99, pp. 70-71]—**Anthony J. Adam**

299. Patrick, Diane. **The New York Public Library Amazing African American History: A Book of Answers for Kids.** New York, John Wiley, 1998. 170p. illus. index. (New York Public Library Answer Books for Kids Series). $12.95pa. ISBN 0-471-19217-1.

This latest New York Public Library (NYPL) adolescent reference work tells the story of African Americans from the beginning of the slave trade through the mid-1990s in a refreshing, balanced manner. Every aspect of African American history is covered, from politics to arts and business, with attention paid to significant personalities and events in each era. Patrick does not aim for comprehensiveness, but it is impressive to see just how much she includes without bogging down. Although the subtitle proclaims this book is written for kids, the audience is closer to at least junior high level and above. The language and writing style throughout are simple and direct, but never condescending.

Patrick's Socratic approach offers one brief definition or explanation to a question (e.g., "What is the Ku Klux Klan?") that automatically leads to another ("What other white hate groups existed?"). It is easy to get caught up in the flow of expositions and the reader will undoubtedly accidentally learn new facts along the way. However, as a dictionary, the format does not hold together well. The numerous photographs, reproductions, and insets with quick information only add to the quality of this volume. Public and high school libraries will be well served by this text, but academics will find it too juvenile.—**Anthony J. Adam**

300. Torres-Saillant, Silvio, and Ramona Hernández. **The Dominican Americans.** Westport, Conn., Greenwood Press, 1998. 184p. illus. index. (The New Americans). $39.95. ISBN 0-313-29839-4.

During the 1930 to 1961 dictatorship of Trujillo, the Dominican Republic's population increased from 900,000 to 3,000,000. During recent decades, the United States has supported Western-leaning but unpopular dictators of this island by allowing entry visas to revolutionaries. These dictators have taken international loans and accepted global corporations but neither have increased the incomes of the poorer class—the majority of the population. Since the 1970s as many as 20,000 uneducated people migrate each year, usually to New York City. Because the United States has changed economically from industrial to service oriented, low-level jobs are not common and when found are low paying. The 1990s cutoff of welfare money is parallel to youth being attracted to the drug culture. Some Dominicans write and create music and art but Latin American professional organizations have been slow to acknowledge this. This story is clearly and coherent told by two Dominican Americans, emphasizing gender, race, and class issues. Although religion, health, and family perspectives might be the genesis of a solution, they are not developed; instead social determinism has precedence. Education, work, and political muscle are believed to be the paths to rectitude of dire circumstances. The prevalence of poverty around the world and the problem of how to curtail it, say nothing of escape it, make this book valuable. Self-respect and validation from neighbors and communities are well supported by these writers and their data. The bibliography, created by a separate scholar, is a treasure in itself.—**Elizabeth L. Anderson**

Indians of North America

Bibliography

301. Bahr, Howard M. **Diné Bibliography to the 1990s: A Companion to the Navajo Bibliography of 1969.** Lanham, Md., Scarecrow, 1999. 739p. index. (Native American Bibliography Series, no.23). $95.00. ISBN 0-8108-3651-3.

Whenever choices are made in compiling a bibliography of this type, whether to include, exclude, annotate, or just list, the author is pivotal to the quality and usefulness of the book. To understand the scholarship, sensitivity, and sensibility that Bahr brings to the task, it is imperative to read the introduction of this work. He explains the complexity of studying a culture different from your own cultural values, time, and training; clearly discusses observer-related liabilities in Navajo studies; presents his sensible guidelines to inclusion and exclusion; and then adds a straightforward acknowledgment of the imperfection of this comprehensive work. In fact, if one were to read only this part of the bibliography, he or she would find a lucid explanation of why the study of Navajo peoples is inherently flawed, why it is necessary to probe beyond and between academic disciplines to gain a more complete understanding, and why multiple perspectives are critical in attempting to form a reasonable sense of the culture.

One of the greatest strengths of the book is the extension of the entries beyond the academic disciplines. For example, entries from popular magazines are included as well as from academic journals. Some children's literature and popular literature (e.g., Tony Hillerman) are included as well as the books of renowned scholars, such as N. Scott Momaday. The bibliography "is an invitation to relax further some already attenuated disciplinary boundaries, to heighten awareness and analysis of underutilized Navajo source materials, and to explore sources that may formerly have been defined as irrelevant, esoteric, ideological or otherwise unrespectable." This honesty and courage is often hard to come by.

It is important to note that the entries complement and extend an earlier bibliography and do not include works written after 1990. The works included in the two bibliographies provide more than 12,000 textual glimpses of Navajo life, culture, art, economics, and history. The author intends to compile another volume to include these later works, but he notes that they are available through online sources. The study of the Navajo is a journey, not a destination, and this bibliography provides a comprehensive, if not complete, map for the traveler.—**Karen D. Harvey**

302. Osterreich, Shelley Anne, comp. **Native North American Shamanism: An Annotated Bibliography.** Westport, Conn., Greenwood Press, 1998. 109p. index. (Bibliographies and Indexes in American History, no.38). $55.00. ISBN 0313-30168-9.

There is probably no part of American Indian cultures that is as misunderstood (or simply not understood at all) as American Indian spirituality. This book should make the journey toward developing an understanding easier; it does not. Several significant faults mar what could have been a valuable work that would make a notable contribution.

First, and perhaps most importantly, there is no information given regarding the qualifications of the compiler to attempt such a complex endeavor. The issue of accuracy or authenticity seems critical. In the past, many American Indian tribes either did not provide sacred information to non-Indians or just made up something to satisfy the interviewer. Much information is truly most sacred and hidden, unavailable to the outsider even today. In addition, the anthropologist or observer also views and explains spiritual practices of other cultures through his or her own cultural lenses and particular generation and often simply sees or interprets the wrong meaning and significance. The non-Indian person frequently must accept that only partial knowledge and limited understanding may be available.

Second, and just as important for the reader, no criteria are listed for the inclusion or exclusion of any particular work. Third, the audience or market for the book is unclear. Lastly, there is an awkwardness about the language in the book. The term "Native North Americans" is clumsy; the preferred language usually refers to the "indigenous people of North America." Further, the word "shaman" is generally not a term used by tribal people. The text does not clarify if a "shaman" is the same as a medicine man. And even if it were clear, there is still confusion, for medicine men are not all alike. An informed explanation of the terms used—healer, medicine man (or woman), and shaman—would be useful.

Perhaps, depending on the intended audience, a contemporary reference work such as *The Encyclopedia of Native American Religions* (see ARBA 93, entry 432) would be more useful even though the scope of an encyclopedia is larger. Further, the inclusion of additional works about contemporary medicine people and the enduring nature of Indian spiritual practices would help to establish in the reader's mind that traditional beliefs are still practiced and help maintain cultural identity for many American Indian people. The annotations are quite lengthy and give the compiler's perspective on what the book or article included, making it convenient to locate particular information, and many of the book selections are readily available in many bookstores and most libraries. [R: Choice, Oct 99, p. 315]—**Karen D. Harvey**

303. White, Phillip M., comp. **The Kickapoo Indians, Their History and Culture: An Annotated Bibliography.** Westport, Conn., Greenwood Press, 1999. 118p. index. (Bibliographies and Indexes in American History, no.41). $55.00. ISBN 0-313-30927-2.

Kickapoo Indians are one of the more widely traveled of the native peoples in North America since Europeans arrived. Their first European encounter took place in what is now northern Wisconsin and the upper Michigan peninsula sometime in the early seventeenth century. By the mid-eighteenth century they were in Illinois and Indiana. During the period of "Indian Removal" (1820-1840) they were forced first to Missouri, then to Kansas, and finally to the Indian Territory (Oklahoma). Today there are Kickapoo reservations in Oklahoma, Texas, and the state of Coahuila, just south of the U.S.-Mexican border. Thus, while their numbers are small, there may be a surprising number of states with individuals who would have an interest in this title.

Like White's other bibliographies on native peoples—*American Indian Studies: A Bibliographic Guide* (see ARBA 96, entry 421), *Bibliography of Indians of San Diego County* (see ARBA 99, entry 383), and *The Native American Sun Dance Religion and Ceremony: An Annotated Bibliography* (see ARBA 99, entry 384)—the introductory essay provides an excellent overview of the topic. In this case, he included a 17-item "Core Collection." His bibliography provides annotations to 366 books, journal articles, online materials, chapters in books, doctoral dissertations, proceedings, government publications, and some newspaper articles published between 1800 and 1998. Coverage focuses on traditional culture and history. Given the book's scope it is somewhat surprising that he excluded—and so noted the fact—contemporary issues of economic development as well as contemporary social issues. Entries are alphabetically arranged by author within 27 broad topics such as education, land tenure, and religion. Annotations vary in length from a few sentences to as much as 600-plus words and are descriptive in character. The index covers subjects, people, authors, and editors. A quick check against material contained in the 1997 CD-ROM version of *Bibliography of Native North Americans* suggests White was comprehensive in his recording of books and journal articles for the topics he covered. Unfortunately, the rather high price for a slender volume may keep it from being added to as many collections as would otherwise find this a useful volume. [R: Choice, Nov 99, pp. 520-521]—**G. Edward Evans**

Biography

304. **American Indian Biographies.** Harvey Markowitz, ed. Englewood Cliffs, N.J., Salem Press, 1999. 436p. illus. index. (Magill's Choice). $68.75. ISBN 0-89356-972-0.

One might wonder how many more Native American biographical works the market can absorb. There has been at least 1 new work every year for the past 10 years. Admittedly, some are for the middle and high school market (for example, *Native American Biography* [see ARBA 97, entry 339]) and some for a class of person (for example, *Biographical Directory of Native American Painters* [see ARBA 97, entry 807]). Most of the titles are more general in character. In this case much of the material (a total of 329 entries) has appeared elsewhere. "The majority of these essays first appeared in Salem Press's *Ready Reference: American Indians* (1995). Other entries are from Salem Press's Great Lives in History series. Only 22 entries are newly prepared for this volume and all are for twentieth-century individuals. One page is the average length of an entry; a few are much longer, such as the five-page entry for Wilma Mankiller. Coverage is from European contact to the present, with something of a bias toward the contemporary. One will find all of the expected names represented in the volume but with limited coverage for individuals north of the U.S.-Canadian border. The content is good and coverage is reasonable for a small single volume. The question is how much one is willing to pay for convenience. *The Encyclopedia of Native American Biography* (see ARBA 98, entry 350) provides almost double the coverage of this volume. If one has *Notable Native Americans* (see ARBA 96, entry 416), one has almost the same coverage with a stronger contemporary bias. Certainly, if one has the other Salem Press publications from which this volume draws upon, one would want to think long and hard before buying this volume. [R: LJ, 15 Mar 99, p. 66; Choice, May 99, p. 1587]—**G. Edward Evans**

Dictionaries and Encyclopedias

305. **The Encyclopedia of Native American Economic History.** Bruce E. Johansen, ed. Westport, Conn., Greenwood Press, 1999. 301p. index. $85.00. ISBN 0-313-30623-0.

Any student or scholar of Native American history understands that economic interests were and are the driving force in the relationship between Native Americans and the white race. These interests are not always clearly articulated in Native American studies, but they underlie almost all interactions. This volume provides a sound single source for an overview of many of the economic issues. Johansen suggests, in the introduction, there is no active body of scholarship addressing economic issues; however, his 18-page selected bibliography suggests there is a rather large literature by Linda Barrington titled *The Other Side of the Frontier: Economic Explorations into Native American History* (Westview Press, 1999). Topics range in scope from place names to broad areas, such as contemporary economic development; from precontact economic activities to modern mining operations. Coverage also includes people (Popé) and national organizations (National Center for American Indian Enterprise Development). The majority of entries end with a reference or two to other resources on the topic. There is no claim that the work is comprehensive. The index is useful but does not provide any insight as to why some topics are or are not included. One can find reasonably concise summaries of many but not all tribal economics; the problem is which ones. For example, for the southwestern United States there are entries for the Apaches, Navajos, and Pueblos but none for the Pima or any of the Pai–speaking groups. There is a long entry for the Yamasee but nothing for the Yakima. Some of the information can be found in other general encyclopedias dealing with Native Americans. However, this reviewer is unaware of any other single source covering such a wide range of Native American economic issues. This work will be most useful in an undergraduate reference collection. [R: BL, 1 May 99, p. 1616; Choice, Oct 99, p. 312]—**G. Edward Evans**

306. Green, Rayna, with Melanie Fernandez. **The British Museum Encyclopedia of Native North America.** Bloomington, Ind., Indiana University Press, 1999. 213p. illus. $39.95; $27.95pa. ISBN 0-253-33597-3; 0-253-21339-8pa.

This is not your grandfather's encyclopedia. Instead, in an unusual format, it is an exciting reference on American Indian history and cultures from a Native perspective. Extraordinarily readable, it extends beyond the common purpose of an encyclopedia to a different kind of reference. Difficult to explain in many ways, it addresses many widely divergent topics important to Indian people such as Africans, African Americans and Indians, diplomacy, dams, coyotes, clans, land, pipes, population, Pocahontas, the Bureau of Indian Affairs, self-determination, self-government, squash, and stomp dance. Abundantly illustrated with historical and contemporary photographs, art, and historical documents, it is fascinating reading. Many of the entries are explained through essays; historical and current quotations from poetry, literature, and newspapers; and even some "Indian" jokes.

Readers should caution that because the book was first published in Britain, British spellings and grammatical structure prevail. Teachers might wish that the maps were more clear and abundant. But this could be remedied easily in the classroom.

In addition to providing a new and compelling perspective on Native America, the book is well organized and convenient, with words in bold typeface to note where there are entries on that particular subject. There is a comprehensive general index and an index of individuals. Also for those who want to know more, there are sections that provide the sources of information, picture credits, and the sources of all quotations. The list of errata is longer than one would like, but it is a small issue in a book that meets a great need.

The authors state that this encyclopedia "offer[s] some introduction to the people's issues and ideas (past and present) that make up Native North American history and culture." As such, and because of its urgently needed Native perspective, it should be in every high school, college, and public school library. [R: LJ, Aug 99, pp. 76-78]—**Karen D. Harvey**

307. Johnson, Michael. **Macmillan Encyclopedia of Native American Tribes.** 2d ed. New York, Macmillan Library Reference USA, 1999. 288p. illus. maps. index. $80.00. ISBN 0-02-865409-9.

Much of North American society has been influenced by Native American culture. This beautifully illustrated encyclopedia presents an overview of 400 separately identifiable tribes. The presentation has been largely improved in this new edition. The previous edition was printed in black-and-white with a short, central section of Robert Hook's color illustrations. The editors have now integrated these illustrations into the text along with the captions that were missing from the 1st edition. The text itself, aside from a few corrections, remains mostly the same. The glossary has been expanded and the appendixes now include a list of pow-wows, another of Native American museum exhibits, and tables of Native American populations in North American (based on the 1990 census). Also new to this edition is a useful almanac of Native

American holidays and festivals and a list of Websites relating to the study of Native Americans. Johnson has researched the material, culture, demography, and linguistic relationships of Native Americans for more than 30 years, and has led numerous field studies with the cooperation of many present-day Native American communities. He is also a former associate editor of *American Indian Crafts and Culture* as well as *Pow-wow Trails*. This encyclopedia is recommended for all Native American collections.—**Cari Ringelheim**

308. Lyon, William S. **Encyclopedia of Native American Shamanism: Sacred Ceremonies of North America.** Santa Barbara, Calif., ABC-CLIO, 1998. 468p. illus. maps. index. $64.00. ISBN 0-87436-933-9.

Over the past six years there has been a surprising interest in publishing reference works dealing with various aspects of Native American spirituality and religion. Undoubtedly, some of that interest comes from the market potential for "New Age" publications and some from a true interest in understanding Native American spiritual/religious beliefs and practices. Lyon has compiled an interesting, if narrowly focused, book that draws on anthropological data on Shamanism. According to the preface, it is also a continuation of the *Encyclopedia of Native American Healing* (see ARBA 97, entry 340). Entries range in length from fewer than 50 words to 2 or 3 pages. Most of the entries contain several quotations and references to ethnographic monographs. Full bibliographic information for the material cited in entries is provided in an appendix. Approximately two-thirds of the entries relate to specific aspects of Shamanism and other Native American terms. Thus, this volume will be of greatest value to a person who has some prior knowledge of the topic rather than a person seeking general information. One useful aspect of the index is it brings together information about Shamanism by group (Fox, Hopi) and broad topics such as dreams, ghosts, and hunting medicine. There is very little overlap between this title and *The Encyclopedia of Native American Religions* (see ARBA 93, entry 432) or the *Dictionary of Native American Mythology* (see ARBA 94, entry 418). Given that this is a continuation of the author's previous book on healing, there is little overlap between the two titles. A 7-page ethnobotanical bibliography and 27-page index round out the volume. Coverage also includes Canadian and Inuit material (some listed under Eskimo). This will be a useful volume for collections supporting anthropology course work. [R: LJ, 1 Mar 99, p. 74; BL, 15 April 99, p. 1353; Choice, Oct 99, p. 314; RUSQ, Fall 99, p. 89]—**G. Edward Evans**

309. Rudes, Blair A. **Tuscarora-English/English-Tuscarora Dictionary.** Buffalo, N.Y., University of Toronto Press, 1999. 700p. $80.00. ISBN 0-8020-4336-4.

The Tuscarora are an Iroquoian tribe who once lived in North Carolina. In the eighteenth century they were forced to flee to New York State, where they became the Sixth Nation of the Iroquois Confederacy. Today they live in two communities in New York and Ontario. Only four or five fluent speakers of the language remain. Rudes has drawn on documentary sources, as well as on his own fieldwork, to compile this very detailed dictionary, intended for use by the Tuscarora people in reclaiming their language, as well as for reference by scholars.

Like some other American Indian languages, Tuscarora presents a special problem for dictionary makers. Most of its basic roots do not occur as independent words—which could conveniently be alphabetized as dictionary entries—but only combined with a large number of prefixes and suffixes (e.g., the root for garden is "hehn," but the word for garden is "uhéhneh"). Rudes deals with this by devoting his first 539 pages to an alphabetic listing of Tuscarora roots, with full grammatical information and examples for each. The English-to-Tuscarora section that follows refers users to the roots of the first section. For example, garden is listed as "Garden: uhéhneh (-hehn-)."

The volume as a whole is meticulously prepared and a model of lexicography for American Indian languages of such complex structure as those of the Iroquoian family.—**William Bright**

310. **U*X*L Encyclopedia of Native American Tribes.** Sharon Malinowski, Anna Sheets, and Linda Schmittroth, eds. Farmington Hills, Mich., U*X*L/Gale, 1999. 4v. illus. maps. $99.00/set. ISBN 0-7876-2838-7.

This encyclopedia, written at a 5th grade reading level, contains entries on 80 Native American tribes, confederacies, or groups. The entries are divided into 10 sections in 4 volumes: The Northeast and Southeast; The Great Basin and Southwest; The Arctic, Subarctic, Great Plains, and Plateau; and California and the Pacific Northwest. Each section begins with an essay that introduces the area's history and shared cultural experiences. The entries for individual groups follow. Each begins with basic information, such as name, location, population, language family, and group affiliations. This is followed by specific topics, such as history, language, religion, government, and arts. Suggestions for further reading conclude each entry.

One problem with this title is that there are simply not enough tribal entries. For example, the Southeast includes six tribal entries: Caddo, Cherokee, Chickasaw, Choctaw, Creek, and Seminole. On the map entitled "Historic Locations of U.S. Native Groups," there are 10 tribes in Georgia alone. Six is not representative of the region as a whole.

"Moundbuilders" is an extremely curious entry considering it combines 4 distinctively different cultures, dating from 1500 to 1751 B.C.E., into 1 group. The Creeks and Cherokees had much more in common than these four groups but they certainly merit separate entries. The Mississippian Culture also extended further west than Arkansas. Some of the finest examples of Mississippian shell engravings come from the Spiro Mound Group in Eastern Oklahoma. Readers interested in the moundbuilders would be better served by *Archaeology of Prehistoric Native America: An Encyclopedia* (see ARBA 99, entry 443).

Sections entitled "Words to Know" and "Timeline" are included, along with many maps and pictures that supplement the text nicely. Each volume also contains a complete bibliography of books, periodicals, Websites, and CD-ROMs. The volumes uses continuous pagination and each contains the index for the entire set.

Future editions of this work are planned to expand on the number of Native American groups profiled. Rather than wait and buy each subsequent edition, interested individuals should just purchase *The Gale Encyclopedia of Native American Tribes* (see ARBA 99, entry 389). It shares both general format and two editors with this volume. It also contains nearly 400 tribal entries in much more detail. [R: BR, Nov/Dec 99, pp. 79-80]—**John R. Burch Jr.**

311. Waldman, Carl. Illustrated by Molly Braun. **Encyclopedia of Native American Tribes.** rev. ed. New York, Facts on File, 1999. 312p. illus. maps. index. $65.00. ISBN 0-8160-3963-1.

Carl Waldman has prepared several reference books about Native Americans for Facts on File—*Who Was Who In Native American History* (see ARBA 91, entry 402) and *Word Dance: Language of Native American Cultures* (see ARBA 95, entry 437). In addition to the preceding titles, he has compiled two other titles in collaboration with illustrator Molly Braun—*Atlas of the North American Indian* (see ARBA 86, entry 380) and *Encyclopedia of Native American Tribes* (see ARBA 89, entry 364). This is a revised edition of the latter title and is 20 pages longer. Entries and illustrations that appeared in the 1st edition appear to be only slightly changed. This is based on checking eight entries selected at random. Most of the changes are in the form of rewording the same information and in one case a new sentence about current economic conditions. Some of the increase in length is due to an extra 10 pages of front matter, additional entries in the glossary, as well as an updated and expanded bibliography. The question for libraries with the 1st edition is, is there enough new information to make this a worthwhile purchase? For libraries with only limited customer interest in Native Americans the answer is probably no. Where there is a strong interest in Native American studies and the library holds the 1988 edition, it would be best to get an examination copy before making a final decision. For libraries that did not buy the 1st edition the answer is clearly this is a worthwhile addition to a general reference collection.—**G. Edward Evans**

Directories

312. Meiners, Phyllis A. **National Directory of Foundation Grants for Native Americans.** Kansas City, Mo., CRC Publishing, 1998. 205p. index. $99.95pa. ISBN 0-9633694-8-2.

This volume is one of four titles in the Native American Series of Multicultural Grant Guides, including the *National Directory of Philanthropy for Native Americans*, the *Corporate and Foundation Fundraising Manual for Native Americans*, and *Church Philanthropy for Native Americans and Other Minorities*. The preface states that "in less than a decade, funding from large private foundations for Native American programs grew by 608 percent ($10,713,000 in 1998 vs. $65,084,000 in 1996)." Assuming that this is true, and knowing that American Indian organizations are always struggling for additional outside funding, it seems clear that this particular volume fills a need.

Information included is convenient and easy to understand. Information is given on 56 foundations that now make grants to Native American projects and studies programs. Data include addresses, telephone numbers, contacts for each foundation, sample grants (names of organizations and amount of funding awarded) actually made by each foundation, foundation deadlines, procedures, materials required for application packets, e-mail addresses and Websites for each foundation (if they have them), and foundation geographic preferences. A subject index and geographic index make it easier to locate the information desired.

Some of the foundations cited are large, well-known foundations who award millions of dollars annually, such as the Ford Foundation, William Randolph Hearst Foundation, Robert Wood Johnson Foundation, W. K. Kellogg Foundation, and Lilly Endowment Inc. So it is particularly useful to have information available that cites the number of grants and the high and low amounts of funding for grants awarded in a particular year. Those seeking smaller amounts can more readily determine what foundations might be appropriate for their requests. Libraries that serve native populations should surely provide this resource. [R: Choice, June 99, p. 1765]—**Karen D. Harvey**

Handbooks and Yearbooks

313. Carrasco, Davíd, with Scott Sessions. **Daily Life of the Aztecs: People of the Sun and Earth.** Westport, Conn., Greenwood Press, 1998. 282p. illus. maps. index. (The Greenwood Press "Daily Life Through History" Series). $45.00. ISBN 0-313-29558-1.

Carrasco, director of the Moses Mesoamerican Archive and professor of history of religions at Princeton University, and Sessions, doctoral candidate in the department of religion at Princeton University, have combined their talents to present this overview of pre-Columbian Aztec culture that reflects the latest scholarship while remaining accessible to lay readers. It provides a glimpse of Aztec life that is often overlooked in texts that tend to dwell on subjects such as ritualistic human sacrifice and cannibalism. These subjects are also included in this book but are examined in context with their role in society as a whole.

The first two chapters are designed as an introduction to the geography and cosmology of the Aztec world. Chapter 3 focuses on life in the community in general. Three chapters focusing on education, societal dynamics, and aesthetics supplement it. Chapter 7 is extremely informative and focuses on human sacrifice and its role in Aztec religion. The authors carefully explain the role of priests and the function of sacrifice in an effort to dispel the stereotypical view of bloodthirsty priests that has dominated the literature on the subject. The 10th chapter focuses on the clash of cultures between the Aztecs and Spaniards that proved to be the end of the Aztec Empire. The 11th chapter serves as an epilogue, which examines the impact of the Aztecs on Mexican culture today. All of the chapters are greatly enhanced by the large number of pictures and photographs scattered throughout the text. The book also includes both an index and a selected bibliography. Especially noteworthy is a glossary, which includes a pronunciation guide for Nahuatl terms. This excellent book is recommended for public and academic libraries.—**John R. Burch Jr.**

314. Lovett, John R., Jr., and Donald L. DeWitt, comps. **Guide to Native American Ledger Drawings and Pictographs in United States Museums, Libraries, and Archives.** Westport, Conn., Greenwood Press, 1998. 135p. illus. index. (Bibliographies and Indexes in American History, no.39). $55.00. ISBN 0-313-30693-1.

Ledger drawings of the Great Plains native peoples served to clarify oral interpretations of an event. Prior to having European materials on which to record the visual history, native recorders or artists used animal hides. Most of the drawings are what Europeans would call egocentric, as the recorder, warrior, or artist almost always was the central player in the drawing. Although most of the drawings were produced by individuals living on the Great Plains, they are housed in museums and archives in 38 states and the District of Columbia. As might be expected, the Smithsonian holds the greatest number, perhaps as many as 2,000. Most of the institutions (90) that reported holdings have 5 or fewer drawings. The main body of the book is the state-by-state directory of institutions. Each entry has the basic address and telephone information, data about artist and tribal affiliation, number of drawings and medium, dates covered by the drawings, thematic and geographic locations represented in the drawings, any published material about the drawing, and comments (usually in the form of accession number or collection name). There is an annotated bibliography (244 items) of publications about ledger drawings. The two or three sentence annotations are descriptive in character. An index of subjects, tribal affiliation, artists, and institutional names concludes the volume. Although the number of persons interested in this topic is small, having a volume like this may in fact generate more interest as it will now be easier to locate similar items. This work is clearly for the specialized Native American studies libraries.—**G. Edward Evans**

315. Pritzker, Barry M. **Native America Today: A Guide to Community Politics and Culture.** Santa Barbara, Calif., ABC-CLIO, 1999. 453p. illus. maps. index. $75.00. ISBN 1-57607-077-8.

Although it is common to find reference sources on how Native Americans lived hundreds of years ago, it is more difficult to find up-to-date information on the current situations of Native tribes today. This work from ABC-CLIO examines education, health, and tribal identity issues. After a brief introduction the book is arranged into 3 sections: "Contemporary Issues"; Contemporary Profiles of Tribes and Groups"; and "Documents: Acts of Congress, Executive Orders, Court Decisions, Laws, and Resolutions." Each section has entries that are arranged alphabetically. "Contemporary Issues" explains in detail the current situations of Native tribes concerning things like arts and crafts, education, land acquisition or reacquisition, economic development, sacred sites, and control of natural resources. "Contemporary Profiles of Tribes and Groups" examines the current status of 32 tribes within the United States today. Each tribe is described within two to three pages and topics of most concern to that particular tribe are noted. The 3d section provides reproductions of political documents, including Congressional acts, executive orders, court decisions, laws, and resolutions. The three-page bibliography that follows will be useful for researchers. The four appendixes at the end of the volume provide names of federally recognized tribes, Indian groups who have petitioned for federal recognition, first nations in Canada, and maps of federal Indian lands.

This work will serve as a basic tool for those researching the current status of Native American affairs. It will be useful in school, undergraduate, and public libraries.—**Shannon M. Graff**

Jews

316. **American Jewish Desk Reference.** By the American Jewish Historical Society. New York, Random House, 1999. 642p. illus. index. $39.95. ISBN 0-375-40243-8.

This compilation of information, principally biographical, focuses on the Jewish experience in America from the sixteenth century to the present day. It is a comprehensive guide to the history, religious observances, culture, and achievements of the Jewish people in the United States. The publication is sponsored by the American Jewish Historical Society, which since 1893 has been publishing works documenting and recording the Jewish experience in America. The 12 contributors include well-known scholars and academics. However, the authors of the nearly 900 entries are not identified, which is a limitation of the book. The book includes a short guide to its use, which is helpful.

The entries are arranged in 13 thematic parts, each dealing with 1 aspect of American Jewish life and culture. The book begins with history—a useful brief chronology of the history of Jews in America from 1585 to 1999. Other parts include "Judaism and Community in America"; "Rituals, Celebrations, Holidays and Family Life"; "Law, Government and Politics"; "American Zionism and United States Relations with Israel"; "Business, Labor and Finance"; "Education and Intellectual Life"; "Sports and Games"; "Art, Architecture and Photography"; "Music, Dance and Theater"; "Radio, Television and Film"; "Books, Newspapers and Magazines"; "Language and Literature"; and "Science, Medicine and Social Science." Each part begins with a brief overview, and includes background descriptive information, biographies of key figures in the subject area, and a bibliography. The biographical information predominates. The biographies include dates, a brief identification of the person, and his or her major contributions. The structure and organization of each part are not clearly evident, which is sometimes puzzling.

It is useful that the table of contents lists all the main entries. Each part also lists the entries included in that section of the book. This improves access to information included in the text. There is also a detailed, comprehensive index that provides easy access to specific entries. Entries in the text are printed in bold typeface. The numerous interesting black-and-white photographs are another strong feature of the book.

The 2 appendixes, "Finding Out About Jews Around the World" and "Organizations and Resources," are useful guides for further study and research. They include recommended titles and brief descriptions of books as well as names and addresses of selected organizations, research institutes, museums, libraries, local historical societies, and newspapers and magazines.

Even though the scope of the book is broad, its coverage is uneven. The section on music, dance, and theater has the greatest number of entries, followed by radio, television, and film. The science, medicine, and social science section is the weakest, with many notable omissions, including Jewish Nobel Prize-winners such as Stephen Weinberg, Josh Lederberg, and Salvador Luria. The section on Judaism and community in American fails to include mention of the Jewish Renewal Movement, and does not include biographies of important contributors to Jewish Renewal, such as Rabbi Zalman Schacter Shalomi and Rabbi Arthur Waskow.

The book is aimed more toward a popular rather than scholarly audience. It is an interesting, convenient compilation, balancing its strong and weak points, and a useful addition to public, school, temple, and synagogue libraries.—**Susan J. Freiband**

317. Burstein, Chaya M. **A Kid's Catalog of Israel.** rev. ed. Philadelphia, Jewish Publication Society, 1998. 279p. illus. maps. index. $16.95pa. ISBN 0-8276-0651-6.

First published in 1988, the revised edition of *A Kid's Catalog of Israel* provides an overview of the land and its cultures and peoples. Israel is a young country with an ancient history and a diverse population. The 17 chapters of this book are a trip through time and the land. They point out historical sites, geographic features, and wildlife. Interviews with Arab and Jewish adults and children provide a personal connection between readers and their Israeli peers. Maps, quizzes, games, songs, stories, recipes, and craft projects offer opportunities for hands-on activities that increase understanding of the country and its rich heritage. Although this is a children's book, adults will enjoy it. The reading level is appropriate for ages 10 and up. It is an excellent source of projects for classes, youth groups, and families. *A Kid's Catalog of Israel* is recommended for school, synagogue, and public libraries. Families with young children will want it for their homes as well.—**Barbara M. Bibel**

318. Orleck, Annelise. **The Soviet Jewish Americans.** Westport, Conn., Greenwood Press, 1999. 216p. illus. index. (The New Americans). $39.95. ISBN 0-313-30074-7.

One of a series of books that study recent groups of immigrants to the United States, this lively, moving narrative provides the first comprehensive account of the immigration of nearly 500,000 Soviet Jews to the United States between 1967 and 1997. By weaving immigrant voices and numerous photographs together with historical, journalistic, social service, and psychological studies, this book offers a highly readable introduction to the history, politics, and culture of this important new American population. Following a format similar to other books in the series (see ARBA 99, entry 374, for a review of *The Korean Americans*), topics covered include the varied reasons for the exodus of Soviet Jews from the Soviet Union, their experiences in the United States, the communities they have created, and the cultural problems they have encountered. Readers will find fascinating details on religion, politics, foods, festivals, gender roles, employment trends, and general community life. The author, an expert on this group, dispels stereotypical notions about Soviet Jewish immigrants by exploring their tremendous social, political, and cultural diversity, and also shows the impact this ethnic group has had on their adopted country. An appendix profiles some noted Soviet Jewish Americans and is followed by an extensive bibliography and an index. The book is targeted toward the high–school–age and general reader; this might seem overambitious, but due to the scarcity of books dealing with this subject and to its engaging style, it achieves its goal admirably.—**Larry Lobel**

319. **The Shengold Jewish Encyclopedia.** Mordecai Schreiber, ed. Rockville, Md., Shengold Books/Schreiber Publishing, 1998. 301p. illus. $36.00. ISBN 1-887563-43-1.

First published as the *Junior Jewish Encyclopedia* (14th rev. ed., Shengold Books/Schreiber Publishing, 1997), this source has been revised and rewritten as a tool for all age groups. It is a ready-reference source with brief entries on a wide variety of Judaica-related subjects. Users are encouraged to consult other sources for more comprehensive, in-depth information.

The layout is attractive with double columns and ample margins. The alphabetic entries range in length from a few sentences to four pages. They cover people (Abraham, Martin Buber, Jeremiah), places (Iowa, Poland, Uruguay), religious concepts (heaven and hell, Kabbalah, Teshuvah), holidays (Passover, Sukkot), historical events (Holocaust, Yom Kippur War), and arts and letters (music, Hebrew literature, stage and screen). There are also articles on diverse subjects such as stamps, sports, and education. Maps, charts, and illustrations augment the text. Cross-references appear in bold typeface within the entries. *See* references direct users to the proper entry when necessary. As in any general work, there are some inconsistencies. Well-known musicians Isaac Stern, Andre Previn, and Jan Peerce are in the article on Jews in music, while Artur Rubinstein, Itzhak Perlman, and Pinchas Zuckerman have their own entries. Reconstructionism has an article, but the Orthodox, Conservative, and Reform denominations are covered under Judaism. There is no entry for the term *kosher*, but if one looks up *kashrut*, there is a *see* reference to dietary laws.

Although less comprehensive than *The New Standard Jewish Encyclopedia* (7th ed.; see ARBA 93, entry 448) or *The Encyclopedia of Judaism* (see ARBA 91, entry 1449), this is an excellent, inexpensive ready-reference source. With articles on exotic groups such as the Karaites and the Khazers as well as the mythical golem, it is a good choice for school, synagogue, and small public libraries as well as home collections. [R: BL, 15 Nov 98, pp. 613-614; Choice, May 99, p. 1594]—**Barbara M. Bibel**

Latin Americans

320. **Bibliographic Guide to Latin American Studies 1998.** New York, G. K. Hall/Macmillan Library Reference, 1999. 3v. $795.00/set. ISBN 0-7838-0217-X. ISSN 0162-5314.

This subject bibliography includes publications cataloged during the past year by the Nettie Lee Benson Latin American Collection at the University of Texas in Austin, one of the richest and most important libraries in this field in the United States. The records were taken from the University of Texas Online Computer Library (OCLC) tapes. The guide also includes Latin American publications cataloged by the Library of Congress selected from the MARC database on the basis of geographic area codes (for subject coverage), along with country of publication codes (for imprint coverage).

The guide contains bibliographic citations to materials in all languages, as well as to works written by Latin American authors on any subject. Books as well as nonbook materials, but not serials, are included. This bibliography serves in part as an annual supplement to the *Catalog of the Latin American Collection of the University of Texas at Austin* (G. K. Hall, 1969) and its four supplements (1971, 1973, 1975, 1977).

The scope of the guide is broad, including representation from South, Central, Middle and Latin America, the West Indies, the Caribbean, Circumcaribbean, and Intercontinental areas (Western Hemisphere). Individual countries in these geographic areas are represented in the guide. The organization of the entries is in one alphabetic sequence, author, title, and subject. Access is by main entry, with full bibliographic information (including tracings), complete LC cataloging information, ISBN, and identification of library. Cross-references are included. The entries are presented in three columns for ease of reading. Subject headings appear in capitals, also improving readability. The type, although small, is clear. The paper meets the minimum standards of the American National Standards for Information Science—Permanence of Paper for Printed Library Materials.

The guide is bilingual, with title page, preface, and introduction in both Spanish and English. It is a useful reference tool for students, scholars, and researchers in Latin American studies, as well as a valuable, important resource for library acquisitions, reference, and cataloging in this field.—**Susan J. Freiband**

321. Fernández-Shaw, Carlos M. Alfonso Bertodano Stourton, and others. **The Hispanic Presence in North America from 1492 to Today.** updated ed. New York, Facts on File, 1999. 396p. illus. maps. index. $45.00. ISBN 0-8160-4010-9.

This book traces the Spanish presence in the United States from the sixteenth-century explorers and explorations. It is organized geographically by state with separate chapters for those states with a significant Hispanic community: Florida, Arizona, Colorado, California, New Mexico, Texas, Louisiana, and Missouri. The first part presents a general history of Spain's influence in the United States, including the missionaries, colonization, present Hispanic population, outstanding Americans of Spanish origin, Hispanic culture, and contributions to the economy and the law. The second part focuses on the Atlantic Coast states with a historical overview and a section on Spanish place-names for each state. Part 3 covers the states on the east bank of the Mississippi River; part 4 the states on the west bank; part 5 states of the Southwest; part 6 the Rocky Mountain states; and part 7 Pacific Coast states.

The book includes several appendixes: a chronology, a listing of Spanish governors, Spanish missions, Spanish forts and presidios, historical societies, national parks, monuments and other sites of historic interest, North American universities and colleges with chapters of the National Collegiate Hispanic Honor Society, state chapters of the American Association of Teachers of Spanish and Portuguese, Hispanic associations, holidays and festivals, periodicals published in Spanish that highlight Hispanic history and culture, and radio and television stations that broadcast in Spanish. In addition, there is a list of selected readings and an index. The illustrations include black-and-white photographs and maps.

The author is a Spaniard, historian, lawyer, writer, and diplomat. The work was originally written in Spanish (in 1987) and translated in 1991. This edition includes updated appendixes prepared by Dr. Gerardo Piña Rosales, a professor of Spanish language and literature at City University of New York. The handbook is a useful reference tool for high school, community college, and public library collections, particularly in institutions and communities with notable Hispanic populations.—**Susan J. Freiband**

322. **Latin American Lives.** New York, Macmillan Library Reference/Simon & Schuster Macmillan, 1998. 1189p. illus. index. (Macmillan Compendium). $125.00. ISBN 0-02-865060-3.

Latin American Lives presents 3,000 biographical entries that "explore the life and work of the people who had an impact on the history and culture of Latin America." This one-volume reference work draws its content from the five-volume *Encyclopedia of Latin American History and Culture* (see ARBA 97, entry 349). The entries were reproduced in their entirety, and photographs found in the original work were also included in *Latin American Lives*. An alphabetic index allows one to locate additional references to individuals within other entries in the book. There is also an index that groups names into general topical categories, such as "Exploration and Conquest," "Music and Dance," "Revolutionary Leadership," and "Women." The only information that was not reproduced in this new volume was the references to source materials at the end of each entry. The omission of bibliographic references reduces the usefulness of this work as a tool for those wanting to do further research.

Despite this shortcoming, the separate publication of this volume provides a comprehensive source of English-language biographical information on Latin American personalities. Libraries that would hesitate to invest in the more expensive *Encyclopedia of Latin American History and Culture* will find *Latin American Lives* to be an affordable alternative that provides access to much of the former work's richest material. The ease of accessing biographical information in a single volume makes this work a useful complement to collections that already own the larger work. [R: SLJ, Aug 99, p. 184]—**Pamela M. Graham**

323. Ochoa, George. **The New York Public Library Amazing Hispanic American History: A Book of Answers for Kids.** New York, John Wiley, 1998. 192p. illus. maps. index. (New York Public Library Answer Books for Kids Series). $12.95pa. ISBN 0-471-19204-X.

Amazing Hispanic American History is an easy-to-read book of questions and answers for young adults, covering historical and cultural topics. The glossary, recommended reading list, and index are all clear and helpful. Several ruled boxes contain short paragraphs of additional information. Shorter factual notes of one or two sentences enhance the broad margins of the page, providing trivia related to the topic being discussed.

Ochoa provides chapters with broad overviews, such as "Who are Hispanic Americans?" and "Hispanic American Life." He also looks at specific immigrant groups from Mexico, Puerto Rico, Cuba, Dominican Republic, Central America, South America, and Spain in seven separate "Coming From" chapters. He focuses on historical topics in "Before the United States" and "The Lost Land."

The book is for the most part successful in presenting balanced answers to difficult questions, such as "Are Hispanics a race?" and "Why are so many Hispanic Americans poor?" However, there are a few occasions where trends have been missed, or somewhat under-discussed. For example, in answering a question about the rise of Spanish-language church services, Ochoa mentions that there is a growing minority of Protestant Latinos. Yet in answering a question about how Hispanic Americans get along with each other, he writes that while there are many differences, Hispanic Americans share many things, including a "wide-spread Catholic faith."

This book is an important resource for self-understanding and acceptance of others. It is also a good reference book for quick historical facts and social trivia. [R: SLJ, Nov 98, p. 141]—**Sandra E. Fuentes**

324. Smith, Carter, III, and David Lindroth. **Hispanic-American Experience on File.** New York, Facts on File, 1999. 1v. (various paging). illus. maps. index. $125.00. ISBN 0-8160-3695-0.

This compilation, part of a 3-volume series titled Ethnic Minorities in America, presents clear, concise information from graphic sources on the history of Hispanics in the United States. The binder consists of 7 major sections: a background, Spanish and Mexican Settlement in North America (1565-1835), Manifest Destiny and Hispanic American (1836-1900), the Early Twentieth Century (1901-1945), La Raza Unida (1945-1974), Hispanic America Today (1975-present), and Hispanic American Cultural Contributions. The information, taken from many different sources, is presented in a series of black-and-white maps, graphs, diagrams, drawings, photographs, and timelines, along with accompanying brief text.

The scope is broad, providing an overview of Hispanic American history rather than an in-depth coverage of any topic. Although there is a list of sources used for each, the complete bibliographic information for every source is not included. The binder also contains a bibliography (with many Websites) and an index. Access to specific information is facilitated by the detailed table of contents, which lists the subdivisions in each section. Tabs are included to separate and mark each of the sections. There is a brief introduction that describes each section.

Because the format of the work is a looseleaf binder, each page can easily be removed for photocopying. The type, although small in some of the graphics, is clear and easy to read. This reference tool, like others in the Facts on File series, is aimed at students and teachers in need of visual resources for reports, papers, handouts, or oral presentations. It is a convenient, useful resource for reference collections in public, school, and academic libraries.—**Susan J. Freiband**

7 Genealogy and Heraldry

GENEALOGY

Dictionaries and Encyclopedias

325. Schaefer, Christina K. **Genealogical Encyclopedia of the Colonial Americas: A Complete Digest of the Records of All the Countries of the Western Hemisphere.** Baltimore, Md., Genealogical Publishing, 1998. 814p. illus. maps. index. $49.95. ISBN 0-8063-1576-8.

This ambitious project covers Colonial history from European colonization to the American Revolution and presents many interesting records. Some of the work is divided into "Colonies Founded by Spain" and "Colonies Founded by England, France, Netherlands, and Portugal." The original 13 colonies of America, plus Maine and Vermont, are each given extensive coverage in their respective chapters, with some important sources listed for each town or county of the state; frequently including the Family History Library (Salt Lake City) microfilm numbers. More confusing is the section titled "Other U.S. States with Settlements Prior to the Revolution." The 18 states listed did have genuine settlements in pre-Revolutionary times, and in some cases there are fascinating diaries and journals that survived. A few sources, such as "Ohio Vital Records, 1750-1880s," are misleading with a starting date of 1750, which may be a birth date taken from some of the cemetery records included, rather than genuine vital records as named.

Other helpful information appears in a section titled "Colonial Sources in Great Britain." There are also similar sections for France, Germany, Spain, and so on, along with some beneficial maps. There is an intriguing chapter on foreign records at the Library of Congress, including many in microform; for example, "Reformed Protestant Sources, German and Dutch, 1600s and 1700s." This extensive compilation will suggest numerous original and printed sources, leading the serious researcher to new and exciting works. [R: BL, 15 Dec 98, p. 764]—**Carol Willsey Bell**

Directories

326. Arends, Marthe. **Genealogy on CD-ROM.** Baltimore, Md., Genealogical Publishing, 1999. 258p. index. $29.95pa. ISBN 0-8063-1623-3.

The explosion of materials available on CD-ROM has led to the creation of this guide to assist users. Included in this publication are topics such as biographies and historical references, journals, newspapers and periodicals, as well as special-interest items. Following these topics the reader will find an alphabetic state listing and lists for territories, U.S. possessions, and foreign countries. Each entry typically gives the title, publisher and price, system requirements, and a description. Nearly all of the descriptions are taken directly from publishers' lists. A few selected items were examined by the author and are highlighted by a "closer look."

The introductory material includes a section on pros and cons of genealogical CD-ROMs that discusses accuracy, completeness, and sources. Some comments on specific discs would have been helpful, such as "Ohio 1800 Census Index, Selected Countries," which includes Lake Co. (created 1840), Mahoning Co. (created 1846), and Summit Co. (created 1840). One wonders where data were found for the 1810 census index of Ohio, since it was destroyed in the War of 1812 fire. An index to the 1860 census of Pennsylvania claims to be "for the entire state," when in actuality at least six counties are missing.

Nevertheless, this guide is very useful, containing a detailed index and a list of addresses for publishers and vendors of CD-ROM products. Numerous illustrations show visual examples of data on screen.

—**Carol Willsey Bell**

327. Arends, Marthe. **Genealogy Software Guide.** Baltimore, Md., Genealogical Publishing, 1998. 269p. index. $24.95pa. ISBN 0-8064-1581-4.

An impressive compendium of software resources and related information, this work opens with a discussion of the basic issues regarding hardware and software, followed by an overview of what genealogy software can and cannot do. A brief chapter on locating software leads into sequential chapters focused on evaluation of 27 individual genealogy database programs, as well as 43 genealogy utilities and research tools. A separate chapter discusses 12 Macintosh databases and utility programs, as well as older products. Screen snapshots enhance the explanations and evaluations throughout the work.

Several appendixes provide a database comparison chart; a list of genealogy software vendors; guides to older and superseded files; Internet software resources; a list of programs not reviewed; an explanation of Genealogy Data Communication (GEDCOM), a genealogy product created by the Church of Jesus Christ of Latter-day Saints; and a bibliography of computer genealogy publications. A glossary and index supplement the main text. Both the novice and the seasoned researcher should find this work immensely valuable just for the sheer variety of options it provides. [R: LJ, 1 Feb 99, p. 76]—**Edmund F. SantaVicca**

328. Bentley, Elizabeth Petty. **The Genealogist's Address Book.** 4th ed. Baltimore, Md., Genealogical Publishing, 1998. 832p. index. $39.95pa. ISBN 0-8063-1580-6.

Earlier editions of the *The Genealogist's Address Book* have been very popular with genealogists and genealogical librarians. The 4th edition has 182 more pages than the 1995, 3rd edition (see ARBA 96, entry 428). The introduction states that the work "is based largely upon data received in response to direct-mail questionnaires, supplemented by information from printed and Internet sources." "Still, a few organizations, especially religious archives, cited the inability of their limited staff to cope with the mounting demands of genealogists—hobbyists, in their view, rather than serious scholars" (p. v). Coping with and not being "serious scholars" is understandable, because some genealogists are not scholars. However, labeling genealogists as "hobbyists" is a mischaracterization and discriminatory.

Because of the above-admitted prejudices of some organizations, users of Bentley's book should also check other appropriate directories such as the *American Library Directory* (49th ed.; see ARBA 98, entry 572); the *Directory of Historical Societies and Agencies in the United States and Canada* (see ARBA 79, entry 413); the *Directory of Archives and Manuscript Repositories in the United States* (see ARBA 89, entry 424); and the *Hereditary Society Blue Book* (Historic Trust, 1994).

The major portion of the book is arranged by state, then subdivided into topics, such as archives and libraries, historical societies, and genealogical societies. These are arranged alphabetically by the name of the institution, agency, or society, with some inconsistencies in its alphabetizing. Because most genealogists research geographically, many of the topical sections of this work would serve their users better if they were sub-arranged geographically by city. For example, if a genealogist were looking for libraries in the communities where his ancestors resided, the *American Library Directory* would be the better of the two sources to consult, because it is arranged by city. In Bentley's work, libraries that use the name of their city or county are easy to find; but the Monterey Park, California, public library is listed under its memorial name, Bruggemeyer Memorial Library.

The first index is for periodical titles; the second, for the names of the institutions, agencies, and societies. One Website that should be added to the section of antiquarian book dealers is www.bibliofind.com. There are also a few bookstores that should be added to the booksellers section. [R: Choice, July/Aug 99, p. 1915]—**J. Carlyle Parker**

329. **The County Locator: The Guide to Locating Places and Finding the Right County for Public Record Searching.** Michael L. Sankey and Carl R. Ernst, eds. Tempe, Ariz., BRB, 1998. 473p. index. $19.50pa. ISBN 1-879792-39-7.

Whether one is searching for genealogical or business records, it is important to first find where the records for the transaction are kept. This is sometimes difficult to answer. This publication will help.

The work is divided into 3 sections. Section 1 is zip code to county cross-reference, section 2 is the place-name index, and section 3 is a county index. Section 1 includes all the zip codes assigned as of January 1998 as well as zip codes in existence as of May 1992. Each of the possible 99,999 zip codes is listed in this section so the searcher can determine if a zip code is valid or not. The low and high zip codes are listed at the bottom of each page, and the state for those zip codes is listed at the top of the page. Some zip codes are not geographic, and this is indicated by the codes.

Section 2 contains more than 100,000 place-name/zip code combinations. It is ordered alphabetically first by place-name and then by state in order to help distinguish between the same place-names in different states, giving the zip codes for each place. Section 3 lists counties by state alphabetically, along with some basic information about the state and the counties, such as the zip code range for the state, the 1997 population estimate, and capital of the state. The entries for the county include the 1997 estimated county population and the county seat.

There is a detailed introductory section telling how to use this work along with the exceptions to the ways public records are handled. This will be a tremendous resource for locating records.

—**Robert L. Turner Jr.**

330. Howells, Cyndi. **Cyndi's List: A Comprehensive List of 40,000 Genealogy Sites on the Internet.** Baltimore, Md., Genealogical Publishing, 1999. 858p. $49.95pa. ISBN 0-8063-1556-3.

This very extensive guide to at least 40,000 sites on the Internet is organized by major topics, as listed in the table of contents. Among some of the intriguing topics are "Citing Sources," "Calendars and Dates," "Obituaries," "Queries & Message Boards," "Societies & Groups," and "Supplies, Charts & Forms." The "Forms to Print" section gives the URL addresses for census forms, checklists, ancestor charts and family group sheets, and more.

Given the size of this work, creating an index would have been a formidable task. Using the contents' list of topics seems to work well. Once the topic has been selected, a category index appears listing each subtopic covered in that section. It may take a little while to navigate through all of the choices, but it certainly would have taken as much time, or more, to peruse the same material on the computer.

The choice of places to explore is almost overwhelming. For the busy librarian who may not have quick and easy access to the Internet, *Cyndi's List* is an excellent place to look for answers for the genealogical patron. This is an excellent reference tool for electronic media. [R: LJ, 1 Sept 99, pp. 178-180; BL, 15 Nov 99, p. 644]—**Carol Willsey Bell**

331. Schaefer, Christina K. **Instant Information on the Internet! A Genealogist's No-Frills Guide to the 50 States & the District of Columbia.** Baltimore, Md., Genealogical Publishing, 1999. 86p. $9.95pa. ISBN 0-8063-1608-X.

This is a compilation of URLs of the author's choice of genealogy resources on the Internet. The preface states that the book was designed for speed and convenience, and it is indeed a compact paperback that would fit in a researcher's briefcase. The book is organized alphabetically by state. Grouped together under each state's listing are URLs for the state department of vital records; the state archive, library, and historical society; any National Archives Branch located in the state; and other important library and archival resources. Separate headings follow for local information sites; indexes, searchable databases, and digitized documents; and comprehensive Websites with multiple links to relevant resources. There are no annotations.

Designed for individual genealogists and family historians who want to harness the Internet for their research, this guide will be a good addition to a library's circulating collection. However, librarians serving genealogists will be better advised to acquire Thomas Jay Kemp's *Virtual Roots: A Guide to Genealogy* and *Local History on the World Wide Web* (see ARBA 98, entry 366). A more comprehensive resource, this work is international in scope and also includes sites maintained by family associations. Unlike the book under review, Kemp lists sub-addresses for sites, provides postal addresses and telephone numbers to facilitate reference contact, and flags some sites as "outstanding" or "extraordinary." [R: LJ, 1 Sept 99, pp. 178-180]—**Ruth A. Carr**

Handbooks and Yearbooks

332. Szucs, Loretto Dennis. **They Became Americans: Finding Naturalization Records and Ethnic Origins.** Orem, Utah, Ancestry, 1998. 294p. illus. maps. index. $19.95pa. ISBN 0-916489-71-X.

This well-written guidebook to naturalization records and ethnic origin leads the user through a multitude of varying records created in differing time spans. It is imperative for the researcher to understand the naturalization process and to learn where to find surviving records. It is noted that "perhaps only about one-quarter of the foreign-born were naturalized," creating a problem in trying to find alternative records. This work explores the other types of documents to be found, and presents visual examples of them.

The author carefully and methodically leads the reader through early time periods into the twentieth century with samplings of the wide range of various sources. Each new discussion provides creative ideas and possibilities of places to search for additional data. Information about the many different ports of entry is given, plus facts on Castle Garden, the predecessor to the more recent Ellis Island in New York Harbor. Szucs' excellent and well-written research guide should quickly become the epitome of the subject in the field of genealogy.—**Carol Willsey Bell**

333. Woodtor, Dee Parmer. **Finding a Place Called Home: A Guide to African-American Genealogy and Historical Identity.** New York, Random House, 1999. 499p. illus. index. $25.00; $18.00pa. ISBN 0-375-40595-X; 0-375-70843-Xpa.

This nicely done research guide is arranged into logical chapters, and provides an excellent pattern for the novice genealogist to follow. Among some of the topics presented are "Searching for Your Ancestors During Reconstruction," " The Genealogy of Your Slave Ancestors," "The Records of Slavery," and "African American Institutional Records."

The author directs the new researcher through the various mazes common to anyone starting work on family history, with helpful suggestions for ways to proceed. Special instructions are given for using sources that are unique to African American genealogy, as well as how to efficiently use other records common to everyone. There are many illustrations showing good examples of special records.

In addition, information is provided on African American genealogical societies and Internet sites. There is a good index and a lengthy bibliography included. This reviewer would have preferred more importance placed on documenting and citing sources. This is an excellent book and is highly recommended. [R: LJ, 15 Mar 99, p. 73]—**Carol Willsey Bell**

HERALDRY

334. **Flags.** New York, DK Publishing, 1998. 240p. illus. maps. index. (Eyewitness Handbooks). $18.95 flexibinding. ISBN 0-7894-4224-8.

This handbook for the study of flags throughout the world is delightfully illustrated in color and enhanced with the use of world maps as endpapers. The introduction gives thumbnail sketches about historical usage of flags for identification, and later for political reasons. Today, many private and professional organizations are adopting flags.

Typical entries inform the reader of the date the current flag was adopted, a description of the colors used and why, a complete explanation of the coats of arms if used, and other distinguishing facts. Regional flags, if used by a country, are also described. In the case of the United Kingdom, there are subnational flags for England, Scotland, Isle of Man, Jersey, Wales, and Guernsey. The U.S. section shows some of the historical flags, as well as all of the state flags with brief descriptions. Some international flags are presented, such as the North Atlantic Treaty Organization (NATO), Olympic Movement, United Nations (UN), and Red Cross. Signal flags for each alphabet letter and numbers are included. This is a nicely done handbook on the subject, and will surely help to answer many questions in a quick and concise manner.—**Carol Willsey Bell**

PERSONAL NAMES

335. Reaney, P. H., and R.M. Wilson. **Dictionary of English Surnames.** 3d ed. New York, Oxford University Press, 1997. 520p. maps. $15.95pa. ISBN 0-19-860092-5.

A close examination of the present volume reveals it to be a reprint of the 3d edition published in 1995. The prefaces, introduction, and A to Z name entries appear to be identical, the sole apparent changes being the cover illustration and a new 10-page appendix essay by David Hey titled "Locating the Home of a Family Name."

A favorable review for the 3d edition will be found in ARBA 96 (entry 427). This reprint is not recommended for libraries that already possess it. It is, however, recommended for other libraries with an interest in English genealogy.—**Donald E. Collins**

8 Geography and Travel Guides

GEOGRAPHY

General Works

Atlases

336. **Collins Essential Atlas of the World.** London, HarperCollins; distr., North Pomfret, Vt., Trafalgar Square, 1998. 159p. maps. $22.95pa. ISBN 0-00-448611-0.

HarperCollins has published an inexpensive atlas on quality paper using maps by Bartholomew Ltd. The atlas is visually pleasing, from the clarity of the maps to the presentation of the information associated with the maps. The table of contents not only gives the name of the map and page location, but also the scale and a visual depiction of the maps on an outline map of the continent or region. The reference section is arranged by continent and gives the name of each country followed by area, population, capital city, languages, religions, and currency. This is followed by information on world economic groups, international organizations, time zones, physical features, vegetation, climate, population patterns, world health, travel and tourism, global telecommunications, and political changes through the world during the twentieth century. The vegetation section not only uses maps to show the locations of the various types of vegetation in the world but also gives a definition and a picture of the type of vegetation. The six pages of "Century of Change" will be useful to students studying the influence of wars and revolutions on political boundaries. A segment on how to use the atlas precedes the main body of maps. Both relief and political maps are included, with major cities, roadways, railways, and physical features noted. Boundaries are marked according to their location at press time with disputed and cease-fire lines also marked. Maps of oceans are included. The volume concludes with a glossary, list of abbreviations, and extensive index. This is a user-friendly, affordable atlas for home, schools, and libraries. [R: Choice, Sept 99, p. 103]—**Elaine Ezell**

337. Cumming, William P. Louis De Vorsey Jr. **The Southeast in Early Maps.** 3d ed. Chapel Hill, N.C., University of North Carolina Press, 1998. 362p. maps. index. $90.00. ISBN 0-8078-2371-6.

A classic book on cartography has come back to life. First published in 1958, *The Southeast in Early Maps* is a tribute to its originator, deceased cartographer and collector William Cumming. A 2d edition appeared in 1962 but the 3d edition is more complete with 95 maps, 24 color plates, and a new essay by the editor on mapping by Native Americans. The majority of the volume is a descriptive bibliography of 449 maps of the colonial southeastern United States. Entries include map topic, size, an extensive description, where reproductions were published, and location of the original. Indication is made if the map is reproduced in the volume. Cumming's original introductory essay on early maps is reprinted. There are brief listings—a chronological list and a short-title list—as well as an index to the two essays. The volume is handsome and the reproduction quality of the maps is excellent. Maps of early settlement and civilization are a key research element for the historian, sociologist, and cartographer, and a new edition of this volume is welcome. Earlier editions are out of print and quite expensive on the open market. Reviews of the 1st edition praised the work and, although expensive, this new edition of *The Southeast in Early Maps* is a must for research libraries and collections focusing on colonial history. [R: LJ, 1 Oct 98, p. 76]

—**Boyd Childress**

338. **National Geographic Atlas of the World.** 7th ed. Washington, D.C., National Geographic Society, 1999. 134p. maps. index. $125.00. ISBN 0-7922-7528-4.

This 7th edition of National Geographic's *Atlas of the World* is completely updated and will continue to serve as a standard source for all types of libraries—college, public, special, and school. Extending National Geographic's cartographic expertise to the Web, National Geographic has teamed up with the Environmental Systems Research Institute (ESRI) to develop a highly innovative Website to access maps and geographic data online. The comprehensive index offers some 140,000 entries and there are new maps of major cities of the world. This atlas is highly recommended.—**Bohdan S. Wynar**

339. **National Geographic Beginner's World Atlas.** Washington, D.C., National Geographic Society, 1999. 64p. illus. maps. index. $17.95. ISBN 0-7922-7502-0.

340. **National Geographic United States Atlas for Young Explorers.** Washington, D.C., National Geographic Society, 1999. 176p. illus. maps. index. $24.95. ISBN 0-7922-7115-7.

Both the *National Geographic Beginner's World Atlas* (for children ages 5 to 8) and the *National Geographic United States Atlas for Young Explorers* (for children ages 8 to 12) are excellent atlases designed specifically for use by young people and families. The atlases are the most recent addition to a children's series begun by the National Geographic Society in 1998 with *National Geographic World Atlas for Young Explorers*.

The *Beginner's World Atlas* focuses on the seven continents. There is an introductory chapter called "Understanding Your World," which provides age-appropriate explanations about maps and mapmaking as well as vivid illustrations portraying the physical world map, physical world map symbols, and the political world map. Completing the introduction are two pages describing "what this atlas will teach you." The seven sections that follow describe each of the seven continents. A young child introduces each continent and a scenic vista portrays a beautiful part of the landscape. The section called "The Land" describes major land regions, waterways, climate, plants, and animals in brief, fact-filled text. Another division, "The People," tells about various countries, cities, native peoples, languages, and products for each continent.

Accompanying the large-format, easy-to-read maps are more than 100 color photographs with great appeal to young children. A page of world facts, a glossary, and an index complete the atlas. The *United States Atlas for Young Explorers* combines beautiful photographs, two-dimensional maps, and information presented in colorful, fact-filled pages. Two introductory pages explain how to use the atlas and show that the United States has been divided into five regions. The following two sections contain in-depth information about the physical and political U.S. areas. These pages have excellent maps, beautiful photographs, and clear and brief explanations—all with the younger student in mind. Another brief section has a map and information about our nation's capital. The main portion of the atlas is devoted to each of the five regions of the United States. A panoramic photograph with a list of the states in the margin introduces each region. A physical map of the area is followed by clear and concise descriptions and photographs of the region. To complete the regional coverage, each state is portrayed with a map, fact capsules, and a brief summary. Completing the atlas are several pages covering the U.S. territories, facts and figures, a glossary of terms, abbreviations and Websites, and a comprehensive index.

National Geographic's high standards are evident throughout both volumes. Their world-renowned quality and accuracy are further validated by a collaboration of education consultants and geographers. Both atlases should be on every shelf at home as well as school and public libraries.—**Mary L. Trenerry**

341. **New Millennium World Atlas Deluxe.** [CD-ROM]. Skokie, Ill., Rand McNally, 1998. Minimum system requirements: IBM or compatible Pentium processor with 100MHz. Eight-speed CD-ROM drive. Windows 95 or Windows NT 4.0. 16MB RAM. 40MB hard disk space. Video adapter card. Monitor. Internet service. $44.95.

User-friendly and highly interactive, this flexible atlas provides a variety of features that will likely be appreciated by many high school and college students. More than 1.6 million place-names are included as part of a sophisticated three-dimensional model that provides impressive shaded relief. In addition, interactive city center street maps are provided for 65 major cities of the world. Pan and zoom navigational tools allow the user to roam about the street; to search for key sites; and to connect with texts that describe a country's geography, people, economy, history, and politics.

Other features include thematic maps that highlight significant social, economic, and environmental themes; "exploration" maps that cover such topics as the oceans, glaciation, volcanoes, and historic empires; comparison tools that allow the user to compile statistics for up to four countries; dynamic links between map and nonmap content; hyperlinks and cross-references; drawing tools and map markers; and online connectivity to pertinent Internet links. The user is also able to use any of these capabilities to create personal notebooks.

Although data are current only through 1997, this product is a strong value for its price. This CD-ROM is recommended for school and public library reference collections. [R: LJ, 15 Mar 98, pp.103-104; SLJ, Mar 99, p. 134]—**Edmund F. SantaVicca**

342. **People and the Earth: An Environmental Atlas.** Andrea Dué, ed. Danbury, Conn., Grolier, 1999. 6v. illus. maps. $225.00/set. ISBN 0-7172-9204-5.

No introductory material anywhere in the set explains the editor's intent. But the range of this colorfully illustrated set, designed for middle school and somewhat older students, is the history of the world; the development of animal, plant, and human life; and the effect human activity has had on the environment. The volumes are titled Prehistoric Times, Ancient Times, Medieval Times, Age of Expansion, Age of Revolutions, and The Modern World. Numerous two-page spreads deal with life and human development in the indicated time period, but may or may not have anything to do with the environment. Coverage is often not in proportion to events' relative importance. The final volume, in the printed material surrounding glitzy illustrations, hits very hard at modern humans' degradation of the environment, and may leave young people with hopeless feelings. This set is not especially useful for reference (despite a list of topics, a source list, a glossary, and an index in each volume), but it would serve as an excellent general browser for students who may then refer to other sources. For example, the Prehistoric Times volume has globe-shaped world maps showing the positions of the world's plates throughout its history. Medieval Times has a spread on the design of windmills and another on wars, plagues, and famines that would catch the interest of many young students despite their inexact fit with the theme of the set. [R: BR, Sept/Oct 99, p. 70]

—**Edna M. Boardman**

Bibliographies

343. **Bibliographic Guide to Maps and Atlases 1998.** Thorndike, Maine, G. K. Hall/ Macmillan, 1999. 1039p. $395.00. ISBN 0-7838-0225-0. ISSN 0360-5889.

This hefty volume contains a comprehensive listing of publications cataloged by the New York Public Library and the Library of Congress from January 1 through December 31, 1998. The materials selected are limited to imprint dates of 1990 to the present. The bibliography has works of various languages and formats, including books, serials, and nonbook items. Examples of types of material covered include U.S. geological survey maps, Belgium topographical maps, Chicago street and road maps, nautical charts of Tasmania, dictionaries of cartography, India guidebooks, aerial views of Zabreb (Croatia), remote-sensing images of Washington, D.C., and world and celestial globes. This bibliographic guide is arranged into one integrated alphabet by main entry (usually author or corporate author), added entry, title, series title, and subject. Each entry contains full bibliographic information and complete Library of Congress cataloging information.

The 1996 edition, published in 1997, was the last one on maps and atlases to be reviewed in ARBA (see ARBA 98, entry 391). It had more than 200 fewer pages and its price was $35 less. As one of the most complete bibliographies in the field, research libraries in areas related to geography, geology, cartography, and maps should find this volumes extremely useful. A cumulative Web version of the title would be even more appealing, especially if the price were kept reasonable.—**O. Gene Norman**

Biography

344. **Explorers: From Ancient Times to the Space Age.** John Logan Allen, E. Julius Dasch, and Barry M. Gough, eds. New York, Macmillan Library Reference/Simon & Schuster Macmillan, 1999. 3v. illus. maps. $275.00/set. ISBN 0-02-864893-5.

Younger readers are always enthusiastic about the adventure and drama of exploration. They are inspired by the men and women who ventured into unknown territory on land, sea, and into space. Explorers from ancient times to the space age are the kind of reference material designed for students at middle school level or above. This 3-volume set contains profiles of 333 early adventurers, such as geographers, merchants, navigators, botanists, archaeologists, and treasure hunters. Readers will also find people who made essential contributions to the progress of discovery by working in their own countries as cartographers, inventors, and historians.

A group of experts in history, geography, and space science selected the subjects of these profiles. They are arranged alphabetically by the explorer's last name. Each profile begins with a note that lists the explorer's nationality, dates of birth and death, and main activities. The text of the profile summarizes the explorer's accomplishments and the cause and the effect of the exploration. A list of suggested readings is placed at the end of each profile. There are 3 introductory essays at the beginning of volume 1—"The Technology of Exploration," "Causes and Effects of Exploration," and "The History of Exploration." These articles "provide technical and historical background and help students to understand how each explorer's efforts were a part of the long and complex process of discovery." A glossary, list of explorers by nationality, list of explorers by area of exploration, bibliography, and index are at the end of the profiles to help readers search from different aspects. The editors have included many pictures and maps with the purpose of trying to help readers gain a better understanding. Like other new students' encyclopedias from Macmillan Library Reference, this well-designed reference source is curriculum focused and written at an appropriate reading level. It is an essential for school libraries, public libraries, and academic libraries. [R: BL, 15 April 99, pp. 1354-1356; Choice, July/Aug 99, pp. 1926-1928]—**Xiao (Shelley) Yan Zhang**

345. Pear, Nancy, and Daniel B. Baker. **Explorers & Discoverers, Volume 6: From Alexander the Great to Sally Ride.** Farmington Hills, Mich., U*X*L/Gale, 1998. 265p. illus. maps. index. $39.00. ISBN 0-7876-2946-4.

This additional volume to the *Explorers & Discoverers* set (see ARBA 96, entry 454, for a review of the original 4-volume set) features an additional 30 biographies of 19 men, 9 women, 1 facility, and 1 machine. Those chosen span a time period from approximately 1520 B.C.E. to the present. Except for one person, all individuals included are deceased. The men and women included were selected based on their contributions to human knowledge about the earth and its life-forms. The reader learns who these adventurers were, when and how they lived and traveled, and the significance and consequences of their discoveries. The introduction provides insight into the reasons that motivate people to enter the unknown, including information on what motivated 19 of those included in the volume.

Entries are alphabetically arranged and enhanced with extensive photographs, illustrations, and maps. The volume concludes with a cumulative chronology of exploration by region, a list of explorers by country of birth, and a cumulative index to volumes 1 through 6. Libraries holding the original series will want to expand the set with this additional volume.—**Elaine Ezell**

346. Pear, Nancy, and Daniel B. Baker. **Explorers & Discoverers, Volume 7: From Alexander the Great to Sally Ride.** Edited by Jane Hoehner. Farmington Hills, Mich., U*X*L/Gale, 1999. 295p. illus. maps. index. $39.00. ISBN 0-7876-3681-9. ISSN 1522-9947.

The latest supplement to this set, volume 7, adds 30 biographies of men, women, and machines that have expanded our horizons. The 20 men, 8 women, 1 museum, and 1 ship newly inducted into the set include Thor Heyerdahl, Nearchus, Mel Fisher, John Bryon, Helen Thayer, and the National Air and Space Museum. Although they represent a time range from ancient to modern, they are mainly European or American. Arranged alphabetically, the entries focus on the motivation driving these explorers and discoverers and the journeys themselves. There is little information about family or early life. Sources are included for each entry. Entries do include items such as illustrations, maps, geographic details of journeys, and similar information. The volume begins with a section of 16 black-and-white maps of major world regions. The end sheets provide a general world map. The section on chronology and exploration covers all seven volumes by area explored. The index is cumulative. This is a nice supplement to upper elementary and middle school history classes. It brings to the forefront some figures who might otherwise be forgotten and will provide additional information for research. [R: BR, Nov/Dec 99, p. 72]—**Esther R. Sinofsky**

Chronology

347. **Worldmark Chronology of the Nations.** Timothy L. Gall and Susan B. Gall, eds. Farmington Hills, Mich., Gale, 1999. 4v. illus. maps. index. $249.00/set. ISBN 0-7876-0521-2.

The four volumes in this set are arranged geographically (Africa, Americas, Asia, and Europe), and include entries for the 192 nations that exist at the end of the twentieth century. Volumes contain maps and black-and-white photographs. Each volume begins with the same, brief 6-page timeline of world history and ends with the same 107 pages of glossary, bibliography, and index. This work follows the organization of similar works by the same publisher—*Worldmark Encyclopedia of the Nations* (8th ed.; see ARBA 96, entry 105) and the *Nations and Worldmark Encyclopedia of Cultures and Daily Life* (see ARBA 99, entry 364).

Each national entry begins with a one- to two-page overview describing the location, general geography (illustrated with a map showing cities, rivers, and mountains), and broad historical description. Although the publisher's notes describe a graphical timeline for each entry, there are no linear-type graphic time-lines that most students are familiar with. Rather, the "timeline" is a chronological listing of important events in that nation's social and cultural history beginning, for many nations, with prehistory and focusing on the twentieth century. The historical timeline forms the bulk of each chapter and often contains additional maps showing political history or illustrating military operations. Within each timeline emphasis is given to notable individuals. Each chapter concludes with a bibliography, which is a useful source of information for students conducting additional research. Some of the bibliographic entries at the end of each chapter are repeated in the comprehensive bibliography at the end of each volume.

In any such work, debate about why "X" was included and why "Z" was omitted is inevitable. Under the United States of America, for example, readers might question the historical significance of including the "nondiscovery" of the United States by Christopher Columbus, the running of the first Kentucky Derby, or the inclusion of Herman Melville (a great American writer to be sure) while the only mention of Mark Twain is as an opponent of U.S. imperialism (under the entry for Puerto Rico).

This set could serve as an addition to a reference library or perhaps in an individual classroom. Its virtues are the chronological listing of historical events within each entry and the specific national bibliographies. "Written by experts and edited for student researchers who are just beginning to tackle complex issues..." the work would be suitable for secondary school students and beyond. It could be used to provide an introduction to a country or as a "first step" to more comprehensive student research.

—Craig A. Munsart

Dictionaries and Encyclopedias

348. **Merriam-Webster's Geographical Dictionary.** 3d ed. Springfield, Mass., Merriam-Webster, 1998. 1361p. maps. $29.95. ISBN 0-87779-546-0.

Librarians will welcome this new edition of a standard reference source, one that is relatively inexpensive for the amount of information provided. More than 48,000 entries are arranged in alphabetic order and include countries, cities, towns, villages, mountains, oceans, islands, rivers, lakes, deserts, valleys, major buildings, large constructions, and other significant human additions to the landscape. As for the United States, nearly all incorporated places with a population of 2,500 or more have been included, as well as all county seats regardless of population size. Information in entries includes variant spellings, pronunciations, size, population, and location. Entries for significant topics (larger cities, countries, significant landforms) provide additional information such as description and history. There are more than 252 maps and hundreds of tables throughout the book. Introductory material includes explanatory notes, abbreviations and symbols, map projections and symbols, a list of maps, a world map, and pronunciation symbols. There are two appendixes—a glossary and a list of geographical terms in other languages.

Other aids that make this a user-friendly reference are guide words at the top of each page, bold letters for entry words and references, a pronunciation guide key at the bottom of each odd-numbered text page, references to other entries, and map legends. This is a highly recommended reference source for those needing quick, easy access to basic geographical information.—**Dana McDougald**

349. Skinner, Malcolm, David Redfern, and Geoff Farmer. **Dictionary of Geography.** Chicago, Fitzroy Dearborn, 1999. 311p. illus. $40.00. ISBN 1-57958-154-4.

Geography is a rather large topic to be the subject of a dictionary. With no limitations on the subject, fairly large definitions, and a modest number of pages, it is any wonder that there are gaps in this work.

No particular audience is given for this dictionary, so it is difficult to say whether it meets the target expectations. The book is relatively small, so one assumes that the work is not necessarily for professionals, and yet it is not the sort of thing to buy for Christmas presents either. Definitions are clear enough for the intelligent, novice reader, although an understanding of the entries does require some application. The range of coverage is broad but not deep—even though geography is not this reviewer's subject, some entries prompted me to look for others, and I was surprised at the number of listings not found.

Some of the terms are a bit surprising, although a moment's thought can explain the inclusion of terms for topological mathematics and other fields. Further contemplation suggests that because this is a geographical dictionary rather than a geological one, political and economic concepts do have a place. The reason that these latter terms seem odd becomes clear after a more thorough perusal. Right–wing political and social views seem to have a definite preponderance. This is a business-oriented geographical glossary.

It is not clear who this dictionary is aimed at, and it is difficult to think of an appropriate group. It may do for a high school reference, but some work may have to go into plugging the holes. [R: LJ, 15 Nov 99, p. 62]—**Robert M. Slade**

Handbooks and Yearbooks

350. **America from Space.** By Thomas B. Allen. Willowdale, Ont., Firefly Books, 1998. 160p. illus. maps. $29.95. ISBN 1-55209-280-1.

Allen, a former associate director of National Geographic Books and the prolific author of books and articles on the natural world, has gathered 128 computer-generated satellite images and nearly 100 other photographs to show what our country looks like from the heavens. The pictures are exquisite, with vibrant color and astounding detail filling each page. An excellent introduction gives a brief history of the technology that has made such images possible and explains their value to modern-day society. The book is organized into eight chapters, each featuring a different area of the county: Alaska and Hawaii ("fire and ice"), the West Coast, the West, the Rockies, the Heartland, the Land of Lakes, the Southland, and the Northeast Corridor. Each chapter begins with a short essay, and each illustration has an informative caption. The pictures are not intended to be comprehensive, but show unique natural or artificial features. There is a relatively brief, but adequate, index. The value of the book lies in its ability to bring such geographical features as fjords and mountain ranges to life and to demonstrate how farms and cities have altered the natural landscape. *America from Space* is just the thing to add that element of wonder to geography and geology courses. It would also be a lovely coffee-table book, and at the remarkable price, an affordable one. This work is recommended for the circulating collections of high school, public, and larger academic libraries.

—Hope Yelich

351. **The Columbia Gazetteer of the World.** Saul B. Cohen, ed. New York, Columbia University Press, 1998. 3v. $750.00/set. ISBN 0-231-11040-5.

For many years *The Columbia-Lippincott Gazetteer of the World* (1952) was the standard reference source for geographic names and data. For many years to come, the standard source will be *The Columbia Gazetteer of the World*. Indeed, the new gazetteer should rank among the most important reference books currently in print.

Under the editorship of Saul B. Cohen, one of the world's most recognized geographers, a staff of more than 150 geographers, editors, and advisors compiled a list of some 165,000 entries that reflect the massive changes in the geopolitical landscape since the early 1950s. Since publication of the previous gazetteer, widespread colonialism ended resulting in the recognition of scores of new countries, towns, and cities; Eastern Europe was freed from Soviet domination; and the United Nations grew threefold. Renewed nationalism inspired thousands of name changes and spelling changes. Of the 165,000 entries in *The Columbia Gazetteer of the World*, 30,000 are new.

Entries reflect the geopolitical world (countries, provinces, states, regions, and cities), the physical world (continents, regions, lakes, islands, valleys, and peninsulas), and so-called special places (national parks, airports, harbors, dams, and shopping malls). Where appropriate, physical, economic, political, historical, and cultural descriptions are included as are population, latitude, longitude, and elevation. Pronunciations and changed and variant spellings are also included. A monumental work of great authority and utility, *The Columbia Gazetteer of the World* should be in the core reference collections of virtually every library. [R: Choice, Oct 98, p. 283-284; C&RL, Sept 98, p. 613; BL, 15 Oct 98, pp. 437-438; RUSQ, Spring 99, p. 316]—**Edward Kurdyla**

352. **The National Geographic Desk Reference.** Washington, D.C., National Geographic Society, 1999. 699p. illus. maps. index. $40.00. ISBN 0-7922-7082-7.

The National Geographic Society may be most widely known for its maps, monthly magazine, and television specials, but it is also an organization responsible for serious scientific research. For those among us who feel that "geographic expertise" may be demonstrated by reciting the names of 25 African nations and their capitals, this book may be overwhelming; for the rest of us it is a comprehensive reference to what geography is all about. If a working definition of geography is the interaction of a population and its environment, then a single-volume guide to geography must be a combination of almanac, atlas, and textbook about earth science, history, politics, and economics. This is a book about how humans are influenced by the Earth and how, in turn, our activities affect the Earth and each other.

It is divided into 4 parts (each with multiple chapters); the 1st and last can almost be considered appendixes to the middle 2. Part 1, "What Is Geography?" is an introduction to the interactions of people and the Earth, a history of geography, and a survey of the differences among maps and globes and how they are made. Part 2, "Physical Geography," is essentially a 200-page earth science textbook describing the physical nature of the Earth that forms the stage upon which the human drama occurs. It includes an overview of the Earth, weather, climate, geology (materials and processes, landforms and landscapes, and soils and bioregions). Part 3, "Human Geography," is a 200-page description of that drama. It includes sections about population; migrations; cultural, economic, urban, and political geography; and the environment and society. Part 4, "Places," provides a list of independent countries and dependencies by region, almanac-type information on all the world's 191 countries (as counted by the Society), and a mini-atlas for quick reference. The end matter includes a glossary and an index.

Each chapter is well illustrated with color photographs, maps, diagrams, and charts and contains highlighted text sections of special interest, such as how the meter was originally defined as a fraction of the Earth's circumference, the development of the Pentecostal movement, and how the zebra mussel is affecting water supplies. Terms in bold typeface are included in the glossary. Each chapter is followed by a summary and a list of sources of further information (there is no bibliography).

The publishers consider this a "prodigious volume" that defines "the world and all that's in it." As immodest as that claim may sound, this book comes arguably close to meeting it. It is an affordable and useful volume for the home, office, or school library and can be enjoyed as both a readable text and a desktop reference.—**Craig A. Munsart**

TRAVEL GUIDES

General Works

353. **City Profiles USA 1999: A Traveler's Guide to Major U.S. and Canadian Cities.** 4th ed. Dawn Bokenkamp Toth, ed. Detroit, Omnigraphics, 1999. 847p. index. $110.00. ISBN 0-7808-0280-2. ISSN 1082-9938.

City Profiles USA is designed for the business traveler, providing general travel-related information and specific information on 212 major cities throughout the United States and Canada. *City Profiles USA* is organized into 2 parts. The 1st section on special features is made up of useful quick-lookup features. There is a list of major airline companies, airport codes, airports, area codes, car rental agencies, convention centers, credit card companies, and hotel chains. In the 2d section, information for specific states and cities is listed.

City Profiles USA offers a huge amount of contact information—phone numbers and Web addresses—for government agencies, airports, car rentals, lodging, restaurants, stores, banks, newspapers, television stations, radio stations, colleges, hospitals, sports teams, attractions, and more for each city. Web addresses for 12,500 sites are included. Besides city information, information on the states is listed, such as online government resources, time zones, population, and area codes. All information was gathered by direct contact and then independently verified.

This book would be a useful purchase for libraries needing this kind of travel information. Since city telephone books have become too costly for the average library, *City Profiles* would also be a good substitute. [R: Choice, Nov 99, p. 502]—**Carol D. Henry**

354. McMillon, Bill. **Volunteer Vacations: Short-Term Adventures That Will Benefit You and Others.** 7th ed. Chicago, Chicago Review Press, 1999. 391p. illus. index. $16.95pa. ISBN 1-55652-363-7.

Ever since President John F. Kennedy gave hope and sense of purpose to young people by founding the Peace Corps, there have been others eager to follow in that idealistic tradition, although that particular avenue is latterly closed to them. If readers would like to serve others on their vacation or at other times, this directory of opportunities is going to prove stimulating as well as useful. McMillon is an old hand at this sort of thing, having in 1992 compiled a list of programs of outdoor education in geology, rain forests, birds, and so on entitled *Wilderness U: Opportunities for Outdoor Education in the U. S. and Abroad* (see ARBA 93, entry 335). The current book lists sponsoring organizations with address, telephone, fax, Website and e-mail addresses, and details on the programs themselves. For example, information includes project location, costs to the participant, type, and dates. Further, brief entries provide information on how to apply, work done by volunteers (should they be accepted), special skills or requirements needed, and additional comments. Many of these projects will take youths and adults. As one may imagine, most of these programs are heavily related to environmental matters, but others out of the 2,000 included will satisfy cravings in agriculture, archaeology, community development, outdoor recreation, religion, science, and social work. All sponsors have been vetted by the author and are on the up and up, but no guarantees of an all-positive experience are given. Not enough information is given on the nature of the living accommodations. Testimonials from volunteers who did find fulfillment and more are included. This book compares well with Gale's *Community Resources Directory* (2d ed.; see ARBA 85, entry 706). This is a compact, affordable reference book for the service minded that is made more convenient by its multiple indexes (by project cost, project length, location, season, and type).—**Randall Rafferty**

355. Paris, Jay, and Carmi Zona-Paris. **100 Best All-Inclusive Resorts of the World.** Old Saybrook, Conn., Globe Pequot Press, 1999. 336p. illus. maps. (100 Best Resorts Series). $16.95pa. ISBN 0-7627-0415-2.

This travel guidebook, written by two travel experts and copublishers of *Outbound Traveler Magazine*, is a comprehensive, yet selective, guide to all-inclusive resorts. The book focuses on North America, the Caribbean, Africa, Asia, and the Pacific. Europe has been omitted because the authors feel that travelers with that destination in mind tend to look for heritage and culture over relaxation and entertainment.

The book is first divided into chapters: "North America"; "The Caribbean"; and "Africa, Asia, and The Pacific." From there specific regions, islands, or countries are addressed. For each featured resort there is a three- to four-paragraph description of the area, which focuses on things such as accommodations, points of distinction, when it is open, how long the vacation runs, nearest airport, and what to bring. Each featured site also is provided a sidebar that lists the all-inclusive activities (e.g., food and beverages, activities, facilities, entertainment, what is available for an additional fee). Symbols associated with each resort indicate whether the resort is intended for couples, families, or singles, as well as if it is a spa, sport site, or for the adventurous. For each site an address, telephone number, and Website and e-mail addresses are listed. The two appendixes at the end include an at-a-glance chart to determine which all-inclusive resort will suit the reader's needs and a country-by-country list of all-inclusive resorts around the world.

The organization of this volume will make it easy for readers to narrow their choices of travel destinations. By providing descriptions and highlights of the resort, the authors have done the research for travelers. This guide will be a welcome addition to any public library travel collection.—**Shannon M. Graff**

356. Reif, Joe, and others. **The Global Road Warrior: 85-Country Handbook for the International Business Traveler.** San Rafael, Calif., World Trade Press, 1999. 666p. maps. $29.95pa. ISBN 1-885073-49-6.

The growth of global trade has resulted in a great increase in international business travel. Travelers usually have a lot of questions before they travel to a place they have never been. Questions may vary from "How do I get from the airport to the city center?" to "How do I hook up to the Internet and check my e-mail?" to "How do I use local telephone?" To find out the answers to all of these questions and many more, a traveler should have in hand *The Global Road Warrior*—a compact worldwide reference resource for the traveling international entrepreneur. This handbook contains travel and business information critical to daily survival and success while travel abroad.

The book starts with a general introduction about international travel, visas and passports, staying healthy, traveling to a country, communications, the technical traveler, travel Websites, business culture, emergencies, time zone map, international dialing guide, and currencies of the world. The top 85 countries of the world most traveled to are covered within this handbook. Information on each country includes background on the people; the economy, holidays, and money; travel facts; communications; business services; technical support; business culture; and city centers. Information in this guide is accurate and up-to-date. Materials for this publication were obtained from information supplied by U.S. government agencies, foreign government embassies, consulates and agencies, and industry and trade organizations. *The Global Road Warrior* will be an asset to any library collection because of its general information on business travel as well as its concise information on many areas of the world.—**Xiao (Shelley) Yan Zhang**

357. Sakach, Deborah Edwards. **Bed & Breakfasts and Country Inns.** 10th ed. Dana Point, Calif., American Historic Inns, 1999. 469p. illus. maps. $21.95pa. ISBN 1-888050-04-7.

The unique pitch used to promote this travel guide to guest establishments is a certificate included that guarantees one free night of lodging. Librarians and bookstore owners can breathe easily, however. The certificate is void if torn from the book and may be taken from it and completed only by the representative innkeeper. More than 1,800 guest inns found in all 50 states and Canada are profiled in the guide. The organization of the book is alphabetic, first by states and provinces, then by towns and cities within states, and finally by inn names within the respective locations. Each state or province is introduced with a map that is simple but helpful; only major highways and locales represented within the directory are listed. Hence, a quick glance at the maps allows the user to determine the location of lodging sites in any given state or province featured.

The guide's publisher, American Historic Inns, makes a point of seeking and featuring guesthouses that have unique architecture and histories. Converted schoolhouses, stone castles, adobe lodges, and lighthouses are among the buildings featured in this 10th edition of the guide. Indeed, the first thing listed in the colorful and historical descriptions found in the separate entries is the known or approximate age of the buildings. Each entry is accompanied by a pen-and-ink sketch of the building. The entries include all pertinent information about the number of rooms, rates, availability, food offerings, and special amenities such as hot tubs and pools as well as the availability of equipment such as fax machines, copy machines, and VCRs. Entries include information about local history and any record of celebrated visitors or famous former guests to the establishment itself. For example, The Stonehouse Inn in Carmel, California, was originally owned by "Nana" Foster who delighted in playing hostess to writers such as Jack London and Sinclair Lewis. For travelers who enjoy history, literature, and local color, *Bed & Breakfasts and Country Inns* will be a welcome and highly useful find.—**Jerry D. Flack**

358. Sakach, Deborah Edwards, and Tiffany Crosswy. **Bed & Breakfast Encyclopedia.** 2d ed. Dana Point, Calif., American Historic Inns, 1999. 980p. illus. maps. $18.95pa. ISBN 1-888050-03-9.

Bed & Breakfast Encyclopedia is a compilation of B&B inns, country inns, and homestays in both the United States and Canada. There are 2,300 individual inn listings with accompanying descriptions (and illustrations), which include location, address and telephone number, rates, number of rooms, types of beds, innkeeper's name, e-mail and Website address, amenities and activities, and other pertinent factors. Canada gets slighted in this group as the book only covers 54 Canadian inns. The volume also lists another 13,000 inns without descriptions, mentioning only the city and telephone number; Canada is better represented here with hundreds of entries. The term "bed & breakfast inn" implies that the inn focuses primarily on lodging and will have from 3 to 20 rooms or more and serves breakfast. Country inns are primarily found on the East Coast and generally serve breakfast and dinner. A homestay is simply a room available in a private home. Years ago this type of room would have been called a tourist home. The authors are specialists in the field and have authored many books on B&Bs and have visited many of the Bed & Breakfast inns listed in this present volume.

Bed & Breakfast Encyclopedia offers a lot of information on the 2,300 selected inns and is quite helpful in the selection of an appropriate inn for a special occasion. Some chapters are worthy of note in this book. For example, "Hot Spots" highlights 20 often-visited locations in the United States, offering short descriptions or the area and recommending a few restaurants. "Culinary Inns" lists some 50 inns that serve fine cuisine. "Low-Stress Travel" has tips on making trips more relaxing. "Ghostly Inns" lists 13 inns that either feature a ghostly past or where guests participate in the solving of a murder mystery. "Dude Ranches" lists a few dude ranches and there is also an interesting chapter on how to start running a B&B business. The volume also lists the top 50 inns in the United States and the top 40 most romantic inns in the

United States (25 selected by *Road Best Traveled*). All in all, the volume is fascinating reading and most helpful in selecting the most appropriate inn for that special event or in simply selecting a place to relax and enjoy for a short time in a home that has a history of its own. This guide is highly recommended to all travelers and those who love old homes and enjoy people.—**Robert Palmieri**

359. Smith, Harold F. **American Travellers Abroad: A Bibliography of Accounts Published Before 1900.** 2d ed. Lanham, Md., Scarecrow, 1999. 383p. index. $60.00. ISBN 0-8108-3554-1.

Americans from all walks of life have traveled extensively throughout the world and not just during the twentieth century. This volume showcases not only the observations of the well known (e.g., Mark Twain, Nathaniel Hawthorne, Wendell Holmes), but also those of the lesser-known travelers, such as Lillian Leland's account of a 25-year-old's solo trip around the world, Francis Clark's 1874 book on how to travel inexpensively, William J. Flag's account of European vineyards in the years after the Civil War, and others who offer equally interesting accounts of places and peoples visited. The writers encompass architects, artists, diplomats, explorers, musicians, presidents, sailors, soldiers, and more. All entries are limited to published books and authors of American citizenship. Foreign travel is defined as that outside the lower 48, hence the inclusion of Alaska and Hawaii. The work is organized alphabetically by author, with full bibliographic information. A brief annotation summarizes each title. Two excellent indexes of places (countries) and occupations help locate content. This is a useful tool for the researcher, historian, scholar, and interested traveler who wants firsthand accounts of faraway places with strange-sounding names. Research institutions and large travel collections should reserve a place for this book. [R: Choice, Nov 99, p. 502]
—**Joy Hastings**

360. **Whale Watching.** Nicky Leach, ed. London, Discovery Communications; distr., Maspeth, N.Y., Langenscheidt Publishers, 1999. 224p. illus. maps. index. (Discovery Travel Adventures). $19.95pa. ISBN 1-56331-836-9.

This joint collaboration between Insight Guides and Discovery Communications produces a guidebook featuring some of the best whale, dolphin, and porpoise watching sites in North America. The team of cowriters, all with previous experience in covering whale or marine issues in other publications or in films, focus on the upbeat and positive side of watching these species of cetaceans. Little mention is made of the negative impact that has ensued with the increased human traffic and interference within these mammals' environment.

The publication includes 3 main sections, with corresponding chapters in each, along with several appendixes. The introductory sections deal with tales of cetaceans through history, some background information about them, and a look at the American whaling industry. A helpful chapter is also included on what to wear and suggested equipment and supplies to bring along to a whale-watching trip. The main section deals with the top places in North America to view whales, dolphins, and porpoises. Thirteen locations are featured, including sites in Canada, Mexico, Alaska, and Hawaii. Each site description includes a variety of information about the site, the cetaceans found there, and travel tips regarding the types of lodgings, excursions, and tours available there. Interesting tidbits of information about each site or the cetaceans are inserted throughout the pages as well as maps and fabulous color photographs. A resource directory listing further readings and addresses for various marine organizations and tourist sites, as well as an index and identification guide round out the publication.

This book is recommended for libraries that have travel guide collections or a general interest in whales, dolphins, or porpoises. It is also recommended for personal collections. This guidebook is full of information about cetaceans, where to view them, and features stunning photography.—**Julia Perez**

United States

361. **Alaskan Wilderness.** Tricia Brown, ed. London, Discovery Communications; distr., Maspeth, N.Y., Langenscheidt Publishers, 1999. 224p. illus. maps. index. (Discovery Travel Adventures). $19.95pa. ISBN 1-56331-837-7.

Alaskan Wilderness is a culmination of two of the most well-known and respected resources of geographic information—Insight Guides, a series of visual travel guides, and Discovery Communications, a source of nonfiction television programming. The result is a beautifully photographed and informative guide to traveling adventures in Alaska.

The book begins with a short introduction describing Alaska's history and rugged terrain. Section 1, titled "Adventuring in Alaska," provides information on Alaska's many natural wonders, tips on surviving the wilderness, and suggestions for adventurous activities (e.g., cross-country skiing, sledding, ice climbing). Section 2, titled "Wilderness Destinations," provides detailed travel tips and guidelines for 16 popular destinations, including Glacier Bay National Park, Prince William Sound, and Kodiak Island. Each featured destination is given information on lodging, tours and outfitters, when to visit, a detailed map, and superb photographs. The book concludes with a resource directory and an index.

This guide is written specifically for the adventurous traveler looking for an Alaskan destination. It will not appeal to everyone, but is perfectly suited for its intended audience. Public libraries may want to add it as a supplement to their travel collections.—**Shannon M. Graff**

362. Baldwin, Jack, and Winnie Baldwin. **Baldwin's Guide to Museums of Louisiana.** Gretna, La., Pelican Publishing, 1999. 303p. illus. maps. $14.95pa. ISBN 1-56554-272-X.

Louisiana is known variously as the Bayou State, the Pelican State, the Magnolia State, and the Creole State. Featured in this book are museums that display a similar wide variety of Louisiana themes. The Baldwins, a husband-and-wife team, convey enthusiasm with every entry. They obviously enjoy sharing facts about their home state, and they have personally visited most of the more than 170 museums listed in this guidebook. The introduction offers tips on using museum visiting time to one's advantage with experienced advice, such as considering the museum map or floor plan as soon as you arrive, keeping in mind your personal interests, and above all having fun. There is an alphabetic table of contents of cities; however, the book would benefit from a subject index. A short summary of each town precedes the museum descriptions and for some towns the Baldwins also recommend restaurants. A map of the state gives general locations with major highways.

Louisiana is definitely unique among the southern states with its complex history blending French, Spanish, Creole, African, German, English, and Native American cultures. Louisiana has a museum for practically every interest and these museums are nicely scattered throughout the state, from the low hill country of the northern parishes to the sugarcane country in the south. A museum may be a well-known plantation house (e.g., Oak Alley or Shadows-on-the-Teche) but there are lesser-known museums mentioned as well (e.g., Louisiana Cotton Museum, Burk Log Cabin and Museum, and the Bayou Lafourche Heritage and Folklife Museum). There are 9 museums of interest in Lafayette, Baton Rouge has 10 entries, and New Orleans has more than 20. A number of towns have museums devoted to their Acadian (Cajun) heritage. Those in New Orleans range from art displays to voodoo. At the historic Cabildo and Presbytere, both adjoining the 200-year-old St. Louis Cathedral, one can see a variety of exhibits. Several active military bases have collections on display to visitors. There are nature center museums, music museums, a sports museum, and a petroleum museum. The book is well researched through on-site visits, and the authors' concise style helps to lead the visitor to pleasant and interesting experiences while traveling through Louisiana. This paperback is recommended as a general reference book.—**Louis G. Zelenka**

363. Bennett, Paul. **The Garden Lover's Guide to the Northeast.** New York, Princeton Architectural Press, 1999. 180p. illus. maps. index. $21.95pa. ISBN 1-56898-163-5.

Besides profiling horticultural oases throughout New England, New York, New Jersey, and Pennsylvania, this guide dips below the Mason-Dixon Line to take in botanical gardens, arboretums, museums, plantations, conservatories, and verdant estates in Delaware, Maryland, the District of Columbia, and northern Virginia. The latest issuance in Princeton's Garden Lover's Guide series, this volume showcases 139 public and semiprivate sites whose manicured flora and classic landscape architecture command awe.

Arranged into five chapters, progression is that of a south-going tour down the Atlantic seaboard. This book is of pleasing heft and presentation of the subject matter. Entries typically run about 500 words each, although substantially longer articles treat such places as Philadelphia's Kennett Square, Massachusetts' Naumkeag estate, and Delaware's Winterthur Museum. Fewer than two dozen of this directory's entries are not graced with resplendent photographs, and seven entries (including Washington D.C.'s Dumbarton Oaks and Cambridge's Mount Auburn Cemetery) are also accompanied by helpful watercolor maps.

Two rival publications cover much of the same ground: Mary Zuazua Jenkins' *National Geographic Guide to America's Public Gardens: 300 of the Best Gardens to Visit in the U.S. and Canada* (The National Geographic Society, 1998) and Marina Harrison's *Gardenwalks: 101 of the Best Gardens from Maine to Virginia and Recommended Gardens Throughout the Country* (Michael Kesend Publishing, 1997). Although these competitors are indexed more thoroughly by garden type and floral collection, Bennett's resource is superior to either with regard to comprehensiveness and depth of coverage of gardens of the northeastern United States. For the same geographic area, Jenkins and Harrison's books offer, respectively, about 35 and 60 fewer full-length entries than Bennett's.

Aside from its index's unfortunate subject deficiency (as well as its maddeningly tiny typescript), Bennett's survey draws up short of its rivals in few respects. For instance, the *National Geographic Guide* clearly indicates whether a given site is handicap-accessible, whether lot parking is available, whether pets are allowed, and whether a horticultural reference library is available to the public. Harrison's book exceeds Bennett's in its glossary of terms (e.g., "bosquet," "espalier," "ha-ha," "knot garden"), but lacks Bennett's thumbnail biographical sketches of such figures as Frederick Law Olmsted and Gertrude Jekyll. Despite its paucity of illustrations, Harrison's volume embarrasses both Bennett and Jenkins with its insightful essays on the "Colonial Garden," "Formal and Informal Garden," and "Walled Garden." On balance, however, Bennett's guide remains unmatched as a source of information to botanical riches of the northeastern United States.—**Jeffrey E. Long**

364. Cook, Samantha, Tim Perry, and Greg Ward. **USA: The Rough Guide.** 4th ed. New York, Rough Guides; distr., New York, Penguin Books, 1998. 1152p. illus. maps. index. $19.95pa. ISBN 1-85828-307-8.

USA: The Rough Guide is one of a series of some 85 guidebooks to travel in various locations of the globe. The 4th edition of the U.S. guidebook is tightly packed with practical and background information, with emphasis on sites and scenes of most interest to travelers. Before discussing each region of the country on a state-by-state basis, useful information of a general nature is given, such as arrival in the United States, distances, average temperatures, useful telephone numbers, and other practical insights. The book is directed largely to those who seek modestly priced living and traveling arrangements. Therefore, relatively few references are made to deluxe accommodations and restaurants. The guide contains references to hostels, motels, and bed & breakfasts, as well as modestly priced hotels. Brief but pertinent notes related to historical background are included; however, greater emphasis is placed on contemporary life and culture. Consequently, the book describes not only what to see, but what to do as well. The authors assume that, although sightseeing is of paramount interest, travelers will also want to enjoy recreational activities (e.g., beaches, nightlife). Information is provided on modes of travel, not only by car, but insights into the use of buses and trains are also included. Suggestions for shopping are notably excluded. The book contains a table of contents, an index, and a list of the more than 75 maps placed in the guide. The guide is an excellent source of information on travel as well as contemporary life in the United States, especially for the young or the young at heart.—**William C. Struning**

365. **Empire State Railway Museum's 34th Annual Guide to Tourist Railroads and Museums.** 1999 ed. Waukesha, Wis., Kalmbach Publishing, 1999. 460p. illus. index. $15.95pa. ISBN 0-89024-404-9. ISSN 0081-542X.

Rail fans of all ages, interest levels, motive-power predilections (steam vs. diesel), and financial means should find something in this guide to tempt them from home for a few hours, days, or even weeks—if only, in some cases, in their fantasies. The diversity of its attractions is nicely epitomized on facing pages 116 and 117. One side features the Little Toot Railroad in Flora, Illinois, offering 20-minute, 1.25-mile rides on a 15-inch gauge mini-steam train for only $3. The opposing page touts the Illinois-based American Orient Express Rail Expeditions, offering extended tours "through America's most scenic regions" aboard a train consisting of "15 vintage carriages, which glisten with polished mahogany and brass," pulled by 2 Amtrak locomotives—prices ranging from $1,890 to $4,990 per person. Altogether, some 450 rail-related attractions in the U.S. and Canada, arranged by state or province, are described here. More than half are rail rides of every sort, including live-steam and diesel-powered, electric trolleys, and even one-horse-drawn railroad. There are also standard gauge and narrow gauge, a few theme-park train rides (obligatory train robbery included), a few dinner trains, jaunts of a few minutes, and journeys of several weeks. Information on museums encompasses attractions of many different sizes and degrees of sophistication, from major assemblages of rolling stock to small displays of memorabilia and models, typically housed in decommissioned depots or restored train cars, as well as extensive model railroad layouts open to the public.

Each attraction, regardless of scope, is allotted one full page including one photograph. Standard data include a brief description, schedule, admission price or fare, nearby attractions and accommodations, location and directions, and contact information; plus, where applicable, listings of motive and rolling stock and of special events. Libraries purchasing this guide (as many should) may face a minor conundrum—what to do about those tear-out discount coupons gathered at the volume's center?—**Hans E. Bynagle**

366. **Guide to Martha's Vineyard.** 8th ed. Burroughs, Polly. Guilford, Conn., Globe Pequot Press, 1999. 226p. illus. maps. index. $12.95pa. ISBN 0-7627-0432-2.

Guide to Martha's Vineyard, now in its 8th edition, is an informative travel guide to the historic and famous island. The book begins with a profile and history of the island and its communities: Vineyard Haven, Oak Bluffs, Edgartown, the island of Chappaquiddick, North and West Tisbury, Chilmark, and Aquinnah. It provides travel tips such as what time of the year is the best to visit and methods of transportation to and on the island. Descriptions of hotels, inns, bed and breakfasts, and restaurants include addresses and telephone numbers and price ratings from inexpensive to very expensive. There are also telephone numbers and addresses for emergencies, churches, conservation organizations, general and historical information, libraries, museums, post offices, and translation services. The guide points out a multitude of leisure activities, from shopping and museums to the beaches and island tours. A calendar of annual special events is also provided and an index concludes the work. Black-and-white photographs complement the guide, but some are clearly outdated and color photographs would be more eye-catching for interested travelers.

—**Cari Ringelheim**

367. **Hawaii.** New York, DK Publishing, 1998. 208p. illus. maps. index. (Eyewitness Travel Guides). $22.95 flexibinding. ISBN 0-7894-2750-8.

Travel guidebooks comprise a best-selling portion of the book market, and the destination of Hawaii is the subject of no small number of them. The Eyewitness series of guidebooks looks for a distinctive edge in this market by providing profusely illustrated volumes. This guide to Hawaii, for example, contains more than 400 color photographs in a little more than 200 pages. The photographs are accompanied by a variety of maps and three-dimensional aerial views of major tourist locations. Interspersed among these excellent images are textual descriptions of the geography and history of the Hawaiian Islands, a more detailed investigation of the key areas of Honolulu and Waikiki, and an island-by-island description of each major link in the island chain and its attractions. The writing style is clear and upbeat.

A central section of this book is its lists of places to eat, sleep, shop, and recreate. All of the usual details are provided for these elements in a clean graphical style. The restaurants and hotels are described sufficiently to provide a sense of their character, but they are almost universally given uncritical reviews. The coverage of hotels and eating establishments matches that found in many competing guides.

This guide is similar in look to Hawaii in the Insight Guide series (Langenscheidt, 1999), another well-illustrated guide, though the Eyewitness guide has slightly superior maps. Either provides a nice pictorial balance to the useful, but more textually oriented Lonely Planet guidebook *Hawaii* (Oakland, 1999) or the almost textual yet classic *Fodor's Hawaii* (New York, 1999). The latter gives the most thorough descriptive information but cannot provide the aesthetic sense of location that the photograph-based guides can. Purchasers should be aware that most of the major series also include more specific guides focusing on single islands instead of the entire state.—**Christopher W. Nolan**

368. Lewis, Anne Gillespie. **The Minnesota Guide.** Golden, Colo., Fulcrum, 1999. 367p. illus. maps. index. $21.95pa. ISBN 1-55591-362-8.

Minnesota author Anne Gillespie Lewis compiled this handy guide to Minnesota, which offers a colorful overview of the state. It is evident that the author is proud of her state, as she writes with unmistakable enthusiasm. *The Minnesota Guide* examines eight different regions of the state, from the Twin Cities (Minneapolis–St. Paul) to the east-central portion (St. Cloud, Little Falls, the St. Croix Valley). Each region of the state is described by an overview and a history, with attention to major attractions and festivals, outdoor activities (e.g., skiing, snowmobiling, snowshoeing, ice-skating, ice fishing, boating), sightseeing, where to stay, where to dine, shopping, tours, services, and where to get local information. There are handy maps of each region as well as directions on how to get to a particular destination. The volume has full-color illustrations, includes bibliographical material, and is well indexed. Minnesota is a beautiful state and well worth touring. The use of this book will make it even more interesting. *The Minnesota Guide* is highly recommended.—**Robert Palmieri**

369. McMillan, Cecily. **The Charleston, Savannah, & Coastal Islands Book: A Complete Guide.** 3d ed. Lee, Mass., Berkshire House, 1998. 293p. illus. maps. index. (The Great Destination Series). $17.95pa. ISBN 1-58157-001-5.

This is the 3d edition of McMillan's travel guide to the low country of the southeastern United States, stretching from Charleston to Savannah. After a historical introduction to the area, the book is divided into chapters on Charleston, Savannah, Hilton Head and Beaufort, and Edisto and Bluffton. Each lists lodging, restaurants, tourist sites, recreational activities, and shopping. Coverage of lodging and restaurants is sparse—only 13 hotels and 20 restaurants for Savannah and 16 hotels and 25 restaurants for the Charleston area—with almost all of them in the "large" or "luxury" category. Discussions of museums, cultural attractions, and shopping destinations are good; recreational opportunities are often just listings with golf courses receiving the best treatment. A final chapter gives basic travel information and telephone numbers, and an excellent bibliography for those who want to read up on the area before they visit. This work is fine for the upscale traveler with a cultural bent; however, tourists with other needs should try other guides.

—**Deborah Hammer**

370. **National Audubon Society Field Guide to the Southeastern States.** By Peter Alden and others. New York, Alfred A. Knopf/Random House, 1999. 447p. illus. maps. index. $19.95pa. ISBN 0-679-44683-4.

One of a new series of regional guides to the United States, this title covers Alabama, Arkansas, Georgia, Kentucky, Louisiana, Mississippi, North and South Carolina, and Tennessee. In the typical compact format, the book provides a lot of information in 3 major sections: an overview covering topography, geology, wildlife habitats, conservation, ecology, weather, and astronomy; a section on flora and fauna; and a section on parks and preserves. For illustration there are 1,500 color photographs, maps, and drawings. A political boundary map with major highways and cities is inside the front cover, with a physical map in the back.

The overview section provides excellent topical summaries, including the Mississippi River Valley and coastal water areas. In the flora section are mushrooms, algae, lichens, spore plants, trees, shrubs, and wildflowers. The large fauna section has invertebrates and vertebrates (marine and land), ranging from sponges and insects to reptiles and mammals. Each illustrated description is concise but definitive enough for identification and location.

The section on parks and preserves has a selected list of 50 state or national parks or forests as well as nature preserves arranged by state. Major areas are described in one to two pages, with a half page or short paragraphs for others. Longer descriptions include unique natural areas, recreational opportunities, trails, and native plants and animals. Every entry has an address and telephone number for contact information.

Authors are identified by a brief vita, with acknowledgment of the sections they authored. The sturdy plastic cover, sewn binding, and slick paper offer a lasting quality. The index is limited to major entries (i.e., the Joyce Kilmer Memorial Forest is not indexed, but is the first subdivision mentioned in the entry for the Nantahala National Forest in North Carolina). Although not as comprehensive as a specific subject guide, this all-in-one source is a handy reference for personal use and is recommended for all libraries, especially those in the Southeast.—**Margo B. Mead**

371. **National Audubon Society Field Guide to the Southwestern States.** By Peter Alden and others. New York, Alfred A. Knopf/Random House, 1999. 447p. illus. maps. index. $19.95pa. ISBN 0-679-44680-X.

As is the case with other National Audubon Field Guides (California, Florida, Mid-Atlantic, New England, Pacific Northwest, Rocky Mountain, and Southeastern states), this guide to the Southwestern states is impeccably done and fulfills its intended purpose with gusto. The states included are Arizona, Nevada, New Mexico, and Utah. The guide is organized into 3 parts. Part 1 is an overview of natural highlights, topography, geology, habitats, ecology, and weather. Night sky charts will appeal to amateur astronomers. Part 2 focuses on flora and fauna, and this is clearly the emphasis of the field guide. In-depth coverage of trees, shrubs, wildflowers, mushrooms, lichens, ferns, insects, fishes, amphibians, reptiles, birds, and mammals is provided in this section. Hundreds of excellent color photographs illustrate the flora and fauna. The only deficiency here pertains to ease of use as a field guide. Grouping wildflowers by color rather than alphabetic by common name, for example, would allow for easier use. Part 3 briefly covers the parks and preserves in the region. There are listings for 50 selected national parks, monuments, forests, riparian areas, tribal parks, recreation areas, and so on, each with a color photograph, general location, and telephone number of the managing agency. An adequate index and list of photographers round out the guide. This is highly recommended, in fact essential, for all libraries in the region and any major public and academic library in the country.—**Thomas K. Fry**

372. O'Brien, Tim. **Amusement Park Guide: Coast to Coast Thrills.** 3d ed. Old Saybrook, Conn., Globe Pequot Press, 1999. 305p. index. $14.95pa. ISBN 0-7627-0437-3.

This book is exactly as it is titled. It is a complete guide to amusement and theme parks across the United States and Canada. The background color of the pages in this guide is bright orange and tends to work on the nerves a bit, but it is still useful once you get past that. The author is a self-confessed roller coaster fanatic, who is the southeast editor of *Amusement Business* magazine. His background and enthusiasm show in each of his park descriptions. Every entry includes park telephone numbers, along with driving directions and hours of operation. A brief description of the park, including rides and attractions, is followed by detailed sections on extras such as paddle boats and miniature golf. Other sections included are Season Specials, Operating Hours, Admission Policy, Plan to Stay, and Top Rides. There are also descriptions of roller coasters for the extreme thrill enthusiast. At the front of the guide is a brief history of the amusement park, followed by a chapter of tips from the author that offers advice to getting the most enjoyment out of an amusement park adventure, such as wearing the right shoes and clothing and planning the day to include any shows and other in-park entertainment. A quick-find index is also included in this book. In general, the guide is helpful as both a vacation companion and planner.—**Michael Florman**

373. Sakach, Deborah Edwards. **The Official Guide to American Historic Inns, Bed & Breakfasts, and Country Inns.** 6th ed. Dana Point, Calif., American Historic Inns, 1998. 582p. illus. maps. $15.95pa. ISBN 1-888050-02-0.

Although technically inns built before 1940 are considered "historic," the majority of the inns in this directory are of seventeenth- through nineteenth-century vintage. The lodgings are located predominantly in the United States and Canada, but there is also one inn in Puerto Rico and another in St. Croix. The lodgings described are either "Country Inns," usually including breakfast and dinner, or "Bed and Breakfast" establishments that may have 3 to 20 rooms or more and usually provide some type of breakfast from simple to sumptuous. "Homestay inns," a private home that has one or two rooms, are not included. Although the inns have paid a fee to be listed, all establishments are examined from time to time and only those meeting quality standards are accepted for inclusion.

The 2,300 inns are arranged by city and state. Most cities listed have only one inn, but a few locations have as many as five or six. The usual directory information is also accompanied by an e-mail address when available (but, oddly, Websites are not given) and the approximate date of construction. The narrative descriptions of each lodge are compiled from experiences of guests and are not written by the innkeeper. These are far more informative than those of standard lodging directories such as AAA or Mobil guides, and should be helpful for selecting the right site. The third segment of each entry gives the specifics of price ranges, room types, nearby conveniences and tourism, and amenities. If an inn has been featured in a magazine, it is noted, but no specific references are provided. An enthusiastic comment by a past visitor may also be included. For most sites there is also a line drawing sketch of the inn, and a sketch-map for each state noting each city with an inn.

The index is specialized. There is unfortunately no overall alphabetic index of inns, but rather only groupings of "interest" areas such as inns that are converted barns, log cabins, or old taverns. Of interest primarily for public libraries, this guide will be an important resource for those who are selective when seeking authentic historic lodgings.—**Gary R. Cocozzoli**

374. Swirsky, Judith. **On Exhibit 1999: Art Lover's Travel Guide to American Museums.** New York, Abbeville Press, 1999. 428p. index. $24.95pa. ISBN 0-7892-0454-1.

In the 7th edition of this annual publication, this work continues to provide the art lover on tour or on a business trip with the opportunity to preview what will be on display in more than 700 museums and galleries in the United States for the coming year. The work is arranged alphabetically by state and location. Each entry includes telephone numbers, hours, addresses, group tour information, and information about the permanent collection. The main section of each entry is devoted to what exhibition is on display with dates of display as well. Also included are lists of museums, permanent collections on display in the museums, and traveling exhibits with museums visited and the dates of the exhibition at the various museums. This is an invaluable work for any library with a need for up-to-date art–related information. A great companion volume would be a guide to Canadian museums.—**Gregory Curtis**

Asia

375. **Insight Guide: India.** Verlag, KG, APA Publications; distr., Maspeth, N.Y., Langenscheidt Publishers, 1999. 410p. illus. maps. index. (India Series). $22.95 flexibinding. ISBN 0-88729-133-3.

This is perhaps the most valuable introductory book on India now available and a must for those planning to visit the country. It is far more than a typical tourist's guide, covering the history of the whole region (with particular focus on present-day India), the religions, the main tourist destinations, the national parks, ashrama, and travel information—in fact, almost every aspect of Indian sociology. Brief coverage of press, literature (both local and Diaspora), and education would have added to the usefulness of this guide. Dance, music, art, and movies are well treated. Particularly helpful are warnings that certain urban and archeological sites are unsafe for individuals (e.g., Tughlaquabad Fort on the outskirts of Delhi). The photographic illustrations are plentiful, apposite, and of the highest quality. Information on hotels, temples, and museums is detailed, though in a few cases it is somewhat selective. For example, in Mysore, the cathedral's old name is offered, the two Dasaprakash hotels are not differentiated, the Brindavan Gardens (India's Versailles) is not mentioned, and the Metropole hotel is now closed. But such shortcomings are few and not serious; they are inevitable in a wide-ranging guide that must be selective. The style of writing is neither demonic nor pedantic; it is aimed at a rather sophisticated readership. Like many travel guides, this one tends to list more high-end than tourist-quality accommodations. However, it offers ample lists of low-budget places to stay. Advice on language, food, festivals, and shopping is, like the numerous maps, most helpful. Many informational boxes supplement the main text and an ample index facilitates discovery of contents. Historical material is very fair-minded.—**Marian B. McLeod**

376. **Insight Guide: Japan.** 3d ed. Verlal, KG, APA Publications; distr., Maspeth, N.Y., Langenscheidt Publishers, 1999. 395p. illus. maps. index. (East Asia Series). $23.95 flexibinding. ISBN 0-88729-588-6.

This is an updated, 3d edition of Insight's guidebook to Japan. Basic information is presented in 3 color-coded sections. The features section covers Japan's history, geography, religion, arts, cinema, sports, cuisine, and people in articles that the preface states were written by specialists, but are unsigned. The places section divides the islands into four areas: Central Honshu, the North, Kansai, and the South. Contributing writers to this section are credited in the preface. Many colored maps and street maps of major cities are provided. Places mentioned in the text are numerically keyed to the maps. The travel tips section gives information on transportation, accommodations, shopping, museums, sports events, and so on. It has its own index. The guide is lavishly illustrated with excellent color photographs (many full page or double page), showing views, buildings, statues, city street scenes, and country panoramas. Photographs show Japanese people—the Hokkaido egg seller and the Sendai shellfish harvester at work in realistic settings. Sidebars give bits of interesting information on topics such as haiku poetry, historical events, the *Godzilla* cult, and thousand-year-old music. Short travel tips in the margins warn of overcrowded places, unsavory characters and hustlers, and inflated prices, but also suggests pleasant or intriguing places to visit or economical places to eat. Seven information panels give more detailed information on a variety of topics of general interest. A six-page index, a short bibliography, and a list of Internet sites complete the offerings. Because of its extensive coverage, the book will be of interest to the armchair traveler and to students of Japanese life and culture as well as to its primary audience, the traveler.—**Shirley L. Hopkinson**

Australia

377. **Australia 2000.** New York, Fodor's Travel Publications/Random House, 1999. 624p. illus. maps. index. $21.00pa. ISBN 0-679-00326-6.

This easy-to-use travel guide will help readers successfully plan a trip to any of the beautiful areas of Australia. It begins with a short section outlining all of the regions featured in the book. This section presents a short description of the city or region and provides beautiful photographs of the area. The main part of the work is divided into sections or regions, including Sydney, New South Wales, Canberra and the A.C.T., Melbourne and Victoria, Tasmania, Queensland, the Great Barrier Reef, Adelaide and South Australia, the Red Centre, and Perth and Western Australia. Each section provides information on the city's or region's sites to see, restaurants, hotels, travel information, nightlife, and maps. Following this is a short section with vacation destinations and ideas for adventurous travelers, with activities such as horseback riding, cross-country skiing, and bushwalking (hiking). The chapter titled "Background and Essentials" gives practical advice on such topics as travel insurance, medical emergencies, and tipping. The volume concludes with an index and pullout map.

This guide will provide readers with a lot of practical travel tips and information about traveling to Australia. It is very up-to-date and easy to use and will be a valuable edition to the travel collection of public libraries or the personal libraries of travel enthusiasts.—**Shannon M. Graff**

Europe

378. Abbs, Barbara. **The Garden Lover's Guide to The Netherlands and Belgium.** New York, Princeton Architectural Press, 1999. 144p. illus. index. $19.95pa. ISBN 1-56898-162-7.

There is only one serious omission to this book—a plane ticket. It would be lovely to find one tucked away within the glossary, index to gardens, and short biographies of architects. After all, the accounts of varied green spaces—cottage and castle, demonstration and topiary, native plant, and water among them—stir a powerful desire for an immersion experience.

Lucid descriptions of the 122 gardens are laced with tantalizing bits of history. For example, Mariemont Park near La Louvière in Belgium took root from the inspiration of Mary of Hungary, the widowed sister of Emperor Charles V; Mary imparted an Italian style. By the late sixteenth century, a new occupant, the daughter of Philip II (and the wife of Archduke Albert), introduced a Spanish style. When Louis XIV took the estate, French style predominated. But in 1850 an English industrialist prevailed and an English landscape defines the place now.

Hours for public viewing, telephone numbers for more information, and a guide to amenities (icons) are given for each garden. A photograph that captures the unique aspect of the garden accompanies the description of it in most cases. Road and site maps are models of clarity.—**Diane M. Calabrese**

379. Abram, Dave, and others. **Britain: The Rough Guide.** 2d ed. New York, Rough Guides; distr., New York, Penguin Books, 1998. 1074p. illus. maps. index. $23.95pa. ISBN 1-85828-312-4.

This travel series has been around since 1982 and has become a standard for the independent budget traveler. The guides are fun to read, excellent to use during the planning stage of a trip, and useful while traveling. This volume covers England, Scotland, and Wales. Information is given for each country by broad geographic area and then by specific locations within the area. The descriptions of towns and cities, while succinct, manage to impart a sense of place. An example is the description of South Uist (Outer Hebrides), which describes the area as "a whole series of country lanes lead[ing] west from the island's one main road to the old crofters' villages that straggle along the coast."

Each section of the guide begins with a brief history of the area and highlights of significant sites to visit. Limited lodging and dining recommendations are provided. Rough Guides also publishes individual guides to England, Scotland, and Wales. These guides give more in-depth information about the areas and accommodations. Users are advised not to look for four-star hotels or restaurants in this book. Hostels, bed-and-breakfasts, budget hotels, and self-catering accommodations are featured, as are pubs and moderately priced restaurants. Except for large cities, recommended services are integrated within the text of the town's description. Those who prefer lists and demarcations between sections will find this arrangement takes some getting used to.

There are useful sections on modes of transportation. Especially helpful is the explanation of the numerous types of rail tickets available. Ferry schedules are also listed. There are climate charts, safety tips, and information boxes with practical information and interesting sidelights. Maps are detailed and there are some lovely color photographs. A history of Britain and a bibliography for further reading complete the book.

All Rough Guides are available online (http://www.roughguides.com) free of charge. Travelers can easily print out just what they need and forgo packing a tour guide. But then those interesting off-the-beaten-track places found while browsing on a seven-hour flight would be missed, and that would be a shame.—**Marlene M. Kuhl**

380. **Eurail and Train Travel Guide to Europe.** 3d ed. Westminster, Md., Houghton Mifflin, 1998. 720p. index. $15.00pa. ISBN 0-395-88161-7. ISSN 0085-0330.

The *Eurail and Train Travel Guide to Europe* is the updated version of the former *Eurail Guide*, first published in 1971. The title was changed to allow coverage of all European and British Isles train information.

The coverage is train travel information for 36 countries of Eastern and Western Europe, Britain, and Ireland. Eurail, Britrail, and more than 100 other passes are described and priced. The prices are in U.S. dollars and other European currencies are based on October 1997 exchange rates.

The first five chapters discuss the advantages of rail travel. The different rail passes are described as well as where to purchase them and the qualifications for discounts. It also discusses how to plan a rail itinerary and delivers valuable train travel tips.

The countries of Europe and Britain train information are describe in an alphabetic country listing. In this section one will find tourist office addresses and telephone and fax numbers, public holidays, standard time and daylight time changes, currency, and a helpful overview of the country's trains. A highlight of this section is the descriptions and sightseeing suggestions for more than 800 rail trips. An appendix of route charts and a directory of the best Websites geared for train travel is available. This is an essential guide for travel collections in public and academic libraries.—**Kay M. Stebbins**

381. **Europe 2000.** Nancy van Itallie, ed. New York, Fodor's Travel Publications/Random House, 1999. 1176p. maps. index. $22.00pa. ISBN 0-679-00328-2. ISSN 0362-0204.

Always a pleasure to use, this years edition of *Europe* continues Fodor's long-standing tradition of providing quality travel information at a reasonable price. As with other Fodor's publications this edition is easy to use; it is arranged alphabetically by country, region, and city. A wealth of detail on accommodations, expenses, what to see, what to avoid, and local customs aids the traveler in planning and pursuing an interesting, safe, and enjoyable European adventure. The well-illustrated volume includes basic maps of the country and city street maps. A Rand McNally color map of the region complements the other illustrations well, serving as a pull out guide. Any library will find this guidebook of continuing interest to its clientele and rarely will it be found on the shelf, but rather in the hand of a potential traveler.—**Gregory Curtis**

382. **Fodor's Upclose Germany.** Tania Inowlocki, ed. New York, Fodor's Travel Publications/Random House, 1999. 483p. illus. index. $18.00pa. ISBN 0-679-00442-4.

In its previous incarnation, this book was entitled *The Berkeley Guide to Germany & Austria* (Fodor's, 1994) and written by Berkeley students. It is now revised and published in Fodor's Upclose series and includes only Germany, while retaining the original orientation as a guide for students and other low-budget travelers. The authors set out to offer readers advice on how to experience Germany "up close"—the local culture, the offbeat places to stay, eat, drink, and have fun without spending too much money. The book is divided into 2 major sections. One is an alphabetic "Basics" section that offers almost 40 pages of general information on how to travel cheaply to and in Germany, along with tips on packing, tipping, working, and so on in Germany. There are also entries on a variety of topics such as hay hotels, ride-share offices, and women's centers. The major part of the guide is made up of descriptions of regions, cities, and other sites. Each chapter begins with an overview of the region or city (accompanied by a map), information on where to sleep and eat cheaply, what to do after dark, and a description of all the major tourist attractions. Also included are dozens of interesting tidbits on local history, customs, and other useful current information. There is even a German to English vocabulary appendix and an index. Although geared toward student travelers, *Upclose Germany* offers useful information for virtually all tourists.—**Leena Siegelbaum**

383. Franco, L. N. **Literary Landscapes: Walking Tours in Great Britain and Ireland.** New York, George Braziller, 1998. 151p. illus. maps. $15.95pa. ISBN 0-8076-1438-6.

This is an interesting guide to "walking" the landscapes that inspired such writers as D. H. Lawrence and James Joyce. Franco has focused on English and Irish writers who chose actual and identifiable settings for their works, and on those settings that are currently accessible to visitors. The author also avoided writers who set their works in London because there are already a number of literary tours in that city.

Each chapter contains a brief biographical sketch of the writers and their connection to a particular place, along with descriptions of walks in and around the literary sites. Maps are provided as general guides, but Franco recommends the use of the all-purpose maps provided by the British Ordnance Survey Landranger series, which show public rights-of-way.

This work is an interesting guide for readers who would like to travel to these sites and learn more about the life and works of the featured authors. However, the work is limited to only a handful of critically acclaimed writers. Thus, it is only useful to readers who are knowledgeable of the literary works discussed.—**Cari Ringelheim**

384. Karr, Paul, with Martha Coombs. **Hostels France & Italy.** Guilford, Conn., Globe Pequot Press, 1999. 314p. illus. maps. $14.95pa. ISBN 0-7627-0395-4.

Students and European travelers on a budget will enjoy this amusing guide to hostels in France and Italy. As the cover states, this is an "opinionated guide," making it very useful to travelers who are unfamiliar with the area. The editors comment on important topics, such as cleanliness, safety, hospitality, and privacy. Information is also provided about rates, hours, kitchen availability, and other various significant factors. The guide also explains what a hostel is, how information was gathered, hostel etiquette, how to pay, what to bring, and how to get there. Advice is given about making telephone calls (buy a phone card), exchanging money, and speaking French and Italian. Each entry provides the hostel's address, telephone number, fax number, and e-mail and Website addresses (if available). Karr and Coombs use a humorous and entertaining style of presenting the information. They have also noted which hostels are their best picks. This guide is more appropriate for personal collections as travelers will want to bring it with them on their trips. Libraries need not acquire it.—**Cari Ringelheim**

385. Karr, Paul, with Martha Coombs. **Hostels U.K.: The Only Comprehensive, Unofficial, Opinionated Guide.** Old Saybrook, Conn., Globe Pequot Press, 1999. 321p. illus. maps. (Hostels Series). $14.95pa. ISBN 0-7627-0396-2.

For years hostels have been known to be a cheap and efficient way to travel, not to mention adventurous. *Hostels U.K.* is a guidebook to the hostels of the United Kingdom and Northern Ireland. Part of the Hostels Series by Globe Pequot Press, these books list each of the hostels by region and give travelers insight into what the hostel offers and at what price.

The book begins by explaining what information can be found for each listing, then goes on to explain the history of hostels and rules of "hostelling." The book is divided into regions, and hostels are listed under their region and located on a map at the beginning of the chapter. Each entry contains such information as address, telephone number, and Website address; cost; number of beds; curfew; season it is open (if applicable); and affiliation (e.g., Youth Hostel Association or independent). There are icons located with the hostel indicating such things as whether it is wheelchair accessible, good for families, a good value, or one of the authors' favorites, among other things. Finally, the hostel is rated with thumbs up if it is extremely worthwhile, thumbs down if it is only recommended in case of emergency, or no thumbs at all if it is standard. The book concludes with the authors' top 10 hostels. This book is a worthwhile guide for students or anyone who plans to travel as cheaply as possible through the United Kingdom.—**Shannon M. Graff**

386. **Naples with Pompeii & the Amalfi Coast.** New York, DK Publishing, 1998. 240p. illus. maps. index. (Eyewitness Travel Guides). $22.95 flexibinding. ISBN 0-7894-2752-4.

The beauty and history of Naples and its surroundings are fascinating and captivating, and the new Eyewitness Travel Guide on Naples truly captures the essence of the area. The volume covers Naples, Pompeii, Amalfi Coast, Sorrento Coast, Ischia, Capri, Caserta, and other spots in that general vicinity. The guide includes historical materials; maps; 3-D illustrations; architectural overviews; cultural highlights; street-by-street overviews; and lists of recommended hotels, restaurants, shops and markets, and entertainment spots, as well as everyday practical information, travel data, a street finder (with a map), and an excellent index. The volume's strength is that it is small and easy to carry, has an abundance of beautiful illustrations and diagrams, is well laid out and easy to follow, and the descriptions are short and to the point. The chapter on what to eat and drink in Naples has actual photographs of typical dishes of the area that should entice many people to pack up and take the first plane to Naples. The Eyewitness Travel Guides are always fun to view and use, and this one on the Naples area is highly recommended.—**Robert Palmieri**

387. **Sardinia.** New York, DK Publishing, 1998. 224p. illus. maps. index. (Eyewitness Travel Guides). $22.95 flexibinding. ISBN 0-7894-2868-7.

The Eyewitness Travel Guides are distinctive in that their numerous color illustrations feature three-dimensional drawings of historical buildings and districts. If readers need illustrated travel guides, these are the ones to consult. The Eyewitness volume on Sardinia offers historical and cultural overviews; describes important sites, with helpful maps and illustrations; covers food specialties; supplies data on hotels and restaurants; and gives practical information concerning transportation, shopping, banking, and currency. The general index is helpful, which is something not easy to find in many travel guides.

The guide rightfully focuses on the rich history of Sardinia. Historically the island was occupied by Phoenicians, Romans, the Spanish, and Austrians, and experienced fierce struggles with Byzantines and Arabs. Today, Sardinia is an interesting tourist destination with many impressive sites. The volume is well designed, with a durable binding that is sewn together and defies splitting. Many travel guides that are glued together are apt to come apart easily; not so with the Eyewitness books. Another useful feature is that this volume fits perfectly in a back pocket or travel bag. The editorial staff has put together an excellent volume that will endure for many voyages.—**Robert Palmieri**

388. Segall, Barbara. **The Garden Lover's Guide to Spain and Portugal.** New York, Princeton Architectural Press, 1999. 144p. illus. maps. index. $19.95pa. ISBN 1-56898-161-9.

The publisher of this unique travel guide series has focused their attention on exploring the beauty and originality of gardens in different countries. *The Garden Lover's Guide to Spain and Portugal* gives the reader an up-close view of the gardens of these two countries, which are both extremely rich in culture and tradition. One does not have to be an experienced gardener to appreciate the beauty and history to be found in the photographs and descriptions within this guidebook.

The book is first divided into five major sections and then separated by region: Northern Spain, Southern Spain, Central Spain, the Spanish Islands, and Portugal. Each chapter begins with an introduction describing the climate and any historical information that may have influenced that region's garden design. A map is given that shows the area being examined. The following pages in each section feature entries with specific gardens that give readers information, such as when the garden is open to the public, whether there is a cost of admission, nearby sites of interest, and the distinguishing features of the garden. The photographs are beautiful and the maps will give travelers the general idea of where the sites are located. A glossary, bibliography, and index conclude the volume.

The guides in this series will give travelers fresh ideas when planning their vacations. This book is more than just a travel guide; its beautiful photographs and well-written text offer new insight into the culture and history of Spain and Portugal. This will be a worthwhile volume to add to the travel collection of any public library.—**Shannon M. Graff**

Latin America and the Caribbean

389. **Insight Guide: Venezuela.** Verlag, KG, APA Publications; distr., Maspeth, N.Y., Langenscheidt Publishers, 1999. 369p. illus. maps. index. (South America Series). $22.95 flexibinding. ISBN 0-88729-160-0.

Each of these guides is written by several British and American authors who specialize in specific regions or topics related to the countries in question. They are well illustrated, with numerous color photographs of tourist attractions and daily life, and maps of cities, metropolitan areas, and regions. Although they emphasize coverage of the best-known cities and areas of interest to tourists, such as national parks, they provide limited information about most, but not all, areas of the countries. For example, the Brazil volume does not cover the state of Tocantins, or its capital, Palmas.

Topics covered include history and culture (e.g., festivals, cuisine, sports, subjects unique to each country). Depth of coverage of the same topic varies; for example, *Venezuela* devotes six pages to food, whereas *Brazil*, with its rich tradition of regional cuisines, is limited to three pages. "Information panels" interspersed throughout the text focus on a variety of topics. Two examples from *Venezuela* are "Cacao" and "Amazon Peoples," and topics about Brazil range from "The Disappearing Rainforest" to "Wild Bus Rides." Although the focus of these guides is on substantive information about the countries rather than serving as directories of hotels and restaurants, a section on travel tips completes each volume, with information about planning the trip; general information, such as concerns about tipping and internal travel; and listings of hotels, campsites, and restaurants that describe and evaluate them.

These titles join a growing collection of travel guides devoted to specific countries of Latin America. General guides are exemplified by those that comprise the Lonely Planet Travel Survival Kit series, and those published by Fodor's Travel Publications and Fielding Travel Books. Guides catering to particular interests also abound. *Eat Smart in Brazil: How to Decipher the Menu, Know Market Foods, & Embark on a Tasting Adventure* (Gingko Press, 1995) by Joan Peterson and David Peterson and *Trekking in Bolivia: A Traveler's Guide* by Yossi Brain, Andrew North, and Isobel Stoddart (Mountaineers, 1997) are two recent examples. These guides nicely complement other travel books about the same countries that a library may already have on its shelves, because of their excellent illustrations and information about topics that may not be covered in other books.—**Ann Hartness**

390. **Mexico 2000.** New York, Fodor's Travel Publications/Random House, 1999. 656p. illus. maps. index. $20.00pa. ISBN 0-679-00319-3.

Fodor's *Mexico 2000* offers all the information one will need to know when traveling to this exotic country. The book begins with a short section of beautiful photographs of the highlights of each of the areas discussed in the book. It is then divided into 13 chapters that explore different regions of the country, including Mexico City, side trips from Mexico City, Baja California, Sonora, Copper Canyon, Guadalajara, the heartland of the country, Pacific coast resorts, Acapulco, Oaxaca, Chiapas and Tabasco, Veracruz and the Northeast area, and the Yucatan Peninsula. For each region recommendations for dining, lodging, nightlife, shopping, beaches, outdoor activities, and sightseeing are listed. Many of the hotels and restaurants have prices listed and there are addresses, telephone numbers, and Website and e-mail addresses given for many locales. Maps are located throughout the book as well. A small section on the history of Mexico is given toward the end of the book in a chronological format, which will be worthwhile to readers wanting to do more than sunbathe. An important chapter at the end of the volume titled "Essential Information" gives readers tips for safe and efficient travel, including such information as the various forms of travel (e.g., air, bike, bus), customs and duties, accessibility for travelers with disabilities, and language. Because Mexico is such a popular destination for Americans this travel guide will be welcome in the reference section of almost any size public library.—**Shannon M. Graff**

Middle East

391. **Insight Guide: Israel.** Verlag, KG, APA Publications; distr., Maspeth, N.Y., Langenscheidt Publishers, 1999. 377p. illus. maps. (Middle East Series). $22.95 flexibinding. ISBN 0-88729-157-0.

This travel guide provides an excellent overview of Israel past and present with the primary focus on today. A chronology and historical summary outline key events in the country's history and provide a foundation for understanding the culture and politics. Clearly written text and numerous color photographs and maps explore significant features of various geographic regions. Also included are extensive travel tips on everything from public transportation to advice on restaurants, money, and accommodations; and information on local media and customs. Quick-find indexes on the end flaps of the compact guide make it a very user-friendly source.—**Ahmad Gamaluddin**

392.　**Istanbul.** New York, DK Publishing, 1998. 272p. illus. maps. index. (Eyewitness Travel Guides). $24.99 flexibinding. ISBN 0-7894-2751-6.

　　This attractive book packs an amazing amount of information into its compact format. Well-organized sections describe tourist sites, restaurants, hotels, Turkish food, entertainment, and transportation options. Travelers will appreciate the attention to detail throughout the volume, ranging from color-coded tabs and street map finders to basic vocabulary lists and descriptions of street food. Color photographs, maps, and three-dimensional illustrations complement the text. The guide is an excellent purchase for travelers and library travel collections.—**Ahmad Gamaluddin**

9 History

ARCHAEOLOGY

393. **A Dictionary of Archaeology.** Ian Shaw and Robert Jameson, eds. Malden, Mass., Blackwell, 1999. 624p. illus. maps. $99.95. ISBN 0-631-17423-0.

Shaw and Jameson's volume is the latest in a line of works in archaeological reference publishing that began with the appearance of *Adeline's Art Dictionary* in 1883, and has seen increased emphasis on regional archaeology (mainly biblical and Egyptian) since 1950. An editorial approach reflecting the definition of archaeology as both a process and a discipline in constant change has been adopted in the crafting of the articles. Content selection, while emphasizing traditional topics (such as terminology, theoretical concepts, field techniques, and summaries of important sites worldwide), also incorporates practical applications of theory and method as well as terms from the fields of art history, sociology, human biology, and philosophy. A significant difference from similar volumes, such as the *Collins Dictionary of Archaeology* (ABC-CLIO, 1993), is the lengthy overview essays on individual continents, which provide expanded coverage of the archaeology of areas less thoroughly covered in previous Western dictionaries such as Oceania, China, and Japan. Each entry is followed by a short chronological bibliography of significant primary and secondary publications, including major subdiscipline periodicals such as *Azania*. Illustrations are limited to high-quality maps, charts, and line drawings reproducing artifact designs. This volume is most applicable to university library reference collections supporting undergraduate and graduate degree programs in archaeology. However, given its scope and accessible writing style, large public libraries should consider it for acquisition as well. [R: Choice, July/Aug 99, p. 1926]—**Robert B. Marks Ridinger**

394. Empereur, Jean-Yves. **Alexandria Rediscovered.** New York, George Braziller, 1998. 253p. illus. maps. index. $60.00. ISBN 0-8076-1442-4.

This fascinating book is Empereur's preliminary assessment of his 10 years of experiences as an archaeologist working in Alexandria. The author's intention is to provide a work that is accessible to a wide public audience. The book is lavishly illustrated by the color photography of Stéphane Compoint. Many readers will find the chapters on the Pharos Lighthouse, the seventh wonder of the world, and on the quest for Alexander's tomb to be the most fascinating. In addition to the interesting descriptions of the excavated areas of Hellenistic Alexandria, Empereur provides insight into the vagaries of archaeological discovery. The author has provided a modest set of notes to the text as well as and index of persons, gods, and places. The author's credentials, including his roles as a director of research at France's National Center for Scientific Research and director of the Center for Alexandrian Studies that he founded in 1990, give the book an authoritative scholarly dimension. Scholars and archaeologists interested in Hellenistic Alexandria will look forward to the more detailed archaeological reports.—**Harold O. Forshey**

395. **Encyclopedia of Archaeology: The Great Archaeologists.** Tim Murray, ed. Santa Barbara, Calif., ABC-CLIO, 1999. 2v. illus. index. $150.00/set. ISBN 1-57607-199-5.

This superb 2-volume set (part of an envisioned 5-volume *Encyclopedia of Archaeology* conceived in 1992) significantly augments the pool of scientific biography extant within anthropology. It presents highly readable accounts of 58 men and women active in the study of the past as antiquarians, prehistorians, or archaeologists from the sixteenth and the twentieth centuries. Written by practicing archaeologists from Australia, the United States, France, England, New Zealand, Wales, India, and Mexico, these essays (chronologically arranged by birth year) interweave personal biography with the gradual development of distinctive professional geographic, temporal, and theoretical interests. Of special value are their bibliographies, divided into primary writings by the individual, followed by a sampling of commentary and criticism regarding their significance. The editor provides a historical overview of evolving approaches to writing an effective autobiography in his epilogue, "The Art of Archaeological Biography," that users should read despite its awkward placement at the end of the 2d volume. A short glossary and detailed author, title, and subject index are included. Seventeen of these individuals are also reviewed in shorter pieces in the 1991 *International Dictionary of Anthropologists* produced by the Library-Anthropology Resources Group (LARG). Useful for social science reference collections in public and undergraduate libraries of all sizes.
—**Robert B. Marks Ridinger**

396. **Encyclopedia of the Archaeology of Ancient Egypt.** Kathryn A. Bard, with Steven Blake Shubert, eds. New York, Routledge, 1999. 938p. index. $250.00. ISBN 0-415-18589-0.

This encyclopedia, compiled by modern Egyptologists, contains valuable resources for researchers and others interested in the ancient Near East, most especially ancient Egypt. It provides succinct, accurate and up-to-date overviews of 13 different historical periods of ancient Egypt, ranging from prehistory through the end of the Roman period. The entries themselves address many, though not all, of the details mentioned in those overviews as well as presenting archeological sites, social and political organizations, flora and fauna, kingship, various deities, many historical persons from ancient Egypt, some modern Egyptologists, and other assorted pertinent topics. Many site maps, temple and tomb plans, and photos of artifacts serve to illustrate in greater detail the topic under discussion. Each article concludes with a current bibliography, utilizing mostly English sources. The volume is completed with a short glossary of Egyptological terms and a very extensive and useful index.

The one problem with this volume lies in the apparent misplacement of an overlay map showing the different archeological sites. Virtually all sites, except those named (i.e., Cairo, El Minia, Thebes, and Aswan/Elephantine), appear to the west and some south of their proper location. Hopefully, the publishers will develop a correction page to rectify this extraordinary error in an otherwise truly remarkable collection of articles on the archaeology of ancient Egypt. Despite this problem, the volume should become a part of every library with an interest in archaeology and ancient history. [R: BL, 1 Sept 99, pp. 178-179]—**Susan Tower Hollis**

AMERICAN HISTORY

Almanacs

397. Burg, David F., and L. Edward Purcell. **Almanac of World War I.** Lexington, Ky., University Press of Kentucky, 1998. 320p. illus. maps. index. $22.00. ISBN 0-8131-2072-1.

World War I continues to fascinate the public and the media, just as its sequel a short two decades later has recently rekindled the imagination of novelists and filmmakers. Given the enormous number of publications on the Great War, it is difficult to conceive that another new book might offer something not covered in previous studies. However, the *Almanac of World War I* does precisely that in a surprising but extremely effective way.

The book consists of a series of entries arranged chronologically from the start of the war in 1914 to its tragic, exhausting finish in 1918. Each entry compresses the battle or campaign of the day in a succinct and readable fashion. In addition, the last 50 or so pages offer brief biographies of the major political and military leaders as well as a selected bibliography. The index is well organized and easy to use.

Another welcome feature in this volume is the large number of maps, illustrations, and photographs (many from the Library of Congress), which add interest and prevent the almost diary-like narrative from becoming too tedious. The reproduction of the maps is not as clear as readers would like, but the photographs are sharp and detailed. Moreover, authors Burg and Purcell, who previously produced *The World Almanac of the American Revolution* (World Almanac Books, 1992), include a host of intriguing sidebars on such diverse topics as World War I technology, tactics, weaponry, and cultural life (including the machine gun, tanks, poison gas, and patriotic songs). Finally, it should be noted that William Manchester's introduction is an eloquent piece of writing about World War I. It captures the pathos and absurdity of the conflict in a way that few others have. [R: BL, 1 Feb 99, p. 990]—**John B. Romeiser**

398. Engelbert, Phillis. Chenes, Betz Des, ed. **American Civil Rights: Almanac.** Farmington Hills, Mich., U*X*L/Gale, 1999. 4v. illus. index. $127.00/set. ISBN 0-7876-3172-8.

The *American Civil Rights Reference Library* is composed of four volumes and three titles: *American Civil Rights Almanac* (2 vols.), *Biographies*, and *Primary Sources*. They are designed for use at a fifth-grade and above reading level. The Advisory Board lacks the usual distinguished names; rather, it includes mostly junior faculty (one professor, three assistant professors, and one graduate student), two public school representatives, and one from the American-Arab Anti-Discrimination Committee. The *Primary Sources* volume includes 22 documents with brief profiles of their authors; the *Biographies* volume includes short biographies of 32 individuals. The *Almanac* volumes include major sections covering Africans, Asians, Hispanics, and Native Americans, with much briefer coverage for Irish, Italians, Germans, Jewish, and Arab Americans and for women, gays and lesbians, and persons with disabilities.

The *Almanac* includes much too brief bibliographies at the end of major sections and all volumes are profusely illustrated. Both volumes of the *Almanac* repeat the same chronology, glossary, and "Research and Activity Ideas." The *Primary Sources* and *Biographies* volumes have different versions (though largely the same) of the chronology and glossary. Overall this set serves its purpose well, but it would have been improved by an adequate bibliography and more precise (e.g., location, date) picture captions. Few errors have crept into the text (but there are some, e.g., Highlander Folk School was not founded near New Market, its current location; its founder, Myles Horton, was not African American; and Andrew Young was born in 1932, not 1921). The greatest problem with this set is what has been excluded: groups (e.g., Haitian Americans who are misleadingly classified as "Latinos," Hmong, Appalachians, Greeks, and Polish), individuals (from *Biographies*), and their words (from *Primary Sources*), such as Frederick Douglass, W. E. B. DuBois, and Russell Means.—**Fred J. Hay**

399. Purvis, Thomas L. **Colonial America to 1763.** Balkin, Richard, ed. New York, Facts on File, 1999. 381p. illus. maps. index. (Almanacs of American Life). $75.00. ISBN 0-8160-2527-4.

Purvis' volume offers an interesting and entertaining look at the American colonial period using charts and statistics. His topical approach includes essays that interpret the information offered on climate, education, crime, science, the arts, Native Americans, and the like. Among the facts that can be learned from this statistical approach are that the colonists were relatively healthy, having a nutritionally complete diet, that the average worker earned considerably more than his counterpart in England, and that New York City and New England suffered several significant earthquakes during this early period. Fully indexed and illustrated, this is an excellent source for a variety of information. The only sections that seem unrelated are the eight biographical sketches that seem to have been randomly selected and a similar brief selection of historic documents. Although not an essential volume, this is an appealing and provocative look at the colonial period.—**Deborah Hammer**

Atlases

400. **Atlas of the Official Records of the Civil War.** [CD-ROM]. Carmel, Ind., Guild Press, 1999. Minimum system requirements: IBM or compatible 386. Four-speed CD-ROM. Windows 3.1, Windows 95, or Windows 98. 16MB RAM. $59.95. ISBN 1-57860-028-6.

This work was originally published to accompany the monumental *The Civil War CD-ROM: The War of the Rebellion* (see ARBA 97, entry 401). Although it is primarily an atlas devoted to military aspects of the Civil War, its uses extend beyond that. The detail of these maps enable users to identify creeks, towns, and other geographical features that have since changed names or ceased to exist. Family historians will appreciate the fact that the names of landowners are shown on many maps. And, although there is no text beyond the one-page preface, the atlas is interspersed with numerous illustrations of Civil War military scenes and equipment. Color charts show Union and Confederate uniforms, ranks, and buttons. Numerous charts illustrate types of bridge construction; weapons; medical equipment; plans of forts; defensive structures; means of transportation; and federal, southern national, and military flags. Multicolor maps show the entire theater of the war, military divisions and departments, military operations in the field, campaigns, battles, and skirmishes.

Access to the contents is good via the subject search window to the CD-ROM itself as well as the several indexes within the original volume. An authority index guides users to maps according to the person or persons responsible for creating them. A geographic and topical index provides locations of various topical and pictorial materials as well as to maps by geographic location or military action. Of particular value is a separate index to maps contained not on this CD-ROM. Such items might be overlooked if one relies solely on the atlas as a source. Maps are reproduced in the same size and colors as the original, making them easily read. Because of the sizes of the various maps, however, scroll bars must be used to view an entire map. Because these maps are solely for military purposes, users should not expect to find every geographic name indexed. Nevertheless, when the general area is known from another source, scanning will produce good results. Many users will also appreciate the ability to bookmark, annotate, and store maps for future use. This title is highly recommended and should be considered by libraries and individuals with an interest in the American Civil War, or that already possess the print or CD-ROM versions of the Army or Navy editions.—**Donald E. Collins**

Bibliography

401. Barbuto, Domenica M., comp. **The American Settlement Movement: A Bibliography.** Westport, Conn., Greenwood Press, 1999. 123p. index. (Bibliographies and Indexes in American History, no.42). $59.95. ISBN 0-313-30756-3.

Written by an expert on the American Settlement Movement in the United States, this slender, 123-page volume presents a selected bibliography that pertains to this part of the Progressive Era. A brief introduction explains the American Settlement Movement. The 185 sources are arranged into the following sections: English antecedents, general surveys and studies, settlement-focused studies, autobiographies, biographies and memoirs, settlement workers' research and case studies, and reference guides. Of great use are the concise, 150- to 300-word abstracts written by the author that describe the content of these books and summarize their value to the student or researcher. The material is conveniently indexed by author, title, and subject, which is especially important to the researcher. For example, social service agencies are discussed in six of the sources.

Barbuto's book is a valuable contribution to the analysis of the American Settlement Movement. The titles she has selected provide a solid overview of this part of U.S. history and it would be a fine addition to any library or historical collection.—**Mark J. Crawford**

402. **Bibliographic Guide to North American History 1998.** Thorndike, Maine, G. K. Hall/ Macmillan, 1999. 807p. $385.00. ISBN 0-7838-0227-7. ISSN 0147-6491.

This 8½-by-11-inch volume contains lists of publications about the United States and Canada that were cataloged during 1998 by The New York Public Library and the Library of Congress. The lists include all of the "E" and part of the "F" titles in the Library of Congress classification system, and all the "I" and part of the "H" titles in the New York Public Library classification system. The guide also includes some additional classification numbers for North American directories. The major areas covered in the guide are works on American Indians; the era of the European discovery of America; American colonial and revolutionary history; the antebellum period; the American Civil War; the late nineteenth century; the twentieth century; U.S., state, and local constitutional, diplomatic, political, and social history; and Canadian history. The lists include works in all languages and all forms—nonbook materials as well as books and serials.

The alphabetically arranged entries are cross-listed by author, title, and subject. Each entry contains a complete set of the Library of Congress cataloging information. These data include author's name and (when available) date of birth; a short title and subtitle; place, date, and publisher of the work; pagination; illustration and series information; subject headings; and ISBN, DDC, and Library of Congress call numbers.

This volume, along with 20 other G. K. Hall Bibliographic Guides that cover fields ranging from business to theater arts, is intended to serve as an authoritative reference source for librarians and scholars. It is most useful as a technical aid for library acquisition and cataloging.—**Terry D. Bilhartz**

403. Etter, Patricia A., ed. **To California on the Southern Route 1849: A History and Annotated Bibliography.** Spokane, Wash., Arthur H. Clark, 1998. 178p. illus. maps. index. (American Trail Series, 18). $37.50. ISBN 0-87062-270-6.

California's gold rush of 1849 may be one of the best-documented migrations in human history. There are thousands of letters, journals, and diaries in archival collections in the U.S. Most of the published items from this period are from individuals who traveled west on the Oregon-California trail (over 300,000 persons made that trek). There was a less traveled route across what is now the Southwest; some 20,000 persons made that journey. What has been published about the southern routes has appeared primarily in local history journals and private or small presses. Etter provides a description and location of 181 published and unpublished items. The first 40 pages of the volume outline the historical setting of the immigration and identify major published works about the trails as well as describing the "Southern Trails." Her bibliography is arranged by the trails (8 sections) that the journals and letters cover. Each trail has an introduction that describes the trail in some depth. This arrangement makes the 10-page index critical to locating information, unless the user knows the subject very well and would not need the bibliography. Within each section entries are in alphabetic order by author. Each entry starts with basic bibliographic data and holding institution information followed by short descriptive annotations. An appendix listing the authors by trail is another aid in locating material. A glossary provides additional information about people, places, and things mentioned briefly in the annotations. Three maps and a number of photographs help users visualize the trails. One shortcoming is there is no listing of the institutions that hold the material. The only way to determine that is to check each entry and make a list. Without that information it is difficult to know how comprehensive the author's coverage is of the unpublished materials. A useful addition to western history reference collections. [R: Choice, July/Aug 99, p. 1926]—**G. Edward Evans**

Biography

404. Chipman, Donald E., and Harriett Denise Joseph. **Notable Men and Women of Spanish Texas.** Austin, Tex., University of Texas Press, 1999. 359p. illus. maps. index. $40.00; $17.95pa. ISBN 0-292-71217-0; 0-292-71218-9pa.

Two historians at the University of North Texas and the University of Texas at Brownsville have combined their talents to produce a lively volume about a fascinating cast of characters who made the

Spanish colonial era in Texas (1528-1821) such a colorful period of history. The work contains 11 chapters that cover 15 famous or infamous men who cast a large shadow over Texas during the Spanish colonial period. The list of notables includes such figures as Cabeza de Vaca, Alonso de Leon, Father Miguel Hidalgo, Felipe de Rabago y Teran, and Domingo Cabello y Robles. Chapter 12, entitled "Colonial Women: Rigors, Responsibilities, and Rights," introduces readers to a few high-profile Latinos as well as a host of heretofore "faceless" colonial Texas women who contributed to a society well known for its male chauvinism.

Each chapter consists of an 8,000- to 11,000-word biographical essay that brings to life these legendary figures who discovered and settled Spanish Texas. The volume is entertainingly readable, yet erudite, containing 58 pages of endnotes and bibliographies that direct readers to the pertinent primary sources of the period. It also includes two dozen maps and illustrations and an index. A winner of several history awards, this volume would make a welcome addition to all research and public libraries with collections in Texas history and life.—**Terry D. Bilhartz**

Chronology

405. **The American Scene: Events.** Danbury, Conn., Grolier, 1999. 9v. illus. maps. index. $265.00/set. ISBN 0-7172-9448-X.

This 9-volume set is designed for young readers (grades 4 and up) and highlights many of the important events and people who have helped shape U.S. history. With a total of more than 1,000 pages, an important subject is portrayed on each page. Ranging from the Watson Brake Mounds in Louisiana that were built 3,500 years ago by Native Americans to the Clinton scandal, the books are packed with key information about the United States that will educate students and teachers alike.

The well-designed pages start with a colorful photograph or image of the subject at the top, a location map, and a handy U.S. history timeline along the right margin. Written descriptions vary in length from 200 to 300 words and adequately cover the significance of the event. The page concludes with highly interesting facts in bold typeface under the heading "Did you know . . ."

Including *all* of the important events of U.S. history in a series of this scope is impossible, and selection must be somewhat subjective. For the most part the coverage is thorough, but some glaring omissions are Sitting Bull, Crazy Horse, and the Reconstruction era. Blank space is left at the bottom of each page that would have been a perfect spot for further reading citations or an extra 100 words of text, either of which would have enriched the entries. Occasional oddities also crop up; for example, volume 4, "The Civil War and Its Aftermath," begins in 1863 (the 1861–1862 war years are covered in "Growth and Conflicts"—it would have been more logical to have all the Civil War in one volume). The image for "The Battle of Wounded Knee" actually has nothing to do with the battle—there are far better historical events to choose from that better illustrate this tragedy. These inconsistencies aside, the set serves as an adequate introduction to U.S. history for the young reader. [R: BL, 1 Sept 99, p. 178; BR, Nov/Dec 99, pp. 76-77]—**Mark J. Crawford**

406. **Events That Shaped the Century.** Alexandria, Va., Time-Life Books, 1998. 192p. illus. index. $19.95. ISBN 0-7835-5502-4.

This volume cites all of the events one would expect to find in a work with this title and by this publisher. Besides the predictable catastrophic, momentous, or triumphant events, there are the less obvious trends, inventions, and personalities that have likewise impacted our everyday lives at the end of this century. As usual for a Time-Life series, it is the striking, poignant, or intentionally repugnant photographs (some famous and familiar) that tell much of the story and make the book a visual archival summary of the past 100 years in the United States.

The treatment is more superficial than Peter Jennings and Todd Brewster's *The Century* (Doubleday, 1998) or Harold Evans' *The American Century* (Knopf, 1998) by necessity of its size. Although the text lacks the eyewitness accounts of ordinary persons' reactions found in other books, the sources of information reflect both contemporary and historical interpretations.

Of the 125 events included, the majority deal with political affairs, although the economy, society, science, education, medicine, fine arts, and sports are also covered. Notable by its absence is any significant comment on religion, considering it is a right as sacred to Americans as the other freedoms in the Bill of Rights. Many of the happenings emphasize controversial, debatable issues that serve to illustrate or test the tenets of the Constitution as the nation has progressed through the twentieth century. This work, along with many others appearing on the market that deal with important people and events in the 1900s, is sure to be of interest, and provides a concise look at the United States' direction as the new century approaches. [R: BR, Nov/Dec 98, p. 72]—**Janet J. Kosky**

407. Gross, Ernie. **The American Years: A Chronology of United States History.** New York, Charles Scribner's Sons/Macmillan Library Reference, 1999. 655p. illus. index. $95.00. ISBN 0-684-80590-1.

This is a general chronology of U.S. history, beginning with 1776 and ending in the year 1997. Arranged with much white space, each year get two to three pages, with at least one illustration (usually a black-and-white photograph). Events of the year are classified under "International," "National," "Business/Industry/ Inventions," "Transportation," "Science/Medicine," and similar subjects, ending with a brief "Miscellaneous" category. Under each subject are a number of subcategories, such as plays, movies, and deaths, all under entertainment.

There is no apparent rhyme or reason for the selection, nor does the author give any selection criteria, except for a statement that he has included "the most important events of each year." Although one might question whether Joni Mitchell's *Turbulent Indigo* is one of the most significant records of 1994 or of her career (it is the only work of hers listed), lacking anything resembling selection criteria or any citations to sources whatsoever, it is hard to quibble.

The matter of the index is another issue—it is awful. For example, although there is a coal miner's strike listed in the entries for 1948, there is no index entry for *miners* or *coal*. The entry for *hairstyles—bobbed* is listed as on page 268, not page 269 where it appears, and both the index and the actual entry have Isaac Asimov's classic *I, Robot* as *I, Robert*.

A number of standard reference sources include chronologies of some sort; there would be some value to an index by date to these or, for that matter, to a well-designed chronology that emphasizes popular culture (the apparent point of this book). Unfortunately, the complete lack of documentation, along with the brief entries and the poor indexing, suggests this book belongs on the coffee table or in the general collection. [R: Choice, Sept 99, p. 118; BR, Sept/Oct 99, pp. 71-72; SLJ, Aug 99, p. 182]—**James H. Sweetland**

408. **ResourceLink: 20th-Century American History.** [CD-ROM]. Santa Barbara, Calif., ABC-CLIO, 1998. Minimum system requirements (Windows version): Pentium-compatible processor at 75MHz or faster. Four-speed CD-ROM drive. Windows 95. 8MB RAM. 10MB hard disk space. SVGA monitor 640x480 (256 colors). 16-bit sound card with Windows drivers. Mouse. Minimum system requirements (Macintosh version): 68040 processor with 25MHz or faster. Double-speed CD-ROM drive. System 7.5.3 or later. 8MB RAM. 10MB hard disk space. SVGA monitor 640x480 (256 colors). $79.00 (standalone); $199.00 (lab pack); $389.00 (site license). ISBN 1-57607-013-1.

This is essentially an encyclopedia of twentieth-century U.S. history. Approximately 1,500 entries on this subject are presented in the form of video and audio clips, still photographs, maps, definitions, biographical sketches, documents, statistical tables, quotations, and articles of varying length. The term "encyclopedia" is used in this review because of the manner in which users access the contents. Information is in alphabetic lists in which topics may be located either in a single list or via separate lists organized by type (e.g., video clip, audio clip, maps, biographies, organizations).

There is much to be said about this title that is good. Most of the contents will be found useful by both teachers and students. Access to the contents is simple. Users are guided through the various features, search procedures, and methods for carrying out functions in a clearly written and well-organized onscreen manual. A useful feature is the ability to group items for an orderly presentation, to add or edit text to illustrations, and to manipulate and move about text and illustrations in various ways. Topics cover the broad spectrum of the century's history, with emphasis, as one might expect, on the latter half, because this is where the interest of most users probably is. The 27 audio clips are generally excellent, and include such outstanding incidents as Richard Nixon's "Checkers" speech, a "fireside chat by Franklin D. Roosevelt, and Neil Armstrong's moon landing. The same may be said for the 27 video clips, which feature such events as Lyndon Johnson's infamous "Daisy spot" campaign commercial, Woodrow Wilson's 1918 visit to Europe, and scenes from World Wars I and II. The editors also did well in the selection of the 186 biographies and the many still photographs contained in this work.

The content of this CD-ROM is also subject to criticism. With only 1,500 entries, there is not enough information to cover a century as eventful as the twentieth. Related to this criticism is the fact that a significant number of these seem irrelevant. For example, one questions the value of including separate entries for the official seals of 68 government agencies, and illustrations of the flags of all the states and territories. Similarly, few of the 75 state, territorial, and other maps do more than simply list a few of the more populous cities. And, although many of the 178 quotes by famous Americans are interesting, this reviewer does not see their value or need when so many historical events and persons might have been added in their place. A reference work is only as good as its contents, and this one offers less than it could or should have. Despite the above criticisms, this title still has value for teachers and students in secondary schools, and would be a useful addition to their libraries. [R: BR, May/June 99, p. 92]—**Donald E. Collins**

Dictionaries and Encyclopedias

409. **American History.** Mark C. Carnes, ed. New York, Macmillan Library Reference/Simon & Schuster Macmillan, 1998. 1198p. illus. index. (Macmillan Compendium). $125.00. ISBN 0-02-864978-8.

Covering the American experience in one volume has always been an exciting challenge. The standard work in this field, the *Dictionary of American History*, consists of eight volumes and a 2-volume supplement (see ARBA 77, entry 384). *American History* is an attempt at producing a 1-volume version of the *Dictionary of American History* for ready-reference use.

This work, although published in 1998, contains no bibliographical material after 1994. Some articles, such as the one on the hydrogen bomb, contain only older references, the latest being Henry Kissinger's 1957 work, *Nuclear Weapons and Foreign Policy*. The hydrogen bomb article, alas, ends with the following virtually worthless piece of information, probably from the 1950s: "The ultimate threat of such weapons to national security is matched only by the potential benefits of thermonuclear reaction as a source of controlled energy for peaceful purposes."

Other articles, such as the one on the antinomian controversy, are summaries by well-known historians, this one being done by Perry Miller. The Civil War article, for further example, is written by J. G. Randall. If this 1-volume source to American history is not brief enough, the editors have in some cases reduced the topics to one sentence. For instance, Andersonville Prison is mentioned as follows: "To the Union Prisoners at Andersonville and their northern friends it appeared that the Confederates were deliberately murdering the captives through deprivation." Similarly, the 19th Amendment is reduced to: "The Nineteenth Amendment, which gives women the vote, grew out of pressures for equal rights set in motion at the 1848 Seneca Falls Convention organized by Elizabeth Cady Stanton."

There are no entries for individuals, but instead topics such as "Burr Conspiracy," "Burr-Hamilton Duel," and "Burr Trial" are given. Individuals must be researched through the indexed entries under their names. For example, there are extensive entries under "Washington, George" in the index, but only one article, "Washington's Farewell Address," is alphabetically in this compendium. There are a few minor not very well-selected illustrations accompanying the text. A table of contents provides an alphabetic listing of the entries. This is supplemented, as mentioned by the index, at the conclusion of the volume. This work is hardbound, but it is doubtful the binding will stand up to extensive use. Most libraries will want to order this as a 1-volume companion to the *Dictionary of American History*. [R: SLJ, Aug 99, p. 181]—**Ralph Lee Scott**

410. **American Social Issues: An Interactive Encyclopedia.** [CD-ROM]. Santa Barbara, Calif., ABC-CLIO, 1999. Minimum system requirements (Windows 95 or Windows 98): IBM or compatible at 75MHz or faster. Four-speed CD-ROM drive. Windows 95 or Windows 98. 24MB RAM. 40MB hard disk space. SVGA monitor (640 x 480). 16-bit sound card with Windows drivers. Mouse. Minimum system requirements (Windows NT): IBM or compatible at 90MHz or faster. Four-speed CD-ROM drive. Windows NT 4.0. 32MB RAM. 40MB hard disk space. SVGA monitor (640 x 480). 16-bit sound card with Windows drivers. Mouse. $69.00 (standalone); $339.00 (network). ISBN 1-57607-136-7.

Focusing on a range of important social issues of the twentieth century, this CD-ROM provides 850 articles of varying lengths (250 to 1,500 words) that combine text with images, video, audio, and statistics. Through extensive cross-references users are able to access related entries on the CD-ROM as well as an interactive Website produced by the publisher. Included are primary source documents, concepts, events, social and political movements, organizations, and biographies. Topics range from AIDS and abortion to medical use of marijuana and the Women's Educational Equity Act.

A separate illustrated timetable displays selected entries in the context of historical events. Another separate link provides access to eight extensive thematic entries—crime, discrimination, education, environment, family, labor, pacifism, and sexuality. The product is easy to navigate, and provides numerous possibilities for manipulation, customization, and storage of information. An extensive glossary and citation guide are provided.

High school and college students should appreciate the ready-reference information provided by this work, and although some subject areas such as communism, McCarthyism, and war are not included, those that are included provide adequate facts and data for the beginning researcher. This resource is recommended as a complement to journal and monograph research in the area of social issues.—**Edmund F. SantaVicca**

411. Barbuto, Domenica M. **American Settlement Houses and Progressive Social Reform: An Encyclopedia of the American Settlement Movement.** Phoenix, Ariz., Oryx Press, 1999. 270p. illus. index. $74.95. ISBN 1-57356-146-0.

The settlement movement in the United States was a product of Americans trying to provide the housing needs of many urban poor, including the stream of immigrants who arrived in the United States at the rate of one million per year from 1890 to 1905. As the movement grew, more men and women, such as Lillian D. Wald, Charles B. Stover, and Stanton Coit, took active leadership roles in the social reform, and the settlement movement spread over urban centers. From these experiments, individual settlement houses became part of our progressive reform vocabulary, including South End House in Boston, Hartley House in New York, and College Settlement in Philadelphia, and the movement spread internationally. Barbuto provides a small but extensive encyclopedia on the settlement house movement, where biography is the obvious strength, but issues, individual houses, agencies and associations, and publications such as Jacob Riis's *How the Other Half Lives* are also featured. Entries are concise and include cross-references in bold typeface and references where appropriate. A brief bibliography and useful 25-page index conclude the volume. This unique volume belongs in reference collections of academic and larger public libraries. [R: LJ, 15 Sept 99, p. 68; Choice, Dec 99, p. 698]—**Boyd Childress**

412. Crawford, Mark. **Encyclopedia of the Mexican-American War.** Santa Barbara, Calif., ABC-CLIO, 1999. 350p. illus. maps. index. $75.00. ISBN 1-57607-059-X.

Recently, in celebration of the 150th anniversary of the Treaty of Guadalupe Hidalgo ending the Mexican-American War, 1846 to 1848, several reference books have been published. This reasonably priced encyclopedia provides an informative presentation of key persons, battles, treaties, health issues, cities and states, and groups (e.g., abolitionists, the Texas Rangers). There are 459 entries of which 275 are biographical—mostly of U.S. persons. Special features include a selected bibliography, an annotated chronology from 1830 to 1848, portraits and pictures of battles from collections at the Library of Congress, and an introduction outlining the author's 11 causes of the war. There are only six maps; more would have improved the work. The encyclopedia entitled *The United States and Mexico at War: Nineteenth Century*

Expansionism and Conflict (1998) has nearly 600 entries and includes more pictures, maps, and bibliographic citations; however, it is more expensive ($175). The *Historical Dictionary of the United States–Mexican War* (see ARBA 99, entry 462) includes 840 entries, of which 567 are biographical. All three of these works are biased toward the United States. This work is recommended for high school, public, and academic libraries. [R: BL, 15 Nov 99, p. 649]—**Karen Y. Stabler**

413. **Everyday Life: American Social History.** New York, Macmillan Library Reference/Simon & Schuster Macmillan, 1998. 1078p. illus. index. (Macmillan Compendium). $125.00. ISBN 0-02-864976-1.

This extensive volume is a compilation of selections from the three-volume *Encyclopedia of American Social History* published in 1993 (see ARBA 94, entry 505). Articles have been excerpted in their entirety and have not been updated; therefore, statistical tables and charts are not as current as one might wish, which is a major weakness of this volume. Organized alphabetically, the book chronicles the history of daily life in the United States. Addressing such topics as African American music, death, film, gender roles and relations, manners and etiquette, public health, slavery, and sports, each entry gives an extensive historical overview of the social institution addressed. Included with each entry are chronological bibliographies and cross-references to other articles in the volume. Alternate tables of contents—one alphabetic and one synoptic—aid the reader in locating topics. The topical index is lengthy and complete. The volume also includes black-and-white photographs and quotations. Written in a lively manner by leading experts in the field, each entry is both a valuable research source as well as fascinating reading. The only real drawback to the volume is the lack of up-to-date information.—**Janet Hilbun**

414. Hatch, Thom. **Encyclopedia of the Alamo and the Texas Revolution.** Jefferson, N.C., McFarland, 1999. 229p. index. $55.00. ISBN 0-7864-0593-7.

As memorable as the cry "Remember the Alamo," Hatch's latest specialized reference volume is another example of a first-rate reference book. Centered around the March 6, 1836, fall of the Alamo garrison to Mexican troops under Antonio Lopez de Santa Anna after a 13-day siege, the book is a chronology and encyclopedia of prominent Alamo events and people on both sides of the Texas Revolution. In a dictionary format, Hatch provides brief notes on all 188 Alamo defenders, with longer sketches of leaders such as Jim Bowie, Davy Crockett, Bill Travis, and Santa Anna. Entries on subjects such as the Golidad massacre, the battle of San Antonio, and the decisive battle of San Jacinto are in greater depth, often with a chronology, maps, and troop strengths. Significant figures in Texas independence like Sam Houston and Stephen F. Austin are included, as are a handful of Mexican generals. A brief bibliography and index conclude the volume. Hatch's work, like that in his *Custer and the Battle of Little Bighorn* (see ARBA 98, entry 441), is accurate, readable, and comprehensive—all essential traits of a reliable reference work. [R: BL, 1 Dec 99, p. 721]—**Boyd Childress**

415. Mays, Terry M. **Historical Dictionary of the American Revolution.** Lanham, Md., Scarecrow, 1999. 555p. illus. index. (Historical Dictionaries of Wars, Revolutions, and Civil Unrest, no.7). $125.00. ISBN 0-8108-3404-9.

This source provides over 1,000 articles, covering people, places, battles, events, individual countries (France, Spain), and issues related to the Revolutionary period from the mid-1760s to 1783. Articles are arranged alphabetically and, except for a few longer ones (George Washington, for example), tend to be very brief—Thomas Paine and Thomas Jefferson merit only three sentences each. There are numerous *see* references, but the author uses "q.v." in parentheses instead of bold typeface to indicate "see also," which some readers may find intrusive. While the book covers a wide range of topics, the author favors the military aspects of the Revolution, providing entries for many forts, vessels, minor battles, and not-so-famous patriots, such as William Washington, whose entry is four times the length of that for James Otis. There is a select chronology of the period, a general introduction, and an appendix containing six documents and four maps, but no overall index. The bibliography (books, articles, and dissertations) is arranged by subject, and gives full bibliographic information. Although the bibliography is a remarkable 190 pages long, part of that is because items appear repeatedly. For example, Christopher Ward's *The War of the Revolution* (1952) is included in 59 separate sections. While the articles are briefer than those in Mark Mayo Boatner's *Encyclopedia of the American Revolution* (see ARBA 96, entry 506), Mays' bibliography is much more up-to-date, making this a valuable source for all reference collections. Due to this book's high price, however, libraries that already own the (also expensive) 2-volume *The American Revolution, 1775-1783: An Encyclopedia*, edited by Richard L. Blanco (see ARBA 94, entry 503), with much longer articles, should be able to pass on this one, unless they have comprehensive American history collections. [R: Choice, July/Aug 99, pp. 1928-1929]—**John A. Drobnicki**

416. **Scholastic Encyclopedia of the Civil War.** By Catherine Clinton. New York, Scholastic, 1999. 112p. illus. maps. index. $18.95. ISBN 0-590-37227-0.

The title, *Scholastic Encyclopedia of the Civil War*, is somewhat misleading if one accepts the traditional definition of an encyclopedia as alphabetically arranged information. Written for juveniles, this slender volume skims the surface, yet contains a great deal of information, much of which is not the kind usually seen in such texts.

The table of contents lists six chapters, which are arranged chronologically. The first, "Before the War," is followed by others for each year, 1861 to 1864. The final chapter, "1865 and After," places much emphasis on the Reconstruction period and the Civil Rights Movement of the 1960s. The volume also includes an alphabetic index. The inside covers provide a clear, color-keyed map showing Union and Confederate capital cities, state capitals, major cities, other locales, places where major battles occurred, and the route of Sherman's March to the Sea.

The text is illustrated with an abundance of period art and photographs, including political cartoons and sketches made by soldiers on the scene. Sidebars with labels like "Eyewitness" (diary excerpts), "Battle-at-a-Glance" (number of troops and casualties on each side and the winner), and "Did You Know" (facts and anecdotes) can be found on nearly every page.

The vocabulary is often above juvenile level, and some might question the author's dwelling on the extended post-war period in a work ostensibly about the war itself. However, the *Scholastic Encyclopedia of the Civil War* provides a lively introduction to a complex subject at a reasonable cost.—**Kay O. Cornelius**

417. Sifakis, Carl. **The Mafia Encyclopedia.** 2d ed. New York, Facts on File, 1999. 414p. illus. index. $40.00; $19.95pa. ISBN 0-8160-3856-2; 0-8160-3857-0pa.

This volume, an expanded and updated version of the 1987 1st edition (see ARBA 88, entry 589), is part of a continuing series of popular criminology reference works on aspects of organized crime by former wire service reporter Sifakis. It is written for a nonspecialist audience, its principal focus remaining the provision of biographical data on major figures belonging to or associated with the Mafia in the United States. Other categories covered include the Mafia's public history and mythology, slang terms and their meanings, and types of businesses run by members of various crime families. Contents are arranged alphabetically, with indexing by proper name and subject. The addition of index headings for specific court proceedings and the wide range of colorful nicknames used by mob figures would have improved the work considerably. This volume will be most useful for large public libraries wishing to augment their biography holdings and university collections supporting degree programs in criminology. [R: LJ, 1 Apr 99, pp. 88-89; BR, Nov/Dec 99, p. 85]—**Robert B. Marks Ridinger**

Handbooks and Yearbooks

418. **American Eras: The Colonial Era 1600-1754.** Jessica Kross, ed. Farmington Hills, Mich., Gale, 1998. 455p. illus. index. $85.00. ISBN 0-7876-1479-3.

This volume contains a smorgasbord of information about everyday life in colonial America. The work is divided into 12 chapters: "World Events," "The Arts," "Business and Communications," "Colonial

Americans," "Education," "Government and Politics," "Law and Justice," "Lifestyles, Social Trends and Fashion," "Native Americans," "Religion," "Science and Medicine," and "Sports and Recreation." Each chapter opens with a section that presents a chronological list of important events related to the theme of the chapter. In most of the chapters, the chart of chronological events is followed by a two- to four-page chapter overview, a "Topics in the News" section that provides brief discussions of selected events and issues of the period, a "Headline Makers" section that offers biographical sketches of prominent colonials, and a "Publications" section that lists pertinent sources that were published during colonial times. Most of the sections conclude with a bibliography of related secondary sources. The volume also includes an illustration, map, or chart on almost every page, and a 20-page index of subjects and photographs.

With 10 authors contributing to the volume, the chapters are uniform in format but not in quality or depth of coverage. Despite its bulk and unevenness, the volume contains many entertaining facts and figures about colonial America. This work is recommended for middle school and high school libraries.

—**Terry D. Bilhartz**

419. **American Immigration.** Danbury, Conn., Grolier, 1999. 10v. illus. index. $325.00/set. ISBN 0-7172-9283-5.

American Immigration is a 10-volume encyclopedia dealing with the topic of immigration from the earliest Asian settlers of 30,000 years ago to modern-day immigrants such as the Kurds, Haitians, and Bosnians. Volume 1 provides an overview of the subject, discussing immigration in a historical context— immigration laws, patterns, and issues. Volume 2 is dedicated to Ellis Island. The remaining volumes contain topical entries, covering individual ethnic groups, terms associated with immigration, and social issues. Each volume is the same length and each contains a bibliography as an index to the entire work.

The coverage of the individual groups will prove valuable. The history of the group in its native land is provided as well as the issues prompting the exodus. Problems encountered by the group are discussed, the names of famous members are given, and, in the case of recent immigrants, some idea of their progress and future is projected. Numerous photographs add interest, and sidebars and inserts giving highlights and little-known facts will get readers' attention.

No one is given total editorial credit for the work, although names of a project coordinator, writers and editors, and researchers are listed. Also included here are the names of several individuals associated with Ellis Island. No credentials are given for any of the participants.

American Immigration is a fascinating and useful overview of a basic thread in U.S. history. Although not scholarly in nature (data is not footnoted and interviews have been "lightly edited for readability"), the work will prove to be a helpful tool for middle and high school students. [R: BL, 1 Mar 99, p. 1234]

—**Michele Tyrrell**

420. **Campaigns of the Civil War and the Navy in the Civil War.** [CD-ROM]. Carmel, Ind., Guild Press, 1999. Minimum system requirements: IBM or compatible 386. Four-speed CD-ROM drive. Windows 3.1, Windows 95, or Windows 98. 16MB RAM. $39.95. ISBN 1-57860-030-8.

This CD-ROM presents the military history of the Civil War as witnessed and written about by Union Army and Navy participants and contemporaries. Written in the decades immediately following the war, these 19 volumes describe the land and water campaigns and battles of that conflict from a decidedly Northern viewpoint. Authors include such noted individuals as famed Naval historian and Union Admiral Alfred T. Mahan, General Abner Doubleday of baseball fame, and John G. Nicolay (private secretary to Abraham Lincoln), as well as lesser-known Naval and Army officers and civilians. The final volume is devoted to statistical data on the war. Most of these works include maps and appendixes, and some contain bibliographies of other Civil War era books. Although most of these writers attempted to present an unbiased treatment of the war, some do not attempt to hide their hostility towards the Southern Confederacy. This is particularly true in the intemperate writing of Lincoln's private secretary. Despite the bias, these works provide valuable information about the military history of the war. Purchasers may, however, wish to provide some balance to these titles by also considering the acquisition of the same publisher's CD-ROM

Confederate Military History (1997), in which Southern authors of Confederate sentiment describe the war from the opposite point of view.

This CD-ROM is easy to install and use. The onscreen manual, available via the help menu, provides clear instructions on its various features and search methods. Information retrieval is excellent through the use of Boolean operators as well as field searching of documents by signer, addressee, greeting, and date. Searching may also be constrained to a single document or the entire database. Highlighting enables fast and easy retrieval of specific information within often lengthy documents. These and other features enable users to read entire books or to find very precise information with ease. The availability of bookmarking and file folders facilitate organization and storage, as well as retrieval, by topic. This CD-ROM offers a significant number of books not normally available in most libraries, and is highly recommended for any library, person, or institution with an interest in the Civil War.—**Donald E. Collins**

421. **Civil War CD-ROM II: Official Records of the Union and Confederate Navies in the War of the Rebellion.** [CD-ROM]. Carmel, Ind., Guild Press, 1999. Minimum system requirements: IBM or compatible 386. Four-speed CD-ROM drive. Windows 3.1, Windows 95, or Windows 98. 16MB RAM. $69.95. ISBN 1-57860-027-8.

This title contains the official records of the Union and Confederate Navies during the American Civil War as reported by the officers and government officials involved in the naval actions and activities of that war. Although these are frequently regarded as less historically important than land warfare in the popular mind, this is nevertheless an extremely important work. The Union Navy was responsible for blockading Southern ports while the Navies of both sides were used to aid their respective armies in actions that took place along the rivers and sounds of the Confederacy. As a rule, the army that was supported by Naval craft on either side was able to dominate that action.

This is a companion piece to Guild Press's *The Civil War CD-ROM: The War of the Rebellion* (see ARBA 97, entry 401), which included the official records of the Union and Confederate armies. While the original compilers failed to include all the written reports of the war, and the documents are subject to the biases of the Union and Confederate officials who wrote them, the two titles taken together contain the best available collection of primary source, official records relating to the Civil War. As such, they are essential to any serious research on the war.

This is a well-done product. Search methods and procedures are clearly explained onscreen via the help function that guides users through all aspects and features of this title. Information is easily found and printed. Both simple and complex searching enables users to perform precise searches via the Boolean operators of "and," "or," and "not." Proximity searches may be set for as little as two or as many as 32,000 words. Field searching allows users to retrieve documents by signer, addressee, date sent, or by range of dates. Highlighting of search topics make them easy to retrieve within often lengthy documents. File folders enable the grouping of topics and searches, while the availability of highlighting makes the location of specific search terms simple within often lengthy documents. This is an extremely important work and is highly recommended for all libraries, groups, and individuals with an interest in the American Civil War.

—**Donald E. Collins**

422. Dent, David W. **The Legacy of the Monroe Doctrine: A Reference Guide to U.S. Involvement in Latin America and the Caribbean.** Westport, Conn., Greenwood Press, 1999. 418p. index. $59.95. ISBN 0-313-30109-3.

This is a collection of essays discussing the history of the foreign relations between the United States and 24 Latin American and Caribbean nations with emphasis on the influence of the Monroe Doctrine that was promulgated in 1823. Independent nations are emphasized—Grenada and Guyana receive essays, whereas the Bahamas and Surinam do not. An introductory essay is followed by individual essays of 8 to 22 pages devoted to individual nations, from Argentina to Venezuela. Each essay starts with a timeline or chronology of events in the country's history and a four to six item list of suggested reading. The volume also includes a 40-item glossary of terms, a fairly extensive index, and an appendix containing excerpts from President Monroe's original message and several editorial cartoons by Thomas Flannery of the Baltimore Sun.

Dent, from Towson University, wrote all of the essays. His historical expositions are quite clear and readable and contain all the important events in the political history of the nation covered and its relationship with the United States. His judgements are temperate but often critical of U.S. policy, particularly during the Reagan years. Although several well-regarded volumes have been written on U.S. Latin American and Caribbean relations, *The Legacy of the Monroe Doctrine* is the most accessible. It is the most current and best organized single volume available for reference purposes. *The Encyclopedia of U.S. Foreign Relations* (see ARBA 98, entry 660) also contains articles on the Monroe Doctrine and U.S. relations with the nations covered in *The Legacy of the Monroe Doctrine*. The former should be a first choice for any library with a reference collection covering U.S. foreign policy, but the latter would be a useful supplementary volume in general libraries and a necessity in libraries with collections on Latin America. [R: Choice, July/Aug 99, pp. 1925-1926]—**Jonathan F. Husband**

423. Genovese, Michael A. **The Watergate Crisis.** Westport, Conn., Greenwood Press, 1999. 197p. illus. index. (Greenwood Press Guides to Historic Events of the Twentieth Century). $39.95. ISBN 0-313-29878-5.

As an addition to the Greenwood Press Guides to Historic Events of the Twentieth Century, this highly readable and interpretive study takes its place alongside entries on matters such as civil rights, Islamic fundamentalism, German unification, and the Cold War. The series makes no attempt to impose some unifying theme on, or to discover some comprehensive meaning of, the twentieth century, but rather strives more modestly to identify and analyze developments of ongoing influences. Genovese, an established authority on the era of President Richard Nixon, easily meets expectations with this effort. He skillfully unfolds not only the story of Watergate, that umbrella term which encompasses all the varied misdeeds of the Nixon presidency, but also attributes to Watergate much of the contemporary cynicism toward government and politics, an increasingly adversarial relationship between the press and political leaders, a decline in civility in public discourse, and the constant scrutiny of public officials by special prosecutors. So, to understand modern politics in this country, Genovese correctly asserts, one should begin with Watergate.

As with all studies in the series, this one adheres to a prescribed format. A detailed chronology is followed by a historical narrative and interpretive essays, brief biographies of key players, a sampling of documents, a glossary of terms, an annotated bibliography, and an index. Rather than finding something startlingly new here, one will be reminded of the connection between Vietnam and Watergate, Nixon's paranoia and the frightening extent to which he was prepared to go to get his "enemies," and the president's knowledge of and involvement in the cover-up. Reference librarians should add this one to their collections, for students and interested laypersons will find it an excellent guide to this nation's most serious political scandal.—**John W. Storey**

424. **The Southern Historical Society Papers.** [CD-ROM]. Carmel, Ind., Guild Press, 1998. Minimum system requirements (Windows version): IBM or compatible 386. Four-speed CD-ROM drive. Windows 3.1 or Windows 95 with Pentium 100. 16MB RAM. Minimum system requirements (Macintosh version): System 7.0 or higher. 8MB RAM. $69.95. ISBN 1-57860-058-8.

As a source of published primary material on the Civil War, these papers are perhaps secondary only to the monumental *The War of the Rebellion: A Compilation of Official Records of the Union and Confederate Armies* and that work's corresponding volumes of Naval records. From 1876 until its conclusion in 1959, the Southern Historical Society collected and published records of the Confederate side of the Civil War in 52 annual volumes. Among the most significant of its contents are the multivolume proceedings of the Confederate Congress and the roster of the 26,300 soldiers who surrendered at Appomattox with Robert E. Lee. The contents tell the stories of leaders and common people of the Confederacy in the form of lengthy monographs, essays, biographies, diaries, rosters, correspondence, speeches, statistics, and even poetry. The topics treated include large and small battles, treatment of war prisoners, the life of the average soldier, justification for secession, and various controversies coming out of the war. All of these materials were collected through the efforts of members of the Southern Historical Society, which included some of the biggest names in the Confederate government and military as well as such imminent historians as Douglas Southall Freeman. Because of the miscellaneous nature of the contents, not all aspects and battles of the war are included. However, the material that is found here is first rate and should be consulted alongside the titles mentioned above.

As a rule, search features and strategies are standard on CD-ROM products from this publisher. Typical users will find them easy to understand and follow. As in its other Civil War CD-ROMs, searchers are guided through every step by onscreen help instructions. Searching is precise and easy via Boolean operators and such field searching features as proximity, dates, and addressees and signers of documents. This is highly recommended for any collection where the Civil War is a significant interest.—**Donald E. Collins**

425. Volo, Dorothy Denneen, and James M. Volo. **Daily Life in Civil War America.** Westport, Conn., Greenwood Press, 1998. 321p. illus. index. (The Greenwood Press "Daily Life Through History" Series). $45.00. ISBN 0-313-30516-1.

Based upon journals, newspapers, and diaries, this title provides an account of the daily life of civilians, ordinary soldiers, and slaves, including such information as how they obtained and prepared food and dealt with food shortages, how clothing and fashion were affected by the war, and the role of popular books and magazines, housing, leisure activities, and political ideas. The 1st of the 3 major parts provides the setting by discussing historical and political events and the attitudes of the day in both the North and South. The 2d part concerns all aspects of the lives of soldiers. Part 3 focuses on the lives of civilians. The work begins with a chronology; concludes with a bibliography and an index; and includes some period photographs, illustrations, and original artwork.

Most publications that deal with this time period focus on political and military matters. The introduction to this work makes it clear that it is envisioned as a supplement to other works—to flesh out the bones of statistics and descriptions of battles. Although the intended audience is not clarified in the introduction, this work seems suitable for readers from 8th grade to adulthood. Students will benefit by gaining an understanding of the culture of the day; teachers will find that this information about daily life will enrich the Civil War curriculum.—**Vandelia L. VanMeter**

AFRICAN HISTORY

426. Bobb, F. Scott. **Historical Dictionary of Democratic Republic of the Congo.** rev. ed. Lanham, Md., Scarecrow, 1999. 598p. (African Historical Dictionaries, no.76). $75.00. ISBN 0-8108-3571-1.

The previous edition of this work, also compiled by Bobb, appeared in 1988. A lot has happened in the interim, as the country changed names (from Zaire), changed governments (from Mobutu Sese Seko to Laurent Kabila), and changed character (from moderate disorder to virtual chaos). Despite his protests that his "intent is historical and not political" (p. xi), the compiler has credentials for understanding the contemporary Congo, but no obvious ones for being qualified to write on its history. As a result, this volume continues the tradition of the Historical Dictionaries series to banish part of its own name from the contents.

The usual accoutrements are present: a list of abbreviations; guide to name changes; chronology (mostly since the 1950s); two tiny maps for the second-largest country in Africa; a 20-page introduction; a 134-page bibliography; a few statistical tables; and no index. I glanced at Table 1, titled "Administrative Regions by Area and Population, 1970-1995," and noticed that the country doubled in population between 1970 and 1995. Given the chaos and terrorism for much of this period, the growth rate seems impossible. However, this extraordinary development—if true—is not explained anywhere that this reviewer could find.

Many post-independence persons and events rate several pages, but the "estimated 200 languages and 450 dialects" earns only a 1-page overview, although a few are treated briefly elsewhere. Oddly, Mobutu Sese Seko, the living embodiment of the country for more than 30 years, is treated in a little more than 3 pages, scarcely more than the space given to Laurent Kabila, in office for a year and apparently in control of little outside the capital of Kinshasa, suggesting that even the recent past is too old to receive proportionate treatment. Bobb's lack of credentials for offering information on Congo's earlier history shows itself in the literal way in which he treats culture heroes from oral tradition as living, breathing human beings, a view once shared by some historians, but not for many years.

Useful then in certain respects, the overall judgment has, once again, to be that except for its bibliography this historical dictionary falls short of what it ought to be—indeed, what it could be. Most certainly it does not fulfill the general editor's sentiment that "we look forward to future editions that will answer many of today's open questions" (p. vii).—**David Henige**

427. Eades, Lindsay Michie. **The End of Apartheid in South Africa.** Westport, Conn., Greenwood Press, 1999. 209p. illus. index. (Greenwood Press Guides to Historic Events of the Twentieth Century). $39.95. ISBN 0-313-29938-2.

For decades the world had feared that the black majority of South Africa would rise up violently against the oppressive white-run government, leading to a massive bloodbath and possible foreign military intervention. What a pleasant surprise it was when Prime Minister F. W. deKlerk willingly gave up his office in a relatively peaceful change of power in the middle of 1994 after the electoral defeat by the African National Congress (ANC), led by Nelson Mandela. This was one of the great political events of the 1990s, right up there with the fall of Communism. This guide contains a variety of information that readers can use for quick answers to questions before they do more in-depth research. Five chapters explain how the end of the apartheid came about. The historical background of apartheid, the structure of racial separation, the parties and the process of painful transition, and internal and external pressures on the parties are all examined. The last chapter on the challenges facing the new country can be complemented by *Security and State in Southern Africa*, written by Agostinho Zacarias (Tauris Academic Studies, 1999). There are reference notes at the end of each chapter. Following this are biographical essays for 16 key players in these momentous events; unfortunately, there are no suggested reading notes for these essays. Then come reprints of 13 important documents of the ending of the apartheid that can be hard to find. The chronology goes from 1652 to 1997, but there is not enough detail for the entries. Interested readers should examine Jacqueline A. Kalley's *South Africa Political History: A Chronology of Key Political Events from Independence to Mid-1997* (Greenwood, 1999). The work is supplemented with a glossary, an index, and a five-page annotated bibliography of resources. There are also two outline maps of the old and new South Africa on one page; matters would have been improved had these maps each had a separate page, with more detail. The author previously published *A Case Study of an Appeaser: Robert Hadow in the Foreign Office, 1931-1939* (Praeger, 1996). The title under review is suitable for the reference and circulating collections of academic and public libraries.
—**Daniel K. Blewett**

428. Kalley, Jacqueline A., Elna Schoeman, and L. E. Andor, comps. **Southern African Political History: A Chronology of Key Political Events from Independence to Mid-1997.** Westport, Conn., Greenwood Press, 1999. 904p. maps. index. $145.00. ISBN 0-313-30247-2.

This work covers the 12 countries of the South African Development Community, ranging as far north as Tanzania as of 1997. Coverage is appropriately uneven, with the trouble spots getting the most attention. Thus Swaziland has only 15 pages and South Africa has more than 15 times as many. The chronology begins at various dates, from 1961 (South Africa and Tanzania) to 1990 (Namibia), and ends in mid-1997. Coverage is enormously detailed, often day-by-day, and sometimes there are many ungrouped entries for the same day, which in cases (e.g., Namibia for 1990) leads to tedious and repetitive entries. There is the usual and necessary list of acronyms.

The indexes—one for subjects and one for names of persons—appear to be computer-generated and are not particularly user-friendly. For instance, subentries under the entry "Diplomatic and Consular Relations" are arranged alphabetically by SADC country but not under other countries, forcing someone interested in, for example, Nigeria's interplay with the relevant countries to look in many places. There are no cross-references; thus users interested in speeches will find nothing under that word and nothing to tell them that the entry for these is "talks." Indexes are immeasurably important and need more than a dollop of human intervention. Nonetheless, anyone interested in the chronology of political, military, educational, and other events for these 12 countries will want to come here first for at least a basic orientation. [R: Choice, Oct 99, p. 314]—**David Henige**

429. Musiker, Naomi, and Reuben Musiker. **Historical Dictionary of Greater Johannesburg.** Lanham, Md., Scarecrow, 1999. 480p. maps. (Historical Dictionaries of Cities of the World, no.7). $98.50. ISBN 0-8108-3520-7.

It seems odd to have a dictionary covering an African city, albeit an extremely large city, that is longer than any of its county-specific counterparts, but such is the case. As a consequence, it is possible to treat the subject with greater depth. The result suggests that cities should always have been the appropriate target for these dictionaries.

Although the ambit is smaller, the arrangement typifies the Historical Dictionaries series: a list of acronyms, 5 interesting historical maps, a chronology of more than 25 pages, the dictionary proper, a list of mayors, a 2-page stab at statistics, and a classified bibliography. The last is shorter than typical in this series, less than 40 pages. There is no index, continuing an unfortunate tradition. The entries are also longer and more detailed than usual, with many of them running to several pages. There are numerous "q.v." references but not a full-scale attempt at cross-referencing. Newspapers are treated in the entry for "Press," but a more systematic list of these would have been helpful, as would information on local archives. Both the bibliography and the chronology could have been keyed to the entries in some way, facilitating traffic in both directions.

The compilers are long-time students of the subject and have done a more than competent job. As a result, this is the first historical dictionary where the dictionary is actually of more use than the bibliography. Even the casual caveat about too little history and much present information does not apply well.

—**David Henige**

430. Stewart, John. **African States and Rulers.** 2d ed. Jefferson, N.C., McFarland, 1999. 420p. index. $75.00. ISBN 0-7864-0613-5.

Although more substantial and accurate than the 1st edition, this new edition still falls well short of being a reliable reference work. The preface and bibliography illustrate why. The author relies on one public and one small university library for his material. As a result, the bibliography is fairly short and includes only books and only materials in English, making his objective an impossible one. Even relevant books in English are missing, such as C. E. Bosworth's *The New Islamic Dynasties: A Chronological and Genealogical Manual* (Columbia University Press, 1996). This lack of serious research shines throughout the work, nowhere more so than in the longest entry "Egypt." Stewart struggles with the Old Kingdom and the First and Second Intermediate periods, surely because much of the work appears in articles and in German. The tendency to oversimplify typifies many other entries, such as Africa Proconsularis, where the evidence is almost entirely epigraphic and does not allow anything like the continuity Stewart displays in his own lists. Conversely, for many states Stewart falls well short of the available information. For Ife he shows only three Onis and for Kongo and Mwene Mutapa he again omits many rulers, particularly for the nineteenth century. Stewart carries on a tradition that needs to end by providing dates for early and problematic rulers of many of the major states—Benin, Buganda, Bunyoro, Kano, and so on.

There are other flaws that would spoil a better work than this. In the index, "de" and "von" affect the alphabetization and Stewart is ill at ease with the Latin, Spanish, Portuguese, and Islamic conventions for alphabetizing personal names. Above all, there are no bibliographic references attached to entries. A user wondering how Stewart came up with his lists of the rulers of Brakna or Masina or Tagant, or the governors of the Caanries of the Swedish Gold Coast will have no way to find out. This is unacceptable in a reference work of this nature.

A pity to find so much wrong with this edition, since African historians would find much value in a well-researched, well-arrayed, and well-documented presentation of dynastic and other lists of rulers. If nothing else, this work underscores the fact that such a work would require many hands and a commitment to a degree of accuracy so high that the effort would not need repeating. Speaking or repeating, one hopes that a 3d edition is not on the drawing board.—**David Henige**

431. Vernus, Pascal. **The Gods of Ancient Egypt.** Translated by Jane Marie Todd. New York, George Braziller, 1998. 202p. illus. maps. $75.00. ISBN 0-8076-1435-1.

This lavishly illustrated volume consists of a very readable text surrounded by pages of photographs, each of which is completely described. Beginning by elaborating the deities' functions, the author continues by discussing various general ideas such as cult organization, the different ways that deities manifested themselves, and the coherence among the deities, followed by a presentation on the practice of syncretism, by which Egyptian deities combined to share traits or foreground specific traits. Next, one learns about the creation of the world, including the creation of humanity as well as its end, with brief discussions of the different narratives, cosmogonies, and the various deities involved, finishing with a brief description of Akhenaten, the heretic king who proscribed gods other than the Aten.

The final two chapters present the intersection of the human and divine worlds. The first of these examines beliefs and practices relating to the afterlife, such as tombs, mummification, and the different mortuary texts designed to assist the individual to the afterworld at his or her death. The final chapter describes how the ancient Egyptians approached the world of the divine, including a considerable discussion of personal piety and dialogues with the gods.

This volume provides a clear, comprehensible, and accurate presentation of ancient Egyptian deities. The excellent and up-to-date annotated bibliography, the clear texts and generally smooth translation, the fine glossary combined with an index of the deities, and the superb photographs of objects not commonly seen in books on ancient Egypt make it deserving of a place in public, private, art, and academic libraries.

—**Susan Tower Hollis**

ASIAN HISTORY

Azerbaijan

432. Swietochowski, Tadeusz, and Brian C. Collins. **Historical Dictionary of Azerbaijan.** Lanham, Md., Scarecrow, 1999. 145p. (Asian/Oceanian Historical Dictionaries, no.31). $40.00. ISBN 0-8108-3550-9.

Until the fall of communism this small country in the Caucasus was long under the control of rulers in Moscow. It has been in the news due to its petroleum industry centered around the capitol city of Baku, and its long-standing conflicts with neighboring Armenia (the Nagorno-Karabagh dispute). Although there are many reference sources on Russia and the Soviet Union, there are fewer sources that are focused on this region. As with the other volumes in this series, there are entries for people, places, events, political parties, concepts, and ideas. In addition to *see also* references at the end of each entry, cross-references within the text of an entry use bold typeface, which makes it easier to pick out important terms. There is one not very detailed map of the country, a three-page historical chronology, and an eight-page bibliography (with most sources published after 1989). A copy of the country's constitution and perhaps some historical statistics, would also have been helpful. Swietochowski (professor of Russian and Middle Eastern history at Monmouth University) previously published *Russia and Azerbaijan: A Borderland in Transition* (Columbia University Press, 1995). Collins, executive director of the Cedar Falls Historical Society, recently published *Cedar Falls, Iowa* (Arcadia Press, 1998). The item under review complements *Armenia, Azerbaijan, and Georgia: Country Studies* by Glenn E. Curtis (Library of Congress, 1995). It is suitable for the reference collections of academic and large public libraries as well as special collections dealing with this region.—**Daniel K. Blewett**

China

433. Chang, Tony H., comp. **China During the Cultural Revolution, 1966-1976: A Selected Bibliography of English Language Works.** Westport, Conn., Greenwood Press, 1999. 199p. index. (Bibliographies and Indexes in Asian Studies, no.3). $65.00. ISBN 0-313-30905-1.

The Chinese Cultural Revolution was one of the most tumultuous periods in modern Chinese history. It affected virtually all aspects of Chinese life, including economic planning, art, music, drama, education, and even the daily life of many Chinese people. This bibliography includes more than 1,000 titles of monographs, dissertations, theses, and audiovisual materials. The arrangement consists of 8 divisions, including "Documents and Reference Works"; "General Works"; "Special Periods"; "Cultural Revolution in Provinces and Municipalities"; "Special Subjects"; "Biographies, Memoirs, and Firsthand Observations"; "Travelers' Reports"; and "Audio-Visual and Microform Materials." Each entry contains a full bibliographic description of the author, title, edition, imprint, and pagination. Also included are brief annotations for most entries along with special notes where appropriate. Entries are numbered consecutively. There are title, subject, and author indexes.

Several bibliographies on the Cultural Revolution in China have been published. Robert Goehlert published *The Chinese Cultural Revolution: A Selected Bibliography*, which was only 10 pages, but included the major works to that time (Vance Bibliographies, 1988); even earlier, Stewart E. Fraser published *Chinese Education and Society, a Bibliographic Guide: The Cultural Revolution and Its Aftermath*, which included major books, articles, and other items to about 1970 (International Arts and Sciences Press, 1972); and finally, James Wang published *The Cultural Revolution in China: An Annotated Bibliography* (see ARBA 97, entry 320), which was the most inclusive treatment to date. Wang's bibliography included more than 300 items and was the major list for a number of years. The present work is a much-needed addition to the bibliographic coverage of the Cultural Revolution begun by these other works. Also, the scope of this present work makes it a valuable addition to Cultural Revolution research.

This book is highly recommended for all larger public and academic libraries with Chinese history and culture collections. It would also be a valuable addition to smaller academic libraries that wish to maintain a Chinese research collection. Because of the cost it would probably not be a logical addition to personal collections. [R: Choice, Sept 99, p. 117]—**Robert L. Wick**

434. Johnson, Graham E., and Glen D. Peterson. **Historical Dictionary of Guangzhou (Canton) and Guangdong.** Lanham, Md., Scarecrow, 1999. 277p. (Historical Dictionary of Cities of the World, no.6). $78.00. ISBN 0-8108-3516-9.

Among China's major cities and provinces, Guangzhou City and Guangdong Province have been significant in its history, culture, politics, economy, commerce, and international affairs. Guangzhou, also known outside of China as Canton, is the capital of Guangdong Province. Cantonese cuisine is a prominent cooking style within and outside of China. Emigrants from Guangdong comprised a major element of the Chinese diaspora in the nineteenth and first half of the twentieth centuries, with the result that the Cantonese dialect is the most pervasive dialect in Hong Kong and in many Chinese communities in the U.S. and other parts of the world.

This concise historical dictionary is divided into two parts, one on Guangzhou and the other on Guangdong, albeit with numerous cross-references. Each begins with an introductory essay and is followed by entries for the people, places, events, and cultural activities significant to the modern period. A chronology of Guangzhou and Guangdong preceding the dictionary entries is helpful. Concluding the volume are two useful bibliographies, on Guangzhou and Guangdong, providing citations to English-language sources mostly published since 1950. This well-researched and concise reference work is very useful for the study of modern China, especially on one of its most populous, vibrant, and prosperous regions.

—**Hwa-Wei Lee**

435. Wortzel, Larry M. **Dictionary of Contemporary Chinese Military History.** Westport, Conn., Greenwood Press, 1999. 334p. maps. index. $95.00. ISBN 0-313-29337-6.

Despite its title, this dictionary is more of a concise encyclopedia in its treatment of each entry. Although the word "contemporary" is not strictly defined, the author initially intended to limit treatment to the twentieth century and does focus on communist forces in earlier periods and on the People's Republic of China. However, the dictionary includes earlier historical information on China and the Chinese military as background information. This is especially evident in the introduction, where there is a brief history of dynastic succession and sections such as "the philosophical basis of Chinese society develops," and "China is unified for the first time." The author, a colonel in the U.S. Army and a military intelligence officer specializing in China and East Asia, has a Ph.D. in political science and has served twice at senior levels in the Army Attaché Office in the American Embassy in Beijing. Three other identified contributors are equally qualified in education and experience. The length of entries varies according to the subject, with some running several pages and others a single paragraph. In addition to bibliographic references at the end of each entry, an extensive selected bibliography concludes the volume. This dictionary on the recent military history of China is a useful reference tool for the study of contemporary China.—**Hwa-Wei Lee**

Japanese

436. **The Columbia Guide to Modern Japanese History.** By Gary D. Allison. New York, Columbia University Press, 1999. 259p. maps. index. (The Columbia Guides to Asian History). $45.00. ISBN 0-231-11144-4.

Even during its current recession, Japan somehow manages to capture the curiosity and interest of scholars and the general public. In 125 pages, University of Virginia professor of East Asian Studies Gary D. Allison has boiled down the essence of Japan's transformations since the Meiji Revolution and the opening of its ports to the West. In addition to this abbreviated historical narrative, Allison has created 13 topical brief essays (ranging from 1 to 13 pages), introducing key players and themes in Japanese modern literature, politics, and business. A resource guide to published studies in English, brief lists of Japanese films, and a sprinkling of electronic resources follow. As a reference guide, the appendix is valuable for its inclusion of translated full-texts and extracts of several key documents in Japanese history. The chronology is also helpful. Public, high school, and undergraduate libraries are encouraged to purchase this book—but not for their reference collection. The bibliography is uneven and the remainder of the work is not helpful as a reference source—unlike *The Kodansha Encyclopedia of Japan* (see ARBA 84, entry 305) or *Japan: An Illustrated Encyclopedia* (see ARBA 94, entry 115). However, a casual reader could certainly peruse the guide in about as much time as the actual flight to Japan and would arrive at Narita with a basic understanding of modern Japanese history.—**Andrew B. Wertheimer**

437. Perez, Louis G. **The History of Japan.** Westport, Conn., Greenwood Press, 1998. 244p. maps. index. (The Greenwood Histories of the Modern Nations). $35.00. ISBN 0-313-30296-0.

This sturdily bound title is a concise primer for Japanese history, and not really a reference book. The author's preface states that it is intended for the general public and secondary school students. Although there are chapters on feudal Japan and the Tokugawa era, most of the pages of text deal with the last 150 years, which have the most relevance to today's situation. The timeline in the front could have had more entries and a bit more detail. The three line maps are of Japan's empire, modern Japan, and feudal Japan. More maps, and with more detail, would have been nice. Appendix A has a sentence of information for each of 73 "notable people in the history of Japan." America's first minister of Japan, Townsend Harris, is mentioned, but not General Douglas MacArthur, who certainly had a much bigger impact on Japanese history. Appendix B is a listing of the nine Sat-Cho Oligarchy (Genro, the main political advisors), while appendix C is a list of premiers and their years in office. The bibliographic essay is disappointing. Many more titles could have been included, such as the *Cultural Atlas of Japan* (see ARBA 89, entry 108), the 9-volume

Kodansha Encyclopedia of Japan (see ARBA 84, entry 305), *The Allied Occupation of Japan, 1945–1952: An Annotated Bibliography of Western Language Materials* by Robert Edward Ward and Frank J. Shulman (see ARBA 75, entry 544), and Frank Joseph Shulman's bibliography simply entitled *Japan* (see ARBA 91, entry 103). A glossary of selected terms can be found at the end of the book. Perez (Illinois State University) recently published *Japan Come of Age: Mutsu Munsmitsu and the Revision of the Unequal Treaties* (Fairleigh Dickinson University, 1999). There are many other titles in this series, including Arnold Blumberg's *The History of Israel* (see ARBA 99, entry 509). This volume is suitable for the circulating collections of public and school libraries. [R: BR, Mar/April 99, p. 74]—**Daniel K. Blewett**

438. Röpke, Ian Martin. **Historical Dictionary of Osaka and Kyoto.** Lanham, Md., Scarecrow, 1999. 273p. maps. (Historical Dictionaries of Cities of the World, no.9). $89.50. ISBN 0-8108-3622-X.

The Historical Dictionaries of Cities of the World series, launched in 1997, is a most interesting project that should be commended for its worldwide geographical diversity. Following the initial volume on Tokyo, the current series includes Paris, Warsaw, Vienna, Johannesburg, Guangzhou (Canton) and Guangdong, Stockholm, and Honolulu. The rationale for including Osaka and Kyoto in this series is understandable. The two cities' history far outshines that of Tokyo, an obscure fishing village until the middle of the last century. However, it is doubtful the market for this particular volume will be very great. It might have been better to treat the other major cities of the world and to establish this series as an essential reference source for most libraries before introducing volumes on important but lesser-known urban areas.

Market concerns aside, this volume contains an immense amount of information, including chronologies of each city, informative narrative introductions to the urban areas, maps, photographs, useful bibliographies, and appendixes that provide other economic, historical, cultural, and statistical information. The heart of each section of the book is the dictionary of people, places, events, and so on. The paragraph entries—by a most knowledgeable author, a Canadian and German citizen, freelance writer, editor, and novelist who has lived in Kyoto and Osaka for 12 years—are well done.

This series will be useful for large research libraries. However, few other collections will be able to justify this particular volume. Most smaller libraries will have to limit their acquisitions to meet the needs and interests of a significant number of their patrons.—**Joe P. Dunn**

Korean

439. Hoare, James, and Susan Pares. **Conflict in Korea: An Encyclopedia.** Santa Barbara, Calif., ABC-CLIO, 1999. 260p. illus. index. (Roots of Modern Conflict). $65.00. ISBN 0-87436-978-9.

"Korean War" and "Korean Conflict" are often used as synonyms. However, this title uses "conflict" to indicate a broader perspective than previous substantial works on the Korean War, such as the *Historical Dictionary of the Korean War* (see ARBA 92, entry 648), *Korean War Almanac* (see ARBA 92, entry 660), and the *Historical Dictionary of the Republic of Korea* (see ARBA 94, entry 117). The British authors (one a diplomat and one a freelance writer) do greatly credit these other volumes. Strikingly, not included in the credits or bibliography is *The Korean War: An Encyclopedia* (see ARBA 95, entry 538). The choice of "conflict" is intended to broaden the subject matter to treat, but extend beyond, the war and warfare, and include diplomacy and terrorism, with a timeframe beginning with the division of the peninsula in 1945 (some entries touch earlier in the century) and continuing to the present. As an example of its orientation, it has references, but no entry, for Lin Biao (commander of the Chinese People's Liberation Army in the 1950s) and a one-page entry for Zhou En-Lai (Chinese premier and foreign minister). In contrast, *The Korean War: An Encyclopedia* has references, but no entry, for Zhou and a 1½-page entry for Lin (albeit using a different romanization system). The volume's eight-page introduction offers skimpy context as one-half covers geographic and historical background and the remainder is a summary of post-World War II developments. Alphabetically arranged entries cover 220 pages, with a bibliography, chronology, and index adding a further 40 pages. If readers are primarily interested in the Korean War, this volume has far less detail (especially on military units) than *The Korean War: An Encyclopedia*, but if they are looking for a wider context still with substantial information on the war, this volume would serve. Larger libraries will want to add this to supplement *The Korean War: An Encyclopedia*, but smaller libraries can probably be content with the latter.—**K. Mulliner**

Pakistan

440. Burki, Shahid Javed. **Historical Dictionary of Pakistan.** 2d ed. Lanham, Md., Scarecrow, 1999. 403p. (Asian/Oceanian Historical Dictionaries, no.33). $89.50. ISBN 0-8108-3634-3.

In 1947 India and Pakistan became independent countries, with Pakistan containing two wings on either side of India. In 1971, after a brief civil war, Pakistan's east wing became Bangladesh. This book contains information for anyone wishing to know more about the before and after independence west wing or today's Pakistan. The volume begins with a chronology and brief narrative history of Pakistan, starting with the arrival of Islam on the subcontinent. The main body of the book contains entries of a paragraph or more about important personages, such as groups like the Ahmadiya, events such as the 22 Families Speech, geographical locations like Lahore or Taxila, and items such as cotton and the Great Game. Entries range from a sentence or two to several paragraphs depending upon the importance of the entry. Included are topics such as China-Pakistan relations, the fifth Cricket World Cup, and the Lahore-Islamabad Motorway. The book concludes with an extensive, useful bibliography and an appendix containing a list of Governors General, Presidents and Prime Ministers, and Chiefs of the Army Staff. A few Urdu entries are not translated (e.g., Bait-ul-maal and Tehrik-e-Istiqlal), forcing the reader to discern the literal meaning of the term from the description. The entries are cross-referenced to make the volume useful for the expert and novice alike. This volume should be in all research libraries.—**David L. White**

441. Long, Roger D. **The Founding of Pakistan: An Annotated Bibliography.** Pasadena, Calif., Salem Press and Lanham, Md., Scarecrow, 1998. 327p. index. (Magill Bibliographies). $45.00. ISBN 0-8108-3557-6.

Although titled the "founding" of Pakistan, this bibliography contains material relevant to the founding of Pakistan in the widest sense and will be useful for those interested in the nationalist movement(s) that led to the independence of India and Bangladesh as well as Pakistan. The works referenced include imperial histories, subaltern interpretations, biographies, and novels, some dating from the 1930s, but with most material from the 1960s to the present. The first part contains general reference materials, many useful for further searches. Here, readers find dissertations, guides to government archives in the subcontinent and the U.S., gazetteers, and guides to special collections (like the Hartley Library, which contains the Mountbatten papers). A selection on "Political Studies" contains books, articles, and some dissertations and reference works. A third section contains books, articles, bibliographies, microform catalogs, and government white papers dealing with the provinces of pre-independence India. The fourth section is devoted to works on Mohammad Ali Jinnah, including collections of his speeches, letters, newspaper reports, and papers as well as other bibliographies and books. The last section contains references to biographies of other players, both Indian and English, in the subcontinent's independence movement. There is material here on the Aga Khan, Stafford Cripps, Gandhi, the Nizam of Hyderabad, and many others who were connected with the independence movement. Each entry in the book is annotated, placing the work within its historical and historiographical framework, making the bibliography useful for both nonspecialists and specialists. Given the works contained in the bibliography, the annotations, and the useful author and subject indexes, this should be the one bibliography consulted by anyone investigating the processes of Pakistan's independence from Britain in 1947. [R: Choice, Feb 99, p. 1045]—**David L. White**

AUSTRALIAN HISTORY

442. Docherty, James C. **Historical Dictionary of Australia.** 2d ed. Lanham, Md., Scarecrow, 1999. 425p. (Asian/Oceanian Historical Dictionaries, no.32). $65.00. ISBN 0-8108-3592-4.

The size of this useful guide to the history of Australia has increased substantially since the 1st edition in 1992 (see ARBA 94, entry 124). The 2d edition contains some 371 cross-referenced entries as well as a bibliography of more than 1,000 items. The main body of alphabetic entries covers a wide variety of people, places, and topics. The numerous cross-references lead the user back and forth through Australian history in a meaningful way. The historical chronology at the beginning, and the three appendixes that provide a wide range of historical listings and statistics, offer a good general perspective. Although this edition places Australia into a broader international perspective than the 1st edition, it seems to still be somewhat parochial in its treatment of the Aborigines and Australia's relationship with its Pacific neighbors (e.g., there is no entry for New Guinea). Despite those flaws, it is the best short guide to Australian history and many American academic and public libraries will find this work of continuing value.—**Norman D. Stevens**

CANADIAN HISTORY

443. Gough, Barry M. **Historical Dictionary of Canada.** Lanham, Md., Scarecrow, 1999. 271p. maps. $55.00. ISBN 0-8108-3541-X.

This dictionary provides a historical and cultural context to understand Canada and its contributions to the world. The majority of the entries center on the people, places, and events of the twentieth century, from Nobel Prize winner Sir Frederick Grant Banting, who discovered insulin, to Agnes Campbell Macphail, first female member of Parliament.

The introductory essay discusses four continuities of Canadian history: the imperial connections to both Britain and France, the interrelationship and conflicts of the French and English as the founding European influences, provincial relations and Canada's success as a federation, and the undeniably profound effect of the United States as Canada's neighbor. Other features include a chronology, maps, acronym definitions, a bibliography, and lists of past governors general and prime ministers. This reference gives the serious scholar as well as the casual visitor to Canada a better appreciation for the uniqueness of this interesting country.—**Adrienne Antink Bendel**

444. Henderson, George F. **W. L. Mackenzie King: A Bibliography and Research Guide.** Buffalo, N.Y., University of Toronto Press, 1998. 367p. index. $95.00. ISBN 0-8020-4157-4.

There are a couple of facts about William Lyon Mackenzie King that every Canadian child learns. First, he believed in ghosts and talked with his dead mother as well as with the late Sir Wilfred Laurier during séances. Second, he was fond of his little terrier, Pat, with whom he also communicated during séances. King was also a faithful diarist, sometime journalist, and author of books as well as Canada's Prime Minister during some of the most difficult days of the twentieth century.

The scholar who approaches King as a subject will find Henderson's bibliography and research guide an excellent resource to the primary sources of King's life and work. A foreword by John N. Turner explains briefly the importance of King in Canadian political and social history and Turner's relationship with King. Henderson's preface discusses the reasons for the interest in King's life, the organization of the bibliography, and some of the detective work that went into the identification of many unsigned articles from King's work as a journalist. The bibliographic materials are divided into two parts. The first, works by King, are itemized into books, articles, government reports, diaries, published speeches, assorted compiled government documents, archives, theses, sound recordings, and other miscellanea. Every edition of each book title has a complete bibliographic description. The second part, works about King, are itemized into books and pamphlets, articles, King in fiction, theses, newsreels, sound recordings, photographs, poems and plays, and unpublished material. Each item has a alpha-numeric tag to identify it within its subject category. In addition, six appendixes describe materials such as King's proposed books, the official biography, books in King's personal library, and other useful and interesting bibliographic facts. A detailed index provides access to entries for authors of books, articles, and theses, as well as for subjects.

Henderson has made use of King's own diaries and other archival materials, interviews with archivists and bibliographers, and Reginald Hardy's biography to enrich the bibliography with scenes from King's life and excerpts from his writings. The researcher who uses Henderson's bibliography and research guide as a springboard to a closer examination of this remarkable politician will find this an indispensable aid.—**Kerie L. Nickel**

CUBAN HISTORY

445. Leonard, Thomas M. **Castro and the Cuban Revolution.** Westport, Conn., Greenwood Press, 1999. 188p. illus. index. (Greenwood Press Guides to Historic Events of the Twentieth Century). $39.95. ISBN 0-313-29979-X.

Historian Thomas M. Leonard has compiled and written a useful overview of Cuba during the second half of the twentieth century. He examines many elements of the history of Cuba, including Cuba as a Spanish colony and a slave society; post-slavery plantocracy; after the Cuban War for independence and the Spanish-American War; and Cuba as a U.S.-dominated, sugar- and tourism-dependent country. He also discusses Cuba's society as highly stratified with a small economic and mostly lighter-skinned elite and masses of impoverished and mostly darker-skinned workers—the independent Cuban nation. This "independent" Cuba was run for the elite by the dictator Fulgencio Batista.

In the fight against Batista, the plantocracy, and U.S. economic domination, Fidel Castro emerged as a leader. Leonard is evenhanded in his description of the events that led up to the revolution and the revolution itself. He also describes Castro's adoption of communism and his consolidation of power in post-Batista Cuba, Cuba's fractious relations with the United States and supportive relationship with the Soviet Union, the experiences and impact of the Cuban exile community, and the relative successes and failures of the Castro regime.

In addition to nearly 90 pages of historical description, this volume includes a chronology (1492-1998) and 23 biographies of key players in twentieth-century Cuban affairs. The text also includes 15 primary documents related to the revolution, Castro's Cuba, and U.S. perceptions of it (from José Martí to Che Guevara, Bill Clinton, and Pope John Paul II). A glossary and a classified and briefly annotated bibliography conclude the work. Black-and-white photographs and an index also enhance this historical study.

This book is a well-written introduction to Castro's Cuba. It will be extremely useful for undergraduate research, though it would have benefited from the inclusion of more illustrations.—**Fred J. Hay**

EUROPEAN HISTORY

General Works

446. **The Hutchinson Encyclopedia of the Renaissance.** David Rundle, ed. Boulder, Colo., Westview Press, 1999. 434p. illus. maps. index. $65.00. ISBN 0-8133-3670-8.

This volume has more than 1,500 entries on all aspects of the Italian and Northern Renaissances of the fourteenth through sixteenth centuries. Its well illustrated, $7\frac{1}{2}$-by-10-inch page makes a welcome addition to European history and humanities reference works available for library collections. The encyclopedia is the U.S. edition of a 1999 imprint first published in Britain. The editor is an Oxford academic and the other contributors are drawn principally from Oxbridge colleges and London University.

Entries range in length from a long paragraph to a double-columned page or more for important figures such as Michelangelo, Raphael, or Erasmus families like the Medici and concepts like exploration or reform and Reformation. The arrangement is alphabetic. In addition to the main articles, there are 20 "Feature Entries" boxed and set apart from the main text, although roughly in the right alphabetic position. These longer entries are perhaps one to two pages long. The extensive cross-references appear thorough. Topics range from antiquarianism and azulejos to botany, climate change, art history, and homosexuality. There are 17 gloss pages with full-color plates of major art and architectural works accompanied by 4 pages of explanatory text. There are eight maps and nine pages of schematic dynastic charts. The latter deal mainly with key Italian families, plus Burgundy, the Habsburgs, the Anjous, and the Tudors. Many black-and-white illustrations and portraits accompany the text. The thematic index is somewhat confusingly laid out with main headings and subheadings without apparent alphabetic or other organization. The contents and lists of maps and genealogies are useful. The general editor provides a useful but brief introductory essay.

The work is admirable. Where budgets permit, it deserves strong consideration as an addition to collections needing reinforcement in its perennially popular topic. [R: Choice, Dec 99, pp. 702-703]—**Nigel Tappin**

447. Singman, Jeffrey L. **Daily Life in Medieval Europe.** Westport, Conn., Greenwood Press, 1999. 268p. illus. index. (The Greenwood Press "Daily Life Through History" Series). $45.00. ISBN 0-313-30273-1.

The subtitle of this work might well read "Northwestern Europe in the High Middle Ages, 1100-1300," for such is its scope. Because the so-called Middle Ages extended over such a long time, Singman concentrates on the period when feudal and manorial systems predominated. He selects specific examples of medieval institutions, each of which embodies the character of the period: Cuxham, a small English village; Dover Castle in England; the monastery of Cluny in France; and Paris as an exemplar of the town. The result is an intriguing view of life and thought in medieval society and the world of that time. This social history approach delves into practical aspects of everyday life; for example, the structure of medieval society; the life cycle; and material culture with practical discussions on food, sanitation and personal hygiene, and sleeping accommodations, among others. Although Singman's research incorporates important sources, the text of this introductory study is both lively and enlightening and not weighed down with footnotes. This is not a scholarly work, but one that will hold the fascination of the ordinary reader interested in the living history of another time and place. A selected bibliography of English-language materials is appended, along with a brief glossary and appendixes on games, recipes, and music. This book and others in the series are recommended for public, high school, and college libraries.—**Bernice Bergup**

448. Vanthoor, Wim F. V. **A Chronological History of the European Union 1946-1998.** Northhampton, Mass., Edward Elgar, 1999. 244p. index. $90.00. ISBN 1-84064-125-8.

This book is just what the title says: a historical chronology of the European Union (EU). Entries for the dates can range from a paragraph to a single sentence. Quotations and excerpts from reports or statements are included. The author has italicized those words or phrases that he considers important. There are informative footnotes with bibliographic citations that provide further explanation of an entry or phrase. The introduction provides a short narrative overview of the history of this important international organization. A helpful list of abbreviations can be found at the front of the book. The appendix is subtitled "Articles of the Treaty Establishing the European Economic Community (Rome, 25 March 1957)." Perhaps the text of more important documents could have been included, along with an organization chart, a map of Europe, and a list of the member countries and date of admission. This volume complements other recent reference books, such as *The European Union Encyclopedia and Directory* (2d ed.; see ARBA 97, entry 607), and Desmond Dinan's *Encyclopedia of the European Union* (see ARBA 99, entry 691). The author, from the historical section at De Nederlandsche Bank in Amsterdam, previously published *European Monetary Union Since 1848: A Political and Historical Analysis* (Edward Elgar, 1996). Although expensive, this item is suitable for the reference collections of all academic, large public, and interested special collections.—**Daniel K. Blewett**

Austrian

449. Csendes, Peter. **Historical Dictionary of Vienna.** Lanham, Md., Scarecrow, 1999. 259p. illus. (Historical Dictionaries of Cities of the World, no.8). $49.50. ISBN 0-8108-3562-2.

This small volume is the eighth in the historical dictionaries of the cities of the world and is an interesting and adequate dictionary of historical Vienna. Vienna has been one of the most important cities in Europe, both as a center of Hapsburg power and one of culture. Csendes provides a broad spectrum of architectural, cultural, geographical, historical, and political entries in this small book.

There are some omissions from these entries, which seem to avoid the dark side of Viennese and Austrian life. There is no mention of the Kurt Waldheim controversy. Nor is there any mention of the organization of Vienna for the German war effort during World War II. In the timeline Vienna is shown as liberated. In the text of the book it states that the Red Army conquered Vienna. Was Vienna conquered or liberated? What was Vienna's status under the Greater German Reich? Very little is said about how the population of Vienna was affected by the war. There is no mention of how many men were conscripted into the German army or how many casualties there were. How did the war experience affect the demographics of the city? The other glaring deficiency in this book is the awkward, stilted tone of the narrative, as if it were not a polished translation from German.

This volume is an adequate resource on historical Vienna, but it needs a substantial revision and, perhaps like Vienna after the Cold War, is trying to find a point of view.—**Norman L. Kincaide**

450. Fichtner, Paula Sutter. **Historical Dictionary of Austria.** Lanham, Md., Scarecrow, 1999. 301p. (European Historical Dictionary Series, no.36). $65.00. ISBN 0-8108-3639-4.

Fichtner, an eminent scholar in the field of Austrian and Central European studies, has produced an outstanding general dictionary of the history of Austria from the earliest times to the present. Fichtner has served on the executive committee of the Society for the Study of Austrian and Habsburg History. She has also been a member of the editorial board of the Austrian History Yearbook, and has taught in the department of history at Brooklyn College for three decades.

The structure of this work includes a chronology, covering the period 5000 B.C.E. to 1998. This is followed by a thorough and superbly written introduction, stressing Austria's land and people, the economy, Austrian prehistory and antiquity, the Austrian medieval period, the Habsburg lands from 1273 to 1490, the Turkish period, the Reformation and Counterreformation, the Revolutionary era (1789 to 1848), Neoabsolutism to the Ausgleich of 1867, Austria from 1867 to 1918, the First Austrian Republic (1918 to 1938), World War II to 1955, and Austria from 1955 to the present. There are four general maps depicting Austria from 1848 to the late twentieth century.

The dictionary section contains entries on the major themes of Austrian history. It covers the country's Habsburg and pre-Habsburg legacy, its political and culture elite, its component provinces, and leading cities. Each entry, meticulously researched and well organized, contains numerous references to other entries in bold typeface; additionally, there are *see also* references at the end of most entries. For example, the entry "Habsburg, House of," describes the origins of the Habsburg dynasty and their early history. The entry continues the historical narrative with the Central European Habsburg period, providing bold typeface references to the Holy Roman Empire, the Babenberg dynasty, Maximilian I, Ferdinand I, Emperor Friedrich III, Protestantism, World War I, and Archduke Franz Ferdinand. The work also contains an appendix section on Austrian heads of state from the Babenberg era to the Second Austrian Republic, providing dates for monarchs, presidents, and chancellors from 976 to the present.

Perhaps the most useful section of the volume other than the dictionary entries is the concise bibliography. Designed with the English reader in mind, Fichtner has provided a bibliographic essay, including various Austrian Websites, and a list of the most significant works on Austria by historical period from antiquity to the present.

This reviewer, an Austrian history buff who studied at the University of Vienna, would like to emphatically state that Fichtner's *Historical Dictionary of Austria* is one of the best general reference works on the subject available. It is a mandatory selection for undergraduate collections, and would be welcome in graduate and research collections as well.—**Mark Padnos**

Belgium

451. Stallaerts, Robert. **Historical Dictionary of Belgium.** Lanham, Md., Scarecrow, 1999. 303p. (European Historical Dictionaries, no.35). $59.50. ISBN 0-8108-3603-3.

The number of English-language reference books on Belgium is small, so this is a welcome and much-needed addition to that collection. People, places, groups, events, themes and organizations of Belgian history, and current events are all covered in approximately 450 entries. Users should read the introduction for a short historical narrative of the country. French and Dutch words are provided where necessary, and helpful cross-references are plentiful. The 6 appendixes list the kings and governments of the country, along with some economic statistical information. Those interested in more recent data should look at the latest edition of the *Europa World Year Book* (1998, 39th ed.; see ARBA 99, entry 66) or a Belgian government Website. No index is provided, and there are no suggestions for further reading at the end of the entries. There are many bibliographic citations to foreign-language materials in the 117-page bibliography, which comes with its own introduction. There is also a table of contents of the index's many topic subdivisions, 4 pages of acronyms and abbreviations, and a 14-page chronology that stretches from 58 B.C. to 1998 B.C.E. The author is a native of Belgium, and previously wrote (with Jeannine Laurens) the dictionary in this series on the Republic of Croatia (see ARBA 96, entry 549). This book is the companion to similar works in this series on the Netherlands and Luxembourg (see ARBA 97, entry 119). This work is recommended for the reference shelves of academic and larger public libraries.—**Daniel K. Blewett**

Dutch

452. Hooker, Mark T. **The History of Holland.** Westport, Conn., Greenwood Press, 1999. 236p. index. (The Greenwood Histories of the Modern Nations). $35.00. ISBN 0-313-30658-3.

In keeping with the policy of the Greenwood Histories of the Modern Nations editors, this work was designed to provide students and interested laypersons with concise, up-to-date information on the history of Holland, officially known as "The Kingdom of the Netherlands," and its people. While it summarizes the country's entire history, particular emphasis is placed on events of the last 30 years that have helped to shape contemporary social issues with worldwide impact. An introductory section gives brief coverage to Holland's geography, natural resources, transportation and communications, major cities, the 12 provinces, the economy, political systems, society, and culture. Holland's history is traced from the Ice Age through the Golden Age of exploration and colonization, the war crisis and recovery, the rise and fall of the welfare state, and the post-Cold War era. The text is especially well-written for its intended audience—it is readable, interesting, and informative. The indexing is thorough. Supplementary sections provide additional reference information. A timeline lists important events from 57 B.C.E., when Julius Caesar began the conquest of the Belgian tribes, to the projected 65th birthday of Queen Beatrix in 2003. A biographical dictionary gives brief sketches of the lives of 33 notable men and women from all periods of Dutch history. A bibliographic essay comments on selected works in the English language and leads the reader to sources of chronologies, documents, narrative histories, and works on the Dutch government, educational system, geography, and literature. A list of abbreviations gives full-name identification for the many acronyms used in the text. Also included are a bibliography of English-language translations of works by twentieth-century Dutch authors and a list of Dutch print media companies.—**Shirley L. Hopkinson**

French

453. Evleth, Donna, comp. **The Authorized Press in Vichy & German-Occupied France, 1940-1944: A Bibliography.** Westport, Conn., Greenwood Press, 1999. 234p. index. (Bibliographies and Indexes in World History, no.48). $69.50. ISBN 0-313-30784-9.

France was the only major European country during World War II with the dubious distinction of being both occupied by the Nazis and, to a large extent, a willing participant of its own occupation. During the past two decades, French, British, and U.S. scholars have looked closely at archival material that tends to validate the view that collaboration was a fact of daily life in both the occupied and unoccupied zones among all classes of people. Evleth's useful bibliography provides further evidence of this sordid chapter of modern French history.

Evleth examines 2,500 periodicals that were published on a daily, weekly, or monthly basis throughout the period of France's occupation. The bibliography is organized alphabetically for the departments or regions of the country and by subject heading for Paris. Each entry indicates the name of the publication, where it was published, its frequency, and, if available, its political or religious orientation. In addition, the bibliography provides each periodical's approximate beginning and ending dates, the library or archive where it is held, and any books or articles that have been written about it. There is truly a wealth of information here for the scholar or student interested in delving into the convoluted politics of collaboration during "les années noires" (the dark years) in France.

What is particularly striking in this reference work is the enormous number of newspapers and magazines that ceased publication after France was liberated by the Allies in August 1944. Either the periodical disappeared altogether or it was replaced by a new publication with a different title and management. It is equally intriguing to note the large number of ephemeral publications, especially in Paris, that came to life after the Nazis marched in (June 1940) and that survived for only 4 years. For the most part, these publications tended to be rabidly right-wing, fascist newspapers that welcomed the German occupiers with open arms and assisted them in their efforts to integrate France into the Third Reich.

The Authorized Press in Vichy & German-Occupied France, 1940-1944 is more than just a niche work about wartime France. It will prove to be a vital resource for researchers who seek to explore the tribulations of a great democratic country engulfed by totalitarianism.—**John B. Romeiser**

454. Nicholls, David. **Napoleon: A Biographical Companion.** Santa Barbara, Calif., ABC-CLIO, 1999. 318p. illus. index. (ABC-CLIO Biographical Companion). $55.00. ISBN 0-87436-957-6.

This encyclopedia outlines the personalities, places, battles, institutions, and events in Napoleon's life as a soldier, ruler, administrator, and legend. Each notation indicates related entries and suggestions for further reading. The editor gives a well-rounded view of Napoleon by including not only major historical figures, such as Charles Talleyrand-Périgord, but also lesser-known influences like François Joseph Talma, an acclaimed French actor who coached Napoleon in oratory. Useful features include an introductory biographical essay on Napoleon, a bibliography, a chronology, an index, and a selection of documents written by Napoleon and others that give a flavor of the subject and his times. The selections provide insight into different facets of the Napoleonic myth and are a helpful companion to narrative biographies and other readings of this period. [R: LJ, 1 Nov 99, p. 74]—**Adrienne Antink Bendel**

455. Raymond, Gino. **Historical Dictionary of France.** Lanham, Md., Scarecrow, 1998. 347p. (European Historical Dictionaries, no.30). $55.00. ISBN 0-8108-3467-7.

The organization of this work is fairly typical of Scarecrow's historical dictionaries: a section on abbreviations and acronyms, a list of monarchs and presidents, a chronology, the dictionary proper, and a select bibliography. There is no index but there are references from one related article to another. The dictionary pays most attention to political issues but does not ignore cultural topics. Entries for political parties, political philosophies, and politicians join entries on revolutions; wars; kings; movie stars; singers; intellectual, social, and cultural movements; and broad topics such as finance, economy, religion, art, and urbanization. Can 2,000 years of French history be covered in the 265 pages of the dictionary proper? Perhaps the answer would be clearer if there were a statement somewhere concerning the audience for which this work was written and the criteria used for selecting topics. The dictionary is certainly interesting and informative reading, but its coverage is uneven. It is almost completely devoted to topics occurring during and after the Revolution. In fact, a quite disproportionate number of these are from the last 20 years. It is significant that the entry for Edith Cresson is only a few lines shorter than that for Napoleon I. Indeed, the number of biographies of Mitterrand-era politicians suggests an importance perhaps not yet justified by history. The selected bibliography runs 65 pages and cites mostly English-language titles. It is quite worthwhile. However, the lack of an index to the dictionary penalizes the reader who does not already have a pretty good knowledge of French history and culture. This is not the English-language dictionary that French history needs, but it is cheap and available. Libraries owning the Greenwood Press Historical Dictionaries of French History series (see ARBA 86, entries 493-494; ARBA 87, entries 512-513; ARBA 88, entry 536; ARBA 93, entry 537; and ARBA 99, entry 498) will not need this work. Other libraries will find this book useful if their and their readers' interests happen to coincide. [R: Choice, June 99, p. 1766]—**Eric R. Nitschke**

German

456. Cosner, Shaaron, and Victoria Cosner. **Women Under the Third Reich: A Biographical Dictionary.** Westport, Conn., Greenwood Press, 1998. 203p. illus. index. $55.00. ISBN 0-313-30315-0.

This volume provides introductory biographies for more than 100 women who lived during the period of Nazi rule in Germany, or the German assault on Europe during World War II. People included range from the obscure (e.g., Emmy Goering) to the famous (e.g., Anne Frank) and the notorious (e.g., Eva Braun). Content emphasizes events during the period 1933 to 1945; postwar experiences are described for some persons but not others (e.g., Leni Riefenstahl). Articles on named individuals are arranged in alphabetic order, averaging one to two pages in length. Appendixes categorize women by the roles they played, such as Nazi sympathizers or spies, and their nationality. Entries conclude with short lists of sources and there is a general bibliography, which does not repeat most of the titles in those lists. Cited works are limited to those in English. There is a brief index.

The book's utility is marred by inconsistencies, in the stringency of indexing, the presentation of bibliographies, and the presence or absence of photographic portraits and post-1945 coverage. However, no other source—including *The Encyclopedia of the Third Reich* (see ARBA 92, entry 493), *The Oxford Companion to World War II* (see ARBA 97, entry 571), and *Who's Who in World War II* (see ARBA 96, entry 681)—brings together comparable information about women and their part in supporting or opposing Nazism. This work could help readers with introductory or preliminary research or identification of lesser-known figures, especially in smaller libraries without access to a wide array of reference sources.
—**Steven W. Sowards**

457. Leiby, Richard A. **The Unification of Germany, 1989-1990.** Westport, Conn., Greenwood Press, 1999. 197p. illus. index. (Greenwood Press Guides to Historic Events of the Twentieth Century). $39.95. ISBN 0-313-29969-2.

The titles in this series all conform to a standard format and this work follows the norm in relation to its subject. It offers a chronology of the events from 1946 to 1995 that bear on German reunification. There is a narrative of these events that provides an overview of the history of postwar and modern Germany and its unification. In following chapters, five related topics are investigated: emigration and escape, the influence of the clergy, the influence of the major powers, the effects of unification on the former West and East Germanys, and the settling of accounts. A final essay attempts to put the whole in perspective. This work also includes a biographical section, a selection of primary documents, a short glossary of terms, and a selective bibliography of English-language sources and studies.

The work succeeds because the topic is not too broad for the space allotted and the writing is good. All of the primary sources are in English and most are translations of German documents and speeches and thus accessible to American students. Strictly speaking, this is not a reference but a subject monograph. Academic and public libraries will probably wish to include this title in their circulating collection because it is one to be read through. It is appropriate for readers from upper-class high school students to adults.—**Eric R. Nitschke**

458. Turk, Eleanor L. **The History of Germany.** Westport, Conn., Greenwood Press, 1999. 231p. maps. index. (The Greenwood Histories of the Modern Nations). $35.00. ISBN 0-313-30274-X.

Germany's reunification in 1989-1990 is one of the most important events of the late twentieth century. The recently completed relocation of Germany's capital from Bonn to its traditional location in Berlin provides further demonstration of Germany's renewed importance in Europe. This compendium provides a succinct overview of German historical development from antiquity to the present for readers desirous of a quick and painless introduction to German history.

The History of Germany opens with a historical event timeline and introduction to contemporary Germany's geography, government, economy, and culture. It proceeds to cover prominent events in Germany's historical development through chapters on historical periods, such as the growth of Prussia, the Weimar Republic, Hitler and World War II, postwar occupation, the development of East and West Germany, and events after reunification.

Entries on key individuals and events are highlighted in black within these chapters. Examples of such emphasis include feudalism, Charlemagne, Thirty Years War, Joseph II of Austria, Congress of Vienna (1814-1815), Frankfurt Parliament, Bismarck's Domestic Politics, Triple Entente, Weimar Constitution, Nuremburg Laws, Sudeten Germans, Russian Front, Marshall Plan, Ludwig Erhard, Walter Ulbricht, and the European Union. The work concludes with a list of notable personalities in German history and an annotated bibliography.

Succinct works of this nature will undoubtedly contain omissions that will displease German history specialists. Works of this nature, however, are not intended to be comprehensive scholarly monographs or appraisals. Instead, they serve as concise introductions to events on important developments in the topic being covered. Recognizing this fact and the scope of this work, one can recommend it as a useful introduction to the historical personalities and events that have formed and continue to influence Germany at the close of the twentieth century.—**Bert Chapman**

Greek

459. Ashley, James R. **The Macedonian Empire: The Era of Warfare Under Philip II and Alexander the Great, 359-323 B.C.** Jefferson, N.C., McFarland, 1998. 486p. index. $55.00. ISBN 0-7864-0407-8.

Historians, the author of this massive study argues, have stressed political and cultural aspects of the Macedonian era, but have relegated the military ones to secondary importance. The intent of the author is to right this deficiency. To the degree historians have written about Macedonian military affairs, the author thinks, have been derivative borrowings from secondary sources. The book consists of 3 parts: ancient warfare, the reign of Philip II and III, and campaigns of Alexander the Great. Further, the subject is subordinated into 12 chapters. The author studies Macedonian armies, siege operations, logistics, and naval operations. It is a well-argued study and the author sets a standard for all future studies of Macedonian warfare to be measured by. The work is thoroughly footnoted and contains nine appendixes, a lengthy glossary, and a bibliography and index.—**Andrew Ezergailis**

Italian

460. Gilbert, Mark F., and K. Robert Nilsson. **Historical Dictionary of Modern Italy.** Lanham, Md., Scarecrow, 1999. 463p. (European Historical Dictionaries, no.34). $65.00. ISBN 0-8108-3584-3.

Continuing Scarecrow's series of historical dictionaries, Italian studies scholars Gilbert, of the University of Bath, England, and Nilsson, Professor Emeritus of Dickinson College, offer this contribution to the history reference shelf. Containing more than 350 cross-referenced entries, Gilbert and Nilsson's dictionary furnishes information regarding the historical odyssey of modern Italy from the mid-nineteenth century to the present. It spans the liberation and political unification of the Risorgimento, through the dark years of fascism, to the present-day Italy born of the "Italian miracle"—a country that is one of the largest industrial nations in the world. The authors transport the reader through the labyrinth of modern Italian history. Unlike Frank J. Coppa's *Dictionary of Modern Italian History* (Greenwood Press, 1985), which provides coverage of Italian history from the eighteenth century to the modern period, this work focuses more upon the twentieth century. While addressing political and economic matters, the authors pay particular attention to notable individuals, intellectual movements, and events relating to modern Italian cultural and social experience that are not addressed by the Coppa work. For example, in terms of cultural/artistic figures, entries are provided for the authors, directors, and painters.

A detailed bibliography in English and Italian, as well as 18 tables of appendixes, complements this excellent work of Italian studies scholarship. This work is highly recommended for academic and public libraries.—**Glenn S. McGuigan**

Polish

461. Wróbel, Piotr. **Historical Dictionary of Poland, 1945-1996.** Westport, Conn., Greenwood Press, 1998. 423p. maps. index. $85.00. ISBN 0-313-29772-X.

Poland, as the eighth largest country of Europe, is of increasing strategic, economic, and political importance. This historical dictionary, covering the period 1945 to 1996, is a sequel to a similar dictionary, issued by the same publisher in 1996. Personalities, events, and concepts are arranged alphabetically. An indication is given if terms appearing in the texts of entries are themselves accorded a separate listing. Each entry provides basic information about the term or personality in question and also includes bibliographic references to items in both English and Polish that contain a more complete exposition of the topic. The reference work also includes several useful maps, a chronology of important events, a selected bibliography of books in English on Poland, and an index to the contents of the entries themselves. Wróbel has compiled an extremely useful volume that will serve as a handy desk reference for anyone studying contemporary Polish politics, economics, and current affairs in general.—**Robert H. Burger**

Russian

462. Rappaport, Helen. **Joseph Stalin: A Biographical Companion.** Santa Barbara, Calif., ABC-CLIO, 1999. 372p. illus. maps. index. (ABC-CLIO Biographical Companions). $55.00. ISBN 1-57607-084-0.

Soviet dictator Joseph Stalin was one of the twentieth century's most important political leaders. His shadow still remains over Russian and international politics nearly five decades after his death. This compendium provides detailed yet succinct portraits of Stalin and the individuals, events, and policies contributing to his career and historical legacy.

Following an introductory preface, this work consists of entries arranged alphabetically by subject that describe and analyze the personalities and forces that were part of Stalin's life and career. Topics covered in these individual entries include Stalin's daughter Svetlana Allilueva, art and architecture, Lavrenty Beria, Nikolai Bukharin, Finland, Georgia, the Great Terror, historiography, the Korean War, nomemklatura, religion, science, the Shakhty Trial, the United Nations, and the White Sea-Baltic Canal. Entries range from one to six pages in length and include cross-references to related entries as well as bibliographic references.

Concluding sections provide a chronology of Stalin's life and important Stalin-related events after his death; a glossary of Stalinist political institutions; and a selected bibliography featuring Stalin's writings, writings about Stalin and his career (broken down into historical and political works), and assessments of his cultural and literary policies.

Joseph Stalin: A Biographical Companion is a helpful addition to those interested in learning more about Stalin's career. The entries are well written and informative, with the historiography entry being a particularly noteworthy example in this regard. Although this volume is not intended for Stalinist historians (as the preface indicates), it represents a substantive and scholarly contribution to further our understanding of a political leader whose policies and personality had and continue to have a strong influence on Russian and international political development. [R: LJ, 15 Nov 99, p. 62]—**Bert Chapman**

463. Ziegler, Charles E. **The History of Russia.** Westport, Conn., Greenwood Press, 1999. 242p. maps. index. (The Greenwood Histories of the Modern Nations Series). $35.00. ISBN 0-313-30393-2.

This brief book is conveniently designed for schools on the 10-week quarter system or, if supplemented with additional material, perhaps for 1-semester courses. Although its brevity may be commendable, the book attempts too much in too little space. However, it has the great virtue of covering events into 1999. In fact, the final chapter, which treats the Boris Yeltsin era, is the best in the volume.

Ziegler is obviously a political scientist rather than a historian, for his work strongly emphasizes policy at the expense of other aspects of Russian history. The treatment of social history and culture is badly scanted and, on occasion, inaccurate. There are also errors of fact in the political history. Terms are often introduced without adequate explanation or background. To some extent, this is partly offset by features such as a glossary of selected terms (all political), a chronology, and a "who's who" of important people (22 of the 36 are political figures). A bibliographic essay provides the reader with information on more specialized works on several aspects of Russian history.—**D. Barton Johnson**

Slovakia

464. Kirschbaum, Stanislav J. **Historical Dictionary of Slovakia.** Lanham, Md., Scarecrow, 1999. 213p. maps. (European Historical Dictionaries, no.31). $55.00. ISBN 0-8108-3506-1.

Kirschbaum, who was born in Bratislava, Slovakia, has written an excellent dictionary that focuses on the territory that now comprises the country of Slovakia. The politics and history of this region from 1790 to 1997 are the center of the volume, even though there are entries for notable social and cultural topics. Special attention is paid to both the first Slovak Republic, which existed briefly from 1939 to 1945, and the second Slovak Republic, which came into existence January 1, 1993.

There are five maps provided, which are reproduced from a previous work by Kirschbaum entitled *A History of Slovakia: The Struggle for Survival* (St. Martin's Press, 1995). The maps are titled "The Great Moravian Empire," "Slovak Counties in Hungary," "The First Czecho-Slovak Republic 1918-1938," "The Slovak Republic of 1939," and "The Slovak Republic of 1993." The inclusion of additional maps showing the region in all its incarnations would have been extremely useful. A 31-page "Chronology of Slovak History" follows the maps. The chronology is supplemented by an introduction that puts the various events into context for the user. The dictionary portion of the text comprises 188 pages and makes limited use of cross-references. The appendix, entitled "Ruler, King, or Head of State on Slovak Territory," begins with Samo (623 to 658 C.E.) and ends with Vladimir Meciar. The volume concludes with a 17-page bibliography that begins with a short bibliographic essay. The author's work fulfills its mission admirably and is recommended for large public and academic libraries. [R: Choice, June 99, p. 1765]—**John R. Burch Jr.**

Spanish

465. Pierson, Peter. **The History of Spain.** Westport, Conn., Greenwood Press, 1999. 223p. maps. index. (The Greenwood Histories of the Modern Nations). $35.00. ISBN 0-313-30272-3.

Good, relatively concise histories of Spain covering the whole range of its history are difficult to find, so this work is welcome. Pierson, a history professor at Santa Clara University and noted scholar on early modern Spain, is well qualified to write such a work. He begins by giving an overview of Spain today, including geography, languages, government, religion, and culture, and then proceeds with a succinct chronological account of the major influences and events on Spanish history from the peninsula's first inhabitants. Spain provides a particular problem for the historian because for so much of its history it was divided into a large number of separate political and cultural entities. For this reason, and the concise format of the book, Pierson at times seems to be reciting a list of kings and political events; the whole reign of Philip II is covered in a mere six pages. But he does bring out the major influences on Spanish history and culture, including Iberian, Celtic, Roman, Visigothic, and particularly Moorish contributions, as well as the influence of the Catholic Church and Spain's European and American empires. The second half of the book, covering the last two centuries, is considerably more detailed on economic, social and cultural, and political issues. The book lacks notes but provides a bibliographic essay, timeline of historical events, directory of important historical characters, and index. Pierson's writing style is clear and concise. The book is recommended for all types of libraries as a good, brief introduction to all of Spain's history.—**Marit S. MacArthur**

United Kingdom

466. **The Blackwell Encyclopaedia of Anglo-Saxon England.** Michael Lapidge, John Blair, Simon Keynes, and Donald Scragg, eds. Malden, Mass., Blackwell, 1999. 537p. illus. maps. $99.95. ISBN 0-631-15565-1.

The Blackwell Encyclopaedia of Anglo-Saxon England is a comprehensive reference work covering every aspect of its subject: art, literature, archaeology, history, and linguistics. There are 150 contributors, including some of the most prominent scholars in the field, who have joined to create this valuable resource. Anglo-Saxon studies is a huge and active area of study, producing some 1,000 publications every year, and this volume is a useful addition, especially for nonspecialists in need of a brief but reliable treatment of a particular subject. Readers will find that the editors have served them well in the breadth of the book. Articles are brief (that on King Alfred is about a page; Northumbria is spread over two columns) but coverage is wide and includes standards such as Bede, Beowulf, and Sutton Hoo as well as an article on dragons and a host of lesser-known kings, princes, and saints. Each article is signed and accompanied by an up-to-date bibliography; some articles are illustrated.

This work sets a high standard for its genre. Articles are informative and well written; browsing through its pages is a real pleasure. Although the single-volume format limits the depth of information presented, those needing more detail can follow the bibliographic citations provided. Blackwell's encyclopaedia is a volume well worth having. [R: Choice, June 99, pp. 1761-1762]—**Victor L. Stater**

467. **Britain in the Hanoverian Age, 1714-1837.** Gerald Newman and others, eds. New York, Garland, 1997. 871p. illus. index. (Garland Reference Library of the Humanities, v.1481). $125.00. ISBN 0-8153-0396-3.

Britain in the Hanoverian Age is a welcome addition to Garland's earlier volumes covering the twentieth century and Victorian eras. With more than 1,100 articles, it is as comprehensive as a single volume can be, ranging across the entire "long eighteenth century." From Robert Harley to Wellington and the South Sea Company to the Liverpool and Manchester Railway, this encyclopedia provides the reader with brief but useful information. In addition to the usual suspects—Hanoverian monarchs, politicians, and major cultural figures like David Hume and Adam Smith—the editors also provide articles on lesser-known figures, such as the poet Sarah Dixon and the Scottish inventor Andrew Meikle. This is not merely a biographical dictionary. There are entries for "dramatic arts," "middle class," and even "pornography," among many others relating to the culture, society, and economy of eighteenth-century Britain. Although the focus of the book is on England, there are many articles concerned with Irish, Scottish, and Welsh subjects, as well as a few on the overseas empire. Thanks to these attempts to extend the range of coverage, the editors have produced a truly British encyclopedia. Inevitably, some articles seem too brief, but all provide a short bibliography directing readers to more in-depth sources. The entries are the work of 250 authors scattered across the globe, including many well-known scholars. Handsomely produced and enhanced by nearly 800 illustrations, *Britain in the Hanoverian Age* will be an exceptionally useful reference for casual readers and experts alike. [R: Choice, July/Aug 98, pp. 1835-1836]—**Victor L. Stater**

468. **The Hutchinson Illustrated Encyclopedia of British History.** Chicago, Fitzroy Dearborn, 1998. 384p. illus. maps. $75.00. ISBN 1-57958-107-2.

This book is a model historical encyclopedia. It is easy to use, attractively illustrated, accurate, politically-balanced, and has a good bibliography. Too many such volumes fail by either being so comprehensive they are unwieldy, or so light in content they are unusable. An encyclopedia should hold readers with each reference, tempting them to read all the related entries, and then to pursue the topic in other resources. This book does it. Any library with history collections will do its readers a service by carrying this title.

British history is a complex and tangled narrative including the ancient Celts and Romans in Britain; the origins of England, Wales, Scotland, and Ireland; colonization of the world; maintenance of the empire; and the development of the Commonwealth. A short book like this can only touch on this rich heritage, but it can provide effective introductions to the many stories. This encyclopedia succeeds by keeping its individual entries relatively short and tying them together with almost two dozen historical essays by noted experts and detailed chronologies. The Civil War, for example, is covered by a half-page entry; at least a dozen specific entries on battles, documents, and personalities; a full-page chronology of events; and a thoughtful essay that provides connecting concepts. The many maps in the book are clearly drawn and well planned. No summary of British history is complete without some explanations of the tortuous relationships among the royal houses, and this book meets the task with numerous genealogies, the earliest stretching back to distant and mysterious Scots. Adding to the interest of the book, the editors have included pertinent quotations from various characters in the otherwise unused page margins.

Encyclopedias are by definition eclectic, and the best will provoke readers to learn more about topics they did not know existed. This encyclopedia will draw people to the drama of British history, and to history in general, by making it fascinating. [R: Choice, Nov 99, p. 518]—**Mark A. Wilson**

469. Langworth, Richard M. **A Connoisseur's Guide to the Books of Sir Winston Churchill.** Herndon, Va., Brassey's (U.S.), 1998. 372p. illus. $39.95. ISBN 1-85753-246-5.

Simply put, this volume seeks to be the authoritative listing of the complete collected works of Sir Winston S. Churchill—the most visible statesman of this country. The order of the entries is based upon those in "Woods" and "Cohen" respectively, plus additional manuscript entries the respective authors have provided. "Woods" is short for the 1975 "bibliography of the works of Sir Winston Churchill, AG, OM, CH, by the late Frederick Woods, second revised edition." "Cohen" refers to the forthcoming bibliography to be published by the Cassell's firm in London. It too is supplemented by the author's manuscript entries provided by the compiler. Certain other entries from the International Churchill Society's files are also included as appropriate. It is necessary to state that the partial title "A Connoisseur's Guide" needs to be taken quite literally—the book should be used by the advanced specialist on Churchill-related matters. Other persons would find the lack of an index to be most inconvenient.

To end on a positive note, the page facing the book's title page lists some 40 works authored by Richard M. Langworth that are descriptive of makes and models of automotive manufacturers' products. These items were much used in the two major automobile-engineering libraries where he has worked in past years. He is currently a founding member, Faculty Seminar on British Studies, at the University of Texas in Austin.

—**Eugene B. Jackson**

470. **Medieval England: An Encyclopedia.** Paul F. Szarmach, M. Teresa Tavormina, and Joel T. Rosenthal, eds. New York, Garland, 1998. 882p. illus. maps. index. (Garland Reference Library of the Humanities, v.907; Garland Encyclopedias of the Middle Ages, v.3). $135.00. ISBN 0-8240-5786-4.

Medieval England forms an important subject area within many disciplines—art, music, literature, and history. That circumstance creates a demand for ready-reference information, which this new title in the successful series Garland Encyclopedias of the Middle Ages fills. *Medieval England: An Encyclopedia* contains 708 alphabetically arranged entries written by an international group of more than 300 expert contributors. The entries cover various topics of importance from the years 500 to 1500 B.C.E. concerning England, Anglo-Saxon and English language, and Continental influences on English culture and history. Political, religious, social, and economic history dealt with, as are music, art, and literature. Many entries are biographical and range from Abbo of Fleury to Andrew Wyntoun, with Roger Bacon, Julian of Norwich, and William Marshall along with many others featured in between. Individual entries are signed and range from about 200 words to several thousand. The entries are uniformly well written and researched. A bibliography concludes each entry and, where appropriate, is divided into primary and secondary sources. Lists of kings, popes, and archbishops of Canterbury and York; a glossary of musical and liturgical terms; diagrams of castles and churches; and maps supplement the volume. *Medieval England* is especially strong in its coverage of cultural topics. Traditional historical topics do not fare as well. The statutes of Provisors and the Praemunire are not even listed in the index, let alone treated in their own entries. It is debatable as to whether the decision to cover both pre- and post-Conquest England in one volume was wise. Although the encyclopedia deals with Continental influences on England, it gives only minimal mention to connections with Wales, Scotland, and Ireland. What is the justification for having entries on Aquitaine and Normandy but not Wales? The amount of space devoted to individual topics is sometimes problematic. Margery Kempe's entry is longer than Archbishop Thomas Becket's, and Archbishop Thomas Arundel has no entry at all. Compared to the overall usefulness of this volume, these criticisms, although not isolated instances, become venial sins. *Medieval England* is a highly useful and well-done work that students and professors working in the area will want to consult frequently. [R: BL, 1 May 99, pp. 1634-1636; Choice, Sept 99, p. 120; RUSQ, Fall 99, pp. 97-98]—**Ronald H. Fritze**

471. Olsen, Kirstin. **Daily Life in 18th-Century England.** Westport, Conn., Greenwood Press, 1999. 395p. illus. index. (The Greenwood Press "Daily Life Through History" Series). $45.00. ISBN 0-313-29933-1.

This volume is a narrative with 19 chapters on aspects of daily life in eighteenth-century England, including such topics as food, religion, politics, entertainment, and behavior. Each chapter (with the single exception of the food and drink chapter, which contains recipes) ends with a short chronology of important events. The volume also includes more than 40 pages of source notes, a short glossary of terms, a bibliography of more than 75 primary and secondary sources for further reading, an extensive subject index (nearly 40 pages), approximately 50 reproductions of contemporary engravings, and several tables (e.g., cost of living, income by profession). Olsen is the author of several books, including *Chronology of Women's History* (Greenwood, 1994).

Although some excellent specialized studies are available, very few general studies of social life and customs in eighteenth-century England have been published in the past 75 years. None of them have the scope and detail of the present volume, which can be read through with pleasure or (due to its arrangement and extensive index) used for reference purposes. There are a few relatively unimportant errors and infelicities of style, but *Daily Life in 18th-Century England* is recommended for circulating collections of public and academic libraries and for reference collections of libraries that support English or European history curricula.

—**Jonathan F. Husband**

Yugoslavia

472. **Conflict in the Former Yugoslavia: An Encyclopedia.** John B. Allcock, Marko Milivojevic, and John J. Horton, eds. Santa Barbara, Calif., ABC-CLIO, 1998. 410p. illus. maps. index. (Roots of Modern Conflict). $55.00. ISBN 0-87436-935-5.

The articles for this encyclopedia are all by recognized authorities on Yugoslavia. The purpose of the encyclopedia is to bring together a wide range of information about the conflict in Yugoslavia in order to understand the basis for the tragedy that occurred there. This information includes articles on people; geographic terms (important towns, rivers, and so on); political terms such as citizenship and democratization; Dayton Agreements; and names of plans, actions, and economic terms. In short, almost every conceivable aspect of the Yugoslav conflict, including an article on the Cyrillic alphabet, is included. The editors note that in spite of the large number of contributors, there are themes that recur again and again throughout the articles. One of these themes is the unbalanced press treatment that saw on one hand the conflict as an inevitable outcome of the region's ethnic diversity and on the other as the result of actions and intentions of powerful individuals.

As the editors indicate, however, "there is no simple explanation of the roots of the Yugoslav conflict, only a complex braid of explanatory factors, the nature, interdependence, and significance of which still have to be fully evaluated" (p. xv). The articles are brief; very few extend beyond one page. Terms and names used in the articles that are themselves entries are presented in bold typeface. Appendixes include a chronology covering events from the 1941 Axis invasion of Yugoslavia to November 26, 1995, when Commissioner Westendorp announced that a UN presence would be necessary in Bosnia-Herzegovina for two to three more years, and a copy of the Dayton Agreements. This encyclopedia is an extremely useful reference source for providing brief summary information on almost any aspect of this tragic conflict. [R: LJ, 1 Mar 99, p. 72; BL, 15 April 99, p. 1543; Choice, July/Aug 99, p. 1925]—**Robert H. Burger**

473. Šušter, Zeljan E. **Historical Dictionary of the Federal Republic of Yugoslavia.** Lanham, Md., Scarecrow, 1999. 419p. maps. (European Historical Dictionaries, no.29). $65.00. ISBN 0-8108-3466-9.

Following Scarecrow's familiar format for historical dictionaries, Šušter begins with a chronology (5th century-June 1999) and an introductory overview of Yugoslav history. Although the present-day Federal Republic of Yugoslavia dates from 1992, comprises only Serbia and Montenegro, and has smaller boundaries than in the past, the region's long history is capably covered by the author, and he includes articles on areas that have long ties to the country, such as Croatia, Slovenia, and Bosnia-Herzegovina. There are more than 1,100 entries, which range in length from 1 sentence to several pages, with *see, see also*, and cross-references (the latter in bold typeface), and English translations are given for foreign words and phrases. Articles are arranged alphabetically according to the Serbian alphabet, which might confuse users who have not read the helpful instructions in the front. Topics covered include people, events, places, concepts, and organizations, but there are some curious omissions. Surprisingly, there are no articles on Albanians, Jews, or Gypsies (or ethnic minorities in general), nor are there entries on either foreign relations or the economy. There is nothing listed under either "Religion" or "Church" to refer users to "Serbian Orthodox Church," which is compounded since the book lacks an index. Several articles appear to have a decidedly pro-Serbian viewpoint. For example, the entry on Slobodan Milosevic, an admittedly controversial figure, mentions his "supposedly nationalist agenda," states that he "became the major proponent of a peaceful settlement in 1993," and that he was indicted by The Hague Tribunal "for the alleged crimes against the Albanian population in Kosovo and Metohija" (p. 201). The Kosovars will be happy to know that the crimes are only *alleged* to have occurred. Similarly, the article on World War I states that Serbia replied to Austria-Hungary's ultimatum and "accepted all the Austro-Hungarian demands, except a provision that would violate international law and the Serbian constitution" (p. 332), when, in fact, Serbia's reply to the ultimatum was deliberately evasive to 4 of the demands, aside from the 1 refusal. The 30-page bibliography contains secondary source materials (books and journal articles), primarily in English, Serbian, and German, but surprisingly does not include any materials by R. W. Seton-Watson, an early and influential historian of the region. There are 14 black-and-white maps, a statistical addendum, and an appendix of United Nations Security Council Resolutions dealing with Yugoslavia from 1991 to 1998.—**John A. Drobnicki**

MIDDLE EASTERN HISTORY

474. Bierbrier, Morris L. **Historical Dictionary of Ancient Egypt.** Lanham, Md., Scarecrow, 1999. 303p. maps. (Historical Dictionaries of Ancient Civilizations and Historical Eras, no.1). $49.50. ISBN 0-8108-3614-9.

This little volume shows some very real strengths with its short pithy descriptions of sites, kings, deities, and artifacts such as canopic jars; key Egyptological concepts such as god's father; and a very limited number of modern archeologists. Within the entries for the different archeological sites, the author includes the archeological history, who and what teams have worked on the site over the years, and what current activity, if any, is under way by what team. It thus provides a ready-reference with definition and description as the individual encounters the topics in other contexts. In addition, the terse introduction to Egyptian history from earliest times through the seventh century (with some reference to the discoveries of the nineteenth and twentieth centuries) provides a good backdrop to the dictionary itself. The reader is reminded the book will not substitute for reading a full history of the civilization.

The dictionary also includes an extensive 82-page bibliography containing references to other bibliographies. Other very useful resources included are a detailed list of the rulers of Egypt by dynasty with approximate dates (there are no firm dates earlier than 690 B.C.E.) and a list of museums with Egyptological materials in them, those with a particularly large or important collection so designated.

In sum, this is a valuable volume, particularly for the academic and theological library, and strongly recommended for major public libraries. The reasonable price and its usefulness make it a good investment.
—**Susan Tower Hollis**

475. Brier, Bob, and Hoyt Hobbs. **Daily Life of the Ancient Egyptians.** Westport, Conn., Greenwood Press, 1999. 253p. illus. maps. index. (The Greenwood Press "Daily Life Through History" Series). $45.00. ISBN 0-313-30313-4.

This book attempts to describe ancient Egyptians—a paradoxical society of startling modern accomplishments with incredibly ancient thought processes, people who looked both forward and back. Ancient Egyptians were stunningly advanced in architecture, food, clothing, and medicine, but their view of the world was closer to that of a prehistoric caveman. Egyptians were among the first people to develop writing, and these writings, along with their accurate tomb paintings, enable archaeologists and historians to study Egyptian life. Egyptians made lists of what they owned, recorded court cases, described battles, preserved recipes, wrote books on medicine and religion, and told stories. Tomb paintings illustrated the clothing, the conduct of professions, and the leisure activities of actual people. Thanks to the recovered objects, inscriptions, paintings, and surviving temples and tombs, today's society knows a great deal about how these ancient people lived and what they thought. The book provides a chronology followed by 10 chapters on various subjects: history, religion, government and society, work and play, food, clothes and other adornments, architecture, arts and crafts, warfare, and medicine and mathematics. An annotated bibliography and an index conclude the work. This is a good introductory reference for archaeology and ancient history students to better understand the Egyptian culture.—**Cari Ringelheim**

476. Kamoo, Ray. **Ancient and Modern Chaldean History: A Comprehensive Bibliography of Sources.** Lanham, Md., Scarecrow, 1999. 199p. (The ATLA Bibliography Series, no.43). $47.50. ISBN 0-8108-3653-X.

This modest volume intends to provide a bibliographic resource for modern Chaldeans, people from present-day Iran and Iraq, who are living in the United States. This group, linked to the Aramaic-speaking people of ancient Mesopotamia, thereby relates itself to ancient Mesopotamia and its culture. The author opens with a brief narrative summary of the protohistory and history of Mesopotamia, becoming increasingly detailed as he reaches the period of his concern. Then, he discusses the spread of Christianity in the area and Chaldean immigration to the United States in the late nineteenth and twentieth centuries.

The bibliography is arranged into 5 sections of alphabetic entries by author: English books; non-English books; English journal articles; non-English journal articles; and dissertations, theses, and papers. Lacking a topical index, although providing an author index, the researcher will have difficulty finding references to specific topics without knowledge of the author's name. Thus, the greatest value of the book lying in its references to the Chaldean Christian Church and to the Chaldeans in the Detroit, Michigan, area, is sadly diminished. The other topics are similarly hampered but are available from other sources. Thus, it is unlikely that this volume belongs in libraries other than those specifically concerned with the Chaldeans in the United States.—**Susan Tower Hollis**

WORLD HISTORY

Bibliography

477.   **Slavery and Slaving in World History: A Bibliography.** Joseph C. Miller, ed. Armonk, N.Y., M. E. Sharpe, 1999. 2v. index. $175.00/set. ISBN 0-7656-0281-4.

Compiling a bibliography on scholarly writings of the twentieth century from 1900 to 1991 on slavery and the slave trade was, no doubt, a daunting task. Updating such a work was no less daunting and in that effort the simple addition of a supplemental volume for writing from 1992 to 1996 extends the usefulness of this growing bibliography. Sections deal with slavery and the slave trade, geographically and chronologically. Works on slavery in western European languages are arranged alphabetically by author without annotation. The introduction discusses the general level of scholarship on slavery in the different geographic regions covered, but does not delve too deeply into the nature of the historiography of slavery and the slave trade. This 2-volume set is well organized and serves to bring the state of scholarship on slavery up to 1996. A more detailed analysis of the historiographical progress on this topic would add much to this bibliography. Recommended for public, college, and university reference collections.—**Norman L. Kincaide**

Biography

478.   Berson, Robin Kadison. **Young Heroes in World History.** Westport, Conn., Greenwood Press, 1999. 269p. illus. index. $45.00. ISBN 0-313-30257-X.

This book of historical narratives chronicles the lives of 17 young heroes, both male and female, whose ages ranged from 12 to 23 at the time of their heroic actions. The heroes profiled were selected from a wide range of cultures and countries and lived during the past 250 years. The biographical entries place the deeds in their historical perspective by giving detailed background information about the times and events leading up to the actions. Each entry includes a bibliography for further reading. Black-and-white photographs of either the hero or an artist's rendition of the hero accompany each section. The appendix categorizes each of the young heroes by gender, century, nationality, and ethnicity within the United States. The book also includes an index. Berson, a former history teacher and the director of the Upper School Library of Riverdale County School in New York City, states that one purpose of these historical narratives is the development of empathy, the root of compassion and compassionate behavior. Although the writing is somewhat uneven, with some entries sounding like a novel and some reading more like a textbook, each person's story is compelling and worthy of being told.—**Janet Hilbun**

479. **Dictionary of World Biography: The 20th Century.** Frank N. Magill, ed. Chicago, Fitzroy Dearborn and Hackensack, N.J., Salem Press, 1999. 3v. illus. index. $295.00/set. ISBN 0-89356-320-X.

The latest contribution to the mass of biographical reference tools available for twentieth-century individuals, the 3 volumes of *Dictionary of World Biography: The 20th Century* are only part of a larger projected 10-volume set. Although 921 of the 1,054 essays originally appeared in Salem Press's Great Lives from History series, this new project (covering 1901-2000) adds 133 personalities and updates older entries, with expanded annotated bibliographies and illustrations. Each entry begins with birth and death dates, area of specialization, and a brief statement of the contribution made to the era. A section on early life outlines the environment within which the person was born and educated, followed by a detailed discussion of his or her life's work and a summary placing their complete life experience within the century's context. Indexes by area of achievement, geographical region, and surname are provided at the end of the 3d volume. School, public, and academic libraries possessing the earlier sets may wish to add this collection to their biographical holdings but should consider that much of the data are duplicated and that there is no indication of which names have been added.—**Robert B. Marks Ridinger**

480. **Dictionary of World Biography, Volume 3: The Renaissance.** Frank N. Magill, ed. Chicago, Fitzroy Dearborn and Englewood Cliffs, N.J., Salem Press, 1999. 813p. illus. index. $125.00. ISBN 0-89356-315-3.

This work follows the same format as the previously published first two volumes (see ARBA 99, entries 519 and 520). It contains 211 essays, 185 of which were drawn from Salem Press's 30-volume Great Lives from History series and 26 new ones. The cutoff point between this volume and the *Dictionary of World Biography, Volume 2: Middle Ages* is 1400 C.E., with 1600 C.E. being the point of demarcation with the next volume in the series. Like the previously published volumes, this one includes three indexes: "Area of Achievement," "Geographical Location," and "Name Index." This is an excellent dictionary for those libraries that do not own the Great Lives from History series, but those that do need to be aware that the essays that have been reprinted have not been updated, with the exception of their bibliographies. [R: Choice, Oct 99, p. 301]—**John R. Burch Jr.**

481. **Dictionary of World Biography, Volume 4: The 17th and 18th Centuries.** Frank N. Magill, ed. Chicago, Fitzroy Dearborn and Englewood Cliffs, N.J., Salem Press, 1999. 1515p. illus. index. $125.00. ISBN 0-89356-316-1.

Part of a projected 10-volume set, volume 4 of the *Dictionary of World Biography* includes 377 essays covering important figures from 1601 to 1800. Most of the essays were originally published in the Great Lives from History series (see ARBA 96, entry 942), but 40 are new, as is the arrangement.

The scope of selections is diverse and broad. Major world leaders, religious figures, artists, authors, scholars, scientists, and explorers are included if they were important in shaping civilization in the seventeenth and eighteenth centuries. Examples are Catherine the Great, James Madison, Abas the Great, Betsy Ross, George Fox, Pocahontas, K'ang-His, and Leeuwenhoek. Neither Shakespeare (1564-1616) nor Malthus (1766-1834) is included because their major accomplishments came in different centuries.

The format of the alphabetic entries (consisting of 2,000-3,000 words) includes an initial "ready-reference" paragraph with birth and death dates, areas of achievement, and statement of major contributions. The main body of the entry is an essay divided into three parts: Early Life, Life's Work, and a Summary or "overview of the individual's place in history." More than 200 scholars contributed the entries and they are listed with their academic affiliations. The entries vary in quality but most are engaging and easy to read.

Each biography concludes with a briefly annotated bibliography of 8 to 10 citations. Most entries also have a quarter- to full-page black-and-white portrait; 95 percent of these are from the Library of Congress. Indexes include an area of achievement (with handy cross-references), geographical locations (24 countries), and a name index.

This set is one of the last editorial works of the late Frank Magill, who was a respected and experienced editor of scores of useful reference titles. His chronological arrangement of this set allows individual purchase as well as quicker and easier access to specific historical time periods. This is not possible with the similar *Encyclopedia of World Biography* (see ARBA 99, entry 23). [R: LJ, 15 Nov 99, p. 58]

—Georgia Briscoe

482. **Dictionary of World Biography, Volumes 5 and 6: The 19th Century.** Frank N. Magill, ed. Chicago, Fitzroy Dearborn and Englewood Cliffs, N.J., Salem Press, 1999. 2v. illus. index. $195.00/set. ISBN 0-89356-317-X.

Volume 5 and 6 of *The Dictionary of World Biography* are part of a 10-volume series. The series covers the lives of important personages from the ancient world through the twentieth century. These two volumes cover some of the important people in the nineteenth century. In addition to the 544 essays from the *Great Lives from History* series, there are 69 new biographies. A total of 613 essays cover biographical information on the important figures who flourished in the nineteenth century. Each essay begins with a summary of facts, such as the birth and death dates and place and areas of achievement and contribution. The body of the articles is divided into 3 parts: early life, life's work, then a concluding overview of the individual's place in history. Articles are supplemented by annotated bibliographies that can be useful for those interested in conducting further research on the individuals.

This new series is a reformatted version of Salem Press's 30-volume *Great Lives from History* series. The contents from the earlier series have been rearranged from a geographical perspective into a chronological one. Regretfully, the world as defined is limited to the European countries; therefore the scope of the dictionary heavily emphasizes those in the Western Hemisphere. Very few important people in Asian and African countries are included. However, the editors of the *Dictionary of World Biography* are successful in including people who are distinguished in one of the broad areas of achievement. People such as political and religious leaders, scholars, philosophers, scientists, explorers, and artists were selected because they have shaped the history and civilization in their own time.

The uniform format of the essays offers users quick and easy access to the information needed. For convenience of reference, these volumes are indexed by areas of achievement, geographical areas, as well as by names. This dictionary is definitely a useful reference tool for those who are interested in finding quick information about the nineteenth century and the important figures who shaped history during that time. Recommended for both academic and public libraries. [R: LJ, 15 Nov 99, p. 58]—**Eveline L. Yang**

483. **Founding Leaders: Shapers of Modern Nations.** [CD-ROM]. Santa Barbara, Calif., ABC-CLIO, 1998. Minimum system requirements (Windows version): Pentium-compatible processor at 75MHz or faster. Four-speed CD-ROM drive. 8MB RAM. 30MB hard disk space. SVGA monitor 650x480 (256 colors). 16-bit sound card with Windows drivers. Mouse. Minimum system requirements (Macintosh version): 68040 processor with 25MHz or faster. Double-speed CD-ROM drive. System 7.5.3 or higher. 8MB RAM. 30MB hard disk space. SVGA monitor 640x480 (256 colors). $49.00 (standalone); $129.00 (lab pack); $249.00 (site license). ISBN 1-57607-014-X.

This title contains 304 biographies, many previously published in Neal A. Hamilton's *Founders of Modern Nations: A Biographical Dictionary* (see ARBA 95, entry 556) by the same publisher. Unfortunately, this CD-ROM also features many of the same problems that plagued its predecessors, such as not defining its criteria for inclusion. This title does include an entry for Franklin D. Roosevelt, an omission that was noted in ARBA's earlier review of Hamilton's title.

The CD-ROM does provide some value-added features to differentiate between the two titles. It has a toolbar on the right side of the screen that facilitates searching. It contains seven buttons: Access, Go Back, Trail, Reference, Tools, Help, and Exit. Among the options presented under "Access" are four indexes—name, subject, attribute, and text. Selecting attributes allows one to search by place of birth, year of birth or death, or gender. The "Reference" button on the toolbar allows the user to bring up a short overview of a country's history, glossary, maps, and timeline. The maps bear little relation to the information contained within the entries, other than showing a map of the country. For example, under Omar Torrijos Herrera, Santiago de Veragua is listed as his place of birth but its location is not shown on the map of Panama. Places not listed in either of the two entries under Panama are included on the map. The timeline feature is used to put the individual into historical context by showing his or her place in world history.

Despite all the bells and whistles on the CD-ROM, there is simply little information here that cannot be found elsewhere. There is also little logic as to what merits inclusion in this title and thus libraries would be better off selecting a different biographical resource. [R: SLJ, June 99, p. 63]—**John R. Burch Jr.**

484. **Kings and Queens.** New York, Macmillan Library Reference/Simon & Schuster Macmillan, 1999. 500p. illus. index. (Macmillan Profiles). $75.00. ISBN 0-02-865375-0.

Written for high school students, this title in the Macmillan Profiles series provides short biographies of some 170 monarchs in world history, including those ruling at the end of the twentieth century. Choices were made based on curricular relevance and historical importance, and a broad range of cultures is represented. Alphabetically ordered, the biographical essays run two to three pages, and are attractively enhanced by such marginalia as quotations, important historical facts, definitions of political terms, and biographical timelines. Black-and-white photographs and special topic boxes add further appeal. A list of suggested reading, a 15-page glossary, and a thorough index finish the book. *Kings and Queens* is a well-designed reference and should find a much-deserved place in high school and public libraries.—**Lori D. Kranz**

485. **Rescue and Resistance: Portraits of the Holocaust.** New York, Macmillan Library Reference/Simon & Schuster Macmillan, 1999. 399p. illus. index. (Macmillan Profiles). $80.00. ISBN 0-02-865362-9.

This volume in the Macmillan Profiles series contains 167 brief biographies of men and women who fought and survived the Holocaust. The alphabetic entries are one to two pages long. The material has been adapted from articles in *The Encyclopedia of the Holocaust* (see ARBA 91, entry 520). Most contain a photograph if available, a timeline of major events in the subject's life, and a brief quotation from relevant literature. Short definitions of unfamiliar terms appear in the margins. The profiles of well-known rescuers and survivors such as Oskar Schindler, Elie Wiesel, Simon Wiesenthal, Raoul Wallenberg appear with those who are less famous such as Joseph D. Schwartz, Aristides de Sousa Mendes, Giuseppe Nicolini, and Janis Lipke. Anne Frank, neither survivor nor rescuer, has a six-page entry, but Miep Gies, who hid the Frank family, is omitted from this book.

Sidebars in shaded boxes offer supplementary material such as a brief account of the voyage of the St. Louis and descriptions of the Simon Wiesenthal Center and the Zydowska Organizacja Bojowa (Jewish Fighting Organization). A series of appendixes provide biographies of Nazi leaders, a timeline of the Holocaust, a glossary, and a bibliography.

Rescue and Resistance offers a basic introduction to the Holocaust. Students will need to consult works by and about those profiled in this book and sources that cover the Holocaust in greater depth to gain any understanding of this event. This work is suitable for school, synagogue, and public libraries as a supplemental resource.—**Barbara M. Bibel**

486. **Who's Who in Political Revolutions: Seventy-Three Men and Women Who Changed the World.** Jack A. Goldstone, ed. Washington, D.C., Congressional Quarterly, 1999. 164p. illus. index. $29.95pa. ISBN 1-56802-461-4.

The importance of revolutionary leaders and visionaries in shaping world events over the past 200 years is the focus of this authoritative and extremely accessible biographical dictionary. The editor is an acknowledged expert in the field of international politics and government. An international cadre of scholars contributed the signed essays, which are drawn from Congressional Quarterly's acclaimed *Encyclopedia of Political Revolutions* (see entry 491).

Introductory material includes an essay on the nature of revolutionary leaders and a useful timeline by region of events and leaders. Each essay contains a picture and a short bibliography. From the well-known to lesser-known leaders such as Rigoberta Menchú Tum or Hong Xiuquan, the descriptions are lively and thorough. This volume is a valuable addition for most libraries wanting a smaller cumulation of biographies of political revolutionary leaders for students and general patrons. [R: BR, Sept/Oct 99, p. 65]

—**Ingrid Schierling Burnett**

Chronology

487. Mellersh, H. E. L., and Neville Williams. **Chronology of World History.** Santa Barbara, Calif., ABC-CLIO, 1999. 4v. index. $375.00/set. ISBN 1-57607-155-3.

This set is a major revision of the companion volumes *Chronology of the Ancient World* (see ARBA 96, entry 559), *Chronology of the Medieval World* (see ARBA 96, entry 561), *Chronology of the Expanding World* (see ARBA 96, entry 560), and *Chronology of the Modern World* (see ARBA 96, entry 562). Like the earlier volumes, these cover specific eras: volume 1, the Ancient and Medieval World, covers prehistory to 1491; volume 2, the Expanding World, 1492-1775; volume 3, the Changing World, 1776-1900; and volume 4, the Modern World, 1901-1998.

Arranged year by year, the information is organized into four broad topics (Politics, Government, and Economics; Science, Technology, and Medicine; Society; and Arts and Ideas), and then is subdivided into 25 specific topics. This arrangement is handy for the person seeking subject-specific information but less useful for the person who wants a general overview. To provide additional access, the authors have provided in each volume a main index and an index of titles. Unfortunately, there is no cumulative index. Some sections (e.g., Politics, Government, and Economics) tend to give very specific dates, while within others (e.g. Arts and Ideas) no more than the year is identified. This inconsistency somewhat lessens the work's reference value. There are also several "mini-chronologies" of important people, trends, and events (early tools, Martin Luther, the Napoleonic Wars, the personal computer). A box listing births and deaths completes the coverage of each year.

This 4-volume work is very handsome, both inside and out. With glossy, colorful book covers, it practically begs to be pulled off the shelf. Compared against the earlier volumes, the *Chronology of World History* de-emphasizes political history in favor of the other subjects, includes many more entries (more than 70,000), and features more details within each entry. There is nothing comparable currently available. These factors make it a worthy purchase for all libraries that can afford the $375 price. [R: Choice, Nov 99, p. 518]—**Hope Yelich**

488. Rodriguez, Junius P. **Chronology of World Slavery.** Santa Barbara, Calif., ABC-CLIO, 1999. 580p. illus. index. $99.00. ISBN 0-57607-155-3.

Despite its preachiness, which quickly becomes wearisome, this is a useful reference. It illustrates the universality of slavery. The institution is as old as humanity, has existed in some form in every part of the world, has involved all major racial groups, and continues to this day in some areas of the world. Of course, the nature of slavery has varied considerably from place to place over time. For Muslims, it served primarily household, administrative, and military objectives. For certain premodern peoples, such as the Carthaginians, some Africans, and the Aztecs of Mexico, its purpose was largely ritualistic. The Aztecs, for example, regularly "adopted" captives, thereby enabling them to sacrifice "beloved family members" to the gods. And in the West, particularly Latin America and the southern United States, slavery became a major economic institution, ultimately affecting all aspects of society.

Sensibly organized, the study begins with the ancient world (the first entry dates from 6800 B.C.E.), then moves in successive chapters through Europe, Asia, Africa, Latin America, and the United States. A concluding chapter treats contemporary developments, beginning with an 1880 entry on slavery in China and ending with a 1998 note on the end of slavery in Mauritania. Adding to the volume's overall appeal are numerous maps, sketches, and photographs, a substantial bibliography, and an extensive section of documents (almost 20 percent of the text). An exhaustive index facilitates access to this material. Given the ongoing interest in this subject, this work should be added to the reference collections of high school and college libraries. [R: LJ, 1 Oct 99, p. 82; BR, Nov/Dec 99, p. 87]—**John W. Storey**

489. **The Wilson Calendar of World History.** John Paxton and Edward W. Knappman, eds. Bronx, N.Y., H. W. Wilson, 1999. 460p. illus. index. (Wilson Chronology Series). $70.00. ISBN 0-8242-0937-0.

This chronology begins at 3500 B.C.E. and continues to 1998. A massive undertaking, more than 25,000 historical landmarks are listed under 6 categories—4 geographic regions, science and technology, and culture and the arts. Entries cover people, places, concepts, inventions, discoveries, and titles of specific artworks and literary pieces. This timeline provides balanced representation for Europe, Asia, the Americas, and Africa including the Middle East. The notations are formatted to allow readers to scan down a vertical column to follow related items or across to track the same date around the world.

The authors provide a detailed index allowing ready access to a specific subject. For example, when readers look up "printing," they will learn that the 1st printed newsletter circulated in China in 748 C.E. Later developments ending with Guttenberg in 1457 C.E. are also noted. This reference is a helpful research tool and complements narrative histories by showing the interrelationship of ideas and events occurring simultaneously.—**Adrienne Antink Bendel**

Dictionaries and Encyclopedias

490. **Encyclopedia of North American History.** John C. Super, ed. Tarrytown, N.Y., Marshall Cavendish, 1999. 11v. illus. maps. index. $459.95/set. ISBN 0-7614-7084-0.

This multivolume encyclopedia will be accessible to at least the well educated among the seventh graders who are its target audience, although many entries are sophisticated enough to be useful to high school students and general readers. The work contains 493 alphabetically arranged entries by a broad array of scholars. Not surprisingly, it is heavily weighted toward U.S. history. Entries range from one to seven pages, all include "causes and effects" sidebars, and the longer ones feature summaries; bibliographies; and six types of sidebars dealing with turning points, daily life, laws and cases, profiles of individuals, temper of the times, and viewpoints. Each volume is indexed, but there is a comprehensive index in volume 11, which also includes biographical, geographical, and various subject indexes; a rather brief bibliography; a glossary; and a timeline. The illustrations are excellent, although it would be nice to have more maps. The selection of topics for entries at times reveals the lack of a sense of proportion (e.g., "Branch Davidian Complex Burns" and "Million Man March" are included, but the presidencies of John Adams and James Madison are not); in fact, a number of U.S. presidents fail to rate individual entries. The choice of battles and treaties is also a bit idiosyncratic. The same is true of religious topics. Although religion is dealt with under several general headings (e.g., Great Awakening, Great Puritan Migration, Separation of Church and State), there are no separate entries on major denominations. All this notwithstanding, there is much useful information in this user-friendly set, and it should help make middle school students more interested in and informed about North American history. [R: BL, 1 Sept 99, p. 179]—**William B. Robison**

491. **The Encyclopedia of Political Revolutions.** By Jack A. Goldstone. Washington, D.C., Congressional Quarterly, 1998. 580p. illus. maps. index. $125.00. ISBN 1-56802-206-9.

This is a well-done, one-volume encyclopedia that supplies information on today's revolutionary world. While the coverage is broad, 1500 to the present, it nevertheless provides articles on revolutions, civil wars, and similar uprisings worldwide—large and small, bloody and bloodless, cultural and political. The quality of entries varies. Most of the articles are generally excellent.

The title does not do justice to the topic. The term "revolution" is treated broadly to include civil wars, cultural revolutions, guerrilla movements, and popular uprisings. The alphabetically arranged articles cover not only the events, but also include biographical entries on prominent revolutionary leaders. Concept articles are included to help readers understand how class, race, politics, and other factors relate to such movements. Specific events include the American Revolution and Civil War, the Palestinian Intifada, the Shining Path Revolt in Peru, the Chinese Cultural Revolution and the Tiananmen Square uprising, numerous Irish rebellions, the recent wars in Yugoslavia, and the sixteenth-century Aztec and Inca revolts against the Spanish. Biographical entries include such recent and past revolutionary leaders as Ho Chi Minh, Ernesto "Che" Guevara, Lech Walesa, Thomas Jefferson, Martin Luther, Martin Luther King, Jose Marti, Patrice Lumumba, and Oliver Cromwell. More than 50 articles discuss revolutionary movement concepts such as gender, class, colonialism, capitalism, elitism, fundamentalism, race, student protest, tyranny, and terrorism. Each entry was written by an expert in the field, and is accompanied by a bibliography for further reading.

From an organizational standpoint, this encyclopedia is all one could ask for. Separate alphabetic lists identify contributors and articles, while a third lists entries in biographical, event, and concept categories. The introduction provides readers with a general history of revolutions. A geographical timeline gives overviews of the revolutions described in the main body of the work. The text is further enhanced by a good selection of maps and pictures. Overall access to the contents is excellent via an extensive subject index, while the articles themselves are more easily scanned through the use of interior subheadings.

This is a first-rate work on a topic that will always be of current interest as long as unrest continues in the world. Highly recommended for public, college, university, and any other library with an interest in this topic. [R: BL, 1 May 99, pp. 1622-1624; Choice, Oct 99, p. 312]—**Donald E. Collins**

492. **Encyclopedia of Violence, Peace, & Conflict.** Lester Kurtz and Jennifer Turpin, eds. San Diego, Calif., Academic Press, 1999. 3v. index. $625.00/set. ISBN 0-12-227010-X.

This 3-volume set was a massive undertaking by contributors from universities and research groups from around the world. Almost 200 articles on violence, peace, and conflict resolution range in topic from peace education, trends in warfare, mental illness, and violence toward animals to ethnic conflict, hate crimes, drug control policies, and child abuse. Considerable discussion is made of how attitudes in children are formed by video games and violence on television. At the core of this whole work is how attitudes toward violence are formed and how people are desensitized to violence. Chapters are arranged alphabetically by subject. There is a list of contributors, listing academic affiliation but not department.

This work is supposed to be the first reference work to address the full range of topics in the fields of violence, peace, and conflict studies. But nowhere in this massive work is there a separate article on violence toward private property and how it correlates to violence against humans. Readers should keep in mind this work is politically correct.—**Norman L. Kincaide**

493. Fischel, Jack R. **Historical Dictionary of the Holocaust.** Lanham, Md., Scarecrow, 1999. 321p. (Historical Dictionaries of War, Revolution, and Civil Unrest, no.10). $55.00. ISBN 0-8108-3611-4.

Following Scarecrow's familiar format for historical dictionaries, Fischel begins with a chronology (1879 to 1998) and an introductory overview of the subject, detailing the Nazis' progression from anti-Semitism to genocide. The facts of the Holocaust are then presented in more than 330 alphabetically arranged articles, ranging in length from 1 sentence to several pages, with *see, see also*, and cross-references (the latter in bold typeface). Topics covered include people (victims, perpetrators, collaborators), places, concepts, organizations, and events, and the book is up-to-date, discussing the recent Swiss bank controversy. Although English translations are given for foreign words and phrases, the use of diacritical marks is inconsistent; for example, Rudolf Höss is anglicized as Hoss rather than Hoess. There are also some notable omissions: no articles on Albert Speer, Martin Bormann, or Rudolf Höss; and although there are entries for both gypsies and homosexuals, there is nothing for Jehovah's Witnesses or religious persecution.

The 47-page bibliography of primary and secondary sources is valuable, but the author includes only 2 of the 3 published Nuremberg sets, and fails to mention the 2 valuable supplements to Abraham J. Edelheit and Hershel Edelheit's *Bibliography of Holocaust Literature* (see ARBA 94, entry 532; ARBA 91, entry 519; ARBA 87, entry 522). Fischel also lists Thomas Keneally's *Schindler's List* in the bibliography under "Righteous Gentiles and Other Acts of Rescue," although it is a fictionalized account of Schindler's activities. Although it contains fewer articles than *Dictionary of the Holocaust: Biography, Geography, and Terminology* by Eric Joseph Epstein and Philip Rosen (see ARBA 99, entry 528), Fischel is to be commended for providing information on more "controversial" Holocaust-related topics, such as human soap and the ongoing debate between functionalists and intentionalists. Numerous typographical errors (e.g., Sally Mayer instead of Saly, and Felip Muller instead of Filip) do not mar this book's overall value. Epstein and Rosen's book, however, is very handy because each article has its own bibliography. Neither of them is as comprehensive as Israel Gutman's 4-volume *Encyclopedia of the Holocaust* (see ARBA 91, entry 520). [R: Choice, Dec 99, p. 702]—**John A. Drobnicki**

494. Howard, Roger. **Great Escapes and Rescues: An Encyclopedia.** Santa Barbara, Calif., ABC-CLIO, 1999. 256p. illus. index. $65.00. ISBN 1-57607-032-8; 1-57607-190-1pa.

Many books have been published about escape and rescue missions (both successful and unsuccessful), often by a participant, but they are usually limited to an individual event or a particular type (e.g., prisoners of war). This source contains more than 200 articles on the topic, but what makes the book most valuable (and enjoyable) is that it includes not only events that one would expect to find, such as "The Great Escape" during World War II, but also many little-known events, such as the missionary Gladys Aylward who rescued 100 Chinese orphans from the Japanese Army in 1938 and led them to safety through the mountains. Articles are arranged alphabetically and are in essay form, ranging in length from a paragraph to several pages. Users are referred to related entries by *see also* references, and each entry contains bibliographic references. There are an overall bibliography, an index, a table of contents (which lists each article), and a table of entries by broad subject (e.g., "Civil Prisoners," "Soldiers and Military"). Aside from historical persons (Casanova, Louis XVIII), the author has included numerous recent figures and events, such as U.S. Air Force pilot Scott O'Grady, who was shot down over Bosnia in 1995, and the Peruvian embassy siege of 1997. Some articles are awkwardly labeled or arranged, however, such as "Medieval England, Imprisonment in," and Charles Edward Stuart ("Bonnie Prince Charlie"), pretender to the British throne, appears under "C" instead of Stuart. Also, the Waco siege is discussed under a generic "Rescue Attempts" article, but there is no listing in the index for Branch Davidians.

Although the essays are very well written, often with dramatic language, some are superficial; for example, the article on Auschwitz mentions the famous escape by Vrba and Wetzler, but the author does not mention its tremendous importance (i.e., the report that they wrote, the so-called Auschwitz protocol, provided early firsthand evidence to the world of the Final Solution). The material in this book, which includes many black-and-white illustrations, is ideally suited for browsing, and public libraries might want to consider an additional copy for their circulating collections. [R: LJ, 1 Sept 99, p. 178; BL, 1 Dec 99, p. 722]—**John A. Drobnicki**

495. Kohn, George Childs. **Dictionary of Wars.** rev. ed. New York, Facts on File, 1999. 614p. index. $50.00. ISBN 0-8160-3928-3.

This ambitious volume provides concise information on more than 1,800 global conflicts, civil wars, mutinies, punitive expeditions, undeclared wars, rebellions, and revolutions as well as religious, sectarian, ethnic, and racial conflicts from all parts of the world. The book spans 4,000 years of history from 2000 B.C.E. to the present, including "The Kosovo Uprising of 1998," in a revision that includes more than 70 new entries. Arranged alphabetically, each entry gives the conflict's name(s), dates it spanned, how it began, the opposing sides involved in the conflict, a summary or description of events, and the outcome or significance. Each entry also discusses the political, social, economic, and cultural influences on the military actions. Entries are cross-referenced to related conflicts. When known by more than one name, all names are included and cross-referenced to the most familiar name. A geographic index gives a chronological listing of all the wars for each country. The book also includes an alphabetic index.

The scope of this volume is impressive, especially with the addition of conflicts that have occurred since its first publication more than 12 years ago. The narrative style of each entry makes for easy reading while providing a lot of information in a concise format. No bibliography is included, however, so the reader has no suggestions of where to go for further information. Although the inclusion would have increased the length of the volume considerably, its lack makes the book less valuable as a research tool. As a starting place or for general information, this work should prove quite useful. [R: LJ, 15 June 99, p. 72; BL, 15 Nov 99, pp. 644-646]—**Janet Hilbun**

496. **Oxford Encyclopedia of World History.** Market House Books, comp. New York, Oxford University Press, 1998. 775p. illus. maps. $30.00. ISBN 0-19-860223-5.

The more than 4,000 entries in this work cover the major events and figures of world history. The world's nation-states are also included, with tables of geographic and demographic data. A reference book of this size and scope would necessarily be very general, but abundant cross-references set off typographically within the text expand its utility. Each entry introduces a topic and touches upon causes and effects related to the subject for a succinct presentation. Two-color, shaded maps and black-and-white illustrations enhance some entries.

Written in British English, this encyclopedia focuses more on the Western than the Eastern world, but politically it is fairly neutral (e.g., the entry on Richard Nixon is devoted mostly to his foreign policy, with only brief mention of Watergate—although Watergate has its own entry). The 26-page chronology at the end of the book lists events in Europe and the Mediterranean region with corresponding information on history and culture in other parts of the world. Up to date through 1996, this reference would be most useful to high school students or general readers in need of background material. It would also serve as a handy desk reference. [R: BL, 1 May 99, p. 1636]—**Lori D. Kranz**

497. Schechter, Michael G. **Historical Dictionary of International Organizations.** Lanham, Md., Scarecrow, 1998. 247p. (Historical Dictionaries of International Organizations, no.16). $60.00. ISBN 0-8108-3479-0.

This volume is the 16th of the historical dictionaries of international organizations. Schechter has clarified the often confusing world of international organizations by providing a brief overall history of their origins and functions. There are a list of acronyms, a selected chronology of the founding of international organizations, an introduction, the dictionary itself, and an extensive bibliography. International organizations grew out of conferences of sovereign states that met to discuss and resolve certain issues of peace or war or to standardize weights and measures in a discordant and distant world.

International travel and communications have altered the meaning and purpose of international organizations. There is a vast array of organizations with an equally vast array of motivations and agendas. The only real clear notion for the future of these organizations is change. There is no longer a cold war to polarize international organizations into east, west, or nonaligned. International organizations deal with a wide variety of economic, environmental, humanitarian, social, diplomatic, and military issues. Schechter's work helps sort these issues and organizations and provides an understanding of the changing international scene. This small informative volume is a valuable addition to any public, college, university, or government reference collection. [R: Choice, June 99, p. 1767]—**Norman L. Kincaide**

498. Shaffer, Jack. **Historical Dictionary of the Cooperative Movement.** Lanham, Md., Scarecrow, 1999. 610p. (Historical Dictionaries of Religions, Philosophies, and Movements, no.26). $110.00. ISBN 0-8108-3666-1.

Modern cooperative organizations date back to the eighteenth century when cheese makers' cooperatives were formed in France, followed by fire insurance societies in England and the United States. Since then the cooperative movement has expanded into nearly every nation of the world with many different goals and purposes, including commercial, religious, philosophical, social, and political reasons. Shaffer's remarkable dictionary pulls together the historical sweep of cooperative activities in a useful and accessible manner. Shaffer begins with a chronology from 1750 to 1998, which highlights major events and the emergence of national movements. A long, 100-page introductory essay touches on cooperative theories and principles, types and definitions, the social and economic impact, political relationships, and regional cooperative developments.

The heart of the dictionary is an alphabetic arrangement of names of places, people, organizations, and events. Most of the entries are brief, ranging from a few sentences to one or two full pages. Shaffer has appended three useful tables that link countries to types and number of cooperatives. By far the most impressive feature of this book is a comprehensive bibliography of 160 pages, which is organized into 8 major sections and limited to books and monographs. This will stand as the essential reference work on cooperatives and is highly recommended for all academic libraries.—**Thomas A. Karel**

499. Wagner, John A. **Historical Dictionary of the Elizabethan World: Britain, Ireland, Europe, and America.** Phoenix, Ariz., Oryx Press, 1999. 392p. illus. maps. index. $59.95. ISBN 1-57356-200-9.

Audiences of the recent films *Elizabeth* and *Shakespeare in Love* who want to know more about the era of the Virgin Queen will profit from this volume. In a comparatively brief space for a work of this breadth, Wagner provides useful entries under such general aspects of Elizabeth's England as government, religion, education, women, and science, to name a few. To each entry is appended a brief bibliographic supplement of several current secondary titles for further reading. Inevitably, some "major minor" figures have been omitted; for example, the entry on music cites longer entries on Peter Carew, William Byrd, and Thomas Tallis, but there is no reference to John Bull or John Dowland. Literary entries tend to be more historically factual than critically summative; Ben Jonson's hallmark neoclassicism is not mentioned. For broader biographical coverage of this period one should supplement this volume with R. H. Fritze's biographical dictionaries of the Tudor and Stuart periods (1991, 1996).

But these shortcomings are minor in a book intended "primarily for students and other nonspecialists." Such readers will be impressed by the book's overall design and layout, and its wealth of ancillary tables, charts, maps, bibliography, and seven appendixes, one of which includes the two quite recent movies cited above. Others tabulate genealogies, archbishops, popes, monarchs, plus selected historical fiction and sound recordings. Frequent black-and-white illustrations enhance the text. Those coming to this historical era for the first time will be enticed to further study by the book's attractive format and user-friendly organization. More experienced students of the period will also appreciate the appendix on selected Elizabethan and Tudor Websites. This is an appropriate acquisition for all libraries from the secondary level on up. [R: BL, 1 Dec 99, pp. 722-724]—**Christopher Baker**

Handbooks and Yearbooks

500. Brogan, Patrick. **World Conflicts.** Lanham, Md., Scarecrow, 1998. 682p. index. $49.50. ISBN 0-8108-3551-7.

It is refreshing to come across a reference work that is well-organized, meaningful, and well written. Patrick Brogan has provided a lively, informative, and entertaining narrative style for this work on world strife and conflict since 1945. The world did not remain at peace after World War II, and perhaps there have been as many casualties of war, rebellion, and revolution in the second half of the century as there were in the first half. Five sections deal with world conflict regionally: Africa, Asia, Middle East, Europe, and Latin America. The last section deals with terrorism and provides a timeline of wars, coups and revolutions, and assassinations since 1945. This thick but manageable volume has a lively historical narrative style, making it a joy to read. Anecdotal material and lively quotes make the topic come alive and carry the reader from topic to topic as easily as one flips through the pages. Patrick Brogan is to be commended on this fine work. It is highly recommended for private, public, college, university, and government reference collections. [R: Choice, Dec 99, p. 699]—**Norman L. Kincaide**

501. **Daily Life Through History.** [CD-ROM]. Westport, Conn., Greenwood Press, 1999. Minimum system requirements: IBM or compatible 386. CD-ROM drive. Windows 3.1x or Windows NT 3.51. 8MB RAM. 15MB hard disk space. VGA with 14-inch monitor. Mouse. $395.00 (single user); $495.00 (2 to 10 users); $595.00 (11-20 users); $695.00 (21-30 users). ISBN 0-313-31367-9.

A valuable enhancement of a noteworthy series, this product is the electronic equivalent of the publisher's The Greenwood Press "Daily Life Through History" Series. As such, it includes the full-text equivalent of 10 volumes, each treating a different time period or culture: Mesopotamia, the Ancient Greeks, the Aztecs, the Inca Empire, Mayan civilization, Chaucer's England, Elizabethan England, Civil War America, the Nineteenth-Century American Frontier, and Victorian England. Each volume is arranged by chapter, and most volumes include a preface, historical timeline, introduction, glossary, bibliography, and illustrations. The text itself has been indexed to provide greater exactness in the retrieval process.

Search software allows a variety of options: searching single or multiple volumes for a keyword or concept, searching only specific chapters or sections of single or multiple volumes, searching illustrations, natural language searching, advanced queries, synonym searching, and proximity searching. Results can be sorted by relevance, and there are also numerous print options available.

This social history database provides a lot of information for students of history, literature, the humanities, and social sciences. Its real value is to be found in the detail of daily life of the culture in question. Well-documented and presented in the context of a highly efficient search architecture, this resource is highly recommended for high school and college collections. Some public and special libraries might also give this title serious consideration.—**Edmund F. SantaVicca**

502. Delgado, James P. **Across the Top of the World: The Quest for the Northwest Passage.** New York, Facts on File, 1999. 228p. illus. maps. index. $35.00. ISBN 0-8160-4124-5.

The search for the Northwest Passage across the top of North America was fraught with death and danger, and Delgado captures well the struggles involved in this quest that spanned more than 600 years. This search for the Northwest Passage—or passages, since several possible routes have been mapped—probably began with Norsemen about 1267 and was not successful until Amundsen completed the journey in 1905. During these years, innumerable men gave their lives in pursuit of the dream. Delgado, the executive director of the Vancouver Maritime Museum, chronicles each of the expeditions that led to the discovery and mapping of the passage in well-documented detail with quotes from the explorers' journals, letters, and published accounts. The volume contains 180 illustrations, 80 of them in color, with historic pictures, documents, and current images of the area included. Both modern and historical maps of the region show the extent of the explorations. Descriptions of archaeological findings add insight into the travails the explorers suffered. The extensive bibliography and chapter notes make this a work of serious scholarship, but its narrative nature and compelling images make it a thoroughly enjoyable read. This well-indexed volume is an exceptional contribution, and the only addition that would make it more readable would be a timeline or chart of the expeditions to help in keeping dates, outcomes, and persons straight.—**Janet Hilbun**

503. George, Linda S. **The Golden Age of Islam.** Tarrytown, N.Y., Marshall Cavendish, 1998. 80p. illus. maps. index. (Cultures of the Past). $19.95. ISBN 0-7614-0273-X.

504. Hinds, Kathryn. **The Incas.** Tarrytown, N.Y., Marshall Cavendish, 1998. 80p. illus. maps. index. (Cultures of the Past). $19.95. ISBN 0-7614-0270-5.

505. Hinds, Kathryn. **The Vikings.** Tarrytown, N.Y., Marshall Cavendish, 1998. 80p. illus. index. (Cultures of the Past). $19.95. ISBN 0-7614-0271-3.

506. Service, Pamela F. **The Ancient African Kingdom of Kush.** Tarrytown, N.Y., Marshall Cavendish, 1998. 80p. illus. index. (Cultures of the Past). $19.95. ISBN 0-7614-0272-1.

These 4 books of an attractive 14-volume series, designed for older elementary through high school readers, bring key vanished cultures to life as they were at the height of their development. The authors, who are either authorities or persons with a special interest in the culture, use narrative, sidebars, descriptive captions, photographs of places, works of art, and sometimes persons, all currently in existence, to discuss these cultures. The daily lives of the people, including their religions, are brought into focus, as are the culture's legends and political history. The authors note the lives of women and the place of slavery. A chronology, glossary, and two bibliographies—one aimed at the younger student and one for use by the teacher or older student—assist readers in each volume. The titles can be purchased singly as can other titles in the series, including *The Ancient Egyptians*, *The Ancient Greeks*, *The Ancient Maya*, *The Ancient Romans*, *The Aztec Empire*, *The Celts of Northern Europe*, *China's Tang Dynasty*, *India's Gupta Dynasty*, *The Kingdom of Benin in West Africa*, and *The Persian Empire*.—**Edna M. Boardman**

507. **The Holocaust: Memories, Research, Reference.** Robert Hauptman and Susan Hubbs Motin, eds. Binghamton, N.Y., Haworth Press, 1998. 320p. index. $49.95. ISBN 0-7890-0379-1.

The Holocaust: Memories, Research, Reference is a collection of essays exploring this historical tragedy from three different directions. The first part, "Memories," emphasizes the memories of those who witnessed the Holocaust and the importance of documenting and recalling those memories in order to preserve an accurate record of historical facts. For example, Arnost Lustig writes a powerful essay recalling his own experiences at Auschwitz-Birkenau. Part 2 concentrates on research and methods of studying and investigating the Holocaust. This section also discusses different methods of integrating Holocaust study into high school and college curriculum. The final part contains essays discussing different sources for reference in the study of the Holocaust. This section provides direction for researchers both in the library and on the Internet. An index is also provided to guide users in their research. This work is a significant reference tool in itself as well as a guide to further research. This is a must-have for all libraries, especially those with patrons interested in Holocaust documentation and research.—**Cari Ringelheim**

508. Kaufman, Burton I. **The Korean Conflict.** Westport, Conn., Greenwood Press, 1999. 193p. illus. index. (Greenwood Press Guides to Historic Events of the Twentieth Century). $39.95. ISBN 0-313-29909-9.

Unlike the Vietnam War, the Korean conflict, as the author and the editor of the series have aptly pointed out, has been a "neglected war in the history of the United States." However, interest in the Korean War has resurfaced recently, perhaps because of the end of the Cold War, which has enabled scholars to examine the exact nature of the roles of Russia and China—the enduring questions of more than 30 years—in this conflict with the opening of their archives to the public.

The Korean Conflict, like other volumes in the series of Greenwood Press Guides to Historic Events of the Twentieth Century, includes a chronology of events, six topical essays, biographical entries on important or key individuals in the conflict, primary documents of the conflict, and a topical annotated bibliography. In the reviewer's mind, the most valuable features of the work are the 6 topical and 15 primary documents. The essays examine the causes, events, and implications of the war; they are brief but thorough, balanced, up-to-date, and readable. The inclusion of the primary documents, however, has further illuminated the views presented in the text. What is missing from the biographical section is the exclusion of Zho En-lai, a major figure in the conflict.

This work should prove to be a useful tool for high school students, especially students taking advanced high school American and Asian history courses, and beginning undergraduates. School, public, and academic libraries should purchase this work.—**Binh P. Le**

509. Konstam, Angus. **History of Pirates.** New York, Lyons Press, 1999. 192p. illus. maps. index. $53.00. ISBN 1-55821-969-2.

Angus Konstam, chief curator of the Mel Fisher Maritime Museum in Key West, Florida, has produced a lavishly illustrated work that is both informative and entertaining. It is not meant to be comprehensive but rather provides interesting bits of information about piracy through the ages.

The book is divided into 11 chapters, focusing on either a specific period of time or region. Each of the chapters begins with a map and a brief synopsis of the subject matter. The one- or two-page entries that follow focus either on pirate ships of the day or biographies of infamous rogues. Scattered throughout the chapters are entries, unique to the period or locale in question, that examine subjects such as the history of pirate flags or their favorite weapons.

As a reference title, the usefulness of the book is limited. It contains excellent maps but an academic framework is missing. There are no cross-references or bibliographic citations, but there is an index. This entertaining work would instead be an excellent choice for the circulating collection of school or public libraries.
—**John R. Burch Jr.**

510. Konstam, Angus. **The History of Shipwrecks.** New York, Lyons Press, 1999. 192p. illus. maps. index. $35.00. ISBN 1-55821-970-6.

Although the title might indicate that this is a catalog of famous maritime disasters (and the dust jacket, inevitably, depicts the *Titanic* and the iceberg), it is in fact a monograph for the general reader on how sunken ships are located and salvaged for scholarly and commercial reasons, and how such operations contribute to knowledge of maritime history. An initial section covers such topics as how shipwrecks happen, the techniques of underwater research and salvage, and the ethical issues involved in such activities. Most of the book covers the shipwreck and individual vessels that have been studied, mainly chronologically by date of shipwreck. Subjects include the anonymous (probably Syrian) merchant vessel that sank off the south coast of Turkey around 1300 B.C.E. and the *Andrea Doria* disaster in 1956. The text is well written and easy to read, and the extensive illustrations (e.g., photographs, maps, facsimiles) are well chosen and nicely printed. There is a good index, but no bibliography or notes.

Although this book can be consulted as a reference work thanks to the good indexing, it can also be read through as a monograph; libraries will have to decide whether it is best placed in the reference or the general collection. The level of treatment is suitable for both public and high school libraries.—**Paul B. Cors**

511. Lang, Sean. **The Twentieth Century World: War, Revolution, and Technology.** New York, Cambridge University Press, 1998. 160p. illus. maps. index. $15.95pa. ISBN 0-521-48324-7.

This book is aimed at the school-age audience and encompasses the history of the twentieth century—a daunting objective for 160 pages. The narrative is simplistic and superficial. The text is minimal and would need to be amplified by extensive teacher input. The majority of the book focuses on World War I and World War II. Undeniably these are pivotal events of the century, but the author leaves glaring gaps. For example, there is no coverage of the explosive advances in technology and science during the past 20 years of the twentieth century (e.g., the Internet, genome research). On the plus side, the author effectively uses quotes from contemporary sources, maps, photographs, and painting reproductions to engage the reader's attention. Sound bites of history are offered when an expanded presentation would be more instructive.
—**Adrienne Antink Bendel**

Quotation Books

512. Langer, Howard J., comp. **World War II: An Encyclopedia of Quotations.** Westport, Conn., Greenwood Press, 1999. 449p. illus. index. $75.00. ISBN 0-313-30018-6.

This reference provides more than 1,000 quotes from more than 300 individuals about World War II. The selections come from heads of state, military officers, diplomats, government officials, chaplains, intelligence officers, scientists, journalists, historians, civilians, and soldiers and sailors speaking from the heat of battle. Both the Allied and the Axis sides of the conflict are represented. Entries come from public addresses, military orders, secret documents released after the war, press reports, private diaries and letters, published histories, memoirs, and many other sources. These excerpts take the reader back in time and impart a visceral understanding of what the war meant to those who lived through it. The most chilling and telling comments are those from ordinary citizens—again from both sides of the war.

Very short coverage is given to the Holocaust in this volume. The editor has done a companion piece dedicated to this tragic dimension of the war. An extensive bibliography is provided as well as two indexes in which pieces are listed by category and by subject and name. Additional features are an inventory of movies made about World War II during the war and a guide to slang, code names, and other terms used during the period. This work brings alive the tenor of the war years and portrays an inspiring time in our history. [R: LJ, 1 Mar 99, p. 76; BL, June 99, p. 1884]—**Adrienne Antink Bendel**

10 Law

GENERAL WORKS

Dictionaries and Encyclopedias

513. **Burton's Legal Thesaurus.** 3d ed. By William C. Burton. New York, Macmillan Library Reference/Simon & Schuster Macmillan, 1998. 1012p. $152.75. ISBN 0-02-864986-9.

Like the two earlier editions, this thesaurus is organized into two parts—main entries and an index. The main entry for a word includes a definition, its part of speech, synonyms, associated legal concepts, and foreign phrases and translations. Do not confuse this with a combination dictionary and thesaurus; the brief definitions are only given when there is more than one meaning. The author cautions the user to consult a dictionary to determine precise meanings. The purpose of the publication is to enable the legal writer to locate a full range of synonyms and words related in meaning. This will promote writing that is more precise, effective, and persuasive.

Four criteria were used by the authors to select entries for the book: those words that are strictly legal, those words that are not strictly legal but are commonly used by members of the legal profession, those words that are neither legal nor widely used by lawyers but are sufficiently sophisticated to warrant their use by attorneys, and those words regularly used by attorneys. The foreign phrases and translations are helpful because they are organized by related concepts rather than alphabetically by the first word of the phrase. The associated concepts show how words are usually found in their legal context. The index entries contain words with only a few synonyms. Index words covered more fully in the main entries are so indicated.

The author gives no indication of how many entries have been added since the 2d edition in 1992 (see ARBA 93, entry 574). *Burton's Legal Thesaurus* may not be helpful to those who are only occasional legal writers, but it definitely will be appreciated by those patrons who do legal writing often.
—**Bev Cummings Agnew**

514. **Dictionary of Law.** 2d ed. P. H. Collin, ed. Chicago, Fitzroy Dearborn, 1999. 258p. $55.00. ISBN 1-57958-155-2.

Although this book purports to cover both British and U.S. law, its emphasis seems to be on the former; indeed the 1st edition was titled *English Law Dictionary*. It is a handy volume containing 6,000 main words and phrases that cover criminal, civil, commercial, and international law. According to the 1st edition's preface (reprinted in this edition), the level of vocabulary ranges from the very formal to prison slang. In addition to their definitions, examples are given of words and phrases used in context. Words with particular grammatical challenges have short grammar notes and explanations of differences between British and U.S. use. Particularly useful are the comments on certain words that explain particular points of law.

The 1st edition's preface curiously refers to a supplement not found in the 2d edition. The 2d edition's preface explains that the text has been completely updated with an emphasis on adding legislative process materials.

Although the book is extremely interesting, it is unclear what audience would appreciate comparing the British and U.S. systems of law in a dictionary format. Other titles must surely cover British legal terms at a less expensive price.—**Bev Cummings Agnew**

515. **The Philosophy of Law: An Encyclopedia.** Christopher Berry Gray, ed. New York, Garland, 1999. 2v. index. (Garland Reference Library of the Humanities, v.1743). $250.00/set. ISBN 0-8153-1344-6.

This 2-volume encyclopedia should become one of the most frequently visited reference works for people interested in virtually any aspect of jurisprudence. As the editor notes in the introduction, this encyclopedia "covers virtually all topics under discussion in the recent literature in philosophy of law" (p. vii). A 10-page list of subjects covered reveals the scope of coverage and includes such headings as Roman Philosophy of Law, Socialist Philosophy of Law, Chinese Philosophy of Law, Natural Law, Legal Positivism, Feminist Philosophy of Law, Critical Legal Studies, Philosophy of Penal Law, Crimes, Punishment, and Morality and Law. Philosophers and jurists who have made substantive contributions to legal theory are extremely well represented here and include such notables as Plato, Aristotle, St. Thomas Aquinas, Thomas Hobbes, John Locke, Jeremy Bentham, J. L. Austin, Immanuel Kant, and more recent representative thinkers such as Wesley Hohfeld, Melville Fuller, H. L. A. Hart, and John Rawls. The substantive presentation begins with "Aboriginal Legal Culture" and ends with "Wrongful Life and Wrongful Death." Each entry concludes with a list of references. The references are by no means substantial (they were not intended to be) but they will lead researchers in the right direction. The encyclopedia includes several excellent indexes, namely an index of names, an index of cases, an index of legislation and legislative-type materials, and an index of topics. The entries are clearly written and coherently organized. Entries include subdivisions where appropriate. For example, "Plea Bargaining" includes the subheadings of "Involuntariness," "Unreliability," "Injustice in Sentencing," and "The Contract Model." This encyclopedia should be a part of all reference collections.—**Michael A. Foley**

Directories

516. **Directory of State Court Clerks & County Courthouses.** 1999 ed. Robert S. Want and Jennifer M. Dowell, eds. New York, WANT Publishing, 1998. 351p. $65.00pa. ISBN 0-942008-85-5. ISSN 1042-4172.

The latest edition of an annual publication begun in 1990 and published each October, this volume offers concise access to contact information for a complex class of public offices arranged alphabetically by state name. Each state entry provides an organization chart of the local court system (together with names and contact information for all related governmental positions and their current occupants), postal addresses, phone and fax numbers for clerks' and registrars' offices, and a listing of all counties lying within specific judicial districts. A separate directory of all probate and recording offices is included. Of additional value for users unfamiliar with legal records and their management are the sections covering the process of trying a court case, state offices of vital statistics and how to request documents from them, information on corporate filings, and trends in state court litigation.

The information on state court Websites permits users to select available electronic resources specific to individual jurisdictions. Most useful for large public, college, and university library reference collections.
—**Robert B. Marks Ridinger**

517. Eis, Arlene L., comp. **Directory of Law-Related CD-ROMs 1999.** Teaneck, N.J., Infosources, 1999. 328p. index. $75.00pa. ISBN 0-939486-5309. ISSN 1065-0334.

Directory of Law-Related CD-ROMs 1999 is published by one of the foremost compilers of legal reference products, Infosources Publishing. Eis, MLS and former law librarian, began publishing annual titles for this niche market as early as 1981 with *Legal Looseleafs in Print* (see ARBA 84, entry 484). The CD-ROM directory has been issued annually since 1993. Paper quality and the inclusion of advertisements in this work suggest that currency of information is valued above a formal presentation style, which is appropriate for such a rapidly changing subject area.

This one-of-a-kind directory is a collection of almost everything law librarians and lawyers need to know about the purchase of domestic and international law-related CD-ROMs. Compiled and edited by Eis, this directory provides multiple access points through several detailed indexes. Entries for each of the CD-ROMs (more than 1,500) contains up to 19 information fields and are uniformly formatted for easy comparison.

The *Directory of Law-Related CD-ROMS* is really part of a suite of products. A newsletter/update service released three times a year may be purchased separately and a Web site, partly accessible only to this directory's subscribers, is also available. The *Internet Guide for the Legal Researcher* (2d ed.; Infosources), by Don MacLeod, may be used as a companion reference.

Although CD-ROM technology usage appears to be waning, it is still being used in conjunction with legal online subscription sources, such as LEXIS-NEXIS and "free" Internet sites such as findlaw.com. When Website subscriptions decrease in price and can guarantee more privacy, stability, and ease of access, CD-ROMs may go the way of many paper subscriptions. For the time being, legal research seems best conducted using a combination of formats: print, CD-ROM, and Internet. Internet addresses of most CD-ROM vendors are provided, an indication that publishers themselves are trying to balance the cost effectiveness, stability, and comprehensiveness of CD-ROMs against the timeliness and sophisticated retrieval features of commercial Web products.

The *Directory of Law-Related CD-ROMs* should be considered an indispensable tool for law offices and law libraries that continue to subscribe to CD-ROM products. As the only reference work of its kind, it is well worth the price.—**Linda D. Tietjen**

518. **Law Firms Yellow Book: Who's Who in the Management of the Leading U.S. Law Firms.** Summer 1998 ed. New York, Leadership Directories, 1998. 1276p. index. $235.00pa. ISSN 1054-4054.

This book is part of a series published by the Leadership Library of who's who in the leadership of the United States. It provides in-depth coverage of the organizational structure of the largest U.S. law firms practicing general corporate law and is published semiannually. The current edition profiles 802 law firms, with emphasis on the personnel responsible for decision making and management. It includes more than 16,000 attorneys listed with their titles, functions, telephone numbers, and law schools they attended, as well as names, titles, and telephone numbers of some 6,000 of the nation's top legal administrative personnel. It includes U.S. law firms and their foreign offices. It includes 46 new firms not previously listed. The book also includes mergers, firm name changes, deletions, branch office openings and closings, managing partner changes, managing partners by law schools, firm locations, largest firms, and domestic and international law firm networks. There is also an excellent user's guide. The largest section of the book is devoted to an alphabetic list of law firms. There are numerous and useful indexes for departments, law schools, personnel, law firms, and subsidiaries and geographic indexes. It has some similarities to the *Martindale-Hubbell Law Directory* (K. G. Saur), but this directory is more limited in its coverage. For all but the largest public libraries, the *Martindale-Hubbell Law Directory* is a better choice. Academic libraries, large public libraries, and law firms will be most likely to purchase this publication.—**Theresa Maggio**

519. **Want's Federal-State Court Directory.** 1999 ed. Robert S. Want and Jennifer M. Dowell, eds. New York, WANT Publishing, 1998. 247p. index. $35.00pa. ISBN 0-942008-84-7. ISSN 0742-1095.

Want's Federal-State Court Directory is an annual publication that is published each October. The material for this edition was compiled from April through August 1998. Thus, this edition is not current for any positions elected in November 1998. However, this limitation is minor compared to the amount of information covered.

No new features were added to the 1999 directory. The list for the International Supreme Courts, found in the 1998 edition, has been removed. This directory, along with the *Directory of State Court Clerks and County Courthouses* (see entry 516), are the main titles in the Your Nation's Courts Series.

The purposes of this series are to provide easy access to state and federal courts and to state enforcement officials and to provide a guide to the operation of the state and federal judicial systems. Besides the obvious directory information, *Want's Federal-State Court Directory* provides a list of federal court vacancies, electronic access to court documents, and diagrams of the judicial systems in each state.

The Bureau of National Affairs publishes a comparable annual publication, *BNA's Directory of State and Federal Courts, Judges, and Clerks* (1997 ed.; see ARBA 98, entry 521). It covers, in one somewhat more expensive publication, more than Want covers in the two mentioned above. The BNA directory also ended its verification efforts in August 1998, so the timeliness is the same as in Want.

The BNA publication includes more state coverage; Want's emphasis is on the federal courts. This predominant federal court coverage was noted in the two prior ARBA reviews of earlier editions (see ARBA 94, entry 564, and ARBA 91, entry 582). The BNA directory, for example, has a personal name index for all judges, clerks, reporters, and administrators. Want's court directory index covers only federal appellate and district court judges.

Want's court directory's coverage for state courts is limited to an organizational chart for each state and information for only the state–level court positions, including the Clerk of the Supreme Court, the Attorney General, and the Court Administrator. The BNA directory list is much more comprehensive, giving names and addresses for the state level as well as the county judges. Both the Want and the BNA directories contain useful information on electronic access to judicial decisions and records. However, the BNA directory has far more Internet sites for the federal and state courts. Want's companion *Directory of State Court Clerks and County Courthouses* does have state court Websites.

If library patrons' needs do not include information on the lower state courts, Want's publication would be sufficient. It does contain useful court information even if purchased without the more expensive companion publication.—**Bev Cummings Agnew**

Handbooks and Yearbooks

520. **American Law Yearbook 1998.** Kris E. Palmer and others, eds. Farmington Hills, Mich., Gale, 1999. 337p. illus. index. $140.00. ISBN 0-7876-3783-1. ISSN 1521-0901.

The *American Law Yearbook 1998*, a supplement to West Publishing's *Encyclopedia of American Law* (1997), updates the contents of the encyclopedia with material through May 1998 and adds additional subjects, largely biographies. An appendix gives descriptions of lobbying organizations. Articles include definitions and discussions of legal terms and concepts; descriptions of events and legal cases; and biographies of people who are significant in American law, politics, and government. The articles are well written, and variations in type size and subheadings make the work easy to use. Special "In Focus" pieces highlight issues of particular interest, importance, or controversy (e.g., campaign financing reform). Black-and-white photographs, a table of cases cited, an excellent index, and cross-references to articles in the encyclopedia are included.

This is an excellent resource for the layperson who wants information on issues (e.g., school prayer) and events (e.g., Whitewater) from a legal perspective that is often lacking in the media, or for the reader, layperson, or professional who is interested in an overview of American legal developments in the period covered by the yearbook. This is a necessary purchase for libraries that own the encyclopedia, where it would be most useful, and it would find users in other libraries with substantial budgets where there is a strong interest in current events and American politics and government.—**Gari-Anne Patzwald**

521. Eisaguirre, Lynne. **Affirmative Action: A Reference Handbook.** Santa Barbara, Calif., ABC-CLIO, 1999. 222p. index. (Contemporary World Issues). $45.00. ISBN 0-87436-854-5.

This is another introductory overview and guide in the Contemporary World Issues series designed to address critical issues current in public policy debate. Similar publications in this series include topics such as hate crimes, feminism, and sexual harassment, the latter guide written by Eisaguirre as well. The series provides people beginning research on a contemporary social issue an objective and clear overview and guide to the issue's history, development, and current status. The series succeeds admirably. High school and college students should begin their research on these issues with the relevant text from the series.

Affirmative Action is divided into 7 chapters. The introductory chapter introduces the reader to a clear and concise overview of the historical development of the affirmative action debate. The chapter moves from the roots of affirmative action, including a definition, through the developments and realities of the 1980s and 1990s. The chapter concludes with a short but useful list of references. Chapter 2 provides a brief but equally useful chronology of important historical events. Chapter 3 presents brief biographical sketches of some of the key players in the debate. Students new to the debate will profit immensely from these sketches. Chapter 4, the longest and arguably the most important chapter, consists of sundry facts and statistics that help focus the debate. This chapter concludes with a helpful list of references. Chapter 5 lists numerous organizations that address the issue. Chapter 6 offers an annotated list of select print resources. Chapter 7 lists select nonprint resources, including several Internet addresses. Any but the most advanced researcher will profit from the clarity and brevity of presentation. A glossary and an index complete this excellent overview and guide to this highly contentious public debate. This volume is highly recommended for all libraries.—**Michael A. Foley**

522. Gibson, Ellen M., and William H. Manz. **New York Legal Research Guide.** 2d ed. Buffalo, N.Y., William S. Hein, 1998. 1v. (various paging). index. $68.00. ISBN 1-57588-220-5.

The authors claim that this is the first comprehensive legal research guide for New York State, New York City, and New York Indian law. They have enlarged the materials on New York City and Indian law for this 2d edition. This is, as the title implies, a guide to finding both primary and secondary New York legal resources. For example, the New York State Constitution is not reproduced here, but an entire chapter is devoted to sources covering all aspects of the constitution and to historical constitutional interpretation from its origin in 1777.

The book is divided into part 1, "New York State," and part 2, "New York City." Part 1 covers the constitutions, state legislation and legislative histories, the judicial system, court reports, and case finders. It also covers administrative regulations and decisions, procedure acts, and court rules. The chapter on local legislation contains resources for local entities or municipal corporations—counties, cities, towns, and villages. The chapter on Indian law gives a brief history of the Iroquois Confederacy (the Haudenosaunee), as well as sources for treaties and documents, a directory of Indian nations, and information on the rights of indigenous peoples in international law. Particularly useful are the chapters on databases and Internet sites, practice books, and forms. The appendixes include lists of New York law reviews, bar associations, publishers, law libraries, and abbreviations.

Part 2 covers the same topics as part 1 (charters, legislation, and judicial system) for New York City. There are no appendixes in part 2. This seems like a valuable addition for any library in need of New York legal resources. The brief histories are also interesting and easy to read.—**Bev Cummings Agnew**

523. **Great American Court Cases.** Mark Mikula, L. Mpho Mabunda, and Allison McClintic Marion, eds. Farmington Hills, Mich., Gale, 1999. 4v. illus. index. $350.00/set. ISBN 0-7876-2947-0.

This is a lavish four-volume set that covers nearly 800 cases and contains 300 photographs. The first volume on individual liberties highlights cases concerning First and Second Amendment issues such as privacy, press, religion, and the right to bear arms. The second volume on criminal justice focuses on cases about defendants' rights, criminal law and procedure, and capital punishment. The third volume on equal protection and family law presents such cases involving affirmative action and sexual harassment. The last volume is on business and government and includes cases related to contracts, consumer protection, and Native American issues.

The purpose of the set seems to be to bring the judicial system and its impact on society to average citizens in a thoroughly readable manner. Most of the cases covered are U.S. Supreme Court cases from the twentieth century. However, 60 cases are from lower courts and some nineteenth-century cases are necessary to show the development of government. "Sensationalistic" trials such as that of O. J. Simpson and Ted Kaczynski are covered in sidebars rather than the main text.

No actual cases appear in the set. These are much more readable case discussions whose language is aimed at high school, college, and public library readers. The case discussions are 750 to 2,000 words. Each case profile contains the legal citation of the actual case and a fact box that lists the party names, the attorneys and judges, a one-sentence summary, and a description of the significance of the case. Following the case discussions are a list of related cases and a bibliography. A preface describing the set and a short article describing the content, process, and procedure of the American legal system introduce each volume. Each topic within the volume begins with a few pages of general information about that particular area of law.

This set is extremely easy to use. Each volume has a detailed table of contents for that volume plus abbreviated tables of contents for the other three volumes. At the end of each volume there are an alphabetic list of court cases and a chronological list of court cases for that volume only. Each volume has an identical 30-page glossary containing 600 words and phrases. A valuable feature is the cumulative index that appears in and covers all four volumes. The index includes case names; however, an attorney index would have been helpful.

This is a valuable and interesting set for reference or browsing. The editors do explain that less than 10 percent of the cases were previously covered in *Women's Rights on Trial* (see ARBA 98, entry 563) or *Great American Trials* (see ARBA 96, entry 613). Considering the cost of this set, the popularity of those titles might dictate the necessity of its purchase. [R: BR, Nov/Dec 99, p. 87]—**Bev Cummings Agnew**

524. Jost, Kenneth. **The Supreme Court Yearbook 1997-1998.** Washington, D.C., Congressional Quarterly, 1999. 325p. illus. index. $38.95; $30.95pa. ISBN 1-56802-411-8; 1-56802-411-Xpa. ISSN 1054-2701.

The Supreme Court Yearbook 1995-1996 was reviewed in ARBA 97 (see entry 603), and the format and style of this source has not changed since then. Jost has been the author since the 1992-1993 edition. Highlighted cases in the overview chapter include several that concerned sexual harassment, one that considered the rights of people with HIV under the Americans with Disabilities Act, and the nullification of the Line Item Veto Act. The chapter that provides case summaries of all the Court's decisions in this term is divided into 13 broad subject areas, such as environmental law, First Amendment, and torts. The text is supplemented by several tables and graphs as well as a few photographs (including one of performance artist Karen Finley with her body partly covered in chocolate to dramatize the sexual oppression of women). Jost writes in a clear and incisive style that is consistent with that of other Congressional Quarterly reporters and researchers. Although there are evaluative and analytic statements made, these are nonpartisan in tone and are generally supported by factual evidence or quotations from sources. Although all public and academic libraries will find it useful, this yearbook should be particularly helpful for smaller libraries where the complete texts of Supreme Court decisions are not available.—**Jack Ray**

525. Lively, Donald E. **Landmark Supreme Court Cases: A Reference Guide.** Westport, Conn., Greenwood Press, 1999. 374p. index. $59.95. ISBN 0-313-30602-8.

This book provides overviews (averaging 4 pages each) of 75 Supreme Court decisions, and is thematically organized in 4 broad areas—separation and distribution of powers, power to regulate or affect the national economy, equality concepts, and individual rights and liberties. Each broad area is further subdivided into several chapters that allow readers to focus on particular topics (e.g., the power of the president, racial issues, freedom of the press). "Landmark" decisions, as defined by Lively, are those that "both mark how governmental power is exercised and point the way toward economic, social, or political change." Not all of these cases are the current law of the land, such as the 1857 *Dred Scott v. Sanford* decision, which held that no person of African descent could be a citizen, but all of them were instrumental in the historical shaping of the law. Lively's discussions of the cases are clearly written and have sidebars that give basic data (e.g., citation, issue, year of decision, outcome, author of the opinion, the vote) that will make this source a helpful study guide.

There are bibliographic notes at the end of each case, although citations to books do not include publisher information. Perhaps the most serious drawback of this book is that there is no easy way to locate a particular case; although an appendix lists the cases alphabetically, there are no page references, and the cases are not listed in either the table of contents or index. Nevertheless, this will be a useful resource for academic and public library reference collections. [R: BR, Nov/Dec 99, p. 87]—**Jack Ray**

526. Olson, Kent C. **Legal Information: How to Find It, How to Use It.** Phoenix, Ariz., Oryx Press, 1999. 333p. index. $59.00; $39.95pa. ISBN 0-89774-961-8; 0-89774-963-4pa.

Modeled on Michael R. Lavin's *Business Information* (Oryx, 1992), "this volume aims to explain where legal information is located, whether in general libraries, in law libraries, or electronically, and to provide the background knowledge necessary to make effective use of that information" (p. vii). It emphasizes materials available in general libraries and on the Internet. Part 1 provides an overview of the U.S. legal system, dictionaries and guides to legal language, legal citations and abbreviations, and research guides. Part 2 covers general reference sources, law books, journals and periodicals, and finding lawyers and institutions. Part 3 turns to federal law, including the U.S. Constitution and the Supreme Court, federal legislation, federal courts, and federal administrative law. Part 4 focuses on state law, including state legislation, administrative law, and state courts. In each part, specific resources are analyzed for their good and bad points. For example *Black's Law Dictionary* (West Publishing, 1990) is one of the most extensive legal dictionaries, but contains many obsolete terms and needs modernization. Illustrations from various resources complement the text. The $8\frac{1}{2}$-by-11-inch page size, two-column-per-page, clean layout is easy to read. Olson nicely weaves discussion of the materials' points into an easily understood narrative. Budding lawyers and laypersons seeking insights into legal research will find this volume helpful. It may also be used for specialized library school reference courses. [R: Choice, July/Aug 99, p. 1929]—**Esther R. Sinofsky**

527. Palmer, Louis J., Jr. **The Death Penalty: An American Citizen's Guide to Understanding Federal and State Laws.** Jefferson, N.C., McFarland, 1998. 285p. index. $39.95. ISBN 0-7864-0444-2.

Palmer's book provides a clear and coherent guide to the death penalty in the United States. To paraphrase Supreme Court Justice Thurgood Marshall's opinion in the 1972 Supreme Court capital punishment case *Furman v. Georgia*, the American public does not understand the reality of the death penalty. Palmer's book will help anyone come to understand the legal complexities that surround the capital punishment debate in today's society. There is no attempt to proselytize here. The material presents information relevant to the legal realities of the death penalty. The book is divided into four parts. Part 1 provides a brief background on the common-law influences on the death penalty, the position of the Eighth Amendment on the death penalty, and death-eligible offenses. Part 2 examines prosecutorial issues, such as the role of the prosecutor in criminal justice cases, the discretionary power prosecutors have in bringing a penalty case to trial, the indictment, and prosecuting a "nontriggerman." Part 3 offers information relating to the court proceedings, including the capital penalty phase of a capital trial, aggravating and mitigating circumstances relevant to a determination of sentence, and the appellate review of a death sentence. Part 4 explains barriers to execution, witnessing an execution, and execution methods. There are tables and boxes throughout the book that make points and issues dramatically clear. For example, there is a murder time clock, a table of murder weapons used from 1990 to 1994, a table of aggravating circumstances of murder from 1990 to 1995, and age and gender of murderers in 1994. The book contains an appendix of eight tables of selected death penalty provisions, an appendix of federal death penalty laws, and concludes with a glossary, chapter notes, a bibliography (including death penalty sentencing statutes, books, articles, and cases), and an index. This work is highly recommended. [R: BR, Sept/Oct 98, p. 76]—**Michael A. Foley**

528. Renstrom, Peter G. **Constitutional Rights Sourcebook.** Santa Barbara, Calif., ABC-CLIO, 1999. 770p. index. $75.00. ISBN 1-57607-061-1.

The constitutional rights treated in this book are found in 5 of the first 10 amendments (the 1st, 4th, 5th, 6th, and 8th) to the Constitution as well as the 14th Amendment. The Bill of Rights amendments not discussed have not played a critical role in the defining of individual constitutional rights, with the possible exception of the 2d Amendment, which concerns the controversial right to bear arms. Each amendment is accorded its own chapter; each of the various rights protected by the amendment is given a separate section that includes a synopsis of the salient Supreme Court cases that have gone into defining the right. The Equal Protection clause of the 14th Amendment and the right of privacy, which has been construed from various parts of the Bill of Rights, are treated in a separate chapter.

Although the text is clearly organized and written, the short overviews that briefly mention each court case that is discussed later in the chapter are not very helpful. The book begins with an introduction to the Constitution and Supreme Court; appendixes feature the text of the Constitution, a list of Supreme Court justices, and a fascinating chart that shows the changing composition of the Supreme Court since 1900. Altogether, this is a well-executed introduction to basic constitutional rights. It would be equally appropriate for the reference or general collection in most public and academic libraries. [R: LJ, 1 Sept 99, pp. 182-183]—**Jack Ray**

529. Sitarz, Daniel. **Laws of the United States: Corporations.** Carbondale, Ill., Nova Publishing, 1999. 223p. (Quick Reference Law). $16.95pa. ISBN 0-935755-67-5.

This is a useful reference book that contains not the laws relevant to corporations, but where to find those laws in every state and the District of Columbia. This title is part of the Quick Reference Law series, whose purpose is to provide concise, comprehensive, and authoritative guides to the laws of the states in specific legal areas. Certainly this title has fulfilled the purpose of the series.

Four or five pages for each state include the following helpful information: the address (but not the telephone number) for the appropriate corporation department, such as the Secretary of State's office; a citation to that state's statute; the title of the corporate filing document; and the fees. Listed are the requirements for the corporate name, the corporate purpose, the director, paid-in capital, publication, assumed name, shareholder, and records. Also included are the corporation's duration, the stock share regulations, corporate powers, amendments, and bylaws. The information from the statutes "has been abridged for clarity and succinctness."

A caveat suggests checking for the most current information. Although the publishing date of 1999 is some guidance, it would have been useful to include in the introduction the date upon which the compiled information was current.

A 1998 Investor Responsibility Research Center publication by Grant A. Gartman and Jack D. Isaacs entitled "Corporate Governance State by State: A Guide to Selected Statutes," will be more useful for legal patrons. It does not, however, contain the information on the corporation's office for each state. More sophisticated patrons may want Websites and e-mail addresses for the appropriate offices; neither are found here. Nevertheless, this handy and inexpensive compilation will be useful in any public library.
—**Bev Cummings Agnew**

530. Sitarz, Daniel. **Laws of the United States: Divorce.** Carbondale, Ill., Nova Publishing, 1999. 191p. (Quick Reference Law Series). $16.95pa. ISBN 0-935755-68-3.

The purpose of this book is to provide concise, comprehensive, and authoritative guides to the law of all states regarding divorce. The publication is alphabetic by state and gives residency requirements and where to file, legal grounds for divorce, name of court in which to file for divorce, legal separation, simplified or special divorce procedures, meditation or counseling requirements, alimony or maintenance spousal agreements, spouse name change, child custody, child support, and premarital agreements. The major drawback of legal publications is that laws can and do change, so one must always check to see if laws have changed since the material was published. The language of the publication is more geared to the layperson than is the *Martindale-Hubbell Law Digest: United States*, whose language is much more legalistic. The subject covered here is more complete than in the above-mentioned publication. This is an inexpensive book that all public libraries ought to purchase for their collection.—**Theresa Maggio**

531. **U.S. Court Cases.** Englewood Cliffs, N.J., Salem Press, 1999. 2v. illus. index. (Magill's Choice). $95.00/set. ISBN 0-89356-422-2.

This source consists of 2 principal parts: 13 essays on "Law and the Courts," and 212 overviews of court cases, arranged alphabetically. The essays are mostly on very broad topics (e.g., justice, jurisprudence, Anglo-American legal systems), but taken as a whole they provide a fairly comprehensive introduction to the American justice system. They comprise about 20 percent of the 2-volume source. The U.S. Supreme Court decided most of the cases that are outlined, but some are from lower federal or state courts. While the length varies, the case articles average about 500 words. Each has a pithy one-sentence summary of the significance of the decision at its beginning. All of the general essays, as well as a few of the more important cases, have bibliographies. There is a more extensive bibliography at the end of the set. Other supplementary materials include the text of the U.S. Constitution and an annotated list of Supreme Court justices. The articles and essays are all signed by a total of 86 scholars, whose names and affiliations are separately listed. The writing is clear and intended for general readers. Readers should note that the alphabetic arrangement makes this source, at least in part, a kind of "Masterplots" for court cases, rather than one that is organized by topic and uses case outlines to show the development of legal doctrine. Also, as acknowledged in the publisher's note, "all articles in these volumes originally appeared in other Salem Press publications." In particular, "the thirteen overview chapters are taken from *American Justice and Survey of Social Science: Government and Politics* (1995)." Eight other Salem Press publications are named as sources of the court case articles. Hence, although it is useful to have all these pieces gathered together in this set, buyers should be aware that it is largely repackaged material. With that caveat, it is highly recommended for most public and academic libraries. [R: BR, Nov/Dec 99, pp. 87-88]—**Jack Ray**

CRIMINOLOGY AND CRIMINAL JUSTICE

Biography

532. Bijlefeld, Marjolijn. **People for and Against Gun Control: A Biographical Reference.** Westport, Conn., Greenwood Press, 1999. 324p. illus. index. (The Greenwood Press "People Making a Difference" Series). $49.95. ISBN 0-313-30690-7.

As both accidental and deliberate shootings occur more frequently in upscale neighborhoods and young people are increasingly the targets, gun control becomes a more intense controversy. It is often a topic for student papers and debates. This volume, part of a series titled "People Making a Difference," is intended to help high school and college students involved in such projects to explore the complex issue of gun control through the lives of 50 people who are very much involved in the debate. They include doctors, elected officials, lobbyists for various organizations, and victims. The one trait they all have in common is their dedication to making a safer society.

Preceding the biographies is an excellent introduction by the author that covers the main elements of the gun control debate; the roles of law enforcement, gun manufacturers, health professionals, and others; statistics; and public opinion. The profiles contain such information as where and when the person was born, family background, education, and present position. More important, however, is the story of how each of these persons became involved in the gun control debate, the contributions they have made to the movement, and the obstacles they have faced from the opposition. Readings by or about the person are appended to each profile and photos frequently accompany the text. Material appended to the main section is helpful in itself, but also to a certain extent in evaluating the evenhandedness of the author. Included are summaries of state and federal gun control laws and state constitutional clauses relating to the right to bear arms; lists of the biographies by pro- and anti-gun control legislation, by profession, and by states represented; a general bibliography; and an index.

All of the profiles were written by the author, a freelance writer and former director of the Educational Fund to End Gun Violence. She also worked with the Coalition to End Gun Violence—activities that obviously put her in the pro-gun control category and would most likely raise questions about her objectivity in presenting both sides of the issue fairly. The text itself, however, gives no indication of bias. Neither is any bias shown in the selection of those profiled—25 for gun control and 25 against it—nor was any detected in the types of persons or geographical locations, as both showed a wide variation. The value of this work is that it presents gun control issues from a different perspective than what students usually find available. The profiles are well written and compelling; they enable the student to consider a reasoned presentation of an opposing viewpoint. It would be particularly helpful for students taking a pro or con side in the gun control debate. Although recommended for school and college libraries, it would also be useful for public libraries where interest in the subject is high.—**Lucille Whalen**

Handbooks and Yearbooks

533. Altschiller, Donald. **Hate Crimes: A Reference Handbook.** Santa Barbara, Calif., ABC-CLIO, 1999. 204p. index. (Contemporary World Issues). $45.00. ISBN 0-87436-937-1.

ABC-CLIO's Contemporary World Issues series offers authoritative and clear guides to some of the most critical social issues. For example, the series includes guides to affirmative action, censorship, feminism, victims' rights, and welfare reform, to name a few. These guides are useful at all levels of research, including high school. In general, the guides share the same basic format and organization. *Hate Crimes* begins with some general background information on a few major targeted groups (e.g., African Americans, gay men and lesbians, Asian Americans). This brief but useful chapter ends with a history of hate crimes legislation (both federal and state), U.S. Supreme Court decisions, and a brief overview of the opponents of hate crime legislation. Chapter 2 provides an excellent chronology of hate crimes from 1955 to 1999. Chapter 3 lists biographical sketches of some prominent individuals engaged in confronting and challenging racism and bigotry in our society. One of the more interesting sketches is that of Floyd Cochran, an avowed racist who came to recognize the destructiveness of hate and now speaks out against hate groups. Chapter 4 offers vital statistics and documents on hate crimes. This section is extremely useful and informative. Chapter 5 is a directory of organizations that monitor hate crimes and extremist groups. Chapters 6 and 7, covering some 50 pages, list print and nonprint resources on hate crimes. These two chapters are vital to people beginning research on this issue. The book concludes with a good index. This resource is highly recommended for al libraries and anyone seeking information about hate crimes.—**Michael A. Foley**

534. **Capital Punishment in the United States: A Documentary History.** Bryan Vila and Cynthia Morris, eds. Westport, Conn., Greenwood Press, 1997. 337p. index. (Primary Documents in American History and Contemporary Issues). $49.95. ISBN 0-313-29942-0.

This excellent volume features over 100 documents relating to various aspects of the capital punishment debate in the U.S. The book is arranged in six chronological sections, starting with the colonial era and the biblical arguments on which colonial capital punishment laws were based. The book includes a brief but informative introduction and each chronological section begins with a discussion of the trends in capital punishment in the period. Each document is preceded by a statement that places the document in context and identifies the author where appropriate. The documents are well chosen and include scholarly articles, book excerpts, position statements, legislation, court documents such as Supreme Court rulings, items relating to high-profile cases (e.g., the Rosenbergs, Gary Gilmore), and newspaper articles. There is a glossary of legal terms, a list of federal and state capital offenses, a table of numbers of executions from 1600 to 1995, a directory of relevant organizations, and a select bibliography.

The compilers have met their goal to provide a variety of perspectives on the major issues relating to capital punishment (e.g., religious and moral arguments, deterrence, irrevocability) and users will find a wide range of materials. The volume provides an excellent overview of the debate on capital punishment and may well meet the documents needs of the general public and high school and college students, while providing a good starting place for more advanced researchers. This book is highly recommended for public, academic, and special libraries.—**Gari-Anne Patzwald**

535. **City Crime Rankings: Crime in Metropolitan America.** 5th ed. Kathleen O'Leary Morgan and Scott Morgan, eds. Lawrence, Kans., Morgan Quitno Press, 1999. 400p. index. $19.95pa. ISBN 1-56692-331-X. ISSN 1081-6453.

Based on data taken from *Crime in the United States 1997*, published by the Federal Bureau of Investigation, *City Crime Rankings* is an analysis of eight types of crime (murder, rape, robbery, aggravated assault, property, burglary, larceny/theft, and motor vehicle theft) in metropolitan areas with a population exceeding 75,000. As such, it provides a ready-reference source of statistical data. Unfortunately, because information was not available for some cities (e.g., Chicago, Cleveland, Philadelphia), the results are incomplete.

The editors manipulate the data in a variety of ways. The tables are arranged in rank and alphabetic order, for both city and metro areas, for each of the eight specific crimes. Appendixes include demographics on metropolitan and major cities.

Morgan Quitno Press awards one community each year its "Safest City and Metropolitan Area" award. The award is the result of comparing the community's crime rates in six areas against national rates, with an undisclosed formula. A subjective telephone survey was also employed. This year's winner, Amherst, New York, has won three times in a row.

Much of the material included in this work can be found in other sources, including the World Wide Web. This work does provide a unified approach to disparate information. The researcher who uses the book, however, must keep in mind that the statistics are from 1997, and that at least seven major metropolitan areas are not included in the rankings.—**Michele Tyrrell**

536. **Crime State Rankings 1999: Crime in the 50 United States.** 6th ed. Kathleen O'Leary Morgan and Scott Morgan, eds. Lawrence, Kans., Morgan Quitno Press, 1999. 508p. index. $49.95pa. ISBN 1-56692-334-4. ISSN 1077-4408.

At century's end the overall drop in the rate of conventional crime, including violent crime, has been quite remarkable. Various possible reasons for this drop have been offered, but it remains to be seen whether this trend will continue in the new century. Nevertheless, concern with crime endures. This reference work, now in its 6th edition, seeks to provide users with a wealth of statistical data pertaining to crime and criminal justice, and is formatted to facilitate interstate comparisons. Single state volumes are also available from this publisher, and a companion volume, now in its 5th edition, compares crime data for major American cities. Altogether, the present volume includes 508 tables. The data for most of these tables are current through 1997, although in some cases only through earlier years (1993 to 1996).

This volume includes seven major sections: arrests, corrections, drug and alcohol, finance, juveniles, law enforcement, and offenses. Additional sections make comparisons between urban and rural crime, and provide data comparing crime rates in 1993 and 1997—highlighting changes. An appendix includes several tables on population data. The section on arrest rates for conventional crimes (and some nonpredatory crimes, such as prostitution) includes tables on ranks between the states for each offense, absolute numbers, and the state's percentage of all such arrests nationally. The corrections section documents the enormous, current size of the correctional populations, with breakdowns on such variables as race and gender, correctional facility and status, and the death penalty. With 82 tables, this is the largest section. A 3d section on drugs and alcohol provides data on attributes of patients in treatment programs (i.e., by gender and race), and on expenditures for such programs. The finance section documents the substantial governmental expenditures on justice-related activities (with per capita expenditures highlighted). The tables in this section specifically compare state and local government expenditures. A section on juveniles, which was not part of the original volume published in 1994, consists mainly of juvenile arrest rates for conventional offenses, with some tables on treatment admissions and rates of reported abuse of children. The section on law enforcement agencies provides breakdowns on such matters as number of different categories of law enforcement officers, percentages of full and part-time workers, and criminal case filings. The final major section, on a range of conventional offenses, includes information on percent changes between 1996 and 1997, and on the use of different weapons. In light of the debate on gun control some of this data should be of particular interest.

This volume opens with a ranking of the 50 states, from most dangerous (Nevada) to least dangerous (North Dakota). This ranking is based upon data for six major conventional crimes, and weights assigned to these different crimes. Altogether, the 508 tables published here are laid out in an easy-to-read format, and a variety of information finding tools are provided. State rankings are a uniform feature of the tables.

The major limitation of this volume is the absence of any interpretive discussion of the limitations of all such statistical, comparative data on crime and criminal justice. Accordingly, those who consult these tables may be prone to unsophisticated and distorted readings of the data contained therein. With that caveat in mind *Crime State Rankings 1999* can certainly be said to contain a wealth of useful information about crime and criminal justice in the United States at the end of the twentieth century.—**David O. Friedrichs**

537. Hearn, Daniel Allen. **Legal Executions in New England: A Comprehensive Reference, 1623-1960.** Jefferson, N.C., McFarland, 1999. 444p. index. $75.00. ISBN 0-7864-0670-4.

Both sides of the capital punishment debate are interested in records of who has been executed and for what reason. Such records can help one decide or argue that past executions have or have not been fairly and appropriately applied, for instance, across ethnic or socioeconomic groups. Hearn is one of several authors who have researched archives and court records to make information on those executed readily available; he previously published a book on executions in New York State (see ARBA 98, entry 554). Those executed are listed by year, then alphabetically; information on each person executed ranges from a paragraph to several pages. For each, Hearn writes a brief that includes a biographical sketch, a description of the crime and its apparent motivation, and surrounding circumstances (e.g., public attitudes toward the event as evidenced in newspaper accounts), and circumstances of the execution. All information from contemporary sources is summarized by Hearn for the reader's convenience, but he cites the sources of information for each person at the end of the book. Hearn's accounts appear to be relatively impartial. He makes a point of withholding his personal opinion on capital punishment, which he feels is not relevant. The accounts themselves are sometimes quite interesting. Most are seemingly straightforward, repulsive cases of crimes like murder and rape; a few are for offenses not now considered capital crimes, such as adultery and bestiality. The famous witchcraft executions are also included here. This is a useful, interesting, and well-documented resource for researchers on capital punishment and the history of social attitudes; it will be a useful addition to law, public, and academic libraries.—**Marit S. MacArthur**

538. Mack, Raneta Lawson. **A Layperson's Guide to Criminal Law.** Westport, Conn., Greenwood Press, 1999. 201p. index. $65.00. ISBN 0-313-30556-0.

Mack, a law professor at the Creighton University School of Law and a media legal consultant, has produced a straightforward, well-written, and comprehensible guide to criminal law for the nonlawyer. Following a brief explanation of the origins of criminal law and statutes, Mack clearly and concisely explains some of the fundamental concepts (voluntary act, mental states, liability, and so on) that serve as the basis for most criminal statutes. Case studies (hypothetical and actual) are often included to further illustrate and elucidate the concepts. Different categories of specific criminal cases (murder, manslaughter, sexual assault, and theft) are also thoughtfully examined, as is the criminal process itself from arrest, trial, and verdict. Each chapter concludes with a few questions designed to stimulate thought and discussion on the various concepts under consideration. A glossary of 76 terms relating to criminal law is also provided.

CNN, Court TV, and other television media outlets now commonly televise high-profile criminal cases. Who can forget the O.J. Simpson trial and its attendant mind-numbing "legalese" spouted by attorneys like Greta Van Susteren and Roger Cossack? Mack's guide would have proved useful in cutting through the rhetoric to a real understanding of the basic legal principles of the controversial case. Academic, public, and law libraries already owning Dean J. Champion's *Dictionary of American Criminal Justice: Key Terms and Major Supreme Court Cases* (see ARBA 99, entry 576) will want to purchase Mack's guide for the layperson.—**David K. Frasier**

539. Rafter, Nicole Hahn, and Debra L. Stanley. **Prisons in America: A Reference Handbook.** Santa Barbara, Calif., ABC-CLIO, 1999. 226p. index. (Contemporary World Issues). $45.00. ISBN 1-57607-102-2.

A few startling facts: the United States spends an estimated $30 billion a year to house in excess of 1 million men and women in more than 1,000 state and federal penal institutions. With 450 people for each 100,000 in the general population behind bars, the United States has the highest rate of incarceration in the world. In this volume in ABC-CLIO's well-regarded Contemporary World Issues series, Rafter, chair of the Crime, Law, and Deviance section of the American Sociological Association, and Stanley, an assistant professor of criminology and criminal justice at Central Connecticut State University, present a concise and useful starting point for research on this timely topic. Following a brief historical overview of the prison system since colonial times, including various attempts at penal reform, the authors examine the on-going debate over rehabilitation versus punishment. Of particular interest is a chapter on issues and controversies that identify and address conflicting positions in penology. These include the purposes of incarceration, sentencing options, prisoners' rights, health care in prisons, and the trend toward private prisons run by corporations. Short biographies are presented for 23 individuals (philosophers, jurists, prisoners, reformers, administrators, researchers) who have contributed to the development of American prisons. Other sections include documents and statistics (with heavy emphasis on prisoners' rights cases), prison data (sentencing, prisoner characteristics), an annotated list with contact information for 52 agencies and organizations, annotated bibliographies for print and nonprint resources, Internet addresses, and a short glossary. Rafter and Stanley have done a creditable job packaging a mountain of information into a clear, well-written introduction to the topic geared toward the high school and undergraduate researcher. [R: LJ, 15 Nov 99, pp. 61-62]—**David K. Frasier**

540. **The Role of Police in American Society: A Documentary History.** Bryan Vila and Cynthia Morris, eds. Westport, Conn., Greenwood Press, 1999. 318p. index. (Primary Documents in American History and Contemporary Issues). $49.95. ISBN 0-313-30164-6.

Throughout the twentieth century the American police played the frontline role in the war on conventional crime, but the police also assumed great significance at the center of social controversies involving such matters as race relations and ideological dissidence. Furthermore, both the character of policing and the demographic composition of the police force underwent some measurable changes during this century, especially in its final decades. The present volume, written and compiled by a criminal justice professor with a policing background and a professional writer, provides readers with a valuable overview of the interesting, if contentious, history of the police in America, beginning in the seventeenth century.

The Role of Police in American Society is divided into seven parts, each representing a noteworthy period in the development of American policing. The first three parts address the seminal origins of policing, beginning with implementation of the Boston Night Watch in 1631 through critiques of the police in the 1920s. The period between 1930 and 1959 is characterized by a growing emphasis on police training, professionalism, efficiency, and ethics. In the 1960s and 1970s the police experienced rapid and sometimes tumultuous social change, and confronted conflicting expectations. The 1980s were identified as a period of reexamination and redefining of the police role. A concluding part considers the role of the police in the final decade of the twentieth century. Each part reprints diverse documents pertaining to police history during these periods, including excerpts from laws or legal proclamations, constitutional amendments and appellate court opinions, journalistic accounts, autobiographical works, and social science or interpretive studies.

Altogether the authors and editors of this volume have done a fine job of selecting pertinent and informative documents from the long history of policing in America. They have surely succeeded in meeting their own criteria of reprinting both historically representative documents and documents addressing a broad array of issues relating to the police. They have also provided substantial introductory comments that place documents in an appropriate sociohistorical context. Glossaries list U.S. Supreme Court cases bearing on police work, and police-related groups, organizations, and Websites. The selective bibliography includes many essential books and articles.

Perhaps the weakest feature in this volume is a list of significant dates, since for recent years the publication of an article included in this volume is identified as a significant event in police history. But altogether a wealth of useful and often interesting information for students of American policing can be found here.

—David O. Friedrichs

ENVIRONMENTAL LAW

541. Abbey, Buck. **U.S. Landscape Ordinances: An Annotated Reference Handbook.** New York, John Wiley, 1998. 438p. index. $74.95. ISBN 0-471-29276-1.

This publication makes available for the first time a national listing of community landscape ordinances and serves as a valuable reference for professionals who work with this type of legislation. In addition, this resource provides an opportunity to analyze existing "green laws" to demonstrate the impact that they have had on our environment and urban design. A greater understanding of these planning tools could assist city planners, architects, landscape architects, and engineers who are responsible for directing growth and preserving the native landscape character of developing urban areas.

The table of contents includes entries for 41 states. The main body of the text includes an alphabetic list of annotated ordinances for some 300 cities within these states. The annotations are summaries that explain the main purpose and regulatory function of each ordinance in a manner that emphasizes its spirit and uniqueness. Many of the annotations are accompanied by useful tables and illustrations. An appendix entitled "Model and Specimen Green Laws" is provided to assist communities in planning their own landscape ordinances. Another appendix is a directory of city planning agencies, with contact information for readers seeking the full text of a given ordinance. There is a concluding glossary, selected bibliography, and subject index. A particular strength of this book is the preface and introduction, which clearly articulate the goals and significance of this work, the background and history of landscape ordinances, the methodology employed in the compilation of the work, and a complete description of how to read and understand the annotations provided. This work is highly recommended for all students and professionals involved in landscape design and municipal planning.—**Michael Weinberg**

542. Bryner, Gary C. **U.S. Land and Natural Resources Policy: A Public Issues Handbook.** Westport, Conn., Greenwood Press, 1998. 292p. index. $95.00. ISBN 0-313-29688-X.

The national debate over how best to administer and use public lands in America is vital, whether citizens realize it or not. This is because public lands provide the resources that contribute to ecological sustainability of all living systems. Long viewed only as an economic base for extractive resources, public lands are now seen by many as a resource for recreation or renewal and environmental stability. At conflict with this are others who are most concerned with the protection of private property rights. At this turn of the century, governmental policies on grazing, mining, timber, water, and wilderness are as conflicted and important as ever. Bryner's handbook on public lands and natural resources policy is an important contribution to understanding and debating these crucial issues.

"The purpose [of this handbook] is to bring together the relevant data and to outline the major issues that are at the heart of the debate over public lands." A comprehensive and systematic assessment of the issues includes environmental conditions, problems, trends, major laws and regulations, policy-making structures, and political context. The strengths and weaknesses of alternative positions are informative to readers and focus their opinions. Bryner was director of the Public Policy Program and professor of political science at Brigham Young University. He recently became director of the Natural Resource Law Center at the University of Colorado.

The book is well organized, easy to read, well documented, and has many informative charts. Chapter 1 gives an overview of the politics of public lands; chapter 2 traces their history while chapter 3 reviews legal issues and the governmental bureaucracy affecting natural resources and public lands. Chapters 4 through 9 analyze policy goals for specific natural resource topics (biodiversity, logging, grazing, mining, water, and wilderness). Chapter 10 is a summary that also explores the values underlying the national debate over public lands and natural resource policy. Anyone concerned with the future, especially policy makers and environmental studies students, will find this book a valuable resource and reference.—**Georgia Briscoe**

543. **Environmental Law Handbook.** 15th ed. Thomas F. P. Sullivan, ed. Rockville, Md., Government Institutes, 1999. 697p. index. $79.00. ISBN 0-86587-650-9. ISSN 0147-7714.

Although environmental law in some form has existed for many years, the field has become enormously more complex in the last 30 years or so, primarily because of the greatly increased statutory and regulatory involvement at the federal level. This handbook is intended as an overview of the major areas of the law for persons without a legal background, particularly those who are working in areas in which compliance with environmental laws is necessary. The book succeeds in this objective for two reasons: first, the authors, although they are all attorneys who specialize in environmental law, write in a clear and straightforward style that will be understandable to educated general readers; and second, the book is admirably organized. Each of the 16 chapters is written by one of the handbook's 15 authors and deals with either a general topic (e.g., underground storage tanks, pesticides) or a specific federal act (e.g., Clean Water Act, Toxic Substances Control Act). The chapters are divided into short subparts and sub-subparts, and all of these chapter subunits are listed in the table of contents, making scanning of detailed contents easy. Nearly every page has footnotes to regulations, statutes, and court cases, obviating the need for a lot of flipping around. One understandable limitation that the editor makes clear at the beginning is that this book does not cover natural resource laws (e.g., Endangered Species Act), but only those that are intended to protect human environment, health, and safety. Most public and academic libraries will find this handbook useful.—**Jack Ray**

544. Goldsteen, Joel B. **ABCs of Environmental Regulation.** Rockville, Md., Government Institutes, 1999. 294p. illus. index. $49.00pa. ISBN 0-86587-629-0.

There are few books written to make sense of the multitude of environmental laws and regulations of the United States. This book, however, does a commendable job of providing the basics of the bewildering set of government programs and laws that have multiplied over the years. Goldsteen, a professor of urban affairs at the University of Texas, wrote the book to provide his students with a comprehensive structure of the regulations and their controlling agencies. To do this, he uses clear and succinct explanations, brevity, large print, and frequent bold section headings. Photographs and sidebars enhance the ease of usage, as do endnotes, a glossary, an appendix, and an index.

The book is organized into seven sections. Section 1 gives the governmental programmatic framework and outlines the major environmental laws in 2 to 4 pages, such as the "National Environmental Policy Act." The remaining six sections have laws on the subjects of air, water, waste and tanks, safety, responding to contaminant releases, and nature and natural resources. For example, section 2 on air has a chapter on the Clean Air Act, the Noise Control Act, and the Airport Noise Abatement Act. Each chapter is further organized for easy understanding, with an overview at the start of the chapter and a chronology of the laws with full citations at the end.

Although the book presents only elemental information, it does so with enough references that a researcher could easily move into more detail with other sources such as the *Environmental Law Handbook* (see entry 543), or a similarly titled book published by the Bureau of National Affairs. This book will be useful in many types of libraries, which need to provide the "big picture" of the U.S. environmental scene.—**Georgia Briscoe**

HUMAN RIGHTS

545. **Human Rights: The Essential Reference.** Hilary Poole, ed. Phoenix, Ariz., Oryx Press, 1999. 311p. illus. index. $89.95. ISBN 1-57356-205-X.

Human rights, both as a social and a legal concept, has been very much in the news in the latter part of the twentieth century. Not surprisingly, many books and articles have attempted to clarify this concept, particularly as conflicts arise from varying perceptions of what is included in human rights. This volume, compiled by international scholars from different fields and human rights activists, provides an overall view of human rights and its role in the modern world. The work is organized into 4 parts, with the 1st being devoted to a history of human rights from the classical world up to 1948, the time of the adoption of the Universal Declaration of Human Rights (UDHR), which is generally considered to be the beginning of modern human rights theory. The 2d part is a discussion of the background of the UDHR and each of its 30 articles. Part 3 covers the contemporary human rights movement, including an overview of events, policies, and controversies; information on related organizations, both governmental and nongovernmental; and biographies of people associated with the movement, such as Aung San Suu Kyi, who was awarded the Nobel Peace Prize for her struggle for human rights in her native Burma (Myanmar), and Wang Dan, a student activist who was imprisoned for his role in the 1989 Tiananmen Square uprising. The last part presents a discussion of contemporary human rights issues, such as child soldiers, police brutality, and the death penalty. Appendixes provide a timeline of important human rights events throughout history, texts of selected United Nations documents, a bibliography, and a list identifying each of the nine contributors to the volume.

The material is organized in a way that makes it relatively easy to find specific information on any aspect of human rights but also to get a more detailed view of areas such as history and current issues. The articles are well written and generally free of technical jargon. The sections explaining the various articles of the UDHR, for example, would be useful for teaching this basic document on all levels—a practice that has only recently been incorporated into academic curricula. One section raises a serious question, however, and that is the section on the full-text documents included. While the inclusion of documents adds considerably to the value of the work, it is curious that of the eight UN documents included, most are "Declarations," which are considered nonbinding principles, even though there are now "Conventions," or legally binding agreements, covering these topics. For example, the Declaration of the Rights of the Child, consisting of 10 principles set forth in 1959, is included, but the Convention on the Rights of the Child, with its greatly expanded 54 articles, adopted in 1989 and legally binding on all states that ratified it, is not. Anyone wanting to discuss the rights of the child would most certainly prefer to see what is actually the present law rather than a set of principles compiled 30 years earlier. Interestingly, there are several references to the Convention in the index, but none to the Declaration. Perhaps a glossary would be helpful in this regard.

Aside from this omission, the book is an excellent source of information on the many facets of human rights. It should be valuable not only for human rights workers and activists but also for teachers, students, journalists, and anyone interested in the subject. [R: BR, Nov/Dec 99, p. 87; LJ, 1 Nov 99, p. 71; Choice, Dec 99, p. 700]—**Lucille Whalen**

546. Langley, Winston E. **Encyclopedia of Human Rights Issues Since 1945.** Westport, Conn., Greenwood Press, 1999. 392p. index. $65.00. ISBN 0-313-30163-8.

Anyone in need of a succinct account of the chief provisions of the United Nations Declaration on the Rights of Mentally Retarded Persons, the Nuremberg war crimes trials, or the mission of Amnesty International is likely to find what they need in this reference tool. Specific entries answering any of these needs typify the range of topics covered in Langley's concise encyclopedia. Important documents, events, organizations, agencies, concepts, individual countries, persons, and issues are all presented here. The articles are well written and authoritative, although sometimes a little too deferential to current United Nations positions. They are also on the brief side—on average, a bit less than 1 page or 300 to 400 words. Except for very basic information or ready-reference needs, they will usually serve only as starting points for inquiry. It is fortunate, therefore, that each concludes with at least one to five references for further reading. Appendixes include the full texts of four declarations and covenants comprising the International Bill of Human Rights, plus the Convention on the Rights of the Child.

Most libraries apt to consider acquiring this work will already have alternative sources for much of the information gathered here. Still, the convenience of a single source may be compelling—where it is affordable and not redundant to an unjustifiable degree. Edward Lawson's far bulkier and pricier *Encyclopedia of Human Rights* (2d ed.; see ARBA 97, entry 517) covers much the same ground in greater depth, especially by including full texts of many more documents. Nonetheless, this work has a fair number of entries not offered by Lawson (the reverse is also true). R. Gorman and E. Mihalkanin's *Historical Dictionary of Human Rights and Humanitarian Organizations* (see ARBA 98, entry 564) also has considerable overlap in coverage, but takes in a broader sweep of history and is less in-depth on the post–World War II period.—**Hans E. Bynagle**

547. Redman, Nina, and Lucille Whalen. **Human Rights: A Reference Handbook.** 2d ed. Santa Barbara, Calif., ABC-CLIO, 1998. 301p. index. (Contemporary World Issues). $45.00. ISBN 1-57607-041-7.

Human Rights: A Reference Handbook is a well-written and timely monograph dealing with the many aspects and issues that concern human rights. A fairly comprehensive introductory chapter attempts to define human rights and to include historical, religious, legal, political, and philosophical foundations and development. A summary of the development of international human rights is included along with discussions of the United Nations, the United States, nongovernmental organizations, and human rights. International law and human rights and current human rights issues complete the introductory section.

Chapters include a chronology of the major human rights documents and events with brief descriptions that begin with 1941, and another has concise biographical sketches of individuals who have made significant contributions to human rights advancement. The majority of the book is devoted to chapter 4, which includes complete text for many selected human rights documents. The remaining chapters are bibliographies of organizations, print resources, and nonprint resources (including computer networks and databases). An index is included to aid the researcher. Redman and Whalen have produced an excellent resource for researchers or anyone needing information on a variety of human rights issues.—**Mary L. Trenerry**

548. Saha, Santosh. **Dictionary of Human Rights Advocacy Organizations in Africa.** Westport, Conn., Greenwood Press, 1999. 200p. index. $69.50. ISBN 0-313-30945-0.

The number of nongovernmental organizations (NGOs) has grown to such an extent that in 1999 a spring conference drew 8,000 NGO representatives from around the world. The impact of these groups has also resulted in two recently published books, *State of the World* (Norton Co., 1999) and *Civil Society* (NYU Press, 1999). Both of these titles examine the role of NGOs in society.

The focus of this dictionary is African NGOs currently active in human rights advocacy work. Of the 335 organizations listed, only 10 are non–African based. All the groups are concerned with ensuring civil, political, and economic human rights. Groups working for the rights of women and children are heavily represented. The range of organizations provides insight into the African human rights agenda, the current status of those rights, and the strategies of the groups.

Dictionary entries are in bold typeface. Acronyms and country of activity are also given. Annotations, ranging in length from a single sentence to 500 words, describe the purpose of the group, its relation to the country's government, and the effectiveness of its work to date. Citations to sources are provided. There is an appendix of African states with constitutional human rights provisions and one listing human rights declarations beginning with the Magna Carta. NGOs are indexed alphabetically and also by country. A subject index is not included.

This title should not be mistaken for a directory. No names, addresses, or other contact information is provided. The *Encyclopedia of Human Rights* (2d ed.; see ARBA 97, entry 517) and the *African Directory* (HRI, SIM, 1996) are excellent sources for this type of information. Human Rights Internet (HRI) also publishes a master list of human rights organizations. Afronet is an excellent source that can be searched online by geographic region and then by country. Many of the groups listed in this dictionary are included along with links to those having Websites.

For up-to-date information, in an area that changes with the political winds, Web sources are critical. For students and scholars of African history, political science, and Third World studies the dictionary is a record of African human rights issues and progress over the past 30 years. [R: Choice, Dec 99, p. 704]

—**Marlene M. Kuhl**

549. Sigler, Jay A. **Civil Rights in America: 1500 to the Present.** Farmington Hills, Mich., Gale, 1998. 710p. illus. index. $95.00. ISBN 0-7876-0612-X.

A comprehensive source on the struggle for civil rights in the United States, *Civil Rights in America* offers researchers broad coverage of ethnic, minority, and religious groups and the laws, people, events, court cases, and documents involved in their experience. Among the groups covered in this unique source are African, Asian, Hispanic, and Native North Americans, as well as immigrants, handicaps, gays and lesbians, teens, children, men, and women.

After the preface, introduction, acknowledgments, and credits, this book includes an extensive chronology beginning pre-1600s (5,000 to 8,000 B.C.E.) with events such as the finding of the Aztec's city of Tenochtitlán, Columbus's discovery of the Americas, Jacques Cartier's exploration of the Gulf of St. Lawrence, and the establishment of Quebec. The years 1600 to 1699 include such events as the Jamestown colony established by English settlers in Virginia and the Dutch founded colony of New Amsterdam. The years 1700 to 1799, 1800 to 1899, and 1900 to the present provide information on the Religious Freedom Act of 1993, which was declared unconstitutional by the Supreme Court in 1997.

The book is divided into 4 sections. The 1st section deals with civil rights through United States history, with the origins and limits of American rights and human rights in the twentieth-century United States. The 2d section deals with the civil rights of minority groups, such as African Americans; Asian Americans; Hispanic Americans; Native Americans; and immigrant groups of the Irish, Italians, Germans, Poles, Jews, Japanese, and Arabs. Section 3 discusses civil rights and government, including politics, policy-making, and the legal system. Topics explored are the politics of civil rights, including ending racial segregation in the United States, civil rights and government, the right to vote, education rights, housing rights, the criminal justice system, and the future of civil rights. The last section treats significant documents and major civil rights cases and includes historical documents and major civil rights case decisions. A glossary is provided as well as a table of the cases cited and a general bibliography.

Special biographical profiles are presented in the form of sidebars throughout the text. These focal points add interest and are useful for providing hard-to-find background information on contemporary figures.

Civil Rights in America goes beyond the scope of most existing civil rights titles, giving significant attention to nineteenth- and early twentieth-century U.S. civil rights as well as post-1950s civil rights issues. It offers an authoritative overview, discussion, and documentation. Once again, Gale has presented an excellent book on this most important subject. [R: BL, 15 Nov 98, p. 609]—**Barbara B. Goldstein**

550. Stein, Laura W. **Sexual Harassment in America: A Documentary History.** Westport, Conn., Greenwood Press, 1999. 297p. index. (Primary Documents in American History and Contemporary Issues). $49.95. ISBN 0-313-30184-0.

This collection of documents relating to the history of sexual harassment policy and litigation features 96 documents arranged in sections, including a general overview and definitions, employment, the military, education, housing, and 1998 U.S. Supreme Court cases. The emphasis is on federal law and policy, and major high-profile events are included (e.g., the Clarence Thomas hearing, Tailhook) as well as lesser-known but often equally important cases. Among the documents are laws, court decisions, government reports, congressional hearings, and newspaper and periodical articles. Each series of related documents begins with a brief introductory statement that places the documents in context. Each section concludes with a brief but potentially useful bibliography. The documents are carefully selected and well edited. This work provides an excellent introduction to resources for the study of a complex and evolving area in which there is wide interest. *Sexual Harassment in America* is highly recommended for libraries serving the general public and high school and college students. [R: BR, Sept/Oct 99, p. 82]—**Gari-Anne Patzwald**

11 Library and Information Science and Publishing and Bookselling

LIBRARY AND INFORMATION SCIENCE

Reference Works

Bibliographies

551. *Choice*'s **Outstanding Academic Books 1992-1997: Reviews of Scholarly Titles that Every Library Should Own.** Rebecca Ann Bartlett, ed. Chicago, American Library Association, Association of College and Research Libraries, 1998. 618p. index. $85.00. ISBN 0-8389-7929-7.

This compilation of 3,112 highly recommended books for undergraduate libraries was selected from titles previously reviewed in *Choice* magazine. According to the editor, the books were chosen from more than 22,000 scholarly and trade books examined annually, hence the present compilation consists of roughly $2\frac{1}{2}$ percent of all titles reviewed in the 6-year period. The selections cover most but not all academic subject areas. For example, there were no outstanding books listed for that period directly in either information science or librarianship.

The major criteria for selection are excellence of presentation, scholarship, overall significance, uniqueness, and importance to undergraduate library collection. However, because the process of applying these criteria was not fully described, it is not clear how the "outstanding" titles were distinguished from other important but perhaps less prominent publications. The reprinted, unabridged reviews are grouped in 5 categories: Reference, General, Humanities, Science and Technology, and Social and Behavioral Sciences, with discipline-specific subject subdivisions. Within each category the entries are arranged alphabetically by author. The indexes consist of book, author, title, and topical listings. Names of the reviewers, although printed, are not indexed. The individual sections are not limited by a predetermined number of reviews. Social and Behavioral Sciences is by far the largest category. The most numerous are the books in "Women's Studies," followed by "African and African American Studies."

This is an important compilation for undergraduate collections but not necessarily for every library, as its subtitle suggests. It will be particularly useful for any acquisition librarians who did not previously subscribe to the 1992 to 1997 editions of *Choice* magazine.—**Joseph Z. Nitecki**

552. **International Bibliography of Bibliographies in Library and Information Science and Related Fields. Volume 2, 1979-1990.** New Providence, N.J., K. G. Saur, 1999. 3v. index. $180.00/set. ISBN 3-598-11145-2.

One of the main critiques of American LIS literature is that it tends to ignore events beyond its borders. The profession's main index, *Library Literature* (1995 ed.; see ARBA 97, entry 529), can only mirror the situation. This tool to reviews one decade's worth of research in LIS and cognate fields. Sawoniak provides access to around 10,000 bibliographies in LIS from around the world. These bibliographies are more often review articles or original research, but Sawoniak lists the number of references per citation, and often a brief descriptive annotation. Maria Witt, Mediathèque de la Cité des Sciences (Paris), aided Sawoniak in the bibliography. The two also edited the *New International Dictionary of Acronyms in LIS and Related Fields* (2nd ed.; see ARBA 93, entry 621).

The value of the work is multiplied by the existence of indexes by author, title, personal name (subject), subject, and geographical place. These indexes are helpful, but not without several typographical flaws, such as the spelling of Wayne A. Wiegand as Wayne A. Wigand, John M. Tucker as Tukker, and Yoshitaka Kawasaki as Kavasaki in the bibliography. This high number of typographical errors detracts from the value of the work.

The geographical index is helpful, but also shows its linguistic limitations. For example, all 28 of the entries on Japan, and 8 on Israel, are limited to English-language articles appearing in journals published outside those countries, ignoring the fine LIS journals published in those countries. Many other countries are in similar situations. The number of such exceptions, and the fact that these were not critically evaluated (not even all citations were seen by the editors), make the bibliography somewhat weaker. Sawoniak's 1st volume covering 1945 to 1978 should be much more valuable for researchers. This work was published in 1985 in Poland as *Miedzynarodowa bibliografia bibliografii z zakresu informacji naukowej I dziedzin pokrewnych*, and contains over 7,000 entries. K. G. Saur will publish this more valuable work in the future as volume 1 with an addition of English-language notes.—**Andrew B. Wertheimer**

553. Meho, Lokman I., and Mona A. Nsouli, comps. **Libraries and Information in the Arab World: An Annotated Bibliography.** Westport, Conn., Greenwood Press, 1999. 349p. index. (Bibliographies and Indexes in Library and Information Science, no.12). $79.50. ISBN 0-313-31098-X.

This comprehensive bibliography was compiled to fill a major gap in the coverage of world librarianship. In the search for Arab-related library and information science one encounters a lack of comprehensive and current specialized bibliographies, regional indexing and abstracting services, and poor coverage in international databases. One needs to use many databases and different search strategies to identify relevant materials. This bibliography is intended as a comprehensive resource of published works on library and information science in the Arab world, covering Algeria, Bahrain, Djibouti, Egypt, Iraq, Jordan, Kuwait, Lebanon, Libya, Mauritania, Morocco, Oman, Qatar, Palestine, Saudi Arabia, Somalia, Sudan, Syria, Tunisia, United Arab Emirates, and Yemen. The more than 1,000 items listed include books, journal articles, book chapters, dissertations, conference papers, and expert reports. The items included are mainly in Arabic, English, and French, covering the period between 1977 and 1998.

The introduction provides a well-written history of libraries and information technology from the earliest times to the present and a description of the current state of librarianship in the Arab world, including the effects of censorship and wars in some countries of the region. Following is a general section on the Arabian Gulf and a section for each country of the region, all with entries arranged alphabetically within subject categories. Each entry has an informative annotation ranging from 50 to 250 words. Some countries have a limited number of entries due to the number of published works dealing with these countries. Author, title, and subject indexes provide access to all of the entries. This book fills an important need in librarianship, bringing together published works from all of the Arab nations.—**David A. Baldwin**

554. Safford, Barbara Ripp, comp. **Guide to Reference Materials for School Library Media Centers.** 5th ed. Englewood, Colo., Libraries Unlimited, 1998. 353p. index. $45.00. ISBN 1-56308-545-3.

This is a useful, if limited, guide to reference books suitable for elementary and secondary school library media centers in the United States. There has been a concentrated effort to include materials in a variety of formats. The author states that she previously thought that books would be eclipsed by CD-ROMs and the Web, but, as she announces in the introduction, identifying new titles available in book form, finding one new book source after the other, was like surfing the reference shelves. The limitation therefore is not in the format of the reference materials, but in the necessary paring down of items to fit into 350 pages. All resources are currently available (as of the time of publication) and most were published between 1992 and 1997. As this is the 5th edition of the title, it will probably be a familiar resource to most school library personnel. Safford discusses the changes from the former volumes that have occurred in organization in the introduction. As before, however, all included items are recommended, although some titles have been highlighted for their excellence. All entries include full bibliographic citations, grade level codes, annotations, and citations to reviews.

The book itself is divided into 5 major parts: collection management tools, general reference, social sciences (subdivided further into 25 varied subject headings), humanities (13 subdivisions), and science and technology (15 subdivisions). Author/title and subject indexes round out the volume. Each descriptive annotation is an adequate length to give the reader a basic understanding of the resource being discussed. The volume is attractively put together and is organized for easy access.—**Gail de Vos**

Directories

555. **The Aslib Directory of Information Sources in the United Kingdom.** 10th ed. Keith W. Reynard and Jeremy M. E. Reynard, eds. London, Aslib Publications, 1998. 1505p. index. £295.00. ISBN 0-85142-409-0.

This directory provides subject access to and contact information on more than 11,500 associations, clubs, societies, companies, educational institutions, government bodies, and other organizations that provide information services in the United Kingdom. Both free and fee-based services are included.

Entries are arranged alphabetically and include the organization name, contact information (including fax and e-mail if available), the type of organization, the person to whom to address inquiries, hours, subject coverage of the information service provided, and a listing of any printed publications the organization produces. Cross-references direct readers to appropriate headings and a separate subject index allows researchers to identify collections or services of interest.

This 10th edition contains 500 new entries and its coverage of local history is expanded. It also features over 3,500 e-mail addresses, 3,200 Websites, and an expanded subject index. The greatest strength of the directory is its broad scope. The range of organizations included runs the gamut from very specialized U.K. groups like the Northern Hamster Club to more traditional and comprehensive sources of information like the British Museum.

Although not examined for this review, a visit to the Aslib Website informs prospective buyers that a CD-ROM version of this directory is available to purchasers of the print version for a nominal extra fee. Persons planning to make heavy use of the tool may wish to consider this added option.

Does every library's reference collection need this? Probably not, but large and specialized reference collections will find it useful for identifying sources of information in the United Kingdom.
—**Gordon J. Aamot**

556. **Directory of Special Libraries and Information Centers.** 23d ed. Marc Faerber and Matthew Miskelly, eds. Farmington Hills, Mich., Gale, 1999. 3v. index. $830.00/set. ISBN 0-7876-2094-7. ISSN 0731-633X.

The 23d edition of this well-known work lists 23,600 special and research libraries; information centers; data centers maintained by governmental agencies; and libraries in businesses, corporations, industries, educational institutions, and nonprofit organizations in several subject areas (e.g., medicine, law, and religion). It complements R. R. Bowker's *American Library Directory* (49th ed.; see ARBA 98, entry 572), with more detailed entries on special libraries. The 21st edition was reviewed in ARBA 98 (see entries 589 and 590) with the price tag of $535 for both volumes.—**Bohdan S. Wynar**

557. **National Guide to Funding for Libraries and Information Services.** 5th ed. Gina-Marie Cantarella, ed. New York, Foundation Center, 1999. 285p. index. $75.00pa. ISBN 0-87954-878-9.

Millions of dollars in grants and donations are available to librarians every year: in fact, nearly $16 billion was awarded to nonprofit organizations in 1999. Finding the right source for the right project can be difficult, but funding directories will help. Most entries in this directory are drawn from the Foundation Center's 2-volume *Foundation Directory* (19th ed.; see ARBA 98, entry 787). Entries are organized by state and then alphabetically, and various subject indexes, such as "Types of Support," "Grants by Subject," and "Grantmaker Name," also provide access to the entries. Descriptions of recent grants provide useful help in determining if an institution's needs meet with the foundation's goals.

Although the 5th edition of the *National Guide to Funding for Libraries and Information Services* has grown from 644 to 880 entries, it does not approach the 2,193 entries included in the 1,400-page *Big Book of Library Grant Money* (1998-1999 ed.; American Library Association, 1998). The latter includes many major library donors not in the former, including some of the largest, such as the Gates Library Foundation. The foundation profiles in the *Big Book* are more informative than entries in the *National Guide to Funding*, and unlike the Foundation Center's volume, the *Big Book* omits programs that will not consider unsolicited proposals. Since nearly 20 percent of the foundations in the *National Guide to Funding* "contribute only to pre-selected organizations," the volume contains only about 700 viable grant sources.

Although the *Big Book* provides better access to more funding sources, any listing could prove invaluable to library grant officers and administrators. This volume, as a supplement to the *Big Book*, should be useful to anyone seeking extra support for their library.—**Peter H. McCracken**

558. **World Guide to Libraries.** 14th ed. New Providence, N.J., K. G. Saur, 1999. 2v. index. $425.00/set. ISBN 3-598-20725-5. ISSN 09336-008.

World Guide to Libraries, the 14th edition, covers 43,570 libraries from 196 countries. The entries are arranged by country with alphabetic listings in the table of contents. In general, in the listing for Ukraine (pp. 697–718), the information and classification of libraries are accurate. However, there are some exceptions. The National Parliamentary Library in Kyiv is not a national library in the sense of Vernadsky's Library and the compiler is unfortunately not sufficiently familiar with Ukrainian (or even Russian) language (e.g., entries 30612 and 30613). Nevertheless, in spite of its high price, the directory will be of substantial assistance to larger and scientific libraries.—**Bohdan S. Wynar**

Handbooks and Yearbooks

559. **Annual Review of Information Science and Technology. Volume 33, 1998.** Martha E. Williams, ed. Medford, N.J., for American Society for Information Science by Information Today, 1999. 460p. index. $99.95. ISBN 1-57387-065-X. ISSN 0066-4200.

The *Annual Review of Information Science and Technology* (ARIST) is an annual publication that publishes in-depth reviews of topics within the broad field of information science and technology. Topics vary from year to year and no single topic is treated on an annual basis. Topics are selected on the basis of timeliness and an assessment of reader interest. The 33d volume of ARIST covers 8 topics in 8 separate chapters: information ownership and control, pricing and marketing online information services, design of interfaces for information seeking, socio-cognitive perspectives on representation, metadata, cross-language information retrieval, computer-supported cooperative work in information search and retrieval, and electronic scholarly journal publishing. ARIST enlists authors who are not only experts on the topics they write about, but who are also frequent contributors to the literature in their chosen topic. Chapters undergo rigorous review by teams of content editors and chapter reviewers who themselves are active contributors to the professional literature. If there is a negative to ARIST, it is that chapter authors are sometimes limited to discussing the literature within a certain time period and thus find the literature shaping their treatment of the topic rather than presenting their topics using the theoretical model or framework that shapes the topic. When an ARIST review is available for a topic of interest, researchers and practitioners are best served by starting their literature review with ARIST because they can depend on its reviews to be scholarly, thorough, up-to-date, and well written. Reviews also aim to be critical in that authors give their expert opinion and appraisal of developments, activities, and trends on the topics their chapters cover.

—**Karen Markey Drabenstott**

560. **The Bowker Annual Library and Book Trade Almanac 1999.** 44th ed. Dave Bogart, ed. New Providence, N.J., R. R. Bowker, 1999. 863p. index. $185.00. ISBN 0-8352-4222-6. ISSN 0068-0540.

This standard almanac serves as a convenient one-stop source for busy reference librarians and the book trade. It has six parts: "Reports from the Field," "Legislation, Funding, and Grants," "Library Information Science and Education, Procurement and Salaries," "Research and Statistics," "Reference Information," and "Directory of Organizations." This volume is edited by Dave Bogart and is a collection of essays written by many contributors. The statistics and directory-type information are most helpful and will probably justify the rather high price of this volume.—**Bohdan S. Wynar**

561. Hull, Mary E. **Censorship in America: A Reference Handbook.** Santa Barbara, Calif., ABC-CLIO, 1999. 233p. index. (Contemporary World Issues). $45.00. ISBN 1-57607-057-3.

Hull has written a well–balanced and up-to-date summary of censorship. A history of censorship is presented, but only as a brief chronology. This work is written to emphasize modern problems and cases. The first chapter deals with current controversies. Censorship in the arts, music (rap), news (Sudan slavery atrocities), textbooks, and the Internet (pornography, filters, v-chip) are all discussed. These essays are well balanced and the rest of the book excels in areas where others do not.

The biographies of major current players in this arena are presented. Some are in the current political area, such as Gary Bauer and Tipper Gore. The short biographies, about a page in length, are well balanced and objective. The next section presents summaries of the major court cases in this area, such as Janet Reno's CDA suit of 1996. The author follows with a full-text section of opinion documents from the various organizations involved. The last document is surprisingly mild and has much to say about the purposes of media in the effects of entertainment on the human mind and soul. The book concludes with about 50 pages of the author's selected reference books, magazines, videos, and Websites. A list of all the major organizations involved in this issue and their Websites concludes the work.

This book is a modern and well-done examination of censorship. As a part of the Contemporary Issues Series from ABC-CLIO, it is a solid choice for any library from high school on up.—**Gary L. Parsons**

562. Karolides, Nicholas J., Margaret Bald, and Dawn Sova. **100 Banned Books: Censorship Histories of World Literature.** New York, Facts on File, 1999. 420p. index. $18.95pa. ISBN 0-8160-4059-1.

This volume is an abridged version of the 4-volume Banned Books Series published by Facts on File in 1998 (see ARBA 99, entries 603, 604, 605, and 606). The 4 sections of the book each have 25 entries covering works banned on political, religious, sexual, or social grounds. Each entry has a summary of the book's contents followed by a censorship history. The books include novels, histories, biographies, children's books, polemics, and religious and philosophical works from all over the world. The Bible, Talmud, Koran, *All Quiet on the Western Front*, *Candide*, *The Autobiography of Benjamin Franklin*, and *The Diary of Anne Frank* are among the banned works included. They accompany the censored works of Henry Miller, James Joyce, D. H. Lawrence, William S. Burroughs, and Judy Blume, which have been involved in highly publicized court cases.

Because censorship is a major concern in schools and libraries, this book is very timely. It demonstrates the wide variety of works that have been condemned. A look at the table of contents will serve as proof that the efforts of censors are futile and ineffective. All of these books are still readily available and many are classics. *100 Banned Books* is an excellent choice for school and public libraries that do not own the 4-volume set. [R: LJ, July 99, p. 83]—**Barbara M. Bibel**

Special Topics

Archives and Manuscripts

563. **Encoded Archival Description: Context, Theory, and Case Studies.** Jackie M. Dooley, ed. Chicago, Society of American Archivists, 1998. 178p. index. $40.00pa. ISBN 0-931828-43-0.

Encoded Archival Description (EAD), first developed in 1993, is now one of the most important trends in archival description. It has emerged as quite possibly what will become *the* tool for making archival finding aids such as inventories and registers available for search and display in an electronic format, especially on the World Wide Web. Indeed, there has been strong interest in the development of EAD even beyond the American archival community because EAD is really a combination of things. First of all, it is a descriptive standard for finding aids that enables multiple uses of the information they contain, their interchange, and their long-term accessibility. Second, it is a communication format for finding aids that enables archives to deliver them electronically to distant users. And third, it is a technology that is standards based; computer platform independent; and employs powerful tools for the searching, retrieval, display, and navigation of finding aids.

The book under review (originally published as volume 60, numbers 3 and 4 of *American Archivist*) consists of 12 chapters divided into 2 parts. The 1st part consists of 6 chapters (some written by its very developers) designed to introduce the major issues that led EAD's developers to design an encoding standard for finding aids, its intended purpose in an integrated system of archival description and access, and the role it is meant to play as an archival descriptive standard. The 2d part also consists of 6 chapters that describe the experiences of archival repositories that began experimenting as "early implementers" of EAD as early as 1996. They do an excellent job in providing the reader with what to expect in terms both of the problems of implementation and resulting final products.

This book is must reading for anyone involved in the archival profession and really should be read by librarians and other information professionals who are keeping abreast of the latest developments in information access. EAD is too important to be missed, and this work should be a first step to understanding and contemplating what it is all about.—**Paul H. Thomas**

564. **Encoded Archival Description Tag Library Version 1.0.** By the Encoded Archival Description Working Group of the Society of American Archivists and Network Development and MARC Standards Office of the Library of Congress. Chicago, Society of American Archivists, 1998. 262p. $25.00pa. ISBN 0-931828-44-9.

Readers familiar with the Standard Generalized Markup Language (SGML) will recognize its great flexibility with respect to organizing data. The Encoded Archival Description (EAD) is an SGML "application" for filing information about archival materials and other collections. This book takes the EAD Document Type Definition (DTD), and presents it in a more "people readable" form.

The content is still highly formal and technical. Those without a strong SGML background will find it very heavy going. However, the persistent reader will be able to pick up some interesting points while slogging through the text.

There is some explanation of the tag library conventions and a listing of attributes. The main body of the work, of course, is the library of EAD elements and their descriptions. This really is merely a reformatting of the DTD.—**Robert M. Slade**

Information Science

565. Healy, Leigh Watson. **Library Systems: Current Developments and Future Directions.** Washington, D.C., Council on Library and Information Resources, 1998. 186p. $25.00 spiralbound. ISBN 1-887334-58-0.

Library Systems: Current Developments and Future Directions is the report that resulted when the Council on Library and Information Resources commissioned Healy to study the gap between institutional digital library initiatives and the products offered by library systems vendors. From September 1997 to January 1998, Healy interviewed individuals from 17 college, research, and public libraries, and top executives of 12 library systems vendors. Healy wanted to determine what libraries need from library systems vendors and to discover each vendor's vision and goals. Healy's report summarizes the information gleaned from these interviews and contrasts librarians' needs with the development philosophies of the vendors. The report is not intended to be a comparative study of library systems, but rather provides an overview of the "state of the art" in the library systems industry during late 1997 and early 1998. The clearly and concisely written sections make this report easy to understand and quick to read. Thorough profiles of the 12 library systems comprise the major portion of the work. The profiles focus on areas of strategic importance to libraries (e.g., markets served, product development) rather than exploring specific software features. The report also includes four case studies of different types of libraries to provide a snapshot of how library systems were implemented through late 1997 and the extent to which vendors met the needs of these libraries. Because the report, published in May 1998, provides an overview of libraries' needs and vendors' solutions at a certain point in time, it becomes a historical work as time progresses. Healy's well-organized, concise, and readable report will be useful as a benchmark to compare subsequent progress by vendors toward meeting libraries' automation needs.—**Karen Selden**

566. **Information Landscapes for a Learning Society: Networking and the Future of Libraries 3.** Sally Criddle, Lorcan Dempsey, and Richard Heseltine, eds. London, Library Association; distr., Lanham, Md., Bernan Associates, 1999. 280p. index. $75.00. ISBN 1-85604-310-X.

Edited works are often interesting because of the variability of the arguments presented in the work. Edited conference proceedings are even more interesting for the same reason. This volume does not disappoint. As the most glaring and obvious example of this point, the opening keynote address by Richard Heseltine makes a rather startling prediction given the theme of the conference, the sponsor, and the publisher. Having noticed that children of the information age are unperturbed by the ambiguity of computer games, he predicts: "Our children, however, will do things differently, and will not invent digital libraries" (p. xx). The volume is focused on digital libraries, networked environments, and the future of libraries. This is a strange beginning for a conference such as this.

It is unclear how the editors obtained manuscripts from the participants. It is clear, however, that some of the participants actively rewrote elements of their papers in response to other papers presented. For instance, some mention is made in a number of the papers of the keynote address, especially the "Alice in Wonderland" motif. Only a few papers challenged the basic notion that libraries are ordained to pilot society into the information age by transforming themselves (and potentially others) into digital libraries.

Quite a few of the papers make the entirely gossamer claim that there has already been a change. The purported change is primarily in terminology and some effort to make that terminology philosophy. There is a usual amount of wishful thinking here, or from the perspective of a pessimist, whistling in the dark. The value of the work is that there is no clear voice and no clearly articulated direction for the work, as evidenced by the keynote address to begin the conference. The authors were allowed by the editors to address the components they, the authors, wished to address. Although this gives the work a bit of an eclectic nature, the end result is a volume that is undoubtedly true to the conference.

There are a series of themes running through the papers. One of the more interesting, for example, is the notion of democracy and availability of information. This issue is normally not dealt with in the depth or with the clear thinking that the papers evidence. This is a refreshing change and one that enriches the book substantially.

On the surface this book is a reasonable piece of work that is yet another product of a conference looking at the future of libraries and digital libraries. Seen from a more critical perspective, it is an excellent example of the dialogue and the debate that some have thought was over and done with some time ago. In point of fact, the true worth of this book is its pointing out of the continuing dialogue and debate in this area. Not to be overlooked is some of the excellent dialogue and debate that is contained in this volume.

This book will find good use among anyone interested in the future of digital libraries or libraries in general. However, it will take some effort on the reader's part to pull some of the disparate themes together. The editors have done an excellent job of pulling together a good set of themes. The richness of conference papers is that there is virtually unlimited lode of themes available. Readers are encouraged to make the effort—it is worth it.—**C. D. Hurt**

567. Junion-Metz, Gail, and Brad Stephens. **Creating a Power Web Site: HTML, Tables, Imagemaps, Frames, and Forms.** New York, Neal-Schuman, 1998. 199p. index. $125.00pa. (with CD-ROM). ISBN 1-55570-323-2.

The authors have provided a remarkably organized how-to manual that presents a basic approach to Web development for librarians. They use language that is familiar to the novice Website developer rather than communicating the topic with undefined terms that many authors assume that the reader will recognize. The book also increases the comfort level for librarians by explaining examples and scripts with content and tasks that are related to their work.

The chapters are organized according to the sequence of skills needed to build different aspects of a Website. The book begins with the basic information about HTML and ends with details for creating Web forms with CGI scripts and PERL. Pictures and hints are presented along with the text to provide further insight into the examples and discussion. Each chapter includes reviews of the chapter information and practice activities.

There are five appendixes, including a glossary of HTML, PERL, and Web terms and a list of recent books and Websites. There is also a list of common HTML equivalent characters for symbols and diacritical marks that can be added to Web pages, but do not show up on the computer's keyboard. The other two appendixes are a list of browser-safe hexadecimal color codes and a PERL command cheat sheet to use for PERL scripts.

A valuable addition to the textbook is the CD-ROM that includes HTML examples, PERL scripts, PERL interpreter software, and an evaluation copy of an imagemap program called Mapedit. This book is a useful tool for librarians as well as others creating Websites. [R: C&RL News, Mar 99, p. 205]

—**Bryce L. Allen**

568. Spitzer, Kathleen L. **Information Literacy: Essential Skills for the Information Age.** Syracuse, N.Y., ERIC Clearinghouse on Information & Technology/Syracuse University Press, 1998. 377p. index. $18.00pa. ISBN 0-937597-44-9.

This comprehensive book, published by the ERIC Clearinghouse on Information & Technology, defines information literacy, traces the history and development of the concept, examines the economic necessity of being information literate, discusses past and present research in this area, and describes information literacy projects and programs in both K-12 and higher education. It also covers national and state goals and standards and assessments of information literacy skills. The 9th chapter focuses on technology and its relationship to information literacy as well as describes two instructional approaches. The final chapter offers suggestions for expansion into arenas other than academic and school libraries.

Each chapter is well organized and clearly written. Many charts and lists help elucidate the text. Seven appendixes contain the American Association of School Librarians and Association of Educational Communication and Technology Information Literacy Standards for Student Learning, the foundations and definitions of competencies from the Secretary's Commission of Achieving Necessary Skills (SCANS) report, a chronology of the development of information literacy from 1974 to 1998 with an accompanying bibliography, correlations of information literacy skills to national subject matter standards and national content standards, and an explanation of rubrics and their application in standards education. An extensive bibliography of books (48 books), journal articles, and ERIC documents completes the book.

The acknowledgments state that the book "draws from, builds upon, and extends the work done by Christina S. Doyle in *Information Literacy in an Information Society: A Concept for the Information Age* (ERIC Clearinghouse, 1994)." The authors of this volume are experts in the fields of information literacy, information skills, information problem solving, and educational technology. This comprehensive book should be required reading for all school and public service academic librarians and would be useful for all other librarians as well.—**Carol Krismann**

Information Systems

569. Deans, P. Candace, and Kirk R. Karwan. **Global Information Systems and Technology: Focus on the Organization and Its Functional Areas.** Hershey, Pa., Idea Group Publishing, 1997. 580p. index. (Series on Global Information Technology Management). $59.95. ISBN 1-878289-21-7.

This scholarly and theoretical work is a third publication in the Series on Global Information Technology Management, with the earlier works having discussed overall global issues and global issues and trends in technology education. The focus narrows with this resource, which examines theories and current views on the emerging global information systems and their subsystem applications at the functional levels of organizations.

The editors have compiled and organized the writings of numerous academicians and business people into 27 chapters that are arranged under 8 sections. These sections include an overview of perspectives concerning the globalization and management of technology, discussion of marketing issues and concerns, analysis of financial services and systems, review of international accounting issues, outline of information management of manufacturing and logistics, impact of information technology on research and development, management of human resources information systems, and a summary of implications and challenges for the future.

Although the primary audience for this work is clearly information systems academicians and practitioners, other individuals in international business and education as well as executives and mid-level managers in international businesses may find this analytical publication is worth acquiring in order to understand the concepts and issues supporting international planning for development of integrated systems. Academic research and global business libraries may also find that this text, in conjunction with the other two volumes in this series, is a valuable addition to their collections.—**James M. Murray**

570. Larsen, Tor J., and Eugene McGuire. **Information Systems Innovation and Diffusion: Issues and Directions.** Hershey, Pa., Idea Group Publishing, 1998. 454p. index. (Series in Information Technology Management). $69.95; $49.95pa. ISBN 1-878289-43-8; 1-878289-46-2pa.

Information Systems Innovation and Diffusion is a collection of academic papers on the processes involved in the adoption and spread of new technologies, mainly new software systems. Given this focus, it is not surprising that the material is presented in a style more suited to the needs and expectations of other academics than of those of us involved in the day-to-day development and implementation of these technologies.

The 1st section, consisting of 4 theoretical papers and 1 study of the use of a specific, proprietary product, is generally written in the turgid, jargon style common to academic research. Although this may facilitate communication among academics, it serves as a barrier to outsiders, causing this section to be of little value to nonacademics. The 2d section, a series of empirical studies, follows the same pattern. The occasional "real world" application here reads as a bland platitude.

The 3d section, a series of case studies, is more interesting. Generally more clearly written, these five papers focus on the concrete, exploring ways small numbers of well-described firms have adopted new technologies. Specific comparisons illuminate the effect of different style of interaction with the larger community of software users, shifts from custom to prepackaged software, and the growth of online services. The papers here are valuable contributions to the growing academic literature on technology adoption and diffusion, but generally offer too little concrete advice to be useful to those of us outside the academic community.—**Ray Olszewski**

Library Management

571. Managing Overdues: A How-To-Do-It Manual for Librarians. Patsy J. Hansel, ed. New York, Neal-Schuman, 1998. 131p. index. (How-To-Do-It Manuals for Librarians, no.83). $39.95pa. ISBN 1-55570-291-0.

This publication provides practical advice to public librarians on how to minimize problems inherent in managing library overdues, including how to significantly lower the number of overdues. Based on findings from four surveys of public library systems across the United States conducted by the editor, herself an esteemed public library director, this comprehensive work contains tips and techniques currently in use. She claims that automation saves huge amounts of money each year because it enables librarians to reduce losses from overdues.

Nine authors contributed nine chapters to the work. The chapters are liberally illustrated with black-and-white figures consisting of numerical charts and textual data. Some of the chapters contain references and appendixes. The chapters are organized into 3 parts. Part 1 contains information describing 4 methods used for retrieving overdue books—prosecution, electronic notification, credit bureaus, and collection agencies. Part 2 describes 3 state Setoff Debt Collection Programs used to collect overdue accounts. Setoff debt programs allow debts to be paid from money that a state owes its citizens from such things as income tax refunds or lottery winnings. Part 3 contains an essay on the philosophy of charging overdue fines and a selected annotated bibliography on overdues. An index and notes about the editor complete the volume, which is recommended for the professional shelves of circulation librarians. [R: BL, 15 Oct 98, p. 398]
—**Lois Gilmer**

572. Martin, Murray S., and Betsy Park. **Charging and Collecting Fees and Fines: A Handbook for Libraries.** New York, Neal-Schuman, 1998. 146p. index. $49.95pa. ISBN 1-55570-318-6.

Although subtitled *A Handbook for Libraries*, this volume on the thorny issue of fees and fines provides more discussion than direction. Like much of the library literature it asks many good questions and identifies many challenges, but does not offer solutions. Some suggestions are important and useful, particularly regarding the need to clearly publicize fee- and fine-related policies. Other topics seem moot, such as discussion about taxes incurred from Internet purchases made on library computers. This is equivalent to using the library's telephones to order merchandise, and the suggested solution that users should have their own Web pages makes little sense given the lack of connection between a purchaser and his or her personal Web page. The authors note the "urgent need" for guidelines, but, unfortunately, do not offer them. Had Martin and Park suggested guidelines and recommendations that librarians could use in setting and supporting library policies, they could have made a significant contribution toward resolving a difficult issue. The need to charge for printing at public workstations, for example, is a challenge facing every library, and solved by some. A compilation of specific examples, showing what several libraries charge and how they do it, plus discussion of potential solutions, would have made this book indispensable. This topic is one of vital importance to librarians today, but practicing librarians seeking policy advice need a combination of discussion and concrete examples. This book provides the first part, but not the second. [R: RUSQ, v. 38 no. 1, p. 115]—**Peter H. McCracken**

573. Siess, Judith A. **The SOLO Librarian's Sourcebook.** Medford, N.J., Information Today, 1997. 246p. index. $39.50. ISBN 1-57387-032-3.

Siess, an experienced SOLO librarian and former chair of the SOLO Librarians Division of the Special Libraries Association, understands the unique needs of librarians who wok in environments without other professional librarians. In part 1 of *The SOLO Librarian's Sourcebook*, she addresses the basics of SOLO librarianship and provides suggestions for serving employers who may not understand the need for and function of a library. She provides concise, interesting discussions of issues of particular importance to SOLO librarians, such as time management and networking, and gives advice on ways to stretch budgets through interlibrary loan and exchange programs and to reduce workloads through outsourcing. Some of the chapters are strongly influenced by Siess' informed opinions on the status and future of SOLO librarians. Siess concludes with a discussion of the role of technology in SOLO librarianship and the future of the profession. Part 2 lists resources for the SOLO librarian: organization; job hotlines; library and related educational programs, including distance learning and continuing education opportunities; vendors, including book jobbers, subscription services, automation services, and consultants; relevant books and journals; and Internet sites and listservs.

This outstanding addition to the library science literature will be essential for new or experienced SOLO librarians and will be an excellent tool for library educators to use to present SOLO librarianship as a career option. This is a necessary purchase for library school libraries and libraries with small staffs. Librarians in larger libraries will also profit from consulting it.—**Gari Anne Patzwald**

Periodicals and Serials

574. **E-Serials: Publishers, Libraries, Users, and Standards.** Wayne Jones, ed. Binghamton, N.Y., Haworth Press, 1998. 363p. index. $55.96. ISBN 0-7890-0514-X.

Jones, the editor of *E-Serials*, has covered the field of electronic serials very nicely indeed with the articles he has chosen for this book. The book has been published simultaneously as *The Serials Librarian*, volume 33, numbers 1/2 and 3/4 1998. Ordinarily, this reviewer is not pleased when publishers make four issues into one and charge for a full volume. This book, however, has substance. There is something here for all serials librarians; catalogers and reference librarians will also find much of value here.

There are 10 sections, most of which have several articles, on various aspects of electronic serials: publishing; pricing; copyright; acquisitions and collection development; cataloging and metadata; preservation and archiving; local, national, and international projects; indexing; uniform resource identifiers; and citation.

The articles on acquisitions and collection development and preservation will be particularly valuable to serials librarians struggling with the questions of how to move into this not-so-brave new world, how to rethink everything from changing comfortable old habits and staff practices to dealing with licensing problems, record-keeping, and maintaining archival materials. Most of the articles discuss the theoretical implications as well as offer practical illustrations, and useful Websites are noted within articles and in the endnotes. Those wishing to contact an author can make use of the e-mail address included in the biographical sketch. Although the book provides many answers, it will undoubtedly raise almost as many questions. This solid piece of work will give serials librarians much to think about.—**Diane K. Podell**

Philosophy and Theory

575. **Books, Bricks, & Bytes: Libraries in the Twenty-First Century.** Stephen R. Graubard and Paul LeClerc, eds. New Brunswick, N.J., Transaction Publishers, 1999. 361p. $24.95pa. ISBN 1-56000-986-1.

First published as the special Fall 1996 issue of *Daedalus*, this collection of 19 essays commemorate the centennial of the New York Public Library. It was a project of the late president of the library, Father Timothy Healy, and the current president, Paul LeClerc, and was supported by the American Academy of Arts and Sciences that included it in its proceedings and whose editor, historian Stephen R. Graubard, was coeditor. The volume includes papers that continue the customary, and now well-rehearsed, mantra of revolutionary changes in libraries as a result of technological innovations, but extend well beyond the expected repetitions into thoughtful essays that treat the various roles of libraries with respect to the communities and the communication developments that they embrace. Although the basis of selection of the invited contributors or their topics is not clear, the common theme that runs through their pieces seems to be change, transition, and transformation. LeClerc's succinct introduction provides the unifying thread with its statement that "what differentiates one library from another is the attitude its proprietors adopt in relation to the traditional functions of acquisition, conservation, and access. What sets the present era apart from virtually all others in history of libraries is the rapid—indeed revolutionary—ways in which information technology is transforming each of these core functions" (pp. xi-xii). Two of the less predictable chapters are those of Kenneth E. Carpenter, "A Library Historian Looks at Librarianship," and Brian Lang's "Bricks and Bytes: Libraries in Flux," which comes closest to embodying the collection's title. The final third of the volume consists of eight essays treating various aspects of libraries in Great Britain, South Africa, Brazil, France, Russia, Germany, and India. That the volume has warranted a second printing may be significant, although it is less focused than two other collected works on related themes also appearing in the late 1990s, reviewed as "Books and Libraries in the New Millennium: A Review Essay" (*Choice*, 37/1 [Sept. 1999]: 87-97).—**Donald G. Davis Jr.**

School Library Media Centers

576. Rankin, Virginia. **The Thoughtful Researcher: Teaching the Research Process to Middle School Students.** Englewood, Colo., Libraries Unlimited, 1999. 211p. index. (Information Literacy Series). $27.00pa. ISBN 1-56308-698-0.

Rankin has written an excellent book that teachers and librarians will find extremely useful in teaching research skills to middle school students. She emphasizes that research is a thoughtful process and provides a variety of techniques for becoming a reflective practitioner, drawing on Carol Kuhlthau's work. She also gives strong arguments for teachers and librarians to collaborate throughout the research process.

Each step in the research process is covered beginning with strategies in performing a pre-search and moving on to generating questions, managing time, searching for and evaluating information, note taking, reading for information, and thinking skills. The final steps include creating a quality product and assessing the process and the product. Rankin carefully explains the rationale of each step and gives a number of possible methods teachers and librarians can use to teach these steps. For example, she discusses how to adjust topics for high risk, low skill students and how to coach students to overcome their fear of failure. Also, one section of the book covers what should be taught in an age of technology and change. Again, she emphasizes that research is a problem-solving process that can be used regardless of the software or search engines being used.

From the many examples Rankin uses throughout the book, it is quite evident that she writes from years of experience in working with this difficult age group. She provides the rationale, the techniques, and handouts that will help other middle school librarians succeed in preparing their students to become lifelong learners.—**Michele Russo**

577. Wasman, Ann M. **New Steps to Service: Common-Sense Advice for the School Library Media Specialist.** Chicago, American Library Association, 1998. 228p. index. $20.00pa.; $18.00pa. (ALA members). ISBN 0-8389-3483-8.

This introduction to the field is addressed to individuals taking first steps to develop a quality media program and those who are "committed to doing a good job in his or her position and is willing to use other resources to activate their commitment" (p. xii). These words set the tone for a handbook that anticipates realistic situations and offers practical suggestions for how to handle them.

The language is positive and encouraging. Terms are defined with clear explanations. The subject range is wide, including the first week on a new job, administrative responsibilities, handling complaints and establishing discipline procedures, and seeking professional growth. An example of the approach is a section dispelling the myths about weeding. Other practical aids include examples of forms and a checklist to use on the first visit to a school.

The appendixes provide addresses for organizations and businesses as well as reprints of documents important to school library media specialists. In summary, this is indeed a helpful resource for the beginner and the person who wants helpful suggestions.—**Phyllis J. Van Orden**

Special Libraries

578. **Business Reference Services and Sources: How End Users and Librarians Work Together.** Katherine M. Shelfer, ed. Binghamton, N.Y., Haworth Press, 1997. 113p. index. (The Reference Librarian Series). $39.95. ISBN 0-7890-0359-7.

This volume brings together nine essays on the topic of reference services in support of business schools and corporate America. The special focus of the articles is related to opportunities for end-users and librarians to collaborate on the delivery of relevant information services and bibliographic instruction. The articles cover such topics as business service on the Internet, developing an Internet site for school business officials, company information on the World Wide Web, networking with community business resources, the information specialist–customer partnership, information-seeking behavior of business students, reference librarians and the business professor, bibliographic instruction for business classes, and reference service and collection development faculty outreach. The essays are rather uneven in quality, but two deserve special mention for their insight and overall value. Readers should consult the essay on "Information-Seeking Behavior," by Joseph D. Atkinson III and Miguel Figueroa, and the "Reference Librarian and the Business Professor, a Strategic Alliance that Works," by Paula J. Crawford and Thomas P. Barrett. Readers desiring a comprehensive examination of business sources should look elsewhere, but those seeking ideas about optimizing end-user and librarian relationships should consult this volume. This work is recommended for all academic libraries serving business education. [R: JAL, Mar 99, p. 144]—**Arthur P. Young**

579. Butcher, Helen. **Meeting Managers' Information Needs.** London, Aslib Publications, 1998. 106p. (A Managing Information Report). $59.95pa. ISBN 0-85142-405-8.

The 6 chapters of this book could serve as a primer for management of the corporate library. Chapter 1, "The Organization, the Environment, and Information," discusses barriers to the flow of information and their causes. They include the corporate culture, the fact that management has tended to value technology above the use of technology for information, and librarians and information officers frequently fail to provide management with information in a useful and timely manner. The productivity of the "knowledge worker" is difficult to determine because the value of a good idea to the organization is probably incalculable. The author states later that in times of recession, functions providing information are often the first to be cut, since they may be perceived as not making a contribution. In chapter 2 the traditional planning, directing, and budgeting is discussed. More significant is the reference to Koch and Godden and their suggestion that most of the time, managers pursue activities that have little value to customers, investors, or any non-management constituency. They propose that most management is unnecessary except in the very largest and most complex organizations. The attainment of "information literacy" implies that the manager understands that it is the information-based needs of the organization that must determine technology and not visa-versa.

Sources of managerial information include formal and informal environment scanning. This is defined as searching for information that will benefit the company and includes customer information; competition information; industry information; and information about specific economic climate, regulatory factors, and sociocultural factors. To be useful, information must be perceived as relevant, which means timeliness, accuracy, and reliability. Managers of information in the future can expect changes in the nature of what constitutes the managers role and information needs. Cost cutting, flattering of hierarchies, and business process re-engineering will likely leave fewer functions needing to be managed. This book is an interesting blend of the traditional managerial thought with the new. Chapter bibliographies include many established writers. In a small volume, we are challenged to consider the future of management, information-related activities as seen by management, and our future roles as knowledge managers.—**Robert M. Ballard**

PUBLISHING AND BOOKSELLING

Bibliography

580. Fleming, Patricia Lockhart, and Sandra Alston. **Early Canadian Printing: A Supplement to Marie Tremaine's** *A Bibliography of Canadian Imprints 1751-1800*. Buffalo, N.Y., University of Toronto Press, 1999. 629p. illus. index. $125.00. ISBN 0-8020-4218-X.

581. Tremaine, Marie. **A Bibliography of Canadian Imprints 1751-1800.** Buffalo, N.Y., University of Toronto Press, 1999. 705p. index. $125.00. ISBN 0-8020-4219-8.

Tremaine's classic bibliography of eighteenth-century Canadian imprints has been made available again in this photographic reprint as a companion to Fleming and Alston's supplement to Tremaine's work called *Early Canadian Printing*, originally published in 1952. Tremaine described all of the printing—books, pamphlets, leaflets, broadsides, magazines, and newspapers—produced in Canada from 1751 through 1800. Entries are arranged by year and alphabetically within each year by author or issuing agency, and consist of a transcription of the title page, collation, contents, historical notes (an especially valuable feature), and a list of locations of copies. Tremaine provides a detailed account of her method of bibliographic description and the introduction is a brief history of printing in Canada in the eighteenth century. There are accounts of all printing offices operating in Canada from 1751 to 1800; a list of all authorities, both manuscript and printed; a list of locations of imprints described; 16 illustrations; and an index.

Fleming and Alston have added many items not in Tremaine's work and they have corrected errors found in her descriptions. They provide a reference to the location of all copies they examined and cite bibliographies in which a work is listed or described. If an imprint is available on microfiche through the film project of the Canadian Institute for Historical Microreproductions, that is noted as well. Other features of *Early Canadian Printing* are especially valuable. Appendix A reproduces all entries pertaining to printing in the shop records of Brown/Neilson of Quebec from 1764 to the end of 1800, and appendix B transcribes printers' vouchers and other bills for official printing found in the Audited Public Accounts for Quebec to 1791 and for Lower and Upper Canada to 1800 for imprints that are not described in Tremaine or in the main body of *Early Canadian Printing*. Five indexes provide access to all entries in *Early Canadian Printing*, except for Tremaine's chapters on "Newspapers and Magazines" and "Printing-Offices and Biographical Notes on Printers," which can be accessed through her original index. The five indexes include a name index; title index; genre, language, and subject index; printer index; and index of copies located. These volumes together constitute an outstanding contribution to bibliographic scholarship.—**Dean H. Keller**

Biography

582. **Dictionary of Literary Biography, Volume 201: Twentieth-Century British Book Collectors and Bibliographers.** William Baker and Kenneth Womack, eds. Farmington Hills, Mich., Gale, 1999. 393p. illus. index. $151.00. ISBN 0-7876-3072-1.

This is a reference for university research collections. The entries describe the holdings of private libraries in Great Britain and give founders' biography information. Collectors include scholars, wealthy collectors, and incunabulists (predecessors of twenty-first-century librarians and archivists). The amount of material in these collections is impressive and valuable to researchers, especially those studying history, literature, biography, and the evolution of ideas. Readers will use this reference to locate rare, often one-of-a-kind books and periodicals. A glance at the list of previous volumes, the first published in 1978, shows that they contain an abundance of information about American and British writers and their works. A few volumes list writers in Canada, Germany, Latin America, Italy, Russia, Japan, and other countries. Volume 41, published in 1984, is devoted to African American poets since 1955, and volume 175, published in 1997, treats Native American writers. This standard resource collects information that is increasingly difficult to find. This reviewer was happy to rediscover a source not touched since university reference classes, and hopes it is purchased widely enough to enable it to stay in business.—**Edna M. Boardman**

Catalogs and Collections

583. Kallendorf, Craig W., and Maria X. Wells. **Aldine Press Books at the Harry Ransom Humanities Research Center: A Descriptive Catalogue.** Austin, Tex., University of Texas Press, 1998. 415p. index. $75.00; $50.00pa. ISBN 0-292-74335-1; 0-292-74334-3pa.

Aldus Manutius was a Venetian publisher from the time of his first book in 1494 until his death in 1515. The press he established, which became known as the Aldine Press, revolutionized book production in the sixteenth century and helped to shape the history of the modern book. Aldine titles included early Greek, Latin, and Italian texts. The Aldine Press collection at the Ransom Humanities Research Center at the University of Texas is one of the most significant collections of Aldine books in the United States. There are 526 titles and more than 900 volumes housed at the Texas site. In this highly specialized, descriptive bibliography, the titles are listed chronologically, with author, binder, and provenance indexes. Each entry includes extensive notes on content, binding, lubrication, notations (where applicable), and relevant book notes. Although this is a superior reference work and a model for other such projects and collections, the potential audience for such a bibliography is limited.—**Boyd Childress**

Dictionaries and Encyclopedias

584. Hartmann, R. R. K., and Gregory James. **Dictionary of Lexicography.** New York, Routledge, 1998. 176p. $75.00. ISBN 0-415-14143-5.

The purpose of the *Dictionary of Lexicography* is to highlight the history, criticism, typology, structures, and use of dictionaries through a comprehensive dictionary on this important type of reference source. Through the entries, it is possible to obtain definitions of working terms for dictionary construction, as well as to better understand this area of literary scholarship. The authors are R.R.K. Hartmann, director of the Dictionary Research Centre at the University of Exeter, and Gregory James, director of the Language Centre at the Hong Kong University of Science and Technology. Hartmann founded the European Association of Lexicography. The primary emphasis of the *Dictionary of Lexicography* is on the English language, but compilations from other cultures are also included.

The *Dictionary of Lexicography* begins with an introduction to the discipline of lexicography, defined as both the art of dictionary making and the scholarly field of dictionary research. A brief section then explains the working methods used in the creation of the *Dictionary of Lexicography*, including the sources consulted and the development of the list of entries. Sources include glossaries, textbooks, treatises, scholarly organizations, and other dictionaries. The remaining pages of the volume are devoted to entries for more than 2,000 terms related to dictionary history and construction. A comprehensive bibliography is provided to give the full citations to sources cited in the entries. This bibliography has been restricted to English-language publications.

Entries in the *Dictionary of Lexicography* include the headword in boldface type, the formulaic definition, expansion of the definition, examples taken from a variety of sources, cross-references to other headwords in the volume, cross-references to related terms, abbreviated references to English-language publications, sample reference works arranged by date that illustrate the headword's context, and references to electronic data, such as Internet sites. Graphic symbols within the entries make the material easier to use. Many entries in the *Dictionary of Lexicography* are cross-references and entries typically have definitions of 10 to 15 lines of text, in addition to bibliographic citations and cross-references.

A search of the literature revealed numerous works on lexicography, but these texts concentrate on the history and methodology of dictionary construction (*The Professor and the Madman: A Tale of Murder, Insanity, and the Making of the Oxford English Dictionary*, New York, HarperCollins, 1998). None of these works are comparable to the *Dictionary of Lexicography* in defining the terms used in dictionary construction. Thus, the volume fills a niche in an interesting area of scholarship, being a dictionary of the field of lexicography as well as revealing a glimpse at the development of this specialized field.

The *Dictionary of Lexicography* is a carefully conceived, attractively presented, comprehensive view of the field of dictionary construction and scholarship. It would be an appropriate addition to academic or special libraries that serve students, faculty, or researchers in the liberal and fine arts. It would be a good choice for public libraries responding to the needs of lifelong scholars and historians.—**Sara Anne Hook**

Directories

585. **American Book Trade Directory 1999-2000.** 45th ed. New Providence, N.J., R. R. Bowker, 1999. 1774p. index. $249.95. ISBN 0-8352-4221-8. ISSN 0065-759X.

The 45th edition of this standard reference source covers the book trade in the United States and Canada. The 43d edition was reviewed in ARBA 98, entry 596. Apart from the increase in price, the information that is provided in this edition is basically the same. This important directory will be of substantial assistance to all interested parties—public and college libraries, publishers, and retail bookstores.—**Bohdan S. Wynar**

586. **Directory of Small Press/Magazine Editors and Publishers 1999-2000.** 30th ed. Len Fulton, ed. Paradise, Calif., Dustbooks, 1999. 328p. $23.95pa. ISBN 0-916685-75-6.

There are thousands of publishers in the world but it is difficult to find the information about all of them, especially small publishers, in one place. Dustbooks, the leader in the small press information field, certainly has done a great service to the profession by publishing *Directory of Small Press/Magazine Editors and Publishers*. The 30th edition of the book lists more than 6,000 names of editors and publishers in alphabetical order. This comprehensive list includes name of editor or publisher, complete address of the company, telephone and fax numbers, and e-mail addresses. Even Web page addresses have been included, if available. Another excellent feature of the directory that will be helpful to users is the cross-references for many entries. Although the emphasis in this well-prepared directory is on the United States, many entries from foreign countries have also been included. It is certainly an excellent source for finding the information on those editors and publishers who are employed by small presses. It is recommended for reference collections of all types of libraries.—**Ravindra Nath Sharma**

587. **The International Directory of Little Magazines & Small Presses 1998-99.** 34th ed. Len Fulton, ed. Paradise, Calif., Dustbooks, 1998. 946p. index. $55.00; $34.95pa. ISBN 0-916685-66-7; 0-916685-70-5pa.

Although not stated in the text, this is obviously a reference work aimed at freelance writers who want to find out where to submit material. It lists publishers of both books and periodicals. Each list has contact information, plus an indication of the market to which the publisher sells, the type of printing done, and some pricing information.

Two indexes support the main entries. A regional index is set forth by states within the United States, and by country for non-American listings. (The vast majority of the houses are in the United States; there are almost twice as many records for California alone as for all non-U.S. countries combined.) There is also a subject index, but no indication as to how topical divisions were decided upon. There is, for example, a section for "Dada," but computers are lumped in with calculators, technology has exactly six entries, and there is no entry at all for telecommunications or any related subject.

The information is based on self–report. There is a slight allusion to this in the key to directory listings, and slightly stronger evidence in the fact that many descriptions of the operation, scope, and interests of the house are enclosed in quotation marks. Only one of the small presses and little magazines of which this reviewer has personal knowledge was listed, and many were not. The question of what constitutes a small press is going to be subjective, but at least one fairly major player was included.—**Robert M. Slade**

588. **Literary Market Place 1999.** 59th ed. New Providence, N.J., R. R. Bowker, 1998. 3v. $189.95. ISBN 0-8352-4053-3.

Literary Market Place has been reviewed in ARBA on many occasions and there is no need to repeat previous comments. It serves as a useful and handy tool to many booksellers, bookstores, and larger libraries that need information about publishers, book manufacturers, societies, pertinent associations, books, and magazines associated with book trade and other items.

The 1999 edition marks the 59th annual publication of this work and contains some 15,000 entries, 584 of which are listed for the 1st time. The information is based on a questionnaire and is about one or two years old.—**Bohdan S. Wynar**

589. **Literary Market Place on Disc.** [CD-ROM]. New Providence, N.J., R. R. Bowker, 1999. Minimum system requirements: IBM or compatible. CD-ROM drive. Windows 3.1x or higher. 4MB RAM. 10MB hard disk space. $289.95. ISBN 0-8352-4211-0.

Literary Market Place on Disc combines two Bowker mainstays: *Literary Market Place* (see entry 588), the well-known directory of the publishing industry, and Bowker's aging search and retrieval software. It should be noted that *International Literary Market Place* data are also included.

The major complaint about *Literary Market Place* for many years has been its tendency to become outdated very quickly. People move around too often and too quickly in the publishing and related industries and many publishers and associated companies are negligent in keeping their data current via Bowker's annual questionnaires and data collection Website. Although the disc version is more current than the traditional print version, some quick searches revealed the problem still exists.

Searching the disc with Bowker's traditional search and retrieval software reveals some flaws common to most Bowker directory and database products. There is too much reliance on strictly software and not enough human intervention or editorial work. The software still is not overly intuitive and the interface remains busy and confusing at times. There is some benefit to the searchable disc version, particularly searching for common data among publishers or for such specific information as which company owns imprint X. Among the major sections are book publishers, small presses, literary agents, lecture agents, book reviewers, manufacturers, and so on. A nice feature of the disc version is the capability to create and print mailing labels to one or many selected persons or companies. This could be of great use by publishing industry personnel, librarians, potential authors, and many other persons.

If library staff and or patrons use *Literary Market Place* frequently, the disc version is recommended. If it is used infrequently, the print version would work as well as the disc.—**Edward Kurdyla**

590. **The Lithuanian Publishers Directory.** Dale T. Lukas, ed. Arlington, Va., Assist International; distr., Medford, N.J., Information Today, 1999. 207p. index. $49.50pa. ISBN 1-57387-076-5.

Although 1997 was declared the year of the book in Lithuania, at that time there was no comprehensive directory of publishers and publishing houses. Recognizing this dearth of information, a team of American and Lithuanian librarians, with the support of the International Research and Exchange Board, undertook the project of compiling such a directory. Based on a survey sent to 700 known publishers at the time, the resulting product includes responses from approximately one-half of them. The directory is divided into 5 parts. Part 1 consists of 6 informative articles about Lithuanian publishing—"Book Publishing in Lithuania," "Lithuanian Publishing Market," "Lithuanian Book Market," "Book Publishing in Reestablished Lithuania: Is Lithuania a Literary Province?" "Book Import Situation in Lithuania," and "Bookselling Through the Publishers' Eyes." Part 2 contains the listings of the publishers themselves, including name, address, telephone and fax number, ISBN, and other information when available (e.g., marketing, distribution, sales representative, ordering information, series, languages, subjects). Part 3 lists publishers by type of literature and subjects. Part 4, an appendix, contains information about related organizations, distributors, bookstores, printers, and other available reference materials about Lithuanian publishing.

The directory is a much-needed resource for Lithuania. Its execution, both in terms of inclusiveness, type of information provided, and presentation, is admirable. It should serve as an excellent example of what can be done cooperatively to create useful reference works about publishing activities in other countries that formerly were incorporated within the Soviet Union.—**Robert H. Burger**

Handbooks and Yearbooks

591. **The American Book Buyers Study.** New York, Book Industry Study Group, 1997. 1v. (various paging). $295.00pa. ISBN 0-940016-68-0.

This study of adult American book-buying habits is based on a representative group of 801 adults who were interviewed by telephone in February and March 1997, 201 Internet questionnaires, and 32 face-to-face exit interviews conducted outside of bookstores. There are 38 pages of summary tables followed by several hundred pages of detailed tabulations. Unfortunately, there is no subject index. This is certainly a major study filled with practical, useful, and interesting information for booksellers, media sociologists, and anyone with an interest in the factors influencing the consumer purchasing of books in the United States. The major limitation of this study is that it was conducted in the early stages of the Internet era before Amazon.com, BarnesandNoble.com, and Border.com had become major suppliers of new books and before Bibliofind.com and ABE.com had revolutionized the finding and purchasing of used and out-of-print books. Thus, although the data on what influences people to buy books remain valid, the data on the sources from which Americans obtain books are outdated. And as the Internet spawns a variety of electronic books, such as Rocket books, and continues to amass an ever larger pool of free, online classics in the humanities, Americans' book-buying habits may well undergo profound change.—**Joseph Cataio**

592. **By the Numbers: Electronic and Online Publishing.** Annemarie Muth, ed. Farmington Hills, Mich., Gale, 1998. 481p. index. $79.00pa. ISBN 0-7876-1858-6. ISSN 1096-4967.

Most librarians are familiar with the technology statistics and graphs portrayed in sources such as *USA Today* citing industry spokesmen, polls, or trade associations. This installment in the Gale series culls these elusive reports and publishes them in uniform, easy-to-read tables, occasionally accompanied by pie charts. Other entries in the By the Numbers series focus on other single industries or sectors. This snapshot is for those readers who want to know where we've been, even as we forge ahead.

This volume on electronic and online publishing uses 593 tables to document the broad topic of high technology, including demographics, industry trends and costs, markets and market share, employment and compensation, computer crime, e-commerce, international trade, and education. A handy glossary and an industry timetable accompany a detailed index.

The subtitle may be slightly misleading because the book ranges well beyond electronic publishing to cover the online world. The section on demographics offers tables treating online users by age, gender, income, and ethnicity, as well as how much time they spend online and whether they access the Web from home, the office, or school. Other tables indicate what it costs the average company to deal with a virus, as well as offering a clear definition of what a virus is and how it usually works. Another section lists each technology-related SIC and breaks down employees, revenues, and payroll for each state. In short, the scope of the work is greater than the title suggests.

Sources tapped for this useful compendium include trade periodicals and newsletters, magazines and newspapers, polling data, the Census, and several government agencies. Most of the data cover 1995 to 1997, although the economic census data are from 1992. When projections are called for, they usually extend to 2000. Clearly in an industry where whole technologies may vanish, there is likely to be a ready market of librarians and information providers awaiting the next edition of this valuable statistical handbook. [R: BL, 15 May 98, pp. 1651, 1654; RUSQ, Summer 98, p. 344]—**John P. Schmitt**

12 Military Studies

GENERAL WORKS

Atlases

593. **The Hutchinson Atlas of Battle Plans: Before and After.** John Pimlott, ed. Chicago, Fitzroy Dearborn, 1998. 237p. maps. index. $55.00. ISBN 1-57958-203-6.

Although this small, attractive volume is called an atlas, it is more correctly a case study of battle plans, before and after. It was not intended to be a comprehensive work on battle plans. Instead, this book looks at types of military action and how plans were implemented and what was the result. There are six headings: classic ploys, surprise, misunderstanding, mission impossible, underestimating the enemy, and narrow margins. Battles from ancient times to World War II are covered. Included among them are Cannae, Crecy, Balaklava, Battle of the Bulge, Austerlitz, and Gettysburg.

Most of the contributors are lecturers at the Royal Military Academy at Sandhurst. The main thrust of the work delves into the variables that come into play during battle, not the least of which is the human variable. Battle is a dynamic activity with two sides acting and responding to each other's moves. This small volume is an excellent introduction to analyzing battle plans and the battles themselves and is highly recommended for private, public, high school, and college and university library reference collections.
—**Norman L. Kincaide**

Bibliography

594. Calder, James D., comp. **Intelligence, Espionage, and Related Topics: An Annotated Bibliography of Serial Journal and Magazine Scholarship, 1844-1998.** Westport, Conn., Greenwood Press, 1999. 1330p. index. (Bibliographies and Indexes in Military Studies, no.11). $150.00. ISBN 0-313-29290-6.

With the end of the twentieth century came a flood of concerns about terrorist activity, causing Seattle to cancel much-awaited millennium celebrations and domestic airports to increase security. The intelligence community was in profile across all media and terrorists and spies were once again in vogue—not just your James Bond-types—but those international terrorists who cause massive death and destruction. Calder's bibliography documents the intelligence and espionage journal literature spanning 150 years. Arranged alphabetically by author, this extensive bibliography (nearly 10,000 citations) includes mostly scholarly literature with a considerable number of popular press references. Literally hundreds of serial publications are covered and many of the entries are annotated. A section of "late entries" includes more than 1,500 additions from July 1997 through 1998. The emphasis is on spy literature, although terrorists and international incidents are included. There are even eight references to the ubiquitous Bond. The primary focus is on more recent studies, but subjects covered include Abraham Lincoln, George Washington, and the American Revolution (60 references). A 60-page index is essential to the volume. This work is a useful addition for reference collections.—**Boyd Childress**

Biography

595. American Military Leaders. [CD-ROM]. Santa Barbara, Calif., ABC-CLIO, 1998. Minimum system requirements: Pentium-compatible processor at 75MHz or faster. Four-speed CD-ROM drive. Windows 95. 8MB RAM. 30MB hard disk space. SVGA monitor 640x480 (256 colors). 16-bit sound card with Windows drivers. $49.00 (single user); $129.00 (lab pack). ISBN 1-57607-021-2.

The interactive CD-ROM version of *American Military Leaders* largely replicates the content of the 2-volume printed edition. More than 420 individuals are featured, including some who were not military leaders (e.g., Clara Barton and Ernie Pyle). There are four means of access to the biographical sketches: an alphabetic list of biographees; a list of 27 subject headings; combining "attributes" (individual title, birth and death date ranges, gender, ethnicity, and place of birth); and "Text Search" (Boolean combinations of up to four terms). Use of assigned subject headings is less than satisfactory, a situation duplicated in the printed edition. The manual gives installation instructions only, as other assistance with the product is with ever-present online help buttons. Supplementary reference materials are a basic glossary, very basic maps, and a timeline that permits users to superimpose the individual timelines of the members of a group (e.g., doctors) on other military and nonmilitary events. There are bibliographic references at the ends of the sketches.

Although the product works in a Windows environment, the user cannot run anything else at the same time, and cutting and pasting to Windows applications is difficult. Some preferences can be set (e.g., export to floppy only and the size of the displayed type). The printed set is priced at $150.00. The minimal enhancements of the CD-ROM will limit demand to those institutions preferring the economy of the single-user license over the printed set. [R: BR, Sept/Oct 99, pp. 83-84; BL, 15 Nov 99, p. 644]

—**Kenneth W. Berger**

596. Fredriksen, John C. **American Military Leaders: From Colonial Times to the Present.** Santa Barbara, Calif., ABC-CLIO, 1999. 2v. illus. index. $150.00/set. ISBN 1-57607-001-8.

Few subjects attract more readers than military history and, when combined with a biography, the result is more often than not a successful book. In *American Military Leaders*, Fredriksen offers 422 sketches of the men and women who make up the leadership of the U.S. military experience. Included are 2- to 3-page biographies spanning time from the colonial period to Norman Schwarzkopf and Colin Powell. The 2-volume set also includes names such as Native Americans Sitting Bull and Geronimo. Military leadership, not military heroism, is the primary criterion for inclusion, thus names like Abraham Lincoln, William Gorgas (who found a cure for yellow fever during the building of the Panama Canal), and Russian-born aeronautical engineer Alexander De Seversky are included. Women include aviator Jackie Cochran and Civil War nurse Dorothea Dix. Some may argue against the inclusion of Benedict Arnold and Jefferson Davis, yet both excelled at leadership. Notes for further reading are added after each biography. A 15-page index provides ample access to individuals, battles, and events throughout the text of all the sketches. Fredriksen's work surpasses the *Dictionary of Military Biography* (see ARBA 86, entry 620) and should be an asset to military history in all libraries. [R: LJ, 15 Sept 99, pp. 68-70]—**Boyd Childress**

597. Leaders of the American Civil War: A Biographical and Historiographical Dictionary. Charles F. Ritter and Jon L. Wakelyn, eds. Westport, Conn., Greenwood Press, 1998. 465p. index. $85.00. ISBN 0-313-29560-3.

This is a biographical work with a significant difference. Not only does it provide biographical information about a selected group of Civil War leaders, but traces the ups and downs of their reputations over a period of more than 130 years, as recorded by themselves and historians.

The basic layout of this book is simple, and it is a wonder that there are not more works of this kind. The editors selected 47 men and women that they consider to have been leaders during the Civil War. These include not only persons in the military, but others in such fields as the press, industry, nursing, literature, politics, the abolition movement, and one wife of a political leader (i.e., Varina Howell Davis, the wife of Jefferson Davis). Arranged in alphabetic order, each entry tells of an individual's life, with emphasis on the war years, followed by his or her treatment in history from the Civil War to the present. This novel approach provides a balanced picture of these men and women that is not possible when examining the literature on an individual written during a specific period when that person's reputation was at its high or low point.

This book includes a 17-page essay on the writing of biographical history. Access to the contents is gained through a good index. The authors of these biographical and historiographical essays are generally reputable historians of the Civil War era. There are 25 (more than half) written by Wakelyn, while 8 were written by Ritter and only 1 each by a variety of graduate students and nationally known scholars.

This volume makes good reading for pleasure by any Civil War buff, of which there are many. History students in colleges and universities will find it invaluable for course and research assignments. As a reference work, however, it suffers from the fact that it is a single volume containing a comparatively small number of Civil War leaders, many of whom are lesser individuals in which few researchers will have an interest. If, however, the editors choose to do this as a series, which this reviewer recommends, it will become a major reference tool that would be indispensable in the library of any institution that teaches the Civil War era. Even with this one criticism, this book is highly recommended for all libraries and individuals with an interest in the Civil War. [R: Choice, May 99, p. 1600]—**Donald E. Collins**

Dictionaries and Encyclopedias

598. **America at War.** New York, Macmillan Library Reference/Simon & Schuster Macmillan, 1998. 846p. illus. maps. index. (Macmillan Compendium). $125.00. ISBN 0-02-865061-1.

This is a 1-volume military history of the United States, dating from the earliest days of colonization to the Gulf War of 1991. It is not a new work, as it is made up entirely from selections taken from an earlier 3-volume set titled *The Encyclopedia of the American Military* published in 1994 and edited by John E. Jessup of the American Military University (see ARBA 95, entry 688).

Despite the abridgement, this is a good work, one that smaller libraries will appreciate for its size, affordability, and usefulness. The book begins with an overview of American history provided in a 3-column chronological chart that lists leading persons, general history, and military history. The remainder of the volume is divided into 3 parts. The 1st part, covering more than half the contents, provides a clear, generally well-written military history of this country. Each chapter is written by a historian, with the writing ranging from average to excellent depending on the author. There are some errors, and some may disagree with the fullness or interpretation of certain events. However, in a work of this magnitude, this is a minor consideration. A particularly valuable characteristic of this book is its coverage of military aspects of the periods between wars.

The 2d part provides brief histories of each of the armed forces, while the 3d part gives brief biographies of 39 military leaders, including 2 Native Americans, Crazy Horse and Sitting Bull. One might question the inclusion, however, of Davy Crockett in such a short list of great military personages of the United States. Three appendixes provide lists of Medal of Honor recipients arranged according to the war it was received in, a selection of wartime speeches and documents, and the texts of 11 peace treaties, although 3 are included in excerpts only. Access to the contents is solely through a 20-page general index that, despite its length, could be improved upon.

This is a reference book that anyone with an interest in history will enjoy. It is recommended for all libraries with an interest in American history, and to those history-minded persons in the general public as well. [R: SLJ, Aug 99, p. 181]—**Donald E. Collins**

599. Beckett, Ian F. W. **Encyclopedia of Guerrilla Warfare.** Santa Barbara, Calif., ABC-CLIO, 1999. 303p. illus. index. $75.00. ISBN 0-87436-929-0.

This is a timely book given the increasing rise in guerrilla warfare during the twentieth century. Readers are introduced to the topic through a well-written bibliographic and explanatory essay that provides a good understanding of the topic and the major literature related to it. Users are provided information on a variety of terms and persons related to guerrilla movements over the past two centuries, with emphasis on the present and recent past.

The book is well organized for ease of use. Access to information is excellent through a detailed subject index and an alphabetic list of subject entries. A list of acronyms helps users identify specific guerrilla and related organizations when only their letter designations are known. A chronology of events from 1755 to 1998 is also useful, while a substantial bibliography leads to further reading on the topic. The main body of the book consists of brief to moderate-length essays that are generally well written and that are followed by *see also* references and suggested books for further reading.

There are criticisms, however. The articles vary in quality. Biographical entries are particularly well done, whereas many others lack sufficient depth and are too sketchy. This reviewer wonders why such persons as General George A. Custer, a regular army officer, are included, while well-known guerrilla leaders like William C. Quantrill and John Singleton Mosby are relegated to a few lines in a survey article. There are also a number of factual errors. For example, Andrew Jackson's Indian removal policy was not limited, as stated, to the "five civilized tribes of the southeast" (p. 214), nor did the Wounded Knee massacre take place at Big Foot's "village," but at a temporary stopping place forced upon the tribe by the U.S. cavalry (p. 11). Also, the First Seminole War (1816-1818) was not connected to an Indian removal policy (p. 11). With the noted exceptions, however, this is a good and useful reference work and is recommended for school, college, university, and public libraries with an interest in history and current events. [R: BL, Aug 99, pp. 2106-2107; Choice, Oct 99, p. 311; BR, Nov/Dec 99, p. 86]—**Donald E. Collins**

600. Davis, Paul K., and Allen Lee Hamilton. **Encyclopedia of Warrior Peoples and Fighting Groups.** Santa Barbara, Calif., ABC-CLIO, 1998. 294p. illus. index. $75.00. ISBN 0-87436-961-4; 1-57607-046-8pa.

The authors of this encyclopedia took a core sampling of military history and chose more than a hundred people or groups of people noted for their fighting qualities. The selection begins with the Assyrians of the ninth and seventh centuries B.C.E. (As Lord Byron wrote: "The Assyrians came down like a wolf on the fold, and his cohorts were gleaming in purple and gold.") The latest entry is the Viet Minh and their successors who won their freedom by defeating two Western military powers, France and the United States. Included are mythical or near-mythical subjects.

The entries are organized alphabetically in true encyclopedia fashion, from Afghans to Zulus. Unfortunately, there are no cross-references. Each entry varies in length from a page to several pages. Leading off each entry is a definition of what and when, followed by the exposition written in a clear, brisk manner and citing two or three sources. Here are the works of such distinguished historians as David Chandler, Shelby Foote, and John Keegan. There is also a nine-page bibliography. The two authors have written an interesting reference work that is fun to read. [R: BL, 1 Feb 99, p. 996; LJ, 15 Feb 99, p. 142; Choice, June 99, p. 1762]—**David Eggenberger**

601. Schwartz, Richard Alan. **Encyclopedia of the Persian Gulf War.** Jefferson, N.C., McFarland, 1998. 216p. illus. maps. index. $45.00. ISBN 0-7864-0451-5.

The brief six-week Persian Gulf War in January and February 1991 has been the subject of a rather large number of reference volumes, including chronologies, fact books, bibliographies, almanacs, and encyclopedias. This slim volume, from a leading publisher of reference sources, is one of the best. The entries are lengthy and the comprehensive coverage includes people, places, events, weapons, operations, and other matters. The volume also has an extensive chronology of major events, from the overthrow of the Iraqi monarchy in 1958 through the aftermath of the 1991 war. The text is augmented by numerous pictures, maps, and portraits; and the book contains a bibliography on the conflict and a good index. The style

and layout make the volume easy to use by specialist and laypersons alike. The attractive volume would be a good addition to public and general use libraries. Compare it to Mark Grossman's *Encyclopedia of the Persian Gulf War* (ABC-CLIO, 1995), Harry G. Summers Jr.'s *Persian Gulf War Almanac* (Facts on File, 1995), and Kevin Don Hutchinson's *Operation Desert Shield/Desert Storm: Chronology and Fact Book* (see ARBA 96, entry 563). [R: BL, 15 Sept 98, p. 262; SLJ, Aug 98, p. 195; Choice, Sept 98, p. 101]
—**Joe P. Dunn**

602. **World War II in Europe: An Encyclopedia.** David T. Zabecki, Carl O. Schuster, Paul J. Rose, and William H. Van Husen, eds. New York, Garland, 1999. 2v. illus. maps. index. (Garland Reference Library of the Humanities, v.1254; Military History of the United States, v.6). $195.00/set. ISBN 0-8240-7029-1.

A truly international effort brought about the creation of this wonderful 2-volume set on World War II in Europe. Contributors totaling 155 from 8 different countries helped make these volumes a part of the Garland series on Military History of the United States. These volumes are well organized, well written, and beautifully produced. Volume 1 contains 3 sections: social and political issues and events; leaders and individuals; and units and organizations. Volume 2 also has 3 sections, plus appendixes. It details weapons and equipment; strategy, tactics, and operational techniques; and battles, campaigns, and operations. The appendixes provide a chronology of events; tables of comparative ranks; a glossary of acronyms, abbreviations, and foreign and military terms; Allied and Axis code names; and a selected bibliography. There are 2 indexes—one of military units and warships and a general index.

This work deals with all aspects of one of the most significant event in the twentieth century. Individual combat soldiers, sailors, and airmen are not forgotten in this well-conceived encyclopedia. The whole concept of the war in Europe is contained in two moderately sized volumes. Well-written and -organized entries provide enough information to get a student or enthusiast of the subject started on a journey of investigation that will probably never end. The editorial staff needs to be commended for their excellent work. This set is highly recommended for high school, college, university, and private reference collections. [R: Choice, July/Aug 99, p. 1930]—**Norman L. Kincaide**

Directories

603. **Jane's World Defense Industry.** John Reed, ed. Alexandria, Va., Jane's Information Group, 1998. 1v. (various paging). $930.00 looseleaf w/binder. ISBN 0-7106-1631-7.

Jane's World Defense Industry contains detailed information on the 300 most important defense companies and includes directory information, main personnel, organizational structure, summary financial data, main contracting agreements, product range and descriptions, subsidiaries and divisions, and news developments. Companies are arranged alphabetically by company within seven regions of the world. There is no index, but all the companies are listed in the table of contents.

There are some quality control and access concerns with the reviewed copy. The volume contained pages from "Issue 0" (May 1997) and "Issue 3" (September 1998) updates. There was no divider tab for "Africa and the Middle East." (There are no entries for "Latin America," but this was because a Brazilian company, part of "Issue 1," was the only one listed in the table of contents.) Commentaries preceding each regional grouping had not been updated since May 1997; and although updates are scheduled quarterly, as of the third update many original entries have never been revised. The lack of page numbers, even within the sections for individual companies, makes it more likely that there will be errors in filing updates, or when users replace pages after use. Furthermore, the names of the companies are not listed as page headers or footers, making access more difficult, especially for those countries with many companies. As with many other Jane's publications, the directory is available either as a CD-ROM ($1,475.00) or through Internet access ($1,550.00). This is potentially a very useful source for those involved in defense industry research or commercial activities, but its high price will probably limit acquisition to comprehensive research collections and appropriate special and corporate libraries.—**Kenneth W. Berger**

Handbooks and Yearbooks

604. Davidson, Michael J. **A Guide to Military Criminal Law.** Annapolis, Md., Naval Institute Press, 1999. 191p. index. $27.95. ISBN 1-55750-155-6.

The title and subtitle aptly describe the purpose and the market for this handy, quick-reference guide. The author, a West Point graduate, was an artillery officer prior to joining the Army Judge Advocate Generals Corps, where he served as military prosecutor, federal prosecutor, civil litigator, and contract and administrative law attorney. Deftly written with a wry sense of humor, the slim volume translates the labyrinth of military law under the Uniform Code of Military Justice into easily comprehensible layperson's terms. Topics include jurisdiction, nonjudicial punishment, the court-martial process, military crimes, the law of war, and much more. Throughout, the author cites specific cases to illustrate his points. For someone who had little prior knowledge or interest in this subject, this reviewer found the book interesting, even captivating, reading. Clearly, this volume should be available in every military library, in civilian libraries where there are military communities, and in all law school collections. Furthermore, its inexpensive price and readability make it worthy of consideration for other general collections as well.—**Joe P. Dunn**

605. Edmonds, Anthony O. **The War in Vietnam.** Westport, Conn., Greenwood Press, 1998. 192p. illus. maps. index. (Greenwood Press Guides to Historic Events of the Twentieth Century). $39.95. ISBN 0-313-29847-5.

America's painfully long, difficult military involvement in Vietnam continues to provoke controversy and debate. Probably no war before or since has polarized the American people to the same extent, which poses a challenge for compilers of reference books on the subject. Edmonds, a professor of history at Ball State University who has authored articles and curriculum guides about the Vietnam War, has decided here to use an objective, nonjudgmental approach in analyzing the complexities of the war and its effects. His perspective on President Lyndon Johnson is typical. He casts Johnson "as neither a war monger nor a noble defender of freedom, but rather as a complex leader who was caught in circumstances difficult to control."

Like the other books in the Greenwood Press Guides series, this work is intended to serve as both a reference book and a history in its own right. First there is a good "Chronology of Events" section, followed by seven perceptive essays, including "Ho Chi Minh and the Vietnamese Tradition of Rebellion" and "Legacies of the War." The section of short biographies is well rounded, covering key figures at home and abroad, including General Westmoreland, Abbie Hoffman, and Robert McNamara, although it is puzzling why there is a biography of entertainer Martha Raye, while Bob Hope (whose Christmas shows for the troops were legendary) is absent. In addition, there are sections including primary documents from the war, a glossary of terms, and an annotated bibliography. A dozen photograph illustrations enhance the work.

Although the stated audience is high school and college students, the approach seems more appropriate for high school. Several controversial issues are avoided or glossed over, including the Vietnamese use of booby traps, widespread drug abuse among American servicemen, the subculture of massage parlors and prostitution, and the increasing incidence of insubordination and even attempted murder ("fragging") of superior officers. However, the divisiveness of antiwar demonstrations is covered, as is the massacre at My Lai.

A more adult perspective is achieved by Harry Summers Jr. in his *Vietnam War Almanac* (see ARBA 86, entry 519), which is the reference book that appears most comparable in scope and format to the present work. Summers, an infantry colonel who served in Vietnam, pulls no punches in his coverage of the distasteful aspects of war, and although he provides the valuable insights of a career soldier, he sensitively examines the many concerns expressed by the antiwar movement. His work will continue to be the standard reference handbook for college libraries, while Edmonds will be best in high school libraries.

—**Richard W. Grefrath**

606.   Lesinski, Jeanne M. **MIAs: A Reference Handbook.** Santa Barbara, Calif., ABC-CLIO, 1998. 238p. index. (Contemporary World Issues). $45.00. ISBN 0-87436-954-1.

Despite the series title, the Contemporary World Issues books, now a total of 28 volumes, deal primarily with U.S. domestic problems such as crime, violence, environmental issues, and drug abuse. The books serve as a basic starting point for high school and college students' research and for general readers. The series follows a uniform pattern that includes on overview of the subject, a detailed chronology, biographical sketches, facts and statistics, documents, a directory of organizations and agencies, an annotated bibliography, a glossary, and an index.

Although the subject of this volume is a bit outside the series norm, it is a useful reference source. The introductory overview of the MIA topic during and after the Vietnam War does a good job of tracing the complex history of an issue that has been characterized more by emotion than dispassion. However, it is not clear what function the chronology of the Vietnam War serves, and the selections for biographical sketches are curious. Although her annotations of the selected books in the annotated bibliography are good, it is not clear why some POW and MIA books are included and other equally important volumes are not. Also, the periodical literature on the subject is virtually ignored. The most valuable section is the list of organizations involved in POW and MIA issues and the copious Internet sources available. The latter references alone justify the book.

Although what is not in this volume may cause some frustration, it nevertheless contains a lot of information for the novice student, and it is offered in an easy and accessible format. This volume is recommended for public and high school libraries and for many undergraduate college collections as well.—**Joe P. Dunn**

607.   **SIPRI Yearbook 1998: Armaments, Disarmament, and International Security.** By the Stockholm International Peace Research Institute. New York, Oxford University Press, 1998. 638p. index. $115.00. ISBN 0-19-829454-9. ISSN 0953-0282.

This resource attempts to cover the wide range of recent military activities and affairs and their impacts on regional and world peace and security. There are three major sections covering development for 1997: security and conflicts; military spending and armaments; and nonproliferation, arms control, and disarmament. The sections are subdivided into various themes, each with an analytical survey essay. The numerous tables and text are heavily documented, more than making up for the lack of a bibliography. The tabular data are current, in most instances through 1996 or 1997, and several offer coverage back into the 1980s. Other supplementary materials include a list of acronyms, glossary of terms and organizations, a list of international organizations and their membership, summary statements and signatories for dozens of relevant international agreement, a chronology for 1997, abstracts of the major articles in the volume, notes on contributors, and a subject index. There is also an errata page of corrections to the 1997 volume. The annual remains a standard resource for students and scholars of international relations and defense studies, and is highly recommended for academic and research libraries.—**Kenneth W. Berger**

AIR FORCE

608.   Terry, Michael Robert. **Historical Dictionary of the United States Air Force and Its Antecedents.** Lanham, Md., Scarecrow, 1999. 460p. maps. (Historical Dictionaries of War, Revolution, and Civil Unrest, no.11). $89.50. ISBN 0-8108-3631-9.

This compact volume gives an excellent overview of Air Force history through its comprehensive chronology and introduction and list of well-selected and encyclopedic definitions. The chronology begins with the 1903 flight 97 years ago by Orville Wright at Kitty Hawk, North Carolina, and ends with the show of force over the Adriatic in 1998 in response to the Serbian shelling of Kosovo. The 22-page introduction outlines the growth of the Air Force from its inception in 1914 as the Aviation Section, U.S. Army Signal Corps, to the U.S. Army Service (1918-1926), to the U.S. Army Air Corps (1926-1941), to the U.S. Army Air Forces (1941-1947), to the present U.S. Air Force.

The major part of the volume is the alphabetically arranged dictionary. The terms range from the well known, such as *ace, air power, B-17 Flying Fortress, Eighth Air Force*, and *Generals Doolittle, LeMay, Spatz*, and *Arnold* to the less familiar, including *Operations Bolo* and *Barrel Roll*. Virtually every aircraft used in combat operations and every officer who played a major role in any of the air wars is listed. Each entry includes cross-references. Thus in the entry for "Persian Gulf War (1990-1991)" one will find *Desert Shield, Berlin Airlift, AIM-7*, and *ordnance*. The volume concludes with an extensive bibliography and 10 appendixes, 5 of which identify aces of air wars. Reference departments with even a modest military history collection will likely want to purchase this outstanding, yet expensive, dictionary.—**Charles R. Andrews**

609. Williams, Nicholas M. **Aircraft of the United States' Military Air Transport Service 1948 to 1966.** Leicester, England, Midland Publishing; distr., Stillwater, Minn., Voyageur Press, 1999. 192p. illus. $39.95. ISBN 1-87780-087-7.

The first third of this work covers the history of the Military Air Transport Service (MATS) from its prewar origins in the 1930s to 1966, when the service was renamed and reorganized as the Military Airlift Command. The rest of the book is devoted to descriptions and service histories of the various aircraft used by MATS during its existence. The book is printed on heavy, coated paper that brings out details in the fine black-and-white and color photographs used to illustrate the history. Few of these photographs, by the way, are the ones readers are used to seeing over and over again in aircraft publications; these have been selected from a variety of sources and are remarkable for their quality and freshness. A brief bibliography concludes the work.

While MATS may not be as glamorous as the combat branches of the Air Force, this extremely well-produced book does justice to a unit who made possible many of this country's successes in World War II, Korea, and the Cold War. While it is more a history than a reference book, libraries with readers interested in the Air Force and its aircraft will want to have this title.—**Eric R. Nitschke**

NAVY

610. **Jane's Naval Construction and Retrofit Markets.** E. R. Hooton, ed. Alexandria, Va., Jane's Information Group, 1998. 1v. (various paging). $810.00 looseleaf w/binder. ISBN 0-7106-1397-0.

A significant support infrastructure is required to construct, maintain, and develop the world's naval fleets. Updated three times a year, this new compendium from Jane's Information Group focuses on the market for naval shipping and the facilities responsible for meeting the needs of this specialized market.

Like other Jane's publications, an editorial foreword covers important events, trends, and developments within this field. The heart of *Naval Construction and Retrofit Markets* is broken into sections dealing with various sectors of the shipping arena. These sectors, separated by binder tables, include shipyards, propulsion/management systems, sensors/communication manufacturers, weapons/weapon control systems manufacturers, ship designs, construction programs, upgrades and refits, and market data.

Individual entries include location and basic contact information for individual companies broken down by country, descriptions of individual facilities and plant infrastructure, workforce size, company financial information (if available), recently awarded contracts, national shipbuilding market condition analysis, and technical descriptions about various propulsion systems. Photographs of selected ships and weapons systems are also included.

This work adheres to the high standards of other Jane's reference works in its information coverage and production quality. It contains insightful descriptions and analysis of trends and developments in this important but overlooked area of economic and military activity. One improvement for individual company entries would be including e-mail and Website addresses when available. This work will be most suited for libraries with comprehensive shipping or naval literature collections, such as armed service academies or libraries in areas where shipping and naval construction play important roles in the local economy.—**Bert Chapman**

WEAPONS AND EQUIPMENT

611. Fredriksen, John C. **Warbirds: An Illustrated Guide to U.S. Military Aircraft, 1915-2000.** Santa Barbara, Calif., ABC-CLIO, 1999. 363p. illus. $75.00. ISBN 1-57607-131-6.

The development of manned aircraft has revolutionized twentieth-century military operations and will continue to play a major role in future military operations. The success achieved by military aircraft has evolved through trial and error and involved several generations of military aircraft that have been created to meet the perceived national security needs of a variety of nations.

Warbirds is a guide to aircraft used by U.S. military forces during the twentieth century. It opens with a preface and contextual introduction. The main part of the book is a guide to important U.S. military aircraft arranged in alphabetic order by the company producing the individual planes. Entries for these aircraft include a black-and-white photograph; type of airplane; plane dimensions; weight; power source; performance including maximum speed, altitude ceiling, and maximum range; armament; service dates; and a succinct summary of major developments during the plane's lifetime.

Examples of aircraft profiled within this compilation are the Bell AH-1J SeaCobra/SuperCobra helicopter gunship, Boeing B-17 Flying Fortress, Curtiss P-36 Hawk, General Dynamics F-16 Fighting Falcon, Grumman A-6 Intruder, Lockheed C-130 Hercules, McDonnell-Douglas AV-8 Harrier, North American F-86 Sabre, Sikorsky CH-53/HH-53 Sea Stallion transport helicopter, and Vought O2U Corsair. Additional contents include an aircraft bibliography arranged by the production company and a general military aircraft bibliography. Concluding appendixes feature aircraft arranged by mission, including electronic warfare and strategic bomber, a chronological listing of aircraft by historical period, U.S. and Canadian aircraft museums, and aircraft journals and magazines.

Warbirds is a good general introduction to military aircraft. Its bibliography is adequate but could be strengthened by the addition of primary sources such as the *Encyclopedia of U.S. Air Force Aircraft and Missile Systems*. Although *Warbirds* does not provide the detail of *Jane's All the World's Aircraft* (89th ed.; see ARBA 99, entry 1575) or armed services-produced compendia, it is still a worthwhile investment for any library desiring to enhancing its military aircraft collections. [R: LJ, 15 Nov 99, p. 61]
—**Bert Chapman**

612. **Jane's Market Intelligence Library.** [CD-ROM]. Alexandria, Va., Jane's Information Group, 1997. Minimum system requirements: IBM or compatible 486. Double-speed CD-ROM drive. Windows 3.1. 8MB RAM. 2MB hard disk space. SVGA monitor. $12,000. ISBN 0-7106-1512-4.

The name "Jane's" is now proverbial to anyone who knows anything about the military, or rather wishes to know anything about the military. *Market Intelligence* (MI) is no exception, full of wonderfully enchanting, staggeringly frightening information impossible to find elsewhere.

Loading MI is quite easy. The tutorial that runs off of Lotus ScreenCam is a pleasure to watch. Not only is it informative, but it is also carefully wrought to provide even the wariest users with all they need to know. The "tooltips" that appear when the cursor is placed on an icon add to the CD's presentation. This CD contains two new reports, "Modernisation [sic] Markets, Western Europe," and "Radars for Combat Aircraft." The heart of the disk, however, is the fabulous specification material on military equipment, from nuclear superiority to Apache helicopters. Not only are diagrams available with a click of the mouse, but in many cases, graphic files allow users to see the viewed equipment in action. A casual scroll through the topics reminds users just how unsafe the modern world is, and how easily its balance can be upset into conflict.

The amount of data on the disk is mind-boggling, the ease of use a delight. Its user-friendliness should become a model for all CD makers. Of course the price will keep it out of the hands of most users. But for libraries who have a need for it, nothing else will do.—**Mark Y. Herring**

613. Massman, Emory A. **Hospital Ships of World War II: An Illustrated Reference to 39 United States Military Vessels.** Jefferson, N.C., McFarland, 1999. 499p. illus. index. $75.00. ISBN 0-7864-0556-2.

There were 39 vessels that served as U.S. hospital ships during World War II. Only one was designed as a hospital ship; some were converted while still being built, whereas others were converted from passenger liners, troop ships, or even freighters. Such vessels provided important service during the war, bringing home thousands of American and Allied soldiers, plus many enemy troops. Massman provides extensive information about each of the 39 ships that served in the U.S. Army or Navy during the war. The work is highlighted with numerous excellent photographs of the vessels and their crews in action. Entries are organized by branch of service and type of ship, and give an overview of each vessel's entire life, not just service during the war. Several vessels also served during the Korean and Vietnam conflicts. Ship histories range from specific information on a voyage to the impact a particular vessel had on wartime America. The entries are well written and informative, and often include firsthand narratives of life on board specific ships. An extensive index provides access to every former or future name of the hospital ships, plus captains, warships, and more. A long bibliography is also included.

Although the subject may seem obscure and even irrelevant to some, it is certainly not to those aided by these ships. The entries are an example of the sort of ship biography one would like to see more often. The book is a useful addition to military and medical history collections, and given the lack of other volumes on the subject, it may find interested readers in academic and some public libraries as well.

—**Peter H. McCracken**

13 Political Science

GENERAL WORKS

Biography

614. **Biographical Dictionary of British Prime Ministers.** Robert Eccleshall and Graham Walker, eds. New York, Routledge, 1998. 428p. index. $110.00; $35.00pa. ISBN 0-415-10830-6; 0-415-18721-4pa.

The evolutionary nature of British political institutions makes it difficult to state with precision when a particular position came into existence. That is true of the post of prime minister, now by far the key political leader in modern Britain. The editors have started their biographical dictionary with Robert Walpole (1676-1745), although he was not the first to be referred to as "prime minister." But the position assumed many of its modern attributes during Walpole's political career. From Walpole to Tony Blair, 49 other men and one woman who have served as prime minister. Each is accorded a separate entry in this biographical dictionary. The editors have not imposed a rigorous framework of analysis on the authors of the 51 "portraits" of British prime ministers. Instead, each entry reflects the particular concerns—institutional or political—and the personality and style of an individual political leader and his or her era. The editors admit that this may not make good "political science" but it does allow quick reference to the individuals who have held the position of prime minister over a period of nearly 300 years. The entries stand alone as good reference material; they can be read sequentially to obtain a sense of the evolution of the office of prime minister and the political history of modern Britain. The entries are concise and accessible. They provide references for further reading or research on each of the prime ministers. An index facilitates cross-referencing of prime ministers and other individuals and topics. This is a useful reference for both scholars and interested general readers. [R: BL, 1 Mar 99, p. 1246]—**Frank L. Wilson**

615. **The Hutchinson Encyclopedia of Modern Political Biography.** Boulder, Colo., Westview Press, 1999. 527p. illus. index. $65.00. ISBN 0-8133-3741-0.

This reference showcases more than 2,000 twentieth-century political figures who have shaped the world. The editors present a broad representation outside of North America and Europe. Using an expanded definition of political activity and influence, leaders from the arts, sports, and the media are also recognized.

The biographical sketches are listed alphabetically by name of personality. The text is enlivened by generous use of quotations and photographs. The quotations humanize the volume and capture the spirit and tenor of the historical figure beyond the brief notation. Annotations are given for further reading. Appendixes include a list of political leaders by country showing presidents, prime ministers, and monarchs for the major countries of the world; a chronological index by year of birth for each leader profiled; and an index by country, noting each individual by the nation with which he or she is primarily associated.

There are a few discrepancies. For example, although the book was published in 1999, the entry for Ron Brown does not list him as deceased. Despite this, it is a readable and accessible resource for general reference.—**Adrienne Antink Bendel**

616. Lentz, Harris M., III. **Encyclopedia of Heads of States and Governments, 1900 Through 1945.** Jefferson, N.C., McFarland, 1999. 508p. index. $75.00. ISBN 0-7864-0500-7.

A companion volume to *Heads of States and Governments: A Worldwide Encyclopedia of over 2,300 Leaders 19445 Through 1992* (see ARBA 95, entry 706), this work covers about 1,200 emperors, kings, queens, presidents, prime ministers, and other heads of government and state serving from 1900 to 1945. Only a "handful of acting presidents" are included. The countries are arranged alphabetically by the English-language name, followed by the biographical entries. Heads of state (i.e., monarch, president, military leader) are arranged chronologically and succeeded by heads of government (i.e., prime minister, premier). Each entry includes birth and death dates, full name, and brief career descriptions. The compiler tried to verify facts from at least two sources when available and used official government documents to authenticate spelling and diacritical marks. The work includes a bibliography and a combined subject, place, and personal name index. Although this volume contains only very cursory information on major world leaders, such as President Harry S. Truman, Emperor Hirohito, and Sir Winston Churchill, students, researchers, and general library users will be able to locate hard-to-find information on a much larger number of obscure government leaders who ruled during the first half of the twentieth century.

This work complements the multivolume *Rulers and Governments of the World*. Although this set covers a much longer chronology, it does not contain the useful biographical descriptions that make the other two volumes such an essential ready-reference source. [R: BL, 15 Nov 99, p. 649; Choice, Dec 99, p. 703]
—**Donald Altschiller**

617. **World Political Leaders.** [CD-ROM]. Santa Barbara, Calif., ABC-CLIO, 1999. Minimum system requirements: Pentium-compatible processor at 75MHz or faster. Four-speed CD-ROM drive. Windows 95. 16MB RAM. 30MB hard disk space. SVGA monitor 640x480 (256 colors). Mouse. $49.00 (standalone); $249.00 (network). ISBN 1-57607-164-2.

World Political Leaders (WPL), while a masterful set of 600 current biographical sketches, may be providing excellent material in an outdated format. Although the CD-ROM set is competitively priced, it is unlikely, given the ease and power of the Web, that many libraries will reserve an area of CD-ROMs at the ready when the vast majority of what they offer is offered over the Web.

It is a pity, too, for WPL provides users with up-to-date biographies of some of the world's important leaders. Ronald Reagan, Dean Acheson, Margaret Thatcher, Zulfikar Ali Bhutto, and Boutros Boutros-Ghali are but a few of the many offered to the wary seeker. ABC-CLIO's stellar reputation is upheld in these biographies. Critical social issues that focused the attention of the world on a leader, or, as is more often the case, that focused a would-be leader on the world, are discussed and fully ventilated. Personal facts abound in these sketches, humanizing the seemingly superhuman.

Access points are numerous and easy to use. Boolean text searching, along with the usual suspects of name, subject indexing, and attribute searching, makes WPL a delight to open. Other features enhance the item: "CLIOview" allows a user to compare and contrast excerpted information in a sortable list. A handy notebook feature allows users to keep crib notes and prepare their own sketch while researching various leaders. A useful timeline allows users to know at a glance where in history one leader is from another. In point of fact there is very little in WPL not to commend it, just a questionable shortsightedness that led to its compilation on CD-ROM rather than a Website that could be updated regularly while being combined with other sources.—**Mark Y. Herring**

Dictionaries and Encyclopedias

618. **World Encyclopedia of Political Systems and Parties.** 3d ed. George E. Delury and Deborah A. Kaple, eds. New York, Facts on File, 1999. 3v. index. $225.00/set. ISBN 0-8160-2874-5.

Optimally, one would like to see Facts on File publish a looseleaf service based on the contents of this encyclopedia to remain as current as possible with the rapid changes that govern most of the world's political systems. This would be especially welcome because this is an excellent resource for students and researchers at all levels. The encyclopedia maintains its format, organization, and purpose from previous editions, while expanding to three volumes that now include many of the countries of the former Soviet Union. Alphabetically arranged by country, each essay is written by one of more than 100 distinguished scholars profiled in the beginning of the 1st volume. Each entry covers essentially the same information about a country's political system and political parties, including a historical overview of the system of government, a description of key political parties, an exploration of the country's electoral process, and an analysis of the nation's prospects for continuing or achieving political stability. Embedded in many of the essays are statistical tables showing past election results and percentage of votes for specific parties. Although useful, most of these enhancements are in entries for developed nations. In many cases, entries mention the names of political leaders and their relationship to the internal political power distribution within the country. All of the entries include an updated bibliography of further readings. Volume 3 includes a list of acronyms and abbreviations that would be more useful if it were placed in the beginning of volume 1 of the encyclopedia, and a comprehensive index.

Although it could be argued that it is beyond the scope of this work, the information provided in many of the essays lacks a cultural framework in defining a nation's political system. The politics of nations and the institutional systems that shape the political environment where leaders share and compete for power is unalterably linked to a nation's cultural belief system and normative rules and regulations. However, absence of this perspective does not diminish from the overall quality or value of this research tool. It is highly recommended. [R: BL, 1 Dec 99, p. 730]—**Robert V. Labaree**

Directories

619. Hernon, Peter, John A. Shuler, and Robert E. Dugan. **U.S. Government on the Web: Getting the Information You Need.** Englewood, Colo., Libraries Unlimited, 1999. 349p. illus. index. $39.50pa. ISBN 1-56308-757-X.

The occasional user needs more than a general search engine to find the vast scope of material available from the U.S. government online. Currently there is no single access point for finding the specific data desired. This guide provides a construct for understanding how to find federal sources on the World Wide Web.

The key is understanding how the three branches of government are structured. The major agencies within each arm are detailed, with descriptions of the information found on each site with Web identifiers and appropriate links. Independent commissions and quasi-government agencies are also listed. Within the text, Web addresses are highlighted boldly in blue. Each chapter ends with easily spotted "blue pages" consolidating the URLs referred to in that section. There are also an extensive table of contents and two indexes, one by the organizations within each branch of government and the other by the title of the listings on each site. The appendix gives Web pages for public-interest groups, universities, and libraries. This book is further enhanced by the publisher's commitment to post updates on its Web page. [R: BR, Nov/Dec 99, p. 84; BL, 1 Dec 99, p. 728; JAL, Nov 99, pp. 496-497]—**Adrienne Antink Bendel**

620. **The International Directory of Government 1999.** 3d ed. Chicago, Euromonitor International; distr., Farmington Hills, Mich., Gale, 1998. 901p. $475.00. ISBN 1-85743-057-3.

With the sudden collapse of communism, many "old" states (e.g., Estonia, Lithuania, Latvia) and new ones (e.g., Bosnia, Croatia, Czech Republic) reentered or came into existence as independent entities in the world community. Although the emergence or reemergence of these states was one of the major political events of the twentieth century, searching for basic, up-to-date, and reliable governmental and related information on these states is not an easy task for many library users. Thus, the revised edition of this directory is a welcome development.

This directory, as pointed out in the foreword, is "intended to provide a comprehensive guide to government ministries, departments, agencies and corporations for every country and dependency in the world." Indeed, under each entry, which is organized alphabetically by country, one can easily find sufficient information such as address, telephone number, and e-mail address (if available) on key personnel and important organizations. The revised edition also includes a listing of "the principal organs of government in the states and provinces of federal nations, in autonomous areas and territories not under effective central control." Other useful features are lists of abbreviations and international telephone codes.

Some entries, however, should have been clarified. For instance, the role of communist parties and their leaders in countries such as Cuba, Cambodia, China, North Korea, and Vietnam are not mentioned in the text, despite the fact that they are the most powerful leaders in their countries. In addition, it would have been helpful if the date when the states covered in the directory became independent, especially the new ones, was provided. In the next edition, the editors may consider providing information relating to demography, religion, and foreign diplomatic mission.

The binding, printing, and organization are attractive; and the information is useful for students, government officials, businessmen or women, and tourists. However, before purchasing this work, libraries may want to compare it with *Worldwide Government Directory with International Organizations 1999* (see entry 625), which is more comprehensive and less expensive.—**Binh P. Le**

621. Kurian, George Thomas, and Jeffrey D. Schultz. **Political Market Place USA.** Phoenix, Ariz., Oryx Press, 1998. 345p. index. $65.00pa. ISBN 1-57356-226-2.

Many libraries will find this tool invaluable in locating addresses, names, facts, and organizations. Kurian is president of Kurian Reference Books in New York and brings to the table dozens of years of experience, not to mention his won voluminous political work. His co-compiler, Schultz, is also president of his own company (Schultz & Co., Inc.) and has taught political science and history at a number of colleges and universities. His previous works were two excellent encyclopedias on the Democratic and Republican Parties.

Political Market Place (PMP) is an annual tool that attempts to satisfy all things political. The first three chapters discuss the two major and third parties. Each section has a geographical listing of party headquarters and their chairs. Other chapters discuss political associations, think tanks, media consultants, political journals and newsletters, reference books, and important documents. A section on political statistics covers various state and national issues (e.g., referenda, term limits, and financial activities for the two major parties).

While certainly fulsome, there is no pretense at comprehensiveness. For example, in the section on organizations, there is no mention of the Women's Independent Forum. Neither *The Women's Quarterly* (Danielle Crittenden's magazine) nor any of the Rockford publications (e.g., *Family in America, Religion and Society Report, Chronicles: A Magazine of Culture*) are named in the magazine and newsletter section. But these oversights, while significant, do not vitiate what is an otherwise useful tool. [R: LJ, 1 May 99, pp. 69-70; BL, 1 May 99, p. 1636; Choice, Nov 99, p. 518; RUSQ, Fall 99, p. 99]—**Mark Y. Herring**

622. **The Leadership Library on CD-ROM: Who's Who in the Leadership of the United States.** Fall 1998 ed. [CD-ROM]. New York, Leadership Directories, 1998. Minimum system requirements: IBM or compatible 386. CD-ROM drive. Windows 3.1. 8MB RAM. Mouse. $2,750.00. ISSN 1075-3869.

This is a selective list of U.S. individuals in the Congress, House, and Senate; Executive Office of the President; the 50 state governments; cities, counties, and local authorities; federal decision-makers outside of Washington, D.C.; and federal and state judges, staff, and law clerks. Other leaders included are corporate executives and board members, financial leaders, news media, trade and professional association officers, law firm partners of 700 leading law firms, government affairs experts, foreign representatives in the United States, 1,250 corporations, and 350 foreign financial institutions. There are 350,000 individuals that made the list, all from the 13 yellow books.

Even though the coverage is large, it is a very selective list, and maybe arbitrary (e.g., which trade association and which law firm are leaders?). Only 66 persons from West Virginia are listed in the 13 yellow books. This work would be useful in a few places, but is costly. Users may rather depend upon the more comprehensive tools, such as the *Encyclopedia of Associations* (see ARBA 99, entry 50), *Statesman Yearbook* (1998-99 ed.; see ARBA 99, entry 82), or the *Congressional Staff Directory* (Fall 1997 ed.; see ARBA 98, entry 652).

Setup is simple enough and use is direct. It is hard to search for one entry if you have no idea which book that entry is in. The setup should allow a global search as the default, not the 13 separate directories. It is an excellent idea, but how many have a need for such a library at such a high cost of 50 percent more than the paper directories? The quarterly updates are an excellent feature. However, much of this information is searchable via the Internet and not at such a high cost. [R: LJ, 15 Mar 98, p. 103]—**Gerald D. Moran**

623. Maxwell, Bruce. **How to Access the Federal Government on the Internet.** 4th ed. Washington, D.C., Congressional Quarterly, 1999. 328p. index. $28.95pa. ISBN 1-56802-387-1. ISSN 1088-7466.

The author notes correctly that whatever one's occupation, interests, or hobbies, one is likely to find important information at federal government sites. This directory is intended to assist one in making those discoveries. It covers some 900 different sites offering information from the federal government. Although most of these sites are run by the government, many of the more useful ones are indexes and catalogs maintained by university scholars and archivists. Each entry includes a brief summary of the site's contents and often some assessments on its usefulness and accessibility. The focus is on information available at no cost, although a few services available by paid subscriptions are also noted. The entry includes Website information and, when available, e-mail addresses for the Webmaster or the site. Information on the site is presented in a straightforward manner and accessible to those still learning to use the World Wide Web. Entries are listed by category (e.g., agriculture, libraries, education). There is also a comprehensive index that allows users to search for specific needs in even greater detail. This is a useful volume; however, many Web surfers will prefer looking for this same information, less the evaluative comments, by using search engines such as Yahoo! or AltaVista.—**Frank L. Wilson**

624. **Public Record Research System.** [CD-ROM]. Tempe, Ariz., BRB, 1999. Minimum system requirements: $299.00 (individual use); $4,800.00 (unlimited network users).

The Windows version of the *Public Record Research System* (PRRS) in CD-ROM format provides information on agencies and institutions that hold public records, and is a combination of databases currently published in seven print sources. The convenience of automated searching comes at a cost of $299.00 for an annual subscription, and is more expensive than the 3-volume print version plus updates for $169.00. Aimed primarily at searchers interested in obtaining public background information for companies or personnel, this reference tool has addresses, hours of operation, contact persons, methods of search, and search costs listed for various public institutions. It ranges from the smallest town court up to federal record centers; using the Locus Power Finder the investigator may identify the most appropriate institution holding public records. Placing the cursor on a gray box, windows open to indicate searching capability by county, state, city or place, zip code, and area code. The authors have included a category of "Public Record Retrievers," listing agencies in a particular geographical area willing to undertake searches. The general reference database for state agencies lists addresses and phone numbers for state officials, along with general search information on agencies responsible for such categories as death records, vehicle ownership, and accident reports. The database for state licenses offers searchable career headings such as teacher, court reporter, and architect. Transcript information and contact persons can be found in the Degree Granting Schools database.

Packaged with a user's manual, this version of PRRS was easy for a novice to install, having a choice of several types of installation, but the practice of contacting another company for the activation key is cumbersome. Fortunately a section designated as a tour of the software instructs the user on the database search strategies that cannot be classified as intuitive. In fact, it is recommended that all users investigate the "Introduction" function button prior to use for each database affording a better understanding of the capabilities available. Several extra features have been included, such as the "Add Page Notes," allowing the user to customize information on a particular search and making it is possible to update information or include conversation notes at will. Lengthy descriptions of categories such as business records, where and how to search for them, and an overview of the federal court structure are some of the hidden jewels that add to the tool's usefulness. Updated three times a year, it appears to fulfill its claim to provide current information. Most suitable for a sophisticated user, this tool would be beneficial for business and legal libraries.

—**Marianne B. Eimer**

625. **Worldwide Government Directory with International Organizations 1999.** D. S. Lewis, D. J. Sagar, and Richard Thomas, eds. Washington, D.C., Keesing's Worldwide; distr., Farmington Hills, Mich., Gale, 1998. 1540p. $368.00. ISBN 1-886994-22-6. ISSN 0894-1521.

Worldwide Government Directory with International Organizations 1999 provides names and addresses of top officials of the major agencies and departments of every country and territory of the world. Each entry is arranged alphabetically by country and organized under the headings "Head of State," "Central Committee" (communist governments), "Cabinet" (presidential or parliamentary governments), "Defense Forces," "State Agencies," "Legislature," "Judiciary," "Central Bank," "United Nations Missions," "General Data," "International and Regional Memberships," "Forms Address," and "Foreign Diplomatic Missions."

Several features included in this directory should prove particularly useful. One is the inclusion of the official names of countries in English, French (if appropriate), and indigenous language. For example, Vietnam is Socialist Republic of Vietnam in English and Cong-Hoa Xa-Hoi Chu-Nghia Viet-Nam in Vietnamese; or Madagascar is Republic of Madagascar in English, Repoblikan'i Madagasikara in Malagasy, and République de Madagascar in French. This feature is especially helpful when one needs to prepare formal documents. Another feature is the names and addresses of foreign diplomatic missions located in each country, a convenient source to find out more information on other countries. Although the "General Data" section is brief, one can easily locate information on the name of the capital, language(s), ethnic composition, religion(s), currency, major political parties, and national holidays for a particular country. There is also a list of international organizations including economic (Arab Band for Economic Development in Africa), regional (Andean Community), international (International Civil Aviation Organization), and United Nations (United Nations Children's Fund) organizations.

All in all, this is the most comprehensive directory available. It should prove useful for large public, law, business, and academic libraries.—**Binh P. Le**

POLITICS AND GOVERNMENT

United States

Almanacs

626. Lilley, William, III, Laurence J. DeFranco, and Mark F. Bernstein. **The Almanac of State Legislatures: Changing Patterns, 1990-1997.** 2d ed. Washington, D.C., Congressional Quarterly, 1998. 387p. maps. $135.00. ISBN 1-56802-434-7.

Synthesizing and updating information previously published in the 1st edition of *The Almanac of State Legislatures* (see ARBA 95, entry 710), *The State Atlas of Political and Cultural Diversity* (see ARBA 98, entry 329), and *State Legislative Elections* (see ARBA 99, entry 674), this work presents a vivid picture of the socioeconomic and demographic composition of state legislative districts in the United States for the period 1990 to 1997. Data are derived primarily from 1997 sources. The almanac begins with a brief introductory essay highlighting trends in rural and urban growth and the changing racial and ethnic populations throughout the United States. Three charts of selected legislative house districts in Chicago,

Los Angeles, and Philadelphia provide statistics to support the descriptive analysis. What follows are detailed entries for each state. The entries begin with a well-written, concise essay that summarizes the changes in the political and demographic makeup of the state since the 1990 census. The essays provide an efficacious framework for placing the statistical data in proper context. Each entry also includes two-color maps showing the boundaries of state legislative districts color-coded according to population growth. Where appropriate, similar maps provide district breakdowns within metropolitan areas. The cartographic boundaries are easily discernible and well produced. Finally, the entries contain statistical charts intended to illustrate the shifting geo-demographic status of each district, broken down by ethnicity, income, and population. The editors properly acknowledge the underlying challenges to the manner in which the Census Bureau gathers data. These issues have been addressed by relying on a variety of legally mandated federal sources. Overall, this is an excellent resource for both students and researchers. This reviewer is looking forward to the post-2000 decennial census edition. Together with this edition, it will provide invaluable research tools that clearly delineate the changing demographic, political, and socioeconomic landscape at the state level as America enters the next millennium. [R: Choice, July/Aug 99, p. 1928]—**Robert V. Labaree**

627. Tucker, Harvey J., and Gary M. Halter. **Texas Legislative Almanac 1999.** College Station, Tex., Texas A&M University Press, 1999. 431p. illus. $19.95pa. ISBN 0-89096-868-3. ISSN 1092-9843.

This political almanac is the 2d volume in an ongoing biennial series on Texas state legislatures that is published by Texas A&M University Press. Much of the information in the volume has been gathered from official state documents that are available on World Wide Web sites. The purpose of the work is to provide this key information in a single ready-reference volume.

The Texas Legislature consists of 2 chambers—a 31-member Senate and a 150-member House of Representatives. This volume includes a mailing address, photograph, and political vita for each state senator and state representative. It also includes population, education, wealth, urbanization, employment, and election statistics for each house and senatorial district. Because the volume went to press immediately after the November 1998 elections, it does not include information on legislative committee assignments, data that were included in the 1997 edition. The volume, however, does provide a listing of Internet sites where these data can be ascertained.

Although the almanac was created with the legislators, lobbyists, and Texas administration agencies in mind, it will also be of interest to lay readers who wish to learn more about the organization and political processes of the Texas legislature. This volume is recommended for high school and college libraries in Texas.—**Terry D. Bilhartz**

Biography

628. **American Legislative Leaders in the South, 1911-1994.** James Roger Sharp and Nancy Weatherly Sharp, eds. Westport, Conn., Greenwood Press, 1999. 361p. index. $115.00. ISBN 0-313-30213-8.

This is the 3d of a 4-volume set designed to provide biographical and career information on state house speakers from 1911 to 1994. Each covers a different region of the country. States covered in this work include Alabama, Arkansas, Florida, Georgia, Kentucky, Louisiana, Maryland, Mississippi, North Carolina, Oklahoma, South Carolina, Tennessee, Texas, Virginia, and West Virginia. Volumes on the Midwest and West have already been published (see ARBA 98, entry 650), with the one on the Northeast slated for publication in 2000. Together, they continue *American Legislative Leaders 1850-1910*, by Charles F. Ritter and Jon L. Wakelyn (see ARBA 90, entry 692).

An excellent introduction traces the history of politics during the twentieth century. However, except for minor changes, the text is the same in all three volumes of the set. Interspersed are 12 statistical tables, and some of these, such as party affiliation, are specific to individual states, but most offer statistics according to the Midwest, Northeast, South, and West regions.

The editors, who are on the faculty at Syracuse University, also edited the two earlier volumes. They have enlisted the expertise of 63 contributors to provide signed entries, which are alphabetically arranged and generally 2 to 3 paragraphs in length, for 1,472 speakers. Many of the entries include brief bibliographies, and there is a general bibliography for each state at the end. Facts about the speakers, such as education, racial background, and occupation, are listed by state in 10 appendixes that precede a name and subject index.

This work, like the others, consolidates information that otherwise would be time-consuming to retrieve. Using the bibliographies, interested researchers can pursue an individual or state in more depth. This work is recommended for academic and state libraries.—**Hope Yelich**

629. Foerstel, Karen. **Biographical Dictionary of Congressional Women.** Westport, Conn., Greenwood Press, 1999. 300p. illus. index. $65.00. ISBN 0-313-30290-1.

In the literature on women who have served in Congress, there is generally a direct correlation between the availability of information on that person and the amount of attention they received while in office. This biographical dictionary is a welcome research tool because it provides detailed information on all women who have been elected to Congress. The introductory chapter outlines the history of women in Congress and the challenges they face in getting elected and being accepted as equals in creating policy. The chapter is well written and concludes with two charts—a list of women who have chaired full House and Senate committees (one indication of who has wielded the most power among congressional women) and a chart showing the number of women who have served in each Congress since 1917. In the future, charts showing a list of congressional women by state and a chronology of service in the House and Senate could help enhance the presentation of data. Each biographical profile includes a description of the individual's political career, highlighting important public policy initiatives and, in many cases, placing the person's term in office in greater historical perspective. Personal anecdotes and excerpts from interviews are used to enhance the content of many profiles. A set of black-and-white photographs is included in the center of the book but is unnecessary. A selective bibliography and a name and subject index complete this work.

This is an accessible and informative research tool. The author steps beyond the dry writing style of most traditional biographical dictionaries by telling the story of each woman's rise to power in our nation's legislative branch and the personal challenges they had to overcome in becoming meaningful participants in our nation's legislative process. This work is especially useful to students. [R: LJ, 1 Sept 99, pp. 176-178]
—**Robert V. Labaree**

Dictionaries and Encyclopedias

630. Binning, William C., Larry E. Esterly, and Paul A. Sracic. **Encyclopedia of American Parties, Campaigns, and Elections.** Westport, Conn., Greenwood Press, 1999. 467p. index. $99.50. ISBN 0-313-30312-6.

The authors provide a comprehensive survey of key information on U.S. politics, politicians, parties, and elections in a short volume accessible to the general reader. Entries range from short biographies of the presidents and key congressional leaders to brief accounts of presidential elections from 1789 to 1996 to summaries of major Supreme Court rulings. Although the encyclopedia covers U.S. national politics since 1789, it gives more attention to recent personalities and issues. Inevitably in a volume designed to be of convenient size, some terms or people are given slight attention or omitted. For example, a curious omission is "impeachment." But the authors seem to have found a good balance between compactness and comprehensiveness in the selection of their entries.

This encyclopedia is recommended for public libraries, secondary schools, and university libraries. It is accessible to the general reader but provides details and bibliographies to the reader who wants additional information. [R: LJ, 1 Mar 99, p. 68]—**Frank L. Wilson**

631. **Congress A to Z.** 3d ed. David R. Tarr and Ann O'Connor, eds. Washington, D.C., Congressional Quarterly, 1999. 592p. illus. index. (CQ's Ready Reference Encyclopedia of American Government). $95.00. ISBN 1-56802-388-X.

This volume, along with similar volumes on the presidency, the Supreme Court, and elections, makes up Congressional Quarterly's *Encyclopedia of American Government*. Congressional Quarterly is the most reliable and complete review of the U.S. government. This volume is an excellent example of their readable, accessible, comprehensive, and unbiased coverage of American politics. Entries range from specific events—such as the Teapot Dome scandal—to prominent past and current congressional leaders, rules and procedures, and specific issues. There are short, but excellent, entries on blacks, Hispanics, and women in Congress. A long entry on "Historic Milestones" provides a chronological listing and brief description of major developments in Congress since 1787.

This revision includes developments through early 1999. Entries are well organized and an index allows easy locating of issues or individuals. Many of the major entries include a listing of additional readings. There is also an extensive bibliography that includes scholarly works, political commentaries, and memoirs.

In addition to the encyclopedia entries, there are several appendixes. They include lists of past and present leaders, statistics on vetoes and expulsions, and figures on reelection of incumbents.

Congress A to Z is illustrated generously with photos, cartoons, tables, and figures. It is written at a level that general readers will find understandable, but includes information that will be useful also to specialists on American government. This is perhaps the best one-volume reference work on the U.S. Congress.

—Frank L. Wilson

632. **Encyclopedia of Women in American Politics.** Jeffrey D. Schultz and Laura van Assendelft, eds. Phoenix, Ariz., Oryx Press, 1999. 354p. illus. index. (The American Political Landscape Series). $99.00. ISBN 1-57356-131-2.

The preface to *Encyclopedia of Women in American Politics* states that it "attempts to be the most comprehensive single source on women in American politics." Other than perhaps the bibliographic compilations of Elizabeth M. Cox that concentrates on twentieth century women, this encyclopedia stands nearly alone. With the December 1999 publication of ABC-CLIO's *Encyclopedia of American Women in Politics*, a 2-volume work by Suzanne O'Dea Schenken, this is probably about to change. Hopefully the similarly titled encyclopedias will complement rather than duplicate each other.

Encyclopedia of Women in American Politics is the first title in the Oryx Press American Political Landscape Series. Schultz, a former college professor of history and political science, is editing several volumes in this series and van Assendelft is assistant professor of political science at Mary Baldwin College. More than 700 entries arranged dictionary style, comprise this encyclopedia. Entries are signed by one of 56 scholars from various U.S. colleges and universities. The introduction, arranged by historical periods, provides a scholarly overview of women in American politics from Colonial times to the present. Encyclopedia entries cover concepts, movements, issues, legislation, case law, and biographical information related to women in American politics. Entry titles include affirmative action, feminism and antifeminism, Reed v. Reed (1971), Elizabeth Cady Stanton, and one for the movie *Thelma and Louise*. Entry size ranges from a paragraph (biographical entries) to several pages and each ends with one or more bibliographic references. Generous cross-referencing and a thorough index enhance retrieval of specific topics. Four valuable appendixes conclude this volume. One covers speeches and documents, including the proposed Equal Rights Amendment to the U.S. Constitution. The tables appendix covers women members of Congress, cabinet members, and a list of First Ladies. Another appendix provides information for organizations, including addresses, URLs and e-mail addresses for various groups, PACs, and donor networks. The final appendix is a particularly useful timeline from 1848 to 1998.

The *Encyclopedia of Women in American Politics* is a valuable reference work that should be included in academic and medium- to large-sized public and high school library collections. This Oryx publication should be joined by other reference works covering the history, statistics, demographics, and biographies of the many women who have entered the political arena, both in the United States and internationally. [R: LJ, 15 Mar 99, p. 70; BL, 1 Mar 99, pp. 1248-1249; Choice, June 99, p. 1764; RUSQ, Fall 99, pp. 89-90]—**Linda D. Tietjen**

633. Moore, John L. **Elections A to Z.** Washington, D.C., Congressional Quarterly, 1999. 560p. illus. index. (CQ's Ready Reference Encyclopedia of American Government). $95.00. ISBN 1-56802-207-7.

This newest addition to the series offers more than 200 short to lengthy entries dealing with electoral politics in the United States. Subjects covered include such matters as districting concerns; party regulations and involvement, including the role specific parties have played in American political history; primaries; relevant legislation, Constitutional provisions, and Supreme Court decisions; suffrage issues; and campaign finance and strategy. There are 25 appendixes included that provide information on such subjects as major party conventions; presidential election results; party representation in Congress and the presidency; the number of Blacks, Hispanics, and women in Congress since the 1870s; and pertinent Websites. A short bibliography and an index conclude the volume.

Although cross-references are plentiful, this otherwise thorough reference work might be faulted for not providing brief lists of references at the end of each entry. For instance, the entry "Realignments and Dealignments" mentions the seminal works of V. O. Key and Walter Dean Burnham, among others, but leaves to the reader the burden of uncovering the bibliographic details concerning these items. This criticism aside, the volume is a fine addition to CQ's Ready Reference Encyclopedia of American Government series and belongs in most libraries. [R: Choice, Dec 99, pp. 703-704]—**Lee Weston**

634. **The Presidency A to Z.** 2d ed. Michael Nelson, ed. Washington, D.C., Congressional Quarterly, 1998. 603p. illus. index. (CQ's Encyclopedia of American Government, v.2). $95.00. ISBN 1-56802-359-6.

One of four volumes in CQ's Encyclopedia of American Government series, this second volume on the presidency includes several new entries and updates of selected essays and appendixes through mid-1998. Among the new entries are descriptions of key presidential policy issues, such as the line-item veto and an examination of the 1996 elections and their impact; an analysis of historical initiatives, such as the New Frontier and the Square Deal; biographical profiles of Bob Dole and Colin Powell and an update of Bill Clinton's term in office; and entries on ceremonial aspects of the presidency, such as national presidential memorials and the Presidential Medal of Honor. Also new in the 2d volume is an annotated list of four comprehensive Internet directories of federal Websites and a description of how to search for federal job opportunities. The remaining contents are essentially the same as in the previous revised edition, including the appendixes. The essays are well written and provide basic information on a particular issue, concept, or key figure in presidential politics. A number of essays are enhanced by the inclusion of photographs, charts, and illustrations. One deficiency should be noted. Some essays, such as the entry on the presidential cabinet, conclude with a brief bibliography of additional readings. However, most other entries do not include a list of further reading. For example, a user researching the issue of presidential elections and campaigns would find no bibliography of suggested reading, even though a number of comprehensive works have been recently published. Aside from this complaint, however, *The Presidency A to Z* remains a resource of high quality and the additional information in the second volume justifies its availability in a broad spectrum of libraries.—**Robert V. Labaree**

635. **The Supreme Court A to Z.** 2d ed. Kenneth Jost, ed. Washington, D.C., Congressional Quarterly, 1998. 582p. illus. index. (CQ's Ready Reference Encyclopedia of American Government). $95.00. ISBN 1-56802-357-X.

One of a 4-volume series entitled *Encyclopedia of American Government*, with the other volumes covering the presidency, Congress, and elections, this 2d edition incorporates significant Supreme Court decisions from 1997 to 1998. More than 300 easy-to-read essays are included in the nearly 600-page text. As the title states, subjects are alphabetically arranged with pictures, lists, and diagrams appropriately included. Although it appears that the work is not intended to be as scholarly, informative, or detailed as a number of other publications, such as Joan Biskupic's and Elder Witt's 2-volume *Guide to the U.S. Supreme Court* (3d ed.; see ARBA 98, entry 526), it includes a great deal of potentially useful information covering all significant events since the Supreme Court's inception. It also provides information on matters such as listings of all of the Reporters of Decisions, Librarians of the Court, and Supreme Court Justices' salaries. It cites a good number of other resources in a selected bibliography following the text.

As an initial or introductory source for conducting research on one or more aspects of the U.S. Supreme Court, this encyclopedia is a good starting point as long as readers and researchers keep in mind that there are a myriad of other in-depth articles and publications concerning the Supreme Court, its history, and its judges and their decisions. Public and school libraries may find that this book is a fairly inexpensive and helpful addition to their reference collections; and this could include any number of law libraries that are open to the public. [R: Choice, July/Aug 99, pp. 1929-1930]—**James M. Murray**

Directories

636. Andriot, Laurie, comp. **The Internet Blue Pages: The Guide to Federal Government Web Sites.** 1999 ed. Medford, N.J., CyberAge Books/Information Today, 1999. 359p. index. $34.95pa. ISBN 0-910965-29-3.

This directory provides the Website addresses for more than 900 federal government offices. Each entry provides the site address, a brief description of materials on the Website, and the links available through the site. Entries are organized by federal department or agency. There is an alphabetic list of all agencies with their URL address. Unfortunately, this list does not cross-reference to the numbered, annotated entries in the main guide. The index allows searching by topic, agency, or program providing the entry number for relevant matches. There is a companion Website to the volume, allowing readers to get new listings, corrections, and updates online.

This resource will help readers gain access to the Website; however, the value of the Website depends on its own construction, maintenance, and creativity, and that varies widely. This work is recommended for press libraries and government relations offices as well as public and education libraries. [R: Choice, Oct 99, p. 301]—**Frank L. Wilson**

637. **Federal Staff Directory, Summer 1999.** 30th ed. Washington, D.C., Congressional Quarterly, 1999. 1779p. index. $109.00. ISBN 0-87289-166-6. ISSN 0589-3178.

This work supplies a wealth of directional and biographical information about the U.S. government, related bodies, and political appointees. As such it is a valuable tool for students of government, businesspeople, professionals, and librarians.

The directory aspect of the work divides into 4 sections. The 1st lists officials and offices connected with the presidency, including a separate table of contents. Subsections deal with the executive offices of the president and vice president, White House agencies, and advisory organizations. The 2d part starts with a list of cabinet members. Executive departments follow alphabetically, beginning with agriculture. Each subsection starts with table of contents, directory details on its main D.C.-area buildings, and table of main information services. Staff listings begin with the secretary, including a picture. The 3d section provides material on independent federal regulatory agencies, boards, and commissions, alphabetically from the African Development Foundation through the U.S. Soldiers' and Airmen's Home. A last directory section groups quasi-official federal agencies, bilateral or multilateral intergovernmental bodies, and bodies including corporations like the Tennessee Valley Authority. One minor irritant is that not all bodies have a "responsibilities" paragraph. Thus, if readers do not know what Freddie Mac does, they remain unenlightened. The 5th section includes brief biographical and career information on 2,600 staffers. Appointees with biographies are marked by asterisks in the directory sections. The final two sections provide additional access. One is a thorough subject index using 14,000 keywords or phrases. The other is a 40,000-name index with phone numbers and page references.

This is a valuable, professionally produced reference tool. Libraries with the budget and relevant clientele should seriously consider purchasing it at regular intervals.—**Nigel Tappin**

638. **Government Phone Book USA 1999: A Comprehensive Guide to Federal, State, County, and Local Government Offices in the United States.** 7th ed. Detroit, Omnigraphics, 1999. 2186p. $225.00. ISBN 0-7808-0360-4. ISSN 1062-1466.

At first glance, the proliferation of government agency homepages on the Internet would appear to render a directory such as this superfluous. However, the 7th edition of the *Government Phone Book USA* (formally the *Government Directory of Addresses and Telephone Numbers*) provides an easy-access, one-stop resource for over 168,000 listings of federal, state, county, and municipal government agencies. The directory is divided into 3 parts: federal offices, state offices, and county and city offices. Each part begins with a quick-reference section that provides, among other things, key phone numbers and addresses, state offices and their personnel, and county and municipal associations. Federal listings include executive agencies and the Executive Office of the President, all members of Congress and their staff, and all federal agencies and departments. The section concludes with regional maps and a keyword index. The state listings give information on state officials, state agencies, and national organizations concerned with state government affairs. A number of state executive office organizational charts are included. This is followed by listings of individual agencies and departments arranged alphabetically by state. The county and municipal listings include county maps, a thorough list of county agencies, and a comprehensive list of city offices, arranged alphabetically first by cities with a population over 15,000, then alphabetically for cities below 15,000 residents. Given the complexity of the information presented, the table of contents provides a useful framework to access information in the directory. The strength of this work lies in its inclusion of e-mail and Website addresses at each level of coverage. This will lead the user to the more comprehensive, and likely more current, information now contained on many government homepages. This volume is highly recommended.—**Robert V. Labaree**

639. **The Sourcebook to Public Record Information: The Comprehensive Guide to County, State, & Federal Public Records Sources.** professional ed. Tempe, Ariz., BRB, 1999. 702p. $69.95pa. ISBN 1-879792-55-9.

This is the 1st edition of a work that incorporates and replaces 4 BRB publications—*The Sourcebook of County Court Records* (3d ed.; see ARBA 98, entry 524), *The Sourcebook of State Public Records* (4th ed.; BRB, 1998), *The Sourcebook of Federal Courts* (2d ed.; see ARBA 97, entry 500), and *The Sourcebook of County Asset/Lien Records*. This work is filled with useful information, along with how-to-use-this-book instructions. The term *public records* is defined. Every state varies as to how they handle public record information. Various agencies within a state may interpret the Freedom of Information Act differently. This sourcebook guides users through the maze. Agencies may be accessed by U.S. mail, telephone, fax, or computer. The appropriate addresses and call-up numbers are listed. This is a work that should prove useful to genealogists, law enforcement and social agencies, attorneys, private investigators, and librarians, among others.—**Frank J. Anderson**

640. **Washington Information Directory 1999-2000.** Mary Burke Marshall, ed. Washington, D.C., Congressional Quarterly, 1999. 1010p. index. $115.00. ISBN 1-56802-083-X. ISSN 0887-8064.

The *Washington Information Directory 1999-2000* continues to be a vital source for basic information concerning the federal agencies; the U.S. Congress; not-for-profit groups located in Washington, D.C.; and state agencies and regional organizations. Specifically, the directory is designed to help users quickly locate the names and addresses of governmental and nongovernmental organizations from the Commission on Civil Rights to the political action committees (PACs) to the names of the chairpersons and the ranking minority members of all congressional committees and subcommittees.

The directory is organized into 20 broad subject categories, ranging from "Advocacy and Public Service" to "Employment and Labor" to "U.S. Congress and Politics." Under each broad subject, information is organized into specific subject areas. Each entry includes name, address, and telephone number of the organization; name and title of the director or the best person to contact for information; fax and press number, hotlines, and Internet addresses, when available; and a description of the work performed by the organization. Arguably, the most comprehensive feature is the coverage on the U.S. Congress and politics. Under this section, one can easily locate, among many other things, information on campaigns and elections, a brief description of the responsibilities of each House and Senate committee, and committee and subcommittee assignment of the 106th Congress.

Also included in the directory is the "Ready Reference List," which provides information on regional organization, governors and other state officials, foreign embassies, U.S. ambassadors, and country desk officers. The name index (more than 100 pages) and the subject index should prove to be useful features in helping users find information in the main text. All in all, this is an essential information source for school, public, and academic libraries.—**Binh P. Le**

Handbooks and Yearbooks

641. **Budget of the United States Government, Fiscal Year 2000.** Washington, D.C., U.S. Government Printing Office; distr., Lanham, Md., Bernan Associates, 1999. 405p. $30.00pa. ISBN 0-16-049890-2.

This document summarizes President Clinton's administrations proposed budget for the 2000 fiscal year. As such it is an important part of the budget negotiating process, but does not necessarily reflect the actual budget to be finally passed by Congress and agreed to by the president. Six other series titles complete the executive's budget documents publications. A cheap, searchable CD-ROM format of all seven documents is available. Internet users can also access and download the material from http://www.gpo.gov/usbudget.

The book contains the text of the "Budget Message of the President" to Congress delivered with the executive's budget proposals, plus detailed summary numbers accompanied by extensive text advocating and explaining them. In addition, it includes the administration's "Government-wide Performance Plan." Text and tables are divided into nine sections, with the first being the presidential letter to congress. Other sections deal with the administration view of what to do with possible future surpluses; its general economic strategy and how to secure social security's future; priorities in specific areas from education and training through families, the environment, and law enforcement to defense and foreign affairs; performance reviews of specific administration programs; and summary statistical tables. The main access points are the contents and a list of charts and tables. There is also a list of Office of Management and Budget personnel who worked on the document, plus price and order information on other budget series publications.

This report will be useful to larger institutions collecting U.S. federal government documents, although the CD-ROM version may prove an attractive alternative at half the price ($14) for more material in a searchable form. Smaller libraries and those facing difficult budget choices (or with no need for back runs) may prefer to provide access through the Internet.—**Nigel Tappin**

642. **Compensation 98: An Annual Report on Local Government Executive Salaries and Fringe Benefits.** Washington, D.C., International City/County Management Association, 1998. 271p. $125.00pa. (members); $180.00pa. (nonmembers). ISBN 0-87326-976-4. ISSN 0732-5282.

The information reported in this annual results from a salary survey conducted in July 1997 by International City/County Management Association. The survey targeted all cities and counties with 2,500 or more in population, and those under 2,500 that are recognized by the Association as having the council-manager form of government, or as providing for a professional management position. Of the 6,394 cities, towns, villages, boroughs, and townships that received the survey, 63.3 percent responded. Of the 3,052 counties, 44.9 percent responded.

The salary information is organized as follows: average salaries by state, by population group within geographic division, executive fringe benefits, job security benefits, individual city salary listing, and finally individual country salary listings. Some of the salary and benefit information is categorized by geographic divisions. These divisions are the New England and mid-Atlantic Divisions, the East North Central and West North Central Divisions, the South Atlantic and East South Central Divisions, and the Mountain and Pacific Coast Divisions.

It is interesting to glimpse at the various salary information and gain some knowledge about the range of cost-of-living standards in various divisions and states. For those who are interested in employment and recruitment of employees for city and county agencies, and for those who are responsible for city and county program planning, this is a useful resource. The value of this resource is made greater due to its timeliness and inclusiveness of the information. *Compensation 98* is recommended for city and county libraries.—**Eveline L. Yang**

643. **Congressional Quarterly Almanac 1998: 105th Congress, 2d Session. Volume 54.** Washington, D.C., Congressional Quarterly, 1999. 1v. (various paging). index. $370.00. ISBN 1-56802-269-7. ISSN 0095-6007.

The *Congressional Quarterly Almanac*, published annually, has been indisputably one of the most essential reference tools for congressional information in particular and U.S. politics in general for more than five decades. The 1998 almanac is organized under 24 major subject areas, ranging from abortion to health to taxes; interestingly, the longest chapter (chapter 2) covers governmental appropriations. Under each major topic category, the almanac provides numerous articles encapsulating the activities on legislation and other issues that were debated during the 105th Congress. The articles are concise, informative, and insightful. Accompanying the text are "Box Scores," serving as quick references to the status of the legislation that were being discussed in Congress in 1998; each consists of the Bill Numbers(s), the House Action, and the Senate Action. The almanac also contains appendixes, which include roll-call votes, texts of presidential messages, public laws enacted by Congress during this session, and an extensive index. It is worthwhile to recall, however, that the 105th Congress was not an ordinary one; the House did impeach President Clinton; and that many of the documents relating to the impeachment, including the articles of impeachment (H.R. 611) against President Clinton, are provided in the almanac. All in all, the 1998 almanac is a useful reference source for a variety of audiences. Public and academic libraries ought to purchase the almanac.—**Binh P. Le**

644. **Congressional Quarterly Almanac, 105th Congress, 1st Session ... 1997. Volume 53.** 53d ed. Washington, D.C., Congressional Quarterly, 1998. 1v. (various paging). index. $514.00. ISBN 1-56802-268-9. ISSN 0095-6007.

There may be a few librarians who do not recognize Congressional Quarterly as the gold standard when it comes to the nonpartisan chronicling of U.S. politics and government. The basic format of this almanac has not varied a great deal over the last decade. An opening chapter, "Inside Congress," gives an overview of the session and highlights events of particular interest (e.g., the ethics case involving Speaker of the House Newt Gingrich). The eight chapters that follow cover congressional developments in broad subject areas, such as economics and finance; government and commerce; environment and energy; law and judiciary; health and human services; education, housing, labor, and veterans; defense and foreign policy; and appropriations. Each of these chapters has a detailed table of contents and separate paging prefaced by the chapter number. The last chapter, "Political Report," focuses on different issues from year to year. This edition features an analysis of the U.S. electorate and a rundown on 1997 political contests. A long series of appendixes (approximately one-half of the book) include a glossary of congressional terms; an overview of the legislative process; a list of members and committee assignments; vote studies; important texts (e.g., State of the Union Address); a list of public laws passed in numerical order; House and Senate roll call votes; and a general index. In all of this, considerable use is made of statistical tables and highlighted sidebars. Quotations are provided to support evaluative statements, such as "Lott's support was grudging."

Not only is this almanac a gold mine for researchers, but it is also a primary tool for the advancement of democracy. As such, it should be considered an essential component of every public and academic library's reference collection.—**Jack Ray**

645. **Congressional Quarterly's Federal PAC Directory 1998-1999.** Dan Gainor, Peter Roybal, and Derek Willis, eds. Washington, D.C., Congressional Quarterly, 1998. 630p. index. $195.00. ISBN 1-56802-425-8. ISSN 1099-0097.

This directory profiles the political action committees (PACs) that gave $5,000 or more to congressional candidates during the 1995–96 election. The PACs featured come from a broad spectrum of industries, unions, trade associations, and special interests. Each entry provides a brief description of the sponsoring entity, plus a contact name with address, phone, fax, and e-mail. Total cash and in-kind donations are listed for 1993–94, 1995–96, and 1997. The amount going to Republican and Democratic candidates, whether these individuals were running for the Senate or the House, and if they were incumbents or challengers, winners, or losers, are not noted.

The introductory essay summarizes the history of PACs and their current impact on U.S. political campaigning. The appendix provides tables listing the top PAC contributors overall by major industry classification. Congressional recipients of the largest amounts of funding are also identified. The indexes list PACs by city within each state, by PAC name, and by the PAC's sponsoring organization.

This reference is not only a valuable resource for those working in the legislative arena, but is also an eye-opener for the average citizen. Even with all of the recent publicity on the need for campaign reform, it is staggering to learn that in the last 25 years the number of PACs has grown from 608 to 3,844. In the 1996 election, PACs gave $217.8 million to federal candidates.—**Adrienne Antink Bendel**

646. **The Constitution and Its Amendments.** Roger K. Newman, ed. New York, Macmillan Library Reference/Simon & Schuster Macmillan, 1999. 4v. illus. index. $225.00/set. ISBN 0-02-864858-7.

This illustrated, 4-volume introduction to the Constitution and its amendments is suitable for students studying the Constitution for the first time—regardless of age. After a chapter that provides the setting for the Constitutional Convention (1787), the work introduces persons and events critical to its success and concise essays clarify each article, including explanations of the intent of the founders and examples of application throughout the nation's history. Illustration, definitions of highlighted words, and enriching or explanatory sidebars all add to the accessibility of this important resource. For example, the 19th Amendment receives five pages of coverage. The exact wording of the amendment begins the chapter (with definitions as needed), along with a brief explanation of its meaning in layperson's terms. The explanation of the history of the amendment begins at Seneca Falls, New York, in 1948; explains several points of view; and reveals the tactics of both supporters and opponents, including jail time for women who picketed for the right to vote. The essay does not conclude with the passage of the amendment in 1920, but continues the discussion with information about those who were still denied the vote—women in territories, African Americans, and nonwhite immigrants.

The first three volumes cover the Constitution and the Bill of Rights. The final volume covers the remaining amendments. Each volume concludes with its own index; preceding the index to volume 4 is an inclusive glossary. This excellent set is recommended for all libraries servicing students grade 7 and up. [R: BL, 15 April 99, p. 1353; BR, Sept/Oct 99, p. 80; SLJ, Aug 99, p. 186]—**Vandelia L. VanMeter**

647. **CQ's Politics in America 2000: The 106th Congress.** Philip D. Duncan and Brian Nutting, eds. Washington, D.C., Congressional Quarterly, 1999. 1564p. illus. maps. $98.95; 55.95pa. (with disc). ISBN 1-56802-470-3; 1-56802-471-1pa. ISSN 1064-6809.

This voluminous 10th edition of a biennial work produced by the publisher's editorial and reporting staff is an excellent resource for describing the men and women who make up the United States Congress. Although the publisher seeks to provide the best assessment of each member of Congress, the emphasis is not on where each politician stands on issues, but rather how his or her views are expressed and how effectively individual goals are accomplished.

This resource begins with an informative preface that outlines the current state of politics as well as an easy-to-read table of contents and an explanation of statistics section. Under the alphabetic listing of each state are the following three sections: the name and picture of the governor as well as relevant additional state and demographic information, including an outline of that state's congressional districts, pictures, and detailed background descriptions of each senator; and pictures and detailed descriptions of each representative. The text is supplemented with a useful index that indicates the page where members of Congress have been mentioned or described. A nice feature included with the publication is a CD-ROM with the full text in Adobe Acrobat format, which can be used with either Macintosh or Windows versions.

Although this resource is not the only publication covering the U.S. Congress, and there are other related publications such as *Congress and Its Members* (Congressional Quarterly) and various almanacs, this work is among those introductory and informative sources that most public, school, and university libraries should include within their reference collections largely because of its relatively inexpensive cost. This item is also likely to be considered a must-have resource for any number of businesses, special interest groups, lobbyists, and political consultants whose livelihood depends upon predicting or responding to the actions of Congress.—**James M. Murray**

648. **The FBI: A Comprehensive Reference Guide.** Athan G. Theoharis, Tony G. Poveda, Susan Rosenfeld, and Richard Gid Powers, eds. Phoenix, Ariz., Oryx Press, 1999. 409p. illus. index. $85.00. ISBN 0-89774-991-X.

Anyone doing research involving the FBI will find this reference work indispensable. Chapter 1 presents a brief, but highly informative, guide to the history of the FBI. The chapter is divided into eight chronological divisions that enable the reader to obtain a sense of the FBI's development. Chapter 2, "Notable Cases," examines many of the high-profile cases in the FBI's history. The chapter is divided into three historical periods that help define the FBI's evolutionary development. As one might expect, this is the longest chapter in the book, and culminates with the Unabomber case. Chapter 3 divides into the same three historical periods as used in chapter 2. Here, however, the leading controversies and issues involving the FBI are examined, including COINTELPRO, ABSCAM, Ruby Ridge, and Waco. Chapter 4 is appropriately entitled "FBI Oversight and Liaison Relationships." The reader will gain an elementary understanding of the FBI and its interactions with the Attorney General, the White House, and Congress. Chapters 5 through 7 are equally self-explanatory ("The Traditions and Cultures of the FBI," "Organization and Day-to-Day Activities," and "Buildings and Physical Plant"). Chapter 8 will find a large audience as it reviews the FBI in popular culture, including reviews of movies, both negative and positive, that depict FBI operations. Chapter 9 contains brief biographies of leading FBI personalities. Chapter 10 offers a chronology of leading events from 1789 to 1998. An annotated bibliography, accessible FBI files, and an index conclude this highly useful and practical guide to understanding the FBI more fully. [R: LJ, Dec 98, p. 90; BL, 15 Feb 99, p. 1090; Choice, Sept 99, p. 118; RUSQ, Spring 99, p. 304; BR, Sept/Oct 99, p. 81]—**Michael A. Foley**

649. **Federal Agency Profiles for Students.** Kelle S. Sisung, ed. Farmington Hills, Mich., Gale, 1999. 1070p. illus. index. $65.00. ISBN 0-7876-2795-X.

This anticipated volume provides a comprehensive overview of more than 175 federal agencies from each branch of government, including departments, government corporations, administrations, and commissions. In addition, more than 200 independent agencies are described. Agency profiles are arranged alphabetically according to the official name given in the *United States Government Manual* (1996/97 ed.; see ARBA 97, entry 604). Each profile contains information about the agency's mission or purpose and its organization, primary functions, and current programs. The editors have paid special attention to placing each agency in proper historical and political context. All the profiles include entries that outline the history of the agency and review important contemporary political issues that have empowered or constrained the agency's ability to carry out its mission. Profiles also include a brief entry describing possible future directions of the organization and its successes and failures based upon self-assessments of the organization.

More profiles conclude with a description of agency resources, with public affairs contact numbers, e-mail and Internet addresses, a list of agency publications, and a brief bibliography for further reading. A select number of profiles may also include information on how individuals can become involved with the agency, "fast facts" about a specific agency function, or biographical sketches of key agency personnel.

The volume begins with a chronology of events in U.S. history and concludes with four brief appendixes, a glossary, and a subject index. Illustrations, photographs, and pie charts of agency budget allocations are used throughout the encyclopedia to enhance its textual presentation. The essays are well written and should be easily understood by most students. Although of limited value to scholars, this work succeeds in providing students with an in-depth understanding of the agencies that make up our system of government. This, and most likely future volumes in this series, should be available in every school and public library. [R: Choice, Oct 99, p. 314; BR, Sept/Oct 99, p. 81]—**Robert V. Labaree**

650. **Gubernatorial Elections 1787-1997.** Washington, D.C., Congressional Quarterly, 1998. 183p. index. $34.95pa. ISBN 1-56802-396-0.

This volume is part of a group of Congressional Quarterly summaries of U.S. elections over history. Another volume includes *Presidential Elections 1789-1996* (see ARBA 99, entry 682). This volume begins with a brief summary of the nature of gubernatorial elections across the country and a short discussion of the importance of primary elections in the South where Democratic party dominance rendered the general elections meaningless until recently. Separate sections then provide a list of the governors of each state from 1789 to 1998, general election returns by state from 1787 to 1997 (e.g., candidates, votes, percentage of vote), and primary election returns from 1919 to 1997. Separate indexes allow the user to track candidates in general elections and in primaries by name. Among the virtues of this Congressional Quarterly volume is the ready access to data over a long period of time. This work is recommended for general, high school, and higher education libraries.—**Frank L. Wilson**

651. **How Congress Works.** 3d ed. Washington, D.C., Congressional Quarterly, 1998. 184p. illus. index. $29.95pa. ISBN 1-56802-391-X.

This is the first revision of Congressional Quarterly's *How Congress Works* since 1991. Since then, much has changed in Congress and this volume captures and identifies those changes. However, its historical sweep allows the reader to recognize how much remains the same in this venerable political institution. It describes leadership in Congress, the legislative process, and the committee system. A reference section at the end provides useful information on party representation, leadership, and votes in Congress from 1789 to 1997. A useful addition is a section on Websites providing information on Congress on the Internet. Congressional Quarterly (CQ) is a reliable and thorough publisher on U.S. national politics. This volume continues CQ's tradition for useful, accurate, and accessible information on national politics. Information is presented clearly in nontechnical language. This volume is highly recommended for public libraries and school libraries at all levels.—**Frank L. Wilson**

652. **How Government Works.** New York, Macmillan Library Reference/Simon & Schuster Macmillan, 1999. 1108p. illus. index. (Macmillan Compendium). $125.00. ISBN 0-02-864975-3.

The purpose of this latest work in the Macmillan Compendium series is to provide students and researchers with a one-volume compendium of information on all aspects of U.S. government. The compendium is divided into three parts that correspond to each branch of government, each alphabetically arranged. The essays covering the legislative branch are selected from *The Encyclopedia of the United States Congress* (see ARBA 96, entry 720). Coverage of the executive branch is derived from *The Encyclopedia of the American Presidency* (see ARBA 95, entry 542). Part 3 concerns the judicial branch and includes essays from the *Encyclopedia of the American Judicial System* (see ARBA 88, entry 562) and the *Encyclopedia of the American Constitution* (see ARBA 87, entry 711). Each part is introduced by several articles that provide an overview of the branch's functions, authority, and purpose. Several features have been added to the compendium to enhance its presentation. Call-out quotations (quotes lifted from the text intended to solicit interest from the reader) are included throughout. When deemed appropriate, the editors have chosen a number of photographs, reproductions, and illustrations to accompany the text. A comprehensive index concludes the volume. The bibliographies have been retained from the original articles, but the opportunity to update them has been missed. This work is recommended for researchers who do not own the original works or for those libraries that cannot afford the other encyclopedias. [R: Choice, Sept 99, pp. 118-119]—**Robert V. Labaree**

653. Kemp, Roger L. **Managing America's Cities: A Handbook for Local Government Productivity.** Jefferson, N.C., McFarland, 1998. 460p. index. $55.00. ISBN 0-7864-0408-6.

The modest goal of this volume is to provide an overview of municipal government to interested parties. It proceeds to do so in a thorough if uninteresting manner. A historical overview and chapters on areas of municipal government provide an uncontroversial background to the topic as well as a list of pertinent issues, possible approaches, and concerns. A variety of sensible strategies are noted for everything from finances to parks and recreation. Unfortunately, the author ignores developing computer technology and its ramifications for local governance. The volume provides a resource directory that is adequate, but does not provide Web addresses for any association mentioned. The bibliography is dated, the most recent citations dating from 1995. Oddly, it has little relationship to the text and contains at least one topic, "retrenchment management," not mentioned in the volume. The book is an adequate but not dynamic introduction to municipal government. It is suitable for public and academic libraries. Libraries supporting more concentrated municipal studies programs will want to supplement this with a more scholarly work.—**Ann E. Miller**

654. **Local Government Election Practices: A Handbook for Public Officials and Citizens.** Roger L. Kemp, ed. Jefferson, N.C., McFarland, 1999. 495p. index. $48.50. ISBN 0-7864-0567-8.

This is an exceptional handbook on local government. It is an encyclopedic compilation of essays on various aspects of local U.S. election issues and systems. One of the important issues is the system of the election, whether district wide or use of wards. The first four essays review alternative local election systems, at-large vs. district election systems, alternative election systems as voting rights remedies, and mixed election systems (the newest reform structure).

Six essays review the laws and the systems in local government election practices, including issues of the U.S. Supreme Court, Voting Rights Act, vote dilution, and voting rights litigation. Nine essays review national studies and trends of election processes, minority representation, diversity, vote dilution, urban politics, municipal employee unions, term limits, and turnover of elected officials. Four essays deal with state studies and trends on home-rule charters, cumulative voting, women, and term limits. Six essays cover county and city studies and trends concerning women, minorities, win at large elections, vote dilution, voting patterns in tri-ethnic communities, proportional representation, and term limits. Only three essays focus on the future of the creation of effective local citizenship.

There are 2 appendixes—one on model city charter election guidelines and another on county charter election guidelines. This is an outstanding presentation of current issues and possible solution in local government effectiveness, not only in the electoral process but in governance and representation in U.S. communities. This volume is essential for all political science collections in every public library and academic library.—**Gerald D. Moran**

655. Lyn, Ragsdale. **Vital Statistics on the Presidency: Washington to Clinton.** rev. ed. Washington, D.C., Congressional Quarterly, 1998. 464p. index. $50.95; $35.95pa. ISBN 1-56802-393-6; 1-56802-427-4pa.

This newly revised volume retains the comprehensiveness and thorough descriptive analysis of the 1st edition while at the same time providing updated data on all the post–World War II presidents, from Harry Truman to William Clinton. The revised edition includes 170 tables and figures (20 more than the previous edition) and 9 introductory chapter essays. The chapters cover the following topics: personal information about the presidents, presidential elections, public appearances, public opinion, presidential organization and the executive branch, presidential policy making, congressional relations, and the relationship between the president and the judicial branch of government. Although brief, the essays are concise and well written. They succeed in highlighting key issues and summarizing important trends of the modern presidency as well as providing a descriptive interpretation of the data. The presentation of statistical data remains consistent with the 1st edition. The sources of information, usually obtained from government documents or compiled and formulated by the author, are cited for each table, followed by appropriate explanatory notes. The newly revised edition succeeds in updating both its statistical and descriptive information to reflect the beginning of Clinton's second term in office and the 1996 elections. The revised edition is also more reader-friendly with a list of tables and figures under each chapter heading in the table of contents. Although the book includes an index and a bibliography of references, the author has added few new citations from the previous edition. Despite the fact that most of the content is the same as the 1st edition, the book's availability in paperback justifies purchase of the new edition for the added information.

—**Robert V. Labaree**

656. Maddex, Robert L. **State Constitutions of the United States.** Washington, D.C., Congressional Quarterly, 1998. 518p. index. $115.00. ISBN 1-56802-373-1.

Focusing on "topics of major importance and interest" Maddex presents an outline of the current constitutions of the 50 states and 3 U.S. territories. In most cases, the actual text is used (so noted by the frequent use of quotation marks). Topics such as citizens' rights, and the role of legislatures, presiding officers, governors, and the Supreme Court dominate the work. Each entry follows a similar pattern beginning with a brief overview of the state, including square miles, size, and rank of the state. A brief outline of the constitutional history is included, followed by the preamble; fundamental rights; division of powers; the legislative, executive, and judicial branches; and ending with impeachment, taxation and finance, education, and the amendment procedures. Entries end with special topics that vary from state to state depending on their relative significance in that state.

After the introduction, the volume opens with a very interesting set of tables. These include state government structure, state constitutions and amendments, and new state rights and special provisions. Very quickly the reader can determine the term for the governor, term limits, whether item veto power exists, and so forth. Under the legislative branch, the memberships of the upper and lower houses are given, and whether term limits are in place. For the judicial branch, court size is cited, and whether officials are elected or appointed. The state constitution table presents the date of statehood and the effective date of the current constitution, along with amendments (Alabama leads with 618). Rights considered include privacy, sexual discrimination, disabled persons, victims, and taxpayers. Examples of special provisions considered include direct democracy, official language, and abortion. These tables are very useful and provide a splendid ready-reference resource.

Overall the volume presents a quick overview of state constitutions in a single volume—something not seen in recent times (with the possible exception of summaries found in law libraries). Most typically, such resources consist of one or more volumes devoted to the state constitution of each state. These are, of course, excellent for the legal profession and constitutional historians. But for the wider public, Maddex's volume merits a place in all general collections, as well as specialized political science libraries. Law libraries might find the book useful as a fast ready-reference tool. The work helps simplify a vast body of literature and will permit students to get quick answers without being put off by a massive series of state-by-state volumes. Highly recommended.—**Graham R. Walden**

657. Martin, Mart. **The Almanac of Women and Minorities in American Politics.** Boulder, Colo., Westview Press, 1999. 293p. index. $49.95. ISBN 0-8133-6870-7.

This almanac reconstructs the chronological histories of women and other minorities in the United States since its early history as a republic. The history begins with the first woman to cast a vote in the New World in 1655 and records minorities' interaction in U.S. politics until 1998.

The minorities include women, Afro-Americans, Hispanics, Asian Americans, native minorities, and gays and lesbians. Each of these groups has a chapter that begins with a brief chronology, political power defined through discussions of how each of the minorities achieved power through appointments to presidential cabinet, national party level, and congressional members. Statistics for voting percentages, ethnic representation, and first notables of the various minority groups are available. Academic libraries with a need for women and minority materials will find this almanac valuable to their collections. It contains information that is not readily available anywhere else. [R: Choice, Oct 99, p. 314]—**Kay M. Stebbins**

658. McGillivray, Alice V., Richard M. Scammon, and Rhodes Cook. **America at the Polls 1960-1996: A Handbook of American Presidential Election Statistics.** Washington, D.C., Congressional Quarterly, 1998. 1002p. $158.00. ISBN 1-56802-322-7.

Published in two volumes in 1994, *America at the Polls* provided a comprehensive statistical compendium of presidential election results from 1920 through 1992 (see ARBA 95, entry 737, for a review). The volume under review is an update of volume 2 and captures the results from the 1996 presidential election. The pattern of organization remains the same. National summary of the state-by-state vote and the Electoral College vote is provided for each election from 1920 to 1996. The remaining chapters, arranged alphabetically, cover each state. They include a table of popular vote and Electoral College vote for each president since John F. Kennedy, a county outline map, and detailed tables of presidential election results arranged by county. Each table includes total population based on the most recent Bureau of the Census data at the time, the total vote distribution, and vote distribution by major party and as a percentage. Each chapter concludes with a note giving a more detailed breakdown of votes by minor party for each election. The same high quality has been maintained in this updated volume, but ready access to the 1996 presidential election results makes this purchase necessary only for those institutions that can afford the convenience.
—**Robert V. Labaree**

659. Milkis, Sidney M., and Michael Nelson. **The American Presidency: Origins and Development, 1776-1998.** 3d ed. Washington, D.C., Congressional Quarterly, 1999. 474p. illus. index. $31.95pa. ISBN 1-56802-432-0.

As stated in the preface, the authors saw the need for a 3d edition of this work based on 2 reasons: to update the history of the presidency to include the political events of the Clinton administration, most notably with regard to the 1994 and 1996 elections and congressional attempts to impeach the president, and "to refine the writing and analysis throughout the book." *The American Presidency* remains the only 1-volume analysis of the American presidency and, as such, continues to serve as a rich source of information about the history of the Executive Office. Although this resource could be considered more a comprehensive handbook than a ready-reference tool, it still serves as an important chronological survey of the American presidency.

As in the two previous editions, the book opens with an introductory chapter that examines the Constitutional Convention and the conceptual framework of the presidential office. The 2d chapter builds on this introduction by analyzing various organizational structures, such as enumerated powers, that characterize the institution of the presidency. Subsequent chapters are arranged in conceptual categories that mark transitional stages in the history of the presidency or encompass a term in office dominated by one individual. The majority of new information is in the chapter devoted to the Clinton administration. This chapter takes the reader from Clinton's election to office through the events of mid-1998 during the period when Clinton was engulfed in the Monica Lewinsky scandal and attempted impeachment trial. The book concludes with an updated chapter on the history of the vice presidency. Also included is an appendix with the text of the Constitution of the United States and a list of the presidents and vice presidents and their terms in office, as well as a comprehensive index. This work remains very dense, with some photographs but no other visual supplements to the book's contents. Nevertheless, this is a highly recommended research tool because the authors have produced a well-written book that is relatively free of author bias and organized in a logical manner that facilitates a clear understanding of the American presidency throughout history.
—**Robert V. Labaree**

660. **Special Interest Group Profiles for Students.** Kelle S. Sisung, ed. Farmington Hills, Mich., Gale, 1999. 883p. illus. index. $85.00. ISBN 0-7876-2794-1.

Special Interest Group Profiles is one volume in a series cited in the preface as the U.S. Government for Students series. Although directed primarily at high school students and college undergraduates, the information and quality of the text make it just as suitable for the general public. Included are 150 groups; the final selection was based in part on information from teachers and textbooks indicating that the group is a broad one, covering "any organized group of individuals, united together [sic] for a common cause, that attempts to influence public policy." The selection seems reasonably balanced, with groups from both the right and the left. The goal is not to critique the organizations included, but enough information is provided so that readers can make judgments on their own. The entries are four to six pages in length, and all are structured in the same way, with sections on the organization's mission, structure, primary functions, programs, budget, history, current political issues, future directions, group resources and publications, and a bibliography of secondary sources. Each profile includes a "case study" of a recent controversial issue in which the organization was involved; these add interest and are helpful in understanding the organization's activities. There are some other sources for this kind of information already available on the market. David Wall's *Activist's Almanac* (see ARBA 94, entry 865) is perhaps the most similar, although the choice of organizations differs substantially: International and foreign policy issues are emphasized, while labor unions (many included in the present volume) are omitted entirely. Congressional Quarterly's *Public Interest Profiles* (see entry 42) is another and some more general encyclopedias like the *Encyclopedia of American Activism: 1960 to the Present* by Margaret DiCanio (see entry 667) can also be useful. This work is recommended for school, public, and academic libraries.—**V. W. Hill**

661. **State Government 1998-99: CQ's Guide to Current Issues and Activities.** Thad L. Beyle, ed. Washington, D.C., Congressional Quarterly, 1998. 225p. index. $19.95pa. ISBN 1-56802-098-8. ISSN 0888-8590.

This new edition of *State Government* contains recent articles that define and analyze some current issues and agendas of state and local governments. Those problems have grown considerably in scope and size during the past 40 years. A total of 10 parts present articles of relevance, although they are not always exhaustive. The parts include "Politics in the 1990s"; "Politics: Direct Democracy"; "Politics: Parties, Interest Groups, and PACs"; "Media and the States"; "State Legislatures"; "Governors and the Executive Branch"; and eight articles on state issues. For instance, the 2d part has articles on "Direct Democracy Works," "Voter Initiatives on Race and Sex Preferences," and "Time Line of Term Limits." There are 13 boxes that provide interesting side views and examples of topics under discussion. Only some of the articles found here include notes, which decreases the textbook value of this volume. Some important topics, such as the federal-state fiscal and political relations and federal revenue sharing, are not included in this edition. This source is recommended as a starter for discussions in political science classes, although the instructor would have to do supplementary reading. The book can also serve as a guide for state legislators.

—**Bogdan Mieczkowski**

662. **States' Rights and American Federalism: A Documentary History.** Frederick D. Drake and Lynn R. Nelson, eds. Westport, Conn., Greenwood Press, 1999. 232p. index. (Primary Documents in American History and Contemporary Issues). $49.95. ISBN 0-313-30573-0.

This research guide represents the latest volume in the Primary Documents in American History and Contemporary Issues series from Greenwood Press. As with earlier books, this work is intended to provide in one volume the full-text of key documents on a particular event or issue in U.S. history. This particular work traces the relationship between state's rights and the American system of federalism. The editors have chosen a total of 72 documents that they believe best illustrate the struggle between public good and private rights in our nation. An introductory essay gives a brief but concise overview of the birth and development of American federalism. The instruction concludes with a chronology of events.

The documents are arranged chronologically in 5 parts. Part 1 examines the drafting of the Constitution and the related debates between Federalists and Antifederalists. Part 2 contains documents concerning the writing of the Bill of Rights. Part 3 focuses on the debate between advocates of state's rights and federalists who viewed the Declaration of Independence "as a source of higher law to thwart states' rights arguments" (p. xxii). Part 4 highlights the rights of women and African American as citizens. Part 5 focuses on the issues of state's rights and federalism from the New Deal to the present. Each part is introduced by a brief essay that places the time period covered in proper historical context. Brief essays also introduce each document and include a bibliography for further reading. These essays are well written and help to tell the story of state's rights and federalism as represented by the documents in this volume. The book concludes with a comprehensive name and subject index.

Beyond the convenience of having all of these documents in one guide, the true value of this work centers on the fact that it helps bring to light those historical documents that no doubt represent significant contributions to our nation's history but remain in the shadows of those few documents found in almost every text book published on U.S. history. This book is highly recommended.—**Robert V. Labaree**

663. **The United States Government Manual 1998/1999.** Lanham, Md., Bernan Associates, 1999. 869p. index. $41.00pa. ISBN 0-16-049690-X.

This manual is the official handbook of the U.S. federal government. In essence, the manual provides a detailed description of the legislative, judicial, and executive branches of government. For example, the section on the judicial branch is divided into 6 sections, namely the Supreme Court, the lower federal courts, special courts, the Administrative Office of the United States Courts, the Federal Judicial Center, and the United States Sentencing Commission. The researcher will find not only the purpose, nature, and function of these divisions but also a list of the positions and the personnel in those positions. Throughout this indispensable resource are additional sources of information, including office addresses, electronic access, and publications. In addition, all executive agencies are defined and described. The major departments are delineated here (e.g., Agriculture, Commerce, Defense, Interior, Justice, Labor, Transportation, and Treasury) as well as "independent establishments and government corporations." Some of the agencies under this last heading are the Central Intelligence Agency, Farm Credit Administration, Federal Labor Relations Authority, Federal Reserve System, Merit Systems, Protection Board, National Labor Relations Board, Nuclear Regulatory Commission, Office of Government Ethics, Social Security Administration, United States Commission on Civil Rights, and United States Postal System, to name only a few. There are other categories as well, including quasi-official agencies and multilateral organizations. There are two indexes—name and agency/subject. Every library should have a copy of this easy-to-use guide to the U.S. government.—**Michael A. Foley**

664. Van Tassel, Emily Field, and Paul Finkelman. **Impeachable Offenses: A Documentary History from 1787 to the Present.** Washington, D.C., Congressional Quarterly, 1999. 326p. illus. index. $34.95; $19.95pa. ISBN 1-56802-479-7; 1-56802-480-0pa.

When nearly half of the American adult population does not know that a vote on the articles of impeachment by the House does not automatically dismiss the president, something is amiss. Congressional Quarterly has turned its formidable skills to report on impeachable offenses since the early founding of our country.

Impeachable Offenses (IO) offers readers a basal primer on the U.S. Constitution. There was a time when every child in America learned this in grade school. Today, however, with so much education given over to reeducation—diversity, multiculturalism, hate crimes, and so on—there apparently is no time to cover the basics of our country and how it works. The beauty of IO is that it provides readers with a simple and easy-to-follow guide written in easy-to-understand language.

The introduction chronicles the evolution of impeachment, both how the law works and the process by which Congress does its duty, or not. Then follows a lively discussion of that fateful phrase "high crimes and misdemeanors." It is clear from the 16 impeachment proceedings that have occurred since 1787, every impeached officer has claimed no crime was committed. It is also clear from those 16 proceedings that a "crime" did not have to occur for the impeached officer to be removed (favoritism, for example, removed a district judge in the 1930s).

Chapters then follow on the framers' intent, the scope of impeachable offenses, and those who could stand for impeachment. Following these very entertaining pages are biographies of judges, senators, and presidents who stood for impeachment. Special, separate treatment is given to Andrew Johnson, Richard Nixon, and William Clinton.

Not only is this book easy and necessary reading, but its text is also peppered with illustrations and photographs to make it even more entertaining and informative. A bibliography and index close out this excellent reference tool.—**Mark Y. Herring**

European

665. **The History of Parliament on CD-ROM.** [CD-ROM]. New York, Cambridge University Press, 1998. Minimum system requirements (Windows version): IBM or compatible 486. Double-speed CD-ROM drive. Windows 3.1 or Windows 95. 8MB RAM. Minimum system requirements (Macintosh version): System 7.0 or later. Double-speed CD-ROM drive. 4MB RAM. $895.00. ISBN 0-521-62907-1.

This is truly a remarkable CD-ROM and a remarkable research tool. While expensive, its virtual ubiquity means tens of thousands of libraries that may have passed up the 23-volume print incarnation will openly welcome the single CD-ROM advent.

It is not just the ease of use that will have scholars, laity, and librarians alike cheering, but the presence of hundreds of thumbnails will also delight the eyes of many users. What is more, these thumbnails (both embedded in the text and in the index of illustrations) have been reproduced exquisitely. Some adjustments may be necessary to the video output of certain machines, but most PCs will display these pictures with perfect, astonishing clarity. Herein included is everything from medieval floor plans to paintings depicting parliament in all its various guises.

As for the CD-ROM itself, the usual aspects are present: easy searching, keyword use, and a table display of where the hits are and how many in each section, as well as cut and paste notebooks for the researcher. Moreover, cross-referencing was never easier or better. A click on the red-lettered text and users are off and researching. Book marking is as easy as ever, as is hypertext navigation.

It would appear the name of Cambridge University Press is not only unparalleled when it comes to print, but also when it comes to CD-ROMs. Almost. Using the CD-ROM requires printing off the near 50-page user guide. This CD-ROM is not intuitive. Students will not figure out that under the "view" rubric on the toolbar resides the word "enlarge" that will take grainy text and make it perfect. Nor will users intuit what each icon means. Some tables will display poorly but adjustments to the display (as explained in the guide) will correct most if not all of them. This really is a CD-ROM created with a scholar in mind. Its residence on a library PC will vary from location to location, depending on collection strengths. By all means, wherever it is placed, a laminated version of the user guide nearby will greatly enhance its use.—**Mark Y. Herring**

Middle Eastern

666. **Political Encyclopedia of the Middle East.** Avraham Sela, ed. New York, Continuum Publishing, 1999. 815p. $125.00. ISBN 0-8264-1053-7.

That another such work is needed, despite the recent spate, is clear from events: the Israel-Egypt peace treaty of 1979, the eight year Iran-Iraq war, the invasion of Kuwait and the subsequent Gulf War, the collapse of the Evil Empire, the end of the Cold War, and new, if often failed, peacemaking ventures between Arab and Israeli officials. Sela, an expert on the Palestinians at Hebrew University, has assembled a veritable who's who of figures on all the issues concerned. And the hefty volume covers everything from conflicts, wars, and rumors of war, to water politics, nuclear weapons, OPEC, and the EC. There is even a chapter on women in the Middle East.

The book compares well with its predecessors. *The Cambridge Encyclopedia of the Middle East and Africa* (see ARBA 89, entry 141) is still excellent if dated. Hiro's *Dictionary of the Middle East* (see ARBA 97, entry 138) is good for ready-reference but Sela's offering is by definition more complete, of course. Ziring's *The Middle East: A Political Dictionary* (see ARBA 93, entry 776) takes a different tact than Sela but both cover similar ground. And Congressional Quarterly's wonderful 8th edition of *The Middle East* (see ARBA 96, entry 764) covers much the same ground and even a bit more.

What makes Sela's work a useful and necessary contribution is both the range of topics and the space devoted to each. Each article serves as more than a snapshot; it is a veritable primary source for information. Tables, charts, maps, political intrigue, GNPs, debts, and more are all accounted for. Although cross-references abound, there is, sadly, neither an index nor a bibliography. [R: LJ, 15 Oct 98, p. 63]—**Mark Y. Herring**

IDEOLOGIES

667. DiCanio, Margaret B. **Encyclopedia of American Activism, 1960 to the Present.** Santa Barbara, Calif., ABC-CLIO, 1998. 322p. illus. index. $75.00. ISBN 0-87436-899-5.

This encyclopedic volume attempts to document the spectrum of alternative activist movements in the United States since 1960. An introductory essay provides context for the development of the civil rights and antiwar movements, and the protest movements that evolved from them. The entries vary in length from one paragraph to several pages. Sources follow each entry, and sometimes *see also* references are provided.

The volume leans toward left-wing thinking, but a search for some prominent figures of the 1960s and 1970s revealed some significant absences. The Berrigan brothers, Philip and Daniel, do not get entries. Although there is an entry for "Chicago Seven Trial," only Tom Hayden and Abbie Hoffman get personal entries, and these lack *see also* references to the trial. Codefendants Jerry Rubin and Rennie Davis get no entries, nor does defendant eight, Bobby Seale. And in what might be the unkindest cut, Richard Daley does. It could be argued that, unlike Hayden and Hoffman, these men dropped out of the movement, but Dave Delliger was an activist until his death and he has no entry either. Chicago Seven lawyer William Kuntsler, another lifetime activist, has no entry and is not in the index, although he does appear in a photograph illustrating the entry on Russell Means.

Other examples of omissions: Earth Day is included but Earth First! is not and Kent State is included but similar events on the black campus of Jackson State are not. A long entry is devoted to Jane Fonda, but Carl Oglesby, a founder of Students for a Democratic Society (SDS), does not even appear in the index. Angela Davis and Al Sharpton are not here either. Even stranger, entries appear for Ho Chi Minh, Gandhi, Mao Zedong, and Jacques Cousteau. The information given is general and not particularly relevant.

This is a disappointing work. Although much of what it includes would be useful for ready-reference, what it does not include might fill a second volume. [R: BL, 1 Mar 99, pp. 1246-1247; Choice, July/Aug 99, p. 1926]—**Ruth A. Carr**

668. Gay, Kathlyn, and Martin K. Gay. **Encyclopedia of Political Anarchy.** Santa Barbara, Calif., ABC-CLIO, 1999. 242p. index. $60.00. ISBN 0-87436-982-7.

Most people will associate anarchism with terrorism, radicals, socialists, or communism, but the authors contend that they are not the same. Some anarchists used terrorism to make a point, but many groups publicly adopt some of the themes of anarchism to advance their particular radical goal. Using this book can help one differentiate between anarchism and other political movements. The 172 entries are in alphabetic order and are not arranged by broad subject categories. There is a detailed table of contents and index to help one find relevant entries. Events, political groups, themes, and movements are all covered, but most of the text is related to people. This is to be expected since it is individuals who are the most important aspect of this movement. Cross-references and citations for suggested readings are found at the end of the entries. Helpful Web addresses are also included. Quotations and extracts from other important writings are embedded in many of the entries. The glossary is much appreciated, saving the reader from having to search through other political science dictionaries. Photographs and a chronology of events would have increased the value of this reference tool. The appendix discusses the new field of Internet anarchism that is potentially very dangerous. There are no corresponding entries for anarchism as it might be utilized through journals, newspapers, television, or the radio. This title complements *The Encyclopedia of Revolutions and Revolutionaries: From Anarchism to Zhou Enlai* (see ARBA 97, entry 477), which is much broader in scope. The authors previously collaborated on *Heroes of Conscience: A Biographical Dictionary* (see ARBA 97, entry 22). This easy-to-read encyclopedia is recommended for the reference collections of public, academic, and school libraries. [R: LJ, July 99, pp. 80-83; Choice, Nov 99, p. 516; BR, Nov/Dec 99, p. 86]—**Daniel K. Blewett**

669. Nash, Jay Robert. **Terrorism in the 20th Century: A Narrative Encyclopedia from the Anarchists, Through the Weathermen, to the Unabomber.** New York, M. Evans, 1998. 468p. illus. index. $24.95pa. ISBN 0-87131-855-5.

This work on terrorism in this century begins with the statement that "terrorism comes in all forms." This descriptive account provides an esoteric array of individuals, terrorist groups, and organizations. The chapters follow chronologically, from 1900 to 1990. The book includes a chapter titled "The 1920s, Ghost Governments: Beneath the White Hood," which includes a section on Leo Frank; "The 1960s, Malcontents, Misfits, and the American Left: Havoc in Chicago," which includes a section on Yippies, SDS, and MOBE; "The 1980s, Day of the Arab: A Murder in Egypt, which includes a section on Anwar Sadat's assassination; and "The 1990s, Rage from the Right: At the Lunatic Fringe, which includes a section on the Zodiac Killer who terrorized New York City. A number of photographs are provided, although the layout could have been improved. Also provided is a thorough chronology of twentieth-century terrorism, a glossary of terrorist organizations, a bibliography, and an index. This work is recommended for public libraries and undergraduate users.—**Leslie R. Homzie**

INTERNATIONAL ORGANIZATIONS

670. **The Europa Directory of International Organizations.** London, Europa; distr., Farmington Hills, Mich., Gale, 1999. 568p. index. $230.00. ISBN 1-85743-068-9. ISSN 1465-4628.

The 1st edition of this 1-volume research guide gives information on international organizations around the world. More than 1,700 international organizations that encourage international peace, security, and cooperation in economic, social, cultural, and humanitarian areas are included. It also includes extensive background information to give a historical and legal perspective on the international system. Organizations such as the United Nations, the League of Arab States, and the Organization of American States have a lot of information provided, such as addresses, telephone and fax numbers, e-mail and Website addresses, date of formation, principal objectives, leadership, structure and principal officials, detailed accounts of recent activities, financial background, and a list of publications. Other organizations are covered in briefer descriptions, with activities, membership, principal officers, and publications.

The 1st chapter is an introductory essay on developing roles of international organizations and challenges facing the international community. Texts of significant international charters, treaties, and documents are also included. Biographical information is also supplied for leading officials of international organizations and a chronology outlines historical developments. Also included are lists of U.S. Security Council and general assembly resolutions, plus information about UN peacekeeping activities and a calendar of international observances. A comprehensive index of international organizations is included. The printing, binding, and paper are of average quality and the font is large enough for periodic reading. The book would be useful for anyone interested in the international area.—**Herbert W. Ockerman**

671. Humphreys, Norman K. **Historical Dictionary of the International Monetary Fund.** 2d ed. Lanham, Md., Scarecrow, 1999. 330p. (Historical Dictionaries of International Organizations, no.17). $60.00. ISBN 0-8108-3659-9.

The International Monetary Fund was established in 1945 as a relatively obscure organization. The Fund, commonly know as the IMF, has evolved to a central position in the global effort to orchestrate the workings of the international monetary system and to maintain a recognized code of behavior among its 182 member nations. In addition to its program related to economic and financial policies and assistance, the Fund now has an extensive information and publications program with an extensive array of reports and a Website (http://www.inf.org). In this book the editor, Norman K. Humphreys, the former chief editor of the Fund and longtime staff member, provides definitions and historical information about financial and economic concepts, operational policies, and the IMF's structure and staffing, its decision-making authority, and the relationship of member countries to the Fund over the years. Each definition or entry, which can run several pages, is a small historical essay on the concept addressed. In addition to this main section that provides alphabetic access to concepts, the introductory sections and appendixes are of equal importance. The chronology and introduction, covering 55 pages, provide an overview of the history and development of the Fund. There is also a section on abbreviations and acronyms, a statistical appendix, and a bibliography of IMF publications and publications about the Fund. This title is a very useful dictionary, or really a handbook, for anyone needing more information about the International Monetary Fund than is available on the Website. Its strong point is the historical context that is concisely provided for each term in the dictionary. It will also be of use to persons not interested specifically in the IMF but in such topics as the recent Asian economic crisis, Third World debt payments, or the economic development of eastern Europe after communism.

—Henry E. York

INTERNATIONAL RELATIONS

672. **Encyclopedia of Conflicts Since World War II.** James Ciment, ed. Armonk, N.Y., M. E. Sharpe, 1999. 4v. illus. maps. index. $359.00/set. ISBN 0-7656-8004-1.

The twentieth century has been one of the bloodiest eras in human history. This violence is most vividly demonstrated by the two world wars and has also been dramatized by regional conflicts throughout the world, from conflicts such as the Korean War and Iran-Iraq war in the 1980s to the current NATO-Serbian confrontation over Bosnia. *Encyclopedia of Conflicts* seeks to describe these conflicts in a succinct fashion accessible to the first-time student as well as the seasoned scholar.

Its initial volume opens with an introduction describing the immediate aftermath of World War II and an essay on the origins of the Cold War and the differing schools of thought on this conflict's genesis. Other introductory essays stress the role of anti-Colonialism after World War II; the influence of "people's wars" in Marxist-Leninist military strategy, coups, invasions, and border disputes; coverage of ethnic and religious conflicts; terrorism; and the international arms trade. Other features of the first volume include coverage of international organizations, such as the Arab League; key events, such as U.S. diplomatic recognition of China; the creation of West Germany; Middle East peace negotiations; and the role of the Marshall Plan in fostering postwar European reconstruction.

The main section of this book includes concise coverage of significant twentieth-century international and regional conflicts. Examples of profiled conflicts include the Soviet invasion of Afghanistan in the 1970s and 1980s, the Falkland Islands war between Argentina and the United Kingdom, the Chinese civil war between 1927 and 1949, the Kabila uprising in Zaire/Democratic Republic of the Congo in 1996 to 1997, El Salvador's civil wars in the 1970s and 1980s, Iran's Islamic Revolution of the late 1970s, Israel's 1973 Yom Kippur war, Nigeria's Biafran conflict between 1967 and 1970, the Uganda civil conflict, and the ongoing disintegration of the former Yugoslavia. Entries on these conflicts provide historical background information, key personalities and events, factors precipitating conflict, developments during the conflict, and a bibliography of selected readings concluding each entry.

Encyclopedia of Conflicts Since World War II is a good introduction for undergraduates to the myriad international and regional conflicts that have marked the twentieth century's history. Individual entries are well written and may stimulate additional research on these events. A significant weakness is the nostalgic tone taken toward the U.S.-Soviet alliance during World War II in the introduction and a tendency in this same section to engage in the uncritical criticism of free market economics and anti-Western rhetoric that regrettably mars numerous scholarly assessments of these conflicts. Coverage of emerging arenas of conflict, such as nuclear proliferation, biological and chemical warfare, information warfare, and urban conflict would provide further enhancement to this work. Despite the presence of such regrettable polemics in the introduction, this work will serve as a useful introductory primer to students of these multifaceted conflicts. [R: LJ, July 99, p. 80; BL, Aug 99, pp. 2104-2106; Choice, Oct 99, pp. 311-312; SLJ, Aug 99, p. 181]
—**Bert Chapman**

673. Ramsbotham, Oliver, and Tom Woodhouse. **Encyclopedia of International Peacekeeping Operations.** Santa Barbara, Calif., ABC-CLIO, 1999. maps. index. $75.00. ISBN 0-87436-892-8.

Military forces perform peacekeeping operations for the United Nations (UN) and other international organizations in areas as diverse as the Sinai Peninsula, Kosovo, and Rwanda. These forces are called upon to separate warring factions from each other, promote social stability, rebuild and maintain the physical infrastructures of individual nation-states, and perform a variety of other responsibilities.

Encyclopedia of International Peacekeeping Operations covers the multifaceted operations and recent history of international peacekeeping forces. An introduction defines peacekeeping's continually evolving nature, historical development since World War II, strengths and weaknesses with the current international peacekeeping system, and an assessment of possible future developments within this field. The main part of this work is an alphabetically arranged collection of entries covering the countries, individuals, and organizations involved in international peacekeeping.

Entries include UN missions in Bosnia and Herzegovina, conflict prevention, first-generation peacekeeping, humanitarian intervention, Irish peacekeeping, Canadian general and UN Protection Force Commander for the former Yugoslavia Lewis Mackenzie, current UN Secretary General Kofi Annan, the Western Union, and relevant Websites. Appendixes list force commanders of UN peacekeeping missions for 1948 to 1998, UN Secretary General Special Representatives for this same period, and international peacekeeping acronyms.

Encyclopedia of International Peacekeeping Operations is a valuable introduction to an increasingly important and controversial aspect of international security and the debate over the future direction of U.S. foreign policy. Individual entries are well written, make references to applicable cross-references, and supply references to appropriate bibliographic sources. Although it does not deal with recent issues, this is a useful addition to academic library reference collections. [R: Choice, Nov 99, p. 520]—**Bert Chapman**

674. Silverburg, Sanford R., and Bernard Reich. **U.S. Foreign Relations with the Middle East and North Africa: A Bibliography, Supplement 1998.** Lanham, Md., Scarecrow, 1999. 518p. index. (Scarecrow Area Bibliographies, no.19). $95.00. ISBN 0-8108-3615-7.

This bibliography adds to the collections titled *United States Foreign Policy and the Middle East/North Africa: Bibliography of 20th Century Research* (see ARBA 91, entry 770) and *United States Foreign Policy Toward the Middle East and North Africa: A Bibliography* (see ARBA 95, entry 764). It contains more than 3,500 discrete sources that come from professional and scholarly material published in Western languages. Nonprint media sources such as video production, CD-ROMs, URLs, and the Internet are also included. The information is organized by topic descriptors and covers areas such as Arab/Israel conflict, Lebanese civil war, Iran hostages, Gulf War, and Intifada. Key persons such as U.S. presidents as well as Arab leaders are also included. There is an author and subject index to make the information easier to locate. The paper, printing, and binding are of average quality and the font is large enough to be easily readable. The biographic information would be a tremendous source and time-saver for anyone studying or writing about relations in this area of the world.—**Herbert W. Ockerman**

PUBLIC POLICY AND ADMINISTRATION

675. Brown, Mary Elizabeth. **Shapers of the Great Debate on Immigration: A Biographical Dictionary.** Westport, Conn., Greenwood Press, 1999. 322p. illus. index. (Shapers of the Great American Debates, no.1). $59.95. ISBN 0-313-30339-8.

Brown offers the reader a wonderful opportunity to know something about the lives of 20 people who have contributed, positively or negatively, to the immigration debate. The biographies range from 12 to 15 pages, including endnotes and a bibliographic narrative to direct readers wanting to examine the life of a "shaper" more fully. The bibliographic sketches include Thomas Jefferson, Lyman Beecher, Booker T. Washington, Jacob Riis, Jane Addams, A. Mitchell Palmer, Henry Ford, and Cesar Chavez. In addition, an appendix provides brief biographical sketches of other players in the history of the immigration debate. The book concludes with a selected bibliography and a useful index. The biographies are clearly and coherently written, and they are fair and informative. Although this book is not designed to set forth arguments for and against immigration philosophies, it succeeds admirably in putting some faces on the debate, which is the author's intent. The biographies also incorporate the social and political climate present in these lives, for "shapers" are themselves shaped by the world in which they live. The life of Laura Fermi presents a clear example of the cause–and–effect relationship. The biographies are a joy to peruse. This work is highly recommended for any reference collection. [R: Choice, July/Aug 99, p. 1925]—**Michael A. Foley**

676. Hing, Bill Ong. **Immigration and the Law: A Dictionary.** Santa Barbara, Calif., ABC-CLIO, 1999. 400p. index. (Contemporary Legal Issues). $55.00. ISBN 1-57607-120-0.

ABC-CLIO's Contemporary Legal Issues series is designed for high school and college students seeking introductory information on U.S. legal issues. This volume focuses on the often-confusing issue of immigration law in the United States. The book begins with an introduction that addresses the history of immigration and explains how the laws and their amendments have created the complexities of current immigration procedures. It also discusses current laws and how family reunification, employment, labor certification, and the number of immigrants allowed into the United States a year come into play. The bulk of the book is arranged into A to Z entries that cover historical terms, laws, court cases, key people in immigration history, and basic terms (e.g., orphans, visa, picture bride). Each entry is one-half page to one page in length and all words contained within an entry that are provided their own entry are in bold typeface. The appendix that follows provides eight reproductions of government immigration documents including a form for employment eligibility verification; an application for naturalization; and 100 typical questions of the Department of Justice, Immigration, and Naturalization Service. An index concludes the volume.

This is a good introduction to immigration law for high school and undergraduate students. Anyone needing more information will need to consult more comprehensive legal sources. This work will be a valuable addition to high school and university libraries.—**Shannon M. Graff**

677. **Issues for Debate in American Public Policy.** Sandra L. Stencel, ed. Washington, D.C., Congressional Quarterly, 1999. 320p. illus. index. $25.95pa. ISBN 1-56802-463-0.

This helpful guide to public policy debate reprints 16 issues of *The CQ Researcher* published between 1996 and 1998. The issues selected for inclusion focus on concerns central in public policy today and are likely to remain policy issues well into the next decade. The debates profiled here include school choice, teacher education, patients' rights, welfare, Social Security, population and the environment, environmental justice, gun control, Internet privacy, drug testing, promoting democracy in Asia, and U.S.-Russian relations, among others. Each topic is presented in the following well-defined and coherent format. First, the issue itself is defined and explained. Then relevant background information on the issue is presented. For example, to get a clear and immediate sense of where an issue has been, there is a separate one-page chronology briefly outlining key historical developments. After this the current situation is assessed, with different sides to the issues receiving fair and equal treatment. Each issue concludes with an outlook, notes, and a useful bibliography. The material is presented in a clear, straightforward, and nonpartisan manner. The collection concludes with a helpful index. *The CQ Researcher* has no agenda other than to help people become more informed, critically thinking citizens. People who are interested in any of these issues are advised to read these guides. Each issue is approximately 20 pages in length.—**Michael A. Foley**

678. Jackson, Byron M. **Encyclopedia of American Public Policy.** Santa Barbara, Calif., ABC-CLIO, 1999. 230p. index. $65.00. ISBN 1-57607-023-9.

Jackson, a political scientist, has written approximately 500 entries describing key concepts in the field of American police, as well as major legislation, Supreme Court cases, terms, agencies, and figures relating to 13 American public policy domains, such as agriculture, civil rights, commerce and transportation, communications, crime, economics, education, energy, entitlement programs, environment, health, housing, and labor. The entries include short lists of references, and each section begins with a chronology of major events affecting policy in the domain. Cross-references are plentiful. A short introductory essay provides an overview of the subject, and the volume concludes with a bibliography and index. Although brief, the entries provide a comprehensive and authoritative introduction to U.S. public policy, making it a useful tool for undergraduates and high school students.—**Lee Weston**

679. **U.S. Immigration and Naturalization Laws and Issues: A Documentary History.** Michael Lemay and Elliott Robert Barkan, eds. Westport, Conn., Greenwood Press, 1999. 336p. index. (Primary Documents in American History and Contemporary Issues). $49.95. ISBN 0-313-30156-5.

As part of the Greenwood series on documents and issues in American history, this book is designed to meet the needs of high school and college students by providing background material and documents on immigration history. It purports to trace the controversial aspects of the topic through documents representing a variety of viewpoints. Although there has been controversy about immigration and citizenship throughout American history, it is perhaps more intense in the present time when both legal and illegal immigrants so clearly impact on the nation's economic, social, and political life. The editors remind readers that in order to understand this phenomenon, it is necessary to examine the ways our immigration and naturalization laws have shaped this complex process.

A lengthy introduction to the work provides an overview of immigration policy from 1790, when Congress restricted citizenship to free white persons of good character, to 1996, when it enacted laws that authorized stricter border controls and attempted to deny all benefits to noncitizens. A list of significant dates and events follows the introduction. The main text comprises more than 100 primary documents divided into 4 periods of history and arranged chronologically. The documents include the major laws and court opinions relating to immigration, either in their entirety or as excerpts of the key provisions, and also such documents as presidential proclamations, Congressional remarks, and statements of various organizations such as the Ku Klux Klan. A glossary, selected bibliography, and index are appended.

The editors (both of whom are college professors in the fields of history, political science, and ethnic studies) have made readily available the most significant laws and opinions relating to immigration history. Additionally, through the excellent introductory summaries of each of the four periods, they have highlighted many of the recurrent themes of that history (e.g., the methods used to exclude certain groups and the close relationship of immigration laws to foreign policy). A feature that is particularly useful in this work is the table of contents, which allows the user to quickly review the documents as they developed throughout history, since they are arranged chronologically either by the name of the act or a more popular title. The convenience of having this sometimes difficult-to-find information in one volume, the ease of access to particular documents, and the helpful added features, particularly the introduction and period summaries, should make this book a welcome addition not only to school and academic libraries, but also to those public libraries having immigrant populations among their users.—**Lucille Whalen**

14 Psychology, Parapsychology, and Occultism

PSYCHOLOGY

Bibliography

680. **Bibliographic Guide to Psychology 1998.** Thorndike, Maine, G. K. Hall/Macmillan, 1999. 452p. $295.00. ISBN 0-7838-0228-5. ISSN 0360-277X.

G. K. Hall has once again compiled a comprehensive annual subject bibliography devoted to select psychology materials that were cataloged in 1998 but may have been published between 1990 and the present. The guide is made up of recent publications cataloged by The Research Libraries of The New York Public Library (NYPL), which share two or more Library of Congress subject headings from MARC psychology records. Other materials included have been cataloged by the Library of Congress in the same time period and retrieved from the LC MARC tapes with a "BF" classification.

Alphabetically arranged in a dictionary format, all main entries supply full bibliographic information, conveniently including call numbers and subject tracings. Another way to access information is to use the added entries, such as titles, editors, and compilers, which are also supplemented with cross-references to proper LC headings. These valuable features enhance the guide's usefulness not only as an authoritative reference source of recently published psychology materials, but also as a research tool for students and other research-oriented patrons. It is recognizable as a collection development tool, providing the means to maintain current awareness of noteworthy resources within the field. Having such complete technical information easily accessible, catalogers and acquisitions librarians will also find it worthwhile to consult. Visually pleasing, the entries are in bold typeface and include all languages and formats. Major subject areas include such topics as child psychology, applied psychology, temperament, character, personality, the occult sciences, and parapsychology, to name a few.

Unfortunately, the omission of the NYPL holdings indicator and Classmark for appropriate records as promised in the preface is a definite flaw. The overall quality of the guide, which is intended for librarians, students, and researchers, meets previous high standards established in G. K. Hall's series. This resource is appropriate for libraries serving research needs, but it may have limited appeal due to its increased cost.
—**Marianne B. Eimer**

681. Van Whitlock, Rodney, and Bernard Lubin, comps. **Mental Health Services in Criminal Justice System Settings: A Selectively Annotated Bibliography, 1970-1997.** Westport, Conn., Greenwood Press, 1999. 190p. index. (Research and Bibliographical Guides in Criminal Justice, no.6). $65.00. ISBN 0-313-30186-7.

Van Whitlock and Lubin have addressed nearly three decades of a very specialized but key subject area within the criminal justice setting. The volume is divided into 15 independent sections, covering such topics as individual psychotherapy, sex offenders, and female mentally ill offenders. In total, 1,264 citations are provided, of which 150 are for books. The annotated entries number 542. The authors note that most of the empirically based works received annotations, and those vary from one to five sentences, with most on the shorter side. Material was collected from a number of disciplines, such as psychology, psychiatry, nursing, education, and social work, producing a reference tool covering a wide variety of journal sources, books, and book chapters. As Stanley Brodsky notes in the foreword, since the early 1970s much has changed in attitude toward and treatment of the mentally ill, incarcerated criminal. The articles within each of the chapters reflect this transition. Both authors are psychologists, Whitlock in private practice and Lubin as a university professor, each with prior experience as bio-bibliographers of annotated publications.

Clearly the work would be enhanced by more substantial annotations as well as by increasing the number of entries receiving annotations from the current 43 percent. Ideally the annotated entries should near the 100 percent mark. Nevertheless, because the authors have presented a new compilation in an area that has recently gained considerable mass media attention, and have clearly used the phrase "selectively annotated" in their subtitle, it would appear that the work is very useful and represents a solid beginning. The subject presented is one that will grow in interest both within academia and in the wider general public. This bibliography will serve both audiences well as a starting point, and is an appropriate title for the variety of subject areas from which the materials have been drawn. General collections would also want to have the book as greater societal focus is drawn toward prisons and the nature of services provided to their inhabitants. [R: Choice, Sept 99, p. 124]—**Graham R. Walden**

Biography

682. **Portraits of Pioneers in Psychology, Volume 3.** Gregory A. Kimble and Michael Wertheimer, eds. Washington, D.C., American Psychological Association, 1998. 363p. index. $79.95pa. ISBN 1-55798-479-4.

The preface of *Portraits of Pioneers in Psychology* states that the set presents "informal portraits of some of the giants in the history of psychology." The editors' purpose for this book is to provide collateral source material for undergraduate and graduate courses in the history of psychology. There are 20 portraits in the book ranging in length from 16 to 24 pages. Following the preface, the editors include a section containing brief sketches of the authors and editors.

The subjects of the biographies run the gamut from those whose names are instantly recognized by almost anyone, such as Alfred Binet and B. F. Skinner, to others to whom this reviewer was introduced for the first time in this volume. Because a different author or authors write each review, the writing varies from chapter to chapter, as does the organization of each chapter. Each chapter contains information about the personal life of the psychologist, his or her professional life, and a description of the contributions he or she made to the field of psychology. Some of the biographers did not know their subject personally because they died in the late nineteenth or early twentieth century. Others were coworkers, students, or relatives of the subjects. Myrtle McGraw's chapter contains her life story in her own words, a window into the thought processes of an important influence in modern psychology.

This reference book provides the information the editors intended it to: supplementary information on seminal figures in the history of psychology. Although the entire set would be more useful in a reference collection, volume 3 can stand alone if necessary. It will be useful for student researchers or anyone interested in the history of psychology. [R: Choice, Sept 98, p. 224]—**Nancy P. Reed**

Dictionaries and Encyclopedias

683. **Baker Encyclopedia of Psychology and Counseling.** 2d ed. David G. Benner and Peter C. Hill, eds. Grand Rapids, Mich., Baker Book House, 1999. 1276p. (Baker Reference Library). $59.99. ISBN 0-8010-2100-6.

This is the 2d edition of a work born out of an awareness of the need for a comprehensive treatment of psychology from a Christian point of view. Not only do articles present psychology in its own terms, but many also contain a biblical or theological perspective. This new edition gives more attention to pastoral care and counseling than the 1st edition, and includes a large number of new articles that explore issues of particular interest to clergy, Christian counselors, and mental health practitioners.

Included in this edition are articles covering psychological fields of specialization and professional organizations; people who have contributed to the field of psychology; systems and theories; human development; learning, cognition, and intelligence; sexuality, marriage, and family; social behavior; personality; psychopathology; and pastoral psychology and counseling. The signed articles are arranged alphabetically and most conclude with reference or reading lists. Article contributors include academicians and practitioners who specialize in psychology, psychiatry, social work, and pastoral care. Each was chosen for his or her involvement in the current discussion of the relationship between psychology and Christianity. Aids for use of the book include guide words at the top of each page, headings for articles and subdivisions of articles in bold typeface, and a category index. [R: Choice, Nov 99, p. 506]—**Dana McDougald**

684. **Encyclopedia of Creativity.** Mark A. Runco and Steven R. Pritzker, eds. San Diego, Calif., Academic Press, 1999. 2v. illus. index. $250.00/set. ISBN 0-12-227075-4.

Runco and coeditor Pritzker have created a massive, 2-volume encyclopedia that attempts to survey and to a degree, define, this most important yet intangible psychological construct. Given the imprecise nature of the subject matter, they succeed to a remarkable degree in bringing forth a valuable reference work that will serve both general and scholarly audiences.

Of course, no survey of a field will meet everyone's needs. Scholars of particular fields will no doubt find greater depth in individual resources within their respective disciplines. Yet *Encyclopedia of Creativity* is a remarkable survey distinguished by both the quality of the essays and the sheer breadth of its approach to its subject. The nearly 200 articles included are written by authors from around the world. Although a majority of the writers are U.S. experts in their respective fields (e.g., acting, motivation, problem solving), authors from 15 other nations such as India, Sweden, Israel, Slovenia, and Hungary are also represented.

All articles share several standard features: an outline, a glossary, cross-references, and a bibliography. An outline gives a quick overview of the article's scope and contents. The glossary lists and defines terms as utilized in the article. Cross-references call attention to other subjects examined in greater detail elsewhere in the encyclopedia, and the bibliography directs readers to resources for further inquiry on the subject. Authors note how the construct of creativity is understood in their respective fields or areas of study, but also note how their disciplines, or concept-specific notions of the subject, relate to more universal understandings.

Articles cross many disciplines and represent a broad survey of human interests, knowledge, and pursuits. Articles represent specific domain fields of study, such as art, music, dance, design, architecture, and political science. Another classification of articles examines interrelationships between creativity and other diverse phenomena such as humor, morality, and motivation. Still other articles examine creativity related to circumstances, such as genetics, birth order, and cultural differences. Authors explain how these separate phenomena interrelate with creativity. Thought processes such as incubation, attention, flexibility, and memory make up yet another category of investigation, as do specific techniques commonly associated with creativity and creative thinking, such as brainstorming and problem solving. Educational programs and courses that purport to teach creativity are also examined. In addition to the research, theoretical, and discipline-specific articles that comprise most of the encyclopedia, a number of biographies are included of figures whose lives and works exemplify creative productivity. The biographical studies present some of the liveliest reading.

Articles are arranged alphabetically by subject. The complete table of contents appears in both volumes, and name and subject indexes are found in volume 2. Two appendixes are also found in the second volume, both constructed by Runco. The first provides a timeline of notable events in the history of the formal study of creativity and the second describes major tests of creativity. The *Encyclopedia of Creativity* is an estimable contribution to scholarship related to the study of creativity and innovation that both deserves and will serve wide reading audiences.—**Jerry D. Flack**

685. **Encyclopedia of Human Emotions.** David Levinson, James J. Ponzetti Jr., and Peter F. Jorgensen, eds. New York, Macmillan Library Reference/Simon & Schuster Macmillan, 1999. 2v. illus. index. $200.00/set. ISBN 0-02-864767-X.

The *Encyclopedia of Human Emotions* brings together information from psychologists and other experts on the definition, causes, and expression of human emotions. The article on anger, for example, begins with a paragraph-long definition of anger. Then the origin of anger is covered with nine basic types of anger described and listed in a chart. Different theories of anger follow with varying psychological studies described from the 1960s to the 1990s. A photograph showing an argument in Milan, Italy, and a quote from a Faulkner short story further illustrate the emotion. The article ends with a lengthy conclusion, several *see also* references to other articles, and an extensive bibliography. The *Encyclopedia of Human Emotions* covers popular topics such as anxiety disorders, the psychology of color, gender and emotion, emotional intelligence, and flirtation as well as more scholarly topics such as actualization, biochemistry of emotion, and cross-cultural patterns. Famous experts in the field, both past and present, are also included.

Unique in its coverage of a subject that is hard to get a handle on, the *Encyclopedia of Human Emotions* is highly recommended for high school students. Students doing research in psychology, sociology, and even literature will find it very useful.—**Carol D. Henry**

686. **Key Words in Multicultural Interventions: A Dictionary.** Jeffery Scott Mio and others, eds. Westport, Conn., Greenwood Press, 1999. 306p. index. $89.50. ISBN 0-313-29547-6.

As multiculturalism in our society continues to increase and evolve, so does the volume of terms used within different cultures and in interactions between and among cultures. Almost 300 common terms and concepts used in multicultural counseling and psychotherapy are included in this dictionary, providing not only definitions, but also information about word origins and usage. This resource is intended for anyone interested in multicultural issues and research.

Extensive entries, averaging about a page, include references to significant writings about the term and a list of references for further research. A selected bibliography and an index follow, enhancing future research and present access.

It would have been beneficial for the word "multicultural," by itself, with all its myriad connotations, to be included. Nevertheless, this book is a valuable resource in explaining the increasing number of terms, concepts, and theories associated with multicultural counseling. As such, it will help clarify an important issue in our society and a growing concern in psychotherapy.—**Anita Zutis**

687. **The MIT Encyclopedia of the Cognitive Sciences.** Robert A. Wilson and Frank C. Keil, eds. Cambridge, Mass., MIT Press, 1999. 964p. illus. index. $145.00. ISBN 0-262-23200-6.

The cognitive sciences are a new interdisciplinary effort developed in the past 25 years to allow scholars and scientists in 6 fields of study to share information and collaborate in their studies. This encyclopedia is a landmark work that pulls together in one location reference materials on the six areas of this new discipline relating to the mind and cognition, including philosophy; psychology; neurosciences; computational intelligence; linguistics and language; and culture, cognition, and evolution. *The MIT Encyclopedia of the Cognitive Sciences* contains 471 essays arranged in alphabetic order written by a leading researcher in the field of study represented. Two experts, one from the same field of study, one from one of the other cognitive sciences, and at least one of the general editors, reviewed each essay. Each entry contains *see* and *see also* references to other pertinent entries along with a list of references for further reading. An alphabetic list of articles acts as a table of contents. This list is followed by six introductory essays written by the advisory editors for that discipline, which serve to lead the reader into the area of study and give a perspective on the way it relates to the cognitive sciences. These essays vary in length from 10 to 25 pages. Finally, the encyclopedia contains two indexes—one of names and the other with subjects. In addition, purchase of this reference in either the print or CD-ROM version gives free access to *The MIT Encyclopedia of Cognitive Sciences Online Version*. This is an impressive volume that will be valuable in any collection designed for an adult population. It contains much information invaluable to an individual investigating any of the cognitive sciences. [R: Choice, Dec 99, p. 696]—**Nancy P. Reed**

Directories

688. **APA Membership Register 1999.** Washington, D.C., American Psychological Association, 1999. 1044p. $35.00pa. ISBN 1-55798-577-4. ISSN 0737-1446.

689. **Directory of the American Psychological Association.** 1997 ed. Washington, D.C., American Psychological Association, 1997. 2110p. index. $70.00pa. ISBN 1-55798-423-9.

Considered standard biographical reference tools, the American Psychological Associations' (APA) *Membership Register* should be used in conjunction with the *Directory of the American Psychological Association* in order to derive the maximum information about the practitioners included. The 1999 *Membership Register* as reported for the 1991 edition (see ARBA 93, entry 803; ARBA 80, entry 1460) provides up-to-date enrollment information on the American Psychological Association, totaling 83,617 members as of February 1999. Two sections provide most of the information, that of new and continuing members and the international affiliates, with type of membership; year of joining; and address and telephone numbers comprising the biographical sketch of each entry. Additional sections contain the categories of membership statistics, and a geographical breakdown according to state residence or country. APA divisions also have statistical information listed. A very useful tool at the back is the glossary of abbreviations, which offers guides to acronyms, frequently used terms, and geographical locations.

Complementing this brief sketch is the fairly detailed information found in the *Directory*, following earlier published edition formats, which has been elicited through the membership survey sent to its 82,387 members in 1997. Listing such facts as the highest degree achieved, date of birth, major field, psychological specialty area, licensure as a psychologist, employment information, and membership status, in addition to common personal facts, each entry offers pertinent information for evaluation of the member as a professional to both practitioner and layperson. More importantly, the criteria for membership at each level are explained here, facilitating the comprehension of each category for the layperson. As a reference guide to the organization, this tool also includes the bylaws of the APA, ethical principles of psychologists endorsed by the APA, and the Code of Conduct to be followed by all practicing members. Other useful features are such guides as an explanation of entries, an alphabetic name index, and a division membership roster, all of which can be located using the table of contents. As a primary source of information for this prominent organization, both the *Membership Register* and the *Directory* should be considered necessary purchases for large academic, medical, and research libraries.—**Marianne B. Eimer**

690. **The Complete Mental Health Directory, 2000: A Comprehensive Source Book for Individuals and Professionals.** Lakeville, Conn., Grey House Publishing, 1999. 559p. index. $190.00; $165.00pa. ISBN 0-939300-94-X; 0-939300-85-0pa.

The distinguishing feature of this volume is that it was written to address both the needs of individuals with mental health challenges as well as persons who devote themselves to assisting as a career choice. There are 7 sections, the 1st covers 24 specific categories, such as depression, schizophrenia, and suicide. Each topic is briefly described, with an outline of symptoms followed by associated features; issues related to age, gender, and prevalence; and treatment options. After these observations, associations and agencies, books, video and audio, and Web resources are listed, usually with an abstract. The next category is a 42-page directory of the national and state health associations and organizations. The national entries have abstracts, but most of the state listings do not. Government agencies are considered, again with abstracts at the federal level and very few at the state level.

The section on professional support services, containing a section for books, consumes more than 25 percent of the volume. Oddly, 20 of the 24 categories considered under the specific areas of the 1st section are presented, but bipolar and sleep disorders, tardive dyskinesia, and Tourette's syndrome are not. The omission is peculiar since each subject has been the basis for multiple books. Also considered here are accreditation and quality assurance, conferences and meetings, consulting services, periodicals (an interesting and useful listing but it should not be considered exhaustive), testing and evaluation, training and recruiting, video and audio, and Websites, as well as workbooks and manuals. Considerable effort has been taken to represent both the spectrum of services as well as the differing modes available.

Clinical management is the last major category, consisting of directories and databases, management and software companies, and information services. Some of these items are abstracted. A three-page summary of the major pharmaceutical companies closes the book with name, address, telephone and fax numbers only. Three separate indexes are provided: disability, geographic, and title/entry.

Overall, Grey House Publishing has produced a valuable contribution with this 1st edition. The 4,889 entries would benefit by additional abstracting as well as a greater attempt at inclusiveness in sections such as the periodicals directory and the listing of pharmaceutical companies. These adjustments would help the text approach the "Complete" found in the title. It is recommended for medium- to large-size libraries.—**Graham R. Walden**

691. Simonian, Susan J., and Kenneth J. Tarnowski. **Directory of Internship and Post-Doctoral Fellowships in Clinical Child/Pediatric Psychology, 1999-2000.** 3d ed. Mahwah, N.J., Lawrence Erlbaum, 1999. 129p. $39.95pa. ISBN 0-8058-3595-4.

Focusing on clinical child psychology and pediatric psychology, this directory fills a need in identifying specific training programs devoted to these areas of expertise. Aimed at graduate students, faculty, and clinical supervisors, the programs are "self-defined" by the participating agency, according to the authors. The goal of the authors for this 3d edition was to supplement, but not replace, the American Psychological Association's (APA) *Directory of Internship and Post-Doctoral Programs in Professional Psychology*. Psychologists who are members of Section 1 and Section 5 in the Division of Clinical Psychology of the APA have given their support for this directory, but it has not been officially sanctioned by the APA.

Divided into pre- and postdoctoral internship sections, the format is alphabetically arranged by state, with the last section devoted to Canadian provinces. Each program entry supplies information about the faculty and agency, and details pertinent to the program such as the number of positions available, amount of stipend, application deadlines, type of clinical training provided, and what types of patient contact the candidate will experience. Requirements for applicants are also listed, such as the minimum number of graduate school years necessary for the candidate to have completed. Supervisors, contact personnel, addresses, phone and fax numbers, and in some cases e-mail addresses and Websites have been included in the entry.

Unfortunately, the authors neglected to include a table of contents, providing the only access through an alphabetic index in the back of the book. However, the content of the information provided will be very useful for those libraries serving graduate psychology programs and it can be recommended for purchase by all libraries for this level.—**Marianne B. Eimer**

Handbooks and Yearbooks

692. Boucher, C. Robin. **Students in Discord: Adolescents with Emotional and Behavioral Disorders.** Westport, Conn., Greenwood Press, 1999. 395p. index. (The Greenwood Educators' Reference Collection). $75.00. ISBN 0-313-30799-7.

Students in Discord fills a significant gap in mental health literature, made even more pressing by the recent violence in U.S. high schools. The book covers the psychological problems of students, with emphasis on the teenage years. Personality disorders in student behavior, eating, mood, anxiety, communication, learning, and other disorders are covered with sensitivity to adolescent development. Disorders are arranged into chapters where each is defined clearly, giving a research summary and history of the disorder, precursors of the disorder in the younger years, criteria used to identify a student with the disorder, and suggested educational strategies. The author also includes information on how these disorders may overlap. Actual student histories are often used to illustrate the diagnosis. For each disorder, the federal definitional guidelines are given.

Students in Discord would be a priority purchase for all schools whose social workers, counselors, special education, and classroom teachers would certainly find it useful. Public libraries would also find this book appropriate in their psychology sections both as a supplement to the DSM-IV and as a resource for parents.—**Carol D. Henry**

693. **Handbook of Work and Organizational Psychology.** 2d ed. Pieter J. D. Drenth, Henk Thierry, and Charles J. de Wolff, eds. Bristol, Pa., Psychology Press/Taylor & Francis, 1998. 4v. index. $200.00/set. ISBN 0-86377-528-4.

In 1984, the *Handbook of Industrial and Organizational Psychology*, edited by the present editorial team and their former colleague Paul Willems, appeared as the first comprehensive European handbook in this field. Since then, the rapid development of the discipline led the editors to produce a revision. The result is not just an updated book, but a completely rewritten one, including a title change and an expansion from two to four volumes.

The introductory volume, *Introduction to Work and Organizational Psychology*, deals with the definition, history, research methods, and the role of the work and organizational psychologist. Volume 2, *Work and Psychology*, concentrates on the issues of the direct relationship of the worker to the organization, or the "human factors." *Personnel Psychology*, the 3d volume of the handbook, examines the differences of individuals and the consequences for the organization. The last volume, *Organizational Psychology*, concerns itself with how organizational and environmental characteristics affect the behavior of individuals and groups, and how those characteristics are in turn influenced by behavioral features.

All 4 volumes are arranged in standard chapters, each chapter beginning with an introduction and concluding with a list of references. Tables and figures are interspersed throughout the text. Each volume ends with an author and subject index. There is no cumulative index for the entire set, presumably because each volume works equally well as a stand-alone title and can, in fact, be purchased separately. With the multitude of new studies and research, the changes in organizational psychology have been extensive enough that this new work will be a much-needed addition to any academic or large public reference collection.
—**Rachael Green**

OCCULTISM

694. Guiley, Rosemary Ellen. **The Encyclopedia of Witches and Witchcraft.** 2d ed. New York, Checkmark Books/Facts on File, 1999. 417p. illus. index. $50.00; $24.95pa. ISBN 0-8160-3849-X.

Guiley knows her witches. In the book's acknowledgements she thanks a "Who's Who" list of today's major leaders of Neo-Paganism (of which Witchcraft, or Wicca, is a denomination). Guiley is the author of more than 20 books, most dealing with aspects of Eastern and Western metaphysics. Her books are shining examples of professionalism in fields plagued by books that are poorly researched and written.

The book focuses on the magic and witchcraft in Western culture, covering classical to modern witchcraft. Classical witchcraft is a term often applied to the medieval conception of witches who worshipped Satan and performed vile deeds. The encyclopedia applies modern research to the concepts and cases of medieval witchcraft. Modern Neo-Pagan Wicca is a nature religion centering on the worship of a mother Goddess, her consort God, and the practice of self-empowering and transformative white magic. Another category of articles are on folk magic and include topics such as village wise women and Pennsylvania Dutch hex witches. Guiley also covers related religions such as Santeria and Vodoun (or Voodoo), which are usually treated by the media as inaccurately as it treats witchcraft.

The articles are arranged in alphabetic order. There are many *see also* references, although many more could be added. Most of the articles include a further reading list, and the book has an extensive bibliography. The index looks rather sparse, but is adequate to an encyclopedia that is already organized alphabetically.

The 2d edition adds new articles and updates many of those from the original 1989 edition (see ARBA 90, entry 755). New articles primarily deal with the modern religions and their developments since the earlier edition, although Guiley also reviewed new publications on classical witchcraft. Any encyclopedia deals with the problem of being out-of-date as soon as it is in print. For example, the wonderful Doreen Valiente, author of some of the most widely cherished Wiccan rituals, died in 1999 after the book went to press. Guiley might also want to consider if she publishes another edition adding an article about the dynamic Neo-Pagan Internet presence in newsgroups, mailing lists, and Web pages. *The Encyclopedia of Witches and Witchcraft* is highly recommended. It is a comprehensive source of accurate information concerning topics too often misunderstood. [R: LJ, 1 Oct 99, p. 80]—**Mary A. Axford**

695. Lewis, James R. **Witchcraft Today: An Encyclopedia of Wiccan and Neopagan Traditions.** Santa Barbara, Calif., ABC-CLIO, 1999. 377p. illus. index. $75.00. ISBN 1-57607-134-0.

As one of the oldest and fastest-growing religions in the world, Wiccan and Neopagan traditions are of interest to many people. *Witchcraft Today* is a reference work written in encyclopedic format that attempts to define the traditions, rituals, and people associated with this often-misunderstood form of religion.

The book begins with a lengthy introduction that describes the many forms of witchcraft and the thinking behind them. It describes in depth the way the Wiccan religion of centuries past influences the practice today and abolishes the myths associated with Wiccan and Neopagan traditions. It also describes the many forms of the religion—similar to the concept of different denominations in the Christian church—such as Druid groups, Norse Paganism, and the Women's Spirituality Movement. The next section of the book is the encyclopedia. The entries are generally two to three paragraphs in length, with the more significant terms sometimes being several pages. Each entry is given a list of *see also* references to consult and book or periodical articles to consult for further reading. The entries are well written and thorough enough for readers to grasp the general idea even about the most difficult concepts. A 25-page list of resources is located near the end of the book as well as an appendix that chronologically takes the reader through the history of the religion. A second appendix is a reproduction of two common documents used in Wiccan ceremonies.

This book is a well researched tool that will be helpful to anyone researching Wiccan or Neopagan traditions. Its definitions are extremely thorough and the information on the religion's history will be useful to both students and laypersons alike.—**Shannon M. Graff**

PARAPSYCHOLOGY

696. Abraham, Lyndy. **A Dictionary of Alchemical Imagery.** New York, Cambridge University Press, 1998. 249p. illus. index. $80.00. ISBN 0-521-63185-8.

Presenting a wealth of information for the specialist as well as the general reader, this compact volume provides curiosity after curiosity, drawing as it does upon the rich traditions of alchemical symbolism that date from the early centuries through the twentieth century. Arranged alphabetically, each entry includes a definition of the symbol, including literal (physical) and figurative (spiritual) meanings; an example of how the symbol has been used in alchemical writing; and a quotation from a literary source when possible. Variations in usage that are contingent on context are indicated.

The focus of the volume is on literary and intellectual works current in the sixteenth and seventeenth centuries, in the Western tradition, and written or translated into English. Fifty black-and-white images enhance the text, and include graphic woodcuts, copperplate engravings, and hand-painted emblems. Clearly, both the compiler and the editor have invested some interest in producing a quality product.

Accessible and well formatted, this work will find an audience with historians of literary culture, philosophy, science, and visual arts, as well as armchair scholars with an interest in alchemy and hermeticism. This book is recommended for large public and academic collections.—**Edmund F. SantaVicca**

697. Clark, Jerome. **The UFO Encyclopedia: The Phenomenon from the Beginning.** 2d ed. Detroit, Omnigraphics, 1998. 2v. illus. index. $140.00/set. ISBN 0-7808-0097-4.

This reference work revises the 3-volume 1st edition published between 1990 and 1996 titled *The UFO Encyclopedia in the 1980s* (1990), *The Emergence of the Phenomenon: UFOs from the Beginning Through 1959* (1992), and *High Strangeness: The UFOs from 1960 Through 1979* (1996). Entries include some popular topics, such as abductions, as well as crashes and retrievals of UFOs. All but 12 of the 273 entries in this 2d edition are written by award-winning author and ufologist, Jerome Clark, who has studied the UFO phenomenon for decades. Clark has published several other books on physical phenomena and sightings. He points out that this work covers the study of the UFO phenomenon, which exists undeniably—as opposed to UFOs, which may or may not exist. The thorough coverage is from ancient times to the present. The major difference from the 1st to the 2d edition seems to be the consolidation of the entries from the 3 volumes arranged by distinct time periods into 2 volumes, with 1 alphabetic listing of 273 entries, and also the inclusion of new material from the 1990s as well as e-mail and Web addresses. There is an impressive, nearly 100-page bibliography of more than 4,000 books, articles, letters government documents, and other sources, as well as a much appreciated list of abbreviations and acronyms of the higher technical and specialized jargon (e.g., CE1, CE2, CE3—"close encounters of the first, second, and third kind," and SETI—"search for extraterrestrial intelligence." There is also a "Webliography" of 27 UFO-related Websites. In addition, there are black-and-white photographs as well as line drawing and diagrams. This revised reference work is highly recommended. [R: Choice, Nov 98, pp. 495-496; BR, Nov/Dec 98, p. 76]

—**Edward Erazo**

15 Recreation and Sports

GENERAL WORKS

698. **Beyond the National Parks: A Recreation Guide to Public Lands in the West.** Mary E. Tisdale and Bibi Booth, eds. Washington, D.C., Smithsonian Institution Press, 1998. 395p. illus. maps. index. $19.95pa. ISBN 1-56098-566-6.

This book provides both a history and a guide to the 264 million acres of land that has been managed by the Bureau of Land Management (BLM) for the past 50 years. This land, which lies in 14 western states and several eastern states, belongs to U.S. citizens and is meant to be enjoyed by the public. Tourism to these beautiful areas generates $1 billion in revenue for the nation each year and provides such necessities as lumber, coal, grazing lands, and oil and gas. This work's goal is to highlight some of the most beautiful and popular of the areas and provide maps and descriptions in order to facilitate their use.

The book begins with an introduction explaining the role of the BLM. It then goes on to describe the many ways in which these public lands benefit U.S. citizens—by providing areas of recreation (e.g., camping, fishing, sports) and by providing a place to observe wildlife in their natural habitat. From there the book is divided up by state, with each trail, river, or canyon described in detail. Every site is given a small map; beautiful photographs; and information on its location, fee of admission, activities to be enjoyed, and anything else specific to the area. There are activity codes for each site indicating whether the area allows camping, fishing, hiking, hunting, horseback riding, wildlife and plant viewing, boating, or other special activities. There is an emphasis throughout the book on respecting the land and leaving it clean and in its natural condition. The book concludes with two appendixes that provide BLM state addresses and telephone numbers as well as contact information for other organizations mentioned in the work, such as the National Geographic Society and the National Audubon Society.

This guidebook is sure to provide readers with new information on exploring U.S. public lands. It will be of most value to public libraries in the western United States, where the majority of the featured sites are located.—**Shannon M. Graff**

699. Crothers, Tim, and John Garrity. **Greatest Athletes of the 20th Century.** Kingston, N.Y., Total/Sports Illustrated; distr., Emeryville, Calif., Publishers Group West, 1999. illus. index. $19.95pa. ISBN 1-892129-18-3.

As the century ends, there has been a flood of books that take stock of what has occurred in the last 100 years. Best and worst lists abound. This book is a "best" list for athletes and is a great deal of fun, but it is difficult to imagine what reference questions it would answer that cannot be answered better by other sources. The authors admirably admit to their prejudices (no race car drivers or jockeys; short shrift to the early years of the century) and note that they are aware that among the highly qualified names that ended up on the cutting-room floor are Mark Spitz, Oscar Robertson, Gordie Howe, Ty Cobb, Jerry Rice, Billie Jean King, and Kareem Abdul-Jabbar. However, they persuasively argue that none of the 25 athletes chosen by the 2 authors and 3 editors and researchers involved in this project could be said to be a bad choice.

The athletes are arranged into three categories. The "Transcendent Three" consists of Babe Ruth, Muhammad Ali, and Michael Jordan. There is no argument there—the impact of each of the three went well beyond the sports world. Next are the "Peerless Performers," which include Wilt Chamberlain, Bill Russell, Wayne Gretzky, Pele, Jack Nicklaus, and five others. The final grouping is "Greatness Visible," which includes Hank Aaron, Willie Mays, Mickey Mantle, Jim Brown, Joe Montana, Martina Navratilova, and seven others. Each athlete is given a breezy, magazine-style write-up, along with sidebars of interest and the individual's statistical record. It is a lovely, lavishly illustrated, well-laid-out book that any public library would welcome, but not in their reference shelves.—**John Maxymuk**

700. Hastings, Penny. **Sports for Her: A Reference Guide for Teenage Girls.** Westport, Conn., Greenwood Press, 1999. 254p. illus. index. $45.00. ISBN 0-313-30551-X.

As this book notes, one in three high school girls are involved in a sport and this number is growing each year. The number of athletics offered to young women is growing as well. The author of this work wrote this book in an attempt to get information about sports and their benefits out to young women. Besides the obvious benefit of promoting good health, sports also provide young women with self-confidence, socialization skills, leadership skills, and time management skills.

The top eight most popular sports among teenage girls are given their own chapters. These include basketball, field hockey, soccer, softball, swimming and diving, tennis, track and field, and volleyball. Another chapter titled "Other Sports to Try" includes less familiar sports, such as badminton and crew, and male-dominated sports, such as football and baseball. Each of these chapters provides practical advice on trying out for the team, equipment used, and most common injuries of the sport, among others. One of the most interesting chapters discusses the special issues that can arise from participating in athletics, such as eating disorders, over-involved parents, and problems with coaches. The book concludes with a list of resources and an index. This book will be a valuable addition to any middle or high school library.—**Shannon M. Graff**

701. Paré, Michael A. Carnagie, Julie L., ed. **Sports Stars, Series 5.** Farmington Hills, Mich., U*X*L/Gale, 1999. 348p. illus. index. $39.00. ISBN 0-7876-3683-5.

The fifth volume in this series continues the format that has been generally praised in reviews appearing in *Book Report*, *School Library Journal*, and *Booklist*. In this volume, 22 athletes have been profiled, and 12 others have had their entries in earlier volumes brought up-to-date (late 1999). The comprehension level is pitched at young people. The biographies, though called "full-length" in the introductory matter, run only 8 to 10 pages of text and pictorial matter; they are written in an undemanding style. While many of the subjects here may be thought of as role models for the young, the author has not left out examples of past indiscretions, such as law-breaking and drug use. Entries include the athlete's address and a list of sources for the essays (most often newspapers and magazines, including *Sports Illustrated*, *USA Today*, *Newsweek*, *People*, *Ebony*, and the occasional book.

The *Sports Stars* series does, in general, most of what it sets out to do. The essays are sometimes too praising. To be sure, athletes who have "overcome physical obstacles or social constraints" are most likely to be chosen for inclusion, along with stars who are merely currently active or at the top of their games. Minor sports, such as those that do not get much press and media attention, are also included: track and field, yachting, swimming (with its teenage heroes), and skiing. Girls and women are given an equal place. Even some of the "bad boys" of sports, such as the media-wary Albert Belle of baseball, are recognized. Except for some minor and rare editing miscues (e.g., Nyland Stadium for Neyland Stadium and Washington State "Huskies" instead of "Cougars"), *Sports Stars, Series 5*, along with its predecessors, deserves consideration for school libraries and young adult areas in public libraries.—**Randall Rafferty**

702. Sparano, Vin T. **Complete Outdoors Encyclopedia.** 4th ed. New York, St. Martin's Press, 1998. 830p. index. $39.95. ISBN 0-312-19190-1.

Now in its 4th edition, the *Complete Outdoors Encyclopedia* continues to be a reliable and up-to-date resource for the outdoor sportsman. The entries illustrate the new technologies and trends in outdoor recreation. This edition includes more than 1,300 illustrations and diagrams, 500 of which are new to this volume. Several new topics of interest are discussed, including kayaking and waterskiing, and more information is provided for sports that have found a wider audience (e.g., fly-fishing).

The book is divided into 11 chapters, which are further divided into more specific topics. The chapters cover topics such as hunting and shooting, game animals and birds, fishing, camping, survival, boating, archery, hunting dogs, and first aid. The author, a writer for *Outdoor Life* and the *Los Angeles Times*, has taken the updated information he has researched for these other publications and added it to this volume in one easy-to-use reference. Especially important are the new facts and procedures involved in first aid and survival. Many of these procedures are illustrated in the text for ease of understanding. The book concludes with a chapter titled "Outdoor Information Sources," which provides addresses and telephone numbers for U.S. Fish and Game Departments, U.S. National Parks and Forests, outdoor recreation organizations, and travel information. The book concludes with a subject index.

The update of this valuable resource will be an important purchase for any public library. Because it has not been updated since 1988, much of the information is new and there are many new outdoor activities included. [R: LJ, July 98, p. 100]—**Shannon M. Graff**

BASEBALL

703. **Bill James Presents ... STATS All-Time Baseball Sourcebook.** Bill James, John Dewan, Neil Munro, and Don Zminda, eds. Skokie, Ill., STATS Publishing, 1998. 2653p. $79.95. ISBN 1-884064-53-1.

Weighing in at more than 8 pounds and some 2,600 pages (all in 1 volume), this companion to the equally large *Bill James Presents STATS All-Time Major League Handbook* (ARBA 99, entry 715) sets a new record for statistical data. Together the two volumes provide more information about baseball than even the most dedicated fan will be able to absorb. The handbook concentrates on individual player statistics; the sourcebook concentrates on season standings and related information, leaders in 14 different categories, teams, post-season data, all-star games, awards, "greats," ballparks, situational statistics, managers, the amateur draft, and umpires. As with the handbook, James and his team create new statistical measures and analyze virtually every possible statistic in the minutest detail. Their analysis of these data takes some of the fun out of the usual arguments about individual performances, such as who was the best manager. The lack of an index makes it especially hard to locate all of the information about an individual but, in the long run, this tome is intended not so much as a ready-reference tool as it is a volume to be studied and absorbed. As the ARBA review of the Bill James handbook commented, "libraries will have to judge for themselves their particular need for this exhaustively researched yet overindulgent work." These two handbooks are too much of a good thing. Together they can best be compared to a doubleheader in which both games last 18 innings. Nobody cares in the end what the results are. Like the players in such an exhausting doubleheader, the bindings of both volumes are not likely to hold up under regular library use.—**Norman D. Stevens**

704. **Bill James Presents ... STATS Minor League Handbook 1999.** 8th ed. Skokie, Ill., STATS Publishing, 1998. 420p. $19.95pa. ISBN 1-884064-57-4.

This is the 8th edition of what has become the standard guide to the year-by-year statistics for the hundreds of players and teams who compete each year in organized minor league baseball. For the true baseball fanatic, this guide is an indispensable source of information about players who are on their way up to, or down from, the major leagues or are only minor league players. Otherwise, this guide is of primary interest to those who follow the fortunes of a particular minor league team or league. Therefore, it can only be recommended for libraries with extensive baseball collections and for public libraries in cities with an active minor league team.

The excellent arrangement of this guide is designed to assist the most likely user who is apt to be interested in the career of a particular player. It begins with an extensive alphabetic listing (with career statistics) of every player who appeared in Double-A or Triple-A baseball in 1998; only players who also appeared in the major leagues are excluded, as they are included in *STATS Major League Handbook* (1998 ed.; STATS Publishing, 1997). From there a variety of other charts and tables are presented covering Class-A and rookie statistics and other individual and team statistics and records of all kinds. The most intriguing set of statistics is one that computes the major league equivalencies that, through a complex formula, suggest what a minor league player might have accomplished had he played in the major leagues in 1998. There is also an appendix that lists all current minor league teams by city with their major league team affiliation. This is a fine complement to the 2d edition of *The Encyclopedia of Minor League Baseball* (see ARBA 98, entry 729) that provides a historical compilation of statistical and other information about minor league baseball.—**Norman D. Stevens**

705. Dickson, Paul. **The New Dickson Baseball Dictionary.** San Diego, Calif., Harcourt Brace Jovanovich, 1999. 579p. illus. $35.00; $20.00pa. ISBN 0-15-100380-7; 0-15-600580-8pa.

Dickson, a baseball fan and author of other books on the national pastime, has revised and updated the 1st edition of his book that was published in 1989 (see ARBA 90, entry 766). Unlike most dictionaries, this volume is entertaining to browse, even if one is not an avid baseball fan because no other sport has introduced so many words and phrases into our everyday language. Like the original edition, this reference work is filled with words and phrases associated with the game of baseball, and is written to satisfy an audience ranging from the little leaguer to the lover of language to the baseball fanatic. The entries, arranged alphabetically, provide definitions, etymology, the citation of a word's first use in print, and, if known, a term's first use outside of baseball. As appropriate, the entries also offer synonyms or signify whether a term is considered archaic or obsolete. As in the 1st edition, this volume provides a section on how to use the book and a bibliography. The new edition expands the number of terms from roughly 5,000 to 7,000, and is improved by the addition of a thesaurus, and a list of abbreviations and symbols commonly used in the game. Also included are hundreds of interesting reproductions of historic photographs and illustrations depicting the personalities and culture of the game.

The lingo of the "grand old game" is constantly changing. In addition to expanding the definitions of words and phrases included in the 1st edition, Dickson added terms that recently became associated with the game, such as "interleague play," "go yard," and the "400-400 club." This reviewer was able to find almost every baseball term imaginable in this absorbing work. However, being a loyal Red Sox fan, I was disappointed that the term "Pesky's pole" was missing. (For the record, Pesky's pole is the short right field foul pole in Boston's Fenway Park, named after Red Sox player Johnny Pesky, who hit more than one "cheap" home run barely 300 feet down the first base line.) Nevertheless, this fun, informative, and authoritative work is highly recommended for every general sports collection. [R: BL, 1 May 99, p. 1636; Choice, Sept 99, p. 114]—**David Selden**

706. Freese, Mel R. **Magic Numbers: Baseball's Best Single-Season Hitters, Decade-by-Decade.** Jefferson, N.C., McFarland, 1998. 310p. index. $35.00pa. ISBN 0-7864-0298-9.

Magic Numbers: Baseball's Best Single-Season Hitters, Decade-by-Decade encapsulates the question of what makes an MVP—strictly numbers or the personality that leads a team to the playoffs, no matter the numbers?

Each chapter covers one decade, from 1901 (the first year of the American League) to 1997 (the year before Mark McGwire and Sammy Sosa began their jaw-dropping home run race). Each chapter is split between American League (AL) and National League (NL), then year-by-year. Mel R. Freese lists players by "Super Season" or "Near Miss," a "Super Season" being at least 30 home runs plus a .330 batting average plus 100 RBIs. A "Near Miss" is any two of these three.

Appendix A recaps "Super Seasons" (players ranked by number of "Super Seasons" achieved and career statistics, AL and NL teams ranked by number of "Super Seasons" achieved, and "Super Seasons" per decade). Appendix B uses the same recaps for "Near Miss" seasons. What these numbers show, besides how rare a "Super Season" (or even a "Near Miss") is, is how baseball has changed, from batting for average (with few home runs) to batting for power. For a couple of decades (the 1920s and 1930s) players hit for average and power, but that is truly rare these days.

Magic Numbers sorely needs a bibliography. Freese presents his numbers with very little historical context or player biography that would add perspective to the data. This book is recommended, but only as part of larger baseball collections.—**R. S. Lehmann**

707. Johnson, Daniel E. **Japanese Baseball: A Statistical Handbook.** Jefferson, N.C., McFarland, 1999. 355p. index. $49.95. ISBN 07864-0678-X.

Japan ranks high among the foreign countries that have adopted American baseball in a big way. Organized Japanese baseball has been played since 1936. However, few Americans really know much about Japanese baseball teams or their superstars. In fact we often joke about the "World Series" of baseball since other countries are not involved. Even the English-language media pays scant attention to baseball in Japan except for occasional mention of an exhibition game or an American player who joins a Japanese team. One reason for a relatively ignorant American public is the language barrier. Most publications giving information about Japanese baseball are in Japanese. This book may help remedy the situation by providing information about Japanese baseball that can be used to compare against teams from other countries. The book is the only English-language publication to do so in a substantive manner.

The statistics and lists are drawn from the Japanese Professional Baseball League, beginning with its formation in 1936. The data include the two-league system that was established in 1950, consisting of the Central and Pacific Leagues. The Japanese National Baseball League that existed only in 1947 is not included. The bulk of the book is devoted to season summaries for the teams as well as for individual players. Statistics include the usual ones, such as batting average, home runs, runs batted in, and other team and individual performances. The remainder of the book provides individual career records, single-season records, miscellaneous records, members of the Japanese Hall of Fame, tours of Japan by foreign teams, a bibliography, and an index.

The initial reaction of "who cares" to this volume is soon lost upon realizing that the Japanese teams have their share of great players and games that equal and sometimes surpass those in other countries. Readers may realize that if it were not for the language and geographic barriers, Japanese players might share the same spot on American teams as players from Costa Rica, the Dominican Republic, and Cuba. The American public deserves exposure to this book in public and school libraries, as do sports and fitness majors and researchers in academic institutions.—**Andrew G. Torok**

708. **Official Major League Baseball Fact Book.** 1999 ed. Ron Smith, ed. St. Louis, Mo., Sporting News Publishing, 1999. 502p. illus. $19.95pa. ISBN 0-89204-606-6.

709. *The Sporting News* **Baseball Guide.** 1999 ed. Craig Carter and Dave Sloan, eds. St. Louis, Mo., Sporting News Publishing, 1999. 615p. index. $15.95pa. ISBN 0-89204-604-X.

The Sporting News Official Major League Baseball Fact Book, which began in 1997 (see ARBA 98, entry 736), and *The Sporting News Baseball Guide*, which began in 1991 (see ARBA 97, entry 648, and ARBA 92, entry 776), have established them as two of the premier annual compilations of information about major league baseball. They are particularly useful because, given the amount of information each contains, they are reasonably priced. That is presumably because all of the ongoing information is maintained in computers and it is relatively simple to incorporate the previous year's statistics and print new editions. That is of particular advantage to libraries that acquire these kinds of tools because avid users will be satisfied with nothing less than the most up-to-date statistics. Citing a library policy of purchasing new editions of handbooks only every two or three years to a disgruntled user may not work in this case.

The older baseball guide is intended primarily as a guide to the current—in this case 1999—baseball season. It concentrates on the current year schedules and rosters in the first quarter of the book. The second quarter of the book is a recap of the previous season that provides comprehensive information on all of the details of that year, including team and individual performances. Next there is a short historical section that is followed by a longer recap of minor league team and player statistics for the previous year. Designed to be primarily a statistical tool, this is perhaps the more useful library purchase.

The newer *Official Major League Baseball Fact Book* takes a more historical approach, although it incorporates some of the same information. It begins with a preview of the present year that includes team rosters and other information. It too contains an extensive review of the previous year but then adds three sections: "Who's Who," "History," and "For the Record." Here one finds detailed information about a wide range of players, a season-by-season review of baseball history, and all of the many all-time records that baseball keeps such meticulous track of. Designed more for the baseball fan, this is perhaps a less essential library purchase.

As an examination of past volumes of ARBA indicates, there is no shortage of statistical baseball guides. There is, naturally, a great deal of repetition in those guides. Most libraries will need only one, and are perhaps best advised to select the one or two that seem to best meet their needs and then to purchase the new editions on a year-by-year basis.—**Norman D. Stevens**

710. Palacios, Oscar A., with others. **The Ballpark Sourcebook: Diamond Programs.** 2d ed. Skokie, Ill., STATS Publishing, 1998. 220p. illus. $24.95pa. ISBN 1-884064-65-5.

Park diagrams follow the history of a particular team—all the team's parks, all the team's permutations (Atlanta Braves to Milwaukee Braves to Boston Braves, for example). But there is no logical order in the table of contents (not alphabetic by team name, for example, or broken down by current American League and National League division alignment).

Diagrams are either gray checked (for grass) or solid (for artificial turf), accompanied by boxes on "Park Factors" and "Park Dimensions" (years dimensions existed, fence heights, altitude, capacity, area of fair territory, size of foul territory) and an often humorous essay on the park's history and quirks. Independent essays also comment on such diverse topics as Roberto Clemente and using pitchers' batting averages to measure whether the expansion has truly diluted pitching talent.

A second section on the minor leagues seems an afterthought. Few teams are covered, and only one has an actual ballpark diagram included. Its theme is a common one—the joyful simplicity of baseball on a budget. Really, this requires a book of its own.

The Ballpark Sourcebook looks as if it were done in a hurry. The many typos and the desktop publishing appearance add to this. But it is also obvious that a great deal of love went into this subject, and with a bit of prettying up (maybe color or sepia photos and using ballpark green instead of gray for the diagrams), future editions could be spectacular. As is, still recommended.—**R. S. Lehmann**

711. *The Sporting News* **Baseball Register.** 1999 ed. Mark Bonavita, Brendan Roberts, and John Duxbury, eds. St. Louis, Mo., Sporting News Publishing, 1999. 662p. $15.95pa. ISBN 0-89204-605-8.

The 1999 edition of *The Sporting News Baseball Register* belongs in any library if only because 1998 was such a remarkable baseball year: Mark McGwire's and Sammy Sosa's chase of Roger Maris' homerun record; David Wells' perfect gam and the New York Yankees run at the season record for team wins; rookie Kerry Wood's tie for the record of strikeouts in a 9-inning game (20); and the owner of that record, Roger Clemens, with a pitching triple crown (e.g., ERAs, strikeouts, victories), wins a record fifth Cy Young Award. One page explains the footnotes and abbreviations used with the statistical entries. Entries are in alphabetic order by last name, both 1998 minor and major league players. A separate section contains the career playing statistics of all 1999 major league managers. Entries give full names, with pronunciation guides for unusual or difficult names in most cases. A short introduction to explain how the statistics were gathered would have been helpful. At the end of the volume are a list of the 1998 statistical leaders and a list of the career statistics for this year's Hall of Fame inductees. This work is recommended for historical value alone.—**R. S. Lehmann**

712. **Total Baseball: The Official Encyclopedia of Major League Baseball.** 6th ed. John Thorn and others, eds. New York, Total Sports; distr., Emeryville, Calif., Publishers Group West, 1999. 2538p. $59.95. ISBN 1-892129-03-5.

The publication of the *Macmillan Baseball Encyclopedia* in 1969 was a landmark event for baseball fans, particularly those of a statistical bent. Gathered for the first time in print was the cumulated statistical record of every professional who ever played the game. Subsequent editions updated the figures every few years, but the next publishing landmark was the 1st edition of *Total Baseball* in 1989. *Total Baseball* expanded the concept of a baseball encyclopedia in 2 ways. The statistics were expanded with the addition of many new complicated measures created from the traditional "counting" statistics compiled by Macmillan. Furthermore, the work was enlarged to include a greater preponderance of prose materials, essays on history, the players, and the game on and off the field. In 1995, Major League Baseball recognized the added value of *Total Baseball* and named it the game's official encyclopedia.

This 6th edition continues successfully in that vein. In the text section, established articles remain—team histories, baseball families, streaks and feats, awards and honors, black baseball, baseball in Japan, and so forth. These are supplemented by a new chronology of baseball records; essays on baseball in Korea, Taiwan, and Australia; and an analysis of home run records. The book jacket also touts the expansion of player biographies from 100 to 400, but this feature is merely an updated reinstatement of the 400 biographies originally published in the 1st edition.

The bulk of the work remains the pitcher and player statistical registers that are as complete, clearly arranged and accurate as ever. There are also rosters of all managers, coaches, umpires, team owners and officials, lists of all-time and year-by-year leaders, as well as a rundown of post-season play. Last year, statistical maven Bill James and STATS Inc. came out with a wonderful 2-volume set—*STATS All-Time Major League Handbook* and *STATS All-Time Baseball Sourcebook*—(see ARBA 99 entry 715) with even more detailed historical statistics. But *Total Baseball* is as thorough a baseball encyclopedia as any library is likely to need. This volume is highly recommended for all libraries.—**John Maxymuk**

713. Wright, Russell O. **Crossing the Plate: The Upswing in Runs Scored by Major League Teams, 1993 to 1997.** Jefferson, N.C., McFarland, 1998. 194p. index. $24.95pa. ISBN 0-7864-0536-8.

In *Crossing the Plate: The Upswing in Runs Scored by Major League Teams, 1993 to 1997* Wright states his premise on page 33: "Pitchers are blowing away hitters at record levels while hitters are torching pitchers at near-record levels." He uses a mind-numbing number of tables and graphs to prove his point.

The preface states the author's case, while the introduction explains what statistics he used, why, and how. Wright contends modern pitching is not as poor as commonly thought; the biggest change in the game is the all or nothing mentality of hitters (in the 1920s and 1930s hitters hit for average; today they swing for the fences—higher levels of strikeouts are traded for the big run). He also uses this to push for the National League to adapt the designated hitter rule, as the National League lags the American League in runs scored and doubles.

Because his book only goes up to 1997, Wright misses the Sosa/McGwire race and most recent round of expansion. A reader wonders how these events would (and will) affect his numbers. *Crossing the Plate* is more of a companion book for other books on modern hitters, such as *Magic Numbers* (see entry 706), and is recommended as such only.—**R. S. Lehmann**

BASKETBALL

714. Brenner, Morgan G. **College Basketball's National Championships: The Complete Record of Every Tournament Ever Played.** Lanham, Md., Scarecrow, 1999. 1036p. (American Sports History Series, no.13). $98.50. ISBN 0-8108-3474-X.

Every March, literally thousands of college basketball fans jump at the opportunity to attend "March madness," or basketball's national tournaments. The excitement created is unmatched. Brenner's extensive compilation of basketball tournament records held by eight collegiate associations includes men's and women's play in the NCAA and NAIA. Others include lesser-recognized associations and several incorporated into existing national alliances, such as the Association for Intercollegiate Athletics for Women (now part of the NCAA). Nearly 500 tournaments are recorded. Other national tournaments, such as the National Invitation Tournament (NIT), are also covered. The two major sections are the NCAA tournament, for men and women at all three divisions, and a school-by-school list of all the participants. Only records are given, including the name of the coach, but there are no scores or individual game results. Although the information is extensive, the book is disappointing. Without a record of which teams played and when, only numbers remain, and the excitement that is "March madness" is lost. Considering the price and other available sources, not to mention the Internet, book selectors may well want to pass on this volume. [R: Choice, Sept 99, p. 103; RUSQ, Fall 99, pp. 86-87]--**Boyd Childress**

715. *The Sporting News* **Official NBA Guide.** 1999-2000 ed. Mark Broussard and Craig Carter, eds. St. Louis, Mo., Sporting News Publishing, 1999. 712p. illus. index. $15.95pa. ISBN 0-89204-618-X.

716. *The Sporting News* **Official NBA Register.** 1999-2000 ed. Mark Broussard and Brendan Roberts, eds. St. Louis, Mo., Sporting News Publishing, 1999. 462p. illus. $15.95pa. ISBN 0-89204-620-1.

These companion volumes contain practically any type of statistical information an NBA basketball aficionado, sports fan, or casual observer could ever want or expect to gleam from one source. The 1999-2000 edition contains such useful information as complete 1999-2000 roosters for every NBA and ABA team; day-to-day schedules that include all television and radio broadcasts; team histories, records, and statistics; year-by-year team statistical histories (1946-1947 to 1998-1999); career statistics of every player currently on a NBA roster; and a section on the all-time great NBA/ABA coaches and players. Each volume has been meticulously researched and compiled to offer professional basketball fans statistics on any category of interest, from the typical statistic such as "points per game," minutes played, rebounds, and 3-point shots attempted to the minutia such as player personal data, arena size, and team orthopedic surgeon(s). Each volume is fully stocked to satisfy any fan's curiosity or need.

The *Guide* contains a useful one-page index at the end of the volume. Statistics on all-star games, the ABA, coaches, end-of-year team and individual statistics for every NBA team since its inception (1947-1948) can be easily accessed. The *Guide* also has a table of contents, which lists the major categories under which information can be found. The contents are well organized and easy to access and use. Each entry contains a wealth of information, including complete team schedules, rosters, game-by-game score, highlights, and team leaders and records. Other sections include award winners from the 1998-1999 season, team histories since their inception into the NBA, records for the regular season and playoffs, and all-star games. The *Guide* has a current rules manual as enforced by the NBA officials and a detailed diagram of the basketball court.

The *Register* is the companion volume to the *Guide*. There are several sections in this volume broken down as follows: veteran players, including veteran NBA players who appeared in at least one game during the 1998-1999 season; individual career highs; statistics on the regular- and post-season games; promising newcomers; rookies, international players, or those rising up from other professional basketball associations; head coaches; statistical information on each including their career as a head coach, professional, or college player; and all-time great players. All-time great coaches and non-active coaches who compiled

400 or more wins are listed as well. Each section is alphabetically arranged by individual. One will also find an explanation of footnotes and abbreviations used throughout.

One must taken into consideration that these tomes are cumulated from statistics generated during a strike-shortened season. Therefore, each statistical category deserves an "*" next to the entry (although it does not exist it does deserve mention). Asterisk or not, these volumes are well researched, compiled, and edited. *The Sporting News* is noted for its in-depth coverage of sports and their NBA *Guide* and *Register* are no exception to their publishing standards. This is a must for all sports fans and reference libraries supporting extensive sports collections.—**Daniel C. Barkley**

BODYBUILDING

717. *Ironman*'s **Ultimate Bodybuilding Encyclopedia.** By *Ironman* Magazine and Peter Sisco. Chicago, Contemporary Books, 1999. 451p. illus. index. (Ironman Series, Book 1). $19.95pa. ISBN 0-8092-2811-4.

For more than 60 years *Ironman* magazine has been the leading source of information in the newest techniques and advances in bodybuilding. This book combines photographs of the top bodybuilders in the sport along with the best techniques for training they recommend. It is not a traditional encyclopedia in the fact that the information in this book is not listed alphabetically. More accurately, the book is arranged in the form of a handbook, with each chapter addressing a specific area of the sport. The work begins with two sections titled "Bodybuilding Fundamentals and "Bodybuilding Physiology," which discuss how to select a bodybuilding program based on the athlete's body type and desired rate of progress. The next six chapters each focus on training a specific part of the body—shoulders, chest, back, arms, abdominal muscles, and legs. These chapters feature specific training techniques and detailed photographs of the part of the body being discussed. The remaining chapters teach about training for muscle mass or power, the mental aspects of bodybuilding, natural bodybuilding, nutrition, drugs associated with the sport, and common injuries to the sport.

Although *Ironman* magazine and the author call this work an encyclopedia it is written in the format of a handbook. Because there are many terms defined here and specific muscle groups and bodybuilding techniques discussed in detail, it may have some use in the reference section but most libraries will find it will be more widely used in the circulating section where readers can benefit from taking it home or to the gym and copying the well-illustrated techniques.—**Shannon M. Graff**

FOOTBALL

718. Barber, Phil. **Superstars of the NFL.** Kansas City, Mo., Andrews McMeel Publishing, 1998. 160p. illus. index. $19.95pa. ISBN 0-8362-7115-7.

The cover pretty much tells the whole story of this book. A large, poster-like photograph of famous quarterback John Elway and the headline—"featuring the 35 best players in the NFL"—plainly indicate that the book consists of lavishly illustrated profiles of the best (or at least the most celebrated) players in the National Football League.

The profiles are "intimate," that is, they emphasize the "human interest" aspect of the players' careers and personalities. The author has cannily included a good many quotations from fellow players and coaches; these lend color and authenticity to the praises that are constantly sung in each profile. Even so, the tone that Barber maintains will be hard to take if one is not a fan. But then this book is clearly intended for fans who want stirring accounts of their heroes, not some dour reference book. Each profile does include a statistical table of its subject's achievements, but otherwise *Superstars of the NFL* is of little value for consultation purposes. Libraries will not want this book for their reference shelves, but people (especially kids) with a keen interest in football will find it a pleasure to look at and, given some suspension of disbelief, readable as well.—**Samuel Rothstein**

719. **The Official National Football League 1999 Record & Fact Book.** New York, Workman Publishing, 1998. 488p. illus. $15.95pa. ISBN 0-7611-1319-3.

The 488-page *Official National Football League 1999 Record & Fact Book* lives up to its claim to being the "definitive source for NFL information"—complete 1998 statistical information is available for each team, as well as 1999 rosters and draft choices. It is also the premier source that many pro football television commentators rely on. It is the only record book authorized by the NFL that is distributed to news organizations around the world for their coverage of NFL games.

The book opens with a colorful collection of NFL team helmets and logos, followed by a 1999 weekly schedule for each team. Pages 27 to 152 contain 4-page sections on each team with management information, schedules, record holders, coaching history, 1998 team records and team and individual statistics, 1999 roster, and coaching staff. The 1998 season is reviewed in detail from pages 153 to 242, including preseason and regular season standings and results, game summaries, All-Pro teams, attendance records, and team and individual statistics.

Extras include NFL team Internet sites, tie-breaking procedures, an explanation of the NFL passer rating system, a discussion of instant replay, and 1999 draft lists. Perhaps the most interesting part covers less well-known accomplishments, such as the coldest NFL games, longest winning streaks, greatest comebacks, and career statistics for standout performers such as Warren Moon, Cris Carter, and Barry Sanders. Other sections include a chronology of the history of football, past standings as far back as 1920, all-time team-versus-team results, playoff and Super Bowl summaries, and AFC-NFC Pro Bowl results. A brief summary of rules is also included. The *1999 Record & Fact Book* is an indispensable and affordable source for any football fan or professional broadcaster.—**Mark J. Crawford**

720. ***The Sporting News* Pro Football Guide.** 1999 ed. Craig Carter and Dave Sloan, eds. St. Louis, Mo., Sporting News Publishing, 1999. 408p. illus. $15.95pa. ISBN 0-89204-613-9.

721. ***The Sporting News* Pro Football Register.** 1999 ed. Brendan Roberts, ed. St. Louis, Mo., Sporting News Publishing, 1999. 512p. $15.95pa. ISBN 0-89204-614-7.

The National Football League (NFL) is the success story of American professional sports and commands the largest television audiences in the country. There are probably millions of serious NFL fans and these books are made for them. Constituting a pair (although they are usable separately), these volumes can tell readers all that they will want to know with regard to statistics and other data about the NFL teams and their players and coaches.

The *Register* deals with the individuals and the *Guide* deals with the teams. The former offers career statistics and biographical information, including full name and pronunciation. The *Guide* gives team records, current rosters, personnel directories, and schedules. It also offers capsule histories of the team's performance over the years and a recap of the 1998 season, including statistics for every game played.

The Sporting News reference publications have a first-rate reputation for reliability and accuracy. They are also well made physically and reasonably priced. In that tradition of excellence, these latest editions of the *Guide* and the *Register* will command deserved confidence and satisfaction from their audience.
—**Samuel Rothstein**

722. **STATS Pro Football Handbook 1999.** Skokie, Ill., STATS Publishing, 1999. 522p. $19.95pa. ISBN 1-884064-63-9.

Already in its fifth year of publication, this is an impressive statistical resource for professional football. After a brief rundown of the final 1998 conference standings and playoff results, the major section of the book provides an alphabetic list of every player who participated in the 1998 National Football League (NFL) season. Each entry gives the player's vital statistics, position played, college draft placement, and a summary of statistics for each year played in the NFL. Many of the offensive and defensive players and all regular kickers and punters are then statistically profiled for their play in the 1998 season in a separate section.

This analysis provides a breakdown in a variety of categories, allowing the user to gauge and compare individual performances and effectiveness in different situations, such as play on grass versus turf, home and away, in different formations, and by down played. An analysis of each team's offensive line play and a variety of leader board compilations complete the book.

It is hard to imagine a statistic on active players not covered by the compilers. The detailed situational analyses will be of particular interest to anyone with more than a passing interest in the game. This easy-to-use annual is a statistical treasure trove for fans and analysts alike.—**Barbara E. Kemp**

GOLF

723. Tait, Alistair. **Golf: The Legends of the Game.** Willowdale, Ont., Firefly Books, 1999. 352p. illus. $35.00. ISBN 1-55209-435-9.

This is an impressive book with beautiful illustrations. The information it contains is equally extraordinary. The 275 professional golfers profiled within are the best to have ever played the game. Alistair Tait, a golf writer since 1987, has chosen men and women from all parts of the world and all eras in the history of golf. He profiles some of the most famous golf holes in the world, such as the celebrated "Amen Corner" at Augusta National. Tait also describes some of the most famous events in golfing history. One vignette entitled "Palmer Saves the British Open" (pp. 160-61) makes fascinating reading.

The golfers examined range from Tommy Aaron to Fuzzy Zoeller with many interesting mini-biographies along the way. The earliest golfing legend profiled is Allan Robertson of St. Andrews, Scotland, who died in 1859, the year before the first British Open. According to Tait, "Allan Robertson is generally regarded as the first true professional. It is said that his death ... was the impetus behind the creation of the British Open" (p. 263). Each essay includes the golfer's vital statistics, career highlights, and a short resume describing how this individual earned a place as one of the "legends" of golf.

The final pages contain the results of all the major championships and Ryder Cup results from their beginnings. This is a fascinating book for anyone who loves golf, or wants to learn about golfers.

—**Nancy P. Reed**

HOCKEY

724. *The Sporting News* **Hockey Guide.** 1999-2000 ed. Craig Carter, ed. St. Louis, Mo., Sporting News Publishing, 1999. 397p. $15.95pa. ISBN 0-89204-617-1.

725. *The Sporting News* **Hockey Register.** 1999-2000 ed. Brendan Roberts and Larry Wigge, eds. St. Louis, Mo., Sporting News Publishing, 1999. 469p. $15.95pa. ISBN 0-89204-616-3.

The Sporting News guides and registers have long been familiar to and highly esteemed by devoted fans of U.S. professional sports. Such fans hunger for data and *The Sporting News* annuals, in a variety of sports, provide them with a full array of statistics and related factual information on players and coaches (i.e., the registers) and teams (i.e., the guides).

In the present volumes, the *Hockey Register* and the *Hockey Guide* follow the standard model. The IHockey Register provides a full complement of statistics on every player in the National Hockey League along with biographical notes and career highlights. As an extra, it also offers a list of draft choices and information on European players. For its part, the *Hockey Guide* provides complete team rosters, schedules, histories, and personnel directories of management staff. The guide also includes all-time NHL records, a list of award-winners, and even statistics for minor-league and college teams. All of this information is presented in an attractive format, at a good price, and is up-to-date.—**Samuel Rothstein**

726. **Total Hockey: The Official Encyclopedia of the National Hockey League.** Dan Diamond and others, eds. Kansas City, Mo., Andrews McMeel Publishing, 1998. 1878p. $49.95. ISBN 0-8362-7114-9.

Compiled by the publishers of *Total Baseball* (see entry 712) and *Total Football* (see ARBA 98, entry 747), *Total Hockey* follows the successful formula of combining essays on various aspects of hockey with statistics and records that provide an "unprecedented look at the history of the game." The information is broken down into 6 sections: Origins, National Hockey League, Other North American Leagues and Teams, International Games, Other Facets About the Game, and Statistical Biographical Register. Information about the contributors is also included. Photographs are limited to the start of each section and there is no index.

This all-encompassing resource establishes a new standard for sport encyclopedias. The essays highlight or focus on a wide range of topics related to hockey on and off the ice and all around the world. Besides the essays on all areas of the National Hockey League, there is good coverage of international hockey, unique inclusion of African American history, and Web and Internet information. The coverage on women is fairly good, but as excellent as many of the essays are, there are bits and pieces of information that are missing. In the biographical section, it is not clear what the difference is between the biographies in the North American section and those who overlap in Canada and the U.S. section of "International." An explanation would have helped. It also would have helped to have a table reference list to quickly identify various records that are otherwise hidden. However, this is truly a worthwhile resource to purchase for all libraries and for those who love the game.—**Mila C. Su**

OLYMPICS

727. Mallon, Bill. **The 1904 Olympic Games: Results for All Competitors in All Events, with Commentary.** Jefferson, N.C., McFarland, 1999. 271p. index. (Results of the Early Modern Olympics, no.3). $39.50. ISBN 0-7864-0550-3.

728. Mallon, Bill. **The 1906 Olympic Games: Results for All Competitors in All Events, with Commentary.** Jefferson, N.C., McFarland, 1999. 232p. index. (Results of the Early Modern Olympics, no.4). $39.50. ISBN 0-7864-0551-1.

Mallon has undertaken the task of providing an extensive and comprehensive look into the history and background of each Olympic Game. This series currently focuses on the early Modern Olympic Games, and the author has compiled the information from primary and secondary sources to provide the complete record of what happened at the 1904 and 1906 Olympic Games. One of the problems with the early history of the modern Olympics is lack of consistency in the documentation and the contradictions in the information available. What Mallon does in each volume is collect and organize information from original and official documentation, and then pieces together an accurate description of what happened at the Games and the events behind the scene. The format includes an introduction, list of abbreviations, and references and related sources. The author incorporates analysis, summaries, and background of the Games as well as exploring the uniqueness, conflict, and issues with each Olympic Game. In the section on background, facts include the dates, sites, official opening, number of countries competing, and number of athletes, as well as descriptions of numbers of sports and events at the Games. The bibliography and footnotes are extensive. The statistics and results, by sport, include commentary and analysis.

The importance of these two volumes is quickly appreciated for uncovering so much of the murkiness of the early Games. For example, the Intercalated Games or the Intermediate Games of 1906 have been played down by the International Olympic Committee, which was not formed until 1908, and many of the presidencies set at these games have not been acknowledged. The closest title of comparable coverage is Findling's *Historical Dictionary of the Modern Olympic Movement* (see ARBA 97, entry 661). These volumes are highly recommended for Olympic collections of any kind.—**Mila C. Su**

RUNNING

729. Sampson, Ellen E. **The Runner's Sourcebook.** Los Angeles, Calif., Roxbury Park/Lowell House, 1999. 210p. index. $15.95pa. ISBN 1-56565-963-5.

The author of this work states in the introduction that this book is "a hybrid—part how-to and part reference and resource" (p. xii). This work contains up-to-date information for both the novice and experienced runner. Nearly every conceivable facet of the sport is covered, from health and safety concerns to training for competition. The book begins by placing great emphasis on the importance of consulting a doctor before beginning a running program. It then goes on to discuss selecting the right athletic wear (e.g., shoes, appropriate weather apparel) based on comfort, not fashion. The author offers a flexible training schedule that encourages new runners to start out slow, set goals, and incorporate cross training into their workout schedule. The book ends with chapters on how to eat healthy for a running regime, how to include friends and family in the activity, and how to select organized races or runs that are suitable to one's running level and preference.

At the end of the chapter is a list of resources with books or organizations that will further inform the reader on the subject discussed. For example, at the end of the chapter titled "Racing and Running Around" are the address, telephone number, and Website address for the Triathlon Federation USA. The book concludes with an appendix of information on running apparel stores and running publications in the United States. A thorough index follows.

This book contains a lot of information in one easy-to-use resource. The writing is personable and interesting and will have even the most nonathletic reader considering taking up the sport. *The Runner's Sourcebook* will be a valuable addition to any public library.—**Shannon M. Graff**

SOCCER

730. Woog, Dan. **The Ultimate Soccer Encyclopedia.** Los Angeles, Calif., Lowell House, 1999. 144p. illus. maps. $9.95pa. ISBN 0-7373-0399-9.

Intended for young readers, this encyclopedia provides interesting tidbits of information about the game of soccer. It is not a comprehensive or in-depth examination of the game, but is more of a fun and entertaining introduction for young fans and players. Alphabetic entries of only a few sentences cover various players such as Mia Hamm, Thomas Dooley and, Tony Meola; rules and regulations; famous teams; and soccer terminology. Black-and-white photographs and educational maps enhance the work. Sidebars provide interesting facts and trivia, such as how Cobi Jones made a guest appearance on *Beverly Hills 90210* in 1994 and how much distance does an average soccer player cover during an average 90-minute game? (7 miles). Woog was the 1990 National Youth Coach of the Year and has written several other books about the sport, including *The Parent's Guide to Soccer* (Roxbury Park, 1999) and *The Ultimate Soccer Almanac* (Lowell House, 1998). This volume is recommended for juvenile reference and circulating collections.

—**Cari Ringelheim**

TAE KWON DO

731. Park, Yeon Hee, Yeon Hawn Park, and Jon Gerrard. **Tae Kwon Do: The Ultimate Reference Guide to the World's Most Popular Martial Art.** updated ed. New York, Facts on File, 1999. 218p. illus. index. $26.95; $14.95pa. ISBN 0-8160-3838-1; 0-8160-3839-2pa.

A literal translation of Tae Kwon Do (TKD) is "the way of punching and kicking." The term was developed in the late 1950s in an attempt to unify Korean martial arts. It was not until 1973, with the formation of the World Tae Kwon Do Federation (WTF), that a single organization was recognized by the

Korean government as an international regulatory body. However, various systems of TKD continue to be practiced worldwide under the auspices of numerous organizations not endorsed by the WTF.

This book then reflects the TKD as endorsed by the WTF. The volume's principal contribution is a graphic depiction of sequential movements, known as forms, that have been officially sanctioned by the WTF. Practitioners of a particular martial arts style are required to execute forms for advancement through various levels of their art. The rest of the book contains little not included in other books about TKD or martial arts of other countries. Warm-up exercises, sparring, breaking, and self-defense are neither unique nor well covered. Of some value are the various sections on Korean martial arts terminology, officially sanctioned WTF associations worldwide, and rules of competition used for the Olympics. A grossly sexist section on etiquette tells readers how to chew their food and attend to their superiors.

Library collections do not usually carry martial arts books because they are likely to be vandalized. Despite the current emphasis on martial arts in the media, this book will not likely enjoy that notoriety. Unless readers need to be informed on the doings of the WTF, they are better off with books that provide better coverage on self-defense and a balanced view of oriental martial arts.—**Andrew G. Torok**

16 Sociology

GENERAL WORKS

732. **Encyclopedia of Genocide.** Israel W. Charny, ed. Santa Barbara, Calif., ABC-CLIO, 1999. 2v. illus. maps. index. $65.00/set. ISBN 0-87436-928-2.

The 2-volume *Encyclopedia of Genocide* is the first reference work to chart the global extent of this horrific subject with objectivity and authority. It presents the work of more than 90 renowned authorities from countries around the world, including Michael Berenbaum and Elie Wiesel. The alphabetic entries comprehensively cover many known genocides: The Nazi Holocaust; The Armenian Genocide; and genocides in Cambodia, Rwanda, East Timor, and the former Yugoslavia. Entries are also included on the deliberate systematic eradication of indigenous peoples such as the Aborigines in Australia and Native Americans in the Americas. The encyclopedia presents a wide variety of scholarly viewpoints along with tables and black-and-white photographs. Sources are thoroughly documented and most entries are followed by lists of references and recommended reading. There are entries on genocide organizations, art, films, literature, museums, and first-person accounts. This is a good beginning resource for scholars, students, and any individual interested in the subject. Additional sources will need to be acquired for more in-depth information on specific topics.—**Cari Ringelheim**

733. **Required Reading: Sociology's Most Influential Books.** Dan Clawson, ed. Amherst, Mass., University of Massachusetts Press, 1998. 221p. $40.00; $14.95pa. ISBN 1-55849-152-X; 1-55849-158-8pa.

This work started out as a special issue of *Contemporary Sociology* (May 1996), which marked the journal's 25th anniversary. In that issue 10 books were selected by the board of 28 editors as the most influential books published in sociology in the past 25 years. This expanded edition now adds seven more books, along with four essays that discuss the process of selection and what required reading might mean. This has generated much conversation in the field, some of it heated. Most of the books were originally reviewed in *Contemporary Sociology* and brief quotes from the original reviews are included. Each book is examined to determine what influence the work had in the field of sociology. The essays, which are written by other sociologists, are well written and thought provoking. This work is not recommended for the reference collection. It needs to be read, thought about, and discussed. It should be a part of the circulating collection. [R: LJ, Aug 98, p. 119]—**Robert L. Turner Jr.**

734. **Violence in America: An Encyclopedia.** Ronald Gottesman and Richard Maxwell Brown, eds. New York, Charles Scribner's Sons/Gale Group, 1999. 3v. illus. index. $375.00/set. ISBN 0-684-80487-5.

This 3-volume encyclopedia examines the history of violence in America from the 1622 Powhatan uprising against Jamestown to the 1999 massacre at Columbine High School. The aspect of violence in America is approached from many different angles—not just the many different acts of violence that plague American society, but the causes and influences behind the acts. Entries for the Ku Klux Klan, serial killers, and riots are included, along with a wide range of legally authorized violence such as war and capitol punishment. The various ways violence is represented in America is included in entries about dance, music, painting, sculpture, and literature as well as comics, movies, and television.

In all, the encyclopedia included almost 600 entries written by leading historians, psychologists, anthropologists, folklorists, sociologists, criminologists, and medical researchers. Sidebars and black-and-white photographs enhance the work. An 8-page chronology of violence is included in the 1st volume and a comprehensive index concludes the last volume. There is also a list of contributors and an appendix of organizations, publications, and Web resources.

The work is intended to help students and general readers research hundreds of issues relating to violence. Obviously, it would be almost impossible for a work of this magnitude to be all-inclusive. It should be intended for use as a beginning step for further research or to answer simple questions. It is recommended for university and college reference collections.—**Cari Ringelheim**

AGING

735. **Older Americans Information Directory, 1999.** 2d ed. Lakeville, Conn., Grey House Publishing, 1999. 956p. index. $190.00; $165.00pa. ISBN 1-891482-37-8; 1-891482-36-Xpa.

The *Older Americans Information Directory*, now available in its 2d edition, is another fine and useful effort by Grey House Publishing, known for their health and business directories. This directory focuses on a growing segment of population, Americans over 50 years old, and their unique social, health, finance, and recreational interests. The introduction acknowledges that this group includes diverse individuals, from parents with school-aged children and adults with established careers or in transition to retirement to seniors with health challenges. As a result, issues such as age discrimination, adaptive devices, estate planning, health information, and travel are all included in the directory. Chapters include lists related to organizations, special awards for older adults, continuing education opportunities, adaptive devices, government programs, major health problems of older adults (especially chronic illnesses), legal resources, libraries and information resources, and senior discounts for travel and leisure. Attention to health support groups and assistive devices in this edition represent an improvement over the 1st edition, which was published by Gale. Three indexes aid the user's access to listings by name, geographic region, and subject. Many listings include e-mail address and URLs for resources as well as contact information and descriptions. Libraries with gerontology collections or with heavy use by this age demographic will want to purchase this reference source. [R: Choice, Sept 99, p. 122]—**Lynne M. Fox**

DISABLED

736. **The Complete Directory for People with Disabilities, 2000: A Comprehensive Source Book for Individuals and Professionals.** 8th ed. Lakeville, Conn., Grey House Publishing, 1999. 928p. index. $190.00; $165.00pa. ISBN 1-891482-23-8; 1-891482-22-Xpa.

The latest edition of this work, with more than 9,000 entries, is nearly twice the size of the 1st edition published almost a decade ago. Information about the following types of resources is provided: periodicals and books, assistant devices, independent living centers, employment and education programs, rehabilitation facilities, state and federal agencies, associations and support groups, camps and travel groups, clothing, conferences and shows, legal information sources, and referral agencies. Information is organized into 27 chapters, with each composed of subchapters. For example, the chapter on assistant devices has 18 subchapters, including communication; dressing aids; kitchen and eating aids; lifts, ramps, and elevators; and wheelchairs. The chapter on computers boasts 13 subchapters, including keyboards and joysticks, screen enhancement, speech synthesizers, software, and word processors. The chapter on periodicals contains chapters focusing on publications for the elderly, hearing impaired, visually impaired, and others. Chapters listing organizations (rehabilitation centers, camps, support groups, and so on) are organized by state.

Entries provide one-paragraph descriptions of the product or service along with contact information. For example, the subchapter on kitchen and eating aids lists 41 devices; the entry for each includes a description and the source (name, address, and telephone numbers, and when available, fax number and e-mail addresses). All sources are in the United States. Three indexes aid in locating information—a disability index, a geographic index, and a title/entry name index.

Although perhaps not as comprehensive in coverage in any given area as other specific reference sources, this directory is very comprehensive in the breadth of topics addressed and should be a valuable resource to people with disabilities, their family members, and professionals.—**Jan Bakker**

737. Joffee, Elga. **A Practical Guide to the ADA and Visual Impairment.** New York, AFB Press, 1999. 159p. $39.95pa. ISBN 0-89128-318-8.

The purpose of this easy-to-read guidebook is to help "people and institutions design and carry out policies that improve the lives of people who are blind or visually impaired and those of their families, as well as the communities in which they live and work" (p. vii). The language of the book is understandable and identifies the different aspects of the law in an easy-to-follow way. There are four sections to the book. Within each section are helpful checklists, which are used as points for discussing the law and as guides for determining compliance with the law. Section 1 provides an overview of the Americans with Disabilities Act of 1990 (ADA), its five titles, and key points within each title. A discussion of visual impairment and accessibility issues, along with a chart that is a quick guide to getting help on the ADA, is included. Section 2 is designed as a customer service guide in accommodating the blind and visually impaired. Included are discussions on employees interacting with impaired customers, providing service in the areas of cash and credit transactions, and food services. Also discussed is the Americans with Disabilities Act Accessibility Guidelines for Buildings and Facilities (ADAAG) regarding environmental issues. Section 3 is on making the ADA work for your business or organization. It involves making accommodations for employees within the workplace; looking at services within the health care system; and providing service to customers within retail establishments, hotels and motels, dining, and food services.

Section 4 is an annotated list of several sources. There is a section on technical assistance, products and services that include contact and Website information, and a list of recommended readings. The text of the ADA; a section of excerpts from the ADAAG; and excerpts from the Accessible and Usable Buildings and Facilities, Revised 1998 ANSI Standards on Signage and Automatic Teller Machines (ICC/ANSI Standards A117.1) are also included. Several checklists used within the text of the chapters are reproduced at the end. They regard communication with blind and visually impaired individuals; accessibility under the ADA relating to communication barrier removal; accessible food services; employers' rights and responsibilities; and accommodating them as patients, customers, and hotel and motel guests. This is a useful book for all types of libraries.—**Jan S. Squire**

FAMILY, MARRIAGE, AND DIVORCE

738. Agyei-Mensah, Samuel, comp. **Fertility Decline in Developing Countries, 1960-1997: An Annotated Bibliography.** Westport, Conn., Greenwood Press, 1999. 140p. index. (Bibliographies and Indexes in Geography, no.3). $65.00. ISBN 0-313-30242-1.

The 1st edition of this subject–specific bibliography will be useful to researchers and students delving into the area of population studies and fertility decline. Covering the years 1960 to 1997, this source is divided into five chapters. Chapter 1 covers the concepts and theories of fertility decline, and chapters 2 through 4 cover fertility decline in the major geographic regions of Latin America, Asia, and Sub-Saharan Africa. Chapter 5 looks at general literature on fertility decline in developing countries and is followed by an author index and a subject index each being based on the 491 entry numbers. The entries in each chapter are arranged alphabetically by the last name of the first author, and each entry includes either a brief sentence or a short paragraph about the particular resource (i.e., book, journal article, conference paper, dissertation). The author is a lecturer at the University of Ghana in the Department of Geography and Resource Development and writes articles on population and the geography of health. There is a massive amount of information on fertility decline in developing countries located in government publications, journal articles, conference papers, and a variety of electronic databases. Researchers who want to avoid information overload will find this bibliography a good place to begin their work. *Fertility Decline in Developing Countries, 1960-1997* is recommended for academic libraries.—**Diane J. Turner**

739. Carangelo, Lori. **The Ultimate Search Book: Worldwide Adoption and Vital Records.** 1998 ed. Bountiful, Utah, Heritage Quest, 1998. 293p. index. $39.95pa. ISBN 1-877677-85-X.

The author of this work is the president of Americans for Open Records (AmFOR), a group working to reverse or modify laws that keep adoption records unobtainable to adopted persons and birth parents. Portions of letters that she receives from people around the world who are searching for lost biological kin are included in each chapter of this book. Adoption-related newspaper accounts are also included. In spite of its obvious agenda, the book is a unique and valuable resource for anyone involved in or anticipating this type of search. Genealogists and others who may be looking for people with little information to go on will also find this volume useful.

Carangelo summarizes state laws and provides names and addresses of adoption search and support groups in each state as well as agency information for foreign countries. Low-cost strategies are outlined for finding each type of missing person, from runaway children to old war buddies. Detailed descriptions of searches, excerpts from searchers' letters, and reproductions of record types prepare the user for what she or he may encounter. This is a necessary purchase for public libraries.—**Glynys R. Thomas**

740. Cooper, Sonja. **Child Care: A Parent's Guide.** 2d ed. New York, Facts on File, 1999. 183p. index. $24.95; $12.95pa. ISBN 0-8160-3858-9; 0-8160-3859-7pa.

There are many different reasons that people need or use child care: economic necessity, socialization for the child, or even stress reduction for the parents. Today there are many options for child care, including an in-home sitter or nanny, family day care homes, nursery schools or child care centers, employer-sponsored child care, child care co-ops, and relatives. However, even the seemingly best child care option can cause anxiety and stress for both parents and child. This book is a thorough aid for parents to use in determining whether or not to use child care, deciding on the type of child care that will work best for their and their child's needs, what to look for in good child care, and how to deal with the guilt that parents inevitably feel when leaving their child in child care.

A self-test early in the book is designed to help parents determine the best child care options for their family. Other aids include sample questions to ask applicants and references, the kinds of emergency information that a child care provider needs, an employment agreement form, a checklist of things to look for in a child care center, and a child care action plan. A final chapter deals with the long-term effects of child care (the author does not give any conclusions or solutions, pointing out that each child is different; she provides both negative and positive aspects).

Appendixes include a list of national associations and publications for parents and other caregivers, a state-by-state resource list including ratios for the number of qualified care providers required by law per the number of children in a specific age group, and a listing of Websites that may help parents find quality child care. An index is included.—**Dana McDougald**

741. **Divorce: The Best Resources to Help You Survive.** 2d ed. Rich Wemhoff, ed. Issaquah, Wash., Resource Pathways, 1998. 315p. index. (Lifecycles Series). $24.95pa. ISBN 1-892148-00-5.

More than 100 books and online resources on the subject of divorce are reviewed in this work. It is divided into 4 sections and includes title, author, publisher, and subject indexes. The 1st section, "Recommended Resources," lists the top 25 percent of titles for 9 subject areas. The 2d section, "Single

Best Resources for Selected Divorce Topics," gives the best title for 14 different topics. The 3d section, "Resources of Interest to Specific Groups," has only 2 groups listed—women and Christians. All the first 3 sections contain a bibliographic citation, brief description, and rating using a 4-star system for each book reviewed. The last section, "Resource Reviews," gives a full-page review plus an evaluation for each work listed in the 3 previous sections. In addition, it lists information about the author, price, and a rating for the work's design and ease of use. Unfortunately, the last section is the only one that is indexed.

Because of the indexing, the arbitrarily chosen subject areas, and the layout of the first 3 sections, finding works within a particular subject area in this book is often difficult. In addition, one wonders why a bibliography that claims to focus on the best resources would even list a work it describes as having "unscrupulous tactics outlined in a thoroughly unattractive picture of divorce." Despite its shortcomings, the volume gives clear, concise descriptions for each work reviewed. It reviews fewer works and is not as well organized as Cynthia David's *Women on the Brink of Divorce*; however, *Divorce* has a broader scope and covers helpful Internet resources. This work is therefore recommended only for large public libraries and other libraries collecting heavily in the area of divorce.—**Laura K. Blessing**

742. **Encyclopedia of Family Life.** Carl L. Bankston III, ed. Englewood Cliffs, N.J., Salem Press, 1999. 5v. illus. maps. index. $380.00/set. ISBN 0-89356-940-2.

Focusing on the United States and Canada, this 5-volume set comprehensively covers a wide range of issues concerned with family life in North America, both in the past and in the present. Arranged to meet the needs of students, general readers, and professionals, this reference tool will be useful for all levels. The 452 essays included are portrayed as discussions of family issues where terms are defined, controversies are explored, and historical trends and events are documented. In addition, articles on laws, court cases, organizations, and people directly involved in the above-mentioned areas are included. Consulting it for a ready-reference question concerning the Aid to Families with Dependent Children Act, this reviewer was pleased to find a detailed history of the law along with current activity concerning it. Essay lengths range from 250 to 4,000 words, the longest of which deals with core subjects. The articles providing in-depth coverage of a topic have subject bibliographies, photographs, charts, and tables as part of the information included. A helpful feature for these core subjects is that of categories entitled "Relevant Issues," which offer additional subject search strategies, and "Significance," which explains how each entry relates to family life. Cross-references to related articles can also be found at the end of the articles.

Each volume begins with an alphabetically arranged subject index of articles included in that particular volume that is identified as the table of contents. Volume 5 contains an alphabetically arranged keyword index to the entire set, with full articles indicated by pagination in bold typeface. Several more helpful appendixes can be found in this volume, such as a listing of support groups, a timeline of historical events, a glossary of terms used, and a timeline of important legislation and court decisions, to name a few. Due to the ease of use and the worthiness of the content for all levels of researcher, this reference set will be valuable for all libraries to acquire. [R: LJ, 1 April 99, p. 85; BL, 15 April 99, p. 1544; Choice, June 99, p. 1764]—**Marianne B. Eimer**

743. Kinnear, Karen L. **Single Parents: A Reference Handbook.** Santa Barbara, Calif., ABC-CLIO, 1999. 263p. index. (Contemporary World Issues). $45.00. ISBN 1-57607-033-6.

This is the 12th book in ABC-CLIO's Contemporary World Issues series. Kinnear is the author of five other titles in this series—on abused women, on Third World women, on childhood sexual abuse, on gangs, and on violent children. The series' purpose is to draw together basic resources for high school and college students and general researchers studying "vital issues in today's society." This volume's purpose is to provide a survey of available literature and other resources on single parents and to point people in the direction of further information on the topic. *Library Journal* gives it a lukewarm review, pointing out that it is relatively easy to find the information included in the library and that the book focuses mainly on the United States. Books like this one are so helpful and handy for busy reference librarians needing to get students pointed quickly to effective research paths that the reviewer is sure that it will find a home in many libraries, particularly those serving undergraduates needing social science references. On topics such as this one, there are almost too many information possibilities and having a book to recommend further reading and Internet sites will be appreciated.

The book begins with a literature review covering roads to single parenthood, men versus women in this role, the challenges of it, the legal system, and sources of research data. A chronology of significant events in the history of single parenthood since 1797 follows. There are a few biographical sketches of persons noted for their work in this area, such as Jane Addams and Daniel Patrick Moynihan. Facts and statistics on single parents, on teen pregnancy, on welfare participation, and on the legal difficulties (e.g., issues surrounding paternity, child support, adoption) are provided. Synopses of Supreme Court decisions and state statutes on custody and adoption are provided. There is a chapter on representative public, private, and governmental agencies working in the area of single parenthood. The 67-page annotated bibliography contains books and articles from the 1980s and 1990s and media and Internet resources for further research.

—**Agnes H. Widder**

GAY AND LESBIAN STUDIES

744. Hunt, Ronald J. **Historical Dictionary of the Gay Liberation Movement: Gay Men and the Quest for Social Justice.** Lanham, Md., Scarecrow, 1999. 239p. (Historical Dictionaries of Religions, Philosophies, and Movements, no.22). $65.00. ISBN 0-8108-3587-8.

The author of this historical overview of the gay liberation movement is a professor of political science at Ohio University where he teaches a course on gay and lesbian politics. His work, which deals with only male homosexuality (a companion volume on lesbianism is promised in the future), is in 5 parts. The 1st is a list of acronyms and the 2d is an 8-page chronology beginning with 1864 and the publication of Ulrich's volumes on same-sex love and ending with 1999 and the 30th anniversary of Stonewall. This chronology is expanded into a narrative format to form the 3d section, a concise, 29-page international history of the gay liberation movement. The body of the work is an alphabetically arranged series of more than 200 articles, with the coverage concentrating on the twentieth century (although there is an entry for Britain's anti-sodomy law passed in 1533). Articles average a page in length. Most deal with landmark legislation and important organizations. Again the coverage is international. There are also entries on large geographical areas (e.g., Latin America, Asia); prominent gay activists like Harvey Milk; important historical figures, such as Walt Whitman and Oscar Wilde; pioneering sexologists like Havelock Ellis; and general topics, such as Stonewall and "Don't Ask, Don't Tell." Coverage on present-day gay topics is scant. For example, there are no entries for organizations like ACTUP, GLADD, or GLSEN. *One*, the homosexual magazine of the 1950s and 1960s, gets an entry, but *The Advocate* does not. Similarly, there is no coverage on current leaders of the gay movement. Some topics, such as same-sex marriages, are covered through the 1990s. The work ends with a valuable 50-page bibliography of books, articles, and other print materials arranged in 14 topical divisions, including psychology, law, and gay culture. There is no index. In spite of some limitations in coverage, this book contains enough valuable historical information, particularly on international topics, to warrant its purchase where material on this subject is needed. [R: LJ, 15 Mar 99, p. 70; Choice, Sept 99, p. 119]—**John T. Gillespie**

PHILANTHROPY

Directories

745. **The Foundation Grants Index 1999: A Cumulative Listing of Foundation Grants Reported in 1997.** 27th ed. Rebecca MacLean and Denise McLeod, eds. New York, Foundation Center, 1998. 2633p. index. $165.00pa. ISBN 0-87954-812-6. ISSN 0090-1601.

These two volumes, both of which have gone through many editions, have been considered authoritative sources for those in the ever-increasing field of grant seeking for many years. Although both provide information on grant support and sources and both make recommendations for grant seekers, each is distinctive in purpose, as is evident from the subtitles. *The Annual Register* is basically a directory of funding sources, whereas *The Foundation Grants Index* is a cumulative listing of foundation grants reported for a specific year.

The latter includes details on some 86,000 grants of $10,000 or more awarded by over a thousand leading foundations. Most of the data are taken from reports submitted by the foundations to the Foundation Center, the publisher of the index. If these reports were not available, however, other annual reports, newsletters, or records from the Internal Revenue Service were used. The *Grants Index* includes four types of foundations: independent, company-sponsored, operating (those that use resources to conduct research or provide a direct service), and community (those that award grants only for a particular region). It should be noted that no government agencies are included. The fairly lengthy introductory section of the index provides material on trends in funding, using many statistical charts to highlight information for groups that received the largest amounts of funding and how much funding different types of programs received. Thus, it is possible to see that in a particular year, museums received a considerably higher amount of funding and higher percentage of total grants than libraries. Also included in this section is information on how to use the index, a list of reference collections around the country operated by the Foundation Center, and a lengthy description of the 28 major subject fields used in the volume. This is particularly important for new users, as it is not always clear in what category a certain type of program might be found.

The main part of the index is divided into 2 sections. The first, comprising nearly 2,000 pages, is a listing of foundations arranged by the main subject fields and then by the state where the foundation is located. For each foundation a list of the grant recipients with amount awarded and dates covered by the grant is given. The second section is a recipient name index with the designated numbers referring to the first section. The remainder of the volume is devoted to various indexes: a subject index (more detailed than the 28 main categories), a type-of-support and geographic index, a recipient category index, and an index to grants awarded by each foundation. The final section of the volume is an alphabetical listing of the foundations with addresses, phone, fax, e-mail, and Web pages where available, and, especially important, the limitations each of the foundations places on its grant giving.

This latter section most resembles the main part of the *Annual Register*, but there are differences. The register covers 3,323 grant support programs, with some foundations, but also includes government agencies and other types of support clearly defined in the introduction. One of the distinctive sections of this volume is the chapter on program planning and proposal writing. With a description and explanation of each part of a grant proposal, even including a sample budget, it should be especially helpful to first-time applicants. Another introductory chapter provides a list of new grant support programs that could be useful to those seeking new sources of support. The main part of the register covers descriptions of funding organizations arranged by 11 broad subject categories with specific subcategories clearly designated on the contents page. In addition to the types of information given for each foundation in the *Grants Index*, the *Annual Register* includes date of founding, areas of interest, types of programs, legal basis, eligibility requirements, geographic restrictions, financial data, application information, and names of the board and officers. The indexes include a detailed subject index, an organization and program index, and geographical and personnel indexes, making it possible to find almost any information on a granting agency, though not on grant recipients.

The numbers of grant support agencies differ in the 2 volumes. This can be explained not only by the fact that the *Annual Register* covers government agencies while the *Grant Index* does not, but also by the fact that the data in the index are based on a sampling taken from its own Foundation Directory. The arrangement and indexes in both volumes make pertinent information readily accessible. Though the print is necessarily small in both, the bold headings and page layout make searching somewhat easier. The hard cover of the register certainly makes for easier handling, but the ease in handling must be weighed against the cost difference. Both of these works fulfill their purposes well and, ideally, both should be available to all grant seekers. Large academic and public libraries will find both volumes indispensable for the many among their clientele who are engaged in seeking funding sources.—**Lucille Whalen**

746. **Giving by Industry: A Reference Guide to the New Corporate Philanthropy.** 1999-2000 ed. Craig Smith, ed. Gaithersville, Md., Aspen, 1999. 439p. index. $149.00pa. ISBN 0-8342-1658-2.

In the introduction, the author points out the four big trends that corporations are facing. First, corporate philanthropy is not keeping pace with inflation and nonphilanthropic support is rising. Second, technology is a key factor. Third, corporate philanthropy is no longer centered at headquarters. And fourth, corporate philanthropy is now global. Many people are asked to do much more with less than in previous years. Also, many corporations are now giving more to nonprofit organizations through their core business units than they are giving through their charitable activities. How does a nonprofit tap this wealth? This work should help. With this book one can find out which causes are linked with which industries. This describes the giving of over 280 companies. There are 20 different industries discussed—1 in each chapter. Each overview chapter looks at the industry and its giving patterns as well as highlighting some successes. Then, each of these chapters is followed by a chapter that spotlights individual companies. The entries for each company include a name, address, telephone number, fax number, e-mail address, and a Website, if the latter two are available. There is some brief information on the corporation and what it does. The guide also discusses the corporate giving and the types of things the company funds. It includes such information as a brief discussion of past types of giving, what support is given to employees to encourage them to volunteer in and give to, and various community organizations and programs it is already aiding. There is an alphabetic list of all the companies and an index by company and type of giving. All nonprofit organizations will want a copy of this as well as libraries that have many nonprofit corporations as users.—**Robert L. Turner Jr.**

747. **The Grantseeker's Handbook of Essential Internet Sites.** 1999-2000 ed. William Reinhard, ed. Gaithersburg, Md., Aspen, 1999. 301p. index. $95.00pa. ISBN 0-8342-1659-0.

The latest edition of this directory lists more than 500 Websites with grant information. Organized into 5 categories (corporations, foundations and associations, government, research, and resources) with 2 indexes (title and "corporate and foundation sites by major category of giving"), the volume provides a title, URL, annotation, and giving categories for each Website. The editor defines giving categories very generally as arts, civic, culture, documents, education, environment, health, humanities, international, publications, religion, science, social sciences, and sources.

In a 10-page introduction, David Lamb (University of Washington), who is well known for his Prospect Research Page http://staff.washington.edu/dlamb/, gives a potted history of the Internet and a brief guide to doing online research. William Reinhard has done yeoman service in pulling together these resources; however, his work sometimes seems hasty. For instance, the entry on the American Historical Association's Website emphasizes the AHA's work with K–12 education, instead of colleges and universities. The editor also mistakenly lists the organization's giving categories as "art" (which presumably should read "arts") and "civic," rather than "education" and "humanities" or "social sciences."

Although highly useful, *The Grantseeker's Handbook* will frustrate many users. Some of the Website annotations in this volume and many of the Websites themselves are minimally instructive; much grant information is simply not yet available on the Web. There are also some annoying typographical (e.g., "sight" instead of "site," p. 11) and grammatical errors in this pricey handbook. And, alas, it will soon become outdated. In the brief interval since the book's publication, some URLs (including those for the AHA's and Lamb's own Websites) have already changed.

Serious grant seekers should not abandon tried-and-true, annually updated print resources, such as *The Foundation Directory* (19th ed.; see ARBA 98, entry 787). In order to maximize grant-seeking efforts, readers must consult both print and online tools.—**John D. Blackwell**

748. **Guide to Grantseeking on the Web.** New York, Foundation Center, 1998. 392p. illus. $19.95pa. ISBN 0-87954-800-2.

Any guide to resources on the Web is by nature destined to almost immediate obsolescence. That said, readers can still use the information contained here, and update that information through more current Web resources.

The work opens with a basic introduction to the Foundation Center and an overview of functions and navigation through the Web, with the overall goal of providing an array of resources of potential use to grant seekers. Each of the nine chapters explores independent foundations, public charities, corporate giving, government resources, free and proprietary databases, online journals, interactive services, a guided tour of the Foundation Center's Website, and other useful sites. For most organization entries, snapshots of Web pages are presented along with the URL and a summary of the activities and resources available. In many cases, the history of the organization is also presented. Information is generally terse and to the point. Four appendixes detail procedures for Internet connectivity, the history of the Internet, a bibliography on grantseeking, and an Internet glossary.

Lack of indexes provides an obstacle to quick access of information, unless the reader already knows in which category to locate an organization. This resource is recommended for its breadth of information.
—**Edmund F. SantaVicca**

Handbooks and Yearbooks

749. **Practical Guide to Planned Giving 2000.** 8th ed. Paul H. Schneiter, ed. Farmington Hills, Mich., Taft Group/Gale, 1999. 997p. index. $130.00pa. ISBN 1-56995-339-2. ISSN 1045-1951.

Well organized and containing a lot of information, this volume will serve as a key handbook for many individuals and organizations involved in planned giving and other aspects of philanthropy. The focus of the work is on how to start and manage a planned giving program, which might include outright gifts, bequests, charitable gift annuities, deferred payment gifts, pooled income funds, charitable remainder trusts, revocable charitable trusts, trust savings accounts, insurance pollicies, charitable lead trusts, life estate gifts, and sales. Issues, definitions, protocols, and assessment of programs are all explored, along with marketing strategies, tips for success, gift planning methods, and examples of special kinds of giving. A separate section treats federal tax aspects of planning and gifts, and the many considerations involved in types of gifts. Sample case studies are included to assist the reader. Teamwork in planning is also explored, outlining the various roles of financial planners, insurance professionals, attorneys, and accountants.

Appendixes include a glossary, sample forms for planned gifts, resources (including Websites) for further reading, marketing tools, regulations, statement of ethics, and sample disclosure statements. A final appendix, which comprises the majority of the volume, is a compilation of Internal Revenue Service forms and instructional pamphlets. A broad subject index supplements the entire text. Recommended for its scope and comprehensiveness, this volume should prove a valuable administrative and teaching tool for appropriate individuals and organizations.—**Edmund F. SantaVicca**

SOCIAL WELFARE AND SOCIAL WORK

750. Barker, Robert L. **The Social Work Dictionary.** 4th ed. Washington DC, NASW Press, 1999. 584p. $34.95pa. ISBN 0-87101-298-7.

As with every profession, there is a need for a dictionary to standardize the terminology used in social work. Social workers face complexity and potential confusion in using professional terminology because of several factors: increasingly close ties to other professions with their own terminology (psychiatry, psychology, education); divisions within social work itself (policy makers, clinical practitioners); and divergent theoretical approaches to social work practice (behaviorist, cognitive, psychosocial). This volume is the standard social work dictionary, which first appeared in 1987, and clarifies much of the confusion concerning appropriate usage of social work.

This 4th edition, which is part of the National Association of Social Workers' special centennial project, adds almost 2,000 new entries to the previous edition, bringing the total to some 8,000 entries. The author's main goal for this volume "is to give the social worker an abbreviated interpretation of the words, concepts, organizations, historical events, and values that are relevant to the profession" (p. xiv). All diagnostic terms are based on the definitions provided by such accepted standard reference texts as the DSM (4th ed.; American Psychiatric Association, 1999) and the 10th edition of the *International Classification of Diseases* (World Health). The definitions cover a diverse number of entry types, including legislation, individuals, organizations, philosophies, trends concerning social work, and the broader subject of social welfare. The author has relied on the input of hundreds of his colleagues worldwide to make this work as inclusive and accurate as possible. A separate section of historical milestones in social work and social welfare follows the dictionary entries. Regrettably, some of the entries are inaccurate (in 1798 the U.S. government established the Marine Hospital Service, not the USPHS), and some major events are ignored (the 1879 creation of the National Board of Health). The book concludes with the NASW Code of Ethics and the addresses of state boards regulating social workers and NASW chapter offices. This volume is an invaluable reference tool, complementing the *Encyclopedia of Social Work* (19th ed.; see ARBA 96, entry 893) as a central resource for all health care, academic, and large public libraries.—**Jonathon Erlen**

751. Dumouchel, J. Robert. **Government Assistance Almanac 1999-2000: The Guide to Federal Domestic Financial and Other Programs.** 13th ed. Detroit, Omnigraphics, 1999. 884p. index. $190.00. ISBN 0-7808-0369-8. ISSN 0883-8690.

The *Government Assistance Almanac* is an annually updated version of the *Catalog of Federal Domestic Assistance* that is both simpler to use and more thoroughly indexed than the latter title. The almanac provides descriptions of almost 1,400 federal programs providing services and financial assistance to individuals. These programs include scholarships, grants, loans, counseling, training programs, insurance coverage, and more. For each program there is a description of the type of assistance provided, its purpose, the eligible applicants and beneficiaries, the amount of activity for the program, the range of awards (if applicable), and an address and telephone number for the supervising agency.

The program descriptions are arranged numerically according to the system used in the *Catalog of Federal Domestic Assistance*. These numbers correspond to the administrative entity and subunit that provide the program. Although this arrangement roughly groups the programs by agency, it also necessitates using the supplementary indexes for identifying programs by more practical features. The master index includes subjects, program titles, popular titles, acronyms, and other proper names, with an average of 10 index entries per program. The agency index provides an alphabetic list of sponsoring agencies, with cross-references to their programs. There is also a detailed and useful introductory section that explains the most effective means of using the almanac to obtain federal assistance. Supplementary sections include a list of program funding levels for recent years as well as a directory of field office contacts broken down by federal agency or department. As the almanac notes, contacting the closest field office is often an important factor in successfully obtaining assistance.

If a library already owns the *Catalog of Federal Domestic Assistance*, then this almanac may be a rather expensive and needless near duplicate. However, for those willing and able to pay for more user-friendly reference works, this almanac's comprehensiveness and ease of use should make it a valuable addition to the reference collection. [R: Choice, Nov 99, p. 502]—**Stephen H. Aby**

752.   **Mercer Guide to Social Security and Medicare 1998.** 26th ed. By J. Robert Treanor, Dale R. Detlefs, and Robert J. Myers. Louisville, Ky., William M. Mercer; distr., Chicago, Independent Publishers Group, 1999. 200p. illus. index. $12.95pa. ISBN 1-880754-99-1.

All Americans should understand their rights and benefits under Social Security and Medicare, particularly as they approach retirement age when these programs typically become the major source of income and health care for the elderly. This excellent guide clearly explains these complex programs, covering how they were developed, what they do, how they are funded, and how to apply. Disability and survivor benefits are included, and supplement security income, plus many rules and regulations. The Medicare section discusses eligibility for parts A and B, what the individual pays, services covered, how the system works, and how to handle complaints. There is information on the new Medicare-Plus-Choice plans, Medicaid, and Medigap insurance, among others.

All material, including financial, is current to 1999. Through the question-and-answer technique, tables, and brief explanations, a great amount of information is available here. Many changes in Social Security and Medicare occur automatically or by legislation each year; this book is published annually to meet this need. This issue contains a short but thoughtful essay on the future of Social Security (pp. 167-171), summarizing the proposals on reform being debated today.—**Harriette M. Cluxton**

SUBSTANCE ABUSE

753.   Chepesiuk, Ron. **The War on Drugs: An International Encyclopedia.** Santa Barbara, Calif., ABC-CLIO, 1999. 317p. illus. index. $75.00. ISBN 0-87436-985-1.

The War on Drugs is a reference work in encyclopedic format describing and defining major drug dealers, cartels, organizations, smuggling and antismuggling strategies, drug epidemics, legal restraints, and famous incidents concerning drugs. The book begins with a 15-page historical overview on the war on drugs, including its effects on government, economics, and society. It then goes on to the A to Z format of the individual entries. Each entry is anywhere from half a column to one full page in length, depending on how relevant and influential the topic at hand is. There are cross-references and *see also* references located within the entries as well as a list of references and several photographs. There is an 11-page chronology of the history of drug warfare that begins with 2737 B.C.E. and the first references to marijuana in Chinese culture to events in 1998 concerning drugs. The book concludes with lists of 90 relevant Websites, an extensive bibliography, and an index. This book will be a valuable addition to high school and academic libraries where research on this topic is common.—**Shannon M. Graff**

754.   O'Brien, Robert, Morris Chafetz, and Sidney Cohen. **The Encyclopedia of Understanding Alcohol and Other Drugs.** New York, Facts on File, 1999. 2v. maps. index. $195.00/set. ISBN 0-8160-3970-4.

Following the same pattern of earlier publications by Facts on File, *The Encyclopedia of Alcoholism* (2d ed.; see ARBA 92, entry 839) and *The Encyclopedia of Drug Abuse* (2d ed.; see ARBA 93, entry 890) have been combined to form a new encyclopedia entitled *Understanding Alcohol and Other Drugs* with updated and expanded information. In fact, the names of the original compilers remain on the title. Volume 1 is a dictionary of approximately 1,300 terms, including specific drugs, classes of drugs, medical and psychosocial terms, countries, and organizations. Definitions range from one sentence to several pages.

The longest definition is marijuana at 8½ pages. Some of the entries have not changed from the earlier works, but most have. The volume is rich in tables, graphs, and maps. Volume 2 includes a glossary, directory, bibliography, and 6 appendixes. Each appendix is a series of short essays on the following broad topics: appendix 1 covers the history of alcohol and drug usage in the United States by looking at laws and major events; appendix 2 covers social aspects of the use of alcohol and drugs; appendix 3 covers health issues; appendix 4 provides in-depth information on drugs such as heroine and marijuana; appendix 5 covers treatments; and appendix 6 provides statistical information. Although not as comprehensive as the *Encyclopedia of Drugs and Alcohol* (see ARBA 97, entry 707), this new encyclopedia is very readable, up-to-date, and reasonable in price. It is highly recommended for all libraries.—**Karen Y. Stabler**

YOUTH AND CHILD DEVELOPMENT

755. **The Encyclopedia of Parenting Theory and Research.** Charles A. Smith, ed. Westport, Conn., Greenwood Press, 1999. 501p. index. $95.00. ISBN 0-313-29699-5.

This 1-volume encyclopedia provides brief, scholarly pieces on parenting theory and current research. Smith has pulled together a collection of essays whose main focus is the investigation and documentation of the multifaceted roles lived by parents. Most suitable for teachers, researchers, librarians, parent educators, and knowledgeable parents, the 244 entries in this reference work touch upon those issues inherent in relationships between parent and child, exploring the dynamics of social, emotional, and biological relationships.

Starting with a classification of nine groups of categories, the introduction lists primary search terms within the following individual headings: child activity, child outcomes, child states, parent behaviors, a parent state or context, external or community factors, system issues, and resources and people. Alphabetic entries with source references follow, and all articles are signed. If the reader has not made use of the introduction's categories, it is possible to consult a list of *see also* notes assigned to a particular topic, which will guide one to related terms. Located after the entries are a bibliography and an alphabetically arranged subject index. The index in particular enhances the usefulness of the reference tool. Contributors are described in the final section, with all participants having such credentials as that of a university professor, a research institute member, or a practitioner in the field of sociology, social work, psychology, or family studies. For those interested in additional resources, the editor maintains a Website devoted to parenting.

This encyclopedia should be considered adequate but costly as a ready-reference tool. For longer entries the researcher might prefer to consult *The Encyclopedia of Family Life* (see entry 742), which offers more in-depth coverage in a 5-volume set. [R: BL, June 99, p. 1878; Choice, Oct 99, p. 312]
—**Marianne B. Eimer**

756. Hobbs, Sandy, Jim McKechnie, and Michael Lavalette. **Child Labor: A World History Companion.** Santa Barbara, Calif., ABC-CLIO, 1999. 292p. illus. index. (ABC-CLIO's World History Companion Series). $65.00. ISBN 0-87436-956-8.

The title of this work almost says it all. The definition used for child is broad, including young children as well as adolescents. Labor involves nearly any work done for pay, from acting and modeling to carpet weaving and caring for others as well as selling newspapers and delivering milk. It includes, of course, the factory and mine work, chimney sweeps, and sweat shops.

During the English Industrial Revolution the debate on child labor became public. For this reason there are few references to events that occurred before the eighteenth century. The coverage of events is focused on Great Britain and the United States, with other countries being addressed in single entries.

There are more than 250 alphabetically arranged entries. There is a contents page, then an "Entries by Category Index," which lists broad topics and some entries that discuss those topics, such as child labor strategies, people who have worked on behalf of working children, and organizations concerned with child workers. The entries range in size from a paragraph to a couple of pages. Brief references are given for each entry. There are black-and-white pictures of children in various occupations included among the entries. Some of the photographs are difficult to look at. Seeing a child that looks barely three carrying a brink that is almost as big as he is, and realizing that he would be doing that for many hours a day, is hard.

There is an appendix that lists Websites dealing with child labor issues, a glossary, and a list of acronyms that did not include some of the acronyms listed in the text, such as the Brazilian FUNABEM. There is also a chronology that starts in 1724 and continues through 1998. There is a bibliography and an index. This will be useful to those wanting to know about child labor and its history as well as current status.

—Robert L. Turner Jr.

757. **Raising Teenagers: The Best Resources To Help Yours Succeed.** John Ganz, ed. Issaquah, Wash., Resource Pathways, 1998. 256p. index. (Parenting Series). $24.95pa. ISBN 1-892148-04-8.

For parents, having been a teenager is not necessarily sufficient preparation for raising one, particularly in contemporary American culture. This guide provides assistance to those parents looking for help. It includes thorough descriptions and evaluations of books, media, and Internet sites dealing with both general approaches to raising teenagers and specific problems that teenagers and their parents might confront.

The book is arranged into six chapters: an introduction, "Understanding Adolescents" (with subsections for boys and girls), "Parent-Teen Relationships," "Critical Issues and Concerns," "General Overview of Raising Teenagers," and "Terrific Resources" for selected topics. Each chapter begins with an introductory overview of that chapter's subject, followed by the resource reviews. The chapter on critical issues has subsections on major social problems facing teenagers, including pregnancy, eating disorders, gangs, depression and suicide, substance abuse, divorce, and death. The chapter on "terrific resources" deals primarily with communicating values to one's children and cultivating parent-child relationships when dealing with difficult issues (e.g., substance abuse, sexuality, eating disorders). Entries for specific resources include bibliographic details, cost, and availability as well as paragraph-long descriptions and evaluations with ratings for overall quality and ease of use. Title, author, subject, media, and publisher indexes provide additional access to the entries. A directory of helpful organizations, broken down by topic, is appended.

Focusing on teenagers seems valid, given their unique social and developmental characteristics and the promise and peril we associate with that stage of life. However, it is also true that raising teenagers is part of a continuum of child rearing, and the way teenagers and their families deal with issues cannot help but be affected by the relationships and communication established during earlier years. Consequently, this guide legitimately could have, and possibly should have, included more works dealing with raising kids from the beginning. This caveat aside, Ganz has provided a thoughtful guide that is highly recommended for public libraries, counselors, and interested parents.—**Stephen H. Aby**

758. Rollin, Lucy. **Twentieth-Century Teen Culture by the Decades: A Reference Guide.** Westport, Conn., Greenwood Press, 1999. 396p. illus. index. $59.95. ISBN 0-313-30223-5.

The time between childhood and adulthood is one of many transitions. The culture of teenagers often breaks with the past and presages the future. In this book, Rollin does an admirable job in providing a glimpse into the lives and times of teenagers during each decade of the twentieth century. Although she admits that such a division of the trends and events of the century is an artificial exercise, her research and use of a variety of sources does place her work on a firm foundation.

Each chapter delves into the major events and trends that defined the decade, both national and international. Thus, each chapter provides an overview of the historical events of the time, especially as they relate to teens. In addition, each chapter includes a discussion of teens' home life, work, school, fashion, and slang. One of the more interesting sections is that on leisure activities and entertainment in which the author discusses topics such as popular movies, music and dancing, dating and sex, books and reading, and radio and television. Differences between urban and rural teens are emphasized, as is the difference between white and minority teens, especially African Americans and Hispanics. A list of references concludes each chapter. The book also includes an appendix that provides a sample of teen-oriented Websites and a comprehensive index. The many illustrations provide additional support for the text.

This reviewer found the work to be an interesting amalgamation of facts and observations. It is not, however, a true reference guide, but rather a historical narrative. Although each chapter provides references to useful material, the result is a highly selective list of sources presented alphabetically. A major weakness is the inclusion of discussions of main sources in the text but no corresponding entry in the references. A few minor errors, such as an incorrect date for Lindbergh's transatlantic flight and a misstatement on where Martin Luther King Jr. was shot were noted, but these do not detract from the overall quality of the work. This book can be strongly recommended for purchase, but more for the general collection rather than the reference collection.—**Gregory A. Crawford**

17 Statistics, Demography, and Urban Studies

DEMOGRAPHY

General Works

759. **A Demographic Perspective on Women in Development in Cambodia, Lao People's Democratic Republic, Myanmar, and Vietnam.** By the Economic and Social Commission for Asia and the Pacific. New York, United Nations, 1998. 135p. (Asian Population Studies Series, no.148). $15.00pa. ISBN 92-1-119842-9. S/N E.98.II.F.53.

This study assesses the status of women in development in four Southeast Asian countries that share borders: Cambodia, the Lao People's Democratic Republic, Myanmar, and Vietnam. The four countries are the least developed countries in Southeast Asia on most indicators, and their economies are in transition to more open, market-oriented economies. In each of the four countries, women have traditionally played an important social role marked by considerable gender equity.

The study reviews the situation in the four countries, highlights similarities, and notes common patterns. It focuses on women in development rather than the broader goals of gender equality, equity, and empowerment for women. Detailed data and analysis are provided for each country. There are five chapters in the book. The comparative assessment in the first chapter compared findings for the four countries on a number of key indicators of women's involvement in development. The first chapter also includes policy implications of the findings. Each of the other four chapters studied the same six aspects in the four countries—demographic context, family formation, health, education, employment, migration, and conclusion.

Based on data available primarily from national population censuses and demographic surveys, the study was prepared by the ESCAP Population Division, and many offices in the concerned countries provide data. The study will be of benefit to national and international agencies and organizations planning social development programs in these countries.—**Vera Gao**

760. Platt, Lyman D. **Census Records for Latin America and the Hispanic United States.** Baltimore, Md., Genealogical Publishing, 1998. 198p. $19.95pa. ISBN 0-8063-1555-5.

Designed for researchers and family historians, this reference identifies 4,000 separate censuses available for Latin America and the Hispanic United States. Organized alphabetically by country (Argentina through Venezuela), entries consist of five columns offering locality name, province, country, year, and reference acronym or number. Listings cover Mexico, Spanish North America, Central America, and South America, with relevant states or areas of the United States appearing separately (e.g., Florida) or as part of Mexico (e.g., California), depending on their historic relationship to Mexico. Most reference numbers are acronyms connoting a specific archive; however, non-acronym number ranges are identified only in the introduction as being part of the Family History Library microfilm collection.

This has the beginnings of a major reference source as there is increasing interest in exploring family roots and in researching Hispanic population patterns and movements. However, in its present state, it is most useful for knowledgeable genealogical researchers. The current introduction's basic use guidelines within the descriptions of census difficulties are unorganized and unhelpful. The instructions should be clearly separated from the more historical points of interest and research methodologies, and undefined acronyms should be avoided. The bibliographic information on census record locations is inadequate, as beginning researchers require more information (e.g., address, telephone) on location and use requirements than the author provides. Users would also benefit from a geographic index, making it easier for researchers to locate areas within Mexico (e.g., Alta California). This volume is recommended for consideration by academic libraries with the appropriate graduate programs. [R: Choice, Nov 98, p. 502]

—**Sandra E. Belanger**

Dictionaries and Encyclopedias

761. Ness, Immanuel, and James Ciment. **The Encyclopedia of Global Population and Demographics.** Armonk, N.Y., Sharpe Reference/M. E. Sharpe, 1999. 2v. index. $185.00/set. ISBN 1-563240710-0.

This two-volume encyclopedia covers, for each country, information on geography, population and its ethnic distribution, vital statistics, economics, health, and education. It is a standard reference for these demographics. The countries are arranged alphabetically with the break between the books being between Italy and Jamaica. Nine essays preface the first volume and the data seem to date from 1995. This reference compares favorably with other sources of its type. In particular, it is of value to students in that the essays increase comprehension on the use of the tabular material. Limitations include the inevitability that the information becomes dated and a failure to provide metropolitan populations for cities; data are limited to only the central cities. [R: LJ, 15 Mar 99, p. 68; BL, Aug 99, p. 2106; Choice, Oct 99, p. 315]—**Arthur R. Upgren**

Directories

762. **Mobility Plus ... A Reference Guide 1999.** Scottsdale, Ariz., Center for Mobility Resources, 1999. 848p. index. $400.00pa. ISBN 0-9643934-0-9.

This is a catalog of cities and communities of the United States and Canada aimed at the prospective mover and homebuyer. For more than 700 cities in every state and Canadian province, an extensive variety of information is given. Included are specifics on the population, climate, employers and unemployment, housing costs, education details, and crime statistics. The book is prefaced by an introduction, with details on how to go about sizing up a community as a new homeowner. The title, *Mobility Plus . . . A Reference Guide 1999*, is appropriate in this regard. There is much of interest in the features of home ownership that apply to any place. This is a handy reference book for this purpose almost exclusively; it has little of interest for the tourist. But for the new settler, tips on mortgages, managing personal records, selling real estate, and renting are all described in detail. Within these limits it can be a helpful reference. By targeting a rather narrow and well-defined group of readers, the book does not replace more general almanacs and city comparisons but augments them.—**Arthur R. Upgren**

Handbooks and Yearbooks

763. **Demographic Yearbook, 1997.** 49th ed. New York, United Nations, 1999. 582p. $100.00. ISBN 92-1-051088-7.

One of the tasks of the United Nations is the making and keeping of records and estimates of the population of the world and all of its member nations. This volume is a 1997 revision in a series of similar volumes in the past, and supersedes them. It summarizes distributions by age and sex for each country, and for selected countries, over each fifth year beginning in 1950 through 1995. Preceded by explanatory information about the tables, the remainder of the book consists of the tabular data. Thus it is by its very nature a reference volume, a compendium of the population distribution by age and sex along with vital statistics of fertility and mortality. Updated as it is, it comprises the best data available and is a must for any reference library needing to be inclusive in demographics.—**Arthur R. Upgren**

764. **Demographics USA 1999: County Edition.** Lynda Gutierrez, Andrea Yurasits, Angela Hurdle, and Michèle Franklin, eds. New York, Market Statistics, 1999. 1v. (various paging). $435.00pa. ISBN 1-891856-09-X.

This comprehensive resource presents demographic, employment, and buying information on the United States by county, and also by metropolitan area and designated market area. The book is primarily aimed at marketing and sales teams who can use the information for setting sales goals and measuring performance, evaluating new product potential, and developing marketing strategies. Each section utilizes a Buying Power Index (BPI) based on disposable income and consumption patterns. There are separate sections for basic demographics, retail sales by store category and merchandise lines, consumer expenditures by category, occupational data, and five-year projections for change within each category. Easy-to-use tables break each section down by state and county. There is a wealth of useful information here for commercial and manufacturing concerns. Companion CD-ROMs are available, at $995 each, that allow the information, arranged by county or zip code, to be downloaded to spreadsheets. An indispensable resource for corporate and academic libraries, but public libraries will get essentially the same information for their area at much lower cost with the county-specific volumes available from Strategic Mapping.—**Susan B. Hagloch**

765. **Demographics USA 1999: ZIP Edition.** Lynda Gutierrez, Andrea Yurasits, Angela Hurdle, and Michèle Franklin, eds. New York, Market Statistics, 1999. 1v. (various paging). $435.00pa. ISBN 1-891856-10-3.

This annual publication of more than 1,500 pages (for a review of the 1994 edition see ARBA 95, entry 889) is filled with a wide range of demographic and economic data broken down by ZIP code—both by basic codes (i.e., the first 3 digits) and by detailed codes (i.e., all 5 digits). It covers population; race/ethnicity; household data, such as income and educational level; retail sales; consumer expenditures; employment; occupations; and establishments. It is designed for use primarily by people involved in marketing and sales, and the editors even point to certain industries that should find this publication of particular use, such as newspapers, retail merchants, consultants, and media planners. However, with all the data contained in this volume, it certainly should have application to an even wider audience. In addition to data, it includes an expansive "Explanation of Terms" and listings of Designated Market Areas and Metropolitan Area Definitions.

Demographics USA: ZIP Edition is also available on CD-ROM, along with its companion publication, *Demographics USA: County Edition* (see entry 764). Although the publisher of this volume has competition—in print, government, and Internet sources (e.g., the Bureau of the Census and for-profit organizations, such as CACI Marketing Systems)—the publication being reviewed presents a particular range of data in one easy-to-use volume that is not readily available elsewhere. That is to say, its value lies in the fact that no other volume or Website has all these data in such a convenient format. With its ready-reference style, it certainly should prove to be of use to business libraries and to major reference collections or simply as a major source of data for researchers.—**Paul H. Thomas**

766. Exter, Thomas G. **Regional Markets: The Demographics of Growth and Decline.** Ithaca, N.Y., New Strategist, 1999. 2v. index. $160.00/set. ISBN 1-885070-13-6.

Exter, a consultant and trained demographer, presents U.S. population and income figures for policy makers, business planners, and marketers hoping "to get a jump on the 2000 census" (p. 3). Although his numbers are unofficial, they are based on Census Bureau sources, and go beyond any official figures that will be available until after the 2000 count. Added value accrues in two ways, compared with current detailed official data. First, Exter looks ahead to 2003, as well as estimating 1998 numbers. Second, his presentation descends to a finer level of geographic detail for the nation's regions, states, 315 Metropolitan Statistical Areas (MSAs), and largest counties.

Population, fertility, mortality, migration, household, and income figures are analyzed by place, age, or race and Hispanic origin. Some 350 unnumbered tables, ranging in length from 1 to 16 pages, are grouped in 9 chapters, such as "Births, Deaths and Migration" and "Household Income." A detailed table of contents lists those tables. Appendixes identify states in each region and counties in each MSA, followed by a basic glossary. An index covers the names of cities and major demographic categories. Given the number, variety, and complexity of elements combined in the tables, the index is often too simple. A device like the "Table Finding Guides" at the beginning of Census publications might have been more effective.

This set resembles *The Sourcebook of ZIP Code Demographics* (see ARBA 99, entry 786) or Nestor E. Terleckyj's *Regional Economic Growth in the United States* (NPA Data Services, 1997) in content and purpose. Like other works of this kind, it has a specific audience, and will diminish in value as the projections become dated or are replaced by official figures from the 2000 Census. [R: LJ, 1 Apr 99, pp. 85-86; Choice, May 99, p. 1599]—**Steven W. Sowards**

STATISTICS

General Works

Dictionaries and Encyclopedias

767. **Cambridge Dictionary of Statistics.** By B. S. Everitt. New York, Cambridge University Press, 1998. 360p. $39.95. ISBN 0-521-59346-8.

This excellent dictionary provides concise definitions of statistical terms for those working in many disciplines who are users of statistics. Although all areas of statistics are covered, any choice of a specific term is dependent on the author. The author acknowledges that there is a difference in mathematical content and level among the definitions, but hopes that such differences will reflect the type of reader likely to turn to a specific definition. Those looking for students' t-tests, for example, will encounter relatively simple formulae, although those seeking information about spline functions will find the more extensive material required.

In content the dictionary contains 3,000 entries and short biographies of more than 100 important statisticians, all of whom are deceased. Ample cross-referencing is provided throughout the volume. The order of the entries may confuse some readers since the arrangement is letter-by-letter rather than word-by-word (e.g., "NOEL," an abbreviation preceding "N of 1 clinical trial").

For those readers who seek more extensive information about a topic than that provided here, the author has provided many entries with either a reference to one of the texts listed in the preliminaries or a more specific reference to a book or journal article. When entries for software are given, the appropriate address is provided.

The dictionary is well conceived and executed. The author has taken pains not only to provide concise and accurate information, but to ensure that users requiring more assistance are not frustrated in their search for information, either within the dictionary itself or beyond. This volume is useful for any reference collection and especially for those that serve higher educational institutions. [R: Choice, Feb 99, p. 1043]
—**Robert H. Burger**

768. Vogt, W. Paul. **Dictionary of Statistics and Methodology: A Nontechnical Guide for the Social Sciences.** 2d ed. Newbury Park, Calif., Sage, 1999. 318p. $75.00; $34.95pa. ISBN 0-7619-1273-8; 0-7619-1274-6pa.

The current version of this dictionary is a revision and expansion of its 1st edition published in 1994. The author has added 600 new definitions and illustrations to the existing 1,400 entries included in its predecessor. However, the author did not indicate how the 2,000 entries were selected for inclusion in this reference tool.

The most distinctive feature of this dictionary is its simplicity. The author attempts to use plain language to explain rather technical and specialized terms and concepts in statistics and methodologies, which is by no means an easy task. Nevertheless, the author has achieved this objective with success. In addition, the author tries to apply cross-references extensively so that the reader can be directed to preferred and related entries. But the author, probably due to his background in education, did not use the right terminology in labeling the different types of cross-references.

The author offers examples in many entries when defining them to facilitate comprehension from the perspective of dictionary users. But the explanation for some of the entries appears too brief to be helpful. For example, the author allocated only two lines of text as a definition for the entry of "p Value," and also made no cross-reference to any other related entries such as "Alpha Level" and "Level of Significance."

Furthermore, a close examination of the dictionary reveals that a considerable number of entries (e.g., "Artificial Intelligence," "Cognitive Science," "First In–First Out," and "Flow Chart") pertain to computer science and other disciplines rather than statistics and methodologies in the social sciences. To ensure the quality of this reference tool, the author should either eliminate those entries or change the title of this dictionary accordingly. Despite the limitations, this dictionary is highly recommend. It is a valuable reference tool to anyone and any library that has an interest in statistical terminology.—**Heting Chu**

Handbooks and Yearbooks

769. **Annual Abstract of Statistics, Number 135.** 1999 ed. London, Stationary Office; distr., Lanham, Md., Bernan Associates, 1999. 450p. index. $90.00pa. ISBN 0-11-621068-0. ISSN 0072-5730.

This excellent resource is the UK equivalent of the *Statistical Abstract of the United States* (115th ed.; see ARBA 96, entry 920). The table's layout is quite similar, as are the types of statistics. An amazing amount of data has been incorporated into a relatively small space. Included are land area for England, Northern Ireland, Scotland, and Wales; and parliamentary elections' registered voters, votes cast, and winning majorities, as well as statistics on overseas aid; defense; population; vital statistics; education; labor, income and expenditure; health; and social services (e.g., National Health). Most of the figures presented are for the entire United Kingdom, but, where noted, they are broken out for Scotland, England, and Wales, or Northern Ireland. The figures are given for, in most cases, 1992 through 1998, though some go back as far as 1987.

This volume provides more data on the United Kingdom than do any others of comparable price. Highly recommended for academic libraries, as well as for public and school libraries where the need exists.
—**Susan B. Hagloch**

770. **Balance of Payments Statistics Yearbook 1998.** Washington, D.C., International Monetary Fund; distr., Lanham, Md., Bernan Associates, 1998. 2v. $68.00/set. ISBN 1-55775-752-6. ISSN 0252-3035.

The *Balance of Payments Statistics Yearbook 1998* is a 2-volume set in 3 parts. Part 1 is the detailed tables on balance of payments and statistics for 160 countries, and the international investment position data for 48 countries. Part 2 aggregates the country data by major balance of payments components. For each component, data for countries, country groups, and the world are provided. Data for international organizations are also included in part 2. Part 3 is the formulas, practices, and data sources for deriving each country's balance of payments statistics. This part outlines the government agency that provided the statistical information, the currency used, and supporting documentation for calculation of statistics.

The information is presented in three languages—English, French, and German. A CD-ROM is available. This publication is recommended for special government libraries, business libraries, and large academic libraries that have a need for economics statistics information.—**Kay M. Stebbins**

771. **Handbook on Civil Registration and Vital Statistics Systems: Management, Operation, and Maintenance.** By the Department of Economic and Social Affairs, Statistics Division. New York, United Nations, 1998. 199p. (Studies in Methods, Series F, no.72). $35.00pa. ISBN 92-1-161405-8. S/N E.98.XVII.11.

It is important to have available accurate statistics concerning vital events (e.g., births, deaths, marriages, and divorces) in the world population. Recognizing that importance, the International Programme for Accelerating the Improvement of Vital Statistics and Civil Registration Systems was created under the auspices of five United Nations bodies about a decade ago. It is intended that five handbooks will eventually be published under the international program to assist in the establishment of civil registration and vital statistics systems where they do not exist, and to provide guidelines for improving current systems. The present volume, *Handbook on Civil Registration and Vital Statistics Systems: Management, Operation, and Maintenance*, published by the United Nations, represents the first volume of the series. Roughly one-half of the book consists of a comprehensive and detailed discussion of procedures for managing, operating, and maintaining an appropriate system. Several annexes contain lists of information to be obtained, examples of systems in selected countries, and numerous samples of civil registration and vital statistics forms drawn from 10 countries. A table of contents and a list of references, largely other UN handbooks, are included. Although designed primarily for those attempting to establish or to improve systems in their countries, the book may well provide insights for those concerned with trends in the growth and structure of world population.—**William C. Struning**

772. **Pocket World in Figures 1999.** 1998 ed. New York, John Wiley, 1998. 224p. $14.95pa. ISBN 0-471-29598-1.

This annual publication now has 62 major country profiles, including Russia and Ukraine. Each profile has a general section that includes information on the area, capital, and the unit of currency. A section on people includes data on population, population per square kilometer, average annual growth, the gross domestic product (GDP), the GDP per head, the GDP purchasing power, the origins of the GDP, and the components of GDP. There are also sections on the structure of employment; energy; inflation and finance; exchange rates; principal exports; principal imports; balance of payments, reserves, and aid; and family life. These profiles comprise almost the last two-thirds of the book.

The first third of the book consists of world rankings of 171 countries. To be included the country has to have a population of at least one million or a GNP of one billion U.S. dollars. The quality of the statistics varies from country to country. The data included are for the year ending December 31, 1996, unless otherwise noted. There are over 200 rankings, which include facts about the geography of the countries, the population, the economy, the quality of life, the economic growth (including inflation and debt, employment, banks, and stock markets), transportation, education, death rates, crime, and the environment. The book is relatively small (pocket size) and could get lost on the reference shelves. If purchased, it should circulate.—**Robert L. Turner Jr.**

773. **Statistical Handbook on Poverty in the Developing World.** Chandrika Kaul and Valerie Tomaselli-Moschovitis, eds. Phoenix, Ariz., Oryx Press, 1999. 425p. index. $69.50. ISBN 1-57356-249-1.

Poverty remains one of the most widespread social ills in the world. Although all countries exhibit poverty, developing countries experience the most severe problems. Poverty can account for other social maladies, such as illiteracy, disease, insufficient health care, high mortality rates, and hunger. This volume provides data on poverty and poverty-related issues for developing countries with a gross national product (GNP) of $785 or less. In some cases data are also provided for higher-income countries. Data are taken from official agencies and sources such as the World Bank, the United Nations, and the World Health Organization. The data from these sources are fairly well coordinated, thus making comparisons more meaningful. Most of the book consists of indicators organized by the 1998 World Bank income levels. Main categories of indicators include land area, population, GNP, life expectancy, education and literacy rates, and mortality rates. Each section begins with an explanation of the indicators. This is followed by various tables and graphs listing the data. Tables and graphs are well annotated and definitions from source materials are frequently provided.

There is a definite need for this type of volume. Data are difficult to find about poverty in developing countries. A bibliography would have been a useful addition. Academic, special, and large public libraries may find this volume useful. [R: LJ, 1 Nov 99, pp. 74-75; BL, 1 Dec 99, pp. 726-728]—**Andrew G. Torok**

774. **Statistical Yearbook for Asia and the Pacific 1998. Annuaire Statistique Pour l'Asi et le Paceifique.** By the Economic and Social Commission for Asia and the Pacific. New York, United Nations, 1999. 631p. $80.00pa. ISBN 92-1-119898-4. ISSN 0252-3655. S/N E/F.99.IIF.1.

This United Nations (UN) sponsored title, from the Economic and Social Commission for Asia and the Pacific, provides data in 11 categories for 56 countries or areas, from Russia in the east to the Cook Islands in the Pacific. Besides such major economies as China and Japan, it includes data from such hard-to-find locales as Vietnam, North Korea, and many former Soviet republics. Data categories are population, manpower, GNP, agriculture, forestry and fisheries, industry, energy, transport and communications, trade, finance, and selected social statistics. Like most UN statistical publications, it attempts to standardize data reporting, though this is not always successful. Data are arranged alphabetically by country and cover 1987 to 1997, though most categories only come up to 1995 or 1996. Organization is clear and the absence of an index should not cause any problems. Descriptions are in English and French. With data from such small entities as Fiji, New Caledonia, and Uzbekistan, a lot of data are available here that are not available elsewhere. This title can be supplemented by the periodical *Statistical Indicators for Asia and the Pacific* (vol. 27, no. 2, June 1997; see ARBA 99, entry 788) and it can be used in conjunction with *International Historical Statistics: Africa, Asia and Oceania, 1750-1988* (see ARBA 96, entry 917). At $80, this title is quite reasonably priced for data compilation of its breadth and authority. It occupies a unique niche and, as such, can be highly recommended for academic, special, and larger public libraries building collections on Russia, Asia, and the Pacific.—**Patrick J. Brunet**

775. **Trends in Europe and North America 1998/1999: The Statistical Yearbook of the Economic Commission for Europe.** By the Economic Commission for Europe. New York, United Nations, 1999. 262p. maps. index. $40.00pa. ISBN 92-1-116698-5. ISSN 1020-5799. S/N E.98.II.E.22.

This is the 3d edition of this publication, which presents both social and economic data, although the emphasis is more on social rather than economic trends. Readers desiring more economic statistical data are referred to the Commission's periodical, *Economic Survey of Europe*.

Trends in Europe and North America is divided into 2 parts. The 1st part gives a general overview of each country, including a map; basic data, such as the unemployment rate, population, and official language; and four graphs on trading partners, GDP change, consumer price index, and infant mortality. This 1st part is currently also available online at http://www.unece.org/stats.

The 2d part is comprised of 13 chapters, each devoted to a general theme (e.g., housing, education, environment). A page listing major trends in the theme under consideration starts each chapter, which is then followed by specific topics whose data for each country are presented by graphs, maps, or tables. Under education, for example, one can compare relative rates of literacy or expenditure per student. The sources for the data are conveniently given below each table, map, or chart. It should be noted that exact comparisons are not always available due to inconsistencies in the data sources. A useful and expanded glossary of definitions is appended, along with a somewhat minimal index. New materials and some updated topics have also been added to this edition, which helps to increase its usefulness.

This work is intended for a general audience and is suitable for public and school libraries, although it should be quite useful as a ready-reference source for academic and business libraries as well. All readers should find it easy to use, readable, and interesting.—**Paul H. Thomas**

776. **World Cost of Living Survey: A Compilation of Price Data….** 2d ed. Robert S. Lazich, ed. Farmington Hills, Mich., Gale, 1999. 618p. $235.00. ISBN 0-7876-2470-5. ISSN 1092-1702.

This survey is quite a fascinating compilation of data concerning the cost of goods and services around the world. Because the prices are generally given in U.S. dollars, it makes for a very useful way to compare relative costs. While fun for anyone to peruse, its intended audience is people who plan to relocate or travel to another area of the world, or businesses that wish to know the cost of operations in various places around the globe. The information in this volume should also be of value to anyone studying or researching international economic conditions. The data have been drawn from over 500 sources and provide information on 209 countries and 458 cities worldwide for over 30,000 prices on more than 3,900 goods and services.

Some of the major topics covered are clothing, fuels, health care, entertainment, food, housing, and education. It is important to note that not every geographical location has prices for all the same goods and services, so searching for the comparative costs of a given item can be frustrating. Also, one cannot help but wonder how it was decided that lunch at a snack bar in Kigali, Rwanda, costs, on the average, $12.37. Still, it is doubtful many people outside of Kigali would have a clue about such a cost, so it is useful to have. The data are arranged by country and within each country by city or other geographical entity. The topics are listed in the same order each time, and under each "major topic" are listed specific items. For each item the cost is provided for a given amount (e.g., 1 kg of bananas), the date the cost was ascertained, and a reference to the source from which the information was taken. The data are preceded by a useful introduction, a listing of cities covered, and a listing of items covered (in the same order as found under each country). The list of sources used is found at the end of the book. Most major collections, especially business and research libraries, should find the information in this book invaluable, as it would be virtually impossible to find such an assemblage of information so conveniently arranged anywhere else.—**Paul H. Thomas**

Indexes

777. **Statistics Sources 2000: A Subject Guide to Data on Industrial, Business, Social, Educational, Financial, and Other Topics….** 23d ed. Wasserman Jacqueline O'Brien and Steven R. Wasserman, eds. Farmington Hills, Mich., Gale, 1999. 2v. $445.00/set. ISBN 0-7876-2462-4. ISSN 0585-198X.

For those not familiar with this work, it is not a compilation of statistics themselves, but rather a subject index to statistical sources. Its basic arrangement continues as it has in the past—a straight alphabetic list of over 20,000 subjects each sub-arranged alphabetically by issuing organization. It includes over 100,000 citations from more than 2,000 sources, in print and nonprint format, both published and unpublished, and in electronic and other forms as well.

This edition has updated, revised, and expanded the scope and content of previous editions, incorporating a wider range of current national and international data sources. It has also expanded the potentially very useful sections on federal statistical telephone contacts and federal statistical databases. Also included in this work are a dictionary of statistics sources and appendixes for source publications and sources on unpublished statistical data.

If this work has a drawback, it is that it is vague on citation details. After one searches for and locates a subject, its reference will be to a source that does not have a publication date (useful for annual publications) or page number. A reference simply to *World Book Almanac* without additional details can mean a lot of searching, and one can only assume it means the latest issue. Greater specifics would be more useful for the user than repeating the information (address and telephone number usually) that is given in the appendix.

This work should be valuable for research libraries whose patrons have a need to do statistical research. There is nothing else quite like it for statistical subject searches in size or scope and, despite the shortcomings mentioned above, it should at least save time by pointing a researcher in the right direction.—**Paul H. Thomas**

United States

778. **County and City Extra, 1999: Annual Metro, City, and County Data Book.** 8th ed. Deirdre A. Gaquin and Mark S. Littman, eds. Lanham, Md., Bernan Associates, 1999. 1v. (various paging). maps. $109.00. ISBN 0-89059-161-X. ISSN 1059-9096.

This new edition of summary statistical data continues Bernan Associates' effort to provide an annual update to the *County and City Data Book*, published irregularly by the U.S. Bureau of the Census and last produced in 1994. Compiled by a data use consultant and a senior analyst, this massive volume contains statistical data on population, land area, health, crime, education, income and taxes, construction and housing, labor and employment, agriculture, manufactures, wholesale and retail trade, transportation, federal funding and finance, voting, and climate. The work is then arranged in five tables for states, counties, metropolitan areas, cities, and congressional districts for the 105th Congress. The arrangement of the 7th edition of *County and City Extra* has changed little from the 6th edition and closely follows that of the government product. A helpful introduction, a table of the subjects covered by type of geographic area, column headings for the tabular data, and a current highlights section that includes 16 color maps that thematically display a variety of demographics and statistical change are also included. The tabular statistics are arranged alphabetically by geographic area and include total numbers, percent change, and relative breakdowns for each category as well as comparable figures for the country as a whole. Most of these statistics are derived from federal agencies, including the Census Bureau, the Centers for Disease Control, the U.S. Department of Education, the Bureau of Economic Analysis, and the Bureau of Labor Statistics. The currency of statistics range from 1990 census data to 1996 population estimates. A set of appendixes, which define geographic concepts and codes, provides maps of statistical areas. A list of cities by county completes the volume. Although more current information may be obtained online via government Websites, the organization and ready access provided by this work will appeal to many types of data users.—**Debra S. Van Tassel**

779. **CQ's State Fact Finder 1998: Rankings Across America.** By Kendra A. Hovey and Harold A. Hovey. Washington, D.C., Congressional Quarterly, 1999. 406p. index. $79.95; $44.95pa. ISBN 1-56802-453-3; 1-56802-454-1pa. ISSN 1079-7149.

For anyone doing research that involves comparing the various states and Washington, D.C., or who may just wish for a convenient, up-to-date compendium of statistical data on a state-by-state basis, this volume will be quite welcome. It is the 5th edition, but it retains much of the arrangement found in its 4 predecessors, which will allow people having access to them to compare numbers over the years covered in the earlier editions. Each volume, as it is published, attempts to present the most recent figures the publisher can amass. For example, in this 1999 edition, the data for state health rankings are from 1998, but for AIDS cases they are from 1997. Nevertheless, it is estimated this edition consists of approximately 90 percent new data in comparison to the 1998 edition—a trend the publishers hope to maintain with each subsequent volume. The data are presented in 240 tables and are arranged under 12 general categories, such as population trends, health, crime, transportation, and taxation, among others. The tables also provide a numerical ranking for each state in the subject being treated so that one can see at a glance where a state ranks nationally. When available, each table also gives the national average and total for its particular subject. This publication is especially useful because it compiles statistical data not always readily available from standard sources, or if available, converts such data so that they can be used for meaningful comparisons within the context of this title. The source for the data presented in each table is carefully noted at the end of the section in which it appears along with any pertinent information about its usefulness or what to beware of when using it.

This volume is prefaced by a useful introduction that explains how best to make use of the data contained within, including some of the general questions it will help answer. It finishes with a final and convenient section that provides a state-by-state list of how each state ranks in all the categories listed by topic in the main section of the book. Thus, one can turn to the two pages for California and see at a glance that in 1997 California ranked number one in population, personal income, and number of prisoners, whereas it ranked number 40 in education spending per capita and number 50 in high school completion rates.

As fascinating as it is informative, this work belongs in any reference collection that wants to provide in one easy-to-use volume statistical data for students, researchers, or ordinary citizens.—**Paul H. Thomas**

780. **Housing Statistics of the United States.** 2d ed. Patrick A. Simmons, ed. Lanham, Md., Bernan Associates, 1999. 538p. index. $65.00pa. ISBN 0-89059-108-3. ISSN 1521-5601.

This reference contains 250 tables on housing stock, demand, production, investment, market data, financing, and utilization of federal housing programs. Examples of the information provided are the number of owned housing units versus those rented, broken out by state. Other variables are included, such as how many rooms the house has and the ethnic and age composition of the households. The reader will find median rents and sale prices reported by state. Even the nature of the neighborhood (e.g., vandalism, trash, bars on the windows) and the condition of the units (e.g., broken windows, sagging roofs, exposed wiring) are noted.

The statistics reflect a range of dates, but the majority are multiyear indicators with 1996 and 1997 being the most recent years available. The table of contents and detailed index give easy access to the broad array of information available. The two appendixes identify the reporting source for each table, definitions for the headings used in each figure, and descriptions of the surveys and censuses used to collect the data. Everything one will ever want to know about housing can be found in this useful resource. It will be useful for those in the industry as well as general users needing insight into current living conditions across the country. [R: Choice, July/Aug 99, p. 1928]—**Adrienne Antink Bendel**

781. **State and Metropolitan Area Data Book 1997-98: A Statistical Abstract Supplement.** 5th ed. Washington, D.C., U.S. Bureau of the Census; distr., Lanham, Md., Bernan Associates, 1998. 1v. (various paging). maps. index. $24.00pa. ISBN 0-934213-54-2.

This is the 5th edition of a summary of statistics on the social, political, and economic organization of the states and metropolitan areas in the United States, and it serves as a supplement to the *Statistical Abstract of the United States* (115th ed.; see ARBA 96, entry 920). Source citations allow it to act as a statistical reference and guide to other statistical publications and sources form the U.S. Bureau of the Census. Emphasis is, of course, one the states and metropolitan areas, but tables are also included that provide data for the counties that comprise the metropolitan area as well as its central city. A few changes in format have been made from previous editions. The order of tables has been changed so that state tables appear first, state data is presented in alphabetic order, and one data table for all the metropolitan areas is shown before the next data table. Source notes now appear at the bottom of each page of tables and also in the source notes and explanations appendix. Also included is a "Telephone Contact List" of federal agencies with major statistical programs. Each agency's mailing address, telephone number, and Internet address is given. As fact-filled and easy to use as its predecessors, this inexpensive volume belongs in every library.
—**Susan B. Hagloch**

782. **State Profiles 1999: The Population and Economy of Each U.S. State.** Courtenay M. Slater, Martha G. Davis, and Elizabeth Rogers, eds. Lanham, Md., Bernan Associates, 1999. 469p. index. $65.00pa. ISBN 0-89059-159-8. ISSN 1524-3958.

This reference book offers a statistical perspective on how different and similar the different states in the United States are. The book has a tight structure; each state and the District of Columbia get eight pages with tables for population and labor force, household and personal income, economic structure, housing, agriculture, education, health, and government. Introductory paragraphs offer overviews of the state's economic and demographic profile and highlight important recent trends. The information covers the 1990s and is supplemented by basic information for earlier years. While users may want more detail from State Data Centers for their individual states, as a comparative tool, *State Profiles* is tremendously revealing. Probably the pages that will be relied upon most are the opening section on the "United States" that explores the relation of states to one another and to the nation. Maps and charts suggest shifting regional lines by economic and social trends of the 1990s, and the narrative delves into recent events possibly causing shifts such as welfare and finance reforms. The section then closes with a table of rankings, sure to be quoted by politicians and interpreted by scholars. Whether finding out that Arkansas has the lowest percentage of residents reaching college or that Connecticut has the highest personal income per capita, users have a gauge of state patterns, although they may be sometimes used as tests of success and failure. This section could be easily expanded and given more discussion, even though as it stands, it will probably be turned to the most for reference. The structure of the work makes turning to the category in a particular state easy, and if one cannot immediately put his or her finger on the statistic, a detailed index with easy-to-read highlights is provided.—**Simon J. Bronner**

783. **State Rankings 1999: A Statistical View of the 50 United States.** 10th ed. Kathleen O'Leary Morgan and Scott Morgan, eds. Lawrence, Kans., Morgan Quitno Press, 1999. 569p. index. price not reported pa. ISBN 1-56692-332-8. ISSN 1057-3623.

If one is curious about where the U.S. Defense Department spends the most money (California), which state has the lowest crime rate (Vermont), or who is the top soybean producer in the United States (Illinois), this book is the source to consult. This book contains 569 tables of state comparisons—1 per page. The same rankings are reported twice—in an alphabetic list beginning with Alabama and ending with Wyoming and in an accompanying ranking list beginning with 1 and typically ending at 50. The District of Columbia is included where applicable. Running alongside both lists are the data on which the 1996 to 1998 rankings were based and each state's percentage. In a few cases, only percentages or data are reported. Sources, typically federal government publications, are given for each table. As a bonus, the publisher combined 24 negative variables (e.g., poverty rate) and 19 positive ones (e.g., books per capita in public libraries) to discover the country's most livable state. Minnesota won the distinction in 1998 and again in 1999. Each state's nickname, capital, population, area, song, flower, tree, and bird are included. *State Rankings 1999* makes for fascinating browsing. The work is highly recommended for middle and high school libraries.—**Pete Prunkl**

784. **Statistical Abstract of the United States 1998.** 118th lib ed. By the U.S. Department of Commerce, the Economics and Statistics Administration, and the Bureau of the Census. Lanham, Md., Bernan Associates, 1998. 1020p. index. $50.00. ISBN 0-89059-123-7. ISSN 1063-1690.

This publication is one of the standard reference sources found in library collections and should need no introduction to anyone who has ever used a library's services. The volume under review is the library edition, meaning that it is hardbound and has larger print, making it easier for users to read (unless one finds reading a computer screen easier and wishes to resort to the CD-ROM version of this title).

Published continuously since 1878, this is the 118th edition of this venerable and indispensable title. As usual, its statistics are taken from a mix of government and private sources and, unless otherwise noted, cover the United States as presently constituted. (For data on specific states and metropolitan areas, one must consult other sources such as the *State and Metropolitan Area Data Book* [see entry 781] or *CQ's State Fact Finder* [1997 ed.; see ARBA 97, entry 817]).

This edition of *Statistical Abstract of the United States* consists of 1,487 tables containing statistics for the most recent year or period available by spring 1998. This edition contains 94 new tables that cover subjects ranging from the number of male sexual partners in lifetime, by selected characteristics 1995, to public library use of the Internet 1997, to age of driver and number of accidents 1996. Several of the new tables are the result of information taken from the National Survey of Family Growth. Eighty-eight tables removed that appeared in the previous edition, making it a good idea to retain past editions of this title when possible.

As in past editions, the data are followed by several useful appendixes. They provide further sources for statistical information, on both a national and a state level, a list of metropolitan areas with their population estimates, a discussion of the limitation of the data listed in this book, and lists of the new and deleted tables. Given the importance of this publication, especially the inclusion of both the new tables and of newer data in general, this is a title that any reference collection will need to include on its shelves.

—**Paul H. Thomas**

785. **Statistical Handbook on Consumption and Wealth in the United States.** Chandrika Kaul and Valerie Tomaselli-Moschovitis, eds. Phoenix, Ariz., Oryx Press, 1999. 290p. index. $65.00. ISBN 1-57356-251-3.

This excellent resource provides a comprehensive statistical examination of wealth and consumption in the United States. It includes 8 sections: General Economic Data; Personal, Family, and Household Income and Wealth; Business and Corporate Wealth; Overview of Consumption; Consumption of Material Goods; Consumption of Services; Consumption of Travel, Leisure, and Other Non-Essentials; and The Role of Government. Each is summarized with a wide variety of tables showing the patterns of income, disposable income, and consumption over a number of years. Each section is briefly prefaced by a general overview of the topic and an explanation of the indicators, and the tables and graphs used to illustrate them. The book tracks consumer trends across recent years and also gives, in some instances, historical comparisons. The graphs and tables for federal government percentage of the Gross Domestic Product (GDP), for instance, cover the years 1945 through 1992. Most of the consumption data cover the 1970s or 1980s through the mid-1990s. Due to the lag time in gathering data, there are no figures on e-commerce because the most recent data available are projections for 1998. An appendix compares the 1997 GDP in U.S. dollars of 178 nations, both alphabetically and ranked by the size of the GDP. An excellent index makes specific information easy to find. This will be extremely valuable for economic researchers, forecasters, and students. This resource is recommended for public, academic, and corporate libraries.—**Susan B. Hagloch**

786. **Statistical Handbook on the American Family.** 2d ed. Bruce A. Chadwick and Tim B. Heaton, eds. Phoenix, Ariz., Oryx Press, 1999. 326p. index. $62.50. ISBN 1-57356-169-X.

This book addresses the current state of U.S. families through 340 tables and graphs covering the categories of marriage, quality of family life, divorce, child raising, working women, child care, and sexual behavior. The editors give an interesting combination of census data as well as the results of opinion polls. For example, the section on children not only shows birthrates by age and education of the mother, but explores the hours parents spend with their children in leisure activities, parental disagreements over clothes and friends, and discipline issues. One survey asks how often the family had meals together in the last 3 months; 44 percent reported once a month or never.

Each section is introduced with a narrative that briefly summarizes major trends. The list of tables and the index make it easy to locate a specific statistic. The data are primarily drawn from 1995 and 1996 with information comparative to earlier years. The appendix lists the source for each table and graph. Although this resource provides pertinent material for the reader to assess the condition of today's American family, it is flawed because the reporting date for many of the tables is not stated. [R: Choice, Sept 99, pp. 122-123]—**Adrienne Antink Bendel**

URBAN STUDIES

787. **America's Top-Rated Cities, 2000: A Statistical Handbook.** 7th ed. David Garoogian, ed. Lakeville, Conn., Grey House Publishing, 1999. 4v. $195.00/set; $59.95/vol. ISBN 1-891482-50-5.

The 7th edition of *America's Top-Rated Cities* (see ARBA 98, entry 820 for a review of the 5th edition) is designed for persons considering relocating to a new city, professionals considering expanding their business to a new city, corporations relocating offices, market researchers, real estate consultants, urban planners, and investors. The set is divided into 4 volumes, which cover the southern, western, central, and eastern regions of the United States. The book focuses on the largest 76 cities of the United States; this new edition includes 17 new cities, including Louisville, Kentucky, Providence, Rhode Island, and Reno, Nevada. Each city has information provided on their background, statistical rankings, business environment (e.g., state economy, employment, real estate, population, taxes), and living environment (e.g., cost of living, housing, education, major employers, recreation, air and water quality). In addition there are 4 appendixes, which provide data on comparative statistics and metropolitan statistics as well as addresses and telephone and fax numbers for chambers of commerce and economic development organizations and state departments of labor and employment organizations. The information is gathered from magazines (e.g., *Money*, *Fortune*), federal and state statistics, newspapers, and Websites.

Obviously, much of the information found here can be found in other sources but this is the only source of its kind that brings together all of this information into one easy-to-use source. It will be beneficial to many business and public libraries.—**Shannon M. Graff**

18 Women's Studies

BIBLIOGRAPHY

788. **Interdisciplinary Bibliographic Guide to Women's Studies 1998.** New York, G. K. Hall/Macmillan Library Reference, 1999. 2v. $295.00/set. ISBN 0-7838-0405-9. ISSN 0896-8101.

This 21st addition to G. K. Hall's *Bibliographic Guides* for 1998 is a welcome finding tool for libraries supporting Women's Studies curriculum. Not only are these guides a useful research tool for scholars, but they are also a valuable aid for library acquisitions. These 2 volumes are a compilation of women's materials, in all languages and formats, cataloged by the New York Public Library and the Library of Congress (LC) in the 1998 calendar year.

The entries are arranged in one alphabetic sequence with numbers preceding letters. The cataloging for each main entry includes the author's name, short or main title, subtitle or other title page information, place of publication, publisher, date of publication, pagination, illustration statement, series, notes, ISBN and DDC numbers, subject headings, added entry, LC call number, and New York Public Library indicator. There are also condensed citations for secondary entries. In some instances the term "in process" is used to denote titles not yet assigned call numbers by the Library of Congress. Subject entries appear in boldface capital letters.—**Sue Brown**

BIOGRAPHY

789. Adamson, Lynda G. **Notable Women in American History: A Guide to Recommended Biographies and Autobiographies.** Westport, Conn., Greenwood Press, 1999. 540p. index. $49.95. ISBN 0-313-29584-0.

There are 500 notable women from more than 100 different fields discussed in this volume. The three criteria for inclusion are that they "must have lived in the United States or one of its territories, and if born abroad after 1900, be a naturalized American citizen; have enriched life for other Americans in some way; and have a full-length biography or autobiography for either adults or mature young adults published since 1970 which is available by interlibrary loan" (pp. xi-xii). Adamson includes up to five citations to autobiographical monographs per person. The entries provide readers a tight, albeit short, summary of each women's life and are listed alphabetically. The appendixes include the women by date of birth (the earliest being Pocahontas in 1617); by occupation or main area of interest, such as activist, nurse, missionary, tribal leader; and by ethnicity, including African Americans, Asian Americans, Latino Americans, and Native Americans. This work is recommended as an excellent starting point for biographical research. [R: BL, 1 Dec 99, p. 726]—**Leslie R. Homzie**

790. Anderson, Alice Hellstrom. **Extraordinary Ordinary Women.** San Carlos, Calif., Ladybug Press, 1998. 238p. illus. $27.95pa. ISBN 1-889-40920-0.

The title tells the whole plot and purpose of this publication. There are 39 women, ranging in age from 16 to 97, described in these pages. Each entry provides a photograph and a brief biography, plus a description of the problem and how the woman provided a solution.

These women are from all parts of the country and all walks of life. The only characteristic they have in common is the ability to see the situation that needed changing and the courage to change it and help others in the process. There is Anna Gould who used her family's resort and resources to provide a respite for families with critically ill children; or Colene Daniel who was reared in a ghetto and spent her time making life better for inner-city children; and another who certainly deserved honorable mention, Margaret Chase Smith. The stories go on from the very poor to the not so poor, but all have a strong public service ethic.

The entries are not alphabetic and there is no discernible order to these biographies. However, there is a table of contents that lists each name along with her accomplishment. There is an endnote inviting the readers to submit their own nominations for the next publication of *Extraordinary Ordinary Women*. This would be a welcome addition to any sociology department with an emphasis on women.—**Sue Brown**

791. Jackson, Guida M. **Women Rulers Throughout the Ages.** Santa Barbara, Calif., ABC-CLIO, 1999. 471p. illus. index. $75.00. ISBN 1-57607-091-3.

According to the author of the volume, *Women Rulers Throughout the Ages* includes a biographical listing of "every known ruling queen, empress, prime minister, president, regent ruler, de facto ruler, constitutional monarch, and verifiable ruler who was female, from the oral tradition and written history of the world's kingdoms, islands, empires, nations, and tribes down to present time" (p. xxxi). Each of the 508 alphabetically arranged entries contains a 50- to 350-word overview of the life and career of the woman ruler, and a brief reference section that includes a bibliography of 1 to 6 sources. About one in five entries also contains an illustration. The volume also contains a 12-page introduction that discusses the role of women in political history; a 15-page geographical chronology of entries, which lists the subjects by country and century; a 16-page bibliography that lists the references cited in the text; and a 17-page general index.

Although the entries include some interesting information and are generally well written, much of the material in the volume is drawn from world history textbooks, dated monographs, encyclopedias, almanacs, and newspapers. The brevity of the entries also limits their usefulness. The work is more a reference text for nonspecialists than a guide for scholars in the field of women's history. This work is recommended for high school libraries. [R: BL, 15 Dec 99, pp. 804-805]—**Terry D. Bilhartz**

792. **Significant Contemporary American Feminists: A Biographical Sourcebook.** Jennifer Scanlon, ed. Westport, Conn., Greenwood Press, 1999. 361p. index. $79.50. ISBN 0-313-30125-5.

This work is a collection of 50 short essays on second-wave feminists in the United States. Each essay contains biographical information about the individual and her accomplishments in regard to feminism. At the end of each entry, a bibliographical section is included that contains a selective list of publications by and about the individual and her work. A selected bibliography on second- and third-wave feminists, an index, and information on the editors and contributors are listed at the end of the book.

One of the collection's stated criticisms is that it concentrates only on a small number of feminists who have influenced the second-wave movement in the United States. However, unlike *Feminist Writers* (see ARBA 97, entry 886), this work reviews women of all professions. A sampling of women included are Judy Chicago, Pearl Cleage, Gloria Steinem, Kate Clinton, Ruth Bader Ginsburg, Florynce Kennedy, and Olga Madar. Its biographical entries are by no means comprehensive. However, those wishing to find a brief overview of the most influential contemporary U.S. feminists will not be disappointed. [R: Choice, Sept 99, p. 104; BL, 1 May 99, pp. 1636-1638; RUSQ, Fall 99, pp. 100-101]—**Laura K. Blessing**

793. **Women in World History, Volumes 1-3: A Biographical Encyclopedia.** Anne Commire and Deborah Klezmer, eds. Farmington Hills, Mich., Gale, 1999. 15v. illus. index. $995.00/set. ISBN 0-7876-4080-8.

Women have been major contributors to history since the beginning of time, but the historians have chosen to omit these contributions in historical writings. The editors, Commire and Klezmer, found this omission while editing a multivolume work on historic leaders. They found that women had been "denied their history, denied the momentum of their accomplishments." Therefore, they decided to compile a multi-volume biographical encyclopedia devoted 100 percent to women's lives.

There are approximately 10,000 biographies in alphabetic order presented here. The coverage includes women's biographies from the earliest known women through women living in modern times—approximately 310 B.C.E. through women born before 1926. If specific birth and death dates are not known, the era the woman flourished is given.

It is international in scope, and includes those women who are revered in their own country, but may not be well known in the United States. Artists, pirates, scientists, athletes, philanthropists, adventurers, politicians, pacifists, saints, and courtesans are examples of the lives discussed in this encyclopedia. The achievements, awards, advancements, discoveries, and "legacies left for future generations" are listed in chronological order. All of the possible variations of a woman's name are provided for the researcher to perform a thorough search for that person. Photographs of the person and illustrations that help to identify the biographee are present. Quotations spoken by that person are interspersed in the text. Genealogical charts are provided to help the researcher place the woman in history. There are numerous *see* and *see also* references, and bibliographic sources are provided at the end of the entry.

This is the most comprehensive women's biographical encyclopedia. Academic and public libraries, large and small, should make this a priority purchase for their biography collections.—**Kay M. Stebbins**

794. **Women Leaders: Rulers Throughout History.** [CD-ROM]. Santa Barbara, Calif., ABC-CLIO, 1998. Minimum system requirements (Windows version): Pentium-compatible processor at 75MHz or faster. Four-speed CD-ROM drive. 8MB RAM. 30MB hard disk space. SVGA monitor 650x480 (256 colors). 16-bit sound card with Windows drivers. Mouse. Minimum system requirements (Macintosh version): 68040 processor with 25MHz or faster. Double-speed CD-ROM drive. System 7.5.3 or higher. 8MB RAM. 30MB hard disk space. SVGA monitor 640x480 (256 colors). $49.00 (single user); $149.00 (networks). ISBN 1-57607-016-6.

This CD-ROM provides biographies about the lives as well as accomplishments and controversies of 380 female rulers; de facto rulers; and constitutional monarchs of the world's kingdoms, empires, nations, islands, and tribes. These leaders were elected, rose to eminence, or were the power behind the throne, some more legendary than historical.

The leaders and their domains are listed alphabetically within the CD-ROM as well as in the accompanying documentation. Each entry provides a name, attribute, country, and title. There are hyperlinks to an overview of the country and a color topographic map. Bibliographies are provided for each biography.

ClioView provides the name of the leader, title, beginning year of rule, and the highlight of the reign in chart form. A summary of each biography can be brought to screen with a mouse click. Documentation provides clear directions for installation and even how to uninstall the CD-ROM. This is an interesting source of information for those lesser-known women leaders.—**Sue Brown**

CHRONOLOGY

795. Franck, Irene M., and David M. Brownstone. **Illustrated History of Women.** Danbury, Conn., Grolier, 1999. 10v. illus. index. $295.00/set. ISBN 0-7172-7497-7.

The *Illustrated History of Women* is a comprehensive, well-written history of women from ancient times through the twentieth century. The text is enriched with illustrations, photographs, charts, sidebars, and many timelines and boxes. There is a set index in each of the 10 volumes. The reading level is appropriate for middle school and high school students.

The topics discussed in "HerStory" are religious battles, childbirth and midwives, education, women of power, women of medicine, scientists and inventors, slaves, art patrons, writers, and heroines and villains. Each of the volumes presents an overview of the period and a timeline for that period. A short bibliography and cross-references are provided and a cumulative index is provided in each of the volumes. This set is recommended for middle and high school libraries due to the reading levels and the limited bibliographies. [R: BR, Nov/Dec 99, pp. 88-89]—**Kay M. Stebbins**

DICTIONARIES AND ENCYCLOPEDIAS

796. **The Women's Movement in the United States: An Interactive Encyclopedia.** [CD-ROM]. Santa Barbara, Calif., ABC-CLIO, 1999. Minimum system requirements: Pentium-compatible processor at 75MHz or faster. Four-speed CD-ROM drive. Windows 95, Windows NT, 4.0, or Windows 98. 16MB RAM. 40MB hard disk space. SVGA monitor 640x480. Mouse. $69.00 (standalone); $279.00 (network). ISBN 1-57607-135-9.

"From reference to research, from research to knowledge" is the slogan of ABC-CLIO's new series of interactive encyclopedias with companion Websites. The purpose of the series is to enable students with the simple touch of a key to find, select, organize, and evaluate information that can be used to research relevant historical subjects. Along with the CD-ROM products, ABC-CLIO provides Websites with learning activities for students and instructional aids for teachers. Students are encouraged to use the resources on the CD-ROM to write their own biographies, and then submit their works to ABC-CLIO editors for posting on the Website's "Hall of Fame."

The inaugural publication in this interactive encyclopedia series is *The Women's Movement in the United States*. The CD-ROM includes about 700 articles that trace the long struggle for gender equality in America from colonial times to the present. Included in the entries are articles on pertinent movements (abolition, feminism), events (Triangle Shirtwaist Fire, Seneca Falls Convention), individuals (Abigail Adams, Anna Shaw), court cases (*Adams v. Kellogg, Roe v. Wade*), organizations (League of Women Voters, YWCA), legislation (Pregnancy Discrimination Act, Title IV of the 1972 Higher Education Act), publications (The Woman's Bible, Ladies' Home Journal), and definitions (biological clock, equity law). A large number of the entries have photographs, video or audio segments, statistical tables, or primary source documents that accompany the text.

The CD-ROM is easy to use, and its content can be searched by article, keyword, text, media type, and research theme. Most materials can be exported to a word processing program and printed. Although it is prepared for a 7th to 12th grade readership, college students and adults will also find considerable value in this innovative introduction to American women's history.—**Terry D. Bilhartz**

797. **Women's Studies Encyclopedia.** rev. ed. Helen Tierney, ed. Westport, Conn., Greenwood Press, 1999. 3v. index. $295.00/set. ISBN 0-313-29620-0.

In view of the male-centered coverage of general encyclopedias, the 2d edition of Helen Tierney's vast compendium on gender issues affecting women is a welcome addition to the reference shelf. The project coordinates the work of 457 consultants and contributors in a series of articles that range from arcana (couvade, shadow price, imposter phenomenon) to such central gender issues as violence, cult of womanhood, sports, semiotics, abortion, patriarchy, and veiling. Because the layout is straightforward and the diction generally unencumbered with technical terms, the 3-volume set will appeal to students and average readers, who would be put off by the daunting machinery of academe.

The typeface is pleasing and the subheads and articles well spaced. The whole is consecutively paginated. Guide words at the top of facing pages name the entries below (e.g., Epics, Medieval and Equal Employment Opportunity Laws). References are brief, but substantial and up-to-date, as with Ruth Firestone's citation of Joseph R. Strayer's *Dictionary of the Middle Ages* and Kathy Fletcher's mention of Sheila Stowell's *A Stage of Their Own*.

As is common with combined efforts, the finished product varies in texture, style, and coverage. The most damaging flaw of this set is the variance in specificity. Some essays, like those on ancient Rome, filmmakers and mainstream production, contraception, and Native American writers, abound with names of individuals, events, titles, and dates. Others, in particular the articles on Mormons and Native American women, are irritatingly generalized and devoid of names, events, and dates. Two other weaknesses are the lack of comprehensive indexing, which fails to cover specific people, and the absence of women usually glossed over or omitted from other sources (such as Elizabeth Ann Seton, the first American saint canonized by the Roman Catholic Church, and Auguste-Charlotte Bartholdi, activist and model for the Statue of Liberty project). [R: BL, 15 Dec 99, p. 805]—**Mary Ellen Snodgrass**

798. **Women's Studies Encyclopedia.** rev. ed. [CD-ROM]. Helen Tierney, ed. Westport, Conn., Greenwood Press, 1999. Minimum system requirements: IBM or compatible 386. CD-ROM drive. Windows 3.1x or Windows NT 3.51 or later. 8MB RAM. 15MB hard disk space. VGA video adapter with 14-inch monitor. Mouse. $295.00. ISBN 0-313-31074-2.

This edition boasts revised articles as well as an increase in the number of entries. Written in a language and style understandable to all, the *Women's Studies Encyclopedia* on CD-ROM contains information about women from all fields and disciplines of study. Included are "women's contributions to literature, art, science, learning, philosophy, religion, and their place in history." There is a focus on the American experience but there are articles on individuals and incidents from abroad as well.

The arrangement is alphabetic with ample hyperlinks to related subjects and articles. The references at the end of each entry direct researchers to works for additional information and different perspectives. Documentation accompanying this CD-ROM provides installation directions as well as search methods and strategies, allowing even a "technophobe" easy access to information. In addition, the opening screens lead the user into the program. As a tool for researchers in the field of women's studies as well as history, this will be a valuable addition to any library. [R: LJ, 1 Feb 99, p. 80; BR, Nov/Dec 99, p. 92]—**Sue Brown**

HANDBOOKS AND YEARBOOKS

799. **Arab Women 1995: Trends, Statistics, and Indicators.** By the Economic and Social Commission for Western Asia. New York, United Nations, 1997. 126p. $45.00pa. ISBN 92-1-128187-3. S/N 97.II.L.12.

Arab Women 1995 discusses important social and cultural trends in the Arab world, not the Middle East or Muslim states. The text is an analysis of roughly 70 studies published by various organizations including the World Bank, several universities, the United Nations Economic and Social Commission for Western Asia (ESCWA), and the UN Center of Arab Women for Training and Research (CAWTAR). The latter two groups are the primary sources of raw statistical data for this book. More than 50 graphs and tables support the points of the written text. Small articles discuss several key social issues including AIDS, an impending water crisis in Arab states, family planning, and sanitation facilities and their noticeable absence in some countries.

The primary topics of the work include populations and families, discrepancies between urban and rural populations, health issues such as infant and maternal mortality and female genital mutilation, education of men and women, opportunities for women to work outside the home, and women in politics. Each section lists policy recommendations to improve the health and welfare of the people. The writing is not preachy or biased toward Western political philosophy or Judeo-Christian religious views; rather they emphasize commonsense health, political, economic, and social reasoning to empower men, women, and children of all social positions in these states. Any special collection for government publications, women, Islam, Arabs, or the Middle East would value this text.—**Susan D. Baird-Joshi**

800. Berkeley, Kathleen C. **The Women's Liberation Movement in America.** Westport, Conn., Greenwood Press, 1999. 225p. illus. index. (Greenwood Press Guides to Historic Events of the Twentieth Century). $39.95. ISBN 0-313-29875-0.

Berkeley's book is a concise critique of the major issues and events of twentieth-century feminism in the United States. Berkeley, the chairperson of the history department at the University of North Carolina at Wilmington, specializes in women's issues and recent history. The book consists of a chronology, a critical history, biographies, excerpted writings, a glossary, an annotated bibliography, and an index.

The chronology lists major events between 1848 and 1963, then adds more details between 1963 and February 1999. Textual coverage of 1998 and 1999 is scanty, however. Although 5 or 10 events concern the scandal of President Clinton and Monica Lewinsky, neither is mentioned in the text. Clinton's resulting inability to promote women's issues would have been well within Berkeley's political focus. The history begins with an overview of women's emancipation before the twentieth century. Most of the text focuses on the events from 1960 to present. Berkeley touches on a number of the internal conflicts in the movement, including racism among white feminists and sexism among male radical activists. Thirteen biographies include activists promoting feminism, as well as one opposing it, Phyllis Schlafly. The writings present the complexity of women's liberation, including lesbianism, ethnicity and race, law, politics, and social tradition. Authors range from Betty Friedan to Marabel Morgan.

Students will find very helpful the annotated bibliography of 90 books, 25 articles and essays, and 8 Websites. The sources are commonly carried by both academic and public libraries. Most of the Websites appear to be ongoing sites supported by universities. A recent work of comparable approach to Berkeley's would be hard to find.—**Nancy L. Van Atta**

801. Harlan, Judith. **Feminism: A Reference Handbook.** Santa Barbara, Calif., ABC-CLIO, 1998. 308p. index. (Contemporary World Issues). $39.50. ISBN 0-87436-894-4.

Harlan has written on girls' self-esteem and on U.S.–Puerto Rican politics. In *Feminism: A Reference Handbook* she offers a broad overview of feminism in the United States from 1920 to today. This guide appropriately offers no surprises. It contains a brief history of feminism in the United States, a chronology, an attempt to define the basic tenets of feminism in all its broadness, biographical sketches of key people, and an extensive explanation of key issues.

Harlan defines feminist issues by asserting that there are two kinds of feminists: those who seek "access" for women and those who seek "control." She then names the primary areas feminists feel access and control are needed, including education, economics, politics, reproduction, sexuality, violence, and society in general. She touches on global feminist issues such as population control and genital mutilation.

A tiny slice of a pie chart displays the 1.9 percent of women representing the top earners at Fortune 500 companies. Such useful charts and statistical tables are included throughout this volume. An extensive section of organizations, books, Web pages, videotapes, and other media concludes the volume, along with an essential index. This reference could have used more imaginative photographic illustrations. Although visually dull, it offers a basic, general grounding in feminism and should be purchased by public, school, and academic libraries. [R: Choice, Dec 98, p. 668; BL, 1 Nov 98, p. 532]—**Glynys R. Thomas**

802. Heinemann, Sue. **The New York Public Library Amazing Women in American History: A Book of Answers for Kids.** New York, John Wiley, 1998. 192p. illus. index. (New York Public Library Answer Books for Kids Series). $12.95pa. ISBN 0-471-19216-3.

A chronological history of women is presented in the latest reference text from the New York Public Library. The format is in questions and answers, with informative sidebars and numerous black-and-white photographs for kids grades 6 through 10. Women from political activism and slavery to fine arts and sports are explored. Notable women, such as Eleanor Roosevelt and Amelia Earhart, and less notable ones, such as Emma Goldman, Nelly Bly, and Ida B. Wells, are discussed. Their achievements and controversies are included in each of the women's stories.

There is a selected bibliography and a "New York Public Library's Recommended Reading List." This work is recommended for school libraries and public libraries for their women's studies collections or biography collections. [R: BR, Nov/Dec 98 , p. 83]—**Kay M. Stebbins**

803. **Women in India: A Country Profile.** By the Economic and Social Commission for Asia and the Pacific. New York, United Nations, 1997. 103p. (Statistical Profiles, no.12). $24.00pa. ISBN 92-1-119760-0. S/N E.97.II.F.24.

Women in India is one in a series of profiles emphasizing social and economic issues for men and women in 19 Asian and Pacific countries. The introduction is a useful explanation of India, explaining the role of women from a religious and social perspective and how they often contradict each other. It also discusses the bureaucratic structure of the Indian government that provides support for women.

The highlights section summarizes the key points of each section that further analyzes the plethora of statistics quoted. The other detailed sections cover the political and social structure of India, an overall profile of women in India, family life, economic life, public life of women, and special concerns regarding violent crimes within and outside the family committed against women. Most of the discussion in the detailed sections offer some explanation of applicable social prejudices, historical background, and social systems (such as the education system) when discussing the literacy of women and school-age girls.

More than 100 tables and figures from several sources provide the bulk of the data for analysis. The primary sources are the Office of the Registrar General, India; the International Institute for Population Sciences; the National Sample Survey Organization; the Ministry of Labour, Government of India; and the Election Commission of India. Unfortunately, there is no explanation of what these organizations do or how they gathered the statistics.—**Susan D. Baird-Joshi**

804. **Women's Roles in Ancient Civilizations: A Reference Guide.** Bella Vivante, ed. Westport, Conn., Greenwood Press, 1999. 389p. maps. index. $59.95. ISBN 0-313-30127-1.

The role of women in 12 ancient civilizations is analyzed from a feminist perspective in this title. The Far and Near East, Africa, Egypt, Greece, Rome, Mesoamerica, the ancient Andes, and North America are covered. The lengthy essays reflect the multidisciplinary makeup of the authors, who include archeologists, art historians, literary analysts, religious studies researchers, and art historians. Although the essays approach the topic from the author's area of expertise, they all discuss the roles of women, how those roles were fulfilled, and how women were regarded by their society.

Each essay begins with a discussion of sources, a timeline, and a map. Source information pays particular attention to the significance of archeological sources and the authorship of written texts and makes the point that although historical records are valuable, they do not always tell the whole story.

Most essays cover the role of women in the family, in politics, and in religion. Creation myths and goddesses, details of domestic life, women rulers, and warriors are used to illustrate the position and activities of women in the ancient world. Literature by women is used to shed light on their lives if such works exist. The strongest entries are those of the Asian, African, and Mediterranean civilizations for which extensive primary sources have been found. The ancient Americas, particularly the Andean and North American cultures, lack such sources and thus depend on sixteenth-, seventeenth-, and eighteenth-century accounts written by European men.

This is a solid work that gives insight into ancient civilizations and allows the reader to compare female roles across cultures. It is a scholarly yet accessible work that is a valuable addition to the field of women's studies.—**Marlene M. Kuhl**

INDEXES

805. **Women's Studies Index 1997.** New York, G. K. Hall/Simon & Schuster Macmillan, 1998. 899p. $295.00. ISBN 0-7838-0077-0. ISSN 1058-8369.

The 1997 edition has expanded its coverage from 65 to 78 periodicals, including a diverse set of scholarly journals as well as some popular literature titles. New journals indexed include *Nora*, *Sex Roles*, *Women's International News Network*, and *Women's Rights Law Reporter*. Also added are two young women's magazines, *Teen Voices* and *New Moon*. Coverage focuses on U.S. publications, but also includes periodicals published in Canada, the United Kingdom, Europe, India, and Australia. Nearly all journals are indexed comprehensively, while articles from popular magazines such as *Redbook* and *Good Housekeeping* are indexed selectively. The multitude of topics—spanning careers, health, politics, literature, business, art, aging, family, sports, and sexuality—illustrates the diversity of pursuits and perspectives operating within the area of women's studies.

The authority for subject headings in this specialized index is Library of Congress subject headings, although terms appearing in a women's studies thesaurus have been integrated. The arrangement is a simple one: Rather than separate alphabetic indexes for subjects and authors, a single alphabetic arrangement is provided. If an indexed article is about a person, the term "about" follows the personal name in the index. Reviews (book, fiction, film, music, and theater) are also covered. The index itself is preceded by a list of periodicals indexed (including volume, issues, or month) as well as a list of publishers' mailing addresses. Students, scholars, and researchers in the area of women's studies will appreciate this comprehensive reference tool.—**Jan Bakker**

Part III
HUMANITIES

19 Humanities in General

HUMANITIES IN GENERAL

806. Sedge, Michael H. **The Writer's and Photographer's Guide to Global Markets.** New York, Allworth Press, 1998. 275p. index. $19.95. ISBN 1-58115-002-4.

Sedge, founder of Strawberry Media and publisher of the quarterly *Markets Abroad* newsletter, has written this indispensable guide to global publishing markets. Intended for experienced freelancers, it explains the benefits and advantages of working with foreign publishers, including in-flight magazines. He gives important cultural advice, such as spelling "correctly" for British publications and learning specific taboos for individual countries.

Sedge also explains the success he has found by using aggressive business tactics. For example, even though many freelancers have been taught not to, Sedge encourages multiple simultaneous submissions. He also advises people to work as both writers and photographers to increase their income and deliver a more complete package.

There is an extensive list of periodicals and book publishers around the world. Each entry contains contact information and a basic description of what they publish. Appendixes include international media e-mail addresses, reference materials, clubs and associations, foreign agencies, and foreign stock photograph agencies. Writers and photographers will appreciate the markets that this guide opens for them, but keep in mind that Sedge has geared this book toward experienced freelancers.—**Cari Ringelheim**

807. **Walford's Guide to Reference Material, Volume 3: Generalia, Language and Literature, the Arts.** 7th ed. Anthony Chalcraft, Ray Prytherch, and Stephen Willis, eds. Lanham, Md., Bernan Associates, 1998. 1186p. index. $279.00. ISBN 1-85604-300-2.

Walford's guide has a long tradition and has been reviewed in ARBA many times. This is the 7th edition of the work covering generalia, language, literature, and the arts, with several new libraries consulted, as mentioned in the introduction (pp. ix–x). In the section on generalities there are 350 new items, "with every item checked and, if necessary, revised" (p. ix). In the arts section there are 400 new entries and about the same number of new entries in the language and literature section. In most cases, brief annotations are based on prefaces or introductions to individual books covered in this guide and, in general, they are adequate. In comparison to the *Guide to Reference Books* published by the American Library Association, Walford is more comprehensive, especially for European materials. Nevertheless, several items listed here are quite obsolete, but Walford is still the best resource for general orientation.—**Bohdan S. Wynar**

20 Communication and Mass Media

GENERAL WORKS

808. **Bacon's Media Source: A Comprehensive Media Management System.** [CD-ROM]. Chicago, Bacon's Information, 1999. Minimum system requirements (Windows version): Pentium processor. CD-ROM drive. Windows 95 or Windows NT 4.0. 32MB RAM. 30MB hard disk space. SVGA monitor. Minimum system requirements (Macintosh version): Power PC. CD-ROM drive. System 7.1.3. 32MB RAM. 30MB hard disk space. Foreign File Access extension active. $1,495.00/year (single user); $200.00/user (2-10 users); $175.00/user (11-25 users); $150.00/user (26+ users).

An amazing reference tool as well as a media management system, this product provides the user with detailed directory-type profiles of more than 50,000 media outlets, including every U.S. and Canadian daily newspaper; all U.S. community newspapers; more than 12,000 magazines and newsletters; newswires and news syndicates; syndicated columnists, by beat; all U.S. radio, television, and cable networks and stations; television, radio, and cable syndicators and independent producers; news, talk, interview, and public affairs programming; and online news outlets. In sum, more than 300,000 editorial contacts are provided, along with the editorial calendars of 2,400 major magazines and newspapers. Keyword searching and field searching provide a variety of options to meet user needs.

This product also allows the user to build on the database by creating personalized records regarding almost any public relations initiative (e.g., contacts with editors, advertising, clip art). In essence, a highly efficient and comprehensive media management system is at one's fingertips. Quarterly updates, technical support, and training are offered as part of the purchase. Pricing varies between single-user and networked versions. A Web-based version will be available in early 2000. An intranet version can also be implemented.

This resource is recommended for all institutions needing quick and effective access to directory-type information, coupled with the need to manage media initiatives. Academic schools of journalism, communications, and marketing might especially benefit from this product.—**Edmund F. SantaVicca**

809. **The Power of the Press.** Beth Levy and Denise M. Bonilla, eds. Bronx, N.Y., H. W. Wilson, 1999. 187p. index. (The Reference Shelf, v.71, no.1). $30.00pa. ISBN 0-8242-0962-1.

The Reference Shelf is a series of six books covering social issues in the United States and other countries that can be purchased separately or as a subscription. Five books are topical; the last of the series is a compilation of recent speeches. This first book in the series is a collection of critical articles, excerpts of books, and addresses about recent issues of importance in news reporting. The first chapter defines the press by exploring public perception of the media, the trend toward human-interest stories, news organizations as corporate entities, and the Internet as a news source. Next the book discusses the media's involvement in celebrity, or high-interest events, such as the O. J. Simpson trial, as well as the drive for journalists themselves to become celebrities. A chapter on ethics discusses the quality of investigating and reporting versus the need to "scoop" competitive news agencies. Subsequent chapters cover media scandals and their effects on the profession's credibility, and a look at freedom of the press as it exists in several countries. The contents are selective, but provide a good contemporary view of the profession, both its problems and its potential. The bibliography will lead readers to other sources and additional periodical articles. It is indexed for easy reference. School and public libraries may want this in both the reference and circulating collections.—**Jean Engler**

810. Shilling, Lilless McPherson, and Linda K. Fuller, comps. **Dictionary of Quotations in Communications.** Westport, Conn., Greenwood Press, 1997. 315p. index. $65.00. ISBN 0-313-30430-0.

There are several subject-specific collections of quotations for the edification of writers and speakers (or the merely curious), and despite the title, this collection covers an immense field. The compilers have considered communications in the broadest sense of this increasingly popular area of specialization: reading, writing, journalism, photography, advertising, computers, listening, film, and public relations are just some of them. In all there are more than 3,000 quotations from 2,000 sources arranged under some 200 subject headings, ranging from acting, the Bible, conflict, dreams, money, peace, science, time, and women. There are Ibo proverbs, Oriental aphorisms, Greek and Latin quotations, and contemporary Western snippets, all offered in the interests of multiculturalism. But some of the quotations are of only tangible connection to communications, even when broadly defined. For example, Indira Gandhi's observation, "My theory is that men are no more liberated than women." And the questionable inclusion of Gorgias of Leontini on the subject of speech itself, "Logos dunastes megas," translated as "Speech is a mighty ruler," when Latin is no longer familiar to audiences, even of a scholarly nature. One of the commendable aspects of this anthology is the representation of women (about 15 percent of the quotations are drawn from their works) and somewhat surprisingly, the most-quoted author is Mark Twain, followed by Ralph Waldo Emerson, G. B. Shaw, and William Shakespeare. A great many low-culture sources have been included to advantage, for readers and listeners have long been led to believe that only canonical authors are worthy of quotation. This is a compilation that represents indefatigable searching by the compilers. One that will be a continuous source of help and pleasure to its users.—**Marian B. McLeod**

AUTHORSHIP

General Works

811. Bates, Jem. **The Canadian Writer's Market.** 13th rev. ed. Toronto, McClelland & Stewart, 1998. 378p. index. $19.99pa. ISBN 0-7710-8770-5. ISSN 1193-3305.

This book is roughly the Canadian equivalent to *Literary Market Place* (1995 ed.; see ARBA 95, entry 672). It is revised every two years, and now consists of mainly English-language publications and publishers only, plus many of the important bilingual publishers in Canada. Its sole purpose is to aid readers in how to get published in Canadian periodicals and Canadian books.

Most of the book is a directory, with many listings for magazines (e.g., consumer, literary, trade), daily newspapers, and book publishers. For each of the periodical listings, there are data on the title, address, telephone number, e-mail and Website addresses, editorial content, circulation and frequency, and payment fees. Other useful directory sections include lists of agents, awards, government support programs, writer organizations, and creative writing and journalism programs in Canada.

There is no section on writing or research, only markets and marketing. As well, there is nothing about the Internet, such as potential markets for selling a story or writing online. E-mail and Websites are mentioned only as a database field in the directory. Still, the book is as useful as it always has been.

—**Dean Tudor**

812. Fabio, William F. and James M. Plagianos, comps. **The Complete Guide to Literary Contests 1999.** Buffalo, N.Y., Prometheus Books, 1999. 525p. $22.95pa. ISBN 1-57392-261-7.

The purpose of this directory is to provide a comprehensive guide to literary contests, including those sponsored by national as well as local organizations. The compilers do not present their credentials for assuming this task beyond their affiliation with the Literary Fountain which, according to the entry in this publication, awards a small cash prize for creative writing to those applicants willing to submit their work for an entry fee. The directory is organized for browsing through an alphabetic table of contents arranged by sponsoring organization. However, without a detailed index, it is difficult for a writer with a particular focus to find an appropriate contest. Each directory entry contains address and contact information for the organization with submission guidelines and deadline for the contest. In some cases, an application form is provided. In spite of this extensive entry, it is understood that the applicant must take the responsibility to verify the accuracy of the information in this directory by contacting the sponsoring organization before submission to obtain current submission requirements and an official application form. Moreover, the appendixes do not represent a value-added feature to this directory. On the contrary, they reproduce information that is freely available on the Internet. Appendix A (copyright basics with the application form TX) has been lifted from the Copyright Office link on the Library of Congress homepage. Likewise, the canon of ethics of the Association of Authors' Representatives (appendix B) is accessible through the organizational Website. Clearly, the compilers do little more than offer an assemblage of material available through other publications. For example, appendix C, a directory of arts councils, is customarily included as a section of the *Writer's Market* (see entry 818). Librarians with patrons interested in literary contests are advised to consult the awards, prize contests, fellowships, and grants chapters of the most recent editions of the *Literary Market Place* (see entry 588) or the *Writer's Market*. They should also check out more specialized directories with awards information for fiction writers, such as the *Poet's Market* (see entry 818) or the *Novel & Short Story Writer's Market* (see entry 814). [R: LJ, 1 May 99, p. 68; Choice, July/Aug 99, p. 1920]—**David G. Nowak**

813. **Guide to Literary Agents, 1999: 500 Agents Who Sell What You Write.** Donya Dickerson, ed. Cincinnati, Ohio, Writer's Digest Books/F & W Publications, 1999. 360p. index. $19.99pa. ISBN 0-89879-878-7. ISSN 1078-6945.

Writers endlessly debate whether literary agents are necessary for publication. This book will not settle the issue, but it does offer practical advice and information to those who wish to find an agent. It identifies more than 500 literary or script agents who sell freelance writing. There are four sections of listings—literary agents, non–fee charging; literary agents, fee charging; script agents, non–fee charging and fee charging; and writer's conferences. With each agent listing, the publisher provides contact information, directions on how to contact, a list of the type of material represented, current needs, recent sales, terms, conferences they attend, and other helpful tips. In addition, agents are rated according to their openness to new writers. Other symbols identify changes in contact information, new listings, Canadian markets, closed markets, and whether the agent charges a fee to new writers. Some of the symbols are new to this edition or modified from previous symbols. The publishers have also added subheads to the listings, and section pages are striped for quick and easy reference. As in other Writer's Digest publications, the book contains articles that address practical concerns and pertinent issues, such as how to write query letters, how to outline a manuscript, and the conglomeration of publishing. Writer's conferences and other resources (e.g., professional organizations, Websites) are included as well and there are a number of indexes, some at the end of the book and some at the end of specific sections. Users may need to familiarize themselves with the organization of the book and its indexes, but the amount of current information will make the effort worthwhile. Although there are other guides that cover agents, this is the only annual publication and therefore an up-to-date and valuable resource for writers and the libraries that serve them.—**Barbara Ittner**

814. **Novel & Short Story Writer's Market, 1999: 2,000 Places to Sell Your Fiction.** Barbara Kuroff, ed. Cincinnati, Ohio, Writer's Digest Books/F & W Publications, 1999. 678p. illus. index. $22.99pa. ISBN 0-89879-876-0. ISSN 0897-9812.

Novel and Short Story Writer's Market offers so much more than a directory of fiction markets that perusing its pages is practically a prerequisite to getting published. This annual compilation of advice, essays, and listings is already a bible for many writers, and this edition's new features and topic sections further ranks it as a must-have.

Three new sections are geared especially to writers of mystery, romance, and science fiction and fantasy. These chapters begin with pearls of wisdom from successful writers including Mary Higgins Clark (suspense), Amanda Scott (romance), and Terry Brooks (fantasy). New alphabetic market listings by genre make it easy to flip right to the markets that publish in the area readers are interested in. Finally, individual genre resource groups—magazines, books, organizations, and online resources—are given.

Another new feature to ease the user's selection of possible publishers is the use of symbols at the beginning of each market entry that denote everything from easier markets for unpublished writers to markets that pay. A symbol of a briefcase with an "A" helps writers without agents avoid wasting time on markets where they are shut out. These same writers might find the new literary agent listings provide an excellent starting point to getting published. As always, markets listed include literary magazines, small circulation magazines, consumer magazines, small press houses, book publishers, and contests and awards. New to this edition is a section on markets for television and movie scripts.

Two extensive indexes, one by category (e.g., adventure, lesbian, military, religious) and another by medium (e.g., magazine, book publisher) make accessing information on relevant publishing outlets quick and easy. Quite a bit of relevant information is given for each of the more than 2,000 markets. This includes who to contact and how, average print order of a book, specific types of fiction needed, general contract terms, and advice from individuals within the specific publishing outlet.

Novel and Short Story Writer's Market offers a succinct alternative to the all-encompassing writers guides where the fiction market is just a niché amongst all the trade and journalistic outlets (see entry 818 for a review of *Writer's Market 2000*). The book's attention to providing such useful detail on the novel and short story market will keep this guide in the forefront of its own market for years to come.—**Deborah Cottin**

815. **Poet's Market, 1999: 1,800 Places to Publish Your Poetry.** Chantelle Bentley, ed. Cincinnati, Ohio, Writer's Digest Books/F & W Publications, 1998. 604p. index. $22.99pa. ISBN 0-89879-854-X. ISSN 0883-5470.

In the tradition of other Writer's Digest publications, this key guide to publishing opportunities for poets offers a wealth of useful information, clearly presented and affordably priced. The 1999 edition boasts listings for 1,100 journals and magazines, 200 chapbook publishers, 500 book publishers, and 200 contests. According to the publisher, that all adds up to 1,800 places to publish poetry, including 400 publishing opportunities new to this edition. The book also includes a guide to poetry submission etiquette, a key to symbols and abbreviations, and information on other resources (conferences and workshops, organizations, publications, Websites, and glossaries). Twelve "Insider Report" interviews with poets and publishing professionals offer readers insight into the business of poetry. To clarify the text, the editors have added subheads (e.g., editorial needs, submission requirements) to the publishers of poetry listings, and they have changed and added symbols (e.g., new, Canadian market, publishers who pay). General, geographical, subject, and chapbook indexes assist users in locating information for specific needs. As was noted in a previous review, the *Directory of Poetry Publishers* (see ARBA 98, entry 868) is a similar work with more specific subject indexes and several other helpful features. Most larger libraries should have both books.—**Barbara Ittner**

816. Woodward, Jeannette A. **Writing Research Papers: Investigating Resources in Cyberspace.** 2d ed. Lincolnwood, Ill., National Textbook, 1999. 317p. illus. index. $16.95 spiralbound. ISBN 0-8442-0332-7.

This is a basic undergraduate research paper or report writing text, with an overlay of Internet search strategies. Perhaps a major difference from other such books is the fact that the author is a librarian. This means a de-emphasis on writing styles and a re-emphasis on searching styles. That is a good thing. Topics include general research processes; selecting a topic; planning search strategies; reading, evaluating, and note taking; library resources; Internet resources; writing the paper through drafting and revising; and documentation styles. There is also an instructor's edition, which was not available for review.

Although LEXIS/NEXIS is mentioned, there is not much coverage of CD-ROMs or online databases in general. There still needs to be some material written here about computer applications, such as databases and spreadsheets (perhaps mapping software as well), clearly showing their roles in creating a definitive paper. And, of course, the section on the Internet is already outdated. Of the four proprietary services discussed on pages 182 to 183, three have already been blown away. Some Websites do not exist anymore. Other similar textbooks have listed the URL, which one can visit to download updates, but Woodward's does not (there is not even an e-mail address for the author or publisher). The best place to find out about the Internet is on the Internet itself, where all such updated materials are freely offered. Nevertheless, the binding is well done for a spiral book, the index is good (as you would expect from a librarian), there are useful reproductions of computer screens, and the price is certainly decent. [R: C&RL, July 98, pp. 390-392]—**Dean Tudor**

817. **The Writer's Handbook.** 2000 ed. Sylvia K. Burack, ed. Boston, Writer, 1999. 919p. index. $32.95. ISBN 0-87116-187-7.

For more than 60 years this handbook has served as a comprehensive resource for freelance writers seeking guidance on writing and marketing manuscripts (see ARBA 99, entry 832; ARBA 94, entry 999; ARBA 91, entry 945). Organized into 2 parts, the volume's strongest section continues to be section 1, with 110 chapters of how-to information from leading writers. The techniques, directed toward writing kinds of literature (e.g., poetry, mystery novels, greeting cards) and addressing specific audiences (e.g., young adults), remain enlightening, informative, and inspirational. The conversational interviews with eight famous writers (e.g., Doris Lessing) report on their experience and unique perspective as successful authors.

Part 2, resources for writers, offers 3,300 places to send manuscripts, along with useful listings of literary agents, writers' colonies, conferences, and arts councils. The articles market is divided into topical categories (e.g., travel, true crime) to aid the writer in locating a publisher. The brief descriptive entries are less informative than those found in *Writer's Market* (see entry 818). A glossary of key terms and an alphabetic index to the material in part 2 complete the volume. A detailed table of contents facilitates access to the volume's resources. The handbook is recommended for acquisition by public libraries. College and university libraries from institutions with writing programs should also consider its purchase.—**Sandra E. Belanger**

818. **Writer's Market, 2000: 8,000 Editors Who Buy What You Write.** electronic ed. Kirsten C. Holm and Donya Dickerson, eds. Cincinnati, Ohio, F & W Publications, 1999. 1112p. index. $49.99pa. (with disc). ISBN 0-89879-916-3.

The latest edition of this must-have handbook for the writing market gives more information than ever before on how to get published. The three largest sections of the book are market listings of book publishers; consumer magazines; and trade, technical, and professional journals. Users will also find market listings for scriptwriting, syndicates, greeting cards, and contests and awards. Each listing contains information about the editorial focus of the market, how it prefers material to be submitted, payment information, and other helpful tips. The editors have also indicated whether or not markets will accept queries by e-mail.

This edition has been revised to include a list of 60 literary and 20 script agents. All of these agents have indicated a willingness to work with new, previously unpublished writers as well as more established authors. Most are members of the Association of Authors' Representatives (AAR) or the Writers Guild of America (WGA). As in previous editions the editors have included articles from professionals in the writing field with helpful tips and information on getting published. For example, the "Query Letter Clinic" showcases "good" and "bad" letters with comments straight from editors about what attracted and what distracted.

Seeing as how there is no user guide provided for the CD-ROM, it is recommended that users who are not computer savvy stick to the print version. Otherwise, users who have a general knowledge of navigating computer programs will have no problem installing and using the *Writer's Market* CD-ROM. Searching for the appropriate market for a writer's work is greatly improved on the CD-ROM as opposed to the print version. User's need only select specific criterion and their computer will select the most promising market opportunities along with all of the submission information provided in the print version. As an added bonus the CD-ROM also provides a submission tracker for writers to save time and stay organized. This work is highly recommended for all reference collections in university and public libraries. Serious writers should consider obtaining their own personal copies.—**Cari Ringelheim**

Style Manuals

819. Gibaldi, Joseph. **MLA Handbook for Writers of Research Papers.** 5th ed. New York, Modern Language Association of America, 1999. 332p. index. $14.50pa. ISBN 0-87352-975-8.

There were 7 years between the 3d and 4th (1995) editions of this classic style manual. Now the 5th edition has made its debut. As in previous editions, the handbook takes the reader through the mechanics of the research paper. It covers selection and narrowing a topic, outlining, note taking, spelling, punctuation, and formatting. It also covers the use of print and online library catalogs and indexes. The documentation and citation sections cover all types of sources, both print and nonprint. Section headings are in red and citation examples are in a different font, making them easy to locate and identify.

Although the information about print sources remains unchanged, this edition expands the coverage of electronic sources. What was called "Citing Online Databases" has become "Citing Electronic Publications" and has tripled in length. The section now includes instructions on citing information databases, online books and periodicals, and Websites including personal Web pages. There are also guidelines (as yet there are no agreed-upon standards) for works that will be submitted electronically.

Another valuable revision is the updated list of selected reference works by field. New titles and editions are included as well as online sources and CD-ROM products.

This new edition of a standard reference tool addresses the rapidly evolving needs of today's students and will once again prove its value in college and public libraries.—**Marlene M. Kuhl**

820. Kinzie, Mary. **A Poet's Guide to Poetry.** Chicago, University of Chicago Press, 1999. 561p. index. (Chicago Guide to Writing, Editing, and Publishing). $47.00; $18.00pa. ISBN 0-226-43738-8; 0-226-43739-6pa.

Best suited for academic and public libraries that interact with campus and community creative writing programs, this highly detailed guide will benefit beginning poets, poets to be, and those readers who enjoy reading and analyzing poetry. Written by a poet, critic, and editor who founded the creative writing program at Northwestern University, this excellent guide will enrich those who have the time and the determination to work with it. It is clearly not fare for freshman English programs.

Following a helpful and necessary introduction, the volume is divided into three parts: "Elements of Relation and Resemblance," which discusses syntax, diction, rhetoric and rhythm; "Elements, Controlled in Time," which addresses meter, stanza, rhyme, and rhythm; and "Writing in Form," which carries exercises for beginning and advanced writers, a 100–page section of poetic terms that are all listed in bold typeface throughout the preceding two parts, and an excellent well–annotated bibliography for further reading. Concluding the volume are a "List of Poems by Form," where poems (and parts of poems) cited in the text are listed according to their form (e.g., couplets, quatrains, sonnets, free verse). An author/title index and a subject index follow. Because this volume walks that thin line between a reference and a circulating book, libraries intending it for their reference collection would please their users by adding a paper copy or two as well to their circulating collection.—**Charles R. Andrews**

821. Todd, Loreto. **The Cassell Guide to Punctuation.** repr. ed. New York, Cassell, 1998. 128p. index. $9.95pa. ISBN 0-304-34961-5.

Using correct and consistent punctuation in one's writing is imperative to ensuring that it will be understood by readers. This simple guide helps explains some of the more confusing rules of punctuation. Its slim and concise style makes it ideal as a ready-reference.

The book begins with an introduction that explains how rules of writing have changed over the past few centuries and what the latest trends in writing are today—mainly that writing is simpler with fewer punctuation marks. It then provides a dictionary of the marks discussed in the guide and gives examples of how and when they are to be used. The majority of the punctuation marks discussed are common, but there are a few (e.g., obelisk, virgule) that were new to this reviewer, suggesting they are very rarely used in current writing. The last section of the guide, "Punctuation in Use," compares how the use of punctuation varies from American writing to British writing.

This style guide will be helpful for those needing a ready-reference just on this particular subject. Other more comprehensive style manuals, such as *The Chicago Manual of Style* (14th ed.; see ARBA 94, entry 1001), will most likely be used by the typical writer who will probably have style questions that go beyond just punctuation.—**Shannon M. Graff**

822. Walker, Janice R., and Todd Taylor. **The Columbia Guide to Online Style.** New York, Columbia University Press, 1998. 218p. index. $17.50pa. ISBN 0-231-10788-9; 0-231-10789-7.

In cyberdom, there are no title pages, versos, or colophons—few of the familiar bibliographic signposts and conventions by which scholars and students have traditionally charted and documented the course of their research and writing. In fact, as Janice Walker and Todd Taylor discuss in their perceptive preface and introduction to *The Columbia Guide to Online Style*, the very notions of single authorship and linear discourse often fall by the wayside once that property is staked on the Web or other online venues. In the face of this complex and often inchoate new communications landscape, Walker and Taylor have made commendable strides toward establishing effective new standards for "ensuring scholarly integrity" in terms of both publishing and citing online academic research and correspondence. *The Columbia Guide* differs in a number of significant respects from the established style manual trinity—the MLA, Chicago, and APA. While the most recent editions of those venerable publications deal cautiously with some electronic sources, they unfortunately miss the precipitous rise of academic publishing on the Web in the last five years. In contrast, *The Columbia Guide* devotes a substantial chapter to WWW citation, as well as to a panoply of other electronic sources missed (or neglected) by the other manuals, including video games, graphic files, chat rooms, and other electronic ephemera. A bolder and generally less successful attempt is also made to establish standards and guidelines for academic Web authors (there is something slightly off in addressing standard publishing conventions in a hypertextual world). Perhaps the most notable innovation of *The Columbia Guide*—distinguishing it most from the other style guides—is its "element oriented" approach to style. Rather than prescribing a hard-and-fast, discipline-oriented citation style, *The Columbia Guide* attempts to define a core of essential bibliographic elements that can be applied to a variety of already established style guides and used in a wide variety of situations. While the MLA, APA, and Chicago manuals may eventually catch up to the realities of new scholarly media, it is unlikely that they will match Walker and Taylor's comprehensiveness, or their levelheaded grasp of what it means to do academic business in an increasingly online world. An essential addition to all libraries, portions of *The Columbia Guide* can be viewed online at http://www.columbia.edu/cu/cup/cgos/idx_basic.html. [R: LJ, 1 Sept 98, p. 175]
—**Gary Handman**

RADIO, TELEVISION, AUDIO, AND VIDEO

823. **AV Market Place 1999: The Complete Business Directory of Products & Services for the Audio Video Industry....** New Providence, N.J., R. R. Bowker, 1999. 1489p. index. $165.00pa. ISBN 0-8352-4098-3. ISSN 1044-0445.

Somehow it seems a bit presumptuous in this age of information, technology, and rapid change to use the word "complete" instead of, perhaps, "comprehensive." However, the editor gracefully acknowledges that, in a project of such magnitude, there may be errors and omissions and asks to be informed about the errors and changes. An updating method is available on the Internet and directions are given to obtain a correction form. In addition, an editorial revision form is included within the volume.

An introductory page clearly explains how to use this volume, and another page lists the section contents with a brief and useful explanation of what information is contained in each section. For guidance, an example is provided. The sections—associations, film and television commissions, awards and festivals, calendar, periodicals, reference books, and industry yellow pages—contain logically organized and user-friendly information. Again, comments or suggestions regarding the content and format are encouraged. Industry-specific acronyms are given.

In a reference of such size, not only is it imperative to have accurate information, but it must be the information needed by potential users. Further, the organization of each section and the indexes is critical; they must be logical and easily understood. This reference admirably meets these criteria and will be welcomed by those in and working with the industry.—**Karen D. Harvey**

824. **Bacon's Radio Directory 1999: Directory of Radio Networks and Stations with Program Contacts.** 13th ed. Chicago, Bacon's Information, 1998. 1662p. index. $285.00pa. ISSN 1088-9647.

Now in its 13th edition, *Bacon's Radio Directory* provides a listing of more than 27,000 station, network, and radio show outlets and some 141,000 broadcast personnel. The 1999 edition contains several additional features, including "lead times," radio guest information, product usage, contact preferences for shows, and an expanded television and radio advertising listing. Also included is a list of television and video news releases used by individual television stations. Additional features that are continued include Arbitron Ratings for the top 100 markets and a list of all available Web pages and e-mail addresses. The work is cross-referenced using a number of separate lists, including an index of radio station counts by state, an index of radio station counts by format, national radio networks, regional radio networks, radio syndicators, and radio stations. Additional indexes include radio programs by title, radio programs by topic, syndicated radio programs, an index of call letters, and an alphabetic index of multiple radio owners.

Bacon's Radio Directory has very quickly become the standard reference source in the industry. The typical entry contains the call letters of the station, the address and telephone numbers, Web page and e-mail information, information on the audience and coverage of the station, Arbitron rankings, the name of the owner or owners, a profile of the type of broadcasting, and a list of the name of the major management personnel.

Other directories that cover radio include *Broadcasting & Cable Market Place: The Industry Source for Radio, Television, and Cable* (see ARBA 93, entry 992), *The Broadcasting & Cable Yearbook* (R. R. Bowker, 1993-), and the *FM Atlas and Station Directory* (FM Atlas Publications, 1977-). None of these sources have the coverage of *Bacon's Radio Directory*, and all tend to fill a smaller niche in the broadcasting world. *Bacon's Radio Directory* is recommended for all larger public and academic libraries, and especially for college libraries that serve communications departments that offer degrees in radio and television.
—**Robert L. Wick**

825. **Bacon's TV/Cable Directory 1999: Directory of TV/Cable Networks and Stations with Program Contacts.** 13th ed. Chicago, Bacon's Information, 1998. 926p. maps. index. $285.00pa. ISSN 1088-9655.

According to the publisher of this work, the purpose of *Bacon's TV/Cable Directory 1999* is to "provide the most extensive broadcast industry listings in the U.S." With more than 27,700 network, station, and show outlets and some 141,000 broadcast personnel included, the volume seems to have met its goal. The directory provides lists by television and cable networks, television syndicators, television stations, and cable satellite systems. Other information includes television and cable systems counts by state, an index of television and cable programs by title and by topic, television stations by network affiliation, a call letter index, major market maps, syndicated programming, and satellite and PBS networks. The listings for national and regional networks include addresses, telephone numbers, fax numbers, and Website addresses. Personnel listings with titles, telephone numbers, and e-mail addresses are also included. Entries for local stations provide information pertaining to address, executive personnel, locally produced programming, and personnel and affiliations. The directory lists regional cable satellite systems that have locally produced programs or public access channels. The volume also gives the Arbitron ratings for the top 100 markets. This extensive volume provides a lot of information for a variety of uses. A table of contents makes for easier use, especially because there is no comprehensive index, only indexes of television programs by title, topic, and syndication.—**Janet Hilbun**

826. Cox, Jim. **The Great Radio Soap Operas.** Jefferson, N.C., McFarland, 1999. 331p. illus. index. $55.00. ISBN 0-7864-0589-9.

This reference work provides detailed descriptions of 31 radio soap operas that graced the airwaves from 1930 to 1960. As the predecessor of the popular television version of soap operas today, the radio received the same kind of attention and following in their day. This work discusses each series' story line; provides in-depth information on each character; lists producers, directors, writers, announcers, casts, sponsors, ratings, and broadcast dates; and provides the times of day and network on which the show was featured. The author is a lifelong fan of radio and his enthusiasm for the medium is apparent through his clear writing and in-depth research. An annotated bibliography and an index conclude the volume. This resource has a rather limited audience but will be welcome in libraries that have patrons researching radio or communications history.—**Shannon M. Graff**

827. **Encyclopedia of Television News.** Michael D. Murray, ed. Phoenix, Ariz., Oryx Press, 1999. 315p. illus. index. $69.00. ISBN 1-57356-108-8.

The *Encyclopedia of Television News* is a compilation of profiles of national-level, U.S. television news journalists and personalities, articles on the history of network and major cable news operations, articles on the involvement of television news in major historical events, and summaries of major trends in television journalism. Coverage stretches back to the early days of television news. The alphabetically arranged entries are written by nearly 100 faculty of communications or journalism from throughout the United States. The entries are, for the most part, uncritical, engaging, and superficial. A resource list at the end of each entry provides suggestions for further reading. A thorough index provides access to people and events not given their own entries, but mentioned as significant in another entry. Some thought has been given to coverage of major events and the news' impact on those events. Some articles also address when the profession has become newsworthy, such as the trend toward "happy news" or "tabloid television." Focus on individuals is significantly skewed toward on-air personalities, although some coverage is given to news directors or other off-air personnel who have had impact on the medium. Profiles are often inconsistent with an individual's impact in the profession. Daniel Schorr's impressive 60-year career is distilled down to less than a one-half–page entry, whereas Willard Scott receives nearly a full page. There are other inconsistencies in selection of individuals for coverage. Deborah Norville merits an entry and photograph, yet Paula Zahn receives a brief mention in the article on women in television news.

The *Encyclopedia of Television News* provides value by gathering information into one resource, eliminating the need to consult biographical, historical, or technical reference works separately. Unfortunately, this encyclopedia does not expand on its subject with enough depth to effectively substitute for these other works. [R: BL, 15 Feb 99, pp. 1088-1089; Choice, June 1999, p. 1752; BR, Sept/Oct 99, p. 81]—**Lynne M. Fox**

828. Payton, Gordon, and Martin Grams Jr. **The CBS Radio Mystery Theater: An Episode Guide and Handbook to Nine Years of Broadcasting, 1974-1982.** Jefferson, N.C., McFarland, 1999. 475p. index. $65.00. ISBN 0-7864-0559-7.

For almost a decade, radio audiences were entertained and enthralled by the sinister stories and scary sounds brought to them by the "CBS Radio Mystery Theater." This award-winning series, produced and directed by Himan Brown and hosted initially by E. G. Marshall and later by Tammy Grimes, featured a number of actors who are better known for their television or film roles, for instance, Keir Dullea, Celeste Holm, John Lithgow, and Mercedes McCambridge. During its nine-year run it was a daily staple in thousands of homes, and it has earned many new fans in syndication.

Obviously a labor of love for the compilers, who gathered their information from an archive of CBS press releases and interviews with a number of individuals involved with the show's production, this compendium lists and describes all the programs that were broadcast during the original run of the series. Arranged in chronological sequence, the 2,970 numbered entries provide the title of the episode, the date it originally aired, and its rebroadcast date. The first listing for each of the 1,404 original episodes also identifies the cast and the writer and includes a brief synopsis of the plot. In addition, many entries include interesting notes and anecdotes regarding the performers or the episode. Appendixes provide logs for the "CBS/General Mills Radio Adventure Theater," which was a spin-off of "Mystery Theater" intended for a younger audience, and the 6-month revival of "Mystery Theater" in 1998. The volume also features a 6-page history of the series and an excellent index to titles, actors and actresses, and writers.

Providing a fascinating glimpse into the history of radio and radio drama, this compilation will be of greatest interest to libraries that are developing comprehensive collections in the area of popular culture or mass media.—**Marie Ellis**

829. Terrace, Vincent. **Radio Programs, 1924-1984: A Catalog of Over 1800 Shows.** Jefferson, N.C., McFarland, 1999. 399p. illus. index. $75.00. ISBN 0-7864-0351-9.

Because the field of radio programs is characterized by a relative dearth of reference tools, any addition to that small corpus should be greeted with almost automatic acceptance. *Radio Programs, 1924-1984* might do just that. It provides the most current and broadest coverage of any of its competing titles.

The more than 1,800 listings provide casts, character relationships, story lines, announcers, musicians, producers, hosts, regulars, dates, networks, running times, and many program openings and closings. A unique feature is the appendix of "lost" programs—those about which very little is known. Illustrations generously (and delightfully) pepper the text. Cross-references consistently point to the more appropriate heading; for example, "Topper," the more common name, directs the user to the official "Adventures of Topper." Because the cross-references and the alphabetic arrangement facilitate access to the titles of the radio shows, it would appear that the sole purpose of the index is to provide access to the names of those involved in all areas of production and performance. The index falls short, however, in that it lacks references to the names of characters in shows. For example, this reference tool is absolutely useless if one needs to look up "Ish Kabibble" but knows neither the show nor the actor who portrayed him.

Otherwise shadowed by the exhaustive comprehensiveness of John Dunning's *On the Air: The Encyclopedia of Old-Time Radio* (Oxford University Press, 1998), the tool this directory most closely resembles is Terrace's earlier *Radio's Golden Years* (see ARBA 82, entry 1242). One important difference between the two is that *Radio Programs* expands the time coverage by retrogressing 6 years at the beginning and appending 24 at the other. Its scope is still restricted, however, to national programs; coverage of local programming, a massive undertaking, would be fertile ground for a future endeavor. One has the feeling that considering the ephemeral oral nature of the radio medium, it would be best to compile as much as possible while it is still possible to cull it from actual programs. *Radio Programs* is a step forward in that direction. [R: Choice, April 99, p. 1435; BL, 15 Feb 99, pp. 1092-1093]—**Lawrence Olszewski**

21 Decorative Arts

COLLECTING

General Works

830. **The Charlton Standard Catalogue of Royal Doulton Beswick Figurines.** 6th ed. By Jean Dale. Toronto, Charlton Press, 1998. 476p. illus. index. $24.95pa. ISBN 0-88968-212-7. ISSN 0228-6947.

First published more than 15 years ago and now in its 6th edition, this catalog covers over 100 years of Royal Doulton figurines. Listing over 3,500 models, this edition covers vellum and stoneware figures produced at the Lambeth studio; HN, CL, and M series models; and Beswick figurines. Entries contain a black-and-white photograph (when available), descriptions, and cross-references. The descriptions include height, color, issue date, the HN number for all variations, series information, and current market value price. The catalog also features a history of Royal Doulton figures, tips on building a collection, and a guide to back-stamps and dating. In addition, the book provides information on places to buy figurines and on the Royal Doulton International Collectors Club. The work concludes with and alphabetic index and another by type or series.—**Cari Ringelheim**

831. *Collector's Mart* **Magazine Price Guide to Limited Edition Collectibles, 1999.** Mary L. Sieber, ed. Iola, Wis., Krause Publications, 1998. 894p. illus. index. $17.95pa. ISBN 0-87341-646-5.

This book is the 4th edition of *Collector's Mart Magazine Price Guide to Limited Edition Collectibles*. The editors and staff have taken the information from the 3d edition, studied it, added to it, and updated it to create an incredible resource of nearly 60,000 prices that covers the broad spectrum of limited edition collectibles.

The goal of the book is to provide a guide listing thousands of secondary market (the market collectibles enter after they have left the original, primary point of retail sales) prices covering the gamut of limited edition collectibles including bells, cottages, dolls, figurines, ornaments, plates, prints, and steins. The book has been divided into categories that make it easy for readers to find the information relevant to the items they collect. An introduction precedes each section and summarizes many of the trends occurring in today's marketplace. Items within the listings are arranged alphabetically, first by company name, then by series name, and finally by the artist's last name. They are further organized chronologically by the year the collectible was issued, then alphabetically by the title of the piece. Folios at the top of each page mark each section and make flipping through the book quick and easy. Two indexes at the back of the book help readers locate items for which they may not have the necessary information.

This one-of-a-kind resource gives the reader almost 60,000 listings, with more than 200 photographs for easy identification. This book would be a help to those who are interested in collecting and seeing the market value of their collectibles.—**Barbara B. Goldstein**

832. Maloney, David J., Jr. **Maloney's Antiques & Collectibles Resource Directory.** 5th ed. Dubuque, Iowa, Antique Trader Books, 1999. 856p. $29.95pa. ISBN 1-58221-016-0. ISSN 1083-8449.

David J. Maloney, the author of this resource, is a nationally known appraiser, author, radio talk show guest, and lecturer. He is a full-time professional personal property appraiser, specializing in the valuation of antiques and collectibles.

Many people look at *Maloney's Antiques & Collectibles Resource Directory* as just a place to find a contact in order to buy or sell an item, but the book is much more than that. The book also provides valuable information on the legalities of buying and selling certain types of items as well as resources for learning more about fakes and reproductions. Readers will be able to find appraisers, repair services, matching services, suppliers of parts, and even auction services within the pages of this book. The best part of all this is that everything in *Maloney's* is also online in an easily searchable format.

In addition to thousands of new and updated listings and scores of new categories, the 5th edition of *Maloney's* includes the following important features: a greatly expanded cross-referencing system where readers are directed to the relevant categories that might contain information of interest; four important appendixes for educated and tested appraisers, auction services, general-interest periodicals, and repair firms; a redesigned and highly detailed index; and nearly 7,500 listings with Websites and more than 9,500 e-mail addresses. The goal of this book is to place as much information as possible at users' fingertips to allow them to make decisions based on knowledge and fact.

Prior to *Maloney's*, there was no organized method to capture, preserve, collate, and distribute collector resource information to efficiently keep the public accurately informed on a continuing basis. *Maloney's* is designed to overcome this shortfall through frequent updating and regular publication.

This is the reader's one-stop reference for contacting fellow collectors who might want to buy items they own. It also helps readers in identifying the recognized experts in thousands of collectibles categories and locating an appraiser or auction house that specializes in antiques and collectibles. Furthermore, it will help readers in seeking out and joining the most popular collector clubs and organizations, and subscribing to books and magazines devoted to the special areas of interest. It can also be used to find out where to get parts, have repairs done, and where to go to match a pattern.

Maloney's Antiques & Collectibles Resource Directory is the one book that savvy collectors, knowledgeable dealers, and professional appraisers and claims adjusters depend on as a basis for their research. Whether readers buy, sell, trade, or collect contemporary, traditional, or the most rare and unusual items, *Maloney's Directory* has the information they want and need.—**Barbara B. Goldstein**

Antiques

833. Adams, Carol, comp. **Guide to the Antique Shops of Britain 1997/8.** Wappingers Falls, N.Y., Antique Collectors' Club, 1997. 763p. illus. maps. index. $29.50. ISBN 1-85149-264-X.

Sturdily bound and printed on glossy stock, this guide provides detailed information about shops in England, the Channel Islands, Northern Ireland, Scotland, and Wales. Arrangement is geographic, opening with the London shops filed by name within postal districts. The counties are in alphabetic sequence with entries grouped by town. A map of each county indicates the distribution of shops; for towns with more than 25, there is also a street plan. Each entry, nearly 6,000 in total, follows a standard format based on the questionnaire printed at the back of the book: shop name and address, owner name, professional affiliation, date of establishment, hours, stock with price range (and sometimes items not stocked), parking information, directions, telephone, fax, fairs the dealer participates in, and services such as valuations. For multiple-dealer shops, individual coverage varies with some London markets (Alfies, Grays, and Antiquarius) each listing more than 100 dealers, while others, particularly at Portobello, only indicate total numbers and the nature of the stock. Following the entries (pp. 32–592) are geographic directories of packers and shippers, auctioneers, a calendar of fairs, and services including The Dummy Book Company, which supply faux book spines (p. 641). There is an alphabetic index of towns with county name to get the reader into the correct section, although "N. Yorks" in the index is Yorkshire North in the directory. Two indexes complete the work, both with geographic rather than page references: a classified list grouping specialist dealers in about 60 categories and a list of the dealers by both business and personal name. Published by specialists in the decorative arts, this guide is a standard sourcebook for collectors and the trade.—**Patricia Fleming**

834. **Antique Trader's Books, Antiques, & Collectibles Price Guide.** 2000 annual ed. Kyle Husfloen, ed. Dubuque, Iowa, Antique Trader Books, 1999. 882p. illus. index. $15.95pa. ISBN 1-58221-017-9.

Now in its 16th edition, this guide is alphabetically arranged by type of item to provide descriptions and current market prices for antiques and "hot" collectibles. Under such broad categories as ceramics, glass, and furniture, items are subdivided by type or manufacturer, and again alphabetically. As in other editions, contributors to the guide are listed, and a general index leads users to items of interest. What sets the 2000 edition apart from previous years is its more numerous black-and-white photographs of items listed as well as a special full-color supplement, a 32-page essay entitled "A Century of Collecting" by appraiser Emyl Jenkins. Here she gives an interesting overview of the history of collecting—a twentieth-century phenomenon that is rapidly growing in popularity.—**Lori D. Kranz**

Autographs

835. Keating, Kevin, and Michael Kolleth. **The Negro League Autograph Guide.** Norfolk, Va., Tuff Stuff Publications/Landmark Specialty Books, 1999. 271p. illus. $24.95pa. ISBN 0-930625-51-X.

Autograph collecting, particularly of athletes, has always been a popular hobby. In *The Negro League Autograph Guide* the authors provide a detailed look at a subset of the hobby, collecting signatures of former Negro league players. The book consists of 3 parts: "Negro Leagues Baseball: The Game . . . and the Hobby," "Autograph Collecting Basics," and "Negro Leagues Autographs." Appendixes include a glossary of sports autograph terms, a guide to grading signature condition, "Namesakes and Ghosts," collectors' challenges, and selected reference sources.

Following a brief history of the Negro leagues, the authors discuss the development of collecting Negro league autographs. They date the beginning of the specialized hobby from 1971, when Satchel Paige was inducted into the Baseball Hall of Fame. By the 1990s, following Negro league reunions and an Upper Deck Company promotion, demand for Negro league signatures increased. Reunion shows have become part of the hobby calendar, and some dealers have begun specializing in Negro league items. Collectors are urged to set goals for their hobby, and not necessarily to view them as an investment. Chapters on detecting forgeries, valuing and pricing autographs, and acquiring signatures by mail will be useful to neophytes in the hobby as a whole as well as those choosing Negro league players as a niche.

The main part of the book focuses on 110 historically significant Negro league players and administrators. They do not include stars such as Hank Aaron, Ernie Banks, Jim Gilliam, Willie Mays, or Don Newscombe who debuted in the Negro leagues but are best known for their accomplishments in the major leagues. For the players listed in chapter 8, information for each includes player names (the name by which each was known and his legal name), the years he was active in baseball, year and place of birth and death, a brief overview of his career, and a photograph. The meat of each entry is at least one carefully analyzed signature example. A glossary of terms used in the analyses is also included. The entries conclude with scarcity ratings of signatures within the hobby and price guidelines. Signature samples are noted with their source (team-signed sheets, postal requests, checks, and legal documents). The bibliography includes books on the Negro leagues; baseball in general; autograph collecting; and Websites for the Baseball Hall of Fame, the Negro leagues, and Negro league collectors.

Because of the specialized nature of this title, it is recommended primarily for libraries with extensive baseball or African American interest collections. The information on autograph collecting in general, however, makes the book a suggested acquisition for libraries whose clientele is interested in the hobby. This is an excellent resource for its niche.—**Sue Kamm**

Books

836. Bookman's Price Index, Volume 60: A Guide to the Values of Rare and Other Out of Print Books. Anne F. McGrath, ed. Farmington Hills, Mich., Gale, 1999. 1073p. $280.00. ISBN 0-7876-3314-3. ISSN 0068-0141.

Published three times per year, this price guide to the U.S., Canadian, and British market in antiquarian books is of primary interest to book dealers and collectors. Most of the 15,000 or so books in the volume at hand are priced in the 3 figures, as reflected in the recent inventories of 83 antiquarian booksellers. Each volume of *Bookman's Price Index* (BPI) lists approximately 15,000 books alphabetically by author and then by title. Multiple editions of a title are listed by publication date, from earliest to latest. Anonymous works are arranged alphabetically by title. As in all BPI volumes, condition (edition, size, illustrations, binding, author signature) is fully described. The bookseller's name, catalog number, and price (which can be higher than the price charged to a walk-in customer) follow each description. At the end of BPI are three short sections: association copies (books with prominent owners), fine bindings, and books with fore-edge paintings. Although the latter features are also noted in the main alphabetic section of BPI, these listings notify dealers and collectors of the existence and pricing of such special books.

Only the most successful antiquarian book dealers can afford to purchase the BPI series. Many prefer the annual *Book Prices, Used and Rare* (Spoon River Press), whose 1999 edition lists 32,000 books and costs only $75. In light of the time-sensitive nature of the antiquarian book market, and the increasing prevalence of booksellers' Websites that tend to be updated frequently, the need for "hard-copy" book-pricing references is dwindling rapidly and will probably vanish altogether.—**Lori D. Kranz**

837. Huxford's Old Book Value Guide: 25,000 Listings of Old Books with Current Values. 11th ed. Paducah, Ky., Collector Books, 1999. 442p. $19.95. ISBN 1-57432-119-6.

Not only does this book place values that an interested party would be willing to pay to obtain possession of nearly 25,000 books, it also lists scores of buyers along with the type of material each is interested in purchasing. These prices are taken from dealers' selling lists that have been issued within the past year.

Huxford's Old Book Value Guide places values on the more common holdings that many seem to accumulate. The majority of books listed in this guide are in the $10 to $40 range. The format of this guide is very simple: Listings are alphabetized first by the name of the author, translator, editor, or illustrator, and if more than one book is listed for a particular author, each title is listed alphabetically under his or her name. When pseudonyms are known, names have been cross-referenced. Dust jackets or wrappers are noted when present, and sizes (when given) are approximate. Condition is usually noted as well. If the condition is not stated, it is assumed to be very good. Dates within parentheses indicate the copyright dates while dates without parentheses are dates found on title pages or are the actual publication dates.

There is also a listing of book buyers according to the topic or theme of the book (i.e., art, aviation, bibliographies, civil war, farming, and so on). These topics are arranged alphabetically for ease of use. This book would prove worthwhile to those who have books they want to either learn the value of or sell.

—**Barbara B. Goldstein**

Coins (and Paper Money)

838. Bressett, Kenneth. **Guide Book of United States Currency.** 3d ed. New York, Golden Books; distr., New York, St. Martin's Press, 1999. 336p. illus. $15.95pa. ISBN 0-307-48003-8.

This work is similar in format to other Whitman products, such as the *Guide Book of United States Coins* (see entry 841). This 3d edition has been extensively revised from the previous version. Within the first few pages are explanatory material on grades, terminology, various collection specialties, detecting counterfeits, and a brief history of U.S. currency. Nearly 30 recognized authorities contributed to this work.

The rest of the book is devoted to listing, in chronological order, every type and major variety of U.S. paper money from the Treasury Notes of 1812 to date. Included are large-size, small-size, and fractional currency. Each entry includes a black-and-white photograph, description, and a value for a few representative grades. Some historical discussion of design and engraving variations begins each major section. Due to the volatility of the collectibles market, these values should be considered approximate only. A bibliography is provided at the end of the book.

The book is packed with information. Even if one is not a collector of currency, the historical insight here is well worth the reading. Color photographs would have been nice, but the black-and-white photographs are as sharp as the original objects would allow. The *Guide Book of United States Currency* is highly recommended for public and general academic collections.—**Margaret F. Dominy**

839. Bressett, Kenneth. **The Whitman Guide to Coin Collecting: A Beginner's Guide to the World of Coins.** New York, St. Martin's Press, 1999. 246p. illus. index. $11.95pa. ISBN 0-307-48008-9.

As the subtitle "A Beginner's Guide to the World of Coins" reveals, this guidebook is aimed at the beginning coin collector, and is designed to fill a need for basic information about how to get started in the coin collecting hobby and how to avoid costly mistakes. Guidebooks of this nature have appeared frequently, but many of them are out of print or out of date. The author's credentials are impressive; he is a former president of the American Numismatic Association and long-time coeditor of the renowned *Guide Book of United States Coins* (see entry 841) and the *Handbook of United States Coins* (see entry 842), also known respectively as "the red book" and "the blue book," the most trusted and most used references in the field of numismatics for decades.

The reader is introduced to coin collecting as a hobby. The book includes such information as where collectible coins can be obtained, sources for learning the history of coins, how to care for a collection, how coins are graded and priced, and information about special coins (e.g., commemorative issues, counterfeits, other interesting and collectible coinage). A chapter addressing an area that has generated more interest in recent years is devoted to coins as an investment and discusses when it is time to sell. A catalog chapter gives current values for all U.S. coins that sell for substantial premiums over their face value. Explanations are well written and the black-and-white illustrations are excellent. There are occasional errors, as where it is stated that "Barber design coins dated back to the late eighteenth century were still in circulation in the 1940s and '50s." Barber-designed coins were issued in the late nineteenth century, from 1892 to 1916, as shown in the catalog chapter of this book. The widespread interest in coins as collectibles and investments makes this book a welcome addition to any library.—**Larry Lobel**

840. Friedberg, Arthur L., and Ira S. Friedberg. **Paper Money of the United States: A Complete Illustrated Guide with Valuations.** 15th ed. Clifton, N.J., Coin & Currency Institute, 1998. 336p. illus. $35.00. ISBN 0-87184-515-6.

Everyone is excited by the look and feel of money because of the unlimited possibilities presented by having a fistful of greenbacks. But paper money is also fascinating to many for the rich glimpses of history, art, finance, politics, and culture it provides. This guide lives up to its claim to being a complete pictorial, descriptive, and numismatic history of the currency of the United States. The fronts and backs of all types of currency are illustrated, accompanied by descriptive text and current market pricing for every variety issued. Included are large- and small-size notes, fractional currency and encased postage stamps, colonial and continental currency, and Confederate states notes. Appendixes include a complete list of the thousands of national banks throughout the United States that used to issue their own legal tender currency and tables showing signatures and dates of issue. A unique section, new to this edition, pictures a nearly complete collection of United States large-size currency. It consists of color replications of 192 bank notes from the collection of the Federal Reserve Bank of San Francisco.

Revised and updated many times during the last 45 years, this 15th edition continues to be an invaluable reference work for numismatists and currency collectors; and also possesses an appeal to students and devotees of Americana, the art of engraving, history, and economics. While there have been welcome improvements, it is disappointing that the quality of paper and printing seems to have declined, despite claims to the contrary. Compared to the 11th edition, the currency reproductions in the newer edition appear dark and muddy, and the paper is thinner and not as bright. For this reason, it may be preferable to keep an older edition until the problem is corrected in future editions.—**Larry Lobel**

841. Yeoman, R. S. **A Guide Book of United States Coins 2000.** 53d ed. New York, St. Martin's Press, 1999. 336p. illus. index. $8.95 spiralbound. ISBN 0-307-48004-6.

This work is the standard for the numismatist. In its 53d annual edition, it provides illustrations, suggested prices for a variety of coin grades, and mintage history of U.S. coins 1616 to date. A history of U.S. coinage, a description of the American Numismatic Association (ANA) grading system, and a frank discussion of rare coin investing can be found at the beginning of the book. More than 90 contributors, who are recognized authorities, are also included within the first few pages.

The main part of the book is the listing, chronologically, of all U.S. coinage used or minted from the earliest colonial period to the present time. Each listing is accompanied by a high-resolution photograph for identification purposes, a description, and a value for various grades of the object. Due to the volatility of the coin market it must be pointed out that these values should be treated purely as benchmarks. The collector should not depend on the literal values in any kind of trade or transaction.

This edition has maintained the high quality of the previous versions. The type font is clear and crisp and the color photographs are sharp, including enlargements for clarification of marks or errors. A bibliography is provided at the end of each section. The spiral binding allows for flat viewing, a convenience when holding a coin. This resource is highly recommended for public and general academic collections.

—**Margaret F. Dominy**

842. Yeoman, R. S. **Handbook of United States Coins, 2000.** 57th ed. Edited by Kenneth Bressett. New York, St. Martin's Press, 1999. 208p. illus. index. $7.95pa. ISBN 0-307-48006-2.

This book, informally called the "blue book," is published annually and lists the average prices paid by coin dealers by coin condition or grade; in effect, the wholesale prices for coins. This book is a useful guide to the collector who expects to sell coins to a dealer, although there is no guarantee that any dealer would pay the prices as listed. The prices are an average and are meant to be guidelines only.

The book covers U.S. coins and is chronologically arranged from 1616 to the present time. Photographs of each coin type accompany the entry and frequently details are highlighted to aid identification. Historical commentary adds richness to each entry. Each coin type is provided with complete mintage information, and prices are provided for a range of coin grades or conditions. Also included are listings for commemorative coins and gold, platinum, and silver bullion pieces.

This book is considered the standard reference wholesale price guide in the U.S. coin collecting market along with its companion volume, *A Guide Book of United States Coins* (see entry 841), which is the retail price guide. This book is recommended for public and college library collections.—**Margaret F. Dominy**

Memorabilia

843. **Tuff Stuff's Baseball Memorabilia Price Guide.** By Jim Warren II, Dennis Madigan, Melanie Haynie, and Jerry Shaver. Norfolk, Va., Tuff Stuff Books/Landmark Specialty Books, 1998. 384p. illus. $18.95pa. ISBN 0-930625-24-2.

This is a comprehensive guide that can be used as a valuable resource for anyone who collects treasures related to the United States' national pastime. The book consists of 16 chapters, each one dealing with a separate type of memorabilia.

Chapter 1 deals with autographs. This expanded list includes current stars, retired players, and Hall of Fame members. Also included in this chapter is a section on collecting signatures of some of the game's best managers, announcers, commissioners, and owners. Chapter 2 deals with multiple signed items, with inclusions of memorabilia signed by members of the 500 Home Run Club, the 3,000 Hit Club, and the 300 Win Club. In addition, there is a list of team-signed baseballs from every ball club from 1920 to 1997. Game-worn uniforms have become a big part of baseball collecting, and this subject is addressed in chapter 3. There is information on what to look for when purchasing authentic player uniforms. Chapter 4 features baseball publications. Included also in the chapter is value of books, media programs, and baseball literature.

The remaining chapters discuss collecting programs and tickets, limited-edition cards and coins, pennants and posters, cereal boxes with baseball heroes on them, and baseball-related movie memorabilia, among other items. Chapter 15 shows all of the items that were auctioned by Ron Oser Enterprises, one of the country's leading auction houses, in a telephone auction held March 14, 1998. The final chapter is devoted to baseball cards. Each set that is listed in *Tuff Stuff* will also be listed here, along with quality ratings, descriptions, current prices, and artwork. Prices, checklists, and artwork for dozens of pre-war sets, including the most popular tobacco issues, have been included as well.

This compendium of baseball memorabilia prices has all the answers. It is a great book for all avid baseball memorabilia collectors.—**Barbara B. Goldstein**

22 Fine Arts

GENERAL WORKS

Bibliography

844. **Bibliographic Guide to Art and Architecture 1998.** New York, G. K. Hall/Macmillan Library Reference, 1999. 2v. $545.00/set. ISBN 0-7838-0188-2. ISSN 0360-2699.

The *Bibliographic Guide to Art and Architecture* is an annual that lists publications with imprint dates of 1990 to the present. The guide has been cataloged during the 1998 calendar year by The Art and Architecture Division of the New York Public Library and the Library of Congress. It also serves as an annual supplement to the *Dictionary Catalog of the Art and Architecture Division* (see ARBA 76, entry 919). The *Bibliographic Guide to Art and Architecture* includes a preface (with a sample entry with explanatory notes), an introduction, and a bibliography.

The Art and Architecture Division of the New York Public Library aspires to be comprehensive, and collects intensively in all languages and all forms. It contains a research collection that includes paintings, drawings, sculptures, and the history of design aspects of architecture and the applied arts from the prehistoric and primitive to the latest art movements.

Access is alphanumerically available by main entry, added entries, titles, series titles, and subject headings (in capital letters in boldface type). Entries have been selected from LC MARC tapes. Cataloging follows the Anglo-American Cataloging Rules.

The preface states that "complete LC cataloging information for each title, as well as ISBN and identification of NYPL holdings," are given. Noticeably missing in most of the titles are the ISBNs, the NYPL holdings, and subject headings. Rarely does one see a DDC call number. Typeface is minute as with most print bibliographies. With all these negatives, the guide is still an authoritative reference source for those in the library and art and architecture fields.—**Nadine Salmons**

845. **Bibliography of Modern Art on Disc.** [CD-ROM]. New York, Macmillan Library Reference/Simon & Schuster Macmillan, 1998. Minimum system requirements (Windows version): IBM or compatible 386. CD-ROM drive. Windows 3.1. Windows 95. 8MB RAM. $995.00. ISBN 0-7838-0320-6.

The *Bibliography of Modern Art on Disc* is derived from the collection of the Museum of Modern Art (MOMA). More than 200,000 records of cataloged works have been included in a fully searchable database. As art historians and other scholars in the art world are aware, the modern art collection at MOMA is the most extensive there is. The CD provides bibliographic records for about 16,000 books, periodicals, exhibition catalogs, and other printed works collected by the museum. This database is a product of the MOMA catalog that was first published by G. K. Hall in 1976, and has since been kept up-to-date at the museum. All departments of MOMA are included (i.e., Architecture and Design, Drawings, Conservation, Film and Video, and Photography). All languages and formats are included. The museum maintains records of more than 40,000 artist files, including many obscure and emerging artists.

Each record provides complete information including title, MOMA's record number, author, uniform title, imprint, description, series, notes, contents, source, subjects, form or genre, added names (added entries), LC call number, LC card number, and ISBN/ISSN. Searching is done through the search command window that comes up upon loading the disc. From this point it is possible to make detailed searches by all the entries points listed above. Also, a search history feature is provided that is useful while doing searches with several parameters. Searches may be saved to disc using the system, downloaded, or printed. Detailed searching information is included under help menus on the disc, but searching is quite logical and easy. Once a search is completed it is possible to use various display options, including a brief display of bibliographic information, and progressively increasing the display information until all information about each item is displayed. Complete displays of a large number of hits will provide almost a half page or more of information for each item.

This CD-ROM has no peer. It is by far the most complete list of materials concerning modern art in machine-readable format. Because of its extensive data this CD will be of great interest to both public and academic libraries with extensive art collections. It would also be of great use to larger museums, and even larger college and university fine arts departments, for reference. Because of the cost it is not recommended for smaller school or branch public library collections. One drawback is the lack of a Macintosh version. Highly recommended.—**Robert L. Wick**

Biography

846. **Contemporary Women Artists.** Laurie Collier Hillstrom and Kevin Hillstrom, eds. Farmington Hills, Mich., St. James Press, 1999. 760p. illus. (Contemporary Arts). $155.00. ISBN 1-55862-372-8.

As part of the Contemporary Arts series, this work is the first to focus exclusively on women artists in the twentieth century. Biographical and career information is provided on more than 350 of the world's most prominent and influential contemporary artists, such as Mary Cassatt and Georgia O'Keefe. Coverage includes artists who have worked or are working in the visual arts. Different media include painting, sculpture, drawing, print making, collage, photography, ceramics, mixed media, electronic media, performance art, video, design, and graphic arts.

Each entry contains basic biographical information, a comprehensive list of individual exhibitions, a selected list of group exhibitions, a list of public collections that include works by the artist, a selected bibliography of works by and about the artist, and a brief critical essay by a specialist in the field. Many entries also include a list of permanent public installations such as murals, outdoor sculptures, and environmental works. Several black and-white photographs illustrate the artist's and their works. A bibliography, a nationality index, and a medium index are also included, as is a list of contributors.

Only 30 years ago a work such as this would have included very few women artists. After the second wave of feminism in the late 1960s there was an emergence of many women artists in the 1970s. The number of women artists has grown dramatically over the past three decades making it impossible to include all of them in this edition. The editors hope to include many more entries in future volumes. This volume is recommended for all art collections. [R: LJ, Aug 99, p. 74; BR, Nov/Dec 99, p. 88; Choice, Dec 99, p. 686]
—**Cari Ringelheim**

847. Grauer, Paula L., and Michael R. Grauer, comps. **Dictionary of Texas Artists, 1800-1945.** College Station, Tex., Texas A&M University Press, 1999. 240p. illus. (The West Texas A&M University Series, no.3). $34.95. ISBN 0-89096-861-6.

Art, like poverty, is always with us. However, the cultivation and accumulation of art require social stability in the form of wealth and leisure time. The last half of the nineteenth century saw the appearance of both of these in the life of Texans, and the burgeoning quest for culture was as vigorous as the earlier search for land and profits. Basing their study on records of art exhibitions and competitions prior to 1945, the authors have created a fine survey of those artists living and working in Texas in a variety of media and styles. The alphabetic listings offer biographical data: dates, places of residence, education, credentials, and exhibition records. This is followed by a section of color illustrations that offer the reader a kaleidoscope of imagery over the years. The final extensive tables are a chronology of exhibitions and competitions, with cross-references to the artists noting the dates of their participation. This is a useful reference work that should certainly be of interest to any Texas collection, as well as to art libraries with holdings in American art. It records a part of the American heritage, the work of immigrant artists who chose to live in Texas, as well as those born there. [R: LJ, 1 Oct 99, p. 80]—**Paula Frosch**

848. Henkes, Robert. **Latin American Women Artists of the United States: The Works of 33 Twentieth-Century Women.** Jefferson, N.C., McFarland, 1999. 245p. illus. index. $40.00. ISBN 0-7864-0519-8.

The 33 artists featured in this study are deserving of attention because they have established strong regional reputations. The range of backgrounds include those born in the United States of Latino backgrounds, to naturalized citizens from countries such as Argentina, Chile, Colombia, Cuba, Mexico, El Salvador, and Puerto Rico. There ages span from those born in the first part of the century to the 1970s, and their artistic formation goes from college graduates to self taught. The collection includes a good representation of regions, media, and approaches. It features muralists, sculptors, architects, photographers, mixed-media artists, and painters—in other words, all representative areas of twentieth-century art. Henkes has achieved his goal of spotlighting a group that has a long way to go before it is adequately represented in the study of American art. The variety in their interests, approaches, and backgrounds is a clear indication that Latin American women artists have earned a place in the mainstream, and deserve to be studied as such. Although suffering from some glaring omissions of consensus top Latino artists (Judith Baca, Amalia Mesa-Bains, and Patssi Valdez come to mind), the study, which includes analytic essays on the work of the 33 women, brief biographies, illustrations of their representative works, and lists of their exhibitions, is an informative, well-executed, and welcome addition to a field that still occupies a small space in academic library shelves. [R: LJ, Aug 99, pp. 74-76; RUSQ, Fall 99, pp. 95-97]—**Stella T. Clark**

849. Jackson, Christine E. **Dictionary of Bird Artists of the World.** Wappingers Falls, N.Y., Antique Collectors' Club, 1999. 550p. illus. index. $89.50. ISBN 1-85149-203-8.

Jackson's ornithological publications are for bird lovers, natural history art buffs, bird artists, and bird art collectors. She has formerly published on art of our feathered friends done by earlier European natural historians and surveys of some fine artists' use of birds as subjects. This dictionary includes seventeenth- to early twentieth-century bird artists of the world plus Asian bird artists of earlier times and the last three centuries of the old masters' names. Short entries and unique descriptions of the artists' birds are in alphabetized entries under the artists. Only lesser-known artists are represented in the satisfying illustrations. The later European and American bird artists are covered thoroughly. More research, expositions, and inspiring pictures could be published regarding Asia's graphic birders to add to the work. Jackson reveals the best facts that can now be said about each bird artist. She has compiled and compared data from catalogs of museums and auction houses. She has visited many bird-focused artworks and occasionally critiqued them. From this we can see her opinions: a preference for naturalistic anatomical detail and distaste for over-sentimentality, abstract form, and religious symbolism. An Englishwoman, Jackson has a homey and direct style. With an ecologist's commitment to the appreciation of birds and a librarian's capacity to juggle details, here is a book that breaks the silence of spring with prints, oils, watercolors, and inks that should increase the distribution of art about the present-day descendants of the dinosaurs. [R: LJ, 15 Oct 99, pp. 62-64]—**Elizabeth L. Anderson**

850. **Who Was Who in American Art 1564-1975: 400 Years of Artists in America.** rev. ed. Peter Hastings Falk, ed. Madison, Conn., Sound View Press, 1999. 3v. $299.00. ISBN 0-932087-57-4.

This long-awaited update of the 1985 1st edition of *Who Was Who in American Art* proves to be all the 1st edition was and more. Now a 3-volume set, Falk has updated this biographical dictionary to include more than 65,000 entries. He researched thousands of sources while updating this resource: early artist dictionaries that are now out of print, monographs, exhibition catalogs, and regional artist directories and dictionaries. The result is a comprehensive reference work that covers 400 years of artists in the United States. Each entry provides the artist's name, birth and death date, profession (e.g., engraver, blockprinter, screenprinter, lithographer, museum curator, designer), state and city of residence, where they studied, associations they are members of, where they have exhibited, where their works are located today, general comments about the artist's life and work, and a list of sources. Then entries average about one column in length and also provide signature examples of the artist's name. This set will be a valuable addition to any public or academic library that would benefit from a thoroughly researched and up-to-date biography on American artists.—**Shannon M. Graff**

851. **Women Artists of Color: A Bio-Critical Sourcebook to 20th Century Artists in the Americas.** Phoebe Farris, ed. Westport, Conn., Greenwood Press, 1999. 496p. index. $95.00. ISBN 0-313-30374-6.

These basic facts on ethnic women artists' lives, art shows, art in permanent collections, publications mentioning them and by them, quotations from the artists, and descriptions and interpretation of artworks are helpful in researching ethnic women's prowess. The authors hope this recognition is in the wake of universal opportunities to have individual and artistic integrity. Feminist editor-writer Phoebe Farris and her collaborators know segregating a type of artist is not a final goal; rather it is half of a paradox with suffering as well as fulfillment at every step. All humans have paradoxical issues of lifestyle, identity, and meaning. Decisions racked with confusion and compromise can lead to the visibility of artists and the agents making them visible in books and exhibition space. Kay Walkingstick, one of the 100 minority and socially active artists presented, has an artwork in the current edition of Horst Janson's text titled *History of Art*. She exemplifies the women artists of color who are appreciated and have spoken up. But justifying others, who are not women artists of color or do not like prophetic art is neglected. Nor is the issue of whether the wealthy and powerful people of any profession have more than average meaning in their lives. One-sidedness makes this a dated book. The excellent index and lists of the vitae of these artists and commentators are a valuable resource for the adult art-conscious (young and old) to study and visit.

—**Elizabeth L. Anderson**

Dictionaries and Encyclopedias

852. Strieter, Terry W. **Nineteenth-Century European Art: A Topical Dictionary.** Westport, Conn., Greenwood Press, 1999. 300p. index. $89.50. ISBN 0-313-29898-X.

As an introduction to nineteenth-century art, especially the artistic development of visual arts in France, this dictionary will fit well on the shelf. Arranged alphabetically by topic, artist, or artwork, the entries average approximately one-quarter of a page in length. Numerous cross-references provide multiple access points for those unfamiliar with the interrelationship of the artists, movements, and works discussed. The biographies are brief with birth and death dates, a sketch of the artist's life, and a few of the artist's more famous works. Not all of the artists working during this time are covered, as is to be expected. Two surprising omissions from consideration of brief biographies are Pissarro and Vuillard. This is further questioned by the inclusion of works by both artists in the discussion of artworks and the mention of their influence on other artists. As stated in the introduction, the years covered are 1789 to 1914, an indication of precursors to the nineteenth-century and effects of that century upon early twentieth-century artistic development.

Any library will find this work of use in answering quick introductory questions relating to nineteenth-century art, especially those questions of French origin. Those looking for further study on the artists, movements, or artwork mentioned in this volume will need to consult additional general and specialized volumes to fully comprehend the artistic development that occurred during this time period. A companion volume on twentieth-century art is planned for the near future. The author states in his introduction that many of the themes touched upon in this volume will be extended there. [R: BL, Aug 99, p. 2109]—**Gregory Curtis**

Directories

853. Painter, Robert. **The Native American Indian Artist Directory.** Albuquerque, N.Mex., First Nations Art Publishing, 1998. 280p. $19.95pa. ISBN 0-9668806-0-9.

This directory includes more than 2,100 artists, sculptors, potters, rug weavers, basket makers, kachina carvers, bead workers, clothing designers, silversmiths, jewelry makers, and other crafts people from some 100 Native American tribes across the United States. The artists are listed according to their tribe (e.g., Cherokee, Hopi, Navajo, Sioux). The author begins each section with a brief overview of the kind of art common to the tribal members and where their art can usually be located. The artists are then listed in alphabetic order and information such as name, address, telephone number, e-mail and Website address, and type of art is included. The author admits that not all Native American artists can be found here but this is a good place to start. Painter also makes suggestions from his personal experience about contacting artists, purchasing art, and locating galleries that feature Native American art. This work will be a useful addition to art libraries or in the reference section of libraries in the southwestern United States, where most of the artists are located. [R: Choice, Sept 99, p. 112]—**Shannon M. Graff**

854. Walker, Sandra C., and Donald W. Beetham. **Image Buyers' Guide: An International Directory of Sources for Slides and Digital Images for Art and Architecture.** 7th ed. Englewood, Colo., Libraries Unlimited, 1999. 186p. index. (Visual Resources Series). $55.00pa. ISBN 1-56308-658-1.

Presentation software, image CD-ROMS, class Websites, and image databases are a few of the new formats that have changed the needs of curators, librarians, teachers, and scholars in their educational use of art and architecture images. Previously titled the *Slide Buyers' Guide*, the current edition marks a fresh direction for the scope of this reference work.

The new guide is well structured with a pleasing and thorough preface that explains the guide's history, methodology, arrangement, conventions, and evaluation procedures. The editors immediately acknowledge the most obvious drawback to any use of URL's in directory entries—the likelihood of change. In an attempt to keep current, the preface includes a URL for the guide's Website, and advises using the Website name as a constant that "can be located in a web index." Although it is confusing that the Website describes itself as "unofficial" when mentioned in the preface, it is clear that the Website is an extremely valuable resource. The Website contains working links to the entries.

The introduction provides a simple overview of the process of image buying that is extremely valuable for the novice. There is advice for inexperienced buyers, statements on slide quality standards, and clarification of copyright issues. The entries themselves include contact information, documentation and catalog information, product notes, purchasing procedures, and evaluations.

While evaluation help is welcome, some entries were assessed by only one committee member, or were assessed many years ago. Quality and consistency of evaluation seems like the main area where the guide could be improved. There is also the usual problem that all directories seem to have of some omitted fields in the entries due to lack of information from the vendor or resource.

This guide is an interesting resource and easy to use. The *Image Buyers' Guide* is highly recommended for those who use slides and digital images of art and architecture, and the staff that assist them to find the materials that they need. Even libraries with more general collections may want to consider this book as an addition to reference.—**Sandra E. Fuentes**

Handbooks and Yearbooks

855. Brown, Michelle P., and Patricia Lovett. **The Historical Source Book for Scribes.** Buffalo, N.Y., University of Toronto Press, 1999. 128p. illus. index. $29.95. ISBN 0-8020-4720-3.

The author's intent for this work is to emphasize the importance of studying and preserving early hand-written and decorated books. Brown and Lovett explain why and how these materials were made to inform and fuel the creative process as well as to provide a historical assessment of script. They set the scribes and their scripts in context while analyzing the way manuscripts were produced and the materials that were used. Visual aids are provided in the form of illustrations, diagrams, exemplar letters, and creative calligraphy. Chapters are provided on tools and materials and analyzing the scripts as well as different script styles such as Uncial, Gothic, and Italian Rotunda. The different script chapters provide a history and analysis of the styles along with illustrations demonstrating how specific letters are created. A list of further reading and an index conclude the work. This is a good introductory work to learn the history behind and the creation of calligraphy.—**Cari Ringelheim**

856. Grant, Daniel. **The Fine Artist's Career Guide.** New York, Allworth Press, 1998. 298p. index. $18.95pa. ISBN 1-58115-013-X.

Potential artists may boost their careers with this resource, a collection of vital information from college listings to practical advice on job-hunting. The author, a contributing editor of *American Artist* magazine, explores a wide range of occupations in the art world and the rudiments of developing the credentials necessary to succeed. He starts with a chapter on selecting an art school, which offers pointers on improving the chances of acceptance and financial aid sources. Chapter 2 discusses networking, resume preparation, interviewing, and a variety of resources for job-hunters, including Websites, books, and professional agencies. Subsequent chapters cover internships, art exhibits, private commissions, and other ways to create a market, as well as the search for art-related positions like teaching that will supplement the beginner's income. Finally, the book deals with specific art careers, such as medical and scientific illustration, art therapy, architecture and interior design, printmaking, sculpture, museum work, art appraisal, and more. A lengthy bibliography and index top off the volume. Certainly, this is a well-rounded artist's resource, suitable for a reference or circulating collection.—**Jean Engler**

857. Vaughan, William. **Arts of the 19th Century: Volume 1, 1780 to 1850.** New York, Abrams, 1998. 625p. illus. index. $195.00. ISBN 0-8109-1982-6.

As the title suggests, this compilation is an attempt to show the arts of the first part of the nineteenth century. It includes not only two-dimensional paintings, but delves a little into sculpture, graphic art, furnishings, and architecture. The volume is huge, offering an abundance of illustrations that aptly cover the taste, flavor, and color of the era.

It is difficult reviewing an art book like this one. Because of this reviewer's deep love of the romanticism and style of nineteenth-century art, the book is held in high esteem simply because of its content. However, because of this personal admiration of all things of this century, I hold a more critical eye of the book's approach and presentation.

The various phases and styles of art during this time period are covered effectively by the narrative. A painting is often explained and categorized by its emotional offering, symbolism, and intent. A painting may be categorized as well by the application of coloring, shadowing, and technique of artistry, but this is not explained as fully.

Arts of the 19th Century includes painting, graphic art, sculpture, furniture and accessories, and architecture, but not theater, dance, music, functional art and design (e.g., bridges, tunnels, vehicles, appliances), and so on. The title *Arts of the 19th Century* suggests the era, not the region. France, England, Spain, the United States, and Italy are well represented. The rest of the world is not here at all, or only receives a footnote mention. The narrative is complete enough, but very dry. The art selected is an excellent representation, although as a whole hints of bias.

Finally, there is the physical book itself. As formatted, the figures are grouped together, which is fine for the majority of figures that have a figure number alongside for easy identification, but some do not. And in many cases, the figure is far away from where it is referenced in the text. Before each grouping of figures four of five captions are placed on a single page. This seems like a waste of space.

The book is 10 by $12\frac{1}{2}$ inches—a nice size for showing details of the art, and the paper used is of a heavyweight, high quality to give a nice faithful reproduction of the pieces selected. But because the paper is of this heavier weight, and because there are more than 600 pages, the volume is extremely heavy and cumbersome to carry or place on the lap. If the captions had been placed on the same page of the pictures, it could have saved bulk and would have aided greatly in instantly identifying the piece.

Although it is clear that expense has been put into the text of the book, the cover and binding appear cheaply done. The cover is a black paper/cloth treatment around boards, and light-colored ink stamps the title, author, and publisher only on the spine. (There is nothing on the front or back to identify the book once the dust jacket is removed.) The fragility of the binding alone will send up red flags to libraries and librarians. After having opened the book less than a half dozen times, the endpaper has split in the back and the cover is now separated from the spine.

This volume is recommended as a reference book. The photographs and reproductions are superior, and the era is nicely covered. [R: Choice, Oct 99, p. 322]—**Joan Garner**

ARCHITECTURE

858. **Architecture: An Interactive Introduction. [CD-ROM].** By Mark Keane and Linda Keane. New York, McGraw-Hill, 1998. Minimum system requirements (Windows version): IBM or compatible 486. Double-speed CD-ROM drive. Windows 3.1. 16MB RAM. VGA 640 x 480 color display monitor. QuickTime software. Sound-card with speakers. Minimum systems requirements (Macintosh version): System 7.0. Double-speed CD-ROM drive. 8MB RAM. 640 x 480 color display. QuickTime software. Sound-card with speakers. $69.95.

Multimedia tools have changed forever the interaction between the machine and viewer, and the educational experience. One outstanding example of the use of this technology in an instructional setting is *Architecture: An Interactive Introduction*. Using an impressive array of flybys, slides, movie clips, pictures, and animation, combined with narration and music, this work brings the world of the architect to the desk of every student with a computer. Basically a college-level survey introduction to the field, viewers are spellbound while examining, in detail, most aspects of architecture. Concepts are illustrated with virtual tours of many examples of the world's outstanding buildings from prehistoric times to the twentieth century. From the Parthenon to the Villa Savoye, students and researchers have ready access to slides and concept drawings of illustrative exemplars of what is best in Western architecture. But the work illustrates no buildings outside of Europe and only a few in the United States.

In addition to a historical survey, the work covers structural principles (wood, steel, stone), technologies (air systems, sanitation, energy sources), design concepts (scale, proportion), the architectural profession (education, practice, drawing), historic preservation, urban planning, landscape architecture, and interior architecture. Appendixes contain timelines, an atlas, sources of information (a list of some major architectural boards), a list of master architects (with some hyperlinks to slides), and a review of terminology.

The work is by and large a fun and interesting introduction to the field. The Windows (3.1, 95, 98, or NT) version, as well as the Macintosh (System 7.0 and up) version loaded for the most part without a problem, especially if the user is familiar with installing new software from a CD-ROM. Monitor and graphic board quality does make a difference with this type of highly visual product. A 60 MHz Pentium machine running Windows 3.1 attached to a Sony H-P monitor looked much better than a Power Mac 9500/132 running Mac OS 8.5 with a Macintosh color display (model 1212). The documentation with the set could be better. Links sometimes just do not work; other times they are not there at all. The navigation icons are not intuitive and require some study, especially when the hyperlinks fail to run. Some links are even mislabeled. For example, when users click on the image of St. Mark's Basilica (Venice), they are immediately taken to an animated clip of the Hagia Sophia (Istanbul). Some images are of poor quality, such as the photo of 860 Lake Shore Dr. (Chicago), largely a reflection of the sun off Lake Michigan. Some older black-and-white movie clips (Eiffel Tower) are clearly of historic interest and show little to the modern viewer. In other cases when users run the hyperlink, parts of the old page remain on the screen due to incomplete screen wipes, rendering the new text confusing.

Processors under 100 MHz have trouble handling the images in a reasonable time. Loading the slide shows takes forever and in some cases users may need to reboot. Viewers with faster machines will, however, find this work a delightful way to study the topic. The text and narration are what one might expect in a survey course (accurate, but not breathtaking). Overall, despite a few faults, this work takes a good shot at the topic and deserves purchase by most libraries with readers interested in architecture.—**Ralph Lee Scott**

859. **Award Winning Architecture 1998/99: International Yearbook.** Frantisek D. Sedlacek, ed. New York, Prestel USA; distr., New York, Neues, 1998. 216p. illus. index. $49.95. ISBN 3-7913-1833-0.

Evaluating a meal from a photograph in a book is an exercise in futility. The aroma must be smelled and the food must be sampled between tongue and palate to determine taste and texture; it is an experience. Sampling architecture from a book is much the same. Good architecture represents a dynamic resolution of function and space, a juxtaposition poorly conveyed in small photographs. To be truly appreciated it, too, must be experienced. Having said that, however, the realities are such that, as a substitute for visiting 19 countries around the world, this book works very well. As Marcus Binney writes in the foreword, "The task of a book such as this...is to show whether world architecture is treading a wide and varied path full of surprises..." (p. 9). The book accomplishes its task and architecture is, indeed, full of surprises.

Each included project has received an award from a national architectural association. Of the 400 worldwide projects that received such awards, 100 were selected for inclusion in this volume, the 3d in the series that began in 1996. Projects are displayed on one or two pages, illustrated by multiple color and black-and-white photographs and accompanied by small site drawings, sections, or elevations, with accompanying details such as design team, structural team, contractors, areas of the project, and additional references. The book is indexed by project location, architect, and building type. The book is inspirational. The spectrum of projects included is broad and spectacular—both secular (residences, museums, hospitals, libraries, transportation facilities, and industrial buildings) and spiritual (synagogues, churches, and convents).

This book is more than a collection of structures; it is a sampling of innovative problem solving that affects populations. In the beginning of the book the editor laments the fact that recent architecture was falling into a boring series of similar solutions to diverse problems, banks appearing like housing projects and architecture reflecting neither site nor social conditions. The projects contained within this volume happily declare that the trend the editor observed may be over. The book is a volume that can easily be placed on the coffee table, but more effectively can be used as a reference to good architecture for those in the field or for students as an example of inventiveness and problem solving at its best.—**Craig A. Munsart**

860. **Encyclopedia of Vernacular Architecture of the World.** Paul Oliver, ed. New York, Cambridge University Press, 1997. 3v. illus. index. $995.00/set. ISBN 0-521-56422-0.

The title page of this 3-volume encyclopedia defines vernacular architecture as "the dwellings and all other buildings of the people. Related to their environmental contexts and available resources, they are customarily owner- or community-built, utilizing traditional technologies...built to meet specific needs, accommodating the values, economies and ways of living of the cultures that produce them." The editor, therefore sets a task for himself and the consultants and contributors to discuss not only the formal aspects of the architecture itself, but to place the architecture in its cultural, historical, environmental, and social contexts.

A preface by Oliver gives the background of the development of the encyclopedia, and also describes his vision of what this encyclopedia was intended to be. Rather than the traditional organization of the alphabetic single sequence, he wanted a form that would demonstrate the relationships between the entries in a logical progression. The preface also notes that a potential problem would be the repetition of information that was common to cultures: building construction and architectural and environmental aspects within culture areas. To that end, he explains that he has chosen to place this information in one volume, and then apply the information to entries in the 2d and 3d volumes that are concerned with the cultural groups and culture areas. The 1st volume, "Theories and Principles," is organized into sections that describe approaches and concepts, culture traits and attributes, environment, materials, services, symbolism and decoration, and functions. The 2d volume, "Cultures and Habitats," covers Asia, Australasia and Oceania, Europe and Eurasia, and the Mediterranean and Southwest Asia. The 3d volume covers Latin America, North America, and Sub-Saharan Africa, and also includes a glossary and lexicon, bibliography, index of cultures, nations and locations, and a general index. It is well illustrated throughout with black-and-white photographs, line drawings, elevations, and maps. The entries are structured and numbered in a triple-sequence system, so that an entry on Atlantic Canada (3.VI.2.a) will have a reference to another entry explaining a service that a building provides for a specific function (1.VI.1). In addition, most entries have a brief list of references printed in the margin, for easy reference in the bibliography.

The list of contributors is eight pages long, and lists not only architects and architectural historians, but also anthropologists, geographers, chemists, ethnologists, urban planners, social scientists, archaeologists, and ecologists, among the expert contributors. Oliver points out that the contributors represent 80 countries; in many cases the authors acted as their own translators, but in other cases the translation was anonymous. This encyclopedia is a wonderful achievement and holds a unique place in architecture, not only for the range of architecture represented, but also for the technical and contextual information about the development of vernacular architecture. It should be in every college library where students and faculty are studying architecture, sociology, geography, and anthropology. [R: C&RL, Sept 98, pp. 471-472]—**Kerie L. Nickel**

861. Guthrie, Pat. **The Architect's Portable Handbook: First Step Rules of Thumb for Building Design.** 2d ed. New York, McGraw-Hill, 1998. 555p. illus. maps. index. $76.50. ISBN 0-07-025303-X.

Any book where the author can sum up its purpose in a one-sentence paragraph at the beginning of an introduction must be praised. Guthrie writes in his introduction, "The concept of this book is that of a personal tool that compacts the 20 [percent] of the data that is needed 80 [percent] of the time by design professionals in the preliminary design of buildings of all types and sizes" (p. xiii). The book then suits this purpose. Now in its 2d edition, this paperback probably will hold up to the abuse it will receive when frequently consulted by architects and designers. It is a consulting tool for these professionals to use daily when starting new projects and working on each new step in the process. Part 1, for instance, highlights all of the preliminary planning one must go through, from construction costs and administration to zoning laws and structural systems.

Other sections include information on site planning, building materials, and interiors. The table of contents is arranged as a quick guide to each section, with places for checkmarking as completed. Within the sections, numerous charts, tables, geometric formulas, and schematic drawings accompany the text. There are also blank pages for notes that the author encourages readers to use to literally make the book their own with additions and changes. The author recognizes that cost information will become outdated, but reminds readers in the introduction that the book is to be used as a starting point. Overall the work makes for a great ready-reference tool, not only for the building professional, but also for the library patron needing a quick answer to technical architectural inquiries.—**Roberto C. Ferrari**

862. Ierley, Merrett. **Open House: A Guided Tour of the American Home, 1637–Present.** New York, Henry Holt, 1999. 317p. illus. index. $32.50. ISBN 0-8050-4837-5.

A fine combination of historical record and personal experiences, this is, simply, a splendid book. Based on an extensive survey sent to curators and managers of historic sites throughout the country, the work offers insight into the American dream via the American house. It documents the technological changes as well as the social, and does so by citing contemporary reference works, advertisements, popular magazines, and personal diaries and correspondence. Using 18 "focus" houses, the author offers the reader a glimpse into the lives of those who designed, built, and inhabited them. The content is scholarly without being stuffy, instructive without being pedantic. There are 100 houses, many of which are more fully discussed in the work, delineated in a timeline, tracing their origin and further development from the mid-seventeenth century to the present time. A section of sources and an extensive bibliography, plus a listing of the "focus" houses with information about their availability to the public, complete this work. The author is to be congratulated upon producing an informative, insightful, and interesting work.—**Paula Frosch**

863. Langmead, Donald. **J. J. P. Oud and the International Style: A Bio-Bibliography.** Westport, Conn., Greenwood Press, 1999. 261p. illus. index. (Bio-Bibliographies in Art and Architecture, no.5). $79.50. ISBN 0-313-30100-X.

J. J. P. Oud was a Dutch architect and one of the founders of the International School. This bio-bibliography lists works by and about Oud, and also attempts to explain his place in international architecture, his contributions to the field, and the reasons for his relative obscurity today. This work will be useful to students and faculty studying the period or the style or his architecture.

Oud established a professional reputation just after World War I, while he was chief housing architect in the city of Rotterdam. He was invited to build a model suburban housing development in Stuttgart in 1926. This project attracted the attention of Philip Johnson in the United States. Johnson was so impressed with Oud, he included Oud in his work *The International Style: Architecture Since 1922*, which was a companion to a major New York exhibition in 1931. In 1938 he won a closed competition for the new headquarters for the Bataatsche Import Maatschappij (the Shell Building) in The Hague. World War II intervened and little communication of a professional sort was possible between Europe and the United States. When back in touch after the war, Johnson and other American architects were shocked and offended to see that Oud had abandoned the international style by including ornamentation in his design of the Shell Building. The disappointment of his colleagues was publicly stated. After this change of heart, Oud built numerous projects in The Netherlands, but was dropped from the international press.

This book includes a preface; a list of abbreviations; an essay with bibliography; a short photograph essay; and an annotated bibliography by decade, which is divided into books and journals, a guide to archives, a list of works (buildings), J. J. P Oud's Library (a provisional list), and an index of personal names. The author is professor of architectural history at the University of South Australia, with several other bibliographies to his credit. This work is recommended for university and public libraries. [R: Choice, July/Aug 99, p 1922]—**Joanna M. Burkhardt**

864. Mace, Angela, comp. **Architecture in Manuscript 1601-1996: Guide to the British Architectural Library Manuscripts and Archives Collection.** New York, Continuum Publishing, 1998. 628p. illus. index. $175.00. ISBN 0-7201-2195-7.

This work is a marvelous guide to an important and fascinating collection of papers and manuscripts that too often fall between the cracks in documentation. Architectural drawings, photographs of sites, and completed images are all carefully preserved. It is these other documents that bring to life the day-to-day activities; the thoughts and concerns of working architects of many decades. The collection includes a wide variety of resources. Specifications of types of materials and methods used provide an invaluable historical record for conservation and restoration projects. The extensive correspondence, between architects themselves as well as between architect and client, offers a range of professional and personal insights. Literary papers, many unpublished, reveal the breadth of interest and knowledge of these professionals, along with many innovations and inventions necessitated by the work at hand and the challenges presented. Additional assets are the collected papers of architectural societies and association organizations. The endeavor to preserve, to organize, and to protect materials while continuing to make them available is a remarkable achievement, and this work is an excellent guide to this continuing effort. It is clearly presented and well indexed, and other pertinent information for potential researchers is included. This is an important addition to any reference collection on social history as well as architecture and its allied arts.

—Paula Frosch

GRAPHIC ARTS

865. Beer, Robert. **The Encyclopedia of Tibetan Symbols and Motifs.** Boston, Shambhala, 1999. 368p. illus. $60.00. ISBN 1-57062-416-X.

The Encyclopedia of Tibetan Symbols and Motifs contains 169 plates, in black-and-white, of paintings done with sable hair brushes and china ink accompanied by 200 pages of explanatory text. Most illustrations are the same size as their originals and usually a dozen or more images are collected onto 1 plate of 7 by 10 inches. The author and illustrator compares his book to a thangka (p. xvi), a teaching tool for the symbols and artistic background of Tibetan religious art, including ritual offerings, landscapes, animals, musical instruments, and decorative borders. The text is an excellent source of definitions of Sanskrit and Tibetan religious terminology and also provides ample explanation of devices and symbols within their religious context. The attention to detail, both artistically and textually, is impressive. Because the table of contents is detailed, this book could be useful as a supplement to dictionaries of Near Eastern symbols (even though it does not have an index). Its value as a tool for artists, both professionals and students, is hard to overestimate. Readers concerned about the ethical issue of publishing Near Eastern art, sometimes available in the West through plunder, may be pleased to know that the author's paintings are the product of his years of painting and study of art and religion in India, Nepal, and Tibet. Upon his return, Beer continued his work for many years. This book would be a good companion to Marylin Rhie and Robert A. F. Thurman's *Worlds of Transformation: Tibetan Art of Wisdom and Compassion* (Abrams, 1999). This book is especially recommended for schools with design programs.—**Nancy L. Van Atta**

PHOTOGRAPHY

866. **International Photography: George Eastman House Index to Photographers, Collections, and Exhibitions.** Andrew H. Eskind, Greg Drake, Kirsti Ringger, and Lynne Rumney, eds. Thorndike, Maine, G. K. Hall/ Macmillan, 1998. 3v. $395.00/set. ISBN 0-7838-0325-7.

An update to the 1996 *Index to American Photographic Collections* (see ARBA 97, entry 789), *International Photography* adds two important features to the earlier work and its predecessors. One is the new international outlook. For the first time, collections in institutions outside of the United States are listed. The other is information on exhibitions, added to the previous listings of photographers and collections.

The one-volume 1996 work has become three volumes. Volume 1 alphabetically lists photographers. As appropriate, each photographer's name is followed by a listing of collections that contain information on the photographer or works of the photographer, and by a listing of exhibitions featuring the photographer. Volume 2 lists collections, both here and abroad, arranged alphabetically by geographic place-name. This volume gives address and telephone and fax numbers for each institution, plus a list of collections. Symbols indicate whether a collection on a particular photographer is major (*) or substantial (#). No symbol attached means that a particular collection is more modest. Volume 3 is the exhibition volume. Arranged by date, then alphabetically by geographic place-name, this lists under each institution the exhibitions it has mounted. The date arrangement makes it possible to see trends in exhibitions over time.

All three volumes cross-reference each other—one can look up a photographer's name in volume 1, then refer to volumes 2 and 3 for more complete information either about the institutions that have germane collections or about those institutions that have had exhibitions. This index does for photography research what guides to archives and manuscripts, such as Philip Hamer's classic *A Guide to Archives and Manuscripts in the United States* (Yale University Press, 1961) have long done for literary and historical studies.

It is not for everyone, but is essential to libraries that support such research. [R: Choice, July/Aug 99, pp. 1920-1922]—**Terry Ann Mood**

867. Kreisel, Martha. **American Women Photographers: A Selected and Annotated Bibliography.** Westport, Conn., Greenwood Press, 1999. 350p. index. (Art Reference Collection, no.18). $79.50. ISBN 0-313-30478-5.

This work will contribute significantly to extending the research avenues for those studying women photographers. The work covers photographers from the late nineteenth century to the present. Most of the approximately 680 photographers listed have several bibliographic references listed. The entries include the bibliographic information for each work, Website addresses, and a list of images included in the work. There is little in the way of annotations for each entry to place the photographer in context. A few of the entries include a short statement about the particular work listed. Some of the lesser-known individuals are cross-referenced to a collected works volume. These collected works (volumes numbering about 75) are listed separately in one section of the work. The list of individual photographers is arranged alphabetically. Indexes include an author list and an index to doctoral dissertations and video recording titles. Libraries with patrons interested in photography, women's studies, or U.S. cultural history will find this work a useful addition to the collection. [R: Choice, Oct 99, p. 305]—**Gregory Curtis**

868. McDarrah, Gloria S., Fred W. McDarrah, and Timothy S. McDarrah. **The Photography Encyclopedia.** New York, Schirmer Books/Simon & Schuster Macmillan, 1999. 689p. illus. index. $80.00. ISBN 0-02-865025-5.

The current interest in photography as an art can be seen in the great number of exhibitions, auctions, and books dealing with the medium. Long regarded as a stepchild of fine arts or thought of as a mechanical process requiring no artistic insight, the photograph has become in integral part of both the aesthetic and the commercial world of art. This excellent reference book offers information on the development of scientific techniques, from daguerreotype to video and digital imaging. Its major contribution lies in the short biographical sketches of photographers, from the pioneers in the field to the photomontage artists of the 1990s. Included are all the expected artists, from Julia Margaret Cameron and William Henry Fox Talbot to Dorothea Lange and Andy Warhol, but the attention, as well, to the less well-known photographers makes this an important reference tool. The accompanying black-and-white photographs are graphic examples of the art of those named and the addition of "photographers photographed" gives a human face to the name and the work. There are additional assets in this work; the sections on book reviews, booksellers, awards and prizes, films and magazines, and galleries and museums are all vital to the researcher in the field. Photography has come a long way from the camera obscura and this volume provides an excellent guide along this path. Treating the technical and the innovative, the people and the pictures, this encyclopedia makes a fine contribution to the literature for students, scholars, and amateurs. [R: C&RL News, June 99, p. 483; BL, 1 Sept 99, p. 183; Choice, Nov 99, p. 508]—**Paula Frosch**

869. **Photographer's Market, 1999: 2,000 Places to Sell Your Photographs.** Megan Lane, ed. Cincinnati, Ohio, Writer's Digest Books/F & W Publications, 1998. 630p. illus. index. $23.99pa. ISBN 0-89879-851-5. ISSN 0147-247X.

Photographer's Market retains its basic organization and purpose in this 1999 edition. As in earlier editions, it is aimed at the person who may be skilled in photography but inexperienced in the business world, one who is looking to move from the amateur to the professional level. The first 45 pages are devoted to such topics as creating a business plan, tax information, copyright information, specific information on dealing with international markets, and charging for one's work—information needed by people trying to succeed in the professional world. Following the 1st section are a series of chapters on various markets, such as consumer publications, trade publications, and stock photography agencies. A section titled "Resources" follows, with lists of helpful Websites, photography workshops, and schools of photography. The main section of the book is titled "Markets." Each entry describes a particular outlet for photographic work, giving name, address, and telephone and fax numbers. Entries may also include information on what types of photographs the outlet purchases, how many each year, and what prices they pay.

Several new features appear in the 1999 edition. Perhaps most significantly, the editors have added a new index on international markets. Another addition is that of sidebars to several of the chapters on specific markets, in which practitioners in various fields write of their experiences and offer helpful hints. The new edition of *Photographer's Market* still provides useful information in a familiar format, with a few new twists.

—**Terry Ann Mood**

23 Language and Linguistics

GENERAL WORKS

870. Dalby, Andrew. **Dictionary of Languages: The Definitive Reference to More Than 400 Languages.** New York, Columbia University Press, 1998. 734p. maps. index. $50.00. ISBN 0-231-11568-7.

The book under review is an excellent survey of the languages of the world. There is no attempt at completeness, but the selection is wide enough to satisfy most searches for information. The numerically smallest languages covered are Bislama (a pidgin of the Western Pacific, about 60,000 speakers), Gaelic (in Scotland, 80,000), Kiribati (Micronesia, 70,000), Marshallese (Micronesia, 30,000), Ojibwa (U.S., Canada, 80,000), and Romansch (Switzerland, 65,000). Hawaiian seems to be the language with the smallest number of speakers (2,000) included in the book. The indication of the number of speakers is useful, although sometimes approximate; however reluctantly, one must accept the number, remembering the constant failures of governmental programs to revive the language. Some extinct languages are also covered, not only Akkadian or Latin, but also some like Sogdian. There are also sections on families of languages, such as Turkic or Afro-Asiatic, that contain more information about languages not mentioned individually. For instance, the "click languages" are summarily treated under the heading "Khoisan Languages."

The information given about the languages pertains mostly to their history, both linguistic (affiliation, cultural attributes) and political (periods of oppression, transplanted varieties, development of the standard variety); their geographic spread; and their scripts (with specimens). There is an indication of a few words (usually the first numerals), frequently compared with their counterparts in genetically related languages. If the language uses a script of its own, a short history of the script and illustration of its characters are given. Different alphabets are mentioned, and so are interesting orthographies. The book also provides interesting bits of information in separate boxes, making the work more readable and attractive. For instance, Makonde secret songs are mentioned on page 385.

One important component of the book is the maps indicating the location of practically all the languages mentioned. They are very informative and were obviously drawn for this book. The user of the book, however, must adjust to particulars. First, the maps indicate the contours of the land, the frontiers of states, the large rivers, a few cities, and the area where the language is spoken. Rivers and states are not mentioned by name. Second, while the maps are good, their printing does not always achieve the technical level of representing every minor detail. But these are mere trifling details; on the whole, the maps are immensely helpful.

For deeper study, the linguist will probably prefer the excellent surveys of the languages of the world in William Bright's *International Encyclopedia of Linguists* (see ARBA 93, entry 1050). But for the general public, this is the best source available, one that will offer, to the linguist as well, much interesting information. [R: LJ, 1 May 99, pp. 68-69; Choice, July/Aug 99, p. 1916; RUSQ, Fall 99, p. 88]—**L. Zgusta**

871. Elster, Charles Harrington. **The Big Book of Beastly Mispronunciations: The Complete Opinioned Guide for the Careful Speaker.** Westminster, Md., Houghton Mifflin, 1999. 426p. $15.00pa. ISBN 0-395-89338-0.

The linguistically challenged, the perfectionists of style, and many a public speaker will find this book to be of immense value and curiosity. The volume incorporates two earlier books by the same author—*There Is No Zoo in Zoology, and Other Beastly Mispronunciations* (1988) and *Is There a Cow in Moscow? More Beastly Mispronunciations and Sound Advice* (1990). However, the author indicates that extensive revision and updating have occurred, along with an expansion of authorities consulted. The value of the latter is to be found in the numerous references and defenses presented under each entry. Where there is doubt regarding correct or alternate pronunciation, Elster presents a variety of viewpoints as well as a final ruling.

Entries are arranged alphabetically and include spelling and pronunciation, the latter keyed to a modified phonetic system that relies upon a pronunciation key. Stress is indicated for oral syllabication, but not for the written word. Following this are the arguments for variant pronunciations and rationales for correct pronunciations. In some cases, the author presents harsh warnings to those who might dare pronounce a word in some unacceptable fashion. Supplementing the whole are a glossary of explicatory terms used, a list of authorities, and a list of other sources cited or consulted. This book is recommended for school and public libraries, and for those academic libraries that have strong collections regarding usage and style. [R: Choice, Sept 99, p. 104]—**Edmund F. SantaVicca**

872. **Encyclopedia of Language and Education.** Norwell, Mass., Kluwer Academic, 1997. 8v. index. $350.00pa./set. ISBN 0-7923-4936-9.

This superb, 8-volume encyclopedia provides cutting edge topical reviews of the literature exploring the central role of language as both a vehicle and mediator of educational processes. More than 200 essays authored by prominent scholars in the fields of language and education provide extensive descriptions of the field's important literature, basic questions, ongoing research, and future developments. Given its worldwide perspective and diverse disciplinary approaches, the *Encyclopedia of Language and Education* is an indispensable resource for understanding the international and interdisciplinary nature of this field.

Volume 1, "Language Policy and Political Issues in Education," addresses issues in language acquisition, language teaching, and minority languages, while volume 2, "Literacy," focuses on reading, writing, the social context of literacy, and literacy teaching in various parts of the world. Volume 3, "Oral Discourse and Education," examines how the place to talk in education can be theorized and how talk is used in educational settings. Volume 4, "Second Language Education," highlights the contributions of linguistic theory and research to understanding second-language instruction and samples innovative L2 pedagogical practices from various parts of the world. A worldwide perspective also strongly informs volume 5 "Bilingual Education," which provides wide-ranging accounts of the implementation of diverse bilingual education programs around the globe. Volume 6, "Knowledge About Language," surveys various aspects of language awareness and the role of metalinguistic knowledge and processes in language development and education in arguing for building an element of language awareness into language education. Volume 7, "Language Testing and Assessment," includes material on assessing both first and second language ability as well as on assessing individual skills; essays also address methodological issues and test validation as well as the affects and ethics of assessment. The final volume, volume 8 "Research Methods in Language and Education," focuses on language and education in relation to society, variation, culture, and interaction. Each individual volume ends with a subject index and a name index, and volume 8 contains cumulative subject and name indexes for the entire encyclopedia. Between the excellence of its scholarship and its synoptic view of the field, the *Encyclopedia of Language and Education* belongs in every reference department patronized by scholars interested in language and education.—**G. Douglas Meyers**

873. Metcalf, Allan. **The World in so Many Words: A Country-By-Country Tour of Words That Have Shaped Our Language.** Westminster, Md., Houghton Mifflin, 1999. 298p. illus. index. $12.00. ISBN 0-395-95920-9.

Through some 200 brief yet discursive essays, Metcalf serves up a multicultural buffet that showcases the foreign and domestic origins of such variously colorful and familiar words as bijou, voodoo, bandicoot, java, and chocolate. The first four chapters focus upon loanwords from Europe, Africa, and Asia that have been assimilated into American English (e.g., geyser from Iceland, bizarre from Basque, arsenic from Syriac, and mogul from Mongolian). Following these chapters is one that examines words whose provenances are indigenous to South and Central America, the United States, and Canada. Without a dry recitation of linguistic theory or etymology, Metcalf has leavened his entries with interesting historical anecdote and informed speculation. For example, paradise originally denoted a particular "walled park of a Persian ruler," and hunky-dory, created by a Japanese entertainer employed in New York City in the 1860s, was derived from "Honcho–dori," the actual name of a street in Japan.

Besides the book's general introduction, each chapter is prefaced by a two- or three-page overview that succinctly yet thoroughly addresses issues concerning linguistic migration; dozens of additional examples of loanwords pepper these pages as well. Metcalf has also supplemented his text with three indexes—a word index (including some 800 words that are not main entries in the dictionary proper), a language index (some 200 entries), and a country index (some 120 entries).

Black-and-white drawings and photos appear infrequently through this volume, and too often are squandered, illustrating entries that are more pedestrian than exotic (e.g., kayak, dunk, penguin, and bikini). That said, for most academic and public library collections, this reference source stands as a modest yet useful supplement or alternative to more exhaustive dictionaries.—**Jeffrey E. Long**

874. **Pocket Guide to Clichés.** Hauppauge, N.Y., Barron's Educational Series, 1999. 155p. $6.95pa. ISBN 0-7641-0672-4.

American English is full of clichés that help speakers and writers express their thoughts and opinions. This guide has been composed with three audiences in mind. The first is native speakers of American English who know the clichés of their generation, but are unfamiliar with clichés from other generations. Second, this dictionary is for nonnative speakers of American English who cannot lookup clichés in standard dictionaries and cannot understand them by literal interpretation. Finally, this guide is intended for writers and speakers who want to familiarize themselves with clichés and use them when appropriate and to avoid them when original expression is called for. Being as how this work is a "pocket" guide it is by no means all-inclusive. Each alphabetic entry provides an easy-to-understand interpretation of the cliché and uses it in a sentence for further understanding. The front cover claims that the guide also contains explanations of the origins of the clichés, but this is nowhere to be found; unless this claim is meant to refer to the brief general description of clichés in the introduction. This is a useful reference for writers, speakers, and ESL students, but the cover text is a little misleading. [R: LJ, Aug 99, p. 74]—**Cari Ringelheim**

875. Trask, R. L. **Key Concepts in Language and Linguistics.** New York, Routledge, 1999. 378p. index. (Key Concepts). $75.00; $18.99pa. ISBN 0-415-15741-2; 0-415-15742-0pa.

Key Concepts in Language and Linguistics is an accessible text for the layperson as well as the specialist. Trask makes the task of explaining such common terms as noun, adjective, and verb, and more esoteric concepts as syntagmatic relation and discourse analysis, both pleasurable and rewarding. The book appears to be the 5th in a series devoted to making current topics (cinema studies, popular music) more understandable to the lay reader.

The book's design is simple yet comprehensive. It is presented as an A to Z guide of the main terms and concepts used in the study of language and linguistics. Clear, readable definitions with multiple examples are provided for the following: terms used in grammatical analysis; branches of linguistics; critical approaches used in studying language; linguistic phenomena, such as code-switching and conversational implicature; and various forms of language from pidgin to standard discourse. Moreover, the entries for each topic trace its origin and mention the key individuals associated with the concept. Extensive cross-references and a lengthy bibliography complement this handy guide to language and linguistics.

One of the more enjoyable aspects of *Key Concepts in Language and Linguistics* is the engaging way in which Trask explains his key concepts. Although clearly demonstrating his mastery of linguistics and language, he succeeds in keeping a sense of humor throughout, even in the more complex sections of the book. Perhaps most helpful are the everyday examples he uses. In discussing connotation, for instance, he notes that "particularly emotive words like *foxhunting*, *lesbian*, *multinational*, and even *vegetarian* may produce connotations for different people that are almost wildly different." In addition, it is somewhat mind-boggling to learn that such languages as Basque and Finnish have a dozen or more case distinctions, while English and Romance languages like French and Spanish have only a few. One wonders how it is possible to learn such difficult languages without being born into them.

Trask has not only done his homework but convincingly demonstrates his extensive knowledge of Indo-European languages. This is a work that is both affordable and essential for anyone interested in the science of linguistics and in how language operates on a day-to-day basis. [R: BL, 1 May 99, pp. 1630-1632; Choice, Sept 99, p. 114]—**John B. Romeiser**

ENGLISH-LANGUAGE DICTIONARIES

General Usage

876. **Cassell Compact Dictionary.** London, Cassell; distr., New York, Continuum Publishing, 1998. 1278p. $15.95. ISBN 0-304-35006-0.

Librarians might well ask whether the world needs another desk dictionary, even one that boasts over 200,000 entries and "up-to-the-minute coverage of all aspects of English" from around the world. Yet here, with much to recommend it, is just such another candidate for the proverbial "better mousetrap" award in its niche of the market. *Cassell Compact* sports a smaller format and price than other standard, clothbound dictionaries on the shelves of book superstores, and its lightness makes it easy to hold in one adult hand while turning pages with the other. The typeface is small but clear, while bold typefacing of entries distinguishes them beautifully in the double columns of print. The front matter, offering simple guidance on abbreviations, symbols, and pronunciation, is scantier than that in Merriam-Webster, Houghton, Chambers, or Oxford publications. *Compact* offers only the bare lexical bones: entry, pronunciation according to a simplified phonetic system, meanings according to parts of speech, compounds and derivatives, and idioms and phrases. British spellings precede U.S. spellings. Stylistic, geographic, and field (of knowledge) labels further guide the reader, and "Xs" mark entries representing frequent misspellings. Words beginning with such common prefixes as "un," "pre," "non," and "anti" are grouped into paragraphs. Usage, spelling, and pronunciation notes or warnings dot the text. *Compact* is plain vanilla, with no features—no essays, etymologies, thumb-indexes, quoted examples, illustrations, personal or geographical names, maps, tables, writing style guides, or CDs. This dictionary is better for domestic than library purchase except perhaps where libraries serve inexperienced users of English-language dictionaries.

—**Robert H. Kieft**

877. **Cassell Concise Dictionary with CD-ROM.** rev. ed. Herndon, Va., Mansell/Cassell, 1998. Minimum system requirements: IBM or compatible PC. CD-ROM drive. Windows 95 or Windows NT 4.0. 256-color video adapter. Mouse. 1711p. $29.95 (with CD-ROM). ISBN 0-304-35003-6; 0-304-35015-X (CD-ROM).

Cassell is an English publisher that has published numerous dictionaries since 1891. The *Cassell Concise English Dictionary* was first published in 1989 (see ARBA 90, entry 995), revised and reprinted with amendments and additions in 1994, 1997, and 1998 respectively. The 1998 edition has both print and CD-ROM format and contains more than 250,000 entries and definitions—more words and phrases than any other concise dictionary. The coverage of this dictionary includes not only standard English but also scientific and technical terms. New words covered, such as *World Wide Web*, *Internet*, *e-mail*, and *cyberpet*, make this dictionary the most current when compared with other concise dictionaries. Being compiled by an English publisher, obviously this dictionary gives first the modern British spellings. North American alternatives are specified where applicable. To help readers choose the right word, this dictionary has more than 500 notes on correct usage. Another unique feature is its misspelling guide. If the reader sees an "x" in front of a word, he or she is informed that this is a misspelled word. Many people will enjoy the CD-ROM version of this dictionary. It gives readers more choices. One can search by headword, full text, idioms, style of use, area of study, origin, and crossword. For example, if one is interested in finding out how many words are from the French language, one need only to consult the origin feature to search and will receive a list of French words. The CD-ROM version also frees users from carrying around the 1,711-page print dictionary. This dictionary is a good reference tool for anyone who speaks or is learning to speak English. It is also a good replacement for the libraries with out-of-date reference materials.—**Xiao (Shelley) Yan Zhang**

878. **The Cassell Dictionary and Thesaurus.** London, Cassell; distr., New York, Continuum Publishing, 1999. 1277p. $49.95. ISBN 0-304-35004-4.

Cassell's latest contribution to the English language combines a dictionary of more than 200,000 words with a thesaurus of more than 250,000 synonyms and antonyms. Words and combinations of words are given in alphabetic order rather than being nested in the definition of the root word. Although the dictionary purports to cover the English language from America to Australia, the emphasis is decidedly British. British spellings precede North American: "favor" follows "favour." A "boot" is, among other things, a compartment in a car. But "trunk" is defined as "the boot of a motor car." "Tomato" has one pronunciation and it is British rather than North American. In other instances, the British pronunciation appears before others. A singular feature is the inclusion of misspellings so the user can find the correct spelling. For example, "freind" refers the user to "friend." One drawback is that the guide to pronunciation appears only in the introductory pages, requiring the user to page back and forth. Synonyms, identified by a black square, follow after definitions, and the number of the synonym corresponds to the numbered definition. However, synonyms and antonyms are merely listed with no attempt to differentiate shades of meaning. The layout is clear and uncluttered with headwords in bold type. The physical volume is a convenient and usable size. Recommended for large public and research libraries with large language collections.—**Bernice Bergup**

879. **The Cassell Paperback Dictionary.** Herndon, Va., Mansell/Cassell, 1998. 1278p. $12.95pa. ISBN 0-304-35016-8.

The Cassell Paperback Dictionary is the paperback version of the *Cassell Compact Dictionary* that was published in 1998. Both are derived from the database that supplied the 1997 edition of the *Cassell Concise Dictionary*, a larger work. The paperback dictionary, with more than 200,000 entries, is intended as a standard desk dictionary but features scientific and technical terms as well as words new to the language. Readers can find definitions for "zero tolerance," "couch potato," "detox," "road rage," "infotainment," "electrophorus," "converse," and "virtual." The definitions and pronunciation guides are clear and easy to understand. Usage notes scattered throughout help readers avoid pronunciation, factual, or linguistic faux pas. Another handy feature is the use of "misspelled" words (sargant, sanwich, unatural, colaborate) preceded by a black box to direct users to the correct spelling. As is to be expected from this British publisher, English spellings are given first (labour, catalogue) with American spellings second (labor, catalog). Although suitable for personal use, this paperback edition would not last in libraries. Its pages are thin and easily ripped out, with a narrow gutter that tempts users to push down on the spine. For about $10 more, libraries can purchase the hardcover *Cassell Compact Dictionary*.—**Hope Yelich**

880. **The Concise Oxford Dictionary.** 10th ed. Judy Pearsall, ed. New York, Oxford University Press, 1999. 1666p. $29.95. ISBN 0-19-860287-1.

This 1-volume dictionary from Oxford University Press is a recommended work. The best reason to recommend this edition is its organization. The dictionary's massive sibling, *The Oxford English Dictionary* (2d ed.; see ARBA 90, entry 1006), is considered the authoritative dictionary of the English language, but is difficult for the layperson to use. *The Oxford English Dictionary* (OED) is massive; definitions can last for pages and are full of information necessary to the linguist but which may otherwise confuse the average user. *The Concise Oxford Dictionary* is written, in contrast, for the remainder of the population. The definitions center on the "core" (most literal and central) use of the word in current English, and are written in clear, precise language. Meanings and sub-meanings are well organized, giving the reader a sense of the relationships between differing definitions of the same term. The origins and derivatives parts of the definition begin, respectively, with the word's "origin" and "derivatives," making it much simpler to understand than the comparable parts of the OED. Labels such as "formal," "archaic," "technical," "humorous," and "euphemistic" give a sense of how the word is currently used. The listings include some grammar guidelines and spelling variations.

The front matter includes a preface, introduction, guide to the use of the dictionary, abbreviations, and a note on trademarks and proprietary status. It is as well organized and written as the rest of the dictionary. Another notable quality of the dictionary is its currency. The 2d edition of the OED was published in 1989. Since then, revolutions in knowledge and knowledge access have taken place, and the 10th edition of *The Concise Oxford Dictionary* reflects the new vocabulary with such words as "webmaster," "wicca," "nanotechnology," and "html." This dictionary is highly recommended for any library or for personal use.

—**Mary A. Axford**

881. **Encarta World English Dictionary.** New York, St. Martin's Press, 1999. 2078p. illus. maps. $50.00. ISBN 0-312-22222-X.

World English is the English language in all its varieties as it is spoken and written around the world. The editors of this work endeavored to create a comprehensive dictionary of American English (that spoken in the United States) written for a diverse, worldwide audience, with the goals of introducing American English to other English speakers, and World English to American English speakers. This large, handsome volume succeeds in fulfilling these goals. The volume's prefatory materials include a detailed user's guide and a pronunciation guide. Because the pronunciation system is unique to this dictionary, reviewing the pronunciation guide is highly recommended. The dictionary contains more than 100,000 headwords and some 400,000 references. More than 4,000 attractive black-and-white illustrations, in the form of photographs, maps, and simple drawings, are also included. Access to the work's 62 tables, charts, and composite pictures is greatly enhanced by an alphabetic list at the end of the volume. Entries are comprehensive and include, as appropriate, spellings, pronunciation, definitions, contextual examples of usage, etymologies, usage notes, and synonyms. More than 2,000 short essays provide extra detail about word history, usage, synonyms, and cultural notes. Some 500 cultural notes, a unique feature of this dictionary, refer to books, movies, plays, and musical pieces to provide cultural context for some words and phrases.

Although the editors created an interesting and useful dictionary, a few slight oversights were noted. Pronunciation was missing from at least two words encountered during a brief examination of the work. More cross-references between related entries would be useful. For example, an essay about African American Vernacular English refers to the alternative term "ebonics" (a term that is probably more familiar to most American English speakers), but the entry for "ebonics" does not contain a cross-reference to the first term, with its associated essay. Although more than 5,000 biographical entries are included in this work, the currency of some of the information is a bit uneven. Bill Clinton's 1999 impeachment and acquittal are noted, but there is no mention of Michael Jordan's retirement year (1998), which is standard in other athletes' entries. This work also contains more than 5,000 geographic entries, but inclusion criteria are absent, and context is rarely provided for the importance of these entries. For example, Bismarck, North Dakota, is included because it is a capital city, but why are Bangor, Maine, and Endicott, New York, included? Overall, however, this ambitious volume succeeds as a useful, unique, and interesting dictionary. [R: LJ, 1 Oct 99, p. 78; BL, 15 Nov 99, pp. 646-648]—**Karen Selden**

882. **Random House Webster's Basic Dictionary of American English.** New York, Random House, 1998. 524p. $10.95pa. ISBN 0-679-78005-X.

Random House Webster's Basic Dictionary of American English has targeted a rather specialized audience for this new version of its dictionary, but the work will almost certainly prove to be a valuable tool for a variety of individuals, including native speakers. Written primarily for beginning learners of English as a second or foreign language, this new dictionary will undoubtedly draw a large readership for both its excellent content and its highly readable format. Moreover, the dictionary is affordable for classroom and individual use.

One of the most exciting aspects of a new edition of a standard work like Webster's is the inclusion of newly minted words. This volume does not disappoint in this respect, including such recent issues as *digerati*, *dweeb*, *soccer mom* (which already appears to be outdated in many circles), and trendy but probably long-lasting abbreviations such as *ATM*, *PIN*, and *PCS*. However, even newer abbreviations spawned by technological leaps, like DVD, are missing and will surely be found in future editions. It was also helpful to include words related to unusual but significant cultural events in the United States, including the December 26–January harvest festival, Kwanzaa, celebrated in some communities by African Americans. Foreign words, most especially those related to popular ethnic cooking, figure prominently in this new dictionary, such as *fajitas*, *tortilla*, and *taco*. The accepted postal service abbreviations for the 50 states are also listed.

As the dictionary is intended for people who are learning American English as a second language, it offers a useful pronunciation guide based on the International Phonetic Alphabet. There is a relevant discussion of the differences between British and American standard English in which the editors note that the 2 languages differ mainly in their pronunciation and that they are actually quite similar considering the 400 years that have elapsed since they went their separate ways. The reader will also find abundant grammatical information, such as a list of intransitive verbs, irregular verb conjugations, and notations on whether nouns are considered "count" (i.e., can be preceded by "a" or "an") or "noncount."

Considering its relative brevity, *Random House Webster's Basic Dictionary of American English* offers a lot of useful information to anyone seeking to update and expand their knowledge of the language. It could also be a valuable reference work for K-12 and college users (both students and teachers), who will always benefit from a reminder of grammatical points and pronunciation rules.—**John B. Romeiser**

883. **Webster's New World College Dictionary.** 4th ed. Michael Agnes, ed. New York, Macmillan General Reference/Simon & Schuster Macmillan, 1999. 1716p. illus. maps. index. $21.95. ISBN 0-02-863119-6.

This latest of the Webster's New World Dictionaries, the 4th edition of the *College Dictionary* is a revision of the 3d edition, originally published in 1988. It continues a line of dictionaries, published since 1951, committed to providing a guide to the vocabulary of general American usage. One therefore seeks and finds modern usage; American pronunciation; definitions written in a current style; American geographical etymology; and attention to American colloquialisms, slang, and idioms, all placed in a context of general English language and not narrowly limited to American colloquial language.

This medium-sized dictionary has 163,000 entries, about 7,500 of them new since the 3d edition. It is illustrated, including some new illustrations since the last edition and a few colored maps. Definitions are clear and concise. The type is small, but easier to read than in the 3rd edition. Perhaps some definitions are too concise: "central processing unit" is an inadequate definition of *cpu*. On the whole, current computer terminology, of the sort frequently needed by typical users of this kind of dictionary, is just adequately but certainly not excellently covered. *E-mail*, *PC*, and *byte* are included; *Unix*, *Y2K*, and *Pentium* are not. The "Reference Supplement" is both expanded and typographically spread out, in comparison to this section in the 3d edition. It contains 45 pages of population statistics (partially updated since 1988), English punctuation, U.S. political documents, meteorological data, chemical elements, and a new section on Mexico, among other things. Its contents are indexed at the end of the dictionary. Biographical and geographical entries are interfiled in the main section of the dictionary.

With its 163,000 entries, this dictionary may be compared in comprehensiveness to the *Oxford Dictionary and Thesaurus* (American ed.; see ARBA 98, entry 994). The later serves a slightly different purpose, with its inclusion of synonyms. It is now outdated by at least three years. In the Oxford dictionary the definitions and synonyms are integrated, but geographical and biographical entries are not. It lacks the etymology and illustrations present in the *New World Dictionary*.

This dictionary is inexpensive for its type and coverage and is apparently well bound. It is recommended for academic, high school, and public libraries, and is also desirable for home purchase and use.
—**Florence W. Jones**

Eponyms

884. Ehrlich, Eugene. **What's in a Name? How Proper Names Became Everyday Words.** New York, Henry Holt, 1999. 238p. $25.00. ISBN 0-8050-5942-3.

Although the word "eponym" is used only in the CIP, *What's in a Name?* is in fact a dictionary of eponyms and is similar to such works as Cyril Beeching's *A Dictionary of Eponyms* (3d ed.; see ARBA 91, entry 1051). In *What's in a Name?*, Ehrlich defines approximately 900 terms that have their origins in proper, literary, religious, and mythological names. Alphabetically, these range from "Aaron's Rod" to "Zöllner Illusion" and include such terms as "boson," "Cassandra," "diophantine equation," "grog," and "pecksniff." Ehrlich's definitions are chatty and amiable, and the volume itself is capably done, with cross-references as necessary. At the same time, enjoyable though it is, *What's in a Name?* is, sadly, far from comprehensive. Those looking for explanations of "Pickwickian," "Lovecraftian," "Tournedos Rossini," the "Schmidt telescope," "Schrödinger's wave equation," and "Shakespearean," to name but a few, will be forced to go elsewhere. This volume is recommended for larger libraries.—**Richard Bleiler**

Etymology

885. Lee, Laura. **The Name's Familiar: Mr. Leotard, Barbie, and Chef Boyardee.** Gretna, La., Pelican Publishing, 1999. 312p. $14.95pa. ISBN 1-56554-394-7.

Many words and phrases in the English language derive from the names of people. Their origin is usually reflected in their capitalization (e.g., a Freudian slip) but sometimes not (e.g., boycott, gerrymander). If one includes commercial products (e.g., Heinz ketchup), geographical features (Mount Rushmore), scientific and medical terms (e.g., Van Allen Belt, Rorschach test), and songs (e.g., Eleanor Rigby), the number comes to thousands, each with its tale to tell. Lee, a journalist and broadcaster who ran a radio program on trivia, offers in this book a selection of such tales in two sections: the main one gives about a half-page to each entry and the "shorts" give about six lines.

Lee directs her work squarely at a popular audience. She emphasizes the story behind the name and makes little attempt to validate her accounts by scholarly evidence. The style is breezy, colloquial, and quite often humorous. There is no index or bibliography. More important from the reference viewpoint, the contents are so miscellaneous that it seems to be quite unpredictable as to whether a given eponym will appear. *The Name's Familiar* is to be used for entertainment rather than research. Libraries will probably not want it for their reference departments but may well choose it for their circulating stock. Many individuals will find it worth buying for their own enjoyment or perhaps as a gift for teenagers who may thereby be stimulated to learn more about language.—**Samuel Rothstein**

886. Sheildlower, Jesse. **Jesse's Word of the Day: From Abacinate to Yonic.** New York, Random House, 1998. 242p. index. $14.95pa. ISBN 0-375-70245-8.

Threats to the future of the book notwithstanding, lexicographer and Random House editor Jesse Sheidlower incarnates in print 300 queries submitted to a Random House online question box during 1996 and 1997. Jesseword.com responds to inquiries about the usage, style, etymology, grammar, and meaning of words or phrases in a few short paragraphs of clear, highly readable prose worthy of the most patron-friendly reference librarian. Indexes of people whose questions are reprinted, of sources quoted as examples, and of main and subsidiary entries conclude the volume. That these questions came to a publisher's Web-site perhaps indicates the number of people who live in cyberspace without a desktop dictionary, who do not think of using their local library, or who prefer consulting an online expert to using the intermediary of a book. A desk dictionary would have gone a long way toward answering these questions. Sheidlower might have profitably included a bibliography of such references along with his annotated list of online lexical resources because, even taken together, the latter do not offer as comprehensive an array of possibilities as a library's reference shelf. A token of the liveliness of people's interest in language, Sheidlower's compilation looks to print in order to archive his responses and reach an even larger audience of curious browsers; that said, his informative work is not systematic or inclusive enough for the reference collection. [R: LJ, Aug 98, p. 79]—**Robert H. Kieft**

Euphemisms

887. Adams, Ramon F. **Western Words: A Dictionary of the Old West.** New York, Hippocrene Books, 1998. 182p. $11.95pa. ISBN 0-7818-0590-2.

The pervasive myth of the American western frontier and the men (and less frequently) the women who tried to tame and exploit it has long fascinated us. Based on 25 years of collection, Ramon Adams (1888-1976), a Dallas, Texas, businessman with a fascination for the vernacular, culture, and folklore of the American cowboy, published *Western Words: A Dictionary of the Range, Cow Camp, and Trail* (University of Oklahoma Press, 1944). Encouraged by readers who wanted a more inclusive dictionary of western terms, he published an expanded edition subtitled *Western Words: A Dictionary of the American West* (University of Oklahoma Press, 1968), doubling its size. To his cowboy and cattle vernacular he added that of sheep men, trappers, buffalo hunters, stagecoach drivers, loggers and sawmill workers, freighters and packers, western river boatmen, miners, gamblers, and Indians.

Why Hippocrene chose to reprint the limited 1944 edition with a misleading, if not deceptive, subtitle is a mystery. Only a brief note that the book was originally published by the University of Oklahoma Press gives a clue that it is even a reprint. But this is not a dictionary of the American West. Its original subtitle more accurately reflects its content. Libraries wanting a dictionary of western vernacular and idioms will be better served by Winfred Blevins' *Dictionary of the American West* (see ARBA 94, entry 1088); Robert Hendrickson's *Happy Trails: A Dictionary of Western Expressions* (see ARBA 95, entry 1043); or Thomas Clark's *Western Lore and Language: A Dictionary for Enthusiasts of the American West* (see ARBA 97, entry 841). These all give better coverage of western culture, both past and present, than this misnamed reprint of Adams' early work. This book is recommended only for libraries who missed the 1944 edition and would like to add it to their collection.—**Blaine H. Hall**

Homophones and Homographs

888. Hobbs, James B., comp. **Homophones and Homographs: An American Dictionary.** 3d ed. Jefferson, N.C., McFarland, 1999. 318p. $32.50. ISBN 0-7864-0610-0.

Homophones are words of similar pronunciation, having disparate meanings and spellings (e.g., write, right, rite). Homographs comprise a more elite group, being words whose spelling is the same, but whose meanings and pronunciations differ (e.g., bass and bass). In this work, Hobbs has enlarged upon his earlier efforts (see ARBA 87, entry 1026, and ARBA 94, entry 1086), with 637 new homophones and 83 new homographs. While maintaining the format and layout of its predecessors, this volume's pages display their text in broader and longer dual columns. Hobbs also supplies three dozen new citations in the annotated bibliography of ancillary sources. Furthermore, this edition adopts a sturdier font for its pronunciation symbols and notations that accompany homophone entries.

Headwords of entries that are classifiable as either a homophone or a homograph are underscored throughout, and are listed together in an appendix. For any given pair or group of homophone entries, their definition appears beside only whichever term precedes all others alphabetically; in such instances, cross-references from the other entries are provided. Among this book's entries, one finds such obscure words as "keeks," "grimmal," "jill," and "scudder." New entries include "freezer/frieser," "aune/own," and "palm/pom/pomme." Some proper adjectives (Swedish), as well as many proper nouns (Sikh, Mainiac, Chow, and McIntosh) are included; however, individual personal names (Paul, Peter, Jean) are not—although there are entries for "Midas" and for such eponyms as "Pattons" (a type of tank) and "Stirling" (a type of engine). To a degree belying it subtitle, this resource contains a liberal number of foreign terms (quete, guib, marichal) as well.

Defects and weaknesses, while minor, do intrude. "Cursor" is defined as "part of a mathematical instrument that moves back and forth," an outdated meaning. Although a cross-referencing notation at "hello" directs one to "hallo," the former term appears nowhere in the entry of the latter. Also, readers consulting this reference may doubt that among typical, educated American speakers, any of the following pairs of entries share the same pronunciation: topology/typology, satem/Sodem, or just/joust. Finally, whether as a result of careless copyediting or a dubious editorial decision, a number of words that were hyphenated in the 2d edition appear unhyphenated in this revision (e.g., closegrained, mediumsized, illusioncreating, NigerCongo, and so forth). Even so, this dictionary remains without peer in its comprehensiveness and general authoritativeness of its subject matter. [R: LJ, 1 Oct 99, p. 80]—**Jeffrey E. Long**

Juvenile

889. **The Merriam-Webster and Garfield Dictionary.** Springfield, Mass., Merriam-Webster, 1999. 800p. illus. $12.95pa. ISBN 0-87779-626-2.

The Merriam-Webster and Garfield Dictionary is the most child-friendly dictionary to be published. This innovative dictionary actually encourages use by utilizing a cartoon character that appeals to children of all ages.

This dictionary features the cartoon cat Garfield, in collaboration with its creator Jim Davis, to highlight featured words in the dictionary. At the bottom of the pages that use the highlighted featured word is a comic strip illustrating that particular word's usage.

This dictionary, inspired by Jim Davis, is designed just like every other dictionary and includes a list of common English given names; a list of foreign words and phrases; a section on biographical, biblical, and mythological names; a section on geographical names; signs and symbols; a handbook of style section; and a section on documentation of sources. There is even a special list of wacky definitions that only Garfield could dream up. In the front is a section of explanatory notes, abbreviations used in the work, and a page devoted to pronunciation symbols. It is an extraordinary combination of both dictionary and comic book and is highly recommended.—**Pamela J. Getchell**

890. **Merriam-Webster's Intermediate Dictionary.** Springfield, Mass., Merriam-Webster, 1998. 943p. illus. $15.95. ISBN 0-87779-479-0.

This dictionary, of about 40,000 word entries, is intended for middle and junior high students. It is preceded by *Merriam-Webster's Elementary Dictionary* (Merriam-Webster, 1994) and followed by *Merriam-Webster's School Dictionary* (see entry 891). All three volumes are highly respected and widely used. For each entry in the main body of this work, syllabification is given, followed by variant spellings, phonetic pronunciation (the pronunciation key is found on each double-page spread), usage indication (e.g., slang, substandard), grammatical classification, and irregular plurals or tense formations when necessary. The definitions follow. They are clear, concise, and suited to the intended audience. As in other Webster dictionaries they are in chronological order. Separate entries are given for homographic words. A few basic words have synonym entries with definitions and usage pointers for each synonym. Some words with interesting origins are given a separate short paragraph called "Word History." There are about 300 "Word Histories" and an equal number of synonym entries. Brief etymologies or usage indicators are sometimes given, but there are no antonyms. The word coverage seems up-to-date. *Dork*, *Internet*, and *World Wide Web* are included, but not *search engine*. Many words considered obscene are absent; for example, *fornicate* is here but not its more frequently used synonyms. Running heads at the top of each page give both the first and last word on the page. Small black-and-white drawings are used to illustrate objects or animals. Special features include several mini-dictionaries at the back; a list of abbreviations, which includes chemical symbols; a biographical directory of more than 1,000 names with one-line identifications; a gazetteer of nearly 3,000 place-names with their pronunciations; and a short section of signs and symbols. The format is attractive, type size is suitable, and the binding is sturdy. This dictionary is highly recommended for students in grades six through nine.—**John T. Gillespie**

891. **Merriam-Webster's School Dictionary.** Springfield, Mass., Merriam-Webster, 1999. 1158p. illus. $15.95. ISBN 0-87779-380-8.

Designed for high school students, this dictionary indicates the expertise of the staff of one of the preeminent dictionary makers in the United States. It compares well with the *Merriam-Webster's Collegiate Dictionary* (10th ed.; see ARBA 94, entry 1076), including about 75 percent of the same words. The definitions, while frequently shorter with few subsections, reflect a strong influence from that volume. The etymologies are also very similar, but with fewer abbreviations, making them easier to understand. The introductory material includes topics such as guidewords, pronunciation, function, form and meaning of words, cross-references, usage, synonyms, abbreviations, and pronunciation symbols. The pronunciation guide also appears on each two-page spread. General abbreviations; a biographical dictionary with historical, biblical, and mythological names; a geographical dictionary; and a brief article on style complete the book.

The back cover of the dictionary claims that it contains 85,000 entries and 91,000 definitions. Terms omitted from this volume that are present in the *Collegiate* volume would probably not be of pressing interest to the average high school student. There are no terms appearing in the *School Dictionary* that are not in the *Collegiate*. Terms such as *CD*, *RAM*, *ROM*, and *grass* as marijuana, are included, as are body parts relating to sexual functions, but not the slang words defined in the *Collegiate* volume.

Nearly every two-page spread includes at least one helpful drawing or chart. The pages have enough white space to be appealing and easy to read. This will be a good dictionary for senior high school students, libraries, and for some middle school students. Libraries and some high school students may also wish to consult the *Collegiate* in book or CD-ROM (see ARBA 98, entry 998) format.—**Betty Jo Buckingham**

New Words

892. **Oxford English Dictionary Additions Series, Volume 3.** Michael Proffitt, ed. New York, Oxford University Press, 1997. 351p. index. $55.00. ISBN 0-19-860027-5.

Reviewing the *Oxford English Dictionary* (OED) is a lot like reviewing the Pacific Ocean; so great is its bulk, so large its presence on the map, that whatever opinions one might hold about it pale into irrelevance because nothing else could fill the space. Those who know the first 2 volumes of *Additions* to OED's 2d edition will recognize its conformity in editorial practice and layout to the 2d edition's, and its purpose of entering 3,000 words or senses of words not entered heretofore in OED. A cumulative index of the roughly 9,000 entries in all 3 additions completes the volume. Conceived with other national-imperial cultural projects, OED reveals the reach of the language now assuming global domination. Entries in these additions derive from all fields of human endeavor, from around the world and from colloquial as well as formal usage. The electronic OED licensed to libraries for local loading does not include the *Additions* volumes. The OED homepage (http://205.229.236.10/dicts.html) allows subscribers to search the 2d edition and its additions as separate databases. Early in 2000, OED will integrate online the 2d edition and additions with the revisions and further additions that will cumulate in the 3d edition in 2010. A necessary purchase for most academic and larger public libraries and a necessary complement to William A. Craigie and James R. Hulbert's *A Dictionary of American English on Historical Principles* (4 vols., University of Chicago Press, 1938), J. E. Lighter's *Historical Dictionary of American Slang* (Random House, 1994), and Frederic G. Cassidy's *Dictionary of American Regional English* (Belknap Press of Harvard University Press, 1985). [R: RUSQ, v. 38 no. 1, p. 101]—**Robert H. Kieft**

Sign Language

893. Tennant, Richard A., and Marianne Gluszak Brown. **The American Sign Language Handshape Dictionary.** Washington, D.C., Clerc Books/Gallaudet University Press, 1998. 407p. illus. index. $35.00. ISBN 1-56368-043-2.

The American Sign Language Handshape Dictionary allows an ASH signer to look up a sign using visual clues instead of English-language ones. It conquers the dilemma of the student who cannot recognize a signed word and is told to "look it up in the dictionary"—a laborious, boring, and often fruitless effort. While other dictionaries are organized by the English alphabet, the authors and artist saw a need for the backdoor approach, which could encourage the students of early or medium proficiency to increase their understanding of the language. To identify a sign using one hand making an open "B," the viewer goes to the one-hand sign section, finds the "Open B" handshape, and remembers the signer touched the stomach; so he or she goes past the sign produced in space, past the sign that touches the head, to signs that touch the body. This limits the viewer to five pages and he or she can easily find the dominant hand making a circular sign on the stomach and see that it means "upset." Those that benefit would be middle school students and beyond, those who already read handsigns but see a sign they do not recognize, those who need a good charted description, those who need a quick refresher of many handsigns, and those who want to hone their skills and increase their vocabulary.

Each handsign has synonyms and variations of form that offer helpful memory devices. There are cross-references and a chart that helps the reader reproduce the sign themselves. The chapter has the handshape, its orientation, location in space, and movement of the hand(s) shown by arrows.

The dictionary contains only about 1,600 signs as opposed to the Random House dictionary, which contains more than 5,600 entries. *The American Sign Language Handshape Dictionary* is on a conversational level. There are helping verbs, personal pronouns, place-names, illnesses, slang, and everyday jobs.

The introduction gives a one-page history of handsigning and explains some of the grammatical differences from English. English uses subject-verb-direct object, but handsigning used direct object-subject-verb. Thus "I like you" becomes "you I like." The introduction also includes five tips on acquiring proficiency in reading handsigns. Users should read the "How To Use" section. The book also contains a glossary of all words and concepts illustrated.—**Constance Harding**

Terms and Phrases

894. Ammer, Christine, comp. **Cool Cats, Top Dogs, and Other Beastly Expressions.** Westminster, Md., Houghton Mifflin, 1999. 266p. illus. index. $14.00pa. ISBN 0-395-95730-3.

Originally published in 1989 as *It's Raining Cats and Dogs—And Other Beastly Expressions*, this tour of the zoological garden of metaphor will entertain the browser or shut-in, the waiting-room idler or drowsy traveler. Ammer arranges approximately 1,200 expressions topically in narrative sections subsumed in chapters by kind (e.g., cats, dogs, insects) or environment (e.g., the barnyard, the wild, the sea). An index allows the reader to find a specific expression without browsing through the chapter where the animal might be found. Occasional line drawings enliven the text. Librarians would certainly be more comfortable with this popular title if it had a bibliography of sources, for although Ammer's preface gestures toward a long line of predecessors, she does not generally cite authorities. With the familiar, historically based dictionaries or volumes of proverbial sayings already on the shelf, Ammer's slight work is not for the scholarly or general reference collection but will amusingly occupy the insomniac or flight-delayed.—**Robert H. Kieft**

895. Homer, William Innes. **The Language of Contemporary Criticism.** Madison, Conn., Sound View Press, 1999. 175p. illus. $15.95pa. ISBN 0-932087-58-2.

The author has written this book as a key for people, especially students, to understand the arcane language and confusing theoretical concepts used in contemporary criticism. The volume consists of two sections that are closely related to each other. The first is a series of text essays that explain larger concepts such as structuralism and poststructuralism, movements such as the Frankfort School, or the teachings of influential thinkers from Marx to Althusser. These essays are meant to explain the complexities of modern and postmodern theoretical and critical writing. They also serve as a background and context for the 2d section of the book, an extensive glossary of currently relevant terminology. The author states in his introduction that in writing this text he has "tried to make complex ideas easy to understand." He has also "used language that is, as much as possible, nontechnical and liberated from jargon." Many disciplines—art criticism, linguistics, literary theory, anthropology, social theory, philosophy, and psychoanalysis—are represented in this book, often overlapping and merging. This is a good reference for college-level criticism students.—**Cari Ringelheim**

Thesauri

896. **The American Heritage Student Thesaurus.** By Paul Hellweg, Joyce LeBaron, and Susannah LeBaron. Westminster, Md., Houghton Mifflin, 1999. 378p. $17.00. ISBN 0-395-93026-X.

According to the cover, *The American Heritage Student Thesaurus* is meant for ages 12 to 16, in grades 7 to 10. A two-page introduction defines a thesaurus as a book of synonyms, or "a book of word choices." According to the authors, more than 6,000 words are listed as main entries, with approximately 100,000 synonyms in all. After explaining how to use the thesaurus, the editors invite readers' comments and questions and provide an address where they may be reached.

Each entry lists the part of speech of the word, followed by several synonyms and a sentence using the entry word. When a word has several uses, the most common are put first. Finally, the word's antonyms are listed. Occasionally, a blue box will give information about word groups. For example, the word *firework* is defined as "an explosive device set off to create bright lights and loud noises for amusement. Firework is a general term with no true synonyms." Then the box lists and describes some specific types of fireworks, such as pinwheel, Roman candle, serpent, skyrocket, and torpedo.

Certainly every writer, no matter what age, should learn to rely on a thesaurus. *The American Heritage Student Thesaurus* seems built to hold up well to classroom use. However, this volume's vocabulary level and content seem more suited to 5th through 7th graders than to those in higher grades.—**Kay O. Cornelius**

897. **DK Dictionary/Thesaurus.** New York, DK Publishing, 1999. 512p. $9.95pa. ISBN 0-7894-3949-2.

Contrary to standard DK practice, the *Dictionary/Thesaurus* has absolutely no illustrations, and, except for one page of abbreviations, no directions for the user. Nor is any user age level suggested. The color blue sets out the letters of the alphabet at the beginning of each section. The same color highlights the synonym lists to separate them from the definitions. Parentheses contain words indicating the sense of the word (e.g., "abandon v 1 [desert sb] dump, jilt, leave, run out on, throw over. 2 [desert a place] evacuate, quit, vacate. 3 [give up altogether] cede, forfeit, resign, surrender" [p. 5]).

According to the back cover, 20,000 dictionary entries and 50,000 synonyms are provided. Definitions are generally one-liners but do include the part(s) of speech. No pronunciation or etymology is included. The book includes less than 40 percent of the words in the *Merriam Webster School Dictionary* (1999) and around 42 percent of the synonym entry words from *Oxford Minireference Thesaurus* (1992).

This is a clear, easy-to-read, and quite portable dictionary/thesaurus. Serious students and libraries might prefer to spend a few more dollars for the *Oxford Desk Dictionary and Thesaurus* (1997 ed.; see ARBA 98, entry 993) or the *Oxford Dictionary and Thesaurus* (1996 American ed.; see ARBA 98, entry 994).

—**Betty Jo Buckingham**

898. **The Oxford American Thesaurus of Current English.** Christine A. Lindberg, ed. New York, Oxford University Press, 1999. 863p. $17.95. ISBN 0-19-513375-7.

With some 15,000 separate entries that provide more than 350,000 synonyms, *The Oxford American Thesaurus of Current English* is a large and engaging volume. As do most thesauruses, it groups and separates its words and their synonymous terms by part of speech, and it separates groups within semantic senses and meaning relationships. Furthermore, there are cross-references as necessary, verb phrases are often included as subentries, and many entries provide antonyms. The volume concludes with a "writer's toolkit," which provides guides to punctuation, usage, diacritical marks, proofreader's marks, and brief discussions of easily confused words.

This thesaurus will assist students and writers, but is also a work that should occasionally be used with caution, for rather than oppose written slovenliness, the compilers have at times offered what is tantamount to an endorsement of it. For example, among the terms given as synonymous for *massacre* is "decimate," which has traditionally meant to kill one of every ten. The toolkit explains that this older meaning "has been superseded by the later more general sense, 'kill or destroy (a large portion of),'" but that a word is commonly misused by the American public does not mean that the makers of thesauruses need endorse the misuse. Oddly, a stand is taken in the discussion of the word *fulsome*, the toolkit stating that it means "excessive, cloying, or insincere," and is "often imprecisely used to mean 'generous.'" A firmer editorial presence throughout would have been welcome, but nevertheless this thesaurus is generally recommended for academic and public libraries. [R: BL, 15 Dec 99, p. 800]—**Richard Bleiler**

899. **Scholastic Children's Thesaurus.** By John K. Bollard. Illustrated by Mike Reed. New York, Scholastic, 1998. 256p. illus. index. $15.95. ISBN 0-590-96785-1.

As an educational resource for young learners, this thesaurus is designed to improve vocabulary, language, and communication skills. It contains more than 500 entries and 2,700 synonyms. One distinguishing feature of this thesaurus is that definitions and example sentences are given to provide more in-depth understanding of the words and their synonyms. Information boxes provide additional data, such as parts of speech and differences in grammatical usage. Entries are also cross-referenced to direct readers to other groups of related synonyms. For example, the entry for "nice" points readers to also look at "friendly," "good," and "great."

The index lists all entry words and synonyms alphabetically, making it easy for users to locate a word they have in mind. Also included in the index for many of the entry words (which are listed in capital letters) are antonyms that are also listed in the thesaurus. This is a great learning tool for young readers and writers. The introduction provides instructions on how to use the thesaurus, but it would be beneficial for a parent or teacher to help children get started. [R: LJ, Dec 98, pp. 540-542; SLJ, Feb 99, pp. 132-134]—**Cari Ringelheim**

NON-ENGLISH-LANGUAGE DICTIONARIES

General Works

900. Adeleye, Gabriel G., Kofi Acquah-Dadzie, Thomas J. Sienkewicz, and James T. McDonough Jr. **World Dictionary of Foreign Expressions: A Resource for Readers and Writers.** Wauconda, Ill., Bolchazy-Carducci, 1999. 411p. $70.00; $19.95pa. ISBN 0-86516-422-3; 0-86516-423-1pa.

This is a dictionary of words and phrases borrowed by English speakers from more than 20 languages. The language most frequently represented, by far, is Latin, perhaps because the work was conceived and first written as a legal dictionary and was later expanded to include philosophical, historical, and literary terms.

For each word or phrase, the user finds part of speech, gender, plural form, language of origin, and both a word-by-word translation (unusual in a dictionary of this type) and a more "polished" definition and translation. There are no pronunciation guides. Where appropriate, a usage note indicates the discipline where the term is used (i.e., law). Illustrative sentences are provided for each entry as well.

It is a handy reference tool as far as it goes, but the work's "strong African focus" (editor's preface) and heavy emphasis on legal terms limit its utility for an American audience. Many foreign words commonly used in the United States (such as mensch, sushi, docent, maillot, Bolshevik, and compadre) are missing. Overall, this is a well-executed work, given its scope, and will be especially useful in libraries needing a source for legal phrases and Latin loanwords. For a general dictionary of foreign terms, *The Oxford Dictionary of Foreign Words and Phrases* edited by Jennifer Speake (see ARBA 99, entry 903) would be a better purchase. [R: LJ, July 99, p. 79]—**Emily L. Werrell**

901. Allen, C. G. **A Manual of European Languages for Librarians.** 2d ed. New Providence, N.J., Bowker-Saur/Reed Reference Publishing, 1999. 994p. $215.00. ISBN 1-85739-241-8.

The 1st edition was published in 1975. In the preface of this new edition, the author states that the release of this 2d edition is due to the great changes taking place in publishing in Eastern Europe, some language changes since the 1st edition, and the linguistic implications of electronic data processing.

This book is remarkably comprehensive and extremely useful for librarians. It treats 38 European languages including ancient and modern Latin and Greek. The languages are treated within the following seven language groups: Germanic; Latin and Romance; Celtic, Greek, and Albanian; Slavonic; Baltic; Finno-Ugrian; and other—Maltese, Turkish, Basque, and Esperanto. Each language has the following sections: general characteristics; bibliographic linguistics; alphabet, phonetics, and spelling; articles; nouns; adjectives; numerals; pronouns; verbs; adverbs; prepositions; conjunctions; particles; and word formation. The small glossaries of library and book terms at the end of each language make for delightful browsing. For example, "llyfrgellydd: librarian" (Welsh), "gebrosjeerd: paperback" (Afrikaans), "tipografie: press" (Rumanian), "iris: journal" (Irish), "wydanie: edition, publication" (Polish), and "ukazatel: index" (Czech).

This remarkable volume is compiled by a former superintendent of readers' service at the British Library of Political and Economic Science. Clarity of arrangement, realistic understanding of problems unique to every language, and an interpretative ability to translate problems into commonsense and understandable examples make the book both a tutorial and a fascinating reference tool. This manual is useful to librarians in college, university, and other research schools. It will be of particular interest to technical service librarians. [R: Choice, Nov 99, p. 501]—**Vera Gao**

Albanian

902. **Albanian-English Dictionary.** Leonard Newmark, ed. New York, Oxford University Press, 1998. 978p. $95.00. ISBN 0-19-864340-3.

The small number of twentieth-century reference works available on the Albanian language have chiefly been published in that country, beginning with the 1957 volume by Nelo Drizari and later dictionaries in the 1980s and 1990s compiled by Ilo Duro and Gaspar Kici. The present volume, created jointly by an American editor and specialists from Albania, was designed to help users "read and understand existing Albanian text . . . not express themselves in speaking or writing Albanian," and as such includes current forms as well as older styles no longer used. This places it in the tradition established by Stuart Mann's earlier tome, *A Historical Albanian and English Dictionary, 1496-1938*. A lengthy users' guide prefaces the body of the dictionary, providing background data (including an overview of the Albanian alphabet), a detailed summary of grammar and usage conventions, and a long list of sources drawn upon for further research on the language. This volume is useful for undergraduate and graduate libraries supporting programs in Slavic studies, although large public libraries may also wish to consider acquiring it to expand their resources for questions dealing with the ongoing crisis in Yugoslavia.—**Robert B. Marks Ridinger**

Chinese

903. **Chinese Character Dictionary: A Guide to the 2,000 Most Frequently-Used Characters.** Wang Huidi, Fan Keyu, Gao Jiaying, and Wang Zhifang, eds. Translated by Kong Jing. Boston, Cheng & Tsui, 1998. 510p. $18.95pa. ISBN 0-88727-314-9.

The Chinese language is very different from English and other languages around the world. Learners experience difficulty especially in the area of learning Chinese characters. This Chinese character dictionary is designed to help learners overcome that difficulty. It contains 2,000 entries, based on the vocabulary list for primary level. Each entry includes the following features: number of writing strokes, correct stroke sequence components that form the character, classifications of the structure of the character, illustrations of the structure in diagram form, two forms of written script (kai script and Song scripts, which are common errors in writing), the phonetic notation to help in pronunciation, common phrases with meanings in English, and the grade level of the word. Students should have no problems with writing Chinese if they can write these characters correctly. There are also four appendixes listed at the end of this dictionary: "Strokes of Chinese Characters," "Components of Chinese Characters," "Types of Character Structures," and "Radical Index." This dictionary is a good resource for teachers when teaching the Chinese language; learners will also find this an indispensable learning aid for achieving a sound level of competence in writing Chinese.—**Xiao (Shelley) Yan Zhang**

904. **Chinese-Pinyin-English Dictionary for Learners.** Wang Huan, ed. Boston, Cheng & Tsui, 1998. 1250p. $28.95pa. ISBN 0-88727-316-5.

This dictionary is exceptional in many ways. The main strength is its focus on learners. Students of the Chinese language are faced with the daunting task of learning to read and write characters, speak and understand, and most importantly for this volume, read transliterations in several styles. The Wade-Giles system, perfected in the nineteenth century, was joined by the French style, and most recently the Pinyin style created by the communist government. Being the most recent, it lacks many reference resources. This well-organized and complete dictionary goes far in correcting that problem. Compiled by teachers of Mandarin Chinese as well as the usual scholars, this 10-year project is extremely accessible and easy for the student to use. The 30,000 entries are presented with useful details. Each entry includes grammar usage and pronunciation, definitions in English and Chinese, sample sentences in Chinese characters, and additional notes. This dictionary is further enhanced by 2 indexes, 10 appendixes, and an overall guide. It is an excellent addition to any library.—**Linda L. Lam-Easton**

Dutch

905. **NTC's Compact Dutch and English Dictionary.** Lincolnwood, Ill., National Textbook, 1998. 288p. $19.95pa. ISBN 0-8442-0101-4.

Although bilingual dictionaries for students of both Dutch and English have been produced at regular intervals since the 1950s in both Europe and the United States, the majority of titles available in this genre predate 1990. The current decade has seen a shift in this genre toward works centering their attention on specific subject areas, while recent general works have been limited to *Cassell's English-Dutch, Dutch-English Dictionary* (1996) and Arseen Rijkaert's 1997 work from Hippocrene Books (see ARBA 99, entry 923). The present work brings coverage of the growth and development of contemporary Dutch up to the century's end and offers 30,000 entries split evenly between the 2 languages (including many compound words and phrases), noting that recent official changes in spelling introduced by the Netherlands government are included. A preface providing background on the date and scope of these changes would have enhanced the value of the dictionary. Tables of symbols and abbreviations used are provided. Suitable for all large public and undergraduate library reference collections.—**Robert B. Marks Ridinger**

Finnish

906. **NTC's Compact Finnish and English Dictionary.** By Sini Sovijärvi. Lincolnwood, Ill., National Textbook, 1998. 794p. $21.95pa. ISBN 0-8442-0325-4.

The subtitle of this work is "The Most Practical and Convenient Finnish and English Dictionary." The characteristics are largely accurate: the font is larger, so it is easy to read, and the entries are not complicated. The latter advantage is somewhat reduced by the diminished number of examples (particularly in the Finnish-English section). However, polysemy is well represented, and in most cases well discriminated. Comparison with other Finnish-language dictionaries shows that the vocabulary here has been updated. For instance, the *Finnish-English Dictionary* by P. E. Halme (Helsinki, Suomalaisen kirjallisuuden seura, 1957) had to list "puna armeija" as "Red army," whereas Sovijärvi could leave it out because the Russian name itself has changed. Whether, however, it was necessary to enrich the new dictionary with "puna-alpi" as "pimpernel" or "Punahilkka" as "Little Red Ridinghood [sic]" is somewhat moot. Compared to Aune Tuomikoski and Anna Slöör's *English-Finnish Dictionary* (Helsinki, Suomalaisen kirjallisuuden seura, 1957), readers can say that it was reasonable to save space by omitting "garrotte," only to add, alas, "gas chamber."

Finnish spelling is regular, with predictable pronunciation; on the other hand, not to indicate English pronunciations will certainly be felt as a lacuna. A list of the normal pronunciations of English letters is hardly sufficient for the task. However, there is also (in the back matter) a list of useful phrases and, what is particularly laudable, a special vocabulary of expressions one needs in a restaurant. The present dictionary can hardly make the two 1957 dictionaries superfluous, but it can render good service for simpler tasks.
—**L. Zgusta**

French

907. Strutz, Henry. **Dictionary of French Slang and Colloquial Expressions.** Hauppauge, N.Y., Barron's Educational Series, 1999. 355p. $8.95pa. ISBN 0-7641-0345-8.

In the ever-changing world of language, slang is one of the most transitory and fleeting forms of communication. In one moment, a word changes from a standard usage to something completely different. New expressions rise and fall as each generation or group tries to distinguish itself from others. No longer does one need to try to discern current slang and colloquial expressions only in English, but in other languages as well. This work fits into that category quite well, with French slang in use currently. A student of

French or current culture will find this an invaluable addition to the shelves, providing access to words and phrases ranging from humorous to earthy. The faint of heart are to be forewarned—all aspects of life and living are covered in detail, but then that too is part of an evolving language. For the price, any academic or public library will find this a useful addition to their collection of dictionaries on slang terms and colloquial expressions.—**Gregory Curtis**

908. Wittels, Harriet, and Joan Greisman. **French Thesaurus for Children.** Hauppauge, N.Y., Barron's Educational Series, 1999. 124p. illus. $6.95pa. ISBN 0-7641-0896-4.

This thesaurus has limited usefulness. It describes itself as designed to help both French-speaking children and those first learning French, but it is the concept of "children" that is the fundamental weakness. What kind of vocabulary should they be assumed to have? 5,000 words? 10,000? 20,000? The search for the exact French word is more a concern to people with an advanced vocabulary. More specifically, the synonyms offered are not always accurate. For instance, "badigeonner" (to whitewash) is not a synonym for "peindre" (to paint), and "rigoler" (to laugh) is a more accurate synonym for "rire" (to laugh) than the suggested "glousser" (to chortle or to cluck like a hen). Antonyms, even dubious ones, are often omitted. No antonym is offered for "obligatoire" (obligatory), although "facultatif" (optional) easily suggests itself, and either "gâter" or "gâcher" (to spoil) seems a clear antonym for "perfectionner" (to improve).

Other dictionaries consistently offer more carefully considered synonyms and antonyms. These are the dictionaries one should and ultimately would turn to.—**John B. Beston**

Gaelic

909. Macbain, Alexander. **Etymological Dictionary of Scottish-Gaelic.** New York, Hippocrene Books, 1998. 412p. $14.95pa. ISBN 0-7818-0632-1.

Originally published in 1896, this is a paperback reprint of the 1911 2d edition of *An Etymological Dictionary of the Gaelic Language*. The author emphasizes his effort to exclude Irish vocabulary from this Scottish-Gaelic dictionary. The 2d edition, published 4 years after the author's death, incorporated his corrections and additions, with final editing by another scholar. Thus it contains fairly pure Scottish-Gaelic of 1900, without the commonly intermingled Irish vocabulary. The author was a nineteenth-century teacher and scholar who wrote on Celtic religion, customs, history, and language. The vocabulary, at 6,900 words, is complete enough for most purposes. Around 70 percent of the words have etymological origins in Celtic, with about 20 percent clearly from other language groups. The dictionary also contains a 20-page introduction to Gaelic philology and separate sections on national names relevant to the British Isles and personal names of historical Celtic personages. The latter is presented as two lists—16 pages of male names and 1 page of female names.

This dictionary is unique in that it is both etymological and limited to Scottish-Gaelic; nothing more modern that satisfies these requirements has been published. As a further plus, the introduction provides fairly detailed and scholarly information on Gaelic grammar and philology. For libraries the book has one significant drawback: with its extremely narrow margins binding would require hand sewing, thus adding perhaps $10 to the price of the book. This dictionary, which has stood the test of time, is useful for scholars or genealogists with an interest in Scottish Gaelic words, names, and places.—**Florence W. Jones**

Irish

910. **Irish-English, English-Irish Easy Reference Dictionary.** Niwot, Colo., Roberts Rinehart Publishers, 1998. 480p. $24.95; $14.95pa. ISBN 1-57098-165-5; 1-57098-184-1pa.

This is a quick-reference dictionary for use by travelers or beginning students. Its main advantage is that its vocabulary is quite up-to-date. This is shown not only by items comprised in the bilingual gazetteer of place-names such as Kosovo or Vojvodina, known by few people just a couple of years ago, but also by items such as "Friends of the Earth–Cairde na Cruinne" (p. 353) that users find in the main vocabulary. There is some disambiguation of senses, treated in the English-Irish by separate entries: one for "foot" as part of the body, another for "foot" as a unit of measurement, and yet another to lead the user to an expression like "to foot the bill" (p. 351). The dictionary is intended for an English user, because the Irish-English section offers more synonyms, but without discrimination (e.g., "iall f2–string, leash, lace, strap"). The abbreviation following the Irish noun informs the reader about its declension. Tables of such grammatical paradigms follow the gazetteer. The vocabulary is generally well selected; only occasionally is there cause to stop and wonder. For example, why do we get "oileáin ilchríche" (continental islands) as the only exemplification in the entry for "ilchríoch" (continent), or "ilchineálacht timpeallachta" (environmental diversity) as the only exemplification of diversity? But no need to object. On the other hand, the absence of any indication of both English and Irish pronunciation is regrettable. Although this dictionary does not offer a massive amount of well-ordered and well-explained information as that offered by de Bhaldraithe's *English-Irish Dictionary* (Baile Átha Cliath, Oifig an tSoláthair, 1959), it will offer help for some simpler purposes.—**L. Zgusta**

Italian

911. Gobetti, Daniela. **Dictionary of Italian Slang and Colloquial Expressions.** Hauppauge, N.Y., Barron's Educational Series, 1999. 331p. $8.95pa. ISBN 0-7641-0432-2.

Gobetti, of the Center for European Studies at the University of Michigan, presents 4,500 common Italian slang words and colloquial expressions, each followed by the definition in English, a sentence or phrase in Italian to illustrate usage, an English translation of the example, and, where applicable, a corresponding English slang expression. She includes slang used by four groups: young people and students, drug addicts, criminals, and the general population.

If you thought languages such as English or Yiddish had a lot of words for "penis," learn that in Italian there are 1,200 vernacular words for the male organ! Gobetti helps readers understand some of the social contexts and connotations of these words so that they will get in less trouble next time they are traveling through Italy.

Have you ever actually tried to read a dictionary, but quickly became bogged down by boredom? Trying to read *Dictionary of Italian Slang and Colloquial Expressions* is difficult because the reader is likely to keep doubling over with laughter. For example, did you think you knew what a *bottega* was? Think again: "Bottega, f.(Lit., shop.) a) slang, rude. 1. Avere la bottega aperta. To have the fly of one's trousers open. E completamente sfatto: gira con la bottega aperta. 'He's completely lost his mind; he wanders around with his fly open.' "

Who will use this little gem of a book? This reviewer will, before my next trip to Italy, when I am reading or writing a novel or play set in the Roman underground, or whenever I am looking for some great laughs. If there exists a funnier dictionary, this reviewer would love to see it.—**Anthony Gottlieb**

Japanese

912. **The Compact Nelson Japanese-English Character Dictionary.** By John H. Haig. North Clarendon, Vt., Tuttle, 1999. 779p. $27.95pa. ISBN 0-8048-2037-6.

This dictionary is an abridged edition of Andrew Nelson's award-winning *The Modern Reader's Japanese-English Character Dictionary*. The dictionary contains more than 3,000 main-entry kanji (Chinese characters) and more than 30,000 *jyukugo* (Chinese character compounds). Unlike an English dictionary, which arranges the entry words alphabetically, this dictionary, like any other kanji dictionary, lists kanji entries in the increasing order of the number of strokes of the radical (the left side of Chinese characters). This arrangement may inherently discourage anyone from looking up any kanji. But to assist the user, the author instructs precisely what radical of kanji the user should search for in order to look up any kanji. The user, who should already know how to read kanji but who does not know the English meaning of a word, can follow the instructions provided, but can also look a word up instead through the *on* (Chinese-derived) or *kun* (native) reading, a section about which is provided in the appendix. Many kanji entries are followed by useful *jyukugo* with an English translation but not by illustrative sentences. The dictionary includes 11 appendixes that contain information about radicals and explanations on how to find kanji and how to determine the radical. Since the number of Japanese words introduced to English-speaking people has been increasing, scholars, business people, or school libraries would benefit from having a Japanese-English dictionary that contains kanji. The brevity and lucidity of this dictionary make it recommendable. For greater comprehensiveness and wider coverage, *NTC's New Japanese-English Character Dictionary* (see ARBA 94, entry 1121) is preferable, if more expensive.—**Seiko Mieczkowski**

913. Suzuki, Reiko, Are Hajikano, and Sayuri Kataoka. **Business Kanji: Over 17,700 Essential Business Terms in Japanese.** North Clarendon, Vt., Tuttle, 1999. 422p. $22.95pa. ISBN 0-8048-2134-8.

This book is intended for both self-study and classroom use. The authors offer 50 steps of instruction, each step consisting of 3 parts. The final part contains a list of Japanese compound words with furigana (Japanese script that assist in reading kanji); English equivalents are also listed for each compound word. In the 2d part, each Japanese compound is followed by a short sentence that uses the word with no English translation. The 3d part, "Reading Practice," comprises 6 to 8 sentences, again without English translation. In the sentences in the 2d and 3d parts the authors use compound words that have already appeared in the preceding steps. The authors have organized their text in this manner to enhance readers' understanding of Japanese, but their efforts fall short for two principal reasons. First, even though many compound words in the 2d and 3d parts have been introduced in earlier steps, most readers will be unable to recall these words. Although an index appears at the end of the steps, finding compound words there may be difficult for most American students because the index is arranged by Japanese alphabetic order. Second, to further confuse the reader, in writing the sentences the authors frequently have not included the subject. An adroit instructor may put the book to satisfactory classroom use, but it cannot be recommended for public or undergraduate college libraries.—**Seiko Mieczkowski**

Polish

914. Grzebieniowski, Tadeusz. **Langenscheidt's Pocket Dictionary: English/Polish, Polish/English.** rev. ed. Revised by Andrzej Kaznowski. Maspeth, N.Y., Langenscheidt Publishers, 1999. 816p. $13.95pa. ISBN 0-88729-017-5.

The revision of this dictionary, first published in 1985 by the distinguished Langenscheidt publishing house, has been allegedly updated to include terms in computer science, leisure activities, sports, business, and finance. With words like "Xerox," "cyberspace," "Walkman," "go-cart," and "talk show," it succeeds admirably in those first three categories. For the last two, its claims of updating are questionable. It includes no entries for such commonplace current lingo as "nonprofit," "outsource," "bottom line" or "mutual fund."

As a pocket dictionary, it by definition sacrifices clarity for brevity. The entry for the English word "elimination" includes four Polish words with no distinction as to usage or differentiation. The Polish section includes the word "olszyna" (a personal favorite), but there is no English-language counterpart for "alder forest." Three other comments are in order. First, it adheres to U.K. spelling. Second, it follows the International Phonetic Alphabet for pronunciation for the English words; the Polish words have no pronunciation key at all. Finally, the usage notes in both sections use Polish abbreviations.

The heart of any dictionary is its vocabulary, of course. With about 50,000 entries, it contains almost 5 times as many entries as the latest Pogonowski concise dictionary (see ARBA 95, entry 1091). That alone validates this dictionary's usefulness for business people, journalists, tourists, and students.

—**Lawrence Olszewski**

Russian

915. **Random House Russian-English, English-Russian Dictionary.** By Howard H. Keller. New York, Random House, 1999. 565p. $25.00. ISBN 0-679-44964-7.

This bilingual dictionary is designed to provide accurate and up-to-date information in regard to the subject matter covered. The aim of this new dictionary is to cover as much current vocabulary as possible. There are 2 major sections in this publication, with about 64,000 entries: the Russian-English dictionary (pp. 1–251), and the English-Russian dictionary (pp. 253–563). In the front and back of the book are pronunciation guides for English and Russian, lists of abbreviations, and tables including irregular verbs. In both sections, all terms are entered in a single alphabetic listing. Some of the main entries contain compounds, phrases, and expressions that appear as boldface subentries that are preceded by a long dash. A number of main entries contain run-on derived words that are formed by adding a prefix or suffix. An explanatory note, gloss, or field label is given in parentheses if the meaning that is being translated is not self-evident. In the English-Russian section, the dictionary shows the pronunciation of English headwords, as a version of the International Phonetic Alphabet (IPA). In the Russian-English section, each Russian word is given in its basic form with the correct stress mark for that form. Comparing to the most popular analogous dictionary by K. Katzner, this publication is better adapted for Russian consumers, because it provides the pronunciation of English words and tables of irregular verbs. On the other hand, a glossary of geographical names and other proper nouns would be more helpful. Also, a number of set expressions and phrases could be expanded sufficiently. However, this dictionary is of valuable assistance to all Russians who would like to use up-to-date English.—**Ludmila N. Ilyina**

SerboCroatian

916. Benson, Morton. **Standard English-SerboCroatian, SerboCroatian-English Dictionary: A Dictionary of Bosnian, Croatian, and Serbian Standards.** New York, Cambridge University Press, 1998. 344p. price not reported. ISBN 0-521-64209-4; 0-521-64553-0pa.

Not so long ago, the languages this dictionary covers belonged to just one actual language: Serbo-Croatian. Differences belonged under the heading of dialects. Now they seem to be separate languages, as indicated by the complicated subheading of this dictionary. As the preface indicates, this volume is intended for use by English speakers who are studying Serbo-Croatian, for Serbo-Croatian speakers who are studying English, and for professional translators. The preface also indicates that this volume is an abridged version of the same authors more extensive dictionaries.

Entries try to cover all possible variations of the dialects, giving priority to the Serbian one that is featured in the Latin, not Cyrillic alphabet. English words adhere to American spelling variants, while also including a few British ones. While transferring entries for the publication of this book, however, some strange conflation occurred. Life, for instance, can be found under livable, while morning is hidden in the Mormon entry. A casual browse revealed several typographical errors that should not exist in a dictionary. These could be minor matters, but not if one is a translator or student of the language and not if one trusts what one finds in a dictionary. In sum, this volume will be useful mainly to persons who are thoroughly familiar with the language and can use it only in order to refresh the memory of some familiar terms.

—**Koraljka Lockhardt**

Spanish

917. Serrano, Juan. Serrano, Susan, comp. **Spanish Idioms, Proverbs, and Slang of Yesterday and Today.** New York, Hippocrene Books, 1999. 196p. $14.95pa. ISBN 0-7818-0675-5.

Students of language, literature, and culture will find this volume to be valuable for its scope, readability, and ease of use. Included are broad overviews of the historical role of proverbs in moral teaching, the linguistic import of brief sayings, and the contrasts of scholarly and homespun wisdom.

Examples provided throughout enhance discussions and treatments. Through these examples, the authors examine the use of religious symbolism in modern Spanish, the use of the vulgar tongue in some classics of Spanish literature, and the relationship between popular speech and literature. In most cases, short (50 to 150 words) annotations are provided to explain the meaning and use of these terms and phrases. The final section of the work groups various proverbs and sayings according to names and places, keywords, and universal themes. This is followed by excerpts from *Sayings Used by Old Women by the Fire* (fifteenth century). Notes and a bibliography supplement the main text.

The rich and varied content of the volume is diminished by a lack of multiple indexes that could provide better access to the information. Nonetheless, it is an entertaining and illuminating reference tool.
—**Edmund F. SantaVicca**

918. Vox Spanish and English Student Dictionary: English-Spanish/Spanish-English. Lincolnwood, Ill., National Textbook, 1999. 672p. maps. $14.95; 10.95pa. ISBN 0-8442-2554-1; 0-8442-2438-3pa.

Compiled with beginning and intermediate students in mind, this volume, in addition to its more than 79,000 headwords, phrases, and examples, offers concise grammar overviews and suffix lists for Spanish and English and a lengthy compilation of idiomatic expressions for each language. Other useful supplements include a list of false cognates, plus tables for monetary units, weights and measures, and maps. Each entry begins with a pronunciation key based on the International Phonetic Alphabet. A distinguishing feature is the inclusion of conjugated forms of irregular verbs within individual entries rather than in an appendix. For example, under *seguir* and *repetir* students are directed to the verb *servir* (the model for this type of stem change), where they will find conjugated forms in the present indicative, present subjunctive, imperfect subjunctive, imperative forms, and the gerund. Despite the dictionary's claim that it contains "current technical, scientific, and business terms," neither *computadora* nor *ordenador* is included in the Spanish section. Similarly, in the English listings the entry for *computer*, in addition to being somewhat misleading, omits one of the two basic Spanish equivalents. The entry reads "máquina de calcular, computadora." Although most new dictionaries arrange words that include "ch" and "ll" in alphabetic order under the "c" and "l" headings, this volume continues the tradition of treating "ch" and "ll" as separate and distinct letters. Markers distinguish between European and American Spanish, but for the latter, users are not told in which countries the New World vocabulary items are used. This dictionary's compact format and clear, easy-to-read type will be appealing to students, but the volume lacks many frequently used words found in comparably sized and priced lexicons.—**Melvin S. Arrington Jr.**

Yiddish

919. Bluestein, Gene. **Anglish/Yinglish: Yiddish in American Life and Literature.** 2d ed. Lincoln, Nebr., University of Nebraska Press, 1998. 164p. $12.00pa. ISBN 0-8032-6147-0.

The term "Yinglish," was coined to describe the entry of Yiddish words like "chutzpa" into popular American English usage. The best exposition of the Yiddish words, phrases, and idioms that have become a part of the English language was Leo Rosten's *The Joys of Yinglish* (see ARBA 90, entry 1062). Bluestein's more academic approach expands on the idea, suggesting that a cross-pollination occurs between the English and Yiddish languages, as Jewish Americans have both assimilated into Anglo culture and simultaneously changed it. He makes a distinction, lacking in Rosten's approach, that "Yinglish" (Yiddish influenced

English) gives English words and expressions the qualities of Yiddish syntax and intonation, while "Anglish" (Anglo influenced Yiddish) turns Yiddish words into colloquial English.

The scholarly approach has its drawbacks. Bluestein acknowledges the difficulty of creating a good pronunciation guide to a language that first has to be transliterated from another alphabet, but his method does not seem to be an improvement on Rosten's. As an example, his "KHOOTSpe" seems difficult both to sound out and to locate alphabetically; Rosten's simpler and more logical "chutzpa" comes closer to commonly used spellings. Likewise, the Bluestein's illustrations of usage and meaning are drawn from academic literature and are mostly devoid of humor, an important component of any Yiddish study, and one of the main reasons for the infiltration of Yiddish words into the English language. Bluestein's exegeses on individual words fail to equal Rosten's pithy illustrations for clarity and humor. For example, "chutzpa" is the quality demonstrated by the defendant in a courtroom who, having murdered his mother and father, threw himself on the mercy of the judge because he was an orphan. *Anglish/Yinglish* can make a worthwhile addition to collections with a focus on language, but does not approach Rosten's book for entertainment value. [R: Choice, April 99, p. 1431]—**Larry Lobel**

24 Literature

GENERAL WORKS

Bibliography

920. **ABELL: Annual Bibliography of English Language and Literature 1920-1995.** [CD-ROM]. Alexandria, Va., Modern Humanities Research Association/Chadwyck-Healey, 1998. IBM or compatible 386/33MHz. High-speed CD-ROM drive with Microsoft CD-ROM Extensions 2.10. MS-DOS 6.0. Windows 3.1. 8MB RAM. 10MB hard disk space. High-density floppy disk drive. VGA color monitor. Microsoft-compatible mouse. $14,500.00/site license. ISSN 1461-7528.

ABELL indexes monographs, periodical articles, critical reviews, collections of essays, and doctoral dissertations. It covers subjects such as the English language, English literature, bibliography, and traditional culture of the English-speaking world. Articles are international in scope.

Installing the CD-ROM is quick and easy on a stand-alone personal computer. Networking appears to be an option but information on the procedure was not contained in the materials received. Instructions in the user's manual were for installing on Windows 3.1 or Windows 95. The CD-ROM does not appear to work on a Macintosh.

The search engine and screen designs are wonderful. They are easy to navigate and do not require a lot of consultation with the user's manual or help functions (although both are available and well written). Searching can be done with a keyword or browse function. The keyword protocols included Boolean and word proximity operators and phrase searching. The best part of the phrase searching was that it does not require special characters to designate it as a phrase. The only disappointing search strategy tried was to limit results to only articles in English. At this time the software does not allow limiting or searching by language.

When results are displayed, they display in reverse chronological order. The brief entry included basic bibliographic information. Full entries included more complete publication information and some descriptors. No full-text or abstracts are included.

This product is available on the World Wide Web and is much less expensive than the CD-ROM network version. However, if the search engine for their Web version is similar to their Literature Online product, the CD-ROM search is easier to use. The advantage of ABELL is easy-to-search literature research back to 1921. The disadvantage is the CD-ROM price and the lack of abstract or full-text information.

—**Suzanne Julian**

921. **The Comparative Reader: A Handlist of Basic Reading in Comparative Literature.** John T. Kirby, ed. New Haven, Conn., Chancery Press, 1998. 211p. (Comparative Studies, v.1). $26.95pa. ISBN 1-890657-01-8.

This book belongs in every library whose patrons include serious students and scholars of literature and rhetoric. *The Comparative Reader* consolidates bibliographies for the study of comparative literature by providing basic reading lists (modules) about the basic foundational texts in the field; about texts that examine the literature of one particular part of the world; and about ones that explore a particular school of literary criticism, era of rhetoric, or visual literacy (the figurative and plastic arts as well as film, television, and video). Each module gives bibliographic information for the most important 30 or 40 texts in a particular area, largely the kind of works that master's students taking written comprehensive exams would be expected to know. Compiled by leading scholars in the field (the majority of whom are colleagues of the editor at Purdue University), each of the 47 modules lists seminal works, the study of which would certainly advance most readers' understanding of the topic—from African literature, French literature, Indian literature, Japanese literature, and Spanish American literature to cultural studies, gay and lesbian studies, rhetoric, and semiotics. Kirby's introduction contextualizes issues of canonicity and multiculturalism in a thought-provoking manner. [R: Choice, Sept 98, p. 86]—**G. Douglas Meyers**

922. Harner, James L. **Literary Research Guide: An Annotated Listing of Reference Sources in English Literary Studies.** 3d ed. New York, Modern Language Association of America, 1998. 772p. index. $37.50; $19.75pa. ISBN 0-87352-573-6; 0-87352-574-4pa.

This outstanding guide, intended for those seriously interested in English literature, has been considered a required purchase for library reference collections since 1990 (see ARBA 94, entry 1139; ARBA 91, entry 1097). Harner, an important scholar and bibliographer, delights in reviewing the strengths and weaknesses of various editions of important works as well as well-known titles that have been around for too long. Librarians will use his comments to make decisions about collection development as well as weeding collections. Indeed, many in academe will use the guide to discover sources that remained unknown to them throughout their graduate studies, including subject bibliographies, abstracts, surveys of research, genre histories, annals, and chronologies. Harner also points to works in progress, giving them the benefit of the doubt now but promising a reevaluation with the next edition (every three to four years).

This is clearly an important work in progress as well. There are 47 titles that have been reevaluated and removed, 560 entries are revised, and 60 new titles are added. This edition contains more than 1,200 entries, and the annotations refer to 1,331 additional books, articles, and electronic resources. For major reference sources, the author cites reviews (approximately 752) that add value to his annotations. And what annotations! Lay users benefit from reading descriptions of a source; scholars will delight in Harner's evaluative comments. It is helpful to read that more than one subscription reference set of long standing is considered "virtually useless" as a critical guide. Recommended works making the cut have their shortcomings as well. On and on they go, encouraging both scholar and serious student to read one entry after another, one section (there are 21 of them) after another. The discussion of database utilities (OCLC, RLIN) is helpful; the discussions of database vendors (Ovid Technologies, Wilsonline, Dialog) are discussions in progress. Pay attention as new editions are made available.

This guide is dense with information. All bibliographic citations are complete, and cross-references, indexes, organization, and pleasing topography contribute to the guide's reference value.

—**Milton H. Crouch**

Bio-bibliography

923. **Contemporary Authors Autobiography Series, Volume 30.** Joyce Nakamura, Sheryl Ciccarelli, and Motoko Fujishiro Huthwaite, eds. Farmington Hills, Mich., Gale, 1999. 442p. illus. index. $140.00. ISBN 0-7876-1975-2. ISSN 0748-0636.

Like its parent publication, *Contemporary Authors* (see entries 924-928), this series includes writers working in many genres—fiction, nonfiction, poetry, drama, journalism, and screenplays. Here, however, individual entries may vary greatly because each contributor has complete freedom in shaping his or her own "mini-autobiography" of approximately 10,000 words. Most of the 16 entries in this volume follow a predictable chronological pattern, but some are more inventive and more challenging for readers. For example, novelist and translator Alison Anderson presents a series of word paintings that cut back and forth in time. Poet Guy Beining focuses on four voices that form his "complete mystical being." Except for the essay by Lisa Alther (reprinted from the anthology *Bloodroot*), all contributions appear here for the first time.

Along with the autobiographical account, each entry provides black-and-white photographs provided by the author and a bibliography of primary works. The back matter consists of an alphabetic list of the 524 authors covered thus far in 30 volumes and a cumulative index citing personal names, titles of literary works, geographic names, and other significant terms.

Readers seeking specific biographical data or a comprehensive view of an author's work can find it more easily in other reference works (e.g., *Contemporary Authors*, *Dictionary of Literary Biography*). This series offers instead individual writers' own reflections on the creative process and experiences that have influenced their work.—**Albert Wilhelm**

924. **Contemporary Authors, Volume 165: A Bio-Bibliographical Guide to Current Writers....** Scot Peacock, ed. Farmington Hills, Mich., Gale, 1999. 450p. $145.00. ISBN 0-7876-2002-5. ISSN 0010-7468.

This serial work remains a reliable source of information on approximately 100,000 current fiction and nonfiction writers, screenwriters, and children's authors, as well as great writers of the early twentieth century who are commonly studied in high schools and colleges. Its most valuable attribute is the inclusion of obscure authors and those who fall outside the scope of other literary reference works. Poet Sascha Feinstein and novelists Paul Claudel and Haruki Murakami are covered in this volume, as well as journalist Damon Runyon and Rick Bragg, critic Adam Gopnik, vegetarian cookbook author Mollie Katzen, and celebrities Whoopi Goldberg, Paul Reubens, Rick Pitino, and Ellen DeGeneres.

Each entry follows the standard *Contempory Authors* format, including personal and career highlights, a list of primary works, a bio-critical section, and a bibliography of secondary materials. Some entries are signed. The bibliographies include Internet sites and are heavy on book reviews and light on criticism. While this is understandable for works of nonfiction or popular fiction, it is less helpful to students who are using the tool as a starting point for literary study. Book citations are complete, but newspaper and magazine article titles are omitted from the bibliographies, leaving users in the dark regarding their content.

Name and title access is provided in a cumulative index, published separately. Because of its broad scope, its ease of use, and the accessibility of its essays, *Contemporary Authors* will undoubtedly continue to be popular in school, academic, and public libraries.—**Emily L. Werrell**

925. **Contemporary Authors, Volume 168: A Bio-Bibliographical Guide to Current Writers....** Scot Peacock, ed. Farmington Hills, Mich., Gale, 1999. 445p. $145.00. ISBN 0-7876-2671-6. ISSN 0275-7176.

With entries for approximately 100,000 authors, this well-established series is a primary source of information about current writers. It covers journalists, screenwriters, dramatists, and poets, as well as writers of fiction and general nonfiction. Although the series focuses on authors currently writing in English, it also includes a few major authors from the early twentieth century and some from other countries whose works have been published in the United States.

Volume 168 follows the same format as earlier volumes. A typical entry provides personal information (usually supported or verified by the author), a bibliography of the author's publications and works in progress, some analysis of major works (frequently including pertinent comments from the author and from published reviews), and a list of biographical and critical sources.

Some notable writers covered for the first time in this volume are cartoonist Scott Adams, actor and screenwriter Ben Affleck, crime novelist Sharyn McCrumb, and Supreme Court Justice Antonin Scalia. This volume also provides updated or expanded information on social theorist V. I. Lenin, literary critic Carl Van Doren, journalist Jacob Riis, and poet Edgar A. Guest.

A very useful cumulative index (issued separately) covers entries in this volume; in earlier volumes of *Contemporary Authors*; and in other complementary Gale publications, such as *Contemporary Literary Criticism* and *Dictionary of Literary Biography*.—**Albert Wilhelm**

926. **Contemporary Authors, Volume 169: A Bio-Bibliographical Guide to Current Writers....** Scot Peacock, ed. Farmington Hills, Mich., Gale, 1999. 448p. $145.00. ISBN 0-7876-2673-2. ISSN 0275-7176.

As the title implies, this work provides information on current writers of fiction, nonfiction, poetry, and drama. Early twentieth-century literary figures who continue to be studied in high school and college are included, as are authors who write in languages other than English, provided their works have been translated into English or have been published in the United States. *Contemporary Authors* is also the place to look for hard-to-find information on prominent print and broadcast journalists, editors, photojournalists, syndicated cartoonists, graphic novelists, screenwriters, television scriptwriters, and other media people.

Sketches of authors containing personal, career, and biographical and critical sources vary from less than one column of text to several pages. Obituary notices for authors whose full-length sketches appeared in the series before their deaths summarize the authors' careers and list other sources of information about the author.

Sketches may be updated in volumes of *Contemporary Authors New Revision Series* or in other Gale publications, such as *Dictionary of Literary Biography*, *Contemporary Literary Criticism*, or *Major Twentieth Century Writers*, among others. The separately published cumulative index is the key to locating an author's most recent entry. Though the index may be somewhat complicated or cumbersome to use, it is a comprehensive location tool for references to all entries in the Gale literary series. As a part of that series, *Contemporary Authors* is a must purchase for academic libraries.—**Lois Gilmer**

927. **Contemporary Authors, Volume 170: A Bio-Bibliographical Guide to Current Writers....** Scot Peacock, ed. Farmington Hills, Mich., Gale, 1999. 443p. $145.00. ISBN 0-7876-2675-9. ISSN 0275-7176.

Contemporary Authors, Volume 170 continues the series that provides information on more than 100,000 writers in a wide range of media. Included are current writers of prose, poetry, and drama whose works have been issued by commercial publishers; print and broadcast journalists, syndicated cartoonists, graphic novelists, screenwriters, television scriptwriters, and other media people; and authors who write in languages other than English who have been published in the United States or in English translations. In addition, the series features literary "greats" of the early twentieth century whose works are still being studied in high school and college and who continue to garner fresh critical attention.

Arranged in alphabetic order, each entry provides available author's personal information and addresses as well as a summary of the person's career and memberships, awards, and honors. A list of writings, adaptations, and works in progress is accompanied by titles of books and periodicals containing additional information on the writer's life and writings. Obituary notices and career recapitulations are provided for authors previously featured in *Contemporary Authors*.

Unlike many literary reference books, the subjects represented here range from current popular romance writers like Linda Howard and Debbie Macomber to Theodore Roosevelt (a "contemporary" author who died in 1919) and "Joe Dogs" Ianuzzi, a self-described member of the Gambino Mafia family. Its attempt to be all-inclusive could lead some readers to question the inclusion of a few entrants. Despite that and its expense, this latest volume in the Contemporary Authors series will be a "must have" acquisition for many reference collections.—**Kay O. Cornelius**

928. **Contemporary Authors, Volume 171: A Bio-Bibliographical Guide to Current Writers....** Scot Peacock, ed. Farmington Hills, Mich., Gale, 1999. 454p. $145.00. ISBN 0-7876-2677-5. ISSN 0275-7176.

This latest entry in Gale's long-running series is subtitled *A Bio-Bibliographical Guide to Current Writers in Fiction, General Nonfiction, Poetry, Journalism, Drama, Motion Pictures, Television, and Other Fields.* It centers on current writers whose works are issued by commercial publishers, risk publishers, or university presses; prominent print and broadcast journalists; editors; photojournalists; syndicated cartoonists; graphic novelists; screenwriters; television scriptwriters; and foreign-language authors whose works have been translated into English or published in the United States. It also picks up early twentieth-century literary greats whose works are studied in high schools and colleges and elicit critical attention. Entries vary in length and include the most complete form of the author's name plus pseudonyms or name variations. Also provided are personal information, addresses, career summary, membership information, and awards and honors. There is also a comprehensive, chronological list of titles; adaptations into films, plays, and other media; works in progress; sidelights (i.e., revealing comments often by the author); and biographical and critical sources. Obituary entries are provided. This volume highlights authors such as Larry Bond, Warren Christopher, Avram Davidson (Ellery Queen, a joint pseudonym), Sally Field, Old Edvart Roelvaag, Elizabeth Cady Stanton, and Quentin Tarantino. All entries are indexed in the *Contemporary Authors* cumulative index that is published separately and distributed with even-numbered *Contemporary Authors* original volumes and odd-numbered *Contemporary Authors New Revision Series* volumes. This volume continues the series' reputation for providing accurate information. The real question is whether secondary, public, and university libraries can continue to provide shelf space for the set or whether an online subscription via GaleNet is more appropriate.—**Esther R. Sinofsky**

929. **Major 20th-Century Writers: A Selection of Sketches from Contemporary Authors.** 2d ed. Kathleen Wilson, ed. Farmington Hills, Mich., Gale, 1999. 5v. index. $315.00/set. ISBN 0-8103-8450-7.

First published in 1991 (see ARBA 92, entry 1097), this set has expanded from 4 volumes to 5 but retains all the important features of the 1st edition and its parent work, *Contemporary Authors*. More than 1,000 authors commonly studied in high school and college and representing more than 60 nations are included. They are primarily writers of fiction, ranging from established literary giants to authors of children's and young adult literature to writers popular in a variety of genres. However, many prominent nonfiction writers (e.g., Stephen Jay Gould, Sigmund Freud, Stephen Hawking, Martin Luther King Jr.) who have influenced twentieth-century thinking are also included.

Arranged in alphabetic order, each entry provides personal, career, and award information as well as a bibliography of the author's works, including media adaptations. An unsigned "Sidelights" essay provides some brief biographical background and summarizes critical reaction to the author's work. A list of additional biographical and critical sources completes the entry. Indexes for nationality/ethnicity and subject/genre enhance accessibility.

Although the introductory material of this edition says there are approximately 200 new and 800 updated entries and indicates that some entries from the 1st edition have been dropped, there are no details on these changes. Thus, owners of the 1st edition might have difficulty in deciding whether to purchase this new edition. This drawback aside, this set remains a useful literary reference source for libraries unable to afford *Contemporary Authors*.—**Barbara E. Kemp**

Dictionaries and Encyclopedias

930. Carey, Gary, and Mary Ellen Snodgrass. **A Multicultural Dictionary of Literary Terms.** Jefferson, N.C., McFarland, 1999. 184p. index. $29.50. ISBN 0-7864-0552-X.

In a mild departure from the standard dictionary of literary terms, this work defines hundreds of words and phrases, then demonstrates their meanings with examples from world literature. The book also includes chronological listings of award-winning books, a timeline of world literature, a bibliography of sources, and a subject index.

Unfortunately, the scope of this book is not clearly focused and coverage is limited. The authors have included some terms from other cultures (e.g., griot, corrido), but most of the entries are of standard literary terms (e.g., ballad, postmodernism) that are treated more thoroughly and adeptly in other sources. Indeed, the number of entries in this book (approximately 450) pales in comparison to that of other dictionaries of literary terms, such as J. A. Cuddon's *A Dictionary of Literary Terms and Literary Theory*, which has more than 2,000 entries. In addition, the inclusion of terms from other cultures is not any more comprehensive than in other standard literary dictionaries, including the *Bedford Glossary of Critical Literary Terms* by Ross Murfin and Supryia M. Ray.

Although the definitions in this book are concise and correct, they sometimes get lost in the lengthy illustrations that accompany them. Furthermore, the titles and authors mentioned as illustrations are not indexed, which limits the use of the feature.

The authors assert that this work has been created for students, scholars, librarians, and researchers, but because of its limited scope and coverage and its poor organization, it is hard to imagine how the book would be used in any serious manner. It may make for interesting reading, but its value as a reference book is marginal. Readers in need of reliable dictionaries of literary terms are advised to explore the many other available sources. [R: LJ, Dec 98, p. 86; Choice, April 99, pp. 1432-1434]—**Barbara Ittner**

931. **Encyclopedia of Literary Critics and Criticism.** Chris Murray, ed. Hackensack, N.J., Salem Press and Chicago, Fitzroy Dearborn, 1999. 2v. index. $285.00/set. ISBN 1-57958-144-7.

The *Encyclopedia of Literary Critics and Criticism* explores the broad diversity of literary criticism and theory past and present, Western and non-Western. Its aim is to "provide a clear, wide-ranging, and authoritative guide to literary theory and criticism..." (introduction). There are 374 entries on individuals, theories, and concepts. Indexes and cross-references are provided to help readers explore themes. All of the entries have bibliographies and suggestions for further reading to direct readers in their research.

The 1st edition of this work was published in 1987 as the *Critical Survey of Literary Theory* (see ARBA 89, entry 993). This edition is completely revised and updated with 117 new entries. It covers a wide scope, including the history of Western literary theory and criticism and familiar figures such as Aristotle and Sir Philip Sidney as well as non-Western traditions and lesser-known figures.

Individual critic's entries include birth and death date and place (when available), a brief bibliography, and a description of their influence or achievements in literary criticism and theory. The bulk of these entries are an analysis of the individual's theories and major works. There are 15 entries on major literary periods and literatures from Plato to postmodernism, 3 entries on the twentieth century, and 4 on non-Western traditions. There are 28 entries providing accounts of many of the major theories, approaches, and movements, such as Deconstruction, Narratology, and Semiotics. Slightly shorter than the other entries, the 39 entries on concepts discuss such topics as intertextuality, style, and translation.

A subject index provides a detailed listing of proper names, concepts, theories, themes, and titles. The title index gives a complete list of the books cited in the "Principal criticism" section of the articles on individuals. This 2-volume set is a good reference source for college and university libraries.

—**Cari Ringelheim**

932. **Encyclopedia of World Literature in the 20th Century.** 3d ed. Steven R. Serafin, ed. Farmington Hills, Mich., St. James Press, 1999. 4v. illus. index. $575.00/set. ISBN 1-55862-373-6.

Previous editions of this important reference work have been favorably reviewed in ARBA. This latest revision continues the tradition of excellence, offering users a comprehensive guide to world literature of the century. The 4-volume set covers more than 2,300 authors, with more than 250 new names added. It provides users with a wealth of information on authors from around the world, as well as on specific national literatures (e.g., Turkish literature, Austrian literature) and on the major literary and intellectual movements of the century (e.g., postmodernism, futurism).

Each author entry provides vital statistics, a biographical and critical essay, a list of the author's publications, and a bibliography of other sources of information. Biographies have been written by qualified subject specialists, and generally speaking the content is accurate and complete. Black-and-white photos accompany many of the biographies and critical excerpts are appended to some essays. To enhance access, the volume is amply cross-referenced and indexed. It is also worth noting that a nationality index has been added to this edition.

As in previous editions, the coverage of European and North American authors is strongest. However, representation of Asian and South American authors is also substantial in this edition. It would be beneficial if subsequent editions continue the effort to achieve a more balanced representation. Although the revisions and additions to this edition are not as extensive as to the last, the book maintains its position as an essential reference for public and academic libraries. [R: BL, 1 May 99, pp. 1624-1628; Choice, July/Aug 99, pp. 1918-1920]—**Barbara Ittner**

933. Ferber, Michael. **A Dictionary of Literary Symbols.** New York, Cambridge University Press, 1999. 263p. $69.95. ISBN 0-521-59128-7.

This book, the first of its kind and long overdue, describes traditional symbols used over many years by many authors. The descriptions are impressive. They explore the derivation of words used as symbols and elaborate on the probable reasons for their symbolism. The words are traced by means of citations and quotations from various writers through biblical and classical works to twentieth-century writings (primarily poetry).

The entries vary in length from approximately one-half of a page to several pages. Because the animal kingdom has been a source of symbols from the earliest literature to the present, for example, there is a one-half page entry for the generic word "beast" and separate entries of varying lengths for the words ape, ass, bat, deer, dog, leopard, lion, serpent, and so on. The author states in his introduction that he includes such words as "dawn, death, dream, nature, and certain other subjects not so much for what they have stood for as for what other things have stood for them." Hundreds of cross-references and quotations add to the body of the work.

The body of the work is preceded by a list of abbreviations. More than nine pages of authors cited, including their birth and death dates and the language or nation they represent, follow the body. A bibliography completes the book. An index is unnecessary, since all entries are arranged in alphabetic order.

Written by a professor of English and humanities, this scholarly work is highly recommended for all students of American and English literature faced with writing papers where they are expected to expound upon the symbolism found in a given poem or story. The author admits that the book was, in fact, inspired by such a student. Suggestions for researching symbols not found in this book are included in the author's introduction. This work will also be a valuable resource for literary scholars and practicing writers. They should be able to find it in any academic library.—**Lois Gilmer**

934. **Merriam-Webster's Dictionary of Allusions.** By Elizabeth Webber and Mike Feinsilber. Springfield, Mass., Merriam-Webster, 1999. 592p. $14.95pa. ISBN 0-87779-628-9.

This is a recent addition to the genre defined by Ebenezer Cobham Brewer in the nineteenth century, when he wrote his *Dictionary of Phrase and Fable*. This book covers about 900 terms, provides a history and definition of each, and provides several illustrative quotations for each, taken mostly from top newspapers and magazines. Other books, such as David Grote's *Common Knowledge: A Reader's Guide to Literary Allusions* (Greenwood Press, 1987), are more comprehensive but lack the currency and depth of this volume.

There are many literary references here ("bliss was it in that dawn to be alive," "Patient Griselda"), but the book also covers a broad spectrum of history, politics, and culture ("Borscht Belt," "Chernobyl," "Children's Crusade," "pas de deux," "pogrom," "zero-sum game"). Although there are some references to classical matters ("Oedipal"), most of the references relate to the twentieth century ("Age of Aquarius," "Pax Americana," "Captain Queeg," "round up the usual suspects"). The illustrative quotations are mostly from the 1980s and 1990s, and give readers an excellent sense of how the words or phrases are currently used.

There is next to no overlap between the entries in this book and others in similar volumes, so this work could well sit on the shelves of any reference department. However, the book is not really a scholarly production, and reads more like a coffee-table item than a reference work. It has virtually no editorial information, and the authors are not lexicographers, although one is a lawyer and the other a news reporter. These two have written a fun-to-read, random walk through a variety of interesting allusions.—**Bill Miller**

935. Netzley, Patricia D. **Social Protest Literature: An Encyclopedia of Works, Characters, Authors, and Themes.** Santa Barbara, Calif., ABC-CLIO, 1999. 295p. illus. index. $65.00. ISBN 0-87436-980-0.

About 75 percent of this reference book covers plot summaries and entries for selected major characters in literary woks of social protest, which the author defines as works that "encourage readers to empathize with those who suffer from a particular social problem." Worldwide in scope, the entries, averaging a bit less than one page each, cover everything from *Gulliver's Travels* and *Hard Times* to relatively unknown titles such as *Close Sesame*, the final book in a trilogy on African dictatorship by Somalian author Nruddin Farah. Although focused mainly on the novel, drama and poetry are also minimally present. There is half a column on Countee Cullen's collection of poems entitled *Color*, and half a column also on George Crabbe, the eighteenth-century English poet who wrote about the plight of the rural poor. Drama is represented by articles on Oscar Wilde, Lillian Hellman, and Arthur Miller.

Although mostly Western in orientation, and mostly English and American within that Western orientation, this book does cover many items in Spanish, French, Italian, German, and Russian, along with a small number of Asian and African titles. However, one is much more likely to encounter John Steinbeck, Margaret Atwood, or Ayn Rand in this volume than to come across anything non-Western. The index does not categorize the entries by country, race, sex, or anything else, so one needs to peruse the entire work from cover to cover to get a sense of its range. An analytic index would have been a valuable addition.

The book also contains occasional subject entries, all of them quite short, but most of them functioning as a kind of index to the other entries in the book relevant to that particular subject. For instance, the half-column on "McCarthyism" refers readers the entries for *The Children's Hour* and *The Crucible* as well as to personal entries on Lillian Hellman, Arthur Miller, and Tillie Olsen; it also refers readers to another subject entry on "Censorship."

This volume makes fascinating reading, and is a wonderful way to remember works one has read in the past, or to learn a bit about other works that one has never read. This volume's focus on social protest makes it particularly valuable to anyone concentrating on this area, especially to the extent that it includes non-Western or little-known works. The plot summaries are succinct and well written.

Social Protest Literature provides a summary and overview of a major subset of works, most of which clearly were written to protest discrimination of one kind or another, and the book does an important service also by integrating its coverage of English and American literature with that of materials from many other nations. The book would have benefited from some additional attention to the definition and scope of its materials, but even as it stands, it is an interesting and valuable compilation. [R: Choice, Nov 99, p. 508]—**Bill Miller**

936. Quinn, Edward. **A Dictionary of Literary and Thematic Terms.** New York, Facts on File, 1999. 360p. index. $45.00. ISBN 0-8160-3232-7.

Since the boundaries between literary study and the larger culture have become more fluid, this dictionary includes many terms from psychology, television, film, and other fields. Quinn offers the expected entries on standard literary terms (e.g., litotes, oxymoron, villanelle) and on literary history (e.g., Augustan age, Harlem Renaissance). He also provides good comments on recent critical theory (e.g., deconstruction, reader response criticism), on film genres and techniques (e.g., screwball comedy, caper film, zoom shot), on theatrical styles (e.g., Bunraku, theater of cruelty), and on many facets of popular culture (e.g., cyberpunk, interactive computer fiction, rap).

Quinn's dictionary uses nontechnical language and addresses a more general audience than does William Harmon's *A Handbook to Literature* (7th ed., Prentice-Hall, 1996). In choosing to be less comprehensive, Quinn naturally omits many esoteric terms (like choriambus), but he also ignores several terms that are more commonplace (e.g., slant rime, rondel). Although Quinn's entries are less numerous and usually shorter, he does include some topics not found in Harmon's book, such as the entry on queer theory. Quinn's treatment of literary terms is more effective than his cursory discussions of major themes in literature. A brief entry may adequately introduce the "Faustian theme" to readers, but trying to cover "evil" in less than a page or "love" in less than two pages seems foolhardy.

Quinn provides useful cross-references within entries and a thorough index of proper names. Entries for critical and thematic terms frequently offer sound suggestions for further reading. Harmon includes a few simple diagrams to clarify his text, but Quinn uses none.—**Albert Wilhelm**

Directories

937. **Directory of Books and Authors.** Englewood Cliffs, N.J., Salem Press, 1999. 3v. $240.00/set. ISBN 0-89356-631-4.

Designed for reference librarians, this 3-volume directory provides information on 2,800 authors and their works. Volumes 1 and 2 are an alphabetic list of more than 50,000 works by title; each entry includes alternate titles, date of publication, and genre designation (e.g., drama, poetry, long fiction, short fiction, nonfiction, children's literature). Foreign titles are included, as are the original names of works translated into English. Authors included in volume 3 are those "most commonly read and studied by juvenile through adult readers." Included for each author are full name, pseudonyms, dates of birth and death, and lists of major publications. Coverage is comprehensive; for example, authors in the drama genre range from Aeschylus and Shakespeare to Neil Simon.

Librarians will find this tool useful for reference or verification purposes. Yet, even though poetry is one of the genres included, the directory is not useful in identifying authors of individual poems if they were published as part of a larger work. Publisher information is not included because it falls outside the purpose of this reference work.

Currency is a concern as it is with any print reference source. Users will not find recent books in this 1999 directory. For example, although earlier Stephen King novels can be found here, one will not find his 1998 release, *Bag of Bones*. Children's librarians may be disappointed by omissions of contemporary works. For example, no works by Lois Lowry, Scott O'Dell, Beverly Cleary, or Dr. Seuss are included. [R: LJ, July 99, p. 80; BL, 1 Sept 99, p. 178; Choice, Oct 99, p. 304]—**Jan Bakker**

938. **MLA Directory of Periodicals 1999: A Guide to Journals and Series in Languages and Literatures.** 9th ed. David Bagnall and Martin A. York, eds. New York, Modern Language Association of America, 1999. 1017p. index. $130.00. ISBN 0-87352-833-6.

This new edition of a trusted resource for information professionals contains vital information about 3,729 language, linguistics, literature, and folklore periodicals. Alphabetically arranged by journal title, annotations are organized into 5 sections—general contact information, editorial personnel, subscription information, advertising information, and submission requirements. Although not all annotations contain all of the information in each category, most are complete and approximately 70 percent of the listings have been verified directly by the publishers. The text is followed by 5 indexes—editorial personnel, languages published (with exception of English, French, German, Italian, and Spanish), sponsoring organizations, periodicals with an author-anonymous submission policy, and subjects.

Vital to serials librarians seeking subscription information as well as to collection development specialists, this book is also a valuable guide for humanities faculty and scholars looking for potential publishers of their work. It is an essential reference for large public and academic libraries. Smaller libraries should consider the paperback version of the book, which covers 1,558 titles and is limited to journals and series of the Americas.—**Barbara Ittner**

Handbooks and Yearbooks

939. Babin, Edith, and Kimberly Harrison. **Contemporary Composition Studies: A Guide to Theorists and Terms.** Westport, Conn., Greenwood Press, 1999. 330p. index. $79.50. ISBN 0-313-30087-9.

Contemporary Composition Studies is intended to define key terms and concepts in composition theory and to provide information about scholars in the field. It is an introductory reference for newcomers who wish to explore and contribute to the discipline, for people in other disciplines who wish to become familiar with composition studies, and for seasoned writing teachers who wish to review the field. The authors have selected about 100 scholars who have contributed to composition studies. Each entry includes a list of areas where the scholar has made important contributions, a brief description of their contributions (focusing on books and articles), and a bibliography of representative works. In-depth definitions are provided for key terms. Each term entry has a working definition of the term, variant definitions or explanations of the term offered by established composition scholars, examples of the term in context, and an alphabetic list of the scholars associated with the term. There is also a list of journal abbreviations, an appendix of scholars outside of composition studies who have influenced the field, a list of works cited, a name index, and a subject index. This work is recommended for college and university reference collections.

—**Cari Ringelheim**

940. **Contemporary Literary Criticism, Volume 110: Excerpts from Criticism of the Works of Today's Novelists, Poets, Playwrights....** Jeffrey W. Hunter, Deborah A. Schmitt, and Timothy J. White, eds. Farmington Hills, Mich., Gale, 1999. 489p. index. $145.00. ISBN 0-7876-2033-5. ISSN 0091-3421.

Volume 110 is a continuation of the Contemporary Literary Criticism series, which is devoted to authors now living or who died after December 31, 1959. Nine writers from six countries are discussed: Cleanth Brooks, Alejo Carpentier, Agatha Christie, Barbara Ehrenreich, Oriana Fallaci, Kazuo Ishiguro, Neil Jordan, Edmund White, and Richard Wilbur. The sections on each contain a portrait of the writer and an introduction consisting of biographical information, a list of major works with dates of publication, and the critical reception. Reviews, critical essays, and interviews appear chronologically, with all titles by the author printed in bold typeface. Each critique is prefaced with complete bibliographic information on the source and a one-sentence summary of the contents. The excerpts have been chosen to provide a good balance of opinions. Suggestions for further reading are followed by cross-references to other publications by Gale. The collection of reviews is extensive; even the shortest, that of Italian journalist and novelist Oriana Fallaci, is 31 pages in length.

This is an essential volume because in addition to its title index for volume 110, it has cumulative indexes divided by author, topic, and nationality. These include cross-references to earlier volumes of *Contemporary Literary Criticism* as well as to other Gale bibliographic and literary series such as the Dictionary of Literary Biography series and Major Twentieth Century Writers series. Every scholar of literature should have access to this extensive series, which is both basic in content and comprehensive in scope.—**Charlotte Lindgren**

941. **Contemporary Literary Criticism, Volume 111: Excerpts from Criticism of the Works of Today's Novelists, Poets, Playwrights....** Jeffrey W. Hunter, Deborah A. Schmitt, and Timothy J. White, eds. Farmington Hills, Mich., Gale, 1999. 527p. index. $145.00. ISBN 0-7876-2208-7. ISSN 0091-3421.

Contemporary Literary Criticism, Volume 111, continues the series that provides critical commentary and other information on more than 2,000 authors now living or who died after December 31, 1959.

Included in this volume are avant-garde exponent of the punk movement Kathy Acker; poet Lawrence Ferlinghetti; novelist and screenwriter S. E. Hinton; Pulitzer Prize-winning novelist Norman Mailer; American poet Sylvia Plath, British novelist Barbara Pym; Polish-born Nobel laureate Isaac Bashevis Singer; novelist Kurt Vonnegut; and playwright, novelist, essayist, short story writer, screenwriter, and poet Tennessee Williams.

As usual, each entry contains a brief biography, information about that writer's principal works, excerpted criticism, explanatory notes, bibliographical citations, author interview, and suggestions for further reading dating through 1997. Each writer in this volume has been previously treated in the series *Contemporary Authors* or other companion volumes; however, there is no duplication of reprinted criticism. With the cumulative topic, author and nationality indexes, and an alphabetic title index, students, teachers, librarians, and researchers will find more than enough material to write a term paper, analyze a work, or lead a discussion group. In addition, helpful citation forms show how to footnote reprinted criticism. *Contemporary Literary Criticism, Volume 111*, continues the tradition of providing a great deal of information in an easy-to-use format for those libraries that can afford it.—**Kay O. Cornelius**

942. **Contemporary Literary Criticism, Volume 113: Excerpts from Criticism of the Works of Today's Novelists, Poets, Playwrights....** Jeffrey W. Hunter, Deborah A. Schmitt, and Timothy J. White, eds. Farmington Hills, Mich., Gale, 1999. 549p. index. $145.00. ISBN 0-7876-2212-5. ISSN 0091-3421.

The criterion for inclusion in *Contemporary Literary Criticism* (CLC) is that the authors it covers have to be living or have died after December 31, 1959. This volume includes material on Edward Albee, Eavan Boland, E. L. Doctorow, T. S. Eliot, Carlos Fuentes, Susan Hill, Stephen King, and Carol Shields, all still alive except for T. S. Eliot who died in 1965. Interestingly, the material on Eliot is all limited to "The Love Song of J. Alfred Prufrock," Eliot in general presumably having been done to death in earlier volumes, and the other broader critical output on him is not a voluminous as it used to be.

For each author in the volume, the article contains the following sections: a full name, with reference to earlier volumes of CLC that discuss the same author; a one-paragraph introduction; one paragraph of biographical information; a one-paragraph summary of major works; a one-paragraph summary of critical reception; a list of principal works; and a generous number of sections of criticism, some being excerpts, but most being the complete texts of newspaper and journal articles and play reviews.

There are minor faults in the entries. For instance, in the introduction to the Albee article, *Seascape* is listed as one of the three plays that he received the Pulitzer Prize for, but it is not one of the plays discussed in the major works section. In general, the short introductory paragraphs on each author's work and life are very satisfactory. In any case, the only really important part of this volume is the reproduction of the voluminous snippets or complete texts of criticism, most of which would be tedious at best for the average student to obtain. In reality, for reasons ranging from vandalism to missing issues to the fact that their libraries do not subscribe to the particular titles for where articles are reproduced, much of this critical material would be otherwise impossible for students to obtain in many libraries.

This volume, and the series it represents, constitutes a real service both to scholarship and to the average student looking for critical materials to write papers with. Every academic library should maintain this series, or its electronic equivalent.—**Bill Miller**

943. **Contemporary Literary Criticism, Volume 114: Excerpts from Criticism of the Works of Today's Novelists, Poets, Playwrights....** Jeffrey W. Hunter, Deborah A. Schmitt, and Timothy J. White, eds. Farmington Hills, Mich., Gale, 1999. 497p. illus. index. $145.00. ISBN 0-7876-2211-7. ISSN 0091-3421.

Since 1973, high school and college students have relied upon the Contemporary Literary Criticism (CLC) series for excerpts to critical commentary on the works of novelists, poets, playwrights, short story writers, scriptwriters, and other creative authors from around the world. Covering living writers or ones who died after December 31, 1959, each volume contains some 500 excerpts of published criticism, including book reviews, interviews, and feature articles from magazines, journals, and books.

The diversity of the authors covered in the series is readily apparent. Authors discussed in volume 114 include Pedro Almodóvar, Stuart Dybek, Ralph Ellison, June Jordan, Miroslav Krleza, Tillie Olsen, Ken Saro-Wiwa, Leslie Marmon Silko, and David Foster Wallace, while volume 115 comprises Amiri Baraka, Donald Barthelme, Nicole Brossard, Annie Dillard, Brian Friel, Garrison Keillor, Milan Kundera, and Bharati Mukherjee.

The easy-to-understand format of CLC makes the set ideal for students. Each lengthy author entry includes a portrait (when available), a biographical and critical introduction, a list of principal works, chronologically arranged excerpts of criticism (with complete bibliographic information for each), and, in many instances, an annotated list of additional critical resources. Explanatory notes accompany many excerpts, and are invaluable summations of the criticism and comments on the critics' reputations. Rounding out each of the two volumes are a cumulative author index (to the entire Gale Literary Criticism series), a cumulative topic index (to five sets in the series), a cumulative nationality index (to the CLC series), and a title index to the particular volume at hand.

Of course, students in both public and academic libraries need more literary criticism than just these excerpts, but the strength of this set lies in the wide range of authors studied and the numerous bibliographic citations it provides. Serious researchers can find much here that will lead them to scholarly books and periodicals—and not just the nearest photocopier.—**Jack Bales**

944. **Contemporary Literary Criticism, Volume 116: Excerpts from Criticism of the Works of Today's Novelists, Poets, Playwrights....** Jeffrey W. Hunter and Timothy J. White, eds. Farmington Hills, Mich., Gale, 1999. 546p. illus. index. $145.00. ISBN 0-7876-3191-4. ISSN 0091-3421.

This is the 116th volume in the Contemporary Literary Criticism series, which "provides readers with critical commentary and general information on more than 2,000 authors now living or who died after December 31, 1959." The strength of this series is in the reproduction of critical articles and significant excerpts from book-length critical studies of the authors in question. This particular volume focuses on eight people: Robert Altman, American filmmaker; Yehuda Amichai, German-born Israeli creative writer; Sven Birkerts, American essayist and critic; Edna O'Brien, Irish creative writer; Georges Perec, French writer of both fiction and nonfiction; Sonia Sanchez, American author; William Trevor, Irish author; and Mona Van Duyn, American poet.

For each figure, the volume includes a short introduction with biographical information, a discussion of the person's critical reception, a bibliography of the principal works, and a photograph. The heart of each author's section, of course, is the series of secondary resources that are reproduced, in whole or in part, arranged chronologically and preceded by a complete bibliographic citation and a summary explanation of each. The volume is composed almost exclusively of long excerpts from books and excerpts or complete texts of journal articles. As such, this volume and its companions would be highly valuable to anyone focusing on the particular authors being covered, especially at smaller institutions that do not offer comprehensive collections.

The section on Sonia Sanchez, examined here as a representative section of the volume, begins with the complete text of a journal article, "The Pain of Women, The Joy of Women, The Sadness and Depth of Women," by John D. Williams, published originally in *Callaloo* in February 1979 (vol. 2, no. 5, pp. 147-49), followed by 10 additional pieces (including 2 interviews with Sanchez), ranging in date from 1979 to 1992. The 1st article and 1 other piece in the Sanchez section, a 12-page essay by David Williams published in a book, *Black Woman Writers (1930-1980): A Critical Evaluation* (Anchor Press, 1984), are not in the electronic version of *Contemporary Literary Criticism*, but all the other excerpts and full-text pieces reproduced here are also in the electronic version. On the other hand, the electronic version contains two articles that are not in this printed version.

Minor features that enhance this volume include a "Literary Criticism Series Cumulative Topic Index," for topical entries included in all volumes of Gale's *Classical and Medieval Literary Criticism*, *Contemporary Literary Criticism*, *Literary Criticism from 1400 to 1800*, *Nineteenth-Century Literary Criticism*, and *Twentieth-Century Literary Criticism*; a "Cumulative Nationality Index" for all volumes of *Contemporary*

Literary Criticism (which gives one an easy way of judging the international coverage of the series); and a cumulated title index to all authors' works discussed in the first 116 volumes of Contemporary Literary Criticism. These indexes, the lengthy list of copyright permissions granted, and the meticulous accuracy of the citations and texts in the book testify to the quality of this volume and of this series, which continues to be a mainstay for students and scholars needing quick reference to a wide range of critical opinion on the world's contemporary authors.—**Bill Miller**

945. **Contemporary Literary Criticism, Volume 117: Criticism of the Works of Today's Novelists, Poets, Playwrights....** Jeffrey W. Hunter and Timothy J. White, eds. Farmington Hills, Mich., Gale, 1999. 508p. illus. index. $145.00. ISBN 0-7876-3192-2. ISSN 0091-3421.

This latest entry in Gale's venerable series, subtitled *Criticism of the Works of Today's Novelists, Poets, Playwrights, Short Story Writers, Scriptwriters, and Other Creative Writers*, continues to provide readers with critical commentary and general information on current authors or those who died after December 31, 1959. This volume covers eight authors: Frederick Barthelme, J. M. Coetzee, Bret Easton Ellis, Nikki Giovanni, Thomas Keneally, Tadeusz Konwicki, Malcolm X, and Mary Stewart. It "contains individual essays and reviews taken from hundreds of book review periodicals, general magazines, scholarly journals, monographs, and books. Entries include critical evaluations spanning from the beginning of an author's career to the most current commentary" (p. vii). It includes interviews, feature articles, and other published insights together with bibliographical citations. A typical author entry provides a portrait, when available; brief biographical and critical introduction; list of principal works; criticism; critical essays prefaced by explanatory notes; bibliographical citation; author interview, when available; and further reading. Entry length varies. For example, the Barthelme essay runs 28 pages while the Coetzee entry runs 74 pages. In addition to the title index, there are cumulative indexes for topic, author, and nationality. This is an excellent resource for high school and college students and staff seeking information for term papers, poem analysis, and even book discussion starters.—**Esther R. Sinofsky**

946. **Masterplots Complete CD-ROM.** 1999 ed. [CD-ROM]. Pasadena, Calif., Salem Press, 1999. Minimum system requirements (Windows version): IBM or compatible 386SX (486 or higher recommended). Double-speed CD-ROM drive. Windows 3.1. 4MB RAM. 4MB hard disk space. VGA 256 color monitor. Printer. Mouse. Minimum system requirements (Macintosh version): Apple Macintosh or compatible 68030 (68040 or higher recommended). Double-speed CD-ROM drive. System 7.1. 12MB RAM. 6MB hard disk space. Monitor. Printer. $750.00. ISBN 0-89356-264-5.

Masterplots Complete CD-ROM provides electronic access to 13,364 articles from the 22 sets of reference book in the Masterplots series. The articles are of three types: critical essays on specific literary works, character sketches, and author biographies. Descriptive details, a bibliography (usually), and links to other related entries supplement each article. Since the same work may be covered from different perspectives in the various sets in the Masterplots series, such as juvenile, women's, or British literature, the links often connect to other treatments of the same work or author.

The CD-ROM does not automatically load on Windows 95 or 98 machines; however, it takes only one minute to install and operates smoothly on most Pentium machines. The toolbar to the right of the display is neither intuitive nor standard and icons do not correlate with commands on the drop-down menus.

Seven topic indexes facilitate searching: titles, authors, text (words or phrases contained in the articles), locale, genre, subject, and principal characters. To use the "AND Complex 3.5" search engine you select the proper index from the drop-down menu and then type the search argument into the input box. Double-clicking the choice in the list displays the desired article on the right. The asterisk (*) for wildcard is the desired search technique from the main display. The asterisk can be placed before and after the search input to indicate which side of the search should be open-ended. Boolean, nested, and proximity searching are all supported, but only from the detailed and global search tabs. While the search techniques are powerful, they are also quite complex. Library staff must master the detailed user's guide and instruct patrons in searching before they can use the product effectively.

Value-added features contribute to the flexibility of the material on the CD. With the simple installation of macros, users may copy selected text to Microsoft Word or WordPerfect. Entire articles may also be exported in text, html, or rich text format for use in other applications. The user may add notes to any article. The obscurely named "spike" feature (similar to bookmarks or favorites in Web browsers) allows the user to maintain a list of articles for speedy access.

Because the content itself is already heavily used in academic, public, and school libraries in the space-intensive paper format, the integration of so many series onto a single CD-ROM is a boon to reference departments, teachers, and students alike. For libraries just purchasing Masterplots, the complete CD-ROM may be less expensive than purchasing more than one series in print. The product may be networked to computers within one building to overcome the single-user dilemma.

The 1999 edition is significantly improved over the original 1997 version, although the user interface needs additional refinement. This resource is highly recommended for public, academic, and large school libraries. [R: BR, Nov/Dec 99, pp. 90-91]—**Anne C. Moore**

CHILDREN'S AND YOUNG ADULT LITERATURE

Children's Literature

Bibliography

947. Anderson, Vicki. **Sequels in Children's Literature: An Annotated Bibliography of Books in Succession or with Shared Themes and Characters, K-6.** Jefferson, N.C., McFarland, 1998. 314p. index. $35.00pa. ISBN 0-7864-0285-7.

A librarian's dream reference source is one that helps answer the question "I loved Paula Danziger's *Amber Brown is not a Crayon*. What do I read now?" This book attempts to provide just such a resource.

This bibliography includes sequels for children in grades K through 6. Anderson defines a sequel as "a book that can stand alone and be read and enjoyed by itself, but is also one of several books written about the same main character following a similar theme" (p. 2). There are 7,500 titles arranged alphabetically by author. The books included in this list were chosen for their age range and publication date (the date criterion was not found). Not all the books in Anderson's bibliography are still in print. Her reasoning for including these titles is to provide a complete list and allow the patron to use interlibrary loan for the titles that are not available.

Each entry includes the author, title, publisher, year of publication, an age range, and a few sentences about the book. An example of a series included in this book is the books by Tamora Pierce. Anderson spelled the author "Tamara Pierce." The titles listed are *Wild Magic*, *Wolf Speaker*, *Emperor's Mage*, and *Realms of the Gods*. These titles are from the Immortals Series but Pierce has three other series, two that are newer than the one included in this bibliography. Another disturbing entry is Lucy Dahl. She is listed as the author of *Matilda* and *Matilda's Movie Adventure*. However, Roald Dahl is the author of *Matilda* and he is not given credit.

A weakness in this bibliography is the lack of series information. A title index is included in the book, but not a series index. In fact, series are not listed in the title entries at all. For example, in looking for books from the *Babysitters Club* the reader would need to know that Ann Martin is the author or the names of some of the books in the series in order to find the complete list of titles. Not all the books in the bibliography were printed with a series title, but for those that do have series titles the information is critical to successfully helping a patron. The concept of the book is excellent, but the editing and lack of series information limit the book's usefulness. [R: SLJ, April 99, p. 43]—**Suzanne Julian**

948. **Best Books for Children: Preschool Through Grade 6.** 6th ed. John T. Gillespie, ed. New Providence, N.J., R. R. Bowker, 1998. 1537p. index. $48.00. ISBN 0-8352-4099-1.

A bibliographic guide to a multitude of fiction and nonfiction books for preschool through sixth grade levels. The editor has aimed this guide to provide a list of books to satisfy both recreational and academic needs for young readers. In this sixth edition, there are more than 18,000 entries, of which over half are new. Each book listed has been recommended from sources such as *Booklist* and *School Library Journal*.

Entries are organized under major subject headings such as mathematics, fairy tales, and sports figures. In each listing, the guide provides basic bibliographic information, a brief synopsis, and review citations for books published between 1985 and March 1998. The editor has also noted any books that have been awarded Caldecott or Newbery medals. The four indexes—author, illustrator, book title, and subject/grade level—make locating specific entries very user-friendly. The preface also gives readers information about how to use the guide, including abbreviations that are utilized.

Readers need to keep in mind that certain types of books have been omitted from the bibliography, including reference books such as dictionaries and encyclopedias, and mass market series such as Nancy Drew and Hardy Boys books. Thus, this work is very extensive, but it is limited and may not contain listings for specific titles that readers may be looking for.—**Cari Ringelheim**

949. **Children's Books in Print on Disc.** [CD-ROM]. New Providence, N.J., R. R. Bowker, 1999. Minimum system requirements (Windows version): IBM or compatible. CD-ROM drive. Windows 3.1x or higher. 4MB RAM. 10MB hard disk space. Minimum system requirements (Macintosh version): System 7.x or higher. SCSI CD-ROM drive. 4MB RAM. 10MB hard disk space. $380.00. ISBN 0-8352-4013-4.

Children's Books in Print (see ARBA 99, entry 992) is now available on CD-ROM and provides the user the ability to search or browse the file of records from R. R. Bowker's bibliographic, audio, and visual databases with ease. The titles included are suitable for children and young adults through grade 12. Records are from Bowker's *Books in Print* and *Books Out of Print* plus audio and video titles and book reviews and annotations from *Bowker's Professional Children's Publications*. Publisher and distributor records are also included, which simplifies ordering.

Installation allows the user to configure portions: passwords, ordering, and display, as well as disabling features. The main screen provides three choices: browse, search, or form search. There are 17 ways to alphabetically browse, which range from the traditional methods of author, title, and subject to language, publisher, award/year, performer, binding, and format. Search allows the same choices as browse with the addition of grade level, price, and publication year. The search form allows for various configurations as well as wildcard and Boolean searches. Titles located can be viewed in nine formats: brief citations, full record, detailed, concise, catalog card, MARC tagged, order form, Custom, and USMARC. Searches can be saved and printed. Reviews and annotations are particularly helpful.

The ordering system of the product can simplify acquisition. The user is provided with 28 ordering systems from which to choose. Ordering may be completed three ways: electronically, special, or purchase. Each may be configured as needed. Publisher contact information is provided. A pull-down help menu giving contents and the ability to search and bookmark sections provide ready assistance with the program. Help topics can be printed.

This product is easy to use with drop-down windows and other features common to products operating in the Windows environment. It allows the user many choices in configurations. The information is displayed in an easy-to-read format allowing the user to change the display at any time. This product will be very useful to anyone searching for book, audio, or video titles for children and young adults pre-K through grade 12.—**Elaine Ezell**

950. Cooper, John, and Jonathan Cooper. **Children's Fiction 1900-1950.** Brookfield, Vt., Ashgate Publishing, 1998. 228p. illus. $76.95. ISBN 1-85928-289-X.

According to the authors, this book, which covers the work of 206 children's fiction authors, is intended for "readers, librarians, parents, scholars, collectors, book dealers, and those interested in artwork during this period." The book is divided by decades, and authors are listed by both birth names and pseudonyms. Illustrations and dust covers are frequently reproduced as black-and-white photographs. Both British and American authors are included. Only the decade from 1900 to 1910 has any introductory material about the period, but all divisions have a list of authors for that section. Within each section, author and illustrator entries are alphabetic and include a short biography and a bibliography of works written or illustrated by the person. Authors and illustrators whose work spans more than one decade are cross-referenced to the time period where they were most prolific. Although the book is extremely comprehensive with a lot of information, its usefulness is hindered by the lack of an index, which makes it time consuming to locate an author or illustrator if one is unsure of the time frame of the individual.—**Janet Hilbun**

951. Dole, Patricia Pearl. **Children's Books About Religion.** Englewood, Colo., Libraries Unlimited, 1999. 230p. index. $32.00. ISBN 1-56308-515-1.

When Dole set out to locate books on religion for children suitable for inclusion in public and school libraries, she found that she had to consult religious and mainstream publishers, church and public libraries, and bookstores. Limited sources within the library science profession were available, although Dole completed a master's degree project on the subject in the 1980s. In this resource, the author devotes sections to the world's major religions (including Native American religions), with subsections on major U.S. faiths and world religions.

Dole lists books on comparative religions, God, prayer, the Bible, biographies of religious leaders, and church history. Each book has an annotation of two to four sentences, and every section has a list called "Old and Noteworthy," most published in the 1980s. These have no annotation, but only the author, title, publisher, and date. She understands our discomfort with "didactic, saccharine, or doctrinaire material." Her lists include many series books, which is not negative because their authors take care to define and summarize, and the books are usually attractively packaged. Dole made unusually bad choices under the heading "Fundamentalism." Exceptionally awkward for the scanning librarian is Dole's omission of recommended age or grade levels; a selector must examine every review for this information. Once public and school librarians are inspired to select from the amount of religion-related books available, this book will provide a boost to publishers of quality religious books for children and a stimulus to authors. Dole states, "Since religion and spirituality are an integral part of every culture in the world, access to information on all types of faiths should be freely available to readers of all ages." Librarians should not suspend judgment when using this book, but choose it for a look at the many possibilities in an often-neglected subject area.
—**Edna M. Boardman**

952. **The Horn Book Guide Interactive.** [CD-ROM]. Westport, Conn., Heinemann, 1999. $35.00 (single user); $115.00 (network).

This CD-ROM is based on the *Horn Book Guide to Children's and Young Adult Books* (vol. 7, no. 2; see ARBA 98, entry 1078), which is published twice a year, and contains approximately 4,000 reviews per year. This product is a collection of all of the reviews published since 1990. Entries include the standard bibliographic information about the book (title, author or illustrator, series, publisher, page length, ISBN, and year). Also included in the entry are the genre, rating, grade level, and subjects. There are more than 29,000 short reviews that are descriptive and critical. The reviews also include notes about color and black-and-white illustrations or photographs. Also noted is whether or not an index, bibliography, or glossary is present. Searchable indexes are provided for all the elements present in the entry. Each book is rated on a six-point rating scale: outstanding and noteworthy, superior well above average, recommended satisfactory, recommended with minor flaws, marginal seriously flawed, and unacceptable.

The database is alphabetically arranged by the author's last name. Reviews can show up for individual books or books that are part of a series. Users are able to search multiple index fields by typing in text or selecting from a list of choices. Searches can be done by grade level (choose from those listed), author (enter last name), and genre (fiction or nonfiction). Searches by rating (1–6, 1 being the highest), review (choose from keywords), subject (type in subjects you want), title (type in title desired), year (choose from years listed), and full-text (allows for searching of all fields) are also available. There are clearly marked navigational buttons and a menu bar. Lists can be displayed that meet the search criteria, and records or portions of records can be marked for printing. This CD-ROM is aimed at the teacher or librarian and would be of benefit to school and public libraries, and those academic libraries that have a teacher education program that offers children's and young adult literature classes.—**Jan S. Squire**

953. Lewis, Valerie V., and Walter M. Mayes. **Valerie & Walter's Best Books for Children: A Lively, Opinionated Guide.** New York, Avon Books, 1998. 708p. index. $15.00pa. ISBN 0-380-79438-1.

The publication of bibliographies of best books for children is, to be sure, not a new concept; however, these authors bring to their readers a somewhat different approach to this literature form, as indicated in their subtitle, *A Lively, Opinionated Guide*. The authors, recognized for their expertise in the world of children's literature, have compiled a list of 2,000 titles (slimmed down from an original list of 8,000) that they profess they "couldn't live without." To achieve their goal and to reach consensus on selections for inclusion, they combined their experiences as storytellers, read-aloud presenters, extensive reviewers of children's books, reactions from their listeners, and their own love of children's books. Acknowledging that most people are more apt to remember a title than an author's name, they entered each book alphabetically by title. The entries are grouped into age categories, including a list of recommended books for all ages and titles for the very young, and conclude with young adult selections. Their chatty, humorous comments accompanying each selection do, in fact, reflect their own biases. However, the resulting annotations make for enjoyable reading and may well pique the curiosity of the reader. Another helpful feature is their comprehensive, cross-referenced theme appendix, which appears to be thorough.

This "pooling of impressions" serves as an extensive and selective guide to both the oldies, such as Tolkien's *The Hobbit*, and books by current authors, such as the prolific and melodious writings of Jane Yolen. For anyone seeking to guide children toward becoming lifetime lovers of books and reading, this qualifies as a worthy purchase. Do not overlook reading the witty introduction; it sets the tone for what is to follow. [R: SLJ, Oct 98, p. 51]—**Margaret Denman-West**

954. Miller, Wanda J. **Teaching U.S. History Through Children's Literature: Post-World War II.** Englewood, Colo., Libraries Unlimited, 1998. 229p. illus. index. $27.50pa. ISBN 1-56308-581-X.

The purpose of this handbook is "to provide teachers with information to begin or expand their use of quality children's literature in the teaching of United States history" (p. xi). To that end the editor, herself a teacher, recommends specific titles for an entire class to read and discuss, offers brief information about the author, suggests group activities, lists discussion questions, and explains vocabulary terms. Additional suggestions are offered for small groups.

Individual chapters cover the Korean War, the Civil Rights movement, the Women's Rights movement, space exploration, the Vietnam War, multicultural heritage, and the Persian Gulf War. The chapter on multicultural heritage provides the most extensive bibliography and gives titles for second through ninth graders. The final chapter identifies professional resources and computer resources and offers ideas for teachers of social studies and English to use in evaluating students.

Unfortunately, the work does not explore the role that the school library media specialist can play in these collaborative efforts. Media specialists can use the annotated bibliographies to identify resources for the collection.—**Phyllis J. Van Orden**

955. **Subject Guide to Children's Books in Print 1999: A Subject Index to Books for Children and Young Adults.** New Providence, N.J., R. R. Bowker, 1999. 1247p. $195.00. ISBN 0-8352-4080-0. ISSN 0069-3480.

The review of the author, title, and illustrator index to *Books for Children and Young Adults* in ARBA 1999 (see entry 992) describes the general value of this primary tool for booksellers, librarians, parents, researchers, and teachers. In this electronic age, the CD-ROM or online versions of all of R. R. Bowker's Books in Print series are more useful and increasingly more widely used. In some ways it seems unlikely that the print versions of these standard guides will have much value to libraries for much longer. In fact, it would not be surprising if the print versions were to disappear in the next few years. That would be unfortunate if only in terms of the status of the print versions as a basic historical record.

This subject index to children's books has, however, a use of its own that many users will still find valuable. Given the enormous range of titles listed and the detailed subject analysis provided, it is one of the best sources for identifying children's books—both fiction and nonfiction—on a particular topic. Many libraries, especially in respect to fiction, do not provide in their catalogs the same level of analysis that is found here. Amazon's Website does provide similar access but it is at present not as straightforward and simple to use. As teachers and researchers look to make wider use of children's books in dealing with topical issues, this remains by far the best starting point for locating basic comprehensive information of this kind.—**Norman D. Stevens**

956. Thiessen, Diane, Margaret Matthias, and Jacquelin Smith. **The Wonderful World of Mathematics: A Critically Annotated List of Children's Books in Mathematics.** 2d ed. Reston, Va., National Council of Teachers of Mathematics, 1998. 355p. index. $17.95pa. ISBN 0-87353-439-5.

Those with a phobia to mathematics and those who love math will appreciate this book. The title of the book may frighten some who do not love math but once inside, the reader finds a wonderful resource of mathematics topics and approximately 550 trade books related to the concept. Parents will have fun using the suggested titles with their children at home, teachers will have some helpful trade books to utilize with a math lesson, and librarians will have a guide to the best mathematics books in print.

In order to be included in this bibliography a book has to be in print and have math for a primary theme. The committee of reviewers arranged the books into topics and then gave them a rating on their usefulness in teaching the math concept. This is the 2d edition of this bibliography but 60 percent of the titles are new and the other 40 percent are still in print. Some of the sections list five or six books that may be out-of-print but are still considered exceptional titles. Textbooks and teacher workbooks were not included.

Each section of the book is arranged by topics that range from counting to measurement to geometry. The introduction of the math topic makes this book better than most bibliographies. It does not teach how to do the math concept, but it gives examples of how parents and teachers have used the books to successfully teach children about math. Some of the topics are unique and interesting, such as using quilts to teach geometry.

Once the topic is introduced, the trade books related to that concept are listed alphabetically by author. Each book is given a complete bibliographic citation, a grade level designation, a rating for its usefulness in teaching the topic, and a paragraph describing the book.

The format of the book is user-friendly with a good table of contents and indexes for author and title. Most of the suggested titles seem to be aimed at preschool and elementary school grades, but some of the picture books may be favorites of older students or adults, such as Jon Scieszka's *Math Curse*.

—**Suzanne Julian**

Biography

957. McElmeel, Sharron L. **100 Most Popular Children's Authors: Biographical Sketches and Bibliographies.** Englewood, Colo., Libraries Unlimited, 1999. 495p. illus. index. (Popular Authors Series). $48.00. ISBN 1-56308-646-8.

The compilation of this volume is based upon more than 3,000 teacher and student responses to a 1997 survey that attempted to identify the top 100 of the most important authors and illustrators of children's literature. Teachers, librarians, and students will find this easy-to-read volume useful in identifying and reading about popular authors' backgrounds and their works. Most of the books listed here are intended for an elementary or middle school audience. Please note that the author has also published a volume entitled *The 100 Most Popular Young Adult Authors: Biographical Sketches and Bibliographies* (see ARBA 98, entry 1102).

Entries are alphabetically arranged by the author's last name, and in some cases include a photograph. Each entry includes a birth and death date, an indication of the broad genre the author's work falls into, any books they have written in a series, and a biographical essay. Under the books and notes section of the entry is a bibliography (sometimes annotated) of the author's books on a certain subject, books in a series, and sources to consult for further information on the author. An appendix is included for photography credits and there are two indexes.

The genre index is alphabetically arranged and includes genres such as adventure fiction, biographies, contemporary realistic fiction, fantasy, historical fiction, humorous stories, mystery, nonfiction, poetry, and sports fiction. Underneath each genre the author is listed in alphabetic order by last name. Page numbers are not included. The general index is an alphabetic list that includes the author's name and titles of works mentioned in the author's biography. Page numbers are provided and the ones that reflect the main entry for an author are in bold typeface. Books listed in the bibliographies of each section and genres are not included in this index. [R: BL, 1 Sept 99, p. 182]—**Jan S. Squire**

958. Murphy, Barbara Thrash. **Black Authors and Illustrators of Books for Children and Young Adults: A Biographical Dictionary.** New York, Garland, 1999. 513p. illus. index. (Garland Reference Library of the Humanities, v.21. $70.00. ISBN 0-8153-2004-3.

It is heartening to witness the growth of this work since its initial publication in 1987. Murphy does an admirable job of continuing the endeavors of the late Barbara Rollock in introducing children and educators to black authors and illustrators. Updating the more than 150 entries from the 2d edition and adding 121 new names to the book, this latest edition contains a total of 274 biographical sketches of modern and contemporary creators of children's books, along with selected bibliographies of their works. Black-and-white photographs (more than 120 new to this volume) accompany many of the sketches. Reproductions (again black-and-white) of a number of book jackets appear in an appendix. A second appendix lists chronologically awards and honor books, and a third contains a state-by-state directory of bookstores and distributors. The book also has two indexes—one for book titles and the other for authors and illustrators.

The biographies range in length from one paragraph to several pages and many were written by the illustrators and authors themselves, so the coverage is not consistent, nor does treatment reflect the importance of the individual. Even birth dates are left out of some of the entries. The biographies would be more useful if they followed a set format that contained similar information for each individual. In addition, the book could be made more attractive by integrating the covers into the biographies, rather than relegating them to an appendix. One hopes that future editions will remedy these rather minor shortcomings. However, in spite of the deficiencies, the book offers an abundance of valuable information to students and educators. It is a worthwhile purchase for school and public libraries.—**Barbara Ittner**

959. **Something About the Author: Facts and Pictures About Authors and Illustrators of Books for Young People. Volume 99.** Alan Hedblad, ed. Farmington Hills, Mich., Gale, 1999. 329p. illus. index. $137.25. ISBN 0-7876-1981-7. ISSN 0276-816X.

This is the latest volume of the excellent series featuring biographies of well-known writers and illustrators of books for young people. It began more than 20 years ago and continues to add several volumes a year. (For recent reviews, see ARBA 97, entries 926-930, and ARBA 96, entries 1172-1174.)

The new addition to the set includes 73 authors (all except 1 are living), plus 7 obituaries of authors previously featured. Most authors are American, some are Canadian and English, and one is Swedish. Length of biographies varies from sketches of 1 page or less to 14 pages. A photograph of the author is usually included. Also included are personal information, address, career description, awards, honors, bibliographies, and "sidelights." The latter is often a longer article that, in addition to biographical information, may include illustrations from the author's works and summaries of the best-known writings. The illustrations index and author index at the end of the volume include references to previously published volumes of this series and also to related series published by Gale. The entire set continues to be highly recommended for all libraries that can afford to keep it up-to-date, especially those that feature a strong children's collection.—**Patricia A. Eskoz**

960. **Something About the Author, Volume 102: Facts and Pictures About Authors and Illustrators of Books for Young People.** Alan Hedblad, ed. Farmington Hills, Mich., Gale, 1999. 232p. illus. $104.00. ISBN 0-7876-1984-1. ISSN 0276-816X.

New volumes of Gale's writers' series are always a treat. The current volume presents 95 subjects from varied publishing backgrounds. The front matter, consisting of a table of contents, "Authors of Forthcoming Volumes," an introduction, and acknowledgments, precedes valuable data on current authors from Diane Ackerman to Paul Zindel. These short, fact-filled biographies begin with name and birth dates and cover personal life, current addresses, education and career, awards and honors, published works (listed chronologically with publisher), and adaptations in print and electronic media. Under "Sidelights," the editor summarizes critical commentary from reliable sources, such as *School Library Journal*, *Publishers Weekly*, *Booklist*, and Gale's own Contemporary Authors series. A detailed bibliography and a list of cross-references provide adequate links for more thorough research. The text includes cross-references to writers such as Sydney Horler, who publishes under two pseudonyms, and lists the obituary of Athelstan Spilhaus.

This series thrives for a number of reasons. Gale has honed the process of capturing a life's work. Another feature that benefits young readers, parents, teachers, librarians, students, and researchers is the generous sprinkling of entry photographs alongside illustration and book covers from their works. In this volume Demi's energized art from *The Stonecutter* coordinates well with the bland but satisfying maple leaves from Loretta Krupinski's self-illustrated *Into the Woods* and a cartoon of children's bathroom antics from Jacqueline Wilson and Nick Sharratt's *Elsa, Star of the Shelter!* Gale deserves credit for furthering multiculturalism with a balanced selection of male and female authors. The volume features Jewish author Miriam Chaikin, black author Angela Johnson, Chinese writer Sophia Blanche Lyon Fahs, Colombian author Lyll Becerra de Jenkins, Canadian writer John Perrie Ibbitson, and Chinese American writer Cynthia D. Chin-Lee. A weakness of this volume is the scant data on Geof Smith and William Boniface. Boniface's four books appear to have generated only one critique (no photographs or art) and not enough details about his life and career are given to warrant inclusion.—**Mary Ellen Snodgrass**

961. **Something About the Author, Volume 103: Facts and Pictures About Authors and Illustrators of Books for Young People.** Alan Hedblad, ed. Farmington Hills, Mich., Gale, 1999. 317p. illus. index. $104.00. ISBN 0-7876-2124-2. ISSN 0276-816X.

Something About the Author is an ongoing series that began more than 20 years ago. It continues to be one of the leading authoritative reference sources for information on authors and illustrators of children's literature. Coverage includes both well-known writers and artists as well as individuals who have entered the field more recently and are becoming known for their works. Primarily the series covers the English-speaking countries, especially the United States, Canada, and the United Kingdom. Beginning with volume 57 the cumulative illustrations and author indexes appear in alternative odd-numbered volumes. Beginning with the current volume, three or more specifically commissioned autobiographical essays of prominent authors and artists will be included in each volume. These entries average 10,000 words in length and are illustrated with many photographs. The autobiographical essays of Emma Bull, Isabelle C. Holland, and Barbara Wersba are both informative and entertaining. The current volume includes 71 other entries and 3 obituaries.

The format and information for the entries are standard in all volumes, which makes it easy for students to use older volumes as well as recent ones. Nine sections comprise each entry and include personal information, addresses (including home and electronic mail), career, awards and honors, writings in a title-by-title chronological bibliography, adaptations, works in progress, a sidelight biographical portrait, and references for further information. Extensive illustrations, including book covers, photographs, and illustrations from the author's or illustrator's books, are provided as well.

This is a well-researched and highly recommended set for school, public, and academic libraries. Students find it easy to use and visually appealing.—**Elaine Ezell**

962. **Something About the Author, Volume 104: Facts and Pictures About Authors and Illustrators of Books for Young People.** Alan Hedblad, ed. Farmington Hills, Mich., Gale, 1999. 229p. illus. $137.25. ISBN 0-7876-2125-0. ISSN 0276-816X.

In 1971, the 1st volume of this biographical dictionary on authors and illustrators of children's books was published as an aid to librarians besieged by students who were required by their teachers to include in their book reports "something about the author." Now, more than 100 volumes and several thousand biographical sketches later, this set has become the most extensive (and expensive) source of material on past and present writers and illustrators of children's books published in English in this country. Each volume contains approximately 70 to 80 entries that are of 2 kinds. The 1st gives a brief (about 2-page) introduction to the subject of his or her work, whereas the 2d provides an in-depth profile extending over several pages illustrated with photographs, jacket art, and examples of the subject's illustrations (when appropriate). In addition to career and personal data, these entries include excerpts from diaries, letters, and interviews; detailed chronologies; and lists of both the writer's works and sources of further information. Beginning with volume 57, a cumulative index to the set appears in odd-numbered volumes. Each volume usually contains a few updated, expanded profiles of important authors covered in previous editions. For example, the volume under review has new entries for the photographer Tana Hoban and Newbery Award-winning authors Susan Copper and Louis Sachar. This volume also inaugurates a policy of featuring 3 or more specially commissioned autobiographical essays per volume, each about 10,000 words in length and heavily illustrated with photographs. The 3 authors featured in volume 104 are Donald R. Gallo, Robert Silverberg, and Maia Wojciechowska. Although this set is a handsome, useful addition to any children's literature collection, its price and the fact that five or six volumes are added per year make it a luxury for school and small public libraries. However, for school district libraries, larger public libraries, and universities that support children's literature collections, it continues to be a quality mainstay in the reference collection.
—**John T. Gillespie**

Handbooks and Yearbooks

963. Barker, Keith. **Outstanding Books for Children and Young People: The LA Guide to Carnegie/ Greenaway Winners 1937-1997.** London, Library Association; distr., Lanham, Md., Bernan Associates, 1998. 135p. index. $35.00pa. ISBN 1-85604-287-1.

This is a detailed guide to books awarded the Carnegie and Kate Greenaway Medals. Published by the Library Association in London, this work depicts winners and commended titles from 1937 to 1997.

The author has tried to provide as much bibliographic information as possible, along with a description of the story of illustration and a critical evaluation of the book's relevance to today's children. The author notes that information has not been included on big books, miniatures, and some educational editions.

The first half of the book lists titles honored for outstanding writing with the Carnegie Medal. *The Borrowers* by Mary Norton and *The Last Battle* by C. S. Lewis are just some of the winners listed. The second half of the book lists works such as *The Snowman*, which is illustrated by Raymond Briggs, and *Gorilla*, illustrated by Anthony Browne. Both were honored for illustration by the Kate Greenaway Medal. The author also provides information on award criteria and author/illustrator and title indexes. One criterion of the awards is that the books must have been first published in the United Kingdom. Thus, some titles may be difficult for U.S. audiences to locate. Also, many titles, including recent publications, are out of print and no longer available.—**Cari Ringelheim**

964. **Children's Literature Review, Volume 50: Excerpts from Reviews, Criticism, and Commentary on Books for Children and Young People.** Deborah J. Morad, ed. Farmington Hills, Mich., Gale, 1999. 295p. illus. index. $131.00. ISBN 0-7876-2078-5. ISSN 0362-4145.

This is an irregularly published series reviewing children's and young adult authors and illustrators. *Children's Literature Review*'s (CLR) intended audience is librarians, parents, teachers, and researchers. It includes a table of contents, a preface, acknowledgments (most sources listed), a review of eight or more authors, and a page on how to use the three cumulative indexes (authors, nationalities, and titles). Although this Gale series is generally international in scope, this particular volume only includes eight American authors and illustrators. Those reviewed are Candy D. Boyd, Barbara Corcoran, Holling C. Holling, Trina Schart Hyman, Jean Lee Latham, Ann McGovern (Scheiner), Andre Norton, and Katherine (Womeldorf) Paterson. Each entry presents a bio-critical introduction; author's portraits, when available; author's commentary; and general commentary, as well as title commentary, explanatory annotations, bibliographic citations, and illustrations. Two or more reviews accompany each title. Unlike some older editions of this series, there is no list of authors who will appear in future volumes. A complete synopsis of each author or illustrator is presented that will assist parents or professionals in their quest to find reading materials for children and young adults.—**Nadine Salmons**

Quotation Books

965. **Scholastic Treasury of Quotations for Children.** By Adrienne Betz. New York, Scholastic, 1998. 254p. $16.95. ISBN 0-590-27146-6.

Scholastic Treasury of Quotations for Children is an outstanding reference work for libraries and classroom use. A wonderful introduction to the concept of quotations, the book is targeted for a younger audience but is equally informative for adults. The book is divided into two main sections. The first section contains the quotations arranged by subjects. The second section has brief biographies of all the people quoted in the book and indicates the subject where they are quoted. The table of contents is arranged alphabetically by subject to help locate quotations about a specific topic. Some sections are highlighted in special boxes that contain more information about special quotations and the people who said them. There are cross-references at the end of some sections that point out similar topics containing related quotations.

Betz has provided an excellent introduction to the book. In it she explains the history of quotations and how books of quotations originated. Betz also discusses how one can use quotations in speaking and writing to introduce an idea; describe a person, place, or concept; add authority and support to opinions; borrow titles from old proverbs and literary works; twist a quotation to make a point; and use a favorite quotation to add style. The author selected quotations for this book because each says a lot in a few words. The goal was to create a balanced collection by including quotations that state clear and direct messages, present a variety of opinions, reflect knowledge and experiences of experts, and present famous statements from English and American literature and history.

Finally, Betz explains the difference between proverbs and quotations and provides several examples of books containing collections of proverbs. *Scholastic Treasury of Quotations for Children* is a compact, concise, and powerful resource book. It is a delightful browse and an equally serious study for those wanting quotations and information about quotations. It is a must-have for all schools and public libraries. [R: SLJ, Feb 99, p. 132]—**Mary L. Trenerry**

Young Adult Literature

966. **Lives and Works: Young Adult Authors.** Danbury, Conn., Grolier, 1999. 8v. illus. index. $255.00/set. ISBN 0-7172-9227-4.

Lives and Works: Young Adult Authors is an eight-volume set of brief author biographies designed especially for the middle school student. The more than 250 authors profiled include both modern and classical writers ranging from William Shakespeare to Anne Frank to Francesca Lia Block. Each three- to four-page biography includes a picture; a quote from a major work; a brief overview of the author's life; a description and brief, critical analysis of the author's major works; a list of selected works by and about the author; and when available, a Web address. All eight volumes include a table of contents for the individual volume and a master index for all volumes. The master index has references to authors, titles, and subjects, which makes it useful for finding multiple books about a topic. Although the set is designed for the middle school reader to learn about individual authors, the design of the index should also prove useful for teachers and librarians looking for additional works on specific subjects.

The format of the volumes makes for easy, interesting reading but does not allow for any in-depth student research. The strength of the set lies in its up-to-date coverage of both modern and historical authors who are frequently read as part of the curriculum or for pleasure reading. [R: BL, 1 May 99, p. 1632; BR, Sept/Oct 99, p. 74]—**Janet Hilbun**

967. Mediavilla, Cindy. **Arthurian Fiction: An Annotated Bibliography.** Lanham, Md., Scarecrow, 1999. 157p. index. $24.50pa. ISBN 0-8108-3644-0.

Arthurian Fiction is a bibliographic guide to novels and short stories based around the myth and lore of King Author, his Knights of the Round Table, Camelot, and the search for the Holy Grail. There is also bibliographic information on fantasy fiction featuring Merlin. Entries are organized under subject headings such as "Romance of Camelot," "The Women of Camelot," and "The Holy Quest." Each entry includes basic bibliographic information along with a brief summary of the work's story line. With more than 200 entries this work does not include all Arthurian fiction works but it is geared to reflect titles that may appeal to and are appropriate for young adults.

Most of the books listed are easily accessible though booksellers and public libraries. The author has chosen to omit older books written in archaic or pedantic prose as well as any that contain overly explicit content intended for more mature audiences. Literary and historical titles have not been included because they are not generally considered fiction. The guide contains three appendixes, including "Books Listed by Reading Level," "Arthurian Fiction: Recommended Core List," and "Recent Short Story Anthologies." This is a good resource for teachers, librarians, and young adults interested in Arthurian fiction, but extended research may be needed to find additional titles and titles that have gone out of print.—**Cari Ringelheim**

968. **Novels for Students, Volume 6: Presenting Analysis, Context, and Criticism on Commonly Studied Novels.** Marie Rose Napierkowski and Deborah A. Stanley, eds. Farmington Hills, Mich., Gale, 1999. 366p. illus. index. $79.25. ISBN 0-7876-2116-1. ISSN 1094-3552.

This is the 6th volume in a set that seeks to provide an in-depth analysis of novels that are frequently studied in the high school and college-level literature classroom. It is designed for use by high school and undergraduate students and teachers. For previous reviews of volumes 1 through 4 see ARBA 98, entries 1109 and 1110, and ARBA 99, entries 1013 and 1014. This set provides detail about the novels included and contains recently published titles. The titles included in each volume were identified from several sources. Books on teaching literature and novels, and course curricula from various school districts were consulted. Reading lists like Reading Lists for College Bound Students, The Books Most Recommended by America's Top Colleges, and surveys like the College Board survey of commonly studied novels in high school were also examined. Information was gathered from different organizations like the National Council of Teachers of English (NCTE) and the Young Adult Library Services Association (YALSA).

The titles included here range from the classic to the contemporary: *The Adventures of Tom Sawyer* and *Uncle Tom's Cabin* to *Beloved* and *The Woman Warrior*. A chronologically arranged literary timeline is provided for the 15 novels included so that one can see what was going on during the author's time period, life and death, and the publication of the novel. Entries are alphabetically arranged by the title of the work. Each entry includes an overview or background on the novel, an author biography, a detailed plot summary, and any media adaptations. A list of characters and a detailed description of them, detailed themes and topics, and style elements contained within the novel are also provided. The historical and cultural context for the novel, a critical overview, and several texts of criticism are there to help in analyzing the novel. There are a list of topics related to the novel for further discussion and an annotated bibliography to assist in further study. Also included is a section on what novels might be read next and a list of sources used to write the entry. Photographs are included, some of authors and some of real-life settings of the novels.

Concluding the volume is a glossary of literary terms and several indexes: a cumulative author/title index for all six volumes, a cumulative nationality/ethnicity index based on the author's heritage, and a subject/theme index that indicates the themes addressed in bold. This set is highly recommended for high school and public libraries, and academic library collections that serve undergraduates.—**Jan S. Squire**

969. **Short Stories for Students, Volume 6: Presenting Analysis, Context, and Criticism on Commonly Studied Short Stories.** Tim Akers, ed. Farmington Hills, Mich., Gale, 1999. 368p. illus. index. $60.00. ISBN 0-7876-3606-1. ISSN 1092-7735.

High school teachers of literature will want this title on their school's standing order. They will be especially pleased with it if they are looking to expand their teaching repertoire beyond a textbook or traditional author group but are concerned about usefulness and literary status. With input from practicing teachers, the editor provides author biographies, plot summaries, characters, themes, styles, and bibliographies. In addition, the information given for each of 17 stories includes a critical overview, sources, media adaptations, complementary works, study questions, and comparison and contrast with the time of the author or the story context and the present. The mix of classic and contemporary titles treated in this volume have been published across more than a century, with the oldest being published in 1877 and the newest in 1989. This work is also for student research projects where teachers see themselves as "guides on the side," not direct purveyors of information. Good students who struggle with scholars' critical treatments will find this readable. This source will feed the interest in expanding the canon of literature "to include international, women, and multicultural authors." A glossary, suggestions for citing stories and critical comments, text of stories not included, and nationality and ethnicity indexes are included.—**Edna M. Boardman**

DRAMA

970. **Drama for Students, Volume 5: Presenting Analysis, Context, and Criticism on Commonly Studied Dramas.** David Galens, ed. Farmington Hills, Mich., Gale, 1999. 331p. illus. index. $60.00. ISBN 0-7876-2754-2. ISSN 1094-9232.

This series' 5th volume faithfully follows its predecessors with discussion of 14 plays frequently encountered in courses taken by high school and undergraduate students. Ph.D. candidates and freelance writers contribute 20-page articles whose conveniently surveyed sections summarize the importance of the play, the author's life, and the plot; discuss characters, themes, stylistic devices, and historical context; provide a "critical overview" with excerpted reviews and Gale-commissioned essays; and list sources, which are usually reviews or essays, and briefly annotated further readings, which are usually monographs. Quotations and illustrations dot the pages, as do sidebars for media adaptations, term paper suggestions, related readings, and ill-conceived lists comparing cultural elements from the period of the play to those of today. Front matter sketches the study of drama and offers a superfluous chronology. The volume concludes with a glossary of literary critical terms, series-cumulative indexes for authors/titles and playwrights' nationality/ethnicity, and an index of themes developed in the 14 plays covered.

The writing is serviceable, but scholars will cringe at the level of generalization and the tendencies to glorify and label; the fastidious will wince at editing oversights and clunky moments in the prose. The amount of repetition in the text suggests either poor editing or the expectation that articles will not be read whole. Such study aids can provide a quick orientation, compensate for small collections, and model the study of literature, but their treatment can also preempt students' responses by encouraging uncritical reporting of what they so neatly package. Whether Gale's series will lure the market from the shorter, more inclusive *Masterplots* (see entry 946 for a review of the CD-ROM edition) remains to be seen, but they are reasonable choices for libraries stocking synoptic study guides.—**Robert H. Kieft**

971. **Drama for Students, Volume 6: Presenting Analysis, Context and Criticism on Commonly Studied Dramas.** David Galens, ed. Farmington Hills, Mich., Gale, 1999. 298p. illus. index. $60.00. ISBN 0-7876-2755-0. ISSN 1094-9232.

This is the 6th volume in a new Gale series designed to provide extensive information on a wide variety of commonly studied plays, both classical and modern, for the secondary school student and beyond. A distinguishing feature of this series is the basic cultural and historical background it provides for the novice reader. Readers really need a daunting amount of information to appreciate a play fully in its historical and cultural context, and young people typically do not have such background; *Drama for Students* was conceived as a tool to bridge this gap.

This volume covers 14 plays, ranging from the classical Greek tragedy *The Bacchae* to modern works by David Mamet, Harvey Fierstein, and Joe Orton. The series as a whole emphasizes international and multicultural contributions in drama by women, represented in this particular volume by authors Zora Neale Hurston and Athol Fugard.

Each play is accorded its own chapter, and each chapter contains the following standard elements: a short overview about the play and its author; a plot summary; an alphabetic description of each chapter; and a discussion of the play's themes, style, and historical and cultural context. There is a critical overview of each play, including its reputation and historical reception; a list of critical sources one could read for further study; a bibliography of the sources used in the chapter; an extensive original essay about the play covering its major themes, followed by multiple excerpts of criticism from secondary sources; a summary of the media adaptation of the play; a comparison and contrast box highlighting the cultural and historical differences between the world of the play and its author, and our current world; a list of other works to read next if one wants enrichment or further reading; and a list of study suggestions.

The plays in these volumes are chosen by surveying sources such as *Reading Lists for College-Bound Students* and by analyzing school district curricula, as well as by consulting with an advisory board consisting largely of current high school teachers. The eclectic mix of titles is refreshing. The volume includes a 34-page glossary of literary terms (not all of them related to drama), a cumulative author/title index, a nationality/ethnicity index, and a subject/theme index. It is also enriched by black-and-white photographs of the authors and of playbills and scenes from the plays. Even though this volume is intended for secondary students, it is not toned down in any sense, nor does it shy away from controversial issues, as evidenced by its graphic depiction of the life of Joe Orton. The writing is mature and the critical judgments are incisive. The extensive critical excerpts are taken from top-flight newspapers, magazines, and reference works.

What makes this work different from the volumes of a set like *Contemporary Literary Criticism* lies mostly in the broader range of material it presents, some of which would be needlessly obvious to scholars but most of which would be interesting and valuable to most readers. Gale is to be congratulated for conceiving of a series such as *Drama for Students*. It should occupy a valuable place on the reference shelves of all academic libraries at every level of institution.—**Bill Miller**

972. Dunton, Chris. **Nigerian Theatre in English: A Critical Bibliography.** New Providence, N.J., R. R. Bowker, 1998. 366p. index. (Bibliographical Research in African Literature). $100.00. ISBN 1-873836-71-6.

This volume assumes great significance with the current awareness of and emphasis on diversity, especially in the arts. It is the 5th publication in the Bibliographical Research in African Literature series. Despite the initial assumption from the title of a narrow scope of the topic, the author cites the publication of over 500 plays from the Nigerian English-language theater. Among these are "dozens of works that are truly impressive, that constitute a major contribution to world drama." These works are covered in eight sections. Following a helpful explanatory introduction is the body of the study: an annotated bibliographic listing of 528 published play texts arranged alphabetically by playwright. The majority of the annotations are descriptive of form and content. All are brief and some are only listings of author and title. The author justifies in the introduction the extensive and broad bases on which titles were selected for inclusion in the study. The remaining sections of the volume include a subject, thematic, and general index; a survey of secondary texts; a bibliography of secondary texts; a dramatists author index; a secondary texts author index; and an index of play titles. The extensive cross-referencing greatly enhances the usefulness of this volume. The author makes a strong case for regarding the position of Nigerian theater as the most vigorous in Africa and justifying its dramatists writing in English as worthy subjects for this unique and extensive study. [R: Choice, July/Aug 99, p. 1918]—**Jackson Kesler**

973. **An Index of Characters in Early Modern English Drama Printed Plays, 1500-1660.** rev. ed. By Thomas L. Berger, William C. Bradford, and Sidney L. Sondergard. New York, Cambridge University Press, 1998. 170p. $59.95. ISBN 0-521-62149-6.

This index is a revised and expanded version of the earlier volume *An Index of Characters in English Printed Drama to the Restoration* (Microcard Editions, 1975). The present edition includes all of the characters who may be found in English-printed drama of the Tudor, Elizabethan, Jacobean, Caroline, and Commonwealth periods. The work is generally based on W. W. Greg's *Bibliography of the English Printed Drama to the Restoration* (Bibliographical Society, 1939-1957), and includes the characters of more than 180 plays. In addition to the inclusion of more plays in English, this new version provides characters found in Latin plays published in England. The work is divided into 2 sections: an alphabetic list of characters and character types (e.g., Generals, Dutchmen) and a "finding list" that includes all plays indexed. Each entry in the "finding list" includes the Greg identifying number, the title (also as it appears in Greg), the author or authors, the date of first publication, the date of the first production (if known), and the STC number of the earliest edition of the play (i.e., *A Short Catalogue of Books Printed in England, Scotland, and Ireland, and of English Books Printed Abroad, 1641-1660* [Bibliographical Society, 1926]). In addition, there is an author index and an alphabetic list of English-printed drama, Latin printed drama, and lost plays.

This is an invaluable reference tool for early modern English drama. Its value lies not only in the list of characters, but also in its complete listing of early modern English drama. The work is easy to use and has an interesting introduction, which provides information on how to use the work, and some interesting information concerning early modern English drama. The work is highly recommended for all public and academic libraries. [R: Choice, Oct 99, p. 302]—**Robert L. Wick**

974. Reynolds, John J., and Szilvia E. Szmuk. **Spanish Golden Age Drama: An Annotated Bibliography of United States Doctoral Dissertations 1899-1992....** New York, Modern Language Association of America, 1998. 573p. index. $35.00. ISBN 0-87352-570-1.

Devoted to the Spanish theater of the sixteenth and seventeenth centuries, this bilingual bibliography follows the arrangement established by the annual compilation on the Comedia in the Bulletin of the Comediantes, begun in the early 1950s. Although the focus of the work is on the drama and the playwrights, the scope extends back to the origins of the Golden Age and forward to its subsequent influences. Divided into 2 parts, the first classifies 784 individual U.S. doctoral dissertations in 853 listings and the second, termed a "supplement," identifies 577 non-U.S. dissertations in 616 listings. "Dissertation" is interpreted in a broad sense, and may include dissertations proper as well as derivative works and articles that appeared in journals or collections. Each section begins with general items on the culture, history, and art of the period and concludes with an alphabetic list of playwrights with a few themes interfiled. Annotations are generally quoted from a published abstract or from the author's introduction to the dissertation. Critical editions identify the text on which they are based. Non-U.S. dissertations are not annotated, although the compilers occasionally add notes for clarification.

Other features adding to the book's usefulness include a list of works consulted, directories and indexes of both U.S. and non-U.S. institutions, an index of dissertation writers and directors, and an index by subject and title. The compilers lay no claim to the comprehensiveness of the bibliography. However, they have meticulously combed their sources with care and judgment. Research collections in Spanish literature will want to acquire this fine, scholarly work. [R: Choice, June 99, p. 1758]—**Bernice Bergup**

FICTION

General Works

975. Barron, Neil, Wayne Barton, Kristin Ramsdell, and Steven A. Stilwell. **What Do I Read Next? A Reader's Guide to Current Genre Fiction, 1999.** Farmington Hills, Mich., Gale, 1999. 656p. index. $158.50. ISBN 0-7876-2151-X. ISSN 1052-2212.

The 1999 edition of this Gale work contains approximately 1,300 entries covering titles published in the last year. These are divided into sections on mystery, romance, western, fantasy, horror, and science fiction. Experts in each of these genres describe each title and offer an overview of the year's writings. The entries include summaries of approximately 100 words, and brief information on story type, series, major characters, time periods, and locales. This is followed by citations of reviews, a list of other works by the same author, and a list of similar books by other authors that the reader might like.

The book's indexes include information on series, time periods, geographic aspects, character names, character descriptions, authors, and titles. The six genre sections are further subdivided. For example, "western" is divided into chase, collection, historical, historical/American Civil War, Indian culture, Indian Wars, man alone, modern, mountain man, mystery, quest, ranch life, revenge, saga, series, traditional trail drive, and young readers.

Rounding out the work is additional information on genre terms and award winners. It should be noted that although this work does not give much space to inspirational literature (Christian fiction), Gale is planning on publishing an entire volume on this type of writing in June 2001.

Overall, this is an invaluable reference tool for reader and librarian alike. The information it contains may be used for readers' advisory, reference questions, and programs and displays. Funds and interest permitting, libraries should consider keeping one copy at the reference desk and another near their fiction collections.
—**January Adams**

976. **Critical Companions to Popular Contemporary Writers.** 1999 ed. [CD-ROM]. Westport, Conn., Greenwood Press, 1999. Minimum system requirements: IBM or compatible 386. CD-ROM drive. Windows 3.1 or later. 8MB RAM. 15MB hard disk space. 14-inch VGA monitor. Mouse. $595.00. ISBN 0-313-30963-9. ISSN 1522-2853.

The authors included in this series were chosen by an advisory board comprised of public and high school librarians as well as high school teachers. The board chose to include 25 best-selling, popular authors who have a proven record of sales and performance: V. C. Andrews, Tom Clancy, Mary Higgins Clark, Arthur C. Clarke, James Clavell, Pat Conroy, Robin Cook, Michael Crichton, John Grisham, Howard Fast, Ken Follett, James Herriot, Tony Hillerman, John Jakes, Stephen King, Dean Koontz, Robert Ludlum, Anne McCaffrey, Colleen McCullough, James Michener, Anne Rice, Tom Robbins, John Saul, Erich Segal, and Gore Vidal.

Volumes in the series are written by scholars with a particular bent for popular fiction. Each volume tries to maintain the same basic format, with chapters focused on author biography, relationship to literary movements or genres, and separate chapters for individual works. Within this latter category, plot development, character development, and theme form the matrix of the chapter, although other perspectives are treated as appropriate. Finally, an "alternative reading" of the novel is presented, followed by a primary and secondary bibliography, including reviews. Search functions allow one to use both Boolean and natural language, with targeted search guides allowing customized searching within author biographies, alternative readings, plot development, character development, literary device and style, or thematic issues. Intuitive printing commands enhance the value.

Available as a one-time purchase or as a standing order with annual updates, the disc is also available to be networked for an additional fee. High school, public, and academic libraries should seriously consider this product for its unique coverage and approach. [R: BR, Sept/Oct 99, p. 85]—**Edmund F. SantaVicca**

977. Pearl, Nancy, with Martha Knappe and Joyce G. Saricks. **Now Read This: A Guide to Mainstream Fiction, 1978-1998.** Englewood, Colo., Libraries Unlimited, 1999. 432p. index. (Genreflecting Advisory Series). $65.00. ISBN 1-56308-659-X.

Readers' advisors or librarians who attempt to make suggestions to their patrons on what to read next will welcome this book. The compilers, who are librarians, library science students, and avid readers, after careful reading and animated discussion decided upon the "appeal characteristics" of mainstream fiction published between 1978 and 1998. According to them, "appeal characteristics" are those qualities that best describe a book's strengths and set it apart from other books. Mainstream fiction omits genre fiction like mysteries, romances, science fiction, westerns, and fantasy, and is limited to that which explores "aspects of human experiences: love, fear, despair, hatred, aging, and death as well as moral and ethical decisions and choices people make" (p. vii). *Now Read This* divides 1,000 titles into 4 categories based on their "appeal characteristics"—setting, story, characters, and language.

For each entry there is a bibliographic citation; a brief annotation; a listing of "second appeal," if applicable; subjects; and an indication if the book is recommended for discussion in book groups. Following this are two to four titles that might be read next.

Indexes include a title, a subject, and an author index. Bold typeface is used for title and author main entries. Because award-winning books are favored for inclusion, a list of book awards appears in the appendix. This volume, with its ease of use and carefully designed format, is not only appealing but invaluable to the readers' advisor who works with adults.—**Sara R. Mack**

978. Simkin, John E., comp. **The Whole Story: 3000 Years of Sequels and Sequences.** 2d ed. Victoria, Australia, D. W. Thorpe; distr., New Providence, N.J., Reed International Books, 1998. 1469p. index. $135.00. ISBN 1-86452-022-1.

This large work covers ground not attempted anywhere else. It lists 106,000 titles in 20,600 sequences and several thousand related titles for adult and juvenile series, both fiction and nonfiction. Listings are not annotated. Unlike *To Be Continued* (see ARBA 97, entry 946) by Merle Jacob and Hope Apple or *Sequels* (see ARBA 99, entry 1029) by Janet and Jonathan Husband, it lists books that do not necessarily need to be read in chronological sequence. Many of the titles listed are connected by recurring characters or specific settings. Pastiches are also included. There are 233 titles by 132 authors listed under the Sherlock Holmes series. When sequences do not have a specific title, Simkin has created one, often using the main character's name for the listing. It is great for answering some of the stumpers readers' advisors are often faced with when patrons remember a series character from long ago. Many of the books listed have never been collected or cataloged in libraries. Paperbacks and dime novels, a source of frustration for those seeking information on them, are included, providing perhaps the most useful attribute of the book—the verification of authors and titles for patrons seeking long-lost favorites.

The book is organized into 3 sections. Section 1 lists sequels and sequences, including known variations on specific titles. Titles are listed in numbered order with the date of first publication under the sequence name. The 2d section lists individual titles with the author, the name of the sequence, and the position in the sequence. The 3d section is an author index that lists pseudonyms and the names of sequences.

Unfortunately, the listings must be taken with a grain of salt. There are many errors, particularly in science fiction series. For example, even though the author index directs the reader looking under the name "Tracy Hickman" to the Starshield trilogy, the entry in the series section only lists coauthor Margaret Weis. It lists *Sentinels* as first and *Mantle of Kendis-Dai* as second in the series, but in actuality they are the same book, only with a title change. Under the series Simkin calls the Miles Naismith Vorkosigan series (more commonly referred to as the Vorkosigan Saga), *Cordelia's Honor*, which is in actuality an omnibus edition of *Shards of Honor* and *Barrayar* featuring Miles's mother Cordelia, is listed as the first volume. *Barrayar* is then listed as the sixth volume and *Shards of Honor* as a companion volume. *The Spirit Ring* is listed as number seven in the sequence but is not part of the sequence at all. *Young Miles* is listed as 10th in the sequence but is actually an omnibus version of *Warrior's Apprentice*, "In the Mountains of Mourning," a story from *Borders of Infinity*, and *Vor Game*. This is a welcome addition to the readers' advisory arsenal in libraries with active readers' advisory services, but does not replace *To Be Continued: An Annotated Guide to Sequels* or *Sequels*.—**Diana Tixier Herald**

Crime and Mystery

979. Bleiler, Richard J. **Reference Guide to Mystery and Detective Fiction.** Englewood, Colo., Libraries Unlimited, 1999. 391p. index. (Reference Sources in the Humanities Series). $55.00. ISBN 1-56308-380-9.

This reference guide is a well-organized compilation of 749 entries, including Websites, on mystery and detective fiction. The introduction explains not only what has been included, but also precisely what has not—thrillers, westerns, adventure stories, true crime, and espionage.

The volume is organized by various types of bibliographies, including encyclopedias; readers' guides; genres (e.g., classic British, locked door, police detective); regional guides; magazine indexes; cataloging guides; media catalogs; and publishers. By far the largest category is that of more than 200 individual authors alphabetically arranged. Books that list awards, such as the Edgar and the Agatha, are mentioned. The "Directory of Dealers and Price Guides" is helpful for writers, and a selective listing of electronic sources is followed by addresses of journals and periodicals specializing in mystery writing as well as the addresses for professional organizations.

Each section is introduced by a scope note explaining what is covered and where the user may turn for more specific information. Following the bibliographic information on each work is a description of its intent, organization, content, and often an evaluative opinion. In the rare cases where the editor has not seen the work, it is so noted. An extensive index, by item number, ensures the finding of material. With this one volume, students and teachers will have all of the information needed to find any aspect of the genre. [R: LJ, 1 Oct 99, p. 78; Choice, Dec 99, p. 686; BL, 15 Dec 99, p. 804]—**Charlotte Lindgren**

980. Landrum, Larry. **American Mystery and Detective Novels: A Reference Guide.** Westport, Conn., Greenwood Press, 1999. 273p. index. (American Popular Culture). $75.00. ISBN 0-313-21387-9.

This book begins with the historical development of the mystery and detective genre in the U.S. from 1799 to today's contemporary authors. Minority writers are included. In addition, literary criticism for this writing category is surveyed with descriptions of key conventions and formulas. Mystery and detective writers are grouped chronologically with pseudonyms, selected titles, and themes. Individuals were selected on the basis of how well known they are, the size of their body of work, and if they had made a significant contribution to the field.

Finally, a guide is given to reference works in this area by title and author with a brief description of each study. Locations for university research collections are also noted. Features include a timeline of the milestones in mystery writing and a bibliography. Cited are criticism pieces as well as works by writers discussing their craft. There is an author, character, and pseudonym index as well as a subject and title index.—**Adrienne Antink Bendel**

981. Murphy, Bruce F. **The Encyclopedia of Murder and Mystery.** New York, St. Martin's Press, 1999. 543p. $75.00. ISBN 0-312-21554-1.

In the words of its introduction, *The Encyclopedia of Murder and Mystery* surveys the "authors, characters, terminology, famous criminal cases, slang, subgenres and plot devices, murder techniques and poisons" (p. viii), which are part of the matter and context of crime and murder literature. To provide this survey, Murphy has written approximately 2,000 articles, ranging in length from 50 to 500 words, and strives to be genuinely encyclopedic: entries begin with "Aarons, Edward S[idney]" and conclude with a cross-reference to "Zubro, Mark Richard." Cross-references are plentiful, and articles frequently conclude with bibliographies. There is no index.

Murphy, editor of the 4th edition of *Benet's Reader's Encyclopedia*, is a very capable writer, and the entries in the encyclopedia frequently sparkle. It is thus unfortunate that the encyclopedia has several lethal shortcomings. First and foremost, the field of mystery and detective literature is simply too large for one person to provide a viable encyclopedia survey of it, and although Murphy's encyclopedia is in many ways superior to the late William DeAndrea's *Encyclopedia Mysteriosa* (see ARBA 95, entry 932), it has many of the earlier work's problems, chief among which is that apart from a few of the major established international writers, the focus is primarily on the Anglo-American writers, history, and terms.

Next, Murphy's encyclopedia is absolutely riddled with errors, on the order of almost one per page. Some of these errors are reasonably minor (critic E. F. Bleiler is not English but American), and some of these errors are typographical (Fredric Brown did not spell his first name "Frederic"). There are errors of omission (Dashiell Hammett's unlisted first name was Samuel), and errors of fact (the first pulp magazine did not appear in 1889). And there are errors that are unforgivable (Doyle's "A Study in Scarlet" was categorically not "serialized in 1887").

The Encyclopedia of Murder and Mystery was published at roughly the same time as *The Oxford Companion to Crime and Mystery Writing* (1999). *The Oxford Companion* is not perfect, but it is more reliable than Murphy's encyclopedia.—**Richard Bleiler**

982. Riley, Dick, and Pam McAllister. **The Bedside, Bathtub, & Armchair Companion to Sherlock Holmes.** New York, Continuum Publishing, 1999. 216p. illus. $29.95; $19.95pa. ISBN 0-8264-1140-1; 0-8264-1116-9pa.

Sherlock Holmes fans will welcome this compendium of facts, trivia, and puzzles. The 60 capsules briefly provide information on the principal predicament and first publication of each of Conan Doyle's 56 short stories and 4 novels featuring Sherlock Holmes. Each capsule also includes notable features, quotations, or oddities and discrepancies. A 16-page biography of Arthur Conan Doyle details his life and interest in spiritualism. Other essays discuss the illustrators who determined Holmes' familiar appearance, actors who created his mannerisms, values of British money in the nineteenth century, life in Victorian England, crime, colonialism, the ranks of English society, Holmes' attitude toward women and drugs, and a glossary of Victorian terms.

Information is provided about many of the almost 400 Sherlock Holmes societies that exist worldwide and their Websites are provided. There are lists of popular mementos and collectibles. Parodies of the great detective are described as well. Black-and-white line drawings and engravings appear on almost every page, depicting actual people such as Doyle, James Bell (the inspiration for Holmes), and the various actors who played the roles of Watson and Holmes, along with cartoons and illustrations for the stories.

One need not be a serious scholar of Sherlock Holmes o enjoy browsing this volume, although the various puzzles presume a thorough knowledge of the mysteries. Even devoted followers will find much that is new in this companion.—**Charlotte Lindgren**

Historical Fiction

983. Adamson, Lynda G. **American Historical Fiction: An Annotated Guide to Novels for Adults and Young Adults.** Phoenix, Ariz., Oryx Press, 1999. 405p. index. $45.50. ISBN 1-57356-067-7.

Adamson has compiled an annotated bibliography of 3,387 fiction titles covering U.S. history from before 1600 through the 1980s. For the purpose of the book, historical fiction is defined as a period earlier than which the reader is familiar. Although labeled for young adults as well as adults, only 25 percent of the titles are designated for the young adult audience of ninth grade or older. Most of these were chosen from lists in *School Library Journal* or *Booklist* and are noted with a diamond symbol. The volume will be more useful to adults seeking U.S. historical fiction or libraries building adult collections. It complements and expands the listings in *Dickinson's American Historical Fiction* (see ARBA 87, entry 1134), which the author originally sought to update. There is some duplication between the two books; however, Adamson includes more popular fiction. Vandelia L. VanMeter's *America in Historical Fiction* (see ARBA 98, entry 1114) will serve the young adult reader better. Titles for this volume were chosen from Library of Congress holdings and review journals since 1980. Copyright dates range from 1820 to 1989.

The titles are organized into 13 time periods and are listed alphabetically by author within each division. Titles are consecutively numbered, making referencing easy. If a title spans more than one era, it was placed in the period in which the book began. Entries provide expected bibliographic information: author; title; date of publication; recent reprint, if applicable; number of pages; setting; main character; genre; and awards. The descriptive annotations are brief and limited to one sentence.

The appendixes and indexes are a major strength of the book. The two appendixes are comprised of a list of award-winning books arranged alphabetically by award and an alphabetic list by author of titles suitable for the young adult audience. Five indexes—author, title, genre, geographic, and subject—provide extensive methods of locating titles. The 23 genre headings are defined in the preface. [R: LJ, Dec 98, p. 84; BR, Sept/Oct 99, p. 76]—**Elaine Ezell**

984. Adamson, Lynda G. **World Historical Fiction: An Annotated Guide to Novels for Adults and Young Adults.** Phoenix, Ariz., Oryx Press, 1999. 719p. index. $45.50. ISBN 1-57356-066-9.

More than 6,000 historical fiction titles set outside the United States are covered in this welcome tool for the readers' advisor. Espousing a reader-friendly definition of historical fiction, Adamson includes works that were contemporary when written but now belong to a bygone time, such as books by Jane Austen as well as books written more than 25 years after the specific time period setting. Each numbered entry (arranged geographically by time period and then alphabetically by author and title) provides bibliographical information, a concise descriptive annotation, and genre descriptors. Thirty-two genre descriptors, defined in the preface, are used. Books that may be suitable for young adult readers are indicated by a diamond-shaped symbol, but historical fiction written specifically for the young adult market is not included. Appendix 2 lists the books suitable for young adult readers and appendix 1 lists award-winning titles. There are also author, title, genre, subject, and place and time indexes. Some books in series have a parenthetical note to series title and number while on others the preceding books are mentioned in the annotation. Others have no series information noted, but the annotations include the character's name indicating a connection.

This does not provide all that a readers' advisor would like, such as cross-references to indicate that Victoria Holt, Jean Plaidy, and Philippa Carr were all one and the same or that the Angelique books by Anne Golon were originally published in the U.S. as being by Sergeanne Golon. Unfortunately, the early books in Winston Graham's Poldark series are excluded, perhaps because they are out-of-print, but they are still found in many libraries and it would have been nice to have them here, as later books in the series are listed. It would have been preferable in the case of series to include all titles regardless of the print status. This is an excellent addition to readers' advisory collections for public, secondary, and academic libraries as well as a good resource for teachers who use fiction in teaching world history. [R: LJ, 1 May 99, p. 68; Choice, May 99, p. 1590; BR, Sept/Oct 99, p. 76]—**Diana Tixier Herald**

Romance

985. Brackett, Virginia. **Classic Love & Romance Literature: An Encyclopedia of Works, Characters, Authors, & Themes.** Santa Barbara, Calif., ABC-CLIO, 1999. 406p. illus. index. $75.00. ISBN 0-87436-955-X.

The term "classic" in the title of this work is the key to understanding its content. It is not an encyclopedia of genre romance fiction; you will not find entries for Barbara Cartland or Danielle Steele. It is instead an encyclopedia of the classic romance, the romance that grew out of the heroic tradition of the *Odyssey* and *Beowulf*. Its historical practitioners include Walter Scott, Jane Austen, Henry James, and D. H. Lawrence. Modern–day exponents of the genre include Anne Tyler, Toni Morrison, and Isabel Allende. The editor's purpose in writing this book is to acquaint readers with the tradition, so that they may better enjoy today's version of the romance novel.

To accomplish this, Brackett includes articles from half a page to two pages long on authors, characters, book titles, and themes. Arrangement is alphabetic. Most of the material was chosen for entry because the book represented is one that is frequently read in high school or college-level literature classes. Here one can find entries not only on Emily Brontë, certainly a classic romance novelist, but also on *Wuthering Heights*, her most famous book, and on the two major characters in it, Heathcliffe and Catherine Earnshaw. Cross-references lead from one entry to a related one. Brackett provides ample illustrations, mostly portraits of authors or stills from movie versions of romance novels. She also provides an index integrating authors, titles, characters, and themes.

Although most if not all of these books and authors are covered in such standard sources as *Contemporary Authors* (see entries 924-928) or *British Writers* (see ARBA 98, entry 1149), this single volume pulls things together usefully. Those needing a source that concentrates on the contemporary genre romance novel might want to consult Kristin Ramsdell's *Romance Fiction: A Guide to the Genre* (see entry 987). [R: BL, 15 Sept 99, p. 301; LJ, Aug 99, p. 74; BR, Nov/Dec 99, p. 79]—**Terry Ann Mood**

986. **North American Romance Writers.** Kay Mussell and Johanna Tuñón, eds. Lanham, Md., Scarecrow, 1999. 279p. index. $39.50. ISBN 0-8108-3604-1.

Primarily a collection of essays, this title has mixed value as a reference source. Kay Mussell traces the romance genre in America from the 1950s on in a brief historical introduction. And Johanna Tuñón concludes the work with an English-language bibliography, more than 40 pages of scholarly and popular titles, on the romance genre in the twentieth century. In between, some 30 practitioners, one a husband–and–wife duo, express their views on certain aspects of the genre. These constitute the major portion of the work.

The award-winning authors were selected on the basis of having "something interesting to say about their own work" (p. xi). A short biographical note precedes each entry, followed by a listing of the author's works and awards. The essays vary in focus, based on the editors' criteria. The three outlined are influences on their work, contributions to the genre, and their work in relation to feminism and the women's movement.

The essays are as varied as the writers themselves. Mary Balogh concentrates on influences and contributions. Jennifer Crusie Smith talks about her love of the genre in "Why I Know I'll Continue to Write Romance Until They Pry My Cold Dead Fingers from Around My Keyboard." Sandra Kitts sees the genre as "the opportunity to examine the complex dynamics between men and women in relationships" (p. 133). Subjects and names of persons mentioned in the text may be located in the index, but it excludes titles listed for individual writers.

Although the personal impressions of the romance writers are interesting, and in some cases even entertaining, they do not constitute a handbook or a guide. For this reason the book is more appropriate for the circulating rather than the reference collection. [R: BL, 15 Sept 99, p. 301; Choice, Dec 99, p. 692]

—**Bernice Bergup**

987. Ramsdell, Kristin. **Romance Fiction: A Guide to the Genre.** Englewood, Colo., Libraries Unlimited, 1999. 435p. index. (Genreflecting Advisory Series). $45.00. ISBN 1-56308-335-3.

A glance at the title of this work might lead one to believe that it is a straightforward bibliography of romance fiction. It is instead a scholarly discussion and review of the literature, aimed principally at librarians who buy this literature and who must satisfy eager romance readers. In this 2d edition of the 1987 *Happily Ever After: A Guide to Reading Interests in Romance Fiction* (see ARBA 88, entry 1147), Ramsdell adds four chapters, including one on ethnic/multicultural romances and one devoted to the popular regency period romances; drops some chapters, including the one on young adult romances, which Ramsdell believes deserves its own book-length review; and revises all other chapters.

Ramsdell begins with a history of the genre, a discussion of its appeal, and some general hints to librarians on how to approach collection development in this area. She recommends that collection development librarians talk to colleagues and to regular readers of the genre, read reviews, and monitor circulation statistics. For those responsible for personnel allocation, she recommends designating a librarian to be responsible for collection building in this area.

The main body of the book is devoted to sections on subgenres of the field: contemporary romance; romantic mysteries; historical romances; regency period romances; alternative reality romance (e.g., vampire, time travel, fantasy); sagas; gay and lesbian romance; inspirational romance; and ethnic/multicultural romance. Each of these sections begins with a lengthy definition of the subgenre, followed by a discussion of its appeal. Hints on advising the reader follow, including such topics as what other subgenres a reader might find appealing and specific series that might be of interest. An annotated bibliography of selected authors rounds out each section.

Other material includes bibliographies of research material on the genre, including dissertations, a list of writers' organizations (e.g., Romance Writers of America), a list of awards, and a list of publishers in the area.

Romance Fiction is not meant to be used for a quick lookup question. For that, the librarian or the reader can use such tools as *What Do I Read Next: A Reader's Guide to Current Genre Fiction* (see ARBA 92, entry 1136) or the electronic product NoveList. This work is for the collection development librarian with a commitment to building a romance collection and the budget to support that commitment as well as for the scholar or student with an interest in the genre. [R: BL, 15 Sept 99, p. 301; Choice, Dec 99, p. 692]

—**Terry Ann Mood**

Science Fiction, Fantasy, and Horror

988. **Fantasy and Horror: A Critical and Historical Guide to Literature, Illustration, Film, TV, Radio, and the Internet.** Neil Barron, ed. Lanham, Md., Scarecrow, 1999. 816p. index. $85.00. ISBN 0-8108-3596-7.

Because fantasy and horror are so closely related, this work is an extensive revision of two separate guides, *Horror Literature* (see ARBA 91, entry 1138) and *Fantasy Literature* (see ARBA 91, entry 1137). This guide directs readers and viewers to works of fantasy and horror, both commendable and historical. There is greater unity in this one–volume guide, whose scope is wider and now includes chapters on fantasy and horror poetry, teaching fantasy and horror literature, fantasy and horror comics, and a comprehensive guide to the most useful Internet sources.

The guide provides both critical interpretations and historical data pertaining to the fantasy and horror genres. Arranged chronologically, more than 2,300 works of fiction and poetry are discussed, each cross-referenced to other works of similar and contrasting themes. There are also lists identifying books in series, award-winning books, translations, and children's and young adult books. Readers, including librarians, should realize that this new guide is selective. In spite of its expanded size, the editor has necessarily limited the guide to include what he feels are the best works representing fantasy and horror. [R: LJ, Aug 99, p. 76; BL, 15 Nov 99, pp. 652-653]—**Cari Ringelheim**

989. Fonseca, Anthony J., and June Michele Pulliam. **Hooked on Horror: A Guide to Reading Interests in Horror Fiction.** Englewood, Colo., Libraries Unlimited, 1999. 332p. index. (Genreflecting Advisory Series). $55.00. ISBN 1-56308-671-9.

This title in the Libraries Unlimited Genreflecting Advisory Series focuses on horror as its own genre rather than as a subgenre of fantasy. As the series title indicates, the purpose is to provide a readers' advisory tool for public librarians. High school and college librarians may find this title useful as patron reading choices and curriculum demands. It looks at books published from 1994 to 1998 that are still available either by purchase or library loan. It does not include young adult titles unless they are read by adults (e.g., Annette Klaus's *The Silver Kiss*).

The book is divided into 4 parts. The 1st introduces horror fiction as a genre. The 2d provides an annotated bibliography of horror short story collections by individual and multiple authors. The 3d part, the main section of the book, consists of an annotated bibliography of horror novels and films divided into chapters. The chapters cover ghosts and haunted houses; golems, mummies, and reanimated stalkers; vampires and werewolves; demonic possession, Satanism, black magic, witches, and warlocks; mythological monsters; telekinesis and hypnosis; small-town horror; maniacs and sociopaths; technohorror; rampant animals and other eco-monsters; psychological horror; splatterpunk; and comic horror. The 4th part focuses on ready-reference, criticism, and other helpful information such as cross-genre fiction, author bibliographies, periodicals, awards, publishers, and Internet sites. The entries are arranged alphabetically by author's last name within a chapter and cross-referenced among the chapters as needed. The book may be searched by the short story, subject, or author/title indexes. The gray and red cover with gargoyle type heads echoes the subject matter within. This is a good source for libraries that must develop their horror collections.—**Esther R. Sinofsky**

990. Herald, Diana Tixier. **Fluent in Fantasy: A Guide to Reading Interests.** Englewood, Colo., Libraries Unlimited, 1999. 260p. index. (Genreflecting Advisory Series). $39.00. ISBN 1-56308-655-7.

Intended for readers, librarians, and booksellers, this volume tries to serve two audiences at once, readers searching for recommended fantasy books and those researching the genre. Books included were published between the nineteenth century and 1998. Using a format employed for other readers' guides (see ARBA 98, entry 1096, and ARBA 96, entry 1186), an introduction defining fantasy literature precedes chapters devoted to a subgenre (e.g., fairy tales, romance, time travel). Although the introduction neglects to explain the subgenres, each chapter offers a brief definition or explanation and titles chosen to represent the subgenre. Where available, bibliographic guides to the literature are noted. The annotations, which hint at the type of subgenre, are selective and chosen for annotating through an unnamed process. Keywords indicate terms employed in the subject index, while symbols identify award-winning and young adult titles. The author has continued the practice of recommending titles, but has neglected to state any criteria beyond personal choice.

Chapter 20, a compendium of resources, lists research tools (e.g., journals, publishers, biographical sources) useful in the pursuit of fantasy literature, with selective annotations. Librarians and researchers, the second audience, will appreciate the guide to research sources, related science fiction resources, and bibliographies. World Wide Web links mentioned throughout are updated at the author's homepage, a definite highlight. Three appendixes offer a glossary of common terminology, recommended young adult titles, and a recommended core collection. Author/title and subject indexes complete the volume. The first is useful for locating additional works by an author represented in different subgenres (e.g., Anne McCaffrey); however, some entries lead to award lists only (e.g., Jack Finney).

With her book designed to accompany forays into the book stacks, the author has made compromises in order to keep the volume relatively small. Most reprehensible is the intentional absence of publication information, a practice that severely limits the use of the guide for other purposes, such as collection development. This work is recommended for public libraries; the research resource section makes this worthy of consideration by academic libraries as well. [R: BL, 15 Nov 99, pp. 652-653]—**Sandra E. Belanger**

991. **Science Fiction Magazine Story Index, 1926-1995.** By Terry A. Murray. Jefferson, N.C., McFarland, 1999. 627p. $65.00. ISBN 0-7864-0691-7.

Had it appeared two years ago, Murray's index to 4,943 science fiction magazines published between 1926 and 1995 would have been lauded. True, Murray's index does not reference pseudonyms, nor does the work index "poetry, nonfiction articles, columns, letters, contests, cover art, interior art, and information on editorial staff, publisher, physical size, page count, price, or story series," but neither did the long out-of-print 2d edition of Donald Day's *Index to the Science Fiction Magazines, 1926-1950* (G. K. Hall, 1982), nor did the various volumes of the new England Science Fiction Association's *Indexes* to science fiction magazines, and both of these were necessary adjuncts to science fiction research. Thus, two years ago Murray's index—alphabetically arranged by magazine title, with an appendix listing prolific authors and their titles, and indexes for author and title—would have been an essential purchase for science fiction lovers desperate to learn what appeared in the magazines that once so dominated the field. They could have ignored Murray's introduction, which has its share of errors (to call Gernsback's *Amazing Stories* a success is to ignore its 1929 bankruptcy in which Gernsback lost control of his magazines), and they could have learned to accommodate Murray's indexing format, which lumps together in paragraph form the authors and titles, using small capitals to differentiate authors and separating different citations by a semicolon.

What a difference a year makes. First, in 1998 William Contento and Stephen T. Miller published on CD-ROM the *Science Fiction, Fantasy, & Weird Fiction Magazine Index, 1890-1997* (Locus Press, 1998), a monumental index to the science fiction in more than 11,000 issues of 730 English-language magazines published between 1890 and 1997. Their index offers access by magazine, author, title, and cover artist. Furthermore, Contento and Miller offer access to the poetry, nonfiction articles, columns, letters, contests, and cover art. Their index is significantly cheaper than Murray's at $49.95. Also in 1998 appeared Bleiler and Bleiler's *Science Fiction: The Gernsback Years* (Kent State University Press), which provides summaries of up to 1,300 words for each of the 1,835 stories in the genre American and English science fiction magazines published from 1926 through 1936. This volume also includes a 15,000-word introduction; reveals pseudonyms and previously unknown biographical data; offers access to the poetry, nonfiction articles, columns, letters, contents, cover art, and interior art; and provides a history of each magazine, including information on editorial staff, publisher, physical size, page count, price, and story series. Furthermore, both Contento and Miller and Bleiler and Bleiler provide access to the contents of *Flash Gordon Strange Adventure Magazine*, which Murray does not. [R: Choice, Sept 99, p. 112; BL, 1 Sept 99, p. 185; LJ, 1 Sept 99, p. 181]—**Richard Bleiler**

992. **Science Fiction Writers.** 2d ed. Richard Bleiler, ed. New York, Charles Scribner's Sons/Macmillan Library Reference, 1999. 1009p. illus. index. (The Scribner Writers Series). $125.00. ISBN 0-684-80593-6.

This revision adds 23 new articles to a well-respected biographical source. Of the original 27 essays, 19 have been updated, as have the individual bibliographies. This book remains a source for "critical studies of the major authors" rather than a comprehensive encyclopedia. Aimed at the science fiction tradition of the United States, most entries cover Americans, but influential British figures are present, as are continental writers widely translated into English. Coverage of female writers (i.e., Octavia Butler and Sheri Tepper) has grown with the importance of women in the genre. Coverage of authors active in fantasy or horror is limited to their science fiction output (e.g., C. S. Lewis or H. P. Lovecraft).

The quality and vitality of the essays justify the wide latitude enjoyed by contributors. Inconsistencies are most apparent in the bibliographies, which range from comprehensive descriptions to summary lists of major titles or best editions. Contributors include academics (H. Bruce Franklin), creative writers (Brian Aldiss, author of *Trillion Year Spree* and *Helliconia Spring*), and other editors (John Clute, coeditor of the *Encyclopedia of Science Fiction* [see ARBA 94, entry 1211]). Bleiler is humanities librarian at the University of Connecticut and the son of E. F. Bleiler, who produced the 1st edition of this work in 1982 (see ARBA 83, entry 1162).

An index covers personal names and book, magazine, and short story titles mentioned in articles, but not subjects. Readers must browse for topics such as "robots" or "cyberpunk," or fictional characters such as E. E. Smith's Kimball Kinnison. The original introduction is reprinted beside a new one. The essays are now in alphabetic order, accompanied by a chronological list of authors. Most articles include a photograph. A general bibliography lists major reference books, current through 1998.

Those seeking comprehensive bibliographies or less prominent authors, or commentary about science fiction films, illustrations, and fandom, should consult the *St. James Guide to Science-Fiction Writers* (see ARBA 97, entry 951) and John Clute and Peter Nicholls' *Encyclopedia of Science Fiction* (St. Martin's Press, 1995), respectively. This volume offers highly readable summary biographies and introductory criticism of major writers for college, university, and adult readers. [R: LJ, 15 June 99, p. 72; Choice, June 99, p. 1758; BR, Sept/Oct 99, p. 74; SLJ, Aug 99, p. 181]—**Steven W. Sowards**

Short Stories

993. Aycock, Wendell M. **Twentieth-Century Short Story Explication: New Series. Volume IV, 1995-1996.** North Haven, Conn., Shoe String Press, 1999. 342p. index. $49.50. ISBN 0-208-02493-X.

This book provides a bibliographic guide to short story interpretation and analysis. The authors highlighted come from all corners of the globe and reflect today's awareness of literary contributions across cultures. Each writer is listed alphabetically, with the title of the short story studied and a citation to the book or journal in which the explication was published. All works referenced appeared from 1995 to 1996. The entries illustrate which short story authors interested scholars during this two-year span. It is an interesting blend of the traditional (Gustave Flaubert and James Fenimore Cooper) and contemporary practitioners of the craft, such as Toni Morrison and Joyce Carol Oates. There is good representation beyond the United States, but only pieces published in the major languages of Western Europe are included. Appendixes give full bibliographic information for the books referenced as well as a list of journals cited. The index lists the profiled authors alphabetically. This compact volume provides easy access to the current writings and thought on the short story genre both in the United States and internationally.—**Adrienne Antink Bendel**

994. **Short Story Criticism: Excerpts from Criticism of the Works of Short Fiction Writers. Volume 30.** Anna J. Sheets, ed. Farmington Hills, Mich., Gale, 1999. 535p. index. $142.50. ISBN 0-7876-2053-X. ISSN 0895-9439.

Volume 30 of *Short Story Criticism* (SSC) features criticism of the works of seven masters of the short-story or novella form: S. Y. Agnon, Gina Berriault, Theodore Dreiser, George (Palmer) Garrett, Conrad Ferdinand Meyer, Emilia Pardo Bazan, and Leo Tolstoy. In the case of Tolstoy, only his novella *Kreutzer Sonata* is included, as his other works are already treated elsewhere in the Literary Criticism Series. The authors under review in the volume are all of the nineteenth and twentieth centuries; two are still alive and, at least in the case of Gina Berriault, still writing.

Provided for each author are a black-and-white photo, a short biographical and literary introduction, a list of principal short-stories and other works, a range of critical excerpts with explanatory and source notes, and the short-story authors' own commentary, if available. Story titles are set in boldface type to make them stand out in the text. At the end of each chapter are a list of further reading and a note directing the reader to other Gale references that cover the author. The editors claim that no more than 20 percent of the criticism in SSC volumes is duplicated in other literary criticism series by this publisher.

In the case of foreign authors, original foreign-language works are listed, with English translations. But only what the editors consider to be the best English-language editions are mentioned, meaning that nonlinguistic readers may need to look elsewhere for such titles. Like all of Gale's literary criticism references, this one ends with cumulative indexes by author (for all of the Literary Criticism Series), nationality (for SSC only), and title (for SSC only).—**Lori D. Kranz**

NATIONAL LITERATURE

American Literature

General Works

Bibliography

995. **Magill's Literary Annual 1999: Essay-Reviews of 200 Outstanding Books Published in the United States During 1998.** John D. Wilson, ed. Hackensack, N.J., Salem Press, 1999. 2v. index. $75.00/set. ISBN 0-89356-299-8.

Each year since 1954 Magill has published an annual of critical essays written by independent scholars and professors on 200 important books published in the United States the previous year. This 2-volume set contains articles on the outstanding books of 1998.

Following a publisher's note explaining philosophy and form, volume 1 lists the contents alphabetically by title and author, with an annotated list of the books divided into 31 categories ranging from fiction, biography, and history to economics, science, and psychology. Each essay is arranged in a set pattern consisting of title, author, publication information including number of pages and price, a brief synopsis, and, when relevant, locale, time period, and a list of the principal personages. In approximately 2,000 words, each signed article contains a discussion of the intent of the work, point of view, and the author's success in achieving his or her goal. Each ends with a source for further reading that consists of a bibliography of published reviews.

Volume 2 concludes with 4 cumulative indexes of the entire Magill series published since 1977. The reviews prior to that have been collected and published in a 12-volume *Survey of Contemporary Literature* (1977). The indexes are divided into biographical works by subject, including the contemporary biographies of people from Henry Adams and Jane Austen to Adolph Zukor, category (autobiography to women's issues), title, and author. In addition to enjoying the consistent quality of the articles, librarians and scholars will appreciate having 200 books selected as outstanding from among the thousands published during the year, although obviously they may question some of the choices or omissions.—**Charlotte Lindgren**

Bio-bibliography

996. **American Women Prose Writers to 1820.** Carla Mulford, Angela Vietto, and Amy E. Winans, eds. Farmington Hills, Mich., Gale, 1999. 541p. illus. index. (Dictionary of Literary Biography, v.200). $151.00. ISBN 0-7876-1855-1.

From Abigail Adams to Sally Sayward Barrell Keating Wood, this resource proves to be a compelling overview of American women writers. The thoughtful selection of nearly 60 writers reflects the recognition that having a book published is not the sole form of legitimate writing. For example, Martha Moore Ballard is recognized for the diary she maintained for more than 27 years. Eliza Lucas Pinckney's publications include a journal, letters, and a recipe book.

Far more than a traditional dictionary, this book offers essays on each of the writers. The essays are articulate and detailed enough to provide a glimpse into both the writer and the times. In addition to portraits of many of the writers, photographs of pertinent sites are included. Reproductions of manuscript pages, title pages, and diary entries add richness and context to the discussions.

A bibliography offers connections for further reading. Of great value to the serious researcher is the extensive cumulative index, which provides the reader with more than 60 pages of citations. This admirable work will be of value to many librarians, researchers, and students as well as anyone interested in American women writers.—**Suzanne I. Barchers**

997. **Contemporary African American Novelists: A Bio-Bibliographical Critical Sourcebook.** Emmanuel S. Nelson, ed. Westport, Conn., Greenwood Press, 1999. 530p. index. $95.00. ISBN 0-313-30501-3.

Following the format of similar titles from the publisher, such as *Nineteenth-Century American Women Writers* (see ARBA 98, entry 1126), this collection of essays provides biographical and critical information on 79 African American novelists, 41 of whom are women. Many of the authors included are actually better known in other arenas, such as poetry or drama, but each has published at least one novel. Their work covers both general and genre fiction. Arranged alphabetically, each entry contains a biographical sketch, an analysis of the author's major works and themes, a summary of the critical response, and a selected bibliography of the author's works and secondary material for further study. A brief bibliography on African American fiction and an index complete the work.

As might be expected in such a compilation, the length, quality, and detail of coverage vary from entry to entry. Most are approximately five pages in length, with well-known authors like James Baldwin and Toni Morrison having more extensive coverage. Some of the thematic analyses and summaries of critical reception are rather cursory, whereas others offer more insight. Similarly, the number and types of secondary material cited vary widely, with some of the newer or lesser-known authors having book reviews cited as the only sources of information. Still, identifying such occasionally elusive material is helpful for the researcher. Overall, the essays are readable and provide a good introduction to many authors who are unfamiliar to the general public. High school students, undergraduates, and general readers will find this a useful companion. [R: Choice, Sept 99, p. 110; BL, June 99, pp. 1872-1874]—**Barbara E. Kemp**

998. **Contemporary Southern Writers.** Roger Matuz, ed. Farmington Hills, Mich., St. James Press/Gale, 1999. 442p. index. $140.00. ISBN 1-55862-370-1.

Reflecting the thriving state of the art of writing in the contemporary American South, this volume discusses 244 southern authors who were either living in the late 1990s or had works published during the 1990s. In making their selections, the editor and his advisory board considered both writers who were born and raised in the South and those who spent a significant period of their lives in the region. The primary emphasis is on novelists, short story writers, poets, and playwrights, but a number of nonfiction writers, including journalists, historians, and critics, are also featured. Among the recently deceased authors included are James Dickey, Ralph Ellison, Charles Kuralt, and Eugenia Price, while living authors include Rita Dove, Shelby Foote, Bobbie Ann Mason, and William Styron.

Contributed by scholars, editors, and freelance writers, the entries range from one to three pages. All include a section of basic biographical information, a list of the author's publications, and a signed critical essay. In addition, many entries provide a selective bibliography of critical studies and other secondary sources. Some also include commentary from the authors themselves. The volume features a useful chronology of southern literary history through 1998 and a title index. Additional indexes categorizing the authors by state and genre would have been helpful.

Although some of the more widely known writers in this work are also covered in other St. James compilations (*Contemporary Dramatists* [6th ed., 1999], *Contemporary Novelists* [6th ed., 1995], *Contemporary Poets* [6th ed., 1995], and *Contemporary Popular Writers* [see ARBA 98, entry 1058]), the overlap is not significant. Only in a few cases are the articles identical. Moreover, all but 20 of these writers are treated in Gale's Contemporary Authors series, but a number of those sketches are now quite dated. Even though this is the most comprehensive reference work to date on contemporary southern writers, it is flawed by the omission of such authors as Donald Hays, Margaret Maron, Bob Shacochis, Louise Shivers, Charlie Smith, and Philip Lee Williams. However, it succeeds in capturing the breadth, diversity, and vitality of contemporary writing in the American South, and it serves as a useful supplement to Joseph Flora and

Robert Bain's *Fifty Southern Writers After 1900* (see ARBA 89, entry 1049), *Contemporary Fiction Writers of the South* (see ARBA 94, entry 1222), and *Contemporary Poets, Dramatists, Essayists and Novelists of the South* (see ARBA 96, entry 1199). Large academic and public libraries, particularly those in southern states, will want to consider adding this volume. [R: LJ, 1 Mar 99, pp. 72-74; BL, June 99, p. 1874; Choice, June 99, p. 1756]—**Marie Ellis**

999. **Nineteenth-Century American Fiction Writers.** Kent P. Ljungquist, ed. Farmington Hills, Mich., Gale, 1999. 380p. illus. index. (Dictionary of Literary Biography, v.202). $151.00. ISBN 0-7876-3096-9.

Here is another well-executed volume in the Dictionary of Literary Biography (DLB) series. The stated objective of volume 202 is to profile American fiction writers of the nineteenth century who have not been covered previously in DLB. Although some of the subjects have received recent critical attention, many others have been neglected or marginalized (justifiably in some cases), and most will be unfamiliar to the average reader. Many of them were successful in their day—humorists; authors of domestic tales published in ladies' magazines; and writers of works in popular new genres, such as historical and romance novels, detective fiction, and regional fiction including the Western.

The introduction provides an enlightening discussion of the climate for American fiction writers during the nineteenth century. It explains the barriers these writers faced in contemporary attitudes about fiction (a frivolous form) and in the preference among American publishers for proven British authors, whose works, in the absence of international copyright laws, they were able to reprint indiscriminately (to the detriment of unknown American writers).

The 47 entries follow the standard format of the DLB series, including bibliographies of primary and secondary works, consistently well-written, bio-critical sketches, and copious illustrations. A list of books for further reading and a cumulative index to all the DLB volumes complete the work. This volume fills a gap very nicely. [R: Choice, Oct 99, p. 306]—**Emily L. Werrell**

1000. **Twentieth-Century American Western Writers, First Series.** Richard H. Cracroft, ed. Farmington Hills, Mich., Gale, 1999. 379p. illus. index. (Dictionary of Literary Biography, v.206). $155.00. ISBN 0-7876-3100-0.

The biographical details and contributions of 31 literary figures are chronicled in the first of a 3-part series about writers of the twentieth century. Nineteenth-century American western authors were covered in volume 186. Students, teachers, and scholars will benefit from the recognized coverage of these writers to include biographical details, interview quotations, critical analysis, cover photographs, writing samples, and a bibliography. Articles examine such notables as Tony Hillerman, Louis L'Amour, Ken Kesey, Barbara Kingsolver, and Wallace Stegner.

The unique diversity of life in the American West is evident in the authors covered here, from the popular westerns of Ernest Haycox to the Native American experiences of Louise Erdrich to the feminist viewpoint of Barbara Kingsolver. The writers selected for treatment in this volume are appropriately representative of the spectrum of writers of the American West. The primary weakness of the volume is that at least 45 percent of the scholars chosen to write about these authors are narrowly focused in Utah and writing from a Mormon perspective. This seems out of proportion to the reality of modern western America. As one resource consulted in the study of these literary figures, this volume of the Dictionary of Literary Biography will be of value to public, school, and academic libraries.—**Anne C. Moore**

Biography

1001. **American Travel Writers, 1850-1915.** Donald Ross and James J. Schramer, eds. Farmington Hills, Mich., Gale, 1998. 454p. illus. index. (Dictionary of Literary Biography, v.189). $192.75. ISBN 0-7876-1844-6.

Like other volumes in the Dictionary of Literary Biography (DLB) series, the essays on these travel writers use biography to provide critical appreciation of literary works. In this volume, 31 North American travel writers whose works were first published between 1850 and 1915 are discussed in individual essays. Besides providing a biographical context for the books and other travel publications, these essays also include select bibliographies, photographs, or other portraits of the writers and, often, illustrations of manuscript pages, book jackets, and other images that enhance the text of the essays. Another volume in the DLB series, *American Travel Writers, 1776-1864* (see ARBA 99, entry 1044), may be seen as a companion to this volume.

The editors have chosen a wide variety of different kinds of travel writers for this volume, including writers primarily known for their non-travel writing, like Henry James, Edith Wharton, and Harriet Beecher Stowe, as well as those whose major writings are in this genre such as Henry Stanley. Although readers today appreciate Mark Twain primarily for his novels, he made his first reputation as a journalist and travel writer. Henry James' fame as a novelist exploring the tensions between the new world of the United States and the old world of Europe was based, as the essay in this volume explores, on first-hand observations from James' years of travel and self-imposed exile in Europe. Motives of these writers include a great and sometimes conflicting variety of approaches and attitudes, ranging from scholarly, scientific detachment and observation to romantic and exaggerated semi-fictional adventure tales. George Catlin, best known as a painter, was also an author of books about his travels among Native Americans. Although Julia Ward Howe is remembered mostly today as the author of the song "Battle Hymn of the Republic," she was also a prolific travel writer. Some of these writers had a gift for encouraging their readers to do their own traveling, while the hair-raising, not always accurate travel stories told by writers like Twain functioned was a surrogate experience for armchair travelers. One of the constant themes throughout these essays concerns the relative degrees of realism versus romanticism of these writers. Fanny Bullock Workman, one of the lesser-known writers covered here, wrote travel books emphasizing details most useful to mountaineers and geographers. Richard Harding Davis was primarily a journalist focusing on Cuba and South America. This book will prove useful both for readers interested in the subject of travel writing as a distinct literary genre as well as for readers interested in comparing the travel writing of some of these authors with their works in other genres.—**David Isaacson**

1002. Brennan, Elizabeth A., and Elizabeth C. Clarage. **Who's Who of Pulitzer Prize Winners.** Phoenix, Ariz., Oryx Press, 1999. 666p. illus. index. $69.00. ISBN 1-57356-111-8.

Who's Who of Pulitzer Prize Winners provides biographical information on the individuals who have been awarded Pulitzer Prizes as well as bibliographic information on the newspapers and publishers that have won the award. At their fullest, the biographical entries provide a picture of the winner; his or her birth date and place; the colleges at which the winner matriculated; the names of the winner's parents, spouse(s), and children (if any); the winner's career history; and the category of Pulitzer Prize that was awarded. Also provided are selective lists of other awards and of sources containing additional biographical information, a statement about the piece that won the prize, and (when relevant) the date of the winner's death. Entries for newspapers and publishers are briefer but provide the reason for which the prize was awarded and, in the case of newspapers, provide changes in name. In all, there are 1,175 entries for the 1,334 awards presented since 1917; data are current as of 1998.

There is much to praise about this work, but it is also a work that can be frustrating, for the body of the book is arranged by the category in which the Pulitzer Prize was awarded. In order to locate specific biographies, users must thus make use of one of the several indexes—newspaper and organization winners, individual winners, educational institutions, and chronology of prizes awarded. Winners who have Pulitzer Prizes in multiple categories—Norman Mailer, for example, has won the General Non-Fiction in 1969 and the Fiction in 1980—are listed in only one section; in Mailer's case, the entry is in "Fiction," with a cross-reference from "General Non-Fiction." There is no entry for Janet Cooke, whose fraudulent reporting necessitated her returning her prize for feature writing, but she is mentioned in the entry on Teresa S. Carpenter, who received the prize after Cooke returned it. Although not perfect, this volume brings together information that is not easily accessible elsewhere, and it belongs in academic libraries and larger public libraries. [R: LJ, 1 Sept 99, p. 176; BR, Sept/Oct 99, pp. 77-78]—**Richard Bleiler**

1003. **Chicano Writers, Third Series.** Francisco A. Lomelí and Carl R. Shirley, eds. Farmington Hills, Mich., Gale, 1999. 418p. illus. index. (Dictionary of Literary Biography, v.209). $155.00. ISBN 0-7876-3103-5.

Chicano Writers is another excellent volume in the Dictionary of Literary Biography series (DLB). The quality and features of this volume will be familiar to all librarians who have used the DLB. The editorial philosophy is summarized in a short "Plan of the Series." This provides readers with a sense of direction and purpose for the DLB. The introduction is specific to Chicano Writers, and describes the development, sources, and tends of Chicano literature. Although brief, the introduction is helpful—particularly to students who may require a better of understanding of Chicano writing.

Attention to detail is displayed in the inclusion of a comprehensive listing of all the DLB series volume titles. This also lists the Documentary, Yearbook, and Concise series titles. Users will also find a 58-page bibliography arranged by genre and author. The illustrations often include pictures of book covers, drafts, writer's revisions, and correspondence, in addition to typical author publicity photographs. As always, the cumulative index is extremely helpful.

This volume is wonderful, but will not seem to be a comprehensive view of Chicano writers without the first, second, and subsequent series. Chicano literature is too great an area to give full attention to the variety of authors' experiences in one series volume that contains only 41 biographies. This work is highly recommended for use in public and academic libraries.—**Sandra E. Fuentes**

Dictionaries and Encyclopedias

1004. **Encyclopedia of American Literature.** Steven R. Serafin and Alfred Bendixen, eds. New York, Continuum; distr., Farmington Hills, Mich., Gale, 1999. 1305p. index. $150.00. ISBN 0-8264-1052-9.

The editors of this satisfying new reference work, between them, have edited seven other literary reference sources. Here, their aim is to offer users topical essays on American literature as well as biographical information and critical comment on major and minor American writers, living or dead. The 70 topical essays are fully realized contributions to literary genres or themes dominating American literature. These essays serve to call attention to important critics, historians, film directors, and media personalities who, although not included in the encyclopedia, have made their own contributions to cultural life. Some of the topics covered are "The City and Literature," "Film and Literature," "Almanacs and Yearbooks," "The Slave Narrative," "Language and Dialect," and "Lesbian Literature." Each essay concludes with a secondary bibliography of books and articles.

Biographical and critical information on individual authors accounts for most of the encyclopedia's 1,100 entries and 1,282 pages of text. These discussions provide biographical information, but an author's primary themes and unique contributions to literary history are emphasized. Indeed, entries for current authors such as Bobbie Ann Mason and E. Annie Proulx concentrate on themes and unique contributions, not biographical background. Longer entries, those for Herman Melville and Walt Whitman, are made fresh by current critical commentary and genre associations. Many entries end with a selective bibliography citing both books and journal articles. Citations to books are incomplete, but librarians will be able to locate complete citations through electronic sources. Critical editions of major authors are not included, a serious oversight. One-volume secondary sources, biographies, and criticism account for most of the suggested readings.

The reference value of the encyclopedia is increased by an outstanding index that enables users to locate all references to any author mentioned within the encyclopedia, serving, among other things, to identify foreign authors whose work impacted the history of American literature. The cross-referencing system is easily followed, helping users to compare authors within genres. The encyclopedia is well produced, but could benefit from a more sturdy binding to help withstand heavy use by students.

This encyclopedia is the best 1-volume work on American writers presently available for purchase. Working with 300 contributors, the editors have perhaps achieved the stated objected: a useful reference work that "may itself be considered a lasting contribution to American literature." This reviewer is reminded of the *Cyclopaedia of American Literature* (William Rutter, 1880) by Evert and George Duyckinck, which remains a useful reference source for locating information on minor early writers. [R: LJ, 1 April 99, p. 85; BL, Aug 99, p. 2104]—**Milton H. Crouch**

1005. Whitson, Kathy J. **Native American Literatures: An Encyclopedia of Works, Characters, Authors, and Themes.** Santa Barbara, Calif., ABC-CLIO, 1999. 295p. illus. index. $45.00. ISBN 0-87436-932-0.

The stated purpose of this volume is to "provide summary and interpretive information on those texts that would most likely be read and studied by high school students and college undergraduates." The entries include four kinds of articles: those on individual authors, on individual works, on important characters in works, and on terms or events of historical importance that figure in many of the works. These words create expectations that are not met.

Given its purpose, this encyclopedia is exceptionally awkward to use, particularly for teachers and students who are new to American Indian literatures. First, these particular texts are not identified in the table of contents. To identify the texts that supposedly are most likely to be read and studied, one must review the entire volume to determine if the particular texts for which one is seeking information are included. A simple list of book titles and authors seems needed. The alphabetized table of contents that begins the book includes the names of both authors and characters and, again, if one is not familiar with American Indian literatures, there are no designations as to which is which.

Next, the characters included are listed alphabetically by their names, which is acceptable once you are certain that you are looking for the Kashpaw family but not acceptable if you want to locate the major characters in Louise Erdrich's *Love Medicine*. The index is more helpful. For example, the listing for *Love Medicine* has the author's last name included in parentheses, and a string of page numbers follow that would undoubtedly (but not certainly) lead to the articles about the characters. It is also confusing when articles on authors of some of the texts are included and others are not. The themes are few and their explanations are short and simple—in fact, too simple. Some of the themes, such as trickster and witchery, are important and complex and they deserve a more thorough explanation.

Finally, when a text offers to provide interpretive information, it is critical to know the professional, academic, or experiential qualifications of the author; this information is absent. For the novice, it is important to know whether or not to rely on or respect the interpretations of the author.

Teachers and students learning about American Indian authors and their works need help in understanding and appreciating their unique and valuable contributions to American and world literatures. Although this volume offers some useful information, it seems unwieldy to use and limited in depth and practicality. The extensive bibliography will lead both teachers and students to more informative books and articles. [R: BL, June 99, p. 1882; LJ, July 99, p. 84; Choice, Oct 99, p. 308]—**Karen D. Harvey**

Handbooks and Yearbooks

1006. **Asian American Literature: Reviews and Criticism of Works by American Writers of Asian Descent.** Lawrence J. Trudeau, ed. Farmington Hills, Mich., Gale, 1999. 536p. illus. index. $99.00. ISBN 0-7876-0296-5.

The rise of multicultural literature assignments in secondary schools has created a demand for biographical and critical information about ethnic authors and their work. This title addresses that need by bringing together in one volume criticism of 45 Asian American novelists, poets, playwrights, essayists, memoirists, and children's book authors. Writers of Chinese and Japanese origin are predominant but Indian, Vietnamese, Korean, and Filipino authors are also included. Fifteen of the writers are included in Contemporary Literary Criticism volumes but different works are discussed by different critics.

Individual entries begin with an introduction that profiles the author's background, ethnic origin, date and place of birth, and provides an overview of the critical response to their body of work. Biographical information is sparse. Students will have to locate other sources for extensive biographical information. Five to seven critical essays follow the introduction. A brief explanatory annotation outlines the scope and significance of the criticism. The essays are substantive and will be useful to students exploring an author's themes, influences, and motifs. Complete bibliographic information is provided for each essay and a photograph of the author accompanies most entries. Other features include a list of major works organized by date of publication, references to information appearing in other Gale publications, a bibliography of sources for additional study, and a title index. Unfortunately there is no nationality index, which will make it a bit more time consuming for the user looking for an author of specific ethnic background.

Despite the weaknesses mentioned, this is a useful resource for students. It pulls together information about major Asian American authors in one volume. It is especially strong in featuring several Filipino writers not included in Contemporary Literary Criticism. It provides in-depth criticism and analysis of the work of contemporary authors that is often hard to find. Secondary school and public libraries will want to add this title. [R: BL, 1 Feb 99, p. 990; RUSQ, Spring 99, pp. 297-298; Choice, June 99, p. 1754]
—**Marlene M. Kuhl**

1007. **Modern American Literature.** 5th ed. Joann Cerrito and Laurie DiMauro, eds. Farmington Hills, Mich., St. James Press, 1999. 3v. index. $450.00/set. ISBN 1-55862-379-5.

The 5th edition of *Modern American Literature* combines all of the entries from the 4th edition (published in 1960 by Continuum), its 3 supplements (1976, 1985, and 1997 by Continuum), and adds 70 new entries. With the new entries the editors have tried to broaden the cultural scope by discussing works by African American, Hispanic, and Native American authors, including many from the earlier part of the century. The editors have also broadened the expanse of literary genre covered to range from novels and stories to essays, humor, and philosophy.

The main purpose of *Modern American Literature* is to enlighten readers on the works of American authors. This is done so through the presentation of notable critiques from a multitude of sources. Each entry has an average of 12 critical excerpts from newspaper reviews, journal articles, and book-length scholarly analytical treatments. Both the entrants and the sources for excerpting have been carefully chosen to provide broad and instructive overviews of the most significant authors of the modern period. Each excerpt is followed by complete bibliographic information, and a brief biography of the author opens each entry.

Libraries that already own the previous edition and its supplements will wish to update their collections, but others should keep in mind this work only contains critical excerpts. As the editors state, the purpose of this work is to provide an overview of critical reactions to authors over the span of their writing career. The excerpts are too brief to provide any in-depth critical study of the authors, but can be used to lead researchers to other more substantial sources. [R: LJ, 1 May 99, p. 70; Choice, July/Aug 99, p. 1922]—**Cari Ringelheim**

Individual Authors

Maya Angelou

1008. Lupton, Mary Jane. **Maya Angelou: A Critical Companion.** Westport, Conn., Greenwood Press, 1998. 180p. index. (Critical Companions to Popular Contemporary Writers). $29.95. ISBN 0-313-30325-8.

Lupton, an experience author, discusses Maya Angelou's five autobiographical works written between 1970 and 1986, beginning with *I Know Why the Caged Bird Sings* (Random House, 1970) and concluding with *All God's Children Need Traveling Shoes* (Random House, 1986). The essays are designed to introduce readers to works made somewhat complex by their having both author biographical and fictional elements. The five essays devoted to the published autobiography are formal literary reviews of structure, plot, character development, and literary style. The final section of each essay is devoted to an alternative reading of the work. Here, the author offers feminist and psychological interpretations.

Lupton's biographical essay benefits from an exclusive interview with Angelou. Her essay, entitled "The Genre of Autobiography," is an outstanding introduction to the genre, worthy of inclusion in the *Essay and General Literature Index* or some collection of thematic essays devoted to autobiographical writings. Here, the author relates Angelou's five titles to works by George Eliot, Gertrude Stein, Black Elk, and James Weldon Johnson, including a discussion of other serial autobiographical works. Lupton compares Angelou's work to travel and slave narratives as well as spirituals; overall, an excellent review of the black literary tradition.

This title represents an important addition to a series designed to provide good introductions to works by popular authors. Lupton respects her subject and is ambitious for those users turning to the companion for information. The companion includes a good bibliography of Angelou's published work as well as references to articles about her work; however, the strength of the work is Lupton's essays, and many librarians will probably select to place the book in the general circulating collection.—**Milton H. Crouch**

James Dickey

1009. **James Dickey.** Judith S. Baughman, ed. Farmington Hills, Mich., Gale, 1999. 395p. illus. index. (Dictionary of Literary Biography Series, v.19). $151.00. ISBN 0-7876-2523-X.

Chiefly recalled by Americans as a southern writer upon whose stark novel the popular film *Deliverance* was based, James Dickey was a passionate wordsmith whose legacy most profoundly depends upon his poetry. Much of his verse explodes with visions of men at war—whether on the battlefield, in the forest primeval, or within the tumult of a guilt-ridden heart. Dickey's critical and personal essays, though less important elements of his canon, burn with similarly fervid energy.

Judith Baughman comes suited very well to the task of surveying and commenting upon Dickey's literary contributions, having collaborated with (DLB series editorial director) Matthew J. Bruccoli on *James Dickey: A Descriptive Bibliography* (see ARBA 91, entry 1161). Bruccoli, himself an invaluable resource here from his longtime personal, academic, and legal affiliations with Dickey, has made available to Baughman certain previously unpublished items that appear in this volume in quoted or facsimile form. Among the various materials from diverse sources that are on display here, in a seamless melding with the editor's discursive analysis, are typescripts and manuscripts, speeches, photographs, personal correspondence, and even lesson plans and programs from poetry readings.

Arranged chronologically in seven sections, the text follows the evolution of James Dickey's poetics and personas, all the while tracing aesthetic influences upon his artistic sensibilities—whether their effect on his work be formative (Dylan Thomas, Theodore Roethke, Howard Nemerov) or nugatory (Lawrence Ferlinghetti, Anne Sexton, Kenneth Rexroth). No scholar new to the study of the early Dickey could do better than to acquaint himself with the vulnerable self revealed in his essay, "Barnstorming for Poetry" (pp. 58-62). Another treasure appearing in this book is Evan S. Connell Jr.'s laudatory *New York Times* review of *Deliverance* (pp. 125-128). Fittingly, nearly 50 pages of this volume focus upon Dickey's 28-year valedictory tenure as a professor of literature at the University of South Carolina. Perhaps more than any other, this final section provides the fullest intellectual measure of the man.

Regrettably, the absence of an index (apart from the usual author/topic index to other DLB volumes) is a decided impediment to the most efficient and exhaustive searching of this reference. For example, to locate discussion on Dickey's important poem "The Firebombing," readers must already be aware that this work was first collected in *Buckdancer's Choice*. Then, they must peruse the three pages of Dickey chronology to determine that this book appeared in 1965 and then turn to the contents to find that the poem in question might be treated somewhere in the chapter (spanning some 45 pages) that covers Dickey's production from 1960 to 1966. Readers can then laboriously scan the chapter for any mention of "The Firebombing." This criticism notwithstanding, this resource will be fruitfully consulted by anyone whose need or desire is to better understand the work of one of America's most significant poets of the latter half of the twentieth century.—**Jeffrey E. Long**

William Faulkner

1010. **A William Faulkner Encyclopedia.** Robert W. Hamblin and Charles A. Peek, eds. Westport, Conn., Greenwood Press, 1999. 490p. index. $89.50. ISBN 0-313-29851-3.

Following the format of other Greenwood Press single-author encyclopedias, this title guides the reader through the maze of Faulkner novels, short stories, characters, themes, and criticism. Like the Greenwood titles on Jane Austen, F. Scott Fitzgerald, and Emily Dickinson, entries in the Faulkner title are alphabetically arranged and cover a wide range of topics. Novels and short stories are summarized. Themes and critical interpretations are clearly and succinctly laid out in signed articles by more than 50 contributors. For example, readers tracing the genealogy of the Sartoris, Compson, Snopes, and Sutpen families can consult their respective entries. The word "Yoknapatawpha" is traced to its origins in the Choctaw and Chickasaw languages. Characters like "Ikkemotubbe" are identified as they appear throughout Faulkner's oeuvre. Plot summaries for individual works are intertwined with interpretive comments. Major critical schools and movements are evaluated on their influence and specific contributions to Faulkner studies. Fairly lengthy subject entries on topics such as race, the South, and Eden elucidate the context of Faulkner's fiction. And the entry on "translations" testifies to Faulkner's influence on the world of letters and the linguistic and cultural problems related to Faulkner texts. Entries are completed with a brief list of works for further reading. A separate bibliography covers books by Faulkner, bibliographic and biographical sources, and general studies. A detailed index provides access to references within the entries. Students, scholars, and Faulkner aficionados should hope to find this treasure in their academic and public libraries.—**Bernice Bergup**

F. Scott Fitzgerald

1011. Gale, Robert L. **An F. Scott Fitzgerald Encyclopedia.** Westport, Conn., Greenwood Press, 1998. 526p. index. $75.00. ISBN 0-313-30139-5.

Gale is the author of five other literary or cultural encyclopedias published by Greenwood. Among his subjects have been Hawthorne, Melville, and Henry James. This title provides brief information on Fitzgerald's friends, associates, poetry, novels, short stories, and characters. It does not treat subjects, themes, or critical reception except incidentally. The book thus serves as something of a reminder for those who have read one of his works in the past or as a quick review for an unread work. Anyone who has ever "misplaced" a Fitzgerald character will find the figure identified and placed in context in this reference work. There are also cross-references, a chronology of Fitzgerald's life, an index, and very brief bibliographies for longer entries.

The book has one alphabetic arrangement for all entries. Gale provides a one-page synopsis for each short story and a four-page summary for each novel. Major figures in his life, like wife Zelda or his agent Max Perkins, are accorded two pages each. Characters from a story might merit a few lines. Numerous luminaries in Fitzgerald's circle appear here, including H. L. Mencken, Dorothy Parker, Ernest Hemingway, Ring Lardner, Heywood Broun, Irving Thalberg, and various Hollywood celebrities. Gale has indicated if any living person was a probable model or inspiration for a fictional character. A work like this might help to shed light on stories and characters, but it fails to answer the question of whom this book is intended for. It is not essential for the needs of specialists, except as a quick review, nor is it particularly useful as an introduction. The encyclopedia is more like a handbook in practice. Readers may be interested in a similar, less expensive work, *F. Scott Fitzgerald A to Z* by Mary Jo Tate (see ARBA 99, entry 1054). Libraries with comprehensive collections or specialties in American fiction between the wars may wish to consider this for their stacks. [R: BL, 1 Feb 99, pp. 996-997; Choice, April 99, p. 1434]—**John P. Schmitt**

Ernest Hemingway

1012. **Ernest Hemingway: A Documentary Volume.** Robert W. Trogdon, ed. Farmington Hills, Mich., Gale, 1999. 426p. illus. index. (Dictionary of Literary Biography, v.210). $151.00. ISBN 0-7876-3104-3.

The publication of *Ernest Hemingway: A Documentary Volume*, is significant for two very important reasons. First, it documents the life and career of one of America's most famous and influential authors and social figures on the centenary of his birth, and second this volume continues in the tradition of scholarship available to scholars and student alike of twentieth-century literature. The impact of Hemingway's writings on American life, popular culture, and letters is unprecedented in the history of the American literary tradition. Hemingway's writing style is considered by many scholars, including the late Carlos Baker, Charles Fenton, and Phillip Young, to be innovative and hard-hitting. Both the serious scholar and the novice student will find *Ernest Hemingway: A Documentary Volume* indispensable for an understanding and appreciation of his life and work. Each chapter (there are 7 in all) is divided into significant periods of his life; for example, chapter 1 covers the years from 1899 to 1925. Included throughout the 400-page volume are many black-and-white photographs, not only of Hemingway but also of the many important acquaintances and editors, as well as stills from the Hollywood films and pages from many of the typescripts, letters, and magazine endorsements. There is an excellent compilation of his completed works and a comprehensive bibliography for further reading. A cumulative index provides cross-references to the Dictionary of Literary Biography series (volumes 1 to 120), Dictionary of Literary Biography Yearbook series (1980 to 1998), and Dictionary of Literary Biography Documentary series (volumes 1 to 19). Without reservations this volume is recommended as a must acquisition for all academic and large public libraries.—**Dario J. Villa**

1013. Oliver, Charles M. **Ernest Hemingway A to Z: The Essential Reference to the Life and Work.** New York, Facts on File, 1999. 452p. illus. index. $50.00; $17.95pa. ISBN 0-8160-3467-2; 0-8160-3934-8pa.

A comprehensive introduction and guide to the life and work of Ernest Hemingway, this title is an excellent resource for everyone from novice readers just learning about the literary icon to Hemingway scholars. There are extensive entries for Hemingway's works, such as *The Old Man and the Sea* and *A Farewell to Arms*, along with entries for short stories and nonfiction works. The entries include plot summaries, publication data, and critical reception. There are also detailed entries for his most famous characters and descriptions of locations and plot devices that he used.

The author has provided extensive biographic data on Hemingway; his family, friends, and acquaintances; and the artistic and political figures of his time. The entry on Hemingway himself is a brief biographical overview. There is no in-depth study or discussion of his life experiences and how they might have influenced his work. Focus is placed on facts rather than critical interpretation, but there is a degree of subjective judgment. The appendixes include a map from the "At Sea" section of *Islands in the Stream*, the Hemingways' family tree, a chronology and dateline, adaptations of Hemingway's works, and a comprehensive bibliography of his works and recommended readings.—**Cari Ringelheim**

John Crowe Ransom

1014. Abbott, Craig S. **John Crowe Ransom: A Descriptive Bibliography.** Troy, N.Y., Whitston Publishing, 1999. 440p. $38.50. ISBN 0-87875-503-9.

The Agrarian or Fugitive Group poet is well served by this scholarly descriptive bibliography. Abbott provides a complete history and description of Ransom's published poems, essays, articles, sound recordings, and bibliographical ghosts, as well as items by Ransom advertised or cited as published, but in fact not published. He also describes anthologies where works by Ransom are published. Ransom considered his poems works-in-progress, revising them throughout a lifetime, compounding the already complex job of compiling a descriptive bibliography. Abbott's mighty effort is worthy of Ransom's impact on American literature.

Abbott's descriptive method is adapted from Fredson Bower's *Principles of Bibliographical Description* (Princeton University Press, 1949). He adds historical commentary, using a method recommended by G. Thomas Tanselle. His description of Ransom's published works includes typeface, signatures, interred pages, ink, binding, and typography. Title pages are completely described and many are included as black-and-white illustrations. Dust jackets are carefully examined. A beautifully organized and complete index guides users to individual works: poems, essays, editorials, book reviews, letters, interviews, and translations.

This definitive bibliography belongs in all academic libraries supporting graduate studies in American literature. T. D. Young's *John Crowe Ransom, an Annotated Bibliography* (see ARBA 84, entry 1174) remains useful for its citations to criticism of Ransom's work. The book itself is well produced—strong cloth binding, headbands, good paper, pleasing typeface and typography.—**Milton H. Crouch**

John Steinbeck

1015. Meyer, Michael J. **The Hayashi Steinbeck Bibliography, 1982-1996.** Lanham, Md., Scarecrow, 1998. 558p. index. (Scarecrow Author Bibliographies, no.99). $59.00. ISBN 0-8108-3482-0.

Meyer, a disciple of long-renowned Steinbeck scholar Tetsumaro Hayashi, has issued a second supplement to his mentor's *A New Steinbeck Bibliography: 1929-1971* (see ARBA 74, entry 1349). Enumerated here with little annotation are citations for some 140 reprints and new editions of works by Steinbeck, as well as nearly 4,000 print, audiovisual, and electronic items that are secondary resources in the evaluation of the man's writings.

Differing somewhat from Hayashi's two previous compilations in terms of its organization of entries, Meyer's volume subsumes monograph and essay series items under the rubrics "Books" and "Articles," while journalists' assessments of Steinbeck have been accorded their own section (newspapers). Works in foreign languages and English translation have been listed apart as well. The omission of some entries from Hayashi's earlier efforts has been redressed, with an addition of 41 citations of reviews of 7 theatrical and film productions. However, Meyer has not supplied any updated information pertaining to the acquisition or dispersion of manuscripts from major library collections.

To his credit, Meyer has fortified Hayashi's rather anemic Steinbeck chronology, thus now trebled to nearly 20 pages. Moreover, within the composite index, the accessibility of bibliographic entries has been enhanced by more analytic subject terms than those in Hayashi. Also, cross-referencing between related index entries is quite thorough in this supplement. Further, each collaboratively produced item receives an entry under the name of each of its authors, editors, or translators.

Unfortunately, Meyer's index contains some inaccuracies and lapses. Under the entry "Grotesque, Steinbeck and," item 1442 mistakenly appears in place of 1441. More than 20 articles by Hayashi (923-945) remain unindexed; and two items (2213 and 2291) attributed to him appear to have been authored instead by Ray Begovich and William Drummond. Other gaffes in the text include "No Entry" declarations (1881, 3927, and 3982). In summary, one must use this bibliography guardedly, despite its numerous contributions to Steinbeck scholarship. [R: Choice, July/Aug 99, p. 1922]—**Jeffrey E. Long**

Mark Twain

1016. Horn, Jason Gary. **Mark Twain: A Descriptive Guide to Biographical Sources.** Lanham, Md., Scarecrow, 1999. 133p. index. $32.50. ISBN 0-8108-3630-0.

This work is an annotated reference guide to biographical material that covers nearly every facet of the life of Mark Twain. The history of scholarship devoted to the popular American writer's life and work is long and rich. This publication is an organized guide to the biographical resources focusing on Twain's life. Sources covered include dictionaries and encyclopedias, essays, and autobiographical material. Emphasis is placed on describing the sources and not on evaluating them, unless facts are in error. The author describes the scope of a particular source by including its aim and the type and extent of its documentation.

Coverage begins with the earliest known biographical sources, including some written during the author's lifetime, and extends to the most current perceptions of Twain's life and career. Horn has opted to exclude significant critical works of little biographical importance and has only included a select section of essays that are predominantly biographical in coverage. This book is not a complete guide and is only aimed at a particular type of study. Other notable biographies may be needed to fill in gaps missed in this work.—**Cari Ringelheim**

Anne Tyler

1017. Bail, Paul. **An Anne Tyler Companion.** Westport, Conn., Greenwood Press, 1998. 302p. maps. index. $75.00. ISBN 0-313-28999-9.

This volume of literary criticism is part of the series Critical Companions to Popular Contemporary Writers. A biographical chapter opens the book and includes published information, autobiographical material, and interviews. Primarily presented in a chronological narrative, experiences within Tyler's life are related to her novels and the characters she develops. The following chapter focuses on literary influences on the author and explains how the author's work fits into the broader literary field. The main body of the volume analyzes Tyler's most important and popular novels in detail. Arranged in chronological order by publication date, each chapter focuses on a single title. The chapters are organized around three central literary elements: plot, characterization, and theme. Other elements often included are comparison and contrast to other titles within the genre, symbolism, and historical and social context. Bail often includes a subsection viewing the novel from a different perspective, such as feminist, mythological, or psychological.

The bibliography of primary and secondary sources is well organized into categories that are either alphabetically or chronologically arranged. Interviews, reviews and criticisms, articles and books about Tyler, and additional works that were cited follow Tyler's writings. A thorough index completes the volume. Bail contradicted himself on the number of novels by Tyler: stating 13 in one paragraph, 14 in the next, and listing only 13 in the bibliography. Tyler has published 14.

High school and college English students will find the book and the series most useful. The arrangement and extensive bibliography make it easy to use and provide the researcher with additional resources. An advisory board consisting of high school English teachers and public and high school librarians chooses authors for the series. Criteria for inclusion include best-selling authors with a succession of successful novels, writers of wide critical acclaim, and writers not receiving academic literary analysis within the past 10 years. Other volumes in the series are similarly arranged and structured. [R: Choice, July/Aug 98, p. 1853]—**Elaine Ezell**

Walt Whitman

1018. **Walt Whitman: An Encyclopedia.** J. R. LeMaster and Donald D. Kummings, eds. New York, Garland, 1998. 847p. illus. index. (Garland Reference Library of the Humanities, v.1877). $125.00. ISBN 0-8153-1876-6.

It only seems right that the American poet who wrote "I am large, I contain multitudes" should deserve an encyclopedia. Editors LeMaster and Kummings have assembled a formidable array of Whitman critics and biographers to contribute to this hefty reference book. The work provides broadly drawn entries treating Whitman's poems, editions, friends, critics, influences, landscapes, themes, subjects, and the cultural milieu. Each entry is signed, and most have bibliographies.

The largest part of the encyclopedia is the alphabetic arrangement of proper names, places, poems, and subjects. More than 800 pages of double-column text cover contemporaries such as Ralph Waldo Emerson, Henry David Thoreau, and Bronson Alcott, and later writers such as Allen Ginsberg and Jack Kerouac, who carried on a dialogue with Whitman within their own works. Among the larger subjects treated here are transcendentalism, romanticism, Abraham Lincoln's death, phrenology, mysticism, individualism, racial attitudes, popular culture, and influences on Whitman. The entry for transcendentalism alone, by noted scholar Roger Asselineau, runs 1,500 words, has a 13-item bibliography, and contains 11 *see also* references. There are individual entries for each edition of *Leaves of Grass* and for dozens of the major and not-so-major poems. The poetry explication and literary biography sections outline the changes in theory and criticism over the course of the century. This alone could make the book a worthy purchase for students encountering Whitman's paradoxical work for the first time.

The editors supplement the volume with a genealogy of the Whitman family; a chronology of the poet's life; his publishing history through 1993; and a detailed index of names, places, and subjects. The book is attractively illustrated with examples of his poems in manuscript, newspaper columns, and nineteenth-century studio photographs. This is a scholarly work that provides context to the life and works of this American poet who is rediscovered by each generation. [R: SLJ, Aug 99, p. 184]—**John P. Schmitt**

British Literature

General Works

Biography

1019. **British Novelists Since 1960, Third Series.** Merritt Moseley, ed. Farmington Hills, Mich., Gale, 1999. 387p. illus. index. (Dictionary of Literary Biography, v.207). $155.00. ISBN 0-7876-3101-9.

This volume in the Dictionary of Literary Biography Series (DLB), like others in the series, uses biography as a means to interpret literary works. In this volume, 33 British novelists who have become prominent since 1960 are discussed in separate essays. Each essay combines facts about the author's life with criticism of his or her fiction. Essays also include select bibliographies, photographs or other portraits of the author, illustrations of manuscript pages, book jackets, and other images that extend the reader's appreciation of the author's work.

Other than the fact that these writers are British and have been most recognized since 1960, there are few other things these writers have in common. Other volumes in the DLB series typically begin with an essay in which that volume's editor discusses common characteristics of the authors included. But Moseley, the editor of this volume, directs his attention to the fact that contemporary British novelists who win prestigious British literary awards like the Booker Prize tend not to be well received by the majority of the reading public. Moseley devotes most of his essay to defending the literary merit of a number of British novelists under the age of 40, finding fault with publishers who do not give these prize-winning authors sufficient attention, criticizing the majority of readers for not sufficiently recognizing this group of "serious writers," and wondering if the trend toward a few large publishing conglomerates (and the death of many small publishers) portends an even smaller number of serious novels and novelists. At the end of this volume an appendix of major British literary prizes lists winning authors and novels since 1960.

Although Moseley's point is well taken, this reviewer would have appreciated more attention to other qualities these 33 authors have in common besides the fact that they have not usually written best-sellers. Among this group some names do stand out as being better known to a wide audience that goes beyond the British Isles, such as Barbara Pym, V. S. Naipaul, Malcolm Bradbury, John Fowles, and Penelope Lively. But others, such as Maggie Gee and Candida Crewe, are not as well known. The editor might have at least noted the fact that although each of these writers has become prominent since 1960, some are deceased and some were born in the 1920s or 1930s and thus belong to a different generation than those born in the 1950s or 1960s, and often that generational differences coincide with stylistic and thematic differences.

Despite this caveat about the introductory essay, the individual essays themselves are quite useful. It is these essays that matter most, not the rather arbitrary commingling of authors chosen for this volume.
—**David Isaacson**

1020. **British Travel Writers, 1940-1997.** Barbara Brothers and Julia M. Gergits, eds. Farmington Hills, Mich., Gale, 1999. 398p. illus. maps. index. (Dictionary of Literary Biography, v.204). $151.00. ISBN 0-7876-3098-5.

The present volume completes the series on British travel writers in Gale's Dictionary of Literary Biography series (see ARBA 97, entry 981, for a review of *British Travel Writers, 1837-1875*). Together with volumes 174 and 195 these volumes survey the history of British travel writers and writing from 1837 through 1997. The introductory essays of these four volumes survey the rise and evolution of the travel industry in the nineteenth century, through its technological changes and its historical and cultural context through the latter half of the twentieth century. As the editors note, the biographees selected for these volumes were more than mere "tourists." They were "travelers" who gradually transformed the travel genre into something of a hybrid, covering geography, archaeology, botany, linguistics, and other fields. The 29 writers in the present volume saw the development of air travel, motion picture technology, and the glossy travel magazine; and their era truly became that of the professional travel writer. Their writings, however, were not limited to travel. Graham Greene's fiction is transfused by his sense of place, as are the works of Lawrence Durrell by their Mediterranean locale. Sarah Hobson, a travel writer and television producer, documents her explorations in other cultures. Each essay begins with a bibliography of the author's works, followed by a lengthy essay detailing the travel aspects of the biographee's life and writings. If the writer is a subject in other volumes of the DLB, they are identified in an introductory note. Each essay is illustrated with photographs, reproductions of title pages, and facsimiles of typescripts as appropriate. Entries conclude with listings of interviews, bibliographies on the writer, biographies, and references to secondary sources. Like its predecessors, this volume exemplifies the excellence of the series, which belongs in every library that can afford it.—**Bernice Bergup**

1021. **An Encyclopedia of British Women Writers.** rev. ed. Paul Schlueter and June Schlueter, eds. New Brunswick, N.J., Rutgers University Press, 1998. 741p. index. $60.00; $28.00pa. ISBN 0-8135-2542-X; 0-8135-2543-8pa.

This ambitious and useful resource contains approximately 600 biographical entries on British women writers. The authors included are an interesting mixture of genres and time periods. Writers of various genres are well represented, such as Agatha Christie, Lynne Reid Banks, and Georgette Heyer. Not all entries are for women who wrote in England; for example, Anne Bradstreet, who is best known for her writings in colonial America, is presented here. Nor do all the writers exist in real life, such as Juliana Berners. The earliest writer found was Marie de France, born approximately 1140 C.E. The newest writer is Jeanette Winterson, born in 1959.

Each entry describes the author and her contributions to literature. A list of references helps the researcher find additional information. Some of the sources used for references include periodical sources and reference book sources. The entries range from a few paragraphs to four pages. The authors used a clever device to save space. The author is not referred to by name but instead by the first initial of her last name. For example, Eliza Acton is listed as "A" in her entry.

The book is easy to use with each author alphabetically listed by last name. Cross-references help the reader find the person when there may have been two or more variations to the name or written under a pseudonym. An index at the back of the book is also a quick way to access the entries on the author.

This is an updated version of a previous edition. There are 200 more entries and many of the existing entries have been updated. The coverage has been extended to cover women who resided in Great Britain, even though they may have been born elsewhere, and women who live in other parts of the British Commonwealth.

This one-volume reference work provides convenient and quick information on an impressive group of women writers. Even though the coverage falls somewhere between a dictionary and an encyclopedia entry, the entries are well written and concise. A chronological list of the authors covered in this work would have been an interesting and useful addition to the book. Perhaps the publisher will include it in the next revision of this work. [R: LJ, Dec 98, pp. 86, 88; BL, June 99, p. 1876; Choice, Nov 99, p. 506]

—**Suzanne Julian**

1022. **Late-Victorian and Edwardian British Novelists, Second Series.** George M. Johnson, ed. Farmington Hills, Mich., Gale, 1999. 396p. illus. index. (Dictionary of Literary Biography, v.197). $151.00. ISBN 0-7876-1852-7.

Any library that owns the entire run of the Dictionary of Literary Biography (DLB) series must be well funded indeed. Now with more than 200 volumes, this set, like many Gale publications, shows no signs of concluding. Libraries thus must be especially selective in collection development in the area of literary biography, or else set up a separate budget category to handle it.

Late Victorian and Edwardian British Novelists, Second Series retains the familiar DLB format. (Even smaller libraries undoubtedly own a couple of volumes.) Blue-bound, with signed articles alphabetically arranged, photographs of authors and their works scattered throughout, bibliographies of their productions, and evaluations of their major works, this volume differs little from the *First Series* (see ARBA 93, entry 1194) or the rest of the set. Several of the authors have been covered previously in earlier DLB titles. Articles average around eight pages and are a mixture of biographical highlights and literary analysis. A cumulative index of 67 pages covers the entire scope of all of the volumes in the set.

Although the *First Series* concerned itself with romantic late-Victorians, the *Second Series* is primarily novelists in the realist tradition. Larger public and university research libraries may find this volume complements their earlier purchases, but smaller institutions may justly wonder how many requests for information on Barry Pain or Gertrude Dix they will receive, and if the money might be better spent on less esoteric materials. Owners of the *First Series* may wish to purchase this volume to complete their holdings. That is, until the *Third Series* is issued. [R: Choice, May 99, p. 1593]—**James Moffet**

Dictionaries and Encyclopedias

1023. Bruce, Christopher W. **The Arthurian Name Dictionary.** New York, Garland, 1999. 504p. (Garland Reference Library of the Humanities, v.2063). $125.00. ISBN 0-8153-2865-6.

Scholars and general readers alike will enjoy and profit from this comprehensive directory of major and minor items in the King Arthur legends. A longtime "aficionado" of the Arthurian world, Christopher Bruce, professor at Pennsylvania State University, treats each entry with thoroughness and "loving care."

Writing about the Round Table, for instance, Bruce states that this famous motif was first introduced by Wace in *Roman de Brut*, who wrote that the table had no "head." As it is later said in *The Grene Knight*, the king "made the Round Table for their behove, that none of them should sitt above, but all should sitt as one." The number of knights at the Round Table varies, according to which legend we choose to embrace. It ranges from 13, in the early Percival tradition, to 50, 60, 130, 150, and 250 in other traditions. In Layamon, the number rises to an astounding 1,600, and we are told that the table was portable, while another early writer (Beroul) claims that the table could "rotate like the earth." In dealing with the huge size of the table, some artists and writers have depicted it as a ring with inner places for servants and entertainers. Relative to the motif of the Holy Grail, some traditions trace the Round Table to the table used at the Last Supper, in the age of Joseph of Arimathea, who was supposed to have brought the Grail to England.

The treatment of the Round Table is indicative of the thoroughness and care that one finds throughout *The Arthurian Name Dictionary*. Similar care is seen in treatments of other major items, such as Excalibur, Lancelot, the Lady of the Lake, the Green Knight, Camelot, the Isle of Avalon, Merlin, Morgan Le Fay, the Fisher King, and the Dolorous Stroke, which created the Waste Land. The entries under "Arthur" occupy 10 double-column pages and touch on historicity, development of the legend, insignia, grave, relatives, battles, and numerous other matter, even "Arthur's cups and saucers," which are "natural rock basins on the side of the headland of Tintagel, on the coast of Cornwall" (p. 46).

It is clear that this "dictionary" was made for browsing, as well as for assistance in serious studies. Its sources number more than 250 in many languages, ranging from the earliest mention of Arthur as "Artorius" in the first-century Roman writings of Tacitus and Juvenal, down to the *Idylls of the King* by Alfred Lord Tennyson, the beginning of the modern era of Arthurian literature.

Bruce acknowledges the usefulness of other similar dictionaries, but adds that they tend to restrict themselves too much by using only texts in English, drawing primarily from Malory, or by centering too much on primary characters, to the exclusion of lesser but significant items. The job that Bruce has done here can only be described as masterful, and what he has created will entertain and inform readers for generations to come. The book is written in a lively, responsible style and is arranged in a manner that is consistently reader-friendly. There are occasional slips, such as calling Winchester "Wichester" (p. 430), but generally *The Arthurian Name Dictionary* is a welcome addition to the scholarship surrounding King Arthur. [R: Choice, Sept 99, p. 106; BL, Aug 99, p. 2103]—**Peter Thorpe**

Handbooks and Yearbooks

1024. **British Writers, Supplement V.** George Stade and Sarah Hannah Goldstein, eds. New York, Scribner's/Simon & Schuster Macmillan, 1999. 571p. index. $125.00. ISBN 0-684-80615-0.

Supplement 5 adds essays on 25 modern writers to the earlier 7 volumes and supplements in the British Writers series. The term "British" is broadly defined to include people who have been awarded British prizes for literature, especially Booker Prize-winners, but who are only peripherally British. For example, Texas-born mystery writer Patricia Highsmith; Ben Okri, a Nigerian living in England; Wilson Harris, a Guyanese; and Anita Desai, raised in India and the daughter of a Bengali father and a German mother, are covered in the supplement. Various genres are covered, from playwrights Alan Ayckbourn and Joe Orton; Irish poets Eavan Boland, Thomas Kinsella, Medbh McGuckian, and Richard Murphy; short story writer Edna O'Brien; children's writer A. A. Milne; and novelist Penelope Fitzgerald to writers in many genres such as Alan Sillitoe.

The volume continues the pattern of the rest of the series. A chronology of both historical and literary achievements begins with the reign of King Edward VII in 1901 and is brought up to the troubles in Kosovo in 1999. The lengthy essays on each author are arranged alphabetically, ending with a selected bibliography of works both by and about each, including critical studies. The master index of titles and authors covers the entire British Writers series with volume numbers printed in bold typeface for quick reference.

Like the rest of the series, the supplement contains highly readable essays on writers both widely recognized and lesser known. It is an invaluable resource for those seeking information or suggestions for further reading on a wide variety of British writers.—**Charlotte Lindgren**

Individual Authors

Geoffrey Chaucer

1025. Rossignol, Rosalyn. **Chaucer A to Z: The Essential Reference to His Life and Works.** New York, Facts on File, 1999. 432p. illus. index. $50.00. ISBN 0-8160-3296-3.

Reading Chaucer can be daunting, especially for students and general audiences who lack a strong background in literary studies. This book will not only ease the anxieties many modern readers experience at the mention of Chaucer's name, it will also help them enjoy his works while expanding their knowledge and understanding of his historical period. More important, the many references to Greek mythology and French and Italian literature emphasize Chaucer's rich intertextuality, thereby introducing readers to other literary traditions via his writings. Specialists in Chaucer will find this feature of the book especially helpful and easy to use as the entries include the number of the line or verse in a work where a given allusion can be found. The entry for *The Canterbury Tales* is an overall summary of Chaucer's most famous work. Each tale is summarized separately. The commentaries that follow these and the summaries of Chaucer's other works end with a concise paragraph suggesting recent scholarly studies for further reading. The author also includes short entries about prominent scholars of Chaucer and medieval literature and lists their most significant books and essays.

As the title of this reference makes clear, entries are arranged alphabetically. Each entry is in bold typeface with cross-referencing within entries indicated by small capital letters. In addition to a much-needed index, there are five appendixes, including a most helpful chronology of Chaucer's life and a map of the 56-mile road described in *The Canterbury Tales*. The brief bibliography will be of interest to non-specialists. It includes adaptations for children and a list of Websites covering everything from food and recipes popular during Chaucer's time to online texts of *The Canterbury Tales*. This is an excellent reference, a real tribute to the scholarly acumen of its author. [R: LJ, 1 Mar 99, p. 76; Choice, Nov 99, p. 509; BL, 1 Dec 99, p. 721]—**Sandra Adell**

Patrick O'Brian

1026. Brown, Anthony Gary. **Persons, Animals, Ships, and Cannon in the Aubrey-Maturin Sea Novels of Patrick O'Brian.** Jefferson, N.C., McFarland, 1999. 342p. $35.00pa. ISBN 0-7864-0684-4.

Useful for casual readers and for ardent fans, this dictionary is an in-depth guide to many factual and fictional aspects of the Aubrey-Maturin series. Over the past 25 years Patrick O'Brian has written 19 novels featuring the adventures of Captain Jack Aubrey and Doctor Stephen Maturin. From *Master and Commander* to *The Hundred Days* this dictionary defines characters such as William Gorges and Nathanial Martin, animals, ships, and cannon (both historical and imaginary). Organized alphabetically, there are approximately 4,500 entries, each containing a brief summary and comprehensive reference to the chapters of the various novels in which they appear. Historical entries also include sources outside of O'Brian's works and are detailed in the bibliography. This work is worth a look for any readers interested in the Aubrey-Maturin sea novels, but it has a limited audience.—**Cari Ringelheim**

William Shakespeare

1027. **The Comprehensive Shakespeare Dictionary.** [CD-ROM]. The Comprehensive Shakespeare Dictionary Project, comp. Phoenix, Ariz., Oryx Press, 1998. Minimum system requirements: IBM or compatible 486. CD-ROM drive. Windows 3.1, Windows 95. 4MB RAM. 1MB hard disk space. $129.95.

Students and researchers from high school through college will find this compendium of information a handy way to locate summaries, characters, scenes, and quotations pertinent to Shakespeare and his works. The disc has been compiled from three sources: Schmidt's *Shakespeare-Lexicon* (1902), Stokes's *Dictionary of the Characters & Proper Names in the Works of Shakespeare* (1924), and *The Works of William Shakespeare* (Henley ed., 1888). The current editors indicate that they have extensively edited, revised, and reformatted much of the original information.

Users can search in six major categories: characters, plays and poems, quotations, lexicon, image (based on nineteenth-century steel engravings), and a biography of Shakespeare. Through extensive cross-references and links, the user can also hop from character to play to lexicon, affording an efficiency that is valued. For each of the plays, an act-by-act synopsis is provided, as well as date of composition, stage history, and sources for the plot. Similar background information is provided for the poems. The lexicon has more than 20,000 entries that include some 50,000 full quotations. All definitions provided are according to Shakespearean usage. Navigation buttons allow one to free-text search, move backward and forward, copy text to a clipboard, and print.

High school, public, and academic libraries should strongly consider this product for its ease of use and accessibility of information. Even with its lack of inclusion of scholarly references or additional reading, it functions as primary source materials. [R: SLJ, Jan 99, p. 51]—**Edmund F. SantaVicca**

1028. Palmer, Alan, and Veronica Palmer. **Who's Who in Shakespeare's England.** New York, St. Martin's Press, 1999. 280p. illus. maps. $17.95pa. ISBN 0-312-22086-3.

This volume is a lightly reedited version of an edition that appeared in 1981. Although the copyright page notes the addition of new materials, it is difficult to spot what might be new, except for the editors' introductory mention of 5 new reference works on the period published during the past 12 years. Individual entries contain brief suggestions for further reading, but these titles do not seem to have been updated. The entries are simply informational, not evaluative or critical, and many are culled from the standard works of Bentley, Chambers, Eccles, and Schoenbaum. The range of entries is broad (more than 700), but some seem less than vital, such as that for Marie Mountjoy, the wife of Shakespeare's London landlord. Others reveal the perennially popular and fruitless desire to find "sources" for Shakespeare's characters, hence the inclusion of Alexander Aspinall, the schoolteacher who "may have inspired Holofernes in *Love's Labor's Lost*."

Despite these limitations, however, the book is a handy and well-organized compendium for ready-reference. A "Classified List of Entries" by subject group helps one locate persons in specific categories. The list of "Printers, Booksellers and Publishers" is lengthy, as is that on theater figures. Maps of London and Stratford and a brief glossary are helpful. Frequent portraits supplement the entries. For more recent and scholarly surveys of this era one should consult R. H. Fritze's historical dictionary of Tudor and Stuart England (1991, 1996) and John Wagner's *Historical Dictionary of the Elizabethan World* (see entry 499). But these more expensive volumes may make this book a reference of choice for smaller libraries. [R: Choice, Dec 99, p. 692]—**Christopher Baker**

1029. **Shakespearean Criticism, Volume 43: Excerpts from the Criticism of William Shakespeare's Plays and Poetry....** Michelle Lee and Kathy D. Darrow, eds. Farmington Hills, Mich., Gale, 1999. 467p. illus. index. $151.00. ISBN 0-7876-1988-4. ISSN 0883-9123.

Volume 43 is the latest in Gale's annual compilations of representative criticism on Shakespeare. Given the magnitude of the "Shakespeare industry," it is an achievement for editors to select a relatively few essays that will provide an accurate sample of contemporary scholarship. This volume, like others in the series, stands up well as a reference gateway to the much larger pool of published work on the author. Since volume 27, each volume has addressed a specific theme for emphasis (for this volume the theme is violence). The volumes present full essays or excerpts on specific works, here *The Rape of Lucrece*, *Titus Andronicus*, and *Troilus and Cressida*, perhaps the most problematic of the so-called "problem plays." Each essay or excerpt is accompanied by its original footnotes. This volume's selected overview essays on violence also display an awareness of current trends in scholarship, noting not only political violence but also infanticide and violence against women.

The organization of the volume makes for efficient use. Each play section contains an introduction, collection of criticism, explanatory notes, illustrations (production photographs), and an annotated bibliography. Cumulative volume indexes cover characters, critics, and topics arranged both alphabetically and by play. Although Shakespeare specialists will probably proceed directly to fuller bibliographies, students, teachers, and others seeking an authoritative and accessible anthology of current critical views will find this volume essential. Although expensive, it is an excellent solution for public, secondary, and undergraduate libraries that lack the space, funds, or need for extensive periodical holdings in Shakespearean research.

—**Christopher Baker**

1030. **Shakespearean Criticism, Volume 44: Excerpts from the Criticism of William Shakespeare's Plays and Poetry....** Michelle Lee and Kathy D. Darrow, eds. Farmington Hills, Mich., Gale, 1999. 467p. illus. index. $151.00. ISBN 0-7876-1989-2. ISSN 0883-9123.

This 44th volume in the Shakespearean Criticism series can stand alone, like all the other volumes in this series, and does not depend on a continuing subscription. Every volume since number 27 has focused on a particular theme; this one centers on psychological interpretations of the plays, with particular reference to *Hamlet* and *Macbeth*. The volume is composed almost exclusively of long excerpts from books and the complete texts of journal articles. As such, this volume and its companions will be highly valuable for anyone focusing on the themes under discussion, especially at smaller institutions that do not offer comprehensive collections.

The opening section, "Psychoanalytic Interpretation of Shakespeare's Works," after its 3-paragraph introduction, provides 100 pages of journal articles and book excerpts that give the reader a general overview of psychoanalytic approaches to Shakespeare. The first half of this opening section of the volume covers more general pieces, such as the complete text of Robert A. Ravich's article "A Psychoanalytic Study of Shakespeare's Early Plays," as originally published in *The Psychoanalytic Quarterly* (vol. 23, no. 3, 1964, pp. 388-410), and an excerpt from Norman Holland's book *Psychoanalysis and Shakespeare* (McGraw-Hill, 1964), which "surveys the patterns of psychological criticism typically applied to Shakespeare's plays."

After this more general part of the introductory section, there are another 50 pages of material grouped into three topics: "Patriarchy, Gender, and Family"; "Jealousy: *Othello* and *The Winter's Tale*"; and "Internal Conflict: *Coriolanus* and *Measure for Measure*." Each section contains two or three items. For instance, "Jealousy: *Othello* and *The Winter's Tale*" includes one journal article on each play.

Most of the volume focuses on *Hamlet* (150 pages) and *Macbeth* (120 pages). Each play has an overview subsection of its own followed by a "Psychoanalytic Interpretations" subsection, including items such as " 'Who's There?': Hamlet," as it originally appeared in *The Compensatory Psyche: A Jungian Approach to Shakespeare* (University Press of America, 1986). Each of the two main sections also contains a two-page bibliography of further reading. The *Hamlet* section includes the following additional subsections, with their associated article or book excerpts: "Gender Issues," "Hamlet and His Dilemma," and "Secondary Characters." The *Macbeth* section includes the subsections "Macbeth as Tragic Hero" and "Religious and Theological Issues."

The volume concludes with several highly useful cumulative indexes to the entire series: a cumulative character index, a cumulative critic index, a cumulative topic index, and a cumulative topic index by play. These indexes and the meticulous accuracy of the citations and texts in the book testify to the quality of this volume. The articles and book excerpts reproduced here are not available in the online Galenet "Literature Resource Center," which does include 375 articles, most of which are from *Notes and Queries*, and all of which are quite recent. The items included in this book are spread across many decades, chiefly focusing on the 1960s through the 1980s.—**Bill Miller**

1031. **Shakespearean Criticism, Volume 45: Excerpts from the Criticism of William Shakespeare's Plays and Poetry....** Michelle Lee and Kathy D. Darrow, eds. Farmington Hills, Mich., Gale, 1999. 470p. illus. index. $151.00. ISBN 0-7876-2421-7. ISSN 0883-9123.

Gale's Shakespearan Criticism series reprints annual volumes of critical essays and other commentary on the Shakespearean canon. The first 26 volumes offered "critical overviews" from the seventeenth century to the present on the plays themselves. Volumes since number 27 have centered on specific themes, plus a sampling of broader criticism published since 1960, the current theme being "dreams." This volume's oldest essay dates from 1974, so the reader is assured of an up-to-date selection. The opening section reviews dreams, imagination, and psychoanalysis in the plays as a whole (volume 44's topics was psychoanalysis), with special attention to *Macbeth* and *Cymbeline*. Curiously omitted is any comment on one of the poet's greatest speeches on dreaming—Clarence's dream of drowning from act one of *Richard III*.

Succeeding chapters address dreams and other issues in *A Midsummer Night's Dream* (11 essays), *The Tempest* (9), and *The Winter's Tale* (7). Each essay or excerpt is printed with its original notes and apparatus. A brief, annotated bibliography for each play offers additional critical references and production photographs supplement the commentary. Cumulative volume indexes cover characters, critics, topics alphabetically and topics by play. This volume, like others in this series, provides an excellent window into current Shakespeare studies and a very useful beginning point for further research. Libraries unable to support large research collections will find this an excellent general-purpose critical reference.

—**Christopher Baker**

1032. **The World Shakespeare Bibliography on CD-ROM, 1983-1995.** [CD-ROM]. New York, Cambridge University Press, 1998. Minimum system requirements (Windows version): IBM or compatible 386 or Pentium. Double-speed CD-ROM drive. Windows 3.1 or Windows 95. 8MB RAM. Minimum system requirements (Macintosh version): System 7.0 or later. Double-speed CD-ROM drive. 4MB RAM. $585.00. ISBN 0-521-62536-X.

This latest update of *The World Shakespeare Bibliography* on CD-ROM provides coverage from 1983 to 1995 and contains over 40,000 entries. To facilitate use, it has a complete user guide and instructional manual on the disk itself. Once inside the application, a split screen displays a table of contents on the left and a detailed view of the contents on the right. To navigate through the table of contents, users can click on various plus signs to open categories. A user may use word, proximity, and Boolean searches. More complex searches require a search form facility via a book menu. Hypertext links bring up even more information. In addition to making use of many interactive facilities, new windows can be created, resized, cascaded, and juxtaposed. Further accessibility of this CD-ROM is described in detail in the instruction manual. Edited and engineered with sustained care and great skill, *The World Shakespeare Bibliography* can be highly recommended for all university reference collections.—**G. A. Cevasco**

Dylan Thomas

1033. Davies, James A. **A Reference Companion to Dylan Thomas.** Westport, Conn., Greenwood Press, 1998. 365p. index. $89.50. ISBN 0-313-28774-0.

This series of biographical and critical essays on Dylan Thomas give a helpful introduction to the man and his work. Davies, senior lecturer in English at the University of Wales, Swansea, begins with a chronology spanning the birth in 1834 of Thomas's great uncle who was a poet and the source of Dylan's middle name, Marlais, to Thomas's death in 1953. The four subsequent chapters chronicle his family and professional life. The next 10 chapters are readable explications of his poetry and critical interpretations of his prose. Finally, Davies writes well-footnoted articles describing critics' reactions to Thomas in England, Wales, and the United States during his life and after his death. The book closes with a six-page bibliography of works by and about Thomas as well as an index.

This reference companion will not replace Georg Gaston's *Dylan Thomas: A Reference Guide* (see ARBA 88, entry 1227), which is an extensive bibliographic treatment of the subject. It will, however, offer a look at Thomas in the context of his family, friends, and the literary establishment and be suitable for most academic collections. [R: Choice, Oct 98, pp. 313-314]—**Juleigh Muirhead Clark**

Australian and New Zealand Literature

1034. **The MUP Encyclopaedia of Australian Science Fiction & Fantasy.** Paul Collins, Steven Paulsen, and Sean McMullen, eds. Victoria, Australia, Melbourne University Press; distr., Concord, Mass., Paul & Company Publishers, 1998. 188p. $39.95; $29.95pa. ISBN 0-522-84771-4; 0-522-84802-8pa.

The MUP Encyclopaedia of Australian Science Fiction & Fantasy was inspired to some extent by the successes of the much-honored 1993 *Encyclopedia of Science Fiction* (see ARBA 94, entry 1211) and the 1997 Encyclopedia of Fantasy (see ARBA 98, entry 1116). These volumes contained entries discussing Australia and its more significant writers, but they were of necessity broader focused and could not limit themselves to the works of one region. *The MUP Encyclopaedia*, on the other hand, concentrates almost exclusively on the Australian and New Zealand writers of science fiction and fantasy whose careers became active following 1950, including novelists as well as short story writers and writers for children in addition to writers for adults. *The MUP Encyclopaedia* also includes a number of thematic articles on subjects such as cinema, dark fantasy, early Australian science fiction and fantasy, magazines, and radio. In all, the volume contains approximately 1,200 signed entries with bibliographies; there are, alas, no illustrations and no index.

A number of critics have excoriated *The MUP Encyclopaedia*. An introductory statement of methodology by Paul Collins states, "It seems superfluous to go back beyond 1950, if only for the reason that most of the works would not be unobtainable and that, apart from being authoritative, such entries would add little to this work" (p. x). This has been used to indicate a lack of editorial commitment and understanding of the nature of literary history. The volume does indeed contain its share of errors and omissions—to say nothing of inadequate cross-references—but in condemning it outright, the critics have been too harsh. The volume is not perfect, but it marks the first time that a comprehensive attempt has been made at identifying and documenting a discrete body of literature and its writers. It is a volume that should be used with some caution, but it is nevertheless a volume that should be used. It belongs in the libraries of all institutions supporting research and studies in Australian literature and in contemporary science fiction and fantasy literature and its writers.—**Richard Bleiler**

1035. **New Zealand Books in Print 1999.** New Providence, N.J., Reed Elsevier, 1999. 728p. $70.00. ISBN 1-86452-028-0. ISSN 0157-7662.

A reference book designed primarily for booksellers and librarians, *New Zealand Books in Print* contains information on New Zealand and Pacific Island books in print through the end of 1998. Books are listed alphabetically in two formats, by author and by title. Subject categories are regularly indicated (e.g., children's nonfiction, women's studies, politics and government). Publishers and distributors are listed, as are New Zealand agents of overseas publishers (e.g., Doubleday is published through Random House in New Zealand).

Because it lists all books published through 1998, this book is a useful sourcebook for scholars of various aspects of present-day New Zealand life. There is a good deal of information that is especially useful to literary scholars, like the lists of New Zealand literary journals, New Zealand literary awards, and past winners of these awards. There is information too on the sources of assistance to writers there. Lists of antiquarian and secondhand booksellers in New Zealand are also useful, particularly to librarians.

—**John B. Beston**

1036. **The Oxford Companion to New Zealand Literature.** Roger Robinson and Nelson Wattie, eds. New York, Oxford University Press, 1998. 608p. $72.00. ISBN 0-19-558348-5.

Designed as a supplementary volume to the *Oxford History of New Zealand Literature* (see ARBA 92, entry 1239), this excellent guide goes well beyond its earlier companion. The earlier Oxford history, which covered only to 1986, is now outdated and provides only broad topical essays on various literary genres (e.g., the short story). This compact new volume deals more directly with 680 individual authors, 110 significant books or other pieces, and a wide range of other topics. Its broad approach provides entries for distinguished writers from other countries with an association, no matter how brief, with New Zealand. Other efforts, including articles on relationships to a number of other countries, have been made to place New Zealand literature in a broader cultural context. There is also good coverage of 125 Maori writers, texts, or topics, which was sadly lacking in the Oxford history. Although designed as a ready-reference source, with relatively brief entries, this Oxford companion is far more than that. The text is liberally sprinkled with cross-references so that almost every article immediately leads the reader to a series of related pieces that, as a whole, provide a broader perspective on an author, a journal, an organization, or a publisher. It is difficult not to follow those leads and the reader is richly rewarded by doing so. Best of all, virtually all of the entries are direct, honest, and critical. Although New Zealand literature is not widely studied in this country, this Oxford companion warrants a place in most college and university libraries and larger public libraries.—**Norman D. Stevens**

French Literature

1037. Frey, John Andrew. **A Victor Hugo Encyclopedia.** Westport, Conn., Greenwood Press, 1999. 305p. index. $89.50. ISBN 0-313-29896-3.

Victor Hugo dominated nineteenth-century French letters; he was a consummate writer who excelled in all three literary genres. He is probably best known to American readers, of course, through two novels written at either end of his career, *The Hunchback of Notre Dame* (1831) and *Les Misérables* (1862). This encyclopedia, compiled by a noted French-literature scholar shortly before his death, provides in one comprehensive volume salient information about all of Hugo's works (e.g., poetry, fiction, drama); major characters in those works; and names, places, and historical figures associated with his life. Contrary to the author's claim, the entries stick to the basics and eschew expansive interpretation. English-reading audiences, so often denied access to decent reference works on foreign authors, will be thrilled with the breadth of coverage. Entries are succinct and well written; longer ones are followed by one- or two-item bibliographies, some of which do not appear in the general bibliography at the end.

The issue of access is yet another matter, especially because the editors claimed to emphasize Hugo's role within the context of the Western cultural tradition. The most glaring fault in this regard is that the encyclopedia provides no headword for the English title *The Hunchback of Notre Dame*, neither as a cross-reference in the text nor in the index; users need to know to consult the work under the original French title, *Notre Dame de Paris*. It should be noted, however, that other lesser-known works are listed under English equivalents with references to the appropriate French-language title. Furthermore, the index cannot be trusted for completeness in regard to Hugo's vast extraliterary influence, especially in music and the performing arts. *Rigoletto*, Verdi's opera based on *Le Roi s'amuse*, lies embedded in the text in at least two separate entries, but neither the piece nor the composer claims a separate entry in the index. Similar direct access points are lacking for Franz Liszt's orchestrations of *Ce qu'on entend sur la montagne* and *Mazeppa*, Berlioz's rendition of *Sara la baigneuse*, and Truffaut's film *The Story of Adele H.*, among others. Aggravating the inconsistency is the fact that the musical play *Les Misérables* merits its own entry within the body of the encyclopedia. If a work is truly defined as an encyclopedia, one should expect no less than complete indexing as well as coverage. Despite these shortcomings, *A Victor Hugo Encyclopedia* fills an important gap for public and academic libraries because nothing similar exists in English.

—Lawrence Olszewski

1038. **Literature of the French and Occitan Middle Ages: Eleventh to Fifteenth Centuries.** Deborah Sinnreich-Levi and Ian S. Laurie, eds. Farmington Hills, Mich., Gale, 1999. 440p. illus. index. (Dictionary of Literary Biography, v.208). $155.00. ISBN 0-7876-3102-7.

The practical audience for this latest entry in the Dictionary of Literary Biography (DLB) series baffles this reviewer. On the one hand, it provides a summary of the literary careers of 31 named authors, plus separate chapters on the epic, Arthurian literature, drama, hagiography, troubadours, and the *Roman de la Rose*. Except for François Villon and the *Song of Roland*, most users with anything less than a declared French undergraduate major have probably never heard of most of them. The entry for the *Song of Roland* is given surprisingly short shrift, however, as to be virtually worthless, especially when compared to the more extensive treatment of several lesser-known writers. On the other hand, its treatment by reputable scholars will appeal to specialists; in some cases this is the fullest available discussion in English for minor authors.

The bibliographic apparatus is consistent and accurate; each entry contains a list of primary works, with location of manuscripts, translations into English, the accepted "scholarly" edition, and a selected bibliography, all enhanced with profusely informative illustrations. This structure provides a solid framework for both "quick and dirty" reference questions and a springboard for further investigation.

The superfluous and self-indulgent, 60-page cumulative index to the DLB series aside, the one major drawback is the price. At $155 libraries are gambling on an investment that may not pay off. Potential low use for this volume, especially in public libraries, may make its access via Galenet a more cost-effective alternative.

This is the sixth DLB dealing with French literature (following surveys of French novelists and dramatists), as the publisher began expanding beyond Anglo-American roots in 1987 to cover all writers of significance to world literary history. Unlike those other volumes, however, the information contained in this source has no direct competitor in English.—**Lawrence Olszewski**

Irish Literature

1039. Conner, Lester I. **A Yeats Dictionary: Persons and Places in the Poetry of William Butler Yeats.** Syracuse, N.Y., Syracuse University Press, 1998. 209p. (Irish Studies). $34.95. ISBN 0-8156-2769-6.

Woven into the texture of Yeats's poems are the names of his friends, theater people, artists, and public figures with whom he frequently associated, as well as the names of locales with which the poet had a relationship. Although some names are well known, there are hundreds of others beyond the knowledge of the average reader of modern poetry. The prime purpose of this dictionary, accordingly, is to identify such persons and places in order to enhance the readability of the poems in which they appear.

Each entry—some as short as a single sentence and others up to 250 words long—is designed to cover the context of each use of a specific name. Included with many of the explications are pronunciations for unfamiliar Goidelicisms. At the end of each entry are the titles of the poems in which the name appears. One appended supplement provides genealogical information on Yeats's family. The 2d is a list of some 200 books consulted by Lester Conner, a notable Yeats scholar, in the compilation of this excellent reference tool.—**G. A. Cevasco**

Italian Literature

1040. **Ancient Roman Writers.** Ward W. Briggs, ed. Farmington Hills, Mich., Gale, 1999. 438p. illus. index. (Dictionary of Literary Biography, v.211). $155.00. ISBN 0-7876-3105-1.

This new addition to a well-known series treats 45 Roman authors who wrote in the Latin language from the third century B.C.E. (Naevius and Plautus) to the fourth century C.E. (Ammianus Marcellinus). Romans who wrote in Greek and the early Christian writers in Latin are not included.

The alphabetically arranged entries include a list of the author's works, both those that survive and those lost works for which credible evidence exists; a bibliography of the standard Latin editions, major English translations, and important commentaries for the extant works; a biographical sketch; an extensive, critical analysis of the author's opus; and a list of references. Because authentic portraits of most of these writers do not exist, the illustrations are mostly facsimiles of manuscripts and early printed editions of their works, although photographs of a few portrait busts and medallions that may date from the author's lifetime are included. All the articles are signed and are written mostly by scholars at American universities. There are three introductory essays and a "Checklist for Further Reading." This volume meets the high standards of scholarship that characterize the series; it will be essential wherever there is any serious interest in classical Latin literature.—**Paul B. Cors**

1041. **Italian Novelists Since World War II, 1965-1995.** Augustus Pallotta, ed. Farmington Hills, Mich., Gale, 1999. 367p. illus. index. (Dictionary of Literary Biography, v.196). $151.00. ISBN 0-7876-1851-9.

Thirty-five Italian novelists who came to prominence in the last third of the twentieth century, most of whom are still active, are profiled in this dictionary. As usual in this series, each of the alphabetically arranged entries includes a bibliography of the author's works, a biographical sketch, an extended analysis of the author's works, a selected list of references, a portrait, and reproductions of one or more book jackets. The articles are all written by scholars at leading U.S., Canadian, and Italian universities. They average 6 to 10 pages in length, except for the article on Italo Calvino, which, suitably for so influential a figure, is much longer. Quotations from the authors' writings are given both in the original Italian and in English translation. An introductory historical article, a general bibliography, and a list of contributors are also provided. This work maintains the high standard of scholarship set by earlier volumes in the series, and will be useful to all libraries supporting programs in Italian or comparative literature. A cumulative index to all titles in the Dictionary of Literary Biography series, the Dictionary of Literary Biography Yearbook series, and the Dictionary of Literary Biography Documentary series is appended.—**Paul B. Cors**

Latin American Literature

1042. Moss, Joyce, and Lorraine Valestuk. **Latin American Literature and Its Times: Profiles of Notable Literary Works and the Historical Events That Influenced Them.** Farmington Hills, Mich., Gale, 1999. 562p. illus. index. (World Literature and Its Times, v.1). $105.00. ISBN 0-7876-3726-2.

This first of a projected 12-volume new series from Gale profiles 50 literary works from Latin America, including a few from the U.S. Hispanic community thrown in for good measure. Each entry follows a standard format—events in history at the time the literary work takes place and was written, the literary work in focus, and references for further information. All major genres are included—fiction, biography, poetry, drama, chronicle, and essay—but the novel is by far the most heavily represented. The time frame spreads from the colonial period to the present, but coverage is heaviest for the twentieth century. At least one work from all major writers is represented; it is not necessarily a major work, just one that fits the editorial parameters. Major political and historical events, such as the Mexican Revolution (The Death of Artemio Cruz) or Perón's presidency (Santa Evita), or social injustices, like the plight of the Indians or the repression of homosexuality, form the backdrop of the works. Contributors are not known authorities in the field (two-thirds are "professional writers" or Ph.D. candidates), but their essays are well researched and reviewed by an impressive spectrum of notable North American scholars.

The bibliographies are probably the weakest element (other than that traditionally high Gale price, of course) in that, despite the editors' claim, they do not serve as springboards for further investigation but rather act more like footnotes in merely documenting the sources used. In fact, more comprehensive, critical information for these works can be gleaned from other sources; Gale's earlier *Modern Latin-American Fiction Writers* (see ARBA 96, entry 1258), Scribner's *Latin American Writers* (see ARBA 90, entry 1208), and *Encyclopedia of Latin American Literature* (see ARBA 98, entry 1178) come immediately to mind. The uniqueness of *Latin American Literature and Its Times* lies in its work-centered, rather than author-centric, approach and its emphasis on historical context.—**Lawrence Olszewski**

Middle Eastern Literature

1043. Makar, Ragai N. **Modern Arabic Literature: A Bibliography.** Lanham, Md., Scarecrow, 1998. 255p. index. (Scarecrow Area Bibliography Series, no.17). $75.00. ISBN 0-8108-3539-8.

The reason for this bibliography is the increasing interest in Arabic literature throughout the world, especially since the awarding of the Nobel Prize for Literature to Naguib Mahfouz in 1988. In this enumerative bibliography Makar provides 2,548 entries organized into 27 major subject categories that include all types of imaginative literature and criticism of Arabic literature. Most of the entries are English-language works, but some are in Arabic and French. The Arabic sources include "works which are not well represented in English translation, such as Israeli Arabic literature and literary studies by prominent Arab literary figures. The French sources cover North African literature." The bibliography itself covers writers who not only come from existing Arabic states but also belong to special groups such as Palestinians and Arabs in North and South America.

Although Makar has produced an impressive comprehensive bibliography, access to it is hampered by the lack of an adequate subject and name index. For example, a book-length work on the modern Egyptian author Yusuf Idris by P. M. Kurpershoek is only accessible through Kurpershoek or by perusing the listing under "Short Stories Study and Criticism." Similarly with authors, several of the entries are individually authored chapters in books, but the editors of the book-length work are not accessible through the author index. These serious shortcomings will detract from Makar's admirable compilation of citations of modern Arabic literature. [R: LJ, 1 Feb 99, p. 78; Choice, Oct 99, p. 306]—**Robert H. Burger**

Russian Literature

1044.   Leighton, Lauren G., comp. **A Bibliography of Alexander Pushkin in English: Studies and Translations.** Lewiston, N.Y., Edwin Mellen Press, 1999. 310p. (Studies in Slavic Languages and Literature, v.12). $99.95. ISBN 0-7734-8170-2.

Alexander Pushkin (1799–1837) is to Russian Literature what Shakespeare is to English literature or Goethe is to German literature. Lauren Leighton, the well-known scholar of the Russian Romantic movement, marks Pushkin's bicentenary with an excellent bibliography of English-language works by and about the Russian writer. Although the earliest English translations of Pushkin's poetry appeared shortly before the poet's death, full-scale translations of his masterpiece, the verse-novel *Eugene Onegin*, were scarce until the 1960s when the versions by Vladimir Nabokov and Walter Arndt inspired still others. The bibliography's translations portion is broken down by genre and then by individual titles.

The much-belated study of Pushkin in the West began after the Russian Revolution thanks to the efforts of émigré scholars in England and the U.S. The anniversary of Pushkin's death (1937) brought forth the first wave. With the professionalization of Slavic studies after World War II, Pushkin studies grew phenomenally. By 1998, some 1,700 English articles and books had been devoted to the Russian writer. Leighton has tracked down almost all of them, many missed by earlier bibliographies, and elegantly organized the material. The studies section is broken down into 23 categories such as "Bio-Literary Studies," "Comparative Studies," "Lyric Poetry," "Narrative Verse," "Drama," "Dissertations," and so on. One can only regret that space did not permit descriptive evaluations.

The volume includes a foreword by J. Thomas Shaw, the dean of American Pushkin scholars. Leighton's introduction briefly surveys the history of English-language Pushkin bibliography and describes the principles of organization. [R: Choice, Oct 99, pp. 305-306]—**D. Barton Johnson**

1045.   **Russian Literature in the Age of Pushkin and Gogol: Poetry and Drama.** Christine A. Rydel, ed. Farmington Hills, Mich., Gale, 1999. 449p. illus. index. (Dictionary of Literary Biography, v.205). $151.00. ISBN 0-7876-3099-3.

The handsome and durable Dictionary of Literary Biography Series (DLB) has only recently launched a Russian series that began with editor Marcus Levitt's volume on seventeenth- and eighteenth-century writers (see ARBA 96, entry 1261). This was followed by *Russian Literature of the Age of Pushkin and Gogol: Prose*, edited by Christine Rydel, a well-known specialist in Russian Romanticism. Rydel now completes her diptych with this volume on the poets of the "Golden Age of Russian Literature," an age that owes its glory far more to poetry than to prose.

Rydel's introduction sketches the historical and cultural context for the early decades of the nineteenth century, with particular attention to the debate over the meaning of "Romanticism," especially in its imported Russian setting. The 33 authors examined here range from giants (Aleksandr Pushkin, Mikhail Lermontov) to second-rank figures to obscure names such as Nestor Kukol'nik and Viktor Tepliakov. The handsomely illustrated essays, ranging from 5 to nearly 40 pages, are mostly by American and Russian literary specialists on their particular author. Russian drama during the period was relatively undeveloped and the few playwrights here are basically poets—with the exception of Aleksandr Griboedov. The best-known play of the time, Gogol's *Inspector-General*, finds no discussion here because Gogol is covered in the earlier volume on prose.

The articles follow the standard DLB format and include good critical bibliographies and reference to archival holdings. Also noteworthy is the "Checklist of Further Readings."—**D. Barton Johnson**

1046. **Russian Literature in the Age of Pushkin and Gogol: Prose.** Christine A. Rydel, ed. Farmington Hills, Mich., Gale, 1999. 432p. illus. index. (Dictionary of Literary Biography, v.198). $151.00. ISBN 0-7876-1853-5.

The impressive *Dictionary of Literary Biography* (DLB) series has only recently undertaken Russian literature. The Russian volumes commenced with *Early Modern Russian Writers, Late Seventeenth and Eighteenth Centuries*, edited by Marcus Levitt (vol. 150; see ARBA 96, entry 1261) and now moves on to early nineteenth-century prose. The subtitle is noteworthy because many of the period's major figures were poets. As a result, Alexander Pushkin, the era's greatest writer, is absent from a volume that bears his name in its title. Presumably, there will soon be a DLB volume devoted to the golden age of Russian poetry, but meanwhile Pushkin's seminal prose writings are scanted.

Rydel, a specialist in Russian Romanticism, provides a succinct introduction where she lucidly sketches the historical and literary background. The 30 well-chosen figures (born circa 1800) range from writers such as Gogol, Aksakov, and Odoevsky to names such as Ivan Gagarin and Elena Gans. Also included are near-forgotten authors of the first Russian "bestsellers." Although a particular strength is the generous inclusion of critics, journalists, and editors, all of which were instrumental in establishing the role of literature for Russia's nascent reading public. Were it not for Vissarion Belinsky, Ivan Panaev, Makhail Pogodin, and Osip Senkovsky, Russian literature would have been much different. This is equally true for historians and philosophers, such as Timofei Granovsky and Nikolai Stankevich.

The handsomely illustrated essays, written mostly by American Slavists, average about a dozen pages. Each contains the author's bibliography (Russian and English translations) and concludes with a critical bibliography and archival sources. As in all DLB volumes, a cumulative series index is included. [R: Choice, April 99, p. 1435]—**D. Barton Johnson**

Scottish Literature

1047. Todd, William B., and Ann Bowden. **Sir Walter Scott: A Bibliographical History 1796-1832.** New Castle, Del., Oak Knoll Press, 1998. 1071p. index. $95.00. ISBN 1-884718-64-7.

The authors of this exhaustive history of Scott's literary career happen to be husband and wife, and it is clear that this mammoth undertaking has been a labor of love. Both hold Ph.D.s and have had academic careers spanning many decades. Todd and Bowden describe this volume as "a comprehensive bibliographical record of Scott's literary career, disclosing further typographical variants among the poems and novels earlier described, and extending to a number of editions not previously considered, and citing innumerable issues by other writers or artisans evidently dependent upon his publications." In other words, this bibliography purports to encompass writings that Scott had contributed to or influenced, and to encompass generally writings that seem to have been influenced strongly by Scott, including "books by others which he substantially edited or revised."

As the foregoing words imply, this massive volume is not meant for the amateur. It is a complex bibliographic tool designed primarily for the professional scholar or the independent researcher. The highly technical nature of this undertaking can be illustrated by a sampling of some of the items under Scott's renowned piece "The Lady of the Lake" (for which, by the way, there are more than 400 entries). It is clear that material of this nature is intended for an audience of considerable sophistication and that the general reader will quickly become "lost in the forest." Probably more useful to the layperson would be John Sutherland's *The Life of Walter Scott: A Critical Biography* (Blackwell, 1995). However, the Todd and Bowden bibliography does present some fascinating printing histories of various works by Scott (particularly the account of the "derivatives" of "Lord of the Isles"), along with some successfully reproduced illustrations, not the least of which are the portrait of Scott by William S. Watson and, on page 455, a detail of "The Monastery, 1820: First Engraving on Steel."

The layout of this large volume is sensible, following a chronological order and furnishing a brief introduction for each section, often with interesting remarks on Scott's career. For instance, in the introduction to "Part Three, 1814-1817," there is a short discussion of the way in which the author published

Waverly anonymously in 1814, probably to escape to some extent the "immoral" reputation that novels had in those days. Reviewing Jane Austen's *Emma* in the same year, however, Scott prepared the way for his own work by suggesting that the novel could have a certain "universal charm of narrative," and that readers might prefer to "yawn" over novels rather than read heavily in the "historian, moralist, or poet."

Sir Walter Scott: A Bibliographical History, 1796-1832 is a successful effort if it is viewed from a traditional scholarly standpoint. As a labor of love it has a peculiar dry sort of charm and is almost free of errors.—**Peter Thorpe**

Spanish Literature

1048. **Hispanic Literature Criticism Supplement.** Susan Salas, ed. Farmington Hills, Mich., Gale, 1999. 2v. illus. index. $199.00/set. ISBN 0-7876-3755-6.

The key word in this title is "supplement." Ostensibly, its purpose is to compensate for some 63 Spanish, Portuguese, Latin American, and Latino authors that *Hispanic Literature Criticism* (HLC) ignored the first time around (see ARBA 95, entry 1242) and thus includes no authors already covered in the first set. Except for seven entries, all are treated in at least one of the several other volumes in the Gale library of literary criticism, just not the earlier HLC. Bibliographic information in the lists of principal works is often incomplete, not current, and in some cases downright inaccurate. The justification for mentioning only the first published English translation is questionable, especially because later editions may be more readily available in libraries or in print. The listings of translations for Dalton, Rojas, Sor Juana, and Guillén all lack the standard modern editions; in the case of Rodó, the editors included a review of one such translation in the readings yet failed to mention it in the list of principal works. The appalling lack of diacritics in two languages that rely heavily on them is one of several instances of a need for better editing.

As for the selection of criticism, the expectation is that users will appreciate the corpus of a writer's work through exposure to snippets of criticism, mostly intact yet often exhumed out of context. Beyond reviews and author interviews, however, the scholarly, if not pedantic, level of the essays may be too academically advanced for the intended high school, college, and general reader audience. The suggestions for further readings are extremely selective considering the fame of most of these writers.

Access through the three indexes is inconsistent and careless. The cumulative author index unearths other relevant material in the Gale panoply for all authors in both HLC series, thereby obviating the space-eating cross-references in the body of the text. The cumulative nationality index strangely and inexplicably duplicates entries for Machado, Dalton, and Rojas. The slapdash approach carries over into the cumulative title index that, despite being labeled the HLC series cumulative title index, in fact does not include a single title from the supplement; they all refer to those in the master set only. In addition, the volume lacks an index to the authors of the anthologized critical works and to the works themselves.—**Lawrence Olszewski**

1049. Meyers, Glenn G. **Miguel Delibes: An Annotated Critical Bibliography.** Lanham, Md., Scarecrow, 1999. 333p. index. (Scarecrow Author Bibliographies, no.102). $50.00. ISBN 0-8108-3626-2.

Meyers, a practicing attorney, presents the published version of his doctoral dissertation in Spanish literature, accepted by the University of Colorado at Boulder in 1998. Its purpose is to survey the literature by and about Delibes, a Spanish post-Civil War author.

The first chapter is a biography of the author followed by an annotated bibliography. Each of the entries in the bibliography contains a bibliographic citation and annotation. The entries in chapter 3 and 4 also include descriptive and critical comments about the contents of the work. Chapter 2 focuses on publications by Delibes, subdivided by type of work. It should be noted that there are no entries for his work as a journalist, a notable omission from a book that claims to be an "exhaustive survey." Bibliographic annotations from books and scholarly articles make up the third chapter. The fourth chapter consists of entries drawn from dissertations, book reviews, and interviews. It is curious that Meyers did not remember to include his own dissertation in his list of dissertations. The book concludes with a chapter examining the trends in Delibes criticism.

The book features both an index of critics and an index of subjects. Unfortunately, readers have to have some knowledge of the literature to be able to use them effectively. This work would have benefited from judicious editing, since the wording in the entries is confusing at times.—**John R. Burch Jr.**

POETRY

1050. **British Poets of the Great War: Sassoon, Graves, Owen.** Patrick Quinn, ed. Farmington Hills, Mich., Gale, 1999. 350p. illus. index. (Dictionary of Literary Biography Documentary Series, v.18). $151.00. ISBN 0-7876-1933-7.

The 18th volume of the Dictionary of Literary Biography Documentary Series is the first of two dealing with six men who fought in World War I and whose literary accomplishment have stood the critical test of time. The next volume will include Rupert Brooke, Edward Thomas, and Isaac Rosenberg. Although of varying ages and backgrounds, all six were profoundly affected by their experiences in the Great War. This volume provides detailed information about the poets' backgrounds and focuses on how the men's war experiences shaped their poetry.

In addition to textual criticism, the entries include many photographs, manuscripts, military and medical records, interviews, essays, poems, reviews, obituaries, literary assessments, prose excerpts, and personal letters both from the writers' lifetime and afterward. Also included are an excellent bibliography and a list of relevant archives and collections, as well as a cumulative index to companion volumes in these series.

Of the 3 writers treated in volume 18, Sassoon and Graves survived the war, while Owen died in action in France one week before the Armistice ended the fighting. A draft of a poem he wrote in July 1918 is poignant proof of his grim acceptance of his coming death.

As expected from this publisher, this work is well done and easy to use. However, with some judicious pruning, all six writers could be fitted into one volume at a great savings to the many libraries who want to acquire both volumes.—**Kay O. Cornelius**

1051. **Index of American Periodical Verse 1997.** By Rafael Català and James D. Anderson. Lanham, Md., Scarecrow, 1999. 675p. $75.00. ISBN 0-8108-3721-8.

This 27th annual volume of the *Index of American Periodical Verse* attests to the fact that poetry is a creative art flourishing throughout North America. Produced with the cooperation of 290 participating periodicals from Canada, the United States, and the Caribbean, it contains more than 7,200 entries for individual poets, with more than 20,000 entries for the titles of their works. Criteria for inclusion include the reputation of the poet and the quality of his or her recent poems. Selection of participating periodicals, which are listed in a separate section together with the names of editors and addresses, is an editorial decision guided by recommendations of librarians, literary scholars, and publishers.

Entrants are arranged alphabetically by surname. Under each poet's name his or her works are further alphabetized by title, or if untitled, by first line. A separate index provides access to each poem by title or first line. Because this index is an important resource for contemporary American poetry and serves as a continuing record of trends in the output of famous as well as lesser-known poets and the cultural influence they represent, it deserves a place in all large literature collections.—**G. A. Cevasco**

1052. **Index to Poetry for Children and Young People 1993-1997: A Title, Subject, Author, and First Line Index to Poetry in Collections for Children and Young People.** G. Meredith Blackburn III, comp. Bronx, N.Y., H. W. Wilson, 1999. 461p. $63.00. ISBN 0-8242-0939-7.

Initiated in 1942 as the *Index to Children's Poetry*, this stalwart guide, now in its sixth five-year supplement, will be welcomed in elementary and secondary school libraries, in academic curriculum centers, and perhaps in radio and television libraries. Professors and students of the literature for children and young people will also find it a useful addition to their own collections.

The 186 collections indexed here are appropriate for children in elementary school grades and intermediate and older students. The volume's broad scope includes new volumes by individual poets (e.g., Lee Bennett Hopkins) and selections from the works of older authors (e.g., Randall Jarrell). The four basic types of entries—title, subject, author, and reference from first line—facilitate searching for a poem after one becomes familiar with the alphabetic word-by-word arrangement. Fullest information is given in the title entry. Particularly helpful here is the means to distinguish between different poems bearing the same title. Following the boldfaced title is the first line of the poem, the poet's name, and the symbol for the book indexes. This worthy new supplement again brings children and poetry together.—**Charles R. Andrews**

1053. **Poetry Criticism, Volume 22: Excerpts from Criticism of the Works of the Most Significant and Widely Studied Poets of World Literature.** Carol T. Gaffke, Anna J. Sheets, and Laura A. Wisner-Broyles, eds. Farmington Hills, Mich., Gale, 1999. 557p. index. $105.00. ISBN 0-7876-2013-0. ISSN 1052-4851.

Collections that already shelve the first 21 volumes of *Poetry Criticism* will of course want this latest addition to a most useful series. The substantial critical excerpts and biographical information on poets throughout the world provided by the series are an excellent source for students required to write papers on poetic technique, delve into a poet's most prominent themes, or lead poetry discussions. Among the poets included in this volume are the contemporaries Ernesto Cardenal, Philip Levine, and Sharon Olds. Representing the recently deceased are Luis Borges and José Garcia Villa. The outstanding Sanskrit poet Kalidasa (fifth century), the unknown poet of *Beowulf* (eighth century), and the earliest known female French writer, Marie de France (twelfth century), exemplify poets of the past. The final figure, one of the most significant authors of the first half of the twentieth century—celebrated for his fiction but usually ignored for his poetry—is James Joyce. These nine figures and their works amply reflect the influence of tradition and innovation, various nationalities, eras, and movements found in every volume of *Poetry Criticism*.—**G. A. Cevasco**

1054. **Poetry Criticism, Volume 24: Excerpts from Criticism of the Works of the Most Significant and Widely Studied Poets of World Literature.** Laura A. Wisner-Broyles, ed. Farmington Hills, Mich., Gale, 1999. 558p. index. $105.00. ISBN 0-7876-2015-7. ISSN 1052-4851.

Libraries subscribing to this series will want to add this newest volume, which includes eight poets—Hilaire Belloc, Rupert Brooke, Dennis Brutus, James Weldon Johnson, Juana Inés de la Cruz, Li-Young Lee, Howard Nemerov, and Algernon Charles Swinburne. Poets chosen for inclusion in *Poetry Criticism* are those frequently studied in high school and undergraduate college courses. Readers may not agree, however, that Juana Inés de la Cruz and Li-Young Lee necessarily meet that criterion.

The arrangement of each author entry includes the name under which the author wrote, followed by the birth and death dates; a brief biographical and critical essay; a photograph or illustration of the author; a list of his or her principal works; chronologically arranged critical excerpts from fully identified published sources, varying in length and dating for the most part from the 1950s through the 1990s; and a list for further reading, arranged by category (i.e., bibliography, biography, criticism). The excerpts constitute the major part of each poet's entry. Three indexes conclude the volume—a cumulative author index (all authors in Gale's Literary Criticism series), a cumulative nationality index (all authors in the Poetry Criticism series), and a cumulative title index (all poems in the Poetry Criticism series).—**Charles R. Andrews**

1055. **Poetry for Students, Volume 5: Presenting Analysis, Context, and Criticism on Commonly Studied Poetry.** Mary K. Ruby, ed. Farmington Hills, Mich., Gale, 1999. 318p. illus. index. $60.00. ISBN 0-7876-3566-9. ISSN 10094-701.

This 5th volume of a series that began in 1998 (see ARBA 99, entries 1106-1109) continues in the same style as its predecessors, adding 19 more poems to the 80 or so already covered in volumes 1-4. Each poem is treated in exhaustive depth, including author information, line-by-line analysis, historical context, essays by various critics, topics for further study, and more. The actual text of the poem, printed in small type, seems lost among the abundance of secondary information.

Poets included range from Shakespeare and Marvell though Yeats and Dickenson to the very recent Yusef Komunyakaa (*Facing It*, 1988) and Louise Glueck (*The Gold Lily*, 1992). Indeed, these latter choices will probably prove the most useful of the whole selection since less will be found on them elsewhere. Aimed at high school and undergraduate college students and their teachers, these lengthy entries do too much of the student's work for them. They could perhaps be more useful as a guide for teachers wanting to cover all the bases, but at $60 per volume it may be too pricey.—**Willa Schmidt**

1056. **Poetry for Students, Volume 6: Presenting Analysis, Context and Criticism on Commonly Studied Poetry.** Mary K. Ruby, ed. Farmington Hills, Mich., Gale, 1999. 296p. illus. index. $60.00. ISBN 0-7876-3567-7. ISSN 1094-7019.

Much value can be seen in this type of teaching tool, poetry being the most difficult genre for literature novices. The series provides a useful method for close reading and a thorough look at poems by its small selection (this volume highlights 18 poems). Each poem is accompanied by a biographical sketch of the author, a historical context, a line-by-line summary, a description of its themes, two critical articles, suggested topics for discussion and composition, and a bibliography of other critical works on the author. In that respect, the instructor has at hand a good choice of approaches and materials to examine individual works in a larger context. The abundance of material can be useful but can also be detrimental. The summaries and the articles provide overpowering a priori interpretations of the poems that can excuse—or even impede—students from a process of discovery. The discussion themes are very broad and seldom reflect back to the poems, which are dwarfed by the huge critical work around them. This is underscored by the fact that they appear in a font much smaller than the rest of the text. However, the biggest omission in this series, and especially in this particular volume, is in the selection that, judging by the cumulative index, does justice only to African Americans among all American ethnic groups, and relies too much on the canon. One can only hope for better representation of non-canonical groups and people of color in future volumes.—**Stella T. Clark**

1057. Sagar, Keith, and Stephen Tabor. **Ted Hughes: A Bibliography, 1946-1995.** 2d ed. New York, Mansell/Cassell; distr., New York, Continuum Publishing, 1998. 470p. index. $120.00. ISBN 0-7201-2337-2.

This 2d edition expands, corrects, and extends Sagar and Tabor's excellent bibliography of Ted Hughes. The 1st edition was published in 1983 (see ARBA 84, entry 1198). Fortunately, Hughes has not gone into retirement. This necessitated additions to the 1st edition and the 2 authors have taken the opportunity to add a considerable amount of material and make corrections to the 2d edition.

The major change in the 2d edition is extending the record up to the end of 1995. Where possible, the original numbering from the 1st edition was retained. This decision may please those who are familiar with the 1st edition, but as Sagar notes in the preface to the 1st edition, the focus is on readers, not scholars. This makes the retention of the numbering from the 1st edition somewhat curious and more cumbersome than helpful. Nonetheless, however the work is numbered, it contains in one place an excellent summary of the works of, works by, and works about Hughes.

There are those, including this reviewer, who would question the authors' assertion that Hughes is the greatest living English poet. What no one who knows English literature would seriously argue is the major impact in so many areas that Hughes has had on literature in general and in bringing literature to an audience that ranges from children to the expert in literature. Hughes has a talent of wide and deep proportions. This bibliography does considerable justice to the talent of Hughes.

Tabor is the acknowledged bibliographer of the two authors. His contributions are in sections A and B. These are without a doubt the most dense of the sections in the book. These are sections that only a traditional bibliographer could love. The problem for the general reader is the problem with any traditional bibliography: somehow managing to wade through the mind-numbing minutia. The bibliography is excellent, however.

Beyond sections A and B, the work becomes considerably more accessible to the general reader. Bibliographic standards are considerably relaxed, concentrating more on the material and less on its description. Section C lists contributions to periodicals, D is a listing of translations, and E is a list of interviews and comments. Hughes' significant body of recording sand broadcasts make up sections F and G.

These are especially important because in a large number of cases these were the first "publications" of Hughes' work, with the written counterpart coming later and sometimes in different or modified forms. Section H contains a miscellany, I includes settings, and section J is a listing of books and articles about Hughes. The final section, K, is a critical part of the compilation, listing manuscripts by Hughes. The extraordinary breadth of Hughes' contributions to literature in general is made even more clear by perusing this section.

Overall, this is an excellent addition to serious literature collections. The small public collection or a school collection would not find this book useful, but the more research-oriented collection will. For those thinking of adding the book to the collection, there is a warning: This compilation will place some strain on even the most research-oriented collections by pointing the reader to some very esoteric but important materials. This book is highly recommended for research-intensive collections interested in literature in general and English literature specifically.—**C. D. Hurt**

1058. **Victorian Women Poets.** William B. Thesing, ed. Farmington Hills, Mich., Gale, 1999. 380p. illus. index. (Dictionary of Literary Biography, v.199). $151.00. ISBN 0-7876-1854-3.

The *Dictionary of Literary Biography* (DLB) is a respected, excellent source for brief biographical information and additional sources for literary figures, major and minor. The volumes of the DLB are arranged around central themes or time periods. This volume follows this tradition, focusing on Victorian women poets. The introduction makes the claim that Elizabeth Barrett Browning is the poet "around whom the volume is organized." The organization of the volume around Browning is difficult to discern, but it is clear that the 33 poets included here all knew, knew of, or were influenced by Browning. That may be enough organization, but any reader expecting some tie to Browning in most or all of the entries will be disappointed. This is not a study of Browning; it is a study of Victorian women poets of whom Browning was the most influential then and today.

As biographies of the poets' careers, entries keep to the traditional form of the DLB. While there is an attempt to cover some literary criticism, the major goal is to enlighten the reader with biographical, as opposed to critical, information. Black-and-white illustrations are used in a majority of the entries. The only minor complaint is that in too many cases the portraits or pictures are of the poets' husbands and not of the poets themselves.

The authors of the individual biographies are noted, but there is no compilation of the authors' credentials. In most cases, this is not a problem given the overall quality the DLB has demonstrated in the past. All but one of the entries appear to have been authored by an academic, with the sole exception of a biography written by a clergyman.

The individual entries range from a short 4 pages to 21 pages for Elizabeth Barrett Browning. Each appears true to the DLB form of supplying birth and death dates, a list of major writings, personal and educational background, a summary of the poet's life and career, a short critical response to the poet's work, and bibliographies of related and additional works.

Libraries that already have an investment in the DLB will wish to add this 199th volume to their collections. Collections that focus on women's studies and feminism should also include this volume; the women it covers helped lay the groundwork for social change both in Victorian England and elsewhere.
—**C. D. Hurt**

25 Music

GENERAL WORKS

Bibliography

1059. **Bibliographic Guide to Music 1998.** Thorndike, Maine, G. K. Hall/Macmillan, 1998. 881p. $295.00. ISBN 0-7838-0226-9. ISSN 0360-2753.

Bibliographic Guide to Music 1998 continues the long series of annual supplements to the New York Public Library music division catalog originally published in 1964. This 33-volume set was once cumulatively supplemented by a 10-volume set in 1973. The 1980 and 1990 music guides were reviewed in ARBA 1932 (see entry 1016) and ARBA 1992 (see entry 1248). Unfortunately, there have been no discernible changes in this publication since these reviews. This volume lists recent music materials of all types cataloged by the New York Public Library during the 1998 calendar year. It also includes additional entries from the Library of Congress MARC tapes.

The introduction to this title claims the G. K. Hall bibliographic guides are comprehensive annual subject bibliographies. This may be true; however, because each annual guide contains a preponderance of materials from the previous 5 years, not just the past year, and there have been no cumulations since 1973, the guide's value as a current acquisitions tool is limited and a thorough exploration by any researcher will prove laborious. Without any cumulation, using just a single volume that includes items with imprint dates from any of the past eight years renders any estimation of completeness nearly impossible for this reviewer.

Online catalogs at both the Library of Congress and the New York Public Library are readily accessible across the Web. Even OCLC's WorldCat is becoming more widely available in academic and public library settings alike. With this in mind, the *Bibliographic Guide to Music 1998* can only be recommended to institutions that can afford to continue their standing orders.—**C. Michael Phillips**

1060. Newman, Marilyn Stephanie Mercedes. **The Comprehensive Catalogue of Duet Literature for Female Voices: Vocal Chamber Duets with Keyboard Accompaniment Composed Between 1820-1995.** Lanham, Md., Scarecrow, 1999. 573p. index. $75.00. ISBN 0-8108-3647-5.

This valuable catalog will be a welcome reference tool for singers, their teachers, and their collaborators. The major portion of this clearly presented volume covers duets for two female voices from the period 1820-1995, a total of 8,800 entries listed alphabetically by composer. Each citation presents the composition's dates (when known), the full title and opus number of the duet, the types of voices for whom it is intended (if specified), the name of the publisher, and comments relating to any aspect of the work. Many of the 8,800 titles are drawn from secondary sources, but many also come from the author's own experience as a frequent performer of chamber duets. All of the pieces cited are concert music; popular duos or duets from operas are not included. Most duets use piano accompaniment, but some require organ, harmonium, or harpsichord. All items are or have been published.

Several appendixes expand the usefulness of the primary catalog: two simple alphabetic lists of all composers and of women composers represented in the catalog; an index of entries according to voice types, when specified (e.g., two sopranos, soprano and alto); a list of composers according to the languages of their texts; a table of duets accompanied by instruments other than piano; a list of publishers and their addresses (when known); and the table of contents of several published collections of duets. A final index lists duets alphabetically by title.

There are many advantages of this catalog. It covers 175 years' worth of repertoire that is otherwise difficult to locate, and it presents the music and related information in several ways. The author also points out the contributions duet literature can make to vocal pedagogy. Even a cursory reading of the catalog reveals a large number of duets written by composers who are hardly heard of today (e.g., Franz Abt, whose opus numbers top 600), but whose music might well be worth learning. However, the prose materials that accompany the catalog are written in an awkward and often unidiomatic style and are repetitious to the point of defensiveness. Historical information is often incorrect, and in the bibliography there are a large number of outdated sources. However, these flaws can be ignored when the basic research and tabulations are sound. [R: LJ, 1 Sept 99, p. 181]—**Karin Pendle**

Biography

1061. Handy, D. Antoinette. **Black Women in American Bands and Orchestras.** 2d ed. Lanham, Md., Scarecrow, 1998. 359p. illus. index. $55.00. ISBN 0-8108-3419-7.

Handy's profiles of orchestra leaders and string, wind, percussion, and keyboard players fill in gaps in women's history with style and an obvious enthusiasm for the field. Her knowledge of band and orchestra formation and performance is considerable. She has organized material under six chapter headings, beginning with a historical overview of the American orchestra. Entries are packed with information on names and nicknames, musical talent, and birth and death dates and places. Chapters conclude with helpful notes offering additional sources and commentary. A middle folio offers 84 photographs depicting people and instruments; for example, Della Sutton and her trombone, concert mistress Rachel Jordan with the Gateway Festival Orchestra, Olivia Cook at the organ, Julie Gardner with an accordion, and a newspaper sketch from 1895 featuring Myrtle Hart at the harp. She concludes the text with an appendix duplicating her letter and questionnaire requesting aid in research. Her bibliography is neatly organized and thorough. The index lists theaters, universities, orchestras, churches, arts councils, festivals, and sources of funds as well as names of performers.

There is a major fault in Handy's updated volume. To further the 1st edition, she has concentrated on correcting omissions and adding details. However, her preface to the 2d edition is disappointingly small. Because it offers no list of entries, photographs, or significant improvements on the old volume, the purchaser has no access to alterations, photographs, or entries that upgrade the work. Overall, this is a thoughtful, useful compendium on a major segment of women's accomplishments.—**Mary Ellen Snodgrass**

1062. Jasen, David A., and Gene Jones. **Spreadin' Rhythm Around: Black Popular Songwriters, 1880-1930.** New York, Schirmer Books/Simon & Schuster Macmillan, 1998. 435p. illus. index. $29.95. ISBN 0-02-864742-4.

Two dozen individuals or songwriting teams are given rather comprehensive biographical entries here, starting with James Bland, the minstrel composer whose "Carry Me Back to Old Virginy" was until recently that region's state song, and continuing into the Harlem Renaissance with Eubie Blake and Noble Sissle, Henry Creamer and Turner Layton, James P. Johnson, and Fats Waller. This is the most recent and reliable treatment of the period. None of the figures are obscure or unimportant, although names (and tunes) might be less known to the novice. The coverage is lucid and fascinating in every regard, and this is a significantly rich source of data on this very important era in American music of ballads, blues, coon songs, musical theater, and publishing. Those who have read about ragtime will already know Jasen's name, and Gene Jones contributes information on the musical stage. Many of the illustrations (individuals and sheet music covers) have not been readily available previously. The back matter lists sources consulted in a brief, excellent bibliography. In addition to a general index, another is offered of song titles that will prove a most helpful reference feature. [R: LJ, 1 Sept 98, p. 172]—**Dominique-René de Lerma**

1063.   **Women Composers: Music Through the Ages, Volume 4. Composers Born 1700-1799 Vocal Music.** Sylvia Glickman and Martha Furman Schleifer, eds. New York, G. K. Hall/Simon & Schuster Macmillan, 1998. 456p. index. $100.00. ISBN 0-7838-1613-8.

1064.   **Women Composers: Music Through the Ages. Volume 5: Composers Born 1700-1799, Large and Small Instrumental Ensembles.** Sylvia Glickman and Martha Furman Schleifer, eds. New York, G. K. Hall/Simon & Schuster Macmillan, 1998. 434p. index. $100.00. ISBN 0-7838-1614-6.

This is one set of reference works that libraries, schools, women's history departments, and musicians do not want to miss. Glickman and Schleifer's *Women Composers* fits neatly into the empty space marked "female musicians." Opening with a detailed table of contents and series introduction, these segments of a 12-volume set attest to an upsurge in feminism and women's history in the last decades of the twentieth century. Volume introductions set the parameters and identify women by their roles in the era, professional careers, and contributions to the canon for women's (and world) composition. Each volume concludes with biographies of editors and contributors, who are primarily Americans with a sprinkling of Europeans. Extensive indexing by composer (e.g., Margaret Essex, Maddalena Lombardini Sirmen), composition (e.g., *Fleur d'épine, Juvenile Rhymes*), and topic (e.g., barcarolle, vocal improvisation, English guitar, Zwinger Theater) directs even novice readers to specific data.

Volume 4 presents 23 composers; volume 5 contains 12. Entries begin with appealing biographies filled with insightful commentary and generous citations. The editors stress the observations, character, talents, and development of female music supporters. For example, Madame Brillon's correspondence with J. C. Bach, Amélie-Julie Candeille's contribution to the Comédie Française, and Isabella Colbran's relationship with Crescentini, Queen of Spain, are all featured here. Lyrics in French, German, and Italian are translated into English. A generous complement of notes on source material, plus a list of works and a bibliography, opens the way to additional research. At the end of the entry are the compositions in clear notation for perusal, performance, and enjoyment. The addition of a glossary would have been helpful to readers unfamiliar with the topic. Overall, the volumes are beautifully arranged and inviting to the reader who has one hand on the keyboard to hear at last how women expressed their joy in music. [R: BL, July 98, p. 1909; RUSQ, v. 38 no. 1, pp. 108-109]—**Mary Ellen Snodgrass**

Dictionaries and Encyclopedias

1065.   Boccagna, David L., comp. **Musical Terminology: A Practical Compendium in Four Languages.** Hillsdale, N.Y., Pendragon Press, 1999. 243p. $24.00pa. ISBN 1-57647-015-6.

This unusual combination of several types of specialized dictionaries is designed for performing musicians. English is not the language of choice for most composers in their instructions to performers on printed music, and it is vital for musicians to understand instructive terminology in the languages they are most commonly found—Italian, German, and French. The purpose of this dictionary is to provide musicians with translations of these terms in four languages. This pocket-size compendium can be invaluable to instrumentalists, conductors, teachers, students, and amateur music lovers who speak any of the languages.

Standard musical dictionaries provide definitions and explanations of the full range of musical terms, but it can be time-consuming and cumbersome to use these broader references when simply trying to find out how a composer wants a piece of music marked to "strepitoso" (to sound noisy). There have been cross-language dictionaries of musical terminology, such as the *Dictionary of Terms in Music:*

English-German, German-English. Wörterbuch Musik (see ARBA 93 entry 1248), but the present volume may be the first multi-language translator of musical performance terminology. Thus, if an English-speaking conductor comes across the German term "ungezwungen" in his score, he can quickly determine that the music should be performed in an "easy going" manner.

A short introduction tells the interesting story of how this dictionary came to be compiled. This would make a useful and interesting addition to any music book collection.—**Larry Lobel**

1066. **The Companion to Irish Traditional Music.** Fintan Vallely, ed. New York, New York University Press, 1999. 478p. illus. maps. $50.00. ISBN 0-8147-8802-5.

In conjunction with the increasing interest in world music, interest in Irish traditional music has blossomed. Groups like the Chieftains, the Clancy Brothers, and Clannad have developed large followings and have piqued interest in other artists. In addition, the recognition of the influence of traditional Irish music on other forms, such as bluegrass and rock, has resulted in tracing the roots back to the original genre. So this companion comes at a valuable time.

Organized alphabetically, the entries include names, styles, dances, musicians, instruments, and regions. Sections on the accordion and bagpipes, for example, provide a full history of the instrument, different types and tunings, and modern uses. The regional influence on the structure and pattern of songs and use of instruments, as well as the development of the music, is explored with illustrations and musical notation of the patterns and melodies.

Well over 100 experts contributed to this volume, including journalists, musicians, and historians, and several hundred books and journals were consulted in the preparation of this work, making it a highly authoritative resource. The editor enlarged the scope to include music that was influenced by traditional Irish music even though it was not necessarily from Ireland. This increases the value of the work so that music from not only other parts of the British Isles are covered but from all over the world, demonstrating the vast range of Irish influence. The entries are well written, giving a clear summation, history, description of influences, and other relevant information.

This volume is a major addition to the world of music. The illustrations and maps, the well-written entries, and the comprehensiveness of the work make it a highly prized, authoritative source for the study of Irish music and other forms of music at a very reasonable price. [R: LJ, 15 Oct 99, p. 62]—**Joshua Cohen**

1067. **A Dictionary of Australian Music.** Warren Bebbington, ed. New York, Oxford University Press, 1998. 361p. $45.00. ISBN 0-19-550839-4.

Bebbington, general editor of the *Oxford Companion to Australian Music* (see ARBA 99, entry 1122), has created a concise and compact version of the *Companion*, which is most useful for finding factual information quickly. Bebbington has contributed approximately two-thirds of the entries in the dictionary; the remainder of the entries are signed, with a list of contributors and their affiliations or authority noted in the introductory materials.

Approximately two-thirds of the entries from the *Companion* have been retained; however, long entries have been shortened. Lists of works, discographies, illustrations, and bibliographies have been eliminated, as have the lengthy articles on historical or cultural topics, institutions, and significant events. Short summaries replace long articles on major topics; for example, the entry on Aboriginal music, including discography and bibliography, was nine pages in the *Companion*, and is four long paragraphs in the *Dictionary*. Corrections and amendments have been made where appropriate (i.e., death dates of persons deceased after the 1997 publication). Bebbington has retained the range of topics covered, from Aboriginal traditions to the latest European influences, from folk and classical to rock and experimental styles. Biographical entries make up the majority of the contents.

A library that owns the *Companion* will not need this resource; however, it would make a useful addition to a large public library collection or a specialized collection. Students looking for further resources or for an overview of music in Australia will find the short entries and lack of bibliographic notes frustrating.

—**Kerie L. Nickel**

1068.   **The Hutchinson Concise Dictionary of Music.** Barrie Jones, ed. Chicago, Fitzroy Dearborn, 1999. 762p. $55.00. ISBN 1-57958-178-1.

This new entry in the crowded field of musical dictionaries has a strong pedigree, having been abridged from the 1995 *Hutchinson Encyclopedia of Music*, which itself descends from the highly regarded *New Everyman Dictionary of Music* (see ARBA 90, entry 1229). What distinguishes this latest entry into the field is its tight focus, defined in the introduction as "the core technical, biographical, organological (study of musical instruments) and other information vital to the comprehension and enjoyment of music." Thus, although it includes entries about musical genres and forms, biographies of composers, instruments and their makers, theorists and musicologists, and conductors, it excludes instrumental performers and singers, publishers, critics, teachers, and choreographers. Illustrations are limited to about 100 musical examples, and there is a 14-page appendix consisting of a chronology of the history of music, emphasizing composers and important works in the musical repertoire.

To this reviewer, some of the inclusions and exclusions seem inconsistent or arbitrary, but these deliberate limitations do keep the number of entries down to about 7,500 and allow for somewhat lengthier and more detailed descriptions than one finds in dictionaries that attempt to encompass the entire musical field. However, the narrow scope does result in the sacrifice of a pronunciation guide and a shortage of definitions of some terms used to define other terms (the definition of *a cappella* says it is characteristic of gospel music and doo-wop, neither of which has an entry). Nevertheless, this volume succeeds admirably in its stated goals and will serve its intended audience of concert–goers, compact disc collectors, radio listeners, and music students well. [R: Choice, Oct 99, p. 305]—**Larry Lobel**

1069.   **International Dictionary of Black Composers.** Samuel A. Floyd Jr., ed. Chicago, Fitzroy Dearborn, 1999. 2v. illus. $270.00/set. ISBN 1-884964-27-3.

There is a surprising scarcity of authoritative, up-to-date, and comprehensive reference works on black composers in print. Fortunately, the *International Dictionary of Black Composers* fills this need admirably.

Cast in 2 tightly packed volumes, but with refreshingly large, full-page portraits, this set profiles 185 composers of African heritage from the eighteenth century to the present. Entries contain a biographical overview, a list of works, bibliographies of writings by and about the composer, archival notes, and several critical essays. All articles are signed. Musical jargon is kept to a minimum, making the entries eminently readable for most researchers or curious browsers. The broad scope of this work, not limited to any single genre (e.g., rock, classical), presents a sweeping view of the contributions of black composers to Western music.

This is a solid, thorough, well-priced reference set that will make an important contribution to any collection on music. It will be years before any other publishing venture bests this set. [R: LJ, 1 Sept 99, p. 180; Choice, Nov 99, pp. 506-508]—**James Moffet**

1070.   **Music in the 20th Century.** Hao Huang and others, eds. Armonk, N.Y., Sharpe Reference/M. E. Sharpe, 1999. 3v. illus. index. $299.00/set. ISBN 0-7656-8012-2.

This 3-volume set is an encyclopedia that will serve as a useful guide to worldwide developments in music over the past 100 years. Entries cover all major genres, techniques, composers, and performers. It is arranged alphabetically with more than 500 main entries. While most of these entries are biographical—generally 1 full page of highly readable information—there are an additional 1,000 biographical entries at the end of volume 3 in the "Biographical Digest" section. These are concise sketches of those individuals or groups who have made major contributions to music but have not been allotted a main entry. Entries discuss various styles or movements in music and also music with origins in geographical areas or nationalistic movements. Entries are for popular as well as classical music. A few examples of subject entries are disco, doo-wop, film music, Latin jazz, modal jazz, opera, operetta, and swing. Musicologists or journalists, experts in their respective fields, are the authors of the main entries. Written in a style that can be understood by students of music at all levels, the entire work is well formatted and nicely arranged, with sufficient photographs dispersed throughout. *See also* references indicate related articles in the encyclopedia and each entry has suggestions for further reading and suggested listening. A glossary of musical terms is followed by an extensive bibliography and a complete index. *Music in the 20th Century* is recommended for general music information and basic music library collections, including middle school, high school, and public libraries. [R: LJ, 1 Mar 99, p. 76; BL, 15 April 99, p. 1546; Choice, July/Aug 99, p. 1922; SLJ, Aug 99, p. 186]

—**Louis G. Zelenka**

1071. **Reader's Guide to Music, History, Theory, Criticism.** Murray Steib, ed. Chicago, Fitzroy Dearborn, 1999. 891p. index. $135.00. ISBN 1-57958-143-9.

The body of this work is a set of around 500 bibliographic essays, arranged alphabetically, on such topics as musical style periods and geographical distribution, forms and genres, performance practice, theory, feminism, and composers. It is written by nearly 200 contributors and assisted by 16 advisers. Each article begins with a list of titles, restricted to English-language texts (or if the text is primarily in a foreign language, with sufficient English to warrant inclusion). Most titles are books, with some periodical articles and even dissertations; however, no topic having fewer than two books in English has an article. The articles continue with one or two introductory paragraphs followed by a description of each title in the list. Lengthier articles are subdivided.

All sources mentioned are briefly listed in the back, with references to articles citing them. An index of names, titles of musical works, places, and general topics is provided. In front are two lists—alphabetic and thematic. The user can scan these lists for topics of interest (and because few library customers are in the habit of scanning lists, they may benefit from advice on this practice). Several articles are listed under more than one topic. Cross-references are provided, but on a somewhat arbitrary basis; for example, within the article sequence, a reference leads from "Persia" to "Mode: Non-Western."

Steib's stated aim ("to provide some help to those who wish to explore the wealth or writing on music," [p. vii]) is very general, as is his intended readership. Although the title words "Reader's Guide" imply an initial orientation, the guide also has an unspoken expectation of an adequate general grasp of musical terminology. Not all titles listed receive full approbation from the contributors. Many titles are dated—some by several decades. However, literature on music (and even more so, musical scores, which are out of scope) ages at a slower rate than many subjects—a fact that collection developers working with music materials should always bear in mind. The book's substantial size and weight are also a deterrent to usage elsewhere than a reference collection. These criticisms notwithstanding, the work constitutes a broad perspective on musical literature, and is particularly useful in commenting on potential resources for course instructors and essay writers.—**Ian Fairclough**

Directories

1072. **Schwann Spectrum: The Guide to Rock, Jazz, World ... And Beyond.** Woodland, Calif., Schwann Publications, 1999. 731p. $16.95pa. ISBN 1-57598-053-3.

Since their inception in the 1940s, the numerous incarnations, title changes, and spinoffs of what have been popularly called "Schwann catalogs" have become the preeminent authority for listing currently available recordings. In years gone by, just about every record store would have copies near the cash register, though nowadays e-commerce and a plethora of relevant Websites are regularly consulted as well.

The *Schwann Spectrum* has been published irregularly for the past decade, and is a testament to the continuing growth of the nonclassical music industry. The present volume claims to list all popular music recordings currently available in the United States on CD, LP, and cassette. The popular music field coverage is extensive, including rock, blues, country, folk, rap, dance, instrumental, and vocal pop. Also covered are jazz, television and cinema soundtracks, gospel and religious, international, and New Age. Most of the sections are arranged by artist or group name, except where other arrangements are more suitable, such as the international section being arranged alphabetically by country.

At the end of the volume is the labels section, with the full name of each record label or distributor for the abbreviations used throughout. Though the "How to Use" introduction says that addresses are furnished for each, this is not the case. The vast majority of listings just provide the name for the abbreviation and not the company's address. This obvious shortcoming may be somewhat alleviated by consulting other directories and Websites. Many record shops, who are a primary audience for this guide, will likely have a distribution network in place, and will not need to contact the record companies directly anyway.

Compared to previous editions, the number of LPs, CDs, and cassettes listed has more than doubled: There are approximately 158,000 entries displayed in the tiniest of typefaces. There are some minor format changes, including the integration of new releases into the main listings (previously, these had been separate). Also included are a few forgettable essays on contemporary music topics, and some reviews of recent recordings.—**Richard W. Grefrath**

Discography

1073. Ruppli, Michel, and Ed Novitsky, comps. **The MGM Labels: A Discography.** Westport, Conn., Greenwood Press, 1998. 3v. (Discographies, no.75). $325.00/set. ISBN 0-313-30052-6.

The varicolored brilliance of the recording giant that was MGM meets a strong organizing force in Greenwood Press's hefty discography. Rarely does one come across a reference work that re-creates such an awe-inspiring entity. Whether the musical numbers be classified as evergreens, popular or folk tunes, jazz, film scores, country ballads, or classical, MGM recorded and released some of the finest and most interesting examples. Volume 1, covering the years 1947 to 1960, includes not only single offerings that were made available to the public, but items that were recorded and never released. Users read of entire recording sessions in one of several cities (later trimmed down to New York, Los Angeles, and Nashville), along with the roster of musicians involved in each session. The unified coding system, which undergoes some changes in volume 2 due to changing circumstances, is clear and easy to decipher. The 2d volume, covering 1961 to 1982, bears witness to the gradual changeover from 78 rpm recordings to 45s in the mid-1950s. Volume 3 covers several areas: pop and jazz sessions filed without master numbers, foreign recordings (largely European) leased by MGM, classical releases (listed alphabetically by composer rather than chronologically), and additional labels distributed by MGM. The repertoire represented in the classical listings is eclectic, not just the tried-and-true, and even includes music by two women (Peggy Glanville-Hicks and Marga Richter), a rarity even on more recent labels. The three indexes reinforce the set's user-friendly attitude.

This work is a model of logic and clarity that can be used by neophyte and professional alike. Though its preface admits the possibility that additional information may come to light, this discography is far more than something to use until a better resource comes along. Despite some (surprisingly few) typographical errors, this is a reliable guide to MGM and its career.—**Karin Pendle**

1074. Whitburn, Joel. **Joel Whitburn Presents a Century of Pop Music: Year-by-Year Top 40 Rankings of the Songs & Artists that Shaped a Century.** Menomonee Falls, Wis., Record Research, 1999. 242p. illus. $39.95pa. ISBN 0-89820-135-7.

A Century of Pop Music charts the top 40 songs for each year from 1900 to 1999 (incorrectly labeled as the twentieth century). Because no definitive chart of popular songs existed for 1900 to 1939, various surveys and sources were incorporated to compile charts for those years, such as *Talking Machine World*, Jim Walsh's columns in *Hobbies* magazine, and *Billboard* and *Variety* commentaries. From 1940 through 1999 all chart data are compiled exclusively from the following *Billboard* pop singles charts: Record Buying Guide, Best Sellers, Juke Box, Disk Jockey, Top 100, and Hot 100. This guide also notes the song's peak position and peak date from the chart where it attained its highest position. In the year-by-year section, before each 10-year division (i.e., 1900 to 1909, 1910 to 1919, and so on), an essay describes the era's news and popular music industry. Following the year-by-year section is an artist section where artists are listed alphabetically with their hits that appear in the year-by-year section. Interestingly, Bing Crosby has the most entries with 93 top 40 hits. This is followed by an alphabetic song title section. There are also charts of number 1 hits by decade and top 40 artists by half century and by decade. No index is provided but charts are easily browsed for pertinent information. This is a good purchase for music collections and enthusiasts.—**Cari Ringelheim**

Handbooks and Yearbooks

1075. Duckworth, William. **20/20: 20 New Sounds of the 20th Century.** New York, Schirmer Books/Simon & Schuster Macmillan, 1999. 214p. illus. index. $45.00pa. (with disc). ISBN 0-02-864864-1.

In this reference source Duckworth describes 20 selected composers and their works that have had profound impact upon twentieth-century music. Four criteria are used for selection: the compositions have made a difference in Duckworth's life, have been performed widely and steadily, are available on compact disc, and are likely to become monuments for decades to come. The book is about musical sounds of our time. He begins with 20 questions, such as "How do I begin to try to understand new music?" and "What is the avant-garde?" These are answered from a composer's perspective. Several times he states, "Let your ears be your guide." The essays are roughly in chronological order of the composition.

Many styles are explored, including the serial music of Arnold Schoenberg, the impressionism of Claude Debussy and Maurice Ravel, and the ragtime of Scott Joplin. Duckworth also exposes the use of dissonance by Igor Stravinsky and Olivier Messiaen; the minimalism of Terry Riley, Philip Glass, and Steve Reich; and the mysticism of Arvo Part. Articles on Charles Ives and Aaron Copland exhibit the use of folk and hymn tunes. Other American composers include George Gershwin and Alan Hovhaness, plus those who experiment with new structures or sound sources, such as Ben Johnston, John Cage, Alvin Lucier, Robert Ashley, Laurie Anderson, and Meredith Monk. Duckworth, a composer himself, describes the recorded composition, includes a few quotations by and about the composer, and presents a brief biography. He uses the translated English titles when possible throughout the narration. Each essay contains a photograph or drawing of the composer. For unfamiliar compositions, Duckworth writes an enticing essay. For more familiar works, he provides new insights. The 1st appendix is a long list of 86 works by 57 composers. The timeline of music, people, and events from 1813 to the present is useful, but has some misalignment, with 1960 as the date of President Kennedy's assassination. A bibliographic essay of further resources follows. The compact disc has 19 samples from 18 of the composers; Laurie Anderson and Steve Reich's works were unavailable. Duckworth succeeds in his objective to introduce students to the various styles pioneered in twentieth-century music.—**Ralph Hartsock**

1076. **Schwann Opus—, Winter 1997-98: Reference Guide to Classical Music.** Woodland, Calif., Valley Record Distributors, 1998. 1196p. $39.95pa./yr. ISBN 1-57598-043-6. ISSN 1066-2138.

Schwann Opus is a comprehensive reference guide for classical music recordings (see ARBA 91, entry 1293 for a review of the summer 1990 edition). This quarterly publication lists more than 45,000 currently available compact discs (CDs), cassette tapes, and laser discs. Lists provide complete descriptions of recordings, which are accessed in three sections—new releases (more than 2,300 in this issue), composers, and collections (e.g., instrumental, vocal, film soundtrack, and musical genre). Each list gives the album title as well as titles of musical selections on the recording, their key signatures and opus numbers, name of performing artist(s), name of recording company, format (whether CD or cassette), and other useful data to enable the reader to order recordings. A final section provides addresses and telephone numbers of the hundreds of labels from which recordings in the lists can be purchased.

Each issue of *Schwann Opus* has a handful of lengthy and well-written book and record reviews, but it is intended mainly as a finder's guide. For reviews and ratings of the majority of recordings one must consult other reference works, such as the *All Music Guide: The Expert's Guide to the Best Recordings...* (see ARBA 98, entry 1228) or the *BBC Music Magazine Top 1000 CDs Guide* (see ARBA 97, entry 1055). The criticisms of the companion to this work, the *Schwann Artist Issue*, voiced by another reviewer (see ARBA 90, entry 1236), apply equally to the work in question, but it remains an essential companion for the classical music aficionado.—**Larry Lobel**

Indexes

1077. Palkovic, Mark, and Paul Cauthen, comps. **Index to CD and Record Reviews 1987-1997.** Thorndike, Maine, G. K. Hall/Macmillan, 1999. 3v. $350.00/set. ISBN 0-7838-8191-6.

In 1948 Kurtz Myers began to compile an index of record reviews for *Notes*. This consisted of 137 monaural LPs from 15 sources and occupied 12 pages of that journal issue. By September of 1997, 1,577 compact discs from 7 sources occupied 119 pages of the same journal. This proliferation of the recording industry and recent technological revolution, similar to that of desktop publishing a few years ago, have made the further accumulation of this list unwieldy. In 1948 there were relatively few companies with the capital and other resources to delve into sound recording production. This edition is dominated by compact discs, but notes LPs when necessary. The index is arranged by record label, then by manufacturer's number, including the contents of the recording. Reviews are indicated by 23 abbreviations to journals, from *American Record Guide* and *Fanfare* to *Stereo Review*. Additional symbols indicate whether the reviewer's opinion of the recording was excellent, adequate, inadequate, or no opinion given.

Musical ensemble's recordings of early music have increased, from Anonymous Four to the Baltimore Consort. Volumes 1 and 2 are paged continuously. Many smaller specialty labels (Capstone and Pilz) have been added. Ljubljana Symphony Orchestra, not part of the original accumulation, has 10 entries. This particular accumulation consolidates 40 issues of *Notes*. It is filed letter by letter, but some abbreviations are used instead of the fuller names (CRI instead of Composes Recording Inc.). A major improvement from earlier editions is the identification method used—item numbering, similar to that of Duckle's *Music Reference and Research Materials* and various bio-bibliographies of Greenwood and Garland. Previous indexes to record reviews used page numbers. A header at the top of each page identifies the label (RCA, Sony Classical) for that page. The index of composers gives exact titles or genre of the works reviewed. The performer index is merely a list of the citation numbers. Although it was growing to an unmanageable size for *Notes*, this final accumulation of the index will be indispensable for music libraries and others documenting sound recordings. [R: Choice, Oct 99, p. 306; RUSQ, Fall 99, pp. 92-93]—**Ralph Hartsock**

1078. **SongCite: An Index to Popular Songs, Supplement 1.** Goodfellow, William D. New York, Garland, 1999. 400p. (Garland Reference Library of the Humanities, v.2127). $75.00. ISBN 0-8153-3298-X.

This updates the 1st edition of *SongCite* (see ARBA 96, entry 1309), indexing more than 6,500 recent and standard songs by title, first line, and composer. An additional section that provides an index of songs popularized by musicals, motion pictures, and television shows is included. Like the 1st edition published in 1994, this supplement is a useful resource for finding the music and words to both classic and contemporary songs. *SongCite* includes various genres, such as rock and roll and country, as well as musical theater and "old favorites." In addition, it catalogs 201 music books that are not listed in any other music index currently available. Public and academic libraries using the 1st edition will want to add this supplement.

—**Jean Engler**

INDIVIDUAL COMPOSERS AND MUSICIANS

1079. Fairtile, Linda B. **Giacomo Puccini: A Guide to Research.** New York, Garland, 1999. 381p. index. (Composer Resource Manuals, v.48; Garland Reference Library of the Humanities, v.1906). $75.00. ISBN 0-8153-2033-7.

As composers go, Giacomo Puccini belongs to a relatively recent vintage (he died in 1924). Nevertheless, he has already caused an extensive number of works dealing with his life and works. This guide to research, part of the valuable Garland series that has thus far yielded 48 composer entries, will be of enormous help to music scholars and writers. The book covers what one would expect in a publication of this nature—an exhaustive listing of books and articles dealing with Puccini's operas and other compositions. Each entry is followed by a concise paragraph summing up the book or article featured, clearly describing what can be found in it. Among the features of the book is a chronological listing of Puccini's life that is remarkable in clarity and the amount of information it provides. Out of necessity, a number of publications had to be excluded, a fact that is explained in the foreword. One particular exclusion, however, stands out—Joseph Kerman's *Opera as Drama* (University of California Press, 1988), in which the author took an extended and highly critical view of the composer, and coined the oft-quoted description of *Tosca* as a shabby little shocker. The rest of the book includes discographies and videographies of commercially available Puccini works; a guide to autograph materials, letters, and doctoral dissertations on Puccinian subjects; as well as a thorough general index. [R: Choice, July/Aug 99, p. 1920]—**Koraljka Lockhardt**

1080. Jones, Harold. **Bobby Hackett: A Bio-Discography.** Westport, Conn., Greenwood Press, 1999. 290p. index. (Discographies, no.80). $69.50. ISBN 0-313-30622-2.

Bobby Hackett (1915–1976) first rose to prominence as a lyrical, rhythmically apt Dixieland-cum-Swing cornetist and trumpeter. He later received widespread popularity as the featured soloist on a series of mood music records released by comedian Jackie Gleason. Before the Gleason recordings, however, Hackett was highly regarded among fellow musicians and jazz audiences alike as one of the best disciples of the first outstanding white jazz artist, Bix Beiderbecke. He remained active as a performer until his death.

Harold Jones is a retired building construction cost consultant and an avid jazz enthusiast. In this bio-discography, he has attempted to "cover all (Hackett's) musical activities." Included are a 25-page biography, a 174-page discography, a persons index, a songs index, and a label index.

The discography is an excellent source of information about the hundreds of commercially released recordings that Hackett appeared on, starting in 1937 and going through February 1976. In addition to Hackett himself, some of the bandleaders whose recordings are listed are Benny Goodman, Glenn Miller (Hackett played the famous trumpet solo on "String of Pearls"), Louis Armstrong, Tommy Dorsey, and Eddie Condon. Among the vocalists are Tony Bennett, Rosemary Clooney, and Frank Sinatra. Personnel, date(s), location, song titles with numbers, and information on releases are provided for each recording session. Regrettably, no instructions for interpreting the numbers is given, nor is there any indication of the present availability of the recordings.

The biographical section of the book deals exclusively with Hackett's musical activities and is, for the most part, a mere listing and description of engagements. Also, the writing is not on the level of that of a professional writer or scholar. Although a true biography of Bobby Hackett has yet to be written, this first comprehensive discography is a valuable addition to the jazz research literature. [R: Choice, Oct 99, p. 305]—**A. David Franklin**

1081. Jordan, Douglas M. **Alfred Reed: A Bio-Bibliography.** Westport, Conn., Greenwood Press, 1999. 282p. index. (Greenwood Press Bio-Bibliographies in Music Series). $69.50. ISBN 0-313-30333-9.

Composer, conductor, and educator Alfred Reed (not to be confused with songwriter Blind Alfred Reed) has more than 250 published compositions that are performed throughout the world, and yet little has been written concerning this prolific musician. Some of what does exist is not readily available to American researchers, and thus this volume is a welcome addition to the literature.

Part of the Greenwood Press Bio-Bibliographies in Music Series, this overview of Reed's life and work will serve as the most complete reference until such time as he ceases to compose. It is divided into chapters featuring a brief biography, a catalog of his works, a discography, a bibliography of writings by and about Reed, and appendixes that chronicle his compositions. The biography appears to be based heavily on oral interviews with the composer. Although further editing would have enlivened the narrative, the biographical section is written with admiration and appreciation of both the man and his music.

Large collections on American music, and any collections concerned with band or wind music, will benefit from the inclusion of this title. With so little in print on this respected and popular composer of twentieth-century band music, this will be the resource to consult.—**James Moffet**

1082. Lambert, Eddie. **Duke Ellington: A Listener's Guide.** Newark, N.J., Institute of Jazz Studies and Lanham, Md., Scarecrow, 1999. 374p. illus. index. (Studies in Jazz Series, no.26). $95.00. ISBN 0-8108-3161-9.

The author of this work writes in a highly subjective style and does not hesitate to express his personal assessment of recordings, his evaluation of individual solos on these recordings, and even the musical merits of whole compositions. This makes for enjoyable reading, and one feels that this work is a series of conversations about the creativity of a remarkable musician. This reference contains a lot of information on a musical career that lasted more than 50 years. Although most of the materials covered consist of records, some broadcast sessions and concerts are included. The records are arranged chronologically by chapter, each of which is unified by related time periods. For example, chapter 7 is title "Cotton Club Days." The early recordings of the Ellington band are acoustical, dating from 1924. The author explains how some of the individual musicians obtained specific sounds with their instruments, especially during those earlier years. All aspects of Ellington's musical genius and career are explored—composer, bandleader, pianist, and arranger. Lambert provides details regarding the evolution of Ellington's style, his creativity, personnel changes of the band, road trips by Pullman car and by bus, and recording sessions. Adequate photographs accompany the text. Indexing is thorough. There are four appendixes: a bibliography, a discography, French RCA transcription information, and one titled "The Ellington Musicians and the Dates They Were with the Band." The author died in 1987, and although the work has LP listings, it has been updated with current CDs being listed. This reference will make a valuable addition to the holdings of contemporary music libraries.—**Louis G. Zelenka**

1083. Mustazza, Leonard. **Sinatra: An Annotated Bibliography, 1939-1998.** Westport, Conn., Greenwood Press, 1999. 293p. index. (Music Reference Collection, no.74). $69.50. ISBN 0-313-30829-2.

Frank Sinatra had a multifaceted career as a musician, actor, and concert performer. This bibliography includes information on 85 books and book chapters about Sinatra, more than 600 articles, liner notes to 80 recordings, and several Internet resources. In his annotations, the author sometimes evaluates the content or quality, such as the "touching and very personal piece" written by Bill Boggs. In others he identifies the authority of the writer, such as when he describes Steve Allen as a "well-known comedian, writer, and television personality," or Leonard Feather as the "distinguished music critic and the author of *The Encyclopedia of Jazz*." For the liner notes, Mustazza has chosen only those albums available on compact disc; however, the citation date of the original issue is noted. The date for the compact disc reissue is embedded in the annotation. More than 1,000 articles appeared in the week following Sinatra's death in May 1998. Mustazza has selected 200 of the better articles for an appendix. The index includes several song titles; book and periodical titles; and all persons who had contact with Sinatra, including Presidents Franklin D. Roosevelt, John F. Kennedy, Richard Nixon, and Ronald Reagan, as well as his opposition to Joseph McCarthy. Index entries refer to pages, not to specific citations. Although one can find references to songs like "My Way," those seeking a list of all Sinatra's recorded songs will find lists in the author's book *Ol' Blue Eyes: A Frank Sinatra Encyclopedia* (see ARBA 99, entry 1118). The bibliography reviewed here is essential for documenting Sinatra's career. [R: LJ, Aug 99, pp. 78-80; Choice, June 99, p. 1758]

—**Ralph Hartsock**

1084. Perone, James E. **Carole King: A Bio-Bibliography.** Westport, Conn., Greenwood Press, 1999. 225p. index. (Bio-Bibliographies in Music, no.71). $65.00. ISBN 0-313-30711-3.

Carole King has made such a mark as a composer and a performer that it takes a substantial book with many subdivisions to cover her activities. She began as one of the composers who worked for the publishers in New York's Brill Building (and the surrounding area) writing songs that the publishers hoped to sell to performers who would make hits out of them. In the 1920s the Tin Pan Alley publishers worked on the same concept using gifted performers such as the young George Gershwin to push their wares. In King's time, the songs were promoted with professionally produced demo discs that got released without further work and hit the charts on their own. She was a groundbreaking woman composer of her era. She has gracefully and skillfully moved through several decades' worth of changing musical styles with great success. Many of her early songs have survived over the years by enjoying new popularity with new performers. Some have even reappeared on the charts of best-sellers more than once.

She also became a singer and pianist. Although she always downplayed her performing as only a means of getting her songs to the public the way she would like them performed, her success was often enormous. Her *Tapestry* album became the best-selling pop album of all time (a record since broken). Despite her accomplishments and fame, she never allowed herself to become a celebrity and has retained her privacy in a very public arena. This bio-bibliography, therefore, is light on the "bio" and heavy on the "bibliography."

To cover her output, this work, apart from the brief biography section, has eight major sections: Performance Discography, Miscellaneous Discography (King performing with others or with others using her songs), Composition Discography, Publications, Discography Bibliography, General Bibliography, Composition List and Index, and Index. Shorter sections are devoted to a videography/filmography and to electronic resources. In the performance discography listings, all titles on an album are identified, as are the backup musicians (by name and instrument). The publication listings are also detailed and the bibliography sections are annotated.

Carole King has been a major force in her part of the music world with her songs performed by Barbra Streisand and Ann-Margret as well as by The Monkees and Blood, Sweat & Tears. An important artist and an important career are well documented here.—**George Louis Mayer**

1085. Perone, James E. **Elvis Costello: A Bio-Bibliography.** Westport, Conn., Greenwood Press, 1998. 206p. index. (Bio-Bibliographies in Music, no.70). $65.00. ISBN 0-313-30399-1.

Part of an eclectic series of bio-bibliographies of composers, this guide will appeal to diehard Elvis Costello fans and is recommended for libraries with contemporary music and popular culture collections. An adulatory 12-page biography focuses on Costello's prolific 25-year recording career. This is followed by discographies, a videography and filmography, a list of musical scores, an annotated discography bibliography (reviews), an annotated general bibliography (interviews, profiles, and brief mentions of Costello), and a short list of World Wide Web and CD-ROM sources. There are three discographies: albums, singles, and miscellaneous. The latter is organized by "Elvis Costello as Primary Performer," "Covers of Elvis Costello Compositions," and "Production Work and Guest Appearances by Elvis Costello."

The author has used an easily mastered mnemonic system for cross-references, and has provided two indexes: an alphabetical list of song titles and a more general index consisting mostly of musicians and record producers mentioned in the book.—**Lori D. Kranz**

1086. Smith, John L. **Another Song to Sing: The Recorded Repertoire of Johnny Cash.** Lanham, Md., Scarecrow, 1999. 1005p. index. $85.00. ISBN 0-8108-3629-7.

The recording career of singer and guitarist Johnny Cash is archived in this treatise by author Smith, a longtime friend of Cash. Any song recorded by Cash, either in the studio or at a live performance, that is available to the general public is included, as are a number of songs for which Cash was producer. Masters recorded in studios but still unissued are also found here. Rather than using the discographical format, the author lists all songs in alphabetic order, listing songs recorded multiple times chronologically.

In the main section more than 2,600 entries provide information pertaining to composer; producers; recording locations; dates of sessions (including all overdub sessions); personnel (singers and musicians); and release dates for singles, extended-play and long-play albums, and compact discs. Supplementing the thorough treatment of all the songs is a section called "The Liner Notes," which reproduces notes Cash wrote for album covers. The final section is a combined chronological listing of 40 years of major releases, with annotation, on both U.S. and foreign labels. As Marty Stuart writes in the foreword, "This book will no doubt serve scholars as a well of research and information and it is bound to inspire and challenge any patron of the arts."—**Jan Bakker**

1087. Stockdale, Robert L. **Jimmy Dorsey: A Study in Contrasts.** Lanham, Md., Scarecrow, 1999. 688p. index. (Studies in Jazz, no.30). $79.50. ISBN 0-8108-3536-3.

Jimmy Dorsey began his musical career early, playing cornet in his father's band at the age of seven. By the time of his premature death from cancer in 1957, he had become one of the most important musicians of the big band era, a master of the alto saxophone, a composer, and leader of his own orchestra.

Organized chronologically, this discography of Dorsey's career is exhaustive. Stockdale, also author of *Tommy Dorsey: On the Side*, volume 19 in this series, has even included Dorsey's "possible" and "probable" participation in musical productions. Each chapter covers a period in the musician's life and begins with a short biographical introduction. Then, listed for each recording session, are studio name, city, date, name of group or artist, names of band personnel, and instruments played. Under each matrix number are the title of recording, lyricist, composer, vocal and Jimmy Dorsey solo (if any), place and type of release (e.g., LP, 45 rpm, compact disc), and recording label. In addition to commercial recordings, radio and television broadcasts and Broadway musical and movie participations are included. The author has used a detailed notation system for these numerous items of information, but his explanation for using the book is clear.

The career of Jimmy's younger brother, trombonist Tommy Dorsey, is also covered, but only insofar as it intersects with Jimmy's. This reference book is accessible to readers, as it ends with five indexes: general (people and places); performing artists; recording groups; titles; and concerts, broadcasts, and telecasts.
—**Lori D. Kranz**

INSTRUMENTS

Guitar

1088. **The Complete Encyclopedia of the Guitar: The Definitive Guide to the World's Most Popular Instrument.** Terry Burrows, ed. New York, Schirmer Books/Simon & Schuster Macmillan, 1998. 224p. illus. index. $75.00. ISBN 0-02-865028-X.

Attractively designed and abundantly illustrated, this guide is a good introduction to the guitar, from early fretted and stringed instruments, such as the lute and the gittern, to the twentieth-century acoustic and electric guitars. Milestones in guitar development and design, such as the Fender Stratocaster, the National Style O, and the Gibson Les Paul, are also described. One chapter presents 16 guitar masters on 2-page spreads describing each player's career and preferred instrument(s) and lists a few "classic recordings." The black-and-white and full-color photographs of instruments and their players are not only large and numerous, but also well reproduced. Nearly one-half of the book is taken up by an A to Z list of 200 guitarists providing brief career profiles. A general index and a bibliography end the book.

The title of this guide is misleading—at 224 pages, it is neither complete nor encyclopedic. There are a number of books that treat the history of the guitar in far greater detail as well as books on individual guitar manufacturers such as Gibson and Martin. Nonetheless, this work is full of information and photographs that will delight the guitar aficionado.—**Lori D. Kranz**

1089. Gruhn, George, and Walter Carter. **Gruhn's Guide to Vintage Guitars: An Identification Guide for American Fretted Instruments.** 2d ed. San Francisco, Calif., Miller Freeman, 1999. 581p. illus. index. $27.95pa. ISBN 0-87930-422-7.

This is the 2d edition of a well-received guide written by the best-known vintage guitar dealer in the United States, located in Nashville, Tennessee. The guide is organized under maker and type of instrument.

For each guitar the author describes in detail the production dates, shape and size, woods, pickups, bindings, neck and fingerboard, inlays, peg head, platings, finish, serial numbers, and identification keys. The guide is illustrated with 100 photos including close-ups of guitar detail. In addition to guitars, vintage basses, banjos, mandolins, and amps from selected manufacturers are covered. The 2d edition provides additional material on the very popular Fender and Gibson Tube amplifiers (considered the finest sound producers made by most players). *Gruhn's Guide* is very important to instrument owners, because price can often change drastically over model years. Using the details supplied in this book, readers can determine the exact rarity of the model they have, and hence its value. No prices are given for instruments, but production serial number information is supplied in many cases. There is a good table of contents and a model index. The author has also supplied a brief two-page bibliography that is both general and manufacturer-specific. The reader will get a lot of information for a modest price in this 581-page volume. Instrument owners will be able to obtain a wealth of information on their specific models. Recommended for general reference collections in all libraries. [R: LJ, 15 Oct 99, p. 62]—**Ralph Lee Scott**

Organ

1090. **The Cambridge Companion to the Organ.** Nicholas Thistlethwaite and Geoffrey Webber, eds. New York, Cambridge University Press, 1998. 340p. illus. index. (Cambridge Companions to Music). $59.95. ISBN 0-521-57309-2.

The Cambridge Companions to Music series offers a concise and useful overview of several musical instruments and a selection of composers. This volume, *The Cambridge Companion to the Organ*, is comprised of 3 sections: "The Instrument," "The Player," and "Selected Repertoires." The section on the instrument examines the organ's history; construction; its sound, pitch, and tuning; its case; and current organ building trends. Section 2 deals with the fundamentals of playing the organ, performance practices, and organ music and its relation to the liturgy. The section dealing with repertoires is intentionally restricted because of the subject's great scope. However, the section is successful in concentrating on the major schools of organ literature, including Italian organ music to Frescobaldi, Iberian organ music before 1700, French classical organ school, English organ music to 1700, Catholic Germany and Austria (1648-1800), north German organ school, organ music of J. S. Bach, German organ music after 1800, French and Belgian organ music after 1800, British organ music after 1800, and North American organ music after 1800.

The chapters of *The Cambridge Companion to the Organ* are written by experts in the field; the majority of the authors are British, with only a few from the United States, Australia, or Italy. The volume is illustrated, contains an appendix titled "The Modes and Their Attributes According to Zarlino," has endnotes, is indexed, and has an excellent bibliography. The volume is well laid out and thorough in its coverage, although intentionally limited because of the instrument's long and expansive history. It certainly will be helpful to keyboard scholars as well as to organ students and teachers. *The Cambridge Companion to the Organ* should be included in reference divisions of music libraries.—**Robert Palmieri**

Piano

1091. **The Cambridge Companion to the Piano.** David Rowland, ed. New York, Cambridge University Press, 1998. 244p. illus. index. (Cambridge Companions to Music). $64.95. ISBN 0-521-47470-1.

The Cambridge Companion to the Piano is comprised of 12 chapters by 9 British musical experts. The body of the title is divided into 2 parts. Part 1 focuses on the evolution of the instrument from early forms to the most recent developments and performance practice through this evolution. Part 2 is a discussion of the repertory of the instrument in social and stylistic contexts. Blues, jazz, and ragtime are even included. The title includes an index, a select bibliography, notes to each chapter, 38 musical examples, and 36 figures.

Actually, this book has been negatively reviewed for its lack of focus and editorial finesse (see *Times Literary Supplement*, April 9, 1999, p. 35 and *Independent*, February 1, 1999, p. 5). However, for this reviewer, two chapters redeem the title's blatant omissions. Chapter 5 is a survey of pianists on sound recordings, with the details of stylistic changes of the twentieth century noted, thereby make for fascinating reading. This information is difficult to find in one place. Chapter 6 contains a treatment of acoustics of the instrument, which makes for an accessible and enjoyable read.

Reviewers should keep in mind that this volume, like most of the titles in the Cambridge Companions to Music series, does not claim to be comprehensive. The editor states this in the introduction. However, as a supplement to a good basic collection on the topic, this title offers much.—**C. Michael Phillips**

MUSICAL FORMS

Blues

1092. **All Music Guide to the Blues: The Experts' Guide to the Best Blues Recordings.** 2d ed. Michael Erlewine and others, eds. San Francisco, Calif., Miller Freeman, 1999. 658p. index. (AMG All Music Guide Series). $22.95pa. ISBN 0-87930-548-7.

Primarily intended for consumers, the guide is encyclopedic in nature and could serve libraries well as a reference tool. While it is essentially a guide to the blues, the editors have included gospel singers and groups as well. Entries are arranged alphabetically by surname for individuals, and group name when appropriate. Some artists, like Harmonica Sam, are entered by their "first" name. This organization is somewhat awkward but not impossible to figure out. Each entry consists of a fairly complete biography, followed by an annotated discography of the artist's recordings. Evaluation symbols have been assigned to the recordings deemed as "essential" (an empty star) and "first purchase" (a filled-in star). Each recording is also rated overall with diamond symbols from one to five. Even those recordings deemed as inferior are listed to give the consumer a "Heads-Up" warning. All items are referred to as "Albums" regardless of format. The specific format of a recording is not given. Only the record label is listed. A section on various artists rounds out the alphabetic listing. Following this are several essays on various topics such as "Memphis Blues," "The Blues as Folklore," and "Focus on the Slide Guitar." The writing style is informal and very readable throughout. Recommended for most public libraries, music libraries, and academic libraries supporting blues, jazz, and gospel history courses. Useful for collection development as well.

—**Roland C. Hansen**

1093. Dicaire, David. **Blues Singers: Biographies of 50 Legendary Artists of the Early 20th Century.** Jefferson, N.C., McFarland, 1999. 292p. index. $29.95pa. ISBN 0-7864-0606-2.

Dicaire has great enthusiasm for the blues, as evidenced in his lively essays on 50 blues musicians and singers born before 1940. The book is divided into five parts, four to cover each of the major blues regions—Mississippi Delta, Chicago, Texas, outside the Delta—plus one section on women who the author claims used a variety of styles rather than any one classic tradition. Each biography fills about six pages and is followed by a selected discography. Within each section, the musicians have been arranged by order of their birth (although in two cases this did not occur). The book ends with an appendix of "Recordings by Three or More Blues Singers" (presumably involving those in the book), a selected bibliography, and an index of people and recording companies mentioned. Photographs of the singers would have been a nice addition.

Blues Singers is a good and interesting introduction to blues greats. Readers wanting more blues history or music criticism will find it in Alan Lomax's *The Land Where the Blues Began* (Pantheon, 1993), Lawrence Cohn's *Nothing but the Blues* (Abbeville, 1993), Samuel Charters's *The Bluesmakers* (Da Capo, 1991), and in biographies of individual artists. In addition, a few of the great blues artists who qualify as composers can be found in the new 2-volume *International Dictionary of Black Composers* (see entry 1069).

The blues formed the basis for much of today's popular music. The contributions to American musical culture made by these pioneers are finally being recognized—in some cases, sadly, long after their deaths. One hopes that Dicaire will also publish a volume on blues artists born since 1940.—**Lori D. Kranz**

1094. **Joel Whitburn's Rhythm & Blues Top R&B Albums 1965-1998.** Menomonee Falls, Wis., Record Research, 1999. 347p. $49.95. ISBN 0-89820-134-9.

Through the years *Billboard* magazine has followed the rise and fall of various rhythm and blues albums. These range from soul, funk, disco, jazz, and rap to soundtracks and comedy routines. Singles are in another book (see ARBA 97, entry 1079). The first sequence is alphabetic by artist, with brief biographical information, including birth date and place. Like *Forever Lounge* (see entry 1118), it provides a catalog of near-mint values for commercial recordings. There is also useful information in the entries, such as the names at birth of Cher, Ray Charles, and Queen Latifah. Symbols indicate peak position, total weeks charted, weeks in top 40 and top 10, and weeks in the peak position. Other symbols indicate whether it was a gold (half a million sold) or platinum (million copies sold) record or title. The user's guide clearly shows these symbols and their usage. Each entry also lists the tunes, if known. The top artists are in lists by rank, alphabetic order, and decade. Other useful appendixes and charts provide pictures of the top 40 album covers (all in black and white), top 40 albums by decade, and the most valuable albums. The list of rhythm and blues albums from 1954 to 1964 includes recordings of Count Basie and Louis Armstrong. These statistical charts make this a useful source for the history of rhythm and blues recordings.—**Ralph Hartsock**

Choral

1095. DeVenney, David P. **Varied Carols: A Survey of American Choral Literature.** Westport, Conn., Greenwood Press, 1999. 315p. index. $89.50. ISBN 0-313-31051-3.

Varied Carols is DeVenney's fourth book on American choral music. The first three, *Nineteenth Century American Choral Music: An Annotated Guide* (see ARBA 88, entry 1302), *Early American Choral Music: An Annotated Guide* (see ARBA 89, entry 1218), and *American Choral Music Since 1920: An Annotated Guide* (see ARBA 95, entry 1280), are bibliographies of choral literature. The fourth, under review here, is a monographic survey of American choral music.

In his newest publication, DeVenney places American choral music in a historical perspective. It is chronologically organized from the seventeenth century (the *Bay Psalm Book*) to the present. Each musical era is described primarily through the works of choral music composers, with many accompanying brief discussions of specific compositions. A selective bibliography and an index to titles of musical works examined in the text conclude the book.

Information on American choral music and its composers can be obscure, so this overview is certainly welcome. *Varied Carols* in some ways offers a monographic summary of the literature listed in the annotated guides, but it also presents material not included in any of them. The guides also enumerate many works not noted in the survey. The bibliographies in the annotated guides are valuable. Although the bibliography in DeVenney's newest book may duplicate some of those sources, there are new sources as well.
—**Allie Wise Goudy**

1096. Orr, N. Lee, and W. Dan Hardin. **Choral Music in Nineteenth-Century America: A Guide to the Sources.** Lanham, Md., Scarecrow, 1999. 135p. index. $25.00. ISBN 0-8108-3664-5.

Choral singing became increasingly popular in the United States during the nineteenth century, both in the churches and in secular settings. There is a substantial body of literature dealing with this topic, but bibliographic access to that literature has heretofore been limited. The authors, respectively a professor of music history and a librarian and organist at Georgia State University, have attempted to address that problem by compiling this initial bibliography. The entries are arranged topically and sub-arranged by main entry, beginning with comprehensive musical reference works and ending with studies of individual musicians and with histories of local churches that contain significant material on their choirs. Both published material (books and journal articles) and unpublished theses are included. Music scores and sound recordings are not covered. The citations employ standard bibliographic format, but they do not include annotations. There is an index of authors and main entries.

Although the authors admit that this is only the beginning of the task of documenting the literature of nineteenth-century choral music in the United States, and should be considered as a foundation for future work, not as definitive in itself, they have been able to bring together a great deal of valuable material that has previously been difficult to locate. This volume should prove useful to academic libraries supporting programs in music history and American studies.—**Paul B. Cors**

Classical

1097. Staines, Joe, and others. **Classical Music: The Rough Guide.** 2d ed. New York, Rough Guides/Penguin Books, 1998. 505p. illus. index. $23.95pa. ISBN 1-85828-257-8.

Classical Music: The Rough Guide introduces readers to classical music composers and their musical compositions. The body of the work contains an alphabetic listing of nearly 200 composers along with their major works. Each entry includes a brief biography of the composer, an overview of major compositions, and a discussion of the composer's most notable pieces. Entries also include a listing of CD recommendations with a description of the musical interpretation and the price.

The chronology of composers at the beginning of this work assists readers in finding contemporaries of their favorite composers. A glossary of musical terminology and an index to composers and their compositions are listed at the end. The index could have been left out considering that the work is already arranged alphabetically.

This work's strength is in bringing together both a mini-encyclopedia of composers and a selective review of CDs. For that reason, classical music listeners may find this a better selection than either *The Dictionary of Composers and Their Music: A Listener's Companion* (Wings Books, 1993) or *All Music Guide: The Best CDs, Albums, & Tapes* (2d ed.; see ARBA 95, entry 1256).—**Laura K. Blessing**

Country Music

1098. Goodman, David. **Modern Twang: An Alternative Country Music Guide & Directory.** Nashville, Tenn., Dowling Press, 1999. 439p. $22.00pa. ISBN 1-891847-03-1.

The first comprehensive guide to the "alternative country" music scene, this encyclopedia and guide is packed with information on the history of alternative country, various artists, record labels, publications, and addresses and Websites. Whether it is insurgent country, western swing, progressive bluegrass, cowpunk, or some other subtype, one is likely to find it in this book.

Modern Twang opens with an informative review of the alternative country field. About three-quarters of the book is devoted to an encyclopedic section of hundreds of alternative country performers. The entries are satisfyingly in-depth and present a chronological history of the performer followed by a complete discography. A browse through this section will turn up interesting names of performers from the rock and pop fields of the 1960s and the 1970s who have changed directions, such as Leon Russell and Mike Nesmith.

For those readers who are serious about this kind of music, other sections include books, articles, and reviews about alternative country; addresses and Websites for performers and record labels; a glossary of terms; venue guides; festivals; and radio and television programs around the world.

With the proliferation of alternative country artists in recent years, this book is a well-timed, comprehensive resource that covers both well-known and obscure performers. Alternative country and music history enthusiasts will want this book.—**Mark J. Crawford**

1099. **Joel Whitburn's Country Annual 1944-1997.** By Joel Whitburn. Menomonee Falls, Wis., Record Research, 1998. 700p. illus. $64.95. ISBN 0-89820-130-6.

This reference work draws on the rankings for country music from the trade magazine *Billboard*. The longest section is arranged by the years from 1944 through 1997, and documents the peak position of song titles. In later years, the peak position is subdivided for charts according to jukeboxes, disc jockeys, and best-sellers. The second section is an alphabetic listing, by song title, of every title to peak on *Billboard*'s country singles charts from 1944 through 1997. More indexes are given for top artists by decade and year. A final section has miscellaneous "chart facts and feats" such as "singles of longevity," "songs with longest titles," "songs with most charted versions," and "top country songwriters." At first glance this abundance of statistical riches for record researchers would lead to the business side of country music. Upon closer inspection, this annual provides great primary data for cultural studies from the impact of individual artist icons in American music, such as Elvis Presley and Hank Williams, to the ways that some songs become part of American consciousness. The annual deserves to be part of reference shelves in American studies, cultural studies, and music history collections.—**Simon J. Bronner**

1100. **Joel Whitburn's Top Country Singles 1944-1997.** 4th ed. By Joel Whitburn. Menomonee Falls, Wis., Record Research, 1998. 541p. illus. $64.95. ISBN 0-89820-129-2.

Following the successful format of earlier editions (see ABRA 95, entry 1299), this 4th edition will be warmly welcomed by enthusiasts. It updates the country chart information through 1997, listing more than 16,00 songs by some 2,100 artists. Whitburn and his research staff have combed through multiple charts published in *Billboard* magazine over the years to identify the topic country music singles. Standard information provided in each artist's entry includes a brief biographical note and a chronological listing of each charted hit. For each hit the debut date on the charts, the peak chart position, the number of weeks on the charts, the title on the flip side, the estimated value of a copy in good condition, and the record label and number are given. A rather complex system of symbols allows the user to learn more about he artist or song, including identification of crossover hits, specialty (e.g., comedy, spoken) recordings, biggest hits, and hot streaks of hits. A song title section and several lists of top artists by category enhance the value of the work. The large amount of information contained in this attractively packaged volume make it an indispensable reference for any country music fan or researcher.—**Barbara E. Kemp**

Jazz

1101. Carver, Reginald, and Lenny Bernstein. **Jazz Profiles: The Spirit of the Nineties.** New York, Billboard Books/Watson-Guptill, 1998. 304p. illus. index. $21.95. ISBN 0-8230-8338-1.

One of Carver's goals for this work was to profile today's top younger-generation jazz artists. Each profile contains a succinct biography, an interview, a brief discography, and a performance photograph, all of which is designed to give a natural, not contrived, view of the musician. Lenny Bernstein has 40 years' experience in photographing jazz performers; he provides some text from his experience. A second goal was to introduce 40 artists, ranging from Wynton and Branford Marsalis to Cindy Blackman and Kevin Mahogany. Carver subdivides these by trumpeters, saxophonists, trombonists, guitarists, pianists and organists, bassists, drummers, and vocalists. Most of the musicians interviewed were born in the 1950s or 1960s. Interviews are dated and thus provide a chronological framework. Carver, a practicing attorney, uses his oral skills well in documenting the lives of these jazz musicians.—**Ralph Hartsock**

Operatic

1102. Almquist, Sharon G., comp. **Opera Singers in Recital, Concert, and Feature Film: A Mediagraphy.** Westport, Conn., Greenwood Press, 1999. 376p. index. (Music Reference Collection, no.73). $79.50. ISBN 0-313-29592-1.

"Mediagraphy" is a term newly coined by analogy with "bibliography" to mean a list of sources of information in various media other than print. This mediagraphy lists concerts, recitals, and nonoperatic feature films by opera singers. It is intended as a companion volume to the same compiler's book titled *Opera Mediagraphy* (Greenwood Press, 1993). Although its primary emphasis is on listing concerts and recitals by opera singers, it also includes symphonies, masses, and other liturgical works. Oratorios seem to be left in limbo.

Although the work has been conscientiously compiled over several years, it has some of the weaknesses of a compilation undertaken by a single person. For example, it lacks a sense of chronology. There are no dates for any of the opera singers; it is as if they are all contemporaries. Proofreading in foreign languages, too, is less than perfect. Accents in French and Italian and umlauts in German are sometimes missing and capitalization in those languages is inconsistent or even wrong. At times a cross-reference is cited but no reference is provided. Nevertheless, the work is highly useful, especially in conjunction with the earlier companion volume cited above. [R: Choice, July/Aug 99, pp. 1915-1916; RUSQ, Fall 99, pp. 98-99]
—**John B. Beston**

1103. Boyden, Matthew. **Opera: The Rough Guide.** 2d ed. Joe Staines and Jonathan Buckley, eds. New York, Rough Guides; distr., New York, Penguin Books, 1999. 715p. illus. index. $24.95pa. ISBN 1-85828-456-2.

The content, format, and reasonable editorial policy ensure that this book should have a long and useful life, although, because of its heavy emphasis on the discussion of available CD recordings of the operas included in the guide, it will need frequent revision. A review of the 1st edition can be found in ARBA 99, entry 1157. The book is divided into 8 historical chapters: the birth of opera; Baroque opera; the reformation of opera; the age of Romanticism; Verdi, Wagner, and their contemporaries; opera in transition; the era of modernism; and opera since World War II. Each chapter opens with a brief historical overview of the period covered. Then the composers to be discussed in the chapter are presented in roughly chronological order. Composer entries begin with a biographical sketch followed by detailed discussion of their operas. The opera entries begin with a statement of the date when the work was composed, the date of its first performance, the name of the librettist, and the source of the libretto. A synopsis of the opera is provided along with a historical and musical analysis of the work. An overview of recordings of the opera follows, then specific recordings on CD are ranked and discussed, usually in order of preference. The volume concludes with a directory of singers and a directory of conductors who are prominently featured in the book, a glossary of terms associated with opera and singing, and an index. Illustrations, usually portraits of composers or photos of CD covers, are scattered throughout the text.

An added attraction are 30 feature boxes of brief stories with titles like "Gluck versus Puccini," "Malibran's Desdemona," "Verdi in Rehearsal," and "Carmen the Bodice Ripper." Many readers will welcome the accounts of the 35 composers in the chapter on opera since World War II, because biographical information and accounts of their operas and recordings are not readily available.—**Dean H. Keller**

1104. Griffel, Margaret Ross. **Operas in English: A Dictionary.** Westport, Conn., Greenwood Press, 1999. 978p. index. $125.00. ISBN 0-313-25310-2.

This scholarly and interesting volume is now the standard reference work in its field. Its succinct preface gives informative surveys of opera in the United States, the British Isles, Canada, South Africa, Australia, and New Zealand. It traces the history of opera from its beginnings in the seventeenth century masque to its transition into musical comedy and musical drama. In opera, as in most art forms now, the lines between genres have crumbled.

The slant of the work is markedly American. Entries for American operas or musicals at times supply details of repeat performances, cast, and even evaluations. English operas do not receive the same attention. What most arouses the editor's warm appreciation is American musical comedy; her entries on the musical comedies to which she accords status comparable to that of operas are excellent for the 1970s, but she loses interest when they decline in the 1980s. Although she acknowledges the emergence of musical dramas like "Harvey Milk," she does not quite warm up to them and lists few before her cutoff point of 1996.

The work is thoroughly cross-indexed. By far the largest section is devoted to an alphabetic list of the operas in English, often giving brief story outlines and, in contemporary American operas, details of cast. There are other important indexes for composers and librettists (both usually with dates), authors and sources of the story, and a chronology of opera performances from 1634 through 1966.—**John B. Beston**

1105. Raeburn, Michael. **The Chronicle of Opera.** New York, Thames and Hudson, 1998. 256p. illus. index. $45.00. ISBN 0-500-01867-7.

This companion volume to Alan Kendall's *The Chronicle of Classical Music* (Thames and Hudson, 1994) is an oversized, handsomely illustrated chronology of 400 years of opera history. It is divided into 4 sections by time periods: 1589-1761 (Baroque Opera), 1762-1850 (Classical and Romantic Opera), 1851-1914 (International Opera), and 1915-1997 (The Age of Recording). Each section is preceded by an overview essay and followed by year-by-year coverage of important opera premieres and landmark productions with brief cast and background notes that sometimes include a plot annotation and mention of the work's reception. Both well-known and obscure operas are included (e.g., Tchaikovsky's lesser-known *Voevoda* and *Oprichnik* are covered). Scattered throughout the text are about 100 sidebars that give additional information on topics like famous opera houses; musical trends; and profiles of composers, singers, and specific operas. There are illustrations on every page: 320 in black and white and more than 100 in full color. They depict famous set designs, important scenes, original posters, opera houses, and pictures of important artists and composers. The work ends with an extensive reference section that contains a glossary of opera terms, biographies of 100 important singers, a discography of recommended recordings, a timeline of composers' productive periods, a list of opera premieres arranged by city, and a thorough index that includes references to the illustrations and sidebars. This is an outstanding reference work, particularly for supplying comparative material on opera developments in Europe and the United States. In larger collections, the purchase of two copies of this work might be considered—one for reference and the other for circulation.—**John T. Gillespie**

1106. Shaman, William, William J. Collins, and Calvin M. Goodwin. **More EJS: Discography of the Edward J. Smith Recordings: "Unique Opera Records Corporation" (1972-1977), "A.N.N.A. Record Company" (1978-1982), "Special-Label" Issues (circa 1954-1981), and** *Addendum* **to "The Golden Age of Opera" Series.** Westport, Conn., Greenwood Press, 1999. 925p. index. (Discographies, no.81). $145.00. ISBN 0-313-29835-1.

This volume completes the documentation of the Edward J. Smith private-label opera recordings begun in the author's *EJS: Discography of the Edward J. Smith Recordings* (see ARBA 95, entry 1286). Whatever one may think about the ethical and legal aspects of these recordings (most were made and sold without the concern for the rights of the individuals and organizations involved in the performances), as well as their technical flaws and careless documentation, they remain a fascinating and valuable historical resource. If the authors were not able to solve every puzzle these recordings present, their scholarship has again been formidable, and the wealth of information in their annotations is impressive. All music libraries, sound archives, and private collectors will welcome the publication of this work.

The indexes cover both volumes and include artists, titles of works, live performances, studio broadcasts and telecasts, radio and television programs, Metropolitan Opera broadcasts and telecasts, EIAR and RAI (Italy) operatic broadcasts and telecasts, film soundtracks, LP matrix numbers, and LP titles. There is also a useful bibliography. All institutions and individuals that purchased the first volume will want to acquire this volume to complete the set.—**Paul B. Cors**

1107. Zietz, Karyl Lynn. **Opera Companies and Houses of Western Europe, Canada, Australia, and New Zealand: A Comprehensive Reference.** Jefferson, N.C., McFarland, 1999. 480p. illus. index. $95.00. ISBN 0-7864-0611-9.

In 1995 this author published her book on opera houses and companies in the United States. For the next three years she spent most of her time preparing this companion volume to cover other parts of the world. The most important quality needed to pry historical and present information from an organization must be tenacity. Fortunately, the author has it and has used it wisely. She admits to having friends in Italy "badger" opera houses until they responded, and also acknowledges "some helpful embassy staff in Washington D.C., who both provided information and scolded the houses until they responded." In the flurry of opera house activities, tomorrow is always more important than yesterday, and getting help to accurately write about their history, their current activities, and listings of their staff is more difficult than can be imagined by one who has not tried.

Another quality of the author that has strengthened the quality of the work is understanding the virtues of inconsistency so that some of the more than 300 opera companies covered get more complete or more detailed entries than others. Companies such as the Vienna State Opera or The Royal Opera of London have been written about extensively and accurately in English and can get less attention than some smaller companies that have not been written about at all. The arrangement is by country. Each opera house and company entry gets a short (and often entertaining) history, a list of the company staff, lists of repertory (often limited to a recent period), information about world premieres, and practical information about obtaining tickets and recommended hotels that can give information about opera house schedules and often even obtain tickets for visitors. Photographs (frequently by the author) of the opera houses accompany many of the entries. A specific bibliography ends most entries. Book recommendations by language identify the best general works and are followed by a more conventional bibliography as well as a good, detailed index.

This guide will well serve travelers, young musicians looking for information leading to work opportunities in foreign opera houses, those in need of specific information about specific companies, and those who just enjoy reading about opera from all angles. Both useful and reliable.—**George Louis Mayer**

Orchestral

1108. Clark, David Lindsey. **Appraisals of Original Wind Music: A Survey and Guide.** Westport, Conn., Greenwood Press, 1999. 555p. index. (Music Reference Collection, no.77). $89.50. ISBN 0-313-30906-X.

Players of wind instruments have traditionally been shortchanged in their repertoire, unlike pianists, violinists, and singers, whose scores are readily available and well covered in all manner of publications. This volume aims to fill that gap, and it does it admirably. No music library or professional wind player should be without this valuable resource. The author, however, a retired librarian, has devised a rather convoluted way of finding items in the book. The index never sends one to the page number, but rather to a series of codes. If readers try to look up what Wallingford Riegger has written for wind instruments, they will be sent to F54 and B103, an entry in the chapter on flutes and an entry in the brass instruments section. These chapters can be located in the front index, but since each one of them also has subheadings, it makes for a fairly exasperating search. Once past this classification headache, the book offers a lot of highly useful information, such as the addresses of music publishers and their agents worldwide, an instrumentation index, and an extensive bibliography. Composers' biographical sketches are not included, except for years of birth and death found in the back of the book, along with a list of their compositions.

—**Koraljka Lockhardt**

Popular

1109. **All Roots Lead to Rock: Legends of Early Rock 'n' Roll.** Colin Escott, ed. New York, Schirmer Books/Macmillan Library Reference, 1999. 257p. illus. index. $24.95. ISBN 0-02-864866-8.

In *All Roots Lead to Rock*, Colin Escott presents a selection of liner notes that originally accompanied multi-CD sets from Bear Family Records. Since 1975, the Bear family from Germany has been in the business of producing high-quality, high-priced CD sets of individual musicians. Under the leadership of Richard Weize they have produced sets of such country performers as Jim Reeves and Hank Snow as well as such early rock and roll greats as Screamin' Jay Hawkins, Freddy Bell and the Bell Boys, Conway Twitty, and Frankie Lymon and the Teenagers. As the title indicates, Escott's collection traces the routes of today's rock and roll. The various selections demonstrate that rock and roll—or what would become rock and roll—emerged from different sections of the country. It came from the South of Smiley Lewis and the Mid-West of Julia Lee, from the Las Vegas act of Louis Prima and the African American traditions of Buddy and Ella Johnson, Charles Calhoun, Screamin' Jay Hawkins, and Frankie Lymon. It was black and white, north and south, and all American. So often liner notes appear in a CD set and are read only by the people who purchase those sets. Colin Escott has done a fine service by collecting these valuable essays and presenting them to a wider audience. Many of these selections present as good a biography as readers are likely to come across for lesser-known artists.—**Randy Roberts**

1110. **Billboard Guide to Tejano and Regional Mexican Music.** By Ramiro Burr. New York, Billboard Books/Watson-Guptill, 1999. 256p. illus. index. $18.95pa. ISBN 0-8230-7691-1.

With the popularity of Latin music continuing to grow in this last decade of the twentieth century, there are sure to be many more books of this nature in the future. Latin music can easily be divided into three categories: Latin pop, salsa, and regional Mexican. The book specifically focuses on regional Mexican music and discusses the top 300 groups in this category that have either had popularity for many years or strong commercial success in the last few years.

Billboard Guide to Tejano and Regional Mexican Music begins with an introduction explaining the scope of the work and the sources of information. It then goes on to two chapters that discuss the new trends in Tejano music and the impact its success is having on American culture. The main section of the work is the "A-Z Encyclopedia," which clearly defines many of the instruments and styles of Mexican music as well as describing many of the bands and individual singers of Mexican style. Each entry ends with the band's or musician's record names and who produced them. Cross-references to other entries are indicated with the name or topic in bold typeface. Length of the entries varies depending on the influence of the band or musician but tends to run about half a page. The book concludes with a chronology of Mexican music (beginning in 1897), Burr's top 10 list of albums in 5 different categories, a glossary, and an index.

Because Latin music has become so popular in the past decade, this work will be useful as a supplement to music collections in public and possibly school libraries. It is not scholarly in nature, which might make it a poor choice for college or university libraries. [R: LJ, 1 Sept 99, p. 176]—**Shannon M. Graff**

1111. Helander, Brock. **The Rockin' '60s: The People Who Made the Music.** New York, Schirmer Books/Macmillan Library Reference, 1999. 461p. illus. index. $20.00pa. ISBN 0-02-864873-0.

This reference is a critical and historical discography of rock and soul music in the 1960s, covering major musical artists who have contributed significantly to the development of contemporary popular music. In addition to musicians and singers there are also songwriters, FM radio pioneers, Motown Records founder Berry Gordy Jr., and others who have made significant contributions.

Helander, also author of *The Rock Who's Who* (1996) and *The Rockin 50s* (1998), provides, in the introduction, a brief history of popular music in the 1960s. The main text of the book is arranged alphabetically by either group name or last name of individual artists. Entries include birth and, when applicable, death dates; instrument(s) played by each artist; a narrative history of the group or individual; and an extensive discography that includes album title, record label, album catalog number, release year, and format the album was or is available in. A black-and-white photograph accompanies many of the entries. Appendixes include a bibliography and comprehensive index.

This well-researched, entertaining reference will satisfy a still-intense interest in the 1960s and the recording artists of that time, many who are still popular today. Students doing reports on the time period, as well as the general reader, will find this an essential source. [R: LJ, 15 Sept 99, p. 70]—**Dana McDougald**

1112. **Joel Whitburn Presents Billboard Top 10 Album Charts 1963-1998.** Menomonee Falls, Wis., Record Research, 1999. 530p. $39.95. ISBN 0-89820-132-2.

Billboard magazine began publishing its Top 10 album charts in August 1963. Previously, albums were charted in 2 separate categories, stereo and mono. Joel Whitburn has compiled a chronological list of the Top 10 charts since the consolidated format emerged, a first-ever collection of over 1,800 charts that *Billboard* published every week from August 17, 1963, through December 1998. This book is a quick fix for observing music trends throughout the last four decades, pulling together the hottest-selling music from all genres. Each chart lists the top album titles, noting artist and label, current and last week's position, and number of weeks on the chart. A chart "bullet" indicates an album that made a substantial gain during the week. As an added feature, music titles shown in bold typeface are at their peak popularity. Whitburn finishes up with an alphabetic index of artists, along with the titles and dates of their Top 10 albums. A section on notable number ones reports the slowest and fastest movers to the number one position and the biggest falls. Other lists show which albums spent the most time on the Top 10 list and which artists had the most albums on the list—great for trivia buffs. Record Research produces a variety of similar books, covering everything from pop, country, and R&B singles to pop memoirs from 1890 to 1954.

—**Jean Engler**

1113. **Joel Whitburn's Bubbling Under Singles & Albums.** 1998 ed. Menomonee Falls, Wis., Record Research, 1998. 413p. illus. $49.95pa. ISBN 0-89820-128-4.

The 1998 edition of *Bubbling Under: Singles & Albums* is a delight for the popular music aficionado. This work focuses on the singles and albums from June 1, 1959, through December 27, 1997, that were "bubbling under" the "Hot 100 Chart" and the "Top Pop Albums" but never made it to these top charts. In addition, "Hot 100 Singles Sales," "Hot 100 Airplay Hits," and promotional picture sleeves are new to this edition.

All singles are listed alphabetically, both by artist and by song title. The peak spot and the total number of weeks it held that spot are indicated for each song. Biographical notes are listed for nearly all artists, and title notes are listed for many songs. The album section lists all 178 albums that hit the number 201 spot but did not go to the top 200 position. This list includes an album price guide, artist notes, title notes, listing of tracks, and an album price guide.

A useful "Facts and Feats" chapter lists "Bubbling Under" songs and artist trivia. In addition, the MVP's (Most Valuable Platters) section lists records in the singles section valued at $40 or more. An extended play photograph section shows pictures of the covers of the EPs that hit "Billboard's Best Selling Pop EP's Chart" between October 7, 1957, and October 10, 1957. This is an interesting work that any popular music historian or trivia buff would be happy to own.—**Laura K. Blessing**

1114. **Popular Music. Volume 23, 1998: An Annotated Guide to American Popular Songs....** Bruce Pollock, ed. Farmington Hills, Mich., Gale, 1999. 168p. index. $75.00. ISBN 0-7876-1507-2. ISSN 0886-442X.

This guide has about 100 pages of song listings, in alphabetic order under the title. Alternative titles are also mentioned as well as country of origin, author and composer, current publisher, and copyright date. If it is appropriate, Pollock also includes an annotation on the song, something about its origins or performance history, awards won, or the writer's inspirations.

The balance of the book is indexes and essays. The indexes cover lyricists; composers; performances in movies, musicals, television, or concerts; albums; and Academy Award and Grammy Award nominations. There is also a list of addresses for publishers. The main essay details trends in popular music in 1998.

Some 500 of the "best" songs have been selected. This is a difficult task, as Pollock searches through the royalty agencies ASCAP, BMI, SOCAN, and SESAC for data. He also ventures into the Library of Congress's Copyright Office, trade journals (e.g., *Billboard*), publishers and writers, and perhaps even osmosis. A tough job, but rewarding in its outcome. *Popular Music* goes back in coverage to 1900. What is remarkable now is that this is a century of data about popular culture and its music.—**Dean Tudor**

1115. **Popular Musicians.** Steve Hochman, ed. Englewood Cliffs, N.J., Salem Press, 1999. 4v. illus. index. $320.00/set. ISBN 0-89356-986-0.

In scope, this pricey work presents some 532 articles on the careers of pop musicians in the U.S. since the late 1950s (solo, bands, and groups). The musicians can come from any country, but they must have had impact on the U.S. In this respect, "impact" also includes "jazz" through such players as Miles Davis, John Coltrane, Charlie Parker, Weather Report, as well as folk-types from the first half of the nineteenth century, such as Bob Wills, Jimmie Rodgers, and Robert Johnson. There are 140 contributors listed, with 4 articles each on average, filling 1,205 consecutively numbered pages of text.

Tombstone data include the names of group members (but no cessation dates), names of the new group members (but no dates on when they joined), life dates for the group, date of first album release (but no tracks are listed), and a note on musical styles (pop, disco, hard rock). After the text of the entry, the data conclude with a select discography of singles and albums, selected awards, and cross-references to other artists where appropriate. But there is no bibliography for further reading.

The importance of each group determines the length of the entry. The Beatles get 5,000 words; Garth Brooks, Bob Dylan, and the Grateful Dead have about 2,500 words each. Most articles are 600 to 1,500 words. About 400 of the articles are accompanied by black-and-white pictures. Chart positions of the major songs are noted in the text, but this might be better appreciated at the end of each article, as part of the tombstone data.

In the text of each entry, there does not seem to be any real appreciation for the music—just a time-line of activities. The timeline is incomplete, since there are really very few tracings of the coming and goings of old and new members.

The articles are straightforward. Even so, in the article on ABBA (the first one in the book), there is no mention of its resurgence since its breakup, or mention of the fact that ABBA is the leading group among gays, featuring prominently in pride day parade floats. It was the soundtrack for the major Australian movie *The Adventures of Priscilla, Queen of the Desert* (1994). Indeed, there is no explanation for what the acronym ABBA even means. The writer assesses that ABBA had little influence, yet they were the most commercially successful pop act in the world, even outselling the Beatles. In the Miles Davis article, too many words are presented on "what is jazz?" and Davis' Juilliard career, and not enough on his recording career (the Prestige years are totally ignored!). But at least there is some discourse on his style.

There is a lot of informative material in the back matter. There is a timeline of first releases (1923, Louis Armstrong as a sideman to King Oliver) to 1950s "Fat Man" (Fats Domino), 1954s "That's All Right" (Presley) to 1997s Hanson (*Middle of Nowhere*) album. There are a glossary and a bibliography of both general books and biographies. There are a list of artists by musical styles (e.g., adult contemporary, new age, bluegrass, latin, disco, ska, jazz), an index of song and album titles, as well as a name and subject index.

On balance, the material is fine enough, but a bit thin for the money—unless there is a deep discount for library purchase. Most young users are already surfing the Web for this type of data, getting (in addition) audio and visual data.—**Dean Tudor**

1116. Unterberger, Richie. Dempsey, Jennifer, ed. **Music USA: The Rough Guide.** New York, Rough Guides; distr., New York, Penguin Books, 1999. 486p. illus. index. $23.95pa. ISBN 1-85828-421-X.

The Rough Guides are a well-thought-out series of handbooks to a variety of topics, including music and travel. The music guides include jazz and rock, and roots music. So it only seems logical that the publisher combined the two topics: a travel guide to musical sources.

There are 21 regions are covered, east to west, beginning with New York and ending with Hawaii. The shortest is Muscle Shoals (5 pages); the longest is New York (66 pages). Most of the text is a critical review of the history and development of the musical style of each area, stressing interaction within and without the region. Elements of jazz, folk, blues, rock, and soul are covered almost everywhere, but there are specifics of local domination, such as New York klezmer, San Francisco psychedelia, New Orleans jazz, Southwest swing, and Appalachia bluegrass.

The rest of the text, under each region, is an annotated listings guide to applicable festivals, radio stations, publications, record stores, books, videos, and museums. Two other components here are extremely useful: photographs (especially of record album covers) and commentaries on definitive recordings. There is an index to artists, record labels, and venues.

There is always room for improvement, and next time out the publishers need to add some maps for each region to pinpoint locations so the reader can visualize where, for example, Memphis is in relation to the rest of the Delta. Also, there is a distressing lack of Website addresses that can be useful in keeping the book up-to-date. Finally, many of the record recommendations come from Rhino. This company has done an excellent job of anthologizing American music (along with the Smithsonian-Folkways label). For the ardent collector, it may only be necessary to just buy them all.

This guide, of course, can only skim the surface, emphasizing the most influential and lasting music alone. But still, the chapter on Texas is a revelation in its scope of Tex-Mex music, western swing, blues, rock, folk, and honky-tonk. It is probably the most pervasive influence on American music, especially when Louisiana is added to the mix. This guide is highly recommended.—**Dean Tudor**

1117. Whitburn, Joel. **Joel Whitburn's 1998 Billboard Music Yearbook.** Menomonee Falls, Wis., Record Research, 1999. 257p. $34.95pa. ISBN 0-89820-131-4.

Throughout the year *Billboard* magazine follows the rise and fall of various new hit tunes. Whitburn has consolidated various charts of popular music. Single titles are divided into hot 100, bubbling under 100, country, rhythm and blues, adult contemporary, mainstream rock tracks, and modern rock tracks. Albums are listed by these categories, plus dance music, reggae, world music, new age, jazz, classical, religious, and Latin music. *Billboard 200* is a list of the top popular albums. The "Pop Annual" section is a listing of the top 100 tunes, arranged by their peak position in the ratings: 346 songs made it to the top 100. The "Country Annual" section has a similar structure, listing 260 songs that made 75th or higher. Symbols indicate peak position, total weeks charted, weeks in top 40 and top 10, and weeks in the peak position. Other symbols indicate gold (half a million sold) and platinum (million copies sold) records or titles. The duration of the track is in the "Pop Annual" section only. The hot 100 list serves as an index by performer and includes record label information. An all-inclusive index of song titles is the only feature unifying the yearbook.—**Ralph Hartsock**

1118. Wooley, John, Thomas Conner, and Mark Brown. **Forever Lounge: A Laid-Back Price Guide to the Languid Sounds of Lounge Music.** Dubuque, Iowa, Antique Trader Books, 1999. 303p. illus. $24.95pa. ISBN 1-58221-004-7.

The long-playing record first appeared in 1948. This guide is for collectors of nostalgic music that conjures memories of cocktail hours. Lounge music evokes romance, has been known as "mood music." and is exemplified by artists such as Percy Faith, Tony Bennett, and Frank Sinatra. The authors begin with a brief introduction to the history of lounge music, and descriptions and definitions of various conditions: near mint, very good, good, and fair. Artist, then record label, and manufacturer's number arrange the discography. It includes the record label information, stereo and mono (if available), and year of release (if known). Because most dealers do not stock records in "good" condition only two prices are listed—"near mint" and "very good." There are color replications of several LP covers and sidebars with anecdotes. Most of the records are from the long-playing days (12- or 10-inch LPs). The authors avoided singles and 78 rpm's. They claim not to have a comprehensive discography, listing only those albums that fit a concept of lounge music. Thus, Elmer Bernstein's soundtracks to *The Great Escape* (1963) and *Hawaii* (1966) are included, but not *The Magnificent Seven*. Others included are Duke Ellington's *Afro Bossa* (1962), Jackie Gleason's *Music for Lovers Only* (1953), and Morton Gould's *Music at Midnight*. Unless there were relevant foreign editions, the authors chose mostly U.S. releases, with notations if the album is now available on compact disc. Appendixes include a list of CD collections, and three essays on Mother's (the lounge created for the film *Peter Gunn*), the Seattle scene, and dinner music. Directories include shops selling vinyl discs, clubs that play lounge music, other publications, radio stations that program lounge music, and Websites devoted to easy listening. Collectors will find this guide useful in making purchases of earlier recordings. The reproductions provide a visual history of the LP.—**Ralph Hartsock**

Sacred

1119. **An Index to African-American Spirituals for the Solo Voice.** Kathleen A. Abromeit, comp. Westport, Conn., Greenwood Press, 1999. 199p. (Music Reference Collection, no.76). $65.00. ISBN 0-313-30577-3.

Abromeit's compilation of African American spirituals is actually the first to be published in more than 50 years. Smaller bibliographies of spirituals have appeared in numerous articles and as parts of several books, but this more complete list is the first to appear since the publication of *The Book of American Negro Spirituals* (1926) by James Weldon Johnson and J. Rosamond Johnson. This was followed by *The Second Book of Negro Spirituals* by the same authors in 1927, and William Fisher published *Seventy Negro Spirituals* in the same year. Also, the Cleveland Public Library published an *Index to Negro Spirituals* in the 1930s that was reprinted by the Center for Black Music Research in 1991 (see ARBA 92, entry 1315). The present work includes all of the listings from these earlier efforts and adds many additional titles. The compiler points out that the present work "is an attempt to systematically index some sixty collections scored for solo voice represented at Oberlin [College], supplemented by more comprehensive literature review in online databases. [The work] is not intended as a current source of available materials" (introduction).

The work begins with a bibliography of collections of spirituals (65 in all) with codes for later identification. This is followed by a title index that uses a "uniform" title, a first line index, an alternate title index, and a topical index that categorizes the spirituals into 20 topics (i.e., Christmas, church, death, and praise). When using the compilation, the first line index is most useful since many spirituals are recognized from their first line over the actual title, and often there is more than one title for the same spiritual. The first line index also contains many *see* references from alternate selections that are actually the same spiritual.

American Negro spirituals are extremely important to the study of American music. Many themes running through the music in the United States and Canada originated in spirituals. While there are many collections of spirituals in print, it has been difficult for musicologists and music scholars to work with them due to the lack of a complete list. Abromeit has compiled a list that casts light on this lack of cataloging.

An Index to African-American Spirituals for the Solo Voice is highly recommended for all music collections. It will be especially valuable to larger public and academic collections that may have a number of the original spiritual collections. It will also be a valuable source to be collected by individuals who work with choirs or otherwise study this form of music. [R: Choice, Sept 99, p. 106]—**Robert L. Wick**

26 Mythology, Folklore, and Popular Culture

FOLKLORE

1120. Coughlan, Margaret N., comp. **Folklore from Africa to the United States: An Annotated Bibliography.** repr. ed. Washington, D.C., Library of Congress; repr., Detroit, Omnigraphics, 1999. 161p. illus. index. $40.00. ISBN 0-7808-0314-0.

This selective annotated bibliography, indexing works available in Library of Congress, was developed to promote understanding of African culture among Americans and Europeans. Many of the items listed were prepared in textbook formats, for government study, and to preserve purity of cultural roots. Arranged geographically by sections of Africa, the West Indies, and the United States, each geographic section begins with an abstract on the tribes, types of stories, and background, and is further broken down into subsections for adults and children. Missionaries, scholars, and others of a culture better known for its oral histories than for its written ones, capture prisms of cultural clarity as still lifes in writing. Most books are compiled research on certain aspects of African society, tradition, and folklore.

This annotated bibliography is an education on the subject of Africa and paints a colorful picture of a culture oozing with vibrancy and life worth preserving. Black-and-white illustrations, while adding atmosphere and validity to the bibliography, show diversity in art styles and forms. This volume is recommended for academic institutions supporting an African curriculum, for specific cultural and linguistic studies, and as an introduction to customs, mythology, legends, poetry, and language patterns of tribes mentioned.
—**Kimberley D. Harris**

1121. **The Folklore of American Holidays.** 3d ed. Hennig Cohen and Tristram Potter Coffin, eds. Farmington Hills, Mich., Gale, 1999. 573p. index. $105.00. ISBN 0-8103-8864-2.

Arranged by the calendar year, this compendium contains 140 religious, political, seasonal, and regional holidays celebrated in the United States and includes more than 630 items. The editors state that the "traditional lore surrounding a given holiday, regardless of its origin, comprises the heart of the book." This certainly seems to be the case. Each entry is unique in that the information presented depends entirely on the type of folklore that could be obtained. For example, the section on St. Valentine's Day consists of eight pages, with entries as diverse as "Valentine's Day in the Classified Ads," "Valentine's and Lupercalia," "Signing an 'X' for a Kiss," recipes, and "Valentine's Massacre and Its Ghosts." The entry for August 16, the anniversary of Elvis Presley's death, is four pages long and is comprised more of excerpts from articles tackling such topics such as "Taking Care of Elvis," "Did Elvis Fake His Death," and "Elvis and an NFL Exhibition Game."

The preface explains the rationale and format of this volume and the introduction covers the development of formal calendars; agricultural communities and the seasonal cycle; the pagan influence on Christian holidays; and the three types of folk festivals, genuine (May Day), revived (Ground Hog Day), and fabricated (Mother's Day). There are five indexes to round out the journey through the year: the subject index; the ethnic and geographic index; the collectors, informants, and translators index; a song titles and first significant lines index with specific indicators to musical scores included in the text; and a motif and tale index. There is no indexing of the holiday entries that include recipes.

This is a volume that is not only informative but also fun to browse. Although some of the holidays are universal and celebrated elsewhere, there are many that are place specific, and for that reason this reference can be recommended for public libraries and school libraries in the United States and for collections in other places that have a strong Americana section.—**Gail de Vos**

1122. Fritze, Ronald H. **Travel, Legend, and Lore: An Encyclopedia.** Santa Barbara, Calif., ABC-CLIO, 1998. 443p. illus. index. $75.00. ISBN 0-87436-759-X; 1-57607-127-8pa.

This eclectic gathering of real and imaginary destinations and people of yore makes fascinating reading for storytellers, educators, and secondary and college students. Fritze asserts that the focus of the entries is on the expectations of travelers before the twentieth century and that the aim is not to be exhaustive but to be comprehensive. Browsing through the encyclopedia takes the reader from the wanderings of Aeneas and other Greek and Trojan heroes to the wagon trains of the American west. It is populated with entries on people and creatures, such as assassins, circuit riders, Gogs and Magogs, Margery Kempe, and St. Christopher. Along with these legendary names nestle commentaries on places such as the Great Sea of Darkness, the Holy Land, the Indian Ocean, and Timbuktu as well as things like the Alexandrian library and museum, the Grand Tour, Griffins, crossing-the-lines ceremonies, and El Dorado.

The entries are of varied length, but each is concluded with cross-references and suggestions for further reading. Imaginary ancient and historic persons, places, and things are alphabetically arranged within the encyclopedia. A bibliography and comprehensive index follow the main body of entries. Various photographs and sketches break the pages of text. The well-written entries are well researched with commentary on the research by the author. The only complaint is that the first part of each entry is a definition presented as a sentence fragment that may be quite complex in structure, but still jarring when first read.—**Gail de Vos**

1123. Knuth, Bruce G. **Gems in Myth, Legend, and Lore.** Thornton, Colo., Jewelers Press, 1999. 296p. illus. index. $45.95pa. ISBN 0-9643550-1-9.

Through the ages gems have been used not only for adornment but as a source of protection and power. The introduction to this volume discusses gems as talismans and amulets, suggests practical explanations for their supposed medicinal uses, and gives the etymology of their names. Description of crystal shapes and forms leads to a historical survey of early writings about gems from Theophrastus and Pliny the Elder to Christian writings and modern times. Not until 1934 did gemology become standardized. Interest in the mythic lore of stones continues today.

The heart of the book is an alphabetized modus lapidarium of 46 gems ranging from agate to zircon and ending with various mythological stones such as the toad stone. Under each gem is a colored photograph of the stones; a table of jeweler's information giving hardness, color, refraction, and chemical composition; and the lore and legends bracketed by large margins that contain a drawing of the crystal system, quotations from literature, illustrations of old woodcuts, and alchemy and chemist signs.

Other sections give quotations about gems from the Bible, the stones of the New Jerusalem as they appear in Marbode of Rennes (1035–1123), and gems in the plays and poetry of Shakespeare. Birthstones in various religions and countries and belief in the power of certain shapes are also discussed. Several appendixes list biblical and Hindu gems, planetary and zodiacal influences, meaning in dreams, and therapeutic use.

Endnotes and a crucial index provide sources for further reading and make the volume easier to use. Students of myth and lovers of jewelry, as well as jewelers, will learn much from this book.

—**Charlotte Lindgren**

1124. Snodgrass, Mary Ellen. **Encyclopedia of Fable.** Santa Barbara, Calif., ABC-CLIO, 1998. 451p. illus. index. (ABC-CLIO Literary Companion). $65.00. ISBN 1-57607-026-3.

This volume represents an ambitious attempt to embrace all aspects of the fable (and major subgenres) as it has developed throughout the ages. Snodgrass defines fables as "witty, comic, and disturbingly accurate morality tales" (p. xiii) illustrating human foibles, national embarrassment, and cultural downfalls through comparing humans to animals. The subgenres identified and discussed by the author include cruelty jokes, exemplary tales, pourquoi stories, and the art of storytelling. "As a character builder, [the fable] has given the parent, preacher, teacher, and political exhorter just the right story to lighten a spiritual load or ease a ticklish situation" (p. xvi).

Organized by alphabetic entries, the book contains articles of various lengths on the different aspects of fable and its relatives. The average entry is three to six pages of well-written and insightful documented text followed by cross-references as well as reference sources including Internet addresses. Large photographs and illustrations dot the volume and add to the understanding of this vast topic. The entries are followed by several appendixes "to assist the student, writer, scholar, and classroom teacher." The first, a timeline of fable, begins at 2300–2200 B.C.E. with a listing of an anonymous Babylonian fable, *The Tamarisk and the Palm*, and retires with several books of fables and animal tales published in 1995. Snodgrass also provides a comprehensive listing of major authors of fable and fable-based literature, films based on fables (such as the 1994 releases *Thumbelina* and *The Lion King*), the major sources of fable, primary sources of texts, audiovisual and Internet material, and a bibliography with Internet resources.

Extensive entries explore the cultural history of Hispanic, Christian, Latin, and Native American fables among other cultures and eras. Several famous characters are also given their own entries, including Brer Rabbit and Reynard the Fox. Readers will discover not only the historical background of the fables, including their publishing history, but will also be led to literary connections both classical and contemporary. From the ancient Greeks to Chaucer to George Orwell's *Animal Farm* and Richard Adams's *Watership Down*, the book canvasses and encompasses all manners of animal tales. These entries also include public reactions to the texts and discussions of audiovisual interpretations. Space is dedicated to the art of storytelling as well as to various internationally acclaimed contemporary tellers from the United States, the United Kingdom, Australia, and Canada. There are surprising, but ultimately logical, entries in this volume, such as articles on tricksters, illustrators, Robert Louis Stevenson, Jacquetta Hopkins Hawkes, and Anansi. This is a fascinating and thorough discussion of fables in their widest sense. [R: LJ, 1 Feb 99, p. 78; Choice, May 99, p. 1594; BL, 1 May 99, pp. 1614-1616; SLJ, Aug 99, p. 187]—**Gail de Vos**

1125. Strauss, Emanuel, comp. **Concise Dictionary of European Proverbs.** New York, Routledge, 1998. 491p. index. $165.00. ISBN 0-415-16050-2.

To provide a reference book more concise and accessible than his previously published 3-volume *Dictionary of European Proverbs* (Routledge, 1994), multilinguist Emanuel Strauss has created this 1-volume edition. Proverbs have been divided into semantic groups and arranged alphabetically by the first word of the English form. Although there are only 1,803 numbered groups, there are thousands of proverbs since each group contains many variations. Some seem interpreted almost too broadly, such as when "a bad bush is better than no shelter" is joined with "there is no little enemy." While there are no proverbs from non-European languages or in any alphabets other than Roman, 29 languages are included, ranging from Catalan to Yiddish.

A lengthy select bibliography contains the major works on proverbs in many languages, including those classified as Latin, Romance, Scandinavian, Slavic, and German as well as English. Even though some proverbs fall into more than one category, they are easy to locate. On the top of each double page the first English quotation listed appears on the verso and the last English quotation on the recto. The quadruple-columned, 117-page index lists the first word of every proverb in whatever language it appears, identified by its abbreviation as listed on the introductory page of the index, and is followed by the number of its semantic group or groups. The volume is designed for serious scholars, but even a casual reader interested in the way different nationalities have coined similar aphorisms would enjoy browsing in this dictionary of common proverbs. [R: Choice, Sept 99, p. 106]—**Charlotte Lindgren**

1126. Van Scott, Miriam. **Encyclopedia of Hell.** New York, St. Martin's Press, 1998. 308p. illus. $16.95pa. ISBN 0-312-24442-8.

The *Encyclopedia of Hell* is an explanation of the underworld, offering depictions of Hell utilizing a wide range of genres including myth, religion, literature, theater, art, music, film, television, and pop culture. Sources for this work include African legends, Asian folktales, and familiar infernal chronicles from Western lore. The encyclopedia's broad range is both its strength and its weakness. Within the volume one can make connections between ideas of Western and non-Western concepts of Hell. However, the publication also contains an unevenness and cursory treatment that will be frustrating to users. Miriam Van Scott created a reference book with many short articles about Hell and the afterlife from various cultural traditions that vary in depth of scholarship. Most of the literature categories contain useful basic information, such as on Blake and Dante, while other genres such as popular culture are sketchy (e.g., tattoos). With entries ranging from Virgil's *Aeneid* to the 1994 noir film *Dark Angel: The Ascent*, the reader is led through a cultural historical journey of Hell. Folklore and its disciplinary relations seem to be avoided, but they create an integral part of thematic areas in this volume, such as the supernatural; magic; alchemy; witches and witchcraft; devil and demons; gods and goddesses; mysterious creatures and lands in myth and legend; creation myths, beliefs, and customs; psychology and paranormal; and rites of passage. All entries are organized alphabetically. Because of the gamut of entries and no index, specific searching is cumbersome. The illustrations, especially graphs and tables, are very useful. This work could provide inspiration for writers, and is recommended for individuals interested in browsing. Appropriate in public libraries and colleges. [R: LJ, 1 Sept 98, p. 175; BL, 15 Feb 99, p. 1088]—**Magda Želinská-Ferl**

MYTHOLOGY

1127. **Cassell's Encyclopedia of Queer Myth, Symbol, and Spirit.** By Randy P. Luncunas Conner, David Hatfield Sparks, and Mariya Sparks. London, Cassell; distr., New York, Continuum Publishing, 1997. 382p. index. $21.95; $15.95pa. ISBN 0-304-33760-9; 0304-70423-7pa.

In the introduction to this unusual and engrossing reference work, its three accomplished authors state that gay mythology, folklore, and religious practices have been distorted or suppressed throughout history. It is their purpose to help "reinscribe" the "narrative, figures, symbols, etc. pertaining to gender and sexual variance." This is accomplished admirably in more than 1,500 alphabetically arranged entries on deities, traditions, customs, and related subjects on the world's spiritual traditions involving gay, lesbian, bisexual, and transgender lore. Although most of the entries are 10 to 20 lines in length, some extend over several pages (the longest, at seven pages, deals with the galli, transgendered priests of Goddess Cybele in ancient Rome, and the efforts of St. Augustine to suppress this sect). Although more than 90 percent of the subjects are mythological or historical in nature, modern writers, artists, and leaders (e.g., Desmond Tutu, Clive Barker, Bill T. Jones, Allen Ginsberg) are included if their work reflects gay spirituality and traditions. In a fascinating 40-page preface titled "Spiritual Traditions," the authors introduce the world's major religions, mythologies, and such related topics as witchcraft and women's spirituality, and describe their attitudes and traditions related to homosexuality. The book concludes with an extensive, valuable bibliography and a thematic index in which entries are arranged under broad subjects like "Amazons, Heroes, Warriors," "Death and Afterlife," and "Judaism." There are no illustrations. This book was not intended to be a substitute for any of the standard reference works on folklore and mythology; however, as a specialized reference that relates these topics to gay spirituality, it succeeds commendably. [R: Choice, April 99, p. 1434]—**John T. Gillespie**

1128. Dixon-Kennedy, Mike. **Encyclopedia of Greco-Roman Mythology.** Santa Barbara, Calif., ABC-CLIO, 1998. 370p. index. $65.00. ISBN 1-57607-094-8; 1-57607-129-4pa.

Although there is no shortage of good encyclopedias of Greek and Roman mythology, this new one is deserving of a place on school and public library shelves. It is a straightforward alphabetic list of all of the gods, people, and places described in the works of the standard classical authors. The brief entries are of varying lengths—from one short sentence to a page or more—depending on the importance of the subject. To simplify matters, Dixon-Kennedy provides no citations but, instead, states that the information is derived primarily from Homer's *Odyssey* and *Iliad*, Virgil's *Aeneid*, and Robert Graves' *The Greek Myths*. That covers just about everyone and every place, and, as Dixon-Kennedy points out, there is a wide range of readily available sources that can be used to obtain additional information. There is a good nine-page bibliography that helps identify those sources. There is also a brief chronology of the history of ancient Greece and Rome, a chronological listing of Roman emperors, and an index. Other works, such as Michael Grant and John Hazel's *Who's Who in Classical Mythology* (ARBA 94, entry 1393), provide similar information and, for the most part, the older standard texts, such as *Bulfinch's Mythology* (Random House), are as useful as newer publications. Despite recent cultural changes, classical mythology remains an educational staple that requires tools that provide basic information. This is an excellent supplemental text that may be, for many smaller libraries, perfectly adequate as a primary source of such information. [R: BL, 15 Feb 99, p. 1088; Choice, June 99, p. 1756]—**Norman D. Stevens**

1129.   Dixon-Kennedy, Mike. **Encyclopedia of Russian & Slavic Myth and Legend.** Santa Barbara, Calif., ABC-CLIO, 1998. 375p. illus. index. $65.00. ISBN 1-57607-063-8.

This book is a general guide to the myth and legends of the Slavic people and neighboring countries such as Hungary, Romania, and Sweden. Some historical, geographical, and biographical information has been included to give cultural and geographical background for cited material. This work is arranged in an encyclopedic format. A short preface is followed by "How to Use this Book," listing several conventions that make cross-referencing easier and the text more decipherable. Headwords with alternative spellings are given under the main entry within the book and variant spellings are given their own shorter entry, referencing the main entry. A separate entry of the people, places, or objects mentioned within an entry are listed at the end of the entry. The end of some entries contains references.

Following is a brief historical and anthropological detail of Balts, Slavs, Finno-Ugric, and other peoples. The main body of the encyclopedia begins with a useful map of the area and continues with alphabetically arranged entries. Subject coverage varies greatly in length, but missing are some important topics such as the legendary Polish and Slovak hero Juro Janosik. References and lists of further readings also omit important information (e.g., 1992 Algirdas J. Greimas's *Of Gods and Men: Studies in Lithuanian Mythology* [Indiana University Press]). The references are followed by four appendixes: a glossary of terms, a transliteration, a list of the rulers of Russia, and a topic finder—organized by country and category. The last section is a useful index. While Dixon-Kennedy's encyclopedia does not have depth for scholars, it is an excellent resource for readers interested in folklore and mythology, and the Slavic and Balto-Slavic areas. It will profit high school students. Recommended for libraries and schools. [R: Choice, May 99, p. 1592; BL, 15 Feb 99, p. 1088; SLJ, Aug 99, p. 182]—**Magda Želinská-Ferl**

POPULAR CULTURE

1130.   Ash, Russell. **Factastic Book of 1001 Lists.** New York, DK Publishing, 1999. 208p. illus. index. $19.95; $14.95pa. ISBN 0-7894-3769-4; 0-7894-3412-1pa.

The world's most famous criminals, countries with the most workers, oldest underground railroad systems, largest flightless birds—these are just 4 of the 1,001 superlative-type lists included in the *Factastic Book of 1001 Lists*. It is divided into 11 general sections such as "The Arts," "World Sports," " and "Science," and further into 2-page spreads such as "Travel and Tourism," "Insects and Spiders," and "Murder and Punishment." The lists are presented in box format and accompanied by colorful illustrations. A general index is provided. Ash, also author of *The Top Ten of Everything* (see ARBA 99, entry 63), has derived his data from many sources—print, online, and "experts"—but for the most part does not provide specific sources. This makes the volume less a reliable reference than a fun book for the browser and the trivia buff. [R: BR, Sept/Oct 99, p. 77]—**Lori D. Kranz**

1131. Christen, Kimberly A. **Clowns & Tricksters: An Encyclopedia of Tradition and Culture.** Sam Gill, ed. Santa Barbara, Calif., ABC-CLIO, 1998. 271p. illus. index. $65.00. ISBN 0-87436-936-3.

Reading an encyclopedia from front to back covers is not usual practice because such volumes are most often fact-filled, formulaic references meant for occasional dipping. Christen's *Clowns & Tricksters* is different, made up of selectively compiled, well-crafted entries written in narrative form. Altogether, more than 200 clown or trickster characters from all regions of the world—antiquity to the present—are presented in what the author modestly calls a starting point. Christen tries to show both similarities and differences among cultural representations of these characters, while at the same time placing them within specific cultures and relating how they were received there. In an insightful and brief introduction, she discusses "bias against humor" as a long-standing tradition in Western intellectualism, only recently broken in the social sciences and humanities.

What makes this encyclopedia exceptional is the way Christen brings these humorous, powerful, greedy, obscene, scary, selfish creatures to life, especially by recounting fascinating tales about them. Some of the characters are rather well known and expected, but there are occasional surprise entries, such as the one on Ken Kesey and the Merry Pranksters of the United States. *Clowns & Tricksters* also benefits from numerous illustrations, an entry list by culture areas, much cross-referencing, and a 17-page bibliography.

This book is more than a starting point; it is an important guide for students, scholars, and anthropologists interested in clowns and tricksters, as well as an interesting compendium for all of us, relating how humans for centuries have used stories to explain their world. [R: LJ, 15 Mar 99, p. 66; BL, 15 Feb 99, p. 1086; Choice, July/Aug 99, p. 1925]—**John A. Lent**

1132. **Festivals and Holidays.** New York, Macmillan Library Reference/Simon & Schuster Macmillan, 1999. 479p. illus. index. (Macmillan Profiles). $75.00. ISBN 0-02-865378-5.

Festivals and Holidays covers the major Buddhist, Christian, Hindu, Islamic, and Jewish holidays; national holidays from around the world; important ancient festivals; and newly established holidays, such as Earth Day and World AIDS Day. The history and significance of each holiday is described in two to three pages in an easy-to-read style and large print.

Festivals and Holidays is one in a new group of reference books published by Macmillan that are written for the social studies and history curriculums of high schools and junior highs. More than one-half of the articles have been selected from other Macmillan titles, such as the *Encyclopedia of Religion* (CD-ROM ed.; see ARBA 98, entry 1353) and rewritten for a younger audience. The remaining articles have been newly written for this title by leading authorities in world history. All the volumes in the group are very readable and include timelines, definitions, a glossary, sidebars with interesting asides, quotations, a suggested reading list, and an extensive index. *Festivals and Holidays* has a useful chronology of holidays by date, an index by holiday and country, and more than 85 photographs illustrating the book. Although the information is not new, the attractiveness and readability of *Festivals and Holidays* make it a popular choice for high school, middle school, and public libraries.—**Carol D. Henry**

1133. **Holidays and Anniversaries of the World: A Comprehensive Catalog Containing Detailed Information on Every Month and Day of the Year....** 3d ed. Beth A. Baker, ed. Farmington Hills, Mich., Gale, 1999. 1184p. index. $105.00. ISBN 0-8103-5477-2.

This resource is for anyone who has ever needed a perpetual calendar to figure out the day of an important event. This work also has a glossary of time words, the projection of movable holidays for the years 1999 through 2004, and a history of the development of our modern calendar.

There is an entry for each date, January 1 through December 31. Each entry lists Saints' days, Blesseds' days, major events in world history, and holidays and anniversaries of most nations as well as special days, birthdays, events, and religious and civil observances. Included are updates to entries in previous editions and new material to cover recent events. A 204-page index of names, terms, and events concludes the volume. This reference work will be a welcomed addition to any collection for finding such information as the exact date of the bombing of the Murrah Building in Oklahoma City, Shaquille O'Neal's birthday, or the date of the siege of Orléans.—**Sue Brown**

1134. Marks, Diana F. **Let's Celebrate Today: Calendars, Events, and Holidays.** Englewood, Colo., Teacher Ideas Press/Libraries Unlimited, 1998. 337p. illus. index. $35.00pa. ISBN 1-56308-558-5.

Let's Celebrate Today: Calendars, Events, and Holidays is a teacher and librarian resource that takes each day of the year and lists important events and birthdays of famous persons for that day. At the beginning of each month, a history of the month's name is given. Month-long events and special days are listed. Following several of each day's individual entries for both events and birthdays, the author suggests activities that can be done with students. Some Website addresses and telephone numbers of organizations to contact for further information are also included. The book contains a table of contents, strategies for using the book, a bibliography, and an index. One interesting inclusion in the book is an introduction to time with calendars listing dates of major holidays for Christians, Jews, Muslims, and Hindus. Although other books have been written that contain much of the same information, this new entry into the field is interesting and should prove useful, especially because of its currency. [R: BR, May/June 99, p. 87]—**Janet Hilbun**

1135. Melton, J. Gordon. **The Vampire Book: The Encyclopedia of the Undead.** Farmington Hills, Mich., Visible Ink Press/Gale, 1999. 919p. illus. index. $19.95pa. ISBN 1-57859-071-X.

This timely volume presents a compendium of myth, folklore, fiction, and purported realities of vampires. With his endorsements from the Count Dracula Society and Vampire Studies, the author presents this collection from inside the perspective of "believers." Melton is the head of the Transylvania Society of Dracula's American Chapter and a traditional scholar and minister as well. The encyclopedic organization of the text and the 250 photographs are brought together with an effective list of organizations, resources, magazines, Websites, and other sources of information. This lighthearted book has a surprising depth of research on the origins and continuity of the tradition. The references are thorough and excellent. The material is fascinating for those who are curious. Fans, students, and the general public will enjoy and learn from this encyclopedia. [R: Choice, June 99, p. 1758]—**Linda L. Lam-Easton**

1136. Spinrad, Leonard, and Thelma Spinrad. **On This Day in History.** Revised by Anistatia R. Miller and Jared M. Brown. Paramus, N.J., Prentice Hall, 1999. 380p. index. $16.00pa. ISBN 0-7352-0064-5.

With more or less one page per entry, this volume is arranged chronologically by month and day of the year. For each date, a brief list of events (e.g., births and deaths of notable persons, wars, legislation, inventions, firsts, and other noteworthy historical facts) is presented, followed by a few sentences of text that explicate a few of the items included in the list. A brief page of introduction is also provided for each month. There are 16 pages of black-and-white photographs or illustrations tucked in the middle of this volume, and an index supplements the major text.

Editorial selection and arbitrary inclusion result in a work that might best find a home in the collections of public and school libraries. By no means exhaustive, the work is marginally comprehensive in that some items are included, whereas others are not. For this reason, it will always need to be complemented by additional reference tools as part of any search. As a quick review of major historical events, or an introduction to what the editors call "intriguing snippets of lore," the work is interesting; however, its reference value is limited.—**Edmund F. SantaVicca**

1137. Taborelli, Giorgio. **Icons of the Century.** Hauppauge, N.Y., Barron's Educational Series, 1999. 262p. illus. index. $29.95. ISBN 0-7641-5201-7.

Heavily illustrated and full of historical and cultural detail, this volume will more likely find its way onto coffee tables and into leisure libraries than into the reference collections of major libraries. Arranged chronologically, the work is divided first into decades. Within each decade it is then divided into individual years. For each year, a particular individual (or group) has been selected as the focused highlight of that year, by virtue of their historical and cultural importance. About 10 to 12 photographs or other artwork accompany each entry, enhancing the print biographies. Two brief introductory essays open the work, while two brief essays provide reflection at the end of the volume. The book concludes with a bibliography and an index of names.

This work has true eye appeal, and indeed its main value may be in capturing the essence of the times through photography and image rather than generalized and objective history. Everyone from Queen Victoria to Marie Curie and Boris Yeltsin to the Beatles is included, along with other artists, scientists, builders, leaders, thinkers, warriors, film stars, music idols, and villains. Given the scope of inclusion, it is obvious that this is an editor-selected list of major contributors to social and cultural history. As such, it is likely to contend with many such retrospective books scheduled to appear at century's end. This volume is recommended for libraries with strong collections in cultural history, and others that might benefit from such a tool.—**Edmund F. SantaVicca**

1138. **The Ultimate Encyclopedia of Fantasy: The Definitive Illustrated Guide.** David Pringle, ed. Woodstock, N.Y., Overlook Press, 1998. 256p. illus. index. $35.00. ISBN 0-87951-037-1.

Though it is mistitled and is far from being an ultimate encyclopedia of anything, much less fantasy, *The Ultimate Encyclopedia of Fantasy* is substantially more than the coffee-table book it resembles. Accompanying the hundreds of lavish and enjoyable illustrations is a text that is more often than not acute, witty, and perceptive. Apart from Pringle—a noted editor and critic in his own right—the authors of the book include David Langford and Brian Stableford, two of the finest and most perceptive critics of the fantastic currently working; what they have to say is worth reading.

The Ultimate Encyclopedia contains essentially 10 sections, providing a discussion of the origins of fantasy; the types of fantasy; notable fantasy movies and television; the notable writers and characters of fantasy; the games, worlds, and magazines of fantasy; and a glossary of fantastic terms. The arrangement of these sections is too often chronological rather than alphabetical, tending to impede rather than facilitate access to the information; and there are occasional factual errors, though these tend toward the trivial. For example, the claim is made that "the 1937 movie *Topper* was based on [Thorne] Smith's *The Trivial Ghosts*," but the movie and television versions of *Topper* were based on the 1926 *Topper: An Improbable Adventure* and the 1932 *Topper Takes a Trip*; *The Jovial Ghosts* is merely the title of the 1933 English edition of the former title.

Though the *Encyclopedia of Fantasy*, edited by John Clute and John Grant (see ARBA 98, entry 1116), remains the definitive reference work on this subject, *The Ultimate Encyclopedia* should not be dismissed out of hand. It belongs in larger academic and public libraries.—**Richard Bleiler**

1139. Victor, Adam. **The Marilyn Encyclopedia.** Woodstock, N.Y., Overlook Press, 1999. 341p. illus. index. $55.00. ISBN 0-87951-718-2.

Undeniably, Marilyn Monroe lives in the minds of many as the most famous and intriguing actress and sex symbol of the twentieth century. This beautifully written and arranged volume, dedicated to her memories and photographs, is a shrine to the famous actress.

Arranged in encyclopedic format, this book has entries ranging from the actress's famous movies to her famous flings—and everything in between. The book includes information about her films, quotes from reviews, anecdotes, gossip, her most famous sayings, catalogs of her clothing, and a play-by-play of her famous relationships. There are more than 350 beautiful photographs interspersed throughout the text, many of which are rare or have never been seen. The book concludes with a bibliography and an index of names.

This encyclopedia will attract the interest of full-fledged Marilyn Monroe fans, film and Hollywood fans, and those interested in American pop culture. Both the text and the photographs of this work are captivating. Although this is not an essential addition for the reference collection, it is sure to be enjoyed by many.—**Shannon M. Graff**

1140. **War and American Popular Culture: A Historical Encyclopedia.** M. Paul Holsinger, ed. Westport, Conn., Greenwood Press, 1999. 479p. index. $89.50. ISBN 0-313-29908-0.

The editor of this work, M. Paul Holsinger, is a professor of history at Illinois State University and founder of the World War II area of the Popular Culture Association. He has authored or edited a number of works about America's wars and popular culture, especially about World War II. This title, however, covers several hundred years of American history, beginning with the early battle between the European colonizers and the Native American tribes. Although all subsequent wars are covered, particularly large sections of the book deal with the popular culture of the American Revolution, the Civil War, the Indian Wars west of the Mississippi, World War II, and Vietnam. Each segment of the book contains half-page entries that describe works of fiction that were selected as significant representations of popular culture that deal with the nation's various wars. Novels, short stories, poems, songs, plays, films, radio and television programs, as well as paintings, cartoons, toys, comic books, and posters, are all included. There are also articles about some of the writers, songwriters, and other artists who created them. There are almost 500 entries in all. Each entry concludes with one or two bibliographic entries for more information.

As always in a compilation like this, it is almost as interesting to consider the entries omitted as those included. After some review of the possibilities, the author concludes that his definition of popular culture is any work "embraced by the people" (Preface). Within this definition, the author also stresses new materials, as they are more readily available for use and because "Americans today are far more attuned to the modern era than they are to the past" (preface). *War and American Popular Culture* is a practical reference tool that conveniently identifies and describes a broad range of resources that reflect how American culture has viewed and portrayed our history replete with wars. In addition to serving as a resource guide for instructors who seek popular culture material, the book could be simply read or browsed through by those interested in American history or some aspect of popular culture such as war movies or Civil War songs. [R: BL, 15 April 99, p. 1550; Choice, July/Aug 99, p. 1930; SLJ, Aug 99, p. 182]—**Henry E. York**

27 Performing Arts

GENERAL WORKS

Biography

1141. **Contemporary Theatre, Film, and Television, Volume 22: A Biographical Guide Featuring Performers, Directors, Writers, Producers.** Joshua Kondek and Angela Yvonne Jones, eds. Farmington Hills, Mich., Gale, 1999. 543p. index. $151.00. ISBN 0-7876-3161-2. ISSN 0749-064X.

This is the latest volume in a biographical reference series designed to provide information on performers, directors, writers, and producers, as well as behind-the-scenes specialists from the United States, Canada, Great Britain, and the world. This volume adds 300 more entries to the series, which in all provides biographies on approximately 9,300 people in theater, film, and television. Primary emphasis is given to people who are currently active, but it also includes entries on personalities who have died but whose work commands lasting interest. For the most part, the editors verify the information given through the respective individuals or their agents. Where this was not possible the editors have so noted in the entries. All of the entries have an easily accessible layout including data on personal information, career, and awards and honors received. The cumulative index covers the entire series and also covers Gale's *Who's Who in the Theatre* and *Who Was Who in the Theatre*. A nice feature of this series is that it is available in electronic format online through LEXIX-NEXIS. Overall, the series is an ample resource tool for students, educators, researchers, librarians, and general readers—but it can be a costly investment to obtain and maintain the series.—**Cari Ringelheim**

1142. Graves, Mark A. **George Kelly: A Research and Production Sourcebook.** Westport, Conn., Greenwood Press, 1999. 211p. index. (Modern Dramatists Research and Production Sourcebooks, no.16). $65.00. ISBN 0-313-29993-5.

This work is a compilation of resources and research on the lengthy career of George Kelly, a major playwright of the Broadway and off-Broadway stage. There are annotated primary and secondary bibliographies. A section on production credits testifies to both the impact of Kelly's plays on early to mid-twentieth-century American theater and to the continuing interest in his works three quarters of a century after his first full-length play appeared on Broadway. An annotated bibliography of his life and career is valuable because it provides citations for a diversity of sources. Coding symbols identify articles, texts, plot summaries of plays, and photographs. Repertory company productions are also listed. This work includes plot summaries and critical overviews of plays for the stage, one act vaudeville plays, and lyrics and sketches for a musical revue. An index enables access to cross-referenced reviews, critical treatments, notices, and photographs mentioned in other section of this text. Kelly was born in 1887 in the Philadelphia area and was one of ten children. Among his siblings were a brother in vaudeville and his brother John, an Olympic sculling champion and father of princess and actress, Grace Kelly. He received the Pulitzer Prize in 1925 for the play "Craig's Wife," that has been made into a motion picture three times. The stars included Rosalind Russell (1937) and Joan Crawford (1950). Although the point is made that Kelly's women were often bossy, nevertheless he provided an opportunity in "drawing room" situation plays for starring roles of a number of leading ladies, including Tallulah Bankhead, Helen Hayes, and Dame Judith Anderson. Productions in New York, North America, London, and Europe are identified. No new Kelly works after the mid-1950s were published, although he was said to be working on several that have never been located in manuscript form, but he continued to work on revisions of previous plays and there were a few revivals of his older works. Kelly retired to Sun City, California, in 1957, dying in Bryn Mawr, Pennsylvania, in 1974. Theatrical and dramatic scholars, as well as individuals interested in American literature in general, will find the text a valuable contribution to not only theatrical history but also as a source to gain an understanding of an aspect of realism in the American theater.—**Louis G. Zelenka**

1143. Lentz, Harris M., III. **Obituaries in the Performing Arts, 1998: Film, Television, Radio, Theatre, Dance, Music, Cartoons, and Pop Culture.** Jefferson, N.C., McFarland, 1999. 245p. illus. $25.00pa. ISBN 0-7864-0748-4. ISSN 1087-9617.

This is a single source for obituaries in film, television, theater, music, and popular literature. It gives essential data of date, place, and cause of death for 566 people, with 380 photographs. Names are filed by the form in which they are best known: Harry Caray (Harry Carabin), Grandpa Jones (Louis Jones), and Sheri Lewis (Sheri Hurwitz). Lentz is a veteran writer of obituaries; all of these are written in the style typical of obituaries. He covers a wide range of individuals, from Russian composer Alfred Schnittke to film composer John Addison. If the person was an actor, Lentz presents as complete a filmography as possible, as in the cases of Sonny Bono, Lloyd Bridges, and E. G. Marshall. For actor Jack Lord, Lentz lists his numerous television programs. Several songs are listed for Frank Sinatra. He includes wrestler Junkyard Dog, runner Florence Joyner, and football player Ray Nitschke, all of whom made film appearances or were considered to be in the entertainment industry. Most articles include citations to major newspapers, such at *The New York Times* and *The Los Angeles Times*, or magazines, such as *Time* and *Newsweek*. For some entries, no citations are given because Lentz provides the only obituary readily accessible.—**Ralph Hartsock**

1144. **Who's Who in Entertainment 1998-1999.** 3d ed. New Providence, N.J., Marquis Who's Who/Reed Reference Publishing, 1997. 817p. $259.95. ISBN 0-8379-1857-X. ISSN 1044-0887.

Obviously this volume is part of the wide-ranging *Who's Who* franchise. Its 19,000 biographical entries cover film, radio, and television production, and music and dance. Creative artists receive the main focus, but notable administrators, critics, and teachers are also included. Curiously, fashion models are considered "entertainment," but not the designers who employ them. The sketches contain standard information—personal data, affiliations and awards, and a selective list of works. Most of them have been supplied by the subjects; exceptions are noted.

As with any project of this sort, there are a few clanging oversights. Tirlok Malik (producer of the video *How to Flirt, Date and Meet Your Mate*) turns up, but major directors like Robert Bresson, David Cronenberg, and Alain Resnais do not. Celebrity sometimes defeats accomplishment (yes to Elizabeth Hurley, no to Juliet Stevenson and Glenda Jackson). All the pop divas are here—Whitney, Mariah, Alanis, and Jewel. Some choices truly baffle. Ingmar Bergman in absent, but not his son, director Daniel. Refined French pianist Anne Queffélec is included, while the more important Maurizio Pollini and Krystian Zimerman are ignored. Still, avant-garde composer Brian Ferneyhough appears, as do Berio, Boulez, and Stockhausen. The Juilliard String Quartet boasts as many entries as Led Zeppelin, which represents parity of a kind.

Nitpicking aside, an enormous amount of information has been collected here, much of it otherwise unavailable. This is a mandatory purchase for libraries.—**Walt Mundkowsky**

Directories

1145. **Peterson's Professional Degree Programs in the Visual & Performing Arts 1999.** 5th ed. Princeton, N.J., Peterson's Guides, 1998. 601p. illus. index. $26.95pa. ISBN 0-7689-0112-X. ISSN 1073-2020.

This latest Peterson's tool is a guide to more than 1,000 professional degree programs in art, dance, music, and theater offered by U.S. and Canadian accredited institutions. It aims to help arts students find the appropriate program that will assist them in furthering their professional goals. Toward this end, guidance from staff at top programs is included, as is detailed information regarding college costs and the relative merits of different types of degrees. The data contained here were supplied by questionnaires submitted by program directors at these institutions.

A "Quick-Reference Chart of Programs" presents an overview in the form of basic information about each school. Program descriptions are divided into the four disciplines, with each preceded by specific advice about auditioning, studying, and evaluating programs. Individual entries provide more detailed descriptions as well as occasional sections with further background information. A "Gallery of Summer Programs" describes those providing learning experiences to high school students. There is a majors index that includes 313 undergraduate professional degree majors and a school index referring to program descriptions.

This guide provides a useful service as a first step in assisting students to identify relevant programs in art, dance, music, and the theater. It is a welcome addition to Peterson's volume of informative educational resources.—**Anita Zutis**

1146. **U.S. Directory of Entertainment Employers.** spring/summer 1999 ed. Van Nuys, Calif., EEJ Publishing, 1999. 184p. index. $55.00pa. ISBN 0-9644353-7-3. ISSN 1079-6797.

This is the 6th edition of the directory and contains more than 3,000 listings of major employers in various areas of the entertainment industry. Its purpose is to aid and assist job-seekers with searches within the industry. The directory uses a broad definition of the term "entertainment industry," therefore enhancing its value considerably. The organization of the major section of the publication is by 41 types of businesses in the broad areas of advertising, broadcasting, film, law, music, talent agencies, and television and video. Each entry is alphabetically listed under the appropriate heading and includes such information as complete name and telephone number; additional information usually includes Website, project highlights, affiliations with larger companies, job hotlines, and stock symbols. The 2d, and considerably shorter section, deals with resources for locating employment: recruiters, publications, unions, and guilds. Entries are arranged alphabetically under each resource type and contain the same information as found in the entries in the first section. There are both alphabetic and regional indexes. In the preface there is a very brief section of several paragraphs on the subjects of applying for jobs, submitting resumes, and relocation considerations. As a catalog of sources this contains much useful information. It is suited for the job-seeker who has passed the basics and is concerned only with information on how to contact prospective employers.—**Jackson Kesler**

Handbooks and Yearbooks

1147. **Dun and Bradstreet/Gale Industry Reference Handbooks: Entertainment.** Stacy A. McConnell and Linda D. Hall, eds. Farmington Hills, Mich., Gale, 1999. 980p. index. $99.00pa. ISBN 0-7876-3773-4.

The entertainment industry as defined here covers a broad spectrum of private and public companies in fields such as movie and video making, theatrical production, health clubs and physical fitness centers, sports teams, golf courses, country clubs, racetracks, casinos, museums, art galleries, amusement parks, zoological gardens, and carnivals. Included are profiles of nearly 5,000 companies. A foreword and the 1st chapter give an overview of the 35 industries within the entertainment classification, along with some helpful definitions. Current trends and future directions are outlined here, followed by federal government statistics and performance indicators covering the past 10 years. These data include classification of establishments, employment, compensation, revenues, and ratios. A major section of the work is the "Company Directory," with entries providing the company name; its parent; address; telephone number; sales; employees; the company's business activity; and the name and title of its chairperson, president, or other high-ranking officers. A separate geographical index lists companies by city and state.

Individual chapters are devoted to an overview of the industry and federal government statistics and projections, with the source of much of this information being the U.S. Department of Commerce. Tables indicate Dun and Bradstreet ranking by sales as well as ranking by total number of employees. Another chapter lists domestic and international associations with Web addresses, which are largely trade related, such as the Piano Manufacturers Association, yet a surprising number are entertainer specific (e.g., the Elvis Presley Fan Club of Luxembourg). The chapter listing consultants and consulting organizations confines its list to those in the United States and Canada. Additional chapters provide names and addresses of trade journals and other information sources, and of trade shows with dates, locations, and types of major exhibitors. Company and organization names plus names of individuals are included in the master index. An appendix converts Standard Industrial Classification codes to North American Industry Classification System codes. [R: LJ, 15 Sept 99, p. 68]—**Louis G. Zelenka**

DANCE

1148. **Bibliographic Guide to Dance 1998.** New York, G. K. Hall/Macmillan Library Reference, 1999. 2v. $545.00/set. ISBN 0-7838-0199-8. ISSN 0360-2737.

The 2-volume *Bibliographic Guide to Dance* is a partial annual supplement to the *Dictionary Catalog of the Dance Collection* (G. K. Hall, 1974). It includes listings for magazine and journal articles, photographs, clippings, videos and films, prints, programs, posters, playbills, and annotated dance scores cataloged at the dance collection of the New York Public Library between January and December 1998. Access is by main entry, title, and subject, with added entries for names of individuals, geographic names, and subject headings covering most aspects of dance. Full bibliographic information is listed under the main entry, while condensed or abbreviated information appears under other headings. Numerous scope notes and cross-references assist researchers. Entries contain extensive content notes and many have brief summaries of a work. Because 97 percent of the dance collection's holdings are nonbook media, this documentation helps make such hard-to-find material more accessible. Although the value of this comprehensive work still remains, the need is lessened by Internet access to the online catalog of the dance collection. The online version is a complete record of the collection's holdings. Yet as an annual record of the additions to the literature, in a format that can be browsed in a way that an online catalog cannot be, the *Bibliographic Guide to Dance* is recommended for larger, comprehensive collections or for collections without easy and stable Internet access.—**Lizbeth Langston**

FILM, TELEVISION, AND VIDEO

Bibliography

1149. Doyle, Billy H. **The Ultimate Directory of Silent and Sound Era Performers: A Necrology of Actors and Actresses.** Lanham, Md., Scarecrow, 1999. 623p. $98.50. ISBN 0-8108-3547-9.

Doyle's 1995 work, *The Ultimate Directory of Silent Screen Performers: A Necrology of Births and Deaths and Essays on 50 Lost Players* (see ARBA 96, entry 1368), supplied vital statistics on some 7,500 performers of the silent era. In this companion volume, the dogged film researcher provides birth and death data on more than 15,00 actors, actresses, and other allied performers whose careers extended into the sound era of motion pictures presented in the United States. A typical entry includes the range of years the person was active in sound films, the place and date of their birth, and their death. Information has been meticulously gathered from a variety of film books, directories, and both trade magazines (*Variety*, *The Hollywood Reporter*) and newspapers (*Los Angeles Times*, *The New York Times*). All of these resources are cited in a short bibliography. Of note, the present volume also serves as a companion to Doyle's other current necrology, *The Ultimate Directory of Film Technicians* (see entry 1167), which covers more than 9,000 producers, screenwriters, directors, and composers. Taken individually or as a group, these necrologies stand as useful reference works for the film scholar or enthusiast. This work is recommended for academic and public libraries that support a strong interest in film studies. [R: LJ, 15 Sept 99, p. 68]

—**David K. Frasier**

Bio-bibliography

1150. Duchovnay, Gerald. **Humphrey Bogart: A Bio-Bibliography.** Westport, Conn., Greenwood Press, 1999. 344p. index. (Popular Culture Bio-Bibliographies). $69.50. ISBN 0-313-22338-6.

Contrary to expectations based on his film roles, Humphrey Bogart (his real name) was the product of a prominent upper-middle-class family. A portrait of the angelic baby Humphrey by his mother, Maud, a well-known children's book author and illustrator, once graced jars of Mellins Baby Food. This later proved hilarious to classmates at the private Trinity School in Manhattan. In fact, this survey of Bogart's life and career reveals that Bogart first played the kind of "juvenile," "tennis anyone" role that he was born to. His transition came about because of his unforgettable performance as Duke Mantee in *The Petrified Forest*, first on stage and then in the 1936 film.

Although Bogart was not a "dead end boy" by birth, he did have to defend himself. His opponent was most often one of his first three wives. The battling Bogarts became famous in Hollywood. His final romance and marriage to Lauren Bacall brought him happiness until his untimely death.

Duchovnay presents a survey of the actor's life, and then reviews Bogart's impact on popular culture (e.g., films, cartoons—his caricature starred opposite Bugs Bunny as Bacall—fashion, commercials, poster art, literature, and even ceiling fans inspired by *Casablanca*). Although notoriously reticent, a selection of self-penned articles and interviews that appeared in popular magazines is included. A bibliographical essay analyzes and comments on biographical and critical sources, including those remarking on his films. A checklist gives full citations for all sources in the essay. Useful appendixes include theatrical performances; filmography, with full credits; radio and television appearances; and Internet sites. This very complete work should be in every performing arts or film studies reference collection. [R: Choice, July/Aug 99, p. 1918]—**Ruth A. Carr**

1151. Levy, Bill. **John Ford: A Bio-Bibliography.** Westport, Conn., Greenwood Press, 1998. 352p. illus. index. (Bio-Bibliographies in the Performing Arts, no.78). $75.00. ISBN 0-313-27514-9.

This latest entry in Greenwood Press's Bio-Bibliographies in the Performing Arts series profiles film director John Ford. Following 60 pages of biography and chronology, Levy devotes a good portion of the rest of the volume to a lengthy filmography and an equally extensive bibliography. The biographical section attempts to relate Ford's childhood experiences and his unhappiness throughout life to the impact these factors may have had on his films. The filmography entries include credits, casts, synopses, review and critique excerpts, and commentaries for Ford's films from 1917 through 1971. Films from 1914 to 1916 with Ford as an actor have shorter entries. Thirteen pages are devoted to similar entries for his radio, television, and theater credits, and to a listing of unrealized projects. The bibliography annotates 850 items treating Ford and his art. Also listed in the volume are Ford archival collections in the United States and elsewhere, and awards and honors bestowed upon him. An index concludes the book. This is a solid reference source that admirably presents the life and work of one of the United States' most respected film directors. Any library with a motion picture collection would do well to purchase this volume. [R: Choice, May 99, pp. 1593-1594]—**Lee Weston**

1152. Pitts, Michael R. **Charles Bronson: The 95 Films and the 156 Television Appearances.** Jefferson, N.C., McFarland, 1999. 368p. illus. index. $45.00. ISBN 0-7864-0601-1.

This work covers Charles Buchinsky's (better known as Charles Bronson) acting career in film and on television and includes many black-and-white film stills and photographs. Choosing to concentrate on Bronson's professional life, this directory does not include any personal biography aside from some brief information in the introduction. Alphabetic entries list film or television episode, complete cast and credits, and year of release. Accompanying each entry's plot synopsis and discussion is a survey of the critical responses to the work. Since early appearances in *Rawhide*, *Bonanza*, and *The Fugitive*, Bronson's career has spanned four decades. His most popular role is as urban vigilante Paul Kersey in the *Death Wish* films. The entries for film and television appearances are divided into two sections. These appearances are also listed in chronological order—films in order of release date and television appearances in order of air date. A list of video releases is provided along with the video companies who released them. An index concludes the work. This is a good reference for extensive film study collections and Bronson fans.

—**Cari Ringelheim**

1153. Rainey, Buck. **Western Gunslingers in Fact and on Film: Hollywood's Famous Lawmen and Outlaws.** Jefferson, N.C., McFarland, 1998. 341p. illus. index. $35.00pa. ISBN 0-7864-0396-9.

Westerns are a much loved and well-documented genre, and Rainey adds another dimension to the field. Billy the Kid, the James-Younger Gang, the Dalton-Doolin Gang, Belle Starr, Wyatt Earp, Wild Bill Hickok, and Bat Masterson are featured in this comparison of their true lives and their Hollywood interpretations. Each subject's life is told informally, without glamour and without footnotes. Their lives are illustrated with well-chosen black-and-white photographs of both the real people and the movie stars who portrayed them. Interestingly, the real people are more memorable than the beautiful people chosen to play them. A photograph of the dead Bill Doolan, his bare chest riddled with bullet holes, is particularly chilling. Following each 6- to 12-page biography is an annotated list of the films and television productions. The annotations include cast listings and plot summaries if the information is available. Often, excerpts from contemporary reviews are included.

A 39-page bibliography, arranged alphabetically by author, and a detailed index of personal names and film titles conclude the work. In the absence of footnotes, this long bibliography would be more helpful to a novice film student if it was divided into sections corresponding to the gunslingers' names or gangs. Most libraries will want this for their circulating collection for the universal appeal of the subject and for the extensive filmographies. It can also be used it in tandem with Don Cusic's *Cowboys and the Wild West* (see ARBA 95, entry 541) and *Encyclopedia of World Crime* (see ARBA 92, entry 552).

—**Juleigh Muirhead Clark**

1154. Sweeney, Kevin. **James Mason: A Bio-Bibliography.** Westport, Conn., Greenwood Press, 1999. 299p. index. (Bio-Bibliographies in the Performing Arts, no.79). $65.00. ISBN 0-313-28496-2.

A consummate actor whose career on stage and screen spanned more than 50 years, James Mason is perhaps best known for his riveting performances in *A Star is Born*, *Georgy Girl*, and *The Verdict*, the films for which he received Academy Award nominations. Unfortunately, however, Mason also lent his considerable talent to a number of undistinguished, even mediocre, projects. Sweeney, a freelance writer and compiler of *Henry Fonda: A Bio-Bibliography* (see ARBA 93, entry 1323), follows the general format established by earlier volumes in this series. Acknowledging that his subject was a complex, often difficult, man, Sweeney provides a lively and balanced 40-page biography that successfully integrates information on Mason's personal and professional life. In addition, he summarizes the highlights of Mason's life and career in a brief chronology. Particularly useful for researchers is the annotated bibliography that identifies more than 200 publications by and about Mason. Because he had access to an extensive private clipping file in compiling this bibliography, Sweeney undoubtedly was able to include materials that would have eluded him otherwise. However, due to the nature of this collection, his citations frequently lack page references and dates, and several even lack the title of the publication. It is surprising that his editor at

Greenwood did not insist that he do the necessary legwork to provide complete bibliographical information. Moreover, a brief search of several standard sources revealed a number of articles on Mason that do not appear in this work. A chronologically arranged filmography includes production information, credits, a synopsis, quotations from selected reviews, and other useful notes on each of Mason's films. Similar sections cover television, stage, and radio productions in which he was involved. Also included are lists of his audio recordings and his currently available video recordings. The index is useful, but quirky. For example, sources in the bibliography are indexed by article title and publication title, but only selectively by author.

The strengths of this volume, however, far outweigh its idiosyncrasies and flaws. As an important and valuable addition to the literature on James Mason, it is particularly appropriate for libraries building strong film and theater collections.—**Marie Ellis**

Biography

1155. Andrew, Geoff. **Stranger Than Paradise: Maverick Film-Makers in Recent American Cinema.** New York, Limelight Editions, 1998. 374p. illus. index. $38.00. ISBN 0-87910-277-2.

As Hollywood movies have increasingly become big-budget extravaganzas with spectacular special effects and highly paid megastars, the coterie of so-called independent filmmakers has flourished. Ignoring market surveys and target groups, the "indies" (as they like to be called) emphasize originality and freshness in themes, characters, and techniques. Andrew, well-known author and film critic in England, analyzed more than 200 of cinema's most famous directors worldwide in his *Film Handbook* (see ARBA 91, entry 1386). Now he turns his attention to the indies, some of whom, such as Spike Lee and Quentin Tarantino, have achieved notoriety, while most have not.

Major chapters are devoted to 10 filmmakers, including David Lynch, Todd Haynes, and Steven Soderbergh, along with an excellent essay on the history of independent cinema. Acknowledging that maverick filmmakers have always been around the motion picture industry, Andrew examines how the achievements of early outsiders such as Orson Welles and John Cassavetes relate to the current wave of independent filmmakers. He is especially good at explaining the qualities that go together to make important independent films. His insightful analysis of the Coen brothers' acclaimed film *Fargo* suggests how the relatively unknown actors, low budget, and quirky plot were successfully transformed into an engrossing film with memorable performances. He lends a light and entertaining tone to the book by picking up on the comic elements of the films.

This will nicely complement the best film-by-film reference book on the subject, *VideoHound's Independent Film Guide* (see entry 1169). This volume is recommended for academic libraries and cinema collections.—**Richard W. Grefrath**

1156. Mank, Gregory William. **Women in Horror Films.** Jefferson, N.C., McFarland, 1999. 2v. illus. index. $75.00/set. ISBN 0-7864-0580-5.

What fun we mortals have in being scared out of our wits, and what better sound to arouse both the fear and the protective instinct in males than a woman's scream? Horror films have been around since the invention of movies, but really hit their apex in the 1930s and 1940s, with adaptations of some of the greatest horror stories ever written. Film directors such as James Whale, Mark Robson, and Erle C. Kenton turned what could very well have been ridiculous stories into hellish views of the underworld, and women were used to transport the audience into those dark places. They represented the innocents caught up in a nightmare; how else could we know the terrors of graves, crypts, castles, and coffins if we had not been dragged there along with some winsome female with a great set of lungs? The author has obviously indulged himself in a labor of love as he painstakingly re-creates the atmosphere of the films, aided in many instances by the recollections of the actresses themselves. His section on Elsa Lanchester, for example, is indicative of his efforts to get behind the movie magic and find out what drove these talented performers to make viewers believe they were being attacked by all sort of Boschian creatures. What he has come up with is a highly entertaining and informative look at the genre of movies that may not have had their start in the United States, but which came to full flower here. His capsule biographies of the damsels in distress are complete, definitive, immensely readable, and successfully transport readers back into the darkened movie theater for another spell of raising goosebumps. Many of the actresses were unfortunately tagged forever as "scream queens"; Mank's filmography shows that some languished in the shadows, whereas others found new starts in other film types. His volumes are great fun to read and would make a welcome addition to all film library collections as well as large public libraries. [R: BL, 1 May 99, p. 1638]—**Joseph L. Carlson**

1157. Maturi, Richard J., and Mary Buckingham Maturi. **Francis X. Bushman: A Biography and Filmography.** Jefferson, N.C., McFarland, 1998. 254p. illus. $38.50. ISBN 0-7864-0485-X.

One of the most popular and best-known stars of the silent screen, Francis X. Bushman was at the peak of his success when a scandal in his personal life, followed by a misunderstanding with Louis B. Mayer, virtually ended his career as a leading man. However, he continued to act in films—albeit sporadically and generally in minor roles—until the end of his life. He also appeared in a variety of radio and television programs. Surprisingly, there is no full-length biography of Bushman, so the 98-page biographical section of this book is the most detailed treatment of his life currently available. Although the authors were granted interviews with family members and had access to personal papers, they have not used these to their best advantage. Their narrative, accompanied by stills from Bushman's films and family photographs, is amateurish and lacks cohesion. Moreover, it is marred by a number of careless errors, such as the muddled picture caption on page 7.

This work's most valuable feature is the filmography that is arranged chronologically and provides production information, credits, and a brief synopsis of each of Bushman's films. Many entries also include excerpts from reviews and additional commentary. Separate listings cover Bushman's radio and television appearances and the film credits for two of his children. The bibliography notes the books, periodicals, and newspapers consulted by the authors, but it would have been much more useful if it had cited specific periodical and newspaper articles rather than merely listing titles of publications. The index includes references to film titles and selected individuals mentioned in the biography and the credits.

Unfortunately, this volume is far from the definitive work on Bushman's life and films. In light of its significant flaws, it will be a marginal purchase except for those libraries that are building extensive collections in the area of motion picture history.—**Marie Ellis**

1158. Weaver, Tom. **John Carradine: The Films.** Jefferson, N.C., McFarland, 1999. 396p. illus. index. $65.00. ISBN 0-7864-0607-0.

John Carradine may well be the most famous actor that Hollywood has produced whom few people recognize. The authors of this work celebrate the man who may be perceived as the king of "B" movies, but whose prolific career spanned 60 years (1930-1990) and included an astonishing number of films, many notable and of great regard. Until the late 1950s, Carradine was primarily a character actor in films of every type, but unfortunately he may be best remembered today for low-budget, teenage-oriented, and horror films, particularly from the final stages of his career. Despite this, he brought full professionalism and seriousness to every job and that impressed the film's cast and crew no matter how seemingly trite the endeavor.

The book starts out with a biographical survey of Carradine and his career. Next, the main section lists his films year by year, each with a list of principals, a story summary, and an assessment of its importance, which usually includes interesting background information. These entries are paragraph-length in the early days and far more extensive as the star's roles grew in importance. There are also quotes from reviews appearing in newspapers and magazines. It would have been helpful if these reviews were documented so the reader could look up the original source, but this has not been provided. A miscellaneous section points out unusual facts and fictions about Carradine's career. The index points to each film, the actor, and the directors, with bold typeface for the many photographs. Libraries with strong film or biography collections will want to add this well-done survey.—**Gary R. Cocozzoli**

Dictionaries and Encyclopedias

1159. Hischak, Thomas S. **The American Musical Film Song Encyclopedia.** Westport, Conn., Greenwood Press, 1999. 521p. index. $69.50. ISBN 0-313-30737-7.

Hischak's *The American Musical Film Song Encyclopedia* is an ambitious, carefully executed, and generally successful attempt to do for movie musicals what the author's excellent *The American Musical Theatre Song Encyclopedia* (see ARBA 96, entry 1416) did for Broadway. The author provides valuable information on more than 1,700 songs from 500 notable Hollywood musicals, from the birth of talkies to filmed rock operas. For the purposes of this work, musicals are defined as "having at least three songs sung by characters in the movie." Songs in films that originated on Broadway or Tin Pan Alley are excluded—an unfortunate but probably necessary editorial decision.

Hischak largely limits his selection to U.S. movies, including animated works but excluding shorts. Each alphabetically listed entry includes lyric and songwriting credits and performing credits, along with a short but lively overview that provides the plot context for the song and other interesting background. Revelations abound on almost every page. Who would have thought, for example, that the old Dixieland chestnut "Do You Know What It Means to Miss New Orleans" was written for the 1947 film *New Orleans!*? In addition to the information in the body of the encyclopedia, the author has thoughtfully provided a number of other useful indexes and appendixes, including a listing of alternative song titles, songs from other sources, best-song Oscars, and a bibliography of works on film musicals and film songwriting. There is also an essential alphabetic list of musicals cited in the body of the work (with songs cited) and a general index. This is an essential addition to music, film studies, and popular culture collections. [R: Choice, Sept 99, p. 110; BL, June 99, p. 1870]—**Gary Handman**

1160. Katz, Ephraim. **The Film Encyclopedia.** 3d ed. New York, HarperCollins, 1998. 1506p. $28.00pa. ISBN 0-06-273492-X.

The tradition of Katz has been well maintained by new editors Klein and Nolen. No entries have been eliminated from the earlier editions nor have other cosmetic changes, such as photographs, been added. It still adheres to Katz's original intent to compile "the most comprehensive one volume encyclopedia on World cinema ever published in the English language."

Entries are presented in alphabetic order and there is still no index. Each entry, however, does contain cross-references to help readers locate other entries that contain related or complementary information. Those cross-references are noted with the use of small capitals.

If the entry is biographic, "FILMS" indicates that what follows is a fairly complete list of credits in a professional capacity or for the function specified (e.g., director, screenplay writer, and so on). If the entry contains "FILMS INCLUDED," the entry is only a partial listing. When it is not apparent, the national origin of a film or the country where the film was produced is given after the title in parentheses and abbreviated.

A slash separating titles in the credits indicates an alternative title, either in the original language produced or in a second or third language for an international distribution. A slash used with country designation indicates film production done in two or more countries that are also noted. Dates following titles are usually the year of first release for a general screening.

Some credits, where a single film is given, usually give the production in the country of origin. Original titles are listed for pictures in the English, French, Spanish, Italian, and German languages. Titles produced in less familiar languages (i.e., Swedish, Japanese, Russian) are given when released in the United States or United Kingdom. If no record of release in an English-speaking country is known, the title given in a lesser-known language is a literal translation or the English rendition of an untranslatable title.

As has been noted in earlier reviews of earlier editions, there are still some failings that continue. Some "rockumentaries" are not listed nor are the rock groups or individual artists appearing in them. For example, The Who's "Tommy" or Elton John, who appeared in the movie, is not listed. Additionally, musicians who appear under a pseudonym are not cross-referenced (e.g., Ice-T, Ice-Cube, and so on).

Nonetheless, this compendium is still a most useful and necessary acquisition for a library or film buff's collection. The new editors have done a reasonable job in maintaining a credible publication, including new entries and updating those already included.—**Daniel C. Barkley**

1161. Lenburg, Jeff. **The Encyclopedia of Animated Cartoons.** 2d ed. New York, Checkmark Books/Facts on File, 1999. 576p. illus. index. $24.95pa. ISBN 0-8160-3832-5.

This 2d edition of a classic work is sure to be a popular item in school, public, and academic libraries. Lenburg has produced a monumental resource chronicling the history and development of a unique art form. Perhaps the most valuable part of the book is the introduction entitled "A Nutshell History of the American Animated Cartoon," which traces the origins of animation from Winsor McCay to *The Simpsons*. The use of the word "American" in the introduction is significant; students of Japanese anime will not find a great deal of information in Lenburg's work. His information is divided into detailed descriptions of every animated silent and sound cartoon, every animated feature film, and every animated television series or special. The more than 2,200 entries provide complete information on creators, directors, release dates, awards received, and—crucial to the success of any animated film—the voice talents behind the characters. Lenburg clearly demonstrates the social and political significance of animated films, showing how they are able to make statements in a few drawings that would take thousands of words in text. His book is also a treasure-trove of trivia where readers can find out such esoteric information as Beavis and Butt-head's first names; what animal provided the inspiration for Betty Boop; and what happened to such forgotten characters as Clint Clobber, Fanny Zilch, and Honey Halfwitch. Not only is this book a great reference, it is a lot of fun to read.—**Joseph L. Carlson**

1162. Lowe, Denise. **Women and American Television: An Encyclopedia.** Santa Barbara, Calif., ABC-CLIO, 1999. 513p. illus. index. $65.00. ISBN 0-87436-970-3.

Women and American Television: An Encyclopedia provides brief descriptions of television actresses and programs that featured strong or historically significant female characters. Most of the entries are short and do not provide any kind of in-depth study of how the actress or series affected how women are portrayed in popular culture mediums. Occasionally, a few entries provide a little more interpretation of how certain shows affected the depiction of women. One exception, for example, the entry for *The Mary Tyler Moore Show* critiques how the lead character, Mary Richards, was a mere mother figure to her friends and was never "viewed" in her producer position. In other words, the author of this entry feels that Mary Richards was still the 1950s television mother/secretary figure and not the feminist icon so many fans view her as. Also, the entry for *Murphy Brown* discusses how the lead character offered a nontraditional role model of female success. Murphy was depicted as a survivor, a strong journalist, and a single mother. This show not only broke the boundaries of how women are portrayed on television, but also was not afraid to address many controversial issues. The text is speckled with various dialog boxes containing essays on subjects such as black female roles, health issues, and older women on television. Lists of directors, writers, Emmy winners, and Television Hall of Fame inductees are also provided. The encyclopedia concludes with a bibliography and an index. This text is limited in length but would be a good quick reference in women's studies and popular culture collections.—**Cari Ringelheim**

1163. McCaffrey, Donald W., and Christopher P. Jacobs. **Guide to the Silent Years of American Cinema.** Westport, Conn., Greenwood Press, 1999. 343p. illus. index. (Reference Guides to the World's Cinema). $79.50. ISBN 0-313-30345-2.

Using a dictionary format, the authors, both of whom have impressive credentials as film historians and university lecturers, have assembled an impressive amount of material on the silent film era in the United States and presented it in about 250 entries of roughly 500 words each—150 entries on key actors, directors, and screenwriters and 100 on important films such as *Birth of a Nation*, *Gold Rush*, and *Ben Hur*. For each of the personalities, there is a brief biography, an assessment of important contributions, a selective filmography, and a brief bibliography listing additional sources. The entries for films (chiefly full-length features) give a short plot summary and an evaluation of the importance of each in film history. There are also two brief narrative chapters; one is introductory and outlines the technical developments during the silent era (for example, use of color) and the other acts as an epilogue and assesses the principal accomplishments of the silent cinema. Criteria for inclusion as an entry in the main body of the work seem arbitrary, often to the point of being capricious at times. For example, foreign-born directors who were also prominent in their native countries and actors who retained importance during the sound era are not included. This means that pioneers like Ernst Lubitsch, Greta Garbo, Joseph Schildkraut, Wallace Berry, and Robert J. Flaherty are not included, yet there are entries for Norma Shearer, Cecil B. de Mille, and Clarence Brown. The filmographies also show erratic coverage; some end with 1929 and others continue into the sound era.

The book concludes with a selected bibliography of books and Internet sources on film history and a subject index. Because of its price, spotty coverage, and the vast wealth of reference material already available on this subject, the usefulness of this book seems doubtful in all but large library collections and those specializing in film studies. Ephraim Katz's *The Film Encyclopedia* (see entry 1160) gives good coverage and more complete filmographies for all the personalities listed in this guide as well as entries on hundreds of other silent and sound film personalities, and the three volumes on silent films in *Magill's Survey of Cinema* (Magill, 1982) supplies more complete coverage on more than four times the films. Such basic references as *Halliwell's Filmgoer's and Video Viewer's Companion* (Harper, 1998) also have brief entries for most of the 100 films included in this guide, plus material on thousands of sound films.—**John T. Gillespie**

1164. Rajadhyaksha, Ashish, and Paul Willemen. **Encyclopaedia of Indian Cinema.** rev. ed. Chicago, Fitzroy Dearborn, 1999. 658p. illus. index. $75.00. ISBN 1-57958-146-3.

The 2d edition, chronicling India's national cinema, adds corrections to the 1st and updates and expands it to 1995. Also new in this edition is a name index that includes entries not found in other sections. As previously, the focus is on the history of cinema from all parts of India, reflecting six major language industries as well as nine others used in films. Many sources were used, both authoritative ones, which may provide only the "most likely" truth, and reader input. The aim throughout is to provide a research tool that can evolve into a work of collective scholarship on India's cinema.

Copious, although often confusing, the introductory notes mention sources and link film to India's turbulent history. The chronicle contains two main sections—dictionary and films. The former contains sketches of actors, directors, producers, composers, lyric writers and scenarists, with filmographies, as well as major film studios, art movements, and genres. Films are listed in chronological order from 1910 to 1995, including those judged important in India's film history by having made a significant contribution to the development of cinema. A full list of credits also appears. Because of the numerous plot convolutions involved, only an overall shape of the story is given. Entries in both sections are necessarily brief and are illustrated by black-and white photographs. An extensive bibliography is followed by a name index and a film index that includes director, language, and the year the film was made.

In composing this monumental work, the authors have had to deal with problems posed by transliteration and with the series of conflicts and compromises presented by the shifting sociocultural process in India. They have managed admirably, with only a little lack of clarity in their final product. As the editors agree, only a continuous collective scholarship can serve as a solid basis for chronicling the severely under-documented and diverse Indian cinema.—**Anita Zutis**

1165. Zhang, Yingjin, and Zhiwei Xiao. **Encyclopedia of Chinese Film.** New York, Routledge, 1998. 475p. illus. index. $140.00. ISBN 0-415-15168-6.

This is a comprehensive coverage of Chinese film in its historical, cultural, geopolitical, generic, thematic, and textual aspects, and a useful guide to assist readers in locating the information needed through these aspects. This encyclopedia consists of two main parts, the historical essays and the main entries. The six historical essays address the evolution of the Chinese film industry by the geographical area of origin: Chinese cinema, Hong Kong cinema, Taiwan cinema, transnational cinema, Chinese film in the West, and foreign film in China. The rich and well-researched information gives a comprehensive perspective on the political, social, and cultural background of the film industry. The essays also highlight the actors, actresses, films, and film producers that were either well-known or relevant representations at that time. Art imitates life. Many films accurately depicted the people and their society at their time. It is helpful that the authors of these essays provide further readings for each subject covered in the essays.

The main entries mirror and further detail the account of the films and film industry-related topics. For those readers caught between the various versions of romanizations of the Chinese film titles and individual names (i.e., Pinyin, Wade-Giles, Cantonese) there is a table that lists the glossary of Chinese characters and English translations. For those who are interested in being updated on the subject, there is a list of select Websites on Chinese cinema.

This is one of the very few concise and comprehensive works on the subject of Chinese films. With its well-organized format and rich source of information, this encyclopedia should satisfy those who are interested in learning about the film industry in China, Taiwan, and Hong Kong. [R: LJ, Aug 98, p. 80; BL, 1 Mar 99, p. 1247; Choice, Nov 99, pp. 509-510]—**Eveline L. Yang**

Directories

1166. **Cinematographers, Production Designers, Costume Designers, and Film Editors Guide 1998.** 6th ed. Los Angeles, Calif., Lone Eagle, 1998. 669p. index. $65.00pa. ISBN 0-943728-94-0. ISSN 0894-8674.

Cinematographers, Production Designers, Costume Designers, and Film Editors Guide provides a reference to cinematographers, production designers, art directors, set directors, costume designers, and film editors. Previous editions did not include set directors and art directors. The 6th edition is completely updated and revised and contains a list of more than 6,000 film professionals and more than 15,000 film listings. The directory contains names of professionals who are currently active in the industry, along with lists of their feature film credits going back 10 years. Commercials, industrials, stage productions, and direct home video productions are not included. The work is heavily indexed, including indexes to film titles, Academy Awards by name, Academy Awards by year, unions and guilds, agents, and advertisers. Each entry includes the name, a list of affiliations, representing agent, and a list of films the individual has worked on. Abbreviations are used to indicate the type of production (e.g., cable documentary, television pilot, theatrical). Also, symbols provide additional information such as whether the film is an Academy Award winner or if the individual is deceased. Alternative names and titles are indicated by parentheses and brackets.

All of the information in this directory is provided by the individuals listed. A special Web page is provided for updating information. *Cinematographers, Production Designers, Costume Designers, and Film Editors Guide* is much larger than the more well-known *Who's Who in the Motion Picture Industry: Cinematographers, Directors, Producers, Writers, Casting Directors, Executives, Studios, Production Companies, Television Networks* (9th ed.; Packard, 1996).

Although this work is mainly directed to the profession as a tool for hiring and "crewing up" a film or television production, it is also valuable as a general reference source for the film industry. This directory is recommended for all larger public and academic libraries with large film collections. It is also recommended for individuals in the film industry and for academics who study film.—**Robert L. Wick**

1167. Doyle, Billy H. **The Ultimate Directory of Film Technicians: A Necrology of Dates and Places of Births and Deaths of More than 9,000 Producers....** Lanham, Md., Scarecrow, 1999. 297p. $65.00. ISBN 0-8108-3546-0.

In a companion volume to his 1999 work *The Ultimate Directory of Silent and Sound Performers: A Necrology of Actors and Actresses* (see entry 1149), Doyle supplies places and dates of birth and death for more than 9,000 film technicians. This group contains producers, directors, screenwriters, composers, costume designers, executives, animators, film and sound editors, and publicists as well as other behind-the-camera professionals who collaborate in the making of film. Doyle, a retired public school teacher, focuses primarily on those technicians who have worked in the American cinema from the late 1800s to 1997. Each entry gives the person's date and place of birth (if known) and place and date of death. His or her contribution to film (i.e., director, cinematographer) is listed in parentheses at the end of the entry.

A work of this scope and magnitude requires an incredible amount of perseverance and dedication. Doyle has painstakingly researched this necrology in numerous trade papers, newspapers, film books, the *California Death Indices*, and the records of the Social Security Administration. The result is an essential starting point for any research in film biography. This resource is recommended for academic and public libraries that own the companion volume and have strong holdings in film studies. [R: LJ, 15 June 99, p. 70]—**David K. Frasier**

1168. **The Motion Picture Guide: 1999 Annual (The Films of 1998).** Edmond Grant and Ken Fox, eds. New York, News America, 1999. 862p. index. $212.50. ISBN 0-933997-43-4.

The 14th supplement to *The Motion Picture Guide* (MPG) covers about 700 films released during 1998, available to the American public. This output is greater than in any previous volume, and ranges from Hollywood blockbusters to the products of individual producers and foreign imports.

Entries in the "Film Reviews" section, besides including the usual credits, plot synopsis, and genre, also list a star rating, Academy Award results, and a critical appraisal. "Academy Awards" presents winners and nominees by category, and "Obituaries" provides biographies of those who were involved with the film and television industries. A master index to all MPG annuals precedes those listing films by country, distributor, genre, and MPAA rating. An exhaustive name index refers individuals to a particular film title or titles.

Overall, the multiple indexes in this annual provide access to the films from virtually every conceivable aspect. In each entry, the critical appraisals supplement other information to give a more accurate impression of the title. It is hoped that these supplements will continue to reflect the output of one of our most prolific and conspicuous industries.—**Anita Zutis**

1169. Sullivan, Monica. **VideoHound's Independent Film Guide.** 2d ed. Farmington Hills, Mich., Visible Ink Press/Gale, 1999. 666p. illus. index. $19.95pa. ISBN 1-57859-090-6.

With the incredible success of such films as *The Blair Witch Project* and *Dick*, coupled with the dismal financial performances of bloated Hollywood films like *Godzilla* and *The Wild, Wild West*, it is no wonder that independent films are growing in popularity. Of course, trying to find a definition of "independent" is not as easy as it seems; most people link it to budgets, whereas others feel it is an attempt of directors and producers to free themselves from the creative demands of major movie studios. The author of this incredible work does not even bother to offer a definition, hoping probably that people will know "indies" when they see them. Sullivan proceeds to present personal reviews of more than 1,000 independent films, some of them familiar (e.g., *Halloween*, *Pulp Fiction*) and some of them only recognizable to devotees of art houses (e.g., *Death and the Maiden*, *Peeping Tom*). In the slightly irreverent style of other VideoHound publications, Sullivan lays on the "WOOF" as often as she does the bones (signaling approval). The style of writing is definitely literate and entertaining. Of course, in any compilation there are bound to be omissions. Comparing her selection with films shown on the Independent Movie Channel during the months of July and August 1999, it was discovered that of the 31 films shown in July, 29 are not reviewed in this work, and for the 42 films shown in August, 28 were not reviewed. Among the absences are such titles as *Rashomon*, *Black Orpheus*, and *The Indian Runner*. It is safe to say that foreign films are largely overlooked, giving this work a definitive Anglo bias. Once again, however, it must be mentioned that this book represents Sullivan's personal experience with independent films and, although her free-spirited comments might disconcert some, it cannot be denied that she knows the subject well. Along with saucy, insightful reviews, there are complete cast lists and information about date of production, running time, rating, and award(s). There are also comprehensive appendixes that include a cast index, alliterative titles, "indie" organizations, and a category index. Purists will quibble over films left out of this guide, but it is definitely a labor of love and deserves a place on all public and school libraries. It will be very popular with a large segment of the library public.—**Joseph L. Carlson**

1170. **The Video Source Book: A Guide to Programs Currently Available on Video in the Areas of Movies/Entertainment, General Interest/Education....** James M. Craddock, Michelle Banks, and Christine Tomassini, eds. Farmington Hills, Mich., Gale, 1999. 2v. index. $325.00/set. ISBN 0-7876-3406-9. ISSN 0748-0881.

The 23d edition of this compilation is just under 4,000 densely printed pages. The updated *Video Source Book* (VSB) includes 122,000 videos, covering 165,000 separate programs, and is the most comprehensive resource in the VideoHound family of products. VSB includes video titles in the categories of "Movies/Entertainment," "General Interest/Education," "Sports/Recreation," "Fine Arts," "Health/Sciences," "Business/Industry," "Children/Juvenile," and "How-To/Instruction."

Arrangement is alphabetic by standard title. Each entry includes (when relevant and available) the release date; MPAA rating; a consensus critical rating of one to four stars; a description giving synopsis and details, such as whether the film is subtitled, dubbed, or colorized; running time; format options; hearing-impaired options; credits (including names of stars, major cast members, director, screenwriter, composer, narrator, and host); television standards; producer; audience level; purpose (e.g., education); subject categories assigned to it; awards won; acquisition type (e.g., rent, purchase); distributor(s); and price. Indexes provide access to alternative titles; credits; special formats (e.g., closed captioned, laser, optical or compact disc); and awards. The subject index includes 500 categories ranging from the general (animation and cartoons, biography, documentary films, how-to films, job training, sex and sexuality) to the specific (death, lymphatic system, Halloween). Some subjects are further subdivided. For example, the "Music" category has the subheadings "Classical," "Country and Western," "Instruction," "Jazz," "Performance," and "Pop/Rock" as well as "Music Video" and "Musical." A section listing program distributors gives complete contact information.

The VSB will be useful for teachers seeking video for classroom use, the general consumer, and the serious collector. It can serve as an excellent collection development tool for libraries selecting in video formats. It is highly recommended for all general reference, education, and performing arts libraries and collections.—**Ruth A. Carr**

Filmography

1171. Andrew, Geoff. **The Director's Vision: A Concise Guide to the Art of 250 Great Filmmakers.** Chicago, A Cappella Books/Chicago Review Press; distr., Chicago, Independent Publishers Group, 1999. 252p. illus. $24.95pa. ISBN 1-55652-366-1.

Andrew, who is associated with London's National Film Theatre, gives readers brief treatments of the work of 250 directors, from Georges Melies (b. 1861) to Todd Haynes (b. 1961). Overall he has selected noteworthy global filmmakers whose work meets the author's criteria of having a distinct visual style. The directors come from a variety of genres: westerns, silents, melodramas, horror, animation, musicals, propaganda, documentary, epics, and shock schlock.

A high-quality, half-page still shot introduces each entry and frames the discussion of the director's work. The narratives run about 250 words each and thus tend to be descriptive, not analytical. They suggest the quality of the director's work by describing a central or typical scene in his or her best film. There are references to the work of other filmmakers and occasionally to painters or playwrights to enlarge the visual understanding. If readers have seen the film, the description might suffice; if not, this is unlikely to inform in any serious way.

Although Andrew's judgments have merit, his prose gets in the way. After a few pages the reader longs for a simple declarative instead of the compound-complex sentences with multiple clauses and a parenthetical aside that are used. The book has a selective filmography and uses British film titles. There is no index or bibliography, but there are cross-references to directors with similar styles. At 252 pages, *The Director's Vision* falls somewhere between a really good movie scrapbook and useful film criticism.

—**John P. Schmitt**

1172. **The BFI Companion to Crime.** Phil Hardy, ed. Berkeley, Calif., University of California Press, 1997. 352p. illus. $29.95pa. ISBN 0-520-21538-9.

This latest volume in The British Film Institute's (BFI) series of genre film books retains all the best and worst qualities of its predecessors. Hardy, editor of numerous excellent Overlook Press film guides, covers hundreds of international crime, gangster, and noir movies, ranging from the silent era through the mid-1990s. By broadly defining "crime," Hardy includes such diverse titles as *Les Vampyres*, *Blade Runner*, and *Psycho*, with some emphasis on non-English-language productions. Entries are brief, focusing on plot, with some production information, but this is not a resource for detailed data or criticism. Some biographies are scattered throughout, as are short surveys of subgenres and topics (e.g., nightclubs), and almost every page features a black-and-white photograph. Movie remakes (e.g., *Breathless*) are touched upon, but only the original receives full attention.

As BFI is not intentionally comprehensive, one expects films and topics to be omitted. However, not to include entries on B movies or the Dead End Kids (or their imitators, or the film *Dead End*) is surprising. Not to include an index or bibliography significantly weakens the overall utility of the work. Much preferable is Hardy's and Jeremy Clarke's *The Overlook Film Encyclopedia: The Gangster Film* (Overlook Press, 1998), which covers more than 1,500 films and includes 650 black-and-white photographs. This work is recommended for all film collections, with reservations. [R: Choice, Sept 98, p. 84]—**Anthony J. Adam**

1173. Braff, Richard E. **The Universal Silents: A Filmography of the Universal Motion Picture Manufacturing Company, 1912-1929.** Jefferson, N.C., McFarland, 1999. 675p. index. $135.00. ISBN 0-7864-0287-3.

This painstakingly researched work is a comprehensive filmography of more than 9,000 silent-era "entertainment" films, including serials produced or distributed by the oldest producer of motion pictures, Universal Motion Picture Manufacturing Company, during the period 1912 to 1929. Not listed in this book are documentaries, newsreels, cartoons, travelogues, education, industrial, medical, agricultural, military, political, and historical films. The format consists of acknowledgments, a table of contents, preface, introduction, the films, an appendix for serials and episodes, a bibliography, and an index. In the section on films, works are listed in alphabetic order in one serially numbered sequence. The index refers to these serial numbers. The title is followed by the release date, copyright date, and available production information listing producer, directory, scenarist, author, length in number of reels, and cast members. This book covers 74 serials released by Universal. The organization of each serial entry includes the main title in bold typeface, release dates, copyright dates, production information, and a listing of all episode titles. Individual episodes are also listed in the main sequence of the book with cross-references to the series (or serial) titles. Braff concludes his work with an appendix showing serials with their complete episode titles in alphabetic order and a release date, a short bibliography, and a cross-reference index. This complete index lists personnel connected with each film in alphabetic order and each film pertaining to that individual in numerical order.

The information in the entries was drawn from publications aimed at film exhibitors such as *The Moving Picture World*, *The Motion Picture News*, and *Motography*. Much of the production information came from the *Buying and Booking Guide* published quarterly by *The Motion Picture News*, which contained a section of "short" films produced with the titles, producers, directors, stars, lengths, and release dates. Braff comments on the dilemma regarding the accuracy of the release dates since various publications would differ. This highly specialized reference book can serve as a tool in cinematic research for scholars, students, and film enthusiasts. Recommended for inclusion in libraries that support performing arts and comprehensive film collections. [R: LJ, 1 Feb 99, p. 76; Choice, April 99, p. 1432; BL, 15 Feb 99, p. 1094]—**Magda Želinská-Ferl**

1174. Fetrow, Alan G. **Feature Films, 1950-1959: A United States Filmography.** Jefferson, N.C., McFarland, 1999. 712p. index. $72.50. ISBN 0-7864-0427-2.

Many changes in the movie industry during the 1950s were promoted by the need to compete with the ubiquitous box appearing in more and more living rooms. Censorship rules were stretched, science fiction and films about teens were on the rise, and westerns and serials declined. This filmography, listing 3,075 U.S. movies, reflects such changes.

Alphabetically arranged entries include title, production company, release year, full cast and credits, songs, running time, video availability, plot synopsis, and production notes. Character names are included for Oscar winners or nominees, top-grossing films, and for nonfictional characters. Cross-references are made to alternate titles. A list of award-winning films and a brief bibliography precede an extensive name index, enhancing access to the movie listing.

The author has published two other volumes documenting American films back to 1927. Hopefully, he will continue this chronological documentation of the U.S. film industry. [R: Choice, Sept 99, p. 110; BL, June 99, p. 1878]—**Anita Zutis**

1175. Freese, Gene Scott. **Hollywood Stunt Performers: A Dictionary and Filmography of over 600 Men and Women, 1922-1996.** Jefferson, N.C., McFarland, 1998. 261p. illus. index. $48.50. ISBN 0-7864-0511-2.

Few people will deny that one of the necessary ingredients for a contemporary action picture is that it be loaded with as many never-before-seen stunts as possible. Producers and directors have devised ingenious ways to blow up buildings, destroy cars, mutilate planes and trains, and generally put the actors in as much peril as can be squeezed into two hours. The audience responds viscerally to these stunts, but has little knowledge of the people who risk their lives to make sure that it looks realistic, incredible, awe-inspiring, and challenging. Many books have been written on how various stunts are done, but this is the first one that focuses on the people behind them. The author, who has been in the industry as both an actor and a screenwriter, presents an alphabetical listing of men and women who have served as stunt performers between 1922 and 1996. If they have appeared in at least 10 major theatrical releases, Freese includes them, and gives a listing of the movies and television programs in which they have substituted for an actor or been involved in significant stunts. Occasionally, he lists brief biographical information, such as birth and death dates, training, and contributions to the art of stunt performance. Freese has certainly done these people a service by listing their accomplishments, but his work is highly specialized and is recommended only for extensive film libraries. Unfortunately, stunt performers are doomed to obscurity in an industry that thrives on personality, and few readers outside of the film business will find this book of interest. [R: BL, 1 Oct 98, p. 364;]—**Joseph L. Carlson**

1176. Harty, Kevin J. **The Reel Middle Ages: American, Western and Eastern European, Middle Eastern and Asian Films About Medieval Europe.** Jefferson, N.C., McFarland, 1999. 316p. illus. $78.50. ISBN 0-7864-0541-4.

After only a few minutes of browsing through Harty's new book, readers may be tempted to rush over to the video store. With its capsule reviews, clean layout, and numerous film stills, *The Reel Middle Ages: Films About Medieval Europe* is an exceptionally reader-friendly survey. Harty takes a broad approach to the time frame of the Middle Ages, covering the fifth through the fifteenth centuries. Listed in alphabetic order are 564 foreign and domestic films from 1897 to 1996. Each entry gives the date, country of origin, director, production or releasing company, cast, a synopsis, alternate titles, and a bibliography of reviews and other discussions of the film. Because they are already well covered in the reference literature, adaptations of Shakespeare's plays are not included. The index, which refers to entry numbers, lists film titles, actors, directors, and only those characters who are household names (e.g., Joan of Arc, Robin Hood, King Arthur, Marco Polo).

In the synopses, the author often gives his own critique of the film, which is especially useful in the case of multiple versions. For example, there are nine film adaptations of Twain's *A Connecticut Yankee in King Arthur's Court*. Unfortunately, except for the occasional mention in a synopsis, he does not provide names of screenwriters—important information for researchers and film buffs. Nevertheless, *The Reel Middle Ages* belongs in all public and academic libraries with cinema collections. [R: BL, June 99, p. 1884]—**Lori D. Kranz**

1177. Joslin, Lyndon W. **Count Dracula Goes to the Movies: Stoker's Novel Adapted, 1922-1995.** Jefferson, N.C., McFarland, 1999. 237p. illus. index. $44.00. ISBN 0-7864-0698-4.

Dracula is an almost universally recognized fictional character and pop culture icon in the Western world. Bram Stoker's never-out-of-print novel *Dracula* started this phenomenon in 1897, but stage adaptations followed by film adaptations, starting in 1922, have kept Count Dracula before the public eye ever since. Hundreds of other films and novels have taken their inspiration from or tried to imitate *Dracula*'s success over the years. Joslin's book confines its attention to the 11 films that are adaptations of Stoker's novel. Starting with *Nosferatu: Eine Sinfonie des Grauens* (1922) with its cadaverous Max Schreck as the vampire and ending with the improbably *Dracula: Dead and Loving It* (1995), Joslin compares each film's plot in detail to that of Stoker's novel, comments on the adaptation, and provides notes on each film's music. Also described individually are the five Universal Studios spin-offs with Bela Lugosi as Dracula, the eight Hammer sequels mostly starring Christopher Lee, and three films that closely mimic or spin off from Stoker's novel—*Jonathan* (1970), *Count Yorga, Vampire* (1970), and *Nadja* (1994). Black-and-white stills from the various movies are scattered throughout the text. An appendix provides the mailing and e-mail addresses and Websites for suppliers of hard-to-find movies, and there are a bibliography and an index for the volume. For those especially interested in Dracula and horror movies, this book is an interesting addition to the literature.—**Ronald H. Fritze**

1178. Jura, Jean-Jacques, and Rodney Norman Bardin II. **Balboa Films: A History of Filmography of the Silent Film Studio.** Jefferson, N.C., McFarland, 1999. 292p. illus. index. $65.00. ISBN 0-7864-0496-5.

The authors document a little-known but influential silent film company that dominated the town of Long Beach, California, between 1913 and 1918, when the owners went bankrupt. The narrative includes a helpful timeline that clearly outlines the business, artistic, and technical achievements of Balboa Amusement Producing Company. Seven major stars, such as Henry King, Ruth Roland, and Baby Marie Osborne, are profiled, with pictures and a list of their box–office hits. Following these biographies is a filmography that describes 230 film titles of the "countless movies produced in Long Beach" with varying depth of coverage. Only 20 of these films still survive. In some cases the entry includes only the title, number of reels, and distributor, but usually there are a list of the cast, a commentary from a secondary source (e.g., newspaper, The American Film Institute), and a summary of the plot. Occasionally there are reviews.

The concluding index is mainly a name index, not a topical one. For instance, a researcher looking for a particular actor or director will likely find the information, but one looking for cinematography or the role of children in films (something that Balboa was supposed to be a pioneer in) will not find a listing in the index. That much love went into the research and writing is shown by both the admiring tone of the prose and the pictures of the authors with a much older "Baby Marie" and with Elwood Horkheimer's daughter, Jackie Saunders Jr. The narrow subject, the incomplete index, and the conversational style make the book more a browsing tool than a quick reference, but one that will find its way into reference and possibly circulating collections of libraries that support film programs.—**Juleigh Muirhead Clark**

1179. Klepper, Robert K. **Silent Films, 1877-1976: A Critical Guide to 646 Movies.** Jefferson, N.C., McFarland, 1999. 586p. illus. index. $45.00. ISBN 0-7864-0595-3.

There are 119 years of silent films, from Edweard Muybridge and the dawn of cinema though 1996's *Taxi Driver*, chronicled in this critical guide. The author's intention is to present a comprehensive history of silent films. Therefore, all types of silents are included, dealing with social issues, light comedy, pornography, and so on. Among sources cited are two silent film player directories from 1995—*The Silent Film Necrology* (see ARBA 96, entry 1369), and *The Ultimate Directory of the Silent Film Performers* (see ARBA 96, entry 1368).

Chronological entries (646 in all) contain the standard production data, dates, cast, and plot summary, and range from several lines to several pages. A rating system (masterpiece to abysmal) is used. However, there are also detailed critiques, commentaries, background information, and updates. These add considerable value and interest to the volume. Nearly 200 black-and-white photographs, comprising stills, posters, and publicity shots, serve as illustrations. The main section is followed by a bibliography and an index with names, titles, and film companies.

Both the arrival of the video revolution, enhancing the availability of silents, and the publication of the aforementioned directories, as sources for dates, have enabled the writing of a guide of this scope. It provides new and useful information about the origins of creating the illusion of images in motion. [R: BL, 1 Sept 99, p. 186]—**Anita Zutis**

1180. Koliodimos, Dimitris. **The Greek Filmography, 1914 Through 1996.** Jefferson, N.C., McFarland, 1999. 773p. illus. index. $135.00. ISBN 0-7864-0546-5.

Long a staple of film festivals, Greek movies have played a major role in defining the history (both political and social) of that nation. Few countries have used cinema as a potent propaganda tool as has Greece, and in this exhaustive study of Greek films, readers will gain important insights into just how the government and other agencies have entwined their values into Greek movies.

The author has been a film historian for more than 20 years and is a member of the Hellenic Film Critics Society. His efforts have unearthed films that were previously never before available to the public as well as some curiosity pieces that were shown only for a brief period of time. Of the 2,302 films covered in this book, most were limited to Greek distribution, but the artistic value of many of them has led to their discovery by the rest of the world. Koliodimos states frankly that his list does not include the several pornographic films that Greece has been known for, nor any purely religious films made for proselytizing reasons. He has listed the original title of the films in both their Greek and Roman alphabets, any titles subsequently used in international distributions, production year, running time, production company, director, screenwriter, director of photography, composer or creator of the music, and main cast members. Following this is a brief synopsis of the films, any special reviews it may have received, and any awards it may have won. The entries are short, but extremely thorough in their analysis of the film. An extensive series of appendixes lists Thessaloniki Film Festival Awards, National Film Awards, names given in the credits of films, and a Greek index of names and titles. This book is a valuable resource in cinema history and will be of significant importance to all film library collections as well as university and college libraries. [R: Choice, Nov 99, p. 508]—**Joseph L. Carlson**

1181. Rainey, Buck. **Serials and Series: A World Filmography, 1912-1956.** Jefferson, N.C., McFarland, 1999. 321p. illus. index. $95.00. ISBN 0-7864-0449-3.

Rainey's interesting introduction to his book invites students to share his love of film serials and series. He puts them in the context of their times and then proceeds to list 471 American serials, 100 American series, 136 foreign serials, and 37 foreign series alphabetically by series title. Each entry includes such information as the director, producer, writer, and cast; descriptions of the plot; and lists the individual episodes. The amount of information on each title varies. Black-and-white pictures accompany the text. The book concludes with a 14-page selected bibliography and an index of personal names and serial/series titles.

A list of the foreign titles, arranged by country, and a list of the silent titles, arranged chronologically, would add to the reference value of the book. However, this is an entertaining look at a memorable part of film history and will be of interest to film studies collections. [R: BL, 1 Sept 99, pp. 185-186; RUSQ, Fall 99, p. 100]—**Juleigh Muirhead Clark**

1182. Reinhart, Mark S. **Abraham Lincoln on Screen: A Filmography of Dramas and Documentaries Including Television, 1903-1998.** Jefferson, N.C., McFarland, 1999. 292p. illus. index. $49.95. ISBN 0-7864-0602-X.

No other figure in U.S. history has been portrayed in films and television shows more than Abraham Lincoln. By now, many scenes from his life have become ingrained in the minds of everyone—his assassination at Ford's Theater, his delivery of the Gettysburg Address, his lonely wanderings through the halls of the White House—but how many of them are accurate or merely fictional re-creations of what really happened? The author is a noted Lincoln scholar as well as a librarian and musician. Readers might expect a reverential treatment of Lincoln films, but Reinhart excoriates the ones he considers to be more fiction than fact in terms that make for fascinating reading. He has apparently scoured the vaults for every film that features Lincoln, ranging from the monumental works to those that are bizarre to those that have virtually disappeared from sight. "Monumental" works include such well-known works as Raymond Massey's 1940 portrayal in *Abe Lincoln in Illinois* ("It is unfortunate that this film which disregards so many facts relating to Lincoln's life has come to be regarded by many as one of the greatest Lincoln screen portrayals"), *Birth of a Nation* ("The sequence depicting Lincoln's assassination at Ford's Theatre is far and away the best Lincoln scene in the production—it is remarkably accurate to the actual event"), and *The Lincoln Conspiracy* from 1977 ("The worst historical abuses ever perpetrated in a Lincoln-related motion picture").

"Bizarre" touches on such films as *Bill and Ted's Excellent Adventure* from 1989 and *Police Squad*. Reinhart mixes in a great deal of Lincoln history in his discussions of the various films, giving readers a better understanding of this remarkable president and his legacy. He notes that the liberties taken with Lincoln's life are made all the more abhorrent because there are so many photographs available that provide filmmakers with primary resources. Reinhart presents an alphabetic list of films, dates of production, Lincoln impersonators, full-cast lists, and production information. His work is suitable for all university libraries because of its historical value, and for all film libraries because of its incredible attention to detail.
—**Joseph L. Carlson**

1183. Renzi, Thomas C. **Jules Verne on Film: A Filmography of the Cinematic Adaptations of His Work, 1902 Through 1997.** Jefferson, N.C., McFarland, 1998. 230p. illus. index. $55.00. ISBN 0-7864-0450-7.

Renzi's goal in *Jules Verne on Film* is to provide a discussion of Jules Verne's *voyages extraordinaires* as well as the motion pictures that have been based on them. The volume is arranged alphabetically by the English titles of Verne's work, with each section opening with a discussion of the novel followed by a discussion of the films that have been based on it. These discussions give the issuing studio, the major cast and credits, the running time, and a sometimes lengthy summary and critique. The volume concludes with two appendixes—a chronological list of Verne's prose fiction and a bibliography of biological and critical sources—and three indexes listing the directors, film titles, and general subjects.

There are some significant strengths in *Jules Verne on Film*, including the information about the motion pictures, for Renzi has not limited himself to English productions, and the data in these sections are frequently obtainable elsewhere only with difficulty. Bibliographically, however, *Jules Verne on Film* is lacking: Verne's 1888 Deux Ans de Vacances has been published as *A Two-Year Holiday*, *Two Year Holiday*, *Adrift in the Pacific*, *A Two Year's Vacation*, *Lost on the Wide Pacific*, *Boy Castaways*, and *A Long Vacation*. Renzi cites only the first title, though the majority of the editions have appeared as *Adrift in the Pacific*. Equally serious, Renzi's conclusions are often suspect: Verne's father may have been domineering, but that Verne *père* prevented his 11-year-old son from running away to sea and punished him for attempting to do so is hardly the act of a "constrictive" parent (p. 4). Similarly, Renzi's desire to make Verne's influence a pervasive one has led him to connect the motion picture of *Lord of the Flies* with Verne's *Adrift in the Pacific* because "the two stories approach the same idea from opposite directions" (p. 210). There are likewise references to such motion pictures as *Barbarella*, *Death Race 2000*, *Blade Runner*, *Back to the Future*, *Black Moon*, and *The Spy Who Loved Me*, all linked to Verne's works because they have a motif that Renzi feels creates a connection. This is a work of dubious value, although academic libraries supporting serious studies in the history of science fiction and film may want to have it. [R: Choice, Oct 98, p. 293]—**Richard Bleiler**

1184. Russell, Sharon A. **Guide to African Cinema.** Westport, Conn., Greenwood Press, 1998. 183p. index. (Reference Guides to the World's Cinema). $75.00. ISBN 0-313-29621-9.

Even an adventurous film buff's experience of African cinema might come down to Ousmane Sembene (Senegal) or Gaston Kabore and Idrissa Ouedraogo (Burkina Faso). This slender but useful guide covers them and a great deal more. It offers essays on 40 individual films and 16 filmmakers, sorted in alphabetic order. Starting with Sembene's *Black Girl* (1966), the movies chosen present a cross-section of filmic activity on the continent during the past 3 decades. Because these works are so obscure, Russell keys her discussions to synopsis and thematic content. The one film whose stylistic agenda is detailed, Raoul Peck's *Lumumba: Death of a Prophet* (1992), sounds fascinating.

Russell's charmingly practical introduction sets out her selection criteria, and the ways African directors differ from Hollywood and European art film models. She has included little from apartheid-era South Africa. Danish director Henning Carlsen's film of a Nadine Gordimer novel, *A World of Strangers* (1962), gets in because it employs clandestinely shot footage. Likewise, 2 celebrated European efforts appear—*The Battle of Algiers* (1966) and *Ramparts of Clay* (1970). Russell seems more alert to their narratives and use of locations than to the remarkable modes of address.

This book's jargon-free prose suggests that it is intended for the real world, not academe. To that end, Russell has compiled a list of film distributors and an unusually extensive bibliography. Her volume is an important addition to world cinema studies. [R: BL, 1 June 98, pp. 1804-1806; Choice, Sept 98, p. 84]

—**Walt Mundkowsky**

1185. Smith, Don G. **The Poe Cinema: A Critical Filmography of Theatrical Releases Based on the Works of Edgar Allan Poe.** Jefferson, N.C., McFarland, 1999. 307p. illus. index. $55.00. ISBN 0-7864-0453-1.

The father of American horror writers, Poe (1809-1849) failed to enjoy the contemporaneous critical and commercial success bestowed upon his best-selling predecessor Stephen King. Literary critics now acknowledge Poe as a master of the genre, while generations of filmmakers have exploited the marquee value of his name to produce numerous adaptations of his work. Smith, a university history professor, has identified 88 such Poe-inspired feature films produced in 14 countries from 1908 to 1992 in this entertaining, informative, and well-illustrated filmography. Films are arranged chronologically with each entry containing information on cast and credits, story synopsis, production and marketing history, and a critique. The 1st, *Sherlock Holmes in the Great Murder Mystery*, a 1908 movie based on the 1841 Poe story "Murders in the Rue Morgue," is indicative of the film fate suffered by much of the writer's works. Often, the only resemblance a film bears to Poe's work is the title or a few scenes suggested by the original story. For example, beginning in 1960 with *The Fall of the House of Usher*, American International Pictures released a series of 8 low-budget, Poe-inspired films produced and directed by Roger Corman starring Vincent Price. In his description of these entertaining and important films (e.g., *The Premature Burial*, 1962; *The Raven*, 1963), Smith uses the AIP pressbooks to add authority and depth to his analysis. The book's reference value is also enhanced by appendixes listing Poe films by their country of origin and Poe titles and the films adapted from them. Recommended for academic libraries. [R: LJ, 1 Feb 99, p. 78]

—**David K. Frasier**

1186. Soister, John T. **Of Gods and Monsters: A Critical Guide to Universal Studios' Science Fiction, Horror, and Mystery Films, 1929-1939.** Jefferson, N.C., McFarland, 1999. 395p. illus. index. $65.00. ISBN 0-7864-0454-X.

It is always a pleasure to read a book by an author who obviously loves his subject. John T. Soister, a teacher in Orwingsburg, Pennsylvania, describes himself as a member of a "close-knit, ever growing coterie of friends who recognize the gift of imagination that was needed to make films such as these and who possess the gift of imagination needed to appreciate them." He has taken the films made during what is now recognized as Universal's "Golden Age" of horror and fantasy and written concise, definitive essays about them. There is nothing pedantic about his writing; his is equally skilled in his praise as well as his criticism.

Along with details such as release dates, cast and credit lists, and film length, Soister also presents in-depth analyses of each film. He relates intimate details about how each film was made, how actors squabbled, how studio heads threatened the artistic quality of certain films, and how flamboyant directors such as James Whale came to rule the horror genre. Soister has his favorites (*The Invisible Man*, *The Old Dark House*, and *The Cat Creeps* among them) and manages to convince readers why they, too, should regard these films as more than mere entertainment. Each essay is accompanied by "window card" art of on-scene pictures of actors, and Soister's wit is as colorful as the drawings used to advertise these films. Film libraries will definitely want a copy of this intense work; large public libraries will find it a popular reference item.—**Joseph L. Carlson**

1187. **TLA Film and Video Guide: The Discerning Film Lover's Guide 2000-2001.** David Bleiler, ed. New York, St. Martin's Press, 1999. 756p. illus. index. $18.95pa. ISBN 0-312-24330-8.

As implied in the subtitle, the compilers of this selective guide to films and videos set out to advise users on the quality of the titles they include. Bleiler is the video columnist for the *Philadelphila Daily News* and he emphasizes that this is a critical survey for cinema lovers, not a comprehensive viewing list. It covers more than 9,500 films, with special focus on independent and international movies and the best of mainstream feature films.

This is a more readable product than one finds in many video guides. The layout is spacious, with nice margins around each entry. Arrangement is alphabetic by title, with the title clearly shown in large, bold print. Each entry includes year of release, running time, country of origin, directory, a short critical review, a rating on a four-star scale, and the film's main actors. All reviews have cost and format information (e.g., VHS, DVD, letterbox) for prospective film purchasers. Almost all the titles are available from the TLA Entertainment Group, the enterprise that lends its initials to the title of the book. An order form and citation for the group's Website make up the final page. Six indexes round out the volume: countries of origin, genres, directors filmographies, stars filmographies, authors and screenwriters, and themes. And finally, there are lists of "TLA Bests" for 1990 to 1998 and "Awards" for 1970 to 1998.

This successful and moderately priced directory will help film lovers make viewing choices among the better movies of the twentieth century. Libraries that support users in film studies programs should find this a popular reference tool.—**Berniece M. Owen**

Handbooks and Yearbooks

1188. **BFI Film and Television Handbook 1999.** Eddie Dyja, ed. London, British Film Institute; distr., Bloomington, Ind., Indiana University Press, 1998. 416p. illus. index. $35.00pa. ISBN 0-85170-682-7.

The British Film Institute's (BFI) *Film and Television Handbook 1999* offers a basic, if not comprehensive, resource on cinema, video, and television production in the United Kingdom. As one would expect from the publishers of *Sight & Sound* (see ARBA 97, entry 1135), the first few chapters of the handbook make entertaining reading for those interested in the British entertainment industry. There are colorful and informative tables on such topics as "Number of UK Films Produced 1912-1997," "The top 20 Films at the Worldwide Box Office 1997," and "What Happened to 1996's UK Films?" (a report on films made but not distributed and those that went straight to television). Along with photos of recent films, these first 50 pages provide an overview of what happened in 1997. The subsequent chapters revert to normal directory information on film libraries, distributors, festivals, film societies, PR companies, and production starts. In addition to the UK listings, there are entries for European film societies and festivals as well.

What differentiates the *BFI Handbook* from other directories on film and television are the bibliographies provided in the chapters on careers, books, and CD-ROMs—a useful addition to any reference book. The chapter on entertainment legislation in the United Kingdom is also unique.

What is missing from the handbook are pointers to the appropriate commonwealth organizations, libraries, Websites, and film societies. Each category is scattered with European entries, but there does not seem to be any consistency as to when the listing will contain non-England, Scotland, or Wales information. This source is best used in conjunction with the Quigley Press publications *International Television and Video Almanac* (41st ed.; see ARBA 97, entry 771) and *International Motion Picture Almanac* (67th ed.; see ARBA 97, entry 770). For example, the Academy of Canadian Cinema and Television can be found in the *International Television and Video Almanac*, but does not appear in the BFI publication. This book is recommended for larger film study collections.—**Elizabeth A. Ginno**

1189. Booker, M. Keith. **Film and the American Left: A Research Guide.** Westport, Conn., Greenwood Press, 1999. 427p. index. $89.50. ISBN 0-313-30980-9.

This work provides detailed entries for 260 films associated with the American left. The films selected contain left themes or were created by directors, screenwriters, or actors with known leftist sympathies. For the purposes of this volume, left themes include the desire for economic, social, or political justice, and a deep suspicion that capitalism is antithetical to reaching these goals. The focus is on mainstream Hollywood films, although some documentaries and independent films are also included.

The films are arranged chronologically beginning with *The Strike* (1904) and ending with *Men with Guns* (1998). This arrangement allows the reader to follow the evolution of left ideals in film. Early pro-worker silent films (sometimes union-financed) disappeared during the World War I period, and by the 1920s the Hollywood entertainment film had become dominant. The Depression created a mood more open to left ideas but by the 1940s, popular front ideology concentrated efforts on supporting the war against fascism. The blacklist put an end to many careers and those still working in film could allude to left values only obliquely. The 1960s saw the end of the blacklist and the reemergence of culturally critical mainstream films.

Each entry places a film in historical context, examines it for left themes, and provides a bibliographic reference. Although one finds obvious left titles, such as *Salt of the Earth* made by blacklisted artists in 1954, on first glance George Cukor's *The Philadelphia Story* could seem out of place. However, its screenplay was written by Donald Ogden Stewart, who would later leave the country because of his politics, and it is cited as an example of the inability of leftists to get their ideas on screen. Ironically, *Tender Comrades* (screenplay by Dalton Trumbo), a patriotic, pro-war film with no obvious leftist agenda other than defeat of fascism, would be cited by those on the blacklist as evidence of communist influence in the motion picture industry.

Appendixes list films alphabetically by title and director. A full bibliography and index are provided. This volume is recommended for performing arts, popular culture, and U.S. history collections.

—**Ruth A. Carr**

1190. Dement, Jeffrey W. **Going for Broke: The Depiction of Compulsive Gambling in Film.** Lanham, Md., Scarecrow, 1999. 192p. index. $39.50. ISBN 0-8108-3624-6.

"Has Hollywood sent an accurate and responsible message about compulsive gambling to viewers?" is the question freelance writer Dement addresses in this slim volume attempting to meld therapeutic insight with film studies. In part 1, Dement examines 11 films that feature a lead character who is a compulsive gambler. These include *Fever Pitch* (1985), *The Gambler* (1974), *Vegas Vacation* (1997), and *The Hustler* (1961). Each film's theme is examined in light of what is currently known about the condition of compulsive gambling. Too often the psychological insights drawn from a film fail to rise above the level of an undergraduate psychology course. For example, at the conclusion of *The Gambler* the title character played by James Caan is slashed across the face with a razor. Dement concludes that this compulsive gambler "has been scarred, both literally and figuratively, for life." Part 2 examines 10 additional films that include some partial aspect of gambling. Appendixes include a chronology of compulsive gambling in films between 1908 and 1998 and a selected filmography. "Has Hollywood been responsible in its depiction of compulsive gambling?" No surprise: of course not. Dement's study maintains that unlike his true-life counterpart, the

Hollywood compulsive gambler usually wins. This misrepresents the disease and its devastating effect on families and society at large. While there have been responsible films on the subject (*The Gambler*), too often, according to Dement the sickness has been glamorized (*Let It Ride*, 1989). Without debating the role movies play in American society, Dement's study serves little use as information about the disease, its depiction in movies, or as a filmography. A sample of 21 movies specifically selected from 90 years of filmmaking to prove a self-evident point does not qualify as a legitimate study. This work is not recommended.
—**David K. Frasier**

1191. Fernandes, David, and Dale Robinson. **A Guide to Television's** *Mayberry R. F. D.* Jefferson, N.C., McFarland, 1999. 235p. illus. index. $35.00. ISBN 0-7864-0426-4.

When Andy Griffith and Don Knotts decided it was time to pack up and leave the comfy confines of Mayberry, the producers of the hit television series did not want to see the corn pone cash cow run dry. A new set of bumpkins was introduced in the sequel called *Mayberry R.F.D.* During its three year run, the show was consistently popular with viewers, but CBS decided to leave the sticks and move to the big city in 1971 with more "reality-based" shows. Now a staple of TV Land and Nick at Night, *Mayberry R.F.D.* serves to remind us of a quieter, gentler time on television. Fernandes and Robinson, who previously paid homage to the original show with their 1996 *The Definitive Andy Griffith Show Reference* (see ARBA 97, entry 1134), turn their attention to the Ken Berry spin-off, which ran from 1969 to 1971. Griffith and Knotts appeared in a few of the early episodes, and Frances Bavier continued to dispense homespun homilies, making the transfer relatively seamless. Fernandes and Robinson have done an incredible job in chronicling this series, offering readers both a complete episode guide (air dates, guest stars, story lines) and an amazingly rich vein of trivia. Their writing is as folksy as the series and fans of both shows (plus the other spin-off, *Gomer Pyle, U.S.M.C.*) will enjoy this nostalgic look back at life in a small fictional North Carolina town hat has become embedded in the American psyche. This book will be most popular in libraries specializing in television history, and most large public libraries will want to consider it as well.—**Joseph L. Carlson**

1192. Langman, Larry. **American Film Cycles: The Silent Era.** Westport, Conn., Greenwood Press, 1998. 400p. index. (Bibliographies and Indexes in the Performing Arts, no.22). $79.50. ISBN 0-313-30657-5.

Silent films form a vast and important resource for the study of American cultural and social history that is often difficult for scholars and students to access. Most silent films are not easily available for viewing while filmographies and guides for silent movies are far less common than similar works for sound films. This circumstance makes *American Film Cycles: The Silent Era* (part of the Bibliographies and Indexes in the Performing Arts series) a valuable addition to reference literature. More than 1,000 films, both shorts and feature length, from 1900 to 1929 form the focus of this book. These various films are classified into 40 common theme cycles. These themes range alphabetically from "abandoned spouse" to "women's rights." Other cycles include "biographies," "capital vs. labor," "drugs," "political corruption," "red scare," and "slums." Each cycle is presented in the form of a filmographical essay that traces the films in each cycle through two basic chronological periods—the early silent years (1900-1919) and the Golden Age (1920-1929). A name index helps the reader to locate actors and directors while a title index identifies the individual films discussed. There is also a brief selective bibliography. Langman's work usefully lists and classifies many silent films but it is not a complete listing. Why some films are discussed while others are not is unclear. Only a few of D. W. Griffith's vast production of titles are included in this volume. Among the missing are his first feature film, *Judith of Bethulia* (1914), its remake, *Her Condoned Sin* (1917), and the classic *Intolerance* (1916). There is also no mention of the famous 1926 version of *Ben Hur* with Francis X. Bushman. *American Film Cycles: The Silent Era* should be considered a comprehensive introduction to the films cycles used during the silent era rather than an exhaustive work.
—**Ronald H. Fritze**

1193. Nollen, Scott Allen. **Robin Hood: A Cinematic History of the English Outlaw and His Scottish Counterparts.** Jefferson, N.C., McFarland, 1999. 259p. illus. index. $36.50. ISBN 0-7864-0643-7.

Although the literature of Robin Hood is fairly extensive, Nollen is the first to solely critically study the film version of the legend. After a useful, nearly 80-page introduction to the character of Robin Hood, Rob Roy, and other English and Scottish outlaws, Nollen examines in chronological order the development of the cinema character, from the silent films of 1908 to 1913 through the well-known portrayals. Nollen's history is informative, if sometimes overly opinionated, and always readable. Television series are not covered, which is unfortunate since there were at least five versions of the legend on the small screen over the decades, and foreign-language films are also omitted. However, Nollen does examine Sinatra's *Robin and the Seven Hoods* (1964), for an interesting take on the story. The volume concludes with a filmography of the English and Scottish Robin Hoods and brief bibliography.

Unfortunately, although the text is highlighted with numerous illustrations, some of the grainier photographs appear to be snapshots taken from television broadcasts. Nollen makes an interesting companion volume to Lois Potter's more extensive collection, *Playing Robin Hood: The Legend as Performance in Five Centuries* (University of Delaware Press, 1998), which includes an essay on the cinematic portrayal. This volume is recommended for all film and cultural history collections.—**Anthony J. Adam**

Indexes

1194. **The Complete Index to Literary Sources in Film.** Alan Goble, ed. New Providence, N.J., Bowker-Saur/Reed Reference Publishing, 1999. 1028p. $130.00. ISBN 1-85739-229-9.

The Complete Index to Literary Sources in Film is an international index to more than 30,000 literary sources of film from 83 countries. It covers from 1895 to 1999 and over 12,000 authors. It has been compiled from the 1998 CD-ROM titled *The Complete Index to World Film Since 1895*, and combined with additional data that has been gathered for the 2000 edition. Documentation on film is often contradictory and the literary origin of a film is sometimes unverifiable. For example, when a source states "from a story by...," the author may have written several stories, making it difficult to track down which story is being referred to. This can also mean the source was a published story or it was merely a story outline produced by the studio.

Information is found in 3 separate indexes: an author index, a film index, and a literary source index. Understandably, a reference work such as this is a large undertaking. It is impossible to make the work all-inclusive. Although the data included are numerous, readers will easily spot glaring omissions; not to mention several typographical and grammatical errors. For example, Stephen King "legally" has his named removed from any connection to the film *The Lawnmower Man*, but this index still lists his short story as the source for the film. Another glaring error is the omission of Disney's adaptation of the Grimm brothers *Cinderella* and *Sleeping Beauty* while *Snow White and the Seven Dwarfs* is included.

This work contains many useful and entertaining facts that may be useful to filmographers and casual readers, but it is not complete. Interested buyers may wish to wait for the 2000 CD-ROM. Perhaps some of these errors will be corrected by then.—**Cari Ringelheim**

1195. **Complete Index to World Film Since 1895 on CD-ROM.** [CD-ROM]. By Alan Goble. New Providence, N.J., Bowker-Saur/Reed Reference Publishing, 1998. Minimum system requirements: IBM or compatible 486 with 66MHz. CD-ROM drive. DOS 5.0 or higher. Windows 3.1. 8MB RAM. 15MB hard disk space. VGA monitor with a minimum of 16 colors. Mouse. $1,295.00. ISBN 1-85739-252-3.

The *Complete Index to World Film Since 1895 on CD-ROM* is one of the most comprehensive film indexes ever published. It contains more than 300,000 entries on film, beginning in 1895 and continuing through 1998. There are more than 1 million actor credits and 45,000 director filmographies. In addition, it references more than 75,000 films, which makes it by far the largest list of film titles in existence. It also provides information on film production companies, music credits, literary origins of films, and listings of more than 100,000 silent films.

The work uses Folio information retrieval software, which allows users to search the entire database by film title, director, music credits, literary origin, year of release, actors' names, production company, and country of origin. The searching is done through keyword and the entries contain hypertext links between the various categories (e.g., if one finds a particular actor, one can link to the entry for each film the individual appeared in). Boolean searching is also possible. The search screens are clear and well organized, and the entry screens present the information in a concise manner. Also, it is possible to reference the several hundred sources used to make up the database.—**Robert L. Wick**

Quotation Books

1196. Kane, Jim, comp. **Western Movie Quotations.** Jefferson, N.C., McFarland, 1999. 550p. illus. index. $75.00. ISBN 0-7864-0594-5.

Although a uniquely American genre of film and fiction, Westerns have long been and continue to remain popular throughout the world and with all generations. In *Western Movie Quotations*, the compiler, Jim Kane, has performed a labor of love by extracting 6,063 quotations from more than 1,000 movies. Kane has culled his quotes from a wide variety of movies, ranging from the silent films of the 1920s to the films of the present, and within that time frame includes not only big-budget pictures but also forgotten to semi-forgotten "B" films. Appearing in this collection are the usual quotations from such classics as *Stagecoach*, *Shane*, *The Treasure of Sierra Madre*, and *The Wild Bunch*.

The quotations are arranged into 41 alphabetically arranged topics starting with "Bad Guys" and concluding with "Women." In between are quotes about "Cattle," "Gold," "Justice," "Marriage and Romance," and "Stagecoaches and Railroad," to name just a few. Within each category, quotes are arranged alphabetically by the title of the film in which they appeared. Three indexes to personal names, film titles, and subjects and keywords are included to assist readers in finding quotations of interest. *Western Movie Quotations* is a browser's delight. Under the category of "Indians" lies a rainbow of opinions that range from hostile to sympathetic and from stereotypical to insightful and empathetic. The text is liberally sprinkled with a well-chosen selection of black-and-white still photographs. It would have been helpful, however, if the compiler had provided a brief note about the context of some individual quotes within their films. While the context is obvious in many cases, in others, additional information would be helpful to readers. Western buffs will covet this volume.—**Ronald H. Fritze**

Videography

1197. Frank, Sam. **Buyer's Guide to Fifty Years of TV on Video.** Buffalo, N.Y., Prometheus Books, 1999. 1498p. index. $22.95pa. ISBN 1-57392-226-9.

This comprehensive directory was written and compiled with the help of many individuals and sources. It covers television series, television movies, and documentaries. The directory aims to be more than just a list of available shows; it was written to give the reader the edge so that they can in assembling the best possible library of favorite and forgotten shows, movies, and miniseries based on content and visual quality. The author provides helpful commentary throughout the book, indicating places where he is stating his personal opinions, observations, and preferences.

The main section of the directory lists shows in alphabetic order. Entries include several elements—an episode title, network, original air dates, cast members and character names, running times, the author's content ratings from "bomb" to "excellent," and format availability of the show. The author also includes comments and memorable highlights from the show or episode that stood out to him, such as whether it is recommended for children or family viewing, available in color or black-and-white, or closed-captioned. Availability in laser disc, pricing, MPAA ratings for movies and television series, and cross-references to several other well-known television directories are also provided. The author points out that several of these "standard" sources do contain inaccuracies. Entries also contain warning labels for shows concerning content, credits for each show, Nielson rankings, Emmy Awards, and other awards.

There are informative and helpful sections of this book. All of the shows listed are available for purchase, so an alphabetic list of mail and telephone order companies is provided with commentary on what is available from each, ease and time frame of purchase and arrival, and the quality of those purchases. There is a section on recommended family shows that Frank categorizes, from adventure to westerns. His introduction is quite informative and contains many components. He provides explanations for his rating scales, shows how to care for video tapes, discusses the different timings there can be for shows, and details the variations of picture quality there can be based on dubbing from original or copies of different formats. The book gives brief histories on the "fourth network" and the "golden age of television" and includes a detailed section on the history of kinescopes, videotape, and color television. The author includes a section on 180 shows that he would like to see made available for purchase as well as a trivia quiz section, a bibliography, and a name index.

An alphabetic running head in the entries section would help with locating items in the directory because entries can go on for several pages. Also, bolding the episode titles instead of enclosing them in quotation marks might also help with identification. Despite these minor suggested changes, this book is highly recommended for those academic, school, and public libraries that are building a collection of television shows and movies and for all general reference collections. [R: LJ, 1 Sept 98, p. 170]—**Jan S. Squire**

1198. Mayo, Mike. **VideoHound's War Movies: Classic Conflict on Film.** Farmington Hills, Visible Ink Press/Gale, 1999. 368p. illus. index. $19.95pa. ISBN 1-57859-089-2.

This is an engagingly written and liberally illustrated discussion of 201 war films. The book strives to be representative rather than exhaustive; for instance, there are some John Wayne films here, but not all (no *Back to Bataan* or *Flying Tigers*). The chapters include "American Wars" (*The Alamo*, *The Red Badge of Courage*), "British Wars" (*Beau Geste*, *Braveheart*, *Zulu*), "French Wars" (*The Battle of Algiers*, *Waterloo*), "Japanese Wars" (*Seven Samurai*, *Yojimbo*), and "Russian Wars" (*Alexander Nevsky*, *Doctor Zhivago*). The major chapters are "Word War I" (*All Quiet on the Western Front*, *The Blue Max*), "Between the World Wars" (*For Whom the Bell Tolls*), "World War II: Europe and North Africa" (*The Dirty Dozen*, *Where Eagles Dare*), "World War II: Pacific" (*Battle Cry*), "World War II: Documentaries" (*Battle of Midway*), "World War II: The Holocaust" (*The Last Metro*, *Life is Beautiful*), "World War II: Homefront" (*Since You Went Away*), "World War II: POWs" (*Bridge on the River Kwai*), "World War II: The Resistance" (*Casablanca*), "Korean War" (*Pork Chop Hill*), "Vietnam War" (*Platoon*), and "Coming Home" (*The Best Years of Our Lives*).

Each film receives two pages of treatment, including an intelligent annotated plot summary; a black-and-white photograph; a cast list; and lists of the writers, cinematographers, producers, and others. There is also a list of awards, the rating, running time, and formats on which the film is currently available. Somewhat surprisingly, considering the book's popular nature, it has an extensive indexing that makes it usable for reference purposes. These include a title index, a cast index, a directory index, a writer index, a cinematographer index, a composer index, and a category index.

The heart of the book, however, is the annotations and plot summaries, which are intelligent and engaging. Mayo is no hero worshipper or uncritical lover of war movies. For instance, he properly notes the rather disturbing lack of concern in *The Dirty Dozen* over the killing of the civilians in the chateau. However, Mayo is not a censor or a moralist; he simply notes the tendency in films of the time to include such violence and states that "the morality is dubious, but the movie sure is fun."

The book is current, covering *Saving Private Ryan* and other recent films along with the classics. Each film section includes a significant quote or two from the film, and occasionally also some fact of historical interest. There is a short list of thematically similar films on the opening page of each review. Mayo has packed a lot of information into this engaging volume, and its reasonable price makes it a great buy for both individuals and reference departments.—**Bill Miller**

1199. **Our Sunday Visitor's Family Guide to Movies and Videos.** Henry Herx, ed. Huntington, Ind., Our Sunday Visitor, 1999. 879p. $29.95pa. ISBN 0-87973-369-1.

The introduction to *Our Sunday Visitor's Family Guide to Movies and Videos* states that it seeks to fill a niche. Most film guides have been targeted to fans and students of the genre but this one is aimed at parents. More than 8,000 films are reviewed for "value and appropriateness." Virtually all of the English-language films featured here have been released since 1966, and a wide selection of subtitled films and notable older films are included. Each entry provides a brief plot summary and an evaluation of the sex, violence, and language content. Ratings awarded by the U.S. Catholic Conference Office of Film and Broadcasting (USCC) and the Motion Picture Association of America (MPAA) are included. The USCC is an outgrowth of the Legion of Decency founded in 1934. Its ratings range from A-I General Patronage to O Morally Offensive.

This volume presents difficulty to a librarian reviewer. Although librarians regularly evaluate and recommend information sources to users, the *Family Guide* goes beyond this. The criteria for judging films "morally offensive" are not always clear. Among the films so judged are obviously exploitative films such as *Valley of the Dolls*, *Striptease*, *Hot Pants Holiday*, and *Mandingo*. But also receiving O ratings are *A Clockwork Orange*, *Birdy*, *Clueless*, *The Handmaid's Tale*, *McCabe and Mrs. Miller*, *Network*, *The Shining*, and *Taxi Driver*. *The Piano*, although rated A-IV (Adults with Reservations), is faulted for exploring "the intensity of sexual desire without placing it in a moral context." The Hollywood prostitute film *Pretty Woman* is rated A-IV, but in contrast Louis Malle's *Pretty Baby* is judged to be O. As a bonus the volume includes the Vatican Best Films List where one finds Malle's *Au Revoir les Enfants*. Based on the titles included among the morally offensive, it seem almost inexplicable that Todd Solandz's *Happiness* (which was released without an MPAA rating) escapes with an A-IV.

There will be an audience for the *Family Guide* and it can be useful in determining levels of sex and violence in films. Its artistic judgments, however, are in many cases deeply flawed.—**Ruth A. Carr**

1200. **VideoHound's Epics: Giants of the Big Screen.** By Glenn Hopp. Farmington Hills, Mich., Visible Ink Press/Gale, 1999. 570p. illus. index. $19.95pa. ISBN 1-57859-174-4.

A new volume to the VideoHound collection, *VideoHound's Epics* is a guide to "big" movies—"big" meaning big budgets, big stars, big promotions, and big stories. The editors use this loose definition of epic to include 200 movies ranging from historical films, such as *Gone with the Wind*, *Ben Hur*, and *Titanic*, to blockbusters, such as *Star Wars*, *Raiders of the Lost Ark*, and *Batman*.

The films covered are categorized into genre chapters. These include adventure, biblical, comedy, crime, disaster, failed, family, fantasy, futuristic, historical, horror, musical, romance, silent, tragedy, wartime, and western. Each chapter includes discussions on a range of films that combine various points of view, attitudes, and subgenres of the epic. The historical chapter, for example, includes biographical epics, such as *Gandhi*; period films more suggestive of the traditional epic, such as *Spartacus*; and films about more contemporary events, such as *Exodus*. The chapter on failed epics examines movies that reached for classic status but bombed at the box office. For example, *Waterworld* and *Ishtar* are included in this chapter.

VideoHound's Epics gives brief overviews of the general plots of the films without much in-depth criticism. Although the reviews give more information than in *VideoHound's Golden Movie Retriever* (1999 ed.; see entry 1201), this volume is meant more for entertainment than academic study. The indexes for cast, director, writer, cinematographer, composer, and alternative titles are good reference sources for factual information, but overall the book is not intended for any penetrating examination of the films. [R: LJ, 15 Mar 99, p. 70; Choice, April 99, p. 1434]—**Cari Ringelheim**

1201. **VideoHound's Golden Movie Retriever 1999.** Martin Connors and Jim Craddock, eds. Farmington Hills, Mich., Visible Ink Press/Gale, 1999. 1815p. index. $21.95pa. ISBN 1-57859-041-8. ISSN 1095-371X.

The editors of this annual publication have extended and improved the ample guide to include movies on videocassette, laser disc, and DVD. Included with the video guide are several informative and useful indexes. An alternate title index provides a list of titles under which older and B-type videos may have been released. There are also a category index and a separate index of lesser-known categories (humorously referred to as "kibbles") combined with a series index. The awards index includes everything from the Academy Awards to the MTV Movie Awards. This guide also provides indexes for foreign films, digital formats, casts, directors, writers, cinematographers, and composers. An added feature to this publication are guides to distributors and Websites for several movie-related topics, such as actors and general entertainment information. Although this work provides extensive information to movies on video, laser disc, and DVD, readers should keep in mind that the guide is informal and is intended to be more entertaining than scholarly. The reviews provide basic plot information and ratings ranging from woof (a bomb) to four bones. They do not provide any sort of academic, in-depth study of the films. [R: LJ, Dec 98, p. 92]

—**Cari Ringelheim**

1202. **VideoHound's World Cinema: The Adventurer's Guide to Movie Watching.** By Elliot Wilhelm. Farmington Hills, Mich., Visible Ink Press/Gale, 1999. 551p. illus. index. $19.95pa. ISBN 1-57859-059-0.

VideoHound's collection of movie guides now adds this volume on world cinema written by Wilhelm, who is the curator of film at the Detroit Institute of Art and the director of the Detroit Film Theatre series. There are more than 800 foreign films reviewed here. Each entry includes the following information: title; alternative title; a review; suggested viewings; the year released; the MPAA rating; the length in minutes; whether the film is in black-and-white or color; foreign film code; the cast, including cameos and voice-overs; the director(s), writer(s), cinematographer(s), and music composer(s) or lyricists(s); awards, including nominations; the format(s), including VHS, laser disc, letterbox, and others; and the distributor code(s) if available on video. The reviews are generally thoughtful, expressing in no uncertain terms the author's feelings about the movie. There are no ratings given like in some of the other VideoHound books, such as stars for good movies and "woofs" for bad movies. However, the review makes it quite clear whether the movie is worthwhile or not. There are several indexes provided, including master title index, country of origin index, cast index, director index, writer index, cinematographer index, composer index, category index, distributor list, and distributor guide.

There are black-and-white pictures throughout the review section as well as 39 sidebars profiling an individual involved in the world cinema, whether actor, director, or producer. There is, however, one great annoyance. In the suggested viewing section called "Next Stop" are names of other films that might be of interest if the viewer enjoyed the first film. The only problem is that several of these are not contained in this volume even though many are, in fact, foreign films. [R: LJ, 15 Mar 99, p. 70; Choice, May 99, p. 1594]

—**Robert L. Turner Jr.**

THEATER

1203. **Bibliographic Guide to Theatre Arts 1998.** Thorndike, Maine, G. K. Hall/Macmillan, 1999. 292p. $295.00. ISBN 0-7838-0237-4. ISSN 0360-2788.

This volume is the annual supplement to the publisher's *Catalog of Theatre and Drama Collections*. It presents bibliographic citations dealing with theater arts publications that appeared between 1990 and January 1999. The citations include all languages and all forms (e.g., books, serials, newspaper clippings). The entries were gathered from the Library of Congress (LC) and the New York Public Library (NYPL) catalog records and tapes. Coverage includes the state, cinema, radio, television, nightclub performance, circus, vaudeville, magic acts, and puppetry.

The citations are in alphabetic order and are composed of author or institutional name, title, subtitle, place of publication, publisher, date of publication, pagination, illustrative statement, series, notes, ISBN number, Dewey Decimal number, subject heading, added entries, NYPL indicator, and NYPL classmark. The last two entries are for catalogers and not all citations have all of the above-cited subcategories.

This work will be useful for reference librarians in directing readers and theater researchers to cogent materials. The volume will be a boon to library catalogers.—**Charles Neuringer**

1204. Charles, Jill, comp. **Summer Theatre Directory 1999: A National Guide to Summer Employment for Professionals and Students....** Dorset, Vt., Theatre Directories, 1999. 148p. index. $17.95pa. ISBN 0-933919-43-3. ISSN 0884-5840.

The *Summer Theatre Directory* is a slim volume with the definite air of kitchen table publishing about it. It is a publication that seems to want to be a useful guide to summer employment or training opportunities for professional and nonprofessional stage actors, directors, technicians, and managers. Weighing in at an exiguous 148 pages (including a couple of appendixes and two short alphabetic indexes of organizations and programs), it seems to fall short of its potential.

The directory provides information about a scant 385 summer theaters, Shakespeare festivals, theme parks, and outdoor drama events across the United States and Canada (10 cruise lines in the market for show business talent are also listed). Entries for each organization include contact information, season dates, facilities information, hiring requirements and needs, union information, salary, transportation and housing, application procedures, availability of internships and apprenticeships, and a narrative description of the program. Training programs are listed in a separate section.

In scanning these lists, it is difficult to determine how the editors gathered their information, or which criteria were used for including or excluding organizations and programs. There is something generally perfunctory and incomplete about the directory in general. For example, this reviewer noticed that a very well-established and well-known regional theater in the neighborhood with a strong summer training program (the Contra Costa [California] Civic Theater) is omitted. None of the big California theme parks (not even Disneyland) are listed (although Walt Disney World in Florida is). The idea behind a summer stock and summer drama training directory is smart; the execution of this particular publication is not.

—**Gary Handman**

1205. Charles, Jill, Barbara Ax, Debra J. Bromley, and Jennifer Matthews, comps. **Regional Theatre Directory 1999-2000: A National Guide to Employment in Regional & Dinner Theatres for Performers....** Dorset, Vt., Theatre Directories, 1999. 175p. index. $18.95pa. ISBN 0-933919-44-1. ISSN 1041-9411.

Readers might assume it impossible for a relatively brief volume of only 175 pages to contain as much data as this one does. However, this guide speaks loudly to the contrary and stands as the foremost resource guide to regional theatrical show business. Arranged alphabetically by state, it offers specific information on hiring and casting procedures at equity, nonequity, and dinner theaters that operate between September and May. Found in each listing is such information as contact names, addresses, season, employment openings, salaries, facilities, staff, mission statements, historical backgrounds, and internship information. The material is presented in a very comprehensible format and a key to listings is provided. Also included are 6 appendixes presenting information on unions and membership; service organizations; useful resources; drama bookstores and book reviews written by working actors of more than 50 recent guides to employment; and last, a guide of procedures to follow in seeking employment. There is an index of companies as well as "specialty" companies. The publication of this guide coincides with the beginning of the employment-seeking season. Anyone contemplating theatrical employment would be well advised to begin with this volume.—**Jackson Kesler**

1206. Dessen, Alan C., and Leslie Thomson. **A Dictionary of Stage Directions in English Drama 1580-1642.** New York, Cambridge University Press, 1999. 289p. $69.95. ISBN 0-521-55250-8.

Culled from more than 500 surviving printed plays and manuscripts by major and minor dramatists and a database of more than 22,000 stage directions, this dictionary defines and explains some 900 terms found in Tudor and early Elizabethan dramas. Such terms include directions for actions, places, objects, and sounds. A typical entry explains or defines the term, gives one or more examples of its use, cites sources in which it appears, and often refers the user to other relevant entries. Many of the terms are fairly common or self-explanatory, whereas others, such as *coranto*, *mattock*, and *pot birds* are less easily understood. Following the main body of the dictionary is a brief section listing the terms by categories, such as

"Actions," "Blocking/Staging," "Eating and Drinking," "Special Effects," and "Weapons." Bibliographies of the plays with their editions cited and works consulted round out the work.

In spite of a few inconsistencies in the cross-referencing of terms, this specialized dictionary will be of value to its intended audience of scholars, directors, actors, and historians. It will also assist serious students of literature struggling to understand the works of English Renaissance drama.—**Barbara E. Kemp**

1207. Lounsbury, Warren C., and Norman C. Boulanger. **Theatre Backstage from A to Z.** 4th ed. Seattle, Wash., University of Washington Press, 1998. 231p. illus. $27.50 spiralbound. ISBN 0-295-97717-5.

First published in 1967, this 4th edition updates theater terms and definitions particularly to include technological advancements in the area of automated lighting and their controls, trusses, and rigging. It also updates computer applications in theater and explains the basic atmosphere of backstage (scenery, construction, stage appliances). Along with the terms and definitions are appendixes of manufacturers and distributors, bibliographies, periodicals, and pertinent Websites.

This is a good basic book for backstage goings-on. The coverage is complete and illustrations are adequate. However, in reviewing its contents, one cannot help but feel—to spite the updates incorporated into this edition—that the book is pretty much confined to representing the stage of 1967 and before. Any indication of advanced technology and its application to the stage after the 1960s is sporadic and minimal. Realizing that many backstage techniques and operations of a hundred years ago (or earlier) are still utilized, the amount of page space used to cover the making of an archaic thunder machine, for example, and other old-time devices seems unnecessary in a book of this sort. The explanation of color, color gels for lighting, and texturing techniques also seems insufficient when explained in black-and-white, not color.

Theatre Backstage from A to Z is a good starting point, but readers would be more impressed if further thought was given to this edition. When taking the effort to revise an edition, it is just as essential and appropriate to remove the old as it is to update it with the new and more valuable.—**Joan Garner**

1208. Rubin, Don. **World Encyclopedia of Contemporary Theatre, Volume 5: Asia/Pacific.** New York, Routledge, 1998. 524p. illus. index. $140.00. ISBN 0-415-05933-X.

This is the 5th volume in a series dealing with international trends and aspects of modern theater. This particular volume covers both Asian and Pacific countries. The previous contributions to the series dealt with Europe, North and South America, Africa, and the Arab world. Six introductory essays give the reader, among other subjects, a history of the aims and construction of the 6-volume series on cross-cultural theater. The other essays deal generally with Asian and Pacific theater and specifically with theater for young people and puppetry.

The heart of this reference work is a set of alphabetically arranged contributions surveying the theater history and current activities of 31 Asian and Pacific nations, starting with Afghanistan, followed by Australia and then Bangladesh, and ending with Vietnam. Over one-half of the surveys are "overviews," which are quite short.

The contributions cover the theater history of the particular nation from the end of World War II in 1945 to the present. The author feels that the essays cover a wide range of cross-cultural theater activities in a country-by-country approach. He also states that the contributions, which were written by individuals native to their particular country, are not necessarily comprehensive, but introductory. This is certainly true for the overviews, which are, in some cases, less than even introductory. Volume 6 will contain a cross-cultural index that will allow the reader to be able to make comparisons across cultures on a number of topics.

Each article is supposed to be divided into 15 sections. Unfortunately, the length and amount of information vary among the contributions. The article concerning Afghanistan is an "overview" of three pages. Yet the contribution on India runs 49 pages. There is a wide range of adherence to the editor's 15-topic plan and some of the contributors ignore it completely. There is a direct relationship between the length of articles and their usefulness.

Volume 5 is profusely illustrated. The editor has thankfully supplied suggestions for further reading in Asian and Pacific theater. A section on international theater references (e.g., bibliographies, dictionaries, encyclopedias) is available, followed by a list of contributors and their national editorial committees. Finally, a name and subject index is included.

This reference work presents somewhat of a problem for readers. If the users are interested in the modern theater of, for example, Australia or India, then they are in luck. The essays are well written, informative, and of great help. If the readers are interested in the contemporary theater of Afghanistan or Bhutan, they are out of luck. The overviews for those nations are just too cursory.

The volume already is 524 pages long. One can understand the author wanting to control length, and one could imagine that the reference work would be twice as large if all of the overviews were full-length contributions. However, the skimpiness of the overviews mars what could be a great reference work. When volume 6 appears, the cross-cultural index will make this a superior and useful reference series (but only for those contributions of adequate length and substance). [R: BL, 15 Nov 98, p. 614; Choice, Oct 98, pp. 392-394; Choice, July/Aug 99, p. 1923]—**Charles Neuringer**

28 Philosophy and Religion

GENERAL WORKS

1209. **Philosophers and Religious Leaders.** Christian D. von Dehsen, ed. Phoenix, Ariz., Oryx Press, 1999. 246p. index. (Lives and Legacies). $69.95. ISBN 1-57356-251-3.

Teachers, researchers, and journalists who seek more than biographical information about significant persons will be pleased to find this series on the library shelves. Thirteen writers profile ancient, medieval, and modern thinkers, philosophers, and religious leaders from the East, the Middle East, and the West. For each person, the authors have written an essay called "Life and Work" and another titled "Legacy." They review the nature of each person's religious and philosophical roots and, in turn, their ongoing influence on thought and human history. Short timelines give world events that parallel each biographee's life. An introductory essay discusses problems involving choice of entries and spelling. Several indexes make the sketches highly accessible. The first volume in this set is *Scientists, Mathematicians, and Inventors* (see entry 1280). The publishers plan to issue the following titles: *Government Leaders, Military Rulers, and Political Activists* and *Artists, Writers, and Musicians*.—**Edna M. Boardman**

PHILOSOPHY

Dictionaries and Encyclopedias

1210. **Bioethics for Students: How Do We Know What's Right?** Stephen G. Post, ed. New York, Macmillan General Reference/Simon & Schuster Macmillan, 1999. 4v. illus. index. $295.00/set. ISBN 0-02-864940-0.

Today's young people want to be knowledgeable about medical technology in order to help them to make personal choices in the future. *Bioethics for Students* examines issues in medical ethics, animal rights, and the environment at a level that will be understood by young people. Easily comprehensible language is used to explain difficult medical terms, procedures, and concepts.

This work is heavily illustrated, with close to 500 photographs. It contains about 200 individual articles. Each volume contains some 50 articles. Feature articles cover topics such as death and dying, fertility and reproduction, one's duties to animals and the environment, genetics, health care, mental health, population control, research on humans, and artificial organs and transplantation. Broad summaries are given for each of the key topics. In the section on transplantation, six key articles are provided. Discussions range from the historical, legal, and social issues involved in organ and tissue transplants to the medical, ethical, and philosophical ones. A full range of topics related to organ transplants include donor death, artificial hearts, and various types of organ transplants, cryonics, kidney dialysis, and the marketing of organs.

This multivolume set examines issues such as euthanasia, along with the associated public debates and court cases. After extensive research, the best of the case studies (e.g., the Karen Ann Quinlan case) were selected to illustrate the complexity of the decisions concerning euthanasia and sustaining life facing the patient's family and physicians. Significant legislation is also noted. The Uniform Determination of Death Act (UDDA), adopted by more than one-half of the states and the District of Columbia, establishes brain death as the standard for determining the time of death.

This reference work is based on the revised edition of the *Encyclopedia of Bioethics* (see ARBA 96, entry 1429). Continuing the tradition, *Bioethics for Students* brings this topical subject to young people because of its easy-to-read style. This work is written at an appropriate reading level for students beginning middle school.

The two-color format (blue and white with black typeface) is clear and concise. Numerous page features include sidebar definitions, quotations, *see also* references, and bold section heads. Overall, the presentation is appealing to the eye. Bibliographical references and an index are included. Volume 4 contains 3 appendixes. The glossary is comprehensive.

A strength of this work is that both sides of controversial issues are presented with equal coverage. A good addition for public libraries in both the young adult and adult reference collection. [R: BL, 1 May 99, p. 1606; BR, Sept/Oct 99, p. 78; SLJ, Aug 99, p. 187]—**Marilynn Green Hopman**

1211. Bunge, Mario. **Dictionary of Philosophy.** Buffalo, N.Y., Prometheus Books, 1999. 316p. $59.95. ISBN 1-57392-257-9.

C. S. Lewis once noted that while philosophy was indeed adversity's sweet milk, philosophy as a vocation would be too drab by a half. It is easy to see why by dipping into a dictionary of philosophy. Terms like "individualism," "idiographic," and "nomothetic" do tend to make the ideas glaze over. Although a well-known and respected philosopher, Bunge offers no new information.

In fact, this offering differs very little from other more recent ones. For example, any of the following compare well or better: Thomas Mautner's *A Dictionary of Philosophy* (3d ed.; see ARBA 97, entry 1164); *Key Ideas in Human Thought* (see ARBA 94, entry 1497); and Lacey's *A Dictionary of Philosophy* (Routledge & K. Paul, 1976). It falls far short, however, of *The Cambridge Dictionary of Philosophy* (see ARBA 97, entry 1159).

The margin of difference claimed here is modernity: ideas, concept problems, principles, and theories in modern philosophy. There can be no doubt that Bunge has filled this claim admirably. Yet, even accounting for the neoteric, and adding in Bunge's further claim that philosophy should not be dull and bovine and thus this offering is lively and entertaining, *Dictionary of Philosophy* does precious little to merit special attention.

Collections that strive for completeness or that support large philosophy programs will find this slender volume of some merit. All others, if they have any of the titles listed above, may pass on this one. [R: Choice, Sept 99, p. 106; LJ, 15 Feb 99, p. 140; BL, 1 May 99, pp. 1608-1614]—**Mark Y. Herring**

1212. **The Cambridge Dictionary of Philosophy.** 2d ed. Robert Audi, ed. New York, Cambridge University Press, 1999. 1001p. $74.95; $29.95pa. ISBN 0-521-63136-X; 0521-63722-8pa.

With the revision of this work (originally reviewed in ARBA 97, entry 1159) into a new edition, it becomes only stronger as a reference work and more worthy of inclusion on the library shelf. This 2d edition includes more than 400 new entries by 50 additional contemporary philosophers. It also expands the coverage of developing fields, such as applied ethics and philosophy of the mind, while at the same time expanding on non-Western and non-European philosophy. A large selection of entries is devoted to African, Arabic, Islamic, Japanese, Jewish, Korean, and Latin American philosophy. This inclusion is especially gratifying with the world becoming smaller all the time. Inclusion of the non-Western philosophies further exemplifies the breadth of discussion currently undertaken in philosophy.

Entries, as the preface to the 1st edition indicates, fall between brief descriptions of the concept and that of an encyclopedic entry consisting of background context and bibliographic information. Each entry attempts to express the nature and content of the concept while illuminating salient related side avenues of the entry. The target of this volume is the well-versed reader in other fields who may need access to definitions of concepts in the field of philosophy to enhance their understanding. A number of philosophers are included in the entries, not as much to define and discuss their biographical information, but to more fully explore the developments of philosophical thought throughout its development as a field of intellectual inquiry. Various related fields and subfields are also included. Some examples include the philosophy of history, computer and artificial intelligence, political philosophy, and the philosophy of science. Modern philosophers are selectively included in the 2d edition, again weighted toward writers whom many non-philosophers may want to look up.—**Gregory Curtis**

1213. **Dictionary of Existentialism.** Haim Gordon, ed. Westport, Conn., Greenwood Press, 1999. 539p. index. $99.50. ISBN 0-313-27404-5.

Some 65 specialists in the field have contributed a series of signed essays arranged in dictionary format, with the primary goal being to provide a key reference tool for scholars and students who are seeking information on particular thinkers, writers, terms, and ideas that have been developed in or linked to existentialism. Entries range in length, with more depth given to significant names and concepts. Each of the entries includes extensive cross-referencing as well as a brief bibliography of primary and secondary sources, as appropriate.

In most cases, topical concepts are discussed as they relate to major and minor thinkers; and where contrasting perspectives of uses are evident, these are explained. By consulting main entries and cross-references, the reader comes to understand the influence that many writers had on each other and the currents of exchange of ideas. A selected bibliography, index, and list of contributors supplement the text. This will be a solid addition to the philosophy section of any reference collection, and a handsome complement to general and subject-specific encyclopedias. [R: Choice, Dec 99, p. 686]—**Edmund F. SantaVicca**

1214. Diethe, Carol. **Historical Dictionary of Nietzscheanism.** Lanham, Md., Scarecrow, 1999. 265p. (Historical Dictionaries of Religions, Philosophies, and Movements, no.21). $62.00. ISBN 0-8108-3512-6.

Understanding the great nineteenth-century German philosopher Nietzsche has never been easy, but this particular work will benefit anyone, especially the novice, who desires to understand and appreciate his philosophy. The book begins with a "curriculum vitae" that highlights his life from 1844 to 1900. A brief but useful glossary of Nietzsche terms follows the vita. A 40-page introduction takes the reader on a tour of Nietzsche's life and works, 30 pages of which outline his effect on the thinking of those in Germany, France, Great Britain, the United States, and Italy. The substance of the book, the dictionary, consists of 190 pages of names (e.g., Lou Andreas-Salome, Elisabeth Forster-Nietzsche), books (e.g., *The Gay Science, On the Genealogy of Morality, Beyond Good and Evil*), and concepts (e.g., German idealism, God, the will to power) identified with Nietzsche. Although most of the entries are brief, the information is sufficient to help advance one's desire to understand Nietzsche. The reference work concludes with an excellent bibliography divided into four sections. Section 1 lists Nietzsche's works; section 2 provides biographies of Nietzsche and his works; section 3 is a guide to Nietzsche scholarship and interpretation and is itself divided into 8 subsections; section 4 consists of works on the reception of Nietzsche's philosophy. Anyone interested in Nietzsche will be guided well by this resource.—**Michael A. Foley**

1215. **The Edinburgh Encyclopedia of Continental Philosophy.** Simon Glendinning, ed. Chicago, Fitzroy Dearborn, 1999. 685p. index. $125.00. ISBN 1-57958-152-8.

This work is a survey of the important figures and "schools of thought" identified with continental as opposed to analytic philosophy. It begins with a brief preface and acknowledgments, notes on contributors, and a 17-page introductory essay by the editor titled "What Is Continental Philosophy?" The introduction serves as an excellent overview to a large portion of modern European intellectual history of the English-speaking world, and, as is predictable to anyone who is familiar with contemporary nonanalytic philosophy, it defines continental philosophy in contrast to the majority of Anglo-American philosophy (which is generally called "analytic" by proponents and opponents). Throughout the encyclopedia, important concepts, such as phenomenology, are asserted to be indefinable as such but rather to be describable in historical or comparative terms. If anything defines "continental philosophy" in contrast to "analytic philosophy," it is that continental philosophy denies the possibility of clarity of definition that the latter holds out as an ideal.

The body of the work is divided into 10 sections, including Classical Idealism; Philosophy of Existence; Philosophies of Life and Understanding; Phenomenology; Politics, Psychoanalysis, and Science; The Frankfurt School and Critical Theory; Structuralism; and Post-Structuralism. Each section includes an introduction written by the section editor, and six or seven essays on important topics and figures. The essays are of a uniformly high quality and include careful accounts of the appropriate historical and cultural connections. Each essay includes a bibliography composed of a list of primary sources and recommendations for further reading. There is a good subject index and an index of names.

This is an excellent place for an intelligent reader to gain a greater understanding of prominent figures and a clearer view of some of the more perplexing contemporary schools of thought (e.g., phenomenology, critical theory, and various forms of philosophical feminism). It provides a deeper view than works such as *The Encyclopedia of Contemporary Literary Theory* (see ARBA 94, entry 1150), as its approach and organization are more conducive to individual study than are larger and more strictly philosophical reference works, such as the *Routledge Encyclopedia of Philosophy* (1998). This work is highly recommended to libraries serving students, scholars, and general readers interested in contemporary philosophy, literary criticism, and cultural studies. [R: Choice, Dec 99, p. 688]—**Richard H. Swain**

1216. **Encyclopedia of Ethics.** Susan Neiburg Terkel and R. Shannon Duval, eds. New York, Facts on File, 1999. 302p. index. $65.00. ISBN 0-8160-3311-0.

This encyclopedia is meant as an unbiased guide to terms and ideas related to ethics and ethical issues. It is particularly aimed at high school and undergraduate users, and the editorial approach is meant to combine the needs of educators with the methods of philosophy. It begins with an editorial preface and acknowledgements, a brief introduction, and a two-page essay by a philosophy professor titled "Ethics in Our Daily Lives." This essay directs the attention of readers to the distinctions among descriptive ethics, metaethics, normative ethics, and applied ethics and recommends this encyclopedia as an introduction to the study of ethics.

Alphabetic entries comprise the vast majority of the work and there is good use of cross-references to connect related people and concepts. The longest entries are about 1,500 words, and the subject matters include philosophy, morality, contemporary issues, general terms, and terms particular to a specific religion. There is a specific attempt to include feminist ethics and there are entries on historical and public figures ranging from Aesara of Lucania to Carol Gilligan.

The editors are clearly working within the "multicultural" framework currently prevalent in U.S. public education and the underlying approach might be called "democratic humanism." Entries are well written and adequate considering the editorial approach, intended audience, and brevity. But, as in all such works, it is hard to understand why certain information in omitted. There is a contemporary focus to the encyclopedia, such that *Satanic Verses* by Salman Rushdie appears in the entry on blasphemy, but the brevity of the entry (approximately 200 words), permits only the statement that Islamic leaders in Iran found Rushdie guilty of blasphemy. There is no explanation of why the novel was found to be blasphemous.

The encyclopedia concludes with a short bibliography and a good index. The work is well made, sturdily bound, and printed on acid-free paper. It is suitable for high school and public libraries within the limits of the editorial approach outlined above. College and university libraries would do well to complement it with more comprehensive and scholarly works, such as the *Encyclopedia of Ethics* (see ARBA 93, entry 1395) and the *Encyclopedia of Applied Ethics* (see ARBA 99, entry 1251). [R: LJ, 1 Oct 99, pp. 78-80]—**Richard H. Swain**

1217. **Ethics and Values.** Danbury, Conn., Grolier, 1999. 8v. illus. index. $265.00/set. ISBN 0-7172-9274-6.

This work is aimed at providing clear, unbiased information about ethical issues and concerns. It is oriented to students of all ages, but is particularly relevant for intermediate and high school levels. It contains more than 200 entries that reflect a broad range of issues related to ethics, morals, and values. A sample of the topics included is abortion, addition, animal rights, anti-Semitism, capital punishment, censorship, cults, discrimination, euthanasia, child abuse, corruption, Nazism, pornography, gun control, genocide, the Holocaust, racism, and sexism.

The entries are arranged alphabetically. Most are only two pages long, with one black-and-white photograph as illustration. The photographs are well chosen and interesting. The articles are subdivided into shorter sections, which makes for easier reading. The type is large and presented in two-column format. Each volume has an index to the entire set; however, individual entries do not include bibliographic information. There is a one-page listing of references ("further reading" in the last volume that focuses on ethics in general rather than on specific topics included.

Individual articles are not signed. There is a list of contributors hidden on the back of the title page of each volume, with no indication of their qualifications or positions. The authority of the work appears to rest on the reputation of the publisher. However, the information included does clarify and present a balanced, objective, easy-to-understand introduction to complex moral and ethical issues. The set is a useful starting point for discussion and work with students on many important, critical issues that impact today's society. It is recommended for children's and young adult collections in public libraries, as well as for intermediate and high school library collections. [R: BL, 15 Nov 98, p. 612]—**Susan J. Freiband**

1218. Trahair, Richard C. S. **Utopias and Utopians: An Historical Dictionary.** Westport, Conn., Greenwood Press, 1999. 480p. $95.00. ISBN 0-313-29465-8.

Over the course of history, utopias as heaven on earth have not fared so well. For example, in the early part of this century, Stalin promised to bring us his version of the New Jerusalem and it ended up being the same old hell. Hitler similarly made a promise that his new Germany would be paradise. It, too, proved a holocaust. Even down to our own day we find leaders like Koresh and others making promises only a god can keep, only to turn around and give us the devil to pay.

Utopias and Utopians provides just the right mix of history and fantasy to lead readers to genuine utopias. Contained herein are utopias of every description: love communes, caravans, brotherhoods, cults, racist settlements, religious groups and *soi-disant* religious groups, schools, economies, and more. In short, any group or association that sought to make the world better is included.

The volume contains more than 600 entries with a suitable mixture of biographical figures (Sidney Webb, James Greaves), places (Grameen Bank, Hampstead Garden), and things (Greenpeace, Lindisfarne Association). A solid attempt has been made to collect utopias long since passed, those of recent origin, and those newly developed on the Internet. The introduction is a solid contribution to the establishment and study of utopias, covering the early ground in Plato, Thomas More, and Francis Bacon. A bibliography and useful index close out this volume of esoteric but helpful scholarship. [R: BL, 15 Nov 99, p. 654]

—**Mark Y. Herring**

Directories

1219. **International Directory of Philosophy and Philosophers 1999-2000.** 11th ed. Ramona Cormier, ed. Bowling Green, Ohio, Philosophy Documentation Center/Bowling Green State University, 1999. 652p. index.$110.00. ISBN 1-889680-03-6. ISSN 0074-4603.

This directory is a comprehensive guide to universities, programs, societies, journals, and faculty throughout the world (excluding the United States and Canada) engaged in philosophical inquiry. The information is divided into 6 major sections. The 1st section lists 1,200 college and university philosophy departments, along with the names, e-mail addresses, and areas of specialization of the faculty. The 2d section lists more than 200 centers and institutes focused on or related to philosophical inquiry. The information in this section includes the data of founding, the purpose, the names of the directors or chairs, and publications (if any) of the organization. The 3d section lists 290 societies and associations of philosophy. The difference between a "center" and a "society" appears to be, in part, that societies and associations oftentimes require dues to be paid. The 4th section lists 610 philosophy and philosophy-related journals. The 5th section lists the names and addresses of 643 philosophy and philosophy-related publishers. All of the information in these sections is organized alphabetically by country. The final major section lists alphabetically by name the names and addresses of 12,380 philosophers. This outstanding directory belongs in all college and university reference collections where graduate programs in philosophy are offered.—**Michael A. Foley**

1220. **Philosopher's Phone and E-Mail Directory 1998/99.** Bowling Green, Ohio, Philosophy Documentation Center/Bowling Green State University, 1998. 261p. $19.95pa. ISBN 0-912632-63-1.

The current edition of this directory includes more than 11,800 individuals identified as philosophers throughout the United States and Canada. Most of the entries for individuals include institutional affiliation; however, there are many listed without this affiliation. More than 5,000 of the philosophers listed also have an e-mail address listed along with their postal address and telephone number. One interesting piece of information missing from entries is the area of interest for the individuals. This work continues to contribute useful information on location of individuals. This type of information is especially useful for contacting individuals after a conference or seminar where users were not able to get the telephone number for a follow-up discussion.—**Gregory Curtis**

Handbooks and Yearbooks

1221. Gutek, Gerald, and Patricia Guteck. **Visiting Utopian Communities: A Guide to the Shakers, Moravians, and Others.** Columbia, S.C., University of South Carolina Press, 1998. 230p. illus. index. $16.95pa. ISBN 1-57003-210-6.

Intentional communities dubbed "utopian" by later students, though seldom by the participants or their contemporaries, sprang up by the hundreds all across the American landscape from the late eighteenth through the early twentieth centuries. Also classified as "communitarian," these social experiments, whether religious or secular in motivation, embraced some form of communal ownership of property, and more generally aspired to a higher degree of social harmony than characterized society at large. Most were short-lived, but a handful endured for decades, a few persisting well into the twentieth century. Most, too, left few or no obvious traces. Some, however, survive today as museum villages or as the historic heart of communities that are living and active though no longer organized on their original utopian premises.

The authors provide a travel guide to many of the best preserved or most visit-worthy remnants of America's utopian impulse. These include Ephrata Cloister, Pennsylvania; Old Salem, North Carolina (Moravians); seven Shaker sites from Maine to Kentucky; Old Economy, Pennsylvania (Rappites); Zoar, Ohio (Separatists); New Harmony, Indiana (Rappites and Owenites); Oneida, New York (Perfectionists); Fruitlands, Massachusetts (Bronson Alcott's Consociate Family); Bethel, Missouri, and Aurora, Oregon (Keilites); Bishop Hill, Illinois (Janssonists); the Amana Colonies, Iowa (Inspirationists); Rugby, Tennessee (Christian Cooperatives); and Estero, Florida (Koreshans). Coverage of each site begins with basic data: address, phone, location, hours, admission fees, and available facilities such as shops, restaurants, research libraries, and so on. A brief descriptive overview follows, then a substantial sketch of the community's history. Collectively, these sketches make a fair history of American utopianism, though more comprehensive and in-depth histories are of course available. Finally, there is a suggested tour itinerary for the site with brief descriptions of buildings or other attractions. For individuals interested in utopianism and for libraries mainly in the Midwest and Northeast where the majority of included sites are concentrated, this is a worthwhile resource.—**Hans E. Bynagle**

1222. Huang, Siu-chi. **Essentials of Neo-Confucianism: Eight Major Philosophers of the Song and Ming Periods.** Westport, Conn., Greenwood Press, 1999. 261p. index. (Resources in Asian Philosophy and Religion). $85.00. ISBN 0-313-26449-X.

This volume is helpful to the student of Neo-Confucian philosophy. Huang presents the major thinkers of the Song and Ming periods of Neo-Confucian thought. Spanning the eleventh to sixteenth centuries, the book presents five major philosophers of the Northern Song, including Zhou Dun-yi, Cheng Hao, and Cheng Yi who are generally presumed to be the founders of the school. Three Southern Song philosophers are presented and then Wang Yang-ming, the most renowned of the later Neo-Confucians, from the Ming Dynasty are studied. Huang emphasizes the historical, metaphysical, epistemological, and ethical issues of these thinkers. The concepts, of tai-ji (supreme ultimate), xin (mind), and ren (humanity) are compared for each of these philosophers. This book is introductory in nature. The scholar will want original materials and a more complex study. The student and general reader will find this a ready-reference for initial inquiry.—**Linda L. Lam-Easton**

1223. Isaacs, Ronald H. **Every Person's Guide to Jewish Philosophy and Philosophers.** Northvale, N.J., Jason Aronson, 1999. 283p. index. (Every Person's Guide Series). $30.00. ISBN 0-7657-6017-7.

This work is part of the author's Every Person's Guide Series that attempts to explain many aspects of Jewish observance, culture, and history to the general reader. It consists of short chapters divided into brief sections presenting an essentially chronological summary of the history and present state of Jewish philosophy. There is a brief introduction, a discussion of monotheism and Philo Judeas, an overview of medieval Jewish philosophy, about 30 chapters on individual philosophers, a very short chapter on theology after the Holocaust, and a final chapter on the 4 branches of Judaism (Orthodox, Reform, Conservative, Reconstructionist). The work ends with a glossary of philosophic terms, a short bibliography of further readings, and an index. The index does not cover the glossary. Surprisingly, the glossary refers to people and philosophical movements otherwise uncovered in the text and unnoted in the index (e.g., Judith Plaskow and feminist spirituality). The role of women in Judaism and Jewish philosophy is presented as an afterthought in the glossary and not covered as an issue of concern in the body of the text.

The title leads readers to think that the work is meant for Jew and gentile alike. However, the work assumes the reader is familiar with traditional Jewish thought and culture and needs guidance on the history of Jewish philosophy and theology. Hebrew words are used throughout the work without explanation in the text or entry in the glossary. The work also assumes a general familiarity with philosophical and theological terminology. The work is not suitable for anyone lacking a basic familiarity with Judaism or the history of European philosophy.

Although the guide can be used as a reference work, it can also be read from cover to cover as a monograph. Most libraries will find it best suited to the general collection. Because it assumes familiarity with Judaism and the history of European philosophy, and because it omits serious consideration of the role of women in Judaism, it should not be a first choice for most libraries. The guide is characterized by the simplification inevitable in a work of this kind, but within the limits described above, it provides even-handed and reliable information on a weighty and complex subject. It is suitable for public and school libraries, but all libraries should first consider works such as *The Oxford Dictionary of the Jewish Religion* (see ARBA 98, entry 1396) and *The Encyclopedia of Judaism* (see ARBA 91, entry 1449) before purchasing this guide for their reference collections. [R: LJ, Dec 98, p. 114]—**Richard H. Swain**

RELIGION

General Works

Bibliography

1224. Hayward, James L. **The Creation/Evolution Controversy: An Annotated Bibliography.** Pasadena, Calif., Salem Press, and Lanham, Md., Scarecrow, 1998. 253p. index. (Magill Bibliographies). $37.50. ISBN 0-8108-3386-7.

This work annotates, at reasonable and useful length, 447 books related to the ongoing fight between those examining the evidence for the origins of life and the universe and those postulating a creation that cannot be ultimately examined. The difficulty in defining those two groups is one measure of the work that had to go into this book.

Chapter 1 provides an introduction to the debate, citing the major players and theories over time. Doing more, however, it establishes that there is no single camp of either evolutionists or creationists, and notes that both perspectives are continual with a fair amount of overlap toward the middle. Still, the mainstream, and a few discredited, theories on both sides are presented as a background to the materials to be tendered later.

Hayward convincingly dates the "modern era" of creationism from 1981. Chapter 2 outlines those important works published prior to that time. Early works include those scientific books that came into conflict with religious authorities over the origin and place of the earth, books examining the nature of science, and arguments (for the existence of God) from design. It is interesting to note that prior to Charles Darwin's *Origin of Species*, the creationist debate was conducted against the evidence of the geological record, still a prime component of the debate today. Following Darwin, a number of works examine the evolution of evolutionary theory itself. Sticking with the historical outlook, books on the history of the debate are covered in chapter 3. The author presents a brief background on each author and, as well as describing the contents of the books, notes obvious biases in the books, even pointing out where these might be of use to the serious student. Chapter 4 deals with what can be seen as 3 separate topics: philosophy, theology, and general references. At times the jump between works can be a bit jarring. Here also the book starts dividing chapters into theistic and nontheistic references, which does not seem to serve much purpose. The discussion of works on physics and cosmology, in chapter 5, seems to have some weaknesses in regard to non-Newtonian mechanics. Given its preeminence, as noted in chapter 2, it is surprising that there is not more material on earth science (chapter 6). As might be expected, chapter 7, on biology and anthropology, is fairly lengthy. Author, title, and subject indexes end the book.—**Robert M. Slade**

1225. Marshall, George J. **Angels: An Indexed and Partially Annotated Bibliography of Over 4,300 Scholarly Books and Articles Since the 7th Century B.C.** Jefferson, N.C., McFarland, 1999. 479p. index. $95.00. ISBN 0-7864-0555-4.

Angels are presently a very popular topic, and the work reviewed here is a compilation of 4,355 items addressing this subject. Marshall, chairman of the philosophy department, Campion College, University of Regina, Saskatchewan, originally hoped to develop a comprehensive and annotated bibliography but quickly realized that such a goal was beyond his reach, so although all items have been indexed, only 750 have been annotated. Marshall conceived of the subject in very broad and inclusive terms, and has included theological and biblical works from Christian, Judaic, Islamic, and other traditions as well as historical, comparative, anthropological, archeological, sociological, and even inspirational writings.

The items are arranged alphabetically by author, and are numbered in two-column format. The author's name is set off in bold typeface; the remainder of the entry appears in light typeface, with book and journal titles italicized. As much information about each work as could be discerned is included (e.g., ISBN, ISSN, LC card number, LC class number, cover title, pagination and dimensions, a library where the item can be found, a source from which the entry was identified, and still other points pertinent to particular items). Subject keywords, of Marshall's own devising, provide content access to subjects and persons as well as historical periods.

The number of entries and amount of indexing (2 to 10 keywords per entry) in this compilation are impressive, and the book is attractive. Still, the work is weak and lacking in focus. First of all, the subtitle of this bibliography is inaccurate—many non-scholarly items are included as well as some media material and even a collection of clippings. Of much greater consequence, the coverage of the subject, even though fairly extensive, is far from complete or exhaustive; numerous signed entries from standard dictionaries and encyclopedias are missing from this compilation. An equally significant number of entries easily identified in various periodical indexes are not included either. It appears that data gathering was haphazard rather than controlled; search guidelines evidently were never established. An audiocassette recording on angels by Walter Wink is recorded but his major 3-volume contribution is not. Bibliographic data are likewise presented inconsistently. In many cases city, publisher, and date are recorded, but in other cases only city and date, or in still other cases only publisher and date information, is presented. *Religion Index One*, commonly abbreviated "RIO," is here cited variously as "RI1," Religion Index, and Religion Index to Periodic Literature. Sometimes an essay is identified by precise pagination, whereas at other times the entire contents of a book are identified without specific pagination. Annotations are uneven in length and quality. In several instances the annotation consists of a long verbatim quotation of the dictionary source entry.

Indexing, too, is troubling. Persons are usually identified with their full name and life dates, although "More" appeared as a keyword and in the index without first name or dates (Henry, 1614–1687). Occasional errors in identification (Genesis, #67 should be #66) and spelling, and omissions (no entries at all for Lucifer, and only one for Iblis) were noted. Biblical references were usually indexed at book level only, even though keywords for the book as well as book chapter were generally supplied with the entry; still a few book chapter entries (for Matthew) appeared in the index. Although title indexing was not included, it is strange that a document entitled "3 Enoch" did not merit a keyword for "Enoch" and thus cannot be found through the index. The distinction between "Revelation" (as a canonical book) and "revelation" as a concept was made at the keyword level but was then negated when both ideas were merged into one index listing.

Much more can be found on this subject than what is identified in this compilation. Any person interested in this subject would be better advised to consult the standard reference works and periodical indexes before using this work. [R: LJ, Aug 99, p. 78; Choice, Nov 99, p. 508]—**Glenn R. Wittig**

1226. McIver, Tom. **The End of the World: An Annotated Bibliography.** Jefferson, N.C., McFarland, 1999. 389p. index. $55.00. ISBN 0-7864-0708-5.

The annotations in this volume are divided into four chronologically defined sections. All works prior to 1800 are listed in chronological order and usually annotated. All works from 1800 onward are divided into three sections—1800 to 1910, 1910 to 1970, and 1970 to the present. The works within these latter three sections are listed alphabetically rather than chronologically and are usually annotated. Most of the works are from Christian sources, although there are a few from Jewish, Muslim, and other religions as well as some from psychic and occult beliefs. A 21-page introduction is good at defining terms like *apocalypse*, *eschatology*, and *rapture*, along with offering a meaningful discussion of the significance of each. A 50-page index lists all the authors and titles. The annotations contain discussions from the sophisticated (Augustine's understanding of the millennium as an allegory) to current popular anxieties (clues on the American dollar bill). It is not clear whether occasional lapses, such as associating Saddam Hussein with Iran in entry 3483, are in the cited work or the annotation. It is a good book for any reader surveying literature on religious interpretations of the end of the world. [R: LJ, 15 Oct 99, p. 64]—**Robert T. Anderson**

Biography

1227. **Augustine Through the Ages: An Encyclopedia.** Allan D. Fitzgerald and others, eds. Grand Rapids, Mich., William B. Eerdmans, 1999. 902p. index. $75.00. ISBN 0-8028-3843-X.

Augustine of Hippo (364-430), who left behind more than 5 million words has greatly influenced life through the years. His *On Christian Teaching*, *City of God*, *Confessions*, and *Sermons* are an important part of the development of Western thought.

This work is an encyclopedia incorporating his life, writings, thoughts, and influence through the ages up to the present time. Nearly 150 international scholars from a variety of backgrounds—history, philosophy, classics, political science, and theology—have produced nearly 500 entries, from "Abortion" to "World." There are articles on individuals, including Abraham, Jerome, Martin Luther, and John Calvin; on Augustine's influence on asceticism, ethics, ministry, and political thought; on his writings (which are carefully analyzed); and on his thoughts on philosophical problems, such as original sin, liberty, love, and redemption. Furthermore, 396 sermons and 269 letters are listed chronologically.

Fitzgerald, the general editor, is a professor of patristics at the Augustinian Patristic Institute in Rome, and editor of Augustinian Studies for Villanova University. Filling a need that has existed for many years, this encyclopedia will be useful not only to scholars but to anyone wishing to know anything about the man, his thoughts, and his influence. Although the scholar will appreciate the general bibliography and the multinational bibliographies attached to each signed article, much of the text is written in everyday language. It is recommended for inclusion in academic, theological, and public libraries. [R: LJ, July 99, p. 79]
—**Sara R. Mack**

1228. Ball, Ann. **Faces of Holiness: Modern Saints in Photos and Words.** Huntington, Ind., Our Sunday Visitor, 1998. 271p. illus. index. $14.95pa. ISBN 0-87973-950-9.

Our age has its brutal aspects. The blood of martyrs has stained the twentieth century, and not since the early days of the church have so many laid down their lives for their faith. Such saintly men and women demonstrate that holiness is flourishing more today than ever before. Their lives, moreover, serve as role models and confirm that sanctity thrives universally. In short, as this well-researched volume makes clear, holiness has many faces. Its 32 brief chapters profile some 75 martyrs and mystics from around the globe. There are, for example, stories of Peter ToRot, a lay catechist from Papua New Guinea, put to death by the Japanese during World War II; Anuarite Nengapeta, a nun from Zaire murdered in 1964 while resisting rape; and Gianna Berretta Molla, an Italian pediatrician who died rather than endanger the life of her unborn daughter. Additionally, there are biographies of Dorothy Day, who led a life of sanctity working in the slums of New York City; Sister Teresa of Jesus Fernandez in the Carmel of the Andes; and Father Emil Kapaun in the prison camps of Korea. This extraordinary compilation of contemporary saints provides a compelling glimpse—in both words and photographs—of a most amazing variety of men and women.—**G. A. Cevasco**

1229. Bunson, Matthew, Margaret Bunson, and Stephen Bunson. **John Paul II's Book of Saints.** Huntington, Ind., Our Sunday Visitor, 1999. 368p. index. $19.95. ISBN 0-87973-934-7.

Pope John Paul II has presided over more than 300 canonizations and 700 beatifications, more than any other pontiff to date. This is enough to earn him the title of "the saint making pope." This book provides biographical profiles of all those canonized or beatified by John Paul II.

Each entry traces the important life events of the person, in particular events that demonstrated their exceptional holiness and spiritual virtues. Most biographies are about two pages in length and also give the class of spiritual contribution, such as founder, martyr, confessor, mystic, religious (order), or priest, among others. Sketches begin with a "headline" that places the biographee in context, such as "discalced Carmelite mystic" or "model religious and evangelist." Included also are the death, beatification, and canonization dates. Two main listings organize the book—a section on saints and one on the beatified, both of which are arranged alphabetically. An index of saints and blesseds is also included. Cross-references are used throughout to link different forms of names or identities.

The biographical entries are well written and reflect diverse exemplary lives from portraits of faith to profiles in courage. Much of the information for this book came from the Vatican's own Congregation of the Causes and the postulators or advocates of the candidates for sainthood and beatification. This book will be valuable in almost any public or academic library.—**Gerald L. Gill**

1230. Melton, J. Gordon. **Religious Leaders of America: A Biographical Guide to Founders and Leaders of Religious Bodies, Churches, and Spiritual Groups in North America.** 2d ed. Farmington Hills, Mich., Gale, 1999. 724p. index. $99.00. ISBN 0-8103-8878-2. ISSN 1057-2961.

Until now a researcher needing a biography of a current religious leader was required to check many different sources. This volume makes the search much simpler. It includes the biographies of 1,200 Americans and Canadians who have had an influence in North American religious life since 1865.

Whereas earlier works were usually limited to Christian figures, the author of this work has chosen to include leaders from Protestant, Roman Catholic, Jewish, Islamic, Eastern, and metaphysical groups (e.g., Humanists, Agnostics, Atheists), as well as some foreign contemporary leaders. Furthermore, Melton made an effort to include women, African Americans, and North American Indians who were omitted from earlier works.

According to the introduction, in order to select the persons to profile, Melton chose leaders of major older religious bodies of America, leaders of ecumenical bodies, founders of newer and smaller religious traditions, and those who are self-proclaimed nonreligious.

In addition to the main body of the work, which contains the profiles of the religious leaders arranged alphabetically according to surname, there is a "List of Profiled Leaders" that gives a quick overview of the persons included, a "Religious Affiliation Appendix," and a "Master Name and Keyword Index."

Each entry contains the name by which the individual is best known, birth date and place (if applicable), affiliation and occupation, and a brief biography encompassing the individual's life and beliefs. Finally, there are bibliographic citations for publications by or about the person. Each entry is numbered for easy reference in the master index. This 2d edition (see ARBA 92, entry 1402, for a review of the 1st edition) is a valuable biographical work for public, academic, and religious libraries.—**Sara R. Mack**

Dictionaries and Encyclopedias

1231. Benedetto, Robert, Darrell L. Guder, and Donald K. McKim. **Historical Dictionary of Reformed Churches.** Lanham, Md., Scarecrow, 1999. 508p. (Historical Dictionaries of Religions, Philosophies, and Movements, no.24). $79.50. ISBN 0-8108-3628-9.

This handy reference work provides a guide to the history of the Reformed tradition of Christianity, from its beginnings in the Reformation of the sixteenth century to the present. More than 750 entries cover people, places, events, and concepts that are important to the Reformed churches. An extensive bibliography of some 100 pages provides guidance for further study. Five appendixes list general councils of the Presbyterian and Congregational denomination; theological comparisons between various Reformed churches; member churches of the World Alliance of Reformed Churches; United Churches with Reformed heritages; and research centers, publishers, and online bookstores. Many entries, such as "John Calvin," "Union Theological Seminary," and "Savoy Declaration," overlap with the *Oxford Dictionary of the Christian Church* (3d ed.; see ARBA 98, entry 1389) or the *Westminster Dictionary of Christian Theology* (Westminster John Knox, 1983). The volume, however, also contains many unique entries, such as "Augusto Armand Hugon," "Hampden C. Dubose," and "Presbyterian Support Services." There are also regional ("Mesoamerica" and "West Africa") and national ("United States of America" and "Canada") entries that provide overviews of the history and current status of the Reformed churches in various locations. It is these more specialized entries that make this volume a useful resource for libraries and individuals interested in the study of Reformed Christianity.—**Ronald H. Fritze**

1232. **Critical Terms for Religious Studies.** Mark C. Taylor, ed. Chicago, University of Chicago Press, 1998. 423p. index. $18.00pa. ISBN 0-226-79157-2.

For the adept student of religion this volume will be essential, but this is not a "basic" reference work. Taylor, a recognized commentator on the interface between religion and contemporary critical theory, has edited a series of essays from accomplished scholars that explore such familiar concepts as "belief," "God," and "sacrifice," and also newer dimensions of the disciplines, such as "performance," "gender," "writing," "territory," and "body." Each of the 22 essays is supplemented with a list of suggested readings. Taylor's introduction is an excellent summary of the current state of religions studies (as opposed to theological studies) and issues contributing to its resurgence. He maintains that the "responsible study of religion today is multidisciplinary and multicultural," and he probes the "complexities entailed in the notion of religion as well as the range of methodological alternatives available for its investigation." This book will appeal especially to those interested in the intersection of religion and cultural studies, but will prove useful to a much broader audience. The essays tend to exfoliate a variety of sophisticated layers of meaning within their subjects; their emphasis is not on arriving at condensed generalizations about the topics, but rather to chart each one's expanding boundaries of definition. The book may well "deconstruct" the familiar understanding of a reference work by provoking more questions than it answers. This is a key addition to any library's holding in religion.—**Christopher Baker**

1233. **The Encyclopedia of Politics and Religion.** Robert Wuthnow, ed. Washington, D.C., Congressional Quarterly, 1998. 2v. illus. maps. index. $250.00/set. ISBN 1-56802-164-X.

The twin passions of much of humanity are religion and politics, and these powerful impulses intersect frequently in complex ways. This country's principle of church and state separation, for instance, has certainly been no impediment to efforts by these two institutions to influence one another. The unsuccessful attempt of President John Kennedy to use U.S.-owned religious facilities abroad for the Peace Corps, and the continuing determination of some religious bodies to shape government policy on abortion, illustrate the point. Around the globe political movements have found justification in religious beliefs, whether it be liberation theology in Latin America or Muslim fundamentalism in Iran.

Edited by Wuthnow, a noted scholar on religion in America, this excellent encyclopedia not only illuminates the interaction of religion and politics in the nineteen and twentieth centuries, but also demonstrates that religion, far from retiring to the insignificant role predicted for it some years ago, remains a vital force in the world. Written by specialists who drew upon the latest research, the study consists of 256 original articles ranging in length from a few hundred to 8,000 words. Included are essays on specific countries such as China and Germany, all the major world religions, topical matters (e.g., abortion, homosexuality), major events such as the Crusades and the Holocaust, and notable figures like Thomas Merton and Friedrich Nietzsche. And, although people such as Meir Kahane and Jerry Falwell are not featured, they are discussed in broader entries on "Morality" and "Nationalism." An alphabetic list of articles and a detailed index make this information readily accessible. This reference will be of value to interested laypersons as well as scholars, and every high school and college library should have a copy.—**John W. Storey**

1234. **The Encyclopedia of World Religions.** Robert S. Ellwood and Gregory D. Alles, eds. New York, Facts on File, 1998. 390p. illus. index. $29.95. ISBN 0-8160-3504-0.

This brief 1-volume encyclopedia is written for young adults in grades 6 through 12. It contains nearly 500 entries covering ancient, modern, and "new" religions as well as symbols, ideas and concepts, general terms, and past and present personages. The work is minimally illustrated with halftone prints, drawings, maps, tables, and charts. A topical outline grouping all entries under 16 main headings, a 3-page selected bibliography of print and electronic texts, and an 8-page index are included at the back of the work.

The text, in two-column format, is clear and easy to read. All the traditional world religions are included, and each is supplemented with an additional entry addressing its status in America. Christianity, however, receives the greatest coverage (80 entries). Judaism (54), Hinduism (54), and Buddhism (30) are represented with fewer entries. Islam is represented by a mere 20 entries. Woefully weak coverage is devoted to

Confucianism, Jainism, Shintoism, Sikhism, and Taoism; none of these exceeds five entries. Only eight new religions were included and all except Scientology were founded prior to the twentieth century. All entries for religions and denominations are generally subdivided under history, beliefs or teachings, practices, organizations, and significance. Entry keywords and running headers are presented in uppercase letters. Cross-references are indicated by words within the text appearing in small capital letters.

The stated purpose of this encyclopedia is "to help readers find information on the world's religious traditions that is simple and interesting to read." The editors have not adequately accomplished that goal. Each bold typeface entry keyword is followed immediately by a definitional clause (rather than a sentence) that is frequently so simplistic or reductional as not to be helpful at all. The remainder of the essay, however, generally supplies enough extra information to derive some sense of the meaning of the term. The encyclopedia covers a broad range of topics, albeit in a fairly cursory and idiosyncratic fashion. The index serves as an important aid to locating topics not addressed by a unique entry, but the listing—in three-column format—appears in a considerably reduced typeface and thus is difficult to read. The predominance of Judeo-Christian topics is specious in that the tradition is held in low esteem; for example, Jesus Christ and Christianity are no more unique than any other religious leader or religion. Biases are displayed in other ways as well. The entry for "Church and State" addresses only the American situation; it does not cover affairs in other parts of the world. "Evangelical and Fundamentalist Christianity" is addressed in a single entry, yet Liberal Christianity or Liberalism is not identified at all. Muslim prohibitions regarding meat are not mentioned in the "Diet and Religion" entry. The entry for "Christianity in America" focuses on Roman Catholicism and Eastern Orthodoxy, but not on Protestantism; the latter is contained in a different entry. Very few illustrations are included in this work but some, such as for the Buddhist bodhi, tree are indecipherable. Halftone prints are included for Gandhi, Martin Luther King, and Malcolm X, but not for Aquainas, Confucius, Luther, Muhammad, and many others. Guru and syncretism are not defined and it is not self-evident why two entries (Pentecostal Christianity and Pentecostalism) were needed to address the charismatic traditions. David Levinson's *Religion: A Cross-Cultural Encyclopedia* (see ARBA 97, entry 1178), with somewhat fewer entries, is a preferred work even for young adults, and *The HarperCollins Dictionary of Religion* (1995), edited by Jonathan Z. Smith, is the definitive scholarly work for the subject. [R: BL, 1 Sept 98, pp. 156-158; SLJ, Nov 98, p. 151]—**Glenn R. Wittig**

1235. Lewis, James R. **The Encyclopedia of Cults, Sects, and New Religions.** Buffalo, N.Y., Prometheus Books, 1998. 595p. illus. $149.95. ISBN 1-57392-222-6.

This remarkable volume includes information on nearly 1,000 cults, sects, and new religions that have appeared in the United States during the past 200 or more years. The book begins with the Aaronic Order and concludes with Zion's Order, followed by 63 pages of bibliography. The entries range from a short paragraph, as for the Emmanuel Association (formed in 1937 with an estimated 400 members today), to entries of four or five pages, as for Mormonism (Church of Jesus Christ of the Latter-day Saints) and Hasidism. Most of the entries have to do with religions that are still active, but some, such as the Shakers, are nearly gone, whereas others, such as A Candle, are actually defunct. Each entry discusses the history and key people involved in the establishment of the group as well as its current beliefs and status. This information was largely confirmed by the groups themselves prior to publication.

The introduction includes a short discussion of the reasons for the rise of these types of groups. Setting them in the lineage of the Great Awakening of the 1740s, the author designates them as "religious awakenings." He also observes that the awakenings of earlier times were generally characterized by a renewal of the mainstream denominations, whereas those of the 1970s and 1980s differ in that such renewal does not appear to be happening.

This volume truly belongs in every city, county, and academic library, as well as in newspaper and magazine libraries for journalists' use as they report on the various activities of these groups. The only suggestions for this volume would have been to have key bibliographic references appended to each entry and to have an index included. [R: BL, 1 Nov 98, p. 538; LJ, 1 Sept 98, p. 172]—**Susan Tower Hollis**

1236. Melton, J. Gordon. **Encyclopedia of American Religions.** 6th ed. Farmington Hills, Mich., Gale, 1999. 1243p. index. $205.00. ISBN 0-8103-8417-5. ISSN 1066-1212.

A Methodist minister educated at Garret Theological Seminary and Northwestern University and a nationally recognized scholar who currently heads the Institute for the Study of American Religion at the University of California, Santa Barbara, Melton has been studying religion in North America for more than 20 years. A result of his labor is this superb encyclopedia, now in its 6th edition. Its organization is logical and straightforward. Part 1 features 2 introductory essays on religion in the United States and Canada. Part 2 offers 24 brief overviews of specific "families," from Anglicanism and Spiritualism to Liberalism and Fundamentalism. Part 3, comprising about 30 percent of the text, describes and gives current information on 2,364 religious bodies—non-Christian as well as Christian. A detailed table of contents, along with geographic, subject, and master name indexes, affords easy access to this information.

A unifying thread in Melton's work is pluralism. From a nation of only 20 denominations in 1800, the United States had some 900 such bodies by 1988. Melton attributed this to separation of church and state, that crowning achievement of the American Revolution that forced all churches to compete on an equal footing for the souls of the lost, and mass immigration in the nineteenth and twentieth centuries, which compelled Protestants to make room for growing numbers of Catholics, Jews, Moslems, and adherents of various Eastern religions. Such diversity, Melton believes, has thus far prevented contemporary Christian conservatives from having their way on issues such as abortion and prayer in public schools. As would be expected in a work of this scope, there are a few mistakes. James McGready never officially joined the Cumberlands, for example, and Baptist associations are not necessarily coterminous with counties. Such trifles aside, this excellent reference should be in every high school and college library. For anyone interested in North American religion it is a treasure trove.—**John W. Storey**

1237. **Merriam-Webster's Encyclopedia of World Religions.** Wendy Doniger, ed. Springfield, Mass., Merriam-Webster, 1999. 1181p. illus. $49.95. ISBN 0-87779-044-2.

This 1-volume encyclopedia is a product of the University of Chicago faculty and alumni. Most of the contributing editors and the consulting editor have earned degrees from or work for the university. The volume is functional and convenient in its format. Containing 3,500 entries and 30 longer articles, it serves the needs of the quick informational check and the in-depth beginning study. The bibliography, illustration, pronunciation guide, maps, and intricate cross-referencing system all add to the value of this text. The audience is the general reader, not the scholar, and it does well in providing information for the curious reader. [R: BL, 15 Dec 99, pp. 799-800]—**Linda L. Lam-Easton**

Handbooks and Yearbooks

1238. Corduan, Winfried. **Neighboring Faiths: A Christian Introduction to World Religions.** Downers Grove, Ill., InterVarsity Press, 1998. 363p. illus. maps. index. $24.99. ISBN 0-8308-1524-4.

This is not a standard reference work, but rather a textbook written to introduce evangelical Christians to other religions. Not only does the author write from an evangelical Christian perspective, but she also writes from the related position of "original monotheism." The work begins with an introductory chapter where the author describes the basis of her position for the study religions and religious practices. The body of the text is organized according to the theory "original monotheism." It begins with three monotheistic religions (Judaism, Islam, and Zoroastrianism) and then moves to "traditional religions" (African, Native American). This is followed by Hinduism and Buddhism and then religions that are heavily influenced by one or another of the religions previously covered (Jainism, Sikhism, Baha'i, Chinese popular religion, and Shintoism). Christianity is not included on the grounds that the work is meant for Christians and they would find a chapter in a work such as this either "patronizing" or "insufficient."

Each chapter concludes with a section called "So you meet a [Jew, Muslim, and so on]" where evangelical Christians are given suggestions on how to approach and talk to adherents of a particular religion as persons and as possible converts. This section often includes a brief analysis of the success and appropriateness of missionary practices. These analyses are notably more sophisticated than the stereotypical evangelical Christian approaches and give the outsider an interesting view into evangelical Christianity. Chapters include relevant maps and illustrations.

Because the bias of the author is so transparent and the organization of the material so straightforward, adherents of other religions, while they might complain of an ultimate lack of sympathy, cannot reasonably complain of hostile distortion. Its structure and organization is such that the work could be included in a high school or public reference collection, but it is really a monograph and not a reference work. Although bias and structure may render it unsuitable for the reference collections of many libraries, the work is recommended as an addition to the general collection of any library interested in comparative religion. Libraries seeking a less committed and idiosyncratic reference work on world religions for high school and general readers should consider *Religions of the World: The Illustrated Guide to Origins, Beliefs, Traditions, & Festivals* (see ARBA 98, entry 1348).—**Richard H. Swain**

1239. Hartz, Paula R. **Zoroastrianism.** New York, Facts on File, 1999. 128p. illus. maps. (World Religions). $26.95. ISBN 0-8160-3877-5.

1240. Lugira, Aloysius M. **African Religion.** New York, Facts on File, 1999. 128p. illus. maps. index. (World Religions). $26.95. ISBN 0-8160-3876-7.

Each of these two small volumes, the most recent in Facts on File's World's Religion series, provides an excellent resource on its topic. *Zoroastrianism* opens with a brief overview of this religion with very few members. In the following chapters, the reader learns about its founder, Zarathushtra, essentially a reformer; the religion's history, including information about its Persian homeland and later Iran; and then Zoroastrianism in India, where its members are termed Parsis, the religion's largest group in the world. The following three chapters expand on the Avesta, the Zoroastrian scripture; its religious ethics and philosophy; and its rites and rituals. Finally, the author explores the future of this non-proselytizing religion, which has stringent rules against intermarriage and converts and whose members are so dispersed throughout the world that many are separated from any significant group of like-minded individuals.

African Religion discusses the indigenous religions present in the 35 reporting nations, while noting as well the presence of Christianity and Islam. Thus its title is something of a misnomer. After opening with a general overview of Africa, the author notes the topics of significance for African religion—oral tradition and creation myths, the Supreme Being, the spirit world, rites and rituals, sacred spaces and places, and mystical forces—addressing each in greater depth in the subsequent chapters. The final chapter reviews African religion in today's world, noting the increased respect accorded the different indigenous beliefs in contrast to the earlier days when these religions were not considered true religion. Currently, missionaries generally recognize that any conversion represents a graft onto the basic "Africanness" of the individual.

In sum, both of these volumes provide excellent introductions to their respective subjects, with useful glossaries, chapter notes, suggestions for further reading, and comprehensive indexes. Thus these two books deserve a place on the shelves of public, high school, and church libraries, if not even those of colleges, due to both their readability and their clarity.—**Susan Tower Hollis**

1241. Lewis, James R. **Cults in America: A Reference Handbook.** Santa Barbara, Calif., ABC-CLIO, 1998. 232p. index. (Contemporary World Issues Series). $45.00. ISBN 1-57607-031-X.

This reference work is part of the series that addresses often controversial, vital issues in today's society. It provides a balanced view of alternative and controversial religions that are sometimes referred to as cults. Sensational news reports of cults periodically dominate the national news—the recent incidents of

Heaven's Gate, the UFO group in San Diego (1997) and the Branch Davidians in Waco (1993) are two examples of highly complex and controversial cults. The fascinating history of cults and sects in America often chronicles the emergence of charismatic leaders, brainwashing and mind control debates, communes, murders, and tax evasion. This reference work is well-organized into chapters that provide a logical presentation of a lot of information, including a historical overview of cults and alternative religions in the United States. There is also a chronology beginning in 1740 of key names and events and important court decisions as well as facts and data and a directory of organizations and Websites. This last section is fully annotated and provides cult information with more than two dozen URLs of Websites as well as some e-mail contacts. A comprehensive and useful index is provided, as is an extensive list of sources, including books, articles, and videotapes. Readers will most likely proceed directly to the 46 entries in the "Controversial Groups and Movements" chapter; some of the especially interesting ones are on Santeria, the Hare Krishna movement, Satanism, Erhard Seminars Training (EST), Voodoo, and the Church of Scientology. This reference work can be used by students, parents, and psychologists. It is highly recommended for all libraries, but especially those serving undergraduate students and the general public. [R: LJ, 1 Feb 99, pp. 76-78]—**Edward Erazo**

1242. Smart, Ninian. **The World's Religions.** 2d ed. New York, Cambridge University Press, 1998. 608p. illus. index. $27.95pa. ISBN 0-521-63748-1.

Revised and updated, this work unravels the world's religions from a historical perspective that takes the reader from early beginnings to the modern world. Divided into 2 major parts, the 1st traces the development of religions through the fifteenth century, with separate chapters on South Asia; China; Japan; Southeast Asia; the Pacific; the Americas; Ancient Near East; Persia and Central Asia; Greece and Rome; classical African religions; and the manifestations of Christianity, Judaism, and Islam in medieval times.

The 2d part covers cultural transformation from 1500 to the present, and is more focused on the evolution of religions and cultural values. Religions are described through their symbols, rituals, followers, architecture, and art. The volume is heavily illustrated with black-and-white photographs and images, with a few color plates. The work opens with an introduction that touts the value of comparative study of religion, and concludes with a glossary, bibliography, and full index.

Students and others who need a basic overview of various religions should find the volume useful for its cultural approach. Those needing more in-depth information can consult religious encyclopedias. *The World's Religions* is recommended as a basic introduction, and quite possibly for the circulating as well as reference collection.—**Edmund F. SantaVicca**

Bible Studies

Atlases

1243. Laney, J. Carl. **Concise Bible Atlas: A Geographical Survey of Bible History.** Peabody, Mass., Hendrickson, 1998. 277p. illus. maps. index. $16.95. ISBN 1-56563-366-0.

Although this book is titled an atlas, its purpose is to provide historical and other background information on towns and regions in the Holy Land to aid interpretation of the Bible. The contents cover Palestine, Asia Minor, Greece, and Egypt, and are divided into 16 categories based on a chronology spanning from creation to present times. The discussion of each locale's history, climate, physical features, economy, and government structure far surpasses the meager data supplied by the simplified maps.

The work's format is similar to other Bible atlases such as the work by Herbert May, *Oxford Bible Atlas* (3d ed.; Oxford University Press, 1984), in regard to its arrangement by historical periods. Although it is easier to use than Yohanan Aharoni's *Macmillan Bible Atlas* (3d ed., Macmillan, 1993), it lacks the details and thoroughness of both works in description and map information. The black-and-white maps and photographs contrast sharply with the richness of works such as Rogerson's Atlas of the Bible (Facts on File, 1991), which relies heavily on color photographs and classic works of art as well as the use of primary written sources to enhance the narrative. Although Laney approaches his work with a devoted interest and belief in its importance, his expertise cannot compare with the authority gained from a lifetime of study in the field by writers such as Aharoni and May.

This volume perhaps more closely resembles Guy P. Duffield's *Handbook of Bible Lands* (Regal Books, 1969) in summarizing events and citing Bible passages relating to each site. Many of the comments have a Christian connotation. In several cases, Laney's work provides an update of recent archaeological finds at specific locations. Perhaps the book's value is in its brevity for those desiring to study the Bible in a contextual aspect, but not wishing to make that more important than the biblical story itself. Subject and scripture indexes facilitate access.—**Janet J. Kosky**

Dictionaries and Encyclopedias

1244. **The Anchor Bible Dictionary on CD-ROM.** [CD-ROM]. Oak Harbor, Wash., Logos Research Systems, 1997. Minimum system requirements: IBM or compatible 386. Double-speed CD-ROM drive. Windows 3.1. 8MB RAM. $360.00.

Because this work was published in 1992, the 6-volume *Anchor Bible Dictionary* (ABD) has become a standard reference work in many academic and public libraries. In spite of the warm reception it received, it suffered from one major shortcoming: lack of an index. The encyclopedic nature of the ABD made an index volume a highly desired follow-up. By converting the dictionary into electronic form and adding a powerful and flexible search engine (and the King James Version and the New Revised Standard Version of the Bible), Logos has gone one better.

As part of the Logos Library System, the ABD can be browsed and searched. The Library Browser at the left of the program window displays in table-of-contents fashion the titles of the articles in the dictionary. Double-clicking on a title displays the article in the Active Document Window. In the displayed text there are links to cross-referenced articles in the ABD (in red type), passages in the Old and New Testaments and the Apocrypha (in blue), and illustrations (in green). Clicking on one of these links displays the referenced text or image in a separate window. There are also links to pop-up explanations of abbreviations and affiliations of contributors (also in green). Unfortunately, clicking on some of the abbreviations of Dead Sea Scrolls documents results in the message "Numbered caves of Qumran, yielding written material; followed by abbreviation of biblical or apocryphal book" rather than the identification of the documents.

Although browsing the ABD CD-ROM is good, and using the links is better, the ability to search is its best feature, and perhaps what really sets it apart from the print version. Users can perform word, phrase, and Boolean searches on the entire text of the dictionary and display the text of any item on the results list by double-clicking on the item. Additionally, any word or phrase in a displayed text can be searched by right-clicking on the word or blocked phrase and using the search options on the shortcut menu that appears. Because of the enhancements Logos has made to the ABD, the CD-ROM version is even more highly recommended for public and academic libraries, even those that already have the print version.

—**Craig W. Beard**

1245. **The Dictionary of Biblical Imagery.** Leland Ryken and others, eds. Downers Grove, Ill., InterVarsity Press, 1998. 1058p. index. $39.99. ISBN 0-8308-1451-5.

Much of the Bible is taken up with story (of ancient Israel in the Old Testament and of Jesus and the early church in the New Testament) and poetry (primarily the Book of Psalms). The stories, poems, and even the nonliterary writings, such as the letters of Paul, are full of images. God is described as a warrior, Israel as an unfaithful wife, and the adversaries of God and his people are portrayed as beasts. Although this aspect of the Bible is not completely ignored in previous Bible dictionaries and encyclopedias, this is the first one to deal specifically with the imagery in the Bible. The more than 150 contributors include both biblical and literary scholars, many of whom are quite at home in both fields.

Among the alphabetically arranged articles are ones on each book of the Bible; typical characters (e.g., hero/heroine, villain, pilgrim), locations (e.g., city, countryside, sea), and motifs (e.g., quest, rags to riches, crime and punishment); and images (e.g., blindness, drought, fruitfulness). In addition, there are survey articles on rhetorical devices: "Character Types," "Plot Motifs," and "Rhetorical Patterns." Often there is interplay among images in Bible passages, and the cross-references within and at the end of articles, the subject index, and the scripture index tie these together well. One could wish for a bit more bibliography; the majority of articles do not have one.

The articles are well written and will inform readers about not only the images and messages of the biblical writings, but also the world and cultural mindset in which they arose. This work is recommended for academic, public, and church libraries.—**Craig W. Beard**

1246. **Dictionary of Biblical Interpretation.** John H. Hayes, ed. Nashville, Tenn., Abingdon Press, 1999. 2v. $195.00/set. ISBN 0-687-05531-8.

Although bearing a title similar to the 1-volume *A Dictionary of Biblical Interpretation* (see ARBA 91, entry 1425), this is an independent work. Because both treat biblical interpretation, there are some similarities. Like the earlier dictionary (DBI-1), this one (DBI-2) presents alphabetically arranged articles dealing with the books and types of literature in the Bible (e.g., parables and poetry), schools and movements of interpretation (e.g., feminist and evangelical interpretation), critical methods and terminology (e.g., canonical and social-scientific criticism), important interpreters (e.g., Rashi, Abraham Heschel, and Joachim Jeremias), and other disciplines that have interpreted the Bible. Unlike the earlier dictionary, this one includes articles on the deuterocanonical writings. Articles include bibliographies, some very brief and others quite full, that are usually well selected and current.

In spite of the generally positive review DBI-1 received, the ARBA reviewer expressed some concerns about the composition of the team of contributors, the assignment of articles, and the focus of some articles. The current work is much less culpable in those regards. The team of contributors is considerably more diverse, with a better balance of American, British, European, and Israeli scholars. It also appears that the editors generally assigned articles within the writers' areas of expertise: Adele Berlin on Hebrew poetry, Hugh Williamson on Ezra and Nehemiah, and Bo Reicke and David Peabody on the synoptic problem. Finally, the articles on biblical books consistently treat the history of their interpretation (though some articles on Old Testament books fail to mention their interpretation/use in New Testament writings).

DBI-2 improves upon (but does not replace) DBI-1, but it is not without its weaknesses as well. This reviewer's main criticism is that some of the articles lack the balance one might expect in such a work as this. Andrew Adam's offering on postmodern biblical interpretation sounds at times more like an editorial than a dictionary article. Edgar McKnight, in an otherwise fine survey, does little to relate reader-response criticism to biblical interpretation. David Jobling does a better job in "Structuralism and Deconstruction." Also, the nearly 10-page article on Acts of the Apostles by the editor and Jurgen Roloff suffers from absence of section headings, which the editor should have noticed. In spite of its shortcomings (which are not numerous), this set deserves a place in seminary libraries, academic libraries with biblical studies collections, and even some larger public libraries.—**Craig W. Beard**

1247. **Dictionary of Deities and Demons in the Bible (DDD).** 2d rev. ed. Karel van der Toorn, Bob Becking, and Pieter W. van der Horst, eds. Grand Rapids, Mich., William B. Eerdmans and Boston, Brill Academic, 1999. 960p. index. $120.00. ISBN 90-04-11119-0.

The title of this dictionary makes predictable its articles on Baal, Baal-zebub, Mammon, Molech, Satan, and Zeus, all explicitly named in the Bible. It hardly hints, however, at the comprehensive breadth—let alone the enormous scholarly depth—of its treatment of beings. This includes diverse names and designations held by some group or other to be divine, quasi-divine, or otherwise supernatural and that are mentioned or alluded to, however indirectly, in the biblical text, including the Apocrypha. This expansive scope takes in deities not mentioned as such, but reflected as an element in place-names (e.g., Shemesh in Beth-shemesh) or personal names (Tyche in Tychicus), plus entities regarded as divine (sun, moon) or associated with divinities (new wine) in some ancient Near Eastern cultures, but not acknowledged in that capacity in biblical references, and deities whose mention in the Bible, while hypothesized by some scholars, is either disputed or discredited. Further included are "human figures [that] rose to attain divine or semi-divine status in a later tradition," a category said to include Jesus, Mary, Enoch, Moses, and Elijah (introduction, p. xvii). Even these broadly inclusive criteria, however, might not lead one to expect individual and substantial entries for the varied biblical designations of God (Yahweh, Lord, Father, King, Mighty One of Jacob) and of Jesus (Christ, Lamb, Messiah, Savior, Son of God, Son of Man).

Most articles consist of distinct sections that discuss the etymology of the deity's or demon's names and its occurrences in various ancient cultures, his or her character and role in the culture of origin, and biblical references and what they portray. A final section gives bibliographic references, quite often dominated by non-English-language publications.

This is a work by and for scholars. It was produced by an international cast of over a hundred contributors (identified by location only, leaving specific institutional affiliation to be guessed at), headed by an editorial team from the Dutch universities of Utrecht and Amsterdam. As for potential users, lay students of the Bible, undergraduates, and so on can undoubtedly glean useful information from it. But they will almost invariably stumble over specialized terminology, untranslated and untransliterated expressions from ancient languages, and arcane references that may even trouble religion scholars who are not experts in the relevant languages and cultures. Nonspecialists may have difficulty, too, discerning governing assumptions in the work as a whole or in individual articles.

The 1st edition of this work (Brill, 1995) did not have an American copublisher and was not reviewed in ARBA. It was selected by *Choice* as an "Outstanding Academic Book" for 1996. This new edition updates a hundred or so of the roughly 600 original articles and adds 30 new ones.—**Hans E. Bynagle**

1248. **The Illustrated Bible Dictionary.** J. D. Douglas, ed. Downers Grove, Ill., InterVarsity Press, 1998. 3v. illus. maps. index. $79.99/set. ISBN 0-8308-1460-4.

As the title implies, this 3-volume book is a dictionary of the Bible. However, given its size and breadth, it could just as easily pass for an encyclopedia. In total, the book is about 2,000 pages long and covers an enormous number of topics.

The cover of the book declares, "A superb three-part dictionary of the Bible filled with pictures, maps, and diagrams, most in full color." This brief, rather subjective description appears to be quite accurate. With respect to the "superb" part of the description, the definitions and articles contained in the book appear to be quite accurate and very detailed. The editors have done a great job of reducing the individual articles to their most essential pieces. In fact, if the book suffers from any chronic faults, it would be its brevity. Abbreviations are used extensively throughout the work, sometimes to an almost absurd degree. For example, directional words are never spelled out. N, W, S, and E are used for North, West, South, and East. One gets the impression that one of the primary goals of the editors was to make the book as small as possible. There is irony here in that this book is anything but small. It is three large, rather substantial volumes. The extensive use of abbreviations and scholarly detail makes the dictionary a little difficult to use for younger readers, although the binding may give one the impression that it is a juvenile reference work. Each volume is bound in 9-by-11-inch glossy covers, each a different primary color.

However, the dictionary was written by some of the finest conservative evangelical scholars in the world. As such it is highly recommended for every library collection that may serve researchers with serious questions about the Bible, its theology, its literature, and its history. Make no mistake, this is a serious reference work, very much at home in a serious adult reference department.—**Richard A. Leiter**

1249. **New International Dictionary of New Testament Theology.** [CD-ROM]. Grand Rapids, Mich., Zondervan Publishing/HarperCollins, 1999. Minimum system requirements: IBM or compatible. CD-ROM drive. Windows 95. 5MB hard disk space. Video card. Printer. $119.95. ISBN 0-310-21665-6.

Almost everyone contemplating purchase of this CD-ROM version of *The International Dictionary of New Testament Theology* (NIDNTT) will already know and perhaps even own the print version (Zondervan, 1986). The new "edition" seems to offer no changes in text but does claim to present considerable advantages in getting at that text and studying it. Thus searching will be faster and more powerful—users can quickly find any word, phrase, or group of words. The results of searches can be easily printed out and edited. Note taking is readily done and the notes can be printed out and attached to the context they apply to.

There is, of course, a considerable price to pay for these advantages, quite apart from the cost of the purchase. The manual explains how to accomplish the above scholarly tasks and is about 150 pages long. Free online help is available from the publisher, but the technologically inexperienced user may find it difficult to even know how to utilize such help.

A fair guess might be that the CD-ROM would be of substantial value to scholars, clergy, and others who intend to spend many hours with the NIDNTT. For casual, intermittent, and unsophisticated reference use, the printed text is probably still best suited.—**Samuel Rothstein**

1250. **Wycliffe Bible Dictionary.** Charles F. Pfeiffer, Howard F. Vos, and John Rea, eds. Peabody, Mass., Hendrickson, 1998. 1851p. maps. index. $34.95. ISBN 156563-362-8.

The volume includes all personal and place-names from the Bible; many doctrinal and theological terms; some historical and cultural background articles; and extended articles on animals, archaeology, biblical texts and interpretations, chronology, and contemporary theological movements, each listed alphabetically. The editors state that all articles must conform to conservative evangelical orthodoxy and be written for informed general readers. For the most part, orthodoxy has not been a serious limitation. Although the documentary hypothesis, a prominent theory discussed by biblical scholars, is dismissed without description or discussion, most relevant issues, such as the Synoptic problem, the authorship of the Pastoral Letters, the dating of the fall of Jericho, and parallels between biblical stories and other Near Eastern literature (e.g., the birth of Sargon and Moses) are adequately treated. The articles are generally well written and scholarly. The only apparent differences between this newly published edition and its 1975 original are the consolidation of two volumes into one and a change of the title from an encyclopedia to a dictionary. There are many black-and-white photographs, generally small and occasionally repeated. Charts and maps are scarce. The most serious limitation is the aging bibliography. Nothing is cited later than the 1960s and much of the literature is from the first half of the century.—**Robert T. Anderson**

Handbooks and Yearbooks

1251. **Historical Handbook of Major Biblical Interpreters.** Donald K. McKim, ed. Downers Grove, Ill., InterVarsity Press, 1998. 643p. index. $29.99. ISBN 0-8308-1452-3.

This is of necessity a selective reference work. The 101 people were included because of their contributions to the field of biblical interpretation over the past two millennia. Few would argue that these individuals—among whom John Chrysostom, John Calvin, J. B. Lightfoot, Adolph Schlatter, and Raymond Brown—are deserving of a place here, although some may think Søren Kierkegaard is more at home among philosophers and Jonathan Edwards among theologians. Other interpreters, the editor readily admits, could have been chosen in place of those who were and should be treated in future handbooks. Most noticeably absent are women (except for Elisabeth Schüssler Fiorenza and Phyllis Trible) and people of color. To the credit of this notably evangelical publisher, various points on the theological spectrum—from liberal to conservative—are represented.

The articles are arranged alphabetically in chronological sections based upon five periods of church history: the early church, the Middle Ages, the sixteenth and seventeenth centuries, the eighteenth and nineteenth centuries, and the twentieth century. The introduction to each section provides an overview of biblical interpretation in the period and mentions some of the other important figures who were not chosen as subjects of the following articles. The contributors, many of whom are themselves well-known biblical scholars, detail the contribution and assess the significance of each interpreter and round out their articles with select bibliographies. This volume will be particularly useful where the history of biblical interpretation is taught.—**Craig W. Beard**

1252. **The International Bible Commentary: A Catholic and Ecumenical Commentary for the Twenty-First Century.** William R. Farmer, Sean McEvenue, Armando J. Levoratti, and David L. Dungan, eds. Collegeville, Minn., Liturgical Press, 1998. 1918p. maps. index. $99.95. ISBN 0-8146-2454-5.

Begun in 1991 and completed in 1998, this biblical commentary represents an ecumenical collaboration of scholars throughout the world. Besides this English edition, publishers are producing editions in Spanish, French, Italian, and Polish. These international scholars bring not only their biblical expertise but their cultural background as well—from Europe, South America, North America, Australia, Africa, Asia, and the Philippines. Their overarching perspective flows from the Roman Catholic tradition of biblical interpretation, while at the same time focusing on the role of scripture in many different cultures. According to its mission statement the commentary is intended to "be a truly Roman Catholic, and also a truly ecumenical, commentary for all nations" (p. xvi).

The quality of the writing makes the content easily accessible. Although incorporating the work of contemporary biblical scholars, the emphasis is pastoral. The commentaries on individual books are meant to accompany a reading of the Bible rather than to elucidate the technical aspects of biblical studies. There are, however, discussions of certain problems in biblical studies; for example, biblical archaeology, biblical interpretation in Qumran, the canonical structure of the New Testament, the Synoptic problem in the Gospels, and the Nag Hammadi Corpus. Other general articles meant to enhance an understanding of the Bible as a whole discuss the history of biblical interpretation, including rabbinic and patristic exegesis; biblical influences on liturgy, preaching, and the charismatic movement; the origins of the Bible and the transmission of texts; and the historic Jesus and his central role in salvation.

To further emphasize its pastoral approach other articles discuss contemporary concerns, such as liberation, justice, violence, ecumenism, ecology, ant-Semitism, and nationalism and Christian faith, all from a biblical point of view. Many articles as well as the commentaries on individual books conclude with bibliographies for further study.

The choice of topics may be somewhat uneven; for example, the article on the Bible in prayer is geographically limited to Africa. However, most topics are more general, for instance, those on the biblical influence on the charismatic and the retreat movements, and the Bible and preaching. The volume concludes with a pastoral guide for using the Bible in preaching, and with a section of maps and its index. Because of its pastoral approach the commentary will be a worthwhile addition both to reference and to circulating collections in theological, academic, and large public libraries.—**Bernice Bergup**

1253. **Quickverse: Life Application Bible.** [CD-ROM]. Hiawatha, Iowa, Parsons Technology, 1997. Minimum system requirements: IBM or compatible 486. 2X CD-ROM drive. Windows 95. 8MB RAM. 640x480 display monitor. Windows-compatible 16-bit sound device. $49.00. ISBN 1-5726-4269-6.

This multimedia version of the Life Application Bible retains the features that make the print version popular—an introduction to each book of the Bible (including an outline and themes), maps, notes on the text emphasizing application, and profiles of major biblical characters. Several other features have been added that enhance the program's utility: a Bible dictionary; hundreds of artworks and photographs (including 30 images that place users virtually in the middle of a scene, giving them a panoramic view as they move the mouse pointer up, down, left, and right); dramatic readings of more than 160 passages, such as the twenty-third Psalm and the Beatitudes; indexes of Bible- and life-related topics; and a two-level (quick and advanced) search program.

The basic layout of the program screen includes a toolbar, which provides access to program components, across the top with two windows side by side below. The left window always displays the text of the New Living Translation; the content of the right window changes depending upon which other program component (e.g., notes, maps) is being used. Right-clicking on any word in the Bible window opens a pop-up menu that allows users to hear the word pronounced, search for occurrences of the word in all program components, and view definitions from the Bible dictionary for many of the words. Accompanying the Bible text in the left window are hyperlinked icons that display related portions of the other components in the right window.

The *QuickVerse: Life Application Bible* cannot be expanded to include multiple Bible translations, Hebrew and Greek texts, or commentaries, like some of the more comprehensive computer Bible programs. However, it is as tightly integrated as any of those programs (and more than some). Due to its purpose, this program will probably not be a high-priority purchase for most academic collections, but for church libraries and some public libraries it is definitely worth a look. [R: LJ, 1 Feb 98, p. 124]—**Craig W. Beard**

1254. Sawyer, M. James. **Taxonomic Charts of Theology and Biblical Studies.** Grand Rapids, Mich., Zondervan Publishing/HarperCollins, 1999. 171p. (Zondervan Charts). $19.99pa. ISBN 0-310-21993-0.

This volume contains 129 charts of theology and biblical studies and a 36-page glossary. The first 95 charts outline theology and the rest, divided by Old Testament and New Testament, outline the Bible. The charts could be helpful in outlining a course, a talk, or a term paper, and they raise questions and invite disagreements that could be quite stimulating. The theological sections involve many issues (for example, various theories associated with millennialism) that would be of rather exclusive interest to evangelicals (particularly because the charts are intended to communicate structure rather than content and much is left unexplained). Very little is made of unique Roman Catholic or Eastern Orthodox Catholic doctrine. The Death of God theology, existentialism, and Vatican II are essentially absent in twentieth-century considerations. Many charts are quite solid, particularly the charts on church history. Some, like Chart 28 (Names of Gods), are lists rather than charts in organization. The glossary is clear and instructive, although many of the topics, particularly ideas as opposed to events, are too complex to treat in this necessarily summary fashion. Because some of the charts are "portrait" and others are "landscape" it can be frustrating moving from one chart to the next.—**Robert T. Anderson**

1255. **Zondervan Handbook to the Bible.** 3d ed. Grand Rapids, Mich., Zondervan Publishing/HarperCollins, 1999. 815p. illus. maps. $39.99. ISBN 0-310-23095-0.

This volume is a revised and expanded edition of the best-selling *Eerdmans Handbook to the Bible* (1st ed.; see ARBA 74, entry 1187). It retains the arrangement of the previous edition: an introduction to the Bible and its study (part 1); a section each on the Old Testament (part 2) and New Testament (part 3), with books arranged in canonical order, outlined, and commented upon; and a reference index (part 4). The introduction is comprised of articles written by some of the 69 contributors. Other articles written by these scholars are strategically placed throughout parts 2 and 3, the text of which was written by Pat Alexander. Among these articles are character portraits (absent from the previous editions), introductions to specific types of biblical literature, and historical sketches of contemporary civilizations. Also, like its predecessors, the handbook is profusely illustrated with maps, timelines, and pictures of artifacts, among other things. Few, if any, similar works approach the quantity and quality of illustrations.

The sections on the Old and New Testaments is revised and many of the 119 articles are either newly written or thoroughly rewritten for this edition. Some of the articles made the transition unchanged. The same is true of the illustrations; they are a combination of old and new. Most of the changes, which resulted in an increase of 135 pages, were indeed improvements. Unfortunately, a few features that were not retained, such as the charts illustrating weights, measures, and coins of biblical times, will be missed.

Not only was the content itself revised and expanded, so was the list of contributors. The number of scholars was expanded from 32 to 69. Several names appear in the list of contributors of both this and the previous edition (e.g., Alan Millard, Howard Marshall, Dick France). Among the new names are, for the first time, about a dozen women, including Katharine Dell, Grace Emmerson, and Claire Powell. Thorough yet concise coverage, appropriate and appealing illustrations, timeliness, and great attention to detail—which, sadly, cannot be said about enough reference works—make this a highly desirable acquisition for congregational, school, public, and undergraduate academic libraries.—**Craig W. Beard**

Christianity

Almanacs

1256. **Our Sunday Visitor's Catholic Almanac, 2000.** Matthew Bunson, ed. Huntington, Ind., Our Sunday Visitor, 1999. 607p. index. $28.95; $23.95pa. ISBN 0-87973-905-3; 0-87973-904-5pa. ISSN 0069-1208.

The range of Catholic data in this 2000 edition impressively adds to the content and style of the previous editions of the *Catholic Almanac* (1994 ed.; see ARBA 95, entry 1471). It includes revisions and updating of standard sections (e.g., doctrine and dogma, Catholic communications, ecumenism and interreligious dialogue, U.S. Catholic history, the Church in the world); new sections, including an annual review of key Church events and reports; and a special supplement, the philosophy of the Jubilee Holy Year 2000 and its significance for American Catholics. The multiple entries give a fine overview of the structure and teachings of the largest Christian denomination in the world at the start of the Christian third millennium. They are composed from canonical texts and authoritative writings and succeed in projecting evolving developments in the life of the Church (e.g., contra longstanding tradition, cremation in extreme situations may be tolerated if the doctrine of the resurrection of the dead is not tampered). However, the authenticity of self-impression reveals insiders' judgment calls, gerrymandering, and flaws. On the latter, for example, Judaism teaches that the weekly Sabbath is more solemn than Rosh Hashanah, the Passover feast begins on Nisan 15 not 14, and the "Ten Words" are integral but not the sum of the Mosaic Covenant. The up-to-date reports are also a testimony of the diversity and richness of the Church and its mandate—to celebrate Christ's presence in history. In sum, this is a compelling invitation to learn about a dynamic faith community.—**Zev Garber**

Bibliography

1257. Bergman, Jerry, comp. **Jehovah's Witnesses: A Comprehensive and Selectively Annotated Bibliography.** Westport, Conn., Greenwood Press, 1999. 351p. index. (Bibliographies and Indexes in Religious Studies, no.48). $69.50. ISBN 0-313-30510-2.

For those unfamiliar with the history and beliefs of Jehovah's Witnesses, the introduction to this book offers and excellent summary—from doctrine to finances (1 billion, 200 million annual income). Some of the statistics and historical notes might surprise some readers. Five million active believers of the Watchtower Bible and Tract Society (the official name of Jehovah's Witnesses) in 233 countries were counted in 1997, plus an additional 113 million sympathizers. The organization has been highly influential in shaping the constitutional law of many countries, from decisions regarding contemporary freedom of speech to pornography. At one point in its history, the Witnesses made extensive use of radio messages and played phonograph recordings as they went door to door. Now they emphasize the dissemination of religious literature. The chief publication, *Watchtower*, averages 19 million copies a month and is printed in 125 languages—more than any other journal in the world.

This bibliography contains almost 10,000 references to the Watchtower movement and the dozen or so major schisms that have occurred since its founding in 1879. The comprehensive and selectively annotated bibliography includes books, book chapters, manuscripts, tracts, newsletters, booklets, dissertations, journal articles, court cases, and magazines. The organization's main office is "not interested" in cooperating with the publication of the listings, so this reference becomes a valuable tool for scholars and researchers.

Bergman, compiler, is professor of general studies at Northwest State Colleges. He has been researching and writing about the movement for nearly four decades and owns one of the most complete collections of Witness literature, much not available elsewhere. [R: Choice, Oct 99, p. 302]—**Jerri Spoehel**

1258. Di Sabatino, David. **The Jesus People Movement: An Annotated Bibliography and General Resource.** Westport, Conn., Greenwood Press, 1999. 257p. illus. index. (Bibliographies and Indexes in Religious Studies, no.49). $69.50. ISBN 0-313-30268-5.

The Jesus Movement began in the United States in the late 1960s as a reaction against the drug and occult counterculture. The movement itself was perceived as a revival. "In essence, the Jesus People believed they had been recruited into a cosmic battle against the powers of evil, where, as with past revivals, the 'saving of souls' was of utmost significance" (p. 4). The members held to a tightly constructed worldview and there was widespread acceptance of Pentecostalism and biblical inerrancy. Members thought their age was the terminal generation. The movement eventually petered out in 1973 and 1974 and many of the Jesus People returned to the religious mainstream or began new denominations (e.g., Vineyard). The author's introductory essay places the bibliography in context of this movement by presenting key events, concepts, and practices of the movement. The introductory essay also provides suggestions for further study. The bibliography itself is in 3 parts: general resources (historical, sociological, messianic, Jewish, book reviews, periodical and newspaper articles, and film and video resources), extremists (general, Children of God, The Way International, and the Alamo Foundation), and a Jesus music discography. Name, title, and subject indexes provide sufficient access to the contents.

This is an excellent resource for the researcher interested in this aspect of twentieth-century religious history. The introductory essay is informative and the arrangement of the bibliography and indexes ensures access for any user. [R: Choice, July/Aug 99, pp. 1916-1918]—**Robert H. Burger**

Biography

1259. **Sister Wendy's Book of Saints.** By Sister Wendy Beckett. New York, DK Publishing, 1998. 96p. illus. index. $19.95. ISBN 0-7894-2398-7.

This is a book to be admired even before opening it. The illuminated pictures are spectacular—beginning with the cover. The crimson dress of St. Dorothy and the golden armor of St. Martin of Tours almost make a reader forget there is also a text.

Combining illustrations drawn from the rarely seen archives of the Italian State Libraries with personal observations, *Sister Wendy's Book of Saints* is a unique account of the lives and works of more than 35 saints. The works chronicle the lives and ordeals of each chosen saint, their feast days, iconographic emblems, and the subjects of their patronage. In addition to the commentary about their lives, most saints have a full page of dramatic color; a few have two pages.

The subjects of the illustrations include martyrs aplenty, with many depicted as they died—about to be beheaded or in the ravages of fire. Others are less threatening: gentle St. Francis, with the wolf he tamed; St. Christopher, bearing a small child across a river; St. Anthony Abbot, pursued by the naked woman of his dreams; and St. Nicholas, the great gift giver.

Sister Wendy Beckett is a member of the Notre Dame order, a teaching order of nuns. She studied for her degree in English at St. Anne's College in Oxford. Her *Book of Saints* well combines her love of art with her words of inspiration encouraging the reader to love as the saints did. The book concludes with an entire calendar of feast days for saints, not just the ones annotated in the book. Even the list is printed with beautiful color illustrations adorning its pages. [R: BR, Nov/Dec 98, p. 77]—**Jerri Spoehel**

Chronology

1260. Peterson, Susan Lynn. **Timeline Charts of the Western Church.** Grand Rapids, Mich., Zondervan Publishing/HarperCollins, 1999. 383p. index. (Zondervan Charts). $24.99pa. ISBN 0-310-22353-9.

The recent outpouring of books on various Christian topics has helped foster the Zondervan Charts series of reference works. Peterson's volume in this group is, as she acknowledges, similar in format to Bernard Grun's familiar *Timetables of History* (S & S Trade, 1991) and is likely to prove just as useful to a wide array of readers, researchers, and students. Her primary church history timeline covers the period from 4 B.C.E. to 1998. It offers information grouped under the headings of "theology, doctrine, and beliefs," "people and events," "history of the wider culture," and "texts." The second section presents three appendixes, which offer overviews of church history; genealogies of (among others) creeds, Bible versions, and liturgies; and denominational charts tracing the growth of major faith communities. An extensive index to all entries follows, and the volume ends with a brief and somewhat eclectic bibliography of reference works in church history and theology (including Websites where applicable).

Peterson has done an admirable job of compressing a staggering amount of information between two paperback covers and this book will find a welcome place in churches and libraries. Everyone's favorite entry is not likely to be present; John Donne can be found but not Gerard Manley Hopkins, Desert Shield and Desert Storm but not Desert Fathers, Jean-Paul Sartre but not Simone Weil, and the Jesus Movement but not the Jesus Seminar. Nevertheless, Peterson does address the major figures, periods, and events of church history, and her charts on denominational growth may well find their way onto many a teacher's overhead projector.—**Christopher Baker**

Dictionaries and Encyclopedias

1261. **Baker Encyclopedia of Christian Apologetics.** By Norman L. Geisler. Grand Rapids, Mich., Baker Books/Baker Book House, 1999. 841p. index. $49.99. ISBN 0-8010-2151-0.

After three paragraphs of acknowledgments and a half page of abbreviations, the book plunges into text—with neither preface nor introduction. It continues for 791 pages until adding a bibliography, article index, and scripture index, ending with a total of 841 pages.

Challenges to Christianity come from a variety a people and belief systems and Christians are continually searching for appropriate responses to critics of their faith, as stated on the commentary on the back cover. This one-volume encyclopedia is designed to equip believers for Christian defense against the full range of opposing arguments. Its purpose is not to be unbiased. The information is offered to pastors and Christian leaders, students on college campuses, and those involved in counter-cult ministries—all Christians who encounter skeptics.

The volume examines every key issue, person, and concept related to Christian apologetics. The extensive coverage includes philosophical systems, contemporary issues, difficult biblical passages, and classic apologetic arguments. Among the individuals covered in the text are Sigmund Freud, Julian Huxley, Francois-Marie Voltaire, Alfred North Whitehead, Martin Buber, and Aristotle. Some of the topics listed are the Essenes and Jesus, the salvation of infants, genealogies, the alleged divine call of Muhammad, resurrection claims in non-Christian religions, and evolution.

The organization is excellent, especially within each of the long sections. Bold typeface, italics, and numbering of lists make reading very easy. Browsing is quite enjoyable. One disturbing feature, however, is the lumping of Hinduism, Buddhism, and other New Age religions together under the title of Pantheism.

Written entirely by leading apologist Norman Geisler, it stands as the culmination of his lifelong career and ministry. The author is dean and professor of theology and apologetics at Southern Evangelical Seminary. [R: Choice, July/Aug 99, p. 1920]—**Jerri Spoehel**

1262. Brackney, William H. **Historical Dictionary of the Baptists.** Lanham, Md., Scarecrow, 1999. 494p. (Historical Dictionaries of Religions, Philosphies, and Movements, no.25). $69.50. ISBN 0-8108-3652-1.

As the author explains in his informative introduction, Baptists are a movement, a denomination, and a tradition. To understand how this can be so, the history of the Baptists has to be explored. Instead of writing a history, however, Brackney has compiled a dictionary that includes a wide variety of terms, including personal names, countries (and a brief sketch of the history of the Baptists within each), organizations and fellowships, names of movements and concepts (e.g., Adventism), theological terms, and artistic and cultural terms and concepts. The terms are arranged in alphabetic order. Bold typeface terms in the text of the annotations indicate that the term so identified has an entry itself in the dictionary. For the most part, entries are brief (i.e., ½ to 1 page in length). In certain cases, such as in the area of architecture, theological education, and women in Baptist life, the entries can run several pages. In addition, a 30-page selective classified bibliography is appended that arranges the works cited into 13 primary subject groupings and 8 geographical subgroups.

The annotations themselves are clearly and concisely written. One remarkable aspect of the dictionary is its truly international character. The author has apparently made every effort to ensure that information about Baptist churches in almost every nation of the world receives some mention here. The dictionary would be useful for anyone desiring information on Baptists or interested in any aspect of church history that has some relation to the Baptists.—**Robert H. Burger**

1263. **Dictionary of the Presbyterian & Reformed Tradition in America.** D. G. Hart and Mark A. Noll, eds. Downers Grove, Ill., InterVarsity Press, 1999. 286p. $16.99pa. ISBN 0-8308-1453-1.

A reference book with an attitude, this work is explicit about its perspective and is an excellent example of repackaging information for a specialized audience. The editors, respected church historians with excellent reputations, have put together an extension of the publisher's acclaimed *Dictionary of Christianity in America* (see ARBA 91, entry 1444) and have pointed it specifically at the Presbyterian community, stating that the fundamental aim "has been to represent the diversity of efforts to propagate, defend and preserve the Reformed tradition in the United States and Canada" (p. vii). This translates into a more comprehensive coverage of evangelically oriented segments of the general Presbyterian community than has been possible in existing works, such as *The Encyclopedia of the Reformed Faith* (see ARBA 93, entry 1422). An introductory essay, "The Presbyterians: A People, a History & an Identity," underscores this perspective. In addition to a nuanced theological difference, there is a difference in the scope of entries—the focus is on biographical entries and those for various denominational groups. However, contrary to the advertised content, one misses entries for renewal movements (e.g., Presbyterians for Renewal, Presbyterian Coalition), for "A Brief Confession of Faith," or for gender issues—suggesting minimal updating since 1990. Although many of the 400 or more entries are taken from the parent work, they are so identified only if they have been modified in some way. Other entries have been written originally for this work. All entries are signed and include bibliographic references, but there is no index for locating embedded proper names. This work will have greatest appeal to institutions needing information of value to conservative Presbyterians.
—**Donald G. Davis Jr.**

1264. **Encyclopedia of Christianity, Volume 1 (A-D).** Erwin Fahlbusch and others, eds. Leiden, the Netherlands, Brill and Grand Rapids, Mich., William B. Eerdmans, 1999. 893p. $100.00. ISBN 0-8028-2413-7.

The end of the millennium and a desire to provide a serious, scholarly reference work on Christianity are the motivations for production of this work, which is in reality a translation into English, with additions described below, of the fine German work, *Evangelisches Kirchenlexicon* (Vandenhoeck and Ruprecht, 1968). There are 4 more volume to come in the next 5 years, making 1,700 dictionary-type entries total, all written and signed by scholars, mostly from Europe and Germany. A suitable number of additional entries on Christianity of interest to British, American, and other English-speakers have been added, and the already extensive bibliographies at the ends of the articles have had English-language citations added.

Intended for use in academic and public libraries, the work invites comparison with the *Oxford Dictionary of the Christian Church* (3d ed.; see ARBA 98, entry 1389) and *New Schaff-Herzog Encyclopedia of Religious Knowledge* (Baker, 1949). The former, with its English-speakers and Anglo-American emphasis of the subject is a much shorter work (one volume), with shorter entries and shorter bibliographies, compared to the work under review, which emphasizes Continental Christianity and has longer entries and bibliographies. A huge effort has been made here to infuse the work with globalization, with articles on Christianity on different continents and in most countries of the world, and articles on worldwide and ecumenical bodies.

The pluses of the work are numerous. First is the provision of statistical information on Christianity's adherents all over the world, from the resources of David Barrett, a noted demographer of Christianity and author of the 1982 *World Christian Encyclopedia*. Second, the spirit of the work is even-handed and ecumenical, although the starting point is a Western Christian Protestant viewpoint. Roman Catholic, Protestant, Anglican, and Orthodox interpretations are provided. Third, articles on ecumenical bodies are provided. Fourth, current sociocultural contexts are provided in the articles on other world religions, secular philosophies, cultural trends, and political and economical forces. Fifth, historical contexts are provided in articles on historical and theological topics. Sixth, there are biographical entries, although not nearly as many as in the *Oxford Dictionary of the Christian Church*. Seventh, the bibliographic references for further reading are extensive and include both books and periodical articles.

Drawbacks have been noted by other reviewers. These include a complete lack of any illustrations and some inaccuracies in articles on U.S. religious groups. This reviewer notes that in comparison to the entry on Congregationalism the entry for Christian Science seems a bit brief. We have only the one volume so far, so there are maddening cross-references to articles in volumes yet to come, such as under "Campus Crusade for Christ *see* Student Work or Youth Work." The reviewer sees no entry for the African Methodist Episcopal Church, nor a cross-reference. The reader must be clever enough to think to look under "Black Church." There are articles on quite secular topics, such as bourgeois society and birth control, but not one on bioethics. This volume has no index; presumably the index will be for the work as a whole and not be available until the whole set is published, a decided disadvantage, particularly as more volumes appear. Think of this as a companion volume to the *Oxford Dictionary of the Christian Church*, particularly good for materials on Western, continental Christianity, less good for Anglo-American topics, with better attention than most such works to the state of Christianity in countries around the world. [R: LJ, 15 Feb 99, pp. 140-142; BL, 1 Mar 99, pp. 1247-1248; Choice, Oct 99, p. 304]—**Agnes H. Widder**

1265. **Encyclopedia of the Vatican and Papacy.** Frank J. Coppa, ed. Westport, Conn., Greenwood Press, 1999. 483p. index. $99.50. ISBN 0-313-28917-4.

The Vatican and Papacy remain both the most familiar and the least understandable institutions of the worldwide Roman Catholic Church. To make the executive, legislative, and judiciary branches of the near one billion strong church accessible to the educated public requires a certain amount of scholarly effort. Coppa and the contributors of this work ably provide capsule-size entries on important events, ideologies, and persons examined within church teachings and against outside influences that clearly shows the interweaving of the Vatican and Papacy with the course of Western civilization in general and European history in particular. Although the emphasis is on Vatican diplomacy and history from the Renaissance through the 1990s, due recognition is given to influential pre-Renaissance issues (e.g., heresy, schism) as well as papal policy on current theology and morality, including liberation theology and biomedical ethics. A valuable feature is background information on all popes, anti-popes, and 21 church councils from Nicea (325) to Vatican Council II (1965). Arguably, certain topics generate controversy (e.g., Pope Pius XII, Vatican on Zionism) but for the most part plausible evaluations are generally presented. In sum, this is a source of verified information on Vatican matters that will prove beneficial to students and scholars alike. [R: LJ, 15 Nov 98, pp. 60-61; BL, Aug 99, pp. 2107-2108; Choice, Oct 99, p. 304]—**Zev Garber**

1266. **Our Sunday Visitor's Encyclopedia of Catholic Doctrine on CD-ROM.** [CD-ROM]. Russell Shaw, ed. Huntington, Ind., Our Sunday Visitor, 1997. Minimum system requirements (Windows version): IBM or compatible. CD-ROM drive. Windows 3.x or Windows 95. Minimum system requirements (Macintosh version): System 7.0 or higher. CD-ROM drive. $49.95. ISBN 0-87973-774-3.

This is a CD-ROM version of the Our Sunday Visitor encyclopedia published by the same name in 1997 (see ARBA 98, entry 1388). Although electronic value has been added, the text remains unchanged. Installation is quick and easy, taking only a few minutes. This may be due in part to the fact that the setup does not offer the option of loading the entire encyclopedia on the hard drive; the CD-ROM must be loaded in order to access the articles.

The interface is simple and uncluttered. A menu bar includes standard drop-down menus. Below that a button bar presents 13 buttons corresponding to the major functions of the program, including print, previous topic, next topic, search, and zoom. The display area is split into two vertical windows—the contents window and the topic window that can be resized. Topics can be selected from the alphabetically arranged table of contents and displayed in the topic window. The cross-references that are listed at the end of each article in the print version have become hypertext links to the articles referenced. A single click on a link replaces the article being viewed in the topic window with the one selected. A "go back" button on the button bar allows users to move back through the articles viewed during a session, but the history is deleted when the program is closed. The program includes a search function that allows users to find words, phrases, and Boolean combinations anywhere in the text of the encyclopedia. By default, the resulting articles are displayed with the search terms highlighted, but the highlights can be cleared from the view menu. In addition to the ability to navigate fairly quickly through the articles in the encyclopedia, the CD-ROM version adds the ability to print articles and to copy full articles or selected portions and paste them into a word processor. All in all, the encyclopedia is quite easy to use without referring to the help menu.

A couple of shortcomings mar the overall quality of this otherwise good product. First, the program was not developed to fully utilize the capabilities of the mouse. For instance, no functions of the program are available via the right mouse button. Also, the scroll wheel on the mouse works in the contents window but not in the topic window. Second, and more problematic, when an article is located with the search feature and search terms that are highlighted are scrolled, the text can become distorted. Apparently, the only solution is to clear the highlights. Dealing with these shortcomings, especially the latter one, will make this a more desirable acquisition.—**Craig W. Beard**

1267. **Our Sunday Visitor's Encyclopedia of Saints.** [CD-ROM]. By Matthew Bunson, Margaret Bunson, and Stephen Bunson. Huntington, Ind., Our Sunday Visitor, 1998. Minimum system requirements (Windows version): IBM or compatible. CD-ROM drive. Windows 3.x or Windows 95. Minimum system requirements (Macintosh version): System 7.0 or higher. CD-ROM drive. $39.95. ISBN 0-87973-291-1.

The *Encyclopedia of Saints* CD-ROM is an ambitious project: an electronic version of the authors' 1998 reference book on all of the Christian saints (see ARBA 99, entry 1261). Ultimately, however, it falls short of one's expectations. In the introduction on the CD-ROM, the authors write that the work is a comprehensive encyclopedia "on virtually the whole of the Catholic Church's teachings on the Communion of Saints, its traditions of veneration, its methods of decision-making concerning saints, and nearly the whole body of those revered as saints throughout the world." Each entry includes not only biographical information on the saint, but also important dates and cross-references to other saints who were their contemporaries. Listings also include the "beati," or "Blesseds," who are individuals who have not yet been canonized.

The encyclopedia is comprehensive. The vast entry on the Virgin Mary, for instance, discusses her life, including her status as a saint throughout history. Yet, in other instances, the authors have neglected information. The authors write about the famous arrow-pierced St. Sebastian, but they fail to mention his status as a patron saint of those suffering from terminal illnesses and homosexuals. With some of the articles, there are line drawings derived from works of art, but no credit is given to the works or artists, nor is there any discussion of copyright regarding these images. Also, the images do not transfer when copying text to a word processor. Even copying seems odd, as users cannot highlight sections and copy or paste them. Users can only copy the entire article. The best sections of the encyclopedia are the supplemental materials, such as full-text documents from Vatican Council II, a calendar of saints' days, and a glossary of terms.

Technically, the intent of the CD-ROM should make searching, marking, and printing of information easier. However, the use of a CD-ROM format would also denote the ability to incorporate multimedia, which it does not, yielding a product that does not take advantage of its potential. The print version of this encyclopedia would surely be useful in all libraries, but the CD-ROM is more appropriate for home use or only in specialized theological libraries.—**Roberto C. Ferrari**

Handbooks and Yearbooks

1268. Buchanan, Paul D. **Historic Places of Worship: Stories of 51 Extraordinary American Religious Sites Since 1300.** Jefferson, N.C., McFarland, 1999. 1999. illus. index. $39.95. ISBN 0-7864-0588-0.

It is a truism that religion has played a significant role in human existence throughout history. What this collection of stories does is look at 51 places of worship that have influenced society and culture far beyond their immediate location. The geographical scope of the book is the United States, whereas chronologically it ranges from the kivas of the Anazazi from many centuries before Columbus to the Chapel of Peace built in 1970. Individual entries tell the story of each place of worship, giving its background and significance in essays of 2,000 to 4,000 words. A bibliography is included in each entry and most entries include a picture of the site being discussed. The selection is ecumenical, including many Christian denominations as well as Jewish, Islamic, and other religious groups. The subjects selected are generally well chosen and cover such diverse places as St. Louis Cathedral in New Orleans, Harmonie Village in Indiana, Kirtland Temple in Ohio, and the Dexter Avenue Church in Alabama. Some entries, however, could have used a bit more editorial intervention to eliminate some inconsistency in style or superfluous content. *Historic Places of Worship* does what it set out to accomplish, and for those interested in its subject matter it will be more than satisfactory.—**Ronald H. Fritze**

Islam

1269. Daiber, Hans. **Bibliography of Islamic Philosophy.** Boston, Brill Academic, 1999. 2v. index. $391.50/set. ISBN 90-04-11347-9. ISSN 0169-9423.

This 2-volume bibliography of Islamic philosophy is a product of Brill Press and, like all of their work, is magnificently produced. Part of the respected series of handbooks for Oriental Studies, this 2-volume work breaks new ground in its thorough coverage of an emerging subject. The author, Hans Daiber, has created a comprehensive overview of a complex field. The 1st volume is functional and convenient in its format. Containing 9,500 entries in alphabetical order, it serves the needs of the quick informational check. The 2d volume is an index of names, terms, and topics. This work is invaluable for the beginning and competent researcher. Written for general readers and scholars, it also does well in providing information for the curious reader. Scholars will note the comprehensiveness of the endeavor.
—**Linda L. Lam-Easton**

1270. Jenkins, Everett, Jr. **The Muslim Diaspora: A Comprehensive Reference to the Spread of Islam in Asia, Africa, Europe, and the Americas. Volume 1, 570-1500.** Jefferson, N.C., McFarland, 1999. 425p. index. $75.00. ISBN 0-7864-0431-0.

This volume is the first in a series on the Muslim diaspora. This first volume covers the period from the birth of Muhammad in 57 C.E. to 1500, the beginning of the era that spread Islam to the Americas. The domination of the Middle East, the conquest of the Persian and Byzantine Empires and of North Africa, the move into Sicily and the Iberian region, as well as the Balkans are examined. Further spread into central Asia and China, as well as the conquest of India and Indonesia, is documented. The book is set forth chronologically and not much detail is given to enhance the bare historical facts. The researcher would find only a start of the process of exploration in this work. The curious reader or quick-reference checker will use this volume most. For them it provides an easy access to a complex subject.
—**Linda L. Lam-Easton**

Judaism

1271. Solomon, Norman. **Historical Dictionary of Judaism.** Lanham, Md., Scarecrow, 1998. 521p. (Historical Dictionaries of Religions, Philosophies, and Movements, no.19). $60.00. ISBN 0-8108-3497-9.

This book is an excellent addition to Scarecrow's volumes of historical dictionaries. Like other volumes in the series, the entries are arranged alphabetically and, in this instance, cover all aspects of Judaism from Orthodox to Reconstructionist. Key articles on liturgy, festivals, and beliefs are identified as such, and each is given added depth through numerous cross-references to other topics in the text as well as books in the bibliography. The bibliography is more than 40 pages long and mainly topical in format. Topics include poetry, music and art, Kabbalah and mysticism, Holocaust theology, and women in Judaism. There are up-to-date sections on Jewish texts available on CD-ROM and on Jewish sources on the Internet. Appendixes include the 613 Commandments of Mitzvot and excerpts from the several platforms defining the Reform movement. British rabbi and scholar Norman Solomon has compiled a wonderful book that can be used for research or browsing by both laypersons and scholars. [R: Choice, May 99, p. 1594]

—**Deborah Hammer**

Part IV
SCIENCE AND TECHNOLOGY

29 Science and Technology in General

BIBLIOGRAPHY

1272. **Bibliographic Guide to Technology 1998.** New York, G. K. Hall/Macmillan Library Reference, 1999. 2v. $545.00/set. ISBN 0-7838-0234-X. ISSN 0360-2761.

The *Bibliographic Guides* are published annually in 21 fields, primarily in the humanities and social sciences. This 2-volume set on technology is a bibliography of selected materials published since 1990 that were cataloged in 1998 by The Research Libraries of The New York Public Library and the Library of Congress. A wide range of topics is included, such as photography, cookery, engineering, and environmental ecology. Each entry provides complete LC cataloging information and whether the item is part of the New York Public Library holdings. Access is by main entry as well as added entries, titles, series titles, and subject headings. All formats and languages are included. In the past, this series has been a useful tool for acquisitions and cataloging; but with the availability of Web access to both catalogs, it may be difficult to justify the price.—**Teresa U. Berry**

1273. Hurt, C. D. **Information Sources in Science and Technology.** 3d ed. Englewood, Colo., Libraries Unlimited, 1998. 346p. index. (Library and Information Science Text Series). $55.00; $45.00pa. ISBN 1-56308-528-3; 1-56308-531-3pa.

Society has come a long way in both science and technology since the turn of the century. In 1900, medicine, for example, was overrun with homeopaths and mountebanks in surfeit. Cars had not yet been born, and computers were not even a figment of anyone's imagination. Indeed, not one dollar had been spent on computers by businesses in 1965, whereas more than a billion was spent last year.

With the 3d edition of this notable work, Hurt takes away the pain of source-hunting in this area by updating his work substantially. More than half of the previous sources have been dropped. Unless the source was a "classic," it has been dropped from this edition. This change, Hurt felt, grew out of necessity—the rapid expansion of both science and technology required a serious updating. But the outline of the work is still intact: multidisciplinary works, biological sources, math and the physical sciences, engineering and computer technology, and the health sciences. Websites abound throughout the work, making it as up-to-date as possible. The usual title and subject indexes close out the work. Because the updating is so extensive, libraries with the 2d edition will want this one, too. They will want to keep the previous editions as well. [R: BL, 1 Dec 98, p. 698]—**Mark Y. Herring**

1274. **Walford's Guide to Reference Material, Volume 1: Science and Technology.** 8th ed. Marilyn Mullay and Priscilla Schlicke, eds. London, Library Association; distr., Lanham, Md., Bernan Associates, 1999. 687p. index. $269.00. ISBN 1-85604-341-X.

Published 3 years after the 7th edition (see ARBA 97, entry 1229), this classic reference work features a larger format and 700 new entries—over 8,000 entries in all. As in previous editions, this one is international in scope both geographically and linguistically, although English-language material predominates. All entries include full bibliographic information and short annotations. The editors intend for *Walford's* to be a "one-stop source of information on all types of reference material, regardless of form" (p. vii). Thus, they have not only included reference books, but periodical articles, microforms, online databases, and CD-ROM products as well. New to this edition is the inclusion of Websites; since the editors' work on the volume continued to mid-1999, the URLs are as accurate as possible. Subject areas given new or expanded attention are telecommunications, multimedia and digitization technology, building and construction, alternative medicine, sports medicine, and paleontology. This work is recommended for large academic and public libraries or special libraries in the sciences.—**Hope Yelich**

BIOGRAPHY

1275. **American Men & Women of Science 1998-99: A Biographical Directory of Today's Leaders in Physical, Biological, and Related Sciences.** 20th ed. New Providence, N.J., R. R. Bowker, 1998. 8v. index. $900.00. ISBN 0-8352-3748-6. ISSN 0192-8570.

Reflecting the importance of women in the sciences, the title of this 20th edition of *American Men & Women of Science* was changed from that of the 1st edition's title of *American Men of Science* (1906). Its original role, however, remains unchanged: "to make men [and women] of science acquainted with one another and with one another's work" (preface). The first 7 volumes contain the alphabetic biographies of 166,565 living North American (U.S. and Canadian) scientists. Those scientists were also included if a significant potion of their work was performed in North America. No attempt was made to include all scientists; rather, the scientists included are limited to those who have made significant contributions to their field.

Each volume begins with a list of recent recipients of major honors and awards; statistical analyses of the scientists, such as numerical and geographic distribution by discipline and age; an explanation of the bibliographic entries; and a list of abbreviations used. Each biographical entry includes birth date, birthplace, family information, specialty, education, honorary degrees, current position, professional and concurrent experience, publications, awards, memberships, research information, and fax numbers and postal and e-mail addresses.

Volume 8 is an index of the scientists by discipline and location. For example, scientists involved in mathematics are listed under their respective specialty, such as geometry, probability, or topology. Within each of the 192 listed specialties, the scientists are listed geographically by state, province, or other country.

American Men & Women of Science is a comprehensive biographical directory of today's leaders of North American science that should be part of any reference library collection that supports science research. The cross-referencing by subject and geography makes the information very accessible. However, its use below secondary grade level in education would likely be very limited. [R: BL, 1 Dec 98, pp. 688-689]
—**Craig A. Munsart**

1276. Ellavich, Marie C. **Scientists: Their Lives and Works, Volume 6.** Farmington Hills, Mich., U*X*L/Gale, 1999. 193p. illus. index. $39.00. ISBN 0-7876-3682-7. ISSN 1522-8630.

Scientists: Their Lives and Works, volume 6 of the series, is a continuation of an excellent work. Information about 34 scientists from around the world and from the Industrial Revolution to the present are covered in such diverse fields as animal ecology, astronomy, biology, climatology, ecology, forestry, mathematics, medicine, oceanography, physics, zoology, and more.

The volume begins with a cumulative list of the scientists by their field of specialization. More than 80 fields are categorized and each scientist is mentioned by name followed by the volume number and page number where the information can be located. A timeline of major scientific breakthroughs follows, with brief descriptions of these events. Parallel to the timeline is another timeline that includes major world historic events. A glossary of "words to know" follows that includes definitions of scientific terms. The explanations are clear, brief, and easy to understand.

The biographies comprise the majority of the text and are in alphabetic order. Each entry begins with the scientist's name, birth date, death date (if deceased), and a photograph. The content focuses on the scientist's early life, formative experiences, and inspirations. When the article refers to the scientist's educational years, it is done candidly and contains details about any difficulties they may have had, which should have great appeal to students. All entries are easy to read and clearly and concisely written.

Impact boxes are located in each article, which contain important information and summaries of why each scientist's work is revolutionary. Other highlighted areas in each article, biographical boxes, have information about other individuals who were influential in the work of the featured scientist or who conducted the same type of research. Finally, each article concludes with an excellent list of sources for further reading so students know where to seek other information.

A wonderful cumulative index to all six volumes completes the book. It is annotated with italic type that indicates volume numbers, boldface type that indicates entries and their page numbers, and "(ill.)," which indicates illustrations.

This volume is an excellent source for all public and school libraries. Marie Ellavich has written an outstanding tool for research work or for personal knowledge seekers that is appropriate for all ages.

—**Mary L. Trenerry**

1277. Haven, Kendall, and Donna Clark. **100 Most Popular Scientists for Young Adults: Biographical Sketches and Professional Paths.** Englewood, Colo., Libraries Unlimited, 1999. 526p. illus. index. (Profiles and Pathways Series). $56.00. ISBN 1-56308-674-3.

This 1-volume resource focuses on uncovering the "early intentions and plans and the early life events that shaped" the lives of the scientists discussed. Each 5-page entry contains 6 sections: Career Highlights, Important Contributions, Career Path, Key Dates, Advice, and References. The advice section explains in the scientist's own words, "how to start a successful career in that field of science" (p. xv). Some entries include a black-and-white photograph of the scientist. The appendix provides Internet references and a list of scientists by field of specialization. The 100 scientists include some of the ones most frequently researched by students in grades 5 through 10 (e.g., Isaac Asimov, Robert Bakkar, Robert Ballard, Luther Burbank, Rachel Carson, Albert Einstein, Enrico Fermi, Dian Fossey, Edwin Hubble, Bill Nye, Sally Ride, and Carl Sagan). The entries are arranged alphabetically by last name, but the table of contents and page guide words, instead of listing last name first to make scanning for a name easier, the names are listed first name then last name, making the reader work a little harder to scan the last names. The emphasis on the scientist's career makes this a useful research tool.—**Esther R. Sinofsky**

1278. **Notable Black American Scientists.** Kristine Krapp, ed. Farmington Hills, Mich., Gale, 1999. 349p. illus. index. $75.00. ISBN 0-7876-2789-5.

This biographical resource records the accomplishments of 254 African American scientists and physicians from colonial times to the present. The selection criteria for inclusion in this book included several areas, such as scientists who have worked or work in the natural, physical, social, and applied sciences; scientists with notable first achievements; those with an overall contribution to scientific progress; and those familiar to the general public. Some well-known scientists as well as lesser-known individuals have been selected for inclusion. The majority of the biographies are of men, although 59 women are featured here.

The book is divided into several sections—an entry list (an alphabetic list of names with page numbers included to locate the individual biographies); a timeline, which includes scientific milestones of the book's entrants; the biographies; and indexes. The biographies are arranged alphabetically with each list beginning with, if available, a photograph or drawing of the individual, then the scientist's name, birth and death dates, and field of specialty. The biographical essays range in length from 400 to 2,000 words and cover the salient points of the person's early life, accomplishments, and current status if still living. Enough information about the person is contained in the essay in order to get a good introductory background about the person's life and achievements. Other items included in the essay are a list of publications written by and about the entrant. Other useful items in the book are the separate indexes used to locate the biographies by gender, specialization, or subject.

The subject content alone will make it a desirable purchase because not many resources gathered in one place are available about the endeavors of African Americans in the sciences. This book is recommended for any library that has use for biographical information, particularly public, school, or academic libraries. [R: BL, 15 Feb 99, p. 1085; Choice, Sept 99, pp. 114-115; RUSQ, Spring 99, p. 311]

—**Julia Perez**

1279. **Notable Twentieth-Century Scientists: Supplement.** Kristine M. Krapp, ed. Farmington Hills, Mich., Gale, 1998. 617p. illus. index. $85.00. ISBN 0-7876-2766-6.

This volume provides biographical information on more than 300 scientists, from well-known figures throughout the century to those now working and making the latest advances in their fields. Information on 65 scientists included in the first 4-volume set is updated, and 250 new biographies of contemporary scientists are included. Special attention has been given to women, minority, and non-Western scientists. The biographies range from 400 to 2,500 words; each includes a section listing selected writings by the scientists and bibliographic suggestions for further reading. Indexes include listings by areas of scientific specialization, a gender index, a nationality or ethnicity index, and a subject index. Many entries are accompanied by black-and-white photographs. There is also a useful "chronology of scientific advancement" from the invention of the cloud chamber by C. T. R. Wilson in 1895 to the cloning of the first mammal, a sheep (Dolly), in 1997. Although this supplement does not offer great detail, this is surely a volume every reference collection concerned with modern science will want to acquire. [R: BL, 1 Dec 98, p. 694]—**Joseph W. Dauben**

1280. **Scientists, Mathematicians, and Inventors: Lives and Legacies, an Encyclopedia of People Who Changed the World.** Doris Simonis, ed. Phoenix, Ariz., Oryx Press, 1999. 244p. illus. index. (Lives and Legacies). $69.95. ISBN 1-57356-151-7.

Biographical reference sources in the sciences continue to be published at a fast pace, at least in part serving the popularity of biographical assignments among children. This volume follows the lead of many other recent titles by striving to include those who have been traditionally ignored in science biographies, especially women and minorities. The work's unique slant is the choice of those scientists whose lives and work had a significant impact on either their own disciplines after their lives or else on society as a whole. Thus, those scientists and inventors who demonstrated influential and creative thinking were included in favor of those who merely made discoveries that followed from accepted knowledge. Most of the 200 subjects lived during the past two centuries, and the scope is broad enough to include key figures in medicine and physiology.

Each subject receives a 1-page treatment, which includes an outline of his or her life and work, an interpretation of that person's legacy, a timeline, and a brief bibliography. The several appendixes include further chronologies, a fuller bibliography, and a solid index. The splitting of life and work from legacy often seems artificial; whereas some essays (such as that on Werner Karl Heisenberg) include a thoughtfully analytical treatment of the subject's impact, many of the other essays (such as that on Nikolaus Otto) continue the same type of historical discussion in the legacy section that appeared in the life section. The writing is usually clear, although not especially lively, and the coverage is fairly brief and thus would be most appropriate for high school or later junior high age on up. The sources in the bibliographies generally indicate an intended audience beyond elementary school as well. Overall, this source is competently executed, but it may have little new information to add to collections that have purchased other recent works. [R: BR, Sept/Oct 99, pp. 66-67]—**Christopher W. Nolan**

DICTIONARIES AND ENCYCLOPEDIAS

1281. **The Facts on File Encyclopedia of Science.** Sharon Brimblecombe, Diana Gallannaugh, and Catherine Thompson, eds. New York, Facts on File, 1999. 2v. illus. $125.00/set. ISBN 0-8160-4008-7.

This 2-volume set was first published in 1998 in England as the *Hutchinson Encyclopedia of Science*. Intended for academic use as well as for the general reader, the encyclopedia is well designed for both quick fact lookup and browsing. The alphabetically arranged entries, more than 10,000 in all, are broad ranging and generally short. Interspersed among them are well-chosen quotations, offbeat facts, and the kind of mnemonic phrases that make memorizing so much easier (e.g., "To remember the order of the planets: My Very Educated Mother Just Served Us Nine Pies" [p. 586]). Also included are short essays on various topics of current interest, such as El Niño, the millennium bug, and cloning as well as topics of perennial interest, such as evolution, dinosaurs, and astronomy; brief biographies of scientists (with a European emphasis); chronologies of the major scientific fields; and seven appendixes covering scientific discoveries, inventions, Nobel Prize winners, the Greek alphabet, and Roman numerals. There are also several Websites featured; some URLs are inevitably already out of date. There is no index, but one is not needed because the reader is guided to related articles by a symbol within the text of the entries. The typography is excellent, with highlighted sections set off in gray. The illustrations consist of clear drawings and less clear photographs, all in black and white. *The Facts on File Encyclopedia of Science* is a handsome resource appropriate for home, school, and public libraries. [R: LJ, 1 May 99, p. 69; BL, 1 Sept 99, pp. 179-180; Choice, Nov 99, p. 510; BR, Nov/Dec 99, p. 85]—**Hope Yelich**

1282. **The Facts on File Encyclopedia of Science, Technology, and Society.** By Rudi Volti. New York, Facts on File, 1999. 3v. illus. index. $225.00/set. ISBN 0-8160-3123-1.

This book offers about 900 alphabetically arranged articles on a wide variety of topics in science and technology (including agriculture and biotechnology) and some medicine. The articles, which are between 400 and 2,500 words, give brief definitions and explanations of the topics, with emphasis on societal context, applications, and influences. Topics are chosen for their practical or intellectual significance for contemporary society and to some extent for past societies (e.g., "Crossbow," "Phlogiston"). There are treatments of inventions and technological processes; natural or artificial substances; concepts and phenomena; and organizations, programs, and social problems. There are smaller numbers of articles on events, scientific methods and activities, scientific instruments, and disciplines and subjects. Medicine is treated sparsely. Smallpox eradication is included, but there are no articles on cholera, malaria, schistosomiasis, or yellow fever.

This work was written by Volti with the advice of an editorial board. There are 95 contributors featured who are responsible for about 45 percent of the articles. The rest are by Volti. Sometimes one or two references to further reading are included with the articles and are collected in a bibliography in volume 3. The work is well indexed, making subjects and personal names within the articles accessible. The index appears in each of the three volumes.

The articles are well written, accurate, and interesting, and the topics are well chosen. The further reading lists are scanty. If the index had been printed just once, there would have been more space for further reading. [R: LJ, 1 April 99, p. 86; BL, 15 April 99, p. 1546; Choice, Sept 99, p. 116; BR, Sept/Oct 99, p. 79; RUSQ, Fall 99, pp. 91-92]—**Frederic F. Burchsted**

1283. **The International Encyclopedia of Science and Technology.** Steve Luck, ed. New York, Oxford University Press, 1999. 471p. illus. $49.95. ISBN 0-19-521531-1.

Colorful, beautifully illustrated, and well written, this 1-volume encyclopedia looks and operates like a hardcover CD-ROM. Articles are short, averaging about 100 words each; superbly cross-referenced; and, with 6,500 of them, numerous.

This book surveys the hard sciences of astronomy, physics, chemistry, biology, medicine, farming/food, transportation, engineering, and communications. Except for when they border physiology, the softer sciences of psychology and sociology are excluded entirely. Included are laudable features, such as brief biographies of more than 850 famous scientists and a chronology from the domestication of the dog (10,000 B.C.E.) to the launch of the lunar prospector (1998). To test the book's consistency, terms form the chronology were checked against the alphabetically listed topics. In each case, the chronology term was found.

Common scientific prefixes, elements, records, constellations, and even the Greek alphabet and Roman numbers are included in a handy ready-reference. Although the names of the book's British academic and curriculum consultants are listed in the preface, no articles are signed. For the money, middle, high school, and community college libraries cannot go wrong with this interesting, introductory encyclopedia of science. [R: LJ, 1 April 99, p. 86; BL, June 99, pp. 1878-1881]—**Pete Prunkl**

1284. **McGraw-Hill Concise Encyclopedia of Science & Technology.** 4th ed. Sybil P. Parker, ed. New York, McGraw-Hill, 1998. 2318p. illus. index. $150.00. ISBN 0-07-052659-1.

This volume is the 4th edition of a single-volume version of the 20-volume *McGraw-Hill Encyclopedia of Science and Technology* and is edited by the staff of its parent volume. It includes 7,800 alphabetically arranged entries that have been edited from the parent source to provide "helpful knowledge without extensive detail." During editing proportional lengths of entries were maintained. All articles are cross-referenced to related entries and subjects. Text entries are often accompanied by color-enhanced line drawings, black-and-white photographs, and pertinent graphs and tables. The authors of articles are cited in the entry and a list of authors and their affiliations is given in the front matter.

Appendixes include a bibliography by subject, tables of physical constants, supporting data for math and science conversions, fundamental particles, geologic time, 3 tables of data about telescopes, and a biography of 1,200 scientists mentioned in the text. This is followed by a comprehensive index. The index, cross-references, and alphabetic entries all serve to make the volume very user-friendly.

Although touted by the publisher as being useful to the general reader, some entries, because of their inherently complex nature, may be less than informative to those without some knowledge of the field; for instance, those entries that include differential equations in their definitions. The meaning of other entries would be clearer with some background. The entry for *Anisomyaria* reads, "an order containing seven superfamilies of marine and brackish bivalves with byssal attachment."

Other single-volume science references are written at a more introductory level, such as the *DK Ultimate Visual Dictionary of Science* (see ARBA 99, entry 1311) or the *DK Science Encyclopedia* (rev. ed.; see ARBA 99, entry 1310). This comprehensive and technically written volume would be more useful to upper secondary or college students and supporting libraries or homes. It is often suggested that a home reference library should contain an almanac, atlas, dictionary, thesaurus, book of quotations, and a single-volume science reference. The *McGraw-Hill Concise Encyclopedia of Science and Technology* could serve well as a science reference for many homes or libraries.—**Craig A. Munsart**

1285. Newton, David E. **Social Issues in Science and Technology: An Encyclopedia.** Santa Barbara, Calif., ABC-CLIO, 1999. 303p. illus. index. $75.00. ISBN 0-87436-920-7.

Advances in science and technology have inundated our lives daily and at such a rapid rate that we have, at times, become immune to their importance and impact on society. Newton has provided a fresh look at the harms and benefits the progress in science and technology brings to us. *Social Issues in Science and Technology: An Encyclopedia* is a "work in progress" because many of the entries presented are not yet resolved and may never be.

The book provides overviews of about 100 subjects where new advances have forced society to define new issues raised by these discoveries. Each of these issues is treated with a three-part approach. First, an overview and brief background of the science or technology involved is presented. Second, some history is provided to map out how the discovery generated a social, economic, political, religious, or ethical impact on society. Third, the positions taken on each issue are presented.

In selecting topics for his book, Newton has sought issues that two or more positions can easily be defined and explained. He chose to eliminate issues that have been heavily covered, such as some environmental topics. Some issues that have been commercially exploited are also not covered. In other cases, the author has covered a specific topic related to and highlighting a more general principle, such as the masked bobwhite quail, an endangered species.

Each entry has a list of references that includes books, magazines, and Websites about the subject presented. Some entries are illustrated. The book is arranged alphabetically with a table of contents. It includes two indexes, a selected bibliography, and a subject index. Some of the issues covered are abortion, assisted reproductive technologies, biological determinism, chemical castration, Chernobyl, DNA fingerprinting, fetal tissue research, global warming, legalization of drugs, privacy and the Internet, and many other topics. *Social Issues in Science and Technology: An Encyclopedia* is an ambitious project that has been done very well. It would be an excellent addition to any reference collection.—**Mary L. Trenerry**

1286. Peschke, Michael and Bearbeitet von Michael Peschke, comps. **International Encyclopedia of Abbreviations and Acronyms in Science and Technology, Volumes 10-12. Internationale Enzyklopädie der Abkürzungen und Akronyme in Wissenschaft und Technik.** rev. ed. New Providence, N.J., K. G. Saur, 1999. 3v. $200.00/volume. ISBN 3-598-22988-7 (v.10); 3-598-22989-5 (v.11); 3-598-22990-9 (v.12).

Abbreviations, acronyms, and initialisms are all around us. This is especially true in the science and technology fields that seem to experience an increase in new words or terms on an on-going basis. Since the flood of information is growing constantly, additional volumes have been added to the earlier published set of this work to greatly expand the list of terms previously used or ways they can be accessed.

Volumes 10 through 12 supplement the previous volumes and are not intended to stand on their own. The number of total entries is not indicated, but each volume is several hundred pages long and includes terms from over 30 languages. Some nonscientific terms are also included as well as journal abbreviations. Volume 10 is labeled as a supplement and covers alphabetic M–Z listings. The abbreviations or acronyms are listed alphabetically with each entry including a language code and its meaning. Volumes 11 and 12 are the reversed edition and cover the listings for A–Dep and Dep–Glaz. In these volumes, the meaning or phrase is first listed alphabetically, followed by its language code and then its abbreviation or acronym.

These additional volumes provide extensive information and update the previous volumes, so purchase is recommended for larger academic libraries that have bought earlier volumes in the set. Smaller libraries need not purchase if patron demand is not high or previous volumes are not in their collection.
—**Julia Perez**

1287. **Rourke's World of Science Encyclopedia.** By Jason Georges and Tracy Irons-Georges. Vero Beach, Fla., Rourke Enterprises, 1999. 10v. illus. index. $426.60/set. ISBN 0-86593-482-7.

Each of the first nine, 640-page volumes in this set is devoted to a specific subject: Human Life, Animal Life, Plant Life, Earth Science, Chemistry, Physics, Astronomy and Space, Mathematics, and Technology. Each volume contains its own index. The final volume contains a guide to using the books, a comprehensive index, research projects, a glossary, and a bibliography. Each of the volumes contains highlighted boxes of special interest—"Getting to Know" provides biographies, "Finding Out More About" provides expanded information about a particular subject (e.g., holograms in the laser discussion), and "Did You Know" gives additional information. The volumes are heavily illustrated with both color photographs and color drawings. Some illustrations could better interact with the text. Under "Injuries and Healing" the discussion of fractures is accompanied by a photograph of a pair of crutches rather than an X ray, which might have been more explanatory. "Digestion" is illustrated with a photograph of "a diabetic injecting insulin." Although insulin is discussed, diabetes is not. A polar bear on an iceberg does a poor job of reinforcing the caption "The Arctic Circle has many glaciers." An illustration of an erosional feature near Monument Valley is captioned "The Grand Canyon has been formed by erosion over millions of years."

Words printed in red are explained in the text and included in the glossary. Difficult words have pronunciation indicated following their appearance in the text. An icon refers readers to applicable science

Words printed in red are explained in the text and included in the glossary. Difficult words have pronunciation indicated following their appearance in the text. An icon refers readers to applicable science projects in volume 10, some of which may have only limited value to students. For example, the "Gravity" project (vol. 10, p. 22) instructs students to drop 6 objects and "see if they all fall at the same speed."

Within each volume subjects are further grouped within a narrower focus. For instance, in volume 9, "Technology," the focus areas are agriculture, transportation, electronics, medicine, communications, entertainment, computers, and people who use technology. Although it is considered an encyclopedia, entries are not arranged alphabetically as they are in most encyclopedias. Although alphabetic entry of subjects may have made this work more user-friendly, the index can help users overcome this problem.

By its very nature the text must be superficial. Attempting to describe human life or technology in under 60 pages is an insurmountable challenge. In general, students beyond elementary school would probably benefit little from the introductory nature of the text. As an introductory-level, first set of science reference books, this encyclopedia might be useful in a home or classroom library. It is overshadowed, however, by many more comprehensive student science encyclopedias that are available.—**Craig A. Munsart**

1288. **Science Navigator Version 4.0.** [CD-ROM] New York, McGraw-Hill, 1998. Minimum system requirements (Windows version): IBM or compatible 386. CD-ROM drive. Windows 3.1, Windows 95, Windows NT 3.51. 8MB RAM. 5MB hard disk space. Minimum system requirements (Macintosh version): 68020 processor. CD-ROM drive. System 7.0 or higher. 8MB RAM. 5MB hard disk space. $224.00 (single user); $375.00 (network). ISBN 0-07-853110-1.

Science Navigator Version 4.0 is a science reference CD-ROM product that makes available three different "books" that a user can access to search for a topic, biography, or definition. These books are the *McGraw-Hill Encyclopedia* (4th ed.); the *McGraw-Hill Dictionary of Scientific and Technical Terms* (5th ed.), with more than 220,000 definitions; and *McGraw-Hill Biographies*, biographical sketches of more than 1,100 scientists and engineers.

Installation of the product is easily and quickly done. The main menu screen has a variety of features to become familiar with. First, is the appearance of two toolbars. One is the typical Windows toolbar at the top and the other, on the right side of the screen, uses icons to identify the most frequently used functions. Under the primary toolbar is a stack of bookshelves containing the three books listed above that can be searched or browsed. Upon first entering the program, the first book on the shelf has already been selected for the user but clicking on the appropriate book icon will change the selection. On the left side of the screen is the "List" window containing a list of all the entries in the active book. Searching can be done by either selecting a category from the pull-down menu in the list, paging down the list of entries in each category, or typing in a term in the input box. The search feature on the toolbars can also be used to do more sophisticated searching using wildcards, Boolean operators, and searching in more than one book. The main entry area where the search results are displayed is located in the middle of the screen. Within this area, manipulation of the material can be done, such as linking to cross-references, bookmarking, finding words within the same document, adding user notes, printing, and so on.

Despite its promising start, *Science Navigator* has some drawbacks. Its searching features are quite thorough but the search results can be sketchy. Apart from the encyclopedia, the biography, and dictionary, options provide scant information—no more than one or two sentences regarding the topic. The product has few illustrations present and no photographs or multimedia features have been added to enhance it. *Science Navigator* is not recommended for purchase by libraries that already have in their collection the books used in this product, as it offers little extra value. Others should take advantage of any trial periods to evaluate the product for their specific use. This product should only be considered for purchase by academic libraries.—**Julia Perez**

1289. **Van Nostrand's Scientific Encyclopedia.** 8th ed. [CD-ROM]. Douglas M. Considine and Glenn D. Considine, eds. New York, John Wiley, 1999. Minimum system requirements: IBM or compatible 386. CD-ROM drive. Windows 3.1. 8MB RAM. 1MB hard disk space. SVGA monitor. $235.00. ISBN 0-471-29323-7.

Comprehensive yet complicated, this latest edition of a standard scientific encyclopedia provides a number of enhancements that users will appreciate. Among these are the ability to customize searching with comprehensive search criteria; links to cross-references that allow easy back and forward movement between articles; search and retrieval software that allows the user to add notes, create bookmarks, and make additional links; 500 tables and charts; and more than 3,500 photographs, illustrations, and diagrams that enhance the entries. In total, there are some 7,000 entries written by more than 250 subject experts.

The encyclopedia covers six major categories of scientific endeavor: earth and space sciences, life sciences, energy and environmental sciences, materials sciences, physics and chemistry, and mathematics and information sciences. Updates and revisions have been made throughout these six categories, including such topics as AIDS, genetics, satellites, television, anorexia, and obesity. The CD-ROM provides a variety of search options, from simple to complex, and the user is provided a series of explanations on effective use of search engines, navigation, image viewing, and printing.

Some may find the multiple search options a bit confusing, and others may be frustrated by the preponderance of black-and-white illustrations over color. However, the encyclopedia still remains an authoritative source of basic information in the sciences. High school, public, and college libraries should consider adding this as part of a ready-reference collection. [R: BR, Nov/Dec 99, p. 91; Choice, Dec 99, p. 696]—**Edmund F. SantaVicca**

DIRECTORIES

1290. **International Directory of Testing Laboratories.** 1999 ed. West Conshohocken, Pa., ASTM, 1998. 397p. index. $69.00pa. ISBN 0-8031-1805-8. ISSN 0895-7886.

Each entry in the 1999 edition of this work published annually by ASTM (see ARBA 94, entry 1578; ARBA 92, entry 1614; and ARBA 89, entry 1354, for reviews of previous volumes) contains laboratory name, address, telephone and fax numbers, e-mail and Website addresses, names of senior staff, specialties, types of tests performed, other laboratory services, specific tests conducted (issuing agency codes), materials and products, special equipment, testing capabilities, number of staff, and location of branches. Half the book consists of indexes by company name, by subject, and by type of test (listed by each test's issuing agency's acronym and test number). The subject categories are defined on a removable reference card. There are 87 entries for laboratories outside of the United States and Canada. There are entries for 1 African, 11 Asian, 15 European, and 6 Latin American and Caribbean countries.

The directory is also available as a free Website at http://www.astm.org/labs/. For simple lookups, the print is quicker and the search results are often better organized. Laboratories pay ASTM a fee for inclusion. ASTM does not vouch for the companies included. The resulting directory is by no means exhaustive but is useful due to its extensive indexing.—**Frederic F. Burchsted**

HANDBOOKS AND YEARBOOKS

1291. Berinstein, Paula. **The Statistical Handbook on Technology.** Phoenix, Ariz., Oryx Press, 1999. 277p. index. $59.95. ISBN 1-57356-208-4.

Anyone who writes as well as Berinstein should be doing textbooks instead of displaying the population of industrial robots (from 6,300 to 82,000 in 15 years) and the industrial consumption of soybean oil (12 million pounds, nearly all edible). Further, we find that the coaxial metal cables for transatlantic service, costing $2 per minute of expected use, have been replaced by fiber-optic cables, at a cost of $0.003 per minute. Why is it hard to get a new "800" number? Because 7 million have been assigned; only 7,000 remain. The subjects covered range from the number of Oryx through the U.S. defense budget to air pollution. In general, the data reported are for the United States only. A short glossary and index are included.

—**Robert B. McKee**

1292. Engelbert, Phillis. **Technology in Action: Science Applied to Everyday Life.** Edited by Jane Hoehner. Farmington Hills, Mich., U*X*L/Gale, 1999. 3v. illus. index. $79.95/set. ISBN 0-7876-2809-3.

This is a valuable and informative 3-volume compendium of most of the major inventions that have transformed modern civilization in dramatic ways and have had significant impacts on the lives of countless people all over the world. It does not forget the roots or the ancestors, both ancient and of the recent past, of the technological world. The volumes are introduced with a timeline that starts from 8000 B.C.E. when the first canoes were used and ends with 2002 when the International Space Station is scheduled to be completed, and lists in between more than 500 items. There is also a glossary of technical terms right at the outset to which the reader may refer to as the need arises. The topics are presented as short essays and arranged under eight broad themes. The essays not only succinctly discuss the principles and functioning of the inventions, but they give brief histories that refer to the countless originators, some of whom who may have amassed much wealth through their patents but would be forgotten otherwise. The writing is clear and crisp and simple enough to be within reach of the average educated person. This book belongs in all public libraries and in homes where there is an interest in learning about the complex technological environment that has become part of our lives today. [R: BL, 15 Feb 99, pp. 1093-1094]—**Varadaraja V. Raman**

1293. Fitzpatrick, Patrick J. **Natural Disasters: Hurricanes. A Reference Handbook.** Santa Barbara, Calif., ABC-CLIO, 1999. 286p. index. (Contemporary World Issues). $45.00. ISBN 1-57607-071-9.

Natural Disasters: Hurricanes is the latest volume of ABC-CLIO's Contemporary World Issues series. Past volumes include topics such as AIDS, feminism, and victim's rights. The purpose of this book is to provide background information on issues, people, organizations, and publications related to hurricanes and to provide guidance on where additional information may be obtained about a specific topic. There are seven chapters. The first provides a broad introduction to hurricanes, ranging from hurricane information to forecasting procedures to mitigation issues. The second chapter provides a chronology of forecast and scientific advances and also a descriptive timetable of significant U.S. land-falling hurricanes during the twentieth century. The third chapter contains biographies of important hurricane scientists and forecasters. The fourth chapter contains tabular data, interesting letters from hurricane survivors, and important documents. The fifth chapter describes relevant organizations that are involved in hurricane forecasting, research, and mitigation. The last two chapters are intended to guide readers to other sources, both in print and electronic format, for further research. A glossary and an index conclude the work. This is a good basic reference for readers interested in learning more about hurricanes, both from a scientific and a survival point of view. With the print and electronic resource sections, this is also a good starting point for further research. This volume is recommended for geology and natural hazard reference collections.—**Cari Ringelheim**

1294. Krebs, Robert E. **Scientific Development and Misconceptions Through the Ages: A Reference Guide.** Westport, Conn., Greenwood Press, 1999. 286p. index. $49.95. ISBN 0-313-30226-X.

Whatever this book actually is, readers can be certain that despite its advertisement as a "reference guide," it is not. It is mostly a set of small essays about various scientific concepts and their "development" through time. The "misconceptions" are a selected group of errors by various people over the millennia in the fields of medicine, life sciences, chemistry, physics, astronomy, cosmology, and ecology. It is a poor reference work because the choice of topics is limited and idiosyncratic, and the citation of sources is rudimentary at best. Seven pages of references are hardly enough for a survey of the development of science and its attendant errors. Even worse, one of the most common sources cited is the *Valley Morning Star* newspaper of Harlingen, Texas.

Defining and then choosing misconceptions in the vast history of science is a daunting task. The author usually starts with ancient societies that are fertile fields for wrong ideas about virtually everything. Then he moves selectively through scientific history, highlighting obvious errors (the geocentric solar system, phlogiston) and the silly and trivial (the Hollow Earth, astrology). It is difficult to discern a theme for these little stories from our scientific past, until we reach the last chapter, "Conservation, Ecology, and Environmentalism." Here the author has a strong point to make—environmentalists are pseudoscientific, irrational, and dangerous. The previous chapters are just prologue for what amounts to a screed against those concerned about global warming, ozone destruction, overpopulation, acid rain, and so forth. Humans, it appears, are just one of 30 million species on the planet, so their impact on the environment "may be overestimated."

Of course, a book about misconceptions is begging for someone to find its own errors. Trace fossils are described as some mysterious technique; ancient people "had no way to measure time at night"; the explanation for tides is wrong; Galileo died in prison; and the introduction of killer bees was entirely natural. Many of the few figures are indecipherable.

There is no reason for any library to purchase this book. A reader wishing to study the development of a scientific concept would be far better served by simply starting with an encyclopedia.—**Mark A. Wilson**

1295. **Science & Technology Almanac.** 1999 ed. William Allstetter, ed. Phoenix, Ariz., Oryx Press, 1999. 490p. index. $65.00pa. ISBN 1-57356-237-8. ISSN 1524-1319.

This almanac is meant to serve as a sourcebook for topical news and references to current information on all aspects of science, technology, and medicine. Subjects included range from articles on UFOs to the "immorality gene." In covering the most prominent science news stories of the past year (1998), topics go beyond the basic sciences to include material relevant to social concerns, new media, popular science, movies, and awards for science writing and journalism. Country-by-country statistics and regional comparisons are provided, covering environmental, technological, and world health data. A section on "history of science and technology" presents, chronologically, a comprehensive list of major individuals, inventors, innovations, and discoveries. Other sections cover "people and prizes" (e.g., the Nobel Prize and other special awards). Brief biographies of some 250 major scientific figures across all periods of history (from Archimedes to Hedeki Yukawa) are also presented with separate coverage allotted to obituaries of notable scientific figures who died in 1998. Especially useful are appendixes that cover the most important science-related events and meetings for 1999, with directories for science museums, zoos, aquariums, observatories, scientific organizations, associations, research institutes, and government agencies devoted to science. If there is any drawback to this comprehensive collection of science items in the news, it is the lack of any identification for sources of the information provided here, which could easily have been given, if only briefly. Nevertheless, as a ready-reference for very succinct information about major items related to science in the news over the past year, this is a handy reference work. [R: LJ, July 99, p. 84; Choice, Oct 99, p. 310; RUSQ, Fall 99, pp. 99-100]—**Joseph W. Dauben**

1296. **Scientific American Science Desk Reference.** New York, John Wiley, 1999. 690p. illus. index. $39.95. ISBN 0-471-35675-1.

The editors of *Scientific American Magazine* have produced a ready-reference for science buffs (and the naturally curious). Arranged thematically, there are chapters on measurement; mathematics; chemistry; physics; astronomy; earth science; environment and ecology; biology; the animal kingdom; the plant kingdom; the human body; health and diseases; computer science; technology; and discoveries, inventions, and prizes. Each chapter follows the same structure (except the final chapter on discoveries): a subject overview, chronology, biographies of important figures, glossary of key vocabulary used within the chapter, and a bibliography for further reading. The volume concludes with a comprehensive index.

Aids to the coverage of each topic include tables, charts, diagrams, and illustrations. Sidebars provide further aids such as factual tidbits, quizzes, and mnemonic aids. Cross-references are self-contained within each chapter. URLs, with descriptions of the Websites, are interspersed throughout the text, offering endless sources of information on topics covered. The amount of information found in this easy-to-use reference makes it a good choice for either secondary school or public libraries, as well as a delightful and useful home reference.—**Dana McDougald**

1297. Webster, Raymond B. **African American Firsts in Science and Technology.** Farmington Hills, Mich., Gale, 1999. 462p. illus. index. $60.00. ISBN 0-7876-3876-5.

Although it is relatively easy to identify African Americans who have made noted contributions in the field of literature and civil rights, a comprehensive list of those individuals in the scientific fields has often meant much searching. Gale now provides a compilation of the pioneering achievements of African Americans in the field of science and technology in a single volume. These noted accomplishments span a period from 1706 to the present. The achievements range from the first person to graduate from a particular university to the first person to accomplish a particular goal. The first persons to discover, invent, found, or establish something significant are also included. Along with providing an extensive list, the author intends to provide role model data for younger African Americans to inspire them to achieve in this area.

Approximately 1,200 entries of 50 to 100 words are arranged in 8 subject chapters: "Agriculture and Everyday Life," "Allied Health," "Dentistry and Nursing," "Life Sciences," "Math and Engineering," "Medicine," "Physical Sciences," and "Transportation." Each chapter is chronologically arranged. "Medicine" is the largest chapter and "Allied Health" is the shortest. Approximately 25 percent of the entries are of African American females. Bibliographic references accompany each entry and provide the researcher direction for additional information. Black-and-white portraits are provided for 108 of the individuals.

The main body is followed by a bibliography and 3 indexes: index by year, occupational index, and a general index. The index by year is a chronological list of the accomplishments from all the chapters, which allows the reader to see that the number of achievements per year increases notably from the early years to the present. The occupational index sorts the individuals into 89 different occupational categories. This is another of Gale's well-researched works that is well indexed and arranged, which makes it easy for the reader to use. This volume is recommended for middle school through college students and public libraries.
—**Elaine Ezell**

30 Agricultural Sciences

GENERAL WORKS

1298. **Agricultural Statistics 1999.** Washington, D.C., U.S. Government Printing Office; distr., Lanham, Md., Bernan Associates, 1999. 1v. (various paging). index. $26.00. ISBN 0-16-049562-8.

Agriculture Statistics is a yearly publication of reliable reference material on agricultural production, supplies, consumption, facilities, costs, and returns. Foreign agricultural trade statistics include government as well as nongovernment shipment of merchandise from the United States and its territories to foreign countries. The world summaries are taken from statistics supplied by foreign governments and foreign source material. The book of tables is particularly valuable to individuals who want a current overview of agricultural production in the United States as well as worldwide, including world trade. This reviewer knows of no other source where this information is so current, readily available, and accurate. This paperback publication is on average paper, with average binding and print large enough to be useful when looking only at specific information. An adequate index is provided to assist in locating specific information desired.

—**Herbert W. Ockerman**

FOOD SCIENCES AND TECHNOLOGY

Bibliographies

1299. Cagle, William R. **A Matter of Taste: A Bibliographical Catalogue of International Books on Food and Drink in The Lilly Library, Indiana University.** 2d rev. ed. New Castle, Del., Oak Knoll Press, 1999. 991p. index. $95.00. ISBN 1-884718-86-8.

Updating the author's previous volume of the same name (see ARBA 91, entry 1482), this edition adds new titles and revises and corrects some earlier entries. Emphasis is again on European cookbooks from the sixteenth to nineteenth centuries, although there are entries from the twentieth century as well as other countries. Excellent introductory notes describe the purpose of the book and collection. Attention to detail is evident in the full bibliographic description (often in its native language), which often includes complete transcription of the table of contents and title page, collation, pagination, record of illustrations, and location of other copies. Author, title, subject, and chronological indexes complete the book. This book covers not just cookery but the diet and health connection, beverage, hotel and food management, food presentation, and gardening, among other topics. Scattered throughout are facsimiles of title pages or frontispieces. The author, a librarian, has prepared a meticulously researched gastronomic bounty. A culinary delight for the epicurean and passionate collector, this indispensable reference belongs in all serious cuisine collections.—**Joy Hastings**

Dictionaries and Encyclopedias

1300. Mariani, John. **The Dictionary of Italian Food and Drink: An A-to-Z Guide with 2,300 Authentic Definitions and 50 Classic Recipes.** New York, Broadway Books, 1998. 313p. index. $17.00pa. ISBN 0-7679-0129-0.

This is a dictionary that gives pronunciations as well as definitions, spelling, and a description of the extensive regional cuisine of Italy. Also featured are fascinating stories about the origins and etymologies of these foods. Covered are such areas as wines, desserts, antipastos, breads, sauces, and more than 200 types of pastas and authentic Italian dishes and how they differ from their Italian-American counterparts. In addition, the book has more than 50 classic recipes.

The dictionary starts with an introduction that covers the history and pronunciation of Italian cuisine, and each entry usually contains a short definition, origin of the word, special flavors, general cooking procedures, and related words. In addition, there is a section leading the reader to other words that may help explain this term. Recipes are sprinkled throughout the book under the various word headings. This is a paperback edition with average paper, binding, and printing quality, and is extremely well done. It has a bibliography and index and contains English names of commonly used food terms as well as Italian terms that do not appear as main entries and recipes. The author has written several culinary reference books and is well qualified for this assignment. The book should be of interest to chefs, food journalists, menu writers, restaurant critics, travelers, and anyone with an interest in Italian cooking. [R: LJ, 15 May 98, p. 80]

—**Herbert W. Ockerman**

1301. Reavley, Nicola. **The New Encyclopedia of Vitamins, Minerals, Supplements, & Herbs.** New York, M. Evans, 1998. 792p. index. $19.95pa. ISBN 0-87131-897-0.

The Encyclopedia of Vitamins, Minerals, Supplements, & Herbs is a gold mine of information on what the human body needs to fuel itself to maintain optimal health. The American public is inundated with new "miracle" vitamins and supplements that promise to enhance our health and longevity. It is nearly impossible for the layperson to keep up with the latest discoveries in how nutrition and health are related. This easy-to-use volume will provide many answers to commonly asked questions about nutrition.

The book begins with a question-and-answer section that features many common concerns among consumers, such as "Is it possible to get enough vitamins and minerals from food?" "Are vitamin and mineral supplements necessary?" and "Who might need supplements?" It is then broken down into chapters, including "Vitamins," "Minerals," "Other Nutrients," and "Herbal Medicines." Each vitamin, mineral, or supplement is listed alphabetically in its chapter, and a "quick guide" describes its role in fueling the body, sources of the nutrient, and daily recommendations, among other facts. The last section, "Health Problems," discusses the role of nutrients in fighting such health concerns as cancer, HIV/AIDS, insomnia, and many more. The book concludes with a glossary, list of references, and comprehensive index.

This book is extremely user-friendly and contains a lot of information that readers will be seeking on the subject of vitamins and nutrition and how they relate to human health. It is written for the layperson seeking quick information; however, the entries are interesting enough that many users will probably find themselves reading up on more than what originally they were looking for. This volume will be a valuable addition to the reference shelves of any public library.—**Shannon M. Graff**

1302. Sharon, Michael. **Nutrients A to Z.** London, Prion Books; distr., North Pomfret, Vt., Trafalgar Square, 1999. 344p. index. $14.95pa. ISBN 1-85375-325-4.

Diet and nutrition have increasingly become hot topics of interest to the general public. The public is bombarded with new information both promoting and diminishing the benefits of vitamins, supplements, and foods. This work is designed for the layperson who is looking for simple definitions to understand better what specific vitamins do, how to get them naturally, and how much is needed to remain healthy.

The book's short preface and introduction explain how the entries were chosen and where to find the vitamins and special foods discussed in the entries. The book then goes on to alphabetically list vitamins, minerals, herbs, and foods that contribute to human health. The entries are generally one to two paragraphs in length and give information such as the nutrient's or food's history, what its benefits or deficiencies are, and where it can be found. The words throughout the entries that are in bold typeface can be found elsewhere in the book under their own entry. The book concludes with a thorough index.

This book provides adequate information on a wide variety of nutritional concerns. It will answer many questions that users will have. For libraries looking for a more complete guide to nutrition, *The New Encyclopedia of Vitamins, Minerals, Supplements, & Herbs* (see entry 1301) may be a better choice because of its more thorough explanations of how nutrients affect human health.—**Shannon M. Graff**

1303. Sullivan, Charles L. **A Companion to California Wine: An Encyclopedia of Wine and Winemaking from the Mission Period to the Present.** Berkeley, Calif., University of California Press, 1998. 441p. illus. maps. index. $39.95. ISBN 0-520-21351-3.

A Companion to California Wine is a reference guide for anyone interested in knowing more about the history and significance of wine production in California. This is an ideal book for both wine writers and wine enthusiasts. This book focuses mainly on the history of wine production in California and not on the present situation of wineries of that region.

The entries include specific wineries, technical terms used in wine making, some of the most popular wines produced in the area, and specific names of individuals influential in the industry. Entry lengths vary from one paragraph to one page depending on the significance of the term. There are many accompanying photographs and maps that enhance the value of this work. The book includes many cross-references that readers will appreciate. The work concludes with a list of further reading and oral histories that can be found at the Regional Oral History Office of the Bancroft Library at the University of California at Berkeley.

There are few if any sources like this on the history of the wine industry in California. It will be a valuable addition to medium- to large-sized public libraries that feature extensive collections in wine or wine tasting. [R: BL, 1 Oct 98, p. 356]—**Shannon M. Graff**

Directories

1304. **Italian Wines 1999.** New York, Gambero Rosso; distr., Wappingers Falls, N.Y., Antique Collectors' Club, 1999. 648p. index. $24.95pa. ISBN 1-890142-02-6.

The 12th Italian edition of this current guide to Italian wines is only the 2nd English version of Vini d'Italia. The book, arranged by region and then alphabetically by estate, evaluates 10,120 wines from 1,536 producers. It identifies 154 labels that won the highest "Tre Bicchieri" (Three Glasses) award this year. A star beside the name of the producer indicates that they have won the Three Glasses award at least 10 times and shows consistent production of high-quality wine. One producer, Gaja, has a double star for having won 21 Three Glasses awards. At the end of the listing of the Three Glasses awards, the book selects the wine of the year, the winery of the year, and the oenologist of the year. On page 14, a key to using the guide explains ratings, prices, and abbreviations. An asterisk beside a price identifies an especially good buy. Indexes to wine and to producers can be found in the back of the book. Readers can access the publisher's Website at http://www.gamberorosso.it for additional information on Italian wine, food, and travel.

Italian Wines expands and updates coverage of Italian wines found in the *Wine Spectator's Ultimate Guide to Buying Wine* (see ARBA 99, entry 1338). The book also supplements and updates Victor Hazan's useful older guide entitled *Italian Wine* (see ARBA 84, entry 1466). This is one of the most important selection tools to identify the best in current Italian wines. **O. Gene Norman**

Handbooks and Yearbooks

1305. **Diet and Nutrition Sourcebook.** 2d ed. Karen Bellenir, ed. Detroit, Omnigraphics, 1999. 650p. index. (Health Reference Series). $78.00. ISBN 0-7808-0228-4.

This book is beautifully done for its stated purpose. It is a consumer's reference book on all things nutritional and dietetic. The writing is excellent. It is at a level that most adults without advanced degrees can read. The sections are very complete and present two sides of a controversy, if there is one (e.g., olestra). The backgrounds and developments of some dietary substances are given (aspartame), regulatory concerns are discussed (food supplements), basic health information is given in relation to diet (asthma), terms are understandably defined (lipoproteins), and some easily confused concepts are explained thoroughly (salt and sodium). One major part of the book even goes into nutritional research.

The book is authoritative. The basis of the writing is a large variety of documents from federal agencies, university medical and nutrition departments, and professional organizations for nutrition and dietetics. There are many bibliographies throughout the book.

The last part of the book is made up of five chapters that give additional help and information. There is a very good glossary of terms, a large section on federal nutritional support programs, online information sources, a sizable list of books for further reading, and a resource list of CDs, books, and computer programs.

The book's format makes it easy to find information. There are large broad categories that are broken down into more specific chapters. The index, however, is really good, making this a valuable reference tool. A test of the page locators indicates that they are accurate, there is liberal use of *see* and *see also* references, there are a substantial number of double postings, and there are qualifiers that explain acronyms. Common terms like "overweight" send users to the more scientific terms (obesity).

This reference document should be in any public library, but it also would be a very good guide for beginning students in the health sciences. If the other books in this publisher's series are as good as this, they should all be in the health sciences collections.—**Lillian R. Mesner**

1306. **Food Safety Sourcebook.** Dawn D. Matthews, ed. Detroit, Omnigraphics, 1999. 339p. index. (Health Reference Series). $48.00. ISBN 0-7808-0326-4.

This volume is part of the Omnigraphics' ongoing Health Reference Series, a series encompassing the fields of food, health, and medicine. The focus of this book takes the complex issues of food safety and foodborne pathogens and presents them in an easily understood manner. Various chapters cover the present status of food safety in the United States; foodborne diseases; food product dating; home-based food illnesses; and the roles of the consumer, food handler, and governments in the safe handling of food. One chapter charts symptoms of various organisms and toxins, then proceeds to a detailed discussion of the various pathogens. Most chapters include further reading materials and government contacts. A useful glossary is provided. There is an excellent list of the numerous federal agencies involved with food safety, and there are directions for locating appropriate agencies to contact with a food safety and product problem. In addition, information is given on how to obtain the 1999 FDA Food Code. This book is very similar to another recently published book on the same topic, *Food Alert: The Ultimate Sourcebook* by Martin Satin (see entry 1308), which covers virtually the same areas. Both books do an excellent job of covering a large and often confusing topic. *Food Safety Sourcebook* is written at a more fundamental level than Satin's book—some might find it easier to read and understand. If a library already has Satin's book, there is no need to purchase this book. Public libraries will probably find this volume more useful due to its shorter chapters and more basic reading level. Other libraries and food collections will probably want the more scholarly coverage of Satin's *Food Alert*.—**Joy Hastings**

1307. Rinzler, Carol Ann. **The New Complete Book of Food: A Nutritional, Medical, and Culinary Guide.** New York, Facts on File, 1999. 440p. index. $40.00. ISBN 0-8160-3987-9.

The New Complete Book of Food: A Nutritional, Medical, and Culinary Guide provides multiple facts about many common foods. It gives basic nutritional information on fat, protein, fiber, and other levels, along with vitamin and mineral contributions and energy value. This information is presented two different formats—with a profile ranking of low, moderate, or high and in a more detailed format with easy-to-follow educational information. Individual food entries go beyond other nutrition works to provide tips on the most nutritious ways to serve, what to look for when buying, and storage and preparation. There is also information on what happens when foods are cooked and how other kinds of processing affect foods, such as canning, drying, and freezing. One of the most important and useful parts of this guide is the information it provides about medical uses and benefits (such as cancer and heart disease prevention), adverse effects associated with specific foods, and food and drug interactions that are possible with certain foods. Important diet information is also provided: first it is noted in the individual entries what diets may restrict or exclude a food, and second, an appendix charts what foods are high in nutrients for specific diets. A bibliography of sources and an index conclude the work. This is a good basic reference for nutritionists and anyone interested in streamlining their diets for their specific health needs.—**Cari Ringelheim**

1308. Satin, Morton. **Food Alert! The Ultimate Sourcebook for Food Safety.** New York, Checkmark Books/Facts on File, 1999. 306p. illus. index. $27.95; $14.95pa. ISBN 0-8160-3935-6; 0-8160-3936-4pa.

With almost daily reports of foodborne illnesses, and even death, filling pages of the newspapers, radio, and television airwaves, the nation's food supply has come under increasing scrutiny. What is happening during processing and handling? Where along the food chain is contamination occurring? What are the pathogens involved and how do they affect us? This volume uses science and fact to explain in understandable terms what is happening to the food we eat and handle and what foodborne diseases occur. There is a good overview of the history of food disease and food poisoning; an informative presentation of the various foodborne pathogens (i.e., bacteria, fungal, parasitic, viral diseases, toxins, and toxic substances); and what technologies and practices are being used to make food safer. An enlightening section notes all the diseases and bacteria that inhabit various foods. The glossary is informative and the appendixes provide further information on causes and symptoms of foodborne disease, storage conditions of selected foods, and additional sources of information (including Websites). Not too scientific or complicated, written not to scare but to inform, this authoritative resource serves up knowledge and understanding on food safety and foodborne disease. Many libraries may want a copy for the reference and circulating collections.
—**Joy Hastings**

1309. **The State of Food and Agriculture 1998.** Rome, Food and Agriculture Organization of the United Nations; distr., Lanham, Md., Bernan Associates, 1998. 371p. illus. maps. (FAO Agriculture Series, no.31). $51.00pa. (with disk). ISBN 92-5-1042204. ISSN 0081-4539.

This volume in the FAO Agriculture Series is an assessment of the world's food supply, especially as it relates to the economic and social welfare of rural nonfarm people in the developing countries. Part 1 covers the world as a whole, dealing with specific issues such as overall food availability, feeding the cities, and fish farming. The growth of Third World cities presents many factors (e.g., economic, demographic, social) that influence the supply and distribution of food to urban residents. Changes in trade, crop production, economic growth, and population are depicted in several graphs. Population growth and the shift toward urban residence are projected to the year 2020.

Part 2, "Regional Review," covers several major regions, including Africa, Asia and the Pacific, Latin America and the Caribbean, the Near East, and Central and Eastern Europe (the latter including the former Soviet republics). For each region as a whole, economics, agriculture performance, and policy developments are covered. One or two countries are singled out in each region for more extensive treatment, with discussions of particular crops and their yields outlined in charts.

Part 3, "Rural Nonfarm Income in Developing Countries," deals with employment of rural nonfarm people, the products they manufacture, the connection between this activity and farms, and household income. There are comparative studies across the major regions. Also included is a diskette with time series data by country derived from the FAOSTAT database. A chart chronicles the percentage of undernourished people in 98 countries for 1969 to 1971, 1990 to 1992, and 1994 to 1996.

For a thorough assessment of the availability of food and the economic status of the rural nonfarm population in the developing countries, this is the definitive source. The writing is excellent and the tables and charts use colors, which provide exceptional clarity and ease of interpretation.—**John Laurence Kelland**

Indexes

1310.   **Healthy Cookery Index.** By Rhonda H. Kleiman. Lanham, Md., Scarecrow, 1999. 315p. $49.50. ISBN 0-8108-3650-5.

This is Kleiman's third cookery index. It assists in the location of 20 English-language cookbooks that are readily accessible in most larger public libraries. They are some of the "most popular and accessible vegetarian, low cholesterol, and other healthy ethnic cookbooks. Recipes are easy to find since the book is subject indexed by well-known dishes, type of dish, major ingredient, preparation and ethnic origin." This index includes the following sections: an introduction, "How To Use This Book," "Books Listed by Key," "Books Listed by Author," "Index To Recipes," and "About the Author." The introduction includes Kleiman's criteria for inclusion, her selection process (which included researching in bookstore and library collections and using advice from librarians and food marketing consultants), special features, and acknowledgments. The author clearly fulfills her major objective to create "a tool for librarians, researchers, chefs, and home cooks" (p. ix). She includes more than 24,000 entries from approximately 8,000 recipes. Each recipe entry has a minimum of two cross-references. The author goes into great detail on how to locate appropriate entries in this alphabetically arranged, subject-heading index. Only dishes that are popularly known under a foreign name have not been translated by the author. This reviewer found this index useful with her own collection. However, she would have liked to see all 45 cookbooks that she reviewed indexed.

—**Nadine Salmons**

FORESTRY

1311.   Allaby, Michael. **Temperate Forests.** New York, Facts on File, 1999. 216p. illus. maps. index. (Ecosystem). $45.00. ISBN 0-8160-3678-0.

Flowing along in great rhythm and sequence, we find, between the beautifully colored cover plates, 216 pages of facts about the world's temperate forests. Today, much attention seems to be focused upon the tropical rain forests. It is a welcome treat to stand back and become reacquainted with the great historic temperate zone forests.

The author, with his telltale English lexicon, does a remarkable job in introducing such a forest. Quickly following are splendid discussions of plate tectonics, a complete course in weather systems and related phenomena, and the puzzling aspects of plant migration. The reader is thus enriched with the essential background necessary to cope with the biological phase of plant life. Some of the planet's well-known species of trees get excellent coverage. The uses of the forest products and a great array of related data such as soil compositions, forest fire problems, and many other matters are expertly covered.

At this point, the reader has an understanding of the forest and then can appreciate a brief review of the history of the forests, which takes the reader back 5,000 years or more. Readers are then brought up gradually to the current milieu with discussions of forest management practices in our own time.

The book has many well-designed charts and tables displaying data to support the text and a series of short paragraphs intended to get a point understood. Above all, the colorful photographs are ideally suited for the text and the whole edition is a gem well worth the investment. [R: BR, Sept/Oct 99, p. 70]

—**James H. Flynn Jr.**

HORTICULTURE

1312. Darke, Rick. **The Color Encyclopedia of Ornamental Grasses: Sedges, Rushes, Restios, Cat-tails, and Selected Bamboos.** Portland, Oreg., Timber Press, 1999. 325p. illus. index. $49.95. ISBN 0-88192-464-4.

Using grasses to accent a garden is not often considered, but it will be after reading this book. Beautiful color photographs show how ornamental grasses can add dramatic color, form, and movement to any landscape.

The book draws the reader from page to page with captivating color photographs showing how grasses can be used effectively in large or small gardens. It begins with illustrating how beautiful these plants can be in gardens, then progresses to describing the families of grasses and their near relatives. After a brief but informative section on their taxonomy and nomenclature, the book moves on to show grasses in their native habitats and then how they can be used in designing a garden with their rich varieties. A good chapter titled "Growing and Maintaining Grasses" proves grasses are not difficult to grow if planted in the correct life zone. The author even points out that he has "gardened for more than two decades without having ever directly fertilized a grass" (p. 117).

The largest chapter, "Encyclopedia of Grasses, Sedges, Rushes, Restios, Cat-tails, and Selected Bamboos," takes up half the book. It arranges the plants in alphabetic order by genus, then species. Each is described in a paragraph that includes information on where the plant originates, a short description of the plant, very brief cultivation information, and the USDA life zone it should be grown in. Color photographs illustrate most plants. A glossary, five-page bibliography, and indexes to common and botanical names complete the work.

It would have been helpful to have a section that lists plants by categories, such as grasses for rock gardens, woodland gardens, mound-forming grasses, or grasses with red foliage or blue foliage. Also, more information than just one paragraph per plant would also have been helpful. Readers can go to *Manual of Grasses* (see ARBA 96, entry 1583) by the same author for more complete descriptions. These suggestions aside, this is a beautiful book that will entice most any gardener to try planting ornamental grasses in their garden.

This book is recommended for all public, academic, and agriculture libraries. Home gardeners and landscape professionals may also want to add this one to their private libraries.—**Diane B. Rhodes**

1313. Pregill, Philip, and Nancy Volkman. **Landscapes in History: Design and Planning in the Eastern and Western Traditions.** 2d ed. New York, John Wiley, 1999. 844p. illus. maps. index. $79.95. ISBN 0-471-29328-8.

This 2d edition of the highly scholarly and thorough analysis of the history of human interaction with landscape as a cultural achievement certainly belongs in academic libraries and many public libraries. The book is in 2 parts. The 1st part looks at European and Asian development of the landscape from earliest settlement to the modern period. It deals with landscape design and human interaction with the landscape before the formal confines of landscape architecture. The 2d part deals with landscape in North America from prehistoric to modern times, with an emphasis on the development of the profession of landscape architecture. The book is heavily documented, has many pictures (somewhat sadly in black and white only), and is well arranged and easy to read. The chapter headings and the subheadings within are highly descriptive. The bibliography alone is 54 pages long, offering a very complete list of sources in the field.

Special libraries of landscape architecture or architecture in general, or special libraries of park history, should most certainly have this title in their reference sections as it provides an almost encyclopedic history of landscapes. General academic and public libraries will wish to acquire this title for their general collections, as it will be consulted. The Library of Congress subject heading "Landscape architecture—History" given in the CIP information is somewhat limiting as an access point, as this books looks at the whole range of how people and their surroundings have interacted through history. This work is highly recommended.—**Paul A. Mogren**

1314. Troshynski-Thomas, Karen. **The Handy Garden Answer Book.** Farmington Hills, Mich., Visible Ink Press/Gale, 1999. 442p. illus. index. $19.95pa. ISBN 1-57859-088-4.

Some gardening books are useful, some are informative, some are interesting, and some are just fun to read. Because of the question-and-answer format of this book, this is a fun and interesting book to read. The reader can pick it up and read from any section, and learn a little from questions like "Are there any plants that Japanese beetles won't eat?" (p. 99).

The author answers more than 1,000 gardening questions that are arranged under headings for plant and soil science, seeding, propagation, and planting; care and feeding; problems; garden design; gardens, gardeners, and gardening; special gardens; perennials, annuals, and biennials; vegetables and fruits; trees and shrubs; lawns, groundcovers, and ornamental grasses and herbs. There are two to five questions and answers per page. A seven-page bibliography of print sources, a list of gardening magazines, and garden Websites are included at the end. A subject index that includes the scientific and common names of plants mentioned in the text helps the reader find specific information in the book. Several black-and-white photographs and six pages of color plates illustrate the text.

Although the book covers a lot of ground, the questions are too scattered to help with basic gardening. It is also geared more for gardening in Michigan, where the author lives, and is not as useful for warmer-climate gardeners in the southern and southwestern United States. It would have been helpful if the author had referenced what source (presumably from the bibliography) the answer to the questions came from, so the reader might be able to read further on the question. Aside from this, the book provides fun reading and information on many aspects of gardening. This work is recommended especially for public libraries.—**Diane B. Rhodes**

VETERINARY SCIENCE

1315. **Black's Veterinary Dictionary.** 19th ed. Edward Boden, ed. Lanham, Md., Barnes & Noble Books, 1998. 595p. illus. $99.50. ISBN 0-7136-4400-1.

Black's Veterinary Dictionary is likely the most known and respected by veterinarians. The 1st edition was printed in 1928. Not only has the 19th edition been extensively updated and revised to reflect changes in legislation, advances in medicine and treatment, veterinary practice, and animal husbandry, it also has become more usable for the practitioners by having less technical jargon than in past editions. Some of the topics addressed in the new edition are resistance to antibiotics, new vaccines for cats and dogs, embryo transfer in cattle breeding, and new findings about BSE and cloning. A positive aspect of this publication is the accuracy and timeliness of the information; the only major drawback is its cost. There are other veterinary dictionaries by various publishers, but they are outdated. All public and academic libraries should make this edition part of their collection.—**Theresa Maggio**

1316. **Dictionary of Veterinary Epidemiology.** Bernard Toma and others, eds. Ames, Iowa, Iowa State University Press, 1999. 284p. $69.95pa. ISBN 0-8138-2639-X.

This highly specialized dictionary is the result of a lot of work by an international group of veterinary scholars. It was originally a translation from a French glossary, but as the French was being translated to English, basic disagreements about the meanings of some terms had to be resolved. Thus it developed an ambitious collaboration of U.S., French, and Canadian veterinarians. The object was "to produce a dictionary of veterinary epidemiology, incorporating the translations of the French glossary, written for a large spectrum of the members of the animal health professions, and jointly presenting the French and the North American perspectives on definitions and terms."

The book has broad coverage that includes pathology, statistics, economics, ecology, and preventative medicine as well as pure epidemiology. The entries can be quite extensive. For instance, the term "monitoring" includes the definition and three comments. The comments state other uses for the term, give a discussion of other interpretations, and add some computer programs that assist monitoring. At the end of the entry, there is a *see also* reference to "epidemiologic surveillance." When appropriate, the terms include illustrations, tables, graphs, and formula.

The book claims to be the only dictionary in this field. Many individual practitioners will want to buy this book, and any collection that covers animal sciences should have it. The definitions are written in a straightforward language and students at any level will be able to use it.—**Lillian R. Mesner**

1317. Plumb, Donald C. **Veterinary Drug Handbook.** 3d ed. White Bear, Minn., Pharma Vet Publishing; distr., Ames, Iowa, Iowa State University Press, 1999. 750p. index. $89.95pa. ISBN 0-8138-2444-3.

This handbook covers drugs approved for veterinary use and nonapproved drugs (human) that are nevertheless used in veterinary practice. There are more than 380 drug monographs, 27 more than in the previous edition (see ARBA 97, entry 1263). Each drug monograph includes chemistry, pharmacology, storage, use, adverse effects, drug interactions, dosage for each of several animal species, and more. Animal species covered in each monograph vary, and include dogs, cats, cattle, sheep, goats, swine, birds, and even reptiles and other animals, depending on the usefulness of each drug for an animal. A lengthy appendix includes more than 30 topical ophthalmic products (several more than the previous edition). The appendix also has chemotherapy protocols, diet tables, estrus and gestation periods for dogs and cats, poison control center listings, and more. The appendix topics are listed in the detailed table of contents. New to the 3d edition is a special index of drug monographs by therapeutic class and animal. A regular index is included.

This handbook contains a lot of practical information for the veterinarian. It is well organized with excellent access to the contents. It is an essential reference for veterinarians and for academic libraries in institutions with veterinary medicine or animal science programs.—**John Laurence Kelland**

31 Biological Sciences

GENERAL WORKS

1318. Kotyk, Arnost, comp. **Quantities, Symbols, Units, and Abbreviations in the Life Sciences: A Guide for Authors and Editors.** Totowa, N.J., Humana Press, 1999. 130p. $39.50pa. ISBN 0-89603-616-2; 0-89603-649-9pa.

Arnost Kotyk, of the Institute of Physiology of the Academy of Sciences of the Czech Republic, has garnered recommendations from the 36 member organizations of the International Council of Scientific Unions, other international societies, journal editors, and other experts on the proper use of "non-words" in the biological sciences. The objectives of the book are to foster standard usages and thus make the literature more understandable. Biochemistry and molecular biology, cell biology, genetics, taxonomy, virology, plant and animal physiology, pharmacology, immunology, medicine, soil biology, paleontology, and psychology are included together with relevant material from mathematics, chemistry, and physics. Several subjects, including ecology, ethnology, and biological oceanography, are not included. There is no index, so one has to know the context of a term to look it up. A term used in more than one discipline is only entered under the first. Abbreviations are spelled out, but not defined.

The criteria for inclusion are unclear. Even a desultory search of biological subject dictionaries yields numerous well-known abbreviations not included here. Perhaps no agreement on the part of the organizations and experts consulted was forthcoming on many items.

This book is an essential resource for authors and editors of biological literature and should be in any library supporting such work. While it will be useful as a convenient, compact work of reference for readers, as opposed to authors and editors, its noncomprehensiveness demands that it be supplemented by biological subject dictionaries.—**Frederic F. Burchsted**

1319. **Life Sciences on File.** rev. ed. By the Diagram Group. New York, Facts on File, 1999. 1v. (various paging). illus. index. $165.00 looseleaf w/binder. ISBN 0-8160-3872-4.

Facts on File has produced another quality product in the *Life Sciences on File* revised edition. The heavy-duty, looseleaf binder contains 300 black-and-white illustrations and images designed for use by educators and lecturers. Permission is granted for reproduction, by photocopying only, of all materials for nonprofit, educational, or private use. The size and clarity of the images are excellent. All illustrations have a title and the parts are labeled using a detailed key to identify each component of the image. The heavy, acid-free paper ensures a long life of repetitive uses.

The six major topics included are unity, continuity, diversity, maintenance, human biology, and ecology. The unity chapter has 69 illustrations. Examples in the unity division include major branches of biology, life activities, levels of organization, units of measurement, classification of carbohydrates, amino acids, protein structures, and much more. There are 76 images and illustrations in the continuity sections including cell division, mitosis, asexual reproduction, meiosis, flower structure, pollination, and plant fertilization.

The diversity chapter deals with the classification of living organisms and has 41 illustrations ranging from Kingdom Protista Ameba, Kingdom Fungi Rhizopus, Kingdom Plantae Bryophta, and Kingdom Animalia Porifera to Kingdom Animalia Mammalia. In the maintenance section 43 images deal with the topics of nutrition, transport, respiration, excretion and osmoregulation, coordination, locomotion, reproduction, and growth and development. The chapter about human biology has 53 masters covering all of the functions of the body from nutrition-digestive system, transport-circulatory system, respiration, excretion, and coordination-nervous system to locomotion. In the final section, ecology, there are eight images. They are terrestrial biomes, carbon cycle, nitrogen cycle, water cycle, energy flow, food chain, pyramid of biomass, and food web.

The back of the binder has a complete index, a chronology, and an excellent glossary. Each of the sections is separated by tabbed and labeled dividers that make finding the various chapters quite easy. An extremely useful book for, but not limited to, the learning environment. The illustrations would make excellent overhead transparencies or simply used on a document camera for wonderful visual aids for professional speakers, teachers, and students alike. *Life Sciences on File* is an outstanding undertaking and an investment worth many years of use in the public or private sector.—**Mary L. Trenerry**

1320. Tiner, Ralph W. **In Search of Swampland: A Wetland Sourcebook and Field Guide.** New Brunswick, N.J., Rutgers University Press, 1998. 264p. illus. index. $55.00; $26.00pa. ISBN 0-8135-2505-5; 0-8135-2506-3pa.

Wetlands are becoming an increasingly scarce commodity in the United States. Our understanding of their function and necessity for a healthy environment ecosystem has changed substantially over the last 20 years. This volume will aid in the understanding of wetlands and their importance to the environmental well-being of all. The author has created a work that will serve two purposes. The first purpose is that of a textbook for use in an introductory biology or ecology course at the undergraduate level; the second purpose is that of a field guide to supplement our understanding of wetlands as we venture into these once forbidding, useless places. The 1st section consists of 8 chapters and act as a primer to wetland hydrology, formation, soils, plant communities, wildlife, and conservation activities. The field guide includes plant and wildlife identification keys, interpretation of hydric soils, and the delineation and limits of wetland areas. The text is supplemented with numerous line drawings, black-and-white photographs, maps, and charts. A few color photographs appear in the center of the volume. The work concludes with a glossary of terms, a bibliography, and an extensive list of wetlands to explore in the northeastern U.S., arranged geographically.

One criticism that might be found with this work is the few color photographs included. A greater number of color photos or illustrations would increase the use of the field guide section to a considerable extent. Viewing line drawings of plants is good for determining form, but leaves open to question other attributes that deal with color. Another criticism is the softcover binding used in producing the work. This will serve well for use in the classroom or the library as a reference tool, but some other form of binding might make more sense for use during field study.

This work will find use in academic, special, and school libraries supporting courses or research in biology, ecology, public policy and planning, environmental ethics, and other related courses. It will also find use in public library collections for similar reasons and for its wealth of data contained in the field guide section. [R: Choice, Nov 98, p. 545]—**Gregory Curtis**

BIOLOGY

Dictionaries and Encyclopedias

1321. **Encyclopedia of Genetics.** Jeffrey A. Knight, ed. Hackensack, N.J., Salem Press, 1999. 2v. illus. index. $200.00/set. ISBN 0-89356-978-X.

This timely 2-volume set on genetics is written in a language that can provide the general reader with an overview of genetics and its related glossary. Mostly this source emphasizes human genetics. Many contributing authors from academia and research institutes put their thoughts together to publish this reference text. The public or school libraries might find this text useful in explaining the various areas in this field of study. Although the encyclopedia is alphabetic in scope it includes 8 related areas; 11 essays on bacteria genetics: topics on classical transmission genetics; developmental genetics; genetic engineering and biotechnology; human genetics; surveys on immunogenetics; molecular genetics discussions; and centers on population genetics. The appendixes include a timeline of major developments in genetics, a biographical dictionary of important geneticists, a glossary, a bibliography, and an index. In addition, this easy-to-read set contains more than 200 photographs, charts, graphs, and illustrations that can further illuminate the complex nature of genetics. Each article has the standard format, such as field of study, significance, key terms, *see also* references, and further reading. It is interesting to find concepts such as fragile X syndrome, knockout genes, gene therapy, and molecular medicine included in this encyclopedia. This is a good starting point for locating introductory information on genetics, but more supplemental readings will be required for more in-depth research findings. [R: Choice, Oct 99, p. 310; SLJ, Aug 99, p. 184]—**Polin P. Lei**

1322. **The Facts on File Dictionary of Biology.** 3d ed. Robert Hine, ed. New York, Checkmark Books/Facts on File, 1999. 361p. $17.95pa. ISBN 0-8160-3908-9.

As the revised, updated, and expanded edition of an established reference work, this dictionary retains the basic format of previous editions, with some 3,300 alphabetically arranged headwords. Appendixes giving succinct diagrams of the animal and plant kingdoms and amino acid structures have been added. Definitions, usually encyclopedic in scope (one or two paragraphs) are clearly written for the intelligent layperson and are fairly nontechnical. Many cross-references are provided. Entries have been revised and updated when needed. A few illustrations of chemical or cellular structures have been included.

The Facts on File Dictionary of Biology remains a good basic dictionary for school and public library use, particularly where budgets are limited and works such as the *McGraw-Hill Dictionary of Scientific and Technical Terms* (5th ed.; see ARBA 95, entry 1493) and the *Concise Encyclopedia Biology* (see ARBA 97, entry 1266) are not readily available.—**Jonathan F. Husband**

1323. Flickinger, Michael C., and Stephen W. Drew. **Encyclopedia of Bioprocess Technology: Fermentation, Biocatalysis, and Bioseparation.** New York, John Wiley, 1999. 5v. illus. index. (Wiley Biotechnology Encyclopedias). $1,500.00/set. ISBN 0-471-13822-3.

This latest addition to he Wiley Biotechnology Encyclopedias series is a 5-volume set that covers facets of bioprocess technology concentrating on fermentation, biocatalysis, and bioseparation. According to the publisher, more than 600 scientists and engineers, representing industry and academe from a multitude of countries, have provided entries in this alphabetic encyclopedia. Biotechnology needs the combination of mathematicians, computer scientists, and biologists to decipher and explain the various types of biological information so it can be used to prevent disease, increase crop output, increase animal productivity for food, or a wide number of other issues related to human survival. Useful bibliographies are provided at the end of each entry for further research. The clear typeface and variety of illustrations and tables enhance many of the entries. Bioprocess technology develops valuable products using natural biological activities but it also raises several important ethical issues, such as genetic engineering, cloning, animal rights, waste treatment, and others. This area of research is extensive and the volumes cover topics ranging from the use of Chinese hamster ovary cells for the production of complex proteins in clinical research to scientific studies on baker's yeast. Because the research covered is both sophisticated and varied, the detailed alphabetic entries and the index in volume 5 are especially useful. Taking the price and highly specific subject matter into consideration, this encyclopedic set is recommended for academic libraries supporting specific programs in biotechnical engineering and biotechnology and select special libraries that aid engineers or scientists advancing the research field. [R: Choice, Dec 99, pp. 694-695]

—Diane J. Turner

1324. Nill, Kimball R. **Glossary of Biotechnology Terms.** 2d ed. Lancaster, Pa., Technomic Publishing, 1998. 264p. $49.95. ISBN 1-56676-580-3.

According to the author, this work introduces nonscientists to an explanation of terms they may encounter while working within some aspect of the biotechnology field. Such people working in the marketing and sales departments, legal departments, and human resource departments of biotechnology firms, along with other interested personnel, comprise a potential audience for this dictionary. The terms included have been taken from the fields of biology, chemistry, and biochemistry.

The length of the explanations varies from term to term. In some instances, one or two sentences complete a definition, while with other words, a few paragraphs may be used in order to provide an explanation. Biotechnology associations and agencies, along with the variety of biotechnology terms, are included. Many of the biotechnology words are explained using analogies to aid nonscientists in the understanding of the definitions presented. It should be noted, however, that some biological knowledge on the part of the reader would be useful as well.

The inclusion of a subject index would have enhanced the usefulness of this work. This volume is recommended for industrial, college, and university libraries. [R: Choice, July/Aug 99, p. 1924]

—George H. Bell

1325. **Wildlife and Plants of the World.** Tarrytown, N.Y., Marshall Cavendish, 1999. 17v. illus. index. $329.95/set. ISBN 0-7614-7099-9.

Wildlife of the World (see ARBA 95, entry 1561) has been updated and expanded for this set. Biomes (e.g., desert, grassland) and moneran, protoctist, fungi, and plants (e.g., bonsai, ginkgo) have been added. The original set was limited to only animals and most of that information has not changed.

The 17-volume set contains more than 400 alphabetically arranged entries. Animals are still the primary focus of the set and comprise approximately 75 percent of the articles. Volume 1 provides general information on the 5 kingdoms, classifying organisms and a table of contents for all volumes. The information on the kingdoms is repeated at the beginning of volumes 2 through 16. Each volume is individually indexed. Articles follow a prescribed format. Each is two pages in length with two color photographs or detailed drawings, a distribution map, cross-references, and a key facts side box. Key facts include but are not limited to scientific name, range, habitat, appearance, life cycle, uses, status, food, and breeding. Color-coding is used to indicate the type of organism, biome, or habitat. A color bar is used at the top of the page and in the key facts box; a legend of the code is provided at the beginning of each volume. Volume 17 has more in-depth information on classifying organisms, including essays on various classes of organisms, which are structured in the same page format as the other articles. A glossary, bibliography, and 5 indexes (geographic, biome, classification, scientific name, and comprehensive) complete volume 17. These indexes aid the user in locating information from various vantage points, such as the plants and animals found in Australia. Although the set is not comprehensive, it does contain lesser-known as well as common plants and animals. The alphabetic, concise format and visually pleasing layout will appeal to elementary and middle school students for research. [R: BL, 1 Mar 99, p. 1254; SLJ, Feb 99, p. 136]—**Elaine Ezell**

1326. Williams, D. F., comp. **The Williams Dictionary of Biomaterials.** Liverpool, England, Liverpool University Press; distr., Portland, Oreg., International Specialized Book Services, 1999. 343p. $79.95. ISBN 0-85323-734-4.

The field of bio-materials has grown rapidly over the last decade, from concern with the design of a relatively small array of biologically inert devices to the current involvement with numerous, often biologically active, materials and devices and with the rapidly growing field of tissue engineering. This growth has brought about a proliferation of new terminology and the importation of terms from other fields, including anatomy, dentistry, engineering, molecular biology, and immunology. Much confusion has arisen because growth has outpaced standardization, and because a term may have different meanings in formerly separate but now confluent fields. Williams's Dictionary attempts to promote order by supplying for each term a brief definition, grammatical usage, associated discipline, and the source on which the definition is based. Whenever a term has more than one sense, these are identified. Phrases with nonobvious meanings are included. There is a listing of sources for definitions and a thorough guide to using the book. This book is essential for any library with significant biological or medical coverage.—**Frederic F. Burchsted**

1327. **World of Biology.** Kimberley A. McGrath, ed. Farmington Hills, Mich., Gale, 1999. 942p. illus. index. $85.00. ISBN 0-7876-3044-6.

This encyclopedia is aimed at the high school market. More than 1,000 subject and biographical entries cover most of the major areas in the life sciences, including some specialized topics. The subject articles are concise and well written, with numerous cross-references. Although the entries naturally lack the detail found in more advanced encyclopedias, they cover a remarkable range of ideas in a manner that should appeal to bright high school students. The biographical articles are a mix of well-known and relatively obscure living and deceased biologists. Scientists who made important discoveries are mentioned in the appropriate subject articles, and most are also discussed in a biographical entry, although there are some surprising gaps. The biographical articles are an excellent source of information on the scientists, including family histories and stories about their education and careers. The biographies are clearly designed to humanize scientists and to provide role models for students. The encyclopedia also includes a bibliography, which is not cross-referenced to individual articles, and a historical chronology. The index is extensive but flawed, leaving out a number of important topics that are covered within the alphabetic entries or in the illustration captions.

Despite the relatively minor flaws mentioned above, the encyclopedia is a useful resource. The breadth of coverage is impressive, the subject articles are well done, the biologists are nicely humanized, and the links of scientists to their discoveries should be of interest to the intended audience. The encyclopedia would be an educational addition to the high school or public library. [R: BL, 1 Sept 99, p. 188; BR, Nov/Dec 99, p. 86; Choice, Dec 99, p. 698]—**Diane Schmidt**

Handbooks and Yearbooks

1328. **Genetic Engineering: A Documentary History.** Thomas A. Shannon, ed. Westport, Conn., Greenwood Press, 1999. 282p. index. (Primary Documents in American History and Contemporary Issues Series). $49.95. ISBN 0-313-30457-2.

Timely, thoughtful, thorough, as well as engaging and provocative, are the descriptors that apply here. By allowing research scientists, science writers, historians, ethicists, and others to tell the story of genetic engineering in their own words, Shannon has produced a book that is difficult to put down.

Most biologists will have read at least half of the material in its original context. It does not matter. The topical arrangement (e.g., debate, animal applications, human genome project, ethical issues, and cloning) unites documents that amplify one another, and the reader sees things in a new light. Perhaps genetically engineered plants that resist insect pests are better than plants doused with chemicals. And Shannon's introduction to each piece is literally just right.

Catherine Hayes writes about why she chose to be tested for Huntington's disease and why she advises that not everyone at risk should be tested. In many ways, her personal tale is a microcosm of the swirling complexities in genetic engineering, such as what happens with test results if there is no cure, and discrimination by employers and insurance companies.

Despite the volatility of the subject, Shannon's approach is balanced and the book is not without humor. We meet the young, flamboyant James Watson straightaway and again many times as he moves beyond the double helix. This is the text equivalent of Paul Gauguin's "Where Do We Come from? What Are We? Where Are We Going?" It deserves as wide an audience as that painting.—**Diane M. Calabrese**

1329.   **Innovations in Biology.** Santa Barbara, Calif., ABC-CLIO, 1999. 345p. illus. index. (Innovations in Science). $50.00. ISBN 1-57607-116-2.

Innovations in Biology covers the major advances in biology during the twentieth century, touching on topics such as the Human Genome Project, genetic engineering, and biotechnology. Once a discipline based upon natural history, biology is now a multidisciplinary study of biological systems, whether they are entire ecosystems or the components within a cell. With new technology and instrumentation, the discoveries made during this century continue to have a major impact on our everyday lives. *Innovations in Biology* attempts to cover all this within a few hundred pages.

The volume begins with an introductory essay providing an overview of important discoveries, followed by a detailed chronology of key events since 1900. The biographical section provides brief information about influential biologists of the twentieth century. The first section then concludes with directories of organizations and Websites and an annotated bibliography of selected reading. The majority of the book is a dictionary of more than 1,200 terms and concepts. The section concludes with a list of Nobel Prize winners for physiology or medicine. The extensive index pertains only to the first part of the book, but it is very useful.

This book provides only a brief overview of twentieth-century biology, but it touches on the major topics that appear in the news media. The text is clearly written and can be easily understood by students or general readers. The black-and-white illustrations are of good quality and cover the standard topics, such as mitosis, the circulatory system, and the Krebs cycle. The information is easily attainable in an encyclopedia or general biology textbook, but *Innovations in Biology* provides a concise and readable account of recent discoveries. This resource is recommended for high school, public, and community college libraries. [R: BL, 1 Dec 99, p. 734]—**Teresa U. Berry**

1330.   LeVine, Harry, III. **Genetic Engineering: A Reference Handbook.** Santa Barbara, Calif., ABC-CLIO, 1999. 264p. index. (Contemporary World Issues). $45.00. ISBN 0-87436-962-2.

This resource represents an excellent introduction to the topic of genetic engineering. Divided into seven sections, this work guides the reader through a number of facets of the topics. Section 1, written in an easy-to-understand manner, presents an overview of genetic engineering. Topics such as what is genetic engineering; its history; and its relationship to health, food, biomanufacturing, and environmental restoration are considered. In addition, the international impact and predictions of genetic engineering are discussed. Section 2 represents a chronological list of important dates in history relating to a variety of aspects of the subject. The chronology begins in 6000 B.C.E. with the Sumerians and Babylonians and ends in 1998 with pending legislation against human cloning.

A series of biographical sketches of scientists who played a role in genetic engineering encompasses section 3. Compiled as text and tables, section 4 provides statistical data, such as federal investment in biotechnology research, regulatory information for environmental release of genetically modified organisms, and much more. A directory of organizations, along with their publications, can be found in section 5, while an annotated list of selected print sources, such as books, periodicals, and government publications, completes section 6. Section 7 provides an overview of selected nonprint sources, such as videocassettes, computer programs, and databases. A glossary, a list of abbreviations and acronyms, and an index can be found at the end of the book.

This resource provides an excellent introduction to the topic, and because of the importance of genetic engineering and cloning in today's society, belongs on the shelf of every public, college, and university library. High school libraries may also wish to purchase it.—**George H. Bell**

1331. Sept, J. Duane. **The Beachcomber's Guide to Seashore Life in the Pacific Northwest.** Madeira Park, Harbour, 1999. 235p. illus. $21.95pa. ISBN 1-55017-204-2.

What an exquisite pleasure it is to walk a lonely coastline and contemplate the hundreds of fascinating plants and animals living in the narrow space between the tides. This book has gorgeous illustrations, clear and succinct prose, and an easily grasped organization. It is also scientifically accurate and remarkably sensitive to the delicate environments of the seashore.

The book begins with simple explanations of tides, coastal environments, and basic ecology. The author shows a laudable concern for the safety of his beachcombing audience and the integrity of these natural systems. The bulk of the guide is a systematic listing of 274 common species found along the Pacific Northwest shorelines. The animals and plants are presented in taxonomic order, from Phylum Porifera (sponges) through Phylum Anthophyta (flowering plants). There are no gimmicks in this systematic section, such as silhouettes of common groups or cute names, just straightforward listings of the features and attributes of the organisms, along with top-quality photographs of seashore life. To his lasting credit, the author has not ignored the inconspicuous taxa, so there are excellent sections on bryozoans, lichens, and even the little crabs that live inside infaunal clams. The brief descriptions of the physiology, reproductive history, and ecology of the species are invariably interesting. The only problem with this systematic section is that some of the color-coded pages have an underlying pattern that makes the text difficult to read.

The last part of this guide contains short descriptions of 39 intertidal sites in British Columbia, Washington, and Oregon, each keyed to the type of exposure and the most common organisms found there. The descriptions even include telephone numbers and the occasional Website addresses of state, national, and provincial parks.

This guidebook is significantly better than most others designed for a casual audience. It is highly recommended for libraries and individuals with any connection to the beautiful seashores of the Pacific Northwest.—**Mark A. Wilson**

BOTANY

General Works

Dictionaries and Encyclopedias

1332. Holliday, Paul. **A Dictionary of Plant Pathology.** 2d ed. New York, Cambridge University Press, 1998. 536p. $155.00. ISBN 0-521-59453-7.

This is a comprehensive list of major and many minor plant pathogens. More than 500 genera of fungi and 800 viruses, bacteria, mollicutes, nematodes, and viroids are described. Entries are also included for diseases and disorders, crops and their pathology, fungicides, taxonomic groups, terminology, toxins, vectors, and past plant pathologists. More than 11,000 entries are included.

The author claims that this 2d edition represents a major revision in that cross-references have been increased and new journal references have been added. The use of common names has also been expanded for those readers unfamiliar with scientific names. An important note is that mycorrhizae are omitted with one exception. A list of approximately 175 major textbooks dealing with plant pathology and related areas is included. Abbreviations and conventions are listed.

Many of the actual entries include literature citations for those readers wanting further information. Most of these citations consist only of the author(s) name and a date so readers will have to do some hunting to find the referenced sources.

This book will be valuable primarily to plant pathologists, mycologists, virologists, and others dealing with microbes and the diseases they cause. It is strictly a dictionary, and will be of no use for diagnosing diseases or studying their etiology and life cycles. However, it will be useful for naming conventions and clarification of meanings when writing scientific papers. [R: Choice, May 99, p. 1596]—**Michael G. Messina**

1333. Mineo, Baldassare. **Rock Garden Plants: A Color Encyclopedia.** Portland, Oreg., Timber Press, 1999. 284p. illus. maps. index. $59.95. ISBN 0-881920432-6.

Rock Garden Plants is a tribute to a form of gardening that almost any garden or nature enthusiast can appreciate. Rock garden plants are generally defined as plants that grow easily in a rock environment and mature to a height of only 24 inches. These include perennials, shrubs, wildflowers, ferns, and ground cover, among other varieties.

The book is arranged alphabetically and each entry contains the scientific and common name of the plant, the family it belongs to, growth habit, suggested exposure amounts to the sun, soil and drainage, whether the plant produces flowers, its dimensions, and a hardiness zone (what areas of the country the plant will thrive). Each plant is given an illustration with a caption and the name of the photographer. Sections at the back of the book include "Families of Rock Garden Plants," which lists the family name and all the plants that fall under it, and "Rock Garden Plants for Specific Purposes and Locations," which provides appropriate plants for alpine houses, troughs and containers, stone walls, moist soil, sandy soil, woodlands, peat gardens, limy soil, heat and drought, heat and high humidity, dry winters, dry summers, and mild climates. The book concludes with an index to common names and synonyms.

This book will be well received in many public libraries that hold collections in gardening. It is well written and illustrated and will be a welcome addition.—**Shannon M. Graff**

1334. Pollock, Michael, and Mark Griffiths. **Shorter Dictionary of Gardening.** London, Macmillan UK; distr., North Pomfret, Vt., Trafalgar Square, 1998. 836p. illus. index. $65.00. ISBN 0-333-65440-4.

The British have a way with gardening books. This abridged version of *The Royal Horticultural Society Dictionary of Gardening* tackles the long and the short of most aspects of planning, execution, and maintenance. Researchers, horticulturists, librarians, botanists, farmers, landscapers, and home gardeners will delight in its straightforward layout and ease of use. The table of contents lists acknowledgments and a foreword accounts for the $3\frac{1}{2}$-year effort to distill the more comprehensive dictionary. An introduction explains tables, climatic zones, nomenclatures, and cultivars. A list of 13 abbreviations and a conversion chart from metric to U.S. measures clarify details requiring interpretation.

The dictionary offers clear presentation in its alphabetized entries. A five-page exposition of pests and diseases charts problems affecting fruit trees, vegetables, and ornamentals. An 11-page graphic guide to leaf arrangements, shapes, lobing, veining, flower forms, and fruit shapes supplies line drawings to exemplify such complex terms as dorsifixed, decussate, and septifragal. A two-column index of common names covers 14 pages. The text ends with a two-page list of synonyms. Impeccable photography highlights seasonal gardening with models of container beds, bog plantings, climbers, and the use of broad-leaved evergreens to brighten winter landscapes.

The heart of the book is its text, which expresses in understandable terms the subject of gardening—how and when to prune, how to naturalize, methods of potting orchids, and how to recognize various types of nematodes. Generous sidebars, line drawings, and cross-referencing as well as guide words simplify advice on particulars. As an adjunct to the well-read gardener, fascinating details are included. All in all, the book is a good read at a reasonable price. [R: LJ, 15 June 99, p. 72; Choice, Nov 99, p. 512]

—**Mary Ellen Snodgrass**

Handbooks and Yearbooks

1335. Magee, Dennis W., and Harry E. Ahles. **Flora of the Northeast: A Manual of the Vascular Flora of New England and Adjacent New York.** Amherst, Mass., University of Massachusetts Press, 1999. 1213p. illus. maps. index. $69.95. ISBN 1-55849-189-9.

The long-awaited *Flora of the Northeast* (from the Hudson River and Lake Champlain east to Maine) is available. Based upon the extensive research of Harry Ahles and completed by Dennis Magee, this is a comprehensive coverage of the vascular plants of the Northeast, updating and complementing M. L. Fernald's *Gray's Manual*, 8th edition, corrected printing (Van Nostrand Reinhold, 1970).

This is a thoroughly professional work. It commences with a nested set of keys to the families. Within families, keys are provided to the genera and within genera, to species. The species descriptions are terse and include salient characters, ecological information, and distribution. Most descriptions are accompanied by a county-level distribution map (a wonderful resource) and many are accompanied by line drawings of diagnostic aspects of the plant in question.

Complementing the systematic portions of the text are several tabular summations, including the generic and specific diversity of the New England flora and two matrices, one to characters of dicots of the area, and a second to woody plants in winter. Both are useful summaries of the distribution of characters within the plants of the Northeast. A glossary and index complete the work.

While *Gray's Manual* often contains more detailed species descriptions, *Flora of the Northeast* updates this material, and provides both more illustrations and, most importantly, updated distribution maps. This volume belongs on every public and academic library shelf in the Northeast, and will be a valuable reference for years to come.—**Bruce H. Tiffney**

1336. Valder, Peter. **The Garden Plants of China.** Portland, Oreg., Timber Press, 1999. 400p. illus. index. $49.95. ISBN 0-88192-470-9.

Combining vast research as well as information and photographs from his many trips to China, Valder presents a comprehensive volume on ornamental plants in the gardens of China. Within the first three chapters are an overview of Chinese horticulture, the use of ornamental plants in Chinese culture, and the introduction of Chinese plants to other countries. The history, occurrence, use, and symbolism of the plants are discussed throughout the volume as individual varieties are focused upon. The discussion of plants in literature and art expands the volume beyond gardening. The work does not include all ornamental plants. Specifically, trees used in forestry and recently introduced and now popular plants were chosen to be excluded. The author does not seek to replicate the many extensive works on Chinese plants, but does provide the reader with extensive references for further exploration and reading, with full bibliographic information given in the lengthy bibliography. Approximately 80 percent of the text is devoted to the plants, with more than 400 being listed. Arrangement of the chapters is seasonal, beginning with the conifers and following in the progression of their blooming or use for ornament. Within the chapters the plants are primarily in alphabetic order. Plant listings include the Latin name, common name, and Chinese name in Chinese characters and romanized. Valder noted that Western botanists have assigned various names to many of the plants and that the taxonomy of many groups has been revised. With this in mind, he chose to be conservative in the use of plant names and to stay with the old family names. The descriptive information provided for each plant is enhanced with the history, literature, myths, and uses associated with the plant. Although not all plants are illustrated, most pages are richly enhanced with several color photographs, many of which the author took on his trips to China. The glossary of botanical terms and an extensive index of common and botanical names, general topics, and horticultural sites complete the volume. This work will be of interest to public and university libraries with botanical collections, a gardener planning a visit to China, or a reader interested in the history of Chinese gardening.—**Elaine Ezell**

Flowering Plants

1337. **500 Popular Annuals and Perennials for American Gardeners.** Loretta Barnard, ed. Hauppauge, N.Y., Barron's Educational Series, 1998. 288p. illus. index. $12.95pa. ISBN 0-7641-1177-9.

Arranged alphabetically, the entries in this work include the species names, any cultivars, brief cultivation instructions, common names, and color photographs. This is preceded by a general introduction that covers more detailed planting directions and basic information on flowers and types of gardens and plantings. Sidebars contain lists of outstanding plants in various categories, such as "winter flowering" and "annuals for cutting." A hardiness zone map and a reference table that arranges the entries into annuals/perennials, growing zones, colors, planting times, and flowering times combine to make this work user-friendly.

The book's size and layout make it a good choice for gardeners to take to nurseries when choosing plants. Another advantage for U.S. gardeners is that other plants are excluded, thus eliminating information on plants that are probably not available to the average gardener. One drawback is the omission of information on why these particular 500 plants were selected. If they are the most popular—or even just popular—it would be helpful to know the source of this information. Also, some of the data in the book differ from those found in other works. Because this book is not comprehensive it should not be the first choice for a reference collection. Excellent sources for libraries to consider include *The American Horticultural Society A-Z Encyclopedia of Garden Plants* (see ARBA 98, entry 1432) and *America's Garden Book* by Louise and James Bush-Brown (Macmillan, 1997). Libraries should, however, buy at least 1 copy of *500 Popular Annuals and Perennials* for their circulating collections.—**January Adams**

1338. **500 Popular Roses for American Gardeners.** Hauppauge, N.Y., Barron's Educational Series, 1999. 288p. illus. index. $12.95pa. ISBN 0-7641-0851-4.

By most accounts, roses are the most popular garden plants in the world. Literally hundreds of books have been written about every aspect of roses; from their culture, use in the landscape, pruning techniques, and folklore to innumerable regional guides of best rose cultivators. This particular book is strictly a reference guide to roses, with color photographs and brief descriptions of each rose.

After a general introductory chapter, the book is further divided into four chapters representing four classifications of roses: species or wild roses, old garden roses, modern garden roses, and miniature roses. The entry for each variety includes the origin of the rose, its shape and flower color, recommendations for its use in the landscape, and other interesting tidbits. Additional information about each rose can be found in a cultivation table at the end of the book. Here readers will find data on each rose with regard to fragrance; suitability for cut flowers, bedding, hedging or climbing; its shade tolerance; susceptibility to rose diseases; plant size; and more. A shortcoming in the book that limits its usefulness is that there is no indication of winter hardiness for each rose.

Two other reference guides to roses that are quite similar in their presentation are *Roses* (see ARBA 97, entry 1277) and the popular *Taylor's Guide to Roses* (rev. ed., Houghton Mifflin, 1995). Both of these guides do indicate the level of winter hardiness, making them more useful to the American gardener. However, the photographs and descriptions in this book are excellent, so it still deserves a place in the public library's gardening collection.—**Elaine F. Jurries**

1339. Grimshaw, John. **The Gardener's Atlas: The Origins, Discovery, and Cultivation of the World's Most Popular Garden Plants.** Willowdale, Ont., Firefly Books, 1998. 224p. illus. maps. index. $29.95. ISBN 1-55209-226-7.

Many gardeners probably do not stop and think of the origins of the flowers they tend so carefully. Yet flowers, in addition to being beautiful, have fascinating histories. Grimshaw, a noted botanist, has selected 20 families of plants and reviews their origins and how they were carried to new areas of the world—ultimately becoming the flowers we enjoy today.

Among those plants Grimshaw includes are narcissus, begonias, gentians, pinks, daisies, heather, geraniums, iris, peas, lilies, oleanders, orchids, poppies, primroses, buttercups, roses, camellias, pansies, and ferns. The text is liberally supplemented with 300 color photographs and illustrations and 50 maps. In addition, there are supplemental articles on such subjects as the gardens of Islam and the medieval garden. Sidebars on botanists and on various aspects of flowers and gardens combine to make this an appealing book to browse through.

The work is not comprehensive, thus limiting its reference value. It is, however, a good source of information on the origins of the included plants. With its reasonable cost, libraries might consider buying a copy for reference and one to circulate. [R: LJ, 1 Nov 98, p. 118]—**January Adams**

1340. Hood, Susan. **National Audubon Society First Field Guide: Wildflowers.** New York, Scholastic, 1998. illus. index. $17.95. ISBN 0-590-05464-3.

As anyone who has seen them classifying and trading Pokemon cards can attest, children are natural classifiers, even to the extent of understanding evolutionary relationships and fine distinctions between similar types. So a series of field guides to the natural world expressly for children is a great idea, if done well. This volume, in a series that includes guides to birds, insects, and rocks and minerals, improves on a similar effort sponsored by the Audubon Society in the early 1980s. Those tiny softcover books, the Audubon Society Beginner Guides, published by Random House in 1982, were perhaps too simple for all but the youngest children. This new effort is much more ambitious. It combines an introductory look at plant anatomy, physiology, and ecology with a beginner's field guide to the most common flowers of North America.

Much of the introductory section is in question-and-answer format, with two-page spreads answering questions such as "What is a fruit?" or "What is the purpose of a flower's color?" The answers are given with colorful illustrations of both common everyday plants and some of the less familiar oddities of nature that are guaranteed to capture children's interest.

The field guide section has 1-page write-ups on 50 of the most common North American wildflowers, plus on the facing page smaller photographs and descriptions of 2 to 3 flowers that either look similar or are closely related. The one flaw is in organization. The main flowers are grouped by color, although the reader is never alerted to this fact. The author has developed a novel identification system based on flower silhouettes, and although a silhouette symbol is included with each flower, no effort is made to group flowers of the same shape. The best way to use this field guide is just to page through the 100 pages of flower photographs, looking for the plant in question. Because the pictures throughout the volume are exquisite, and the choice of flowers is a good sampling of the wildflowers most likely to be found across North America, this system actually works fairly well. Anyone who becomes truly interested in wildflower identification will need a more complete regional or national guidebook, but this volume is a wonderful introduction to the hobby for both children and adults.—**Carol L. Noll**

1341. Markley, Robert. Elizabeth D. Crawford. **Encyclopedia of Roses.** Hauppauge, N.Y., Barron's Educational Series, 1999. 240p. illus. maps. index. $35.00. ISBN 0-7641-5193-2.

Whether this book is used to find a hardy rose that blooms yearly, without fail, or to unearth the most unique varieties, it is an aesthetically pleasing book with illustrations that bring the roses to life. But do not let this pretty cover fool you, for it is also a comprehensive guide to gardening not only roses, but other shrubs, herbs, and flowers as well. A detailed history, from before man into the new millennium, proclaims this queen of flowers throughout the ages in art, music, and literature. General information includes pruning, watering, fertilization, pest and disease control, home remedies, winter protection, right tools to use, and how to cultivate good breeding in ones roses. Colorful charts are full of clearly stated information about growing requirements for a wide variety of roses. Gardening tips for the best lighting, soil, and climate conditions help to match plant and grower temperaments. This work can be used as a manual for planting, cutting, drying, and even cooking with various floral arrangements. The "Rose Atlas" lists statistics on more than 170 varieties grown the world over. Information includes character, year introduced, color, height, and planting requirements of individual species. "Rose Lexicon" is a compact section containing fast facts and definitions about the world of roses. A "Hardiness Zone Map" covers all 50 states. The index, although comprehensive, has some problems with vocabulary representation within the text, which could be due to the translation process from German to English. Even with indexing problems, this book is exquisite and is recommended for all public libraries.—**Kimberley D. Harris**

1342. McMullen, Conley K. **Flowering Plants of the Galápagos.** Ithaca, N.Y., Cornell University Press, 1999. 370p. illus. maps. index. $59.95; $29.95pa. ISBN 0-8014-3710-5; 0-8014-8621-1pa.

For remote, arid islands located 960 kilometers west of Ecuador with no luxury resorts, the Galápagos Islands are becoming a surprisingly popular tourist destination. The reason, of course, is the role their unique wildlife played in Darwin's formulation of the theory of evolution. In the finches and reptiles of the different islands, the principle of adaptive radiation of immigrant species to fill various ecological niches is significant. So too with the flora, although often the vegetation of the islands is ignored when discussing the natural history of the islands. Almost 30 percent of the plants found on the islands are seen nowhere else in the world. This is the first comprehensive field guide to the plant life of the Galápagos meant for the amateur. At the same time, it is detailed enough to be of use to many of the scientists working on the islands.

This guide includes most of the flowering plants likely to be seen by a visitor to the islands—436 different plants, 266 of which are pictured in color photographs. The entries are not arranged in taxonomical order as in most biological keys, but in an easy-to-use arrangement based on growth type (e.g., tree, vine, shrub, herb, cactus). Within growth types, plants are grouped by leaf arrangement (e.g., alternate, opposite), then by flower color. Each entry then includes scientific and common names, and such information as range, which islands the plant inhabits, description, and interesting details of the history and ecology of the variety. Of particular note are the details on the interaction between the vegetation and the famous animal inhabitants of the islands. The author has included several features to make this guide even more user-friendly. There is an extensive glossary of plant terms, and a list of plants that are likely to be encountered at the most popular visitor sites. The index includes both scientific and common names, and there are numerous cross-references between related or similar species within the body of the guide. This work is destined to be a valuable resource for the amateur naturalists who have made the Galápagos their destination of choice.
—**Carol L. Noll**

1343. Millar, Andreé. **Orchids of Papua New Guinea.** Portland, Oreg., Timber Press, 1999. 118p. illus. maps. index. $34.95. ISBN 0-88192-438-5.

The purpose of this book is as a geographic and pictorial work not a botanical record. The author's enthusiasm for the subject is demonstrated in the anecdotal text and her description of Papua New Guinea as a "wonderland for orchids" in the introductory pages. The introduction provides a brief but comprehensive history of the country and its orchids. Throughout, the text is enlivened with superb color photographs and excellent line drawings. This is particularly valuable in the species description section. Following Schlechter's Orchidaceae of German New Guinea this part is organized by group, section, and genus. Most descriptions cover the habitat and a botanical summary of the plant and flowers. Additional information on photographing orchids, climate, orchids and the native peoples, cultivation tips, and a list of famous orchid botanists can be found in the five appendixes.

Unfortunately, there is a small typographical error in the appendixes (appendix V is titled appendix IV). Also, this book would be too unwieldy for the field. However, it would make an excellent home or laboratory reference. Anyone with an interest in orchids would enjoy this book. It is highly recommended.
—**Katherine Margaret Thomas**

Succulents

1344. Grantham, Keith, and Paul Klaassen. **The Plantfinder's Guide to Cacti & Other Succulents.** Portland, Oreg., Timber Press, 1999. 192p. illus. index. $34.95. ISBN 0-88192-425-3.

The Plantfinder's Guide to Cacti & Other Succulents is a short, encyclopedic work about cacti and succulents. Succulents, the more inclusive term, refers to plants that grow chiefly in arid and semiarid parts of the world and includes all families of cacti. In order to preserve moisture and minimize evaporation, succulent species have evolved into many weird, often beautiful, and sometimes downright grotesque shapes in response to the hostile climates they inhabit.

The Plantfinder's Guide to Cacti & Other Succulents is heir apparently to a 1987 book by John Pilbeam entitled *Cacti for the Connoisseur: A Guide for Growers & Collectors*. Timber Press, a house specializing in "better works for gardeners, horticulturists, and botanists," published both. The layout of the books is strikingly similar, although the newer guide has even more eye appeal due to better-quality color plates and a more aesthetically interesting placement of more than 100 color photographs interspersed among the entries. Following the preface, several short chapters address such topics as the history, cultivation, propagation, and conservation of succulents that are threatened in many parts of the world. The chapter devoted to Latin nomenclature and taxonomy emphasizes the evolving nature of the classification of cacti and succulents.

The body of this guide is arranged dictionary style. Nineteen families and numerous genera and species are included. The authors, hobbyists and longtime members of the British Cactus and Succulent Society, have chosen plants they consider to be of the most potential interest to novice through intermediate succulent growers and enthusiasts. Grantham and Klaassen wish to capture the attention of readers who might then pursue a particular genus, such as haworthia, echinocactus, or opuntia, in a separate monograph.

Appendixes list major desert botanical gardens of the world, indicate where to purchase plants, and list locations of societies and specialist groups. An excellent companion Website is pointed out. A glossary, a brief bibliography, and an index of Latin plant names conclude the work. The authors should consider adding a comprehensive subject index to any guide updates.

The Plantfinder's Guide to Cacti & Other Succulents should be considered for purchase by academic, public, and school libraries and for the personal collections of gardeners, botanists, and horticulturists. It would also make an intriguing addition to the bookshelves or coffee tables of sophisticated bibliophiles.
—**Linda D. Tietjen**

Trees and Shrubs

1345. **500 Popular Shrubs and Trees for American Gardeners.** Loretta Barnard, ed. Hauppauge, N.Y., Barron's Educational Series, 1998. 288p. illus. index. $12.95pa. ISBN 0-7641-1178-7.

Editor Barnard and her 3 consultants have adapted *500 Popular Shrubs and Trees for Australian Gardeners* for amateur, contiguous North American gardeners. A helpful hardiness zone map includes 11 zones from 1 (below 50 degrees Fahrenheit) through 11 (above 40 degrees Fahrenheit). Use this work with caution. While advising amateurs planning their first gardens to consider native or exotic plants, attracting birds, and cultivating shrubs and trees, only basics are mentioned. Beginners are urged to consult their agricultural extension agents or nurseries. Ponder each entire discussion from the opening genera statement, to cultivation, and through the species description that concludes with the hardiness zone range. All the genera from Abelia to Ziziphus give two or three labeled, colored photographs on each page. A reference table including scientific name, tree or shrub, zone, height at 5 and 20 years, deciduous or evergreen, and uses is followed by an index that includes popular and scientific names. This volume is part of the Barron's Educational Series. Readers many want to proceed to the more scholarly *Dirr's Hardy Trees and Shrubs: An Illustrated Encyclopedia*, by Michael A. Dirr (see ARBA 98, entry 1456); *Hillier Gardener's Guide to Trees & Shrubs*, edited by John Kelly (R D Association, 1997); and *Plants That Merit Attention, Volume*

II: Shrubs, by Janet Meakin Poor and Nancy Peterson (see ARBA 97, entry 1285). This work is recommended for high schools, public libraries, and garden stores.—**Helen M. Barber**

1346. van Gelderen, C. J., and D. M. van Gelderen. **Maples for Gardens: A Color Encyclopedia.** Portland, Oreg., Timber Press, 1999. 294p. illus. index. $49.95. ISBN 0-88192-472-5.

Maples seem to be a particular favorite of landscapers and horticulturists. Although there are only 124 species of maples in the wild, spread throughout the Northern Hemisphere are now thousands of cultivars and hybrids. Hundreds of these trees are pictured and described in this volume, including an astounding 260 varieties of Japanese maple.

The authors, a father-and-son team of Dutch horticulturists, have traveled the world and their own magnificent family nursery to photograph a wide variety of maples. This book is meant to accompany their 1994 work, *Maples of the World* (see ARBA 95, entry 1554), a more scholarly text also published by Timber Press. Introductory chapters include a discussion of maple taxonomy and uses of maples in gardens. What follows are hundreds of entries, alphabetic by scientific name, with beautiful color pictures of the leaves and bark, sometimes also full views showing the shape of the mature trees, and information on habit, leaves, flowers, fruits, history of discovery or introduction, special attributes for different types of gardens, and hardiness zones. Appendixes include a list of the world's best arboretums and nurseries for viewing maples. Lists of maples for particular purposes are featured as well; for example, "maples suitable for Bonsai," or "maples with purple leaves during spring and summer." Finally, there is a glossary as well as indexes by both scientific name and common name. Many of the trees pictured here are spectacular, but also rare and probably unavailable to the ordinary home gardener. Most of us can only dream of growing these exotic varieties, but perhaps publication of this book will encourage nurseries to be a little more adventurous in their offerings, going beyond the usual silver maple, Norway maple, and Japanese maple. [R: LJ, Aug 99, p. 80]—**Carol L. Noll**

NATURAL HISTORY

1347. **Encyclopedia of Animal Rights and Animal Welfare.** Marc Bekoff and Carron A. Meaney, eds. Westport, Conn., Greenwood Press, 1998. 446p. illus. index. $59.95. ISBN 0-313-29977-3.

This reference work offers an overview of the issues on the use and abuse of animals along with the ways in which different groups are tackling the issue of animal welfare and animal rights. A multidisciplinary collection of contributors from disciplines such as biology, psychology, education, law, and theology have been tapped to provide an essay that discusses the central theme from different perspectives.

Other than the vague manner in which Bekoff indicates how the topics were chosen, the essays cover a wide array of topics pertaining to the subject matter and include animals living in highly controlled laboratory environments to those living in the wild. Each essay is well written and provides a good introduction to the topic. The entries are arranged in alphabetic order, vary in length from one to two pages, and each ends with a bibliography and the author's name. Some of the larger topics have been subdivided into smaller sections written by different contributors. Cross-references are used throughout to lead readers to other relevant topics. Also included are a chronology, an annotated directory of organizations involved in animal welfare or who provide educational materials, an index, and information about the contributors to this resource. Another plus is the well-written foreword by Jane Goodall. Few illustrations are included, although some black-and-white photographs are used.

This work makes an excellent addition to the literature on animal rights and animal welfare. This is a definite purchase for academic libraries, although public libraries may find it useful. [R: Choice, Nov 98, p. 496; LJ, 15 April 98, p. 68; BL, 15 Sept 98, p. 260; SLJ, Feb 99, p. 132; RUSQ, Spring 99, p. 301]
—**Julia Perez**

1348. **Oryx Guide to Natural History: The Earth and All Its Inhabitants.** By Patricia Barnes-Svarney and Thomas E. Svarney. Phoenix, Ariz., Oryx Press, 1999. 252p. illus. index. $62.50. ISBN 1-57356-159-2.

Oryx Press began in the mid-1990s to publish a series of guides to educational training programs (e.g., community colleges and distance learning) and guided to ethnic genealogy (e.g., Chinese American and Jewish American). This latest Oryx guide has been directed to the study of natural history and reflects a major new category of coverage. This volume is a cross-disciplinary approach to the natural world that "offers the reader a condensed version of the most important topics—from the beginnings of the universe and our planet, to the plants and animals inhabiting our world," and is meant only to be "a compendium of the highlights" (p. xi).

Barnes-Svarney and Svarney have strong backgrounds in the physical sciences, geosciences, engineering sciences, physics, and the materials sciences and have written numerous popular science books and articles. This title is organized under 30 topics, each providing a concise introduction; a stand-out tabular presentation of the timeline of the topic; a detailed, encyclopedia-type entry describing the "highlights" of the topic, including discoveries, expeditions, publications, and breakthroughs; and an alphabetic list with definitions of key terms.

Also included are 44 tables (e.g., "Human Taxonomy," "Ocean Trenches" and "Closest Stars Compared"), appendixes on "Careers in Natural History" and "Natural History Sites on the World Wide Web," a glossary, selected references, and an index. Inserted in selected topics is a sidebar that is deemed of significance to the authors. For example, two-thirds of a page is devoted to "Talking Time" under the chapter on the geologic time scale. Although the volume is nicely designed, location of information will depend heavily on experience. No obvious logic dictates the rationale for separate chapters. However, the attractive presentation and readability may be suitable for users in public libraries and school media centers, although advanced students will seek other sources focused on their specialized needs.—**Laurel Grotzinger**

1349. Schmidt, Diane. **A Guide to Field Guides: Identifying the Natural History of North America.** Englewood, Colo., Libraries Unlimited, 1999. 304p. index. (Reference Sources in Science and Technology Series). $65.00. ISBN 1-56308-707-3.

Vacationers, hikers, bird-watchers, and others have long relied on the compact field guide to help them identify and describe features of the natural world. Large numbers of these guides have been produced, creating a potential use for a bibliographic guide to these works. Schmidt's guide provides descriptions of over 1,300 such titles, mostly published since 1980. Only guides that treat North American subjects and can commonly be found in bookstores and libraries are included here, though the author maintains a free Website with considerably more titles that are either more specialized or international in scope. Subjects of the guides range from the expected birds, flowers, and trees to more unusual topics like astronomy and weather, geology, and man-made objects (e.g., windmills and barns). The entries are quite brief and contain no evaluation, but they present sufficient information to judge the depth and approach of each title. The titles are grouped according to type of organism or other subject, then arranged by geographic region.

Schmidt has gathered a significant number and range of guides, though some evaluative comments would allow easier selection between similar titles. The author makes no pretense of this work being comprehensive, yet the sections on astronomy and geology seem a bit thin—excellent series such as the Roadside Geology books (Mountain Press) are not included. The reference usefulness would also have been augmented by a geographic index that would provide more specific locations than the simple division into eastern and western North America found in the text. These minor criticisms aside, this work offers a good starting point for seekers of appropriate guides to take into the field. [R: BL, 1 Dec 99, pp. 733-735]

—**Christopher W. Nolan**

ZOOLOGY

General Works

1350. **Animal Anatomy on File.** rev. ed. By the Diagram Group. New York, Facts on File, 1999. 1v. (various paging). illus. index. $165.00 looseleaf w/binder. ISBN 0-8160-3875-9.

The idea behind this looseleaf collection is very simple: It provides teachers with diagrams of animal anatomy suitable for photocopying, which can be used as study guides and in tests. Starting with invertebrates and moving to mammals (including human anatomy), the animals most often used in classroom study are presented in clear, simple line drawings. Most are pictured on several pages, including an external view, muscles, digestive system, nervous system, circulatory system, and excretory and reproductive systems. Conveniently for the use in testing, the diagrams are labeled with numbers, with the text off to the side where it can be easily covered before photocopying. The collection is large, with 50 different animals represented, grouped in 8 chapters, some of which are pictured on 5 or more pages. All the highlights of high school biology are here: the earthworm, the frog, the fetal pig, plus many animals that are obviously here only for comparison, such as the Portuguese man-of-war and the bald eagle. An introductory chapter gives useful diagrams on animal classification, cell biology, and embryology. This collection will obviously be of great use to biology teachers at all levels, although its usefulness could be increased if accompanied by a CD-ROM where the diagrams could be presented as clip art and easily sized and included in presentations.
—**Carol L. Noll**

1351. **Animals: A Macmillan Illustrated Encyclopedia.** Philip Whitfield, ed. New York, Macmillan Library Reference/Simon & Schuster Macmillan, 1999. 3v. illus. index. $120.00/set. ISBN 0-02-865420-X.

The 1st edition of this encyclopedia, published in 1984, covered mammals, reptiles, birds, amphibians, and fishes in one volume. This edition packages the same information (even the foreword and introduction are the same) in a 3-volume set. More than 2,000 animals are covered in brief field guide entries, organized by taxonomic category of order, family, genus, and species. Each entry includes information on the animal's size, breeding patterns, feeding habits, habitat and range, behaviors, common and scientific names, and conservation status. As in the previous edition, beautiful color illustrations accompany each entry.

Each volume contains a glossary, an alphabetic index and a classification list. Volume 3 has a list of threatened species, world zoos and aquariums, and conservation organizations. A bibliography is also included. New to this edition is an essay on classification and evolution and the presentation of the cladistic method of taxonomy. Unlike the brief species information that is accessible to upper elementary school students, the classification and cladogram explanations are written for an older audience. Libraries owning the older edition should not feel compelled to replace it with this one just for the added information.

Other titles on the topic, although not covering as many species, do provide more in-depth coverage of individual animals. For example, the *Great Book of Animals* (Courage Books, 1997) has double-paged spreads with beautiful illustrations for more than 700 animals. This set would be a good choice for libraries needing to replace a quick reference title or a worn older edition.—**Marlene M. Kuhl**

1352. Dalton, Stephen. **Secret Worlds.** Willowdale, Ont., Firefly Books, 1999. 159p. illus. index. $35.00. ISBN 1-55209-384-0.

This beautiful book is a collection of Dalton's nature photographs. Most of the photographs are of animals near his home in Sussex, England, with a few scattered over the rest of the world. Dalton has a particular interest in photographing animal flight, and there are numerous stunning pictures of flying insects, birds, and bats. There are about 140 photographs of 111 subjects, including 21 mammals, 21 birds, 7 reptiles, 12 amphibians, 1 fish, 38 insects, 4 spiders or spiderwebs, 1 mollusk, 11 plants, and 5 landscapes. The photographs are accompanied by short accounts of the creature or of the taking of the photograph. There is an index in which creatures are listed under both common and scientific names.

Although not primarily a reference work, this book may be useful in reference collections as a source of images of the natural world. As such, it is not comprehensive, and many taxonomic groups are not represented. The quality of the images is quite spectacular.—**Frederic F. Burchsted**

1353.   Nagel, Rob. **Endangered Species.** Farmington Hills, Mich., U*X*L/Gale, 1999. 3v. illus. maps. index. $84.00/set. ISBN 0-7876-1875-6.

This is a nicely laid-out book for middle school students. The general overviews and species accounts are easy to understand. The book covers 200 endangered species from a broad taxonomic range: mammals, birds, reptiles, amphibians, fish, mollusks, insects, arachnids, crustaceans, and plants. There are 3 volumes. The 1st covers mammals; the 2d covers arachnids, birds, crustaceans, insects, and mollusks; and the 3d covers amphibians, fish, plants, and reptiles. Each volume has the same helpful glossary; introductory sections; a further research section with books, journals, and Internet addresses; and an index, making it easy to navigate between books or to review general information.

The introductory sections are titled "Reader's Guide"; "Endangerment and Its Causes: An Overview"; "Endangered Species Fact Boxes and Classification: An Explanation"; "International Union for Conservation of Nature and Natural Resources (IUCN–The World Conservation Union)"; and "Endangered Species Act." Within each book, sections are organized by class and within class. Accounts are alphabetic by common name.

Each species account contains the common and scientific names of the species, classification information, current status in the wild according to the International Union for Conservation of Nature and Natural Resources and the United States Fish and Wildlife Service, the country where the species currently lives, and locator maps with the range. Each account has 3 sections: "Description of Biology," "Habitat and Current Distribution," and "History and Conservation Measures." Most entries have color or black-and-white photographs. This is a good purchase for any school library. [R: BL, 15 April 99, pp. 1544-1546; BR, Sept/Oct 99, p. 70; SLJ, Aug 99, p. 186]—**Constance Rinaldo**

Birds

1354.   Bird, David M. **The Bird Almanac: The Ultimate Guide to Essential Facts and Figures of the World's Birds.** Willowdale, Ont., Firefly Books, 1999. 460p. $19.95pa. ISBN 1-55209-323-9.

This handbook provides a concise, but remarkably inclusive, reference to the world of birds, birdwatchers, and ornithologists. Nearly half of the volume is devoted to an updated world checklist of bird species, with notations of range and, where applicable, conservation status. Traditional taxonomic organization of birds is compared with the latest DNA-based arrangement of orders and families. Basic avian biology is reviewed with anatomical tables and drawings, including, for example, plumage and molt, skeletal systems, and digestive tract. Data on avian reproduction include incubation periods, clutch sizes, and sex ratios. Again, there are helpful diagrams when necessary (e.g., embryonic development of the egg). Survival data and avian diseases are reviewed briefly with management and conservation figures. A substantial "who's who" in bird biology gives very short biographical comments on more than 200 ornithologists from John J. Audubon to the present. For backyard bird-watchers there are tables on bird box dimensions, attractive plantings for birds, and of course detailed listings on bird feeding. Birders will also find useful lists of a wide variety of ornithological resources, from journal and Internet addresses to videos and CDs of birdsong. The handbook concludes with a glossary of terms from avian biology. This handy guide will be a useful reference, especially for enthusiastic amateurs. [R: LJ, 15 June 99, p. 68]

—**Charles Leck**

1355. Hancock, James. **Birds of the Wetlands.** San Diego, Calif., AP Natural World/Academic Press, 1999. 176p. illus. maps. index. $29.95. ISBN 0-12-322727-5.

This is a collection of short essays (10-12 pages), copiously illustrated with color photographs by Hancock, a British ornithologist, conservationist, and author of books about herons and other long-legged wading birds (e.g., *The Herons Handbook*, Harper, 1984). Each essay covers a wetland area where Hancock has visited (e.g., the Everglades). Six of the twelve wetlands covered are in Asia and one is in North America. The essays are somewhat impressionistic: a little history, an account of Hancock's experiences in the area, conservation problems and outlook, and the bird species encountered there. Suggestions for further reading are included as well as an index.

Birds of the Wetlands has limited reference value. Coverage is very selective and the essays are anecdotal rather than purely factual. However, Hancock's excellent color photographs (nearly 200), make it a worthwhile item for the browsing and circulating collections of public, school, and academic libraries.
—**Jonathan F. Husband**

1356. Howell, Steve N. G. **A Bird-Finding Guide to Mexico.** Ithaca, N.Y., Cornell University Press, 1999. 365p. illus. maps. index. $29.95pa. ISBN 0-8014-8581-9.

For many years author Howell has been an active field ornithologist throughout Mexico. With this book he shares knowledge of the best bird-watching sites of the country. Chapters are arranged geographically for 14 regions, from Baja California to the Yucatan Peninsula. Each chapter has a regional overview and several to a dozen specific site discussions. These site reports include information on access, very detailed directions for locations and seasons, and a local map. The reports also include local checklists of birds, with particular note of rarities and other species of special interest. An appendix presents similar information for the entire country by tabular summaries arranged taxonomically. The book's introductory material gives practical information for travel throughout Mexico today, with appropriate recommendations and warning for bird-watchers. With this book visitors can easily tour any of more than 100 top birding spots in Mexico—one needs only to supplement it with a bird identification guide.—**Charles Leck**

1357. Lukas, David. **Watchable Birds of the Great Basin.** Missoula, Mont., Mountain Press, 1999. 162p. illus. maps. index. $16.00pa. ISBN 0-87842-397-4.

Every amateur field naturalist has learned that the most practical identification guide is one that is well illustrated and designed for a specific area. This small field guide for the beginning or casual birder does well on both counts. The Great Basin, which includes the area between the Rockies and the Sierra Nevada mountain ranges, centers on Nevada with outlying fringes in adjacent Oregon, Idaho, Utah, Arizona, and California. The terrain, predominantly desert dotted with a handful of lakes, rivers, and mountain ranges, offers about 70 watchable birds. Lukas groups the birds by three major environment types. The treatment is uniform: common and Latin name plus etymology; "eye-catchers," a sentence or two giving the bird's most obvious features; a paragraph of natural history (i.e., ecological information, behavior, odd facts); and where it can be seen. One novel feature is the treatment of size. Rather than giving each bird's size in inches, Lukas has a "shadowgraph" of seven common bird profiles on each text page. A vertical line inserted along the scale marks the relative size of the described bird. This is far more useful than a bare measurement, which is often nearly useless in the field. The book's design is well thought out and the glossy full- and half-page bird photographs by Brian Small and Don Baccus are excellent. A small-scale map indicates the half-dozen major bird refuges in the Basin.—**D. Barton Johnson**

1358. Schorre, Barth. **The Wood Warblers: An Introductory Guide.** Austin, Tex., University of Texas Press, 1998. 140p. illus. index. (The Corrie Herring Hooks Series, no.35). $35.00; $17.95pa. ISBN 0-292-77729-9; 0-292-77730-2pa.

The wood warblers are one of the most colorful and popular groups of North American birds. This handy book is a beginner's pictorial guide to the 49 species that commonly nest in the United States and

Canada. As such, it is a showcase for the author's outstanding warbler photographs, which were obtained during spring migrations over a period of more than 20 years. Although an amateur ornithologist, Schorre has become well known for his high-quality camera work with birds—the more than 90 color portraits in this book will be enjoyed and admired by many birdwatchers.

In addition to he photographs there is a short, one-page text for each warbler species that briefly reviews identification features, range, and nesting habitats. The text's brief, introductory style is much more limited in detail than that available in other monographs on the wood warbler family. Introductory pages give an overview of warblers, their migration, and conservation. Novice birders will find this to be an informative little book that features a fine gallery of warbler photographs.—**Charles Leck**

Domestic Animals

1359.   **Barron's Encyclopedia of Dog Breeds.** By D. Caroline Coile. Hauppauge, N.Y., Barron's Educational Series, 1998. 328p. illus. index. $26.95. ISBN 0-7641-5097-9.

The *Encyclopedia of Dog Breeds* covers 150 breeds of dogs. This book is divided by groups—"The Sporting Group," "The Hound Group," "The Working Group," "The Terrier Group," "The Toy Group," "The Non-Sporting Group," and "The Herding Group"—and is preceded by a section called "The Right Dog." This section includes some practical advice to consider when choosing a dog, and how to use the Breed Profiles that cover each breed.

Each group is introduced by a short paragraph that gives an overview of the dog breeds in that group. Each breed that is covered has a short history of that breed and insights into the temperament, upkeep, health, and form and function of that breed. There is a boxed sidebar that gives some standards of the breed as well as an "At a Glance" guide that gives insight into that breed's energy level, ease of training, watchdog ability, and other pertinent information that should factor into any decision when choosing a family dog.

In the back of this book are definitions of medical conditions, a guide to hereditary health problems, and a glossary, as well as a section on dog anatomy. This delightful reference book is highly recommended for any public library's reference collection or anyone considering acquiring a dog.—**Pamela J. Getchell**

Fishes

1360.   Hoffman, Glenn L. **Parasites of North American Freshwater Fishes.** 2d ed. Ithaca, N.Y., Comstock Publishing Associates/Cornell University Press, 1999. 539p. illus. index. $90.00. ISBN 0-8014-3409-2.

Hoffman, a leading fish disease expert of the past 50 years, has again produced the definitive guide to the identification of freshwater fish parasites. The 1st edition, considered the "bible" of this subject area, was written over 30 years ago, so the 2d edition has been updated and expanded to include the research and expansion of knowledge that have occurred in the study of these fish parasites over the past few decades. This text includes information from the literature dating from the time of Linnaeus up through 1992.

The manual is intended as an aid to the identification of freshwater fish parasites in North America as well as related foreign species, with the most important parasites covered sufficiently for research background. Alaska and Mexico are not well represented, as little work has been reported from these areas. Hoffman includes introductory chapters on public health aspects of fish parasites, methods used to examine fish, and brief descriptions of fish parasites by location and genera. The main body of the work consists of species summaries that are grouped by family and genus. Each summary includes information on identification, life cycles, host information, prevention, treatment, and eradication. Reference citations for literature pertinent to the species are used throughout each summary. Inserted in each chapter are plates, drawings, illustrations, and black-and-white photographs. Other useful information is also included at the end of the text, such as checklists, miscellaneous information on fishes and disease control, a glossary, an index, and an extensive reference list.

Aimed for use by scientists or hobbyists interested in fish health, this guide will serve the needs of this specialized audience. This revised edition is destined to remain the most important source in this area. This work is recommended for academic or specialized libraries only.—**Julia Perez**

Insects

1361. **Ball Identification Guide to Greenhouse Pests and Beneficials.** By Stanton Gill and John Sanderson. Batavia, Ill., Ball Publishing, 1998. 244p. illus. index. $67.00. ISBN 1-883052-17-3.

This identification guide goes a long way toward helping practitioners control insect and mite organisms in greenhouses. It emphasizes the use of integrated pest management (IPM), an effective way of controlling pests through early detection, identification, and control. For ease of use, the book is divided into 3 sections. The 1st provides a useful primer on IPM and the tools necessary to establish a program in a greenhouse. Of particular interest to users will be the identification guide section that comprises the bulk of the text. A final part discusses pest management to specific crops. A real aid to identification are the more than 450 photographs, and the occasional black-and-white line drawings, that are spread throughout the book as figures. Accompanying each figure is a short, concise annotation. In the identification section, each major pest account includes a general description, plant damage and group characteristics, pest biology, monitoring methods, life cycle information, and biological controls. An interesting chapter in the identification section is entitled "Other Pests in the Greenhouse" and describes invertebrates such as slugs, snails, cockroaches, earwigs, and crickets. Physically, the book is well bound and lies flat for hands-off use. The index provides page references to the photographs and to scientific and common names. The text concludes with a glossary of common terms.

The authors state in the introduction that the guide will be helpful for practitioners working in United States greenhouses. It should be noted that the book will be useful to Canadian professionals as well. The book is highly recommended for specialized libraries.—**Katherine Margaret Thomas**

1362. H. R. Bolland, J. Guttierrez, and C. H. W. Flechtmann. **World Catalogue of the Spider Mite Family (Acari: Tetranychidae).** Boston, Brill Academic, 1998. 392p. index. $147.50. ISBN 90-04-11087-9.

This world catalog is the first comprehensive list of spider (tetranychid) mites since the world revision of Pritchard and Baker in 1955. Tetranychidae mites are interesting to many readers because they are extremely injurious to crops throughout the world and can reek great economic damage. This catalog is very well organized. Typical of many classification texts, the book opens with a key to genera to aid identification. The key includes the names of 84 new combinations and the restoration of 4 species names. This key is followed by an alphabetic listing of 1,189 species of Tetranychidae, representing the total number of mites described in the world and known to the authors at the end of 1996. For each species the authors have meticulously included bibliographic references to the original description, any successive synonyms, a list of host plants, and the geographic locations to the first record with corresponding bibliographic references.

The final four indexes provide further reference points. These include an index to specific designations, species name, host plant and host plant classified by family, and geographic location. Additionally, there is the list of 1,227 bibliographic references. These papers represent a good cross section of the world literature on spider mites, but not all of them are written in English.

The catalog is not cheap but is worth the price for the wealth and organization of the information. It is a highly specialized book that will be invaluable to practitioners working in agricultural control and plant protection.—**Katherine Margaret Thomas**

1363. **Identifying British Insects and Arachnids: An Annotated Bibliography of Key Works.** Peter C. Barnard, ed. London, Natural History Museum and New York, Cambridge University Press, 1999. 353p. index. $80.00. ISBN 0-521-63241-2.

Having encountered an unfamiliar insect or arachnid (i.e., spider, mite, tick), one naturally wishes to identify it or determine its species. Knowing the correct name allows communication with other naturalists and unlocks the wealth of accumulated knowledge in the literature. Field guides and other popular works include only a selection of the insects or arachnids of a given area. Except for butterflies, identification involves knowledge and use of a vast and scattered literature. Finding the currently authoritative source may be more difficult than making the identification and may be impossible for an amateur naturalist. This situation is much eased for Great Britain and Ireland by this excellent bibliography, which, for each insect or arachnid group, indicates the proper sources (books and periodical articles) for identification and lists distributional studies. The citations are briefly annotated. There is a short taxonomic or distributional overview of each group and an initial chapter introducing the taxonomic literature and explaining how to obtain copies of needed publications.

This book is essential for any library dealing with British or Irish fauna. It is also of some wider interest because books of broader regional or worldwide coverage are also included under each insect or arachnid group.—**Frederic F. Burchsted**

1364. Layberry, Ross A., Peter W. Hall, and J. Donald Lafontaine. **The Butterflies of Canada.** Buffalo, N.Y., University of Toronto Press, 1998. 280p. illus. maps. index. $100.00; $29.95pa. ISBN 0-8020-0898-4; 0-8020-7881-8pa.

The Butterflies of Canada is an extensive guide to the butterflies found in Canada. Not to be mistaken for a field guide, this book contains descriptive accounts of close to 300 butterfly species recorded in Canada, with individual distribution maps generated from a database of extensive location records.

For those not familiar with Canadian butterflies, the authors include an introduction to the study and distribution, classification, systematics, and life history of these butterflies. The main body of the work, however, is the species accounts. Each group of accounts is arranged by family then subfamily, with common and scientific names included for all species. Each species account averages from one-half page to a page in length and includes several categories, such as identification of the larva, adult, similar species, and subspecies. All species accounts have plate and figure references. Also included later in the text are color plates, a checklist, a glossary, a bibliography, and indexes to the butterflies and larval food plants.

The authors have certainly done a thorough study of their subject as evidenced by the amount of information found in this book. Even the selection criteria are listed for the butterflies selected for inclusion and the names used for them. This work will be of use for researchers and libraries interested in the topic and the geographic area.—**Julia Perez**

Mammals

1365. Forsyth, Adrian. **Mammals of North America: Temperate and Arctic Regions.** Willowdale, Ont., Firefly Books, 1999. 350p. illus. maps. index. $40.00. ISBN 1-55209-409-X.

The author of this beautifully done resource is well qualified to write on the more than 35 species of North American mammals explored within the book's pages. Forsyth is a specialist in animal behavior and rainforest ecology as well as a researcher for the Smithsonian Institution. He has first divided the animals into taxonomic classification and then grouped them into order and further into family. Each family receives about 10 pages of thorough description. Each animal is represented with photographs and a map that indicates where they live. A sidebar follows that provides information on the animal's proper name and its meaning, a physical description, the weight and height of the animal, its gestation period and number of offspring, its life span, its diet, and its predators. The description that follows features such topics as why certain animals act as they do and how human intervention affects their habitat and therefore their population. Interspersed throughout the text are magnificent photographs of the animals in their natural habitat. An extensive bibliography and thorough index conclude the work.

Mammals of North America is much more than a field guide. It allows readers insight into the lives and history of the animals featured. With its beautiful photographs and well-written text it will be welcome in both school and public libraries.—**Shannon M. Graff**

1366. Garbutt, Nick. **Mammals of Madagascar.** New Haven, Conn., Yale University Press, 1999. 320p. illus. maps. index. $37.50. ISBN 0-300-07751-3.

Madagascar, an island nation located next to the African mainland, has a diversity of ecological environments that helped foster the evolution of the most unusual mammalian species. This publication provides an up-to-date review of the current literature related to the known mammalian fauna that represents the 6 orders of mammals present on the island.

The morphology, behavior, and ecology of 123 species are covered in detail by the author. Particular attention has been paid to the lemurs, with each of the 4 families in this order represented, while also including the area's lesser-known mammals—the carnivores, rodents, tenrecs, and bats. There are 3 main sections in the book. The introductory chapters discuss the creation of the island of Madagascar, the influences its isolation from the mainland has had on its flora and fauna, and the main biogeographic regions and habitat types these areas support. A lengthy section follows regarding the mammalian species accounts. Each species account, ranging in length from 1 to 2 pages, includes such categories as measurements, description, distribution, behavior, and viewing. Illustrations of the species, distribution maps, and striking color photographs are scattered throughout this section. The last section of the book deals with the island's conservation concerns (protected areas, parks, and reserves) and describes the top mammal-watching sites. A glossary, appendixes, an extensive bibliography, and an index are also included.

This guide serves the needs of users (scientist, tourist, or novice) searching for information on the natural history of Madagascar or its mammals. The information included here is informative, entertaining, and supplemented with plenty of beautiful color photographs, line drawings, and the author's own observations, experiences, and passion for the topic. This work is highly recommended for libraries that collect in the area of natural history.—**Julia Perez**

1367. Nowak, Ronald M. **Walker's Mammals of the World.** 6th ed. Baltimore, Md., Johns Hopkins University Press, 1999. 2v. illus. index. $99.95/set. ISBN 0-8018-5789-9.

Since the 1st edition of *Walker's Mammals of the World* was published in 1964, it has been considered by many to be the most comprehensive reference work on mammals ever written. The 6th edition continues that tradition. A comparison of the latest edition to the 5th edition (see ARBA 93, entry 1572), finds a 25 percent increase in text length, 95 percent of previous generic accounts significantly modified, and 81 new generic accounts added. A goal of the work since the beginning has been to provide a quality photograph of a living representative of every genus of mammal. The black-and-white photographs are excellent in quality. Each genus entry contains information on the number of species known, key literature references, physical description, comparison of characteristics of representative species, description of habitat, general behavior, breeding and care of young, and information on the species' endangered status. This edition takes great care in noting whether a species is endangered or in decline based on the International Union for Conservation of Nature's (IUCN) list of threatened animals. Close to one-half of all of the world's living mammal species are in serious to critical decline.

The high quality of scholarship of this work is evidenced not only in the careful descriptions of each genus, but also in the extensive 172-page bibliography of references. The only other reference work on mammals that approaches the excellence of this set is *Grzimek's Encyclopedia of Mammals* (see ARBA 91, entry 1593). Grzimek's work is nearly as comprehensive as Walker's, and includes color photographs and more information on behavior, ecology, and conservation, but with a much higher price tag. As there has been a significant amount of additional and revised material added since the 5th edition, this latest edition of *Walker's Mammals of the World* is recommended for every academic and public library.

—**Elaine F. Jurries**

Marine Animals

1368. Harbo, Rick M. **Whelks to Whales: Coastal Marine Life of the Pacific Northwest.** Madeira Park, Harbour, 1999. 245p. illus. index. $24.95pa. ISBN 1-55017-183-6.

This field guide covers the larger, more conspicuous, and more interesting species of coastal marine animals and plants in the region from Northern California to Alaska, which is one of the world's richest habitats for marine life. There are 420 species included here, out of about 7,000 in the region. Coverage includes animals from sponges to whales, and from seaweeds to seagrasses.

The species entries are arranged taxonomically, starting with the sponges and proceeding to the marine mammals. The last chapter covers the seaweeds and seagrasses. For each species, common, scientific, and alternate names are provided. Size, geographic range, habitat, description, and comments are provided, as well as color photographs. There are general discussions of distribution, habitat, and scientific names in the introduction. An outline of the classification of the animal kingdom and part of the plant kingdom is included. A glossary and index are also included. There are labeled diagrams of the external anatomy of a few of the animals.

The guide is well written, with the species descriptions authoritative but without overreliance on technical terms. The color photographs are clear and excellent. The overall organization is also excellent. Because the number of species covered is limited, some of the more specialized field guides will be needed as one encounters species not covered here. However, this field guide will serve the intelligent layperson well in identifying the more common marine animals and plants of the Pacific Northwest.—**John Laurence Kelland**

1369. Parker, Steve, and Jane Parker. **The Encyclopedia of Sharks.** Willowdale, Ont., Firefly Books, 1999. 192p. illus. index. $24.95pa. ISBN 1-55209-324-7.

The sinister image of a shark rising from the waters with its sharp-toothed jaws wide open strikes a universal chord of terror in all of us. Because we are both repulsed and fascinated by this magnificent group of sea-dwellers, there is no shortage of books about sharks. *The Encyclopedia of Sharks* joins the ranks of numerous overviews of sharks and their relatives.

This is not an encyclopedia in the traditional sense. Rather it is a loosely compiled narrative of shark lore and information, with an emphasis on color photographs. Chapter headings such as "Super Killers," "Who's Afraid of Sharks," "Sharks in War," "Shark Kith and Kin," "Shark Sizes and Numbers," "From Shallows to the Deep," and "The Survival Suite" are not particularly useful in directing one to specific information. This is a book for the recreational reader, not the serious researcher, and is most suitable for the circulating collection of school and public libraries where the demand for general shark books is high. [R: LJ, 15 Sept 99, p. 71]—**Elaine F. Jurries**

1370. Perrine, Doug. **Sharks & Rays of the World.** Stillwater, Minn., Voyageur Press, 1999. 132p. illus. index. $29.95. ISBN 0-89658-448-8.

There are hundreds of picture books on sharks and their cousins, the rays. This is one of the best. Not only does it have superb photographs, but the text is sharp, clear, accurate, and interesting. The author has taken an explicitly evolutionary and Linnaean approach to the cartilaginous fish, which is all too rare in popular books. This book can serve as a reference text in a library as well as coffee-table decoration.

The book starts by recognizing the renaissance in both the study of sharks and their popular image. No longer are they conventionally seen as implacable enemies of humanity and thereby deserving of death on sight. A more sophisticated and sensitive culture now views sharks as essential components of complex ecosystems, and as beautiful animals to be preserved for their own sake. Ironically, as we begin to better appreciate sharks, they are being "harvested" in commercial fishing and "bather protection measures" at a greater rate than ever before. Sharks are also far less lethal than their usual reputation. The author points out that for every human killed by a shark, 20 million sharks are killed by humans. Fear and greed have driven our relationship with sharks; this book is a sign that we are getting smarter and more compassionate.

The evolutionary sections in the text are excellent. Sharks and rays are carefully defined and described, and then their long history is detailed. The author demolishes the myth that the cartilaginous fish have not appreciable changed in 400 million years. They may have evolved more slowly than mammals, but they have evolved. Several color drawings of ancestral sharks make the point that the past was very different from the present for these animals. The physiology and ecology of sharks and rays are also explained well. The reproductive strategies of these animals are fascinating, and the author shows that many mysteries still remain in our understanding of their biology.

The heart of the book is the "ordering the orders" section where the taxonomy and ecology of major groups are discussed. The information is recent and presented in an easy-to-follow and consistent style. The accompanying photographs are beautiful. Any library will want this book, as will anyone with an interest in the oceans and marine life.—**Mark A. Wilson**

1371. Ripple, Jeff. **Manatees and Dugongs of the World.** Stillwater, Minn., Voyageur Press, 1999. 131p. illus. maps. index. (WorldLife Discovery Guides). $29.95. ISBN 0-89658-393-7.

Manatees and Dugongs of the World is an introduction to the natural history of a species of marine animal that is in grave danger of becoming extinct due to human growth and intervention. The author is a natural history writer and photographer who believes strongly in the responsibility of humans to protect natural wildlife.

After a foreword written by the executive director of Save the Manatee Club, the book is divided into five chapters: "A First Glimpse," "Manatees," "The Dugong and Steller's Sea Cow," "Sirens in Myth and Tradition," and "Finding Sanctuary." These chapters describe the manatee and their close relatives, the dugong and the steller sea cow, including such information as their evolution, habitat, physical description, and anatomy and physiology. The final chapter attempts to tell readers how human-related activities kill up to 35 percent of the manatee population each year. It is a plea for residents of southern coastal regions to become involved in the fight for saving marine life in their area or at least to be aware of the problem when doing their own coastal activities.

The interesting text and beautiful photographs of this work make it a joy to read or just browse through. Although not an essential purchase for the reference collection, it will be welcome and well read in libraries with patrons in southeastern coastal states.—**Shannon M. Graff**

1372. **Sharks.** 2d ed. John D. Stevens, ed. New York, Checkmark Books/Facts on File, 1999. 240p. illus. maps. index. $39.95. ISBN 0-8160-3990-9.

Sharks have become cultural icons, much like dinosaurs. The public is fascinated with strange, primitive, and menacing beasts; and scientists have found many clever ways to use this interest to teach physiology, ecology, and evolution. This book is a superb example of how quality science can be presented attractively and effectively. Most libraries have dozens of shark books on their shelves, and this one should join them. It is profusely and beautifully illustrated with color diagrams and photographs, and the text is readable and highly informative.

This book contains the contributions of almost two dozen shark experts, from paleontologists to marine photographers. It is edited so well that the prose flows smoothly between chapters and sections. The first third of the book is devoted to the origin of sharks, their classification, shark physiology and behavior, and shark ecology. The systematic section is especially important, since general readers rarely see the details of a formal classification. One of the basic premises of the book is that the first step in predicting a shark's behavior is knowing what kind of shark it is. And that mistaken identity provokes most shark scares. The diversity of shark adaptations is very impressive, and the authors use this extraordinary variety to dispel many myths about sharks. Only some, for example, must keep moving in order to breathe, and some nourish their unborn young with placentas analogous to our own. The middle third of the book covers "encounters" with sharks around the world. The reader learns that shark attacks are horrible but relatively rare compared to so many other hazards in the water. The last section of the book is an eclectic set of myths, stories, and observations of sharks. Here is where readers see that people are far more of a threat to sharks than they are to people. Sharks are used for meat, fertilizer, biochemicals, abrasives, cosmetics, paint base, and even corneal transplants. Several species of sharks now face extinction because of overexploitation. The book ends with a short guide to shark resources, including reference books, Websites, and a list of institutions with shark exhibits.—**Mark A. Wilson**

1373. Spalding, David A. E. **Whales of the West Coast.** Madeira Park, Harbour, 1998. 211p. illus. maps. index. $18.95pa. ISBN 1-55017-199-2.

Whales have only recently gained a strong image in Western culture as sentient, complex fellow mammals with social systems, high intelligence, and emotions. This book recognizes the special relationship that has developed between whales and many people, but reminds us that whales have also served as an important, often critical resource, and for many aborigines they were the economic foundation of their societies. The author has produced here a rare combination of whale natural history and the human history of whaling in the Pacific Northwest.

This book is first a guide to the common and rare whales found along the western coast of North America, especially off Vancouver Island. Orcas, dolphins, gray whales, humpbacks, and minkes are treated in detail; the less common right whales, blue whales, belugas, and others are briefly covered. Because the text is concentrated on one region, there is considerable information about particular pods of whales, and even individual whales. The middle portion of the book is devoted to the whaling industry of the Pacific Northwest, and the development of academic and cultural interest in whales. An extraordinary number of whales were taken in these waters with technologies ranging from stone-tipped spears of the Native Americans to the exploding harpoons of Russian "factory ships." This history is illustrated with many old photographs and augmented by the recollections of retired whalers. The last one-third of the book covers vanishing "whale cultures" among the aboriginal and European communities, whale conservation issues (which are treated dispassionately), and the joys of whale watching. A chronology of whaling and a list of library resources are appended at the end. The book has many black-and-white photographs, some of which are unfortunately murky and difficult to interpret.

Libraries in the Pacific Northwest will certainly want this book in their collections because of the strong regional emphasis. Other libraries may not find it as appropriate, unless they have special collections of whaling or conservation literature.—**Mark A. Wilson**

1374. **Whales, Dolphins, and Porpoises.** 2d ed. Carwardine, Mark, ed. New York, Checkmark Books/Facts on File, 1999. 240p. illus. maps. index. $39.95. ISBN 0-8160-3991-7.

This encyclopedic work is organized into three parts. The first part, "Whales of the World," has a chapter on the origin and evolution of whales, and a chapter with descriptions of most cetacean species (including dolphins and porpoises as well as whales). Each entry contains a color illustration and covers appearance, size, habitat, distribution, reproduction, and diet. One chapter covers the general biology of baleen (whalebone) whales. The capabilities of these whales for swimming, feeding, and other functions are discussed as well as population, losses due to whaling, and other information. A similar chapter covers the toothed whales, dolphins, and porpoises. Distribution and ecology are treated in depth in another chapter. Each chapter is written by a different contributor—a recognized expert in that area. "Whales up Close" covers anatomy, senses, reproduction, growth, intelligence, and social behavior. The final part, "Whales and People," covers legends about whales, whaling, cetacean training, and other areas such as stranding. A checklist of living species and a guide to further resources are provided.

The coverage of cetaceans is excellent. Written for the general public yet written by experienced researchers in the field, the work contains many original observations and enough material to be useful in academic as well as public libraries. The color illustrations and photographs are excellent. This book is well written and provides the reader with a lot of information about cetacean biology. [R: BL, 1 Dec 98, p. 682]—**John Laurence Kelland**

Reptiles and Amphibians

1375. Badger, David. **Snakes.** Stillwater, Minn., Voyageur Press, 1999. 144p. illus. index. $35.00. ISBN 0-89658-408-9.

Snakes do not inspire much love or affection as the majority of people are repelled by them. Because of this animosity toward them, snakes do not command the high profile other species do. With this book the author tries to dispel unfounded myths about snakes in order to portray them with greater tolerance and sensitivity, and to call attention to current threats to their populations and habitats. This publication is not written as a field guide, but rather focuses on representative species, exotic and commonplace, from the United States and around the world.

Badger, following in the tradition of other natural historians who in the past wrote popular books about reptiles, presents this book in an easy-to-read, nontechnical manner and includes vivid descriptions, colorful anecdotes, and information gleaned from the herpetological literature dating back to more than a century. Information about the relationship of snakes and humans; physical characteristics and behavior of snakes; species accounts of a select variety of snakes in North America and other parts of the world; and snake conservation are all discussed in the text. Featured are 100 excellent color photographs by John Netherton, a renowned nature photographer, with an explanation given in the appendix of how he captured the vivid shots. A bibliography and an index are also included.

Any reptile fan or natural historian will enjoy reading *Snakes* for its engaging text, or if only to peruse the spectacular photographs. This work is recommended for public and academic libraries.—**Julia Perez**

1376. Campbell, Jonathan A. **Amphibians and Reptiles of Northern Guatemala, The Yucatán, and Belize.** Norman, Okla., University of Oklahoma Press, 1998. 380p. illus. index. (Animal Natural History Series, v.4). $29.95pa. ISBN 0-8061-3066-0.

Numerous species of amphibians and reptiles are profiled in this field guide to the Peten region of northern Guatemala and adjoining areas of Mexico and Belize. The little-known natural history and distribution of each species are summarized in the guide by Campbell, and he includes a variety of species that range from the small and delicate frogs and lizards to dangerously venomous snakes.

The guide is divided into 4 parts: an introduction, which includes information on the environment, identification, and conservation; two main sections that include 160 species summaries of the region's amphibians and reptiles; and appendixes. Each species summary ranges from a page to two pages in length and includes common names in English and Spanish, the scientific name, plate number, description, natural history, distribution, and remarks. The amphibian section includes several species of caecilians, salamanders, toads, and frogs. The reptile section covers turtles, lizards, snakes, and crocodilians. Inserted into the species accounts are 189 color plates. Also of use are the appendixes, which include several identification keys (in English and Spanish) for several species and groups of species. A glossary, an extensive list of references, and an index are also included.

Aimed for use by scientists, tourists, and a general audience, this guide can serve the needs of these disparate users. The information included here is informative and entertaining, and is supplemented with plenty of color photographs, line drawings, maps, and the author's own observations, anecdotes, folklore, and experiences. This reference work is recommended for libraries that collect in the area of natural history or in this specific geographical location.—**Julia Perez**

1377. Necas, Petr. **Chameleons: Nature's Hidden Jewels.** Malabar, Fla., Krieger Publishing, 1999. illus. index. $47.50. ISBN 1-57524-137-4.

Originally published in German in 1995, this book is partly a compilation of published information and partly a summary of unpublished data from various breeders, biologists, and veterinarians. Former publications have frequently misspelled many Latin names. This work points out these errors and thoroughly corrects them. Numerous chameleon species are discussed in detail, from Chameleo africanus to Brookesia superciliaris. The species accounts offer the most recent captive husbandry information known as well as how a particular genus is related to the others. The book is divided into 2 sections. The 1st is a general section with information on the origin and biology of chameleons. The 2d section discusses the various species. Appendixes include a list of recent and fossil species; a table of recent species, their habitats, reproductive strategies, and maximum sizes; and a chronology of valid and described taxa. A bibliography is provided along with lists of cited and recommended literature at the end of each chapter. The work concludes with a glossary and an index.—**Cari Ringelheim**

32 Engineering

CHEMICAL ENGINEERING

1378. **Chemical Elements: From Carbon to Krypton.** By David E. Newton. Lawrence W. Baker, ed. Farmington Hills, Mich., U*X*L/Gale, 1999. 3v. illus. $84.00/set. ISBN 0-7876-2844-1.

This young person's guide (high school level) to the chemical elements is thoughtfully designed and attractively produced. Entries are alphabetic by element name, and there is a table of contents by atomic number as well as one by periodic group. Each volume includes the same timeline of the discovery of the elements, glossary, index to the set, and bibliography that includes Websites as well.

Entries are self-contained, and technical terms are explained within them, although that can lead to slight misstatements. For example, the entry for argon defines fractional distillation as the process of letting liquid air slowly warm up, but fractional distillation is a more general term that includes separations of components in any temperature range. Each profusely illustrated entry contains the atomic symbol; atomic number; mass; periodic family; the pronunciation of the element's name; the history of knowledge; and use of the element, physical, and chemical properties, occurrence in nature, isotopes, extraction processes, compounds of the elements, health effects, and more. There are plentiful cross-references and informative sidebars. Each entry also gives a simple shell diagram for the electronic energy levels, but because the meaning of this diagram is not explained it may be simply puzzling. An explanation would also help the reader to understand what is meant by the periodic group into which the element is placed and to understand the periodic table itself, which is printed on the front and back endpapers of each volume. This is my only real quibble about the set, which would be a useful resource in any public or school library.

Finally, the subtitle is a bit of a mystery. Possibly carbon is there as the element forming the largest number of chemical compounds, but krypton is not quite the element forming the fewest compounds, since helium, neon, and argon form no stable compounds at all. [R: BL, 1 May 99, pp. 1606-1608; BR, Sept/Oct 99, p. 79; SLJ, Aug 99, pp. 186-187]—**Robert Michaelson**

1379. Perry, Robert H., and Don W. Green. **Perry's Chemical Engineers Handbook. [CD-ROM].** New York, McGraw-Hill, 1999. Minimum system requirements (Windows version): IBM or compatible 486. Double-speed CD-ROM drive. Windows 3.1, Windows 95, or Windows NT 3.51. 16MB RAM. 10MB hard disk space. SVGA monitor. Mouse. Minimum system requirements (Macintosh version): 68040 processor. Double-speed CD-Rom drive. System 7.5 or later. 16MB RAM. 10MB hard disk space. $149.95. ISBN 0-07-134412-8.

Perry's print handbook, now in its 7th edition, has long been an indispensable part of any library serving chemical engineers. Many academic engineering libraries find it necessary to keep at least two copies of the latest edition on reference in order to serve the heavy demand for this resource. Thus an electronic version is of great potential interest. This CD-ROM edition includes the complete text of the 7th edition of the print version, along with a number of useful enhancements. The text is displayed in Acrobat files with hyperlinks, and Adobe Acrobat Reader 3.0.1 (including the search plug-in) is included on the CD-ROM in case the user does not already have it installed.

Navigation through this product is quite easy, facilitated by a bookmarks frame, page buttons, and hypertext links outlined in red. It is also possible to use the Acrobat "Find" feature and, with the search plug-in, the Acrobat "Search" feature allows Boolean and proximity searches, word stemming, and use of a thesaurus box as well as a "sounds like" box to find synonyms and alternate spellings, respectively.

Some of the handbook's tables and figures are "Active Objects" (indicated by outlining in red). Data from active tables can be copied and pasted into other programs; the user can also create a new interpolated row to easily find interpolated numerical values. Active figures allow the user to move directly to a specific point by designating the x or y coordinate value and also allow zooming in for greater detail. Thus this CD-ROM provides added value to the full text of the print edition.

Because larger science libraries may not want to confine use of this product to a single workstation, it is useful to know that a local area network (LAN) license is available. The LAN product uses the same software (ISBN 0-07-134638-4, $295). For multiple buildings within five miles, a WAN (ISBN 0-07-134639-2, $495) is also available. However, the ease of networking this product is questionable. Libraries interested in multiple-workstation access may wish to wait for an Internet version, which is expected to be available in the first quarter of 2000.—**Robert Michaelson**

CIVIL ENGINEERING

1380. **Standard Handbook for Civil Engineers.** [CD-ROM]. By Frederick S. Merritt, M. Kent Loftin, and Jonathan T. Ricketts. New York, McGraw-Hill, 1999. Minimum system requirements: IBM or compatible 486. Double-speed CD-ROM drive. Windows 3.1, Windows 95, or Windows NT 3.51. 16MB RAM. 10MB hard disk space. SVGA monitor. Mouse. $149.95. ISBN 0-07-134419-5.

According to the packaging, this electronic version is analogous to the 4th edition of a major civil engineering handbook of the same name. However, some sample searches retrieved information from the 5th edition. Taking advantage of the interactive format, the CD version includes 105 active equations that allow users to enter data values and then compute, plot, and copy the results. Active equations are outlined in a red box. A list of active equations can be found in the bookmark section to the left of the text that functions as the table of contents. Text searching is possible using the Adobe Acrobat binoculars icon. Several search options are possible including proximity, word stemming, and a thesaurus. Searches bring up a list of sections by title, unless there is only one occurrence of the word or phrase, and then the actual text is displayed. Sample searches for seismic forces, white pine, wood connections, floor span, and excavator brought up the expected results. One interesting note is that the index is not searchable; while there is a box marked "indexes" on the Adobe search box, this does not search the index. This search possibility seems to be available in case additional handbooks are included. This is not a real liability since the index is nothing really special—it works exactly like the paper index except that users go from an indexed item to the item with a click.

It would be helpful if users could see a count of how many times a word appears and then a list of the subsections rather than just the section names, as they can be quite broad (e.g., "Geotechnical"). Another not so minor complaint is the licensing options. As always, a single-user license is possible as well as an LAN within a single building. However, a wide-area LAN is possible only if all buildings are within five miles of any building included in such a site.

On the plus side, installation is easy and the commands are all standard Acrobat reader. The price is not out of line and it works as advertised.—**Susan B. Ardis**

ELECTRIC ENGINEERING AND ELECTRONICS

1381. **Electronic Engineer's Handbook.** [CD-ROM]. By Donald Christiansen. New York, McGraw-Hill, 1999. Minimum system requirements: IBM or compatible 486. Double-speed CD-ROM drive. Windows 3.1, Windows 95, or Windows NT 3.51. 16MB RAM. 10MB hard disk space. SVGA monitor. Mouse. $149.95. ISBN 0-07-134378-4.

Electronic Engineer's Handbook is a 1999 electronic edition of the 4th print edition published in 1997. The content is divided into 4 main parts: "Principles and Techniques," "Materials and Hardware," "Circuits and Functions," and "Systems and Applications." Users will find that each is divided into chapters (individually authored) and sections. The text is well illustrated with quality figures, tables, and equations. Although it is mainly intended for the experienced engineer, students will find a sufficient introduction to a topic and helpful references. Users will find the index thorough and the cross-references embedded in the text of great assistance. The work is reliable and complements the content of such works as the *Standard Handbook for Electrical Engineers* (14th ed.; McGraw-Hill, 1999) and *IEEE Press's Electrical Engineering Handbook* (2d ed.; see ARBA 99, entry 1405). But it is the merit of the format that may be of equal concern. The introduction of electronic versions of standard engineering handbooks has caused personal users and librarians to evaluate the merits of switching from a print format or perhaps networking a CD-ROM edition. The price of electronic is usually competitive and, considering the ubiquitous presence of the computer, physically more convenient. Both are certainly true for this reference work. The installation of the CD-ROM is simple, and the appropriate version of Adobe Acrobat for viewing the text comes with the CD-ROM. The cross-references mentioned above are hyperlinks in the electronic version, and thus even more useful in quickly moving about the work. One of the chief advantages is the electronic search feature supported by Adobe. Although far from intuitive, the search feature will amply reward the user who takes the time to understand the layout of the text and how this feature works. Another useful feature is called "Active Object," which allows the user to access many tables (not all) to copy and manipulate data. All users should consider the electronic version of this standard reference work.—**John M. Robson**

1382. Graf, Rudolf F., and William Sheets. **Encyclopedia of Electronic Circuits, Volume 7.** New York, McGraw-Hill, 1999. 1128p. illus. index. $65.00. ISBN 0-07-015115-6.

This 7th volume of an excellent series on electronic circuits is a real handbook—useful, practical, with easy reading font size for the text and index. The circuit designs are readable; however, the size of the book would make it difficult to use on the workshop bench.

There are 1,000 new electronic circuits arranged alphabetically into more than 100 basic circuit categories, ranging from active antenna circuits to weather-related circuits. When combined with the previous 6 volumes, Graf and Sheets have compiled more than 7,000 circuits (see ARBA 97, entry 1305). The 1,000 circuits have been meticulously indexed and cross-referenced. There is no other similar resource in this field. The source of each circuit design and description is listed in one appendix.

The index is comprehensive for all 7 volumes. It is readable even with the small font size; however, where else could one find such a comprehensive list of electronic circuits described and drawn. This is an invaluable resource in electronics. This is an excellent handbook and part of an excellent series.
—**Gerald D. Moran**

1383. **Microelectronic Failure Analysis: Desk Reference.** 4th ed. Richard J. Ross, Christian Boit, and Donald Staab, eds. Materials Park, Ohio, ASM International, 1999. 643p. illus. index. $175.00. ISBN 0-87170-638-5.

Failure analysis is a critical component of any field of engineering, and microelectronics is no exception. Now in a 4th edition (3d ed., 1993), this reference tool brings together "the art and science of Electronic Device Failure Analysis." The work is divided into 14 topical sections, with 47 individually written subsections. For each, the user new to the discipline will find an overview of the topic. For example, "plasma delayering" and "wet chemical deprocessing" are followed by concise explanations of the techniques of failure analysis as they exist today. An abundance of high-quality diagrams and photographs and the applicable mathematics are used for each essay. The expert will find a clear distillation of current practice, a convenient way to learn about related topics, and references—general and cited—to the literature for a fuller explanation. Appended sections include standards, definitions, acronyms, and a useful subject index to papers presented at the International Symposium for Testing and Failure Analysis (ISTFA) meetings. The editor makes note of the fact that the "vast majority" of the material is either new or updated in the last 12 to 18 months. Since, to a certain extent, the techniques of failure analysis always lag behind the technology, a plea is made for engineers and scientists to share their experience for the benefit of the discipline and the industry. This is a good purchase for libraries serving a graduate audience of professionals.

—**John M. Robson**

ENVIRONMENTAL ENGINEERING

1384. **Genium's Handbook of Safety, Health, and Environmental Data for Common Hazardous Substances.** New York, McGraw-Hill, 1999. 3v. illus. index. $467.50/set (with disc). ISBN 0-07-024577-0.

Dangerous chemicals surround all of us in our everyday pursuits. This valuable handbook is a quick way to find authoritative information on those chemicals. Profiling more than 4,500 hazardous chemicals, this reference source is indispensable to those in the environmental, health, and safety fields. Pictograms of health and physical hazards, cleanup and disposal methods, toxicity data, regulation listings, and much more are included to help professionals make critical decisions when problems arise. The intent of this work is to include select substances where there was significant data available and to provide key environmental data such as pH values, odor thresholds, and ecotoxicity data, along with health and safety factors. Indexes by material name, chemical formula, Chemical Abstracts Service, Registry of Toxic Effects of Chemical Substances, Department of Transportation, and European Inventory of Existing Chemical Substances numbers are provided to aid in easy access. The CD-ROM included in volume 3 is an excellent complement to this valuable resource. The search software provides a quick way to print out the information on particular dangerous chemicals. This tool, whether one uses the handbook or the CD-ROM, will be a valuable asset to health, safety, and environmental professionals.—**Diane J. Turner**

1385. Woodside, Gayle. **Environmental Health, and Safety Portable Handbook.** New York, McGraw-Hill, 1998. 279p. index. $49.95 flexibinding. ISBN 0-07-071848-2.

This handbook is especially designed for environmental and health safety professionals and covers environmental, occupational health, safety, and regulatory issues, as well as EHS (Environmental Health and Safety) management techniques and audit and inspection guidelines. Features include checklists, figures, equations, and pages left blank for relevant notes. It is not designed to be a replacement for technical EHS books such as Lewis's *Hazardous Chemicals Desk Reference* (4th ed.; see ARBA 98, entry 1635).

It is not recommended for purchase by any library, as it is intended for use in the field. However, this is an important issue and a better purchase would be Gayle Woodside's *Environmental Safety and Health Engineering* (Wiley, 1997) or the *Standard Handbook of Environmental Engineering* (CRC, 1999).

—**Susan B. Ardis**

MATERIALS SCIENCE

1386. **ASM Handbook, Volume 7: Powder Metal Technologies and Applications.** Materials Park, Ohio, ASM International, 1998. 1146p. index. $186.00. ISBN 0-87170-387-4.

ASM has substantially revised the 9th edition (1984) of its powder metal technology reference book, reflecting the "new methods, technologies, and applications." New topics include powder injection molding, binder-assisted extrusion, field-activated sintering, rigid die compaction, and process modeling of injection molding. The layout follows that of the other volumes in the ASM handbook series. There are 4 main sections: metal powder production and characterization; shaping and consolidation technologies; secondary operations and quality control; and materials systems, properties, and applications. Each of these is composed of several dozen individually authored subsections, each with an extensive list of references. The articles are clearly written in lean technical prose and are well edited for conformity of style. The table of contents allows the user to scan quickly the subsections and the constituent topics under each. Approximately 20–25 percent of the text is given to quality photographs, diagrams, charts, and tables. The 32-page index does an excellent job in leading the user quickly to the relevant information. Highly recommended as the basic reference tool in the area.—**John M. Robson**

1387. **Fracture: A Topical Encyclopedia of Current Knowledge.** Genady P. Cherapanov, ed. Malabar, Fla., Krieger Publishing, 1998. 870p. $150.00. ISBN 0-89464-924-8.

This comprehensive book was written with two goals in mind: to provide an almanac of achievements in fracture science and a reference work about methods and ideas. The work is divided into 10 parts: surface energy of solids, mathematical theory of cracks, failure criteria, toughness and other properties of fracture, microfracture mechanics, invariant integrals, computational fracture mechanics, crack dynamics, physical mechanics of fracture, and composites. Each part then contains three to five chapters on each subject, written by leaders in fracture science. Each chapter features information about the author and a list of references for further research. Written for graduate-level students, this book will make a welcome addition to any university engineering or science library, particularly those with graduate–level programs.
—**Kelly M. Jordan**

1388. **Illustrated Dictionary of Metalworking and Manufacturing Technology.** Steve F. Krar, ed. New York, McGraw-Hill, 1999. 325p. $79.95. ISBN 0-07-038302-2.

The development of new technologies has had an important impact on the way products are manufactured, and one of the major driving forces has been computer-controlled numerical machine tools. Any rapidly changing area creates unique terms, some coined especially for a specific technology. This dictionary is an attempt to provide up-to-date definitions for terminology found in this field. Each entry consists of a brief one- or two-sentence definition. Many of the definitions also include an explanation of the main points relating to the term, an illustration, and a cross-reference to related forms.

This work has contributions from seven individuals with substantial experience in the machine tool trade or technical education. The text is divided into 15 sections, including topics such as "Dies, Jugs, and Fixtures"; "Hand Tools"; and "Metallurgy and Heat Treatment." Each section includes a brief introduction and the author's name and address, followed by the definitions in alphabetic order. This means there are 15 alphabetic listings. Because there is no index, users must know what section a term should fall in order to look up the definition. For example, to find *upset*, the user must know to look in the welding section. Although relatively few terms are defined more than once there are some that are; for example, *viscosity* is defined in at least two places—"Fluid Power" and "Plastics."

Although the illustrations are nice and the definitions are clear and helpful, this is an unacceptable reference book. It is too idiosyncratically organized and this makes it difficult and time-consuming to use.
—**Susan B. Ardis**

1389. **Metals Handbook.** 2d ed. J. R. Davis and Davis & Associates, eds. Materials Park, Ohio, ASM International, 1998. 1521p. index. $198.00. ISBN 0-87170-654-7.

This handbook updates the popular 1st desk edition from 1984, a pioneering effort that successfully provided a single-volume reference for all metals technology. Organization is similar to the 1st edition. However, instead of four there are now five sections. The general information glossary has grown by approximately 20 pages. The section on irons, steels, and high-performance alloys has been expanded to include updated and new material on tempered ductile irons, high-strength low-alloy steels, stainless steels including duplex stainless steels, and powder metallurgy steels. The nonferrous alloys and special-purpose materials section includes new information on metal-matrix composites and structural intermetallics. The processing section includes added coverage on recycling technology and an entirely new section on powder metallurgy. And finally, the inspection and materials characterization section has updated information on wear testing, stress corrosion cracking, hydrogen embrittlement, and a completely new section describing selection of characterization methods for bulk elemental analysis, bulk microstructural analysis, and surface analysis. Even if users can afford the full 20-volume *Metals Handbook* set that this resource is based upon, it is still highly recommended as a valuable reference companion for engineering collections both public and private. If users cannot afford the 20-volume set, this is a must-have.—**Barbara Delzell**

1390. Simmons, H. Leslie, and Richard J. Lewis. **Building Materials: Dangerous Properties of Products in MasterFormat Divisions 7 and 9.** New York, Van Nostrand Reinhold, 1997. 421p. index. $240.00. ISBN 0-442-02289-1.

This book provides information on the dangerous properties found in materials (mostly thermal and moisture protection) commonly used by the building industry. Consisting of several indexes, the work allows one to look at the names of chemicals used in the building construction industry, the products containing the chemicals, chemical abbreviations, and product classes. A rather technical and precise work, this book would be useful to those libraries serving engineers (with an emphasis on construction) or those collecting building and environmental materials.—**Kelly M. Jordan**

MECHANICAL ENGINEERING

1391. **Marks' Standard Handbook for Mechanical Engineers.** [CD-ROM]. By Eugene A. Avallone and Theodore Baumeister III. New York, McGraw-Hill, 1999. Minimum system requirements: IBM or compatible 486. Double-speed CD-ROM. Windows 3.1, Windows 95, or Windows NT 3.51. 16MB RAM. 25MB hard disk space. SVGA monitor. Mouse. $149.95. ISBN 0-07-134411-X.

This is the 2d edition of the CD-ROM title of this well-known engineering classic. Installation is easy and, if one is not familiar with CD-ROMs, the instruction booklet is helpful. Marks comes up with a very nice Quick Start Guide to help users navigate through the materials. Users also have the option of installing the Mathcad, but if they choose not to install it, they will not be able to do any of the Live Math features. The magnification capability is a nice feature for reading the text; this needs to be extended to the graphics. A knowledgeable searcher can easily do content searching and can create bookmarks. There are some minor problems, such as not being able to distinguish between the words *gage* and *gauge*. The content of the material in this edition has been expanded to include more of the content of the printed edition, with the added feature of being able to do actual calculations when one finds a formula. This still cannot be considered a complete replacement for the print edition, but it should be acknowledged that engineering students will appreciate the convenience of this electronic version. Because this title can be networked, many engineering libraries will also find this a useful source to have on their local area networks while still having the latest print edition on their reference shelves.—**Judith J. Field**

33 Health Sciences

GENERAL WORKS

Bibliography

1392. **Medical and Health Care Books and Serials in Print 1998: An Index to Literature in the Health Sciences.** 27th ed. New Providence, N.J., R. R. Bowker/Reed Reference Publishing, 1998. 2v. $249.95/set. ISBN 0-8352-3992-6. ISSN 0000-085X.

This 27th edition covers books and serials related to the major health science disciplines, such as medicine, dentistry, nursing, veterinary medicine, psychology, and biomedical sciences. Titles have generally been selected for a professional or college student audience. Author and title indexes to books include 91,753 entries for titles from 5,894 publishers, plus addresses and prices. Under the titles of journals are 43 domains of information on each periodical, from its Dewey Decimal Classification to whether it is refereed.

Medical and Health Care's 3,896 pages are enclosed in 2 volumes. Volume 1 lists books and journals under subject and author indexes. Volume 2 categorizes its contents under a book title index, serial subject index, vendor listings and serials online, serial title index, and publishers' and distributors' symbols and abbreviations. Type is dark, if not large, and quite readable.—**Anthony Gottlieb**

Dictionaries and Encyclopedias

1393. **Encyclopedia of Human Nutrition.** Michele J. Sadler, J. J. Strain, and Benjamin Caballero, eds. San Diego, Calif., Academic Press, 1999. 3v. illus. index. $799.00/set. ISBN 0-12-226694-3.

Nutrition is finally getting recognition as an important biomedical discipline. Diet is a major factor in promoting health and preventing and treating disease. This encyclopedia, compiled by an international group of distinguished academics, research scientists, and food industry professionals, looks at both the scientific and the social aspects of nutrition.

The signed articles in this 3-volume set are alphabetically arranged. The volumes are consecutively paged. Each one contains the complete table of contents and index for the set. Each also has two appendixes. The first appendix consists of data from the Food and Drug Administration's Pesticide Residue Monitoring Program (1995). The second appendix is a group of charts and tables with weights and measures, growth charts, nutritional allowances, nutritional content of foods, and height and weight and other body dimensions.

The articles cover a broad range of subjects: individual nutrients; foods; social issues related to nutrition; nutritional therapy for diseases and conditions; anatomy and physiology; and diverse subjects such as nutrition education, food folklore, and nutrition policies in developed and developing countries. The articles are each 7 to 15 pages long. The longer articles are divided into sections. Some of the material is revised and updated from relevant sections of *The Encyclopedia of Food Science, Food Technology, and Nutrition* (Academic Press, 1993). The coverage of the social and political aspects of food and nutrition is a strength that sets this work apart from other sources, such as *The Concise Encyclopedia of Food and Nutrition* (see ARBA 96, entry 1524).

With its broad coverage of the nutrition field and its clear writing, *The Encyclopedia of Food and Nutrition* is highly recommended for academic and health science collections. Large public libraries with sufficient funds may want to consider it also. Purchase of the print edition includes a subscription to the online version of the encyclopedia. [R: LJ, 15 Mar 99, pp. 68-70; Choice, May 99, p. 1595]

—**Barbara M. Bibel**

1394. Hirschfelder, Arlene B. **Encyclopedia of Smoking and Tobacco.** Phoenix, Ariz., Oryx Press, 1999. 411p. illus. index. $65.00. ISBN 1-57356-202-5.

Consider that each day in the United States alone 3,000 young people under the age of 20 become established smokers, and each year more than 400,000 individuals die from tobacco-related diseases such as lung cancer and heart disease. A book that summarizes information on smoking and tobacco in a way that could be helpful to any interested reader is timely. The book is arranged on topics from A to Z. For example, "A" has *addiction* and *advertising*, "C" has *chewing tobacco* and *Cuba*, "N" has *Native Americans*, "S" has *Surgeon General's Report*, and "Z" has *Zyban* (a smoking-cessation pharmaceutical). Beyond the encyclopedia are essays on relevant topics, such as "Women, Tobacco, and Health," "Warning Labels As a Legal Protection for the Tobacco Industry," and "Surgeon General's Reports from 1964-1998." Appendixes include "Workplace and Smoking: Selected Landmark Cases," and a chronology starting with Christopher Columbus in 1492. This well-written and interesting book could be usefully placed in many locations, including libraries, health workers' offices, and educational institutions.—**Marquita Hill**

1395. Sharma, Rajendra. **The Family Encyclopedia of Health: The Complete Family Reference Guide to Alternative & Orthodox Medical Diagnosis, Treatment, & Preventive Healthcare.** Rockport, Mass., Element Books, 1998. 692p. illus. index. $24.95pa. ISBN 1-86204-426-0.

The Family Encyclopedia of Health is the most thorough resource to date that integrates discussion of alternative therapies within articles on common health concerns and their recommended Western medical treatments. The author is affiliated with the Hale Clinic, a British organization that promotes alternative health care practice. British and European health systems have moved more quickly than U.S. health care to accept and blend alternative therapies into mainstream medical practice. As a result, much of the advice given in this resource is not commonly accepted practice in the United States, and qualified practitioners of some of the recommended alternative modalities may be scarce in this country. Some U.S. libraries may find this work unsuitable for purchase if they strongly emphasize scientific or evidence-based medical information in their collections because only anecdotal evidence is available for many therapies discussed in this work.

However, this reference has many strengths. It is the first work on complementary or alternative care that discusses alternative practice side by side with Western medical practice, allowing the reader to evaluate the pros and cons of both therapies. As well, the multicultural approach of the work helps to ground the theories or rationales behind alternative therapies within the culture of origin. The work also explains the therapies in a clear and forthright manner that is suitable for its intended audience of health care consumers. The resource includes a contents list for a basic alternative medicine chest and recommends providers of the listed preparations. This work is generously illustrated, with diagrams of anatomy and procedures including, for example, a detailed topography of the eye used in iridology. There is an interesting glossary that includes many terms not found in medical dictionaries. The encyclopedia follows an arrangement that subdivides the book into 3 sections. Part 1 contains articles on sexuality, fertility and conception, and pregnancy and childbirth, then addresses health throughout periods of the life span. Part 2 addresses nutrition topics, diagnosis, alternative therapies, and drugs. And finally, part 3 includes a glossary, a recommended readings list, and an address list for alternative medicine information and practitioners. A thorough index provides access to the three parts of the encyclopedia by topic. [R: LJ, July 99, p. 84; Choice, Dec 99, p. 696]—**Lynne M. Fox**

Directories

1396. Canadian Health Facilities Directory. Don Mills, Ont., Southam Information Products, 1999. 1v. (various paging). $199.00. ISBN 1-55257-021-5. ISSN 1481-4463.

The *Canadian Health Facilities Directory* is a Canadian version of the American Health Association Guide, and a companion volume to the *Canadian Medical Directory*. It complements another Canadian publication, the *Guide to Canadian Healthcare Facilities*, by giving different data and key personnel. However, the *Canadian Health Facilities Directory* is not a bilingual publication. This makes it an ideal resource for U.S. libraries, especially in Canadian border states, where this directory is useful in locating medical records of visiting Canadian patients. The directory also is helpful in identifying institutions offering specialized care centers or services. This directory provides information on hospitals, long-term care facilities, and clinics.

Information in the facility listings includes statistical and contact information supplied by the institution. Data include facts such as length of stay, beds, visits, budget, and personnel. Brief profiles of the institution indicate areas of specialty care and whether they are privately or publicly supported. Long-term care providers describe the amenities and strengths of the facility. Organization is in three sections: by facility type, geographically by province, and by city. The directory also contains a supplier list, although company representative contact names are not included in the lists.—**Lynne M. Fox**

1397. Detwiler's Directory of Health and Medical Resources 1990-2000. 7th ed. Susan M. Detwiler, ed. New York, Hatherleigh, 1999. 826p. index. $195.00pa. ISBN 1-880874-57-1. ISSN 1093-3824.

The 7th edition of *Detwiler's Directory of Health and Medical Resources* has once again conveniently compiled a variety of useful contact information into one volume. This resource is a one-stop quick reference resource, whether one is locating associations, gathering health marketing information, identifying publication sources for acquisition, or tackling other types of health questions. Purchasers of the 7th edition are also given password access to the up-to-date database from which *Detwiler's* is produced.

The organization of the volume is in five sections. Most of the directory is devoted to alphabetic profile listings of major health programs, organizations, professional academies, foundations, government agencies, publishers, and information service providers. The entries include contact and Website information, brief descriptions, and services or publications provided. Other sections include indexes to the alphabetic profile listings. A service index is organized by format of the information distributed by the resource. The subject index provides access by topic to the profiles. A publication index helps locate the source for publications mentioned in the alphabetic lists. An acronym list quickly locates the profile by organization abbreviation.

Some librarians may find that *Detwiler's* is a more cost-effective quick reference resource than the multiple titles offering more extensive content. Titles that expand on *Detwiler's* include the *Medical & Health Information Directory* (see ARBA 94, entry 1807; ARBA 90, entry 1620), *The Medical & Healthcare Marketplace Guide* (14th ed.; HCIA, 1999), *Ulrich's International Periodicals Directory* (36th ed.; see ARBA 99, entry 74), and the *Encyclopedia of Associations* (see ARBA 99, entries 50 and 51). *Detwiler's* provides adequate information listings at a reasonable cost, even though the single volume does not have the depth and breadth of these other resources.—**Lynne M. Fox**

1398. Graduate Medical Education Directory 1999/2000. 84th ed. Chicago, American Medical Association, 1999. 1286p. $64.95pa. ISBN 0-89970-984-2.

The 84th edition of this directory lists programs accredited by the Accreditation Council for Graduate Medical Education (ACGME). The goal of this directory is to provide medical students with a list of accredited graduate medical education (GME) programs in the United States. With this information, medical students can make the important decision on which program they will select for their residency training. This source is commonly used by the state licensing boards, specialty societies, and hospitals to verify the authenticity of programs presented by physicians who wish to apply for licensure, certification, or hospital privileges. This directory is updated annually and is a unique medical education resource that is now online at http://www.rsna.org/REG/launchpad/ama-freida.html.

The American Medical Association Fellowship and Residency Electronic Interactive Database Access system is an extensive database that enables users to search by primary and secondary criteria for fellowship and residency programs in North America. The difference between the print and nonprint product is that the online product is interactive and gives additional information, such as city and county population counts, hospital benefits, the areas cost of living statistics, and much more. However, the print version is a must-purchase for medical facilities and libraries. In this directory there are 5 sections. Section 1 lists general information and policies and procedures of the ACGME, including information for international medical graduates. Section 2 is on essentials of accredited residencies in graduate medical education (e.g., institutional and program requirements). Section 3 presents accredited graduate medical education programs, such as pediatrics, oncology, and so on. Section 4 describes new and withdrawn programs. Section 5 is on graduate medical education teaching institutions. There are also several appendixes. Appendix A reports on combined specialty programs, such as internal medicine and emergency medicine. Appendix B lists medical specialty board certification requirements. Appendix C is on medical licensure information. Appendix D lists medial schools in the United States. And finally, appendix E is a graduate medical education glossary. This directory is ultimately a renounced product from the AMA to assist any medical school student to choose his or her future role in medicine.—**Polin P. Lei**

1399. **Major Health Care Policies: 50 State Profiles, 1998.** 7th ed. By Health Policy Tracking Service. Washington, D.C., Health Policy Tracking Service, 1999. 403p. maps. $165.00pa. ISBN 1-55516-796-9.

Aided by a small army of reporters and contacts in state agencies and legislatures, Health Policy Tracking Service (HPTS) compiles data on the status of health-related legislation. This volume is a summary of 1,500 passed and pending legislative efforts in 1998 organized by state.

Each entry begins with two pages of the state's history and recent efforts in health care legislation. Blocked off for easy reading are 13 legislative categories, which include insurance, Medicaid, Children's Health Insurance Program, managed care, patient records, facilities, regulation of physician practice, prescriptive authority, and pharmaceuticals. Programs for the indigent, uninsured, and students are also discussed. Explanations are appropriate, short, and well written.

A 60-page overview puts the state initiatives in perspective. HPTS documents the growing backlash against managed care as well as the increase in state-mandated insurance benefits. Each of the book's 133 major categories is displayed visually in 8 pages of maps and charts. Comparisons between individual states and the country as a whole are easily accomplished and informative. There are nine pages of definitions and abbreviations that round out the overview. HPTS does a nice job of informing in an area where it is easy to become confused. This volume is highly recommended for university libraries.—**Pete Prunkl**

1400. Miner, Lynn E. **Directory of Biomedical and Health Care Grants 1999.** 13th ed. Phoenix, Ariz., Oryx Press, 1998. 1998. index. $84.50pa. ISBN 1-57356-096-0. ISSN 0883-5330.

Now in its 13th edition, this directory continues to be an invaluable guide for biomedical and health services researchers. This is as close to one-stop shopping as the grant-hungry researcher is likely to get. The volume provides concise descriptions of 3,800 health-related grant programs offered by government, foundations, corporations, and other organizations. Each entry lists the purpose of the grant program, application procedures, sponsor information, contacts, application requirements and restrictions, level of grant awards, and a brief description of a recent award. The directory is organized around four interconnected indexes: subject matter, sponsoring organizations, grants by program type, and geographic areas. The subject matter index is extensive and provides good cross-referencing. In addition to individual program entries, the volume provides a helpful guide to proposal planning and writing and a list of sponsors' Websites. Users familiar with previous editions of this work will find the list of new sponsoring organizations to be beneficial. This work remains an essential reference for health science libraries.—**Bruce Stuart**

1401. **The National Directory of Managed Care Organizations.** 2d ed. Allenwood, N.J., Managed Care Information Center, 1998. 863p. index. $293.50pa. ISBN 1-882364-28-7.

This directory provides detailed profiles on health maintenance organization (HMOs), preferred provider organizations (PPOs), specialty HMOs and PPOs, point of service plans (POSs), exclusive provider organizations (EPOs), peer review organizations (PROs), third party administrators (TPAs), utilization review organizations (UROs), pharmacy benefit management companies (PBMs), pharmacy networks (PNs), and provider sponsored organizations (PSOs). The database from which the directory is printed contains more than 1,800 managed care organizations, 120 pharmacy benefit management companies, and 28 PSOs operating under the Medicare+Choice program. Data were collected from the organization's administrative office, news releases, government agency inquiries, Internet searches, annual reports, industry news services and conferences, and interviews with national trade associations.

Profiles are organized alphabetically by company name within the state of origin. An alphabetic index for each type of organization is also available. An entry can contain such information as directory information, key personnel, company profile, plan statistics, enrollment demographics, coverage type, and plan benefits. Many of the entries are not complete and lack data in several categories. The information is also available on diskette (at an additional cost), providing users with the capability of customizing reports.

This directory will have a limited market. Business libraries may want to include it in the reference collection, although the major users of this information would appear to be individuals or corporations involved in managed care.—**Vicki J. Killion**

1402. **National Health Directory 1999.** Lynn Antosz Fantle, ed. Gaithersville, Md., Aspen, 1999. 400p. illus. $129.00pa. ISBN 0-8342-1721-X.

This annual update provides all the communication information needed to get in touch with congressional delegations or staff as well as federal, state, city, and county health officials. It provides a contact to nearly 12,000 health care policy makers and health programs in public health, such as health care reform, funding, AIDS, aging, substance abuse, and child welfare. In short this publication lists the current names at every level of government needed and the information to contact them directly on health issues. There is no index for the entire book and the user has to begin with the table of contents to locate the appropriate information.

The book begins by providing the names and telephone numbers of the senators and representatives of the 106th Congress. The brief biographical details plus photographs of the key congressional health subcommittee senators and representatives follow. The next section lists all the delegations of the standing committees and their subcommittees dealing with health. Also, the complete congressional delegations are listed by states. The section on the federal health agencies has a complete index and a thorough and inclusive list of any department that is even minutely connected with health issues, such as the Department of Transportation where the Office of Aviation Medicine is included. After the federal health agencies section, the state, county, and city health officials are listed by state for easy access. This source would be improved if many of the operating Websites were included.—**Polin P. Lei**

Handbooks and Yearbooks

1403. **Health and Healthcare in the United States 1999: County and Metro Area Data.** Richard K. Thomas, ed. Lanham, Md., Bernan Associates, 1999. 437p. maps. $135.00pa. (with CD-ROM). ISBN 0-89059-188-1. ISSN 1526-1573.

Drawing from information from the National Center for Health Statistics, the Health Care Financing Administration, and the Bureau of the Census, this work represents a compilation of health and health care statistics. More than 80 statistical tables are represented for some 3,000 U.S. counties and 329 metropolitan areas. The statistical tables are arranged by state and county and by metropolitan area.

In the state and county data section and the metropolitan area data section, the statistical items are grouped under population characteristics, vital statistics, health care resources, and Medicare. Much information, such as number of physicians, dental offices, podiatry offices, Medicare statistics, population projections, births and deaths, and deaths caused by a wide variety of diseases or accidents, can be found. The year that reflects a particular type of statistic varies. For example, some statistics reflect 1998, whereas others reflect 1997, 1996, or 1995.

At the end of the work, maps for each of the states of the union can be found. The maps depict the county and metropolitan statistical areas that are listed within the tables. A CD-ROM is included that represents an electronic version of the printed publication. This resource is highly recommended for all medical, college, university, and large public libraries.—**George H. Bell**

1404. **Health Care State Rankings 1999: Health Care in the 50 United States.** 7th ed. Kathleen O'Leary Morgan and Scott Morgan, eds. Lawrence, Kans., Morgan Quitno Press, 1999. 512p. index. $49.95pa. ISBN 1-56692-333-6.

This health state ranking source on the 50 states provides answers to health questions relating to birth, death, incidence of disease, reproductive health, facilities, abortions, insurance and finance, health providers, and physical fitness. The data in more than 500 tables are collected from government agencies and private sectors. This 7th edition is an updated version with a few deletions, additions, and unchanged data. The birth and reproductive health section has 58 tables, including topics such as teenage birthrate, rate of Cesarean delivery, and birth by midwives, among others. There are 17 tables on legal abortions and 119 tables on different causes of death. The section on facilities lists nursing home occupancy rate, Medicare and Medicaid services, community hospital data, and office and clinic visits. Insurance and finance tables provide ranking of health expenditures on prescription drugs, home health care, nursing homes, dental care, physician services, and more. Incidence of disease includes AIDS, cancer, Lyme disease, sexually transmitted diseases, E-Coli, and the like. The "Providers" section gives dental, chiropractic, and different specialty rankings. The "Physical Fitness" section provides ranking of activities such as swimming, golf, tennis, running, beer consumption, wine consumption, mental health, and car safety seats. Each table lists the rank of the states from highest to lowest, and an alphabetic list of states with the ranking is provided. The District of Columbia is placed at the bottom of the listing. There are no analyses of counties, which might be even more convenient to data-seekers who are looking for in-depth research data. Each table includes the source of the data and footnotes to assist users in locating additional information on their search. The 1st edition of this title (see ARBA 94, entry 1816) included bibliographic references, but this 1999 edition has a separate page on the sources for the table data but no bibliography. For libraries with patrons looking for answers to unique health questions, this is a worthwhile purchase.—**Polin P. Lei**

1405. **The Managed Care Yearbook.** 4th ed. Allenwood, N.J., Managed Care Information Center, 1998. 478p. index. $275.00pa. ISBN 1-882364-26-0.

Managed care executives can learn a great deal about the growth and development of their quickly expanding industry (as of 1998), the changes caused by the continuing shift of employer-sponsored health care plans into managed care plans, Medicare managed care, and how to combat the public's "antimanaged care sentiment" in this volume. Trends in the industry, market news, legislation, controlling costs, improving quality and humanizing relationships, and executive compensations are among the subjects covered. There are lists of advertisers as well.

A detailed table of contents makes location of topics fairly easy, but the text is often like a series of headlines, without continuity or bibliographic data. An appendix called "Sources" is merely a directory of health plan organizations and industry-sponsored study centers. Publications are listed in an appendix called "Managed Care Resources." A list of acronyms and a "Managed Care Glossary" are of some general interest, as are some of the case studies. This is an excellent update for those interested in the changing business aspects of managed care.—**Harriette M. Cluxton**

1406. **The Merck Manual of Medical Information.** home ed. Robert Berkow, Mark H. Beers, and Andrew J. Fletcher, eds. New York, McGraw-Hill, 1997. 1509p. illus. index. $29.95. ISBN 0-911910-87-5.

For a hundred years, *The Merck Manual* has been the doctor's bible. Finally, here is a rewriting in everyday language, a translation of the professionals' reference book to be consulted by today's increasingly literate searchers for medical information. It is in no way paternalistic, but maintains a neutral attitude, uses medical terminology, and is not a "how to" self-care manual. Almost all of the content of *The Merck Manual* is given, except for drug dosages, microscopic slide interpretations, and so on, for which the layperson must depend on the professionals.

The home edition enables the patient and family to learn about human disorders and to understand their biological bases, diagnosis, treatment, and even prognosis, as understood by practitioners of orthodox medicine. A tremendous amount of medical information has been carefully arranged into briefly introduced sections, such as blood disorders. The first chapter under each section often covers the biology of the organ, system, or type of disorder (e.g., infections). Following chapters are more specific, such as abscesses under the skin. A pattern of symptoms, diagnosis, treatment options, and outcomes are often used. Cross-references are indicated by small red symbols in the text, repeated at the bottom of the page, with the location of related topics. There are some general sections on topics such as on death and dying. Additional information often appears in sidebars. Original illustrations have been digitized and sparingly colorized, making them easy to understand. The table of contents is detailed, and the index is extensive. There are several appendixes, such as lists of common medical terms and the generic and trade names of often-prescribed drugs.

This is a definitive, authoritative, easy-to-use current medical reference for laypeople, and should be considered for all hospital libraries, consumer health centers, public libraries, and many individual collections. It is presented from the medical viewpoint and compared to books like the *Mayo Clinic Family Health Book* (Morrow, 1996), this is more concise in statement and inclusive in essential information. It is also directed toward helping the user comprehend the basic nature of diseases and disorders and what the treatments and outcomes may be. The reader should be well prepared for more intelligent interaction with his or her doctors after consulting this excellent book.—**Harriette M. Cluxton**

1407. Shannon, Joyce Brennfleck, ed. **Medical Tests Sourcebook.** Detroit, Omnigraphics, 1999. 691p. illus. index. (Health Reference Series). $78.00. ISBN 0-7808-0243-8.

Written for the medical consumer as part of the Health Reference Series, this volume has a wide scope that makes it useful, although its lack of depth in many instances leaves the reader wanting to know more. The book covers basic health information, such as periodic health exams; general screening tests; "at-home" tests, such as tests for diabetes, HIV, and pregnancy; and payment for medical tests, especially through Medicare and Medicaid. The book divides medical tests into several general categories: X-ray and radiology; electrical (ECG, EEG); blood and other body fluids and tissues; scope; lung; genetics, pregnancy, and newborn; and sexually transmitted diseases. Each section is further divided into types of tests within the category and specific tests. Most sections include background information about the history and development of the test, a description, and preparation for the test if important. Black-and-white illustrations, usually of test images, help to explain some of the tests. Most chapters include references for further reading and information and the addresses and telephone numbers for any groups that deal with the medical problem. Additional chapters include information about the Hill-Burton Free Care Program, computer diagnosis and telemedicine, resources for additional help, and a glossary. An extensive topical index aids the reader.

As a whole, the volume is fairly user-friendly despite its tendency to fall into medical terminology without explanation or glossary entries. Many of the entries, especially the introductory materials, are written in a question-and-answer format. Most individual test entries explain what the test shows and how the test is done. Very little information is provided to aid the patient in interpreting test results (i.e., what each of the numbers in a blood test mean—what is normal, low, or high), with cholesterol numbers being the one exception. Many sections dealing with specific tests include a bibliographic reference for the information at the beginning of the section, but this information is provided on an inconsistent basis. Taken as a whole, this volume can be a valuable reference guide despite some inconsistencies in presentation.

—Janet Hilbun

1408. **Socioeconomic Characteristics of Medical Practice 1997.** Martin L. Gonzalez, ed. Chicago, American Medical Association, 1997. 177p. $159.95pa.; $209.95pa. (with disk). ISBN 0-89970-865-X; 0-89970-866-8 (with disk).

This compilation of data from the American Medical Association (AMA) contains information collected from actively practicing physicians who responded to the Center for Health Policy Research Socioeconomic Monitoring System's 1996 survey. An appendix presents the design, a questionnaire summary, and the statistical methods used. Detailed statistics include age profiles of physicians, utilization and fees for visits, and expenses and income. Many of the data are also included in the 1997 survey report, also conducted by the Center for Health Policy Research and published by the AMA.

Four summary articles will interest practicing physicians and those advising physicians finishing training. The first summarizes the data on contractual arrangements with managed care organizations, pointing out that 75 percent of Americans are receiving health care coverage through some kind of managed care mechanism. Data are presented by specialty, detailing type of managed care plan, participation by payer, and reviews by plan type and capitation. The second article addresses practice size by type of employer and distribution of physicians by employer type. These data include academic as well as other kinds of practices. The relationship of size of practice to such variables as efficiency, cost, and productivity is discussed. The next article discusses trends in physician income from 1985 to 1995. Trends in medical liability claims from 1985 to 1995 are the topic of the last article. The decrease in the annual rate of liability claims, the percentage of physicians with claims, and the liability premiums are noted. The articles place the data presented in the context of other published information.—**Margretta Reed Seashore**

1409. **Source Book in Bioethics.** Albert R. Jonsen, Robert M. Veatch, and LeRoy Walters, eds. Washington, D.C., Georgetown University Press, 1998. 510p. index. $95.00. ISBN 0-87840-683-2.

The study of bioethics began in the early 1970s; today it is an important field of academic study. It is concerned with the moral dimensions of the life sciences and health care. Many of the original troublesome topics have evolved into accepted concepts; policies and procedures have been established by research and health care institutions to respect these resolutions. Many documents relating to bioethics have been produced by government bodies, courts, and legislatures. Although most reports and laws are "in the public domain," it is often difficult to locate them in the original form as opposed to book or journal discussions. Recognizing this, the editors have collected many of the most significant documents and reprinted them in full, or occasionally in shortened form. They are arranged under four general headings representing the major fields of concentration of bioethics, thus providing a history of sorts through the major documents produced. These include the ethics of research with human subjects, the ethics of death and dying, ethical issues in human genetics, and those arising from human reproductive technologies and arrangements. Thoughtful editorial comments precede each part and introduce specific documents. Often notes and references have been added.

The final portion of the book considers ethical issues in the changing health care scene. The old Hippocratic oath can no longer fully govern the relationships between doctors, patients, and other laypersons. Changes in attitudes, advances in research, questions and rights, informed consent, transplantation and donation of organs, and so on have been part of the movement toward concepts of social ethics.

As a historical survey of bioethics, this book should be very valuable as a text and as a reference source for investigating the ethical issues surrounding such particular health-related topics as the right to die or to reject treatments, surrogate birth, and so on, and how society has tried to meet them.

—**Harriette M. Cluxton**

1410. **U.S. Medical Licensure Statistics and Requirements by State.** 1998-1999 ed. Chicago, American Medical Association, 1998. 118p. $79.95pa. ISBN 0-89970-924-9.

An AMA serial that has undergone many name changes, this work was first presented in the 1970s under the title *Medical Licensure Statistics*. In 1974, the series was renamed *Physician Distribution and Medical Licensure in the U.S*. By 1982 this title was changed again to *U.S. Medical Licensure Statistics, 1980-1981, and Licensure Requirements, 1982*. In 1989, it was called *U.S. Medical Licensure Statistics and Licensure Requirements*. From 1990 to 1997, the title was *U.S. Medical Licensure Statistics and Current Licensure Requirements*. Now in 1998 it has become *U.S. Medical Licensure Statistics and Requirements by State*. Whatever name is applied, this is an essential information source for the medical profession. The data collected are from a master file that has data coming in from the medical schools, hospitals, medical societies, national board of medical examiners, state licensing boards, Surgeon General of the U.S. Government, American Board of Medical Specialties (ABMS), Drug Enforcement Administration, and other federal agencies and physicians.

There are 7 parts in this series. Part 1 is on licensure policies and regulations of state medical boards that includes CME policies and "telemedicine" practice. Part 2 is on 1996 statistics of state medical board licensure activities. Part 3 is on medical licensing examination and organizations and includes United States Medical Licensing Examination (USMLE), computer-based testing (CBT), computer-based case simulations (CCS), Federation of State Medical Boards of the United States (FSMB), National Board of Medical Examiner (NBME), the FSMB Federation Licensing Examination (FLEX), and Special Purpose Examination (SPEX). Part 4 is on information for international medical graduates such as the Educational Commission for Foreign Medial Graduates (ECFMG). Part 5 is on federal and national programs and activities such as the Air Force, Army, and Navy. Part 6 is on quality assurance organizations and programs. Part 7 is on other organizations and programs. New features included for this issue are a glossary, contact information, Internet addresses, e-mail addresses, and fax numbers. There is no need to elaborate on the importance of this publication. It is a must for medical education.—**Polin P. Lei**

MEDICINE

General Works

1411. **Consumer Issues in Health Care Sourcebook.** Bellenir Karen, ed. Detroit, Omnigraphics, 1999. 618p. index. (Health Reference Series, v.35). $78.00. ISBN 0-7808-0221-7.

In this era of managed health care, it is critical that consumers keep themselves well informed about health issues that affect them. To meet the demand for more information, many books have been published to guide consumers in making good decisions about their health care. This sourcebook is another in the Health Reference Series published by Omnigraphics aimed at educating the layperson.

The book is arranged in seven broad categories covering the gamut of health care issues: health care fundamentals, physicians and hospitals, medications, cautions for health care consumers, managing common health risks in the home, caring for chronically or terminally ill patients and making end-of-life decisions, and a section on resources. Within each part, there are chapters that thoroughly cover the aspects within that section. For example, in the section on physicians and hospitals, there are chapters that describe the types of health care providers, how to check up on a doctor, how to talk to doctors, questions to ask prior to surgery, hospital hints, and a guide to mental health services. Most of the chapters contain sources of additional information. The indexing is excellent.

Among the many other books on this topic, *Health Care Choices for Today's Consumer: Guide to Quality and Cost* by Marc Miller (John Wiley, 1997) has similar coverage to this book. The layout and organization of the information in Miller's book is more pleasing to the eye than the volume at hand, and thus more readable. Aside from the difference in style, the information itself is essentially the same in both books. Both public and academic libraries will want to have a copy of either or both of these fine books in their collection for readers who are interested in self-education on health issues. [R: BL, 1 Dec 98, p. 698; RUSQ, Spring 99, p. 299]—**Elaine F. Jurries**

1412. Dashe, Alfred M. **The Man's Health Sourcebook.** 2d ed. Lincolnwood, Ill., National Textbook, 1999. 288p. illus. index. $17.95pa. ISBN 0-7373-0109-0.

As the title implies, this text discusses men's health issues and should be read by both men and women, just as the author recommends. It includes a preface, introduction, glossary, index, illustrations, and tables. Unfortunately the reference section is limited and Internet and Web addresses are not provided.

In the preface and introduction the author explores recent trends and issues relevant to today's health care system. This includes the author's opinions in regard to the current status, insights, and future trends as seen from the eyes of a practicing physician. Both of these sections are informative and beneficial as they describe the sociological and health care changes taking place in our world.

The main body of the text is divided into two sections. The first section is a general overview of issues such as healthy living, how to choose a physician, and when to call a doctor. This section should be reassuring for those individuals who are either evasive or procrastinate when it is time to visit their physician. In fact, men who have not had a recent physical exam may find this text to be a motivator to take the first step.

The second section provides an overview of selected medical issues relevant to males. Topics include a basic review of the male anatomy, cardiovascular system, respiratory system, skin and hair, gastrointestinal system, endocrine system, male sexuality, male sexual health, the aging process, substance abuse, and mental health. At the end of each topic the author provides the reader with a useful summary of topic highlights.

Within the text are several tables, charts, and illustrations. The tables and charts are presented in a clear and concise manner. Although the illustrations are black-and-white, they are relevant, effective, and correspond with the text. Medical terminology is included and is either defined within the text or in the glossary.

This text contains information that can be of benefit to both sexes. It can be used as a general reference source and in conjunction with a physician's physical examination. A text of this nature is a valuable source of information and would be appropriately available in a variety of environments, including private physician offices, clinics, and home and school libraries.—**Paul M. Murphy III**

1413. **The Gale Encyclopedia of Medicine.** Donna Olendorf, Christine Jeryan, Karen Boyden, and Mary K. Fyke, eds. Farmington Hills, Mich., Gale, 1999. 5v. illus. index. $499.00/set. ISBN 0-7876-1868-3.

Over the years the quest for medical knowledge by the general populace has been greater than ever. In most cases, either a 1-volume family medical encyclopedia or a textbook of medicine is suggested when dealing with reference medical questions from the general public. In many instances, the 1-volume family medical encyclopedia either does not have enough information or has no information on the topic, whereas the textbook of medicine is usually much too difficult for most people to understand. Finally, a 5-volume reference work by Gale has been published that will give the public useful information on medical disorders, conditions, tests, procedures, treatments, and therapies in easy-to-read language.

This 5-volume, alphabetically arranged set provides the reader with 905 disorders and conditions, 235 tests and procedures, and 352 treatments and therapies. According to the introduction, the topics included were compiled from professional medical guides and textbooks, consumer guides, and encyclopedias. The articles were reviewed by certified physicians and medical advisors.

A total of 620 illustrations support and enhance the text. Illustrations consist of photographs, charts, and line drawings. In addition, definitions of key terms are provided and can be found within a shaded box as part of the entry. The length of the entries varies depending on the topic discussed. [R: LJ, 15 Feb 99, pp. 142-143; Choice, May 99, pp. 1595-1596; BL, 1 Mar 99, pp. 1249-1250]—**George H. Bell**

1414. **Men's Health Concerns Sourcebook.** Allan R. Cook, ed. Detroit, Omnigraphics, 1998. 738p. index. (Health Reference Series, v.38). $78.00. ISBN 0-7808-0212-8.

Men's Health Concerns Sourcebook is part of a 38-volume Health Reference Series by Omnigraphics. This sourcebook contains basic information about health issues that affect men. It helps men identify, prevent, detect, treat, and cope with their most common health threats, such as heart disease, stroke, cancer, and AIDS. It also contains facts on impotence, contraception, circumcision, snoring, and other topics. The book includes a gender focus: top 10 causes of death in men, family planning decisions, circumcision, sleep disorders, diet, and fitness. It has an excellent index. Materials have been collected from both governmental and nongovernmental groups. This comprehensive resource and the series are highly recommended for large public libraries for their health and reference collections. [R: BL, 1 Dec 98, p. 698]

—**Theresa Maggio**

Alternative Medicine

1415. **Alternative Medicine Sourcebook.** Allan R. Cook, ed. Detroit, Omnigraphics, 1999. 737p. index. (Health Reference Series). $78.00. ISBN 0-7808-0200-4.

Like the other books in Omnigraphics' Health Reference Series, this work is presented in a format to help the reader understand the basics and the breadth of a particular health issue. The *Alternative Medicine Sourcebook* is designed to help the layperson understand the issues and controversies surrounding alternative and complementary medicine. It presents an overview of the major families of therapies, and includes in-depth descriptions of some of the most common practices, such as Rolfing, aromatherapy, acupuncture, homeopathy, and reflexology.

The book is divided into 9 parts: the issues of alternative medicine; alternative systems of medical practice; "bioelectromagnetics"; diet, nutrition, and lifestyle changes; herbal medicine; manual healing; mind and body control; pharmacological and biological treatments; and additional help and information. A typical essay on an alternative medicine topic includes a brief history, a description of the practice, an objective analysis of the effectiveness of the practice, and any scientific studies that have been conducted on the particular form of alternative medicine. Many of the essays also contain a list of additional references and sources of information. There are few illustrations to aid in presenting the material. A more colorful and visually appealing work with similar information is *The Encyclopedia of Alternative Medicine* (see ARBA 97, entry 1345). As a starting point to introduce readers to alternative medicine practices, this book will be a great addition to the reference collection of every type of library.—**Elaine F. Jurries**

1416. Cassileth, Barrie R. **The Alternative Medicine Handbook: The Complete Reference Guide to Alternative and Complementary Therapies.** New York, W. W. Norton, 1998. 340p. illus. index. $19.95pa. ISBN 0-393-31816-8.

This is an excellent, balanced overview of the numerous alternative and complementary medical therapies that are being practiced today. The author defines "alternative" as a therapy that is used instead of Western mainstream medicine, and "complementary" as a therapy that serves a supplementary role in conventional care. Alternative therapies tend to be unproven and may or may not be harmful. Complementary therapies, usually used alongside conventional treatment, are generally noninvasive and helpful. With great objectivity, the author describes the background, goals, benefits, and risks of each therapy, neither recommending nor condemning any of them.

The book is composed of 7 parts, each part representing a broad category of alternative or complementary medicine. The 7 parts are routes to health and spiritual fulfillment, dietary and herbal remedies, using the mind for emotional relief and physical strength, alternative biological treatments, reducing pain and stress through bodywork, enhancing well-being through the senses, and restoring health with external energy forces. Within each part, 6 to 12 individual therapies are thoroughly described. The description of each therapy contains the following information: what it is, what practitioners say it does, beliefs on which it is based, research evidence to date, what it can do, and where to get it. Among the 54 therapies discussed are acupuncture, homeopathy, Native American healing, Chinese medicine, fasting and juice therapies, macrobiotics, biofeedback, biological dentistry, oxygen therapies, craniosacral therapy, rolfing, aromatherapy, humor therapy, shamanism, and therapeutic touch.

Although there are numerous alternative medicine handbooks on the market, some of which border on the fantastical, this book stands out because it is balanced, rational, and objective. It deserves a place on the reference shelf of both academic and public libraries.—**Elaine F. Jurries**

1417. Goldberg, Burton. **Alternative Medicine Guide to Heart Disease, Stroke, & High Blood Pressure.** Tiburon, Calif., Future Medicine Publishing, 1998. 293p. illus. index. $18.95pa. ISBN 1-887299-10-6.

As increasing numbers of people are turning to alternative methods for the prevention and healing of various illnesses, and are seeking information in guides such as this one. As part of a series published in conjunction with the *Alternative Medicine Digest*, this guide is divided into three main sections treating heart disease, stroke, and high blood pressure. In an introductory statement, the author points out that the book is on alternative methods, and many are not understood or endorsed by the traditional medical community. While he urges readers to discuss the treatments prescribed with their doctors and not to use the book as a substitute for the advice and care of a physician, he also points out that the traditional medical community (including pharmaceutical companies, physicians' trade groups, insurance companies, and some government agencies) is somewhat of a monopoly and has an investment in keeping non-patentable, expensive treatments from the public.

In each of the three areas covered in the guide, the causes of the problem are clearly discussed, along with the self-care options available for prevention related to diet, exercise, and lifestyle changes. The main text describes various alternative therapies, citing both individual cases and research studies that are well documented in standard medical and scientific journals. Accompanying the text are excellent illustrations and diagrams, particularly useful for seeing how certain problems appear in the cardiovascular system. An added feature of the guide is the use of icons in the margins to give further information in smaller print. A small caution sign, for example, alerts the reader to certain risks or contraindications. In addition to the list of citations from footnotes in the text, an index and a list of organizations are found in the appendix. This highly informative, very readable guide should be an excellent introduction to alternative treatments for those with heart problems. The fact that most of the material comes from physicians with traditional training who have turned to alternative methods should be a plus for those who are somewhat fearful of trying something new.—**Lucille Whalen**

1418. **The Illustrated Encyclopedia of Body-Mind Disciplines.** Nancy Allison, ed. New York, Rosen Publishing, 1999. 448p. illus. index. $79.95. ISBN 0-8239-2546-3.

The United States has been experiencing a spiritual awakening in the 1990s that involves linking mind, body, and spirit in an attempt to find greater peace of mind and physical well-being. Many of the techniques used in body-mind disciplines have been practiced for centuries in various parts of the world. *The Illustrated Encyclopedia of Body-Mind Disciplines* describes in detail more than 100 different practices that help link the physical body with the sensing, feeling, and intuitive facilities of the mind.

The book begins by giving short definitions of the techniques covered. After a short introduction to the history and theory behind body-mind disciplines, the book is divided into chapters that supply 5- to 10-page entries on very specific techniques. The chapters include topics such as alternative health models (e.g., holistic, shamanism), sensory therapy (e.g., aromatherapy, light therapy), massage, acupuncture, martial arts, meditation, and body-oriented therapies (psychodrama, rebirthing), among others. The entries are thoroughly described and include the history and theory behind the technique. Many entries include photographs, and all include resources and suggestions for further reading. The work concludes with a name/subject index.

The encyclopedia will be a valuable inclusion in any health, public, or university library. The topic is timely and the entries offer enough information to help readers grasp the idea behind the subject. [R: LJ, July 99, p. 83; BL, 1 Sept 99, pp. 180-181]—**Shannon M. Graff**

1419. Tirtha, Swami Sada Shiva. **The Ayurveda Encyclopedia: Natural Secrets to Healing, Prevention, & Longevity.** Bayville, N.Y., Ayurveda Holistic Center Press; distr., Chicago, Independent Publishers Group, 1998. 669p. illus. index. $32.00. ISBN 0-9658042-2-4.

Although there is no lack of books on alternative health care, few give an overall, in-depth picture of Ayurveda, a holistic health system that originated in India and aims to provide guidance regarding food and lifestyle in order to maintain good health throughout life. This work was intended to fill the need for an authoritative, comprehensive study of the subject, one that could be used as a text for those studying this fairly complicated system. The author, an instructor at the Ayurveda Holistic Center in Bayville, New York, states that he undertook the task of writing this guide at the request of his students, but also points out that the aim of the work is to offer credible evidence to the allopathic community and government health-regulating bodies that Ayurveda can reduce health care costs by more than 50 percent, avoid side effects, and provide effective healing treatments.

In the Ayurvedic system great emphasis is placed on the relationship between the mind and the body, so it is not surprising that much of the text is devoted to this aspect of the subject. According to the author, this encyclopedia is really 3 books in 1: the 1st includes a history of Ayurveda and its basic principles; the 2d is a description of various therapies, including meditation, herbs, and exercise; and the 3d discusses the causes and natural healing remedies for more than 1,000 disorders. From the table of contents, however, one finds the material divided into 4 main sections, with section 4 being divided into chapters on each of the various body systems, such as digestive, respiratory, and nervous systems, and further subdivided into specific diseases. Following the main text are 9 appendixes, including an Ayurvedic glossary, a bibliography, and an index.

The author reminds the reader that the information presented is only a starting point for learning and should not be followed blindly. It would be difficult, however, for most readers to consider this work a starting point. Without some previous training in Ayurveda, finding information on any specific topic would be difficult and tedious. For example, interspersed throughout the text are many words from the Ayurvedic glossary and one must refer to the glossary constantly to read even a few paragraphs in many sections. Some of the terms in the index have too many references without specific page numbers. Kidney, for example, has 19 references, in addition to 6 subheadings with page numbers. Also, some statements seem questionable—that most psychological diseases are said to be healed through color therapy is one instance. Although the volume provides a great deal of helpful information and the author is obviously well educated and knowledgeable about the subject, the way the information is organized, the frequent use of Sanskrit terms, and the sometimes tedious style make it difficult for the ordinary reader. It is recommended only for those libraries having an extensive collection in alternative medicine.—**Lucille Whalen**

Forensic Medicine

1420. **Forensic Medicine Sourcebook.** Annemarie S. Muth, ed. Detroit, Omnigraphics, 1999. 574p. index. (Health Reference Series). $78.00. ISBN 0-7808-0232-2.

This source is another title from the reputable Health Reference Series by Omnigraphics. Apart from offering the layperson information on forensic medicine, there are several items that make this book attractive to consumers who are seeking certain forensic data. One is the death investigation systems in the United States and Canada that list states and provinces, and the death and injury statistics of the United States that include the top 10 leading causes of death. The other is the timeline of forensic medicine and the employment of biotechnology and multimedia for the advances of crime investigation. Also, the forensic glossary and resources listed are helpful additions.

The book's 55 chapters are arranged into 7 parts, including an overview, crime scene and laboratory investigation, forensic medicine/science subspecialties, emerging forensic subspecialties, advances in crime investigation, the courtroom, and additional helpful information. The section on using computer-aided victim identification and new technology inventions for crime detection is intriguing. The various subspecialties, such as forensic odontology, forensic geology, and forensic engineering, are well defined. Timely topics on DNA testing, drug detection, evidence analysis, accident reconstruction, explosives, statistical data, fingerprinting, product tampering, and autopsies are presented. Burns and rape topics are not thoroughly listed, and the principles on the clinical aspects are not fully analyzed. It is noted that materials from this book were collected from governmental and private agencies, as claimed by the publisher. There are references and notes in some chapters for readers to further locate additional information. On the whole, this is a useful current source for those seeking general forensic medical answers.—**Polin P. Lei**

Geriatrics

1421. **Physical and Mental Issues in Aging Sourcebook.** Jenifer Swanson, ed. Detroit, Omnigraphics, 1999. 660p. index. (Health Reference Series). $78.00. ISBN 0-7808-0233-0.

This new volume in Omnigraphics' Health Reference Series is designed to provide the layperson with a convenient source of information about symptoms, conditions, and diseases commonly encountered by the elderly. The main body of the book is divided into 9 sections covering cardiovascular concerns, pulmonary concerns, oral health and digestive concerns, musculoskeletal and skin concerns, metabolic concerns, sexual and reproductive concerns, concerns about the senses, pain and aging, and mental concerns. Many of the 70 individual chapters provide sources for additional information, and 2 chapters are devoted to identifying resource organizations and agencies, including state agencies on aging. Also included are a feeble glossary and a good index. The book's source material is taken primarily from government publications distributed by the National Institutes of Health, the Federal Drug Administration, and the National Institute on Aging. Most of this material is reasonably current although some of the reprinted and excerpted publications have original publication dates from as early as 1993. A major weakness of the work is the lack of cross-referencing from chapter to chapter. Although the major health problems of aging are covered, this is not a comprehensive sourcebook. The level of writing should be accessible to individuals with a high school reading proficiency. Recommended for public libraries.—**Bruce Stuart**

Pediatrics

1422. **American Academy of Pediatrics Guide to Your Child's Nutrition: Making Peace at the Table and Building Healthy Eating Habits for Life.** William H. Dietz and Loraine Stern, eds. New York, Villard/Random House, 1999. 234p. index. $23.00. ISBN 0-375-50187-8.

This helpful guide for parents and other caretakers gives advice on working with the picky eater and myriad other issues involving the nutrition of children from infancy through adolescence. Written in a narrative style with many case studies of common problems, this book is entertaining reading as well as full of authoritative advice from the doctors of the American Academy of Pediatrics. The first five chapters are an overview of nutrition for children through all the stages of their early life. Many of the questions that parents ask their doctors are discussed. For example, breast-feeding and what to order a child when eating out are both discussed here. Chapters on nutrition basics; outside influences (e.g., television, grandparents, childcare providers); eating disorders; alternative diets and supplements; and allergies round out this useful book.

There are a number of other books that address the topic of children's nutrition. An equally authoritative work, *The Yale Guide to Children's Nutrition* (see ARBA 98, entry 1555), contains essentially the same information, with the addition of 100 pages of recipes designed to entice children to eat better. *Mom's Guide to Your Kid's Nutrition* (Alpha Books, 1997) is a popular rendition of advice on children's nutrition.

This guide is a worthy addition to the nutrition collection of all public libraries. Academic libraries that have an education, nutrition, nursing, or medical program will also find it useful.—**Elaine F. Jurries**

1423. **Children's Health.** Dawn P. Dawson, ed. Englewood Cliffs, N.J., Salem Press, 1999. 2v. illus. index. $185.00/set. ISBN 0-89356-944-5.

The vast subject of children's health presents daunting challenges for both parents and health providers. This 2-volume reference tool, although not claiming to be definitive or to be used in place of professional medical advice, does provide excellent overview guidance for those overseeing the health of youngsters, from newborns through age 18.

This encyclopedia is written by 142 authors, mostly M.D.s and Ph.D.s, and contains 324 alphabetically arranged entries, 90 of which have been republished from *Magill's Medical Guide* (rev. ed.; see ARBA 99, entry 1443). Entries vary in length from 100 to 3,500 words and are accompanied by 173 useful photographs, graphs, and charts. The entries range in coverage from broad health concerns (bleeding, discipline) to specific diseases (bulimia, scabies). Some essays deal with basic childhood developmental issues (growth, senses), whereas others describe the responsibilities of pediatric health specialties (dentistry, urology). Entries' contents vary depending on their length. The majority contain the basic description of the disease or topic, key terms, causes and symptoms, treatment and therapy, and possible outcomes. The longer essays also include a list of suggested readings. A separate resources section contains names, addresses, telephone numbers, and URLs for organizations to consult for further information and assistance. Thorough indexing and cross-referencing make these volumes easy to use.

This clearly written reference guide is an important addition to the reference collections of both medical and public libraries and will prove very useful for health professionals and the general public. [R: LJ, 15 Sept 99, p. 68; BL, 1 Dec 99, p. 733]—**Jonathon Erlen**

1424. **Pediatric Cancer Sourcebook.** Edward J. Prucha, ed. Detroit, Omnigraphics, 1999. 587p. index. (Health Reference Series). $78.00. ISBN 0-7808-0245-4.

Although people often think of cancer as being terminal, the fact is that many cancers, especially those often found in children, are treatable and often curable. This sourcebook looks specifically at those cancers that frequently are diagnosed in infants, children, and adolescents. These include leukemias, brain tumors, sarcomas, and lymphomas, among others. The book is divided into 5 parts: "Common Childhood Cancers," "Treatments and Therapies," Coping Strategies and Other Information for Parents," "Financial Information for Families of Children with Cancer," and "Additional Help and Information." The 1st section takes each of the cancers mentioned above and explains their signs and symptoms and how they can be treated. "Treatments and Therapies" discusses chemotherapy, radiation, and transplants as well as discusses what the side effects of these treatment often are. "Coping Strategies and Other Information for Parents" give parents practical information, everything from discussing cancer with children to getting one's health care to cover treatments. "Financial Information for Families of Children with Cancer" gives basic advice on dealing with insurance providers and obtaining financial assistance for treatments. "Additional Help and Information" provides everything from defining terms related to cancer to giving names, addresses, and Websites for foundations that support cancer patients. An index concludes the work. Because of this volume's emphasis on pediatric cancer it will be a valuable addition to all libraries specializing in health services and many public libraries.—**Shannon M. Graff**

1425. **The 3 a.m. Handbook: The Most Commonly Asked Questions About Your Child's Health.** William Feldman, ed. New York, Facts on File, 1998. 224p. illus. index. $17.95pa. ISBN 0-8160-3802-3.

This book comprises 18 chapters on a variety of topics of interest to parents of children of all ages. The editor and the authors, all pediatricians, are associated with Toronto Hospital for Sick Children; some work in pediatric subspecialties. The authors write from the point of view of problems as parents experience them. The chapters address such issues as fever, feeding, crying, rashes, vomiting and diarrhea, behavior and learning, pain, and emergencies. Areas of anticipatory guidance, such as toilet training, safety, and immunizations, are also discussed. One chapter addresses specific common conditions, such as roseola, asthma, bronchiolitis, and chickenpox. In a unique chapter the authors explain clinical research and offer ideas about deciding to have a child participate in a research study.

The book is nicely laid out. The print is pleasant to read, with simple illustrations. Each chapter has a highlighted sidebar illuminating a specific point, such as preventing night awakenings (sleep chapter) and hints on breast-feeding (feeding chapter). Important problems that must be distinguished from normal are pointed out, such as persistent snoring and risks of dehydration (diarrhea and vomiting chapter). Confusing things, like some medical tests, are clearly explained. The emergency chapter is located at the end and easy to find.

Although this book is from a Canadian point of view, nearly everything pertains to U.S. medicine as well. Some terms are not usual American parlance, but that will not confuse the average parent. Most parents will find this a helpful and sensible book. The small list of support telephone numbers is very eclectic. No Websites are listed.—**Margretta Reed Seashore**

1426. Weaver, David D., and Ira K. Brandt. **Catalog of Prenatally Diagnosed Conditions.** 3d ed. Baltimore, Md., Johns Hopkins University Press, 1999. 682p. index. $110.00. ISBN 0-8018-6044-X.

This Johns Hopkins University Press publication was originally published in 1989 listing 445 prenatal diagnosed conditions. The 2d edition arrived in 1992 with 601 conditions. The 3d edition presents 940 conditions, a 56 percent increase over the previous edition. As the identification of new genes is rapidly growing, this book serves as a reference to provide "more diagnostic information to a larger number of women who carry fetuses with a wider array of problems."

Using this reference source is not as difficult as it seems. The book is divided into 3 parts. The 1st is the text, then comes the massive references alphabetically sorted by author, and the last part is the exhaustive index with the numerical index at the end. The text is divided into chapters discussing chromosomal anomalies; congenital malformations, deformations, disruptions, and related disorders; dermatologic disorders; fetal infections; hematologic disorders and hemaglobinopathies; inborn errors of metabolism; other prenatal conditions, tumors, and cysts; and multiple congenital anomalies of unknown etiology. Each condition has been assigned a reference number that is modeled after the one used by Victor A. McKusick in the book *Mendelian Inheritance in Man* (repr. ed.; Books Demand). The change in reference numbers and names since the 2d edition is explained in a short table. When the information on Short Rib-Polydactyly Syndrome, Majewski Type, was compared between the 1st edition and the 3d edition, it was found that not only does the current edition give differential diagnosis and syndrome notes, it also conveys specific information about the conditions or findings by using a list of superscripts attached to the references listed at the end of the condition. This helps in identifying the particularly useful references for readers. Some conditions have extra information, such as treatment modality, methods and findings, prenatal treatment, and prenatal diagnosis. Abbreviations used in this book are also carefully grouped for easy reading.

Prenatal care is important to women and prenatal diagnosis is essential to determine the health of fetuses before birth. With the help of molecular genetic technology, the practice of prenatal care will become more accurate and simple. This book serves as a guide for such information needs.—**Polin P. Lei**

Poisoning

1427. Turkington, Carol. **The Poisons and Antidotes Sourcebook.** New York, Checkmark Books/Facts on File, 1999. 408p. index. $35.00. ISBN 0-8160-3959-3.

The Poisons and Antidotes Sourcebook is designed to inform readers about dangerous materials that may be within their own home without their knowledge of their dangers or of how to treat them in case of deadly contact. The book includes information on such common items as household poisons; insecticides and fertilizers; poisonous spiders and snakes; drugs; and poison ivy and other toxic plants. Part 1 of the work contains tips on what to do in a poison emergency, how to make one's home safe, food poisoning, and what poisons are associated with what symptoms. The book then is arranged into A to Z entries. These entries explain what the poison is, the symptoms that will occur, and treatment. The book is extensively cross-referenced. At the end of the work are several appendixes that provide hotline telephone numbers in case of emergency, newsletters, organizations, regional poison control centers, and Websites for more information. A glossary, reference section, and index conclude the work. The information provided in this guide is both in-depth and valuable. The work will be useful in both personal libraries and public reference collections.

—Shannon M. Graff

Specific Diseases and Conditions

AIDS

1428. **AIDS Sourcebook.** 2d ed. Karen Bellenir, ed. Detroit, Omnigraphics, 1999. 751p. index. (Health Reference Series, v.48). $78.00. ISBN 0-7808-0225-X.

The 63 chapters in *AIDS Sourcebook* are complete or excerpted documents from 16 U.S. government agencies, 3 nonprofit organizations, and 1 United Nations program. Omnigraphics found, compiled, and edited the documents, which were originally published between 1993 and 1998. As one might expect from government publications, the writing style is terse, factual, and advice-based. Quotations and case studies, which might personalize the topics, are almost totally absent. Content is authoritative, scientific, and as complete as one will find. With the exception of the 90-page glossary, articles are quite short, averaging 8 pages, an ideal length for high school and college students. Areas covered include general AIDS information, statistics and trends, information for people living with AIDS, prevention, and research. This work is highly recommended.—**Pete Prunkl**

1429. Lerner, Eric K., and Mary Ellen Hombs. **AIDS Crisis in America: A Reference Handbook.** 2d ed. Santa Barbara, Calif., ABC-CLIO, 1998. 323p. index. (Contemporary World Issues). $45.00. ISBN 1-57607-070-0.

A welcome revision and update of information contained in the original edition, this valuable reference tool serves as a basic introduction to the subject of AIDS, as well as a resource for various facets and issues related to the topic. The work opens with a general overview including history, scientific perspectives, government response, and predictions for the future. This is followed by a quite detailed chapter treating the chronology (through 1997) of significant events related to AIDS. Short biographies of key people who have played some role in the AIDS crisis are also included. The remaining chapters focus in turn on facts and statistics, official government reports, and legal aspects and issues surrounding AIDS. Coverage throughout these chapters is somewhat uneven, generally encompassing 1997, and sometimes 1998.

Of great value to the individual seeking further information are the two final chapters of the work. The first functions as a directory of agencies, organizations, hotlines, and other assistance programs throughout Canada and the United States. Directory information as well as descriptions of purpose and scope are included. The last chapter focuses on reference materials, and includes both print (books, newsletters, pamphlets, anthologies, personal accounts, photographic works) and nonprint (films, videos, CD-ROMs, Websites). The whole is supplemented by a glossary, index, and biographical profile of the authors.

Although the work suffers, by necessity, of not being as up-to-date as possible, it does present a solid overview and introduction to its topic. Recommended for high school, public, and college libraries, with the understanding that it must be complemented by electronic and periodical literature.

—**Edmund F. SantaVicca**

Alzheimer's Disease

1430. **Alzheimer's Disease Sourcebook.** 2d ed. Karen Bellenir, ed. Detroit, Omnigraphics, 1999. 524p. index. (Health Reference Series, v.26). $78.00. ISBN 0-7808-0223-3.

This new edition of the *Alzheimer's, Stroke, and 29 Other Neurological Disorders Sourcebook* (see ARBA 94, entry 1862) is actually a very different book. The 1st edition provided mainly descriptive information about a wide range of neurological diseases; this 2d edition narrows its focus to diseases producing dementia. It is not only more current but also provides more practical assistance to those who fear these diseases or who must deal with an afflicted loved one. The wide-ranging information included is reprinted, like that in its predecessor, but is drawn not only from U.S. government agencies but also from medical journals and organizations, such as the Alzheimer's Association. The initial section summarizes what is known about Alzheimer's and its occurrence. What used to be called senility is far from universal; only 5 to 6 percent of elderly people suffer from Alzheimer's or related dementias. An overview of warning signs and diagnostic information help the consumer understand what are and what are not signs of a serious problem. Another section covers other diseases of the aged causing dementia, such as Huntington's Disease and Multi-Infarct Dementia, which is the result of a series of strokes causing brain damage. Parts 3, 4, and 5 of this work cover recent developments in prevention and treatment research, information on long-term care of patients, and guides to where those caring for an Alzheimer's patient can find assistance (including directories of federal, state, community, and other assistance programs), and a bibliography. Compilations of reprinted articles can be uneven in style and possibly in currency. Nonetheless, this book provides a wealth of useful information not otherwise available in one place. This resource is recommended for all types of libraries.—**Marit S. MacArthur**

Blood and Circulatory Disorders

1431. **Blood and Circulatory Disorders Sourcebook.** Linda M. Shin and Karen Bellenir, eds. Detroit, Omnigraphics, 1999. 554p. index. (Health Reference Series, v.39). $78.00. ISBN 0-7808-0203-9.

This volume is a recent publication in a series of books that bring together and index reprints of articles originally published by government health agencies and private disease-related organizations. Omnigraphics has produced more than 45 of these volumes, on topics ranging from AIDS to learning disabilities. The target audience is patients and their families as well as health professionals who are involved with patient education. In all cases articles are clear and easy to understand, written in lay terminology and often providing illustrations. Some are in question and answer form, which is particularly handy for patient education purposes. The 51 chapters include material on specific blood problems, such as anemia, leukemia and bleeding disorders, and articles on diseases of the circulatory system, such as aneurysms, hypertension, and atherosclerosis. A final section discusses blood transfusions and their risks, autologous transfusion, and progress toward safety of the blood supply. There are a glossary of blood-related terms and a list of private and government agency resources for patients that gives addresses, telephone numbers, e-mail addresses, and Websites. Most articles are fairly recent, with copyright dates of 1995 or later.—**Carol L. Noll**

Brain Disorders

1432. **Brain Disorders Sourcebook.** Karen Bellenir, ed. Detroit, Omnigraphics, 1999. 481p. index. (Health Reference Series). $78.00. ISBN 0-7808-0229-2.

This is a new addition to the Health Reference Series and is a basic consumer guide of health information about functions of the human brain as well as strokes, seizures, Lou Gehrig's disease, Parkinson's disease, cancer, and other brain disorders. The easy reading style provides readers with information on the complex issues surrounding the brain and its disorders. The text explains the causes and treatments of these diseases, and the book further provides symptoms, diagnostic tests, and coping strategies. There are a few black-and-white illustrations. The 46 chapters are arranged in 7 parts: the human brain including anatomy, EEG, MRI, CT, PET, and brain donation; strokes, including age groups, prevention, Warfarin, carotid endarterectomy, asymptomatic carotid atherosclerosis, and emergency; seizure disorders, including epilepsy and pregnancy, drugs, Felbamate, surgery, traumatic brain injury, febrile seizures, and genetics; Amyotrophic Lateral Sclerosis, including drugs and coping with this disease; Parkinson's disease, including drug therapies and coping mechanisms; other brain disorders, such as tumors, cerebral palsy, headache, narcolepsy, neurotrauma, Tourette's syndrome, and Tuberous Sclerosis; and additional help and information including brain terms, organizational resources for patients with brain disorders, and further reading on brain disorders. In addition to a good index, there are copyrighted articles.

Materials are collected from different government agencies, such as the National Cancer Institute, Agency for Health Care Policy and Research, National Center for Research Resources, National Institutes of Health, and from private organizations such as the American Parkinson Disease Association and the American Academy of Neurology. If readers are familiar with the style Health Reference Series offers, they will also find this source useful. However, these series do not replace professional health advice from health care providers.—**Polin P. Lei**

Burns

1433. **Burns Sourcebook.** Allan R. Cook, ed. Detroit, Omnigraphics, 1999. 604p. illus. index. (Health Reference Series). $78.00. ISBN 0-7808-0204-7.

Annually, some 1.25 million burns are reported to medical personnel in the United States, including 5,500 burn fatalities, making burn injuries one of the nation's leading causes of accidental death. This latest volume in the Health Reference Series from Omnigraphics is an important resource for both health professionals and the general public in dealing with the problems created by burn injuries. Drawing from governmental, medical, and scientific literature, the editors provide a lot of knowledge pertaining to the prevention and the appropriate handling of a wide variety of burns.

This book is divided into 7 easy-to-use sections. Beginning with burn statistics, the following segments discuss the types and degrees of burns, the variety of treatment protocols, issues of rehabilitation and living with the long-term effects of burns, preventive measures to safeguard homes and businesses from burn hazards, and emergency and first-aid procedures for burn victims. A final brief section lists some of the major additional societal and institutional burn resources that are available. Illustrations and bibliographies provide additional useful information throughout this volume, which also includes a comprehensive index.

Burns are a serious public health problem in the United States. This key reference guide is an invaluable addition to all health care and public libraries in confronting this ongoing health issue.—**Jonathon Erlen**

Diabetes

1434. **Diabetes Sourcebook.** 2d ed. Karen Bellenir, ed. Detroit, Omnigraphics, 1999. 688p. illus. index. (Health Reference Series, v.3). $78.00. ISBN 0-7808-0224-1.

This giant comprehensive volume is designed as an overview for laypersons to help them recognize the risk factors associated with diabetes, to identify symptoms, and to acquire the proper medical care. Of the 16 million Americans who suffer the illness, there are still 8 million people who remain undiagnosed. Medical professionals recommend that all adults age 45 and older should be tested for diabetes, and high-risk people under 45 should be tested as well. Based on these sheer numbers alone, this book serves a unique purpose for those people who are diabetic or for those who are high-risk candidates.

The new edition takes into account the changes in diabetic care since the first edition in 1994. According to the preface, the new volume contains 95 percent revised or new material. The 67 chapters of the book are divided into 8 parts. The parts of the book focus on broad areas of interest whereas the chapters relate to single topics. Part 1, "Diabetes Prevalence," offers statistical information about diabetes in the United States. Part 2, "Types of Diabetes and Related Disorders," describes the risk factors and symptoms for the major types of diabetes and related disorders. Part 3, "Diabetes Management," provides practical suggestions for managing the disease and reducing complications. Part 4, "The Role of Diet and Exercise in Diabetes Management," examines the relationship between diabetes management and the lifestyle factors of diet and exercise. Part 5, "Insulin and Other Diabetes Medicines," provides information about the different types of insulin, other medications, and drug interactions of special concern to diabetics. Part 6, "Complications of Diabetes," explains the major complications of diabetes, describes how they develop and provides treatment information. Part 7, "Research Initiatives," reports on diabetes research and the path toward further investigation. Part 8, "Additional Help and Information," provides a diabetes dictionary, sources for cookbooks and recipes, a bibliography of diabetes information, financial help sources, and a directory of diabetes organizations.

A comprehensive index provides easy access to information in the book. Material for this volume was collected from a wide array of government and private agencies. Copyrighted articles from a variety of sources have been reprinted throughout the book. In the commitment to provide ongoing coverage of important medical developments in the field of diabetes, the editors ask the readers to share their medical concerns for the next volume. This comprehensive book is an excellent addition for high school, academic, medical, and public libraries serving clientele with a broad range of medical concerns about diabetes. This volume is highly recommended.—**Betty J. Morris**

Eating Disorders

1435. **Eating Disorders: A Reference Sourcebook.** 2d ed. Raymond Lemberg and Leigh Cohn, eds. Phoenix, Ariz., Oryx Press, 1999. 253p. index. $49.50. ISBN 1-57356-156-8.

Eating disorders, such as anorexia nervosa and bulimia, pose a grave danger to the health of thousands of Americans each year. This volume dispels the myths surrounding these disorders and is well grounded in research on the topic. Essays covers such topics as the causes and symptoms of eating disorders, body-size acceptance, eating disorders in males, eating disorders in athletes, feminist perspectives on eating disorders, and the treatment that is available.

Eating Disorders: A Reference Sourcebook is the 2d edition of *Controlling Eating Disorders with Facts, Advice, and Resources* (Oryx, 1992). New to this edition is an updated state-by-state list of facilities and programs for treating eating disorders, and the section on selected resources has been substantially expanded, listing books, articles, audiovisual materials, electronic resources, and Websites. An annotated list of Internet addresses for sites with information on eating disorders is a valuable resource. Also included is a new section on organizations, associations, hotline counseling services, and support groups. Bibliographic references and an index are included.

A personal account by Meredy Humphreys entitled "Death of a Scalesman" depicts the suffering of an anorexic and her struggle day in and day out to overcome it. This poignant account is accompanied by a case study by the editor. This single volume is uplifting and offers hope to anyone seeking assistance with coping with an eating disorder. [R: BR, Sept/Oct 99, pp. 70-71]—**Marilynn Green Hopman**

Endocrine and Metabolic Disorders

1436. **Endocrine and Metabolic Disorders Sourcebook.** Linda M. Shin, ed. Detroit, Omnigraphics, 1999. 574p. index. (Health Reference Series, v.36). $78.00. ISBN 0-7808-0207-1.

Presently there are 44 titles on various medical topics in Omnigraphics' Health Reference Series. Because of the success of this series, Omnigraphics intends to expand the series to 58 volumes in 1999. *Endocrine and Metabolic Disorders Sourcebook* follows a similar format of the other sourcebooks. Generally the sourcebooks are written in easy-to-read text and are designed for consumers seeking health-related information on certain medical disorders. These sourcebooks intend to be comprehensive in scope, but supplementary sources will still need to be acquired for any in-depth clinical information on disorder.

There are a total of 58 chapters in the volume at hand. Part 1 begins with an introduction to the endocrine system and human metabolism. The other 5 parts contain information on the glands and their disorders. Part 2 lists pancreatic and diabetic disorders, with nutritional recommendations and exercise control. Part 3 is on adrenal gland disorders and has only 4 chapters. Part 4 is on pituitary and growth disorders and includes a chapter on acromegaly. Part 5 is on thyroid and parathyroid disorders, which is extremely useful for a percentage of the general public. Part 6 provides information on other disorders of endocrine and metabolic functioning, such as hypercalcemia, PKU, FMEN1, galactosemia, and more. There are a few illustrations and charts to illustrate growth rate and locations of glands. Although some Websites are included for certain organizations and associations, it would be useful if more appropriate links were inserted, such as PDQ, NCI, or NIDDM for the electronic-savvy readers. Some chapters give suggested readings, other resources, or references. The index at the end is thorough, and readers will have no problem in locating "the information on the glands of the endocrine system, its components, the hormones it regulates, and the metabolic consequences of various disorders." Omnigraphics has produced another needed resource for health information consumers.—**Polin P. Lei**

Gynecology and Human Reproduction

1437. **The Encyclopedia of Reproductive Technologies.** Annette Burfoot, ed. Boulder, Colo., Westview Press, 1999. 404p. index. $85.00. ISBN 0-8133-6658-5.

The Encyclopedia of Reproductive Technologies is a rare find, a resource on a technical subject that is both comprehensible and academic. Articles are written in a clear and concise style about a broad variety of medical, technical, legislative, ethical, and historical topics. The credentials of the Canadian sociologist who edited this text and the contributing authors are impressive. The roster of contributors includes medical faculty and researchers, social scientists, ethicists and philosophers, activists, and feminists. The contents are balanced and well researched, with further reading recommendations for each topic.

The text is organized into chapters on the history of reproduction, early reproductive technology, early infertility treatments, advanced infertility technology, and reproductive genetics. Brief articles within chapters discuss the technologies and risks; ethical concerns related to treatments; legislative issues in a variety of developed nations; and genetic topics, such as fetal tissue and embryo research, cloning, and genetic screening. An acronym list provides a quick reference resource for the confusing jumble of shorthand references within this field. The detailed subject index is invaluable because this encyclopedia follows a thematic approach to organization rather than an alphabetic approach. A selective but highly relevant number of illustrations are distributed throughout the text. This overview resource would be an excellent addition to collections serving college students and health consumers researching fertility options.

—**Lynne M. Fox**

Sexually Transmitted Diseases

1438. Marr, Lisa. **Sexually Transmitted Diseases: A Physician Tells You What You Need to Know.** Baltimore, Md., Johns Hopkins University Press, 1998. 341p. index. $39.95; $16.95pa. ISBN 0-8018-6042-3; 0-8018-6043-1pa.

This text addresses a topic that is of increasing importance and yet is still considered by many to be taboo. The book has two primary components. Part 1 discusses what readers need to know about sexually transmitted diseases (STDs) and part 2 is called the "Encyclopedia of STDs." This approach is beneficial because part 1 provides readers with an overview of what they should know regarding anatomy, symptoms, STD examinations, communication skills, and safe sex. Part 2 is a natural transition as it explains the STDs, including STD signs and symptoms, treatment options, and statistics.

The medical terminology and statistics will not be overly complex for the adult reader to understand. The illustrations are easy to interpret and they correspond directly to the contents of the book. The resources, a glossary of terms, and references are provided in the latter portion of the text. Contact information, including telephone numbers, mailing address, and Website, has been included when possible.

This text provides valuable information that has been presented in a professional and concise manner. Although it could be included in any medical library, it could easily complement a number of libraries (i.e., public, home, health care clinic) as a source of valuable information. It may also be useful as a reference resource for individuals involved in teaching courses that discuss sexually transmitted diseases.

—Paul M. Murphy III

Skin Diseases

1439. Boyd, Alan S. **The Skin Sourcebook.** Los Angeles, Calif., Lowell House, 1998. 404p. illus. index. $22.95pa. ISBN 0-7373-0003-5.

The Skin Sourcebook should not be confused with the plethora of beauty and skin care books. This text transcends the beauty book genre, offering instead a clear and easy-to-understand consumer health dermatology resource. *The Skin Sourcebook* would be a valuable addition to any library fielding consumer health inquiries in the area of dermatology. Prior to the publication of this work, consumer health questions on dermatology were referred to more technical dermatology textbooks, or to consumer health magazines with less authoritative sources of information. The author of this work, Alan S. Boyd, is an experienced Vanderbilt University dermatologist with specialties in dermatology and psoriasis care.

The health of the skin is the focus of well-indexed chapters on skin care and therapy, dermatitis, skin cancer, and diseases and conditions affecting the skin. The chapters include short descriptions of conditions; discussions of commonly prescribed topical, ingested, or injectable preparations and medications; and suggestions for self-diagnosis. The color illustrations of skin conditions at the center of this book provide a visual reference guide usually reserved for more expensive and technical atlases of dermatology. Unfortunately, neither the index nor the chapter text refers the reader to the illustrations. Readers must find topics of interest in the index, identify the chapter that includes the topic, then find the group of illustrations under that chapter heading.

Three appendixes provide additional resources, including a list of commonly prescribed medications along with dosage and drug interaction notes. Another appendix suggests possible conditions indicated by major symptoms. The third appendix includes organizations that provide information and support to patients. An extensive bibliography lists resources used in the preparation of the book. This work will be a useful resource for multiple types of libraries serving patrons with health care concerns.—**Lynne M. Fox**

Sleep Disorders

1440. **Sleep Disorders Sourcebook.** Jenifer Swanson, ed. Detroit, Omnigraphics, 1999. 439p. index. (Health Reference Series). $78.00. ISBN 0-7808-0234-9.

This text, which is part of Omnigraphics' Health Reference Series, contains more than 400 pages of useful information relating to sleep. The book is divided into 6 parts and contains 53 chapters.

Part 1, "Understanding Sleep Requirements and the Cost of Sleep Deprivation," discusses topics such as why we need sleep and power napping. Part 2 contains 11 chapters that explore "Sleep Through the Lifespan." Topics include "What Is Sudden Infant Death Syndrome" (SIDS), "Common Bedtime Trauma," and "Sleep in Older Persons." Part 3 discusses major sleep disorders. The 15 chapters cover topics such as sleep apnea, snoring, narcolepsy, insomnia, and sleepwalking. Part 4, "Sleep Medications," focuses on medications that may be used to either enhance or facilitate sleep. Four chapters are dedicated to medications such as Melatonin, benzodiazepines, and over-the-counter options. Part 5 has 9 chapters that focus on "Sleep and Other Disorders." This section of the book explores the effects and relation between sleep and coexisting illnesses. Part 6, the last 4 chapters of the book, provides the reader with a glossary of terms and an extensive list of references. The inside of the front and back covers of this book lists a complete catalog of the Health Reference Series. This text will complement any home or medical library. It is user-friendly and ideal for the adult reader.—**Paul M. Murphy III**

Sports Medicine

1441. **Sports Injuries Sourcebook.** By Heather E. Aldred. Detroit, Omnigraphics, 1999. 606p. index. (Health Reference Series). $78.00. ISBN 0-7808-0218-7.

This new volume in the Omnigraphics Health Reference Series describes the causes, treatments, and rehabilitation of common sports injuries and also provides information about injury prevention in many different sporting activities. Concerns of special groups (i.e., young athletes, senior citizens, and women) are also addressed.

The book's 46 chapters are arranged in 5 parts: understanding common injuries, injury prevention during training, injury prevention for specific sports, rehabilitation and treatment, and a final section with a glossary and directory of organizational resources. The subject index is fairly comprehensive, as is the table of contents.

Sport Injuries Sourcebook provides basic information for the layperson. It is not intended to be a comprehensive resource for diagnosis and treatment. Although the editors state their concern for providing current information in revised and updated volumes, it should be noted that many of the references cited in this book were originally published before 1996. There is also one glaring error: Indiana University is in Bloomington; Indiana State University is in Terre Haute. In health care, information over three to five years old is often obsolete. Public libraries and undergraduate academic libraries will find this book useful for its nontechnical language.—**Vicki J. Killion**

NURSING

1442. **Handbook of Clinical Nursing Research.** Ada Sue Hinshaw, Suzanne L. Feetham, and Joan L. Shaver, eds. Newbury Park, Calif., Sage, 1999. 696p. index. $89.95. ISBN 0-8039-5784-X.

For the past two decades, the nursing scientific community's goal was to generate a body of knowledge that would guide nursing practice in optimizing health care. This first handbook for the clinical nursing research addresses the major areas in which there is significant and reliable research that can be used to guide nursing practice, explores the depth of knowledge to date, and provides specific direction to advance the science of nursing for the future. It establishes a baseline for the evolving discipline and is intended for multiple audiences, including all degree programs in nursing, faculties, clinicians, and other health care professionals with similar issues.

In part 1 of the handbook, a theoretical analysis of the core of the discipline is examined and the methodological perspectives and issues in nursing research are addressed. It provides context for understanding the scientific processes underlying the various research areas. Part 2 presents syntheses of defined areas of clinical research (i.e., health needs of diverse racial and ethnic populations, clinical therapeutic strategies, health and illness in older adults).

As the first attempt to review and critique the state of clinical nursing research, the editors have been most successful in bringing together the foremost scholars, researchers, and educators. Comprehensive in scope, this book deserves a place in every major academic medical library and nursing school.

—**Vicki J. Killion**

1443. **RSP Funding for Nursing Students and Nurses 1998-2000.** By Gail Ann Schlachter and R. David Weber. San Carlos, Calif., Reference Service Press, 1998. 163p. index. $25.00 spiralbound. ISBN 0-918276-74-8.

This is an excellent source of funding information for student nurses and nurses. It is not just scholarships for nursing students. The coverage is for regular credit courses, continuing education classes, research, seminars, workshops, conference attendance, and a category titled creative activities. The funding sources include grants, loans, awards, forgivable loans, fellowships, scholarships, and traineeships. The text of the book is divided by the above categories instead of alphabetically to give it ease of use—no more flipping between the index and text for entries. Each entry includes the book entry number; official name of the funds; the name, address, phone, e-mail and Website of the sponsoring organization; purpose; eligibility; amount of funds; time period of funding; special features; limitations; number awarded; and the deadline for applying. The book does not cover programs that exclude U.S. citizens and residents or funding offered only by a school for their program. There are five indexes in the book: sponsoring organization, residency, tenability, nursing specialty, and calendar. The indexes make the book's information more accessible if one is looking for funding from a specific organization, for geographical areas, or for deadline date. This is an excellent tool, especially for the working nurse, since it provides all types of funding information not related directly to college credit classes. This volume is recommended for all hospital libraries and other libraries that serve nursing clientele.—**Betsy J. Kraus**

1444. Snodgrass, Mary Ellen. **Historical Encyclopedia of Nursing.** Santa Barbara, Calif., ABC-CLIO, 1999. 354p. illus. index. $75.00. ISBN 1-57607-086-7.

The term "nursing" is not used here as the name of a particular profession, but rather to include the personal and medical care given to all ages of people, in all places and time, under many circumstances, by religious and other organizations, and especially by individuals (many of whom are untrained). It is a social history of healers and health care from the earliest times to modern times. The emphasis is on the contributions of individuals, not labor movements, political acts, or educational efforts. Longer, more thoughtful survey articles, such as those on nursing in ancient times or in major wars, are mixed in alphabetically with biographies and brief discussions of trends. For example, "Gender Issues in Nursing" is followed by "Mother Angela Gillespie" of the Navy Nurse Corps. Many letters and memoirs were consulted as well as the usual biographies and histories of nursing and recollections of fellow workers. Sources are listed carefully in the longer items, and there is an extensive bibliography and a list of "Works By and About Healers." The section on the art of midwifery, covering changing attitudes toward it and its practitioners through the centuries, is particularly interesting.

The content is well researched and the author has succeeded in compiling a great deal of historical material about nursing (both good and bad), with a personal style and viewpoint that makes this excellent encyclopedia a worthwhile reference book.—**Harriette M. Cluxton**

PHARMACY AND PHARMACEUTICAL SCIENCES

1445. Garrison, Robert, Jr., and Michael Mannion. **Pharmacist's Guide to Over-the-Counter and Natural Remedies.** Garden City Park, N.Y., Avery Publishing, 1999. 368p. index. $6.95pa. ISBN 0-89529-850-3.

The purpose of this book is to give important information on over-the-counter (OTC) and natural remedies and to explain how they can be used beneficially for treating conditions not requiring prescription drugs. The information provided is clearly and concisely written for understanding by the majority of readers. This book is divided into 2 main sections. Part 1 lists "fifty common herbs and their potential interactions with regular drugs" alphabetically and other broad general information on these remedies, such as what type of labeling information to look for, the units of measurement, and "vitamin and mineral intakes." Part

2 is an alphabetic list of common conditions. Each entry describes the condition, the OTC remedies, the natural remedies, and if there are specific precautions to note. Appendix A is a list of organizations to contact for further information on any of the conditions or remedies listed. Appendix B is a personal medical form, which includes a place to list all medications, making it easier for someone to note if there might be interactions among medications, OTCs, and natural remedies. There is a list of references for further reading and an alphabetic index of all conditions and natural remedies. Cross-references are included in the index. This book is highly recommended for all library collections because more people are looking for alternative treatments.—**Betsy J. Kraus**

1446. Kuhn, Cynthia, Scott Swartzwelder, and Wilkie Wilson. **Buzzed: The Straight Facts About the Most Used and Abused Drugs from Alcohol to Ecstasy.** New York, W. W. Norton, 1998. 317p. illus. index. $14.95pa. ISBN 0-393-31732-3.

Drug education is often incomplete. We tell our young people to "Just Say No," and cite horror stories of relatively rare cocaine deaths and marijuana "addiction." In addition, many of the drugs that young people encounter go by names we do not know or are themselves arcane and little known outside the youth scene. This excellent resource lays out the plain unvarnished facts in language that high school and college students can understand. Part 1 examines broad categories of drugs: alcohol, caffeine, herbal drugs, entactogens, hallucinogens, inhalants, marijuana, nicotine, opiates, sedatives, steroids, and stimulants. It describes how each is introduced into the system (e.g., ingest, inhale, inject), the effects on the body, common terms used for the substance, overdose, interactions with other drugs, and, where applicable, the different effects of different forms. Each substance is thoroughly examined with no inflated scare tactics. Part 2 covers the basics of brain function and drug function in general as well as legal issues. A bibliography is appended and an excellent glossary of slang terms is provided. This resource will be useful for public library reference departments, but be sure to buy several circulating copies too.—**Susan B. Hagloch**

1447. Mathiowitz, Edith. **Encyclopedia of Controlled Drug Delivery.** New York, John Wiley, 1999. 2v. illus. index. $595.00/set. ISBN 0-471-14828-8.

This multi-authored, 2-volume set on controlled drug delivery is an advanced reference text. The audience for this source will most likely be graduate students, biomedical researchers or scientists, medical professionals, and certain business managers. The author has also recently coauthored a text on bioadhesive drug delivery systems. However, this is the first encyclopedia on controlled drug delivery that includes topics such as history from 1975 to date, pros and cons of controlled versus traditional delivery systems, descriptions of types of controlled drug release, pharmaceutical applications, stabilization and characterization of proteins, methods, characterizations, marketing, economics, gene therapy, and polymer technology. Each drug delivery system has keywords listed and an outline and bibliography. Even though there is no table of contents, the thorough index allows readers to search for narrower terms than the broad categories. The timely knowledge provides needed information on new approaches in treating conditions such as cancer, heart disease, alcoholism, infectious diseases, and others. Agents for contraception, orthopedics, and vaccination are discussed. Polymer substances such as polyanhydrides, chitosan polyesters, hydrogels, and bioadhesives are described. Techniques such as gel permeation and X-ray photoelectron spectroscopy are commented on. Gene therapy, blood substitutes, food ingredients, and tissue engineering are explained. Various methods of administration, such as parenteral, intravitreal, oral, rectal, ocular, nasal, buccal, vaginal, and the central nervous system, are discussed. Controlled drug releases, such as osmotic pumps, pendent-chain systems, membrane systems, nanoparticles, and liposomes, are detailed. Patents, regulatory issues, manufacturing approaches, in vitro and in vivo methods, pharmacokinetics, and others are described.

With the large amount of information on controlled drug delivery systems presented here, this text fills a void for those who wish to understand more about how the controlled drug can target a specific body part and what its medical and economic impact is on the health industry. And this text is costly; many academic centers might consider this as a major purchase.—**Polin P. Lei**

1448. Mindell, Earl, and Virginia Hopkins. **Prescription Alternatives: Hundreds of Safe, Natural, Prescription-Free Remedies to Restore and Maintain Your Health.** 2d ed. Lincolnwood, Ill., National Textbook, 1998. 562p. index. $19.95pa. ISBN 0-87983-989-9.

Written in clear, understandable language, the theme of this work is to be aware of alternative ways of treating medical disorders rather than becoming part of what the author suggests is the "drug treadmill." The source is organized into 2 parts. Part 1 consists of laying the foundation for good health, and part 2 considers prescription drugs and their natural alternatives. Such areas as being aware of the pill-popping mindset; how to avoid prescription drug abuse; the interaction of drugs with food, drink, supplements, and other drugs; and how to read drug labels and information inserts are some of the issues that are considered in part 1.

Part 2, which makes up the majority of the work, considers various types of medical problems, the drugs that are usually prescribed to alleviate the problem, and the alternative remedies to prescription drugs. Each of these medical problems is arranged in a chapter-by-chapter format. For example, chapters on diabetes drugs and their natural alternatives and drugs for pain relief and their natural alternatives are present. Other medical areas considered are digestive tract problems, insomnia, eye diseases, osteoporosis, cold, cough, and asthma. For each medical area considered, general information regarding the malady, prescription drugs given for the malady, along with their side effects and natural alternatives for treating the disease, are given. All of this information is written for a layperson in an informal style and does not follow the conventional type of reference book. More then 1,000 simple, safe, nature-based remedies are presented, along with explanations on how to monitor the body as one switches from drugs to natural health. A list of recommended readings, a list of references reflecting each of the chapters presented, and a subject index complete the work. This work is recommended for all high school, public, and college libraries. Persons interested in this topic may wish to purchase the guide for their own home libraries.—**George H. Bell**

1449. **Mosby's Over-the-Counter Medicine Cabinet Medicines.** By Richard P. Donjon. St. Louis, Mo., Mosby, 1997. 127p. index. $12.95 spiralbound. ISBN 0-8151-8053-5.

Mosby's Over-the-Counter Medicine Cabinet Medicines is a guide that tells what you need to know about the over-the-counter medicines you take. The book is divided into various subject areas, including allergies, asthma, colds, flu and coughs, constipation, diarrhea, diet aids, headache, hemorrhoids, nausea and vomiting, pain and fever, quitting smoking, skin problems, sleep aids, and vaginal infections. Each section describes what it is and the symptoms; medicines and products that relieve symptoms, including side effects; interactions and precautions; use in children; use in the elderly; and use in pregnancy and nursing. It also has commonly asked questions about the topic. The publication includes a product index. The book could be more extensive as it is only 127 pages. Most public libraries should purchase this volume for their consumer health collections.—**Theresa Maggio**

1450. **Natural Medicines Comprehensive Database.** 2d ed. Stockton, Calif., Therapeutic Research Faculty, 1999. 1310p. index. $92.00. ISBN 0-9676136-2-0.

The *Natural Medicines Comprehensive Database* is a monumental compilation of nearly every "natural" medicine distributed in the United States today. For this works purpose "natural" refers to all herbal and non-herbal supplements, some of which may not be collected from natural sources but are still categorized along with natural products. The need for this particular resource arose from the influx of natural products into the general market in the past several years and the inability of either pharmacists or laypersons to keep up on the new research and uses for a particular natural product. This book is designed to answer many of the questions that come with using a natural supplement as well as give readers new information on the products.

The book is arranged in alphabetic order and each supplement listed provides information on the product in 15 categories. These categories include providing the name of the product, any names the product may also be known as, its scientific name, what the product is often used for (regardless of whether it is effective in this area or not), its safety and a recommendation of who should not use the product, its effectiveness, the possible mechanism of action and active ingredients, adverse reactions and allergies, what other drugs it may interfere with, the typical dose or how the product is administered, and a section for comments from the publisher about the product. Each entry is generally a page to a page and a half in length. Entries provide references which are provided in the 80-page reference section at the back of the book. The publisher admits that many of the sources list contradicting information on these natural products so the editors take the evidence into consideration to reach a consensus decision on the effects and reliability of the drug. There is also a general index, a brand name listing, an interaction listing, a therapeutically effective products list, and a nutrient depletion chart at the end of the volume. Readers will find much of this information in these charts of value.

This resource is also available in a Web version that is updated daily. The Web version allows health professionals to interact and discuss new findings about natural drugs. It provides a forum for questions, answers, and relevant citations to be posted. The price for this service is $92 per year. This work is an invaluable resource for those in health-related fields or those in the profession of providing information to them. Medical libraries, academic libraries, and many large public libraries will find this a much-used resource.—**Shannon M. Graff**

1451. Pagliaro, Louis A., and Ann Marie Pagliaro. **Psychologists' Psychotropic Desk Reference.** Bristol, Pa., Taylor & Francis, 1999. 704p. index. $59.95. ISBN 0-87630-964-3.

The *Psychologists' Psychotropic Drug Reference* (PPDR) provides essential information on a variety of prescription drugs commonly used in the treatment of psychological disorders. Intended for use by practicing psychologists and as a guide for psychology graduate students, it is a valuable ready-reference source of psychotropic drugs often prescribed in North America. The authors are careful to point out that current guidelines are cited for the prescription of the psychotropic drugs that should be considered supplemental to clinical psychotherapy treatment. Other medical personnel and well-educated family members will also appreciate the comprehensive treatment of each drug included.

Organized in a similar fashion to the *Physician's Desk Reference* (52d ed.; Medical Economics Data, 1998), the main section begins with an alphabetic list of drugs by generic name. Categories range from antidepressants to benzodiazepine and opiate analgesic antagonists. Each entry has several components on such topics as the therapeutic action of the drug, any possible adverse reactions, and toxicity symptoms, which might be confused with and worsened by psychological disorders. There is comprehensive coverage of clinically significant drug interactions, overdose amounts, and the resulting symptoms. Respected authorities in the field of psychology, university professors, or program directors have contributed to a useful category titled "Cautions and Comments." This section delineates increased risk factors in a patient's condition, which may alter the effect of the drug. Other conditions of prescribing each drug are explored, such as the usual dosage and method of administration, and the physical characteristics of the absorption of the drug.

An alphabetically arranged subject index, which includes brand names, is located at the back of the volume. A section devoted to references cited facilitates further research. One of the most helpful appendixes included gives the pharmacologic classification and listing of all drugs included in the PPDR. Also included are the U.S. Drug Enforcement Agency Schedule Designations and the Food and Drug Administration Pregnancy Categories. The final appendix lists the abbreviations and symbols found in the entries. The intended audience will find this and future editions an easy-to-use reference tool.—**Marianne B. Eimer**

1452. **PDR for Nurses Handbook.** 1999 ed. Montvale, N.J., Medical Economics and Albany, N.Y., Delmar, 1999. 1419p. index. $32.95pa. ISBN 0-7668-0913-7.

Although in most cases nurses do not prescribe drugs to a patient, they are usually the ones who must administer them, teach patients and families about them, and recognize adverse side effects and drug interactions. Therefore, knowledge of the ever-increasing pharmacopoeia is essential to any nurse. This new edition of the standard drug handbook for nurses is an invaluable reference on drugs, their uses, and their effects, all with particular consideration of the nurse's role in patient care.

Unlike the original weighty PDR for physicians, this is a true handbook, of a size to be carried around for quick reference. Yet it is packed with information. Previous editions were arranged by drug manufacturers; however, this new edition is arranged by the generic (or chemical) names of drugs, although with access to trade names through the index. There are three chapters. The first describes the best way to use the handbook. The second is an alphabetical listing of particular types of drugs. There are listings, for example, for such therapeutic classes as antihistamines, diuretics, and anticonvulsants. For each entry, there is a list of the individual drugs that appear in chapter 3 and a general discussion of the mode of action, uses, contraindications, side effects, and effectiveness of this type of medication. Under nursing considerations for each class of drugs there are tips on administration, storage, assessment of results, and patient education concerns.

Chapter 3 lists thousands of individual generic drugs, with detailed information on all the above topics and more. Of particular importance are the side effects sections, with life-threatening effects given in bold, and the overdose management section that gives symptoms and treatments. Other drugs that interact with each entry are listed, and the type of interaction is described. There is a lot of information here in very accessible form. The 10 appendixes include the elements of a prescription, the FDA Pregnancy Categories for drugs, and formulas for intravenous rate calculation. The index lists trade names and general subjects. A visual identification guide has full-color, actual-size pictures of 200 of the most common pills and capsules.

Of course, any handbook such as this is instantly out of date, with new drugs and new uses of old drugs being discovered every day. However, the publishers have provided a Website (http://www.nursespdr.com), which effectively solves that problem. There, in addition to daily pharmaceutical news and links to other drug sites, one can find monthly updates to the handbook, with listings for newly introduced drugs as well as new uses or therapeutic combinations of old drugs and newly recognized side effects. The combination of this convenient, information-packed handbook and constant updating through the Internet makes this a powerful tool for nurses and other health professionals.—**Carol L. Noll**

1453. **PDR Generics 1998.** 4th ed. Montvale, N.J., Medical Economics Data, 1998. 2869p. illus. index. $79.95. ISBN 1-56363-253-5.

Designed to provide clinicians with the most comprehensive information on virtually every generic drug product currently on the market, *PDR Generics 1998* is the collaborative effort of the editorial boards of the Medical Economics Company and Micromedex, Inc. Arranged alphabetically by generic name, four different indexes provide easy access: brand and generic name, product category, indications, and international drug name. Prescribing information for each drug includes FDA-approved uses as well as recognized off-label uses. Dosage and administration, indications and usage, adverse reactions, contraindications, and precautions are provided in detail. Additional information on available supplies, pricing, and therapeutic equivalency emphasizes the targeted market for this volume—the health care professional or clinician.
—**Vicki J. Killion**

1454. Shepard, Thomas H. **Catalog of Teratogenic Agents.** 9th ed. Baltimore, Md., Johns Hopkins University Press, 1998. 593p. index. $125.00. ISBN 0-8018-6075-X.

Even seemingly harmless substances can cause malformations in the fetus. The *Catalog of Teratogenic Agents* is a guide to the agents, the studies that determined whether malformations could occur, and the quantities of the agents that cause malformations. This new edition contains 250 entries not listed in the prior edition and the revision of other entries. The catalog is a standard reference text that can be found in many medical and hospital libraries. It is included in electronic form in the Micromedex database that is used as a reference tool by many pharmacists and hospital emergency departments. Arrangement is by agent name, and each entry includes a brief description of recent studies, outcome of the studies, and a list of references. There is an extensive index to the authors of the studies consulted in the preparation of the entries and an agent index for quick location of information. Most medical and hospital libraries find this work indispensable. University libraries with chemical toxicology collections, genetic counselors, and medical institutions without access to Micromedex should find the *Catalog of Teratogenic Agents* an essential purchase. Pregnant women with advanced questions about the effect of substances on the fetus may also find this reference useful. However, the intended audience is professionals with knowledge of chemistry and fetal development.—**Lynne M. Fox**

34 High Technology

GENERAL WORKS

1455. Dillon, Patrick M., and David C. Leonard. **Multimedia and the Web from A to Z.** 2d ed. Phoenix, Ariz., Oryx Press, 1998. 355p. $39.95pa. ISBN 1-57356-132-0.

Acknowledging the impact that the World Wide Web is having on the field of multimedia, the authors decided to revise and enlarge the previous edition of *Multimedia Technology from A to Z* (see ARBA 96, entry 1750). Almost 500 new terms have been added, most of which originated from the language of the Internet, as reflected in the title change. Most of the definitions for the more than 1,000 terms in the 1st edition were rewritten to reflect the relationship to the Web. The authors' desire is to establish a professional vocabulary for the field of multimedia; thus, they focus on terms used by the major disciplines that contribute to the industry.

The terms cover a wide range of topics. Familiar terms, such as *JPEG*, *cookie*, and *search engine* are defined as well as perhaps less familiar terms such as *Neuro-Baby* and *double buffering*. However, this dictionary includes more than just computer jargon. There are terms reflecting the publishing, recording, and video industries, such as *art director*, *refresh rate*, *footage*, and *fair use*. The paragraph-length definitions are clearly written and understandable to the informed layperson. Often the authors include a statement as to how a particular technology impacted the field of multimedia. Italicized words within the definitions are defined elsewhere and serve as cross-references. The authors also include a list of acronyms and their meanings as well as an annotated bibliography of selected books, scholarly articles, magazines, trade journals, and electronic publication collections to help guide the reader to additional sources of information.

This dictionary is geared toward the practitioner and serves its purpose well. Oftentimes, books about technology are dated the minute they are published, but the authors' style of writing keeps the material fresh. This book is recommended for academic and large public libraries. [R: BL, 15 Nov 98, p. 610; BR, Mar/April 99, p. 72]—**Teresa U. Berry**

1456. **Plunkett's InfoTech Industry Almanac 1999-2000.** Jack W. Plunkett and others, eds. Galveston, Tex., Plunkett Research, 1998. 695p. $149.99pa. (with disk). ISBN 1-891775-00-6.

The 2d edition of this work purports to take a "more rounded approach for the general reader" rather than one where "analysts [are] writing only from an investor's point-of-view." Some changes have occurred since the previous edition (see ARBA 97, entry 539). Chapters are more detailed and longer, and an additional index by region was added. Instead of company rankings being provided in five separate charts, one chart was created that shows rankings in each area, making it very easy to be viewed all at once. A noticeable change was in the header for the individual company listings. Sales, profits, sales growth and research, and development budget figures have been omitted from the header and are found farther down on the page under "Financials." It would have been useful if those figures remained in the header for quick identification while looking at an individual company. On the whole, the individual company listings are much easier to read with the new layout and with shading provided for major areas within the page.

The almanac includes a short glossary of terms and several chapters that provide an overview and outlook on the information technology industry. These chapters focus on examining the 14 current trends that are currently affecting the industry, and an examination of the five major industry areas within the industry (computer equipment, computer software and networking, semiconductors, telecommunication services, and telecommunications equipment). A chapter on contact information with Website and street addresses, telephone numbers, and a brief description is provided. Also, there is a detailed chapter that describes the careers that are available in the industry, along with the education and training needed for these careers, and possible future trends.

Most of the almanac contains detailed listings for the "INFOTECH 500." Listings are alphabetically arranged by company name, and fall into several major categories: computer hardware; computer software; telecommunications services; electronic publishing; specialty services; and equipment, manufacturing, distribution, and reselling. Further subject breakdown is provided under each category and there is a corresponding numerical classification, an internal "Industry Code" that is not the North American industry classification code. Companies were chosen based upon several criteria. They had to be based in the United States, have their stock publicly sold, be preeminent in the industry, not necessarily be exclusively in the information technology field, and have readily available, reliable and accurate financial data and statistics. The almanac editors have tried to select companies that they feel represent the most successful companies in the areas of voice, data and video management (including fiber optics), cellular telephone systems, and networked computers. This is based on criteria that include fastest growing, biggest employer, and highest profits.

Before the individual company listings, there is an easy-to-read chart that lists all of the companies alphabetically within their subcategories. The chart provides information on the industry code, sales, profits, average annual sales growth, and development and research budget.

Three indexes follow, an alphabetic list of companies with their industry code; a geographic listing where headquarters are located, by state and region; and firms with international operations. Main listings for each company include type of business, brands, divisions or affiliates, and contact information including names, street address, telephone numbers, and Internet address. Growth plans and special features are also noted. Financial and other information includes sales and profits and their growth, number of employees, salaries and benefits, competitive advantage, number of minorities or women within the company, and stock ticker name. At the end are two additional alphabetically arranged indexes: firms noted as "hot spots" for minorities and women, and one arranged by subsidiary, brand name, and affiliations. There is also a floppy disk with company listings. It can be opened in Microsoft Excel 5.0 to 7.0 for data manipulation.

The almanac is very easy to read and provides a quick way to identify leading companies in the information technology field. The financial information provided is also very useful for folks researching career and investment opportunities. Academic, public, and special libraries will find this a useful acquisition.
—**Jan S. Squire**

COMPUTING

1457. **Dun and Bradstreet/Gale Industry Reference Handbooks: Computers and Software.** Stacy A. McConnell and Linda D. Hall, eds. Farmington Hills, Mich., Gale, 1998. 1071p. index. $99.00pa. ISBN 0-7876-3002-0.

The computer industry seems to be expanding exponentially. This work is a compilation of information on companies, associations, consultants, trade contacts, and trade shows. It includes statistics, financial information, employment, and other trends, and it targets all audiences including analysts, investor planners, marketers, students, and interested members of the public. It is organized into 10 chapters: "Industry Overview," "Industry Statistics and Performance Indicator," "Financial Norms and Rations," "Company Directory," "Rankings and Companies," "Mergers and Acquisitions," "Associations," "Consultant," "Trade Information Sources," and "Trade Shows." It includes a single index alphabetically and an appendix with SIC Conversion guide to NAICS.

For any reference collection of moderate size, this duplicates information found elsewhere. Although the industry overview gives an inclusive history of the computer industry, the Standard & Poors Industry Surveys are more valuable for a knowledgeable person. Similarly, the company, trade, and consultant information is available in other sources that most reference collections own or can access on the Internet. Although the business ratios and rankings are valuable, other publications offer similar information. The amount of information on a company is limited and does not include a URL.

This handbook's only index is sorted alphabetically. If one wishes to find a consultant by region, country, or subject, this is of little value. The differentiation between company and consultant is not clear. GEAC Computer Systems are listed as a company, but GEAC Computers is listed as a consultant. Dynix is listed as a company, but DRA is listed as a consultant. Attempting to search by anything but name is almost impossible. Although the handbook provides a great deal of information in one volume, it does not achieve its stated goal of being a comprehensive guide to the industry.—**Joshua Cohen**

1458. Levine, John, Margaret Levine Young, Doug Muder, and Alison Barrows. **Windows 98: The Complete Reference.** New York, Osborne/McGraw-Hill, 1998. 1001p. illus. index. $39.99pa. (with disc). ISBN 0-07-882343-9.

The authors promise much, beginning with the book's title. At 1,001 pages plus a CD-ROM and updates and supplements at a companion Website, this "package deal" fulfills that promise. *Windows 98: The Complete Reference* will provide answers to most questions regarding the installation, customization, and, most importantly, the day-to-day use of the Windows 98 operating system. Featured authors John Levine and Margaret Levine Young have made practically a cottage industry writing "for dummies" and other computer books that are used worldwide and have been translated into several languages. So when the authors say they intend their book to be useful for beginners through experienced users, they can be believed. Topics range from very basic (icons, the desktop, taskbars) through advanced concepts, such as LAN configurations, network security, and editing the registry.

Windows 98: The Complete Reference is extremely well organized and thoroughly indexed, as befits a book intended primarily for reference use rather than cover-to-cover reading. The book's table of contents alone is an impressive 23 pages. An introduction tells readers how to use the book and its companion CD-ROM most effectively and explains the book's graphic and textual conventions.

The body consists of narrative, tables, charts, and annotated screen prints. A question-and-answer format is also used. The exclusive use of black-and-white print may help ensure this book's reasonable price, but use of color, at least for the screen prints, would really enhance this book's eye appeal and perhaps make it seem less intimidating at first glance. A comprehensive glossary and a detailed index conclude the book.

Windows 98: The Complete Reference is highly recommended for either reference or circulating collections of public, high school, and academic libraries. Companies and individuals currently using or thinking of using Windows 98 should also consider its purchase.—**Linda D. Tietjen**

1459. **The Software Encyclopedia 1998: A Guide for Personal, Professional, and Business Users.** New Providence, N.J., R. R. Bowker, 1998. 2v. index. $255.00pa./set. ISBN 0-8352-4019-3.

The Software Encyclopedia is a directory of over 23,000 microcomputer software titles from over 3,000 publishers. The information is collected from publishers, catalogs, magazines, and brochures. Volume 1 contains the title and publisher/title indexes. Arranged alphabetically, each entry of the title index has version number, publication date, compatible hardware, operating system requirements, memory required, and price. Most entries also have a brief excerpt from the publisher describing the software. The publisher/title index provides publisher information including address, telephone numbers, and distributor information, but no Internet addresses. In the second volume, the system compatibility/applications index, arranges titles by subject under 15 operating systems. The subject classification is a bit unwieldy, making it difficult to locate certain applications, such as HTML authoring software. Titles span a broad range of subject areas in education, hobbies, professional training, and business.

The Software Encyclopedia has several weaknesses. As expected, it is impossible to keep such a source updated, but Bowker does offer an online version through DIALOG. Some of the systems listed (i.e., Apple II, Atari 8-bit micros, and Radio Shack TRS-80) are so outmoded that it raises doubts about the currency of the directory, and one wonders how many titles are actually still available. *CD-ROMs in Print* (1996 ed.; see ARBA 97, entry 17) does not cover the various formats, but it is a better source of information for CD-ROM products and seems more up-to-date. Although *The Software Encyclopedia* could help provide publishing information for obscure titles, consumers needing to purchase software would be wise to peruse the catalogs, magazines, or other directories.—**Teresa U. Berry**

INTERNET

1460. **Directory of Web Sites.** Chicago, Fitzroy Dearborn, 1999. 622p. illus. index. $75.00. ISBN 1-57958-179-X.

There is still a large market for Web directories, but it is hard to imagine why any library would need anything but an inexpensive yellow pages book to get people started. Websites go in and out of existence much too quickly to warrant such an expensive volume. The book is arranged by broad topics, such as animals and plants, and "Thought & Belief." Although this type of arrangement might work for information professionals (who already know how to use search engines and virtual libraries), it is unnecessarily confusing for novices. The sites listed include a title, the URL, and a good description. The lists tend to be specific instead of good places to start to find information. For example, sites for two astronauts (Neil Armstrong and Alan Shepard) are listed instead of a URL that might list many such sites. Although any Internet directory lists fascinating places, there are many more inexpensive and up-to-date methods for getting there. [R: Choice, Dec 99, p. 683]—**Connie Williams**

1461. Gralla, Preston. **Online Kids: A Young Surfer's Guide to Cyberspace.** rev. ed. New York, John Wiley, 1999. 276p. index. $14.95pa. ISBN 0-471-25312-X.

This is the revision of the widely reviewed and widely acquired 1996 edition of the same title. Like the original edition, the more recent effort introduces the young reader (and the reader's parents) to the world of cyberspace. This is not a book filled with unintelligible jargon and technical information. It provides the basics within the context of entertaining, yet informative articles and annotations.

The chapters cover a wide range of topics within the parameters of cyberspace. For instance, one chapter speaks of what cyberspace is and defines its various capabilities, including chat, downloading software, and video or sound clips. But it is not a "how to" guide. Another chapter discusses equipment requirements, but does not delve into detail beyond the basics. It appears the book is written with the assumption that an adult will guide any child embarking into Internet explorations. With adult supervision in mind, an entire chapter is devoted to online etiquette and a child's safety on the Internet. There is discussion on the site blocking software available, plus how various services provide for protecting children.

The best parts of the book are the chapters devoted to Websites. They are chosen with children in mind, but many are equally as interesting to adults. Each entry includes the address of the site, plus brief annotations describing what is on the site. For quick reference, there is the "Usefulness Index" and the "Coolness Index." According to the introduction, the author's children rated each site. Some of these entries did have drawbacks. Not all of them were readily available unless one is a subscriber to a service such as America on Line (AOL) or CompuServe. Also, a random check showed that some sites are no longer active. But then, that is a problem of the medium. No book of this type will be completely accurate.

Like the well-received, earlier edition, this book achieves exactly what it is designed to do. It provides the young reader a well-organized, well-presented, and informational introduction to the cyberworld.

—**Phillip P. Powell**

1462. Moschovitis, Christos J. P., Hilary Poole, Tami Schuyler, and Theresa M. Senft. **History of the Internet: A Chronology, 1843 to the Present.** Santa Barbara, Calif., ABC-CLIO, 1999. 312p. illus. index. $65.00. ISBN 1-57607-118-9.

That the authors of this work are considering the Internet something broader than a connected mass of worldwide computers is evident from the title. ARPAnet is the usual starting place for discussions of Internet history and that dates only to the late 1960s, but this chronology traces back to 1843 when English mathematician Ada Lovelace's wrote an account of Charles Babbage's design for an Analytical Engine (a successor to his Difference Engine) that intimated the fundamentals of computer programming. Significant relevant subsequent advances in the fields of communications, computers, and general science are all included here.

Structurally, entries are arranged within seven chapters in chronological order. An engrossing final chapter covers future trends. Both chapters and entries feature brief overviews, and entries provide a complete discussion of the topic, going well beyond what happened in a particular year. From this work one can safely conclude that not only did Al Gore not invent the Internet as claimed, he did not even coin the term "information superhighway." A sidebar in this book notes that Ralph Lee Smith used the phrase in a 1970 article in *The Nation* to describe the potential of the new medium of cable television. Sidebars like this add a great deal of depth to the main entries on people, ideas, machines, and advances. Illustrations, statistical appendixes, and an index augment the text further.

Aside from an occasional editing lapse (for example, both ENIAC and Colossus are identified as the "first fully operational electronic computer"), this is a terrific reference book, both well-written and thorough. It will be welcome in any library, and in many personal offices as well. [R: BL, Aug 99, p. 2108; Choice, Nov 99, p. 512; BR, Nov/Dec 99, p. 74]—**John Maxymuk**

1463. Polly, Jean Armour. **The Internet Kids & Family Yellow Pages.** 3d ed. New York, McGraw-Hill, 1999. 744p. illus. index. $34.99pa. ISBN 0-07-211849-0.

The 3d edition of these yellow pages is a directory of 4,000 educational or entertainment-oriented Internet sites for children in grades K-8. The arrangement is alphabetic by broad subject headings. An index is provided for those who wish to locate a Web page by specific topic. An electronic CD-ROM version of the yellow pages is furnished with keyword search capability to enable direct access to listed Websites. Special features include a short list of the 100 best sites on the net, a list of Websites for countries of the world, and a "net files" section to illustrate how the Internet can be browsed to locate trivia. The audience for these yellow pages seems to be apprehensive parents with little direct knowledge of the Internet who fear that their children will access inappropriate material while surfing the Web. The compiler, Jean Armour Polly, a former librarian and self-titled "net mom," assures parents that she has personally reviewed each Website to verify that it is "family friendly" and free of any offensive content. Perhaps her distaste for controversy explains why a good number of sites in these yellow pages come under the heading of fun and games. For example, there is a generous list of links to commercial Disney Online sites, which may not be surprising considering that Polly works for the corporation as a private consultant. So great is her maternal concern that she includes advertisements for "net-mom"-endorsed products that parents may purchase to guarantee the safety of their kids on the Internet.

All good intentions aside, currency is the unavoidable problem with all Web directories in print format. To compensate for this weakness, the author directs us to her personal homepage for free updates to track changes to Web addresses listed in the yellow pages. While consulting her Web page for updates, however, one cannot fail to notice the "net-mom" bookstore link where one can purchase the new 4th edition of her yellow pages through Amazon.com just in time for the millennium. For reference staff who use the Internet on a daily basis in public and school libraries to satisfy the information needs of young patrons, these yellow pages will contain no surprises because the educational sites identified by Polly are already well known by librarians and are usually accessible as bookmarks or links on most library homepages.
—**David G. Nowak**

1464. Reese, Jean. **Internet Books for Educators, Parents, and Students.** Englewood, Colo., Libraries Unlimited, 1999. 299p. index. $32.50pa. ISBN 1-56308-697-2.

A useful and relative inexpensive guide to resources that explicate and teach the Internet and its various functions, this volume includes somewhat lengthy (500 to 1,000 words) reviews of books pertinent to the topic. The volume is divided into 6 major sections: General Internet Books; Internet Books for Educators and Librarians; Internet Books for Parents, Children, and Students; Internet Books for Curriculum Development; The Internet in Juvenile Fiction; and Internet Books for Web Page Design and Creation. Within each section, entries are arranged alphabetically by title, followed by author's name, publication information, date, Web address, name of pages, series title, ISBN, type of binding, cost, software information (when available), and an annotation.

As thorough and information-laden as the volume is, it cannot overcome the problems inherent in its scope—namely, that much of the information contained in the books reviewed is already out-of-date. In some cases, newer editions might exist, but there is no guarantee. This work is recommended for astute librarians who are capable of transcending the limitations of the information, and for collections that might not have more recent guides to the Internet.—**Edmund F. SantaVicca**

1465. Schlein, Alan M. **Find It Online: The Complete Guide to Online Research.** 2d ed. Tempe, Ariz., Facts on Demand Press; distr., Lanham, Md., National Book Network, 1999. 506p. index. $19.95pa. ISBN 1-889150-06-1.

The 2d edition of *Find It Online: The Complete Guide to Online Research* is intended to aid those with basic knowledge of the Internet with the tools to research effectively on the World Wide Web. It will help users narrow information searches, find specific background information, access government and business resources, and check on the accuracy of online information.

The book begins by getting readers familiar with Internet terminology and explaining how the terms relate to one another. The following chapters discuss such topics as the various search engines and how to use them; how to use and access more specialized tools (e.g., discussion rooms, mapping tools, newsgroups); how to save results; and how to access government sources, public records, news resources, and business resources. There are special chapters on managing and filtering information as well as the issue of privacy and protection on the Web. Chapter 12 is especially useful to beginning Internet users because it takes the reader through a series of searches and leads them to the right results. The last half of the book consists of indexes, which serve as a kind of directory to government sites, private and public sites, and different Website profiles. A list of contributors, a glossary, and an index conclude the volume.

This book will serve many library patrons that are new to the Internet and particularly to researching on the Internet. Its clarification of Internet-specific terms and no-nonsense approach make it beneficial for both the circulating and reference collections. [R: Choice, Sept 99, p. 104]—**Shannon M. Graff**

1466. Weber, Peter J. **The Incredible Internet Guide to *Star Wars*: The Complete Guide to Everything *Star Wars* Online.** Tempe, Ariz., Facts on Demand Press, 1999. 354p. illus. (The Incredible Internet Guide). $13.95pa. ISBN 1-889150-12-6.

With the thousands of *Star Wars* sites that currently exist on the Internet, this book provides some direction that users may be looking for. It is useful for the serious researcher as well as the casual browser. The author has weeded through many of the sites that currently exist and attempted to list the better or more interesting sites, then organized his findings in two user-friendly formats.

In the first half of the book, sites are categorized under subjects such as entertainment, image galleries, and software, along with a brief description or "profile" and respective URL addresses. The author has also noted which sites he found more useful or of better quality. The back half of the book lists this same information alphabetically by site. Important information is also provided on troubleshooting, child protection, and how to save information to your computer.

Users should keep in mind that there are many more sites in existence on the Web that are not covered in this guide that may contain worthwhile information. Also, as many Internet users are aware, many sites die off or move, so URLs listed in this book will easily become dated.—**Cari Ringelheim**

TELECOMMUNICATIONS

Dictionaries and Encyclopedias

1467. Newton, Harry. **Newton's Telecom Dictionary: The Official Dictionary of Telecommunications & the Internet.** 15th ed. New York, Miller Freeman; distr., Emeryville, Calif., Publishers Group West, 1999. 953p. $32.95pa. ISBN 1-57820-031-8.

The author bills this work as "the official dictionary of telecommunications and the Internet." He pretty much hits the mark. Harry Newton has an MBA from Harvard, 29 years of experience in the telecommunications industry, and has founded a host of leading monthly industry magazines: *Call Center, Computer Telephony, Imaging, LAN* (now *Network*), *Teleconnect,* and *Telecom Gear.* He is in the process of starting another new magazine, *Technology Investor Magazine* (http://www.TechnologyInvestor.com). The 1st edition of this work appeared in 1989 and the current offering is the 15th edition. The 16th will appear in early January 2000. Now some 1,400 pages in length and 5 and a half pounds in weight, *Newton's* is the virtual industry bible, used by engineers, corporate executives, lawyers, accountants, marketing, sales, and advertising staff among many others. In fact, anyone who works in telecom, networking, or the Internet could benefit by the information in *Newton's.*

The dictionary starts out with an essay on recent trends in the industry, followed by an essay on where Newton thinks the industry will go in the next century. The dictionary section contains around 20,000 defined terms, making it the largest dictionary of its kind by far in the world. The entries are excellent and often very detailed—important definitions are actually essays. A typical example is the listing for the new Internet Protocol (IPv6), which will be installed worldwide to everyone's joy on January 1, 2000. Newton gives two long paragraphs describing the essential upgrade features of IPv6. The alphabetic main sequence of the dictionary is preceded by a numbers section. Embedded in the numbers section is a small telecommunications chronology that lists important events that happened from 1453 (Gutenberg) to 2002 (Eurobills). Newton ends the volume with an appendix of organizations, interest groups, publications, international calling codes, plugs, and connectors.

Few will want to be without this up-to-date volume, which also has the keen insight of a leading force in the telecommunications industry. Like many books now on the market, this volume has a Website, but unfortunately it suffers from a typo in the book. The site is http://www.HarryNewton.com, not http://www.Harry_Newton.com as listed on page ix. Do not expect too much from the site, however, for it consists largely of positive reviews of the book. This is a hefty paperback book, both in terms of weight and price, but well worth both.—**Ralph Lee Scott**

1468. **Telecom & Networking Glossary: Understanding Communications Technology.** Robert Mastin, ed. Newport, R.I., Aegis, 1999. 140p. $9.95pa. ISBN 1-890154-09-1.

With the blurb on the front cover of this work stating this work is "a plain English guide to cutting-edge telecommunications technology, terms and acronyms," this compact volume aims to provide nontechnical readers with basic definitions of common technical terms used in the telecommunications industry. Overall, it does so well, maintaining accuracy to an impressive degree and simplicity about as well as one can without sacrificing accuracy.

A compact guide of this sort cannot aim to be comprehensive; instead, it requires a skilled editor to make sensible choices about what to include and what to omit. In this case, Mastin did his job well. In searching out items, this reviewer never encountered a complete omission of a topic thought to be important, and only once was a major cross-reference found missing. "Dual tone multifrequency dialing" was defined well and was cross-referenced as "DTMF," but it was not also cross-referenced as "Touch-Tone"—a trademarked term, but the name under which a nontechnical reader would be most likely to look.

More serious omissions are the lack of cross-referenced entries for many common acronyms in data communications, such as ACK (acknowledge), NAK (negative acknowledge), UDP (User Datagram Protocol), and DSU (Data Service Unit). Someone unfamiliar with the underlying concepts is far more likely to encounter these terms as acronyms than as spelled-out terms, and such readers will be frustrated by the omissions.

Occasionally, clarity is sacrificed in favor of technical accuracy. It is doubtful that the casual reader would make much sense of the book's definition of "erlang," for example. But this problem is rare; most definitions are clear enough to help the beginner move ahead in understanding technical terms. This reference is recommended as a useful desktop companion for someone new to telecommunications jargon.
—**Ray Olszewski**

Directories

1469. MacKie-Mason, Jeffrey K., and Christopher Lee. **Telecommunications Guide to the Internet.** Rockville, Md., Government Institutes, 1999. 241p. index. $59.00pa. ISBN 0-86587-601-0.

The content for this directory was selected from its online counterpart that contains more than 7,000 listings. Roughly 300 of the most valuable resources were chosen. The 1st chapter, "Getting Started," describes how the book is organized and how to use it. The 2d chapter, "Finding Information on the Internet," gives a brief explanation and history of the Internet, different types of resources and searching tools, and suggestions for further reading. Chapters 3 through 8 contain the directory entries.

The book is well organized from the table of contents to the index. The authors followed a standard format for each of three types of information presented: Web pages, newsgroups, and mailing lists. Each entry is clearly titled, followed by its URL, where applicable. Descriptions are brief and can be comprehended by the nonexpert.

The downside of any print publication about the Internet is that information can change before the book goes to print, as has happened to some of the URLs in this book. With a little ingenuity, most users can work around this minor drawback.—**Deborah Sharp**

1470. **Telecommunications Directory 1999: An International Guide to Organizations, Systems, and Services Concerned with the Interactive Electronic Transmission of Voice, Image, and Data.** 10th ed. Ellen Pare, ed. Farmington Hills, Mich., Gale, 1999. 1237p. index. price not reported. ISBN 0-7876-2135-8. ISSN 1055-8454.

Like any other Gale directory, the format of this work is similar. The indexing is thorough. There is the master name and keyword index, personal name index, geographic index, and the function/service index. A glossary is arranged alphabetically to explain the terms, concepts, acronyms, standards, and government rulings. Each entry is assigned a number for easy access. This directory is in its 10th edition, and claims to be a comprehensive source of organization listings of any telecommunications field such as audiotex, teleconferencing, local area networks, Internet access providers, microwave networks, personal communications services, telegram and telex, voice and data communications, satellite services, and more. There are more than 3,700 entries, including some 400 new company and product entries. This source is also available in electronic format for internal data processing. Some entries have e-mail and URL addresses for additional communications. Although this publication is international in scope, most entries are from the United States. Readers can use the function/service index or the geographic index to search for a specific country's telecommunications organizations. It would be useful if the list of categories in the function/service index was displayed in the beginning of the section. Readers would then know how detailed the function/service index is cataloged. United States companies are listed first alphabetically by state, followed by other countries in alphabetic order. Each entry in the descriptive list has annotations, history notes, address, telephone and fax numbers, toll-free numbers (if available), and name of the president. Gale products are known to be high quality and this reference work is no exception.—**Polin P. Lei**

Handbooks and Yearbooks

1471. **Dun and Bradstreet/Gale Industry Reference Handbooks: Telecommunications.** Stacy A. McConnell and Linda D. Hall, eds. Farmington Hills, Mich., Gale, 1998. 893p. index. $99.00pa. ISBN 0-7876-3005-5.

Two major publishers have combined data from their various products to create a series of industry-specific guides. Information on companies, industry norms, associations, consultants, trade contacts, and trade shows has been combined into one resource. This handbook is a reasonably priced directory for the telecommunications industry (e.g., video, telephone), with additional volumes available (e.g., computers, software, and pharmaceuticals).

The volume begins with an industry overview, a chronology of major events, and brief biographies of pioneers and leaders. What follows are nine chapters on data drawn from different Dun & Bradstreet or Gale publications (e.g., *Encyclopedia of Associations* [see ARBA 99, entries 50-51]). The master index offers easy access through an alphabetic list of companies, organizations, and personal names. The appendix consists of a generic guide for converting standard industrial classification codes (SIC) to North American Classification System (NAICS) and vice versa.

This volume's strength lies in the reliability of the data presented and the publishers' reputations. The excellent introduction explains quite clearly the intricacies of the statistics reported, particularly the industry norms and ratios that can be confusing for beginning students. Company capsules (chapter 4) offer basic information (e.g., name, sales, SIC), while chapters 7–10 (e.g., associations, consultants) repeat listings from Gale directories. Researchers and students will enjoy the industry rankings and merger lists. This work is a snapshot of useful information, although parts (e.g., trade shows) are not as current as they should be.

The directory's format suits small, specialized libraries; however, larger public and university libraries already subscribe to publications from which the information is derived. The directory's usefulness must be weighed against budget constraints, the move toward Web-based resources, and the inability to justify redundancy in an era of tight money. [R: BL, 15 April 99, pp. 1543-1544; Choice, July/Aug 99, p. 1928]

—**Sandra E. Belanger**

1472. Muller, Nathan J. **Mobile Telecommunications Factbook.** New York, McGraw-Hill, 1998. 445p. index. $29.95pa. ISBN 0-07-144461-7.

The preface of this work meanders through a variety of topics related to wireless communications, but never really says who the book is written for. Another bad sign is that toward the end it notes that the book will concentrate on "practical" aspects of mobile telecom, rather than the technology, and then mentions some topics that have nothing to do with mobile or wireless at all.

Chapter 1 is primarily concerned with cellular or PCS phone service. Mobile messaging, in chapter 2, is a rather startling grab bag of two-way paging, a somewhat skewed look at e-mail, fax, and even Usenet news. Mobile computing, although based on currently available technologies, seems to assume that certain proposed directions will become fact. Chapter 4 looks at remote access. A rather constricted review of remote monitoring is given in chapter 5, and it is difficult to tell the selection criteria for what was included or left out. Chapter 6 briefly discusses a wide variety of security risks and protections, including such topics as ticket-granting systems and firewalls. Wireless PBX service is examined in chapter 7. The tutorial on wireless local area networks (LANs) in chapter 8 is not bad except for a hilarious incorrect explanation of spread spectrum. Chapter 9 is a brief overview of the wireless local loop. Web-based management in chapter 10 mentions some central protocols, but the emphasis ensures an unfocused approach. Cellular Digital Packet Data (CDPD) has been mentioned is several prior places, so chapter 11 is, essentially, the technical review that the preface promised would be avoided. A number of satellite communications providers are listed in chapter 12. It is intriguing that chapter 13 is given over to descriptions of technologies, but, given the failure to explain spread spectrum earlier, it is completely unsurprising that an exegesis of Code Division Multiple Access (CDMA) is deftly avoided.

Telecommunications users may get some interesting ideas from various sections of this work, but the book covers such a broad range of topics that it seems a bit of a waste to buy it just to get some idea of the various types of voice mail that local providers may or may not offer. Professionals will find that explanations rarely go into sufficient detail, and that topics tend to be viewed from only one of many possible sides.

—**Robert M. Slade**

35 Physical Sciences and Mathematics

PHYSICAL SCIENCES

General Works

1473. **CRC Handbook of Chemistry and Physics 1999-2000: A Ready-Reference Book of Chemical and Physical Data.** 80th ed. David R. Lide, ed. Boca Raton, Fla., CRC Press, 1999. 1v. (various paging). index. $99.95. ISBN 0-8493-0480-6.

The venerable *CRC Handbook of Chemistry and Physics*, first published in 1913 and now appearing in its 80th edition, has long been a cornerstone of science reference collections. Information is drawn from numerous publications, indicated in the "References" section accompanying each table. The handbook has been updated in each edition since its inception, and the new edition has added tables on stratospheric chemical kinetics, high and low temperature properties of water, gas diffusion and solubility of salts in water, and other topics. One table has been eliminated and the contents of several others have been incorporated into other tables. "Tables Removed from CRC Handbook of Chemistry and Physics, 71st through 79th Editions" (CHEMINFO Chemical Information Sources, Indiana University; http://www.indiana.edu/~cheminfo/crc_xtabs_71-79.html) details the disposition of tables appearing in earlier editions but re-titled, removed, or incorporated into other tables in the 80th edition. [R: BL, 1 Dec 98, p. 689; Choice, Dec 99, p. 694]
—**Frederic F. Burchsted**

1474. **Graduate Programs in Physics, Astronomy, and Related Fields, 2000.** Woodbury, N.Y., American Institute of Physics, 1999. 964p. $50.00pa. ISBN 1-56396-887-8. ISSN 0147-1821.

This directory is a useful tool for undergraduate physical science majors seeking information on graduate programs in physics, astronomy, and related fields, such as nuclear engineering, chemical physics, and materials science. A typical entry is at least two pages long and some up to nearly four pages. The information is presented in a consistent format, allowing the student to make easy comparisons. The directory covers the United States, Canada, and an entry for Mexico.

A typical entry includes data about the university as a whole, admission, financial aid, housing, faculty, enrollments, degrees granted, and graduate degree requirements. Financial information concerning research support and budgets within the department is reported. Faculty members are listed by name, including highest degree (with university and date obtained) and research interests. An interesting section is the breakdown of research specialties within the department. Finally, a list of recent publications by faculty rounds out a program entry.

The directory concludes with five appendixes in convenient table format: geographical and alphabetic lists of departments, alphabetic list by highest degree granted, research specialties of doctoral programs, and areas of concentration of master's degrees. Each entry is packed with information to aid undergraduate students to make the best-informed decision on this next step in their career path. This volume is recommended for academic and public library collections.—**Margaret F. Dominy**

1475. **Physical Sciences on File.** rev. ed. By the Diagram Group. New York, Facts on File, 1999. 1v. (various paging). illus. index. $165.00 looseleaf w/binder. ISBN 0-8160-3874-0.

Following the tradition of other Facts on File titles, *Physical Sciences on File* is a three-ring binder of reproducible diagrams illustrating scientific concepts, processes, and apparatus. Geared for the beginning chemistry or physics student, topics are grouped into 11 thematic sections, covering subjects such as force and energy, electricity, the structure of matter, the chemistry of carbon, and chemical reactions. The illustrations are very basic and clearly drawn, with captions and labels positioned below the drawings so that they can be easily used in testing. Users will appreciate the fact that the sturdy pages are removable and fit a standard photocopier. The index is more like an alphabetized table of contents. The lack of adequate cross-references makes it more likely that the user will scan through the appropriate sections rather than use the index. For example, it is not obvious that the structure of glucose is found under "life, chemistry of." The appendixes are simply four pages of diagrams that do not fit into any category, as well as a blank periodic table and blank graph papers. New to this revised edition is a chronology of important discoveries in the physical sciences and a glossary of terms used in the text. Despite its shortcomings, this is still a useful resource for educators and is recommended for school libraries.—**Teresa U. Berry**

Chemistry

Dictionaries and Encyclopedias

1476. Ayres, David, and Desmond Hellier. **Dictionary of Environmentally Important Chemicals.** Chicago, Fitzroy Dearborn, 1998. 332p. $55.00. ISBN 1-57958-206-0.

This volume is addressed to the general public and to those writing for the media on environmental topics. The technical language used may be difficult for someone who has not had at least some undergraduate science courses. It covers approximately 600 substances, which are arranged in alphabetic order. Entries differ in content, but in general they contain name, Chemical Abstracts Service Registry Number, oral lethal dose (rat), lethal concentration in air or water, and alternative names. Some or all of historical and synthetic details, production and use, examples of pollution incidents, examples of acute or chronic toxicity, occupational limits, potential risks on reaction or storage, sources and human exposure, metabolism, evidence of mutagenic or carcinogenic activity, and references to the literature are provided as well. Unfortunately, there are no cross-references.

Although there are comprehensive compilations on hazardous substances, such as *Sax's Dangerous Properties of Industrial Materials* (Van Nostrand Reinhold, 1998) and *Genium's Handbook of Safety, Health, and Environmental Data for Common Hazardous Substances* (see entry 1384), it is useful to have single-volume works addressed to more popular audiences. Some other such works are *1001 Chemicals in Everyday Products* (2d ed.; John Wiley, 1999), which gives far less information on each substance covered, and *Toxics A to Z: A Guide to Everyday Pollution Hazards* (see ARBA 93, entry 1769), with coverage of only about 110 substances. Because this dictionary has more entries than *Toxics A to Z*, although in general briefer ones, it complements that work and will be a useful addition to public libraries and to libraries serving undergraduates. It will also be a useful reference for science journalists and for journalism students.
—**Robert Michaelson**

1477. **Dictionary of Toxicology.** 2d ed. Ernest Hodgson, Richard B. Mailman, Janice E. Chambers, and Robert E. Dow, eds. New York, Macmillan Reference USA/Gale Group, 1998. 504p. $130.00. ISBN 1-56159-216-1.

The 2d edition of the *Dictionary of Toxicology* is a solid work with a broader audience than the title and the editors suggest. The editors write in the introduction that the book is a starting point for scientists or specialists in areas not of their specialty. Certainly, this book will fit that need. It will also serve as a good reference book and starting point for students, nonscientists, and any inquisitive adult who requires concise and informative descriptions and definitions of things toxicologic: processes, materials, chemistry, biochemistry, medicine, and others. There are some 4,000 entries, 800 of which are new to the 2d edition.

The editors are respected academicians and they have assembled an impressive roster of contributors. The editors have also included material that has been adapted or abstracted from other well-known and authoritative Macmillan dictionaries, including Macmillan's *Dictionary of the Environment* (3d ed.; see ARBA 90, entry 1791), the *Dictionary of Chemistry* (Macmillan, 1987), and the *Dictionary of Genetics and Cell Biology* (see ARBA 89, entry 1413).

A selective list of references appears at the back of the book. American spelling is used, but where appropriate, the editors include a cross-reference entry from the British spelling (e.g., oestrus. *See* ESTRUS). Chemical entries include chemical structures and CAS numbers. This is a solid reference book that will be useful to a broad range of libraries: academic, public, scientific, corporate, legal, and medical.

—**Edward Kurdyla**

1478. **Encyclopedia of Computational Chemistry.** Paul von Ragué Schleyer, ed. New York, John Wiley, 1998. 5v. illus. index. $3,150.00/set. ISBN 0-471-96588-X.

Encyclopedia of Computational Chemistry uses computerized models to study molecular structures. Models can consist of computer graphics or numerical information, such as those dealt with in quantum mechanics. Although the history of the field can be traced back for half a century, rapid progress in the last two decades is a result of improvements in computer technology and a commensurate decrease in the cost of hardware and software. Increasingly, research chemists are more than likely to experiment by computer before heading to the laboratory.

It is fitting that computational chemistry be recognized with its own encyclopaedia. This substantial 5-volume work (more than 2,400 total pages) provides an excellent introduction to major topics. In addition to classic concepts associated with physical and organic chemistry, the volumes can be a useful source of information for ancillary areas; for example, chemical aspects of biological systems or expert systems. The volumes are organized in a traditional format. Entries are arranged alphabetically, written by subject experts. There are three types of entries: regular articles, definition entries, and descriptions of software packages. Articles provide a main text, abbreviations, glossary of terms, related articles, and references. Definition entries explain terms commonly used in computational chemistry. An extensive list of general abbreviations is also provided on the front and back cover of each volume. Each volume contains the complete table of contents, and the last volume provides a detailed index. Some articles provide cross-references to related materials. Numerous color and black-and-white illustrations enhance the value of many articles.

These sturdily bound volumes should hold up well under use. Still, to facilitate access, a CD-ROM or DVD version would be desirable. Institutions with graduate programs and research facilities will find this volume a useful addition.—**Andrew G. Torok**

1479. **The Facts on File Dictionary of Chemistry.** 3d ed. John Daintith, ed. New York, Checkmark Books/Facts on File, 1999. 266p. $17.95pa. ISBN 0-8160-3910-0.

Produced for use in schools, this dictionary, first published in 1980 (see ARBA 82, entry 1436), has been revised and extended. It now contains more than 3,000 entries covering the terminology of modern chemistry; some 250 new terms have been added. Line drawings interspersed throughout the text serve to illustrate chemical structures. Useful tables in the appendix include the chemical elements, the Greek alphabet, fundamental constants, elementary particles, and the periodic table.

Arranged in alphabetic order, each page includes guide words. Entry words are in bold typeface, and each entry is separated by a generous space. Type size is sufficient enough to allow for easy reading. Features include cross-references and *see* references. Definitions are presented in a clear and concise style that is accessible to the beginning chemistry student or layperson, and are frequently enhanced with formulas, the above-mentioned line drawings, and practical applications. This is an affordable and useful reference that will be welcome in both secondary school and public libraries.—**Dana McDougald**

1480. **Gardner's Chemical Synonyms and Trade Names.** 11th ed. G. W. A. Milne, ed. Brookfield, Vt., Ashgate Publishing, 1999. 1418p. index. $295.00. ISBN 0-566-08190-3.

A standard reference for chemical trade names, *Gardner's* (10th ed.; see ARBA 95, entry 1714) provides information on definitions, chemical composition, functions, applications, and suppliers of about 35,000 significant and commercially available chemicals. It includes bulk inorganic chemicals, pesticides, dyestuffs, surfactants, metals, and alloys. Drugs are not included because they appear in a separate publication (*Drugs: Synonyms and Properties*). A typical entry provides the Chemical Abstracts Service (CAS) registry number, Merck Index entry number, European Inventory of Existing Commercial Chemical Substances (EINECS) number, molecular formula, up to 50 synonyms, description, origins, and known uses. A new feature in the 11th edition is the inclusion of physical properties data such as melting and boiling points, density or specific gravity, refractive index, ultraviolet absorption, solubility, and acute toxicity. A thesaurus of 85,000 synonyms provides cross-references for the unnumbered entries. Two indexes enable the user to locate trade names and synonyms for a given CAS or EINECS number. The last section is a directory of chemical manufacturers and suppliers.

The additional data and access points make this volume even more valuable. However, in order to fit in more information, the font size is smaller, making it a challenge for aging eyes. However, the increased white space within the entries compensates somewhat. Regardless, this is still an essential source for academic and special libraries.—**Teresa U. Berry**

1481. Hunt, Andrew. **Dictionary of Chemistry.** Chicago, Fitzroy Dearborn, 1999. 365p. $40.00. ISBN 1-57958-140-4.

This dictionary, first published in the United Kingdom in 1998 under the title *The Complete A-Z Chemistry Handbook*, is a wonderful learning tool. Alphabetically arranged entries begin with one-sentence definitions, followed by expanded explanations, equations, examples (including in many cases worked numerical examples), tables, diagrams, and illustrations. Cross-references are indicated by words in italics.

Coverage includes both basic and applied chemistry, with entries for general subjects such as chemotherapy and spectroscopy as well as specific technical terms such as amphoteric oxides, delocalized electrons, and oximes. Where appropriate, such as in the entries for chemotherapy and thermochemistry, there is an historical overview of the subject. The entries are informative and clearly written and include information on why the defined topic is important. For example, immiscible liquids are useful in solvent extraction (a cross-reference). This chemistry dictionary will be especially useful for libraries serving undergraduates, but it is also highly recommended for high school and public libraries, and would even be useful for libraries serving graduate students. [R: LJ, 15 Nov 99, p. 61]—**Robert Michaelson**

1482. **Kirk-Othmer Concise Encyclopedia of Chemical Technology.** 4th ed. New York, John Wiley, 1999. 2196p. $350.00. ISBN 0-471-29698-8.

Those who are familiar with the literature already know that this work has had previous incarnations, and has served the chemistry community exceedingly well. Not everyone may afford to have the entire 27-volume set of the encyclopedia, but this version should be within reach of practicing chemists and chemical engineers. Though it is called an encyclopedia of chemical technology, it includes a solid amount of chemistry and related topics, such as the AIDS virus, contraceptives, contact lenses, properties of elements, lasers, Xerography (electrophotography), and vitamins. There is even an entry on copyrights and trademarks. The articles are clear, concise, and informative; all are written and condensed by experts in the field, whose affiliations are given right away, instead of in an index. Appropriate references are appended to each entry item. There is also a general index. This is the kind of book that every library should have. Professional chemical engineers and scientists in general will also find this a valuable addition to their library. [R: Choice, Nov 99, p. 512]—**Varadaraja V. Raman**

1483. **Ullmann's Encyclopedia of Industrial Chemistry 1998.** 6th ed. [CD-ROM]. New York, John Wiley, 1998. Minimum system requirements: IBM or compatible 386 with 66MHz. CD-ROM drive. Windows 3.1, Windows 95, or Windows NT 3.51. 8MB RAM. 8MB hard disk space. Mouse. $1,150.00. ISBN 3-527-20160-2. ISSN 1435-6007.

First published in German in 1914, this encyclopedia has become a major reference work in industrial chemistry. The 5th edition, published between 1985 and 1996, was the first edition to be made available in the English language (see ARBA 1996, entry 1789). The encyclopedia has grown rapidly in size over the years. The 4th edition contained 25 volumes. The 5th edition consists of 37 volumes, containing more than 800 major articles by 3,000 authors and filling 27,000 pages. The complete 5th edition was made available on CD-ROM in 1997.

Beginning with the 6th edition the encyclopedia is being released only in electronic form. In addition to saving trees, the advantages of the electronic medium are significant. Updates can be made more frequently. For example, more than 80 articles have been revised for the 6th edition in the 1st release. The 1999 2d release update revises an additional 70 articles and includes several new review articles that reflect recent developments in the field. Subsequent updates are planned on an annual basis. Additional advantages have to do with information access. Advanced search queries can be formulated using Boolean operators, proximity searching, truncation, and other methods. Search terms in a document are displayed and results can be ranked for relevance. The search software performs quickly. The user interface is fairly intuitive, with help functions readily available for the novice searcher. Hot links are contained in several articles, enabling the user to link to relevant Websites.

The program can also be installed on a network for access by one user at a time, or a multiuser site license is available. The disk ships with an expiration date. After the expiration date, access is no longer possible unless users obtain an archival license. Naturally, the best option is to subscribe to the new releases.

Current users of the print encyclopedia will definitely want to switch to the electronic version. Geographically diverse institutions will also wish to consider the networked version for access from remote sites. The conclusion is that a great encyclopedia got better.—**Andrew G. Torok**

Directories

1484. Lee, C. C., and Eming Lee. **Chemical Guide to the Internet.** 2d ed. Rockville, Md., Government Institutes, 1999. 340p. index. (Government Institutes Internet Series). $69.00pa. ISBN 0-86587-655-X.

The first question a reviewer must ask about this volume is, does it offer advantages over a good World Wide Web search engine? It does not replace search engines, but it complements these search methods in several ways and is useful for the serious chemistry Web user.

This revision maintains the structure of the 1st edition (see ARBA 97, entry 1382). The main sections include descriptions of chemical organizations (arranged alphabetically); a directory of academic programs in chemistry, chemical engineering, and environmental engineering; a subject guide focused on topics of interest to chemists; and electronic addresses of chemistry newsgroups and gopher sites. This format offers several advantages. For example, readers can identify related sites, even if the relationship is not obvious from a keyword search; they are less likely to have to wade through unrelated sites that may be returned by some search engines; and while going though the list of sites, they may find relationships that might otherwise be missed. To keep the material current, the authors report that they have added over 200 new entries and also checked the information from the previous edition.

As the Web continues to expand rapidly, search methods are constantly attempting to catch up with a moving target. This book should be helpful for a broad range of users, ranging from experienced Web searchers to those who do not feel completely comfortable with online search methods.—**Harry E. Pence**

Handbooks and Yearbooks

1485. **Dun and Bradstreet/Gale Industry Reference Handbooks: Chemicals.** Stacy A. McConnell and Linda D. Hall, eds. Farmington Hills, Mich., Gale, 1999. 738p. index. $99.00pa. ISBN 0-7876-3839-0.

Two widely respected sources of reference information, Dun and Bradstreet and Gale, have combined their resources with government statistics to produce this excellent overview of the U.S. chemical industry. The listings are based on the Standard Industry Classification (SIC) system, because most companies still report using this rather than the newer North American Industry Classification System (NAICS). Pharmaceutical companies, often included with chemicals, are covered in a different handbook (Gale, 1998). The chemical industry is a key measure of national economic activity, and this sector is particularly important in the United States where it is notable for having a consistent trade surplus.

Like the other volumes in the series, this book provides a lot of information. The largest section, a list of more than 4,000 U.S. chemical companies, provides the addresses, concise description of products, annual sales, and other useful data. The industry norms and key business ratios section is a valuable tool for evaluating company performance. Other useful features are a brief history of the chemical industry, concise reviews of the various sectors and major corporations, biographical sketches of some important individuals, and projections about the future of the industry. Additionally, there are lists of recent mergers and acquisitions, professional associations and consultants, and trade shows. An excellent index makes all of these data accessible.

The handbook offers extensive industrial information in a compact format at a moderate price. It can be a key tool for anyone wishing to better understand the chemical industry in this country or to evaluate specific companies. Its purchase is recommended to support both technical and business programs. [R: Choice, July/Aug 99, p. 1926]—**Harry E. Pence**

1486. **Handbook of Reagents for Organic Synthesis: Acidic and Basic Reagents.** Hans J. Reich and James H. Rigby, eds. New York, John Wiley, 1999. 494p. index. $115.00/vol.; $425.00/set. ISBN 0-471-97924-2.

1487. **Handbook of Reagents for Organic Synthesis: Activating Agents and Protecting Groups.** Anthony J. Pearson and William R. Roush, eds. New York, John Wiley, 1999. 513p. index. $115.00/vol.; $425.00/set. ISBN 0-471-97927-9.

1488. **Handbook of Reagents for Organic Synthesis: Oxidizing and Reducing Agents.** Steven D. Burke and Rick L. Danheiser, eds. New York, John Wiley, 1999. 550p. index. $115.00/vol.; $425.00/set. ISBN 0-471-97926-0.

1489. **Handbook of Reagents for Organic Synthesis: Reagents, Auxiliaries, and Catalysts for C-C Bonds.** Robert M. Coates and Scott E. Denmark, eds. New York, John Wiley, 1999. 746p. index. $115.00/vol.; $425.00/set. ISBN 0-471-97924-4.

The four volumes in this set consist mainly of information extracted from the *Encyclopedia of Reagents for Organic Synthesis* (John Wiley, 1995) in order to provide a less expensive and more convenient review of the most popular reagents for organic synthesis. Several editors from that more comprehensive work have identified more than 500 of the most commonly used reagents and organized the information about these chemicals into these four volumes. The titles have been interpreted broadly enough to ensure that useful reagents are included, even though they may not exactly fit under one of the categories.

Within each volume, the various reagents are listed in alphabetic order, with a one- to nine-page description for each reagent. Each listing provides physical properties, methods of preparation, handling and storage recommendations, suggested precautions, and a well-referenced discussion of how the reagent has been used. To make the treatment more up-to-date, the editors have supplemented the articles from the *Encyclopedia of Reagents for Organic Synthesis* by including information from recent reviews and monographs, including *Organic Synthesis*. The chemicals selected for inclusion encompass not only currently popular reagents, but also some that are expected to become important in the future. Cross-references are included when a reagent might be reasonably included in more than one of the volumes. The combination of a subject index and a formula index in each volume makes it relatively easy to find a desired reagent. These volumes will be an excellent reference source for faculty and upper-level students who are doing organic synthesis or are reading the current chemical literature.—**Harry E. Pence**

1490. **Lange's Handbook of Chemistry.** 15th ed. John A. Dean, ed. New York, McGraw-Hill, 1999. 1v. (various paging). index. $115.00. ISBN 0-07-016384-7.

As a result of the extensive indexing enjoyed by chemistry, practitioners and students have the luxury of choosing between numerous reference sources. Among handbooks, *The CRC Handbook of Chemistry and Physics* (see entry 1473) enjoys tremendous popularity, partially because traditionally it has been a required text for chemistry majors, but also because it is published annually. A close second choice is *Lange's Handbook of Chemistry*. One reason for it being less popular is that *Lange's Handbook* is updated less frequently.

Six years have gone by since the 14th edition of *Lange's Handbook* was published (see ARBA 93, entry 1716). As one might expect, the current edition shows numerous additions. The section providing basic descriptions of organic compounds has grown by 300 entries to a total of 4,300. For those desiring more than the basic data, cross-references are provided to *Beilstein* or the *Merck Index*. The section is organized alphabetically according to the senior prefix of compound name. A number of alternate indexes to these compounds make it easier for novices to access data.

Other sections have also shown tremendous growth. Section 2 on general information, conversion tables, and mathematics has had the table on general conversion factors thoroughly reworked. The material on statistics in chemical analysis has more than doubled. Most of the other sections have also been revised and expanded. Of particular note is section 11 on practical laboratory information. This was a weak section in the previous volume. Certain sections of this handbook complement the *CRC Handbook*. Because of this and with the current revisions, *Lange's Handbook* remains a valuable addition to laboratories and libraries.
—**Andrew G. Torok**

1491. Newton, David E. **Chemistry.** Phoenix, Ariz., Oryx Press, 1999. 294p. illus. index. (Oryx Frontiers of Science Series). $44.95. ISBN 1-57356-160-6.

This volume provides readers with an overview of developments in the fields of chemistry and chemical engineering from 1996 to 1998. The author summarizes about two dozen research studies, covering areas such as buckyballs, reactions at the atomic scale, protein folding, nerve cell growth, and chlorofluorocarbon (CFC) disposal. The topics were selected because they appeared in science journals designed for the general reader, such as *Scientific American* and *Science News*. Readers will need to have a basic knowledge of chemistry to understand the text. Since the author intended to provide only a brief synopsis of each topic, the references at the end of each summary are valuable sources of additional information.

The rest of the book has more general information about the field of chemistry. Newton includes a chapter on controversial issues such as pollution, ozone depletion, greenhouse effect, chemical weapons, and food quality protection and a chapter with excerpts from congressional hearings on these controversies. The biography section provides brief biographies of important chemical researchers in recent years, so the names may not be familiar. There are also sections on the future of chemistry, career information, organizations and associations, a glossary, and an index. Newton also includes a section of statistics on various aspects of the chemical industry and a good list of print and electronic information sources.

Even though Newton gives the reader a good overview of recent advances in chemistry, the organization of the book is a bit confusing. The biographical section separates the chapter on social issues from the congressional hearings on the same topics. Although it may not be the intention, Newton's book is a source of career information. He gives a nice overview of the fields of chemistry and chemical engineering, the kinds of people who work in these fields, and several good information sources. Students considering a science career will find his book very useful. Recommended for high school and undergraduate students.—**Teresa U. Berry**

1492. Wells, G. Margaret. **Handbook of Petrochemicals and Processes.** 2d ed. Brookfield, Vt., Ashgate Publishing, 1999. 494p. index. $160.00. ISBN 0-566-08046-X.

Focusing primarily on olefins and aromatics and their derivatives, this handbook provides information on 76 major petrochemicals and their processes in commercial use. This edition has been extensively revised and expanded to include new processes that have been developed in response to pressures of costs and environmental legislation. Entries are arranged alphabetically by common chemical name, but there is no cross-referencing. Each entry includes synonyms, chemical reactions, flow diagrams, raw materials needed, yield, physical property data, commercially available grades, international classifications, applications, health and safety aspects, and lists of the major manufacturers and licensors. Intended to be just an overview of the processes, Wells not only discusses the technological aspects in a clear and concise manner, but also provides business information such as production figures and market potential.

Much of the information can be found in the more comprehensive *Kirk-Othmer Encyclopedia of Chemical Technology* (see entry 1482 for a review of the concise edition), but the handbook is more up-to-date and includes processes due to be commercialized by the year 2000. Although libraries that already own *Kirk-Othmer* may not need this volume, it is a handy source for frequently needed information. This work is recommended for academic and special libraries.—**Teresa U. Berry**

1493. **World Records in Chemistry.** By Ulrich Siemeling. Hans-Jürgen Quadbeck-Seeger, Rüdiger Faust, and Günter Knaus, eds. New York, John Wiley, 1999. 361p. index. $44.95pa. ISBN 3-527-29574-7.

Originally written in German in 1998, this book is intended to stimulate interest in chemistry as an exciting and productive field. This public relations task is accomplished through brief descriptions of interesting and imaginative superlatives in chemistry, somewhat reminiscent of the *Guinness Book of World Records*.

A number of the entries are facts, such as the worst smelling chemical, the longest footnote in a chemistry article, and the strongest chemical bond. More substantive entries include a brief history of the American Chemical Society; a list of the largest pharmaceutical firms; and health care costs in Europe, Japan, and the United States. Appendixes provide a list of Nobel Prize winners in chemistry, medicine, and physics through 1998. A perpetual calendar lists birth and death dates of famous chemists as well as significant events, such as the forming of a society or major company. The volume also contains a name and subject index.

The volume is worth considering by all types of libraries. It will appeal to a mixed audience, ranging from children through chemists. Reference librarians will appreciate it as a source of ready-reference. The only drawbacks are the somewhat capricious choice of content and being rather pricey for a paperback.
—**Andrew G. Torok**

Earth and Planetary Sciences

General Works

1494. **Earth Sciences for Students.** E. Julius Dasch, ed. New York, Macmillan Library Reference/Simon & Schuster Macmillan, 1999. 4v. illus. maps. index. $325.00/set. ISBN 0-02-865308-4.

This 4-volume set is a student version of the *Macmillan Encyclopedia of Earth Sciences* (see ARBA 97, entry 1391) and is designed for students in grades 5 and up. Articles are arranged alphabetically by topic and are cross-referenced. Vocabulary words are identified by bold typeface and defined immediately to the left of the text as well as in the glossary at the end of volume 4. Each volume contains front matter including the geologic timescale, measurements and abbreviations, and contributors. Volume 1 has a table of contents for the entire set. End matter for volume 4 consists of a glossary, bibliography (annotated to indicate references especially useful to students), photograph credits, and a cumulative index; other volumes contain only a volume index.

Biographical entries of scientists are arranged alphabetically within the text. There are 12 articles concerning careers in the earth sciences—an odd choice, however, was to place them under "C" for careers, rather than within their respective subjects. For instance, "Careers in Oceanography" is found under "C" for careers, rather than "O" for oceanography. Certain articles address social issues generally not associated with encyclopedias, such as "Minorities in the Earth Sciences," "Women in the Earth Sciences," or "Public Health and Earth Sciences."

Although there are many color photographs, some might have been better selected to illustrate the topic and some articles might have been more useful to students if illustrated with diagrams. For instance, to illustrate "Prospecting for Oil and Gas" one might have expected an illustration about a seismic crew or a drilling rig, not the construction of a natural gas pipeline. "Global Positioning System" is illustrated with a photograph of a shipboard scientist and a handheld GPS receiver, whereas a diagram of the signal path from satellites to receiver might help students better understand the determination of position. Similarly, diagrams might have made articles such as "Recovery of Oil and Gas" more student friendly. All cross-sections illustrating tectonics would have been even more useful with a vertical scale of kilometers; some have such a scale, some do not. Some supporting data are outdated. To demonstrate that abrasives are big business the "Abrasives" articles cites 1989 income.

This set could serve as an introductory earth sciences encyclopedia for middle grades and up. Although planned for students in fifth grade and above, some students in those lower grade levels may have difficulty with text comprehension.—**Craig A. Munsart**

1495. **Innovations in Earth Sciences.** Santa Barbara, Calif., ABC-CLIO, 1999. 342p. illus. index. (Innovations in Science). price not reported. ISBN 1-57607-115-4.

The introduction to this series states the intent of providing an "overview of the events, scientists and innovations that have shaped the development of a particular field of science." To this end, the first half of the book includes a brief but nicely written summation of Earth science in the past century, a chronology of major events in Earth sciences starting in 1900, a series of biographical sketches of major figures in Earth sciences during this period, a directory of important geological organizations, a list of references for further reading, and a list of Websites in Earth sciences. The remainder of the book is taken up with a dictionary of terms and concepts, terminated by five short appendixes.

Examination of the actual contents reveals a truly quixotic amalgamation. The biographies are too brief to really place a person in context, and are short on citations. Further, many important names are missing. Similarly, the list of major organizations includes several giants, but also lists university departments, some of which are not distinguished. The list of references contains a curious mix of professional and popular texts, with a strong emphasis on global ecology. Again, several areas and possible titles are missing. A similar summation may be given of the listing of Websites. The dictionary portion is nowhere near as good as, for example, the American Geological Institute's *Dictionary of Geological Terms* (1984), and includes several oddities, such as "outback" and "Mangrove swamp," again reflecting an undercurrent of "Earth-system ecology" that runs throughout the book. Further, the dates for the various periods and epochs are not current. A nice touch at the end are lists of "major geologic events" such as storms, eruptions, and earthquakes.

To some degree these problems reflect the nature of the science—the study of the Earth now embraces everything from biology to atmospheric chemistry, solid-state physics, and a host of other topics. Geology has become the "great synthesis" of science. In places, the book reflects this broadening of the field, particularly in its inclusion of biodiversity issues, but "Earth sciences" is just too broad for the space allotted. This book will be helpful to readers if combined with other books, some primary texts, and references works. Again, this is a great idea; perhaps a (larger) second edition is in order. [R: LJ, 1 Sept 99, p. 183]—**Bruce H. Tiffney**

1496. Lambert, David. **Earth Science on File.** rev. ed. New York, Facts on File, 1999. 1v. (various paging). illus. maps. index. $165.00 looseleaf w/binder. ISBN 0-8160-3873-2.

This production bills itself as a "one-stop reference" for "high school and college Earth science courses" that offers "the most comprehensive collection of visuals on Earth science available." What one gets is a collection of line drawings illustrating Earth in space; simple mineralogy, plate tectonics, and structural geology; atmospheric and oceanic circulation and dynamics; geomorphology; Earth history; Earth resources; and a series of outline maps, tables, and scales. It ends with a glossary and index. These are reproduced with heavy lines on heavy paper, suitable for transferring to overhead transparencies for class use (the purchaser is granted the right to reproduce for nonprofit use).

The startling aspect is that, in this day of magnificent visual aids made possible by computer graphics, the majority of diagrams are extraordinarily simple. This is fine in some cases—celestial mechanics, basic lines of force, and block diagrams all benefit by simple and forceful treatment. However, other illustrations of more complex subjects (e.g., plates, circulation patterns) cannot compare with the communicative power of those provided in the average modern textbook. In some cases the simplification is so great as to affect accuracy. The land-sea relationships of North America during the various geologic periods are "approximately" correct except for the Cretaceous, which is way off. The accompanying illustrations of animals convey little of the diagnostic characters necessary to separate the organisms. More disturbingly, the Phanerozoic time scale presented is many years out of date. The Cambrian begins at 540 Ma, not 600 Ma; the Eocene-Oligocene boundary now falls at 33.7 Ma, not 38 Ma. The diagram on extinction suggests archosaurian reptiles virtually disappeared at the end of the Cretaceous, ignoring the many thousand species of flying dinosaurs visiting our bird feeders.

This reviewer might use a few of these diagrams, but doubts that college courses or most high school courses will find the complete book useful enough to warrant its purchase. However, the simplification of presentation in this resource might work well in many cases at the grade-school level to introduce basic principles.—**Bruce H. Tiffney**

1497. Newson, Lesley. **The Atlas of the World's Worst Natural Disasters.** New York, DK Publishing, 1998. 159p. illus. maps. index. $50.00. ISBN 0-670-88330-1.

This book will convince anyone that the world can be a cold, cruel, dangerous place and that civilization does indeed exist only by "geological consent." The diagrams, photographs, and maps are spectacularly horrific and will be a jolt to anyone perusing this book in a quiet library far from nature's wrath.

The atlas is divided into two parts. The 1st and longest is a fully illustrated catalog of the woes visited upon us by our dynamic planet. This section begins with geological hazards, primarily earthquakes and volcanoes, with good but brief introductions to the physical mechanisms behind tremors and eruptions. Particular events are highlighted in text boxes, giving details of timing, magnitudes, damage, and casualties. Weather-related disasters (e.g., hurricanes, cyclones, blizzards) follow, with the same type of coverage and detail. The least cohesive portion is titled "Patterns of Chaos," which is a catch-all term for floods, droughts, fires, avalanches, landslides, mass extinctions, and patterns of global climate change. These are interesting but could have been placed in the geological and weather chapters. This would have provided more integration between natural systems and human catastrophes. The last descriptions cover biological hazards, from pests to disease epidemics. Here is the new frontier for cataclysms in the new century, particularly with the globalization of obscure and deadly tropical viruses.

The 2d part of the book is a gazetteer with maps covering most of the world. Each map is annotated with locations of natural disasters, numbered so that they can be looked up on an extensive descriptive list. The book ends with a short glossary of prominent terms and an index.—**Mark A. Wilson**

Astronomy and Space Sciences

1498. Angelo, Joseph A., Jr. **The Dictionary of Space Technology.** 2d ed. New York, Facts on File, 1999. 487p. illus. $50.00. ISBN 0-8160-3073-1.

The introduction to the 1st edition of this work, published in 1982, calls attention to the recently completed 1st space shuttle mission. Obviously, an updated edition has been long overdue, especially in such a highly volatile discipline. The work follows the standard Facts on File two-column format, and has grown from 380 to 487 pages. There are approximately 3,000 definitions and 135 black-and-white photographs and line drawings. The definitions range from one sentence to highly technical, extending for more than a page and involving calculus and advanced scientific concepts. The placement of illustrations is generally appropriate, though the captions do not always indicate the corresponding definitions. For example, a group portrait of the Challenger crew does not include "Challenger" in the caption, and one must turn the page for the Challenger article. Definitions include recently declassified information, including the Russian space program, and are reasonably current. The discussion of "Mars Surveyor '98" refers to future launches that actually occurred in December 1998 and January 1999, and the SOHO (Solar and Heliospheric Observatory) article does not mention all the technical difficulties this project has experienced in recent months. Longer definitions usually have one or two cross-references. The work includes some slang definitions, including "bird" (a rocket, missile, satellite, or spacecraft) and "barbecue mode" (the slow roll of an aerospace vehicle to equalize the external temperature). More astronomical terminology might be appropriate, such as "right ascension" and "declination" (the standard coordinates for locating astronomical objects). Most appropriate for libraries serving a knowledgeable clientele. [R: BL, June 99, pp. 1874-1876; Choice, Oct 99, p. 308]—**Richard S. Watts**

1499. **The Astronomical Almanac for the Year 1999.** London, Stationery Office; distr., Lanham, Md., Bernan Associates, 1998. 1v. (various paging). index. $38.00. ISBN 0-11-887303-2. ISSN 0737-6421.

The Astronomical Almanac has been a joint annual production of the governments of the United Kingdom and the United States for many years and a separate publication of each government for a century. Its former title, before 1981, was *The American Ephemeris and Nautical Almanac*, which better describes what it is about. The 1999 edition gives highly accurate positions of the Sun, Moon, planets, satellites, and a few asteroids and comets for the year. Positions for the brighter stars are also provided, as are the latitudes and longitudes of the major observatories and much more. This annual publication is essential for navigating, surveying, and observing for skilled, amateur, and professional astronomers. As the information provided becomes out of date at the end of 1999, libraries will need to replace it with next year's edition.
—**Arthur R. Upgren**

1500. Dickinson, Terence. **The Universe and Beyond.** 3d ed. Willowdale, Ont., Firefly Books, 1999. 168p. illus. index. $40.00; $29.95pa. ISBN 1-55209-377-8; 1-55209-361-1pa.

This impressive volume provides an excellent overview of the heavens for the general reader. What sets it apart from a multitude of other books of its type is a lively, informative text and dozens of stunning photographs and illustrations. It is a delight to read and a delight for the eye. The arrangement is fairly standard, starting with the solar system and moving on to stars, galaxies, and beyond. Additional topics include cosmology, the search for extraterrestrial life, and telescopes. Like other introductory works, it emphasizes findings and photographs from recent space explorations. Substantially updated from the previous edition, this volume contains approximately 25 percent new information and 50 percent new images. Although it may not be considered a reference book as such, it does have many tables of numerical data, a bibliography, and an index at the back. This work is highly recommended for the public and home library.
—**Robert A. Seal**

1501. **Innovations in Astronomy.** Santa Barbara, Calif., ABC-CLIO, 1999. 328p. illus. index. (Innovations in Science). $50.00. ISBN 1-57607-114-6.

This book is part of a series whose apparent mission is to present a patchwork of information within various scientific disciplines. It contains an assortment of chapters on the field of astronomy. There are seven chapters. The overview chapter is the only chapter that is signed; however, there are no credentials provided for this author. Through 23 pages, the overview takes the reader on a tour of the various subdisciplines of astronomy; a bit of history, including related space programs milestones; and astronomical instrumentation. It is presented at the level of the interested layperson.

The remainder of the chapters are essentially lists. Chapter 2, "Chronology," lists by year the important advances of astronomy, beginning in 1903. Chapter 3 is a list of brief biographical sketches. Chapter 4 is a directory of organizations, observatories, and facilities. Conspicuously missing is anything about McDonald Observatory of the University of Texas, which has one of the largest land-based optical telescopes. The information here seems out-of-date. For information of this kind, the current volume of the *Astronomical Almanac* published by the U.S. Naval Observatory is reliable. Chapter 5 is a list of astronomy resources, some of which are certainly classics but may no longer be in print. Chapter 6 is a list of Websites. Unfortunately, the Internet changes so rapidly that many sites listed were out-of-date before it was printed. Chapter 7 is a dictionary.

A book like this that tries to bring together many different aspects of a discipline might be appropriate for school libraries where students just need a summary of a discipline for class projects or career information. [R: LJ, 1 Oct 99, pp. 80-82]—**Margaret F. Dominy**

1502. Moore, Patrick. **Atlas of the Universe.** New York, Cambridge University Press, 1998. 288p. illus. maps. index. $39.95. ISBN 0-521-64210-8.

This handsome revision of a classic atlas contains little text from the original edition (1970). The volume reflects contemporary developments in the field of astronomy and related sciences and disciplines, ranging from the generalities of the universe and the solar system to the specifics of each planet, the Sun, the stars, and the various constellations that comprise the borders of outer space. A brief overview chapter opens the work, presenting the history of telescopes, observatories, rockets, and the arrival of man in space. This is followed by detailed discussions of individual phenomena and objects, accompanied by a wealth of color photographs and images. Sidebars are included for many of the articles and explanations, enhancing the discussion through the presentation of statistics or other relevant data. A concluding section presents information on buying a telescope and creating a home observatory. A glossary and index supplement the main text. This volume is highly recommended for its scope, treatment, and readability. Considering the cost, this volume should easily find a place in the atlas collection of any library. [R: LJ, 15 Feb 99, p. 143]—**Edmund F. SantaVicca**

1503. **The Routledge Critical Dictionary of the New Cosmology.** Peter Coles, ed. New York, Routledge, 1999. 392p. index. $22.99pa. ISBN 0-415-92354-9.

The editor of this book has taken a unique approach to the topic of cosmology. The book is presented in 2 parts. The 1st part consists of 6 essays, each on a different aspect of cosmology. A recognized authority in that area of cosmology signs each essay. The 2d part of the book is a dictionary in the more traditional sense. However, the editor, taking a cue from Web pages, defines terminology used in the essays (displayed in bold typeface) in the dictionary half of the book. Also, there are cross-references from the dictionary entries back to the essays. Most of the extensive entries in the dictionary half also contain references for additional readings. There is an index for terms that do not have a separate entry but can be found in related discussions.

At a time when the popular literature is rife with spectacular photographs and speculations about the Universe, its beginning, its end, and everything in between (which is essentially cosmology), this book will inform the reader about the science behind the jargon. The editor and essayists touch on topics such as "Foundations of the New Cosmology," "The Emergence of Cosmic Structure," "The Very Early Universe," "Opening New Windows on the Cosmos," "The Cosmic Microwave Background," and "The Universe

Through Gravity's Lens." Some of the discussions are quite technical as appropriate for the topic, requiring some advanced mathematical knowledge. Others, however, are directed to the informed layperson and can be enjoyed by those with moderate knowledge of mathematics or physics. An extensive bibliography concludes the book.

The book is well designed and integrated, allowing the reader to be as selective or comprehensive as their interest permits. This book is appropriate for public and academic collections.—**Margaret F. Dominy**

1504. **Space Exploration.** Christopher Mari, ed. Bronx, N.Y., H. W. Wilson, 1999. 157p. index. (The Reference Shelf, v.71, no.2). $30.00pa. ISBN 0-8242-0963-X.

This title follows the traditional format of the venerable H.W. Wilson series The Reference Shelf, now in its 71st volume. It contains 25 articles drawn from periodicals such as *Time*, the *New Yorker*, *Astronomy*, and *Aviation Week and Space Technology*, as well as the *New York Times*, covering 5 major space exploration topics. These are as follows: John Glenn's return to space, the exploration of Mars, the International Space Station, private enterprise and space exploration, and new technologies and discoveries. There are also numerous abstracts of additional articles concerned with these topics. Mari generally does a good job of balancing both sides of controversial topics. Was Senator John Glenn's recent mission in the space shuttle a blatant NASA publicity stunt, or was it the triumphant conclusion to an illustrious career with important implications for geriatric research? Is the International Space Station a necessary step for further exploration of the solar system, or is it an enormous waste of tax dollars, having no real scientific value, used to prop up the aerospace industry in key congressional districts while rescuing Russia's industry from oblivion? Unfortunately, in such a rapidly advancing area, events such as the late 1999 loss of the Mars Climate Orbiter and the extended grounding of the shuttle fleet because of wiring problems quickly overtake speculations in the articles. Many libraries have standing orders to this series. Public, high school, and undergraduate libraries without such standing orders should acquire this title if local interest warrants doing so, with the realization that much of the material will date itself rapidly.—**Richard S. Watts**

1505. **The Universe Revealed.** Pam Spence, ed. New York, Cambridge University Press, 1998. 192p. illus. index. $39.95. ISBN 0-521-64239-6.

Assembling an introductory book on the entire universe must be a daunting task these days. Our perspectives on the solar system; stellar evolution; the formation of galaxies; and the origin of time, space, and matter have dramatically changed in just the past decade. The authors of this book succeed spectacularly and give readers a text that is up-to-date, beautifully illustrated, and a model of scientific clarity. School-age children as well as curious adults will find the book highly informative and challenging.

The Universe Revealed is divided into 6 sections, each with color-coded pages. The theme is first to place us in our physical context in the cosmos, starting with the solar system. Each planet is discussed in clear prose, with the latest spacecraft images and colorful block diagrams as illustrations. The authors present standard planetological information (size, orbital and rotation statistics, surface temperatures, and the like), with a few unsolved mysteries, such as the magnetic field of Mercury and the origin of Pluto. The best chapter is on Mars because of the inclusion of the recent Pathfinder images and data. There is a good essay about the "Martian fossils" controversy centered around a meteorite recovered in Antarctica in 1984 and found to be a rock blasted from the surface of Mars. The chapter on Earth is followed by two pages on global warming, which is a timely and useful addition, even if it is unduly alarmist in tone. The end of the solar system section includes short discussions of gravity, light, and the existence of other planetary systems. These provide essential concepts for the following sections on stars and galaxies, which are well supported by dozens of Hubble images and explanatory diagrams.

The section on cosmology provides the only disappointment in this book. Any simple explanation of the Big Bang Theory may be ultimately doomed to fail, and this one certainly does. A few glossary pages are just not enough to convey the depth of the ideas and the extensive evidence that supports them. Readers may be intrigued by the illustrations enough to look for more details elsewhere.

The final section of the book is a brief discussion of "skywatching," followed by simple but useful star and moon maps. After scanning the text and gazing at the marvelous illustrations, it would be a cold reader indeed who did not want to gaze that very evening at the night sky. This book is highly recommended for everyone who reads.—**Mark A. Wilson**

1506. Vanin, Gabriele. **Cosmic Phenomena.** Willowdale, Ont., Firefly Books, 1999. 167p. illus. index. $35.00. ISBN 1-55209-423-5.

For those with an interest in astronomy or the natural wonders of the universe, this book should provide more than adequate information and stimulation. The work is divided into 3 major sections: "Great Comets," "Meteor Showers," and "Eclipses." Each of the sections follows the same format, discussing the phenomena in historical perspective and identifying the great comets, meteor showers, and eclipses of history. This is followed by a section treating the origin and nature of the phenomena, providing a better understanding of how these phenomena have developed. Additional sections are provided that are unique to each phenomenon (e.g., observing comets, lunar eclipses, solar eclipses). More than 300 impressive color photographs and illustrations enhance the text throughout. Some are full-page, whereas others are snapshots. A bibliography and index supplement the text.

High school and college students as well as armchair astronomers will appreciate the readability of the text; the historical treatments; and the in-depth discussions of the more famous and noteworthy comets, meteors, and other natural phenomena. The author uses a commonsense approach to the topic, and provides an excellent learning and reference tool.—**Edmund F. SantaVicca**

1507. **Who's Who in Space.** International Space Station ed. By Michael Cassutt. New York, Macmillan Library Reference/Simon & Schuster Macmillan, 1999. 665p. illus. index. $115.00. ISBN 0-02-864965-6.

This title is the third edition of *Who's Who in Space* and was named the International Space Station (ISS) edition to commemorate the ISS project that is currently under way. Cassutt has compiled biographical information for more than 300 astronauts, including 80 new entries and complete updates of all existing entries. He includes not only the well-known names, but also has entries for those who trained as an astronaut but did not make it to space due to misfortune. The biographies are divided into three main sections: American astronauts, Russian cosmonauts, and international astronauts. Essays providing an overview and short history of the astronaut groups precede each section. The biographical profiles, arranged alphabetically within each section, contain information on notable achievements in space flight, date and place of birth, education, and career. The length of the profiles ranges from a paragraph to a few pages, and most are accompanied by a black-and-white photograph. Special sections feature first-person accounts and transcripts that provide a glimpse of what it is like to be in space. There are also 16 pages of color illustrations of NASA mission crew patches.

An index provides cross-references to guide the user to related articles. There are 10 appendixes that present factual data in tabular form. They include listings of manned spaceflights, shuttle approach and landing tests, space travelers, duration logs, extravehicular activity logs, flight crews, the planned International Space Station missions and crews, and teacher- and journalist-in-space candidates.

Overall, this resource is useful for providing quick information for reference questions about astronauts and space missions. The fact that it includes information about less famous astronauts as well as non-U.S. space programs makes this source even more valuable. This volume is recommended for public and academic libraries. [R: C&RL News, June 99, pp. 483-484; Choice, July/Aug 99, pp. 1923-1924; RUSQ, Fall 99, p. 104]—**Teresa U. Berry**

Climatology and Meteorology

1508. Watts, Alan. **The Weather Handbook.** 2d ed. Dobbs Ferry, N.Y., Sheridan House, 1999. 160p. illus. maps. index. $19.95. ISBN 1-57409-081-X.

Watts is a former British meteorologist and has written several books and articles on weather and weather prediction. *The Weather Handbook* shows the reader how to interpret the skyscape, combine it with information from local weather forecasts, and make predictions. Using a conversational tone, the author provides straightforward explanations of clouds, winds, weather systems, and precipitation. Watts begins with a chapter covering the basics of cloud identification, accompanied by wonderful color photographs taken by the author. He then moves on to other basics, such as understanding wind directions, pressure systems and fronts, and the mechanics of rain and snow. Through the use of photographs and maps, Watts shows the reader what to look for in satellite images and weather maps. These illustrations are labeled so that the reader can easily follow Watts' explanations of lows, fronts, and rain. Useful tips are scattered throughout the text, and in the end he sums up the information into 14 fundamental principles.

Although Watts occasionally mentions weather phenomena in the United States, this handbook definitely has a British slant, and American readers may have some problems with the unfamiliar geography. However, the principles are basically the same. This work is recommended for public libraries.
—**Teresa U. Berry**

Geology

1509. **Geology.** James A. Woodhead, ed. Englewood Cliffs, N.J., Salem Press, 1999. 2v. illus. index. (Magill's Choice). $95.00/set. ISBN 0-89356-522-9.

For the small public or school library, it is often difficult to provide useful coverage of a subject as complex and diverse as geology. The editors of Magill's Survey of Science: Earth Science Series have responded by selecting from their 6-volume work 87 articles on all aspects of earth science. These cameo articles, which tend to be from 8 to 10 pages in length, provide the reader with current information on topics ranging from archaeological geology, permafrost, and minerals to volcanoes and the origins of oil and gas. Each entry provides a summary of the topic, ways in which the topic is studied and how the resulting information is put to use, and context that describes the role played by the topic. The well-selected, brief, annotated bibliography provides sources of additional information. At the beginning of each article there are a definition of the topic and definitions of principal terms that will be discussed in the article. Each article is signed and one can go to the beginning of volume 1 to identify the author's affiliation.

The articles are arranged alphabetically by title. For the reader wishing to locate related topics easily, a list of subject categories is provided in the appendix. A glossary is also provided, which includes a wide variety of terms. The comprehensive index leads the reader to specific items. In a number of cases, the index term leads only to the glossary, which is understandable given that this book represents approximately one-third of the parent work.

This reference book, intended for high school students and college undergraduates, provides a well-written, up-to-date series of articles, each complete in itself, that cover the fundamentals of geology and its subdisciplines. An added bonus is that it is well written and a pleasure to read. [R: LJ, 15 June 99, p. 72; Choice, Sept 99, p. 114; RUSQ, Fall 99, p. 92]—**Ann E. Prentice**

Mineralogy

1510. **Cambridge Guide to Minerals, Rocks, and Fossils.** rev. ed. By A. C. Bishop, A. R. Woolley, and W. R. Hamilton. New York, Cambridge University Press, 1999. 336p. illus. index. $14.95pa. ISBN 0-521-77881-6.

The preface of this book states that its updated data conform to standards of the International Mineralogical Association (IMA). Seventeen new plates have been added to this revised edition. The main introduction includes safety instructions, a basic equipment essentials list, and general instructions for care and storage of specimens. The introduction to each major section (minerals, rocks, and fossils) gives the history and geography of each broad category. The minerals section defines minerals, their symmetry, references axes, form, and aggregates. It also provides a chemical chart, brief descriptions of physical and chemical properties, and where specific minerals are located. Rocks are categorized by their main features: mineralogy, color index, texture, structure, field relationships, and intrusions. Meteorites and tektites are included. The fossils section was developed in conjunction with The Natural History Museum in London. Its scope includes the most common and widespread specimens—those not requiring special training or equipment to see. A bibliography, geological time scale, comprehensive index, and conversion table are included. This book contains similar information and color graphics to that which is presented in the Eye Witness children's science series, but this handbook has been developed in fact sheet format for young adults and adults. This work is recommended for public and high school libraries.—**Kimberley D. Harris**

Oceanography

1511. Day, Trevor. **Oceans.** New York, Facts on File, 1999. 216p. illus. maps. index. (Ecosystem). $45.00. ISBN 0-8160-3647-0.

To know the oceans is to know the future of the Earth and humanity. This book, with its simple format and colorful illustrations, starts with the observation that life flourished in the oceans for billions of years before it only relatively recently ventured onto land, and that 98 percent (by volume) of the biosphere is still in the seas. The author makes it clear throughout the text that only by understanding the physical and biological processes in the oceans will we know how to protect and enjoy this essential resource. With its contemporary environmental focus, this book will make oceanography relevant and interesting to a broad audience. Almost every section includes an analysis of the relationship between its subject and human activities.

Oceans is the 1st volume in the new Ecosystem series from Facts on File. Like other Facts on File books, *Oceans* is designed for easy reference. It is divided into 10 parts, from geography of the oceans to ocean management, and each part has several topical sections. The "Geology of the Oceans" part, for example, has sections on the Earth's interior, plate tectonics, seafloor sediments, shoreline processes, and changing sea levels. The sections are almost all limited to two facing pages, so the reader can see the relevant information at a glance. The illustrations are excellent, again designed so that information is transmitted efficiently and effectively.

Unlike most oceanography books, *Oceans* includes significant discussion of the role of oceans in human history, literature, and culture. There are even two battle maps—one for Actium and the second for the defeat of the Spanish Armada. The sections on oceanic exploration and the developing art of navigation are particularly good.

Inevitably, a book designed to be a ready-reference on a topic as complex as the oceans will have its shortcomings. The sections on marine biology are only teasers—two columns on the "History of Life" will naturally leave out many details—but they will at least encourage the reader to look elsewhere for more in-depth information. There is a short bibliography for each part, and a useful list of marine journals and Websites. Any library with a science reference section will want this book as a simple but sophisticated guide to oceans, oceanography, and the role the sea plays in our lives. [R: BR, Sept/Oct 99, p. 70]
—**Mark A. Wilson**

1512. **Jane's Underwater Technology 1998-99.** Clifford Funnell, ed. Alexandria, Va., Jane's Information Group, 1998. 329p. illus. index. $470.00. ISBN 0-7106-1693-7.

The nonmilitary underwater technology that has developed over the last 25 to 30 years merits a new book. Jane's now documents underwater rescue, and commercial and recreational vehicles in a separate book (previously covered in their Fighting Ships series). There is a "How to use this book" page. The table of contents' main headings give an idea of what is covered (i.e., platforms and vehicles, acoustic systems, imaging systems, oceanographic instruments, navigation and positioning systems, vehicle tools and robotic manipulators, vehicle-handling systems, and diver chambers). There is a glossary of abbreviations, and manufacturer and alphabetic indexes. There are also numerous illustrations and diagrams. Entries contain descriptions of equipment by type with some comments on operational uses. There is a lot of matter under the sea such as power cables, communications cables, oil wells, pipelines, sunken ships, minerals, marine plants, and sea creatures. These things need to be observed, inspected, studied, monitored, mapped, harvested, salvaged, and protected. A bewildering array of vehicles and equipment have been developed to carry out a variety of underwater tasks: ATVs (Advanced Tethered Vehicles), AUVs (Autonomous Underwater Vehicles), ROVs (Remotely Operated Vehicles), and others. All of these have been developed to facilitate the scientific, commercial, military, and recreational use of the sea. The equipment incorporates cutting-edge technology of computers, robotics, electronics, acoustics, and optics. Because of such advances in technology it has been possible to locate, inspect and photograph the sunken ships *Bismark*, *Titanic*, and *Yorktown*. This 1st edition reference work lives up to Jane's reputation for quality and reliability.—**Frank J. Anderson**

Paleontology

1513. **Encyclopedia of Paleontology.** Ronald Singer, ed. Chicago, Fitzroy Dearborn, 1999. 2v. illus. maps. index. $295.00/set. ISBN 1-884964-96-6.

Paleontology is a science that requires a basic knowledge of many other sciences, including biology, chemistry, and geology. It reaches far beyond the dinosaurs that it is associated with to include other vertebrate taxa, invertebrates, plants, and fungi. This 2-volume encyclopedia provides entries pertaining to both the history and the current state of paleontology. With 4 advisers and more than 200 contributors, this work is a great undertaking and provides a lot of information in one reference source.

The work is arranged in alphabetic order. Preceding the entries there is a thematic outline of entries, which divides the entries into 12 categories: Analytical Approaches, Biology and Behavior, Evolutionary Concepts, Geography and Environment, Individuals, Morphology, Paleontology as a Discipline, Patterns in the History of Life, Practical Approaches, Region Overviews, Stratigraphic and Fossil Record, and Taxa. The entries vary in length from one-half page to several pages. Many have black-and-white photographs or illustrations accompanying the text. *See also* references, works cited references, and further reading lists are provided for many of the longer, more intricate entries. Each entry is signed by a contributor and all contributors are listed in the back of volume 2 with their addresses and area of expertise. The work concludes with a comprehensive index.

This well-researched and well-written set will be beneficial to those doing research specifically in the area of paleontology. It will be useful in science, academic, and many large public libraries.

—**Shannon M. Graff**

1514. Glut, Donald F. **Carbon Dates: A Day by Day Almanac of Paleo Anniversaries and Dino Events.** Jefferson, N.C., McFarland, 1999. 296p. illus. index. $28.50pa. ISBN 0-7864-0592-9.

The author writes in the introduction that it has become increasingly difficult "to find a new or fresh approach" to the very popular dinosaur book. He is correct, and his latest dinosaur book is indeed unique, but it demonstrates that fresh approaches are not necessarily good ones. This book is organized by calendar dates with "dino events and paleo anniversaries" recorded for each. As such it should have remained a calendar. Some people may buy the book for amusement, but it certainly should not clutter library shelves.

A text arranged by calendar date order is by definition haphazard, with the events within one day in scattered years, or in successive days, having very little or usually no connection. Reading the book is a painful task, unless your attention span is measured in paragraphs. The apparent value of such a book is that readers can announce to their family, friends, and colleagues that on August 25, 1987, "The Germain

Collection of fossils is accessed by the Carnegie Museum of Natural History," or that on September 5, 1940, actress Raquel Welch is born. (Miss the significance? You must not remember the 1967 movie *One Million Years B.C.*)

This book has an index, so a reader curious about the date of a particular event in the history of paleontology can look it up. It also has a partial bibliography "compiled rather subjectively." A reader steeped in dinosaur trivia who seeks a new challenge may enjoy this book, but no institution with a serious collection need bother.—**Mark A. Wilson**

Volcanology

1515. Lentz, Harris M., III. **The Volcano Registry: Names, Locations, Descriptions, and History for Over 1500 Sites.** Jefferson, N.C., McFarland, 1999. 190p. index. $29.95. ISBN 0-7864-0732-8.

This volume catalogs more than 1,500 of the world's volcanoes, both named and unnamed, including some mountains that have been claimed as volcanoes, but are not. Each entry includes the name of the volcano, its geographic location, its latitude and longitude, and its physical characteristics. In some cases, a brief summation is given of its eruptive history. It is prefaced by a pleasantly discursive introduction, and concludes with appendixes to extraterrestrial volcanoes, a brief summary of some common language terms applied to volcanoes, and a bibliography.

The Volcano Registry is a simplified version of the standard reference in the field, *Volcanoes of the World* by Tom Simkin and Lee Siebert (2d ed.; see ARBA 96 entry 1818). This latter work is far more detailed in many respects (including maps, illustrations, tabular summations of data, references cited, and details of eruptive history), and will provide a more complete reference source to volcanic activity in the last 10,000 years.—**Bruce H. Tiffney**

Physics

1516. **The Cassell Dictionary of Physics.** By Percy Harrison. London, Cassell; distr., New York, Continuum Publishing, 1998. 216p. illus. $27.95. ISBN 0-304-35034-6.

Offering clear and concise definitions and explanations of hundreds of terms used in physics and related subjects, this dictionary is a small gem. It provides students in high school and college with easy-to-understand entries on terms from mainstream physics, inorganic chemistry, quantum theory, mathematics, astronomy, and computer technology. Many entries also include relevant formulas and illustrations. Although the work does not provide depth of coverage, it does succeed in providing a source for quick definitions to aid in understanding academic texts.

The work is arranged in a logical alphabetic arrangement with cross-references to related articles included within entries. *See* references to preferred terms are also included in the alphabetic listing. Most definitions are only one or two sentences long, while major entries may contain several paragraphs. It should be noted that there is no index. In addition, no pronunciations are given with the entries, leaving the reader to guess at the correct pronunciation of many terms. Several appendixes, some useful, others less so, are included: SI units, SI prefixes, SI conversion factors, common measures, physical concepts in SI units, fundamental constants, electromagnetic spectrum, periodic table of the elements, elementary particles, the solar system, common differential coefficients and integrals, and the Greek alphabet.

Although this dictionary will definitely see use in the library, it does not cover its expressed fields completely. For example, terms such as "dark matter," "variance," and "skew" are omitted, while other related terms are included. Although the periodic table of elements is included, the elements themselves are not included in the body of the work and there are no cross-references from the symbols for the elements to their actual names. With these weaknesses noted, libraries that need an inexpensive and current dictionary of physics should consider the work for inclusion in their collections.—**Gregory A. Crawford**

1517. Chapple, Michael. **Dictionary of Physics.** Chicago, Fitzroy Dearborn, 1999. 264p. $35.00. ISBN 1-57958-129-3.

Science dictionaries sometimes fail readers by providing overly brief term definitions and by forgoing appropriate or adequate cross-referencing. This alphabetic dictionary of core physics concepts extends beyond simple one-sentence definitions and fleshes out each entry with a substantive explanation, and in the case of more complex terms, generous examples and diagrams. More complex concepts are afforded lengthier explanations when appropriate. The "electromagnetic spectrum," for example, is afforded a full-page chart, and nearly three pages are devoted to an explanation of "helical spring." The author has further provided well-chosen cross-references to related terms or ideas for many entries.

The text font and layout are appealing to the eye and invite browsing. Charts and graphics are clear and concise. The source concludes with three practical appendixes covering quantities and units, formulas and equations, and physical constants and useful data.

This is a useful addition to the reference shelves of any academic science library. It would also be appropriate for advanced-level high school physics students. [R: LJ, 15 Nov 99, p. 60]—**Judith A. Matthews**

1518. **The Facts on File Dictionary of Physics.** 3d ed. John Daintith and John Clark, eds. New York, Checkmark Books/Facts on File, 1999. 250p. $17.95pa. ISBN 0-8160-3912-7.

This ready-reference dictionary has been substantially updated since its original publication in 1980 and revision in 1989 (see ARBA 89, entry 1677). The comprehensive coverage includes 2,400 entries, which range in length from a sentence to more than 300 words. Black-and-white drawings and tables are interspersed throughout the main body and enhance the text. Both *see* and *see also* references are used extensively in the dictionary. Words and phrases are italicized within an entry when they have an entry of their own. This is a particularly useful feature to the reader. Five appendixes supplement the main body: chemical elements, periodical table, symbols for physical quantities, conversion factors for various measurements, and the Greek alphabet. This is a useful handbook for high school and college, but is not suitable for in-depth research.—**Elaine Ezell**

MATHEMATICS

1519. **Assistantships and Graduate Fellowships in the Mathematical Sciences, 1999-2000.** Providence, R.I., American Mathematical Society, 1999. 129p. $20.00pa. ISBN 0-8218-2011-7.

This directory is a tool for undergraduate mathematics majors seeking information about graduate programs in mathematics. Important information such as type and amount of assistance, fees and service expected from the student, and degrees awarded by the department in the previous academic year are included for each program. Also included is the department's Web address, if any, department head, faculty (both tenured and nontenured), the number of faculty who have been published, a breakdown of graduate students (part-time, full-time, and first year), and deadline for applications.

Some of the larger mathematics programs include "ads," large blocks of space where additional information is promoted. Although most of this information can be gleaned from the Internet, the usefulness of this directory for the prospective graduate student is the consistent format for comparing different mathematics graduate programs without the hype. Published annually, the information is up-to-date, which is more than can be said of some Websites.

Support for graduate students in mathematics is a high priority of the American Mathematical Society, which also provides information for fellowships and grants they offer as well as support from other societies and foundations. This book is highly recommended for academic and public libraries.

—**Margaret F. Dominy**

1520. **Biographical Encyclopedia of Mathematicians.** Donald R. Franceschetti, ed. Tarrytown, N.Y., Marshall Cavendish, 1999. 2v. illus. index. $228.50/set. ISBN 0-7614-7069-7.

The *Biographical Encyclopedia of Mathematicians* is one of several biographical compilations of mathematical biographies available, both in print and on the Web. What sets this work apart from the others is the treatment given to the mathematical contribution of the subject. At least half a page, independent of the biographical article, is devoted to the mathematical research of each person, which may include illustrations but always includes a bibliography. The presentation of the mathematical research is directed to the professional or informed layperson. The articles run two to three pages. Many include an illustration of the subject. A sentence or two pertaining to the areas of achievement and contributions, followed by a timeline of the subject's lifes begin each article. Each entry concludes with a bibliography that may contain references both by and about the subject.

The indexing is extensive. Besides a general index containing numerous *see* references and extensive name and term entries, there is a glossary, a country index (which includes a list of women mathematicians), areas of achievement, and a timeline of all 178 mathematicians. Time of coverage ranges from the fifth century B.C.E. to present day. The selection of subjects is international, but they are predominately Europeans and North Americans. This set is highly recommended for school, public, and academic collections. [R: LJ, 1 Mar 99, p. 72; SLJ, Feb 99, p. 136; Choice, June 99, pp. 1759-1760]—**Margaret F. Dominy**

1521. Bruno, Leonard C. Baker, Lawrence W., ed. **Math and Mathematicians: The History of Math Discoveries Around the World.** Farmington Hills, Mich., U*X*L/Gale, 1999. 2v. illus. index. $63.00/set. ISBN 0-7876-3812-9.

This encyclopedic set contains 50 biographies of mathematicians alternating with 34 essays describing math concepts and principles important in the middle school curriculum. In choosing the mathematicians to include, an effort was made to choose people from many different periods and countries as well as men and women over these same periods. The biographies include representatives from every major part of the world (ancient and modern) as well as mathematicians who are young or old, male or female. Covering the early life, influences, and career of each individual, it summarizes and describes the lives of well-known mathematicians, and also tells the stories of other greats and near-greats whose contributions have become an integral part of our popular mathematical knowledge. The 50 biographies include 14 people who were born or did their major work in the twentieth century, 6 of whom are still living. This should suggest that not all the great mathematicians are musty names found in old history books. The oldest historical figure included, Thales of Miletus, harks back to the seventh century B.C.E., whereas the youngest living mathematician, Andrew Wiles, was born in 1953. The common thread that links all these biographies is that genius, hard work, determination, inspiration, and courage are multicultural, multiracial, and ignorant of gender. The result is a broad spectrum of mathematicians. This broad spectrum is emphasized by a table of contents by mathematical field and ethnicity. Difficult, technical, and scientific words are defined in the text and sidebars.—**Janet Mongan**

1522. **Combined Membership List 1998-1999: American Mathematical Society, American Mathematical Association of Two-Year Colleges.** Providence, R.I., American Mathematical Society, 1998. 376p. $62.00pa. ISBN 0-8218-1089-8.

This directory lists mathematicians by last name and by geographic area. Entries include work address, telephone number, and e-mail address, as well as a letter code indicating the societies of which the person is a member. There is also a listing of institutional members, usually university math departments, arranged by state and country. This directory is appropriate for math and science libraries as well as government and corporate libraries that serve mathematicians. The information is also available on the Web at http://www.ams.org/cml/, which may be reason enough for individuals not to purchase a copy for their own libraries. The book also includes application forms to join each of the four mathematical organizations.

—**Robert A. Seal**

1523. **CRC Concise Encyclopedia of Mathematics.** By Eric W. Weisstein. Boca Raton, Fla., Chapman & Hall/CRC Press, 1999. 1969p. $65.00. ISBN 0-8493-9640-9.

This work attempts to define the field of mathematics, no small feat and no small work at nearly 200 pages. Definitions tend to be concise, usually not much longer than a column page. For clarity, an illustration is often included. Mathematical rigor is maintained in the definitions. For some of the longer entries, references are provided. The cross-referencing is generous to both internal entries and Internet sites.

Of particular interest is the effort to relate the mathematical topic to recognizable everyday life through copious examples. This makes for very appealing reading. Mathematicians, scientists, engineers, and students will find this book useful and a delight to use. The book is also available on CD-ROM. This encyclopedia is highly recommended for academic, public, and school libraries. [R: Choice, June 99, p. 1761]—**Margaret F. Dominy**

1524. Kapitaniak, Tomasz, and Steven R. Bishop. **The Illustrated Dictionary of Nonlinear Dynamics and Chaos.** New York, John Wiley, 1999. 267p. $195.00. ISBN 0-471-98323-3.

According to this title's preface, "intriguing properties and tantalizing possibilities of chaos have…created considerable interest in the mathematics world, thus leading to…new definitions and results in the general field of nonlinear dynamics." Research into the theory of chaos has been done on a number of fronts. This has not only led to advances in a number of scientific disciplines, but to cross-pollination of ideas as well. The authors also state in the preface that until the appearance of this title, a single text that explained required concepts of nonlinear dynamics and chaos theory to students and researchers was practically nonexistent. This title not only addresses the required concepts, but aims to help readers coming from a broad scientific base as well.

After the preface, a two-page list of pertinent mathematical symbols follows. The body of the work is an alphabetic list of entries and the title closes with an 11-page bibliography. In the body, where alternative terms are possible, an entry is placed under the name in most common usage with cross-references given under other names. If further understanding can be gained, then full additional cross-reference entries are provided. The body lists many of the theorems, terms, and equations that arise in the study of nonlinear dynamic systems. Newer mathematical ideas are explained and described with examples that often include illustrations. Remarks are added to emphasize important aspects and simplify meaning. When further proof is required, references from the bibliography are given. The overall approach of the authors is application of mathematical rigor in an engineering context.

The authors describe the intended audience in the preface. This title is appropriate for postgraduate students and researchers in engineering, mathematics, physics, and applied sciences who have some background in the theory of vibrations and dynamic systems. Undergraduates will find this work most helpful if they have knowledge of ordinary differential equations and linear algebra.—**C. Michael Phillips**

1525. Spencer, Donald D. **Dictionary of Mathematical Quotations.** Ormond Beach, Fla., Camelot, 1999. 145p. illus. index. $24.95pa. ISBN 0-89218-294-6.

Humor and mathematics are words not often found in the same sentence. However, this little gem manages to bring together nearly 1,000 quotes by mathematicians and nonmathematicians that convey humor, wisdom, and insight as they relate to mathematics. Particularly humorous are the quotes from anonymous sources. Also, quotes from George Bernard Shaw, Ronald Reagan, Woody Allen, and Martin Luther can be found.

The book is arranged in alphabetic order by the name of the author. Sprinkled throughout the book are 29 illustrations of mathematicians, each accompanied by a brief biography. An index provides a guide to topics of some of the quotes. None of the quotes are cited, so a follow-up for context is not possible. Whether one falls on the side of hate or love of mathematics, this book will be enjoyed and will be considered appropriate for any collection.—**Margaret F. Dominy**

36 Resource Sciences

ENERGY RESOURCES

1526. **Plunkett's Energy Industry Almanac.** Jack W. Plunkett and others, eds. Galveston, Tex., Plunkett Research, 1999. 599p. $149.99pa. ISBN 0-9638268-8-3.

With changes in the energy industry happening almost daily, it is hard to have a truly up-to-date resource, but this almanac does an admirable job of providing recent information on the petroleum, gas, and electric segments of the energy business. Five chapters provide information on major trends affecting the energy industry, outlook for petroleum and natural gas, energy industry contacts, careers in energy, and profiles of the Energy 400—a group of firms considered by the publisher of this source to be the largest and most successful corporations in all segments of the U.S. energy industry. Website addresses, complete mailing addresses and telephone contacts, e-mail addresses, fax numbers, and other pertinent information are provided for each firm. Several areas, such as major oil companies, electric and gas utilities, gas pipelines, refiners, oil field services, cogeneration, and engineering and alternative energy, are covered in this reference source. An energy glossary is provided to help readers become familiar with the terminology, and 46 useful tables, figures, and charts of information are included. These include U.S. Crude Oil Imports, Coal Overview Annual, OPEC Fact Sheet, Selected Electric Utility Data by Ownership, and World Estimated Recoverable Coal. A diskette is provided to create mailing lists or other information a business may need on the energy industry. The indexes are not as useful as they could be because page numbers are not provided. Firms are listed alphabetically, but a better indexing system would enhance this reference. Another valuable addition to Plunkett's reference titles, the 1st edition of this easy-to-read reference on the energy industry will be a useful source for academic libraries, larger public libraries, and select special libraries. [R: Choice, Dec 99, p. 704]
—**Diane J. Turner**

ENVIRONMENTAL SCIENCE

Bibliographies

1527. **Interdisciplinary Bibliographic Guide to Environmental Studies 1998.** Thorndike, Maine, G. K. Hall/Macmillan, 1999. 887p. $295.00. ISBN 0-7838-0408-3. ISSN 1063-6153.

Formerly titled *Bibliographic Guide to the Environment*, this work continues to be an annual compilation of environmental publications in all formats cataloged by the Library of Congress and the New York Public Library (NYPL). (See ARBA 98, entry 1629, and ARBA 94, entry 1988, for reviews of previous editions.) The full AACR2 bibliographic record appears under the main entry, with briefer records (cross-references, in effect) under added name, title, and subject heading entries. All entries are interfiled in a single alphabetic sequence. Although the introductory matter does not specify precise parameters for inclusion in the work, "environmental studies" appears to be defined quite broadly; works dealing with political, social, and economic issues are covered as well as scientific and technical titles. Juvenile literature is included, and the linguistic scope is wide. Individual papers in journals and conference proceedings are not treated.

Because the vast majority of the listings are taken directly from the Library of Congress cataloging database, to which most libraries have ready access online, libraries will have to determine for themselves whether the additional records from NYPL or the utility of the paper version justifies the not inconsiderable purchase price of the work. In any case, it will be primarily of interest to research libraries.—**Paul B. Cors**

1528. Roberts, Jerry. **Rain Forest Bibliography: An Annotated Guide to over 1,600 Nonfiction Books About Central and South American Jungles.** Jefferson, N.C., McFarland, 1999. 312p. index. $48.50. ISBN 0-7864-0717-4.

The *Rain Forest Bibliography* is actually an annotated guide to over 1,500 books about Central and South American jungles. The contents of the bibliography are as follows: Preface (pp. 1–4), Ecology and Conservation—E (pp. 5–40), Flora and Fauna—F (pp. 41–94), People of the Forest—P (pp. 95–165), Travel and Exploration—T (pp. 167–263), Young Adult and Children's Reading—Y (pp. 265–278), and the Index (pp. 279–312). The preface of this book gives insight into its usage, and being written by the author, a newspaper journalist and film critic, it introduces the reader to his point of view. The book is indexed by entry numbers that allow easy reference. These numbers are preceded by letters that refer to specific sections, such as E, F, P, T, and Y. Each of the 5 major sections begins with a brief description of what is to be found, followed by alphabetically arranged entries. Each bibliographic entry contains notes of the book's subject, focus, and scope. The bibliography is designed as a guide for anyone interested in reading about and studying jungles in America. It is written in the spirit of environmentalism and humanist concerns regarding the future of the rain forests and the people who live in them. It could be used as a guide and quick reference for students and scientists who would like to find more information about scientific aspects of jungles. Unfortunately, some of the very interesting books on life in jungles were not included in this bibliography, such as *The Diversity of Life* written by E. O. Wilson, a scientist of international reputation. In addition, the numbering of entries should be more logical.—**Ludmila N. Ilyina**

Dictionaries and Encyclopedias

1529. Crawford, Mark. **Habitats and Ecosystems: An Encyclopedia of Endangered America.** Santa Barbara, Calif., ABC-CLIO, 1999. 398p. index. $75.00. ISBN 0-87436-997-5.

The extraordinary diversity (and fragility) of our wild ecosystems is well documented in this *Habitats and Ecosystems: Encyclopedia of Endangered America*. This book is a compilation of sites in the United States that preserve "original, pristine remnants of vanishing ecosystems," mostly outside the National Park system and on lands open to the public. After brief discussions of conservation terminology, principles, and organizations, the bulk of the text is a state-by-state description of special habitat sites, including a short analysis of the state's geography and ecological regions and lists of notable organisms and endangered species in the sites themselves. Appendixes include postal addresses (but no Web addresses) of national and state conservation organizations and agencies and a useful listing of endangered and threatened flora and fauna (by Federal definitions) in each state. The reference section at the end is thorough and current.

Libraries will want this book for its primary section on special habitats within each state. These descriptions are useful to peruse. For example, readers learn how many states still possess interesting natural sites, even small eastern states such as Rhode Island, and how many endangered species are now confined to small enclaves. Quickly finding a site of interest, however, can be tedious. The habitat descriptions are listed in alphabetic order, followed by the counties where they are located. Simple index maps for each state would have saved the reader much work and illustrated the proximity of sites to each other. Still, with a good state map the sites can be located. This book will be a good addition to any collection with sections on natural resources, conservation, and ecology.—**Mark A. Wilson**

1530. **Encyclopedia of Environmental Analysis and Remediation.** Robert A. Meyers, ed. New York, John Wiley, 1998. 8v. index. $2,500.00/set. ISBN 0-471-11708-0.

The expanding interest in environmental problems during the past few decades has produced a large number of general survey books as well as a plethora of volumes on individual topics. The field has become so broad and yet contains so many specialized topics that it would seem to be impossible to find a single reference work that covers it all. This encyclopedia is a welcome attempt to fulfill this need.

The 8 volumes contain an alphabetic list of about 280 articles written by more than 450 subject matter specialists from industry and academia. The editor summarizes the general subject headings as air pollution control, environmental laws and regulations, environmental sampling and analysis, hazardous waste remediation, pollution in the biosphere, and water reclamation. As indicated by this listing, the coverage is more comprehensive than one might be led to expect from the title. Thus, it is possible to find help on almost any environmental problem, from writing an environmental impact statement to groundwater remediation.

The individual articles are, in essence, short reviews that take the reader from basic principles to a rather sophisticated level. For further study, the articles include excellent reference lists, which seem to be complete through 1996. The numerous illustrations and tables that accompany the various individual articles are carefully selected, clear, and readable. Volume 8 includes a comprehensive index.

The editor states in the preface that he intends this set of volumes for a broad professional audience, including engineers, scientists, and government officials. It should certainly be useful to these groups, but it will also be helpful for nonprofessionals who have some scientific background. These volumes constitute a valuable resource for a broad range of readers interested in environmental problems, and purchase should be considered by any library that supports a significant number of these users.—**Harry E. Pence**

Directories

1531. **Directory of Municipal Water & Wastewater Systems, 1999.** 4th ed. Tulsa, Okla., PennWell Publishing, 1998. 969p. index. $195.00pa. ISSN 1084-7251.

The water systems of the 50 states, from Alabaster, Alabama, to Worland, Wyoming, are listed herein, along with the people who operate them. Both potable and wastewater treatment facilities are included. Larger systems are treated in more detail. For example, St. Louis' wastewater system serves 97 communities and its description requires 30 column inches. The system includes 7,900 miles of lines and the cost of treatment is $.15 per 1,000 gallons. Worland, on the other hand, lists only its technician, Mr. Neufer. The systems are grouped by state and indexed by system name. The names of the people are also indexed.
—**Robert B. McKee**

1532. Matystik, Walter F., Louis Theodore, and Roberto Diaz. **State Environmental Agencies on the Internet.** Rockville, Md., Government Institutes, 1999. 344p. (Government Institutes Internet Series). $59.00pa. ISBN 0-86587-685-1.

This publication is a digitized directory of environmental agencies that assists the reader with navigating the various state environmental agencies by simply pointing and clicking. The table format allows users to get detailed Internet addresses for easy access to specific sections of their Websites. The contents are as follows: an introduction, presented by a few words about the authors and the book itself; preface; agency names; federal and state interaction (the major part presented by state agency tables arranged alphabetically from Alabama to Wyoming); "Quicklinks" (agency homepages); and an epilogue. The comprehensive profile for each state includes agency name, acronym, URL for the home environmental agency page, and date the Website was last updated. There is also a general description of the agency and contact information for each agency with e-mail, telephone, and fax information where available, along with information on separate offices. Information is also provided for online laws, rules, and regulations with links to specific state laws. Details are given about the availability of downloadable forms, files, permits, and publications; specialized information on pollution prevention; and special features of a state's Website.

This directory provides a handy reference guide for the academic, regulatory, business, and professional community to the burgeoning wealth and maze of environmental information—specifically from state agencies—on the Internet. This publication is helpful for everybody who needs to know about environmental agencies.—**Ludmila N. Ilyina**

Handbooks and Yearbooks

1533. **Book of Lists for Regulated Hazardous Substances.** 9th ed. Rockville, Md., Government Institutes, 1999. 621p. $79.00pa. ISBN 0-86587-672-X.

The 9th edition of this manual of regulated hazardous substances is not a comprehensive compilation of all safety, health, and environmental lists from the Code of Federal Regulations (CFR), but it will be useful for anyone dealing with such issues. Hazardous substances in the soil, water, and air remain one of the key issues in the world today. From industries to individuals, we all have to deal with the repercussions from those who fail to comply with regulations and legislation put in place to protect us. Due to the complexities and changes in the law, this manual continues to be valuable. This year it brings together a variety of relevant lists found mostly in the 29 CFR and 40 CFR dated July 1, 1998. The table of contents provides access to the chapters that cover crucial legislation, such as the Clean Air Act; the Clean Water Act; and other crucial laws relating to our environment, safety, and health. As in previous editions, many of the tables are in small print, but they are taken directly from a variety of publications and have appropriate citations, such as Chemical Abstracts numbers for further research. The print in the 9th edition is much clearer than that in the 8th edition. This is not a book for the general public, but it will be useful to anyone trying to comply with environmental laws, as long as they realize that the information is in condensed format and further research could be required.—**Diane J. Turner**

1534. **The Environmental Debate: A Documentary History.** Peninah Neimark and Peter Rhoades Mott, eds. Westport, Conn., Greenwood Press, 1999. 319p. index. (Primary Documents in American History and Contemporary Issues). $125.00. ISBN 0-313-30020-8.

The goal of this unique series is to provide high school and college students researching current topics of interest with background material and information through pivotal primary documents that shaped policy or law and to expose the controversial aspects of the issue through the historical documents. The work at hand, which discusses environmental issues and primary documents, accomplishes this goal. The work covers such topics as overpopulation, land use and property rights, water quality, energy sources, air quality and atmospheric issues, waste production and disposal, the handling of toxic chemicals, forest and wildlife preservation, aquatic preservation, and loss of biodiversity.

The book is divided into 6 broad categories and each section opens with a historical introduction that provides a context for each document and will help readers understand the various sides to the debate. Following the introductions the primary documents are presented and include such items as proposals; government acts; writing of environmentalists, including John Muir and Theodore Roosevelt; and excerpts from popular literature about environmental issues from authors such as Henry David Thoreau and John Steinbeck. The book concludes with a section of notes, a glossary, a further reading section, and an index. Because the topic of environmental conservation will continue to be popular well into this century, this book will be used frequently in high school and university libraries.—**Shannon M. Graff**

1535. **The Global Ecology.** Edward Moran, ed. Bronx, N.Y., H. W. Wilson, 1999. 231p. index. (The Reference Shelf, v.71, no.4). $25.00pa. ISBN 0-8242-0965-6.

The Global Economy is a compendium of chapters from persons with widely differing perspectives, which addresses several major threats to the global ecosystem. Section 1, "Framing the Issues," examines the historical roots of our environmental crisis, provides current perspectives on environmental problems (such as the greater risk faced by disadvantaged people), and looks at possible future scenarios. Section 2,

"Technical Considerations," analyzes global warming and biodiversity, and also includes a chapter written by the skeptic Julian Simon titled "A Dying Planet? How the Media Have Scared the Public." Section 3, "Personal Testimonies," includes several individual perspectives on problems, including an interview with Paul and Anne Ehrlich on population growth. Section 4 examines some solutions to the ecology crisis, including a "Five Hundred Year Plan" and "Incentive Systems that Support Sustainability." This book has many chapters that, individually, are interesting and informative; however, taken together, they do not cohere. The editor briefly introduced each section, but opposing views on the same issues are presented with no critique. This may be no problem for persons already familiar with the issues, but it may leave readers with no background in the subject matter floundering.—**Marquita Hill**

1536. Katz, William B. **The ABCs of Environmental Science.** Rockville, Md., Government Institutes, 1998. 155p. index. $39.00pa. ISBN 0-86587-627-4.

Directed to people of any age with little or no scientific background, Katz's book is enjoyable reading on environmental issues that are in the media today. Although definitely not a textbook, it will be a useful introductory reference for students in high school or college environmental science classes. The book is written in simple, clear, concise language with specific scientific terms in italics the first time they are used. These words are then compiled into a glossary, which follows the text. The book is divided into 4 parts: "Matter, Energy, and Population Growth," "World's Resources," "Pollution," and "Our Planet's Future." The 22 chapters are short, with less than 10 pages each. Chapters are divided into subtopics; for example, "Minerals—A Nonrenewable Resource" covers the Earth's crust, minerals in demand, mineral distribution, cost of minerals, and environmental impact of mineral production. Each chapter is summarized in a "What You Should Remember" box at the end of the chapter. Topics within the chapters range in length from one paragraph to a page. They do not provide detailed discussion of the particular topic but do clearly explain the issue or scientific principle in plain English. Katz explains how the environment works and the impact humans have on it. He stresses renewable and nonrenewable resources and measures we can and need to take to preserve the environment. Graphs and basic black-and-white clip art illustrate the text. A thorough index is provided.—**Elaine Ezell**

1537. Santos, Miguel A. **The Environmental Crisis.** Westport, Conn., Greenwood Press, 1999. 250p. index. (Greenwood Press Guides to Historic Events of the Twentieth Century). $39.95. ISBN 0-313-30151-4.

This book provides an overview of major environmental problems. After a chronology of events, five chapters explain the environmental crisis. The book's appendixes include biographies of significant individuals, primary documents (which describes 16 environmental organizations and summarizes major environmental statues passed since 1970), a glossary of selected terms, and an annotated bibliography. Of the five chapters the most useful are "Historical Overview," "Vanishing Wilderness," and those on overpopulation. The pollution chapter has useful points as well. Disappointing to this reviewer is the chapter titled "The Concept of a Self-Sustainable System." Instead of describing current thinking (including industrial ecology and design for the environment), he describes a model that was developed more than 20 years ago. Also, he comments that energy cannot be recycled, but does not note that up-to-date technologies make it possible for a power plant to utilize 90 percent of fuel's energy (by such means as finding uses for lower-energy steam). Other portions of this chapter are more relevant, such as the relationship between the steady-state economy and sustainability. All the chapters provide useful figures, tables, and historical notes. This could be a useful supplemental text in environmental courses, and also provides useful summary information for individuals already well versed in environmental concerns.—**Marquita Hill**

1538. **Yearbook of International Co-operation on Environment and Development 1998/99.** 7th ed. Helge Ole Bergesen, Georg Parmann, and B. Thommessen Øystein, eds. London, Earthscan Publications; distr., Covelo, Calif., Island Press, 1998. 348p. maps. index. $90.00. ISBN 1-85383-526-9.

The 7th edition of this yearbook, previously titled the *Green Globe Yearbook*, gives readers a picture of global development in specific environmental issues. The book is an independent publication from the Fridtjof Nansen Institute in Norway, which specializes in studies on resource management that cover the international community. The yearbooks try to answer questions about world progress toward sustainable development, achievement of international collaboration, and the barriers that remain. The main focus this year is on the achievements of international cooperation in sustainable development in the past 25 years. Covering forest industries, the International Whaling Commission, prevention of marine pollution by dumping of wastes and other matter, and the UN Commission for Sustainable Development, this reference highlights the obstacles to creating a healthy environment worldwide. The 1st section has 5 excellent, informative articles that deliver an analysis of international government and sustainable development issues. The remaining two thirds of the book provides reference material highlighting key data on the most important international agreements on environment and development in the listings of conventions. Intergovernmental and nongovernmental organizations (IGOs and NGOs) are listed, with most entries including objectives of the organization, activities, addresses, and in many cases, sources on the Internet. OECD (Organization for Economic Co-operation and Development) countries and selected non-OECD countries are also profiled. There are also quick reference tables that list counties and their participation in agreements and organizations. The variety of environmental conventions held and who actually participates would enlighten the average person on the attempts being made to save the earth from humankind. This compact volume is an essential reference for those in government, industry, and international and national organizations that deal with environmental issues, and would be very useful to environmental researchers and academic and large public libraries that provide information to concerned citizens.—**Diane J. Turner**

37 Transportation

GENERAL WORKS

1539. Whitnah, Donald R. **U.S. Department of Transportation: A Reference History.** Westport, Conn., Greenwood Press, 1998. 228p. index. $75.00. ISBN 0-313-28340-0.

This book begins with a broad-brush overview of the historical events resulting in the establishment of the Department of Transportation (DOT) in 1966. This government body is responsible for regulating, both economically and for safety, the country's highways, pipelines, waterways, railroads, urban mass transit systems, airline and trucking industries, and even beautification projects.

The author summarizes the ongoing discussions from the turn of the century to today as to what is the appropriate level of federal control over America's transportation systems. The bulk of the narrative focuses on the airline deregulation debate of the late 1970s, the present status of the airline industry, and current airline and highway safety concerns. Whitnah also describes the activities of the major agencies operating under DOT, such as the U.S. Coast Guard and the Federal Highway Administration. Features include a list of acronyms, bibliography, index, and brief biographical sketches of key past DOT officials, such as department secretaries, USCG commandants and FAA administrators.

The author attempts to cover too large a subject in too short a volume. This limits its usefulness. He also repeatedly injects his personal bias regarding airline deregulation and weakens his presentation.
—**Adrienne Antink Bendel**

AIR

1540. **AIM/FAR 1999: Aeronautical Information Manual/Federal Aviation.** Charles F. Spence, ed. New York, McGraw-Hill, 1999. 780p. index. $29.95; $15.95pa. ISBN 0-07-060156-9; 0-07-060155-0pa.

Pilots use this annual edition of *AIM/FAR 1999* as a handy compendium of essential aviation information. The Federal Aviation Regulations (FAR) section of this book is a compilation of relevant sections of the current U.S. Code of Federal Regulations. It contains all the Federal Aviation Administration rules and regulations that govern pilots, airports, and the operations of aircraft in the United States. The Aeronautical Information Manual (AIM) contains narrative information of use to pilots. By way of illustration the FAR portion would contain the medical rules and regulations for a pilot to obtain a medical certificate, while the AIM section would contain guidelines for determining if a pilot was fit for flight on a daily basis (i.e., current illness). Changes from the prior year's AIM/FAR are highlighted in the text.

This new edition of AIM/FAR also contains the following appendixes: FAA facilities directory, an aviation Website directory, navigation and communication frequencies, a VOR test facility directory, NTSB incident reporting guidelines, NASA aviation safety report form, and "flight forum" excerpts. The appendixes cover about 18 pages and are somewhat limited in scope. For example, the "flight forum" is 2½ pages long and consists of answers to 4 letters, hardly the major feature noted on the back cover of the book. The back cover also lists an appendix of "VOT sites and frequencies." This appendix is not listed in the index. The modest price of this volume will appeal to readers and librarians alike. Most general reference collections will want to add this volume to their collections. Annual purchase would depend on the amount of aviation reader traffic libraries have. Current pilots will need the latest edition.—**Ralph Lee Scott**

GROUND

1541. Bennett, Jim. **The Complete Motorcycle Book: A Consumer's Guide.** 2d ed. New York, Facts on File, 1999. 258p. illus. index. $27.95; $14.95pa. ISBN 0-8160-3853-8; 0-8160-3854-6pa.

A new edition four years after an original publication can be suspect, but not in this instance. Not only is there new information on trends (the rapidly growing number of women riders, for example), new models (including imported ones), prices, and a new section on exotic bikes, but there is even more material in the sections on safety scattered throughout the book. In this reviewer's opinion, the most notable contribution of this volume is the commonsense approach to all aspects of safety, from health to protective clothing and headgear, skill levels, group riding, and many other factors that novices and experienced riders alike need to take into consideration. This, added to basic and sensible chapters on whether to buy a motorcycle in the first place through the selection process (new or used, domestic or imported, what type) and maintenance, makes Bennett's book a useful and effective one. There is even a brief chapter on road driving aimed at car drivers. This book is highly recommended for public and community colleges in particular.—**Walter C. Allen**

1542. de la Rive Box, Rob. **Encyclopaedia of Classic Cars: Sports Cars 1945-1975.** The Netherlands, Rebo Productions; distr., Chicago, Fitzroy Dearborn, 1998. 287p. illus. index. $35.00. ISBN 1-57958-118-8.

In his brief foreword, the author of this attractive and compact volume notes that it is not comprehensive. In a mock conversation, he points out some of the difficulties of defining "sports car," a topic of endless debate. In the end, he does include some borderline cases (e.g., the Bentley R Continental and the Buick Wildcat and Riviera). Are they? Enough people think so that it adds to the value of the book. Coverage is worldwide for the period. Entries are alphabetic by marque and chronological by model. Each entry has a page or two of general background, then details such as years of production, number made, engine specifications, and illustrations of each model. The color illustrations are often small, but they are profuse and of excellent quality. The index puts all the marques and their models in alphabetic order, especially helpful if one does not recall the time sequence. This encyclopedia should be useful in any library with an audience of automobile enthusiasts.—**Walter C. Allen**

1543. Jensen, Todd A. **Automotive Web Sites.** Jefferson, N.C., McFarland, 1999. 175p. index. $25.00pa. ISBN 0-7864-0741-7.

Following a brief preface on the scope of the volume and an introduction on searching the Web for automotive topics, the body of the work consists of 17 sections on various areas relating to automobiles. Topics include aftermarket, automobile buying resources, eZines and publications, and women's groups. Entries are alphabetical within each section. They give full names and acronyms and full Web addresses, along with descriptions of the scope and content of each site. References are numbered sequentially through the entire book, from 1 to 714. The index refers to these numbers, not pages. Presumably, the work will need to be revised fairly frequently to keep up with all the additions and closings. But at the modest price of the 1st edition, it should not be too hard for libraries to keep up with. This should be very useful for hobbyists as well as public and engineering libraries.—**Walter C. Allen**

Author/Title Index

Reference is to entry number.

A to Z of world dvlpmt, 25
Abbey, Buck, 541
Abbott, Craig S., 1014
Abbs, Barbara, 378
ABCs of environmental regulation, 544
ABCs of environmental sci, 1536
ABELL: annual bib of English lang & lit 1920-95 [CD-ROM], 920
Abraham Lincoln on screen, 1182
Abraham, Lyndy, 696
Abram, Dave, 379
Abramson, Hilary S., 261
Abridged ency of world biog, 10
Abromeit, Kathleen A., 1119
Academic yr abroad 1999-2000, 262
Acquah-Dadzie, Kofi, 900
Acronyms, initialisms, & abbrevs dict, 25th ed, 1
Across the top of the world, 502
Adams, Carol, 833
Adams, Ramon F., 887
Adamson, Lynda G., 789, 983, 984
Adeleye, Gabriel G., 900
Affirmative action, 521
Africa S of the Sahara 1999, 28th ed, 81
African-American atlas, 277
African American biog, v.5, 281
African-American culture & hist [CD-ROM], 294
African-American experience on file, 295
African American firsts in sci & tech, 1297
African-American hist, 296
African American info dir 1998-99, 4th ed, 35
African American military heroes, 287
African-American newspapers & pers, 278
African religion, 1240
African states & rulers, 2d ed, 430
Africana, 291
Agnes, Michael, 883
Agricultural stats 1999, 1298
Agyei-Mensah, Samuel, 738
Ahles, Harry E., 1335
AIDS crisis in America, 2d ed, 1429
AIDS sourcebk, 2d ed, 1428
AIM/FAR 1999, 1540
Aircraft of the US military air transport serv 1948-66, 609
Akers, Tim, 969
Alaskan wilderness, 361
Albanian-English dict, 902
Alden, Peter, 370, 371
Aldine press bks at the Harry Ransom Humanities Research Center, 583

Aldred, Heather E., 1441
Alexandria rediscovered, 394
Alfred Reed, 1081
All music gd to the blues, 2d ed, 1092
All roots lead to rock: legends of early rock 'n' roll, 1109
Allaby, Michael, 1311
Allcock, John B., 472
Allen, C. G., 901
Allen, John Logan, 344
Allen, Larry, 148
Allen, Thomas B., 350
Alles, Gregory D., 1234
Allison, Gary D., 436
Allison, Nancy, 1418
Allstetter, William, 1295
Almanac of ...
    state legislatures, 2d ed, 626
    women & minorities in American pol, 657
    WW I, 397
Almquist, Sharon G., 1102
Alston, Sandra, 580
Altenbaugh, Richard J., 220
Alternative medicine gd to heart disease, stroke, & high blood pressure, 1417
Alternative medicine hndbk, 1416
Alternative medicine sourcebk, 1415
Altschiller, Donald, 533
Alzheimer's disease sourcebk, 2d ed, 1430
America at the polls 1960-96, 658
America at war, 598
America from space, 350
American Academy of Pediatrics gd to your child's nutrition, 1422
American big business dir, 1999, 127
American big business disc, 2d ed [CD-ROM], 128
American bk buyers study, 591
American bk trade dir 1999-2000, 45th ed, 585
American business leaders, 119
American business leaders [CD-ROM], 117
American civil rights: almanac, 398
American eras: the Colonial era 1600-1754, 418
American film cycles, 1192
American Heritage student thesaurus, 896
American histl fiction, 983
American hist, 409
American immigration, 419
American Indian biogs, 304
American Jewish desk ref, 316
American Jewish Histl Society, 316
American law yrbk 1998, 520
American legislative leaders in the South, 1911-94, 628

American manufacturers dir, 1999, 154
American manufacturers disc, 2d ed [CD-ROM], 155
American men & women of sci 1998-99, 20th ed, 1275
American military leaders, 596
American military leaders [CD-ROM], 595
American musical film song ency, 1159
American mystery & detective novels, 980
American presidency, 3d ed, 659
American salaries & wages survey, 5th ed, 204
American scene: events, 405
American settlement houses & progressive social reform, 411
American settlement movement, 401
American sign lang handshape dict, 893
American social issues [CD-ROM], 410
American travel writers, 1850-1915, 1001
American travellers abroad, 2d ed, 359
American wholesalers & distrs dir, 7th ed, 156
American women photographers, 867
American women prose writers to 1820, 996
American yrs, 407
America's top jobs for college graduates, 3d ed, 197
America's top medical, educ, & human servs jobs, 4th ed, 198
America's top-rated cities, 2000, 7th ed, 787
Ammer, Christine, 894
Amphibians & reptiles of Northern Guatemala, the Yucatan, & Belize, 1376
Amusement park gd, 3d ed, 372
Anchor Bible dict on CD-ROM [CD-ROM], 1244
Ancient African kingdom of Kush, 506
Ancient & modern Chaldean hist, 476
Ancient Roman writers, 1040
Anderson, Alice Hellstrom, 790
Anderson, James D., 1051
Anderson, Vicki, 947
Andor, L. E., 428
Andrew, Geoff, 1155, 1171
Andriot, Laurie, 229, 636
Angelo, Joseph A., Jr., 1498
Angels: an indexed & partially annot bibliog, 1225
Anglish/Yinglish, 2d ed, 919
Animal anatomy on file, rev ed, 1350
Animals, 1351
Anne Tyler companion, 1017
Annual abstract of stats, no.135, 1999 ed, 769
Annual review of info sci & tech, v.33, 1998, 559
Another song to sing: the recorded repertoire of Johnny Cash, 1086
Anthropological lit on disk 1999 [CD-ROM], 267
Anthropological resources, 268
Antique trader's bks, antiques, & collectibles price gd, 2000 annual ed, 834
APA membership register 1999, 688
Appiah, Kwame Anthony, 291
Appraisals of original wind music, 1108
Arab American biog, 272

Arab women 1995, 799
ARBA gd to biogl resources 1986-97, 11
Architect's portable hndbk, 2d ed, 861
Architecture: an interactive intro [CD-ROM], 858
Architecture in ms 1601-1996, 864
Arends, Marthe, 326, 327
Arrigo, Bruce A., 62
Arthurian fiction, 967
Arthurian name dict, 1023
Arts of the 19th century: v.1, 1780-1850, 857
Artz, Joan W., 52
Asante, Molefi K., 277
Ash, Russell, 1130
Ashley, James R., 459
Asian-American experience on file, 273
Asian American lit, 1006
Aslib dir of info sources in the UK, 10th ed, 555
ASM hndbk, v.7, 1386
Assistantships & graduate fellowships in the mathematical scis, 1999-2000, 1519
Associations unltd [CD-ROM], 36
Astronomical almanac for the yr 1998, 1499
Atlas of ...
    the official records of the Civil War [CD-ROM], 400
    the universe, 1502
    the world's worst natural disasters, 1497
Audi, Robert, 1212
Augustine through the ages, 1227
Australia 2000, 377
Austria, rev ed, 95
Authorized press in Vichy & German-occupied France, 1940-44, 453
Automotive Web sites, 1543
AV market place 1999, 823
Avallone, Eugene A., 1391
Aves, Alison, 169
Award winning architecture 1998/99, 859
Awards, honors, & prizes 1999, 15th ed, 37
Ax, Barbara, 1205
Aycock, Wendell M., 993
Ayres, David, 1476
Ayurveda ency, 1419

Babin, Edith, 939
Bachtler, John, 189
Bacon's mag dir 1999, 47th ed, 50
Bacon's media source [CD-ROM], 808
Bacon's newspaper dir 1999, 47th ed, 51
Bacon's radio dir 1999, 13th ed, 824
Bacon's TV/cable dir 1999, 13th ed, 825
Badger, David, 1375
Bagnall, David, 938
Bahr, Howard M., 301
Bail, Paul, 1017

Baker, Beth A., 1133
Baker, Colin, 219
Baker, Daniel B., 345, 346
Baker ency of Christian apologetics, 1261
Baker ency of psychology & counseling, 2d ed, 683
Baker, Lawrence W., 281, 1378, 1521
Baker, William, 582
Balance of payments stats yrbks 1998, 770
Balboa films, 1178
Bald, Margaret, 562
Baldwin, Jack, 362
Baldwin, Winnie, 362
Baldwin's gd to museums of La., 362
Balkin, Richard, 399
Ball, Ann, 1228
Ball identification gd to greenhouse pests & beneficials, 1361
Ballpark sourcebk, 2d ed, 710
Banks, Michelle, 1170
Bankston, Carl L., III, 742
Barber, Phil, 718
Barbuto, Domenica M., 401, 411
Bard, Kathryn A., 396
Bardin, Rodney Norman, II, 1178
Barkan, Elliott Robert, 679
Barker, Keith, 963
Barker, Robert L., 750
Barnard, Loretta, 1337, 1345
Barnard, Peter C., 1363
Barnes-Svarney, Patricia, 1348
Barron, Neil, 975, 988
Barron's ency of dog breeds, 1359
Barron's gd to distance learning, 227
Barron's profiles of American colleges, 1999 ed [CD-ROM], 233
Barrows, Alison, 1458
Bartlett, Rebecca Ann, 551
Barton, Wayne, 975
Basque region, 96
Bates, Jem, 811
Bauer, David G., 242
Baughman, Judith S., 1009
Baumeister, Theodore, III, 1391
Beachcomber's gd to seashore life in the Pacific NW, 1331
Bebbington, Warren, 1067
Beckett, Ian F. W., 599
Beckett, Sister Wendy, 1259
Becking, Bob, 1247
Bed & breakfast ency, 2d ed, 358
Bed & breakfasts & country inns, 10th ed, 357
Bedside, bathtub, & armchair companion to Sherlock Holmes, 982
Beer, Robert, 865
Beers, Mark H., 1406
Beetham, Donald W., 854
Bekoff, Marc, 1347
Bell, Arthur H., 874

Bellenir, Karen, 1305, 1428, 1430, 1431, 1432, 1434
Bendixen, Alfred, 1004
Benedetto, Robert, 1231
Benford, Robert D., 59
Benner, David G., 683
Bennett, Jim, 1541
Bennett, Paul, 363
Benson, Morton, 916
Bentley, Chantelle, 815
Bentley, Elizabeth Petty, 328
Bentley, V., 171
Berger, Thomas L., 973
Bergesen, Helge Ole, 1538
Bergman, Jerry, 1257
Berinstein, Paula, 1291
Berkeley, Kathleen C., 800
Berkow, Robert, 1406
Bernstein, Lenny, 1101
Bernstein, Mark F., 626
Berson, Robin Kadison, 478
Best bks for children, 6th ed, 948
Best 80 business schools, 2000 ed, 256
Best graduate programs: engineering, 2d ed, 234
Best 331 colleges, 2000 ed, 238
Betz, Adrienne, 965
Beyle, Thad L., 661
Beyond the natl parks, 698
BFI companion to crime, 1172
BFI film & TV hndbk 1999, 1188
Bibliographic gd to ...
    art & architecture 1998, 844
    business & economics 1998, 115
    dance 1998, 1148
    educ 98, 217
    Latin American studies 1998, 320
    maps & atlases 1998, 343
    music 1998, 1059
    N American hist 98, 402
    psychology 98, 680
    tech 1998, 1272
    theatre arts 98, 1203
Bibliography of ...
    Alexander Pushkin in English, 1044
    Canadian imprints 1751-1800, 581
    Fla., v.3: 1881-99, 78
    Islamic philosophy, 1269
    modern art on disc [CD-ROM], 845
    sources on the region of Former Yugoslavia, 101
Bierbrier, Morris L., 474
Big bk of beastly mispronunciations, 871
Bijlefeld, Marjolijn, 532
Bill James presents ... STATS all-time baseball sourcebk, 703
Bill James presents ... STATS minor league hndbk 1999, 8th ed, 704
Billboard gd to tejano & regional Mexican music, 1110
Binning, William C., 630

Bioethics for students, 1210
Biographical dict of ...
  African Americans, 288
  British prime ministers, 614
  congressional women, 629
Biographical ency of mathematicians, 1520
Bird almanac, 1354
Bird, David M., 1354
Bird-finding gd to Mexico, 1356
Birds of the wetlands, 1355
Bishop, A. C., 1510
Bishop, Steven R., 1524
Black authors & illustrators of bks for children & YAs, 958
Black studies on disc 1999 [CD-ROM], 297
Black women in America, 282
Black women in American bands & orchestras, 2d ed, 1061
Blackburn, G. Meredith, III, 1052
Black's vet dict, 19th ed, 1315
Blackwell ency of Anglo-Saxon England, 466
Blair, John, 466
Bleiler, David, 1187
Bleiler, Richard, 992
Bleiler, Richard J., 979
Blood & circulatory disorders sourcebk, 1431
Blues singers, 1093
Bluestein, Gene, 919
Bobb, F. Scott, 426
Bobby Hackett: a bio-discography, 1080
Boccagna, David L., 1065
Boden, Edward, 1315
Boe, Beverly, 77
Bogart, Dave, 560
Boit, Christian, 1383
Bollard, John K., 899
Bonavita, Mark, 711
Bonilla, Denise M., 809
Bonk, Mary Rose, 1, 2
Book of lists for regulated hazardous substances, 9th ed, 1533
Booker, M. Keith, 1189
Bookman's price index, v.60, 836
Books, bricks, & bytes: libs in the 21st century, 575
Books in print 1998-99, 6
Booth, Bibi, 698
Boucher, C. Robin, 692
Boulanger, Norman C., 1207
Bowden, Ann, 1047
Bowker annual lib & bk trade almanac 1999, 44th ed, 560
Boyd, Alan S., 1439
Boyden, Karen, 1413
Boyden, Matthew, 1103
Brackett, Virginia, 985
Brackney, William H., 1262
Bradford, William C., 973

Bradley, Jane, 134
Braff, Richard E., 1173
Brain disorders sourcebk, 1432
Brands & their cos, 18th ed, 157
Brandt, Ira K., 1426
Braun, Molly, 311
Brennan, Elizabeth A., 1002
Brenner, Morgan G., 714
Bressett, Kenneth, 838, 839, 842
Bridge Info Systems America, 141
Brier, Bob, 475
Briggs, Ward W., 1040
Brimblecombe, Sharon, 1281
Britain: the rough gd, 2d ed, 379
Britain in the Hanoverian age, 1714-1837, 467
Britain 1999, 50th ed, 102
British museum ency of native N America, 306
British novelists since 1960, 3d series, 1019
British poets of the Great War: Sassoon, Graves, Owen, 1050
British travel writers, 1940-97, 1020
British writers, suppl 5, 1024
Brogan, Patrick, 500
Bromley, Debra J., 1205
Brothers, Barbara, 1020
Broussard, Mark, 715, 716
Brown, Anthony Gary, 1026
Brown, Jared M., 1136
Brown, Marianne Gluszak, 893
Brown, Mark, 1118
Brown, Mary Elizabeth, 675
Brown, Michelle P., 855
Brown, Richard Maxwell, 734
Brown, Tricia, 361
Brownstone, David M., 795
Bruce, Christopher W., 1023
Bruno, Leonard C., 1521
Bryner, Gary C., 542
Buchanan, Paul D., 1268
Buckley, Jonathan, 1103
Budget of the US govt, fiscal yr 2000, 641
Building materials, 1390
Bulgaria, 97
Bunge, Mario, 1211
Bunson, Margaret, 1229, 1267
Bunson, Matthew, 1229, 1256, 1267
Bunson, Stephen, 1229, 1267
Burack, Sylvia K., 817
Bureau of the Census, 784
Burfoot, Annette, 1437
Burg, David F., 397
Burke, John Gordon, 54
Burke, Steven D., 1488
Burki, Shahid Javed, 440
Burns sourcebk, 1433
Burr, Ramiro, 1110
Burroughs, Polly, 366

Burrows, Terry, 1088
Burstein, Chaya M., 317
Burton, William C., 513
Burton's legal thesaurus, 3d ed, 513
Business ethics, 205
Business kanji, 913
Business leaders for students, 118
Business orgs, agencies, & pubs dir, 10th ed, 129
Business phone bk USA 1999, 21st ed, 130
Business ref servs & sources, 578
Butcher, Helen, 579
Butler, D., 171
Butler, Marian, 7, 8
Butterflies of Canada, 1364
Buyer's gd to 50 yrs of TV on video, 1197
Buzzed: the straight facts about the most used & abused drugs from alcohol to ecstasy, 1446
By the numbers: electronic & online publishing, 592

Caballero, Benjamin, 1393
Cagle, William R., 1299
Calder, James D., 594
Cambridge companion to the organ, 1090
Cambridge companion to the piano, 1091
Cambridge dict of philosophy, 2d ed, 1212
Cambridge dict of stats, 767
Cambridge factfinder, 3d ed, 3
Cambridge gd to minerals, rocks, & fossils, rev ed, 1510
Cameroon, rev ed, 82
Campaigns of the Civil War & the Navy in the Civil War [CD-ROM], 420
Campbell, Jonathan A., 1376
Canadian bks in print 1999: author & title index, 7
Canadian bks in print 1999: subject index, 8
Canadian health facilities dir, 1396
Canadian who's who 1999 [CD-ROM], 22
Canadian who's who 1999, v.34, 23
Canadian writer's market, 13th rev ed, 811
Cantarella, Gina-Marie, 557
Capital punishment in the US, 534
Carangelo, Lori, 739
Carbon dates, 1514
Career exploration on the Internet, 192
Career opportunities in TV, cable, video, & multimedia, 4th ed, 193
Career opportunities in the sports industry, 2d ed, 199
Career opportunities in theater & the performing arts, 2d ed, 200
Carey, Gary, 930
Carlton, Regie A., 2
Carman, Jennifer L., 157, 158
Carmichael, Cathie, 98
Carnagie, Julie L., 701
Carnes, Mark C., 409
Carole King, 1084

Carrasco, David, 313
Carter, Craig, 709, 715, 720, 724
Carter, Walter, 1089
Carver, Reginald, 1101
Carwardine, Mark, 1374
Cassell compact dict, 876
Cassell concise dict with CD-ROM, rev ed [CD-ROM], 877
Cassell dict & thesaurus, 878
Cassell dict of physics, 1516
Cassell gd to punctuation, repr ed, 821
Cassell paperback dict, 879
Cassell's ency of queer myth, symbol, & spirit, 1127
Cassileth, Barrie R., 1416
Cassutt, Michael, 1507
Castro & the Cuban Revolution, 445
Catala, Rafael, 1051
Catalog of catalogs 6, 144
Catalog of prenatally diagnosed conditions, 3d ed, 1426
Catalog of teratogenic agents, 9th ed, 1454
Cauthen, Paul, 1077
Cavazos-Gaither, Alma E., 55
CBS radio mystery theater, 828
Censorship in America, 561
Census records for Latin America & the Hispanic US, 760
Central & equatorial Africa area bibliog, 83
Central Intelligence Agency, 73
Cerrito, Joann, 1007
Certification & accreditation programs dir, 2d ed, 194
Chadwick, Bruce A., 786
Chafetz, Morris, 754
Chalcraft, Anthony, 807
Chambers biogl dict, 6th ed, 12
Chambers, Janice E., 1477
Chameleons, 1377
Chang, Tony H., 433
Chapple, Michael, 1517
Charging & collecting fees & fines, 572
Charles Bronson, 1152
Charles, Jill, 1204, 1205
Charleston, Savannah, & coastal islands bk, 3d ed, 369
Charlton standard catalogue of royal doulton beswick figurines, 6th ed, 830
Charny, Israel W., 732
Chaucer A to Z, 1025
Chemical elements, 1378
Chemical gd to the Internet, 2d ed, 1484
Chemistry, 1491
Chenes, Betz Des, 398
Chepesiuk, Ron, 753
Cherapanov, Genady P., 1387
Chicano writers, 3d series, 1003
Child care: a parent's gd, 2d ed, 740
Child labor, 756
Children's bks about religion, 951
Children's bks in print on disc [CD-ROM], 949

Children's fiction 1900-50, 950
Children's health, 1423
Children's lit review, v.50, 964
China during the cultural revolution, 1966-76, 433
Chinese character dict, 903
Chinese-Pinyin-English dict for learners, 904
Chipman, Donald E., 404
Choice's outstanding academic bks 1992-97, 551
Choral music in 19th-century America, 1096
Christen, Kimberly A., 1131
Christensen, Lawrence O., 18
Christian colleges & universities 1999, 235
Christiansen, Donald, 1381
Chronicle of opera, 1105
Chronological hist of the European Union 1946-98, 448
Chronology of world hist, 487
Chronology of world slavery, 488
Chung, Christine, 238
Ciccarelli, Sheryl, 923
Ciment, James, 672, 761
Cinematographers production designers, costume designers, & film editors gd 1998, 1166
Cities of the US, 3d ed, 74
Cities of the world, 5th ed, 63
City crime rankings, 5th ed, 535
City profiles USA 1999, 4th ed, 353
Civil rights in America: 1500 to the present, 549
Civil War CD-ROM II [CD-ROM], 421
Clarage, Elizabeth C., 1002
Clark, David Lindsey, 1108
Clark, Donna, 1277
Clark, Jerome, 697
Clark, John, 149, 167, 1518
Classic love & romance lit, 985
Classical music: the rough gd, 2d ed, 1097
Clawson, Dan, 733
Clements, Frank A., 112
Clinton, Catherine, 416
Clowns & tricksters, 1131
Coates, Robert M., 1489
Codes of professional responsibility, 4th ed, 208
Coffin, Tristram Potter, 1121
Cohen, Hennig, 1121
Cohen, Saul B., 351
Cohen, Sidney, 754
Cohn, Leigh, 1435
Coile, D. Caroline, 1359
Coles, Peter, 1503
Collector's Mart mag price gd to ltd ed collectibles, 1999, 831
College basketball's natl championships, 714
College blue bk, 27th ed, 236
College Board college costs & financial aid hndbk 2000, 20th ed, 252
College Board college hndbk 2000, 37th ed, 253
College Board scholarship hndbk 2000, 3d ed, 254

College student's gd to merit & other no-need funding 1998-2000, 244
Colleges that encourage character dvlpmt, 237
Collin, P. H., 514
Collins, Brian C., 432
Collins essential atlas of the world, 336
Collins, Paul, 1034
Collins, William J., 1106
Colonial America to 1763, 399
Color ency of ornamental grasses, 1312
Columbia gazetteer of the world, 351
Columbia gd to modern Japanese hist, 436
Columbia gd to online style, 822
Combined membership list 1998-99, 1522
Commire, Anne, 793
Commonwealth Univ yrbk 1999, 74th ed, 255
Compact Nelson Japanese-English character dict, 912
Companies & their brands, 18th ed, 158
Companion to Calif. wine, 1303
Companion to Irish traditional music, 1066
Company profiles for students, 131
Comparative reader, 921
Compensation 98, v.16, 642
Complete dir for people with disabilities, 2000, 8th ed, 736
Complete ency of the guitar, 1088
Complete gd to environmental careers in the 21st century, 195
Complete gd to literary contests 1999, 812
Complete index to literary sources in film, 1194
Complete index to world film since 1895 on CD-ROM [CD-ROM], 1195
Complete mental health dir, 2000, 690
Complete motorcycle bk, 2d ed, 1541
Complete outdoors ency, 4th ed, 702
Comprehensive catalogue of duet lit for female voices, 1060
Comprehensive Shakespeare dict [CD-ROM], 1027
Comprehensive Shakespeare Dict Project, 1027
Concise Bible atlas, 1243
Concise dict of European proverbs, 1125
Concise Oxford dict, 10th ed, 880
Conflict in Korea, 439
Conflict in the Former Yugoslavia, 472
Congress A to Z, 3d ed, 631
Congressional Quarterly almanac 1998, 643
Congressional Quarterly almanac 1997, 53d ed, 644
Congressional Quarterly's desk ref on the states, 75
Congressional Quarterly's fed PAC dir 1998-99, 645
Conner, Lester I., 1039
Conner, Randy P. Luncunas, 1127
Conner, Thomas, 1118
Connoisseur's gd to the bks of Sir Winston Churchill, 469
Connors, Martin, 1201
Considine, Douglas M., 1289
Considine, Glenn D., 1289

Constitution & its amendments, 646
Constitutional rights sourcebk, 528
Consumer fraud, 146
Consumer issues in health care sourcebk, 1411
Consumer Latin America 1999, 6th ed, 190
Consumer sourcebk, 12th ed, 145
Consumer USA 1999, 4th ed, 209
Contemporary African American novelists, 997
Contemporary authors autobiog series, v.30, 923
Contemporary authors, v.165, 924
Contemporary authors, v.168, 925
Contemporary authors, v.169, 926
Contemporary authors, v.170, 927
Contemporary authors, v.171, 928
Contemporary black biog, v.18, 283
Contemporary black biog, v.19, 284
Contemporary black biog, v.20, 285
Contemporary composition studies, 939
Contemporary literary criticism, v.110, 940
Contemporary literary criticism, v.111, 941
Contemporary literary criticism, v.113, 942
Contemporary literary criticism, v.114, 943
Contemporary literary criticism, v.116, 944
Contemporary literary criticism, v.117, 945
Contemporary Southern writers, 998
Contemporary theatre, film, & TV, v.22, 1141
Contemporary women artists, 846
Cook, Allan R., 1414, 1415, 1433
Cook, Ramsay 24
Cook, Rhodes, 658
Cook, Samantha, 364
Cool cats, top dogs, & other beastly expressions, 894
Coombs, Martha, 384
Cooper, John, 950
Cooper, Jonathan, 950
Cooper, Sonja, 740
Coppa, Frank J., 1265
Cordes, Joseph J., 216
Corduan, Winfried, 1238
Cormier, Ramona, 1219
Cosmic phenomena, 1506
Cosner, Shaaron, 456
Cosner, Victoria, 456
Coughlan, Margaret N., 1120
Count Dracula goes to the movies, 1177
County & city extra, 1999, 8th ed, 778
County locator, 329
Cox, Jim, 826
CQ's pol in America 2000, 647
CQ's state fact finder 1999, 779
Cracroft, Richard H., 1000
Craddock, James M., 1170
Craddock, Jim, 1201
Craft, Donna, 131
Crane, Janet, 108
Crawford, Elizabeth D., 1341
Crawford, Mark, 412, 1529

CRB commodity yrbk 1998, 141
CRC concise ency of math, 1523
CRC hndbk of chemistry & physics 1999-2000, 80th ed, 1473
Creating a power Web site, 567
Creation/evolution controversy, 1224
Cremeans, John E., 161
Crete, 104
Criddle, Sally, 566
Crime state rankings 1999, 6th ed, 536
Criscito, Pat, 227
Critical companion to popular contemporary writers, 1999 ed [CD-ROM], 976
Critical terms for religious studies, 1232
Croatia, 98
Crossing the plate: the upswing in runs scored by major league teams, 1993 to 1997, 713
Crosswy, Tiffany, 358
Crothers, Tim, 699
Crump, Andy, 25
Crystal, David, 3
Csendes, Peter, 449
Cubbage, Sue, 196
Cults in America, 1241
Culture & customs of Argentina, 109
Culture & customs of Colombia, 111
Culture & customs of Japan, 89
Culturgrams: the nations around us, 64
Cumming, William P., 337
Curnutt, Jordan, 205
Custard, Edward T., 238
Cyndi's list: a comprehensive list of 40,000 genealogy sites on the Internet, 330

Daiber, Hans, 1269
Daily life in Civil War America, 425
Daily life in 18th-century England, 471
Daily life in medieval Europe, 447
Daily life of the ancient Egyptians, 475
Daily life of the Aztecs, 313
Daily life through hist [CD-ROM], 501
Daintith, John, 1479, 1518
Dalby, Andrew, 870
Dale, Jean, 830
Dalton, Stephen, 1352
Daly, Martin, 91
Danheiser, Rick L., 1488
Danky, James P., 278
Darke, Rick, 1312
Darnay, Arsen J., 163
Darrow, Kathy D., 1029, 1030, 1031
Dasch, E. Julius, 344, 1494
Dashe, Alfred M., 1412
Davidson, Michael J., 604
Davies, James A., 1033

Davis & Assocs., 1389
Davis, J. R., 1389
Davis, Martha G., 782
Davis, Paul K., 600
Dawson, Dawn P., 1423
Day, Trevor, 1511
de la Rive Box, Rob, 1542
De Mente, Boye Lafayette, 186
De Vorsey, Louis, Jr., 337
de Wolff, Charles J., 693
Dean, John A., 1490
DeAngelis, James J., 42
Deans, P. Candace, 569
Death penalty, 527
DeFranco, Laurence J., 626
deJong, Andrea L., 214
DeLancey, Mark D., 82
DeLancey, Mark W., 82
Delgado, James P., 502
Delury, George E., 618
Dement, Jeffrey W., 1190
Demographic perspective on women in dvlpmt in Cambodia ..., 759
Demographic yrbk, 1997, 49th ed, 763
Demographics USA 1999: county ed, 764
Demographics USA 1999: ZIP ed, 765
Dempsey, Jennifer, 1116
Dempsey, Lorcan, 566
Denmark, Scott E., 1489
Dent, David W., 422
Department of Economic & Social Affairs, 771
Derks, Scott, 139
DesJardins, Dawn Conzett, 38
Dessen, Alan C., 1206
Detlefs, Dale R., 752
Detwiler, Susan M., 1397
Detwiler's dir of health & medical resources 1999-2000, 7th ed, 1397
DeVenney, David P., 1095
Dewan, John, 703
DeWitt, Donald L., 314
Di Sabatino, David, 1258
Diabetes sourcebk, 2d ed, 1434
Diagram Group, 1319, 1350, 1475
Diamond, Dan, 726
Diaz, Roberto, 1532
Dicaire, David, 1093
DiCanio, Margaret B., 667
Dickerson, Donya, 813, 818
Dickinson, Terence, 1500
Dickson, Paul, 705
Dictionary & catalog of African American folklife of the south, 292
Dictionary of ...
    alchemical imagery, 696
    archaeology, 393

Australian music, 1067
biblical imagery, 1245
biblical interpretation, 1246
bird artists of the world, 849
Canadian biog, v.14, 24
chemistry, 1481
contemporary Chinese military hist, 435
contemporary quotations, v.9, 4th rev ed, 54
critical social scis, 62
deities & demons in the Bible (DDD), 2d rev ed, 1247
English surnames, 335
environmentally important chemicals, 1476
existentialism, 1213
free-market econs, 124
French slang & colloquial expressions, 907
geography, 349
human rights advocacy orgs in Africa, 548
intl trade hndbk, 3d ed, 168
Italian food & drink, 1300
Italian slang & colloquial expressions, 911
langs, 870
law, 2d ed, 514
lexicography, 584
literary & thematic terms, 936
literary biog, v.201, 582
literary symbols, 933
mathematical quotations, 1525
Mo. Biog, 18
philosophy, 1211
physics, 1517
plant pathology, 2d ed, 1332
quotations in communications, 810
space tech, 2d ed, 1498
stage directions in English drama 1580-1942, 1206
stats & methodology, 2d ed, 768
Tex. artists, 1800-1945, 847
the politics of the People's Republic of China, 86
the presbyterian & reformed tradition in America, 1263
toxicology, 2d ed, 1477
veterinary epidemiology, 1316
wars, rev ed, 495
world biog: the 20th century, 479
world biog, v.3: the Renaissance, 480
world biog, v.4: the 17th & 18th centuries, 481
world biog, vols.5 & 6: the 19th century, 482
Dienhart, John W., 205
Diet & nutrition sourcebk, 2d ed, 1305
Diethe, Carol, 1214
Dietz, William H., 1422
Dillon, Patrick M., 1455
DiMauro, Laurie, 1007
Dine bibliog to the 1990s, 301
Direction of trade stats yrbk, 1998, 210
Directories in print, 17th ed, 38
Director's vision, 1171

Directory of ...
    alternative investment programs, 1998 ed, 142
    American scholars, 9th ed, 239
    biomedical & health care grants 1999, 13th ed, 1400
    bks & authors, 937
    consumer brands & their owners 1998, 170
    contract electronics manufacturers, 1999, 159
    internship & post-doctoral fellowships in clinical child/pediatric psychology, 1999-2000, 3d ed, 691
    law-related CD-ROMs 1999, 517
    municipal water & wastewater systems, 1999, 4th ed, 1531
    small press/mag editors & publishers 1999-2000, 30th ed, 586
    special libs & info centers, 23d ed, 556
    state court clerks & county courthouses, 1999 ed, 516
    the American Psychological Assn, 1997 ed, 689
    venture capital firms, 2000, 4th ed, 150
    Web sites, 1460
Distance learning funding sourcebk, 4th ed, 228
Distinguished African American pol & govtl leaders, 286
Distinguished Asian Americans, 274
Divorce: the best resource to help you survive, 2d ed, 741
Dixon-Kennedy, Mike, 1128, 1129
DK concise ency, 26
DK dict/thesaurus, 897
Docherty, James C., 442
Dole, Patricia Pearl, 951
Dominican Americans, 300
Doniger, Wendy, 1237
Donjon, Richard P., 1449
Dooley, Jackie M., 563
Do's & don'ts around the world: Asia, 85
Douglas, J. D., 1248
Dow, Robert E., 1477
Dow, Sheila M., 118
Dowell, Jennifer M., 516, 519
Doyle, Billy H., 1149, 1167
Doyle, Kevin, 195
Dragoumis, Mark, 105
Drake, Frederick D., 662
Drake, Greg, 866
Drama for students, v.5, 970
Drama for students, v.6, 971
Drenth, Pieter J. D., 693
Drew, Stephen W., 1323
Duchovnay, Gerald, 1150
Duckworth, William, 1075
Due, Andrea, 342
Dugan, Robert E., 619
Duke Ellington, 1082
Dumouchel, J. Robert, 751
Dun & Bradstreet/Gale industry ref hndbks: chemicals, 1485

Dun & Bradstreet/Gale industry ref hndbks: computers & sftwr, 1457
Dun & Bradstreet/Gale industry ref hndbks: entertainment, 1147
Dun & Bradstreet/Gale industry ref hndbks: hospitality, 160
Dun & Bradstreet/Gale industry ref hndbks: telecommunications, 1471
Duncan, Philip D., 647
Dungan, David L., 1252
Dunton, Chris, 972
Dutton, Lee S., 268
Duval, R. Shannon, 1216
Duxbury, John, 711
Dyja, Eddie, 1188

Eades, J. S., 88
Eades, Lindsay Michie, 427
Eads, Michelle E., 41
Earl, Peter E., 121
Early Canadian printing, 580
Earth sci on file, rev ed, 1496
Earth scis for students, 1494
Eating disorders, 2d, 1435
Ebel, Robert D., 216
Eccleshall, Robert, 614
Economic & Social Commission for W Asia, 759, 774, 799, 803
Economic Commission for Europe, 775
Economic Commission for Latin America & the Caribbean, 191
Economic survey of Latin America & the Caribbean 1997-98, 50th ed, 191
Economics & Stats Admin, 784
Economist desk companion, 3d ed, 45
Edinburgh ency of continental philosophy, 1215
Edmonds, Anthony O., 605
Education stats on the US 1999, 225
Educators resource dir 1999, 3d ed, 222
Edwards, Adrian, 104
Ehrlich, Eugene, 884
Ehrlich, Henry, 140
Eis, Arlene L., 517
Eisaguirre, Lynne, 521
Elections A to Z, 633
Electronic engineers hndbk [CD-ROM], 1381
Elgar companion to consumer research & economic psychology, 121
El-hi textbks & serials in print 1999, 127th ed, 218
Ellavich, Marie C., 1276
Ellwood, Robert S., 1234
Ellwood, Wayne, 25
Elsevier dicts on CD-ROM, 1998/99 ed [CD-ROM], 27
Elster, Charles Harrington, 871
Elvis Costello, 1085

Empereur, Jean-Yves, 394
Empire State Railway Museums 34th annual gd to tourist railroads & museums, 1999 ed, 365
Encarta world English dict, 881
Encoded archival description, 563
Encoded archival description tag lib version 1.0, 564
Encoded Archival Description Working Group of the Society of American Archivists, 564
Encyclopaedia Britannica CD-ROM 1999, multimedia ed [CD-ROM], 28
Encyclopaedia of classic cars, 1542
Encyclopaedia of Indian cinema, rev ed, 1164
Encyclopedia Americana on CD-ROM [CD-ROM], 29
Encyclopedia of ...
    African American business hist, 122
    American activism, 1960 to the present, 667
    American lit, 1004
    American parties, campaigns, & elections, 630
    American public policy, 678
    American religions, 6th ed, 1236
    animal rights & animal welfare, 1347
    animated cartoons, 2d ed, 1161
    archaeology, 395
    bilingualism & bilingual educ, 219
    bioprocess tech, 1323
    Britain, 103
    British women writers, rev ed, 1021
    business info sources, 13th ed, 116
    Canada's peoples, 269
    China, 87
    Chinese film, 1165
    Christianity, v.1 (A-D), 1264
    computational chemistry, 1478
    conflicts since WW II, 672
    controlled drug delivery, 1447
    creativity, 684
    cults, sects, & new religions, 1235
    electronic circuits, v.7, 1382
    emerging industries, 153
    environmental analysis & remediation, 1530
    ethics, 1216
    fable, 1124
    family life, 742
    genetics, 1321
    genocide, 732
    global population & demographics, 761
    Greco-Roman mythology, 1128
    guerrilla warfare, 599
    heads of states & govts, 1900-45, 616
    hell, 1126
    human emotions, 685
    human nutrition, 1393
    human rights issues since 1945, 546
    intl peacekeeping operations, 673
    lang & educ, 872
    literary critics & criticism, 931
    money, 148
    multicultural educ, 221
    murder & mystery, 981
    Native American economic hist, 305
    Native American Shamanism, 308
    Native American tribes, rev ed, 311
    North American hist, 490
    paleontology, 1513
    parenting theory & research, 755
    political anarchy, 668
    political economy, 123
    political revolutions, 491
    politics & religion, 1233
    reproductive techs, 1437
    roses, 1341
    Russian & Slavic myth & legend, 1129
    sharks, 1369
    smoking & tobacco, 1394
    taxation & tax policy, 216
    TV news, 827
    the Alamo & the Tex. Revolution, 414
    the archaeology of ancient Egypt, 396
    the Mexican-American war, 412
    the Persian Gulf War, 601
    the Vatican & Papacy, 1265
    Tibetan symbols & motifs, 865
    understanding alcohol & other drugs, 754
    vernacular architecture of the world, 860
    violence, peace, & conflict, 492
    warrior peoples & fighting groups, 600
    witches & witchcraft, 2d ed, 694
    women in American pol, 632
    world biog on CD-ROM [CD-ROM], 13
    world biog suppl, 14
    world cities, 72
    world lit in the 20th century, 3d ed, 932
    world religions, 1234
End of apartheid in S Africa, 427
End of the world: an annot bibliog, 1226
Endangered species, 1353
Endocrine & metabolic disorders sourcebk, 1436
Engelbert, Phillis, 398, 1292
Environmental crisis, 1537
Environmental debate, 1534
Environmental health, & safety portable hndbk, 1385
Environmental law hndbk, 15th ed, 543
Erlewine, Michael, 1092
Ernest Hemingway: a documentary vol, 1012
Ernest Hemingway A to Z, 1013
Ernst, Carl R., 329
Escott, Colin, 1109
E-serials, 574
Eskind, Andrew H., 866
Essentials of neo-Confucianism, 1222
Estell, Kenneth, 35
Esterly, Larry E., 630
Ethics & values, 1217
Etter, Patricia A., 403

Etymological dict of Scottish Gaelic, 909
Eurail & train travel gd to Europe, 3d ed, 380
Europa dir of intl orgs, 670
Europe 2000, 381
European mktg data & stats 1999, 34th ed, 188
European regional incentives 1999, 18th ed, 189
European Union ency & dir 1999, 3d ed, 94
Events that shaped the century, 406
Everett, Carole, 224
Everitt, B. S., 767
Every person's gd to Jewish philosophy & philosophers, 1223
Everyday life: American social hist, 413
Evleth, Donna, 453
Exchange arrangements & exchange restrictions 1998, 176
EXEGY: Current country profiles 2000 [CD-ROM], 65
Explorers: from ancient times to the space age, 344
Explorers & discoverers, v.6, 345
Explorers & discoverers, v.7, 346
Exter, Thomas G., 766
Extraordinary ordinary women, 790

F. Scott Fitzgerald ency, 1011
Fabio, William F., 812
Faces of holiness: modern saints in photos & words, 1228
Factastic bk of 1001 lists, 1130
Facts on file dict of ...
    biology, 3d ed, 1322
    chemistry, 3d ed, 1479
    physics, 3d ed, 1518
    sci, 1281
Facts on file ency of sci, tech, & society, 1282
Faerber, Marc, 556
Fahlbusch, Erwin, 1264
Fairtile, Linda B., 1079
Falk, Peter Hastings, 850
Family ency of health, 1395
Fantasy & horror, 988
Fantle, Lynn Antosz, 1402
Far East & Australasia 1999, 30th ed, 92
Farmer, Geoff, 349
Farmer, William R., 1252
Farndon, John, 26
Farr, J. Michael, 197, 198
Farris, Phoebe, 851
Faust, Rudiger, 1493
FBI: a comprehensive ref gd, 648
Feature films, 1950-59, 1174
Federal agency profiles for students, 649
Federal staff dir, summer 1999, 30th ed, 637
Feetham, Suzanne L., 1442
Feinsilber, Mike, 934
Feldman, William, 1425
Feminism, 801

Ferber, Michael, 933
Fernandes, David, 1191
Fernandez-Shaw, Carlos M., 321
Fertility decline in developing countries, 1960-97, 738
Festivals & holidays, 1132
Fetrow, Alan G., 1174
Fichtner, Paula Sutter, 450
Field, Shelly, 199, 200
Fiesta! 2, 66
Filipino Americans, 276
Film & the American left, 1189
Film ency, 1160
Financial aid for research & creative activities abroad, 1999-2001, 245
Financial aid for study & training abroad 1999-2001, 246
Financial aid for vets, military personnel, & their dependents 1998-2000, 247
Find it online, 2d ed, 1465
Finding a place called home, 333
Fine artist's career gd, 856
Finkelman, Paul, 664
Finkle, Jane, 257
Fischel, Jack R., 493
Fisher, Helen S., 204
Fitzgerald, Allan D., 1227
Fitzpatrick, Kathleen, 159
Fitzpatrick, Patrick J., 1293
Fitzpatrick, Sandra, 293
500 popular annuals & perennials for American gardeners, 1337
500 popular roses for American gardeners, 1338
500 popular shrubs & trees for American gardeners, 1345
Flags, 334
Flechtmann, C. H. W., 1362
Fleming, Patricia Lockhart, 580
Fletcher, Andrew J., 1406
Flickinger, Michael C., 1323
Flora of the northeast, 1335
Flowering plants of the Galapagos, 1342
Floyd, Samuel A., Jr., 1069
Fluent in fantasy: a gd to reading interests, 990
Fodor's upclose Germany, 382
Foerstel, Karen, 629
Foldvary, Fred E., 124
Foley, William E., 18
Folklore from Africa to the US, repr ed, 1120
Folklore of American holidays, 3d ed, 1121
Fonseca, Anthony J., 989
Food alert! the ultimate sourcebk for food safety, 1308
Food safety sourcebk, 1306
Foreign trade of the US 1999, 211
Forensic medicine sourcebk, 1420
Forever lounge, 1118
Forsyth, Adrian, 1365
Foster, David William, 109
Foundation grants index 1999, 27th ed, 745
Founding leaders [CD-ROM], 483

Founding of Pakistan, 441
Fox, Ken, 1168
Fracture: a topical ency of current knowledge, 1387
Franceschetti, Donald R., 1520
Francis X. Bushman, 1157
Franck, Irene M., 795
Franco, L. N., 383
Frank, Sam, 1197
Franklin, Michele, 764, 765
Fredriksen, John C., 596, 611
Freese, Gene Scott, 1175
Freese, Mel R., 706
French Guiana, 108
French thesaurus for children, 908
Frey, John Andrew, 1037
Friedberg, Arthur L., 840
Friedberg, Ira S., 840
Friedman, Robert, 46
Fritze, Ronald H., 1122
Fuller, Linda K., 810
Fulltext sources online, Jan 1999, 39
Fulton, Len, 586, 587
Funding sources for K-12 educ 1999, 2d ed, 231
Funnell, Clifford, 1512
Fyke, Mary K., 1413

Gaffke, Carol T., 1053
Gagnon, Alain-G., 93
Gainor, Dan, 645
Gaither, Carl C., 55
Galante, Steven P., 142
Gale ency of medicine, 1413
Gale, Robert L., 1011
Galens, David, 970, 971
Gall, Susan B., 347
Gall, Timothy L., 347
Gallannaugh, Diana, 1281
Gallup, Alec M., 57
Gallup poll cum index: public opinion, 1935-97, 57
Ganz, John, 757
Gaquin, Deirdre A., 225, 778
Garbutt, Nick, 1366
Garden lover's gd to ...
    Spain & Portugal, 388
    the Netherlands & Belgium, 378
    the northeast, 363
Garden plants of China, 1336
Gardener's atlas, 1339
Gardner's chemical synonyms & trade names, 11th ed, 1480
Garoogian, David, 787
Garrison, Robert, Jr., 1445
Garrity, John, 699
Gates, Henry Louis, Jr., 291

Gay, Kathlyn, 668
Gay, Martin K., 668
Geisler, Norman L., 1261
Gems in myth, legend, & lore, 1123
Genealogical ency of the Colonial Americas, 325
Genealogist's address bk, 4th ed, 328
Genealogy on CD-ROM, 326
Genealogy sftwr gd, 327
Genetic engineering, 1330, 1328
Genium's hndbk of safety, health, & environmental data for common hazardous substances, 1384
Genovese, Michael A., 423
Geology, 1509
George Kelly: a research & production sourcebk, 1142
George, Linda S., 503
Georges, Jason, 1287
Gergits, Julia M., 1020
Gerhart, Eugene C., 56
Gerrard, Jon, 731
Giacomo Puccini, 1079
Gibaldi, Joseph, 819
Gibson, Ellen M., 522
Gilbert, Mark F., 460
Gilbert, Nedda, 256
Gill, Sam, 1131
Gill, Stanton, 1361
Gillespie, John T., 948
Givens, Archie, 280
Giving by industry, 1999-2000 ed, 746
Glendinning, Simon, 1215
Glickman, Sylvia, 1063, 1064
Global ecology, 1535
Global info systems & tech, 569
Global road warrior: 85-country hndbk for the intl business traveler, 356
Glose, Mary B., 39
Glossary of biotech terms, 2d ed, 1324
Glut, Donald F., 1514
Gobetti, Daniela, 911
Goble, Alan, 1194, 1195
Gods of ancient Egypt, 431
Going for broke: the depiction of compulsive gambling in film, 1190
Goldberg, Burton, 1417
Golden age of Islam, 503
Goldsteen, Joel B., 544
Goldstein, Sarah Hannah, 1024
Goldstone, Jack A., 486, 491
Golf: the legends of the game, 723
Golladay, Kendall J., 206
Gonzalez, Martin L., 1408
Goodfellow, William D., 1078
Goodman, David, 1098
Goodwin, Calvin M., 1106
Goodwin, Maria R., 293
Gordon, Haim, 1213
Gorlin, Rena A., 208

Gottesman, Ronald, 734
Gottlieb, Richard, 133, 150, 222
Gough, Barry M., 344, 443
Government assistance almanac 1999-2000, 13th ed, 751
Government phone bk USA 1999, 7th ed, 638
Graduate medical educ dir 1999/2000, 84th ed, 1398
Graduate programs in physics, astronomy, & related fields, 2000, 1474
Graduate school, 257
Graduate study in psychology 1998-99, 32d ed, 240
Graf, Rudolf F., 1382
Gralla, Preston, 1461
Grams, Martin, Jr., 828
Grant, Daniel, 856
Grant, Edmond, 1168
Grantham, Keith, 1344
Grants register 2000, 18th ed, 258
Grantseeker's hndbk of essential Internet sites, 1999-2000 ed, 747
Graubard, Stephen R., 575
Grauer, Michael R., 847
Grauer, Paula L., 847
Gravelle, Jane G., 216
Graves, Mark A., 1142
Gray, Christopher Berry, 515
Great American court cases, 523
Great American Websites, 76
Great escapes & rescues, 494
Great radio soap operas, 826
Greatest athletes of the 20th century, 699
Greece, rev ed, 105
Greek filmography, 1914-96, 1180
Green, Don W., 1379
Green, Rayna, 306
Greisman, Joan, 908
Griffel, Margaret Ross, 1104
Griffiths, Mark, 1334
Grimshaw, John, 1339
Gross, Ernie, 407
Gruhn, George, 1089
Gruhn's gd to vintage guitars, 2d ed, 1089
Grzebieniowski, Tadeusz, 914
Gubernatorial elections 1787-1997, 650
Guder, Darrell L., 1231
Guerrieri, Kevin G., 111
Guide bk of US coins 2000, 53d ed, 841
Guide bk of US currency, 3d ed, 838
Guide to ...
   African cinema, 1184
   American dirs, 14th ed, 40
   American educl dirs, 8th ed, 223
   black Washington, rev ed, 293
   field gds, 1349
   grantseeking on the Web, 748
   literary agents, 1999, 813
   Martha's Vineyard, 366

   microforms in print 1998, 5
   military criminal law, 604
   Native American ledger drawings & pictographs in US museums, libs, & archives, 314
   ref materials for school lib media centers, 5th ed, 554
   TV's Mayberry R.F.D., 1191
   the antique shops of Britain 1997/8, 833
   the silent yrs of American cinema, 1163
Guiley, Rosemary Ellen, 694
Guteck, Patricia, 1221
Gutek, Gerald, 1221
Guthrie, Pat, 861
Gutierrez, Lynda, 764, 765
Gutkin, Terry B., 226

H. R. Bolland, J. Guttierrez, 1362
Habitats & ecosystems, 1529
Hackwood, Sara, 258
Hady, Maureen E., 278
Haig, John H., 912
Hajikano, Are, 913
Hall, Bridget K., 272
Hall, Linda D., 160, 1147, 1457, 1471, 1485
Hall, Loretta, 272
Hall, Peter W., 1364
Halter, Gary M., 627
Hamblin, Robert W., 1010
Hamilton, Allen Lee, 600
Hamilton, Neil A., 119
Hamilton, W. R., 1510
Hancock, James, 1355
Handbook of ...
   clinical nursing research, 1442
   intl trade & dvlpmt stats 1996/97, 212
   North American industry, 2d ed, 161
   petrochemicals & processes, 2d ed, 1492
   reagents for organic synthesis: acidic & basic reagents, 1486
   reagents for organic synthesis: activating agents & protecting groups, 1487
   reagents for organic synthesis: oxidizing & reducing agents, 1488
   reagents for organic synthesis: reagents, auxiliaries, & catalysts for C-C bonds, 1489
   school psychology, 3d ed, 226
   US coins, 2000, 57th ed, 842
   US labor stats 1999, 3d ed, 206
   work & organizational psychology, 2d ed, 693
Handbook on civil registration & vital stats systems, 771
Handy, D. Antoinette, 1061
Handy garden answer bk, 1314
Hansel, Patsy J., 571
Harbo, Rick M., 1368
Hardin, W. Dan, 1096
Hardy, Phil, 1172

Harlan, Judith, 801
Harmer, William H., 129
Harner, James L., 922
Harris, Gordon, 83
Harrison, Kimberly, 939
Harrison, Percy, 1516
Hart, D. G., 1263
Hartmann, R. R. K., 584
Harty, Kevin J., 1176
Hartz, Paula R., 1239
Haskins, James, 286
Haskins, Jim, 287
Hastings, Penny, 700
Hatch, Thom, 414
Hate crimes, 533
Hauptman, Robert, 507
Haven, Kendall, 1277
Hawaii, 367
Hawkins, Donald T., 39
Hayashi Steinbeck bibliog, 1982-96, 1015
Hayes, John H., 1246
Haynie, Melanie, 843
Hayward, James L., 1224
Health & healthcare in the US 1999, 1403
Health care state rankings 1999, 7th ed, 1404
Health Policy Tracking Serv, 1399
Healthy cookery index, 1310
Healy, Leigh Watson, 565
Hearn, Daniel Allen, 537
Heaton, Tim B., 786
Hedblad, Alan, 959, 960, 961, 962
Heinemann, Sue, 802
Helander, Brock, 1111
Hellier, Desmond, 1476
Hellweg, Paul, 896
Henderson, Ashyia N, 290
Henderson, George F., 444
Henkes, Robert, 848
Herald, Diana Tixier, 990
Hernandez, Ramona, 300
Hernon, Peter, 619
Herx, Henry, 1199
Heseltine, Richard, 566
Higher educ dir, 1999, 241
Hill, Peter C., 683
Hill, Sonya D., 145
Hillstrom, Kevin, 846
Hillstrom, Laurie Collier, 846
Hinds, Kathryn, 504, 505
Hine, Robert, 1322
Hing, Bill Ong, 676
Hinkelman, Edward G., 168
Hinshaw, Ada Sue, 1442
Hirschfelder, Arlene B., 1394
Hischak, Thomas S., 1159
Hispanic-American experience on file, 324
Hispanic lit criticism suppl, 1048

Hispanic presence in N America from 1492 to today, updated ed, 321
Historic places of worship, 1268
Historical dict of ...
 American educ, 220
 Ancient Egypt, 474
 Australia, 2d ed, 442
 Austria, 450
 Azerbaijan, 432
 Belgium, 451
 Canada, 443
 Democratic Republic of the Congo, rev ed, 426
 France, 455
 Greater Johannesburg, 429
 Guangzhou (Canton) & Guangdong, 434
 intl orgs, 497
 Judaism, 1271
 modern Italy, 460
 Nietzscheanism, 1214
 Osaka & Kyoto, 438
 Pakistan, 2d ed, 440
 Poland, 1945-96, 461
 reformed churches, 1231
 Slovakia, 464
 the American Revolution, 415
 the Baptists, 1262
 the cooperative movement, 498
 the Elizabethan world, 499
 the Federal Republic of Yugoslavia, 473
 the gay liberation movement, 744
 the Holocaust, 493
 the intl monetary fund, 2d ed, 671
 the Netherlands, 106
 the US Air Force & its antecedents, 608
 Vienna, 449
Historical ency of nursing, 1444
Historical hndbk of major Biblical interpreters, 1251
Historical sourcebk for scribes, 855
History of ...
 Germany, 458
 Holland, 452
 Japan, 437
 Parliament on CD-ROM [CD-ROM], 665
 pirates, 509
 Russia, 463
 shipwrecks, 510
 Spain, 465
 the Internet, 1462
Hoare, James, 439
Hobbs, Hoyt, 475
Hobbs, James B., 888
Hobbs, Sandy, 756
Hochman, Steve, 1115
Hodgson, Ernest, 1477
Hoehner, Jane, 270, 346, 1292
Hoffman, Glenn L., 1360
Holidays & anniversaries of the world, 3d ed, 1133

Holliday, Paul, 1332
Hollywood stunt performers, 1175
Holm, Kirsten C., 818
Holocaust: memories, research, ref, 507
Holsinger, M. Paul, 1140
Hombs, Mary Ellen, 1429
Homer, William Innes, 895
Homophones & homographs, 3d ed, 888
Hood, Susan, 1340
Hooked on horror, 989
Hooker, Mark T., 452
Hooton, E. R., 610
Hoover's masterlist of major US companies 1998-99, 132
Hopkins, Virginia, 1448
Hopp, Glenn, 1200
Horn Bk gd interactive [CD-ROM], 952
Horn, Jason Gary, 1016
Horton, John J., 472
Hospital ships of WW II, 613
Hostels France & Italy, 384
Hostels UK, 385
Houghton, Walter E., 49
Housing stats of the US, 2d ed, 780
Hovey, Harold A., 779
Hovey, Kendra A., 779
How Congress works, 3d ed, 651
How govt works, 652
How products are made, v.4, 162
How to access the fed govt on the Internet, 4th ed, 623
How to find out about financial aid & funding, 243
Howard, Roger, 494
Howell, Steve N. G., 1356
Howells, Cyndi, 330
Hsu, Robert C., 125
Huan, Wang, 904
Huang, Hao, 1070
Huang, Siu-chi, 1222
Hudson's subscription newsletter dir, 14th ed, 52
Huidi, Wang, 903
Hull, Mary E., 561
Human rights, 545
Human rights, 2d ed, 547
Humanitarians & reformers, 58
Humphrey Bogart, 1150
Humphreys, Norman K., 671
Hunt, Andrew, 1481
Hunt, Kimberly N., 120
Hunt, Ronald J., 744
Hunter, Jeffrey W., 940, 941, 942, 943, 944, 945
Hurdle, Angela, 764, 765
Hurt, C. D., 1273
Husfloen, Kyle, 834
Hutchins, Patrick, 213
Hutchinson atlas of battle plans, 593
Hutchinson concise dict of music, 1068
Hutchinson ency of modern pol biog, 615
Hutchinson ency of the Renaissance, 446

Hutchinson illus ency of British hist, 468
Huthwaite, Motoko Fujishiro, 923
Huussen, Arend H., Jr., 106
Huxford's old bk value gd, 11th ed, 837

Icons of the century, 1137
Identifying British insects & arachnids, 1363
Ierley, Merritt, 862
Illustrated Bible dict, 1248
Illustrated dict of metalworking & manufacturing tech, 1388
Illustrated dict of nonlinear dynamics & chaos, 1524
Illustrated ency of body-mind disciplines, 1418
Illustrated hist of women, 795
Image buyers gd, 7th ed, 854
Immigration & the law, 676
Impeachable offenses, 664
In search of swampland, 1320
Incas, 504
Incredible Internet gd to Star Wars, 1466
Index gd to college jls, 53
Index of American per verse 1997, 1051
Index of characters in early modern English drama printed plays, 1500-1660, rev ed, 973
Index to ...
    African-American spirituals for the solo voice, 1119
    CD & record reviews 1987-97, 1077
    poetry for children & young people 1993-97, 1052
Information landscapes for a learning society, 566
Information literacy, 568
Information sources in sci & tech, 3d ed, 1273
Information systems innovation & diffusion, 570
Innovations in astronomy, 1501
Innovations in biology, 1329
Innovations in Earth scis, 1495
Inowlocki, Tania, 382
Insight gd: India, 375
Insight gd: Israel, 391
Insight gd: Japan, 3d ed, 376
Insight gd: Venezuela, 389
Instant info on the Internet, 331
Intelligence, espionage, & related topics, 594
Interdisciplinary bibliog gd to ...
    black studies 98, 279
    environmental studies 1998, 1527
    women's studies 1998, 788
International acronyms, initialisms, & abbrevs dict, 2
International Assn of Univs, 259
International Bible commentary, 1252
International bibliog of bibliogs in lib & info sci & related fields, 552
International dict of ...
    banking & finance, lib ed, 149
    black composers, 1069
    insurance & finance, lib ed, 167
    personal finance, 151

International dir of ...
    govt 1999, 3d ed, 620
    little mags & small presses 1998-99, 34th ed, 587
    philosophy & philosophers 1999-2000, 11th ed, 1219
    testing laboratories, 1999 ed, 1290
International ency of...
    abbrevs & acronyms in sci & tech, rev ed, 1286
    sci & tech, 1283
    the stock market, 169
International exchange locator, 1998 ed, 263
International financial stats yrbk 1999, 177
International hndbk of univs, 15th ed, 259
International histl stats: Africa, Asia, & Oceania 1750-1993, 3d, 69
International histl stats: Europe 1750-1993, 4th ed, 70
International histl stats: the Americas 1750-1993, 4th ed, 71
International mktg data & stats 1999, 23d ed, 178
International photography, 866
International research centers dir 1999, 11th ed, 41
International who's who 1998-99, 62d ed, 15
International yrbk of industrial stats 1998, 179
Internet blue pages, 1999 ed, 636
Internet bks for educators, parents, & students, 1464
Internet kids & family yellow pages, 3d ed, 1463
Internet resource dir for K-12 teachers & librarians, 1999/2000 ed, 230
Irish-English, English-Irish easy ref dict, 910
Ironman's ultimate bodybuilding ency, 717
Irons-Georges, Tracy, 1287
Isaacs, Ronald H., 1223
Islam, Iyanatul, 232
Issues for debate in American public policy, 677
Istanbul, 392
Italian novelists since WW II, 1965-95, 1041
Italian wines 1999, 1304

J. J. P. Oud & the intl style, 863
Jackson, Byron M., 678
Jackson, Christine E., 849
Jackson, Guida M., 791
Jackson, Kenneth T., 19
Jacobs, Christopher P., 1163
Jacobs, Eva E., 206
James, Bill, 703
James Dickey, 1009
James, Gregory, 584
James Mason: a bio-bibliog, 1154
James, Sandra, 172
Jameson, Robert, 393
Jane's market intelligence lib [CD-ROM], 612
Jane's Naval construction & retrofit markets, 610
Jane's underwater tech 1998-99, 1512
Jane's world defense industry, 603
Japanese baseball, 707

Jasen, David A., 1062
Jazz profiles, 1101
Jehovah's witnesses, 1257
Jenkins, Everett, Jr., 1270
Jensen, Todd A., 1543
Jeryan, Christine, 1413
Jesse's word of the day, 886
Jesus people movement, 1258
Jiaying, Gao, 903
Jimmy Dorsey: a study in contrasts, 1087
Jing, Kong, 903
Job hunter's sourcebk, 4th ed, 201
Joel Whitburn presents a century of pop music, 1074
Joel Whitburn presents Billboard top 10 album charts 1963-98, 1112
Joel Whitburn's bubbling under singles & albums, 1998 ed, 1113
Joel Whitburn's country annual 1994-97, 1099
Joel Whitburn's 1998 Billboard music yrbk, 1117
Joel Whitburn's rhythm & blues top R&B albums 1965-98, 1094
Joel Whitburn's top country singles 1944-97, 4th ed, 1100
Joffee, Elga, 737
Johansen, Bruce E., 305
John Carradine, 1158
John Crowe Ransom, 1014
John Ford, 1151
John Paul II's bk of saints, 1229
Johns, Alan, 292
Johnson, Daniel E., 707
Johnson, George M., 1022
Johnson, Graham E., 434
Johnson, Michael, 307
Jones, Angela Yvonne, 1141
Jones, Barrie, 1068
Jones, Gene, 1062
Jones, Harold, 1080
Jones, Sylvia Prys, 219
Jones, Tiffany M., 44
Jones, Wayne, 574
Jonsen, Albert R., 1409
Jordan, Douglas M., 1081
Jorgensen, Peter F., 685
Joseph, Harriett Denise, 404
Joseph Stalin, 462
Joslin, Lyndon W., 1177
Jost, Kenneth, 524, 635
Jules Verne on film, 1183
Junion-Metz, Gail, 567
Junior worldmark ency of world cultures, 270
Jura, Jean-Jacques, 1178

Kagan, Alfred, 84
Kallendorf, Craig W., 583
Kalley, Jacqueline A., 428

Kamachi, Noriko, 89
Kamoo, Ray, 476
Kane, Jim, 1196
Kapitaniak, Tomasz, 1524
Kaple, Deborah A., 618
Karen, Bellenir, 1411
Karolides, Nicholas J., 562
Karr, Paul, 384, 385
Karwan, Kirk R., 569
Kataoka, Sayuri, 913
Katz, Ephraim, 1160
Katz, William B., 1536
Kaufman, Burton I., 508
Kaul, Chandrika, 773, 785
Kaznowski, Andrzej, 914
Keane, Linda, 858
Keane, Mark, 858
Keating, Kevin, 835
Kehde, Ned, 54
Keil, Frank C., 687
Keller, Howard H., 915
Kemp, Roger L., 653, 654
Kemp, Simon, 121
Kesler, Christine A., 157, 158
Key concepts in lang & linguistics, 875
Key words in multicultural interventions, 686
Keyguide to info sources on the polar & cold regions, 114
Keynes, Simon, 466
Keyu, Fan, 903
Kickapoo Indians, their hist & culture, 303
Kid's catalog of Israel, rev ed, 317
Kim, Hyung-Chan, 274
Kimble, Gregory A., 682
Kings & queens, 484
Kinnear, Karen L., 743
Kinzie, Mary, 820
Kirby, John T., 921
Kirk-Othmer Concise ency of chemical tech, 4th ed, 1482
Kirschbaum, Stanislav J., 464
Klaassen, Paul, 1344
Kleiman, Rhonda H., 1310
Klein, Barry, 40, 223
Klepper, Robert K., 1179
Klezmer, Deborah, 793
Knappman, Edward W., 489
Knaus, Gunter, 1493
Knight, Jeffrey A., 1321
Knight, Judson, 281
Knuth, Bruce G., 1123
Kohn, George Childs, 495
Koliodimos, Dimitris, 1180
Kolleth, Michael, 835
Kondek, Joshua, 1141
Konstam, Angus, 509, 510
Korean conflict, 508
Koslow, Philip J., 288

Kotyk, Arnost, 1318
Kranz, Rachel, 288
Krapp, Kristine, 1278
Krapp, Kristine M., 1279
Krar, Steve F., 1388
Krebs, Arlene, 228
Krebs, Robert E., 1294
Kreisel, Martha, 867
Kremer, Gary R., 18
Kross, Jessica, 418
Kuhn, Cynthia, 1446
Kummings, Donald D., 1018
Kurian, George Thomas, 61, 621
Kuroff, Barbara, 814
Kurtz, Lester, 492

Lafontaine, J. Donald, 1364
Lambert, David, 1496
Lambert, Eddie, 1082
Landmark Supreme Court cases, 525
Landrum, Larry, 980
Lands & peoples, 67
Landscapes in hist, 2d ed, 1313
Lane, Megan, 869
Laney, J. Carl, 1243
Lang, Sean, 511
Langenscheidt's pocket dict: English/Polish, Polish/English, rev ed, 914
Langer, Howard J., 512
Lange's hndbk of chemistry, 15th ed, 1490
Langley, Winston E., 546
Langman, Larry, 1192
Langmead, Donald, 863
Language of contemporary criticism, 895
Langworth, Richard M., 469
Lapidge, Michael, 466
Larsen, Tor J., 570
Late Victorian & Edwardian British novelists, 2d series, 1022
Latin American lit & its times, 1042
Latin American lives, 322
Latin American women artists of the US, 848
Laurie, Ian S., 1038
Lavalette, Michael, 756
Law firms yellow bk, summer 1998 ed, 518
Laws of the US: corps, 529
Laws of the US: divorce, 530
Layberry, Ross A., 1364
Layperson's gd to criminal law, 538
Lazich, Robert S., 164, 776
Leach, Nicky, 360
Leaders of the American Civil War, 597
Leadership lib on CD-ROM, fall 1998 ed, 622
Least developed countries 1998 report, 68
LeBaron, Joyce, 896

LeBaron, Susannah, 896
LeClerc, Paul, 575
Lee, C. C., 1484
Lee, Christopher, 1469
Lee, Eming, 1484
Lee, Laura, 885
Lee, Michelle, 1029, 1030, 1031
Legacy of the Monroe Doctrine, 422
Legal executions in New England, 537
Legal info: how to find it, how to use it, 526
Leiby, Richard A., 457
Leighton, Lauren G., 1044
LeMaster, J. R., 1018
Lemay, Michael, 679
Lemberg, Raymond, 1435
Lenburg, Jeff, 1161
Lencsis, Peter M., 207
Lentz, Harris M., III, 616, 1143, 1515
Leonard, David C., 1455
Leonard, Thomas M., 445
Lerner, Eric K., 1429
Lesinski, Jeanne M., 606
Let's celebrate today: calendars, events, & holidays, 1134
LeVine, Harry, III, 1330
Levine, John, 1458
Levinson, David, 685
Levoratti, Armando J., 1252
Levy, Beth, 809
Levy, Bill, 1151
Lewis, Anne Gillespie, 368
Lewis, D. S., 625
Lewis, James R., 695, 1235, 1241
Lewis, Richard J., 1390
Lewis, Valerie V., 953
Lexicon of labor, 202
Libraries & info in the Arab world, 553
Library systems: current dvlpmts & future directions, 565
Library-anthropology resource, 268
Lide, David R., 1473
Life millennium, 46
Life scis on file, rev ed, 1319
Lilley, William, III, 626
Lindberg, Christine A., 898
Lindroth, David, 273, 324
Literary landscapes, 383
Literary market place 1999, 588
Literary market place on disc [CD-ROM], 589
Literary research gd, 3d ed, 922
Literature of the French & Occitan middle ages, 1038
Lithuanian publishers dir, 590
Littman, Mark S., 225, 778
Lively, Donald E., 525
Lives & works: YA authors, 966
Ljungquist, Kent P., 999
Local govt election practices, 654
Lockhart, Darrell B., 109

Lockhart, Melissa Fitch, 109
Loftin, M. Kent, 1380
Loizou, Andreas, 169
Lomeli, Francisco A., 1003
Long, Roger D., 441
Longe, Jacqueline L., 162
Lounsbury, Warren C., 1207
Lovett, John R., Jr., 314
Lovett, Patricia, 855
Lowe, Denise, 1162
Lubin, Bernard, 681
Luck, Steve, 1283
Lugira, Aloysius M., 1240
Lukas, Dale T., 590
Lukas, David, 1357
Lumley, Elizabeth, 23
Lupton, Mary Jane, 1008
Lyn, Ragsdale, 655
Lyon, William S., 308

Mabunda, L. Mpho, 523
Macbain, Alexander, 909
Mace, Angela, 864
Macedonian empire, 459
MacFarlane, Theresa J, 138
Mack, Raneta Lawson, 538
Mackerras, Colin, 86
MacKie-Mason, Jeffrey K., 1469
MacLean, Rebecca, 745
Macmillan ency of Native American tribes, 2d ed, 307
Maddex, Robert L., 656
Madigan, Dennis, 843
Mafia ency, 2d ed, 417
Magee, Dennis W., 1335
Magic nos: baseball's best single-season hitters, decade-by-decade, 706
Magill, Frank N., 479, 480, 481, 482
Magill's literary annual 1999, 995
Magocsi, Paul Robert, 269
Mailman, Richard B., 1477
Major cos of Africa S of the Sahara 1999, 4th ed, 171
Major cos of SW Asia 1999, 3d ed, 172
Major health care policies 1998, 7th ed, 1399
Major mktg campaigns annual 1998, 213
Major 20th-century writers, 2d ed, 929
Makar, Ragai N., 1043
Malia, Elizabeth, 53
Malinowski, Sharon, 310
Mallon, Bill, 727, 728
Maloney, David J., Jr., 832
Maloney's antiques & collectibles resource dir, 5th ed, 832
Malonis, Jane A., 153
Mammals of Madagascar, 1366
Mammals of N America, 1365

Managed care yrbk, 4th ed, 1405
Managing America's cities, 653
Managing overdues, 571
Manatees & dugongs of the world, 1371
Mank, Gregory William, 1156
Mannion, Michael, 1445
Man's health sourcebk, 2d ed, 1412
Manual of European langs for librarians, 2d ed, 901
Manufacturing worldwide, 3d ed, 163
Manz, William H., 522
Maples for gardens, 1346
Mari, Christopher, 1504
Mariani, John, 1300
Marilyn ency, 1139
Marion, Allison McClintic, 523
Mark Twain, 1016
Market House Bks, 496
Market share reporter, 2000, 164
Markley, Robert, 1341
Markoe, Arnold, 19
Markoe, Karen, 19
Markowitz, Harvey, 304
Marks, Diana F., 1134
Marks' standard hndbk for mechanical engineers [CD-ROM], 1391
Marlow-Ferguson, Rebecca, 156
Marr, Lisa, 1438
Marshall, George J., 1225
Marshall, Mary Burke, 640
Martin, Mart, 657
Martin, Murray S., 572
Massman, Emory A., 613
Masterplots complete CD-ROM, 1999 ed [CD-ROM], 946
Mastin, Robert, 1468
Math & mathematicians, 1521
Mathiowitz, Edith, 1447
Matter of taste: a bibliogl catalogue of intl bks on food & drink in the Lilly Lib, Ind. Univ, 2d rev ed, 1299
Matthews, Dawn D., 1306
Matthews, Jennifer, 1205
Matthias, Margaret, 956
Mattson, Mark T., 277
Matulic, Rusko, 101
Maturi, Mary Buckingham, 1157
Maturi, Richard J., 1157
Matuz, Roger, 998
Matystik, Walter F., 1532
Maxwell, Bruce, 623
Maya Angelou, 1008
Mayes, Walter M., 953
Mayo, Mike, 1198
Mays, Terry M., 415
McAllister, Pam, 982
McCaffrey, Donald W., 1163
McConnell, Stacy A., 160, 1147, 1457, 1471, 1485

McDarrah, Fred W., 868
McDarrah, Gloria S., 868
McDarrah, Timothy S., 868
McDonough, James T., Jr., 900
McElmeel, Sharron L., 957
McEvenue, Sean, 1252
McGillivray, Alice V., 658
McGrath, Anne F., 836
McGrath, Kimberley A., 1327
McGraw-Hill concise ency of sci & tech, 4th ed, 1284
McGuire, Eugene, 570
McIver, Tom, 1226
McKechnie, Jim, 756
McKim, Donald K., 1231, 1251
McLelland, Y., 172
McLeod, Denise, 745
McMillan, Cecily, 369
McMillon, Bill, 354
McMullen, Conley K., 1342
McMullen, Sean, 1034
Meaney, Carron A., 1347
Media courses UK 1999, 6th ed, 264
Mediavilla, Cindy, 967
Medical & health care bks & serials in print 1998, 27th ed, 1392
Medical tests sourcebk, 1407
Medieval England, 470
Meeting managers' info needs, 579
Meho, Lokman I., 553
Meiners, Phyllis A., 312
Mellersh, H. E. L., 487
Melton, J. Gordon, 1135, 1230, 1236
Meltzer, Tom, 238
Men's health concerns sourcebk, 1414
Mental health servs in criminal justice system settings, 681
Mercer gd to social security & Medicare 1998, 26th ed, 752
Merck manual of medical info, home ed, 1406
Merriam-Webster & Garfield dict, 889
Merriam-Webster's dict of allusions, 934
Merriam-Webster's ency of world religions, 1237
Merriam-Webster's geographical dict, 3d ed, 348
Merriam-Webster's intermediate dict, 890
Merriam-Webster's school dict, 891
Merritt, Frederick S., 1380
Metals hndbk, desk ed, 2d ed, 1389
Metcalf, Allan, 873
Mexico 2000, 390
Meyer, Michael J., 1015
Meyers, Glenn G., 1049
Meyers, Robert A., 1530
MGM labels, 1073
MIAs: a ref hndbk, 606
Microelectronic failure analysis: desk ref, 4th ed, 1383
Miguel Delibes, 1049
Mikula, Mark, 523

Milivojevic, Marko, 472
Milkis, Sidney M., 659
Millar, Andree, 1343
Miller, Anistatia R., 1136
Miller, Elizabeth B., 230
Miller, Joseph C., 477
Miller, Wanda J., 954
Mills, William, 114
Milne, G. W. A., 1480
Milton, Suzanne, 53
Mindell, Earl, 1448
Mineo, Baldassare, 1333
Miner, Lynn E., 1400
Minnesota gd, 368
Mio, Jeffery Scott, 686
Mirwis, Allan N., 30
Miskelly, Matthew, 556
MIT ency of the cognitive scis, 687
MIT ency of the Japanese economy, 2d ed, 125
Mitchell, B. R., 69, 70, 71
Mitchell, Bruce M., 221
Mitchell, Michael, 95
MLA dir of pers 1999, 9th ed, 938
MLA hndbk for writers of research papers, 5th ed, 819
Mobile telecommunications factbk, 1472
Mobility plus...a ref gd 1999, 762
Modern American lit, 5th ed, 1007
Modern Arabic lit, 1043
Modern twang: an alternative country music gd & dir, 1098
Molitor, Graham T. T., 61
Money for grad students in the humanities 1998-2000, 2d ed, 248
Money for graduate students in the social scis 1998-2000, 2d ed, 249
Mood, Terry Ann, 11
Moore, John L., 633
Moore, Keith W., 142
Moore, Patrick, 1502
Morad, Deborah J., 964
Moran, Edward, 1535
More EJS: discography of the Edward J. Smith recordings, 1106
Morgan, Kathleen O'Leary, 535, 536, 783, 1404
Morgan, Scott, 535, 536, 783, 1404
Morris, Cynthia, 534, 540
Mosby's over-the-counter medicine cabinet medicines, 1449
Moschovitis, Christos J. P., 1462
Moseley, Merritt, 1019
Moss, Joyce, 1042
Motin, Susan Hubbs, 507
Motion picture gd 1999, 1168
Mott, Peter Rhoades, 1534
Muder, Doug, 1458
Mulford, Carla, 996
Mullay, Marilyn, 1274

Muller, Nathan J., 1472
Multicultural dict of literary terms, 930
Multimedia & the Web from A to Z, 2d ed, 1455
Munro, Neil, 703
MUP ency of Australian sci fiction & fantasy, 1034
Murphy, Barbara Thrash, 958
Murphy, Bruce F., 981
Murray, Chris, 931
Murray, Michael D., 827
Murray, R. Emmett, 202
Murray, Terry A., 991
Murray, Tim, 395
Music in the 20th century, 1070
Music USA, 1116
Musical terminology, 1065
Musiker, Naomi, 429
Musiker, Reuben, 429
Muslim Diaspora, 1270
Mussell, Kay, 986
Mustazza, Leonard, 1083
Muth, Annemarie, 592
Muth, Annemarie S., 1420
Myers, Robert J., 752

Nagel, Rob, 1353
Nakamura, Joyce, 923
Name's familiar: Mr. Leotard, Barbie, & Chef Boyardee, 885
Napierkowski, Marie Rose, 968
Naples with Pompeii & the Amalfi coast, 386
Napoleon, 454
Nash, Jay Robert, 669
National Audubon Society field gd to the SE states, 370
National Audubon Society field gd to the SW states, 371
National Audubon Society 1st field gd: wildflowers, 1340
National dir of fndn grants for Native Americans, 312
National dir of managed care orgs, 2d ed, 1401
National Geographic atlas of the world, 7th ed, 338
National Geographic beginner's world atlas, 339
National Geographic desk ref, 352
National Geographic US atlas for young explorers, 340
National gd to funding for libs & info servs, 5th ed, 557
National health dir 1999, 1402
National job hotline dir, 196
Nationalism & ethnicity terminologies, 60
Native America today, 315
Native American Indian artist dir, 853
Native American lits, 1005
Native N American Shamanism, 302
Natural disasters: hurricanes, 1293
Natural medicines comprehensive database, 2d ed, 1450
Necas, Petr, 1377
Negro League autograph gd, 835
Neighboring faiths, 1238
Neimark, Peninah, 1534

Nelson, Emmanuel S., 997
Nelson, Lynn R., 662
Nelson, Michael, 634, 659
Ness, Immanuel, 72, 761
Network Dvlpmt & MARC Standards Office of the LC, 564
Netzley, Patricia D., 935
New bk of knowledge, 1999 deluxe lib ed, 31
New complete bk of food, 1307
New Dickson baseball dict, 705
New ency of vitamins, minerals, suppls, & herbs, 1301
New intl dict of N.T. theology [CD-ROM], 1249
New millennium world atlas deluxe [CD-ROM], 341
New Palgrave dict of economics & the law, 126
New steps to serv, 577
New York legal research gd, 2d ed, 522
New York Public Lib African American desk ref, 298
New York Public Lib amazing African American hist, 299
New York Public Lib amazing Hispanic American hist, 323
New York Public Lib amazing women in American hist, 802
New York Public Lib desk ref, 3d ed, 47
New Zealand bks in print 1999, 1035
Newman, Gerald, 467
Newman, Marilyn Stephanie Mercedes, 1060
Newman, Peter, 126
Newman, Roger K., 646
Newmark, Leonard, 902
Newson, Lesley, 1497
Newton, David E., 1285, 1378, 1491
Newton, Harry, 1467
Newton's telecom dict, 15th ed, 1467
Ng, Franklin, 275
NICEM ref CD-ROM [CD-ROM], 266
Nicholls, David, 454
Nigerian theatre in English, 972
Nill, Kimball R., 1324
Nilsson, K. Robert, 460
1904 Olympic Games, 727
1906 Olympic games, 728
Nineteenth-century American fiction writers, 999
Nineteenth-century European art, 852
Noll, Mark A., 1263
Nollen, Scott Allen, 1193
Norrgard, Julia M., 146
Norrgard, Lee E., 146
North American romance writers, 986
Notable black American men, 289
Notable black American scientists, 1278
Notable corporate chronologies, 2d ed, 120
Notable men & women of Spanish Tex., 404
Notable 20th-century scientists: suppl, 1279
Notable women in American hist, 789
Novel & short story writer's market, 1999, 814
Novels for students, v.6, 968

Novitsky, Ed, 1073
Now read this: a gd to mainstream fiction, 1978-98, 977
Nowak, Ronald M., 1367
Nsouli, Mona A., 553
NTC's compact Dutch & English dict, 905
NTC's compact Finish & English dict, 906
NTC's dict of Korea's business & cultural code words, 186
Nutrients A to Z, 1302
Nutting, Brian, 647
Nwanna, Gladson I., 85

Oakes, Elizabeth, 213
Oakes, Elizabeth H., 192
Obituaries in the performing arts, 1998, 1143
O'Brien, Robert, 754
O'Brien, Tim, 372
O'Brien, Wasserman Jacqueline, 777
Oceans, 1511
Ochoa, George, 323
O'Connor, Ann, 631
Of gods & monsters, 1186
Office for Natl Stats, 102
Official gd to American historic inns, bed & breakfasts, & country inns, 6th ed, 373
Official Major League Baseball fact bk, 1999 ed, 708
Official Natl Football League 99 record & fact bk, 719
O'Hara, Phillip Anthony, 123
Older Americans info dir, 1999, 2d ed, 735
Olendorf, Donna, 1413
Olivastri, Valentina, 107
Oliver, Charles M., 1013
Oliver, Paul, 860
Olsen, Kirstin, 471
Olson, Kent C., 526
On exhibit 1999: art lover's travel gd to American museums, 374
On this day in hist, 1136
100 banned bks, 562
100 best all-inclusive resorts of the world, 355
100 most popular children's authors, 957
100 most popular scientists for YAs, 1277
Online kids: a young surfer's gd to cyberspace, rev ed, 1461
Open house: a guided tour of the American house, 1637-present, 862
Opera: the rough gd, 2d ed, 1103
Opera cos & houses of W Europe, Canada, Australia, & New Zealand, 1107
Opera singers in recital, concert, & feature film, 1102
Operas in English, 1104
Orchids of Papua New Guinea, 1343
Orion blue bk: power tool 1998, 147
Orleck, Annelise, 318
Orr, N. Lee, 1096

Orton, Lavinia, 264
Oryx gd to natural hist, 1348
Osifchin, Gary P., 181
Osterreich, Shelley Anne, 302
Otfinoski, Steven, 97, 99
Our Sunday Visitor's...
  Catholic almanac, 2000, 1256
  ency of the Catholic doctrine on CD-ROM [CD-ROM], 1266
  ency of saints [CD-ROM], 1267
  family gd to movies & videos, 1199
Outstanding bks for children & young people, 963
Owens, Eric, 238
Oxford American thesaurus of current English, 898
Oxford companion to New Zealand lit, 1036
Oxford ency of world hist, 496
Oxford English dict additions series, v.3, 892
Oystein, B. Thommessen, 1538

Pagliaro, Ann Marie, 1451
Pagliaro, Louis A., 1451
Painter, Robert, 853
Palacios, Oscar A., 710
Palder, Edward L., 144
Palkovic, Mark, 1077
Pallotta, Augustus, 1041
Palmer, Alan, 1028
Palmer, Kris E., 520
Palmer, Louis J., Jr., 527
Palmer, Veronica, 1028
Paper money of the US, 15th ed, 840
Parasites of N American freshwater fishes, 2d ed, 1360
Pare, Ellen, 1470
Pare, Michael A., 194, 701
Pares, Susan, 439
Parham, Marisa, 260
Paris, Jay, 355
Park, Betsy, 572
Park, Yeon Hawn, 731
Park, Yeon Hee, 731
Parker, Jane, 1369
Parker, Steve, 1369
Parker, Sybil P., 1284
Parmann, Georg, 1538
Parry, Melanie, 12
Patrick, Diane, 299
Paul, Tessa, 66
Paulsen, Steven, 1034
Paxton, John, 489
Payton, Gordon, 828
PDR for nurses hndbk, 1999 ed, 1452
PDR generics 1998, 4th ed, 1453
Peacock, Scot, 924, 925, 926, 927, 928
Pear, Nancy, 345, 346
Pearl, Nancy, 977

Pearsall, Judy, 880
Pearson, Anthony J., 1487
Pediatric cancer sourcebk, 1424
Peek, Charles A., 1010
People & the Earth, 342
People for & against gun control, 532
Peoples of the Americas, 271
Perez, Louis G., 437
Perkins, Dorothy, 87
Perkins, Jennifer C., 43, 130
Perone, James E., 1084, 1085
Perrine, Doug, 1370
Perry, Robert H., 1379
Perry, Tim, 364
Perry's chemical engineers hndbk [CD-ROM], 1379
Persons, animals, ships, & cannon in the Aubrey-Maturin sea novels of Patrick O'Brian, 1026
Peschke, Bearbeitet von Michael, 1286
Peschke, Michael, 1286
Peterson, Glen D., 434
Peterson, Susan Lynn, 1260
Peterson's professional degree programs in the visual & performing arts 1999, 5th ed, 1145
Peterson's summer study abroad 1999, 265
Pfeiffer, Charles F., 1250
Pharmacists gd to over-the-counter & natural remedies, 1445
Phelps, Shirelle, 283, 284, 285, 290
Phenner, Lee, 193
Philcox, Phil, 77
Philosophers & religious leaders, 1209
Philosopher's phone & e-mail dir 1998/99, 1220
Philosophy of law, 515
Photographer's market, 1999, 869
Photography ency, 868
Physical & mental issues in aging sourcebk, 1421
Physical scis on file, rev ed, 1475
Pierson, Peter, 465
Pimlott, John, 593
Pitts, Michael R., 1152
Plagianos, James M., 812
Plantfinder's gd to cacti & other succulents, 1344
Platt, Lyman D., 760
Plocheck, Robert, 80
Plumb, Donald C., 1317
Plunkett, Jack W., 203, 1456, 1526
Plunkett's employer's Internet sites with careers info, 1999-2000, 203
Plunkett's energy industry almanac, 1526
Plunkett's InfoTech industry almanac 1999-2000, 1456
Pocket gd to cliches, 874
Pocket investor, 143
Pocket world in figures 1999, 772
Poe cinema, 1185
Poetry criticism, v.22, 1053
Poetry criticism, v.24, 1054
Poetry for students, v.5, 1055

Poetry for students, v.6, 1056
Poet's gd to poetry, 820
Poet's market, 1999, 815
Poisons & antidotes sourcebk, 1427
Political ency of the Middle East, 666
Political market place USA, 621
Pollock, Bruce, 1114
Pollock, Michael, 1334
Polly, Jean Armour, 1463
Ponzetti, James J., Jr., 685
Poole, Hilary, 545, 1462
Popular music, v.23, 1114
Popular musicians, 1115
Portraits of pioneers in psychology, v.3, 682
Posadas, Barbara M., 276
Post, Stephen G., 1210
Potts, Kathleen E. Maki, 201
Poveda, Tony G., 648
Power of the press, 809
Powers, Richard Gid, 648
Practical gd to planned giving 2000, 8th ed, 749
Practical gd to the ADA & visual impairment, 737
Practically speaking: a dict of quotations on engineering, tech, & architecture, 55
Pregill, Philip, 1313
Prescription alternatives, 2d ed, 1448
Presidency A to Z, 2d ed, 634
Price, Frantz R., 165
Princeton Review African American student's gd to college, 1999 ed, 260
Princeton Review gd to performing arts programs, 224
Princeton Review student athletes gd to college, 261
Pringle, David, 1138
Prisons in America, 539
Pritzker, Barry M., 315
Pritzker, Steven R., 684
Proffitt, Michael, 892
Prucha, Edward J., 1424
Prytherch, Ray, 807
Psychologists' psychotropic desk ref, 1451
Public interest profiles 1998-99, 42
Public record research system [CD-ROM], 624
Pulliam, June Michele, 989
Purcell, L. Edward, 397
Purvis, Thomas L., 399
Pyatt, Sherman E., 292

Quadbeck-Seeger, Hans-Jurgen, 1493
Quantities, symbols, units, & abbrevs, 1318
Quebec, 93
Quickverse: life application Bible [CD-ROM], 1253
Quilliam, Neil, 113
Quinn, Edward, 936
Quinn, Patrick, 1050
Quote it completely, 56

Radio programs, 1924-84, 829
Raeburn, Michael, 1105
Rafter, Nicole Hahn, 539
Raghunathan, Sankaran, 232
Rain forest bibliog, 1528
Rainey, Buck, 1153, 1181
Raising teenagers, 757
Rajadhyaksha, Ashish, 1164
Ramos, Mary G., 80
Ramsbotham, Oliver, 673
Ramsdell, Kristin, 975, 987
Random House Russian-English, English-Russian dict, 915
Random House Webster's basic dict of American English, 882
Rankin, Virginia, 576
Rappaport, Helen, 462
Raymond, Gino, 455
Rea, John, 1250
Reader's gd to music, hist, theory, criticism, 1071
Reaney, P. H., 335
Reavley, Nicola, 1301
Redfern, David, 349
Redman, Nina, 547
Reed, John, 603
Reed, Maxine K., 193
Reed, Mike, 899
Reed, Robert M., 193
Reel Middle Ages, 1176
Reese, Jean, 1464
Reference companion to Dylan Thomas, 1033
Reference gd to Africa, 84
Reference gd to mystery & detective fiction, 979
Regional markets, 766
Regional theatre dir 1999-2000, 1205
Reich, Bernard, 674
Reich, Hans J., 1486
Reif, Joe, 356
Reinhard, William, 747
Reinhart, Mark S., 1182
Religious leaders of America, 2d ed, 1230
Renehan, Edward J., Jr., 76
Renstrom, Peter G., 528
Renzi, Thomas C., 1183
Required reading: sociology's most influential bks, 733
Rescue & resistance: portraits of the Holocaust, 485
Research servs dir 2000, 7th ed, 133
ResourceLink Ill. [CD-ROM], 79
Reynard, Jeremy M. E., 555
Reynard, Keith W., 555
Reynolds, Cecil R., 226
Reynolds, John J., 974
Rice, James B., 211
Ricketts, Jonathan T., 1380
Rider, A. J., 151
Rigby, James H., 1486
Riggs, Thomas, 213

Riley, Dick, 982
Ringger, Kirsti, 866
Rinzler, Carol Ann, 1307
Ripple, Jeff, 1371
Ritter, Charles F., 597
Roberts, Brendan, 711, 716, 721, 725
Roberts, Jerry, 1528
Robin Hood, 1193
Robinson, Dale, 1191
Robinson, Roger, 1036
Rock garden plants, 1333
Rockin' '60s: the people who made the music, 1111
Rodenhouse, Mary Pat, 241
Rodriguez, Junius P., 488
Rogers, Elizabeth, 782
Role of police in American society, 540
Rollin, Lucy, 758
Romance fiction, 987
Ropke, Ian Martin, 438
Rose, Paul J., 602
Rosenfeld, Susan, 648
Rosenthal, Joel T., 470
Ross, Donald, 1001
Ross, Richard J., 1383
Rossignol, Rosalyn, 1025
Rourkes world of sci ency, 1287
Roush, William R., 1487
Routledge critical dict of the new cosmology, 1503
Rowland, David, 1091
Roybal, Peter, 645
RSP funding for nursing students & nurses 1998-2000, 1443
Rubin, Don, 1208
Ruby, Mary K., 1055, 1056
Rudes, Blair A., 309
Rumney, Lynne, 866
Runco, Mark A., 684
Rundle, David, 446
Runner's sourcebk, 729
Ruppli, Michel, 1073
Russell, Sharon A., 1184
Russian lit in the age of Pushkin & Gogol: poetry & drama, 1045
Russian lit in the age of Pushkin & Gogol: prose, 1046
Rydel, Christine A., 1045, 1046
Ryken, Leland, 1245
Ryland, Philip, 143

Sadler, Michele J., 1393
Safford, Barbara Ripp, 554
Sagar, D. J., 625
Sagar, Keith, 1057
Saha, Santosh, 548
Sakach, Deborah Edwards, 357, 358, 373
Salas, Susan, 1048

Salsbury, Robert E., 221
Salzman, Jack, 296
Sampson, Ellen E., 729
Sanderson, John, 1361
Sankey, Michael L., 329
Santos, Miguel A., 1537
Sardinia, 387
Satin, Morton, 1308
Sawyer, M. James, 1254
Scammon, Richard M., 658
Scanlon, Jennifer, 792
Schaefer, Christina K., 325, 331
Schechter, Michael G., 497
Scheven, Yvette, 84
Schlachter, Gail Ann, 243, 244, 245, 246, 247, 248, 249, 1443
Schleifer, Martha Furman, 1063, 1064
Schlein, Alan M., 1465
Schleyer, Paul von Rague, 1478
Schlicke, Priscilla, 1274
Schlueter, June, 1021
Schlueter, Paul, 1021
Schmidt, Diane, 1349
Schmitt, Deborah A., 940, 941, 942, 943
Schmittroth, Linda, 74, 310
Schneiter, Paul H., 749
Schoeman, Elna, 428
Scholarship advisor, 1999 ed, 251
Scholarships, fellowships, & loans 1999, 14th ed, 250
Scholastic children's thesaurus, 899
Scholastic ency of the Civil War, 416
Scholastic treasury of quotations for children, 965
Schorre, Barth, 1358
Schramer, James J., 1001
Schreiber, Mordecai, 319
Schultz, Jeffrey D., 621, 632
Schuster, Carl O., 602
Schuyler, Tami, 1462
Schwann opus, winter 1997-99: ref gd to classical music, 1076
Schwann spectrum: the gd to rock, jazz, world...& beyond, 1072
Schwartz, Richard Alan, 601
Science & tech almanac, 1999 ed, 1295
Science fiction mag story index, 1926-95, 991
Science fiction writers, 2d ed, 992
Science navigator [CD-ROM], 1288
Scientific American sci desk ref, 1296
Scientific dvlpmt & misconceptions through the ages, 1294
Scientists: their lives & work, v.6, 1276
Scientists, mathematicians, & inventors, 1280
Scott's dirs 1999, 6th ed, 187
Scouton, William O., 181
Scragg, Donald, 466
Scribner ency of American lives 1986-90, v.2, 19
Secret worlds, 1352

Sedge, Michael H., 806
Sedlacek, Frantisek D., 859
Segall, Barbara, 388
Sela, Avraham, 666
Selden, Holly M., 153
Senft, Theresa M., 1462
Sept, J. Duane, 1331
Sequels in children's lit, 947
Serafin, Steven R., 932, 1004
Serials & series, 1181
Serrano, Juan, 917
Serrano, Susan, 917
Service, Pamela F., 506
Servies, James A., 78
Servies, Lana D., 78
Sexual harassment in America, 550
Sexually transmitted diseases, 1438
Shaffer, Jack, 498
Shakespearean criticism, v.43, 1029
Shakespearean criticism, v.44, 1030
Shakespearean criticism, v.45, 1031
Shaman, William, 1106
Shannon, Joyce Brennfleck, 1407
Shannon, Thomas A., 1328
Shapers of the great debate on immigration, 675
Sharks, 2d ed, 1372
Sharks & rays of the world, 1370
Sharma, Rajendra, 1395
Sharon, Michael, 1302
Sharp, James Roger, 628
Sharp, Nancy Weatherly, 628
Shaver, Jerry, 843
Shaver, Joan L., 1442
Shaw, Ian, 393
Shaw, Russell, 1266
Sheets, Anna, 310
Sheets, Anna J., 994, 1053
Sheets, William, 1382
Sheildlower, Jesse, 886
Sheimo, Michael, 169
Sheldon, AnnaMarie L., 120
Shelfer, Katherine M., 578
Shengold Jewish ency, 319
Shepard, Thomas H., 1454
Shepherd, William, 232
Shilling, Lilless McPherson, 810
Shin, Linda M., 1431, 1436
Shirley, Carl R., 1003
Shook, R. J., 152
Short stories for students, v.6, 969
Short story criticism, v.30, 994
Shorter dict of gardening, 1334
Shuler, John A., 619
Sicily, 107
Sieber, Mary L., 831
Siemeling, Ulrich, 1493
Sienkewicz, Thomas J., 900

Siess, Judith A., 573
Sifakis, Carl, 417
Sigler, Jay A., 549
Significant contemporary American feminists, 792
Silent films, 1877-1976, 1179
Silverburg, Sanford R., 674
Simkin, John E., 978
Simmons, H. Leslie, 1390
Simmons, Patrick A., 780
Simonian, Susan J., 691
Simonis, Doris, 1280
Sinatra: an annot bibliog, 1939-98, 1083
Singer, Ronald, 1513
Single parents, 743
Singman, Jeffrey L., 447
Sinnreich-Levi, Deborah, 1038
SIPRI yrbk 1998, 607
Sir Walter Scott: a bibliogl hist 1796-1832, 1047
Sisco, Peter, 717
Sister Wendy's bk of saints, 1259
Sisung, Kelle S., 649, 660
Sitarz, Daniel, 529, 530
Skin sourcebk, 1439
Skinner, Malcolm, 349
Slater, Courtenay M., 211, 782
Slavery & slaving in world hist, 477
Sleep disorders sourcebk, 1440
Sloan, Dave, 709, 720
Small business sourcebk, 13th ed, 138
Smart, Ninian, 1242
Smith, C. Carter, Jr., 295
Smith, Carter, III, 273, 324
Smith, Charles A., 755
Smith, Craig, 746
Smith, Don G., 1185
Smith, Harold F., 359
Smith, Jacquelin, 956
Smith, Jessie Carney, 289
Smith, John L., 1086
Smith, Ron, 708
Smyth, David, 90
Snakes, 1375
Snodgrass, Mary Ellen, 930, 1124, 1444
Social issues, 59
Social issues in sci & tech, 1285
Social panorama of Latin America, 1997 ed, 110
Social protest lit, 935
Social work dict, 4th ed, 750
Socioeconomic characteristics of medical practice 1997, 1408
Software ency 1998, 1459
Soister, John T., 1186
SOLO librarian's sourcebk, 573
Solomon, Norman, 1271
Something about the author, v.99, 959
Something about the author, v.102, 960
Something about the author, v.103, 961

Something about the author, v.104, 962
Sondergard, Sidney L., 973
SongCite: an index to popular songs, suppl 1, 1078
Sourcebk in bioethics, 1409
Sourcebk to public record info, professional ed, 639
Southeast in early maps, 3d ed, 337
Southern African pol hist, 428
Souther histl society papers [CD-ROM], 424
Sova, Dawn, 562
Soviet Jewish Americans, 318
Sovijarvi, Sini, 906
Space exploration, 1504
Spalding, David A. E., 1373
Spanish golden age drama, 974
Spanish idioms, proverbs, & slang of yesterday & today, 917
Sparano, Vin T., 702
Sparks, David Hatfield, 1127
Sparks, Mariya, 1127
Speak, Peter, 114
Special interest group profiles for students, 660
Spence, Charles F., 1540
Spence, Pam, 1505
Spencer, Donald D., 1525
Spinrad, Leonard, 1136
Spinrad, Thelma, 1136
Spira, Thomas, 60
Spitzer, Kathleen L., 568
Sporting News baseball gd, 1999 ed, 709
Sporting News baseball register, 1999 ed, 711
Sporting News hockey gd, 1999-2000 ed, 724
Sporting News hockey register, 1999-2000 ed, 725
Sporting News official NBA gd, 1999-2000 ed, 715
Sporting News official NBA register, 1999-2000 ed, 716
Sporting News pro football gd, 1999 ed, 720
Sporting News pro football register, 1999 ed, 721
Sports for her: a ref gd for teenage girls, 700
Sports injuries sourcebk, 1441
Sports stars, series 5, 701
Spreadin' rhythm around: black popular songwriters, 1880-1930, 1062
Sracic, Paul A., 630
Staab, Donald, 1383
Stade, George, 1024
Staff of the Princeton Review, 234
Staines, Joe, 1097, 1103
Stallaerts, Robert, 451
Standard English-SerboCroatian, SerboCroatian-English dict, 916
Standard hndbk for civil engineers [CD-ROM], 1380
Stanley, Deborah A., 968
Stanley, Debra L., 539
State & metropolitan area data bk 1997-98, 5th ed, 781
State constitutions on the US, 656
State environmental agencies on the Internet, 1532

State govt 1998-99, 661
State of food & agriculture 1998, 1309
State profiles 1999, 782
State rankings 1999, 10th ed, 783
States' rights & American federalism, 662
Statistical abstract of the US 1998, 118th lib ed, 784
Statistical hndbk on...
   consumption & wealth in the US, 785
   poverty in the developing world, 773
   tech, 1291
   the American family, 2d ed, 786
Statistical yrbk for Asia & the Pacific 1998, 774
Statistics sources 2000, 23d ed, 777
STATS pro football hndbk 1999, 722
Steen, Sara J., 262
Steib, Murray, 1071
Stein, Laura W., 550
Stencel, Sandra L., 677
Stephens, Brad, 567
Stern, Loraine, 1422
Stevens, John D., 1372
Stewart, John, 430
Stilwell, Steven A., 975
Stockdale, Robert L., 1087
Stourton, Alfonso Bertodano, 321
Strain, J. J., 1393
Stranger than paradise: maverick film-makers in recent American cinema, 1155
Strauss, Emanuel, 1125
Strieter, Terry W., 852
Strong souls singing: African American bks for our daughters & our sisters, 280
Strutz, Henry, 907
Students in discord, 692
Subject encys: user gd, review citations, & keyword index, 30
Subject gd to children's bks in print 1999, 955
Suchowski, Amy R, 138
Sullivan, Charles L., 1303
Sullivan, Monica, 1169
Sullivan, Thomas F. P., 543
Summer theatre dir 1999, 1204
Sunshine state almanac & bk of Fla.-related stuff, 77
Super, John C., 490
Superstars of the NFL, 718
Supreme Court A to Z, 2d ed, 635
Supreme Court yrbk 1997-98, 524
Suster, Zeljan E., 473
Suzuki, Reiko, 913
Svarney, Thomas E., 1348
Swanson, Jenifer, 1421, 1440
Swartzwelder, Scott, 1446
Sweeney, Kevin, 1154
Swietochowski, Tadeusz, 432
Swirsky, Judith, 374
Syria, rev ed, 113

Szarmach, Paul F., 470
Szmuk, Szilvia E., 974
Szucs, Loretto Dennis, 332

Tabor, Stephen, 1057
Taborelli, Giorgio, 1137
Tae kwon do, updated ed, 731
Tait, Alistair, 723
Taiwanese Americans, 275
Tarnowski, Kenneth J., 691
Tarr, David R., 631
Tavormina, M. Teresa, 470
Taxonomic charts of theology & biblical studies, 1254
Taylor, Mark C., 1232
Taylor, Todd, 822
Teacher's gd to winning grants, 242
Teaching US hist through children's lit, 954
Technology in action, 1292
Ted Hughes: a bibliog, 1946-95, 2d ed, 1057
Telecom & networking glossary, 1468
Telecommunications dir 1999, 10th ed, 1470
Telecommunications gd to the Internet, 1469
Temperate forests, 1311
Tennant, Richard A., 893
Terkel, Susan Neiburg, 1216
Terrace, Vincent, 829
Territories of the Russian Federation, 100
Terrorism in the 20th century, 669
Terry, Michael Robert, 608
Texas almanac, 2000-2001, 60th ed, 80
Texas legislative almanac 1999, 627
Thailand, rev ed, 90
Theatre backstage from A to Z, 4th ed, 1207
Theodore, Louis, 1532
Theoharis, Athan G., 648
Thesing, William B., 1058
They became Americans: finding naturalization records & ethnic origins, 332
Thierry, Henk, 693
Thiessen, Diane, 956
Thistlethwaite, Nicholas, 1090
Thomas, Janet, 134
Thomas, Richard, 625
Thomas, Richard K., 1403
Thompson, Catherine, 1281
Thomson, Leslie, 1206
Thorn, John, 712
Thoughtful researcher, 576
3 a.m. hndbk: the most commonly asked questions about your child's health, 1425
Tierney, Helen, 797, 798
Timeline charts of the western church, 1260
Tiner, Ralph W., 1320
Tirtha, Swami Sada Shiva, 1419
Tisdale, Mary E., 698

TLA film & video gd, 1187
To Calif. on the southern route 1849, 403
Todd, Jane Marie, 431
Todd, Loreto, 821
Todd, William B., 1047
Tokyo, 88
Toll-free phone bk USA 1999, 3d ed, 43
Toma, Bernard, 1316
Tomaselli-Moschovitis, Valerie, 773, 785
Tomassini, Christine, 1170
Tonga, 91
Top 5,000 European cos 1999/2000, 134
Topaz, Muriel, 224
Torregrosa, Constance Healy, 241
Torres-Saillant, Silvio, 300
Total baseball, 6th ed, 712
Total hockey, 726
Toth, Dawn Bokenkamp, 353
Trade & dvlpmt report 1998, 180
Trahair, Richard C. S., 1218
Trask, R. L., 875
Travel, legend, & lore, 1122
Treanor, J. Robert, 752
Tremaine, Marie, 581
Trends in Europe & N America 1998/99, 775
Trogdon, Robert W., 1012
Troshynski-Thomas, Karen, 1314
Trudeau, Lawrence J., 1006
Trumbull, Priscilla, 165
Tucker, Harvey J., 627
Tuff Stuff's baseball memorabilia price gd, 843
Tunon, Johanna, 986
Turk, Eleanor L., 458
Turkington, Carol, 1427
Turpin, Jennifer, 492
Tuscarora-English/English-Tuscarora dict, 309
20th-century American hist [CD-ROM], 408
Twentieth-century American western writers, 1st series, 1000
Twentieth-century short story explication: new series, v.4, 1995-96, 993
Twentieth-century teen culture by the decades, 758
Twentieth century world, 511
21st century, 61
20/20: 20 new sounds of the 20th century, 1075

UFO ency, 2d ed, 697
Ukraine, 99
Ullmann's ency of industrial chemistry 1998, 6th ed [CD-ROM], 1483
Ultimate dict of film technicians, 1167
Ultimate dir of silent & sound era performers, 1149
Ultimate ency of fantasy, 1138
Ultimate search bk: worldwide adoption & vital records, 1998 ed, 739

Ultimate soccer ency, 730
Uncle Sam's K-12 Web, 229
Unification of Germany, 1989-90, 457
United Arab Emirates, 112
United Nations Industrial Dvlpmt Org, 179
United States govt manual 1998/99, 663
Universal silents, 1173
Universe & beyond, 3d ed, 1500
Universe revealed, 1505
Unterberger, Richie, 1116
US business dir, 1999, 135
US court cases, 531
US Dept of Commerce, 784
US dept of transportation, 1539
US dir of entertainment employers, spring/summer 1999 ed, 1146
US foreign relations with the Middle East & N Africa, 674
US govt on the Web, 619
US immigration & naturalization laws & issues, 679
US land & natural resource policy, 542
US landscape ordinances, 541
US market trends & forecasts, 214
US medical licensure stats & requirements by state, 1998-1999 ed, 1410
USA: the rough gd, 4th ed, 364
Utopias & utopians, 1218
U*X*L ency of Native American tribes, 310

Valder, Peter, 1336
Valerie & Walter's best bks for children, 953
Valestuk, Lorraine, 1042
Vallely, Fintan, 1066
Value of a dollar 1860-1999, 2d ed, 139
Vampire bk, 1135
van Assendelft, Laura, 632
van der Horst, Pieter W., 1247
van der Toorn, Karel, 1247
van Gelderen, C. J., 1346
van Gelderen, D. M., 1346
Van Husen, William H., 602
van Itallie, Nancy, 381
Van Nostrand's scientific ency, 8th ed [CD-ROM], 1289
Van Scott, Miriam, 1126
Van Tassel, Emily Field, 664
Van Whitlock, Rodney, 681
Vanin, Gabriele, 1506
Vanthoor, Wim F. V., 448
Varied carols, 1095
Vaughan, William, 857
Veatch, Robert M., 1409
Velazquez, Rita C., 239
Veremis, Thanos, 105
Vernus, Pascal, 431
Veterinary drug hndbk, 3d ed, 1317

Victor, Adam, 1139
Victor Hugo ency, 1037
Victorian women poets, 1058
Video sourcebk, 23d ed, 1170
VideoHound's epics, 1200
VideoHound's golden movie retriever 1999, 1201
VideoHound's independent film gd, 2d ed, 1169
VideoHound's war movies, 1198
VideoHound's world cinema, 1202
Vietto, Angela, 996
Vikings, 505
Vila, Bryan, 534, 540
Violence in America, 734
Visiting utopian communities, 1221
Vital stats on the presidency, rev ed, 655
Vivante, Bella, 804
Vogt, W. Paul, 768
Volcano registry, 1515
Volkman, Nancy, 1313
Volo, Dorothy Denneen, 425
Volo, James M., 425
Volti, Rudi, 1282
Volunteer vacations, 7th ed, 354
von Dehsen, Christian D., 1209
Vos, Howard F., 1250
Vox Spanish & English student dict, 918
Vuturo, Christopher, 251

W. L. Mackenzie King, 444
Wagner, John A., 499
Wakelyn, Jon L., 597
Waldman, Carl, 311
Walford's gd to ref material, v.1: sci & tech, 8th ed, 1274
Walford's gd to ref material, v.3, 7th ed, 807
Walker, Graham, 614
Walker, Janice R., 822
Walker, Juliet E. K., 122
Walker, Sandra C., 854
Walker's mammals of the world, 6th ed, 1367
Wall Street dict, 152
Walt Whitman, 1018
Walters, LeRoy, 1409
Want, Robert S., 516, 519
Want's fed-state court dir, 1999 ed, 519
War & American popular culture, 1140
War in Vietnam, 605
War on drugs, 753
Warbirds, 611
Ward, Greg, 364
Warren, Jim, II, 843
Washington almanac of intl trade & business, 1998, 181
Washington info dir 1999-2000, 640
Washington 1999, 16th ed, 44
Wasman, Ann M., 577
Wasserman, Steven R., 777

Watchable birds of the Great Basin, 1357
Watergate crisis, 423
Wattie, Nelson, 1036
Watts, Alan, 1508
Weather hndbk, 2d ed, 1508
Weaver, David D., 1426
Weaver, Tom, 1158
Webber, Elizabeth, 934
Webber, Geoffrey, 1090
Weber, Peter J., 1466
Weber, R. David, 244, 245, 246, 247, 248, 249, 1443
Webster, Raymond B., 1297
Webster, Valerie J., 37, 250
Webster's new world college dict, 4th ed, 883
WEFA industrial monitor 1999-2000, 165
Weisstein, Eric W., 1523
Wellesley index to Victorian pers 1824-1900, new ed [CD-ROM], 49
Wells, G. Margaret, 1492
Wells, Maria X., 583
Wemhoff, Rich, 741
Wertheimer, Michael, 682
West, Geoffrey, 96
Western gunslingers in fact & on film, 1153
Western movie quotations, 1196
Western words: a dict of the old west, 887
Wetterau, Bruce, 75
Whale watching, 360
Whalen, Lucille, 547
Whales, dolphins, & porpoises, 2d ed, 1374
Whales of the W coast, 1373
What do I read next? 1998, 975
What's in a name? 884
Whelks to whales: coastal marine life of the Pacific NW, 1368
Whitaker's bks in print 1999, 9
Whitburn, Joel, 1074, 1099, 1100, 1112, 1117
White, Phillip M., 303
White, Sarah E., 44
White, Timothy J., 940, 941, 942, 943, 944, 945
Whitfield, Philip, 1351
Whitman gd to coin collecting, 839
Whitnah, Donald R., 1539
Whitson, Kathy J., 1005
Who knows what: a gd to experts, 17th ed, 136
Who was who in American art 1564-1975, rev ed, 850
Whole story: 3000 yrs of sequels & sequences, 2d ed, 978
Who's who among African Americans, 12th ed, 290
Who's who in ...
    America 1999, 53d ed, 20
    entertainment 1998-99, 3d ed, 1144
    intl business educ & research, 232
    political revolutions, 486
    Shakespeare's England, 1028
    space, 1507
    the world 1999, 16th ed, 16

Who's who 1999, 151st ed, 17
Who's who of American women 1999-2000, 21st ed, 21
Who's who of Pulitzer Prize winners, 1002
Wick, Robert L., 11
Wigge, Larry, 725
Wildlife & plants of the world, 1325
Wiley bk of business quotations, 140
Wilhelm, Elliot, 1202
Willemen, Paul, 1164
William Faulkner ency, 1010
Williams, D. F., 1326
Williams dict of biomaterials, 1326
Williams, Marcia, 196
Williams, Martha E., 559
Williams, Neville, 487
Williams, Nicholas M., 609
Williams, Raymond Leslie, 111
Willis, Derek, 645
Willis, Stephen, 807
Wilson calendar of world hist, 489
Wilson, John D., 995
Wilson, Kathleen, 929
Wilson, R. M., 335
Wilson, Robert A., 687
Wilson, Wilkie, 1446
Winans, Amy E., 996
Windows 98: the complete ref, 1458
Winn, Kenneth H., 18
Wishlade, Fiona, 189
Wisner-Broyles, Laura A., 1053, 1054
Witchcraft today, 695
Wittels, Harriet, 908
Womack, Kenneth, 582
Women & American TV, 1162
Women artists of color, 851
Women composers, v.4, 1063
Women composers, v.5, 1064
Women in horror films, 1156
Women in India, 803
Women in world hist, vols.1-3, 793
Women leaders [CD-ROM], 794
Women rulers throughout the ages, 791
Women under the Third Reich, 456
Women's liberation movement in America, 800
Women's movement in the US [CD-ROM], 796
Women's roles in ancient civilizations, 804
Women's studies ency, rev ed, 797
Women's studies ency, rev ed [CD-ROM], 798
Women's studies index 1997, 805
Wonderful world of mathematics, 2d ed, 956
Wood, Andrew G., 44
Wood warblers, 1358
Woodhead, James A., 1509
Woodhouse, Tom, 673
Woodside, Gayle, 1385
Woodtor, Dee Parmer, 333
Woodward, Jeannette A., 816

Woog, Dan, 730
Wooley, John, 1118
Woolley, A. R., 1510
Workers compensation, 207
World almanac & bk of facts 2000, millennium ed, 4
World bk: millennium 2000, deluxe ed [CD-ROM], 32
World bk ency, 1999 ed, 33
World bk multimedia ency: Macintosh ed [CD-ROM], 34
World catalogue of the spider mite family, 1362
World conflicts, 500
World cosmetics & toiletries dir 1999, 173
World cost of living survey, 2d ed, 776
World dvlpmt indicators, 1998, 182
World dict of foreign expressions, 900
World dir of business info Websites, 137
World drinks mktg dir 1999, 174
World economic factbk 1998/99, 6th ed, 183
World ency of contemporary theatre, v.5, 1208
World ency of pol systems & parties, 3d ed, 618
World factbk 1999, 73
World food mktg dir 1999, 175
World gd to libs, 14th ed, 558
World histl fiction, 984
World in so many words, 873
World investment report 1999, 184
World mktg forecasts 1999 on CD-ROM, 2d ed [CD-ROM], 215
World of biology, 1327
World pol leaders [CD-ROM], 617
World records in chemistry, 1493
World retail data & stats 1999, 185
World Shakespeare bibliog on CD-ROM, 1983-95 [CD-ROM], 1032
World War II: an ency of quotations, 512
World War II in Europe, 602
Worldmark chronology of the nations, 347
World's religions, 2d ed, 1242
Worldwide govt dir with intl orgs 1999, 625
Wortzel, Larry M., 435
Woy, James, 116

Wright, Russell O., 713
Writer's & photographer's gd to global markets, 806
Writer's hndbk, 2000 ed, 817
Writer's market, 2000, electronic ed, 818
Writing research papers, 2d ed, 816
Wrobel, Piotr, 461
Wuthnow, Robert, 1233
Wycliffe Bible dict, 1250

Xiao, Zhiwei, 1165

Yearbook of ...
　　experts, authorities, & spokespersons 1999, 17th ed, 48
　　intl co-operation on environment & dvlpmt 1998/99, 7th ed, 1538
　　tourism stats, 50th ed, 166
Yeats dict, 1039
Yeoman, R. S., 841, 842
York, Martin A., 938
Young heroes in world hist, 478
Young, Margaret Levine, 1458
Young, T. R., 62
Yuill, Douglas, 189
Yurasits, Andrea, 764, 765

Zabecki, David T., 602
Zhang, Yingjin, 1165
Zhifang, Wang, 903
Ziegler, Charles E., 463
Zietz, Karyl Lynn, 1107
Zminda, Don, 703
Zona-Paris, Carmi, 355
Zondervan hndbk to the Bible, 3d ed, 1255
Zoroastrianism, 1239

Subject Index

Reference is to entry number.

ABBREVIATIONS
Acronyms, initialisms, & abbrevs dict, 25th ed, 1
International acronyms, initialisms, & abbrevs dict, 2
Quantities, symbols, units, & abbrevs, 1318

ACADEMIC LIBRARIES
Choice's outstanding academic bks 1992-97, 551

ACRONYMS
Acronyms, initialisms, & abbrevs dict, 25th ed, 1
International acronyms, initialisms, & abbrevs dict, 2

ACTORS. *See also* **MOTION PICTURES**
Charles Bronson, 1152
Francis X. Bushman, 1157
Hollywood stunt performers, 1175
Humphrey Bogart, 1150
James Mason: a bio-bibliog, 1154
John Carradine, 1158
Ultimate dir of silent & sound era performers, 1149
Women & American TV, 1162
Women in horror films, 1156

ADMINISTRATIVE AGENCIES
Federal agency profiles for students, 649
State environmental agencies on the Internet, 1532

ADOPTION
Ultimate search bk: worldwide adoption & vital records, 1998 ed, 739

ADVENTURE STORIES
Great escapes & rescues, 494

AERONAUTICS
AIM/FAR 1999, 1540
Aircraft of the US military air transport serv 1948-66, 609
Jane's world defense industry, 603

AFFIRMATIVE ACTION PROGRAMS
Affirmative action, 521

AFRICA
Africa S of the Sahara 1999, 28th ed, 81
Ancient African kingdom of Kush, 506
Dictionary of human rights advocacy orgs in Africa, 548
Major cos of Africa S of the Sahara 1999, 4th ed, 171
US foreign relations with the Middle East & N Africa, 674
Worldmark chronology of the nations, 347

AFRICA - BIBLIOGRAPHY
Central & equatorial Africa area bibliog, 83
Reference gd to Africa, 84

AFRICA - HISTORY
African states & rulers, 2d ed, 430
Historical dict of Democratic Republic of the Congo, rev ed, 426
Southern African political hist, 428

AFRICAN RELIGIONS
African religion, 1240

AFRICANS
Africana, 291
Interdisciplinary bibliog gd to black studies 98, 279

AFRO-AMERICAN AUTHORS
Black authors & illustrators of bks for children & YAs, 958
Contemporary African American novelists, 997
Strong souls singing: African American bks for our daughters & our sisters, 280

AFRO-AMERICAN BUSINESS ENTERPRISES
Encyclopedia of African American business hist, 122

AFRO-AMERICAN - EDUCATION
Black studies on disc 1999 [CD-ROM], 297
Princeton Review African American student's gd to college, 1999 ed, 260

AFRO-AMERICAN - FOLKLORE
Dictionary & catalog of African American folklife of the south, 292

AFRO-AMERICAN - GENEALOGY
Finding a place called home, 333

AFRO-AMERICAN - HISTORY
African-American atlas, 277
African-American culture & hist [CD-ROM], 294
African-American experience on file, 295
African-American hist, 296
Africana, 291
Guide to black Washington, rev ed, 293
New York Public Lib African American desk ref, 298
New York Public Lib amazing African American hist, 299

AFRO-AMERICAN - MILITARY
African American military heroes, 287

AFRO-AMERICAN - MUSIC
Black women in American bands & orchestras, 2d ed, 1061
Index to African-American spirituals for the solo voice, 1119
Spreadin' the music around: black popular songwriters, 1880-1930, 1062

AFRO-AMERICAN - POLITICIANS
Distinguished African American political & govtl leaders, 286

AFRO-AMERICAN - SCIENCE
African American firsts in sci & tech, 1297
Notable black American scientists, 1278

AFRO-AMERICANS
African American biog, v.5, 281
African American info dir 1998-99, 4th ed, 35
Biographical dict of African Americans, 288
Black women in America, 282
Contemporary black biog, v.18, 283
Contemporary black biog, v.19, 284
Contemporary black biog, v.20, 285
Interdisciplinary bibliog gd to black studies 98, 279
Notable black American men, 289
Notable black American scientists, 1278
Who's who among African Americans, 12th ed, 290

AGED
Older Americans info dir, 1999, 2d ed, 735
Physical & mental issues in aging sourcebk, 1421

AGRICULTURE
Agricultural stats 1999, 1298
State of food & agriculture 1998, 1309

AIDS (DISEASE)
AIDS crisis in America, 2d ed, 1429
AIDS sourcebk, 2d ed, 1428

ALASKA
Alaskan wilderness, 361

ALBANIAN LANGUAGE - DICTIONARIES - ENGLISH
Albanian-English dict, 902

ALCOHOLISM
Encyclopedia of understanding alcohol & other drugs, 754

ALEXANDRIA
Alexandria rediscovered, 394

ALLUSIONS IN LITERATURE
Merriam-Webster's dict of allusions, 934

ALMANACS
Cambridge factfinder, 3d ed, 3
Texas almanac, 2000-2001, 60th ed, 80
World almanac & bk of facts 2000, millennium ed, 4

ALTERNATIVE MEDICINE
Alternative medicine gd to heart disease, stroke, & high blood pressure, 1417
Alternative medicine hndbk, 1416
Alternative medicine sourcebk, 1415
Ayurveda ency, 1419
Illustrated ency of body-mind disciplines, 1418
Natural medicines comprehensive database, 2d ed, 1450
Pharmacists gd to over-the-counter & natural remedies, 1445

ALZHEIMER'S DISEASE
Alzheimer's disease sourcebk, 2d ed, 1430

AMERICAN LITERATURE
American travel writers, 1850-1915, 1001
American travellers abroad, 2d ed, 359
American women prose writers to 1820, 996
Anne Tyler companion, 1017
Asian American lit, 1006
Encyclopedia of American lit, 1004
Ernest Hemingway: a documentary vol, 1012
Ernest Hemingway A to Z, 1013
F. Scott Fitzgerald ency, 1011
Hayashi Steinbeck bibliog, 1982-96, 1015
James Dickey, 1009
John Crowe Ransom, 1014
Magill's literary annual 1999, 995
Mark Twain, 1016
Maya Angelou, 1008
Modern American lit, 5th ed, 1007
Nineteenth-century American fiction writers, 999
Twentieth-century American western writers, 1st series, 1000
Walt Whitman, 1018
William Faulkner ency, 1010

AMERICAN LITERATURE - SOUTHERN STATES
Contemporary Southern writers, 998

AMERICAN MATHEMATICAL ASSOCIATION OF TWO-YEAR COLLEGES
Combined membership list 1998-99, 1522

AMERICAN MATHEMATICAL SOCIETY
Combined membership list 1998-99, 1522

AMERICAN PSYCHOLOGICAL ASSOCIATION
APA membership register 1999, 688
Directory of the American Psychological Assn, 1997 ed, 689
Graduate study in psychology 1998-99, 32d ed, 240

AMERICAN SIGN LANGUAGE
American sign lang handshape dict, 893

AMERICANS WITH DISABILITIES ACT
Practical gd to the ADA & visual impairment, 737

AMERICAS
Worldmark chronology of the nations, 347

AMPHIBIANS
Amphibians & reptiles of Northern Guatemala, the Yucatan, & Belize, 1376

AMUSEMENT PARKS
Amusement park gd, 3d ed, 372

ANARCHISM
Encyclopedia of political anarchy, 668

ANGELOU, MAYA
Maya Angelou, 1008

ANGELS
Angels: an indexed & partially annot bibliog, 1225

ANIMAL RIGHTS
Encyclopedia of animal rights & animal welfare, 1347
Endangered species, 1353

ANIMALS. *See also* **MAMMALS; MARINE ANIMALS**
Animal anatomy on file, rev ed, 1350
Animals, 1351
Mammals of N America, 1365
Wildlife & plants of the world, 1325

ANIMATION
Encyclopedia of animated cartoons, 2d ed, 1161

ANTHROPOLOGY
Anthropological lit on disk 1999 [CD-ROM], 267
Anthropological resources, 268

ANTIQUE DEALERS
Guide to the antique shops of Britain 1997/8, 833

ANTIQUES
Antique Trader's bks, antiques, & collectibles price gd, 2000 annual ed, 834
Maloney's antiques & collectibles resource dir, 5th ed, 832

APARTHEID - SOUTH AFRICA
End of apartheid in South Africa, 427

APOLOGETICS - CHRISTIAN
Baker ency of Christian apologetics, 1261

ARAB AMERICANS
Arab American biog, 272

ARAB WOMEN
Arab women 1995, 799

ARABIC LITERATURE
Modern Arabic lit, 1043

ARACHNIDIA
Identifying British insects & arachnids, 1363

ARCHAEOLOGY
Alexandria rediscovered, 394
Dictionary of archaeology, 393
Encyclopedia of archaeology, 395
Encyclopedia of the archaeology of ancient Egypt, 396

ARCHITECTURE
Architect's portable hndbk, 2d ed, 861
Architecture: an interactive intro [CD-ROM], 858
Award winning architecture 1998/99, 859
Bibliographic gd to art & architecture 1998, 844
Bibliography of modern art on disc [CD-ROM], 845
Encyclopedia of vernacular architecture of the world, 860
J. J. P. Oud & the intl style, 863
Open house: a guided tour of the American house, 1637-present, 862
Practically speaking: a dict of quotations on engineering, tech, & architecture, 55

ARCHITECTURE - GREAT BRITAIN
Architecture in ms 1601-1996, 864

ARGENTINA
Culture & customs of Argentina, 109

ART
Bibliographic gd to art & architecture 1998, 844
Guide to Native American ledger drawings & pictographs in US museums, libs, & archives, 314
Historical source bk for scribes, 855

ART - COMPUTER NETWORK RESOURCES
Image buyers gd, 7th ed, 854

ART - DIRECTORIES
Fine artist's career gd, 856
Native American Indian artist dir, 853

ART- MODERN
Bibliography of modern art on disc [CD-ROM], 845

ART MUSEUMS
On exhibit 1999: art lover's travel gd to American museums, 374

ART - 19TH CENTURY
Arts of the 19th century: v.1, 1780-1850, 857
Nineteenth-century European art, 852

ART - SLIDES CATALOGS
Image buyers gd, 7th ed, 854

ART - TIBETAN
Encyclopedia of Tibetan symbols & motifs, 865

ARTHURIAN LEGENDS
Arthurian name dict, 1023

ARTISTS - BIOGRAPHY
Arts of the 19th century: v.1, 1780-1850, 857
Contemporary women artists, 846
Dictionary of bird artists of the world, 849
Dictionary of Tex. artists, 1800-1945, 847
Latin American women artists of the US, 848
Who was who in American art 1564-1975, rev ed, 850
Women artists of color, 851

ARTISTS - NATIVE AMERICAN
Native American Indian artist dir, 853

ARTS
Walford's gd to ref material, v.3, 7th ed, 807

ASIA
Statistical yrbk for Asia & the Pacific 1998, 774
Thailand, rev ed, 90
Worldmark chronology of the nations, 347

ASIA - BUSINESS
Directory of consumer brands & their owners 1998, 170
Major cos of SW Asia 1999, 3d ed, 172

ASIA - SOCIAL LIFE & CUSTOMS
Do's & don'ts around the world: Asia, 85

ASIAN AMERICAN - LITERATURE
Asian American lit, 1006

ASIAN AMERICANS
Asian-American experience on file, 273
Distinguished Asian Americans, 274
Filipino Americans, 276
Taiwanese Americans, 275

ASSOCIATIONS
Public interest profiles 1998-99, 42

ASSYRIA
Ancient & modern Chaldean hist, 476

ASTRONAUTS
Explorers: from ancient times to the space age, 344
Who's who in space, 1507

ASTRONOMY. *See also* **SPACE SCIENCES**
Astronomical almanac for the yr 1998, 1499
Atlas of the universe, 1502
Cosmic phenomena, 1506
Graduate programs in physics, astronomy, & related fields, 2000, 1474
Innovations in astronomy, 1501
Space exploration, 1504
Universe & beyond, 3d ed, 1500
Universe revealed, 1505

ATHLETES
Greatest athletes of the 20th century, 699
Princeton Review student athletes gd to college, 261
Sports stars, series 5, 701

ATLASES
Bibliographic gd to maps & atlases 1998, 343
Collins essential atlas of the world, 336
National Geographic atlas of the world, 7th ed, 338
National Geographic beginner's world atlas, 339
National Geographic US atlas for young explorers, 340
New millennium world atlas deluxe [CD-ROM], 341
People & the Earth, 342

AUDIO RECORDING INDUSTRY
AV market place 1999, 823

AUGUSTINE OF HIPPO (A.D. 354-430)
Augustine through the ages, 1227

AUSTRALASIA
Far East & Australasia 1999, 30th ed, 92

AUSTRALIA
Australia 2000, 377
Historical dict of Australia, 2d ed, 442
Opera cos & houses of W Europe, Canada, Australia, & New Zealand, 1107

AUSTRALIAN LITERATURE
MUP ency of Australian sci fiction & fantasy, 1034

AUSTRIA
Austria, rev ed, 95
Historical dict of Austria, 450

AUTHORS
Contemporary authors autobiog series, v.30, 923
Contemporary authors, v.165, 924
Contemporary authors, v.168, 925
Contemporary authors, v.169, 926
Contemporary authors, v.170, 927
Contemporary authors, v.171, 928
Critical companion to popular contemporary writers, 1999 ed [CD-ROM], 976
Encyclopedia of world lit in the 20th century, 3d ed, 932

Major 20th-century writers, 2d ed, 929
North American romance writers, 986

AUTHORS, AMERICAN
American travel writers, 1850-1915, 1001
Ernest Hemingway: a documentary vol, 1012
Ernest Hemingway A to Z, 1013
F. Scott Fitzgerald ency, 1011
Hayashi Steinbeck bibliog, 1982-96, 1015
James Dickey, 1009
John Crowe Ransom, 1014
Mark Twain, 1016
Maya Angelou, 1008
Twentieth-century American western writers, 1st series, 1000
William Faulkner ency, 1010

AUTHORS - BIOGRAPHY - JUVENILE LITERATURE
Lives & works: YA authors, 966
Something about the author, v.99, 959

AUTHORS, ENGLISH
British novelists since 1960, 3d series, 1019
British writers, suppl 5, 1024
Comprehensive Shakespeare dict [CD-ROM], 1027
Persons, animals, ships, & cannon in the Aubrey-Maturin sea novels of Patrick O'Brian, 1026
Reference companion to Dylan Thomas, 1033
Shakespearean criticism, v.43, 1029
Shakespearean criticism, v.44, 1030
Shakespearean criticism, v.45, 1031
Who's who in Shakespeare's England, 1028
World Shakespeare bibliog on CD-ROM, 1983-95 [CD-ROM], 1032

AUTHORS, FRENCH
Victor Hugo ency, 1037

AUTHORS, ITALIAN
Italian novelists since WW II, 1965-95, 1041

AUTHORS, MEXICAN-AMERICAN
Chicano writers, 3d series, 1003

AUTHORSHIP. *See also* PUBLISHERS & PUBLISHING
Canadian writer's market, 13th rev ed, 811
Complete gd to literary contests 1999, 812
Guide to literary agents, 1999, 813
MLA hndbk for writers of research papers, 5th ed, 819
Novel & short story writer's market, 1999, 814
Poet's market, 1999, 815
Writer's hndbk, 2000 ed, 817
Writer's market, 2000, electronic ed, 818
Writing research papers, 2d ed, 816

AUTHORSHIP - STYLE MANUALS
Cassell gd to punctuation, repr ed, 821
Columbia gd to online style, 822
MLA hndbk for writers of research papers, 5th ed, 819

AUTOGRAPHS
Negro League autograph gd, 835

AUTOMOBILES
Automotive Web sites, 1543
Encyclopaedia of classic cars, 1542

AWARDS
Awards, honors, & prizes 1999, 15th ed, 37
Outstanding bks for children & young people, 963

AYURVEDA MEDICINE
Ayurveda ency, 1419

AZERBAIJAN
Historical dict of Azerbaijan, 432

AZTECS
Daily life of the Aztecs, 313

BABYLONIA
Ancient & modern Chaldean hist, 476

BALBOA AMUSEMENT PRODUCING COMPANY
Balboa films, 1178

BANKS & BANKING. *See also* ECONOMICS; FINANCE
Encyclopedia of money, 148
International dict of banking & finance, lib ed, 149
International dict of personal finance, 151

BAPTISTS
Historical dict of the Baptists, 1262

BASEBALL
Ballpark sourcebk, 2d ed, 710
Bill James presents ... STATS all-time baseball sourcebk, 703
Bill James presents ... STATS Minor League hndbk 1999, 8th ed, 704
Crossing the plate: the upswing in runs scored by major league teams, 1993 to 1997, 713
Japanese baseball, 707
Magic nos: baseball's best single-season hitters, decade-by-decade, 706
New Dickson baseball dict, 705
Official Major League baseball fact bk, 1999 ed, 708
Sporting News baseball gd, 1999 ed, 709
Sporting News baseball register, 1999 ed, 711
Total baseball, 6th ed, 712

BASEBALL MEMORABILIA
Tuff Stuff's baseball memorabilia price gd, 843

BASKETBALL
College basketball's natl championships, 714
Sporting News official NBA gd, 1999-2000 ed, 715
Sporting News official NBA register, 1999-2000 ed, 716

BASQUE REGION
Basque region, 96

BED & BREAKFAST ACCOMMODATIONS
Bed & breakfast ency, 2d ed, 358
Bed & breakfasts & country inns, 10th ed, 357
Official gd to American historic inns, bed & breakfasts, & country inns, 6th ed, 373

BELGIUM
Historical dict of Belgium, 451

BIBLE
International Bible commentary, 1252
Quickverse: life application Bible [CD-ROM], 1253
Taxonomic charts of theology & biblical studies, 1254
Zondervan hndbk to the Bible, 3d ed, 1255

BIBLE - ATLASES
Concise Bible atlas, 1243

BIBLE - DICTIONARIES
Anchor Bible dict on CD-ROM [CD-ROM], 1244
Dictionary of biblical imagery, 1245
Dictionary of biblical interpretation, 1246
Dictionary of deities & demons in the Bible (DDD), 2d rev ed, 1247
Illustrated Bible dict, 1248
New intl dict of N.T. theology [CD-ROM], 1249
Wycliffe Bible dict, 1250

BIBLICAL SCHOLARS
Historical hndbk of major biblical interpreters, 1251

BIBLIOGRAPHY
Bibliography of Canadian imprints 1751-1800, 581
Books in print 1998-99, 6
Canadian bks in print 1999: author & title index, 7
Canadian bks in print 1999: subject index, 8
Literary research gd, 3d ed, 922
New Zealand bks in print 1999, 1035
Whitaker's bks in print 1999, 9

BILINGUAL EDUCATION
Encyclopedia of bilingualism & bilingual educ, 219
Encyclopedia of lang & educ, 872

BIOETHICS
Bioethics for students, 1210

BIOGRAPHY
Abridged ency of world biog, 10
African American biog, v.5, 281
ARBA gd to biogl resources 1986-97, 11
Biographical dict of African Americans, 288
Canadian who's who 1999 [CD-ROM], 22
Canadian who's who 1999, v.34, 23
Chambers biogl dict, 6th ed, 12
Contemporary black biog, v.18, 283
Contemporary black biog, v.19, 284
Contemporary black biog, v.20, 285
Dictionary of Canadian biog, v.14, 24
Dictionary of Mo. biog, 18
Dictionary of world biog: the 20th century, 479
Dictionary of world biog, v.3: the Renaissance, 480
Dictionary of world biog, v.4: the 17th & 18th centuries, 481
Dictionary of world biog, vols. 5 & 6: the 19th century, 482
Encyclopedia of world biog on CD-ROM [CD-ROM], 13
Encyclopedia of world biog suppl, 14
Founding leaders [CD-ROM], 483
Icons of the century, 1137
International who's who 1998-99, 62d ed, 15
Latin American lives, 322
Notable black American men, 289
Notable 20th-century scientists: suppl, 1279
Religious leaders of America, 2d ed, 1230
Scribner ency of American lives 1986-90, v.2, 19
Who's who in America 1999, 53d ed, 20
Who's who in entertainment 1998-99, 3d ed, 1144
Who's who in the world 1999, 16th ed, 16
Who's who 1999, 151st ed, 17
Who's who of American women 1999-2000, 21st ed, 21
Who's who of Pulitzer Prize winners, 1002

BIOLOGY
Animal anatomy on file, rev ed, 1350
Facts on file dict of biology, 3d ed, 1322
Genetic engineering, 1328
Genetic engineering, 1330
Guide to field gds, 1349
In search of swampland, 1320
Innovations in biology, 1329
Life scis on file, rev ed, 1319
Williams dict of biomaterials, 1326
World of biology, 1327

BIOTECHNOLOGY
Encyclopedia of bioprocess tech, 1323
Glossary of biotech terms, 2d ed, 1324

BIRDS
Animals, 1351
Bird almanac, 1354
Bird-finding gd to Mexico, 1356
Birds of the wetlands, 1355

Watchable birds of the Great Basin, 1357
Wood warblers, 1358

BLIND - DEAF
Practical gd to the ADA & visual impairment, 737

BLOOD - DISEASES
Blood & circulatory disorders sourcebk, 1431

BLUES (MUSIC)
All music gd to the blues, 2d ed, 1092
Blues singers, 1093
Joel Whitburn's rhythm & blues top R&B albums 1965-98, 1094

BOATING
Complete outdoors ency, 4th ed, 702

BODYBUILDING
Ironman's ultimate bodybuilding ency, 717

BOGART, HUMPHREY
Humphrey Bogart, 1150

BONAPARTE, NAPOLEON
Napoleon, 454

BOOK COLLECTING
Bookman's price index, v.60, 836
Huxford's old bk value gd, 11th ed, 837

BOOK COLLECTIONS
Aldine press bks at the Harry Ransom Humanities Research Center, 583

BOOK REVIEWS
Children's lit review, v.50, 964

BOOKSELLERS & BOOKSELLING
American bk buyers study, 591
Dictionary of literary biog, v.201, 582
Literary market place 1999, 588
Literary market place on disc [CD-ROM], 589

BRAND NAME PRODUCTS
Brands & their cos, 18th ed, 157
Companies & their brands, 18th ed, 158

BRITISH ARCHITECTURAL LIBRARY
Architecture in ms 1601-1996, 864

BUILDING
Building materials, 1390

BULGARIA
Bulgaria, 97

BURNS
Burns sourcebk, 1433

BUSHMAN, FRANCIS X.
Francis X. Bushman, 1157

BUSINESS. *See also* **BANKS & BANKING; CORPORATIONS; FINANCE; INTERNATINAL BUSINESS**
Bibliographic gd to business & economics 1998, 115
Encyclopedia of business info sources, 13th ed, 116
Foreign trade of the US 1999, 211

BUSINESS - BIOGRAPHY
American business leaders, 119
American business leaders [CD-ROM], 117
Business leaders for students, 118

BUSINESS - DICTIONARIES & ENCYCLOPEDIAS
Business kanji, 913
Encyclopedia of African American business hist, 122
Lexicon of labor, 202
NTC's dict of Korea's business & cultural code words, 186
Wall Street dict, 152

BUSINESS - DIRECTORIES
American big businesses dir, 1999, 127
American big business disc, 2d ed [CD-ROM], 128
Business orgs, agencies, & pubs dir, 10th ed, 129
Business phone bk USA 1999, 21st ed, 130
Hoover's masterlist of major US cos 1998-99, 132
Major cos of Africa S of the Sahara 1999, 4th ed, 171
Major cos of SW Asia 1999, 3d ed, 172
Scott's dirs 1999, 6th ed, 187
Toll-free phone bk USA 1999, 3d ed, 43
Top 5,000 European cos 1999/2000, 134
US business dir, 1999, 135
World dir of business info Websites, 137

BUSINESS - EDUCATION
Best 80 business schools, 2000 ed, 256

BUSINESS ETHICS
Business ethics, 205
Codes of professional responsibility, 4th ed, 208

BUSINESS - HANDBOOKS & YEARBOOKS
Sexual harassment in America, 550
Small business sourcebk, 13th ed, 138
US market trends & forecasts, 214

BUSINESS - HISTORY
Notable corporate chronologies, 2d ed, 120

BUSINESS - INFORMATION SERVICES
Who knows what: a gd to experts, 17th ed, 136

BUSINESS LIBRARIES
Business ref servs & sources, 578
Meeting managers' info needs, 579

BUSINESS - QUOTATIONS
Wiley bk of business quotations, 140

BUTTERFLIES
Butterflies of Canada, 1364

CABLE TELEVISION
Bacon's TV/cable dir 1999, 13th ed, 825
Career opportunities in TV, cable, video, & multimedia, 4th ed, 193

CACTI
Plantfinder's gd to cacti & other succulents, 1344

CAMBODIA
Demographic perspective on women in dvlpmt in Cambodia ..., 759

CAMEROON
Cameroon, rev ed, 82

CAMPING
Beyond the natl parks, 698
Complete outdoors ency, 4th ed, 702

CANADA
Butterflies of Canada, 1364
Opera cos & houses of W Europe, Canada, Australia, & New Zealand, 1107
Quebec, 93
Scott's dirs 1999, 6th ed, 187

CANADA - HISTORY
Encyclopedia of North American hist, 490
Historical dict of Canada, 443
W. L. Mackenzie King, 444

CANADIAN - HEALTH CARE
Canadian health facilities dir, 1396

CANADIAN - IMPRINTS
Bibliography of Canadian imprints 1751-1800, 581
Canadian bks in print 1999: author & title index, 7
Canadian bks in print 1999: subject index, 8
Early Canadian printing, 580

CANADIANS
Canadian who's who 1999 [CD-ROM], 22
Canadian who's who 1999, v.34, 23
Dictionary of Canadian biog, v.14, 24
Encyclopedia of Canada's peoples, 269

CANCER
Pediatric cancer sourcebk, 1424

CAPITAL PUNISHMENT
Capital punishment in the US, 534
Legal executions in New England, 537

CAREERS
America's top jobs for college graduates, 3d ed, 197
America's top medical, educ, & human servs jobs, 4th ed, 198
Career exploration on the Internet, 192
Career opportunities in TV, cable, video, & multimedia, 4th ed, 193
Career opportunities in the sports industry, 2d ed, 199
Career opportunities in theater & the performing arts, 2d ed, 200
Certification & accreditation programs dir, 2d ed, 194
Complete gd to environmental careers in the 21st century, 195
Fine artist's career gd, 856
Job hunter's sourcebk, 4th ed, 201
National job hotline dir, 196
Plunkett's employer's Internet sites with careers info, 1999-2000, 203

CARIBBEAN AREA
Economic survey of Latin America & the Caribbean 1997-98, 50th ed, 191

CARRADINE, JOHN
John Carradine, 1158

CARTOGRAPHY
America from space, 350
Southeast in early maps, 3d ed, 337

CASH, JOHNNY
Another song to sing: the recorded repertoire of Johnny Cash, 1086

CASTRO, FIDEL
Castro & the Cuban Revolution, 445

CATHOLIC CHURCH
Encyclopedia of the Vatican & Papacy, 1265
Our Sunday Visitor's Catholic almanac, 2000, 1256
Our Sunday Visitor's ency of the Catholic doctrine on CD-ROM [CD-ROM], 1266

CD-ROM BOOKS
Directory of law-related CD-ROMs 1999, 517
Genealogy on CD-ROM, 326

CD-ROMS
ABELL: annual bib of English lang & lit 1920-95 [CD-ROM], 920
African-American culture & hist [CD-ROM], 294

American big business disc, 2d ed [CD-ROM], 128
American business leaders [CD-ROM], 117
American manufacturers disc, 2d ed [CD-ROM], 155
American military leaders [CD-ROM], 595
American social issues [CD-ROM], 410
Anchor Bible dict on CD-ROM [CD-ROM], 1244
Anthropological lit on disc [CD-ROM], 267
Architecture: an interactive intro [CD-ROM], 858
Associations unltd [CD-ROM], 36
Atlas of the official records of the Civil War [CD-ROM], 400
Bacon's media source [CD-ROM], 808
Barron's profiles of American colleges, 1999 ed [CD-ROM], 233
Bibliography of modern art on disc [CD-ROM], 845
Black studies on disc 1999 [CD-ROM], 297
Campaigns of the Civil War & the Navy in the Civil War [CD-ROM], 420
Canadian Who's Who 1999 [CD-ROM], 22
Children's bks in print on disc [CD-ROM], 949
Civil War CD-ROM II [CD-ROM], 421
Complete index to world film since 1895 on CD-ROM [CD-ROM], 1195
Comprehensive Shakespeare dict [CD-ROM], 1027
Critical companion to popular contemporary writers, 1999 ed [CD-ROM], 976
Daily life through hist [CD-ROM], 501
Electronic engineers hndbk [CD-ROM], 1381
Elsevier dicts on CD-ROM, 1998/99 ed [CD-ROM], 27
Encyclopaedia Britannica CD-ROM 1999, multimedia ed [CD-ROM], 28
Encyclopedia Americana on CD-ROM [CD-ROM], 29
Encyclopedia of world biog on CD-ROM [CD-ROM], 13
EXEGY: Current country profiles 2000 [CD-ROM], 65
Founding leaders [CD-ROM], 483
History of Parliament on CD-ROM [CD-ROM], 665
Horn Bk gd interactive [CD-ROM], 952
Jane's market intelligence lib [CD-ROM], 612
Leadership lib on CD-ROM, fall 1998 ed [CD-ROM], 622
Literary market place on disc [CD-ROM], 589
Marks' standard hndbk for mechanical engineers [CD-ROM], 1391
Masterplots complete CD-ROM, 1999 ed [CD-ROM], 946
New intl dict of N.T. theology [CD-ROM], 1249
New millennium world atlas deluxe [CD-ROM], 341
NICEM ref CD-ROM [CD-ROM], 266
Our Sunday Visitor's ency of Catholic doctrine on CD-ROM [CD-ROM], 1266
Our Sunday Visitor's ency of saints [CD-ROM], 1267
Perry's chemical engineers hndbk [CD-ROM], 1379
Public record research system [CD-ROM], 624
Quickverse: life application Bible [CD-ROM], 1253
ResourceLink: Ill. [CD-ROM], 79
ResourceLink: 20th-century American hist [CD-ROM], 408
Science navigator [CD-ROM], 1288
Southern histl society papers [CD-ROM], 424
Standard hndbk for civil engineers [CD-ROM], 1380
Ullmann's ency of industrial chemistry 1998, 6th ed [CD-ROM], 1483
Van Nostrand's scientific ency, 8th ed [CD-ROM], 1289
Wellesley index to Victorian pers 1824-1900, new ed, 49
Women leaders [CD-ROM], 794
Women's movement in the US [CD-ROM], 796
Women's studies ency, rev ed [CD-ROM], 798
World bk: millennium 2000, deluxe ed [CD-ROM], 32
World bk multimedia ency: Macintosh ed, 34
World mktg forecasts on CD-ROM, 2d ed [CD-ROM], 215
World political leaders [CD-ROM], 617
World Shakespeare bibliog on CD-ROM, 1983-95 [CD-ROM], 1032

CELEBRITIES
Obituaries in the performing arts, 1998, 1143

CENSORSHIP
Censorship in America, 561
100 banned bks, 562

CENTRAL AMERICA. *See also* LATIN AMERICA
Consumer Latin America 1999, 6th ed, 190
Peoples of the Americas, 271
Social panorama of Latin America, 1997 ed, 110

CHAMBER MUSIC
Comprehensive catalogue of duet lit for female voices, 1060

CHAOS THEORY
Illustrated dict of nonlinear dynamics & chaos, 1524

CHARLESTON (S.C.) - GUIDEBOOKS
Charleston, Savannah, & coastal islands bk, 3d ed, 369

CHAUCER, GEOFFREY
Chaucer A to Z, 1025

CHEMICAL ELEMENTS
Chemical elements, 1378

CHEMICAL ENGINEERING
Kirk-Othmer Concise ency of chemical tech, 4th ed, 1482
Perry's chemical engineers hndbk [CD-ROM], 1379

CHEMICALS
Dictionary of environmentally important chemicals, 1476
Dun & Bradstreet/Gale industry ref hndbks: chemicals, 1485
Gardner's chemical synonyms & trade names, 11th ed, 1480
Handbook of petrochemicals & processes, 2d ed, 1492

CHEMISTRY
Chemical gd to the Internet, 2d ed, 1484
Chemistry, 1491
CRC hndbk of chemistry & physics 1999-2000, 80th ed, 1473
Dictionary of chemistry, 1481
Encyclopedia of computational chemistry, 1478
Facts on file dict of chemistry, 3d ed, 1479
Handbook of reagents for organic synthesis: acidic & basic reagents, 1486
Handbook of reagents for organic synthesis: activating agents & protecting groups, 1487
Handbook of reagents for organic synthesis: oxidizing & reducing agents, 1488
Handbook of reagents for organic synthesis: reagents, auxiliaries, & catalysts for C-C bonds, 1489
Kirk-Othmer Concise ency of chemical tech, 4th ed, 1482
Lange's hndbk of chemistry, 15th ed, 1490
Ullmann's ency of industrial chemistry 1998, 6th ed [CD-ROM], 1483
World records in chemistry, 1493

CHILD CARE
Child care: a parent's gd, 2d ed, 740

CHILD LABOR
Child labor, 756

CHILDREN'S ATLASES
National Geographic beginner's world atlas, 339
National Geographic US atlas for young explorers, 340

CHILDREN'S ENCYCLOPEDIAS & DICTIONARIES
Junior worldmark ency of world cultures, 270
Merriam-Webster's intermediate dict, 890
New bk of knowledge, 1999 deluxe lib ed, 31
Rourkes world of sci ency, 1287

CHILDREN'S LITERATURE
Best bks for children, 6th ed, 948
Children's bks about religion, 951
Children's bks in print on disc [CD-ROM], 949
Children's fiction 1900-50, 950
Children's lit review, v.50, 964
Horn Bk gd interactive [CD-ROM], 952
Outstanding bks for children & young people, 963
Sequels in children's lit, 947
Strong souls singing: African American bks for our daughters & our sisters, 280
Subject gd to children's bks in print 1999, 955
Teaching US hist through children's lit, 954
Valerie & Walter's best bks for children, 953

CHILDREN'S LITERATURE - BIOGRAPHY
Black authors & illustrators of bks for children & YAs, 958
100 most popular children's authors, 957
Something about the author, v.99, 959
Something about the author, v.102, 960
Something about the author, v.103, 961
Something about the author, v.104, 962

CHILDREN'S NONFICTION
Guide to ref materials for school lib media centers, 5th ed, 554

CHILDREN'S ONLINE INFORMATION SOURCES
Online kids: a young surfer's gd to cyberspace, rev ed, 1461

CHILDREN'S REFERENCE BOOKS
Fiesta! 2, 66
National Geographic beginner's world atlas, 339
National Geographic US atlas for young explorers, 340
People & the Earth, 342
Scholastic children's thesaurus, 899
Scholastic treasury of quotations for children, 965

CHINA
China during the cultural revolution, 1966-76, 433
Dictionary of contemporary Chinese military hist, 435
Encyclopedia of China, 87
Historical dict of Guangzhou (Canton) & Guangdong, 434

CHINA - POLITICAL HISTORY
Dictionary of the politics of the People's Republic of China, 86

CHINESE LANGUAGE DICTIONARIES - ENGLISH
Chinese character dict, 903
Chinese-Pinyin-English dict for learners, 904

CHRISTIAN - BIOGRAPHY
Baker ency of Christian apologetics, 1261
Sister Wendy's bk of saints, 1259

CHRISTIAN - DICTIONARIES
Dictionary of the presbyterian & reformed tradition in America, 1263
Historical dict of reformed churches, 1231
Historical dict of the Baptists, 1262

CHRISTIAN EDUCATION
Christian colleges & universities 1999, 235
Colleges that encourage character dvlpmt, 237

CHRISTIANITY
Encyclopedia of Christianity, v.1 (A-D), 1264
Jesus people movement, 1258

Our Sunday Visitor's ency of saints [CD-ROM], 1267
Taxonomic charts of theology & biblical studies, 1254

CHRISTIANITY - CHRONOLOGY
Timeline charts of the western church, 1260

CHRONOLOGY, HISTORICAL
Chronology of world hist, 487

CHURCH BUILDINGS
Historic places of worship, 1268

CHURCHILL, SIR WINSTON
Connoisseur's gd to the bks of Sir Winston Churchill, 469

CITIES & TOWNS
America's top-rated cities, 2000, 7th ed, 787
Cities of the US, 3d ed, 74
Cities of the world, 5th ed, 63
Encyclopedia of world cities, 72

CIVIL REGISTRATION
Handbook on civil registration & vital stats systems, 771

CIVIL RIGHTS
American civil rights: almanac, 398
Civil rights in America: 1500 to the present, 549

CLIMATOLOGY. *See also* **METEOROLOGY; WEATHER**
Atlas of the world's worst natural disasters, 1497

CLOWNS
Clowns & tricksters, 1131

COGNITIVE SCIENCES
MIT ency of the cognitive scis, 687

COINS
Guide bk of US coins 2000, 53d ed, 841
Guide bk of US currency, 3d ed, 838
Handbook of US coins, 2000, 57th ed, 842
Whitman gd to coin collecting, 839

COLLECTIBLES
Antique Trader's bks, antiques, & collectibles price gd, 2000 annual ed, 834
Charlton standard catalogue of royal doulton beswick figurines, 6th ed, 830
Collector's Mart mag price gd to ltd ed collectibles, 1999, 831
Guide bk of US currency, 3d ed, 838
Maloney's antiques & collectibles resource dir, 5th ed, 832
Negro League autograph gd, 835
Tuff Stuff's baseball memorabilia price gd, 843

COLLECTION DEVELOPMENT (LIBRARIES)
Guide to ref materials for school lib media centers, 5th ed, 554

COLLEGE CHOICE
Barron's profiles of American colleges, 1999 ed [CD-ROM], 233
Best 80 business schools, 2000 ed, 256
Best graduate programs: engineering, 2d ed, 234
Best 331 colleges, 2000 ed, 238
Graduate school, 257
Princeton Review African American student's gd to college, 1999 ed, 260

COLLEGE SPORTS
College basketball's natl championships, 714

COLOMBIA
Culture & customs of Colombia, 111

COLONIAL AMERICA
Colonial America to 1763, 399

COMMERCIAL CATALOGS
Catalog of catalogs 6, 144

COMMODITIES
CRB commodity yrbk 1998, 141

COMMUNICATIONS. *See also* **MASS MEDIA**
Dictionary of quotations in communications, 810

COMPARATIVE LITERATURE
Comparative reader, 921

COMPOSERS
Alfred Reed, 1081
Giacomo Puccini, 1079
International dict of black composers, 1069
Schwann opus, winter 1997-99: ref gd to classical music, 1076
Spreadin' rhythm around: black popular songwriters, 1880-1930, 1062
Women composers, v.4, 1063
Women composers, v.5, 1064

COMPUTATIONAL CHEMISTRY
Encyclopedia of computational chemistry, 1478

COMPUTER NETWORKS
Telecom & networking glossary, 1468

COMPUTER SOFTWARE
Dun & Bradstreet/Gale industry ref hndbks: computers & sftwr, 1457
Genealogy sftwr gd, 327
Software ency 1998, 1459
Windows 98: the complete ref, 1458

CONGO (DEMOCRATIC REPUBLIC)
Historical dict of Democratic Republic of the Congo, rev ed, 426

CONSTITUTIONAL AMENDMENTS - UNITED STATES
Constitution & its amendments, 646

CONSUMER BEHAVIOR
American bk buyers study, 591
Consumer Latin America 1999, 6th ed, 190
Elgar companion to consumer research & economic psychology, 121

CONSUMER GUIDES
Catalog of catalogs 6, 144
Consumer issues in health care sourcebk, 1411
Consumer sourcebk, 12th ed, 145
Orion blue bk: power tool 1998, 147
Toll-free phone bk USA 1999, 3d ed, 43

CONSUMER PROTECTION
Consumer fraud, 146

CONSUMPTION (ECONOMICS)
Statistical hndbk on consumption & wealth in the US, 785

COOKING
Healthy cookery index, 1310

COOPERATIVE MOVEMENTS
Historical dict of the cooperative movement, 498

CORPORATE LAW
Laws of the US: corps, 529

CORPORATIONS. *See also* BUSINESS; INTERNATIONAL BUSINESS
Company profiles for students, 131
Jane's world defense industry, 603
Notable corporate chronologies, 2d ed, 120

COSMETICS
World cosmetics & toiletries dir 1999, 173

COSMOLOGY
Routledge critical dict of the new cosmology, 1503

COSTELLO, ELVIS
Elvis Costello, 1085

COST & STANDARD OF LIVING
Value of a dollar 1860-1999, 2d ed, 139
World cost of living survey, 2d ed, 776

COUNSELING. *See also* PSYCHOLOGY
Baker ency of psychology & counseling, 2d ed, 683
Key words in multicultural interventions, 686

COUNTRY MUSIC
Joel Whitburn's country annual 1994-97, 1099
Joel Whitburn's top country singles 1944-97, 4th ed, 1100
Modern twang: an alternative country music gd & dir, 1098

COURT CASES
US court cases, 531

COURT - MARTIAL
Guide to military criminal law, 604

COURT RECORDS
Directory of state court clerks & county courthouses, 1999 ed, 516

CREATIONISM
Creation/evolution controversy, 1224

CREATIVITY
Encyclopedia of creativity, 684

CRETE (GREECE)
Crete, 104

CRIME
City crime rankings, 5th ed, 535
Crime state rankings 1999, 6th ed, 536
Hate crimes, 533
Violence in America, 734

CRIMINAL JUSTICE
Death penalty, 527
Great American court cases, 523
Layperson's gd to criminal law, 538
Mental health servs in criminal justice system settings, 681
Role of police in American society, 540

CRIMINALS
Mafia ency, 2d ed, 417

CROATIA
Croatia, 98

CROSS-CULTURAL COUNSELING
Key words in multicultural interventions, 686

CUBAN REVOLUTION
Castro & the Cuban Revolution, 445

CULTS (RELIGIOUS)
Cults in America, 1241
Encyclopedia of cults, sects, & new religions, 1235

CULTURES
Culturgrams, 64
Daily life through hist [CD-ROM], 501
Lands & peoples, 67

CURIOSITIES & WONDERS
Life millennium, 46

DANCE
Bibliographic gd to dance 1998, 1148

DATABASE SEARCHING
Find it online, 2d ed, 1465

DELIBES, MIGUEL
Miguel Delibes, 1049

DEMOGRAPHICS
County & city extra, 1999, 8th ed, 778
Demographic perspective on women in dvlpmt in Cambodia ..., 759
Demographic yrbk, 1997, 49th ed, 763
Demographics USA 1999: county ed, 764
Demographics USA 1999: ZIP ed, 765
Encyclopedia of global population & demographics, 761
Mobility plus...a ref gd 1999, 762
Regional markets, 766

DEMONOLOGY
Dictionary of deities & demons in the Bible (DDD), 2d rev ed, 1247

DETECTIVE & MYSTERY STORIES
Bedside, bathtub, & armchair companion to Sherlock Holmes, 982
BFI companion to crime, 1172

DEVELOPING COUNTRIES
Fertility decline in developing countries, 1960-97, 738
Statistical hndbk on poverty in the developing world, 773

DIABETES
Diabetes sourcebk, 2d ed, 1434

DICKEY, JAMES
James Dickey, 1009

DICTIONARIES - ENGLISH LANGUAGE
American sign lang handshape dict, 893
Cassell compact dict, 876
Cassell concise dict with CD-ROM, rev ed [CD-ROM], 877
Cassell dict & thesaurus, 878
Cassell paperback dict, 879
Concise Oxford dict, 10th ed, 880
DK dict/thesaurus, 897
Elsevier dicts on CD-ROM, 1998/99 ed [CD-ROM], 27
Encarta world English dict, 881
Merriam-Webster & Garfield dict, 889
Merriam-Webster's intermediate dict, 890
Merriam-Webster's school dict, 891
Oxford English dict additions series, v.3, 892
Random House Webster's basic dict of American
Western words: a dict of the old west, 887

DIGITAL IMAGES
Image buyers gd, 7th ed, 854

DIGITAL LIBRARIES
Books, bricks, & bytes: libs in the 21st century, 575

DINOSAURS
Carbon dates, 1514

DIRECTORIES
Directories in print, 17th ed, 38
Guide to American dirs, 14th ed, 40

DISARMAMENT
SIPRI yrbk 1998, 607

DISTANCE EDUCATION
Barron's gd to distance learning, 227
Distance learning funding sourcebk, 4th ed, 228

DIVORCE
Divorce: the best resource to help you survive, 2d ed, 741
Laws of the US: divorce, 530

DOCUMENT DELIVERY SERVICES. *See* INFORMATION SERVICES

DOGS
Barron's ency of dog breeds, 1359

DOMESTIC RELATIONS
Encyclopedia of family life, 742

DOMINICAN AMERICANS
Dominican Americans, 300

DORSEY, JIMMY
Jimmy Dorsey: a study in contrasts, 1087

DOYLE, ARTHUR CONAN, SIR
Bedside, bathtub, & armchair companion to Sherlock Holmes, 982

DRAMA
Dictionary of stage directions in English drama 1580-1942, 1206

Drama for students, v.5, 970
Drama for students, v.6, 971
Index of characters in early modern English drama printed plays, 1500-1660, rev ed, 973
Nigerian theatre in English, 972
Spanish golden age drama, 974

DRUG ABUSE
Buzzed: the straight facts about the most used & abused drugs from alcohol to ecstasy, 1446
Encyclopedia of understanding alcohol & other drugs, 754
War on drugs, 753

DRUGS
Catalog of teratogenic agents, 9th ed, 1454
Encyclopedia of controlled drug delivery, 1447
Mosby's over-the-counter medicine cabinet medicines, 1449
Natural medicines comprehensive database, 2d ed, 1450
PDR for nurses hndbk, 1999 ed, 1452
PDR generics 1998, 4th ed, 1453
Pharmacists gd to over-the-counter & natural remedies, 1445
Prescription alternatives, 2d ed, 1448
Psychologists' psychotropic desk ref, 1451
Veterinary drug hndbk, 3d ed, 1317

DUTCH LANGUAGE - DICTIONARIES
NTC's compact Dutch & English dict, 905

DYNAMICS
Illustrated dict of nonlinear dynamics & chaos, 1524

EARTH SCIENCES
Earth sci on file, rev ed, 1496
Earth scis for students, 1494
Innovations in Earth scis, 1495

EAST ASIA
Far East & Australasia 1999, 30th ed, 92

EATING DISORDERS
Eating disorders, 2d, 1435

ECOLOGY
Temperate forests, 1311

ECONOMIC DEVELOPMENT
Least developed countries 1998 report, 68
Social panorama of Latin America, 1997 ed, 110

ECONOMICS. *See also* **BANKS & BANKING; BUSINESS; FINANCE**
Bibliographic gd to business & economics 1998, 115
Dictionary of free-market economics, 124

Economic survey of Latin America & the Caribbean 1997-98, 50th ed, 191
Elgar companion to consumer research & economic psychology, 121
Encyclopedia of political economy, 123
New Palgrave dict of economics & the law, 126
Pocket world in figures 1999, 772
Value of a dollar 1860-1999, 2d ed, 139
WEFA industrial monitor 1999-2000, 165
World dvlpmt indicators, 1998, 182

EDUCATION
Bibliographic gd to educ 98, 217
Historical dict of American educ, 220

EDUCATION - BIBLIOGRAPHY
El-hi textbks & serials in print 1999, 127th ed, 218

EDUCATION - DIRECTORIES
Best 331 colleges, 2000 ed, 238
College blue bk, 27th ed, 236
Educators resource dir 1999, 3d ed, 222
Funding sources for K-12 educ 1999, 2d ed, 231
Graduate medical educ dir 1999/2000, 84th ed, 1398
Guide to American educl dirs, 8th ed, 223
Higher educ dir, 1999, 241
NICEM ref CD-ROM [CD-ROM], 266
Princeton Review gd to performing arts programs, 224

EDUCATION, ELEMENTARY
Internet resource dir for K-12 teachers & librarians, 1999/2000 ed, 230
Uncle Sam's K-12 Web, 229

EDUCATION, HIGHER
Academic yr abroad 1999-2000, 262
Barron's gd to distance learning, 227
Barron's profiles of American colleges, 1999 ed [CD-ROM], 233
Best 80 business schools, 2000 ed, 256
Best 331 colleges, 2000 ed, 238
Christian colleges & universities 1999, 235
College blue bk, 27th ed, 236
College Board college costs & financial aid hndbk 2000, 20th ed, 252
College Board college hndbk 2000, 37th ed, 253
College Board scholarship hndbk 2000, 3d ed, 254
Colleges that encourage character dvlpmt, 237
Commonwealth Univ yrbk 1999, 74th ed, 255
Directory of American scholars, 9th ed, 239
International hndbk of univs, 15th ed, 259
Princeton Review African American student's gd to college, 1999 ed, 260
Princeton Review student athletes gd to college, 261
Who's who in intl business educ & research, 232

EDUCATION - HIGHER - GRADUATE WORK
Graduate school, 257
Graduate study in psychology 1998-99, 32d ed, 240
Money for grad students in the humanities 1998-2000, 2d ed, 248

EDUCATION - INTERNATIONAL PROGRAMS
International exchange locator, 1998 ed, 263
Media courses UK 1999, 6th ed, 264
Peterson's summer study abroad 1999, 265

EDUCATION, MULTICULTURAL
Encyclopedia of bilingualism & bilingual educ, 219
Encyclopedia of multicultural educ, 221

EDUCATION, SECONDARY
Internet resource dir for K-12 teachers & librarians, 1999/2000 ed, 230

EDUCATION - STATISTICS
Education stats on the US 1999, 225

EDUCATIONAL ACCREDITATION
Certification & accreditation programs dir, 2d ed, 194

EDUCATIONAL FUND-RAISING
Teacher's gd to winning grants, 242

EDUCATORS
Who's who in intl business educ & research, 232

EGYPT
Daily life of the ancient Egyptians, 475
Encyclopedia of the archaeology of ancient Egypt, 396
Gods of ancient Egypt, 431
Historical dict of ancient Egypt, 474

ELECTIONS - UNITED STATES
Almanac of state legislatures, 2d ed, 626
Elections A to Z, 633
Encyclopedia of American parties, campaigns, & elections, 630

ELECTRICAL ENGINEERING
Electronic engineers hndbk [CD-ROM], 1381
Microelectronic failure analysis: desk ref, 4th ed, 1383

ELECTRONIC PUBLISHING
By the nos: electronic & online publishing, 592
Columbia gd to online style, 822

ELECTRONICS
Directory of contract electronics manufacturers, 1999, 159
Encyclopedia of electronic circuits, v.7, 1382

ELLINGTON, DUKE
Duke Ellington, 1082

EMIGRATION & IMMIGRATION
American immigration, 419
Immigration & the law, 676
Shapers of the great debate on immigration, 675
U.S. immigration & naturalization laws & issues, 679

ENCYCLOPEDIAS & DICTIONARIES. *See also* CHILDREN'S ENCYCLOPEDIAS & DICTIONARIES
DK concise ency, 26
Encyclopaedia Britannica CD-ROM 1999, multimedia ed [CD-ROM], 28
Encyclopedia Americana on CD-ROM [CD-ROM], 29
New bk of knowledge, 1999 deluxe lib ed, 31
Subject encys: user gd, review citations, & keyword index, 30
World bk: millennium 2000, deluxe ed [CD-ROM], 32
World bk ency, 1999 ed, 33
World bk multimedia ency: Macintosh ed, 34

ENDANGERED SPECIES
Endangered species, 1353
Habitats & ecosystems, 1529

ENERGY INDUSTRIES
Plunkett's energy industry almanac, 1526

ENGINEERING
Best graduate programs: engineering, 2d ed, 234
Encyclopedia of bioprocess tech, 1323
Marks' standard hndbk for mechanical engineers [CD-ROM], 1391
Perry's chemical engineers hndbk [CD-ROM], 1379
Practically speaking: a dict of quotations on engineering, tech, & architecture, 55
Standard hndbk for civil engineers [CD-ROM], 1380

ENGLISH DRAMA
Dictionary of stage directions in English drama 1580-1942, 1206
Index of characters in early modern English drama printed plays, 1500-1660, rev ed, 973

ENGLISH LANGUAGE
ABELL: annual bib of English lang & lit 1920-95 [CD-ROM], 920

ENGLISH LANGUAGE - DICTIONARIES
American sign lang handshape dict, 893
Cassell compact dict, 876
Cassell concise dict with CD-ROM, rev ed [CD-ROM], 877
Cassell dict & thesaurus, 878
Cassell paperback dict, 879
Concise Oxford dict, 10th ed, 880
DK dict/thesaurus, 897

Elsevier dicts on CD-ROM, 1998/99 ed [CD-ROM], 27
Encarta world English dict, 881
Homophones & homographs, 3d ed, 888
Merriam-Webster & Garfield dict, 889
Merriam-Webster's intermediate dict, 890
Merriam-Webster's school dict, 891
Oxford English dict additions series, v.3, 892
Random House Webster's basic dict of American English, 882
Webster's new world college dict, 4th ed, 883
Western words: a new dict of the old west, 887

ENGLISH LANGUAGE - DICTIONARIES - ALBANIAN
Albanian-English dict, 902

ENGLISH LANGUAGE - DICTIONARIES - CHINESE
Character Chinese dict, 903
Chinese-Pinyin-English dict for learners, 904

ENGLISH LANGUAGE - DICTIONARIES - DUTCH
NTC's compact Dutch & English dict, 905

ENGLISH LANGUAGE - DICTIONARIES - FINNISH
NTC's compact Finish & English dict, 906

ENGLISH LANGUAGE - DICTIONARIES - FRENCH
Dictionary of French slang & colloquial expressions, 907
French thesaurus for children, 908

ENGLISH LANGUAGE - DICTIONARIES - IRISH
Irish-English, English-Irish easy ref dict, 910

ENGLISH LANGUAGE - DICTIONARIES - ITALIAN
Dictionary of Italian slang & colloquial expressions, 911

ENGLISH LANGUAGE - DICTIONARIES - JAPANESE
Business kanji, 913
Compact Nelson Japanese-English character dict, 912

ENGLISH LANGUAGE - DICTIONARIES - POLISH
Langenscheidt's pocket dict: English/Polish, Polish/English, rev ed, 914

ENGLISH LANGUAGE - DICTIONARIES - RUSSIAN
Random House Russian-English, English-Russian dict, 915

ENGLISH LANGUAGE - DICTIONARIES - SERBOCROATION
Standard English-SerboCroatian, SerboCroatian-English dict, 916

ENGLISH LANGUAGE - DICTIONARIES - SPANISH
Spanish idioms, proverbs, & slang of yesterday & today, 917
Vox Spanish & English student dict, 918

ENGLISH LANGUAGE - DICTIONARIES - TUSCARORA
Tuscarora-English/English-Tuscarora dict, 309

ENGLISH LANGUAGE - DICTIONARIES - YIDDISH
Anglish/Yinglish, 2d ed, 919

ENGLISH LANGUAGE - EPONYMS
What's in a name? 884

ENGLISH LANGUAGE - ETYMOLOGY
Jesse's word of the day, 886
Name's familiar: Mr. Leotard, Barbie, & Chef Boyardee, 885

ENGLISH LANGUAGE - FOREIGN WORDS & PHRASES
World dict of foreign expressions, 900

ENGLISH LANGUAGE - PRONUNCIATION
Big bk of beastly mispronunciations, 871

ENGLISH LANGUAGE - SYNONYMS & ANTONYMS
American Heritage student thesaurus, 896
Cassell dict & thesaurus, 878
DK dict/thesaurus, 897
Oxford American thesaurus of current English, 898
Scholastic children's thesaurus, 899

ENGLISH LANGUAGE - TERMS & PHRASES
Cool cats, top dogs, & other beastly expressions, 894
Language of contemporary criticism, 895

ENTERTAINERS. *See also* **ACTORS**
Who's who in entertainment 1998-99, 3d ed, 1144

ENTERTAINMENT
Dun & Bradstreet/Gale industry ref hndbks: entertainment, 1147
US dir of entertainment employers, spring/summer 1999 ed, 1146

ENVIRONMENTAL ENGINEERING
Environmental health, & safety portable hndbk, 1385

ENVIRONMENTAL LAW
ABCs of environmental regulation, 544
Environmental law hndbk, 15th ed, 543
US land & natural resource policy, 542
US landscape ordinances, 541

ENVIRONMENTAL POLICY
Environmental debate, 1534
State environmental agencies on the Internet, 1532

ENVIRONMENTAL PROTECTION
Book of lists for regulated hazardous substances, 9th ed, 1533
Dictionary of environmentally important chemicals, 1476
Global ecology, 1535
Habitats & ecosystems, 1529
Yearbook of intl co-operation on environment & dvlpmt 1998/99, 7th ed, 1538

ENVIRONMENTAL SCIENCES
ABCs of environmental sci, 1536
Complete gd to environmental careers in the 21st century, 195
Encyclopedia of environmental analysis & remediation, 1530
Environmental crisis, 1537
Interdisciplinary bibliog gd to environmental studies 1998, 1527

ESCAPES
Great escapes & rescues, 494

ESPIONAGE
Intelligence, espionage, & related topics, 594

ESSAYS & PROCEEDINGS
Information landscapes for a learning society, 566

ETHICS
Bioethics for students, 1210
Business ethics, 205
Codes of professional responsibility, 4th ed, 208
Encyclopedia of ethics, 1216
Ethics & values, 1217
Sourcebk in bioethics, 1409

ETHNIC GROUPS. *See also* MINORITIES
Interdisciplinary bibliog gd to black studies 98, 279
Macmillan ency of Native American tribes, 2d ed, 307

ETHNOLOGY
Encyclopedia of Canada's peoples, 269
Nationalism & ethnicity terminologies, 60

ETIQUETTE
Culturgrams: the nations around us, 64
Do's & don'ts around the world: Asia, 85

EUPHEMISMS
Western words: a dict of the old west, 887

EUROPE
Worldmark chronology of the nations, 347

EUROPE - ART
Nineteenth-century European art, 852

EUROPE - BUSINESS
European mktg data & stats 1999, 34th ed, 188

EUROPE - HISTORY
Daily life in medieval Europe, 447
Hutchinson ency of the Renaissance, 446

EUROPE - TRAVEL
Britain: the rough gd, 2d ed, 379
Eurail & train travel gd to Europe, 3d ed, 380
Europe 2000, 381
Garden lover's gd to Spain & Portugal, 388
Garden lover's gd to the Netherlands & Belgium, 378
Hostels France & Italy, 384
Hostels UK, 385
Naples with Pompeii & the Amalfi coast, 386
Sardinia, 387

EUROPEAN LANGUAGES
Manual of European langs for librarians, 2d ed, 901

EUROPEAN UNION
Chronological hist of the European Union 1946-98, 448
European regional incentives 1999, 18th ed, 189
European Union ency & dir 1999, 3d ed, 94

EVOLUTION
Creation/evolution controversy, 1224

EXECUTIVE DEPARTMENTS. UNITED STATES
Federal agency profiles for students, 649

EXISTENTIALISM
Dictionary of existentialism, 1213

EXPERTS
Yearbook of experts, authorities, & spokespersons 1999, 17th ed, 48

EXPLORERS
Across the top of the world, 502
Explorers: from ancient times to the space age, 344
Explorers & discoverers, v.6, 345
Explorers & discoverers, v.7, 346

FABLES
Encyclopedia of fable, 1124

FAMILY. *See also* **PARENTING**
Encyclopedia of family life, 742

FANTASTY
Ultimate ency of fantasy, 1138

FANTASTY FICTION
Fantasy & horror, 988
Fluent in fantasy: a gd to reading interests, 990
MUP ency of Australian sci fiction & fantasy, 1034

FAULKNER, WILLIAM
William Faulkner ency, 1010

FBI. *See* **UNITED STATES - FEDERAL BUREAU OF INVESTIGATION**

FEDERAL GOVERNMENT - UNITED STATES
States' rights & American federalism, 662

FEMINISM
Feminism, 801
Significant contemporary American feminists, 792
Women's liberation movement in America, 800

FERTILITY, HUMAN
Fertility decline in developing countries, 1960-97, 738

FESTIVALS
Festivals & holidays, 1132
Folklore of American holidays, 3d ed, 1121

FICTION
American histl fiction, 983
American mystery & detective novels, 980
Arthurian fiction, 967
Children's fiction 1900-50, 950
Critical companion to popular contemporary writers, 1999 ed [CD-ROM], 976
Fantasy & horror, 988
Fluent in fantasy: a gd to reading interests, 990
Nineteenth-century American fiction writers, 999
Novels for students, v.6, 968
Now read this: a gd to mainstream fiction, 1978-98, 977
Reference gd to mystery & detective fiction, 979
Romance fiction, 987
Science fiction writers, 2d ed, 992
What do I read next? 1998, 975
Whole story: 3000 yrs of sequels & sequences, 2d ed, 978
World histl fiction, 984

FILIPINO AMERICANS
Filipino Americans, 276

FINANCE
Directory of venture capital firms, 2000, 4th ed, 150
International dict of personal finance, 151

FINANCIAL AID & SCHOLARSHIPS. *See also* **GRANTS-IN-AID**
College Board college costs & financial aid hndbk 2000, 20th ed, 252
College Board scholarship hndbk 2000, 3d ed, 254
College student's gd to merit & other no-need funding 1998-2000, 244
Financial aid for research & creative activities abroad, 1999-2001, 245
Financial aid for study & training abroad 1999-2001, 246
Financial aid for veterans, military personnel, & their dependents 1998-2000, 247
How to find out about financial aid & funding, 243
Money for grad students in the humanities 1998-2000, 2d ed, 248
Money for graduate students in the social scis 1998-2000, 2d ed, 249
National dir of fndn grants for Native Americans, 312
RSP funding for nursing students & nurses 1998-2000, 1443
Scholarship advisor, 1999 ed, 251
Scholarships, fellowships, & loans 1999, 14th ed, 250

FINANCIAL STATISTICS
International financial stats yrbk 1999, 177

FINNISH LANGUAGE DICTIONARIES
NTC's compact Finish & English dict, 906

FISHES
Beachcomber's gd to seashore life in the Pacific Northwest, 1331
Parasites of N American freshwater fishes, 2d ed, 1360

FISHING
Complete outdoors ency, 4th ed, 702

FITZGERALD, F. SCOTT
F. Scott Fitzgerald ency, 1011

FLAGS
Flags, 334

FLORIDA
Bibliography of Fla., v.3: 1881-99, 78
Sunshine state almanac & bk of Fla.-related stuff, 77

FLOWERS
Encyclopedia of roses, 1341
500 popular annuals & perennials for American gardeners, 1337
500 popular roses for American gardeners, 1338
Flowering plants of the Galapagos, 1342
Gardener's atlas, 1339
National Audubon Society 1st field gd: wildflowers, 1340

FOLKLORE
Dictionary & catalog of African American folklife of the south, 292
Encyclopedia of fable, 1124
Folklore from Africa to the US, repr ed, 1120
Folklore of American holidays, 3d ed, 1121
Gems in myth, legend, & lore, 1123
Travel, legend, & lore, 1122

FOOD INDUSTRY & TRADE
Food alert! the ultimate sourcebk for food safety, 1308
Food safety sourcebk, 1306
State of food & agriculture 1998, 1309
World drinks mktg dir 1999, 174
World food mktg dir 1999, 175

FOOD SCIENCES
Dictionary of Italian food & drink, 1300
Healthy cookery index, 1310
Matter of taste: a bibliogl catalogue of intl bks on food & drink in the Lilly Lib, Ind. Univ, 2d rev ed, 1299
New complete bk of food, 1307

FOOTBALL
Official natl football league 99 record & fact bk, 719
Sporting News pro football gd, 1999 ed, 720
Sporting News pro football register, 1999 ed, 721
STATS pro football hndbk 1999, 722
Superstars of the NFL, 718

FORD, JOHN
John Ford, 1151

FOREIGN RELATIONS
Legacy of the Monroe Doctrine, 422

FOREIGN STUDY
Academic yr abroad 1999-2000, 262
International exchange locator, 1998 ed, 263
Media courses UK 1999, 6th ed, 264
Peterson's summer study abroad 1999, 265

FORENSIC MEDICINE
Forensic medicine sourcebk, 1420

FORESTRY
Temperate forests, 1311

FORMER SOVIET REPUBLICS. *See also* RUSSIA
Ukraine, 99
Territories of the Russian Federation, 100

FORMER YUGOSLAV REPUBLICS. *See also* YUGOSLAVIA
Bibliography of sources on the region of Former Yugoslavia, 101
Conflict in the Former Yugoslavia, 472

FOUNDATIONS
Foundation grants index 1999, 27th ed, 745

FRACTURE MECHANICS
Fracture: a topical ency of current knowledge, 1387

FRANCE - HISTORY
Authorized press in Vichy & German-occupied France, 1940-44, 453
Historical dict of France, 455
Napoleon, 454

FREE ENTERPRISE
Dictionary of free-market econs, 124

FRENCH GUIANA
French Guiana, 108

FRENCH LANGUAGE - DICTIONARIES
Dictionary of French slang & colloquial expressions, 907

FRENCH LANGUAGE - SYNONYMS & ANTONYMS
French thesaurus for children, 908

FRENCH LITERATURE
Literature of the French & Occitan middle ages, 1038
Victor Hugo ency, 1037

FRENCH PERIODICALS
Authorized press in Vichy & German-occupied France, 1940-44, 453

FRONTIER & PIONEER LIFE
To Calif. on the southern route 1849, 403

GAELIC LANGUAGE
Etymological dict of Scottish Gaelic, 909

GALLUP POLL
Gallup poll cum index: public opinion, 1935-97, 57

GAMBLING
Going for broke: the depiction of compulsive gambling in film, 1190

GARDENING
Ball identification gd to greenhouse pests & beneficials, 1361
500 popular annuals & perennials for American gardeners, 1337
500 popular roses for American gardeners, 1338
Garden plants of China, 1336
Handy garden answer bk, 1314
Rock garden plants, 1333
Shorter dict of gardening, 1334

GARDENS
Garden lover's gd to Spain & Portugal, 388

Garden lover's gd to the Netherlands & Belgium, 378
Garden lover's gd to the Northeast, 363

GARFIELD (FICTITIOUS CHARACTER)
Merriam-Webster & Garfield dict, 889

GAYS
Almanac of women & minorities in American politics, 657
Cassell's ency of queer myth, symbol, & spirit, 1127
Historical dict of the gay liberation movement, 744

GEMS
Gems in myth, legend, & lore, 1123

GENEALOGY
County locator, 329
Finding a place called home, 333
Genealogical ency of the Colonial Americas, 325
Genealogist's address bk, 4th ed, 328
Genealogy sftwr gd, 327
Instant info on the Internet, 331
They became Americans: finding naturalization records & ethnic origins, 332

GENEALOGY - DIRECTORY
Cyndi's list: a comprehensive list of 40,000 genealogy sites on the Internet, 330
Genealogy on CD-ROM, 326

GENETICS
Encyclopedia of genetics, 1321
Genetic engineering, 1328
Genetic engineering, 1330

GEOGRAPHY
Columbia gazetteer of the world, 351
Dictionary of geography, 349
Encyclopedia of world cities, 72
Merriam-Webster's geographical dict, 3d ed, 348
National Geographic desk ref, 352
Worldmark chronology of the nations, 347

GEOLOGY
Cambridge gd to minerals, rocks, & fossils, rev ed, 1510
Geology, 1509

GERIATRICS
Physical & mental issues in aging sourcebk, 1421

GERMANY
Fodor's upclose Germany, 382
History of Germany, 458
Women under the Third Reich, 456

GOLF
Golf: the legends of the game, 723

GOVERNMENT INFORMATION
County locator, 329
Government phone bk USA 1999, 7th ed, 638

GOVERNMENT LEADERS
International dir of govt 1999, 3d ed, 620
Leadership lib on CD-ROM, fall 1998 ed, 622
World political leaders [CD-ROM], 617

GOVERNORS - UNITED STATES
Gubernatorial elections 1787-1997, 650

GRANTS-IN-AID. *See also* **FINANCIAL AID & SCHOLARSHIPS**
Directory of biomedical & health care grants 1999, 13th ed, 1400
Foundation grants index 1999, 27th ed, 745
Government assistance almanac 1999-2000, 13th ed, 751
Grants register 2000, 18th ed, 258
Grantseeker's hndbk of essential Internet sites, 1999-2000 ed, 747
Guide to grantseeking on the Web, 748
National gd to funding for libs & info servs, 5th ed, 557
Teacher's gd to winning grants, 242

GRAPHIC ARTS
Bibliography of modern art on disc [CD-ROM], 845

GRASSES
Color ency of ornamental grasses, 1312

GREAT BRITAIN
Britain: the rough gd, 2d ed, 379
Britain 1999, 50th ed, 102
Encyclopedia of Britain, 103

GREAT BRITAIN - HISTORY
Blackwell ency of Anglo-Saxon England, 466
Britain in the Hanoverian age, 1714-1837, 467
Connoisseur's gd to the bks of Sir Winston Churchill, 469
Daily life in 18th-century England, 471
Hutchinson illus ency of British hist, 468
Medieval England, 470

GREAT BRITAIN - POLITICS
Biographical dict of British prime ministers, 614
History of Parliament on CD-ROM [CD-ROM], 665

GREECE
Crete, 104
Greece, rev ed, 105
Macedonian empire, 459

GUANGDONG
Historical dict of Guangzhou (Canton) & Guangdong, 434

GUANGZHOU (CANTON)
Historical dict of Guangzhou (Canton) & Guangdong, 434

GUERRILLA WARFARE
Encyclopedia of guerrilla warfare, 599

GUITARS
Complete ency of the guitar, 1088
Gruhn's gd to vintage guitars, 2d ed, 1089

GUN CONTROL
People for & against gun control, 532

HACKETT, BOBBY
Bobby Hackett: a bio-discography, 1080

HANDICAPPED. *See* PERSONS WITH DISABILITIES

HARRY RANSOM HUMANITIES RESEARCH CENTER
Aldine press bks at the Harry Ransom Humanities Research Center, 583

HATE CRIMES
Hate crimes, 533

HAWAII
Hawaii, 367

HAZARDOUS SUBSTANCES
Book of lists for regulated hazardous substances, 9th ed, 1533
Dictionary of toxicology, 2d ed, 1477
Geniums hndbk of safety, health, & environmental data for common hazardous substances, 1384

HEALTH CARE. *See also* MEDICINE; NURSING
Health & healthcare in the US 1999, 1403
Managed care yrbk, 4th ed, 1405
Medical & health care bks & serials in print 1998, 27th ed, 1392

HEALTH CARE - DIRECTORIES
Canadian health facilities dir, 1396
Detwiler's dir of health & medical resources 1999-2000, 7th ed, 1397
National dir of managed care orgs, 2d ed, 1401
National health dir 1999, 1402

HEALTH CARE POLICY
Major health care policies 1998, 7th ed, 1399

HEALTH CARE - STATISTICS
Health care state rankings 1999, 7th ed, 1404

HEART DISEASE
Alternative medicine gd to heart disease, stroke, & high blood pressure, 1417

HELL
Encyclopedia of hell, 1126

HEMINGWAY, ERNEST
Ernest Hemingway: a documentary vol, 1012
Ernest Hemingway A to Z, 1013

HIGH TECHNOLOGY. *See also* COMPUTERS; INTERNET; TELECOMMUNICATIONS
Technology in action, 1292

HISPANIC AMERICANS
Bibliographic gd to Latin American studies 1998, 320
Hispanic-American experience on file, 324
Hispanic presence in N America from 1492 to today, updated ed, 321
Latin American lives, 322
Latin American women artists of the US, 848
New York Public Lib amazing Hispanic American hist, 323

HISPANIC AMERICANS - LITERATURE
Chicano writers, 3d series, 1003
Hispanic lit criticism suppl, 1048
Latin American lit & its times, 1042

HISTORY
Dictionary of world biog, v.3: the Renaissance, 480
Dictionary of world biog, v.4: the 17th & 18th centuries, 481
Dictionary of world biog, vols. 5 & 6: the 19th century, 482
Holidays & anniversaries of the world, 3d ed, 1133
Life millennium, 46

HISTORY - AMERICAN
American civil rights: almanac, 398
American immigration, 419
American scene: events, 405
American settlement houses & progressive social reform, 411
American settlement movement, 401
American social issues [CD-ROM], 410
American yrs, 407
Colonial America to 1763, 399
Encyclopedia of North American hist, 490
Events that shaped the century, 406
Leaders of the American Civil War, 597
Notable women in American hist, 789
ResourceLink: 20th-century American hist [CD-ROM], 408
Violence in America, 734
Watergate crisis, 423

HISTORY - ANCIENT
Daily life of the ancient Egyptians, 475
Women's roles in ancient civilizations, 804

HISTORY - BRITISH
Connoisseur's gd to the bks of Sir Winston Churchill, 469
Daily life in 18th-century England, 471
Encyclopedia of Britain, 103
Historical dict of the Elizabethan world, 499
Hutchinson illus ency of British hist, 468
Medieval England, 470

HISTORY - CANADIAN
W. L. Mackenzie King, 444

HISTORY - CHINESE
China during the cultural revolution, 1966-76, 433
Dictionary of contemporary Chinese military hist, 435
Historical dict of Guangzhou (Canton) & Guangdong, 434

HISTORY - DUTCH
History of Holland, 452

HISTORY - EASTERN EUROPEAN
Historical dict of Slovakia, 464
Historical dict of the Federal Republic of Yugoslavia, 473

HISTORY - EUROPEAN
Chronological hist of the European Union 1946-98, 448
Historical dict of the Elizabethan world, 499
Hutchinson ency of the Renaissance, 446
World War II in Europe, 602

HISTORY - FRENCH
Historical dict of France, 455

HISTORY - GERMAN
Unification of Germany, 1989-90, 457

HISTORY - HOLLAND
History of Holland, 452

HISTORY - IRISH
Historical dict of the Elizabethan world, 499

HISTORY - JAPANESE
Columbia gd to modern Japanese hist, 436
Historical dict of Osaka & Kyoto, 438
History of Japan, 437

HISTORY - MEXICAN
Encyclopedia of the Mexican-American war, 412

HISTORY- MODERN
Founding leaders [CD-ROM], 483

HISTORY - RUSSIA
History of Russia, 463

HISTORY - SPANISH
History of Spain, 465

HISTORY - WORLD
Daily life through hist [CD-ROM], 501
Dictionary of wars, rev ed, 495
Dictionary of world biog: the 20th century, 479
Encyclopedia of genocide, 732
Historical dict of the cooperative movement, 498
On this day in hist, 1136
Oxford ency of world hist, 496
Twentieth century world, 511

HOCKEY
Sporting News hockey gd, 1999-2000 ed, 724
Sporting News hockey register, 1999-2000 ed, 725
Total hockey, 726

HOLIDAYS
Festivals & holidays, 1132
Folklore of American holidays, 3d ed, 1121
Holidays & anniversaries of the world, 3d ed, 1133
Let's celebrate today: calendars, events, & holidays, 1134

HOLLAND - HISTORY
History of Holland, 452

HOLMES, SHERLOCK (FICTITIOUS CHARACTER)
Bedside, bathtub, & armchair companion to Sherlock Holmes, 982

HOLOCAUST, JEWISH (1939-1945)
Encyclopedia of genocide, 732
Historical dict of the Holocaust, 493
Holocaust: memories, research, ref, 507
Rescue & resistance: portraits of the Holocaust, 485

HOMOPHONES & HOMOGRAPHS
Homophones & homographs, 3d ed, 888

HORROR FILMS
Count Dracula goes to the movies, 1177
Of gods & monsters, 1186
Women in horror films, 1156

HORROR LITERATURE
Fantasy & horror, 988
Hooked on horror, 989

HOSPITALITY INDUSTRY
Dun & Bradstreet/Gale industry ref hndbks: hospitality, 160

HOSPITAL SHIPS
Hospital ships of WW II, 613

HOUSING
Housing stats of the US, 2d ed, 780

HUGHES, TED
Ted Hughes: a bibliog, 1946-95, 2d ed, 1057

HUGO, VICTOR
Victor Hugo ency, 1037

HUMAN EMOTION
Encyclopedia of human emotions, 685

HUMANITIES
Money for grad students in the humanities 1998-2000, 2d ed, 248
Walford's gd to ref material, v.3, 7th ed, 807

HUMAN REPRODUCTION
Encyclopedia of reproductive technologies, 1437

HUMAN RIGHTS
Dictionary of human rights advocacy orgs in Africa, 548
Encyclopedia of human rights issues since 1945, 546
Human rights, 545
Human rights, 2d ed, 547
Sexual harassment in America, 550

HUNTING
Complete outdoors ency, 4th ed, 702

ILLINOIS
ResourceLink Ill. [CD-ROM], 79

IMMIGRATION. *See also* **EMIGRATION & IMMIGRATION**
American immigration, 419
Shapers of the great debate on immigration, 675

IMPEACHMENTS
Impeachable offenses, 664

INCAS
Incas, 504

INCUNABULA
Aldine press bks at the Harry Ransom Humanities Research Center, 583

INDEPENDENT FILMS
VideoHound's independent film gd, 2d ed, 1169

INDEXES
Complete index to literary sources in film, 1194
Gallup poll cum index: public opinion, 1935-97, 57

Index gd to college jls, 53
Index to CD & record reviews 1987-97, 1077
Science fiction mag story index, 1926-95, 991
Wellesley index to Victorian pers 1824-1900, new ed, 49
Women's studies index 1997, 805

INDIA
Insight gd: India, 375
Women in India, 803

INDIA - FILM
Encyclopaedia of Indian cinema, rev ed, 1164

INDIAN ARTISTS
Guide to Native American ledger drawings & pictographs in US museums, libs, & archives, 314
Native American Indian artist dir, 853

INDIANS OF NORTH AMERICA
American Indian biogs, 304
British museum ency of native North America, 306
Daily life of the Aztecs, 313
Dine bibliog to the 1990s, 301
Encyclopedia of Native American economic hist, 305
Encyclopedia of Native American Shamanism, 308
Encyclopedia of Native American tribes, rev ed, 311
Guide to Native American ledger drawings & pictographs in US museums, libs, & archives, 314
Kickapoo Indians, their hist & culture, 303
Macmillan ency of Native American tribes, 2d ed, 307
Native America today, 315
Native N American Shamanism, 302
Tuscarora-English/English-Tuscarora dict, 309
U*X*L ency of Native American tribes, 310

INDIANS OF NORTH AMERICA - FINANCIAL AID
National dir of fndn grants for Native Americans, 312

INDIANS OF NORTH AMERICA - LITERATURE
Native American lits, 1005

INDIANS OF SOUTH AMERICA
Incas, 504

INDUSTRIAL SAFETY
Environmental health, & safety portable hndbk, 1385

INDUSTRY
American wholesalers & distrs dir, 7th ed, 156
Consumer sourcebk, 12th ed, 145
Encyclopedia of emerging industries, 153
Handbook of North American industry, 2d ed, 161
How products are made, v.4, 162
International yrbk of industrial stats 1998, 179
Manufacturing worldwide, 3d ed, 163
Market share reporter, 2000, 164

Top 5,000 European cos 1999/2000, 134
US business dir, 1999, 135
WEFA industrial monitor 1999-2000, 165
World retail data & stats 1999, 185

INFORMATION LITERACY
Information literacy, 568

INFORMATION SCIENCE
Annual review of info sci & tech, v.33, 1998, 559
Library systems: current dvlpmts & future directions, 565

INFORMATION SERVICES
African American info dir 1998-99, 4th ed, 35

INFORMATION TECHNOLOGY
Global info systems & tech, 569
Information systems innovation & diffusion, 570
Plunkett's InfoTech industry almanac 1999-2000, 1456

INSECTS
Ball identification gd to greenhouse pests & beneficials, 1361
Butterflies of Canada, 1364
Identifying British insects & arachnids, 1363
Secret worlds, 1352
World catalogue for the spider mite family, 1362

INSURANCE
International dict of insurance & finance, lib ed, 167

INTELLIGENCE SERVICE
Intelligence, espionage, & related topics, 594

INTERCULTURAL COMMUNICATION
Culturgrams: the nations around us, 64

INTERNATIONAL AGENCIES
Historical dict of intl orgs, 497
International dir of govt 1999, 3d ed, 620

INTERNATIONAL BUSINESS
Consumer Latin America 1999, 6th ed, 190
Directory of consumer brands & their owners 1998, 170
European mktg data & stats 1999, 34th ed, 188
European regional incentives 1999, 18th ed, 189
Exchange arrangements & exchange restrictions 1998, 176
International ency of the stock market, 169
International mktg data & stats 1999, 23d ed, 178
International yrbk of industrial stats 1998, 179
Jane's world defense industry, 603
Pocket world in figures 1999, 772
Scott's dirs 1999, 6th ed, 187
Washington almanac of intl trade & business, 1998, 181
WEFA industrial monitor 1999-2000, 165

World cosmetics & toiletries dir 1999, 173
World dvlpmt indicators, 1998, 182
World drinks mktg dir 1999, 174
World economic factbk 1998/99, 6th ed, 183
World food mktg dir 1999, 175
World investment report 1999, 184
World retail data & stats 1999, 185

INTERNATIONAL EDUCATION
International exchange locator, 1998 ed, 263

INTERNATIONAL MONETARY FUND
Balance of payments stats yrbks 1998, 770
Historical dict of the intl monetary fund, 2d ed, 671

INTERNATIONAL ORGANIZATIONS
Europa dir of intl orgs, 670

INTERNATIONAL RELATIONS
Encyclopedia of conflicts since WW II, 672
Encyclopedia of intl peacekeeping operations, 673
SIPRI yrbk 1998, 607
US foreign relations with the Middle East & N Africa, 674

INTERNATIONAL SPACE STATION
Who's who in space, 1507

INTERNATIONAL TRADE
Dictionary of intl trade hndbk, 3d ed, 168
Direction of trade stats yrbk, 1998, 210
European regional incentives 1999, 18th ed, 189
Handbook of intl trade & dvlpmt stats 1996/97, 212
Least developed countries 1998 report, 68
Trade & dvlpmt report 1998, 180
World mktg forecasts 1999 on CD-ROM, 2d ed [CD-ROM], 215

INTERNET (COMPUTER NETWORK)
Find it online, 2d ed, 1465
Fulltext sources online, Jan 1999, 39
History of the Internet, 1462
Multimedia & the Web from A to Z, 2d ed, 1455

INTERNET BOOKS (COMPUTER NETWORK) - BIBLIOGRAPHY
Internet bks for educators, parents, & students, 1464

INTERNET (COMPUTER NETWORK) - DIRECTORIES
Automotive Web sites, 1543
Career exploration on the Internet, 192
Chemical gd to the Internet, 2d ed, 1484
Cyndi's list: a comprehensive list of 40,000 genealogy sites on the Internet, 330
Directory of Web sites, 1460
Great American Websites, 76

Guide to grantseeking on the Web, 748
How to access the fed govt on the Internet, 4th ed, 623
Incredible Internet gd to Star Wars, 1466
Instant info on the Internet, 331
Internet blue pages, 1999 ed, 636
Internet kids & family yellow pages, 3d ed, 1463
Internet resource dir for K-12 teachers & librarians, 1999/2000 ed, 230
Online kids: a young surfer's gd to cyberspace, rev ed, 1461
Philosopher's phone & e-mail dir 1998/99, 1220
Plunkett's employer's Internet sites with careers info, 1999-2000, 203
State environmental agencies on the Internet, 1532
Telecommunications gd to the Internet, 1469
Uncle Sam's K-12 Web, 229
US govt on the Web, 619
World dir of business info Websites, 137
Writing research papers, 2d ed, 816

INVENTORS
Scientists, mathematicians, & inventors, 1280

INVESTMENTS
CRB commodity yrbk 1998, 141
Directory of alternative investment programs, 1998 ed, 142
Directory of venture capital firms, 2000, 4th ed, 150
Pocket investor, 143

IRISH LANGUAGE DICTIONARIES
Irish-English, English-Irish easy ref dict, 910

ISLAM
Bibliography of Islamic philosophy, 1269
Golden age of Islam, 503

ISLAMIC COUNTRIES
Muslim Diaspora, 1270

ISRAEL
Insight gd: Israel, 391
Kid's catalog of Israel, rev ed, 317

ISTANBUL (TURKEY)
Istanbul, 392

ITALIAN LANGUAGE - DICTIONARIES
Dictionary of Italian slang & colloquial expressions, 911

ITALIAN LITERATURE
Ancient Roman writers, 1040
Italian novelists since WW II, 1965-95, 1041

ITALY
Dictionary of Italian food & drink, 1300
Naples with Pompeii & the Amalfi coast, 386
Sardinia, 387

ITALY - HISTORY
Historical dict of modern Italy, 460
Hutchinson ency of the Renaissance, 446

JAPAN
Culture & customs of Japan, 89
Insight gd: Japan, 3d ed, 376
Tokyo, 88

JAPAN - ECONOMIC POLICY
MIT ency of the Japanese economy, 2d ed, 125

JAPAN - HISTORY
Columbia gd to modern Japanese hist, 436
Historical dict of Osaka & Kyoto, 438
History of Japan, 437
Japanese baseball, 707

JAPANESE LANGUAGE DICTIONARIES
Business kanji, 913
Compact Nelson Japanese-English character dict, 912

JAZZ MUSICIANS
Bobby Hackett: a bio-discography, 1080
Duke Ellington, 1082
Jazz profiles, 1101

JEHOVAH'S WITNESSES
Jehovah's witnesses, 1257

JESUS PEOPLE
Jesus people movement, 1258

JEWISH PHILOSOPHY
Every person's gd to Jewish philosophy & philosophers, 1223

JEWS
American Jewish desk ref, 316
Shengold Jewish ency, 319
Soviet Jewish Americans, 318

JOB-HUNTING. *See* CAREERS

JOHANNESBURG (SOUTH AFRICA)
Historical dict of Greater Johannesburg, 429

JOURNALISM. *See also* COMMUNICATIONS; MASS MEDIA; NEWSPAPERS
Power of the press, 809

JUDAISM
Historical dict of Judaism, 1271
Kid's catalog of Israel, rev ed, 317

KELLY, GEORGE
George Kelly: a research & production sourcebk, 1142

KICKAPOO INDIANS
Kickapoo Indians, their hist & culture, 303

KING, CAROLE
Carole King, 1084

KING, W. L. MACKENZIE
W. L. Mackenzie King, 444

KINGS
Kings & queens, 484

KOREA - HISTORY
Conflict in Korea, 439

KOREAN LANGUAGE DICTIONARIES
NTC's dict of Korea's business & cultural code words, 186

KOREAN WAR, 1950-1953
Conflict in Korea, 439
Korean conflict, 508

KUSH
Ancient African kingdom of Kush, 506

KYOTO (JAPAN)
Historical dict of Osaka & Kyoto, 438

LABOR
Handbook of US labor stats 1999, 3d ed, 206
Lexicon of labor, 202
Workers Compensation, 207

LABORATORIES
International dir of testing labs, 1999 ed, 1290

LANDSCAPE PROTECTION
U.S. landscape ordinances, 541

LANDSCAPES
Landscapes in hist, 2d ed, 1313

LANGUAGE & LANGUAGES
Dictionary of langs, 870
Encyclopedia of lang & educ, 872
Key concepts in lang & linguistics, 875
Manual of European langs for librarians, 2d ed, 901
Walford's gd to ref material, v.3, 7th ed, 807
World in so many words, 873

LAS PEOPLE'S DEMOCRATIC REPUBLIC
Demographic perspective on women in dvlpmt in Cambodia ..., 759

LATIN AMERICA. *See also* **CENTRAL AMERICA**
Census records for Latin America & the Hispanic US, 760
Culture & customs of Colombia, 111
Economic survey of Latin America & the Caribbean 1997-98, 50th ed, 191

LAW
ABCs of environmental regulation, 544
Great American court cases, 523
Landmark Supreme Court cases, 525
Laws of the US: corps, 529
Philosophy of law, 515
US court cases, 531
Want's fed-state court dir, 1999 cd, 519

LAW - DICTIONARIES
Burton's legal thesaurus, 3d ed, 513
Dictionary of law, 2d ed, 514
New Palgrave dict of economics & the law, 126

LAW - DIRECTORIES
Directory of law-related CD-ROMs 1999, 517
Law firms yellow bk, summer 1998 ed, 518

LAW ENFORCEMENT
Role of police in American society, 540

LAW - HANDBOOKS & YEARBOOKS
American law yrbk 1998, 520
Constitutional rights sourcebk, 528
Death penalty, 527
Layperson's gd to criminal law, 538
New York legal research gd, 2d ed, 522
Supreme Court yrbk 1997-98, 524

LAW SCHOOLS
Law firms yellow bk, summer 1998 ed, 518

LEARNING DISABLED YOUTH
Students in discord, 692

LEGAL RESEARCH
Legal info: how to find it, how to use it, 526

LEGISLATORS - UNITED STATES
American legislative leaders in the South, 1911-94, 628
Texas legislative almanac 1999, 627

LEXICOGRAPHY
Dictionary of lexicography, 584

LIBRARIES
Aslib dir of info sources in the UK, 10th ed, 555
Bowker annual lib & bk trade almanac 1999, 44th ed, 560
Directory of special libs & info centers, 23d ed, 556
Information landscapes for a learning society, 566
International research centers dir 1999, 11th ed, 41
World gd to libs, 14th ed, 558

LIBRARIES - ARAB COUNTRIES
Libraries & info in the Arab world, 553

LIBRARIES - BIBLIOGRAPHIES
International bibliog of bibliogs in lib & info sci & related fields, 552

LIBRARIES - COLLECTION DEVELOPMENT
Choice's outstanding academic bks 1992-97, 551

LIBRARIES - FUNDRAISING
National gd to funding for libs & info servs, 5th ed, 557

LIBRARY ARCHIVES
Encoded archival description, 563
Encoded archival description tag lib version 1.0, 564

LIBRARY AUTOMATION
Library systems: current dvlpmts & future directions, 565

LIBRARY CATALOGING
Encoded archival description, 563
Encoded archival description tag lib version 1.0, 564

LIBRARY MANAGEMENT
Charging & collecting fees & fines, 572
Managing overdues, 571
SOLO librarian's sourcebk, 573

LINCOLN, ABRAHAM
Abraham Lincoln on screen, 1182

LINGUISTICS
Key concepts in lang & linguistics, 875

LITERACY
Encyclopedia of lang & educ, 872
Information literacy, 568

LITERARY AWARDS
Complete gd to literary contests 1999, 812

LITERARY TERMS
Contemporary composition studies, 939
Dictionary of literary & thematic terms, 936
Merriam-Webster's dict of allusions, 934
Multicultural dict of literary terms, 930

LITERATURE
Comparative reader, 921
Complete index to literary sources in film, 1194
Masterplots complete CD-ROM, 1999 ed [CD-ROM], 946

LITERATURE - BIBLIOGRAPHY
Hooked on horror, 989
Now read this: a gd to mainstream fiction, 1978-98, 977
Reference gd to mystery & detective fiction, 979
Sequels in children's lit, 947
Valerie & Walter's best bks for children, 953
What do I read next? 1998, 975

LITERATURE - BIO-BIBLIOGRAPHY
Ancient Roman writers, 1040
Contemporary African American novelists, 997
Contemporary authors, v.168, 925
Contemporary authors, v.169, 926
Contemporary authors, v.170, 927
Contemporary authors, v.171, 928
Ernest Hemingway: a documentary vol, 1012
Russian lit in the age of Pushkin & Gogol: poetry & drama, 1045
Sir Walter Scott: a bibliogl hist 1796-1832, 1047
Twentieth-century American western writers, 1st series, 1000

LITERATURE - BIO-BIBLIOGRAPHY - JUVENILE LITERATURE
Best bks for children, 6th ed, 948
100 most popular children's authors, 957
Outstanding bks for children & young people, 963
Something about the author, v.99, 959
Something about the author, v.102, 960
Something about the author, v.103, 961
Something about the author, v.104, 962

LITERATURE - BIOGRAPHY
British novelists since 1960, 3d series, 1019
British travel writers, 1940-97, 1020
Chicano writers, 3d series, 1003
Encyclopedia of British women writers, rev ed, 1021
Native American lits, 1005

LITERATURE - DICTIONARIES & ENCYCLOPEDIAS
Contemporary composition studies, 939
Encyclopedia of American lit, 1004
Encyclopedia of world lit in the 20th century, 3d ed, 932
Merriam-Webster's dict of allusions, 934
Multicultural dict of literary terms, 930
MUP ency of Australian sci fiction & fantasy, 1034

LITERATURE - ENGLISH
ABELL: annual bib of English lang & lit 1920-95 [CD-ROM], 920
Arthurian fiction, 967
Arthurian name dict, 1023
British novelists since 1960, 3d series, 1019
British travel writers, 1940-97, 1020
Comprehensive Shakespeare dict [CD-ROM], 1027
Encyclopedia of British women writers, rev ed, 1021
Late Victorian & Edwardian British novelists, 2d series, 1022

Persons, animals, ships, & cannon in the Aubrey-Maturin sea novels of Patrick O'Brian, 1026
Shakespearean criticism, v.43, 1029
Shakespearean criticism, v.44, 1030
Shakespearean criticism, v.45, 1031
Who's who in Shakespeare's England, 1028
World Shakespeare bibliog on CD-ROM, 1983-95 [CD-ROM], 1032

LITERATURE - FICTION
American histl fiction, 983
American mystery & detective novels, 980
Arthurian fiction, 967
Children's fiction 1900-50, 950
Critical companion to popular contemporary writers, 1999 ed [CD-ROM], 976
Encyclopedia of murder & mystery, 981
Fantasy & horror, 988
Fluent in fantasy: a gd to reading interests, 990
Hooked on horror, 989
Nineteenth-century American fiction writers, 999
North American romance writers, 986
Novels for students, v.6, 968
Now read this: a gd to mainstream fiction, 1978-98, 977
Reference gd to mystery & detective fiction, 979
Romance fiction, 987
Science fiction writers, 2d ed, 992
Short stories for students, v.6, 969
Short story criticism, v.30, 994
Twentieth-century short story explication: new series, v.4, 1995-96, 993
What do I read next? 1998, 975
Whole story: 3000 yrs of sequels & sequences, 2d ed, 978
World histl fiction, 984

LITERATURE - FRENCH
Literature of the French & Occitan middle ages, 1038
Victor Hugo ency, 1037

LITERATURE - HISTORY & CRITICISM
Contemporary composition studies, 939
Contemporary literary criticism, v.110, 940
Contemporary literary criticism, v.111, 941
Contemporary literary criticism, v.113, 942
Encyclopedia of literary critics & criticism, 931

LITERATURE - INDEXES
Complete index to literary sources in film, 1194
Twentieth-century short story explication: new series, v.4, 1995-96, 993
Wellesley index to Victorian pers 1824-1900, new ed, 49

LITERATURE - LATIN AMERICAN
Chicano writers, 3d series, 1003
Hispanic lit criticism suppl, 1048
Latin American lit & its times, 1042

LITERATURE - MODERN
Contemporary literary criticism, v.114, 943
Contemporary literary criticism, v.116, 944
Contemporary literary criticism, v.117, 945
Contemporary Southern writers, 998
Major 20th-century writers, 2d ed, 929

LITERATURE - MYSTERY
Encyclopedia of murder & mystery, 981
Reference gd to mystery & detective fiction, 979

LITERATURE - NEW ZEALAND
New Zealand bks in print 1999, 1035
Oxford companion to New Zealand lit, 1036

LITERATURE - PROTEST
Social protest lit, 935

LITERATURE - ROMANCE
Classic love & romance lit, 985
Romance fiction, 987

LITHUANIA
Lithuanian publishers dir, 590

LOCAL ELECTIONS - UNITED STATES
Local govt election practices, 654

LOCAL LAWS
Directory of state court clerks & county courthouses, 1999 ed, 516
State govt 1998-99, 661

LOUISIANA
Baldwin's gd to museums of La., 362

MACEDONIA - HISTORY
Macedonian empire, 459

MAFIA
Mafia ency, 2d ed, 417

MAMMALS. *See also* ANIMALS
Animals, 1351
Mammals of Madagascar, 1366
Mammals of N America, 1365
Walker's mammals of the world, 6th ed, 1367

MANNERS & CUSTOMS
Culturgrams: the nations around us, 64

MANUFACTURERS
American manufacturers dir, 1999, 154
American manufacturers disc, 2d ed [CD-ROM], 155
Brands & their cos, 18th ed, 157
Companies & their brands, 18th ed, 158

Directory of contract electronics manufacturers, 1999, 159
Manufacturing worldwide, 3d ed, 163
Top 5,000 European cos 1999/2000, 134

MANUFACTURING
Handbook of North American industry, 2d ed, 161
How products are made, v.4, 162
Market share reporter, 2000, 164

MANUZIO FAMILY
Aldine press bks at the Harry Ransom Humanities Research Center, 583

MAPS
Bibliographic gd to maps & atlases 1998, 343
Southeast in early maps, 3d ed, 337

MARINE ANIMALS
Encyclopedia of sharks, 1369
Manatees & dugongs of the world, 1371
Sharks, 2d ed, 1372
Sharks & rays of the world, 1370
Whales, dolphins, & porpoises, 2d ed, 1374
Whales of the W coast, 1373
Whelks to whales: coastal marine life of the Pacific Northwest, 1368

MARKETING
Consumer USA 1999, 4th ed, 209
European mktg data & stats 1999, 34th ed, 188
International mktg data & stats 1999, 23d ed, 178
Major mktg campaigns annual 1998, 213
World cosmetics & toiletries dir 1999, 173
World drinks mktg dir 1999, 174
World food mktg dir 1999, 175
World mktg forecasts 1999 on CD-ROM, 2d ed [CD-ROM], 215

MASON, JAMES
James Mason: a bio-bibliog, 1154

MASS MEDIA. *See also* **COMMUNICATIONS**
Bacon's media source [CD-ROM], 808

MATERIALS SCIENCE
ASM hndbk, v.7, 1386
Building materials, 1390
Fracture: a topical ency of current knowledge, 1387
Illustrated dict of metalworking & manufacturing tech, 1388
Metals hndbk, desk ed, 2d ed, 1389

MATHEMATICAL ASSOCIATION OF AMERICA
Combined membership list 1998-99, 1522

MATHEMATICIANS
Biographical ency of mathematicians, 1520
Combined membership list 1998-99, 1522
Math & mathematicians, 1521
Scientists, mathematicians, & inventors, 1280

MATHEMATICS
Assistantships & graduate fellowships in the mathematical scis, 1999-2000, 1519
CRC concise ency of math, 1523
Dictionary of mathematical quotations, 1525
Illustrated dict of nonlinear dynamics & chaos, 1524
Math & mathematicians, 1521
Wonderful world of mathematics, 2d ed, 956

MAYBERRY R.F.D.
Guide to TV's Mayberry R.F.D., 1191

MEDIA PROGRAMS
Media courses UK 1999, 6th ed, 264

MEDICAL EDUCATION
Graduate medical educ dir 1999/2000, 84th ed, 1398

MEDICAL ETHICS
Sourcebk in bioethics, 1409

MEDICAL LICENSURE
U.S. medical licensure stats & requirements by state, 1998-99 ed, 1410

MEDICAL SERVICES
Managed care yrbk, 4th ed, 1405
National dir of managed care orgs, 2d ed, 1401

MEDICAL TESTS
Medical tests sourcebk, 1407

MEDICARE
Mercer gd to social security & Medicare 1998, 26th ed, 752

MEDICINE. *See also* **HEALTH CARE**
Forensic medicine sourcebk, 1420
Medical tests sourcebk, 1407
Merck manual of medical info, home ed, 1406
Socioeconomic characteristics of medical practice 1997, 1408

MEDICINE - DICTIONARIES & ENCYCLOPEDIAS
Ayurveda ency, 1419
Encyclopedia of controlled drug delivery, 1447
Encyclopedia of reproductive technologies, 1437
Family ency of health, 1395
Gale ency of medicine, 1413

MEDICINE - DIRECTORIES
Directory of biomedical & health care grants 1999, 13th ed, 1400
Older Americans info dir, 1999, 2d ed, 735
PDR generics 1998, 4th ed, 1453

MEDICINE - GERIATRICS
Older Americans info dir, 1999, 2d ed, 735
Physical & mental issues in aging sourcebk, 1421

MEDICINE - PEDIATRICS
American Academy of Pediatrics gd to your child's nutrition, 1422
Catalog of prenatally diagnosed conditions, 3d ed, 1426
Children's health, 1423
Pediatric cancer sourcebk, 1424
3 a.m. hndbk: the most commonly asked questions about your child's health, 1425

MEDICINE - POPULAR
Alzheimer's disease sourcebk, 2d ed, 1430
Blood & circulatory disorders sourcebk, 1431
Brain disorders sourcebk, 1432
Consumer issues in health care sourcebk, 1411
Diabetes sourcebk, 2d ed, 1434
Eating disorders, 2d, 1435
Endocrine & metabolic disorders sourcebk, 1436
Man's health sourcebk, 2d ed, 1412
Men's health concerns sourcebk, 1414
Skin sourcebk, 1439
Sleep disorders sourcebk, 1440
Sports injuries sourcebk, 1441

MEDICINE - VOCATIONAL GUIDANCE
America's top medical, educ, & human servs jobs, 4th ed, 198

MEN'S HEALTH
Man's health sourcebk, 2d ed, 1412
Men's health concerns sourcebk, 1414

MENTALLY HANDICAPPED YOUTH
Students in discord, 692

METALS
ASM hndbk, v.7, 1386
Illustrated dict of metalworking & manufacturing tech, 1388
Metals hndbk, desk ed, 2d ed, 1389

METEOROLOGY. *See also* WEATHER
Guide to field gds, 1349
Weather hndbk, 2d ed, 1508

MEXICAN-AMERICAN WAR, 1846-1848
Encyclopedia of the Mexican-American war, 412

MEXICO
Bird-finding gd to Mexico, 1356
Mexico 2000, 390

MICROFORMS
Guide to microforms in print 1998, 5

MIDDLE AGES IN MOTION PICTURES
Reel Middle Ages, 1176

MIDDLE EAST
Istanbul, 392
Political ency of the Middle East, 666
US foreign relations with the Middle East & N Africa, 674

MIDDLE EAST - BIBLIOGRAPHY
United Arab Emirates, 112

MIDDLE EASTERN LITERATURE
Modern Arabic lit, 1043

MILITARY AIRCRAFT
Aircraft of the US military air transport serv 1948-66, 609
Warbirds, 611

MILITARY BATTLES
Hutchinson atlas of battle plans, 593

MILITARY - BIOGRAPHY
Almanac of WW I, 397
American military leaders, 596
American military leaders [CD-ROM], 595
Leaders of the American Civil War, 597

MILITARY CONTRACTS
Jane's Naval construction & retrofit markets, 610

MILITARY CRIMINAL LAW
Guide to military criminal law, 604

MILITARY STUDIES
America at war, 598
Dictionary of contemporary Chinese military hist, 435
Encyclopedia of warrior peoples & fighting groups, 600
Historical dict of the American Revolution, 415
MIAs: a ref hndbk, 606
SIPRI yrbk 1998, 607
War & American popular culture, 1140

MILITARY WEAPONS
Jane's market intelligence lib [CD-ROM], 612
Jane's world defense industry, 603

MINEROLOGY
Cambridge gd to minerals, rocks, & fossils, rev ed, 1510
Gems in myth, legend, & lore, 1123

MINNESOTA
Minnesota gd, 368

MINORITIES. *See also* ETHNIC GROUPS
Almanac of women & minorities in American politics, 657
Macmillan ency of Native American tribes, 2d ed, 307

MINOR LEAGUE BASEBALL
Bill James presents ... STATS minor league hndbk 1999, 8th ed, 704

MISSOURI
Dictionary of Mo. biog, 18

MONETARY EXCHANGE
Exchange arrangements & exchange restrictions 1998, 176

MONEY. *See also* COINS
Encyclopedia of money, 148

MONROE, MARILYN
Marilyn ency, 1139

MOTION PICTURE ACTORS & ACTRESSES. *See also* ACTORS
Charles Bronson, 1152
Francis X. Bushman, 1157
Humphrey Bogart, 1150
James Mason: a bio-bibliog, 1154
John Carradine, 1158
Ultimate dir of silent & sound era performers, 1149
Women & American TV, 1162
Women in horror films, 1156

MOTION PICTURE INDUSTRY
Balboa films, 1178
Cinematographers production designers, costume designers, & film editors gd 1998, 1166
Universal silents, 1173

MOTION PICTURES. *See also* SILENT FILMS
Abraham Lincoln on screen, 1182
American film cycles, 1192
AV market place 1999, 823
BFI companion to crime, 1172
BFI film & TV hndbk 1999, 1188
Charles Bronson, 1152
Complete index to literary sources in film, 1194
Complete index to world film since 1895 on CD-ROM [CD-ROM], 1195
Contemporary theatre, film, & TV, v.22, 1141
Count Dracula goes to the movies, 1177
Director's vision, 1171
Encyclopedia of animated cartoons, 2d ed, 1161
Feature films, 1950-59, 1174
Film & the American left, 1189
Film ency, 1160
Francis X. Bushman, 1157
Going for broke: the depiction of compulsive gambling in film, 1190
Greek filmography, 1914-96, 1180
Guide to the silent yrs of American cinema, 1163
Hollywood stunt performers, 1175
Jules Verne on film, 1183
Motion picture gd 1999, 1168
Of gods & monsters, 1186
Our Sunday Visitor's family gd to movies & videos, 1199
Reel Middle Ages, 1176
Robin Hood, 1193
Silent films, 1877-1976, 1179
Stranger than paradise: maverick film-makers in recent American cinema, 1155
TLA film & video gd, 1187
Ultimate dict of film technicians, 1167
Ultimate dir of silent & sound era performers, 1149
VideoHound's epics, 1200
VideoHound's golden movie retriever 1999, 1201
VideoHound's independent film gd, 2d ed, 1169
VideoHound's war movies, 1198
VideoHound's world cinema, 1202
Western gunslingers in fact & on film, 1153
Western movie quotations, 1196

MOTION PICTURES & LITERATURE
Poe cinema, 1185

MOTION PICTURES - AFRICA
Guide to African cinema, 1184

MOTION PICTURES - CHINA
Encyclopedia of Chinese film, 1165

MOTION PICTURES - INDIA
Encyclopaedia of Indian cinema, rev ed, 1164

MOTION PICTURES - POLITICAL ASPECTS
Film & the American left, 1189

MOTION PICTURES - PRODUCTION & DIRECTION
Cinematographers production designers, costume designers, & film editors gd 1998, 1166
John Ford, 1151

MOTION PICTURES - REVIEWS
Charles Bronson, 1152
TLA film & video gd, 1187
VideoHound's epics, 1200

VideoHound's golden movie retriever 1999, 1201
VideoHound's war movies, 1198
VideoHound's world cinema, 1202

MOTION PICTURES - SERIALS
Serials & series, 1181

MOTORCYCLES
Complete motorcycle bk, 2d ed, 1541

MULTICULTURAL EDUCATION
Encyclopedia of bilingualism & bilingual educ, 219
Encyclopedia of multicultural educ, 221

MULTIMEDIA - CAREERS
Career opportunities in TV, cable, video, & multimedia, 4th ed, 193

MULTIMEDIA SYSTEMS
Multimedia & the Web from A to Z, 2d ed, 1455

MUNICIPAL GOVERNMENT
Compensation 98, v.16, 642
Managing America's cities, 653

MUSEUMS
Baldwin's gd to museums of La., 362
On exhibit 1999: art lover's travel gd to American museums, 374

MUSIC. *See also* **COMPOSERS; SONGS**
Bibliographic gd to music 1998, 1059
Classical music: the rough gd, 2d ed, 1097
Hutchinson concise dict of music, 1068
Index to CD & record reviews 1987-97, 1077
MGM labels, 1073
Modern twang: an alternative country music gd & dir, 1098
Reader's gd to music, hist, theory, criticism, 1071
Schwann opus, winter 1997-99: ref gd to classical music, 1076

MUSIC - AUSTRALIA
Dictionary of Australian music, 1067

MUSIC - BIBLIOGRAPHIES
Alfred Reed, 1081
Comprehensive catalogue of duet lit for female voices, 1060
Sinatra: an annot bibliog, 1939-98, 1083

MUSIC - BIOGRAPHIES
Another song to sing: the recorded repertoire of Johnny Cash, 1086
Black women in American bands & orchestras, 2d ed, 1061
Blues singers, 1093
Carole King, 1084
Duke Ellington, 1082
Elvis Costello, 1085
Jazz profiles, 1101
Jimmy Dorsey: a study in contrasts, 1087
Popular musicians, 1115
Rockin' '60s: the people who made the music, 1111

MUSIC - CHORAL
Choral music in 19th-century America, 1096
Varied carols, 1095

MUSIC - DICTIONARIES
Musical terminology, 1065

MUSIC - DIRECTORIES
Schwann Spectrum: the gd to rock, jazz, world...& beyond, 1072

MUSIC - HISTORY
Reader's gd to music, hist, theory, criticism, 1071
Spreadin' rhythm around: black popular songwriters, 1880-1930, 1062

MUSIC - INDEXES
Index to African-American spirituals for the solo voice, 1119
SongCite: an index to popular songs, suppl 1, 1078

MUSIC INDUSTRY
More EJS: discography of the Edward J. Smith recordings, 1106

MUSIC - IRISH
Companion to Irish traditional music, 1066

MUSIC - LATIN AMERICAN
Billboard gd to tejano & regional Mexican music, 1110

MUSIC - OPERA
Chronicle of opera, 1105
More EJS: discography of the Edward J. Smith recordings, 1106
Opera: the rough gd, 2d ed, 1103
Opera singers in recital, concert, & feature film, 1102
Opera cos & houses of W Europe, Canada, Australia, & New Zealand, 1107
Operas in English, 1104

MUSIC - ORCHESTRAL
Appraisals of original wind music, 1108

MUSIC - POPULAR
Joel Whitburn presents a century of pop music, 1074
Joel Whitburn presents Billboard top 10 album charts 1963-98, 1112
Joel Whitburn's 1998 Billboard music yrbk, 1117

Music USA, 1116
Popular music, v.23, 1114
Popular musicians, 1115
Rockin' '60s: the people who made the music, 1111
Schwann Spectrum: the gd to rock, jazz, world...& beyond, 1072
SongCite: an index to popular songs, suppl 1, 1078
20/20: 20 new sounds of the 20th century, 1075

MUSIC - RHYTHM & BLUES
All music gd to the blues, 2d ed, 1092
Blues singers, 1093
Joel Whitburn's rhythm & blues top R&B albums 1965-98, 1094
Schwann Spectrum: the gd to rock, jazz, world...& beyond, 1072

MUSIC - 20TH CENTURY
Forever lounge, 1118
Joel Whitburn presents a century of pop music, 1074
Joel Whitburn's bubbling under singles & albums, 1998 ed, 1113
Music in the 20th century, 1070
20/20: 20 new sounds of the 20th century, 1075

MUSICAL INSTRUMENTS
Cambridge companion to the organ, 1090
Cambridge companion to the piano, 1091
Complete ency of the guitar, 1088
Gruhn's gd to vintage guitars, 2d ed, 1089

MUSICALS
American musical film song ency, 1159

MUSICIANS
All roots lead to rock: legends of early rock 'n' roll, 1109
Another song to sing: the recorded repertoire of Johnny Cash, 1086
Black women in American bands & orchestras, 2d ed, 1061
Blues singers, 1093
Carole King, 1084
Duke Ellington, 1082
Elvis Costello, 1085
Jazz profiles, 1101
Jimmy Dorsey: a study in contrasts, 1087
Music in the 20th century, 1070
Popular musicians, 1115
Rockin' '60s: the people who made the music, 1111
Sinatra: an annot bibliog, 1939-98, 1083

MUSLIM
Muslim Diaspora, 1270

MYANMAR
Demographic perspective on women in dvlpmt in Cambodia ..., 759

MYSTERY & DETECTIVE STORIES. *See* **DETECTIVE & MYSTERY STORIES**

MYTHOLOGY
Cassell's ency of queer myth, symbol, & spirit, 1127
Encyclopedia of Greco-Roman mythology, 1128
Encyclopedia of Russian & Slavic myth & legend, 1129

NAMES
Arthurian name dict, 1023
Dictionary of English surnames, 335

NARCOTICS
Buzzed: the straight facts about the most used & abused drugs from alcohol to ecstasy, 1446
War on drugs, 753

NATIONALISM
Nationalism & ethnicity terminologies, 60

NATURAL DISASTERS
Atlas of the world's worst natural disasters, 1497
Natural disasters: hurricanes, 1293

NATURAL HISTORY
Guide to field gds, 1349
Oryx gd to natural hist, 1348

NATURAL MEDICINE
Natural medicines comprehensive database, 2d ed, 1450
Pharmacists gd to over-the-counter & natural remedies, 1445

NATURAL RESOURCES
US land & natural resource policy, 542

NATURALIZATION RECORDS
They became Americans: finding naturalization records & ethnic origins, 332

NAVAJO
Dine bibliog to the 1990s, 301

NAVAL ART & SCIENCE
Jane's Naval construction & retrofit markets, 610

NEO-CONFUCIANISM
Essentials of neo-Confucianism, 1222

NETHERLANDS
Historical dict of the Netherlands, 106

NEW ENGLAND STATES
Legal executions in New England, 537

NEW YORK PUBLIC LIBRARY
New York Public Lib African American desk ref, 298

New York Public Lib amazing African American hist, 299
New York Public Lib amazing Hispanic American hist, 323
New York Public Lib amazing women in American hist, 802
New York Public Lib desk ref, 3d ed, 47

NEW ZEALAND
New Zealand bks in print 1999, 1035
Opera cos & houses of W Europe, Canada, Australia, & New Zealand, 1107

NEWS AGENCIES
Encyclopedia of TV news, 827

NEWSLETTERS
Fulltext sources online, Jan 1999, 39
Hudson's subscription newsletter dir, 14th ed, 52

NEWSPAPERS. See also **JOURNALISM**
African-American newspapers & pers, 278
Bacon's newspaper dir 1999, 47th ed, 51
Fulltext sources online, Jan 1999, 39

NIETZSCHE, FRIEDRICH WILHELM
Historical dict of Nietzscheanism, 1214

NIGERIAN DRAMA
Nigerian theatre in English, 972

NORTH AMERICA
Encyclopedia of North American hist, 490
Peoples of the Americas, 271

NORTH AMERICAN - HISTORY
Bibliographic gd to N American hist 1998, 402

NORTHWEST PASSAGE
Across the top of the world, 502

NOVELS - AUTHORSHIP
Novel & short story writer's market, 1999, 814

NUBIA
Ancient African kingdom of Kush, 506

NURSING
Handbook of clinical nursing research, 1442
Historical ency of nursing, 1444
PDR for nurses hndbk, 1999 ed, 1452
RSP funding for nursing students & nurses 1998-2000, 1443

NUTRITION
American Academy of Pediatrics gd to your child's nutrition, 1422

Diet & nutrition sourcebk, 2d ed, 1305
Encyclopedia of human nutrition, 1393
New ency of vitamins, minerals, suppls, & herbs, 1301
Nutrients A to Z, 1302

OBITUARIES
Obituaries in the performing arts, 1998, 1143

O'BRIAN, PATRICK
Persons, animals, ships, & cannon in the Aubrey-Maturin sea novels of Patrick O'Brian, 1026

OCCUPATIONS. See **CAREERS**

OCEANOGRAPHY
Jane's underwater tech 1998-99, 1512
Oceans, 1511

OLYMPIC GAMES
1904 Olympic Games, 727
1906 Olympic Games, 728

OPERA
Chronicle of opera, 1105
More EJS: discography of the Edward J. Smith recordings, 1106
Opera: the rough gd, 2d ed, 1103
Opera singers in recital, concert, & feature film, 1102
Operas in English, 1104

OPERA COMPANIES
Opera cos & houses of W Europe, Canada, Australia, & New Zealand, 1107

ORCHIDS
Orchids of Papua New Guinea, 1343

ORGANS
Cambridge companion to the organ, 1090

ORGANIZATIONAL PSYCHOLOGY
Handbook of work & orgl psychology, 2d ed, 693

ORGANIZATIONS
Public interest profiles 1998-99, 42

OSAKA (JAPAN)
Historical dict of Osaka & Kyoto, 438

OUD, J. J. P.
J. J. P. Oud & the intl style, 863

OUTDOOR RECREATION
Beyond the natl parks, 698
Complete outdoors ency, 4th ed, 702

OUTER SPACE. See also ASTRONOMY
Cosmic phenomena, 1506
Dictionary of space tech, 2d ed, 1498
Universe & beyond, 3d ed, 1500
Universe revealed, 1505

PACIFIC AREA
Australia 2000, 377
Far East & Australasia 1999, 30th ed, 92
Tongo, 91

PACIFIC NORTHWEST
Beachcomber's gd to seashore life in the Pacific Northwest, 1331

PAKISTAN
Founding of Pakistan, 441
Historical dict of Pakistan, 2d ed, 440

PALEONTOLOGY
Carbon dates, 1514
Encyclopedia of paleontology, 1513

PAPER MONEY. See also MONEY
Paper money of the US, 15th ed, 840

PAPUA NEW GUINEA
Orchids of Papua New Guinea, 1343

PARASITES
Parasites of N American freshwater fishes, 2d ed, 1360

PARENTING. See also CHILD CARE
Encyclopedia of parenting theory & research, 755
Raising teenagers, 757
Single parents, 743

PEACE
Encyclopedia of intl peacekeeping operations, 673
Encyclopedia of violence, peace, & conflict, 492

PERFORMING ARTS. See also DANCE; MOTION PICTURES; THEATER
Bibliographic gd to theatre arts 98, 1203
Career opportunities in theater & the performing arts, 2d ed, 200
Obituaries in the performing arts, 1998, 1143
Peterson's professional degree programs in the visual & performing arts 1999, 5th ed, 1145
Princeton Review gd to performing arts programs, 224
US dir of entertainment employers, spring/summer 1999 ed, 1146

PERIODICALS
African-American newspapers & pers, 278
Bacon's mag dir 1999, 47th ed, 50
Bacon's newspaper dir 1999, 47th ed, 51
E-serials, 574
Fulltext sources online, Jan 1999, 39
Hudson's subscription newsletter dir, 14th ed, 52
Index gd to college jls, 53
International dir of little mags & small presses 1998-99, 34th ed, 587
MLA dir of pers 1999, 9th ed, 938

PERSIAN GULF WAR, 1991
Encyclopedia of the Persian Gulf War, 601

PERSONS WITH DISABILITIES
Complete dir for people with disabilities, 2000, 8th ed, 736
Older Americans info dir, 1999, 2d ed, 735
Practical gd to the ADA & visual impairment, 737

PHARMACOLOGY. See also DRUGS
Encyclopedia of controlled drug delivery, 1447
Mosby's over-the-counter medicine cabinet medicines, 1449
Natural medicines comprehensive database, 2d ed, 1450
PDR for nurses hndbk, 1999 ed, 1452
PDR generics 1998, 4th ed, 1453
Pharmacists gd to over-the-counter & natural remedies, 1445
Prescription alternatives, 2d ed, 1448
Psychologists' psychotropic desk ref, 1451
Veterinary drug hndbk, 3d ed, 1317

PHILANTHROPISTS
Humanitarians & reformers, 58

PHILANTHROPY. See also GRANTS-IN-AID
Foundation grants index 1999, 27th ed, 745
Giving by industry, 1999-2000 ed, 746
National dir of fndn grants for Native Americans, 312
Practical gd to planned giving 2000, 8th ed, 749

PHILOSOPHERS
Essentials of neo-Confucianism, 1222
International dir of philosophy & philosophers 1999-2000, 11th ed, 1219
Philosophers & religious leaders, 1209
Philosopher's phone & e-mail dir 1998/99, 1220

PHILOSOPHY
Cambridge dict of philosophy, 2d ed, 1212
Dictionary of existentialism, 1213
Dictionary of philosophy, 1211
Edinburgh ency of continental philosophy, 1215
Encyclopedia of ethics, 1216
Every person's gd to Jewish philosophy & philosophers, 1223
Historical dict of Nietzscheanism, 1214

PHOTOGRAPHERS
American women photographers, 867
International photography, 866
Photographer's market, 1999, 869
Writer's & photographer's gd to global markets, 806

PHOTOGRAPHY
Bibliography of modern art on disc [CD-ROM], 845
Photography ency, 868

PHYSICAL DISABILITIES. *See* PERSONS WITH DISABILITIES

PHYSICIANS
Socioeconomic characteristics of medical practice 1997, 1408

PHYSICS
Cassell dict of physics, 1516
CRC hndbk of chemistry & physics 1999-2000, 80th ed, 1473
Dictionary of physics, 1517
Facts on file dict of physics, 3d ed, 1518
Graduate programs in physics, astronomy, & related fields, 2000, 1474

PIANO
Cambridge companion to the piano, 1091

PIRATES
History of pirates, 509

PLANTS. *See also* BOTANY; GARDENING
Dictionary of plant pathology, 2d ed, 1332
500 popular annuals & perennials for American Gardeners, 1337
Flora of the Northeast, 1335
Flowering plants of the Galapagos, 1342
Shorter dict of gardening, 1334
Wildlife & plants of the world, 1325

PLANTS, ORNAMENTAL
Color ency of ornamental grasses, 1312
Garden plants of China, 1336
Rock garden plants, 1333

PLANTS, SUCCULENTS
Plantfinder's gd to cacti & other succulents, 1344

POE, EDGAR ALLAN
Poe cinema, 1185

POETRY
Poetry criticism, v.22, 1053
Poetry criticism, v.24, 1054
Poetry for students, v.5, 1055
Poetry for students, v.6, 1056

POETRY - AUTHORSHIP
Poet's gd to poetry, 820
Poet's market, 1999, 815

POETRY - INDEXES
Index of American per verse 1997, 1051
Index to poetry for children & young people 1993-97, 1052

POETS
British poets of the Great War: Sassoon, Graves, Owen, 1050
Chaucer A to Z, 1025
James Dickey, 1009
Maya Angelou, 1008
Ted Hughes: a bibliog, 1946-95, 2d ed, 1057
Victorian women poets, 1058
Walt Whitman, 1018
Yeats dict, 1039

POISONS
Dictionary of toxicology, 2d ed, 1477
Poisons & antidotes sourcebk, 1427

POLAND
Historical dict of Poland, 1945-96, 461

POLAR REGIONS
Keyguide to info sources on the polar & cold regions, 114

POLISH LANGUAGE DICTIONARIES - ENGLISH
Langenscheidt's pocket dict: English/Polish, Polish/English, rev ed, 914

POLITICAL ACTIVISTS
Humanitarians & reformers, 58

POLITICAL PARTICIPATION
Congressional Quarterly's fed PAC dir 1998-99, 645
Encyclopedia of American activism, 1960 to the present, 667

POLITICAL PARTIES
Encyclopedia of American parties, campaigns, & elections, 630
World ency of pol systems & parties, 3d ed, 618

POLITICAL REVOLUTIONS
Encyclopedia of political revolutions, 491

POLITICAL SCIENCE
CQ's state fact finder 1999, 779
Encyclopedia of women in American politics, 632
Political ency of the Middle East, 666
US govt on the Web, 619
Who's who in political revolutions, 486

POLITICIANS
American legislative leaders in the South, 1911-94, 628
Distinguished African American political & govtl leaders, 286
Encyclopedia of heads of states & govts, 1900-45, 616
Founding leaders [CD-ROM], 483
Hutchinson ency of modern political biog, 615
International dir of govt 1999, 3d ed, 620
Leadership lib on CD-ROM, fall 1998 ed, 622

POLITICS
Encyclopedia of politics & religion, 1233
Political market place USA, 621
Special interest group profiles for students, 660
Washington info dir 1999-2000, 640

POLITICS - INTERNATIONAL
World ency of pol systems & parties, 3d ed, 618

POLITICS - LOCAL
Compensation 98, v.16, 642

POPULAR CULTURE
Clowns & tricksters, 1131
Great American Websites, 76
Icons of the century, 1137
On this day in hist, 1136
War & American popular culture, 1140

POPULAR MUSIC
Joel Whitburn presents a century of pop music, 1074
Joel Whitburn presents Billboard top 10 album charts 1963-98, 1112
Joel Whitburn's 1998 Billboard music yrbk, 1117
Music USA, 1116
Popular music, v.23, 1114
Popular musicians, 1115
Rockin' '60s: the people who made the music, 1111
Schwann Spectrum: the gd to rock, jazz, world...& beyond, 1072
SongCite: an index to popular songs, suppl 1, 1078
20/20: 20 new sounds of the 20th century, 1075

POWER TOOLS
Orion blue bk: power tool 1998, 147

PREGNANCY & CHILDBIRTH. *See also* MEDICINE - PEDIATRICS
Catalog of prenatally diagnosed conditions, 3d ed, 1426
Catalog of teratogenic agents, 9th ed, 1454

PRESIDENTS - UNITED STATES
American presidency, 3d ed, 659
Impeachable offenses, 664
Presidency A to Z, 2d ed, 634
Vital stats on the presidency, rev ed, 655

PRESIDENTS - UNITED STATES - ELECTIONS
America at the polls 1960-96, 658

PRESS. *See also* COMMUNICATIONS; NEWSPAPERS
Power of the press, 809

PRIME MINISTERS
Biographical dict of British prime ministers, 614

PRISONS
Mental health servs in criminal justice system settings, 681
Prisons in America, 539

PROGRESSIVISM
American settlement houses & progressive social reform, 411

PROVERBS
Concise dict of European proverbs, 1125
Spanish idioms, proverbs, & slang of yesterday & today, 917

PSYCHOLOGY
Baker ency of psychology & counseling, 2d ed, 683
Bibliographic gd to psychology 1998, 680
Elgar companion to consumer research & economic psychology, 121
Encyclopedia of creativity, 684
Encyclopedia of human emotions, 685
Handbook of school psychology, 3d ed, 226
Handbook of work & orgl psychology, 2d ed, 693
Key words in multicultural interventions, 686
Mental health servs in criminal justice system settings, 681
Portraits of pioneers in psychology, v.3, 682
Students in discord, 692

PSYCHOLOGY - DIRECTORIES
APA membership register 1999, 688
Complete mental health dir, 2000, 690
Directory of the American Psychological Assn, 1997 ed, 689

PSYCHOLOGY - EDUCATION
Directory of internship & post-doctoral fellowships in clinical child/pediatric psychology, 1999-2000, 3d ed, 691
Graduate study in psychology 1998-99, 32d ed, 240

PSYCHOTROPIC DRUGS
Psychologists' psychotropic desk ref, 1451

PUBLIC POLICY
Encyclopedia of American public policy, 678
Issues for debate in American public policy, 677
Public interest profiles 1998-99, 42

PUBLIC RECORDS
Public record research system [CD-ROM], 624
Sourcebk to public record info, professional ed, 639

PUBLISHERS & PUBLISHING. *See also*
AUTHORSHIP; BOOKSELLERS & BOOKSELLING
American bk trade dir 1999-2000, 45th ed, 585
Canadian writer's market, 13th rev ed, 811
Directory of small press/mag editors & publishers 1999-2000, 30th ed, 586
International dir of little mags & small presses 1998-99, 34th ed, 587
Literary market place 1999, 588
Literary market place on disc [CD-ROM], 589
Lithuanian publishers dir, 590

PUCCINI, GIACOMO
Giacomo Puccini, 1079

PULITZER PRIZES
Who's who of Pulitzer Prize winners, 1002

PUSHKIN, ALEXANDER
Bibliography of Alexander Pushkin in English, 1044

QUEBEC (PROVINCE)
Quebec, 93

QUEENS
Kings & queens, 484

QUOTATIONS
Dictionary of contemporary quotations, v.9, 4th rev ed, 54
Dictionary of mathematical quotations, 1525
Dictionary of quotations in communications, 810
Practically speaking: a dict of quotations on engineering, tech, & architecture, 55
Quote it completely, 56
Scholastic treasury of quotations for children, 965
Western movie quotations, 1196
Wiley bk of business quotations, 140
World War II: an ency of quotations, 512

RADIO PROGRAMS
CBS radio mystery theater, 828
Great radio soap operas, 826
Radio programs, 1924-84, 829

RADIO STATIONS
Bacon's radio dir 1999, 13th ed, 824

RAILROAD MUSEUMS
Empire State Railway Museums 34th annual gd to tourist railroads & museums, 1999 ed, 365

RAIN FORESTS
Rain forest bibliog, 1528

RANSOM, JOHN CROWE
John Crowe Ransom, 1014

RELIGION
African religion, 1240
Children's bks about religion, 951
Creation/evolution controversy, 1224
Critical terms for religious studies, 1232
Dictionary of the presbyterian & reformed tradition in America, 1263
Encyclopedia of American religions, 6th ed, 1236
Encyclopedia of cults, sects, & new religions, 1235
Encyclopedia of politics & religion, 1233
Encyclopedia of world religions, 1234
End of the world: an annot bibliog, 1226
Golden age of Islam, 503
Merriam-Webster's ency of world religions, 1237
Native N American Shamanism, 302
Neighboring faiths, 1238
Religious leaders of America, 2d ed, 1230
World's religions, 2d ed, 1242
Zoroastrianism, 1239

RELIGION & POLITICS
World's religions, 2d ed, 1242

RELIGION - CHRISTIANITY
Augustine through the ages, 1227
Baker ency of Christian apologetics, 1261
Encyclopedia of Christianity, v.1 (A-D), 1264
Our Sunday Visitor's ency of the Catholic doctrine on CD-ROM [CD-ROM], 1266

RELIGION - EGYPTIAN
Gods of ancient Egypt, 431

RELIGIOUS LEADERS
Philosophers & religious leaders, 1209

REPTILES
Amphibians & reptiles of Northern Guatemala, the Yucatan, & Belize, 1376
Animals, 1351
Snakes, 1375

RESCUES
Great escapes & rescues, 494

RESEARCH
Cambridge dict of stats, 767
Encyclopedia of lang & educ, 872
International research centers dir 1999, 11th ed, 41
Research servs dir 2000, 7th ed, 133

RESEARCH LIBRARIES
Choice's outstanding academic bks 1992-97, 551

REVOLUTIONARIES
Who's who in political revolutions, 486

ROBIN HOOD (LEGENDARY CHARACTER)
Robin Hood, 1193

ROCK MUSIC. *See also* **MUSIC; POPULAR MUSIC**
All roots lead to rock: legends of early rock 'n' roll, 1109
Rockin' '60s: the people who made the music, 1111

RUNNING
Runner's sourcebk, 729

RUSSIA. *See also* **SOVIET UNION**
History of Russia, 463

RUSSIAN FEDERATION
Territories of the Russian Federation, 100

RUSSIAN LANGUAGE - DICTIONARIES - ENGLISH
Random House Russian-English, English-Russian dict, 915

RUSSIAN LITERATURE
Bibliography of Alexander Pushkin in English, 1044
Encyclopedia of Russian & Slavic myth & legend, 1129
Russian lit in the age of Pushkin & Gogol: poetry & drama, 1045
Russian lit in the age of Pushkin & Gogol: prose, 1046

SAINTS
Faces of holiness: modern saints in photos & words, 1228
John Paul II's bk of saints, 1229
Our Sunday Visitor's ency of saints [CD-ROM], 1267
Sister Wendy's bk of saints, 1259

SALARY SURVEYS. *See* **WAGE SURVEYS**

SARDINIA
Sardinia, 387

SAVANNAH (GA.) - GUIDEBOOKS
Charleston, Savannah, & coastal islands bk, 3d ed, 369

SCHOLARSHIPS. *See* **FINANCIAL AID & SCHOLARSHIPS**

SCHOOL MEDIA CENTERS
Guide to ref materials for school lib media centers, 5th ed, 554
New steps to serv, 577
Thoughtful researcher, 576

SCHOOL PSYCHOLOGY
Handbook of school psychology, 3d ed, 226

SCIENCE
African American firsts in sci & tech, 1297
Earth sci on file, rev ed, 1496
Guide to field gds, 1349
Information sources in sci & tech, 3d ed, 1273
International dir of testing labs, 1999 ed, 1290
Science navigator [CD-ROM], 1288
Scientific dvlpmt & misconceptions through the ages, 1294
Social issues in sci & tech, 1285
Technology in action, 1292
Walford's gd to ref material, v.1: sci & tech, 8th ed, 1274
Wildlife & plants of the world, 1325

SCIENCE - DICTIONARIES & ENCYCLOPEDIAS
Encyclopedia of bioprocess tech, 1323
Facts on file ency of sci, 1281
Facts on file ency of sci, tech, & society, 1282
International ency of abbrevs & acronyms in sci & tech, rev ed, 1286
International ency of sci & tech, 1283
Kirk-Othmer Concise ency of chemical tech, 4th ed, 1482
McGraw-Hill concise ency of sci & tech, 4th ed, 1284
Quantities, symbols, units, & abbrevs, 1318
Rourkes world of sci ency, 1287
Van Nostrand's scientific ency, 8th ed [CD-ROM], 1289
Williams dict of biomaterials, 1326

SCIENCE FICTION
Incredible Internet gd to Star Wars, 1466
MUP ency of Australian sci fiction & fantasy, 1034
Science fiction mag story index, 1926-95, 991
Science fiction writers, 2d ed, 992

SCIENCE - HANDBOOKS & YEARBOOKS
Innovations in Earth scis, 1495
Physical scis on file, rev ed, 1475
Science & tech almanac, 1999 ed, 1295
Scientific American sci desk ref, 1296

SCIENTISTS
American men & women of sci 1998-99, 20th ed, 1275
Notable black American scientists, 1278
Notable 20th-century scientists: suppl, 1279
100 most popular scientists for YAs, 1277
Scientists: their lives & work, v.6, 1276
Scientists, mathematicians, & inventors, 1280

SCOTLAND
Etymological dict of Scottish Gaelic, 909

SCOTT, SIR WALTER
Sir Walter Scott: a bibliogl hist 1796-1832, 1047

SECTS (RELIGIOUS)
Cults in America, 1241
Encyclopedia of cults, sects, & new religions, 1235

SERBOCROATIAN DICTIONARIES
Standard English-SerboCroatian, SerboCroatian-English dict, 916

SERIALS MANAGEMENT. *See also* **PERIODICALS**
E-serials, 574

SERIES (PUBLICATIONS)
Whole story: 3000 yrs of sequels & sequences, 2d ed, 978

SEXUAL HARASSMENT
Sexual harassment in America, 550

SEXUALLY TRANSMITTED DISEASES
Sexually transmitted diseases, 1438

SHAKESPEARE, WILLIAM
Comprehensive Shakespeare dict [CD-ROM], 1027
Shakespearean criticism, v.43, 1029
Shakespearean criticism, v.44, 1030
Shakespearean criticism, v.45, 1031
Who's who in Shakespeare's England, 1028
World Shakespeare bibliog on CD-ROM, 1983-95 [CD-ROM], 1032

SHAMANISM
Encyclopedia of Native American Shamanism, 308
Native N American Shamanism, 302

SHARKS
Encyclopedia of sharks, 1369
Sharks, 2d ed, 1372
Sharks & rays of the world, 1370

SHELLS
Beachcomber's gd to seashore life in the Pacific Northwest, 1331

SHIPWRECKS
History of shipwrecks, 510

SHORT STORIES
Short stories for students, v.6, 969
Short story criticism, v.30, 994
Twentieth-century short story explication: new series, v.4, 1995-96, 993

SHORT STORIES - AUTHORSHIP
Novel & short story writer's market, 1999, 814

SHRUBS
500 popular shrubs & trees for American gardeners, 1345

SICILY (ITALY)
Sicily, 107

SIGN LANGUAGE
American sign lang handshape dict, 893

SIGNS & SYMBOLS
Quantities, symbols, units, & abbrevs, 1318

SILENT FILMS
American film cycles, 1192
Guide to the silent yrs of American cinema, 1163
Silent films, 1877-1976, 1179
Ultimate dir of silent & sound era performers, 1149

SINATRA, FRANK
Sinatra: an annot bibliog, 1939-98, 1083

SINGLE PARENTS. *See also* **PARENTING**
Single parents, 743

SKIN DISEASES
Skin sourcebk, 1439

SLAVERY
Chronology of world slavery, 488
Slavery & slaving in world hist, 477

SLAVIC LITERATURE
Encyclopedia of Russian & Slavic myth & legend, 1129

SLEEP DISORDERS
Sleep disorders sourcebk, 1440

SLOVAKIA
Historical dict of Slovakia, 464

SMITH, EDWARD J.
More EJS: discography of the Edward J. Smith recordings, 1106

SMOKING
Encyclopedia of smoking & tobacco, 1394

SNAKES
Snakes, 1375

SOAP OPERAS
Great radio soap operas, 826

SOCIAL HISTORY
American social issues [CD-ROM], 410
Encyclopedia of genocide, 732
Everyday life: American social hist, 413

SOCIAL PREDICTION
21st century, 61

SOCIAL PROBLEMS
Social issues, 59

SOCIAL REFORMERS
Encyclopedia of American activism, 1960 to the present, 667
Humanitarians & reformers, 58

SOCIAL SCIENCES
Dictionary of critical social scis, 62
Dictionary of stats & methodology, 2d ed, 768
Gallup poll cum index: public opinion, 1935-97, 57
Money for graduate students in the social scis 1998-2000, 2d ed, 249

SOCIAL SECURITY
Mercer gd to social security & Medicare 1998, 26th ed, 752

SOCIAL WELFARE
Government assistance almanac 1999-2000, 13th ed, 751

SOCIAL WORK
Social work dict, 4th ed, 750

SOCIETY FOR INDUSTRIAL & APPLIED MATHEMATICS
Combined membership list 1998-99, 1522

SOCIOLOGY
Required reading: sociology's most influential bks, 733
Social issues, 59

SONGS
American musical film song ency, 1159
Varied carols, 1095

SOUTH AFRICA
End of apartheid in South Africa, 427
Historical dict of Greater Johannesburg, 429

SOUTH AMERICA
Culture & customs of Argentina, 109
Insight gd: Venezuela, 389
Peoples of the Americas, 271
Social panorama of Latin America, 1997 ed, 110

SOUTH AMERICA - BUSINESS
Consumer Latin America 1999, 6th ed, 190

SOUTH ASIA
Founding of Pakistan, 441

SOUTHERN STATES - LITERATURE
Contemporary Southern writers, 998

SOUTHERN STATES - MAPS
Southeast in early maps, 3d ed, 337

SOVIET JEWISH AMERICANS
Soviet Jewish Americans, 318

SOVIET UNION
History of Russia, 463
Joseph Stalin, 462

SPACE SCIENCES. *See also* ASTRONOMY
Cosmic phenomena, 1506
Routledge critical dict of the new cosmology, 1503
Space exploration, 1504
UFO ency, 2d ed, 697
Universe & beyond, 3d ed, 1500
Universe revealed, 1505

SPANISH - DRAMA
Spanish golden age drama, 974

SPANISH - HISTORY
History of Spain, 465

SPANISH LANGUAGE DICTIONARIES
Spanish idioms, proverbs, & slang of yesterday & today, 917
Vox Spanish & English student dict, 918

SPANISH LITERATURE
Hispanic lit criticism suppl, 1048
Miguel Delibes, 1049

SPECIAL INTEREST GROUPS
Special interest group profiles for students, 660

SPECIAL LIBRARIES
Business ref servs & sources, 578
Meeting managers' info needs, 579

SPIRITUALS
Index to African-American spirituals for the solo voice, 1119

SPOKESPERSONS
Yearbook of experts, authorities, & spokespersons 1999, 17th ed, 48

SPORTS
Career opportunities in the sports industry, 2d ed, 199
Greatest athletes of the 20th century, 699
Sports for her: a ref gd for teenage girls, 700

Sports stars, series 5, 701
Ultimate soccer ency, 730

SPORTS MEDICINE
Sports injuries sourcebk, 1441

STALIN, JOSEPH
Joseph Stalin, 462

STATISTICAL TECHNIQUES
Cambridge dict of stats, 767

STATISTICS
Agricultural stats 1999, 1298
Annual abstract of stats, no.135, 1999 ed, 769
Arab women 1995, 799
County & city extra, 1999, 8th ed, 778
CQ's state fact finder 1999, 779
Dictionary of stats & methodology, 2d ed, 768
Direction of trade stats yrbk, 1998, 210
Education stats on the US 1999, 225
EXEGY: Current country profiles 2000 [CD-ROM], 65
Handbook of US labor stats 1999, 3d ed, 206
Handbook on civil registration & vital stats systems, 771
Housing stats of the US, 2d ed, 780
International histl stats: Africa, Asia, & Oceania 1750-1993, 3d ed, 69
International histl stats: Europe 1750-1993, 4th ed, 70
International histl stats: the Americas 1750-1993, 4th ed, 71
State & metropolitan area data bk 1997-98, 5th ed, 781
State profiles 1999, 782
Statistical abstract of the US 1998, 118th lib ed, 784
Statistical yrbk for Asia & the Pacific 1998, 774
Statistics sources 2000, 23d ed, 777
Trends in Europe & N America 1998/99, 775
Women in India, 803

STATISTICS - FINANCIAL
Balance of payments stats yrbks 1998, 770
International financial stats yrbk 1999, 177
Pocket world in figures 1999, 772
Statistical hndbk on poverty in the developing world, 773
World cost of living survey, 2d ed, 776

STATISTICS - PRESIDENTIAL
Vital stats on the presidency, rev ed, 655

STATISTICS - TOURISM
Yearbook of tourism stats, 50th ed, 166

STEINBECK, JOHN
Hayashi Steinbeck bibliog, 1982-96, 1015

STOCK EXCHANGES
International ency of the stock market, 169

STUNT PERFORMERS
Hollywood stunt performers, 1175

STYLE GUIDES
Cassell gd to punctuation, repr ed, 821
Columbia gd to online style, 822
MLA hndbk for writers of research papers, 5th ed, 819

SUDAN
Ancient African kingdom of Kush, 506

SYMBOLS IN ART
Encyclopedia of Tibetan symbols & motifs, 865

SYMBOLS IN LITERATURE
Dictionary of alchemical imagery, 696
Dictionary of literary symbols, 933

SYRIA
Syria, rev ed, 113

TAE KWON DO
Tae kwon do, updated ed, 731

TAIWANESE AMERICANS
Taiwanese Americans, 275

TAXATION
Encyclopedia of taxation & tax policy, 216

TECHNOLOGY
Information sources in sci & tech, 3d ed, 1273
International dir of testing labs, 1999 ed, 1290
Practically speaking: a dict of quotations on engineering, tech, & architecture, 55
Science navigator [CD-ROM], 1288
Scientific dvlpmt & misconceptions through the ages, 1294
Social issues in sci & tech, 1285
Technology in action, 1292

TECHNOLOGY - BIBLIOGRAPHIES
Bibliographic gd to tech 1998, 1272
Walford's gd to ref material, v.1: sci & tech, 8th ed, 1274

TECHNOLOGY - DICTIONARIES & ENCYCLOPEDIAS
Dictionary of space tech, 2d ed, 1498
Encyclopedia of bioprocess tech, 1323
Facts on file ency of sci, tech, & society, 1282
International ency of abbrevs & acronyms in sci & tech, rev ed, 1286
International ency of sci & tech, 1283
Kirk-Othmer Concise ency of chemical tech, 4th ed, 1482
McGraw-Hill concise ency of sci & tech, 4th ed, 1284
Rourkes world of sci ency, 1287
Van Nostrand's scientific ency, 8th ed [CD-ROM], 1289

TECHNOLOGY - HANDBOOKS & YEARBOOKS
African American firsts in sci & tech, 1297
Plunkett's InfoTech industry almanac 1999-2000, 1456
Science & tech almanac, 1999 ed, 1295
Statistical hndbk on tech, 1291

TEENAGERS
Raising teenagers, 757
Twentieth-century teen culture by the decades, 758

TELECOMMUNICATIONS
Dun & Bradstreet/Gale industry ref hndbks: telecommunications, 1471
History of the Internet, 1462
Mobile telecommunications factbk, 1472
Newton's telecom dict, 15th ed, 1467
Telecom & networking glossary, 1468
Telecommunications dir 1999, 10th ed, 1470
Telecommunications gd to the Internet, 1469

TELEPHONE DIRECTORIES
Business phone bk USA 1999, 21st ed, 130
Philosopher's phone & e-mail dir 1998/99, 1220
Toll-free phone bk USA 1999, 3d ed, 43

TELEVISION
BFI film & TV hndbk 1999, 1188
Contemporary theatre, film, & TV, v.22, 1141
Encyclopedia of TV news, 827
Women & American TV, 1162

TELEVISION - CAREERS
Career opportunities in TV, cable, video, & multimedia, 4th ed, 193

TELEVISION PROGRAMS
Buyer's gd to 50 yrs of TV on video, 1197
Guide to TV's Mayberry R.F.D., 1191
Women & American TV, 1162

TELEVISION STATIONS
Bacon's TV/cable dir 1999, 13th ed, 825

TERATOGENIC AGENTS
Catalog of teratogenic agents, 9th ed, 1454

TERRORISM
Terrorism in the 20th century, 669

TESTING
Fracture: a topical ency of current knowledge, 1387
International dir of testing labs, 1999 ed, 1290

TEXAS
Dictionary of Tex. artists, 1800-1945, 847
Texas almanac, 2000-2001, 60th ed, 80
Texas legislative almanac 1999, 627

TEXAS - HISTORY
Encyclopedia of the Alamo & the Tex. Revolution, 414
Notable men & women of Spanish Tex., 404

TEXTBOOKS
El-hi textbks & serials in print 1999, 127th ed, 218

THAILAND
Thailand, rev ed, 90

THEATER. *See also* DRAMA; PERFORMING ARTS
Bibliographic gd to theatre arts 98, 1203
Career opportunities in theater & the performing arts, 2d ed, 200
Contemporary theatre, film, & TV, v.22, 1141
Dictionary of stage directions in English drama 1580-1942, 1206
Regional theatre dir 1999-2000, 1205
Summer theatre dir 1999, 1204
Theatre backstage from A to Z, 4th ed, 1207
World ency of contemporary theatre, v.5, 1208

THESAURI. *See* ENGLISH LANGUAGE - SYNONYMS & ANTONYMS

THIRD REICH
Women under the Third Reich, 456

THOMAS, DYLAN
Reference companion to Dylan Thomas, 1033

TOBACCO
Encyclopedia of smoking & tobacco, 1394

TONGA
Tonga, 91

TOURISM
Yearbook of tourism stats, 50th ed, 166

TOXICOLOGY. *See also* POISONS
Dictionary of toxicology, 2d ed, 1477

TRADE. *See also* INTERNATIONAL BUSINESS
Foreign trade of the US 1999, 211
US market trends & forecasts, 214
Washington almanac of intl trade & business, 1998, 181

TRADE & PROFESSIONAL ASSOCIATIONS
Associations unltd [CD-ROM], 36

TRANSPORTATION
US dept of transportation, 1539

TRAVEL
Alaskan wilderness, 361
Amusement park gd, 3d ed, 372

Baldwin's gd to museums of La., 362
Bed & breakfast ency, 2d ed, 358
Bed & breakfasts & country inns, 10th ed, 357
Britain: the rough gd, 2d ed, 379
Charleston, Savannah, & coastal islands bk, 3d ed, 369
City profiles USA 1999, 4th ed, 353
Do's & don'ts around the world: Asia, 85
Eurail & train travel gd to Europe, 3d ed, 380
Europe 2000, 381
Garden lover's gd to Spain & Portugal, 388
Garden lover's gd to the Netherlands & Belgium, 378
Garden lover's gd to the Northeast, 363
Global road warrior: 85-country hndbk for the intl business traveler, 356
Guide to Martha's Vineyard, 366
Hawaii, 367
Hostels France & Italy, 384
Hostels UK, 385
Insight gd: India, 375
Insight gd: Israel, 391
Insight gd: Japan, 3d ed, 376
Insight gd: Venezuela, 389
Literary landscapes, 383
Mexico 2000, 390
Minnesota gd, 368
Naples with Pompeii & the Amalfi coast, 386
Official gd to American historic inns, bed & breakfasts, & country inns, 6th ed, 373
On exhibit 1999: art lover's travel gd to American museums, 374
100 best all-inclusive resorts of the world, 355
Sardinia, 387
USA: the rough gd, 4th ed, 364
Volunteer vacations, 7th ed, 354
Whale watching, 360

TRAVEL - FOLKLORE
Travel, legend, & lore, 1122

TRAVELERS' WRITINGS
American travellers abroad, 2d ed, 359
British travel writers, 1940-97, 1020
To Calif. on the southern route 1849, 403

TREES
500 popular shrubs & trees for American gardeners, 1345
Maples for gardens, 1346

TRICKSTERS
Clowns & tricksters, 1131

TURKEY
Istanbul, 392

TUSCARORA LANGUAGE - DICTIONARIES - ENGLISH
Tuscarora-English/English-Tuscarora dict, 309

TWAIN, MARK
Mark Twain, 1016

TWENTY-FIRST CENTURY
21st century, 61

TYLER, ANNE
Anne Tyler companion, 1017

UKRAINE
Ukraine, 99

UNDERWATER TECHNOLOGY
Jane's underwater tech 1998-99, 1512

UNIDENTIFIED FLYING OBJECTS
UFO ency, 2d ed, 697

UNITED ARAB EMIRATES - BIBLIOGRAPHY
United Arab Emirates, 112

UNITED KINGDOM - LIBRARIES
Aslib dir of info sources in the UK, 10th ed, 555

UNITED NATIONS
Worldwide govt dir with intl orgs 1999, 625

UNITED STATES AIR FORCE
Historical dict of the US Air Force & its antecedents, 608

UNITED STATES - CIVILIZATIONS
American eras: the Colonial era 1600-1754, 418

UNITED STATES - CIVIL WAR, 1861-1865
Atlas of the official records of the Civil War [CD-ROM], 400
Campaigns of the Civil War & the Navy in the Civil War [CD-ROM], 420
Civil War CD-ROM II [CD-ROM], 421
Daily life in Civil War America, 425
Leaders of the American Civil War, 597
Scholastic ency of the Civil War, 416
Southern histl society papers [CD-ROM], 424

UNITED STATES - CONGRESS
Biographical dict of congressional women, 629
Congress A to Z, 3d ed, 631
Congressional Quarterly almanac 1997, 53d ed, 644
Congressional Quarterly almanac 1998, 643
CQ's politics in America 2000, 647
How Congress works, 3d ed, 651

UNITED STATES - CONSTITUTION
Constitution & its amendments, 646
Constitutional rights sourcebk, 528
State constitutions on the US, 656

UNITED STATES DEPARTMENT OF TRANSPORTATION
US Dept of Transportation, 1539

UNITED STATES - ECONOMIC CONDITIONS
CQ's state fact finder 1999, 779
Housing stats of the US, 2d ed, 780
State & metropolitan area data bk 1997-98, 5th ed, 781

UNITED STATES - ELECTRONIC RESOURCES
Great American Websites, 76
Internet blue pages, 1999 ed, 636
US govt on the Web, 619

UNITED STATES - FEDERAL BUREAU OF INVESTIGATION
FBI: a comprehensive ref gd, 648

UNITED STATES - FOREIGN RELATIONS
US foreign relations with the Middle East & N Africa, 674

UNITED STATES - GOVERNMENT
Almanac of state legislatures, 2d ed, 626
America at the polls 1960-96, 658
American presidency, 3d ed, 659
Budget of the US govt, fiscal yr 2000, 641
Congressional Quarterly's desk ref on the states, 75
Congressional Quarterly's fed PAC dir 1998-99, 645
Elections A to Z, 633
Federal agency profiles for students, 649
Federal staff dir, summer 1999, 30th ed, 637
Government phone bk USA 1999, 7th ed, 638
Gubernatorial elections 1787-1997, 650
How govt works, 652
How to access the fed govt on the Internet, 4th ed, 623
Impeachable offenses, 664
Local govt election practices, 654
Managing America's cities, 653
Shapers of the great debate on immigration, 675
Special interest group profiles for students, 660
State govt 1998-99, 661
States' rights & American federalism, 662
United States govt manual 1998/99, 663
US govt on the Web, 619
Washington info dir 1999-2000, 640

UNITED STATES - HISTORY
American hist, 409
American immigration, 419
American scene: events, 405
American yrs, 407
Congressional Quarterly's desk ref on the states, 75
Encyclopedia of North American hist, 490
Legacy of the Monroe Doctrine, 422

UNITED STATES - HISTORY - COLONIAL ERA
American eras: the Colonial era 1600-1754, 418
Genealogical ency of the Colonial Americas, 325

UNITED STATES - HISTORY - EDUCATION
Historical dict of American educ, 220
Teaching US hist through children's lit, 954

UNITED STATES - HISTORY - MILITARY
America at war, 598
War & American popular culture, 1140

UNITED STATES - HISTORY - PROGRESSIVISM
American settlement houses & progressive social reform, 411

UNITED STATES - HISTORY - REVOLUTIONARY ERA
Historical dict of the American Revolution, 415

UNITED STATES - HISTORY - 20TH CENTURY
Events that shaped the century, 406

UNITED STATES - MILITARY
American military leaders, 596

UNITED STATES - POLITICS & GOVERNMENT
Encyclopedia of American parties, campaigns, & elections, 630
Encyclopedia of American public policy, 678
Issues for debate in American public policy, 677

UNITED STATES - SOCIAL CONDITIONS
Encyclopedia of American religions, 6th ed, 1236
Everyday life: American social hist, 413

UNITED STATES - STATISTICS
County & city extra, 1999, 8th ed, 778
State profiles 1999, 782
State rankings 1999, 10th ed, 783
Statistical abstract of the US 1998, 118th lib ed, 784
Statistical hndbk on the American family, 2d ed, 786

UNITED STATES - SUPREME COURT
Landmark Supreme Court cases, 525
Supreme Court A to Z, 2d ed, 635
Supreme Court yrbk 1997-98, 524
Want's fed-state court dir, 1999 ed, 519

UNIVERSAL MOTION PICTURE MANUFACTURING COMPANY
Universal silents, 1173

UNIVERSAL PICTURES COMPANY
Of gods & monsters, 1186

UNIVERSITY OF TEXAS
Aldine press bks at the Harry Ransom Humanities Research Center, 583

UTOPIAS
Utopias & Utopians, 1218
Visiting utopian communities, 1221

VAMPIRES
Vampire bk, 1135

VERNE, JULES
Jules Verne on film, 1183

VETERINARY MEDICINE
Black's veterinary dict, 19th ed, 1315
Dictionary of veterinary epidemiology, 1316
Veterinary drug hndbk, 3d ed, 1317

VICTORIAN PERIODICALS
Wellesley index to Victorian pers 1824-1900, new ed [CD-ROM], 49

VIDEO RECORDINGS
AV market place 1999, 823
Buyer's gd to 50 yrs of TV on video, 1197
TLA film & video gd, 1187
Video source bk, 23d ed, 1170
VideoHound's epics, 1200
VideoHound's golden movie retriever 1999, 1201
VideoHound's independent film gd, 2d ed, 1169
VideoHound's war movies, 1198
VideoHound's world cinema, 1202

VIENNA (AUSTRIA)
Historical dict of Vienna, 449

VIETNAM
Demographic perspective on women in dvlpmt in Cambodia ..., 759

VIETNAMESE CONFLICT, 1961-1975
MIAs: a ref hndbk, 606
War in Vietnam, 605

VIKINGS
Vikings, 505

VISUALLY HANDICAPPED
Practical gd to the ADA & visual impairment, 737

VOLCANOLOGY
Volcano registry, 1515

VOLUNTARISM
Volunteer vacations, 7th ed, 354

WAGE SURVEYS
American salaries & wages survey, 5th ed, 204

WAR. *See also* **MILITARY STUDIES; HISTORY**
Dictionary of wars, rev ed, 495
Encyclopedia of conflicts since WW II, 672
Encyclopedia of guerrilla warfare, 599
Encyclopedia of violence, peace, & conflict, 492
Hutchinson atlas of battle plans, 593
ViedoHound's war movies, 1198
Violence in America, 734
War & American popular culture, 1140
World conflicts, 500

WASHINGTON, D.C.
Guide to black Washington, rev ed, 293
Washington 1999, 16th ed, 44

WATER
Directory of municipal water & wastewater systems, 1999, 4th ed, 1531

WATERGATE AFFAIR
Watergate crisis, 423

WEALTH
Statistical hndbk on consumption & wealth in the US, 785

WEAPONS
Jane's market intelligence lib [CD-ROM], 612

WEATHER. *See also* **CLIMATOLOGY; METEOROLOGY**
Natural disasters: hurricanes, 1293
Weather hndbk, 2d ed, 1508

WEB SITE DEVELOPMENT
Creating a power Web site, 567

WEIGHTS & MEASUREMENTS
Economist desk companion, 3d ed, 45

WESTERN CHARACTERS
Western gunslingers in fact & on film, 1153

WESTERN STORIES
Twentieth-century American western writers, 1st series, 1000

WETLANDS
In search of swampland, 1320

WHALE WATCHING
Whale watching, 360

WHITMAN, WALT
Walt Whitman, 1018

WILDFLOWERS. *See also* **FLOWERS**
National Audubon Society 1st field gd: wildflowers, 1340

WIND ENSEMBLES
Appraisals of original wind music, 1108

WINE
Companion to Calif. wine, 1303
Italian wines 1999, 1304

WITCHCRAFT
Encyclopedia of witches & witchcraft, 2d ed, 694
Witchcraft today, 695

WOMEN
Demographic perspective on women in dvlpmt in Cambodia ..., 759
Who's who of American women 1999-2000, 21st ed, 21
Women & American TV, 1162

WOMEN & LITERATURE
American women prose writers to 1820, 996
Encyclopedia of British women writers, rev ed, 1021

WOMEN ARTISTS
American women photographers, 867
Contemporary women artists, 846
Latin American women artists of the US, 848
Women artists of color, 851

WOMEN - BIOGRAPHY
Extraordinary ordinary women, 790
Significant contemporary American feminists, 792
Women rulers throughout the ages, 791
Women under the Third Reich, 456

WOMEN COMPOSERS
Women composers, v.4, 1063
Women composers, v.5, 1064

WOMEN - HISTORY
Illustrated hist of women, 795
New York Public Lib amazing women in American hist, 802
Notable women in American hist, 789
Women in world hist, vols.1-3, 793
Women leaders [CD-ROM], 794
Women's movement in the US [CD-ROM], 796
Women's roles in ancient civilizations, 804
Women's studies ency, rev ed, 797
Women's studies ency, rev ed [CD-ROM], 798

WOMEN IN MUSIC
Black women in American bands & orchestras, 2d ed, 1061

WOMEN IN POLITICS
Almanac of women & minorities in American politics, 657
Biographical dict of congressional women, 629
Encyclopedia of women in American politics, 632

WOMEN IN SCIENCE
American men & women of sci 1998-99, 20th ed, 1275

WOMEN RULERS
Women rulers throughout the ages, 791

WOMEN'S RIGHTS
Women's movement in the US [CD-ROM], 796
Women's liberation movement in America, 800

WOMEN'S STUDIES
Arab women 1995, 799
Feminism, 801
Interdisciplinary bibliog gd to women's studies 1998, 788
Women in India, 803
Women's roles in ancient civilizations, 804
Women's studies index 1997, 805

WORKERS COMPENSATION
Workers Compensation, 207

WORLD DEVELOPMENT
A to Z of world dvlpmt, 25

WORLD GOVERNMENT
Encyclopedia of heads of states & govts, 1900-45, 616
EXEGY: Current country profiles 2000 [CD-ROM], 65
Junior worldmark ency of world cultures, 270
Pocket world in figures 1999, 772

WORLD HISTORY
Ancient African kingdom of Kush, 506
Chronology of world hist, 487
Chronology of world slavery, 488
EXEGY: Current country profiles 2000 [CD-ROM], 65
Golden age of Islam, 503
Incas, 504
Life millennium, 46
Slavery & slaving in world hist, 477
Twentieth century world, 511
Vikings, 505
Wilson calendar of world hist, 489
World conflicts, 500

WORLD HISTORY - BIOGRAPHIES
Dictionary of world biog: the 20th century, 479
Dictionary of world biog, v.3: the Renaissance, 480
Dictionary of world biog, v.4: the 17th & 18th centuries, 481
Dictionary of world biog, vols.5 & 6: the 19th century, 482

Who's who in political revolutions, 486
Young heroes in world hist, 478

WORLD HISTORY - DICTIONARIES & ENCYCLOPEDIAS
Encyclopedia of violence, peace, & conflict, 492
Great escapes & rescues, 494
Oxford ency of world hist, 496

WORLD LEADERS
Abridged ency of world biog, 10
Hutchinson ency of modern political biog, 615
World political leaders [CD-ROM], 617
Who's who 1999, 151st ed, 17

WORLD POLITICS
World factbk 1999, 73

WORLD WAR, 1914-1918
Almanac of WW I, 397

WORLD WAR, 1939-1945
Authorized press in Vichy & German-occupied France, 1940-44, 453
Holocaust: memories, research, ref, 507
Hospital ships of WW II, 613
World War II: an ency of quotations, 512
World War II in Europe, 602

WORLD WIDE WEB. *See also* **INTERNET**
Great American Websites, 76
Multimedia & the Web from A to Z, 2d ed, 1455

WRITING. *See also* **AUTHORSHIP**
Historical source bk for scribes, 855
MLA hndbk for writers of research papers, 5th ed, 819

Writer's & photographer's gd to global markets, 806
Writer's hndbk, 2000 ed, 817
Writer's market, 2000, electronic ed, 818

YEATS, WILLIAM BUTLER
Yeats dict, 1039

YIDDISH LANGUAGE DICTIONARIES
Anglish/Yinglish, 2d ed, 919

YOUNG ADULT LITERATURE
Arthurian fiction, 967
Horn Bk gd interactive [CD-ROM], 952
Novels for students, v.6, 968
Outstanding bks for children & young people, 963
Something about the author, v.104, 962
Strong souls singing: African American bks for our daughters & our sisters, 280
Subject gd to children's bks in print 1999, 955

YOUNG ADULT LITERATURE - BIOGRAPHY
Black authors & illustrators of bks for children & YAs, 958
Lives & works: YA authors, 966
Something about the author, v.99, 959

YUGOSLAVIA
Historical dict of the Federal Republic of Yugoslavia, 473

ZIP CODES
Demographics USA 1999: ZIP ed, 765

ZOROASTRIANISM
Zoroastrianism, 1239